THE OXFORD HANDBOOK OF

JEWISH STUDIES

THE OXFORD HANDBOOK OF

JEWISH STUDIES

Edited by

MARTIN GOODMAN

Associate Editors

JEREMY COHEN

AND

DAVID SORKIN

OXFORD
UNIVERSITY PRESS

OXFORD
UNIVERSITY PRESS

Great Clarendon Street, Oxford OX2 6DP

Oxford University Press is a department of the University of Oxford.
It furthers the University's objective of excellence in research, scholarship,
and education by publishing worldwide in

Oxford New York

Auckland Bangkok Buenos Aires Cape Town Chennai
Dar es Salaam Delhi Hong Kong Istanbul Karachi Kolkata
Kuala Lumpur Madrid Melbourne Mexico City Mumbai Nairobi
São Paulo Shanghai Taipei Tokyo Toronto

Oxford is a registered trade mark of Oxford University Press
in the UK and in certain other countries

Published in the United States
by Oxford University Press Inc., New York

British Library Cataloguing in Publication Data

Data available

Library of Congress Cataloging in Publication Data

The Oxford handbook of Jewish studies / edited by Martin Goodman in association with
Jeremy Cohen and David Sorkin.
p. cm.
Includes bibliographical references and index.
ISBN 0–19–829996–6

1. Judaism—Study and teaching. 2. Jews—Civilization—Study and teaching. I. Goodman,
Martin, 1953– II. Cohen, Jeremy, 1953– III. Sorkin, David J.

BM70. 095 2002   909' 04924—dc21   2002035554

1 3 5 7 9 10 8 6 4 2

Typeset by Kolam Information Services Pvt. Ltd, Pondicherry, India
Printed in Great Britain
on acid-free paper by
T. J. International Padstow, Cornwall.

CONTENTS

LIST OF CONTRIBUTORS

Glenda Abramson is Cowley Lecturer in Post-biblical Hebrew in the University of Oxford and Fellow of the Oxford Centre for Hebrew and Jewish Studies.

Philip S. Alexander is Professor of Postbiblical Jewish Literature at the University of Manchester.

Wolfgang Benz is Professor at the Zentrum für Antisemitismusforschung at the Technische Universität, Berlin.

Ahuva Belkin is Professor of Theatre Studies at Tel Aviv University.

Ram Ben-Shalom is Senior Lecturer in Jewish History at the Open University of Israel.

Philip V. Bohlman is Professor of Music and Jewish Studies at the University of Chicago.

Elisheva Carlebach is Professor of History at Queens College, New York.

Jeremy Cohen is Professor of Jewish History at Tel Aviv University.

Mark R. Cohen is Professor of Near Eastern Studies at Princeton University.

John J. Collins is Holmes Professor of Old Testament Criticism and Interpretation at Yale University.

Alan Cooper is Professor of Bible at the Jewish Theological Seminary of America and Union Theological Seminary.

Joseph Dan is Gershom Scholem Professor of Kabbalah at the Hebrew University of Jerusalem.

Sergio DellaPergola is Professor of Demography and Contemporary Jewish Studies at the Hebrew University of Jerusalem.

Hasia Diner is Professor of American Jewish History at New York University.

Michael Fishbane is Nathan Cummings Professor of Jewish Studies at the University of Chicago.

Saul Friedländer is Professor of History at UCLA and at Tel Aviv University.

Harvey E. **Goldberg** is Professor of Sociology and Anthropology at the Hebrew University of Jerusalem.

Martin Goodman is Professor of Jewish Studies at the University of Oxford and a Fellow of the Oxford Centre for Hebrew and Jewish Studies.

Alyssa Gray is Assistant Professor of Codes and Responsa Literature, Hebrew Union College–Jewish Institute of Religion, New York.

Galit Hasan-Rokem is Max and Margarethe Grunwald Professor of Folklore, Professor of Hebrew Literature, and Head of the Institute for Jewish Studies at the Hebrew University of Jerusalem.

Pablo-Isaac Halevi (**Kirtchuk**) is Professor of Hebrew Language and Linguistics at Ben-Gurion University of the Negev.

Catherine Hezser is Lippert Professor of Jewish Studies at Trinity College, Dublin.

Lawrence A. **Hoffman** is Professor of Liturgy at Hebrew Union College–Jewish Institute of Religion, New York.

Tal Ilan is an independent scholar.

Bernard Jackson is Alliance Professor of Modern Jewish Studies at the University of Manchester.

Gad Kaynar is Senior Lecturer in Theatre Studies at Tel Aviv University.

Geoffrey Khan is Reader in Semitic Philology at the University of Cambridge.

Cecile E. **Kuznitz** is Visiting Assistant Professor of Jewish History/Jewish Studies and Director of the Sam Eig Jewish Studies Initiative at Georgetown University.

Lee I. **Levine** is Professor of Archaeology and Jewish History at the Hebrew University of Jerusalem.

Berachyahu Lifshitz is Professor and sometime Dean of the Faculty of Law at the Hebrew University of Jerusalem.

Paul Mendes-Flohr is Professor of Modern Jewish Thought at the University of Chicago, and is the Director of the Franz Rosenzweig, Research Center for German Jewish Literature and Cultural History at the Hebrew University of Jerusalem.

Meira Polliack is Senior Lecturer in Biblical Studies at Tel Aviv University.

David Rechter is University Research Lecturer in Oriental Studies at the University of Oxford and Fellow of the Oxford Centre for Hebrew and Jewish Studies.

Tova Rosen is Professor of Hebrew Literature at Tel Aviv University.

Seth Schwartz is Professor of Jewish History at the Jewish Theological Seminary of America.

Ora R. Schwarzwald is Professor of Hebrew Language at Bar Ilan University.

Daniel B. Sinclair is Professor of Jewish and Comparative Bio-Medical Law at the College of Management Academic Studies, Rishon Lezion.

David Sorkin is Professor of Jewish Studies at the University of Wisconsin–Madison.

Michael Stanislawski is the Nathan J. Miller Professor of Jewish History at Columbia University.

Ilan Stavans is Lewis-Sebring Professor in Latin American and Latino Culture at Amherst College.

Sarah Abrevaya Stein is Professor of Jewish History at the University of Washington, Seattle.

Israel Ta-Shma is Professor Emeritus of Medieval Rabbinic Literature, Talmud Department, at the Hebrew University of Jerusalem.

S. Ilan Troen is Lopin Professor of Modern History at Ben-Gurion University of the Negev and Senior Fellow at the Ben-Gurion Research Center, Sede Boqer.

Eli Yassif is Professor of Hebrew Literature at Tel Aviv University.

Moshe Zimerman is Professor of Film Studies at Tel Aviv University.

LIST OF ABBREVIATIONS

AIPHOS	*Annuaire de l'Institut de Philologie et d'Histoire Orientales et Slaves*
AJS	*Association of Jewish Studies*
BA	*Biblical Archaeologist*
CRINT	*Compendia Rerum Iudaicarum ad Novum Testamentum*
DJD	*Discoveries in the Judaean Desert*
FJS	*Frankfurter Jüdische Studien*
HTR	*Harvard Theological Review*
HUCA	*Hebrew Union College Annual*
JBL	*Journal of Biblical Literature*
JH	*Jewish History*
JJS	*Journal of Jewish Studies*
JQR	*Jewish Quarterly Review*
JS	*Jewish Studies*
JSJ	*Journal for the Study of Judaism*
JSQ	*Jewish Studies Quarterly*
JSS	*Journal of Semitic Studies*
Ju	*Judaism*
PAAJR	*Proceedings of the American Academy for Jewish Research*
REJ	*Revue des Études Juives*
RevQ	*Revue de Qumran*
SCI	*Scripta Classica Israelica*
SH	*Scripta Hierosolymitana*
TSAJ	*Texts and Studies in Ancient Judaism*
ZRG	*Zeitschrift für Religions-und Geistesgeschichte*

PREFACE

Deciding on the best categories to use in describing Jewish studies has been a complex but instructive task. When Oxford University Press first approached us to produce this Handbook, we devised between us a draft contents list for the Press to send out to its advisers. Our draft list reflected roughly the way that Jewish studies is normally divided up in conferences around the world. The Press's many advisers responded with much enthusiasm for the idea of the Handbook as a whole, but with a multiplicity of strongly expressed and cogent suggestions about how the various areas of Jewish studies should be categorized and where the emphases of the Handbook should lie. Our problem was that many of these suggestions were mutually exclusive. The issues raised by this conflicting advice, which go to the heart of current disputes about what Jewish studies is (or are), were discussed in July 2002 by a panel and audience at the congress of the European Association for Jewish Studies in Amsterdam. It became all too apparent in the course of the session that universal agreement on the best and fairest way to describe the current state of scholarship in Jewish studies is bound to be elusive. We do not expect to have settled such issues. On the contrary, we hope that this Handbook will stimulate further fruitful debate.

For the Handbook to be produced at all we had to make some pragmatic decisions, and it may be useful to clarify here the principles underlying the final shape the Handbook has taken. The Handbook is intended to provide a snapshot of the current state of research in Jewish studies. It does not prescribe for the future, although individual contributors have been encouraged to make suggestions about possible future directions. We have therefore allocated space to subjects on the basis of the extent and interest of current scholarly debate in that area rather than as a reflection of any judgement about the intrinsic importance of any one subject for understanding Jewish culture.

One effect of this policy is that we have been able to allow only scant discussion of some areas which could, and perhaps one day should, receive more attention than the minimal scholarship they currently attract. Similarly, authors of chapters on 'central' areas of Jewish studies which have evoked much writing but little controversy as to how the subject should be approached have not been encouraged to expand their contributions beyond the extent required to clarify the current state of debates. Our desire to reflect only the present state of scholarship has also precluded redefinition in the Handbook of areas within Jewish studies in ways that may well in time become more common. For example, one day 'Jewish Women's studies' may be more widely considered as 'Jewish Gender studies', or the study of anti-Semitism may be better described as the study of Jewish–Gentile relations, but we do not believe that this as yet reflects the state of the literature in these fields.

The letter we sent to those invited to contribute chapters to this Handbook described their work as a mitzvah, a service to the future of Jewish studies. We are very grateful to the many colleagues who have been involved in the production of this volume for entering into their tasks in this spirit. In particular, we thank those contributors (especially Philip Alexander and Cecile Kuznitz) who undertook to write chapters at short notice when the original contributors had to withdraw.

Our categorization of Jewish studies into discrete chapters has inevitably resulted in the dispersal into different chapters of some important topics, such as work on manuscripts and archives, or bibliographic studies, which might in principle have been allocated chapters of their own. Readers of the Handbook are directed to the subject index, which we have made as full as possible to facilitate cross-referencing between chapters. We are grateful to Rosemary Dear for its compilation.

A Handbook of this kind is most useful when it is up to date, and much effort has been expended by the editorial and production teams of Oxford University Press to ensure that the material submitted be processed and published at exceptional speed. We are very grateful to Helenann Francis for an immense amount of work in preparing the typescript for copy-editing, and to the Oxford University Teaching and Research Unit for Hebrew and Jewish Studies and the Oxford Centre for Hebrew and Jewish Studies for generous grants for this purpose. We are particularly indebted to Jeff New for his expert and rapid copy-editing of such a large work. Readers should note the policy we have followed for the transliteration of Hebrew. Since, for good reason, scholars in different areas of Jewish studies use different transliteration systems, we have not imposed stylistic uniformity, but we have taken pains to ensure that, whichever system is used, the text is fully comprehensible.

It remains to thank Oxford University Press, and especially Hilary O'Shea, the commissioning editor, for their initiative in proposing the Handbook and bringing it to fruition.

Martin Goodman
Jeremy Cohen
David Sorkin

Oxford
August 2002

CHAPTER 1

THE NATURE OF JEWISH STUDIES

MARTIN GOODMAN

THE decision to produce a handbook of Jewish studies at this stage in the development of the subject has been felt justified for two reasons. The first is practical: no similar introduction has ever been written and students often find it difficult to find out what issues are worth discussion and where to get an appropriate bibliography to help. The second is more philosophical: practitioners in the field, both researchers and students, all too rarely seek to put their studies into a general perspective in this way, and it is to be hoped that doing so may produce insights of many different kinds. Hence when the proposal for the Handbook was first mooted by Oxford University Press, the distinguished colleagues asked for advice as to whether and how it should proceed responded with much enthusiasm for the project as a whole—albeit, with a great variety of conflicting suggestions as to how it should be carried out. Enthusiasm, conflict, and diversity are indeed characteristic of the subject in its present state, and it will be the task of this Handbook not to resolve but to reflect this state.

The topics included under the rubric of Jewish studies are exceptionally disparate, ranging not only over a long period of time and all the countries in which Jews have lived, but also over a plethora of different aspects of Jewish culture—literature, history, theology, law, sociology, the fine arts, and more. No method of dividing up these topics is without drawbacks, and any method will be the product, at least in part, of an ideological stance of one sort or another, a problem discussed more fully below. The approach taken in this Handbook is therefore necessarily imperfect, but it is pragmatic. Topics have been assigned in the first half of the Handbook roughly by period, in the second half by theme, reflecting current trends both in research and in teaching.

One effect has been some overlap between chapters, although this has been kept to a minimum. Other issues, such as whether to include biblical studies at all within Jewish studies (since to do so might indicate a particular attitude to the Bible), have been tackled head on: thus one of the main problems discussed in Chapter 2 is precisely whether and how biblical studies can be seen within this context. The Handbook thus errs on the side of inclusiveness, but it cannot claim to include every area that might, and sometimes does, crop up at a Jewish studies conference. There is thus, for instance, no separate chapter on the flourishing fields of Jewish geneal-ogy[1] or Judaeo-Greek studies,[2] although it is to be hoped that brief discussions in other chapters and judicious use of the index will provide help to those who wish to investigate these areas further.

The recognition of Jewish studies as an area of knowledge worthy of research and teaching in universities is a quite recent phenomenon. From an exceedingly small base in the first half of the twentieth century, the subject has now burgeoned. The great centres for research and teaching reflect the main contemporary centres of Jewish population, Israel and North America (the United States and Canada), but Jewish studies are also now taught not only in other countries where Jews live in large numbers, such as France and Argentina, but also in countries where few Jews are now found. Fine scholarship in the field can be found in universities in many countries in Western Europe, in South Africa, Australia, Russia, Japan, and Korea—that is, in almost every country that boasts a higher-education system which incorporates humanities and social sciences on the western pattern.[3] This explosion of interest, particularly since the 1960s, has led to a massive increase in the number of teachers and scholars for whom research in Jewish studies forms a significant part of their academic careers, with a concomitant burgeoning of publications. Many of the major academic presses now produce a Jewish studies list, and the subject features with disproportionate prominence in some of the more self-consciously intellectual magazines and newspapers, particularly in the English-speaking world.

The rationale for this rapid spread of interest is rarely spelled out within general academic circles. Often universities adopt the subject because it is fashionable, because there is student or faculty demand, or because a donor offers to fund a faculty post. If pressed, supporters of Jewish studies may claim that the Jews and Judaism deserve intensive study because of their exceptional impact on world civilization. This would not be untrue, but nor would it explain current interest

---

[1] See e.g. the periodical *Shemot*, published since 1993.

[2] See the *Bulletin of Judaeo-Greek Studies*, published since 1987.

[3] For a partial list of places, see Davis 1995: 253–363, partially updated for countries in the former Soviet Union in Chulkova (1996) and for Western Europe in Winkelmann (1998). All such lists go out of date very rapidly.

compared to the general academic neglect of Jewish culture for much of the history of western scholarship since the Renaissance. For a fuller explanation, it is necessary to see the history of Jewish studies against the background of the history of the Jews.

The relevant parts of that history commence with the status of Jews as an oppressed minority in medieval and early modern Europe and then the emancipation of Jews in some parts of Europe during the eighteenth century. Emancipation encouraged both assimilation into the wider society and a search for a distinctive identity within that society. Jewish intellectuals debated the nature of that identity for much of the nineteenth century. In particular, some restricted Jewishness to the religious sphere, others advocated nationalism, leading to the foundation of the Zionist movement at the end of the century. In the twentieth century the impact of these trends was seen in diverse ways, above all in the defining events of the Holocaust and the foundation of the State of Israel in 1948. The majority of Jews in the second half of the twentieth century have found themselves either in Israel, a Jewish nation state in which the pressures of government have encouraged a widening divide between religious and secular Jews, or in the United States, a self-consciously pluralistic, multicultural society in which, at least since the 1960s, ethnic groups have been encouraged to express their distinctiveness rather than just merge themselves into a common culture. This privilege has been especially extended to Jews, along with a great increase in Jewish–Christian dialogue, in the light of the horror felt by a predominantly Christian society about the holocaust of Jews in Europe. A further factor has been the increased awareness among non-Jews of the continuing vitality of Jewish culture demonstrated by the prominent role of the State of Israel in international affairs for much of the second half of the twentieth century.

The history of Jewish studies has been affected by every aspect of this story. The high valuation of learning about the Torah as a pious activity in itself has been a distinctive aspect of rabbinic Judaism since late antiquity. Yeshiva education, centred on expertise in talmudics, has retained a prestigious role among religious Jews down to the present day. But this learning, which aims at the elucidation and reconciliation of texts as the expression of God's law, is to be distinguished from the study of Jews and Judaism without (at least in principle) any objective beyond a search for the truth.

Not that a totally objective approach to Jewish culture has ever been possible. The earliest students of Jewish literature in European universities were Christian professors of classical Hebrew in the medieval period whose concern was to discover the true meaning of the text of the Old Testament. Christian Hebraists in the Renaissance hoped to find in the Jewish mystical texts esoteric insights to match those of the pagan and Christian Neoplatonists of late antiquity. Much of the best scholarship on Jewish history and literature in the Second Temple period has been, since the nineteenth century, the work of Christian theologians primarily interested in the background to the New Testament. Similarly, the first foray by German Jews, in the early nineteenth century, to create what they proclaimed as a 'science of Judaism' had the clearly apologetic aim of demonstrating to the wider world that Jewish culture could and should be analysed with the same tools as that of other peoples, and in particular the classical cultures of Greece and Rome.[4]

The efforts of the creators of the Wissenschaft des Judentums still underpin contemporary study of some aspects of Jewish culture. But in some respects these pioneers may be deemed to have failed for most of the nineteenth and the first half of the twentieth century, in contrast to advocates of other national cultures such as English or German studies whose promotion in universities alongside classics was strikingly successful. Attempts to encourage European universities to establish posts to teach Jewish culture outside the context of Christian theology were only sporadically successful before the mid-twentieth century. Those few attracted into the field were almost exclusively Jews; the lecturers and professors in rabbinics and Jewish studies in places like Oxford, Cambridge, University College London, Paris, Harvard, and Columbia were all Jews before the late twentieth century, whereas teachers of Arabic were rarely Arabs, and teachers of Chinese were not Chinese. Most of what was written was the product of Jewish institutions, rabbinic academies which tried to combine yeshiva learning with the methods of scientific scholarship. Much was defensive, with aspects of Jewish culture singled out for special praise and the history of the Jews described as far as possible on the model of a national state rather than a dispersed religious minority. The non-Jewish world, both within and outside the universities, paid little attention to what was written, and in much of Europe even such modest advances as had been made were brought to an end either by the upheavals of the 1930s or by restrictions within the communist bloc during the Cold War.

Where the Wissenschaft des Judentums took hold most firmly was in the national homeland. In the 1920s the Hebrew University, with its Institute of Jewish Studies, was established on the European, and especially the German, model as a university for the Jewish people, with the task both of researching the nature of Judaism and of describing a living Jewish culture for the Jewish people. With the establishment of the State of Israel in 1948 this educative role became a major task as the new nation strove to create an appropriate collective consciousness out of a (necessarily selective) evocation of the Jewish past.

In North America, by contrast, Jewish studies took off in the last quarter of the twentieth century in an entirely different direction. A general liberal awareness, particularly in the United States, of the sometimes arbitrary and oppressive concentration of traditional scholarship on the achievements of the wealthy and powerful led in the 1960s to encouragement of minority studies, such as women's studies and black studies. Jewish studies have flourished in many universities under the same general rubric, but with a rather firmer intellectual base precisely because of the

---

[4] On the history of the Wissenschaft des Judentums, see e.g. Schorsch (1994).

solid work of the pioneers of the Wissenschaft des Judentums. The claim to intellectual respectability has often been bolstered by describing the subject as Judaic studies or by sheltering (not altogether satisfactorily) under the rubric of Hebrew studies.

These developments have been, of course, only partly the product of the wider social changes just described, since something at least must also be due to the efforts and inclinations of the scholars themselves. Thus discoveries of new evidence such as the Cairo genizah, the Dead Sea scrolls or, more recently, documents about Jews in the state archives of the former Soviet Union, have stimulated whole new fields of research. Types of scholarship which were previously the preserve of the dedicated few have been opened up through the availability of resources such as the Institute of Microfilmed Hebrew Manuscripts in the National and University Library in Jerusalem, or the publication on CD-ROM of rabbinic texts (e.g. *Bar-Ilan's Judaic Library* 1997), talmudic manuscript readings (Lieberman Institute 1998), and computer-enhanced photographs of the Qumran scrolls (Alexander and Lim 1997).

The institutions in which Jewish studies are based in the early twenty-first century reflect this history of the development of the subject. Thus much is achieved by a coterie of university-based institutions dedicated to the subject, both teaching departments and research centres, but most of these are quite small and of recent foundation. Much the most influential has been the oldest, the Institute of Jewish Studies at the Hebrew University set up in 1925, but more recent years have also seen numerous important publications by other Israeli research centres, notably the at Rosenberg school at Tel Aviv University, and in Bar-Ilan University, but also in the many more specialized institutes such as (for example) the Ben-Gurion Research Centre in Beer-Sheva and the Hartman Institute in Jerusalem. Outside Israel, there are also a few specialized institutions, such as YIVO in New York and the research centre at the University of Pennsylvania which, metamorphosed from Dropsie College and the Annenberg Center into a full part of the university, has become a powerhouse for scholarship through a well-developed and well-funded programme of research seminars for visiting scholars. A similar programme is also administered by the Institute for Advanced Study at the Hebrew University and, on a less ambitious scale, by the Oxford Centre for Hebrew and Jewish Studies which, like the Institut für Judaistik at the Freie Universität in Berlin, also provides courses for graduate students.

But these centres are the exception rather than the rule. For the most part, despite the efforts of co-ordinating institutions both on the national scale (the oldest being the Societé des Études Juives, founded in Paris in 1880) and internationally (from the World Union of Jewish Studies, founded in 1947 to hold a congress in Jerusalem every four years, to the Association of Jewish Studies (1968) with its annual meeting, usually held in Boston, and the European Association of Jewish Studies (1982)), many scholars in the field work in isolation from most of their colleagues.

Thus much important scholarship is still done by enthusiastic amateurs outside the university world, particularly in such fields as genealogy and local history, and much is achieved also within the confines of religious institutions. The Jewish theological academies, pre-eminently the Jewish Theological Seminary of America and Hebrew Union College, retain great influence, although less than their counterparts in Central and Western Europe before the Holocaust. In contrast, there is now very little contact between academic Jewish Studies and the yeshiva world, a reflection of the polarization of the religious world which has also created difficulties for universities such as Yeshiva University in New York and Bar-Ilan University in Israel, which was set up in the 1950s precisely to give to orthodox Jewish students the best of both worlds. Similarly, much of Jewish studies is still done under the aegis of Christian faculties of theology, particularly in Europe and in parts of Latin America.

But the bulk of Jewish studies scholars work in quite disparate faculties, in which their interest in Jewish matters constitutes only a small element in their intellectual identity. Thus the academic addresses of most members who attend and speak at the World Congress of Jewish Studies will be faculties of history, sociology, religious studies, oriental languages, politics, and so on—that is, almost any faculty in the humanities and social sciences—and it will be to those disciplines, rather than to their Jewish material, that these scholars may feel their primary allegiance.

Jewish studies have thus developed in a fragmented and amorphous fashion, with concomitant problems. In essence, the subject is not really a specific discipline in its own right. It certainly does not conform to the norms of a classic historical or literary discipline based upon either a specific place or a specific language: Jewish languages are multifarious and the countries Jews have inhabited all too many. All too often it is impossible to understand aspects of Jewish culture without a detailed knowledge also of the surrounding non-Jewish world, so that a total mastery of Jewish studies requires almost encyclopaedic knowledge. Not even the reductive definition of the subject as 'anything to do with Jews and Judaism' is as simple as it looks, since the definition of Jewishness has been slippery in many periods of Jewish history, not least in recent debates in Israel about 'Who is a Jew?' Thus, although Jewish studies may perhaps be best viewed as analogous to a field of area studies to which various disciplines are applied (history, geography, philology, and so on), even that analogy is not exact.

Against this background it is fruitless to expect consistent methods across the whole field. Most of the journals devoted to Jewish studies specialize in particular parts of the subject, either openly as official editorial policy or in practice through the preferences of editors or the growth of traditions. Thus the two most venerable journals ostensibly devoted to the whole of Jewish studies, *Jewish Quarterly Review* (originally published in England from 1889 to 1908, and in a new series in the United States since 1910) and *Revue des Études Juives* (published since 1880), are both quite selective in their coverage. *Hebrew Union College Annual* (published since 1924) has predominantly material about Judaism rather than secular issues, and the *Journal of Jewish Studies* (published since 1949) deals mostly with late antiquity, with only a few articles on medieval or modern issues (although the reviews section is more eclectic). *Tarbiz* (1929), in Hebrew, still covers a broad chronological span. *Sefarad*, founded in Spain by non-Jewish scholars in 1940 and published in Spanish since 1941, has a wide remit in Hebrew topics, with a special interest in Sephardic studies. Perhaps the widest spread of topics is to be found in *Mada'ei haYahadut-Jewish Studies* (1925–6, with gaps in publication), the forum of the World Union of Jewish Studies, now published annually, and the *Association of Jewish Studies Review* (1976), which reflect (if, of necessity, only patchily) all the subjects which interest the members of these associations, and the newer *Jewish Studies Quarterly* (1993). The predominant use of English and Hebrew in such journals is striking: most non-specialized German periodicals, such as the *Monatschrift für Geschichte und Wissenschaft des Judentums*, published in Leipzig in the 1850s, and the *Monatschrift für die Literatur and Wissenschaft des Judenthums*, published in Vienna in the 1880s, have not survived. Most current journals are devoted to particular periods—for example, all the journals on biblical subjects, the *Journal for the Study of Judaism in the Persian, Hellenistic and Roman Period* (1970), and *Modern Judaism* (1981) and the *Journal of Modern Jewish Studies* (2002)— or to particular aspects of Jewish studies, such as Jewish history (*Zion* (1935, in Hebrew); *Jewish History* (1986)); Hebrew literature (*Prooftexts* (1980); *Modern Hebrew Literature* (1975, refounded 1988)); contemporary society (*Jewish Journal of Sociology* (1959), *Jewish Social Studies* (1939); *Israel Affairs* (1994); *Israel Studies* (1996)); the history and current state of Judaism (*Judaism* (1952); *Annual of Rabbinic Judaism* (1998); *The Journal of Jewish Thought and Philosophy* (1991)); law (*Jewish Law Annual* (1978)); art (*Jewish Art*, originally *Journal of Jewish Art* (1974)); politics (*Jewish Political Studies Review* (1989)); the Hebrew language (*Leshonenu* (1928)); Jewish languages other than Hebrew (*Jewish Language Review* (1981)); or bibliography of Jewish studies (*Kiryat Sefer* (1924, in Hebrew) and *Journal of Jewish Bibliography* (1938)). As will emerge from the brief paragraphs of suggested reading at the end of each chapter of the Handbook, many journals have sprung up in recent years devoted exclusively to what might appear to be small corners of the subject when Jewish culture is viewed as a whole—thus (for example) there are two journals for the Dead Sea Scrolls (*Revue de Qumran* (1958) and *Dead Sea Discoveries* (1994)), and a flourishing annual for Polish Jewish studies (*Polin* (1986)).

This proliferation of specialist publications encourages the intellectual disintegration of the subject as a whole. For many scholars in the field, their main intellectual allegiance is to their primary discipline and their concern is as much to bring a Jewish dimension to the attention of their colleagues in these disciplines as it is to use the methods of those disciplines to enlighten students interested in other aspects of Jewish culture. Few boundaries can be clearly set. The traditional investigation of any aspect of Jewish life 'through the ages', such as 'Jewish Thought' or 'Jewish Art', is open to the objection that it reflects an apologetic search for an essence of Jewishness which may have never existed. The common division of the subject into 'ancient', 'medieval', and 'modern' is similarly open to the charge that, for instance, it assumes a major shift from medieval to modern which may be by no means apparent to some who believe that they still live out the unchanged oral Torah as given to Moses on Mount Sinai.

Some scholars, including some who have made important contributions to knowledge of Jewish history and culture, are so impressed by these problems that they refuse to accept that Jewish studies is a field at all, but I think it is unnecessary to despair over such issues of definition and organization. Almost all humanities subjects raise some questions of this kind, although Jewish studies may raise more than most. But they do help to explain some of the current debates among those in the field, such as the distinction in Germany between Judaistik and Jüdische Studien: practitioners of the former have insisted on the necessity to view Jewish culture as a whole, requiring (usually) knowledge of Hebrew and earlier Jewish history and literature even for those specializing in more modern topics; practitioners of the latter have asserted the validity of historical, political, and sociological studies about the lives and institutions of Jews in more recent periods without need for knowledge of the earlier Jewish background.[5] Another debate has centred on the appropriation of the name of Jewish studies by orthodox religious Jews keen to provide an attractive modern gloss to traditional yeshiva learning. This is an extension of an apologetic tendency which, despite pretensions to academic objectivity, Jewish studies has found it difficult to shed, not least because funding for teaching the subject in diaspora universities has often come from donors who see such encouragement as a means to reinforce local Jewish communal identity.

On a more parochial level of the politics of university administration, teaching staff have needed to balance the advantages of the dispersal of Jewish studies posts into the departments or faculties which house their main disciplines (such as history or modern languages)—which may give disciplinary credibility but may also leave the subject vulnerable when the current postholder retires—against the advantages of coalescence into an identifiable Jewish studies department, in which lack of methodological common ground may leave colleagues unable to judge each other's work; a compromise, to create 'programmes' or 'centres' of Jewish studies using teachers with primary allegiance in other departments, has been quite commonly adopted, but it is probably too early to know whether this form of organization will indeed ensure the continued vitality of the subject.

The solutions to these theoretical and practical problems have been different in the different parts of the world where Jewish studies are to be found, not least because sources of funding vary. Regardless of any protestation by both donor and recipient, it would be naive to expect the wishes of the paymaster to have no effect

---

[5] See discussions in *Jewish Studies Quarterly* 2 (1994) and Brenner and Rohrbacher (2000).

whatever on the directions taken in academic research. Thus in Israel the study of Jewish culture is financed primarily by the state, and historically has played an important role in defining (and questioning) national identity in the new state through the creation and demolition of national myths such as the heroic defence of Masada, the ambiguous role of Bar Kochba, and the contribution of archaeology to Jewish claims to the land. Jewish studies in Israel in the past generally tended towards validation of Jewish culture, with the added patina of authenticity derived from publication in Hebrew, although some of the current generation of younger Israeli scholars see their role as 'post-Zionist' and deliberately divorced from the ideology of the state. In some parts of the field orthodoxies laid down by the giants of the early generations at the Hebrew University were for years only slowly challenged, not least because, in a small country with a culture traditionally respectful towards teachers, many Israeli academics were the direct intellectual descendants of these pioneers, but again, this attitude of deference was never universal, and in the current generation younger scholars sometimes make a virtue of radical departures from the consensus. Perhaps for similar reasons Israeli academics within Jewish studies did not always welcome forays into Jewish topics by their colleagues in other departments, and some areas of Jewish studies, particularly the study of rabbinic texts, have been in danger of becoming too esoteric for those outside the field to venture to use such texts at all. It does not help that the academic study of rabbinics within Jewish studies is also in some danger for a different reason, the current sharp divide between the religious and the secular in Israel. For much of the twentieth century the great figures in this area were scholars who had come to academic study only after a deep yeshiva education. People interested in combining yeshiva learning with an academic approach to rabbinic literature are not now common.

In the United States the quite different pressures on the local Jewish population have encouraged widespread adoption of the model of interdepartmental programmes of Jewish studies, not least because many American Jewish students are attracted by the prospect of including an element of Jewish studies within their modular courses as part of a search to establish their identity. The needs of such students have been pre-eminent for many of the private benefactors responsible for the establishment of Jewish studies posts, often combined with a hope that the incumbent of the post may also play a role within the local Jewish community. The interests of such benefactors in promoting specific aspects of Jewish studies, such as research into the Holocaust and the history of anti-Semitism, reflect to a large degree the concerns of North American Jews as a whole. The result has been some odd imbalances. Two examples may illustrate. First, many courses are taught to Jewish students using sources from within the Jewish tradition, but because the students concerned lack time or inclination to learn the Jewish languages in which these texts were written, much is done in translation. One effect of this is that few students who graduate in Jewish studies are qualified without further training to teach Jewish studies at university level. Second, a desire to maintain academic independence from theological pressures, perhaps a reflection of the divide between the religious and the secular in the American constitution, remains strong. It led to a debate when the Association for Jewish Studies was inaugurated as to whether rabbis should even be allowed to join; they were, but when classic rabbinic texts are taught in America universities it is often in departments of religion, where many of the students are not Jews but enthusiastic Christians seeking to understand the background to Christianity.

Elsewhere in the world the pattern of development of Jewish studies has generally followed a similar route to that in the United States (so in Canada, South Africa, and Australia); thus the efflorescence of Jewish studies in Russia has mostly been fuelled by the desire of Russian Jews to explore their identity (and by the willingness of American and Israeli institutions to fund and advise them). The position in Western and Central Europe is rather more varied. In some countries (such as Britain, France, Germany, Italy, Poland, and elsewhere) there has been much scholarship on the history of the local Jewish populations, partly perhaps in an effort to assert the rightful place of Jews within the history of each nation. The large Jewish population in France, many of North African origin, has encouraged an expansion in Sephardic studies, and in many universities Jewish studies are taught by Jews to Jews. By contrast, most teachers and students in Germany are non-Jews, although in recent years there have been more Jewish students in Germany of Russian origin. In the United Kingdom the field is neatly divided between the mostly Jewish staff and students in places such as the Hebrew and Jewish Studies department at University College London, and the mostly non-Jewish teachers and students in other universities where Jewish studies are more fragmented and still often an offshoot of Christian theology—it is not accidental that for the first ten years or so after its inauguration in 1974, the British Association for Jewish Studies timed its annual meeting always to follow on after the meeting of the Society for Old Testament Study.

Regional variety is most clearly expressed in the different trends to be found in the historiography of local diaspora communities. There has been room in the Handbook to discuss in some detail the historiography of Jews in America, but it would have needed a separate chapter on each diaspora country to include an account of all the roughly parallel developments elsewhere over the past century and a half, such as the sterling work on Anglo-Jewish history carried out since 1893 by the Jewish Historical Society of England, and the highly productive efforts in examining German-Jewish history made by (for example) the S. L. Steinheim Institut für Deutsch-Jüdische Geschichte. In many countries the agenda for such study was long driven by enthusiastic, often exceptionally expert, local Jewish amateurs, and the subject has only recently been adopted by professional scholars based in universities. Specialists in such local Jewish history often feel, not without justification, that their discoveries receive less attention than they deserve from colleagues engaged with non-Jewish history of the same time and place, while being marginalized as parochial within Jewish Studies as a whole.

Where should the subject go in the future? A search for total unity and generally accepted norms, either for methods or for a common curricular core of Jewish studies, seems futile. Instead it may make sense to celebrate precisely the diversity within the field. On the one hand more can be done to introduce a Jewish element into the general curricula of history, philology, theology, and other disciplines. On the other, specialists in Jewish studies can make a virtue of the special insights that may come through cross-disciplinarity. Certainly, any tendency to exclude some scholars from serious consideration on the grounds that they cannot 'really' be in Jewish studies because they lack certain (usually linguistic) skills needs to be firmly resisted by the new generation of scholars trained in the 1990s and the present. There remains a great deal to be discovered about Jews and Judaism, and all methods are to be encouraged: proponents both of Judaistik and of Jüdische Studien must learn to cohabit.

But such cohabitation is not without its dangers, particularly where intellectual trends are led by market forces of student demand or donor wishes, which will tend to favour encouragement of subjects which do not require deep immersion into the difficult languages and texts of classical Judaism. Someone has to keep alive the study of classical Hebrew as a language and of the Talmud as a text from late antiquity. There is not as yet any sign that this need is in danger of not being met within the world of Jewish studies as a whole, but in particular countries these central subjects are too often ignored, and those who care for the subject as a whole will need to ensure they are preserved. And in some respects diversity and fragmentation cannot be left to flourish wholly unchecked. On a basic level, it is clearly undesirable that practitioners in the different streams of Jewish studies should simply ignore the work done by others, either on the grounds that their approaches are wholly different (a reason which used to be given for mutual indifference between Israeli and American scholars in some parts of the field) or, even less respectably, because scholars write in different languages. The main languages currently in use in Jewish studies scholarship are Hebrew, English, French, and German, but a good deal is also published in other European languages (particularly on local Jewish subjects), and it is incumbent on all in the field to take due note of whatever is produced. In particular, the development in some areas of Jewish studies of particular Francophone and German specialities is in large part due to the failure of other colleagues to interact sufficiently with those who write in these languages. The failure is two-way: the subjects covered, for instance, in the Revue des Études Juives are primarily those subjects (medieval rabbinics, Sephardi studies, contemporary sociology) in which French colleagues specialize (with, interestingly, more awareness outside Francophone scholarship of what is written in Hebrew than of work in English or German). It is a sign of some desperation that scholars who write only in German find themselves almost wholly ignored by many of their non-German-speaking colleagues, a degree of insularity not to be found in other humanities subjects, such as history or classics.

A second argument for increased unity arises from the newfound success of practitioners of Jewish studies in establishing their subject as worthy of academic attention. The stronger the subject becomes, the less need there is for scholars to be concerned that their efforts will appear only as a branch of apologetics. It is true that some areas of Jewish studies remain too sensitive for entirely free exchanges of ideas. In particular, writing in specific ways about the Holocaust, or Jewish–Christian relations, or the contemporary or recent politics of Israel, may seem to provoke the wrath of an academic establishment more powerful and unified than in other humanities subjects. But despite such pressures revisionist scholarship, even in these areas, does get written, discussed, evaluated, and when appropriate, imbibed into the common stock of knowledge. That is to say, Jewish studies are sufficiently mature to accept the value of dissent without concern that the main foundations of knowledge will be in danger of collapse.

Hence it may be time for all in the field to drop the pretence that there can ever be a fully objective 'science of Judaism' and to confess that, despite all our striving for objectivity, it is unavoidable that we must come to our studies for particular reasons and therefore with particular interests and biases. The trend in other humanities subjects for scholars to state openly what their interests are, so that readers may be aware of what they are getting, is to be encouraged in Jewish studies as well. Such openness also has to confront the undoubted effects of academic insights on the self-perception of Jews in the wider Jewish world. The discoveries and assertions of scholars about aspects of Jewish culture and the Jewish past are as influential in moulding the Jewish self-consciousness of secular diaspora Jews as the writings of Zionist academics have been in the creation of Israeli identity. It is irresponsible of scholars to ignore the undoubted impact of their work on real people: the search for the essence of Judaism or Jewishness may be bound to fail, but it cannot be simply ignored. At the very least, it is incumbent on all those engaged in Jewish studies at least occasionally to indulge in the kind of self-reflection which it is the intention of this Handbook to encourage.

SUGGESTED READING

The fine volume edited by Cohen and Greenstein (1990) contains only a very brief introduction, by Ismar Schorsch, to Jewish studies as a whole, but other topics touched on in this chapter are discussed by other contributors to that volume. There are observations on teaching in Neusner (1981 and 1984) and Garber (2000). Much can be found in Davis (1995: 9–117 and *passim*), with an emphasis as much on how Jewish studies are taught as on trends in research. Other published reflections on the current state of Jewish studies tend to be found in newspaper articles and other ephemeral media rather than more substantial publications.

There is a proliferation of dictionaries and encyclopaedias which can give guidance on specific topics in the field, most importantly Roth and Wigoder (1972). Much can be culled from the internet, but it is of varying quality.

BIBLIOGRAPHY

ALEXANDER, P. S. and LIM, T. H. 1997. *The Dead Sea Scrolls: Electronic Reference Library.* New York and Leiden.

Bar-Ilan's Judaic Library 1997. Spring Valley, NY.

BRENNER, M. and ROHRBACHER, S. eds. 2000. *Wissenschaft vom Judentum. Annäherungen nach dem Holocaust.* Göttingen.

CHULKOVA, L. A. ed. 1996. *University Teaching of Jewish Civilization in the Former Soviet Union.* Moscow.

COHEN, S. J. D. and GREENSTEIN, E. L. eds. 1990. *The State of Jewish Studies.* Detroit, Mich.

DAVIS, M. 1995. *Teaching Jewish Civilization: A Global Approach to HigherEducation.* New York and London.

GARBER, Z. ed. 2000. *Academic Approaches to Teaching Jewish Studies.* Lanham, Md.

Lieberman Institute 1998. *The Sol and Evelyn Henkind Talmud Text Databank With Search Capability.* New York.

NEUSNER, J. 1981. *Judaism in the American Humanities: Essays and Reflections.* Chico, Cal.

——— ed. 1984. *New Humanities and Academic Disciplines: The Case of Jewish Studies.* Madison, Wisc.

ROTH, C. and WIGODER, G. eds. 1972. *Encyclopedia Judaica.* Jerusalem.

SCHORSCH, I. 1994. *From Text to Context: The Turn to History in Modern Judaism.* Hanover, NH.

WINKELMANN, A. 1998. *Directory of Jewish Studies in Europe.* Oxford.

CHAPTER 2

BIBLICAL STUDIES AND JEWISH STUDIES

ALAN COOPER

TWO COMMENTARIES ON LEVITICUS

ONE way to gauge the relationship between Biblical studies and Jewish studies is to examine two key moments in the development of academic Jewish biblical scholarship.[1] As a starting-point, we might note that the twentieth century was framed by two magisterial Jewish commentaries on the Book of Leviticus, the first by David Zevi Hoffmann (2 vols.; 1905/6), and the second by Jacob Milgrom (3 vols.; 1991–2000). These commentaries stand out not only because of their

---

[1] I use this awkward phrase in order to acknowledge that there is an increasing flow of non-academic Jewish biblical scholarship, intended for the popular audience and the synagogue pew. This trend is well exemplified by the ArtScroll biblical commentaries, written for the Orthodox market. For an evaluation, see Levy (1983). One of most successful ArtScroll publications is their *Chumash* (1994), which may be found in many Orthodox synagogues and homes. The commentary is a compendium of traditional interpretations, and avoids engagement with critical issues. The two largest liberal movements in Judaism, the Reform and the Conservative, have produced Torah commentaries for home and synagogue use that do attempt to synthesize traditional and modern scholarship. See Plaut (1981) and Lieber *et al.* (2001), respectively. Both of those commentaries were intended to supersede the Hertz Pentateuch, which had been a mainstay of synagogue life in English-speaking countries for almost three-quarters of a century. For an evaluation of Hertz, see Meirovich (1998).

excellence, but also because they exemplify significant trends in Jewish biblical scholarship.

By the time Hoffmann undertook to write his Leviticus commentary, he already had gained renown for critical studies of rabbinic literature that raised the ire of some Orthodox scholars (see Herr 1971: viii. 808–10; Levine 1999: i. 513). Yet far from bringing his critical sensibility to bear on the Bible, Hoffmann produced a work that, for all its learning and philological acumen, was unabashedly apologetic. His dual aim was to repudiate the 'higher-critical'[2] analysis of Leviticus that was prevalent in mainstream (Protestant) biblical scholarship, and also to demonstrate that the rabbinic understanding of the laws of Leviticus not only was authoritative for Jews, but also reflected the correct interpretation of the biblical text.

In his Preface to the Hebrew translation of Hoffmann's commentary, his son, Moses Hoffmann, singles out his father's discussion of Leviticus 6: 12–16 as characteristic. Christian scholars, he writes, could not understand the passage because they were ignorant of the rabbinic tradition, 'so they broke the pericope into pieces and invented the notion that it was composed of different layers from different eras, the final addition having been added only after the Babylonian Exile'. Hoffmann, in contrast, was able to demonstrate not only the unity and antiquity of the passage, but also the fact that 'the rabbinic tradition conforms perfectly to the plain sense of the text'.[3]

The Protestant biblical scholars of Hoffmann's time generally were antipathetic to Leviticus, as well as ignorant of the rabbinic tradition.[4] According to the regnant critical view, the book's cultic prescriptions reflected a late, decadent phase of Israelite religion, far removed from the noble teachings of the prophets and all but devoid of theological interest. In this view, Leviticus adumbrated the oppressive legalism of Pharisaic Judaism, from which the Christian dispensation provided relief. As Ernest Frerichs comments in his introduction to an important collection of essays by Jewish biblical scholars: 'The least acceptable element in the Wellhausen program for Jewish biblical scholars was the denigration of Jewish history, the elevation of the preexilic period to a prime status and the corresponding reading of the postexilic period as one of darkness and decline.'[5]

---

[2] 'Higher criticism' comprises source criticism, which divides the text into multiple sources on the presumption of composite authorship, and historical criticism, which locates the sources in their particular historical contexts. A higher-critical approach therefore militates against both unitary authorship, and against the traditional attributions and dating of the biblical books.

[3] Hoffmann (1976): second page of the unpaginated Preface by Moses Hoffmann.

[4] In a letter that Abraham Geiger wrote to the great Semitist Theodor Nöldeke in 1872, Geiger remarked that while Jews cannot expect Christians to be scholars of Rabbinics, 'we do have the right to ask that those who are not familiar with this literature should either refrain from passing judgment on it or, at least, be circumspect in expressing their opinions'. See Wiener (1962: 135).

[5] Frerichs (1987: 3). See also Levenson (1987: 281–307). For a more general overview by a leading Jewish biblical scholar, see Greenstein (1990: 23–46).

No wonder, then, that a traditionally educated Jewish scholar would recoil from biblical criticism. In fact, in 1903, the year that Solomon Schechter memorably dubbed the so-called higher criticism the 'higher anti-semitism',[6] Hoffmann published the first volume of a trenchant polemic against biblical criticism under the cumbersome title, *Die wichtigsten Instanzen gegen die Graf–Wellhausenschen Hypothese* ('The Leading Arguments Against the Graf–Wellhausen Hypothesis').[7] In fact, though, the apologetics and objectionism[8] that characterized Hoffmann's biblical writings were the outcome of more than a century of uneasy Jewish engagement with (or avoidance of) biblical criticism.

As Edward Breuer has shown in his study of Jewish biblical scholarship in the Haskalah ('Enlightenment'), the eighteenth-century Jewish maskilim ('enlighteners') were almost totally in sympathy with the intellectual goals and pursuits of the German Enlightenment. The maskilim drew the line, however, where the study of the Bible was concerned. The lower-critical[9] study of the Hebrew text of the Bible in relation to other ancient versions raised doubts about the authenticity and accuracy of the Masoretic Text, which was normative for Jews. The higher criticism generated a reconstruction of the history of Israel that was imbued with anti-Jewish animus. The equivocal Jewish response, as Breuer puts it, was to 'embrace . . . eighteenth-century standards of literary and interpretative analysis', but 'to resist those aspects of European culture that were deemed incompatible with fundamental elements of traditional Judaism' (Breuer 1996: 228).

Hoffmann's work clearly embodied that equivocal attitude. There also were three other factors at work throughout the nineteenth century that furthered the alienation of Jewish scholars from biblical criticism. First, the anti-traditional and anti-Jewish tendencies of such criticism were compounded by the virtual exclusion of Jews from academic discourse on the topic. Biblical criticism was at home in the theological faculties of the European universities, to which no Jews were appointed. Hoffmann, for example, was mainly yeshiva- and seminary-educated. He never held a university appointment, although the German government did award him the title 'professor' on the occasion of his seventy-fifth birthday. He achieved his eminence

---

[6] See Schechter (1959: 35–9). The address was delivered at a banquet honouring Kaufman Kohler on the occasion of his election to the presidency of Hebrew Union College. Even that most liberal of Jewish institutions had a legacy of opposition to biblical criticism, dating back to the anti-critical attitude of its founder, Isaac Mayer Wise.

[7] The scholars Karl Heinrich Graf (1815–69) and Julius Wellhausen (1844–1918) were the most influential proponents of the Documentary Hypothesis. They identified the four Pentateuchal sources, and arranged them in what became their accepted chronological order: J, E, D, P, for (J)ahwist, (E)lohist, (D)euteronomist, and (P)riestly, respectively. Leviticus was considered to be the work of the post-exilic Priestly author.

[8] Baruch Levine applies this felicitous term to Hoffmann.

[9] 'Lower criticism' refers to the effort to establish the most accurate text of the Bible. The principal tools of lower criticism are philological analysis, and careful comparison of the standard Hebrew text (the Masoretic Text) with other texts, such as the Qumran Scrolls and the ancient Greek translation known as the Septuagint.

as a scholar of Bible and Rabbinics while teaching in a rabbinical seminary and serving as a communal rabbi in Berlin.

Second, the development of the progressive streams in Judaism encouraged the retrenchment of traditional Jewish scholars in an anti-critical position. Tentative movement in the direction of a more critical view in the late eighteenth and early nineteenth centuries tended to be reversed later as a result of Orthodox antagonism towards Reform. The two editions of Jacob Zevi Meklenburg's great commentary, *Ha-ketav ve-ha-qabbala* ('Scripture and Tradition', 1839 and 1852 respectively) offer a case in point. As Breuer has demonstrated, in the later edition, because of his 'apparently growing concern for the integrity of rabbinic traditions', Meklenburg 'was propelled towards a more articulate and programmatic position, one that affirmed as a matter of Orthodox creed the Sinaitic origin of the Oral Law' (Breuer 1995: 287).

By the turn of the twentieth century the apologetic tendencies that are so well exemplified by Hoffmann's Leviticus were a given of Orthodox scholarship. The resultant hermeneutic embodied five characteristics that may be termed 'anti-critical': (1) the entire Torah was given at Sinai; (2) the Torah was divinely authored and dictated to Moses; (3) the biblical text has been transmitted accurately; (4) the rabbinic interpretation of the laws is correct; (5) only traditional Jewish sources are required for the proper understanding of Scripture.[10]

A third factor that kept Jewish studies apart from Biblical studies in the nineteenth century was that even progressive Jewish scholars who advocated the 'Scientific Study of Judaism' (*Wissenschaft des Judentums*) tended to eschew biblical criticism (see Soloweitschik and Rubascheff 1925: 122–43; Levine 1992: 15–32). The few isolated instances of Jewish critical scholarship dealt mainly with the later biblical books, thus avoiding the problems of Pentateuchal criticism. In some cases they provided striking anticipations of subsequent developments in biblical scholarship, and lead one to wonder what would have happened had serious interaction been possible between Jewish and Christian scholars, or between the progressives and traditionalists within the Jewish scholarly community.

The first chapter of Leopold Zunz's epoch-making work *Die Gottesdienstlichen Vorträge der Juden historisch entwicklet* ('The Religious Discourse of the Jews Historically Explained', 1832) provides a case in point. Zunz takes up the question of the authorship and dating of the Books of Chronicles, and concludes that Chronicles represents a reworking of earlier biblical historiography that reflects the concerns of the Second Temple period, specifically the third century BCE. In the course of the discussion, he also argues that the composition of the Book of Psalms

---

[10] See Levy (1996: 39–80; 1992: 159–204). I should add that one of my own teachers, Sid (Shnayer) Z. Leiman (now at Brooklyn College and Yeshiva University), is an Orthodox Jew who is thoroughly conversant with biblical criticism. See Leiman (1996: 181–7).

(traditionally assigned to King David) was contemporary with that of Chronicles, and that it included psalms of the exilic and post-exilic periods along with earlier material.

Zunz's views on these matters were compatible with those held by the biblical critics of his time, but in his subsequent work he confined himself to the study of post-biblical Jewish literature almost exclusively. He seemed to believe that his Christian contemporaries were doing adequate critical work on the Bible, so he focused his attention on corpora that had not yet received critical attention. Only near the end of his life, when he published a remarkable series of brief critical studies of several biblical books, did it become clear that Zunz had kept up with biblical criticism all along.

Abraham Geiger, perhaps the greatest of the liberal Jewish scholars after Zunz, offered an even more radical programme for biblical study in his *Urschrift und Übersetzungen der Bibel in ihrer Abhängigkeit von der inneren Entwicklung des Judenthums* ('The Original Text and Translations of the Bible in Relation to the Internal Development of Judaism', 1857). Building on Zunz's work, Geiger attempted to show how the growth and redaction of biblical traditions reflected later authors' ideologically driven reworking of earlier material. Since the authors of the Second Temple period were priests, their work naturally exhibited a pro-priestly, pro-Temple orientation.

Geiger argued that the processes that these authors used to transform their sources were exegetical in character, and could be compared with similar processes that were evident both in the ancient translations of the Bible and in rabbinic interpretation. 'In the days before the final redaction of the Bible,' he wrote, 'that which in later eras was accomplished by exegesis was achieved by means of textual revision' (Wiener 1963: 261). This aspect of Geiger's work anticipated a major development in biblical scholarship that took place more than a century after the publication of *Urschrift*, which I will discuss below. In its own day, however, despite the approbation that it received from both Jewish and Christian scholars, it spawned no successors.

When we turn from the world that produced Hoffmann's Leviticus to the intellectual environment of Milgrom's commentary, we may discern a few similarities but even more pronounced differences. Milgrom received his college education at a public university, but earned both rabbinical ordination and all of his graduate degrees at the Jewish Theological Seminary in New York City (see Hayes' article about Milgrom in Hayes 1999: ii. 157–8; also Sperling 1992: 103–4). Before taking up a full-time academic career, he served for many years as a congregational rabbi while also teaching at a local university. In that dual capacity, he began his scholarly research. He has said, in fact, that what prompted him to devote himself to the study of Leviticus was the difficulty of preaching on that most recondite book of the Torah! When it proved impossible for Milgrom to keep up both his academic and rabbinical work,[11] he secured a professorship at the University of California. At the time (1965, when he was already 42 years old), he was one of a tiny number of Jewish scholars teaching Bible in North American secular universities—a situation that would not change until the late 1970s.

If Hoffmann's Leviticus is a high-water mark of conservative, anti-critical Jewish biblical scholarship at the turn of the twentieth century, Milgrom's commentary epitomizes the eclectic and accommodating mood at the dawn of the twenty-first. Aside from a profound devotion to his subject-matter, undoubtedly motivated by personal religious concerns as well as academic interests, Milgrom's work shares two features with Hoffmann's. First, the bedrock of both commentaries is sound Hebrew philology. Intimate familiarity with the Hebrew language and great reluctance to alter the received text have been distinguishing traits of most Jewish biblical commentators, who carry on the legacy of the great medieval exegetes in that respect.[12]

Second, Milgrom cites traditional Jewish commentary exhaustively, although he does not share Hoffmann's apologetic reasons for doing so. Milgrom's position, rather, is that rabbinic and medieval interpretations often are philologically sound. The rabbinic tradition, moreover, is chronologically and ideologically continuous with the biblical material, and for that reason it may contain accurate understandings and elaborations of the biblical text. This view is a far cry from the dogmatic acceptance of the authority of the rabbinic interpretation, but it is equally remote from the earlier critical insistence on a radical break between Israelite (i.e. biblical) religion and post-biblical Judaism, and it rejects the notion that traditional interpretation can be dismissed out of hand because it is 'non-critical' or 'pre-modern'.

In addition to bringing both philological analysis and traditional exegesis to bear on the text, Milgrom's commentary draws on resources that were unavailable to Hoffmann, including artifactual and textual evidence yielded by archaeological excavations, and social-scientific models for understanding the religious phenomena described in Leviticus. The archaeological evidence was just beginning to make an impact on biblical scholarship in Hoffmann's time, although it had not yet had a discernible effect on Jewish scholarship. The same may be said for the social-scientific approach: Hoffmann's works evinces no sympathy for the groundbreaking work in comparative religion that was appearing during his lifetime. In

---

[11] Milgrom has commented that his role-model was Robert Gordis, his teacher at the Jewish Theological Seminary. Gordis 'successfully divided his time among communal concerns, seminary teaching, and pulpit' (Sperling 1999: i. 456).

[12] On this trait of Jewish biblical scholarship, see Greenberg (1995: 3–8). An exception to the rule was H. L. Ginsberg of the Jewish Theological Seminary, unquestionably one of the greatest Hebrew philologists of the twentieth century, but notorious for freely emending the biblical text. It used to be said in jest that Ginsberg's many emendations in the Book of Isaiah were justified by the fact that his Hebrew was better than Isaiah's.

the century that has passed since that time, of course, archaeological discoveries and social-scientific research have contributed immeasurably to Biblical studies.

Finally, Milgrom embraces the higher-critical approach to Leviticus, taking up precisely those questions about authorship, dating, and social location that were anathema to Hoffmann. He develops his critical model on the basis of his meticulous analysis, and in dialogue with the relevant modern scholarship.[13] In so doing, Milgrom also stands the older critical approach on its head. Instead of 'proving' that Leviticus represents a late, decadent offshoot of biblical religion, Milgrom shows that the book offers a coherent and sophisticated world-view as well as profound theological insight. The book's 'Jewishness', therefore, is not a deficiency, but the source of its strength.

Just as Hoffmann represented the culmination of several cultural and intellectual developments of the century prior to his writing, the same may be said of Milgrom. In the remainder of this essay I will concentrate on three twentieth-century developments that have drawn Biblical studies and Jewish studies together in ways undreamt of in Hoffmann's time.

JEWS IN THE MAINSTREAM

Hoffmann's era was characterized by the exclusion of Jewish scholars from the mainstream of academic Biblical studies. Milgrom's, on the other hand, witnessed the wholesale entry of Jewish scholars into the guild, including the appointment of Jews to the biblical faculties of several Protestant seminaries.[14] One factor contributing to the growth of academic Jewish biblical scholarship was the rapid growth of the university system itself, with an emphasis on the diversification of both faculty and student bodies to include previously under-represented groups (Sperling 1992: 115–17). This expansion had a profound effect on Biblical studies.

In 1976 the Society of Biblical Literature (the SBL) held its annual meeting at Stouffer's Riverfront Towers in St Louis, Missouri. The programme was divided among thirty-four sections, seminars, and groups. All of the chairs and co-chairs of those sections, seminars, and groups were male, as were all of the officers of the Society. Two Jewish men served on the Society's executive council.

---

[13] It is worth noting that Milgrom hardly takes up critical issues at all in his commentary on the Book of Numbers (1990). The Numbers commentary is part of a Torah commentary directed at a popular Jewish audience; the Leviticus commentary is in the Anchor Bible series, which is intended for both scholars and educated laity of all religious persuasions.

[14] This phenomenon is yet to be documented in full, although the Jewish media have taken note of it (see Cattan 2002). Among biblical scholars, one thinks of Alan Cooper at Union Theological Seminary,

Jewish scholars chaired five of the sections, but the picture becomes murkier when we look at the details. Two of the Jewish chairs represented affiliated societies, the International Organization for Masoretic Studies and the National Association of Professors of Hebrew. Another two chaired sections in areas that clearly were on the periphery of Biblical studies—'Early Rabbinic Studies' and 'Art and the Bible'. The remaining Jewish chair was Milgrom, who led the section called 'Worship and Cult in Ancient Israel'. That section was a well-known ghetto for Jewish presenters, the rubric being of scant interest to most non-Jewish biblical scholars at that time. In 1976, in fact, the presenters included H. L. Ginsberg, Baruch Levine, Jack Sasson, and Ziony Zevit, along with Milgrom himself. Milgrom (University of California, now emeritus), Levine (New York University, now emeritus), and Sasson (University of North Carolina, now at Vanderbilt Divinity School) belonged to the tiny coterie of Jewish biblical scholars then holding appointments in Biblical studies in North American secular universities.[15]

By 1999 the situation had changed dramatically: the 1999 programme lists ninety-five sections, groups, seminars, and consultations—almost three times as many as there were in 1976 (the programme book itself grew from 126 pages to 378). Of those ninety-five programme units, thirty-four were chaired or co-chaired by women, an increase from 0 per cent in 1976 to about 36 per cent in 1999. The proliferation of new programme units also manifested the tremendous diversification of the field. The Jewish presence was diffused throughout the programme, not confined to a few special-interest groups. Some Jews were active in relatively *outré* sections, but a Jewish woman co-chaired the Matthew group, which is about as mainstream as one can get, while a non-Jewish woman co-chaired the section dealing with 'Early Rabbinic Judaism'—an interesting turn of events.

In 1976 anyone looking over the list of sections (the largest programme units) could distinguish the centre of Biblical studies—the hard core—from the mushy stuff around the edges. Firmly ensconced at the centre were 'Form Criticism', 'Old Testament Theology', 'Israelite History', and 'Hebrew Scriptures and Cognate Literatures'. At the periphery were the most recent additions to the list of sections, including 'Art and the Bible', 'The Bible and the Humanities', and 'Biblical Criticism

Michael Fishbane and Tikva Frymer-Kensky at the University of Chicago Divinity School, Jon Levenson at Harvard Divinity School, Jack Sasson at Vanderbilt Divinity School, and Marvin Sweeney at Claremont Divinity School.

[15] There were only three Jewish senior professors teaching Bible in secular universities in 1976 (the year I earned my doctorate): Levine, Milgrom, and Nahum Sarna at Brandeis University (now emeritus). There also were a number of Jewish professors involved in Biblical studies whose appointments and research interests were primarily in the area of ancient Near Eastern languages and cultures. These included two of my teachers at Columbia University, David Marcus (now at the Jewish Theological Seminary) and the late Moshe Held, and two of my teachers at Yale University, William W. Hallo and the late J. J. Finkelstein. Sperling notes that most of the Jewish biblical scholars in North America who belonged to what he terms the 'second wave' (that is, those who completed their doctorates in the years 1942–65) were, in fact, specialists in ancient Near Eastern studies (1992: 89–113).

and Literary Criticism'. Somewhere between the centre and the periphery, one could locate Milgrom's section on 'Worship and Cult', among others.

In 1999 one would be hard pressed to distinguish the centre of Biblical studies from the periphery on the basis of the conference programme. The list of sections now was arranged in alphabetical rather than chronological order, so that there was no way of knowing which sub-fields were of long standing and which were more recent additions. Equal time was given to wildly divergent fields of interest—everything from 'Bible in Africa, Asia, Latin America, and the Caribbean' to 'Biblical Lexicography'. Another striking change was that the term 'Old Testament' appeared to have been banished from the programme, probably in deference to Jewish sensibilities. ('New Testament' was alive and well, however.)

It seems clear that the decentring and diversification of Biblical studies during the past quarter-century are directly related to the entry of Jews and women (and, more recently, other visible minorities) into the guild. The fact is that the field is irrevocably changed from what it was. One can express the situation diagrammatically in two different ways: either the centre has become capacious enough to accommodate people and subject-matter that once were excluded or, perhaps, there no longer is a centre at all. There is a direct correlation between diversity and decentring: the more diverse the practitioners are in a given field, the more the alleged core of the field is likely to be problematized and devalued. The assault from the margins, furthermore, is most likely to succeed when it is truly interdisciplinary, as has been the case with the integration of Biblical studies with Jewish studies.

A paradoxical aspect of the present state of affairs is that, while during the last quarter of the twentieth century Jews had notable success in breaking down the barriers of institutionalized Biblical studies, Jewish biblicists did not made comparable headway within organized Jewish studies. Although Jewish studies programmes were on the rise, few of them appointed biblical scholars to their faculties. The reasoning was reminiscent of Zunz's a century-and-a-half earlier: the Bible was covered well enough already by faculty in divinity schools and Religious studies departments, so there was no need to expend Jewish studies resources on it. More than a few Jewish biblicists were disappointed by job advertisements that sought applicants in practically any area of Judaica, as long as it was *post*-biblical.

By 1998 the programme of the Association for Jewish Studies—the largest and most important scholarly society for Jewish studies in North America—had expanded to eighty-four sessions, but only two were devoted to Bible. As one scholar who has been prominent in the Association since its founding wryly commented, 'as long as there are plenty of sessions on the use of the Bible as subtext, pretext, and intertext, I suppose it is safe to ignore the text'. In terms of the *institutional* relationship between Biblical studies and Jewish studies, then, not much has changed since the 1970s, when the application of a Jewish doctoral candidate in Bible for a fellowship in Jewish studies was turned down because Bible did not fall within the purview of Jewish studies. (That particular situation, fortunately, *has* changed.) The *intellectual* relationship between the two areas, however, is another matter, and to that we now turn.

BIBLICAL VERSUS POST-BIBLICAL

One of the most trenchant assaults against older forms of biblical criticism in recent years has been the blurring of distinctions between the biblical and post-biblical periods, or, to put it another way, between Israelite religion and Judaism. It is now generally recognized that there is a linguistic continuum between the Bible and post-biblical rabbinic literature: Late Biblical Hebrew is a transitional dialect between Biblical and Rabbinic Hebrew,[16] and the picture of continuity and organic development is confirmed by the evidence of the Qumran Scrolls as well. That linguistic continuity is complemented by cultural continuity. There is no longer a simple way of distinguishing between what is 'Israelite' and what is 'Jewish'. A consideration of recent scholarship on the Book of Psalms provides a case in point.[17]

One of the axioms of earlier critical scholarship was that the Davidic attribution of the psalms was untenable, but there were many irreconcilable theories concerning the origin and dating of the psalms, and their ultimate compilation into the present collection of 150. Most critical scholars saw the majority of the psalms as post-exilic, which created a logical dilemma for them. Late biblical religion (the priestly religion of Leviticus) was supposed to have been entirely legalistic and spiritually bankrupt. How, then, could it have produced (or even compiled) such noble expressions of piety as the psalms? That question elicited some remarkably absurd answers, such as this one, published in 1907: '[The psalms] mark the reaction of the pious feeling characteristic of old Israel against Judaism, affording a clear proof that the religious genius of Israel was not killed by Ezra and Pharisaism, and thus form in a quite unique sense and degree the building link between the Old and New Testaments' (Cornill 1907: 399). It is amazing that anyone can have taken such nonsense seriously, but in fact the Book of Psalms *is* a 'building link'—not primarily between the Old and New Testaments, however, but between Israelite religion and *Judaism*.

The individual psalms are diverse compositions from diverse times and places, spanning at least five or six centuries, and perhaps longer than that. But the Book of

---

[16] The pioneering work of Avi Hurvitz deserves special mention, especially his 1972 book.

[17] The following comments are based on my own work in progress on the Book of Psalms. On the Qumran psalters, see the definitive study by Flint (1997).

Psalms in its present form, in contrast to many of the psalms that it comprises, is a product of the Hellenistic period at the earliest, as evidenced by the psalters found among the Qumran Scrolls. Those collections show that the contents and order of the Book of Psalms—especially Psalms 90–150—were still in flux between c.150 BCE and 70 CE.

The standard scholarly view concerning the individual psalms is that originally they were used to accompany rituals that took place in Israelite and Judean temples, especially the Temple in Jerusalem. The Book of Psalms, on the other hand, seems to presuppose a Jewish environment in which the psalms were disused as Temple liturgies. Instead of being discarded, the psalms survived as texts for contemplation and study, adaptable for use in all sorts of private and public worship settings. During the same period in which the Book of Psalms was stabilized, the first 'post-biblical' interpretations of psalms were being authored, including the Qumran exegetical texts known as *pesharim*, as well as the interpretations that are implicit in the citations of psalms in Christian Scripture.

Some readers might find it disorienting to learn that 'post-biblical' literature was being written while biblical books were still being composed, but that appears to have been precisely the case. A startling implication of that situation is that careful study of the earliest interpretations of psalms most likely provides a key to the motives behind the final redaction of the Book of Psalms itself. If all of the earliest interpretations are eschatological, then it seems reasonable to assume that the Book of Psalms owes its present shape to eschatological concerns.[18]

The larger point is that there is seamless continuity between the creation of the individual psalms, the compilation of the Book of Psalms, and the beginning of psalms interpretation. In order for scholars to treat the biblical book competently in its historical dimension, they must employ not only the standard methodological tools of biblical scholarship, but must also be competent to work with the Qumran texts, and with early Jewish and Christian psalms interpretation. The biblical and post-biblical corpora cannot be isolated from one another.

The case of Psalms is not unique. Milgrom's Leviticus commentary demonstrates that rabbinic literature preserves data that facilitate an understanding of the Bible's sometimes elliptical and recondite cultic formulations.[19] A similar claim may be made for biblical civil law as well: in a learned study, Samuel Greengus has explored legislation that may be found in ancient Babylonian law and in the Mishnah, but is for some reason absent from the Bible.[20] Once again, establishing

---

[18] See Wacholder (1988: 23–72). With due caution, I would apply many of Wacholder's observations about this Qumran Psalms Scroll to the Book of Psalms itself.

[19] In a similar vein, Baruch Levine's doctoral dissertation showed that the Mishnah preserved elements of second-millennium BCE Canaanite literature that are not found in the Bible (1962).

[20] Greengus (1991: 149–71). Greengus, who is a Professor at Hebrew Union College in Cincinnati, Ohio, is primarily a scholar of the ancient Near East, but prior to embarking on his scholarly career he spent much of his youth and young adulthood learning in a yeshiva.

arbitrary dividing-lines between disciplines would serve only to impede the growth of knowledge.

Recognition of the continuity between biblical and rabbinic literature has led to another important development in Biblical Studies—one that was adumbrated by Geiger in his *Urschrift*. That is the notion that the processes that are evident in the rabbinic interpretation of Scripture may also have been formative of Scripture itself. Geiger's work lay fallow for a century until a professor at Hebrew Union College, Samuel Sandmel, put it back on the scholarly agenda in an article that he provocatively titled 'The Haggada Within Scripture' (Sandmel 1961: 105–22). Sandmel was perfectly suited to the task that he set himself, a successor to Geiger as one of the most prominent scholars of Reform Judaism, and an expert in rabbinic and early Christian literature as well as Bible.

Without actually mentioning Geiger by name, Sandmel advocated Geiger's approach as an alternative to the Documentary Hypothesis. With his typical wry wit, he wrote: 'This essay may seem to some an effort to drive still another nail into the coffin of the Graf Wellhausen hypothesis, but that would be an indirect result rather than a deliberate purpose' (Sandmel 1961: 105). Instead of seeing the growth of Scripture as the result of the compilation and redaction of written sources, Sandmel argued for a continuous organic process of revision by reinterpretation—Scripture interpreting Scripture, in effect, or inner-biblical exegesis, as it came to be called (Zakovitch 1992). Midrash-style hermeneutics, in this view, do not require a closed and fixed scriptural canon, but are substantially responsible for generating that canon in the first place.

Sandmel's work inspired a flood of scholarship, much of it produced by Jewish scholars who were comfortable with the Bible's contiguity with rabbinic literature, and pleased to work with a critical theory untainted by the anti-Judaism of the standard Documentary Hypothesis. The culmination of the trend inaugurated by Sandmel's work was the extraordinary book by Michael Fishbane, *Biblical Interpretation in Ancient Israel* (Fishbane 1985), a comprehensive and methodical presentation of the varieties of proto-rabbinic exegesis that may be found within the Bible. Fishbane, in turn, inspired a number of other important works, further cultivation of this common ground of Biblical and Jewish studies. Two excellent examples started out as dissertations that Fishbane supervised (although Fishbane himself has worked almost exclusively in the areas of midrash and mystical literature in recent years). In one, Bernard Levinson probes the hermeneutics of the author of Deuteronomy as a reviser of the Covenant Code in Exodus (Levinson 1997); in the other, Benjamin Sommer offers a highly nuanced account of the way the author of Isaiah 40–66 reworks earlier biblical material (Sommer 1998).

PRE-CRITICAL, CRITICAL, AND POST-CRITICAL

The integration of Biblical studies and Jewish studies depends on overcoming the bifurcation of biblical and post-biblical literature. There is also another dichotomy that must be addressed, namely that of pre-critical versus critical biblical scholarship. Until recently, the training of biblical scholars entailed the cultivation of a specific set of philological and methodological skills, usually the biblical languages (Biblical Hebrew,[21] Aramaic, and Greek), other ancient Near Eastern languages (especially Akkadian and Ugaritic, as well as Comparative Semitics), a range of lower- and higher-critical methods (source criticism, form criticism, etc.), and some ancillary disciplines, especially archaeology.

Knowledge of the history of biblical interpretation was presumed as well, but that meant knowledge of the history of *critical* interpretation, usually from Spinoza to the present, but often considerably foreshortened. In this context, traditional Jewish and Christian interpretation was evaluated on a scale that ran from quaint to worthless, when it was not simply ignored altogether. Rashi or Ibn Ezra might be cited on some point of philology, but it was only because their insights happened to jibe with the findings of modern scholars.

In North America, the Protestant scholar Brevard Childs's commentary on the Book of Exodus, which was published in 1974, signalled the beginning of a broad change in attitude. In his Preface, Childs (now Professor Emeritus at the Yale Divinity School) wrote that while he was preparing his commentary, 'I discovered that Calvin and Drusius, Rashi and Ibn Ezra, belong among the giants. I have tried to show why these great expositors—the term "pre-critical" is both naive and arrogant—need to be heard in concert with Wellhausen and Gunkel' (Childs 1974: p. x). True to his word, Childs incorporated traditional exegesis into his commentary in a way that emphasized its continuing value and relevance for modern biblical scholarship.

I was a student of Childs at Yale in the early 1970s, and was both impressed and influenced by him. In my own subsequent work, I suggested that the *full* history of interpretation served as an indispensable bridge between the modern reader and the ancient text, and that modern commentators ought to adopt three hermeneutical principles of traditional interpretation: 'the assumption that the text is meaningful;

---

[21]   That is, vocalized Biblical Hebrew, as distinct from the unvocalized post-biblical dialects. Very few doctoral programmes outside Israel other than the ones based in Jewish seminaries require students in Bible to have knowledge of post-biblical Hebrew. The standard required research languages remain English, French, and German, despite the general recognition that Israel is a major centre of biblical scholarship. Many doctoral programmes now encourage students to study in Israel, but that is no guarantee that they will learn Hebrew, since the Israeli universities offer English-language programmes that cater to foreign students.

the demand that interpretation be answerable to the text; and the principle that all interpretations merely realize the text's possibilities: "new" interpretations, if they adhere to the first two principles, then add to the repository of ideas that is the history of interpretation.'[22]

Childs's deference towards traditional interpretation was part of a larger goal to validate the activity of communities of faith as preservers and authentic interpreters of Scripture. From the Jewish side, the most successful attempt to realize that aim has been the work of James Kugel. In two remarkably learned books (actually popular and scholarly versions of the same book), Kugel has attempted to show how the Bible was read and understood in the formative period of Jewish and Christian biblical interpretation at the turn of the Common Era (Kugel 1997 and 1998). While in his earlier work Kugel occasionally showed an explicit anti-critical tendency, here he permits the ancient interpreters to speak for themselves, allowing his readers to draw their own conclusions about where interpretative merit lies.

Kugel's approach, unlike Childs's, is not integrative: he does not attempt to juxtapose traditional interpretation with modern critical commentary. Some of his students, however, have been moving in the direction of such a synthesis. Steven Weitzman, for example, produced an outstanding dissertation on the placement of poems within biblical narrative (Weitzman 1997b); in subsequent work, Weitzman has widened his scope to take in issues in 'rewritten Bible', as well as exegetical elements in late biblical and post-biblical texts (see e.g. Weitzman 1994, 1996, 1997a).

The most thoroughgoing attempt at integration, and the one that has had the greatest influence on Biblical studies, has taken place in the Israeli academy, exemplified by the Department of Bible of the Hebrew University of Jerusalem. The present-day Bible faculty in Jerusalem is the heir to a grand tradition of Biblical studies going back to the founding of the university. The development that concerns us here, however, occurred subsequent to the arrival of Moshe Greenberg at the Hebrew University in 1970 (he retired in 1996.) (On Greenberg, see Tigay's article in Hayes 1999: i. 464–5; Sperling 1992: 92–4; Cogan, Eichler, and Tigay 1997: pp. ix–xxi.)

Greenberg, who established himself at the University of Pennsylvania as one of the leading biblical scholars of his generation, had made a systematic effort to bring both ancient Near Eastern and Jewish sources to bear on the Bible. He naturally sought to achieve a similar synthesis in the work of his department. The controversial issue was: what is the proper location of traditional Jewish interpretation (*parshanut*) in the university? While some argued that *parshanut* was properly a part of Jewish intellectual history, and therefore ought to be under the auspices of the department of Jewish Thought, Greenberg argued successfully that *parshanut* belonged under the aegis of Bible (*miqra*).

---

[22] Cooper (1987: 72). For applications of the methods that I advocate, see e.g. Cooper 1988: 1–22; 1990: 26–44 (text); 188–198 (notes).

The result of Greenberg's success was that the Hebrew University was able to offer an integrated doctoral programme in Bible that placed *parshanut* on a par with philological-critical and historical-critical studies as an essential component of Biblical studies. During the past three decades the department has produced a roster of scholars of extraordinary breadth and versatility, for whom the boundary between Biblical and Jewish studies has been all but obliterated.

A few examples will illustrate the point: Greenberg's first Hebrew University doctoral student, the late Sarah Kamin, wrote her dissertation on Rashi's understanding of literal interpretation (Kamin 1986), but she was a thoroughly trained critical biblical scholar as well; Sara Japhet's dissertation was on the Book of Chronicles,[23] but she has since produced critical editions of medieval commentaries (most recently Japhet 2000); Yair Zakovitch is a prolific master of the literary-critical study of biblical literature (e.g. Zakovitch 1982, 1991), but he also has collaborated with a specialist in midrash to produce a fine series of studies in the history of Jewish biblical interpretation;[24] two outstanding practitioners of latter-day source criticism,[25] Israel Knohl[26] and Baruch Schwartz,[27] also have expertise in Rabbinics.[28]

The Hebrew University has long been a popular destination for foreign scholars—Jews and Christians alike—who wish to gain mastery of Hebrew, and to benefit from the outstanding faculty in Bible, Semitics, Archaeology, and all areas of

[23] Japhet (1989). The Hebrew original of this work was published in 1977, and was based on a dissertation directed by I. L. Seeligmann.

[24] For example, Zakovitch and Shinan (1992). This volume is one of a series of studies of narratives in Genesis.

[25] Israeli source criticism tends to be anchored not so much in the Graf–Wellhausen model as in the dissident approach advocated by Yehezkel Kaufmann, who taught at the Hebrew University from 1949 until his death in 1963 (see Kaufmann 1960). Greenberg's translation and abridgment of Kaufmann's prolix and polemical Hebrew original was a tremendous service to scholarship, making Kaufmann's work accessible to the non-Hebrew-speaking scholarly community. Unfortunately, as J. H. Hayes comments, 'knowledge and use of his work have been rare among Christian commentators' (see Hayes 1999: ii. 16–17).

[26] Knohl (1995). The book is an English translation of a work published in Hebrew in 1992, which was, in turn, based on Knohl's doctoral dissertation (1988), supervised by Moshe Greenberg.

[27] Schwartz (1999). This work evolved out of Schwartz's doctoral dissertation (1987), which was directed by the late Meir Weiss. Weiss favoured a New-Critical approach to the study of biblical literature, which he called 'Total-Interpretation', and he staunchly opposed source-critical analysis. Schwartz adroitly combines Weiss's close reading with a source-critical approach that he learned from another eminent Hebrew University professor, Menahem Haran.

[28] I do not wish to suggest that this breadth of competence is unique to the graduates of the Hebrew University, only that it is systemic there. North American scholars who embody such breadth usually had a combination of seminary and university training, and/or spent considerable time studying in Israel. Some outstanding examples are Adele Berlin (University of Maryland), Marc Brettler (Brandeis University), Stephen A. Kaufman (Hebrew Union College, Cincinnati), Michael V. Fox (University of Wisconsin). Richard Elliott Friedman (University of California at San Diego), Tikva Frymer-Kensky (University of Chicago Divinity School), Edward L. Greenstein (formerly of Jewish Theological Seminary, now at Tel Aviv University), David Sperling (Hebrew Union College, New York), and Jeffrey H. Tigay (University of Pennsylvania).

Judaica. Observing the integration of Biblical and Jewish studies that has been achieved there, some have tried to achieve similar integration on a smaller scale in their own institutions.

A case in point is the Hebrew Union College (HUC) School of Graduate Studies in Cincinnati, Ohio. Until the late 1980s, the doctoral programme in Bible at HUC was exclusively philological-critical in character, with strong emphases on Semitic languages and text criticism. At that time several faculty members with expertise in Judaeo-Hellenistic and Patristic literature, midrash, and *parshanut* joined their colleagues in biblical and ancient Near Eastern studies to create a new doctoral track in Bible, which they dubbed 'History of Biblical Interpretation'. This programme was formally approved by HUC in 1989, and it has since become one of the institution's biggest attractions for prospective graduate students.

HUC's literature describes the course of study as 'an integrated Ph.D. program in the history of biblical interpretation as a sub-discipline of biblical studies', effecting a shift of a prior programmatic focus 'on the so-called "lower criticism" to broader historical, philological, exegetical, and hermeneutical aspects of the history of interpretation (including comparative Jewish and Christian exegesis)'. Students who enroll in the programme are expected to be proficient in Hebrew (biblical and rabbinic), Aramaic (Targumic and Syriac), and Greek, and they must have reading knowledge of Israeli Hebrew, French, and German (as well as other ancient and modern languages as needed).

The programme demands 'general competence in the standard philological and critical disciplines of biblical scholarship', and specifies various course requirements, including seminars on the History of Interpretation, at least four semesters of Targum, midrash, and *parshanut*, surveys of early Christian and Qumran literature, ancient history, and a range of Hebrew and Greek text courses. Students are expected to pass comprehensive examinations in three areas: '(1) Ancient Languages (normally, Hebrew, Greek, and Aramaic); (2) Bible (on the philological and critical disciplines of biblical scholarship); (3) Central Issues in the History of Interpretation.' Finally, dissertation topics generally treat 'historical, philological, exegetical, and hermeneutical issues that arise in the texts of the Greco-Roman period (Alexander to the Islamic Conquest)', especially 'in the area of comparative Jewish and Christian interpretation'.

Many other institutions with faculty strength in both Biblical studies and Jewish studies are developing this sort of programme—not limited to Jewish institutions. It is easy to see how, in contrast to 'traditional' graduate programmes in Bible, it de-emphasizes such subjects as Semitics and archaeology in favour of areas that are usually associated with Jewish studies, such as midrash and *parshanut*. The point that I wish to stress is that the programme demands that students of History of Interpretation be anchored in the 'philological and critical disciplines of biblical scholarship'. Although the HUC programme was designed in response to the burgeoning interest in traditional interpretation, it still seeks to centre that interest within Biblical studies. It unabashedly asserts that History of Interpretation is not a byway of Biblical studies, but one of its highways.

This last notion has found both powerful expression and theoretical justification in the concept of post-critical interpretation which was developed by Peter Ochs in the introduction to a collection of essays that he edited in 1993 (Ochs 1993). Ochs defines what he terms 'postcritical scriptural interpretation' as 'an emergent tendency among Jewish and Christian text scholars and theologians to give rabbinic and ecclesial traditions of interpretation both the benefit of the doubt and the benefit of doubt' (ibid. 3). This stance is *post*-critical, and not merely *anti*-critical, because it seeks an accommodation between traditional hermeneutics and modernist criticism: dimensions of meaning revealed by the former may be 'clarified', as Ochs puts it, by the latter. It is not obvious in this context what such clarification entails, but at least it signals the post-critical scholar's intention to be inclusive, in contrast to the critical scholar's inclination to dismiss traditional interpretation as 'pre-critical' or 'non-critical'.

From a pragmatic standpoint, post-critical interpreters eschew the historicist agenda that originated with Spinoza and dominated critical biblical scholarship until about thirty years ago. Instead of locating the meaning of the text in external referents, such as historical events or authorial intention, they locate it 'within the text' and 'in the relation between the text and its community of interpreters' (ibid. 8). Cut loose from its historicist moorings, the concept of the 'literal meaning' of the text is a lot harder to pin down than it used to be. One no longer can think of 'meaning' as an artefact that may be recovered from the text the way a potsherd is excavated from the ground. Literal meaning in its linguistic/grammatical sense (cf. Ibn Ezra and Rashbam) does provide a check on exegetical fancy, but the authentic meaning of the text, according to Ochs, 'is its meaning for the authoritative community of interpreters' (ibid. 9).

One of the most perspicacious and influential advocates of a post-critical approach to biblical interpretation is Jon Levenson, a Jewish scholar who holds a professorial chair at the Harvard Divinity School. In 1993 Levenson revised and drew together six previously published essays that stake out his position on the relationship between the traditional and historical-critical modes of biblical study (Levenson 1993). His goal, which is to offer a critique of biblical criticism from the standpoint of traditional hermeneutics, is encapsulated in the following two quotations:

[T]he results of the historical-critical study of the Hebrew Bible have rather generally been at odds with the underlying method. The *method* is historical and therefore privileges the period of composition at the expense of all later recontextualizations. The *results* have been skewed toward one of those recontextualizations, the Christian church, as Christian categories, preferences, and priorities have been restated and occasionally re-energized by historical-critical study. (Ibid. 96).

Historical criticism has long posed a major challenge to people with biblical commitments, and for good reason. What I hope to have shown is that the reverse is also the case: the Bible poses a major challenge to people with historical-critical commitments. (Ibid. 126).

Levenson advocates a method of interpretation that has 'operational' (as opposed to 'theological') affinities with traditional Jewish commentary. On the one hand, he rejects fundamentalism by acknowledging that the Bible was a product of historical processes. On the other hand, he would 'relativize' historical investigation, recognizing 'that the cost of restoring textual units to their *historical* context can only be some loss of their *literary* context'. The historical-critical enterprise, he argues, 'must be dialectically checked by a continual awareness of the need to put the text back together in a way that makes it available and in its entirety—not merely in the past and in the form of historically contextualized fragments' (ibid. 78–9).

At first glance, Levenson might appear to be advocating an emphasis on synchronic or holistic analysis at the expense of historical criticism, but that is not the case. Rather, in true post-critical fashion, he sees each of the two modes of interpretation offering checks on each other. Synchronic approaches, he writes, 'are restoring the Bible to Biblical studies'. On the other hand, what is 'emerging nowadays is a scene of rich methodological pluralism', in which more sophisticated forms of diachronic investigation are becoming the norm (Levenson 1990: 52). This attempt to strike a balance, to reconcile the apparently irreconcilable, strikes me as quintessentially Jewish, in the spirit of the famous rabbinic dictum, *eilu ve-eilu divrei elohim hayyim* ('Both the one and the other are the words of the living God').[29]

CONCLUSIONS

In the 'Concluding Extremely Unscientific Postscript' to his valuable history of Jewish biblical scholarship in North America, David Sperling remarks, 'the relocation of Jewish Bible study to the university and the simultaneous diminution of the role of the seminaries in the formative Bible training of Jewish scholars has increased the chances that future Jewish biblical scholarship will be no different than any other' (Sperling 1992: 206). That statement is true, in my view, but it is also one-sided, for it fails to reckon with the changes that Jewish scholars already have wrought within biblical scholarship. It may be fair to say that as Jewish biblical

[29] B. Eruvin 13b; B. Gittin 6b.

scholarship progresses (Orthodox scholarship excepted), it no longer will have to maintain its former distinctiveness because mainstream biblical scholarship will have a more Jewish character, or will at least be increasingly congenial to Jewish interests. The world of Biblical studies that was so alien to David Zevi Hoffmann a century ago has evolved to the point that it welcomes Jacob Milgrom with open arms, and prizes the contributions of the Israeli academy.

As I remarked before, the admission of previously marginalized groups to the guild, and the movement of their special interests from the periphery of Biblical studies to its increasingly capacious centre, have altered the field in dramatic fashion. From the Jewish point of view, the Society of Biblical Literature's renaming the object of study 'Hebrew Bible' instead of 'Old Testament' is more than cosmetic: it acknowledges the integrity of the Jewish Bible as scripture in its own right, not subsumed to the Christian canon. That acknowledgement, in turn, leads naturally to the recognition of continuity between Israelite religion and Judaism, earlier critical prejudices notwithstanding.

In this essay I have described two particular developments within Biblical studies that may be ascribed to the influence of Jewish biblical scholarship. Both of them, broadly speaking, entail the recognition that the Bible (that is, the Tanakh) is a Jewish book, and both therefore legitimate the study of the Bible in its Jewish contexts. This view of the Bible is both a point of entry for Jewish scholars into critical biblical scholarship, and also the potential meeting-ground for biblical scholars with their colleagues in Jewish studies. In the coming years I expect that interaction between specialists in those fields will yield important new insights into the formation of the Jewish Bible, and into the way the Bible, in turn, serves to shape Jewish mentalities and communities throughout the ages.

SUGGESTED READING

A splendid treatment of the Haskalah's encounter with biblical criticism is found in Breuer (1996). Carmy (1996) has a stimulating discussion of recent attempts by Orthodox scholars to come to grips with biblical criticism. Fishbane (1985) is a classic of biblical scholarship, demonstrating that interpretative processes characteristic of post-biblical literature may also be found within the Bible itself. An excellent introduction to source criticism is that by Friedman (1987). Greenberg (1995) is a superb anthology of scholarly essays. Greenberg (1984) is a wonderful collection, including scholarly articles, writings on Jewish education, and personal reflections. Hayes (1999) contains excellent short biographies of notable biblical scholars, and good surveys of major topics in biblical interpretation. Holtz (1984) is an outstanding popular introduction to the 'great books of the Jewish tradition'. I particularly recommend the following essays: Joel Rosenberg, 'Biblical Narrative' (31–81); Edward L. Greenstein, 'Biblical Law' (83–103); Murray H. Lichtenstein, 'Biblical Poetry' (105–27); Edward L. Greenstein, 'Medieval Bible Commentaries' (213–59). All of these essays have excellent bibliographies. The JPS Torah Commentary (1989–96) is an outstanding series of commentaries that synthesizes traditional learning and modern scholarship for a general Jewish audience. The commentaries on Genesis and Exodus are by Nahum Sarna; Leviticus is by Baruch Levine; Numbers is by Jacob Milgrom; and Deuteronomy is by Jeffrey Tigay. Kugel (1997 and 1998) explores the way the Bible was read and understood in the formative era of Judaism and Christianity. Levenson (1993) contains probing discussions of problems in historical criticism in relation to traditional approaches to interpretation. A valuable collection of essays by leading Jewish biblical scholars is found in Neusner (1987). A stimulating collection of essays on the relationship between traditional and critical modes of biblical interpretation may be found in Ochs (1993). Sarna (2000) is an excellent collection of the writings of a great and influential scholar and teacher. Soloweitschik and Rubascheff (1925) contains a fascinating account with a Jewish slant. Sperling (1992) is a comprehensive and well-written survey of the field both past and present.

BIBLIOGRAPHY

BREUER, E. 1995. 'Between Haskalah and Orthodoxy: The Writings of Rabbi Jacob Zvi Meklenburg.' *Hebrew Union College Annual* 66: 259–87.

——1996. *The Limits of Enlightenment: Jews, Germans, and the Eighteenth-Century.* Cambridge, Mass.

CARMY, S. ed. 1996. *Modern Scholarship in the Study of Torah: Contributions and Limitations.* Northvale, NJ.

CATTAN, N. 2002. 'When Jewish Studies Find a Niche at Christian Campuses.' *Forward*, 18 Jan., 2002. (online: http://www.forward.com/issues/2002/02.01.18/education3.html).

CHUMASH 1994. 2nd edn. (Stone Edition). Brooklyn, NY.

CHILDS, B. S. 1974. *The Book of Exodus: A Critical, Theological Commentary.* Philadelphia.

COGAN, M., EICHLER, B. L., and TIGAY, J. H. 1997. 'Moshe Greenberg: An Appreciation', In *Tehillah le-Moshe: Biblical and Judaic Studies in Honor of Moshe Greenberg.* pp. ix–xxi. Cogan *et al.* eds. Winona Lake, Ind.

COHEN, S. J. D. and GREENSTEIN, E. eds. 1990. *The State of Jewish Studies.* Detroit.

COOPER, A. 1987. 'On Reading the Bible Critically and Otherwise.' In Friedman and Williamson (1997): 61–79.

——1988. 'The Plain Sense of Exodus 23:5.' *Hebrew Union College Annual* 59: 1–22.

——1990. 'Imagining Prophecy.' In *Poetry and Prophecy: The Beginnings of a Literary Tradition.* 26–44. J. Kugel ed. Ithaca, NY.

CORNILL, C. H. 1907. *Introduction to the Canonical Books of the Old Testament.* London.

FISHBANE, M. 1985. *Biblical Interpretation in Ancient Israel.* Oxford.

FLINT, P. 1997. *The Dead Sea Psalms Scrolls and the Book of Psalms.* Studies on the Texts of the Desert of Judah 17. Leiden.

FRERICHS, E. S. 1987. 'Introduction: The Jewish School of Biblical Studies.' In Neusner (1987): 1–6.

FRIEDMAN, R. E. 1987. *Who Wrote the Bible?* New York.

—— and WILLIAMSON, H. G. M. eds. 1987. *The Future of Biblical Studies.* Semeia Studies. Atlanta, Ga.

GREENBERG, M. 1984. *Al ha-miqra ve-al ha-yahadut: qovets ketavim.* (English title: *On the Bible and Judaism: A Collection of Writings*) Tel Aviv.

GREENBERG, M. 1995a. *Studies in the Bible and Jewish Thought*. Philadelphia.

—— 1995b. 'Can Modern Critical Bible Scholarship Have a Jewish Character?' In Greenberg (1995a): 3–8.

GREENGUS, S. 1991. 'Filling Gaps: Laws Found in Babylonia and in the Mishna But Absent in the Hebrew Bible.' *Maarav* 7: 149–71.

GREENSTEIN, E. L. 1990. 'Biblical Studies in a State.' In *The State of Jewish Studies*. 23–46. S. J. D. Cohen and E. L. Greenstein eds. Detroit.

HAYES, J. H. ed. 1999. *Dictionary of Biblical Interpretation*. 2 vols. Nashville.

HERR, M. D. 1971. 'Hoffmann, David Zevi.' In *Encyclopedia Judaica*. viii. 808–10. Jerusalem.

HOFFMANN, D. Z. 1976. *Sefer va-yiqra* ('The Book of Leviticus.') Trans. Z. H. Shefer and A. Lieberman). 2nd edn. Jerusalem.

HOLTZ, B. W. ed. 1984. *Back to the Sources: Reading the Classic Jewish Texts*. New York.

HURVITZ, A. 1972. *Bein lashon le-lashon* (*The Transition Period in Biblical Hebrew.*) Jerusalem.

JAPHET, S. 1989. *The Ideology of the Book of Chronicles and Its Place in Biblical Thought*. Beiträge zur Erforschung des Alten Testaments und des antiken Judentums 9. Frankfurt am Main. (Hebrew original 1977).

——2000. *Peirush Rabbi Shemuel ben Meir (Rashbam) le-sefer Iyyov.* (*The Commentary of Rabbi Samuel ben Meir [Rashbam] On the Book of Job.*) Jerusalem.

KAMIN, S. 1986. *Rashi: peshto shel miqra u-midrasho shel miqra*. (*Rashi's Exegetical Categorization in Respect to the Distinction Between Peshat and Derash.*) Jerusalem.

KAUFMAN, Y. 1960. *The Religion of Israel From Its Beginnings to the Babylonian Exile*. Trans. and abridged by M. Greenberg. Chicago.

KNOHL, I. 1995. *The Sanctuary of Silence: The Priestly Torah and the Holiness School*. Minneapolis. (Hebrew original 1992).

KUGEL, J. 1997. *The Bible As It Was*. Cambridge, Mass.

—— 1998. *Traditions of the Bible: A Guide to the Bible As It Was at the Start of the Common Era*. Cambridge, Mass.

LEIMAN, Z. 1996. 'Response to Rabbi Breuer.' In Carmy (1996): 181–7.

LEVENSON, J. D. 1987. 'Why Jews Are Not Interested in Biblical Theology.' In *Judaic Perspectives on Ancient Israel*. 281–307. Neusner *et al.* eds. Philadelphia.

—— 1990. 'Response.' In Cohen and Greenstein (1990): 47–54.

—— 1993. *The Hebrew Bible, the Old Testament, and Historical Criticism: Jews and Christians in Biblical Studies*. Louisville, Ky.

LEVINE, B. A. 1962. 'Survivals of Ancient Canaanite in the Mishnah.' Doctoral thesis submitted to Brandeis University.

—— 1992 'The European Background.' In Sperling (1992): 15–32.

LEVINSON, B. M. 1997. *Deuteronomy and the Hermeneutics of Legal Innovation*. New York.

LEVY, B. B. 1983. 'Artscroll: An Overview.' In *Approaches to Modern Judaism*. Brown Judaic Studies 49: 111–62. Chico, Cal.

—— 1992. 'On the Periphery: North American Orthodox Judaism and Contemporary Scholarship.' In Sperling (1992): 159–204.

—— 1996. 'The State and Direction of Orthodox Bible Study.' In *Modern Scholarship in the Study of Torah: Contributions and Limitations*. 39–80. S. Carmy ed. Northvale, NJ.

LIEBER, D. L. *et al. Etz Hayim: Torah and Commentary* Philadelphia.

MEIROVICH, H. 1998. *A Vindication of Judaism: The Polemics of the Hertz Pentateuch*. New York.

MILGROM, J. 1990. *Numbers: The Traditional Hebrew Text With the New JPS Translation*. Philadelphia.

NEUSNER, J. *et al.* eds. 1987. *Judaic Perspectives on Ancient Israel*. Philadelphia.

OCHS, P. ed. 1993. *The Return to Scripture in Judaism and Christianity: Essays in Postcritical Scriptural Interpretation*. New York.

PLAUT, W. G. ed. 1981. *The Torah: A Modern Commentary*. New York.

RAPHAEL, M. L. ed. 1983. *Approaches to Modern Judaism*. Brown Judaic Studies 49. Chico, Cal.

SANDMEL, S. 1961. 'The Haggada Within Scripture.' *Journal of Biblical Literature* 80: 105–22.

SARNA, N. 2000. *Studies in Biblical Interpretation*. Philadelphia.

SCHWARTZ, B. 1999. *Torat ha-qedusha: iyyunim ba-huqqa ha-kohanit she-ba-tora*. (*The Holiness Legislation: Studies in the Priestly Code*.) Jerusalem.

SCHECHTER, S. 1959. *Seminary Addresses and Other Papers*. New York.

SOLOWEITSCHIK, M. and RUBASCHEFF, S. 1925. *Toledot biqoret ha-miqra* (*History of Biblical Criticism*.) Berlin.

SOMMER, B. D. 1998. *A Prophet Reads Scripture: Allusion in Isaiah 40–66*. Stanford.

SPERLING, S. D. ed. 1992. *Students of the Covenant: A History of Jewish Biblical Scholarship in North America*. Atlanta, Ga.

TIGAY, J. H. 1999. 'Greenberg, Moshe (1928–   ).' In Hayes (1999): i. 464–5.

WACHOLDER, B. Z. 1988. 'David's Eschatological Psalter: 11SALMS[a].' *Hebrew Union College Annual* 59: 23–72.

WIENER, M. 1962. *Abraham Geiger and Liberal Judaism: The Challenge of the Nineteenth Century*. Philadelphia.

WEITZMAN, S. 1994. 'The Song of Abraham.' *Hebrew Union College Annual* 65: 21–33.

—— 1996. 'Allusion, Artifice, and Exile in the Hymn of Tobit.' *Journal of Biblical Literature* 115: 49–61.

—— 1997a. 'Revisiting Myth and Ritual in Early Judaism.' *Dead Sea Discoveries* 4: 21–54.

—— 1997b. *Song and Story in Biblical Narrative: the History of a Literary Convention in Ancient Israel*. Bloomington, Ind.

ZAKOVITCH, Y. 1982. *Hayei Shimshon (Shofetim 13–16): nittuah sifruti-biqorti*. (*The Life of Samson [Judges 13–16]: A Critical-Literary Analysis*). Jerusalem.

—— 1991. '*And You Shall Tell Your Son . . .': The Concept of the Exodus in the Bible*. Jerusalem.

—— 1992. *Mavo le-farshanut penim-miqra'it* (*An Introduction to Inner-Biblical Interpretation*.) Even-Yehuda.

—— and SHINAN, A. 1992. *Ma'ase Yehuda ve-Tamar: Bereshit 38 ba-miqra, ba-targumim ha-attiqim, u-va-sifrut ha yehudit ha-qeduma le sugeha*. (*The Story of Judah and Tamar: Genesis 38 in the Bible, the Old Versions, and the Ancient Jewish Literature*). Jerusalem.

CHAPTER 3

JEWS AND JUDAISM IN THE SECOND TEMPLE PERIOD

MARTIN GOODMAN

AFTER the First Temple was destroyed by the Babylonians in 587 BCE and the inhabitants of Jerusalem carried off into exile, it was many years before a new building was erected on the sacred site, and in its first incarnation the new building was not particularly impressive. But by the time of its destruction by Roman legionaries in 70 CE, the Second Temple had become one of most magnificent edifices in the civilized world, and in retrospect its demise marked a watershed in the history of Jews and Judaism.

Hence the custom to give the name of the Second Temple to the whole period during which it stood. The nomenclature is politically correct but not universal. Particularly in the older literature, other names for Jewish history in these centuries are more common. Accurate, but somewhat demeaning to the Jews, is definition of the era by reference to the superpowers under whose rule Jews lived: these years are thus designated as the Persian, Hellenistic, and (early) Roman period. Or these centuries can be classified in relation to earlier and later religious developments: so, for Christians, either 'Late Judaism' (*Spät Judentum*, by implication a decline in religious values compared to the earlier religion to be found in the Hebrew Bible) or 'intertestamental' (that is, between the Old and New Testaments). Neither of these Christian designations makes much sense for Jews, for whom 'late' Judaism is 'early' compared to rabbinic Judaism, and there is only one 'Testament'. One proposal for avoiding this terminological trap is to describe the Judaism of this period as 'Middle Judaism', as advocated by Boccaccini (Boccaccini 1991), but the practice he advocates has not been widely adopted.

Regardless of the terminology used, the history of the Jews from 587 BCE to 70 CE was to a large extent shaped by the behaviour of the superpowers who controlled the Levant. Exile in Babylonia after 587 BCE was revoked, for those who wished to return to Judah, by the benevolent policies of the Persian kings who conquered Mesopotamia in the mid-sixth century. The Persian state in its turn fell to the Macedonian Alexander the Great in the course of his extraordinarily rapid campaign after 331 BCE. Alexander's successors divided up his kingdom only after much warfare. The two greatest successor states, both reliant on Graeco-Macedonian elites favouring Greek culture, were those of the Ptolemies, whose kingdom was based in Egypt, and the Seleucids, based in Mesopotamia and northern Syria. These two powers disputed control of the southern Levant, including Judaea, in six Syrian wars in the third century BCE, until in 198 BCE the Seleucids gained control. It was a temporary victory. The demise of both kingdoms began from the early years of the second century BCE. The prime cause was increasing interference by Rome, an exceptionally aggressive state, which had conquered the western Mediterranean coastal region in the third century BCE and from 200 BCE turned to Greece and the East.

As Seleucid and Ptolemaic power weakened, an independent Jewish state emerged in the land of Israel. The immediate cause was traumatic. The Jews of Judaea were galvanized into revolt in 167 BCE after an attack on the Temple cult by the Seleucid king Antiochus IV Epiphanes. The priestly leaders of the rebellion, the Maccabees, in time established themselves as rulers over Jerusalem and the surrounding area. Using a dynastic name, 'Hasmonean', which referred back to an earlier ancestor, they presided over a distinctively Jewish state until they too were finally deposed by Rome.

Direct Roman interference in Judaean politics began in 63 BCE, ostensibly in support of one Hasmonean ruler against a rival. In 37 BCE Roman troops deposed the Hasmoneans altogether, installing Herod the Great, an Idumaean, as a client king in their place. Herod ruled with ruthless magnificence, but his sons had less success. In 6 CE Judaea was taken under direct Roman rule. This too proved a failure, for in 66 CE Jerusalem revolted. After four years of independence, the rebel state was crushed and the Temple burned to the ground.

Thus for some of this period Jews enjoyed political independence in their homeland. At the same time the Jewish diaspora increased in size and influence. The descendants of the Jews who had been carried off into Babylonia in the early sixth century BCE retained a distinct Jewish identity throughout the Second Temple period, although little is known about them. But from the third century BCE Jews also began to be found in large numbers in Egypt, Syria, Asia Minor, and many other countries bordering the eastern Mediterranean. The political history of most of these communities is less easy to recover than that of Judaea, but something can be known about their social organization and religious life.

For all Jews in this period, in both diaspora and homeland, the Jerusalem Temple was the central religious institution. The wide dispersal of Jews prevented many from regular participation in Temple worship, and some Jews sometimes reacted unfavourably to the way in which the Temple cult was administered by the priests, but no religious Jews—not even those who established a temple of their own in Elephantine in Egypt in the fifth century BCE or those who built a shrine for worship in Leontopolis in the Egyptian delta in the mid-second century BCE— seem to have ignored the significance of the sacrificial and other offerings in Jerusalem.

The second pillar of common Judaism was the Torah. It was during these centuries that the biblical text took a form resembling that of the present day and acquired something close to its later authority. Alongside the formation of a canon (or something like it), and building upon it, went biblical interpretation, the evolution of new religious ideas by commentary on an accepted text. To some extent such interpretation was primarily a literary phenomenon (see Chapters 4 and 27), with novel religious tendencies (such as the approbation of asceticism, an emphasis on physical purity as a metaphor for spiritual purity, and a belief in life after death) justified through selective citation of biblical passages, but in other cases it may have been a force for religious change in itself.

The evidence on which historians rely for this period comes in the main from medieval manuscripts copied by two continuous religious traditions which pre-served quite separate bodies of material. The rabbinic tradition, all in Hebrew and Aramaic, preserved the biblical texts from the Persian period but no documents from, and only scant information about, late Second Temple times. The absence of information about this period in the schematic account of Jewish history from Moses to the present to be found in Mishnah *Abot* chapter 1 is telling. The rabbis had little to say about the politics of this period beyond generalities and a few romantic tales.

The Christian tradition preserved far more Jewish material from this period, all in Greek or translation from the Greek, including the Greek version of the Hebrew Bible, the Septuagint, produced originally by Jews in the third and second centuries BCE. The religious texts of the early Christian communities in themselves provide useful testimony, not all of it from a favourable perspective, about Jews and Judaism in the first century CE. But for Jewish history much the most important writings copied and thus preserved by Christians were those of the Alexandrian philosopher Philo Judaeus and the historian Flavius Josephus. Philo's voluminous writings provide an insight into the Judaism of at least one Jew deeply imbued with Greek culture: they may not show what Judaism was generally like, but they do demonstrate what was possible. Josephus' historical works provide the narrative framework for the whole period of Jewish history from the Maccabean revolt to the destruction of the Temple in 70 CE. Historians rely almost entirely on this framework: it is hard to imagine what a history of the Jews in these centuries would look like if an account like that written by Josephus had not survived. This reliance in itself may constitute a danger, as Maclaren has argued (Maclaren 1998), since it is difficult to avoid the hindsight which permeates all of Josephus' extant works. Josephus had himself participated in the great war against Rome and saw all previous Jewish history as a prelude to the disaster of 70 CE.

Without the literature preserved by rabbinic Jews and by Christians, knowledge of Jews and Judaism in this period would be only sketchy. (For an estimate of what would be known, see Goodman 1998.) Pagan Greek and Latin authors wrote a little about Jews, sometimes using sound information but more often simply relaying prejudice (see the texts in the classic collection by Menahem Stern: Stern 1974–84). Archaeological findings, prominent among them the Dead Sea scrolls and other manuscript finds from the Judaean desert, give an insight into some aspects of private behaviour and religious thought, but without the context provided by the medieval rabbinic and Christian manuscript texts such material would have been immensely difficult to evaluate.

The scholars who have engaged in study of this subject have rarely been disinterested. Much of the work on the Persian and early Hellenistic periods has been motivated by an interest in the context of the later books of the Hebrew Bible and the social, religious, and political pressures which led to the eventual delimitation of the biblical collection (e.g. explicitly, Davies 1998). Many students of the later Second Temple period have been interested primarily in the background to Jesus and early Christianity (e.g. explicitly, Schürer 1901–11). For the luminaries of the Wissenschaft des Judentums the challenge was to conjure up out of disparate evidence a coherent political and religious narrative which would justify their portrayal of the Jews as a nation with a political history and literary culture similar to that of other people (see discussion in Shavit 1997). For some more recent Jewish scholars the overriding issue has been the topic of Jewish identity in a non-Jewish world, with questions about citizenship and civil rights paramount in the first half of the twentieth century in the writings of Viktor Tcherikover (Tcherikover 1959) and questions of self identification in a pluralistic society more important in American scholarship (e.g. Cohen 1999). For many historians the origins during these centuries of a general Jewish acceptance of converts to Judaism and even, as some would argue, a positive desire to increase their number (see Feldman 1993 and Goodman 1994 for opposing views) make particularly pertinent the debated issue of the location of Jewishness in this period in either race or religion (see e.g. Schiffman 1985).

For Israeli historians, and diaspora Jews committed to Zionism, the most fascinating aspect of the period has generally been the model of Jewish self-rule under the Hasmoneans and Herodians and the leaders of the rebellion against Rome. The names of many streets and places in contemporary Israel recall the great figures of Second Temple times. Archaeological sites such as Masada and the remains of the Temple itself in Jerusalem bear a deep symbolic significance on both religious and nationalistic planes as relics of a previous era of Jewish independent statehood.

Students of the wider Hellenistic and Roman worlds have also frequently made use of the Jewish evidence for these centuries, if only because native Jewish writings survive in much greater abundance than those of most other subject peoples, simply because of the preservation of texts by rabbinic Jews and Christians. So, for instance, the books of Maccabees and parts of Josephus' history provide invaluable evidence about the Seleucid state (see Shipley 2000). If only a few classicists have chosen to specialize in study of the Jews, the most obvious reason is that use of much of the evidence requires knowledge of Semitic languages with which most classicists are unfamiliar, but the reluctance of some of the great Jewish historians of classical antiquity in the twentieth century to delve into Jewish history is less likely to derive from a linguistic barrier. They were perhaps unwilling to be labelled as parochial in their interests, preferring a larger canvas for their historical investigations (see discussion in Goodman 1999). For the attitude of classicists as a whole, two other factors may also be adduced. In many European universities in the nineteenth and twentieth centuries study of Jews in the Graeco-Roman world lay clearly in the province of the theological faculties, and duplication of effort by classicists may have seemed otiose. The other factor was more insidious. For classicists concerned to celebrate the glories of Greece and Rome, the Jewish contribution to and participation in the culture of ancient Europe could easily be seen as marginal, in much the same way as contemporary Jews were being marginalized in twentieth-century Europe.

Scholarship in this field may rarely have been objective, but it has been voluminous, and much progress has been made over the past century. A good insight into some of the changing trends in the twentieth century up to the 1980s can be gained by a comparison of the fourth edition of the classic *Geschichte des Jüdischen Volkes in Zeitalter Jesu Christi* (Schürer 1901–11) with the new material in the revised English edition (Schürer 1973–87; see the studies in Oppenheimer 1999).

Most obvious among the changes has been the impact of new archaeological discoveries. In the land of Israel, excavation of sites with material from this period has been intense for the past half-century. Much archaeological effort has been expended on uncovering impressive remains that can be directly related to evidence in the written texts (Josephus and the New Testament in particular), a technique which attracts much popular interest but does not always add greatly to knowledge (see discussion in Chapter 33, below), but there has also been work on settlement patterns, pottery distribution and manufacture, stoneware vessels, and other such material which reveal information about the economic and cultural life of the period which could not usually be derived from texts (see e.g. the *New Encyclopedia of Archaeological Excavations in the Holy Land* (Stern 1993), and the periodicals *Eretz*

Israel and *Qadmoniot*, both in Hebrew). In any case the most significant archaeological material emerged not by excavation but by accident. The chance discovery in
1947 of the Dead Sea scrolls opened up a new era in the study of late Second Temple
Jews and Judaism (see e.g. Vermes 1997). Further important documents have been
unearthed from further south in the Judaean Desert and Jericho (see Cotton 1998),
while in the diaspora the most important new material has been documents on
papyri. Aramaic papyri from Elephantine, by the first cataract on the Nile, illuminate dramatically the life of a Jewish garrison there in the fifth century BCE (Porten
1996), and publication of later Greek papyri by or about Jews has enabled much to
be written about Egyptian Jews in later periods, from the third century BCE on
(Tcherikover, Fuks, and Stern 1957–64). In the course of the twentieth century many
Jewish inscriptions on stone have also been published (see now Horbury and Noy
1992; Noy 1993–5), encouraging extensive study of the history of some diaspora
communities (e.g. Trebilco 1991 on Asia Minor and, more generally, Barclay 1996),
although since most of this epigraphic evidence dates to after 70 CE its use to
illuminate the Second Temple period is not straightforward. Similarly debated is
the value as evidence for the period before 70 of the later synagogues excavated at
diaspora sites, such as the third-century building at Dura-Europus, found in the
1930s (Kraeling 1956), or the huge fourth-century synagogue discovered in the 1960s
in Sardis (Hanfmann 1983). The issue is unresolved within the burgeoning discipline
of synagogue studies (see Levine 2000; below, Chapter 33).

Other factors encouraging progress have been changes within the different
disciplines concerned with the history of Jews and Judaism in this period and an
erosion of some of the demarcation lines between them. As classicists have increasingly come to see their subject as the study not only of elite culture but also of
ordinary people in the ancient world, so the value of the Jewish evidence has been
more widely appreciated. As some biblical scholars have adopted an increasingly
sceptical view of the historicity of biblical narrative, so use of archaeological
evidence for the Persian period has become more common (cf. E. Stern 1982).
Perhaps the most productive development of the past half-century has been the
widespread (but not yet universal) recognition by specialists both in New Testament
and in Jewish studies that the history of Jewish Christianity is part of the history of
Judaism. Hence the plethora of studies of Jesus the Jew (classically Vermes 1973b;
more recently, with bibliography, Fredriksen 1999) and, in more recent years, of the
Jewish aspects of Paul (Segal 1990; Boyarin 1997). A number of important studies
which cross traditional boundaries in this way have been written by scholars
working in departments of religious studies rather than either Christian theology
or Jewish studies. It is likely that the tendency in such departments to look at a
number of religious traditions will encourage more progress in this direction.

Not that widening the field in this way is unproblematic. So, for instance, use of
Jewish evidence by classicists raises the question of how marginalized Jews were in
the Graeco-Roman world (compare Feldman 1993 to Schäfer 1997; cf. essays in

Goodman 1998); if Jews were always seen as outsiders by themselves and others, it may be hard to learn much about the wider history of ancient society from Jewish evidence. So too the incorporation of some early Christian studies into Jewish studies raises the contentious issue of the date and cause of the eventual 'parting of ways', about which there is no consensus at all (see e.g. Dunn 1992). Both these areas of disagreement can be categorized under the two main themes which have generated most current debate: the relationship of Jews and Judaism to the societies and cultures which surrounded them in this period; and the issue of whether it is a priori preferable to treat separately each disparate item of surviving evidence about Jews and Judaism unless there is strong reason to conflate it with another item of evidence, or to conflate evidence unless there are strong grounds not to do so.

Most of the debate about the relation of Jews to the surrounding culture has concentrated on the Hellenization of Judaism. Since most Jews after the conquest of the Near East by Alexander the Great lived under regimes in which Greek was the prestige language for political and intellectual discourse, the possible impact of Greek culture on Judaism is a reasonable issue to investigate for its own sake, but the motivation for research has mostly been complex. For the Jewish scholars Viktor Tcherikover (Tcherikover 1959) and Elias Bickerman (Bickerman 1937), the under-lying question seems always to have been the extent to which Jews in antiquity responded to the cultural attractions of Greece by formulating a 'civilized' Judaism much like that of many European Jews in their own day. Hellenistic and Roman societies were generally tolerant, in the sense that in principle anyone willing to adopt the prestige culture could thereby gain access to social prestige and political power, and to a large extent the experiences of Jews in the later Second Temple period could thus be seen as similar to those of European Jews after the Enlighten-ment. Particular examples of assimilated behaviour or thought by ancient Jews might thus act as models for either imitation or avoidance (see Shavit 1997). So, for instance, it is highly likely that the increase in interest in Philo among German Jews in the nineteenth century was connected to the emergence of Liberal and Reform Judaism. Studies of Philo still divide into those which portray his philosophy as essentially Greek (classically, Goodenough 1935) and those which emphasize the continuities between his Bible interpretations and those in rabbinic literature (especially Wolfson 1947); the truth lies probably between these extremes.

The motivation of Christian scholars for investigating the relationship of Judaism and Hellenism has naturally been very different, and more concerned with the origins of ideas found in the early Church. It is universally agreed that Christians adopted many ideas found in the surrounding pagan Greek-speaking world, and some have seen this fact as evidence of a sharp break between Christianity and Judaism. But if it can be shown that Palestinian Judaism was itself thoroughly Hellenized, as Martin Hengel has tried to do (Hengel 1974), the Hellenized church could be seen as an continuator of authentic Jewish traditions.

The problem with all such studies of cultural influence is to decide what should count as evidence of Hellenization. That the Greek language was widely used by Jews in this period in the homeland as much as in the diaspora is widely agreed. So too were Greek art and architecture and (probably to a lesser extent) Greek literature and philosophy. The old distinction, regularly found in studies in the first half of the twentieth century, between a Semitic Palestinian and a Hellenistic diaspora Judaism is generally recognized to be too crude. But language, art, and architecture do not always affect ways of thought—a useful comparison may be the contemporary spread of American consumer goods and the English language to societies which retain largely unwesternized cultures under the surface. Only in one major political episode in Jewish history, the revolt of the Maccabees against Antiochus Epiphanes in the 160s BCE, did the protagonists portray their struggle as a contest between *ioudaismos* and *hellenismos.* By contrast, the later Hasmonean rulers behaved much like other Hellenistic monarchs in many of their actions, despite being political heirs of the Maccabean rebels. One Hasmonean monarch could even portray himself as a 'philhellene' (Jos. *Ant.* 13. 318; on the whole issue of the impact of Hellenism, see recently the chapters collected in Collins and Sterling 2001). It is salutary to note, in confirmation of the suspicion that scholarly emphasis on the issue of Hellenism has been prompted by concerns in the modern world, that, although the spread of the Aramaic language at the expense of the national language Hebrew among Judaean Jews from c.300 BCE was an even more striking phenomenon than their partial adoption of Greek, there have been few studies of the Aramaization of Judaism to set alongside the many volumes on the influence of Greek (for one exception, see Wasserstein 1995).

Debate on the political relationship of the Jews to their surrounding societies has mostly focused on two episodes of rebellion in Judaea: the revolt of the Maccabees and the great revolt against Rome in 66–70 CE. The main issue in both cases is an assessment of the correct balance in establishing the causes of events between the internal pressures within Jewish society and the wider policies of the great powers with which they came into conflict. Hence debate over whether the ending of the Temple cult by Antiochus IV was encouraged, perhaps inadvertently, by Jewish Hellenizers (Tcherikover 1959; Bickerman 1937), or should be explained more by the geopolitical ambitions of the Seleucids (cf. Millar 1978). Hence also disputes over the extent to which the destruction of the Temple was brought upon the Jews by their own internal divisions or as a by-product of the ambitions of the new Roman imperial dynasty, or both (cf. Goodman 1987; Price 1992). Such issues are not easily resolved by straightforward perusal of the main narrative sources for either event. The two books of Maccabees and the works of Josephus describe Jewish history essentially from a Jewish perspective, even though Josephus seems primarily to have had in mind a non-Jewish readership for his writings. Jews accustomed to the mode of historical explanation to be found in the Deuteronomistic history looked instinctively for the causes of disaster not in the ambitions of others but in the sins of Israel and the divine punishment they could be expected to elicit. Accordingly, the narratives must be read with considerable sophistication. Many of the most influential studies of the history of the period have been in large part historiographical analyses of these sources (Bar Kochva 1989; Doran 1981; D. R. Schwartz 1990; S. J. D. Cohen 1979; Rajak 1983; on earlier scholarship on Josephus, see Feldman 1984). Such analysis is helped a great deal by the chance that 1 Maccabees and 2 Maccabees covered some of the same ground, and that Josephus on a number of occasions wrote a second version of a narrative already given in an earlier work, so that the different emphases of the versions are manifest from the sometimes striking differences between them (on Josephus, see Bilde 1988; Mason 1998).

The second underlying cause of debate is the question of when it is justified to conflate evidence to produce a fuller—but perhaps misleading—picture of Jewish society and Judaism. The problem is whether references to people, events, and institutions preserved in different languages by different groups for different purposes should be expected to illuminate each other. The optimistic view is that connections should be posited wherever possible. The pessimistic view is that links are only probable in the case of notably public figures and events. Thus no one doubts that the 'King Agrippas' to whom the Mishnah refers in M. Bikk. 3: 4 must be either Agrippa I or II, the grandson or great-grandson of Herod, both well known from Greek sources including Josephus. But there is far less agreement, for instance, over whether the Pharisees in the time of Herod to whom Josephus referred as 'Pollion and Sameas' (Jos. *Ant.* 14. 172–6; 15. 3) should be identified with any of the proto-rabbinic sages in the Mishnah, and, if so, which (Schürer 1973–87: ii. 362–3).

Conflation is at the heart of the narratives of this period written by the great scholars of the Wissenschaft des Judentums. The postulation of congruity between the rabbinic traditions and the Greek sources gave respectability to the rabbis as chroniclers. Conflation was eased by the earlier infiltration of Josephus' writing into rabbinic thought through the work of Josippon, who produced in the ninth century a Hebrew paraphrase of Josephus' *Jewish War.* Conflation of the rabbinic stories still remained an apparent aim in the immensely learned but poorly argued studies of Louis Finkelstein in the middle of the twentieth century (e.g. Finkelstein 1962), but an increasingly sceptical view of the likely historical veracity of those rabbinic stories about the Second Temple period which derive from sources compiled after *c.*200 CE has become widespread since the early 1970s, and justifiably so, since they can often be shown up as fabrications (cf. esp. Neusner 1970), although a backlash against automatic discounting even of very late traditions has been discernible in recent years (cf. e.g. Schäfer 1998). On the level of religious ideas, particularly in biblical interpretation, much scholarship has demonstrated that some notions which appear first in the rabbinic tradition only very late are likely to have much earlier origins because they can be paralleled in the writings of Josephus, Philo, or the Dead Sea scrolls (Vermes 1973a).

The same scholarship that demonstrated the extent of the historical unreliability of late rabbinic texts also showed that early (i.e. tannaitic) rabbinic teachings and sayings about the Second Temple period are far the most likely to be valuable (Neusner 1971): to put the argument in its negative form, it is possible to demonstrate that named sayings in later rabbinic sources are often pseudepigraphic, but pseudepigraphy cannot be similarly shown for named sayings in tannaitic texts. Cautious use of this tannaitic evidence to understand, for instance, the way that the Temple was administered before 70 CE is therefore common (Sanders 1992), and only a few historians can be found who rule all rabbinic material out of court on the grounds that it was composed too late. Practice thus varies considerably, but it is now rare to find historians making indiscriminate use of late rabbinic stories in a way still widely practised as late as the mid-1970s (Safrai and Stern 1974–6).

The argument about conflation affects not just the use of rabbinic texts but that of all the ancient evidence. Some specific examples may be helpful to show the extent of disagreement. One classic case is the continuing debate about the role of Zealots in the political history of first-century Judaea. In a great work of compendious scholarship, Martin Hengel in the 1960s collected all the evidence that might demonstrate that an attitude of religious zeal manifested in political action against Rome was common among Jews in this period (Hengel 1961); all this disparate material together provided a picture of *Die Zeloten*. Other scholars retorted that in the primary extant source for knowledge of the political history of this period, the history of Josephus, it is specifically stated that the Jewish revolutionaries were divided into a number of different groups of which only one was called 'Zealots' (Jos. *BJ* 7. 260–7; Smith 1971; Horsley and Hanson 1999). The issue matters, because if every anti-Roman act is taken to be the product of religious ideology, the causes of revolt become much easier to explain than they otherwise would be.

A second example is the history of the Pharisees, a subject about which agreement has been little in evidence. The image of the Pharisees carries a heavy ideological load for both Jews and Christians. Christians have tended to see the Pharisees through their depiction in the Gospels as a powerful and hypocritical religious group with which Jesus came into contact and conflict. Jews, aware that Rabban Gamaliel, ancestor of Judah haNasi and descendent of Hillel, was described in the New Testament as a Pharisee, have generally seen the Pharisees as proto-rabbis, encouraging apologetic responses to the hostility of Christian accounts. But even without such tendentiousness, agreement on the numbers, teachings, social position, and influence of the Pharisees would have been hard to achieve, simply because the information in the extant sources (the New Testament, Josephus, and rabbinic texts) is not at all easily compatible (cf. the summary of the debate in Goodblatt 1989). At one extreme, everything attributed to rabbinic literature is taken as Pharisaic (e.g. Maccoby 1989). At the other extreme, any connection between the Pharisees and the rabbis is doubted on the grounds that the rabbis never called themselves Pharisees—they prefer to term themselves *talmidei hakha-mim*—even though they did refer to the Pharisees as a group (Schäfer 1991; Goodman 2001). It is noticeable that on every halachic issue about which both the Pharisaic and the rabbinic attitude is known the two turn out to be identical, which suggests much common ground, but it will always require fine judgement to decide how much to use rabbinic literature to understand the Pharisees.

Conflation has been even more rampant in the use by historians of Judaism in this era of the sectarian texts found among the Dead Sea scrolls. From soon after the accidental discovery of the scrolls in 1947, the sect which preserved them has been identified with almost every Jewish religious group of the period already known from the medieval manuscripts preserved by rabbis and Christians. Apart from maverick suggestions, arguments have been put forward by responsible scholars for designating the sect as Pharisees, Zealots, Christians, Sadducees, and Essenes (see summaries of views in Schiffman and Vanderkam 2000). Different arguments have been put forward for each hypothesis. The purity concerns of the group suggested Pharisees (Rabin 1957), hostility to Rome suggested Zealots (Roth 1958), eschatological interests pointed to Jewish Christians (Eisenman 1983), adoption by the sectarians of some halachic views identical to those ascribed to Sadducees in early rabbinic texts encouraged the view that they were Sadducees of some kind (Schiffman 1990). The most common hypothesis, which identifies the sectarians with Essenes, is based primarily on similarities of organizational structure and communal rules (Vermes 1997: 46–9). Each conflationary model is possible, but each requires a certain amount of conflicting evidence to be explained away either as the product of misunderstanding or exaggeration in one or other of the sources of evidence or as testimony to the existence of a number of different groups with the same name. One example will suffice to demonstrate. In the descriptions of Essenes by outsiders such as Philo and Pliny, one of the most striking facets of the group is said to be their avoidance of money, but some of the sectarian rules preserved among the Dead Sea scrolls clearly envisage the use of money (see discussion in Schürer 1973–87: ii. 577): either Philo and Pliny idealized too much, or there were two (at least) types of Essene. Those unwilling to conflate unnecessarily interpret the same sectarian writings as evidence of a sectarian group unknown before the discovery of the scrolls (e.g. Goodman 1995). Such a hypothesis is not unreasonable. No other ancient source apart from Josephus refers even to all the different groups already mentioned (Pharisees, Sadducees, Essenes, Christians, and Zealots), and Josephus himself, whose histories followed Graeco-Roman models and whose apologetic work stressed not variety but unity in Judaism (*Ag. Apion* 2. 179–81), made no claim to provide a complete ethnography of the Jewish religious parties of his time (Goodman 2000).

Outside religious history, analysis of the administration of Jewish society in this period can also be divided into those which conflate the evidence and those which do not. Early rabbinic sources refer to a 'great court' which sat in the Temple under rabbinic control. Josephus and the New Testament refer to Jewish courts and councils under the leadership of High Priests and (occasionally) Jewish kings (Hasmonean or Herodian). Some scholars amalgamate all this evidence as best they can to produce a unified picture of the operations of 'the Sanhedrin' (e.g. Schürer 1973–87: ii. 199–226). Others posit two or even more contemporaneous courts with different remits and personnel (e.g. Mantel 1961), despite the lack of ancient evidence that more than one court coexisted. Yet others suggest that the existence of conflicting evidence about the composition, competence, and proced-ures of the Sandhedrin shows that it was never a regular formal institution (Good-man 1987: 112–16), a view itself open to the objection that some sources presuppose that some types of political behaviour were only acceptable if sanctioned by the authority of 'the' Sanhedrin (Sanders 1992: 472–88).

As a final example, consider the impact of messianism in this period, an issue much in debate particularly over the past two decades. An influential study pub-lished in 1987 argued against the common assumption that messianic expectation and its impact were rife among Jews in the first century CE (Neusner *et al.* 1987). The authors pointed out that the extant literature of the period rarely refers to any individual, present or future, as a messiah. The general tendency to conflate into a single narrative all the disparate references that might (but also might not) refer to the expected actions of a messianic figure was condemned as a product of the importation of Christian concerns into the understanding of Judaism (although in fact, among the best examples of such conflation was the book on *The Messianic Idea in Israel* by the Zionist historian, Joseph Klausner: Klausner 1956). It is better, the authors suggested, to consider each document, or at least each type of Judaism, separately, as a result of which the evidence for messianic beliefs appears much less impressive. Such scepticism has been countered since the mid-1990s by a series of studies claiming that, especially in the light of the eschatological and messianic material in the scrolls of the Dead Sea sectarians which survive quite independently of the Christian tradition, the traditional view should be upheld (Collins 1995; Horbury 1998). The discussion of messianism has thus become an offshoot of a wider question about the legitimacy of generalizing to the rest of Judaism from the views expressed by the Dead Sea sectarians (on which see, for an extreme view, Stegemann 1998).

It is a reflection of the historiographical origin of this debate as a matter of contemporary theological, rather than historical, concern that the question of the relation between indulgence in speculation about a messianic future and political action predicated on a messianic hope is rarely discussed. It is left to students of the political history of Judaea to try to interpret the curious silence of Josephus about messianic movements among first-century Jews (e.g. Rajak 1983). Ascription of this silence to a desire to hide the truth from his gentile readers (e.g. Hengel

1989) encounters the obstacle that, far from concealing the existence of a messianic hope, Josephus positively asserted its importance for the Jewish rebels as an element in motivating resistance during the siege of Jerusalem (Jos. *BJ* 6. 312–14).

The discussion of messianism is in this respect symptomatic of a general problem in study of Second Temple Judaism. Perhaps because they began as students of biblical texts (Old or New Testament), many experts in this field write as if the study of a religion is the study of the theology of texts: they write about the Judaism of 2 Maccabees, or Wisdom of Solomon, or (even) the Jewish Sibylline Oracles. This procedure is hard to avoid when the texts are all that survive, but also hard to justify when one of the more striking facets of Second Temple Judaism was the ability of Jews to accept a common text (the Pentateuch) as totally authoritative, but then interpret it in radically different ways.

What, then, could be done differently? Texts provide a hint about how ancient people thought and practised their religion, but understanding how that religion worked requires the use of a plausible model into which the textual and other evidence can be fitted. From where, then, will that model come? Imaginative empathy is essential but runs the risk of importing anachronistic concerns; here a useful control lies in awareness of the plentiful evidence for the religious lives of non-Jews in the same period (see e.g. Hopkins 1999). More problematic is the systematic application to Judaism of a structural analysis of how other societies and religions work: at best such procedures provide real insight into implicit relations within ancient society which would remain hidden if historians looked only at what ancient people said explicitly about themselves, but at worst they can create an impression of knowledge that is largely illusory (for use of sociological models, see e.g. Saldarini 1988 and, more successfully, Baumgarten 1997). Perhaps the best hope in the study of Jews is that increasing knowledge of their normal, everyday life may make it easier to find a proper context for the theological writings which have dominated study up to now. As more documents emerge from the Judaean desert (on their value for historians, see Cotton 1998), it will become easier to discuss marriage, divorce, property-ownership, and all the other minutiae of everyday life in a way not previously possible. The Jews of the late Second Temple period may come to be seen less as actors in a great drama of portentous significance under divine direction, and more as a small people with an interesting and unique culture in the Mediterranean world.

On the other hand, no one who works in this field would want normalization of Jewish history to go too far. One of the enjoyable aspects of researching and teaching about Jews and Judaism in this period is precisely the interest it engenders among both Jews and Christians because of its implications for the present. Enthusiasm has its dangers but also an undeniable value.

SUGGESTED READING

Grabbe (1992 and 2000) covers the whole period, with an analysis of many of the issues under debate. The standard textbook for the second half of the Second Temple period is Schürer (1973–87). For good general introductions see Cohen (1987), Schiffman (1991), Boccaccini (1991), VanderKam (2001). For a fine attempt to depict the practicalities of Second Temple Judaism, see Sanders (1992).

BIBLIOGRAPHY

BARCLAY, J. M. G. 1996. *Jews in the Mediterranean Diaspora from Alexander to Trajan (323 BCE–117 CE*. Edinburgh.

BAR KOCHVA, B. 1989. *Judas Maccabaeus: The Jewish Struggle Against the Saleucids.* Cambridge.

BAUMGARTEN, A. I. 1997. *The Flourishing of Jewish Sects in the Maccabean Era: An Interpretation.* Leiden.

BICKERMAN, E. J. 1937. *Der Gott der Makkabäer*, Berlin (English trans., *The God of the Maccabees*, Leiden 1979).

BILDE, P. 1988. *Flavius Josephus Between Jerusalem and Rome: His Life, His Works, and Their Importance.* Sheffield.

BOCCACCINI, G. 1991. *Middle Judaism: Jewish Thought, 300 B.C.E to 200 C.E.* Minneapolis.

BOYARIN, D. 1997. *A Radical Jew: Paul and the Politics of Identity.* Berkeley and London.

COHEN, S. J. D. 1979. *Josephus in Galilee and Rome: His Vita and Development as a Historian.* Leiden.

—— 1987. *From the Maccabees to the Mishnah.* Philadelphia.

—— 1999. *The Beginnings of Jewishness: Boundaries, Varieties, Uncertainties.* Berkeley, Los Angeles, and London.

COLLINS, J. J. 1995. *The Scepter and the Star: The Messiahs of the Dead Sea Scrolls and Other Ancient Literature.* New York and London.

—— and STERLING, G. E. eds. 2001. *Hellenism in the land of Israel.* Notre Dame, Ind.

COTTON, H. M. 1998. 'The Rabbis and the Documents.' In *Jews in a Graeco-Roman World.* 167–79. M. D. Goodman ed. Oxford.

DAVIES, P. R. 1998. *Scribes and Schools: The Canonization of the Hebrew Scriptures.* Louisville, Ky. and London.

DORAN, R. 1981. *Temple Propaganda: The Purpose and Character of 2 Maccabees.* Washington, DC.

DUNN, J. D. G. ed. 1992. *Jews and Christians: The Parting of the Ways.* Tübingen.

EISENMAN, R. 1983. *Maccabees, Zadokites, Christians and Qumran: A New Hypothesis.* Leiden.

FELDMAN, L. H. 1984. *Josephus and Modern Scholarship, 1937–1980.* Berlin.

FELDMAN, L. H. 1993. *Jew and Gentile in the Ancient World: Attitudes and Interactions from Alexander to Justinian*. Princeton.

FINKELSTEIN, L. 1962. *The Pharisees. The Sociological Background of their Faith*. 2 vols. 3rd edn. Philadelphia.

FREDRIKSEN, P. 1999. *Jesus of Nazareth, King of the Jews: A Jewish Life and the Emergence of Christianity*. London.

GOODBLATT, D. 1989. 'The Place of Pharisees in First Century Judaism: The State of the Debate.' *JSJ* 20: 12–30.

GOODENOUGH, E. R. 1935. *By Light, Light! The Mystic Gospel of Hellenistic Judaism*. New Haven.

GOODMAN, M. D. 1987. *The Ruling Class of Judaea: the origins of the Jewish War Against Rome, AD 66–70*. Cambridge.

——1994. *Mission and Conversion: Proselytizing in the Religious History of the Roman Empire*. Oxford.

——1995. 'A Note on the Qumran Sectarians, the Essenes and Josephus.' *JJS* 46: 161–6.

——ed. 1998. *Jews in a Graeco-Roman World*. 3–14. Oxford.

——1999. 'Jewish history and Roman History: Changing Methods and Preoccupations.' In Oppenheimer (1999): 75–83.

——2000. 'Josephus and Variety in First Century Judaism.' In *The Israel Academy of Sciences and Humanities*. Vol. VII. 6. 201–13. Jerusalem.

GRABBE, L. L. 1992. *Judaism from Cyrus to Hadrian*. 2 vols. Minneapolis and London.

——2000. *Judaic Religion in the Second Temple Period: Belief and Practice from the Exile to Yavneh*. London and New York.

HANFMANN, G. M. A. 1983. *Sardis from Prehistoric to Roman times*. Cambridge, Mass.

HENGEL, M. 1961. *Die Zeloten: Untersuchungen zur Jüdischen Freiheitsbewegung in der Zeit von Herodes I. bis 70 n. Chr.* Leiden.

——1974. *Judaism and Hellenism*. 2 vols. London and Philadelphia.

——1989. *The Zealots*. (Engl. edn. of Hengel 1961, with new introduction). Edinburgh.

HOPKINS, K. 1999. *A World Full of Gods: Pagans, Jews and Christians in the Roman Empire*, London.

HORBURY, W. 1998. *Jewish Messianism and the Cult of Christ*. London.

——and NOY, D. eds. 1992. *Jewish Inscriptions of Graeco-Roman Egypt*. Cambridge.

HORSLEY, R. A. and HANSON, J. S. 1999. *Bandits, Prophets and Messiahs: Popular Movements at the Time of Jesus*. (First published 1985; rev. edn.) Harrisburg, Pa.

KLAUSNER, J. 1956. *The Messianic Idea in Israel*. London.

KRAELING, C. H. 1956. *The Excavations at Dura-Europus: Final Report, vol. 8, pt.1. The Synagogue*. New Haven.

LEVINE, L. I. 2000. *The Ancient Synagogue: The First Thousand Years*. New Haven and London.

MACCOBY, H. 1989. *Judaism in the First Century*. London.

MACLAREN, J. 1998. *Turbulent Times? Josephus and Scholarship on Judaea in the First Century CE*. Sheffield.

MANTEL, H. 1961. *Studies in the History of the Sanhedrin*. Cambridge, Mass.

MASON, S. ed. 1998. *Understanding Josephus: Seven Perspectives*. Sheffield.

MILLAR, F. 1978. 'The Background to the Maccabean Revolution'. *JJS* 29: 1–21.

NEUSNER, J. 1970. *Development of a Legend: Studies on the Traditions Concerning Yohanan ben Zakkai*. Leiden.

—— 1971. *The Rabbinic Traditions about the Pharisees before 70*. 3 vols. Leiden.

—— GREEN, W. S., and FRERICHS, E. S. eds. 1987. *Judaisms and their Messiahs at the Turn of the Christian Era*. Cambridge.

NOY, D. 1993–5. *Jewish Inscriptions of Western Europe*. 2 vols. Cambridge.

OPPENHEIMER, A. ed. 1999. *Jüdische Geschichte im hellenistisch-römischer Zeit*. Munich.

PORTEN, B. 1996. *The Elephantine Papyri in English: Three Millennia of Cross-Cultural Continuity and Change*. Leiden.

PRICE, J. J. 1992. *Jerusalem Under Siege: The Collapse of the Jewish State 66–70 CE*. Leiden.

RABIN, C. 1957. *Qumran Studies*. Oxford.

RAJAK, T. 1983. *Josephus: The Historian and his Society*. London.

ROTH, C. 1958. *The Historical Background of the Dead Sea Scrolls*. Oxford.

SAFRAI, S. and STERN, M. eds. 1974–6. *The Jewish People in the First Century*. Assen and Philadelphia.

SALDARINI, A. J. 1988. *Pharisees, Scribes and Sadducees in Palestinian Society: A Sociological Approach*. Wilmington, Del. and Edinburgh.

SANDERS, E. P. 1992. *Judaism: Practice and Belief 63 BCE–66CE*. London and Philadelphia.

SCHÄFER, P. 1991. 'Der vorrabbinische Pharisäismus.' In *Paulus und das antike Judentum*. 125–75. Tübingen.

—— 1997. *Judaeophobia: Attitudes Towards the Jews in the Ancient World*. Cambridge, Mass. and London.

—— 1998. 'From Jerusalem the Great to Alexandria the Small.' In P. Schäfer ed. *The Talmud Yerushalmi and Graeco-Roman Culture*. Vol. I: 129–40. Tübingen.

SCHIFFMAN, L. H. 1985. *Who was a Jew?* Hoboken, NJ.

—— 1990. 'The New Halakhic Letter (4QMMT) and the origins of the Dead Sea Sect.' *BA* 53: 64–73.

—— 1991. *From Text to Tradition: A History of Second Temple and Rabbinic Judaism*. Hoboken, NJ.

—— and VANDERKAM, J. C. eds. 2000. *Encyclopedia of the Dead Sea Scrolls*, New York.

SCHÜRER, E. 1901–11. *Geschichte des Jüdischen Volkes im Zeitalter Jesu Christi*. 3rd/4th edn. Leipzig.

—— 1973–87. *The Jewish People in the Age of Jesus Christ*. Rev. and ed. G. Vermes *et al*. Edinburgh.

SCHWARTZ, D. R. 1990. *Agrippa I: The Last King of Judaea*. Tübingen.

SEGAL, A. F. 1990. *Paul the Convert: The Apostolate and Apostasy of Saul the Pharisee*. New Haven and London.

SHAVIT, Y. 1997. *Athens in Jerusalem: Classical Antiquity and Hellenism in the Making of the Modern Secular Jew*. London and Portland, Oreg.

SHIPLEY, G. 2000. *The Greek World after Alexander, 323–30 BC*. London and New York.

SMITH, M. 1971. 'Zealots and Sicarii, Their Origins and Relations.' *HTR* 64: 1–19.

STEGEMANN, H. 1998. *The Library of Qumran: On the Essenes, Qumran, John the Baptist, and Jesus*. Kampen and Grand Rapids, Mich.

STERN, E. 1982. *Material Culture of the Land of the Bible in the Persian Period 538–332 BC*. Jerusalem and Warminster.

—— ed. 1993. *The New Encyclopaedia of Archaeological Excavations in the Holy Land*. Jerusalem.

STERN, M. 1974–84. *Greek and Latin Authors on Jews and Judaism*. 3 vols. Jerusalem.

TCHERIKOVER, V. A. 1959. *Hellenistic Civilization and the Jews*. Philadelphia.

TCHERIKOVER, V. A., FUKS, A., and STERN, M. 1957–64. *Corpus Papyrorum Judaicarum*. Cambridge, Mass.

TREBILCO, P. R. 1991. *Jewish Communities in Asia Minor*. Cambridge.

VANDERKAM, J. C. 2001. *An Introduction to Early Judaism*. Grand Rapids, Mich.

VERMES, G. 1973a. *Scripture and Tradition in Judaism: Haggadic Studies*. 2nd edn. Leiden.

—— 1973b. *Jesus the Jew: a Historian's Reading of the Gospels*. London and New York.

—— 1997. *The Complete Dead Sea Scrolls in English*. Harmondsworth.

WASSERSTEIN, A. 1995. 'Non-Hellenised Jews in the Semi-Hellenised East.' *SCI* 14: 111–37

WOLFSON, H. A. 1947. *Philo: Foundations of Religious Philosophy in Judaism, Christianity and Islam*. 2 vols. Cambridge, Mass.

CHAPTER 4

....

THE LITERATURE
OF THE SECOND
TEMPLE PERIOD

....

JOHN J. COLLINS

STRICTLY speaking, the Second Temple period extends from the construction of the temple at the end of the sixth century BCE to its destruction by the Romans in 70 CE. Some scholars would now argue that the entire biblical corpus belongs in this period. Even if one accepts the more traditional dating of biblical sources, the final edition of the Torah must be placed after the Exile. Several prophetic books (Zechariah, Haggai, Malachi, Joel) and parts of others (Isaiah 24–7, 56–66) date from the Persian period. Extensive portions of the Writings were also composed in the Second Temple period. Older biblical scholarship often tended to look on this period as a dark age, a kind of epilogue to the Bible. It is now recognized that this was a period of great literary productivity, which included the composition and editing of much of the Hebrew Bible.

Nonetheless, the distinction between 'Bible' and 'Second Temple' remains commonplace, and Second Temple literature is commonly taken to refer to the literature between the Bible and the Mishnah, including some that was composed after the destruction by the Romans. We will follow that convention here. It is important to bear in mind that some of the later books of the Bible share a common literary context with this literature, and that the canon has in some cases created artificial distinctions within the literary genres of the Second Temple period.

The literature that concerns us here may be divided into three categories, based on provenance more than on literary genre, although each category has its own characteristics. These are (1) the Apocrypha and Pseudepigrapha; (2) the Dead Sea scrolls; and (3) the literature of the Greek-speaking diaspora. None of this literature was transmitted by rabbinic Judaism. The first and third categories were preserved by Christians, the second was only recently recovered from the caves by the Dead Sea. Consequently, the significance of this literature for Jewish studies has sometimes been controversial. The shifting status of the material is reflected in the changing nomenclature used to designate it over the last century. In the late nineteenth and early twentieth centuries, this period was called *Spätjudentum*, a term that often had pejorative connotations. In the middle part of the century, the label 'intertestamental literature' was common, an indication that this material was primarily of interest to Christians. With the publication of the Dead Sea scrolls, however, more Jewish scholars entered this field of study. 'Early Judaism' was proposed as a corrective to *Spätjudentum*, but this term raised the difficult question of when Judaism might be said to have begun. Finally, by the last decades of the century 'Second Temple' was accepted as a chronological term without ideological overtones (e.g. Stone 1984), even though the distinction between late-biblical and early post-biblical literature remains problematic.

The changing names reflect changing views of the material. The introduction to Schürer's classic history, which is retained in the revised edition, declared that 'the chief characteristic of this period was the growing importance of Pharisaism', arising out of 'the legalistic orientation introduced by Ezra' (Schürer 1973–87: i. 1). For R. H. Charles, in contrast, the Pseudepigrapha provided an alternative to Pharisaism, and illustrated the kind of Judaism from which Christianity arose. Christian scholarship on the Dead Sea scrolls also found strong lines of continuity with Christianity. In contrast, Jewish scholarship at the end of the century focused rather on the affinities of the Scrolls with rabbinic Judaism (Schiffman). One of the major contributions of the last decade or so is the work of James Kugel (1998), who shows the pervasive interest in biblical interpretation across all genres of literature in this period. This interest is clearly related to the rise of midrash, but Kugel draws widely on Christian sources as well as Jewish to establish his thesis.

Even though the last decades of the twentieth century have seen a growing appreciation of the similarities between Second Temple and rabbinic Judaism, few would deny that the differences remain substantial. The Judaism (or Judaisms, as Jacob Neusner would have it; see Neusner in Avery-Peck, Neusner, and Chilton 2001: 3–21) that Second Temple literature portrays is often quite different from that of the rabbis, and it has wide-ranging implications for understanding the literary heritage of Judaism.

THE APOCRYPHA AND PSEUDEPIGRAPHA

The Apocrypha

'Apocrypha' ('hidden books') is the name given by Protestant Christians to those books that were transmitted with the Greek and Latin bibles but were not found in the Hebrew. Most of these books are accepted as canonical scripture by Roman Catholics: 1–2 Maccabees, Ben Sira ('Ecclesiasticus'), Wisdom of Solomon, Baruch (including the Letter of Jeremiah), Tobit, Judith, and additional passages in the books of Esther and Daniel (including the stories of Susanna and Bel and the Dragon). A few others are included in the scriptures of the Eastern Orthodox churches (3 and 4 Maccabees, Psalm 151). Some are not regarded as canonical by any church (1–2 Esdras, Prayer of Manasseh). Two other books, the Odes and Psalms of Solomon, which are normally assigned to the Pseudepigrapha rather than the Apocrypha, are also included in manuscripts of the Greek Bible. With the exceptions of the Odes of Solomon and of parts of 2 Esdras, all these books are clearly Jewish in origin. While a few (Wisdom of Solomon, 2 Maccabees, 3 and 4 Maccabees) were composed in Greek, most are likely to have been written in Hebrew or Aramaic. Only in the cases of Ben Sira, Tobit, and Psalm 151, however, have parts of the Semitic originals been preserved.

It is clear enough that the status of these books in the Christian churches derives from the fact that they were transmitted in collections of Jewish scriptures in antiquity. The scriptures taken over by the Christians were in Greek. So it was thought at one time that Alexandrian Jewry had a larger canon of scriptures than their brethren in the land of Israel. The idea of an Alexandrian canon, however, was decisively refuted by Sundberg (1964). It is now clear that there was no such canon in the sense of a fixed list of books. Throughout the later Second Temple period, the Torah and the Prophets were the common scriptures of all Jews, but there was also an undefined category of writings, which varied from one group to another, as can be seen from the Dead Sea scrolls (see Barton 1986; Collins 1997a: 3–21). It has been suggested that the smaller canon of Hebrew scriptures adopted by the rabbis corresponded to that of the Pharisees before 70 CE (Cross 1998: 219–29).

The group of writings that became the Apocrypha did not by any means contain all the writings that enjoyed popularity in the Second Temple period. Apocalyptic writings are conspicuous by their absence, as they also are in rabbinic Judaism. Neither is there anything here of a halachic nature. Wisdom texts are well represented, as are historical books (Maccabees), pious tales, and prayers. These presumably were books that won the approval of church authorities and gave no offence to Christians. Even the militant nationalism of 1 Maccabees could be endorsed by Christians as part of their own heritage. It is striking that very few of these books are found at Qumran. This is not surprising in the case of books that were written in

Greek, but the absence of such books as 1 Maccabees and Judith is noteworthy. The people who preserved the Dead Sea scrolls had a quarrel with the Hasmoneans, and were unlikely to preserve anything that served their propaganda, but these books were not preserved by rabbinic Judaism either.

The books of the Apocrypha are indicative of some important trends in Second Temple Judaism. Ben Sira famously identified Wisdom with the book of the law of Moses (Sira 24), and appended to his wisdom teaching a review of biblical history in the form of a eulogy of biblical heroes. The Wisdom of Solomon contains a retelling of biblical history down to the Exodus. The Torah of Moses had evidently become part of the curriculum of wisdom teachers in the Hellenistic period, and this reflects its growing stature as a normative book. The main debate on this issue in recent scholarship has concerned the significance of identifying Wisdom with the Book of the Torah. On one interpretation, the identification represented a rejection of alien, specifically Hellenistic, wisdom, and an affirmation of Jewish particularism (Sanders 1977: 331). Alternatively, it was an affirmation that all wisdom was one, and so that genuine wisdom from any source could be correlated with the Torah and used to interpret it (Collins 1997b: 54–6). The latter interpretation finds some support in the scattered allusions to Greek literature and philosophy in Ben Sira's book. Later, we find the particularistic equation of Wisdom and Law in the Book of Baruch, while Hellenistic Jewish writers such as Philo take the identification in its universalistic sense.

The Pseudepigrapha

The selectivity of the traditional Apocrypha becomes clear in comparison with the much larger corpus known as the Pseudepigrapha. These writings are so called because they are typically attributed to famous biblical figures—Enoch, Abraham, Moses, and so on. (Some pseudepigraphic writings from the Hellenistic diaspora are attributed to non-biblical figures, such as Phocylides or the Sibyl.) Only a few of these pseudepigrapha, such as the Psalms of Solomon and the Sibylline Oracles, were known continuously throughout western history. Many of them were pre-served by Eastern Christians, in Ethiopic, Syriac, or Old Church Slavonic. Some Pseudepigrapha that were written in Greek or Latin were long forgotten, and only rediscovered by researchers in the nineteenth century. The modern study of this literature began with the edition of 1 Enoch by Richard Laurence in 1821, and this was followed by a series of editions in the latter half of the nineteenth century (Jubilees, 2 and 3 Baruch, 2 Enoch, the Apocalypse of Abraham, the Testament of Abraham). At the beginning of the twentieth century there were landmark editions of the collected Pseudepigrapha in German (Kautzsch 1900) and English (Charles 1913). Thereafter, interest in this literature lapsed until the discovery of the Dead Sea scrolls. The most comprehensive collection available is that edited by Charlesworth (1983/1985).

These writings have given rise to two main issues in the context of Jewish studies. The first concerns their authenticity as witnesses to ancient Judaism. All these texts have been preserved by Christians, not by Jews. Some scholars have argued that they should first be understood as documents of late antique Christianity, and only secondarily, if at all, as Jewish documents (see e.g. Satran 1995). This debate has been especially acute in the case of texts that include explicit Christian references. In the late nineteenth and early twentieth centuries scholars tended to postulate source documents, and regarded the Christian elements in the Pseudepigrapha as interpolations (for numerous examples see Charles 1913). This tendency went hand in hand with the kind of source criticism then in vogue in biblical studies, which tended to impose modern ideas of clarity and consistency on the ancient texts. In the latter part of the twentieth century the pendulum swung in the opposite direction, and scholars were more inclined to give primacy to the text in its received form.

The case for Christian authorship of pseudepigrapha that are attributed to figures drawn from the Hebrew Bible differs from case to case. In 1 Enoch there are no indisputable Christian references. Debate has centred mainly on the section of the text called the Similitudes or Parables (1 Enoch 37–71). In part, the suspicion of Christian origin has arisen from the fact that this is the only section of 1 Enoch that is not attested in the Dead Sea scrolls. In part it arises from the prominence of a figure called 'that Son of Man'. This figure is clearly derived from the 'one like a son of man' in Daniel 7, but the title 'Son of Man' was appropriated by the early Christians and applied to Jesus in the Gospels. The argument for (late) Christian origins was made above all by the Polish Catholic scholar J. T. Milik (1976: 89–98), but it has not been widely persuasive. Not only is there no explicit reference to Jesus in this book, but at the end of the book (71: 14) an angel tells Enoch that 'you are the Son of Man who has righteousness'. The meaning of this verse has been disputed at length (see Collins 1998a: 187–91). Nowhere else in the Similitudes is there any hint that the figure whom Enoch sees in his visions is none other than himself, and the preceding chapter (70: 1) seems to make a clear distinction between Enoch and the Son of Man. It may be that the passage intended to affirm the similarity of Enoch and the Son of Man rather than their identity, or that it was added secondarily. Nonetheless, the passage lends itself easily to the assumption that the Son of Man is Enoch, and this is in line with a later Jewish tradition that Enoch was elevated to become Metatron, the little YHWH (3 Enoch or Sepher Hekalot; see Alexander in Charlesworth 1983: 223–315; Davila in Newman, Davila, and Lewis 1999: 3–18). It is unthinkable that a Christian author would have allowed any ambiguity as to the identity of the Son of Man. The Similitudes, like the rest of 1 Enoch, are Jewish, even though the kind of Judaism they reflect is more similar in some respects to early Christianity than to the religion of the rabbis.

A much more difficult case is presented by the Testaments of the Twelve Patriarchs, which are preserved in Greek and in Armenian. The Testaments are clearly Christian in their present form. One of their distinctive features is the expectation of a messiah from Levi and Judah who is evidently identified as Christ. According to the Testament of Simeon (7: 2), he will be priest and king, God and man. T. Joseph refers to him as 'the lamb of God' (19: 6). T. Judah 24 speaks of a man from the tribe of Judah. The heavens will be opened for him and no sin will be found in him. Scholars have argued that each of these references can be justified in a Jewish context, or alternatively that they are Christian insertions in a text that is basically Jewish (Charles 1913: 291). The cumulative evidence, however, is far more easily explained on the assumption of Christian authorship (de Jonge 1953).

Nonetheless, there are good reasons to think that the Testaments draw heavily on Jewish traditions. It is not clear why a Christian author should want to associate Christ with both Levi and Judah. The fact that the Jewish authors of the Dead Sea scrolls expected two messiahs, one priestly and one royal, cannot be coincidental. Moreover, partial parallels to the Testament of Levi, in Aramaic, and to the Testament of Naphtali, in Hebrew, have been found among the Dead Sea scrolls. It is possible, however, that these were source documents used by the later authors of the Testaments (de Jonge 2000). The crucial issue here is whether these traditions were already given the form of Testaments by a Jewish author, or whether the work as we know it is essentially the work of Christians. Besides their messianic passages, the Testaments contain lengthy ethical sermons. The ethical teachings can be explained in the context of Hellenistic Judaism, but they can be explained equally well in the context of Christianity. The early Christians took over much of the ethical teaching of the Jewish diaspora, and this already had much in common with the teachings of popular Hellenistic philosophers. In light of this situation, it is often difficult to identify specific passages as either Jewish or Christian.

The Testaments of the Twelve Patriarchs represent an exceptionally difficult case. It is now granted that Christians as well as Jews could compose texts in the name of figures from the Hebrew Bible. The Ascension of Isaiah is a case in point. Attempts to reconstruct an underlying Jewish composition in some of these texts are dubious. At the other end of the spectrum, several texts (1 Enoch, 2 Baruch, 4 Ezra, Psalms of Solomon) have scarcely anything that would suggest Christian authorship at all. (The attempt of J. Efron 1987: 219–86 to deny that the Psalms of Solomon are Jewish strikes most scholars as quixotic.) In other cases, it may be possible to distinguish Jewish and Christian layers, where the distinct emphases of each are still visible in the composite documents (3 Baruch; 1–2 Sibylline Oracles; see Harlow 1996; Collins in Charlesworth 1983: 330–53). While the origin of some material is uncertain and will continue to be debated, there is much material in the Pseudepigrapha that is undeniably Jewish, and that enables us to recover aspects of Jewish literature and religion that were lost to rabbinic tradition.

A second set of issues arising from the Pseudepigrapha concerns the place of apocalypticism in Judaism. Only one fully fledged apocalyptic writing, the Book of Daniel, was included in the Hebrew Bible. Daniel is a composite book, containing tales about Daniel and his companions at the Babylonian court as well as apocalyptic visions. The apocalyptic visions that make up the second half of the book (Daniel 7–12) have much in common with the books of the prophets, especially Ezekiel and Zechariah. In contrast, the book of Enoch presents a view of the world that is remote from either the classical prophets or rabbinic Judaism. It tells of fallen angels and their demonic offspring, and of mythical places at the edges of the earth, where places of judgement are prepared and where the souls of the dead await punishment. Other parts of the collection that makes up 1 Enoch describe the movements of the stars, or narrate the entire course of history, divided into periods. Enoch shares certain crucial features with Daniel, such as the claim of extraordinary revelation, interest in the angelic world, and belief in the judgement of the dead. But these are the very features that make the Book of Daniel exceptional in the Hebrew scriptures. Moreover, apocalyptic literature has figured much more prominently in Christian than in Jewish history, although Christians too have often looked on it with suspicion.

Scholars have tried to deal with the strangeness of apocalyptic literature in various ways. One way was to try to assimilate it to more familiar types of literature. So it was argued that 'apocalyptic' was a child of prophecy (Rowley 1944) or a late form of wisdom literature (von Rad 1965: ii. 315–30). Only in the last quarter of the twentieth century has apocalyptic literature been recognized as a phenomenon in its own right, a new kind of literature developed in Judaism in the Hellenistic and Roman periods. Rowley and von Rad were biblical scholars, whose primary interest was in the Hebrew Scriptures. These scholars, naturally enough, approached the material with biblical categories in mind. From the 1970s onward, however, apocalyptic literature was studied in the context of the Pseudepigrapha or Dead Sea scrolls. Also salutary was a change in focus from 'apocalyptic' as a kind of theology, often with a view to its relevance for the New Testament, to the study of apocalypse as a literary genre, with a more balanced appreciation of the defining features of apocalyptic literature in both Judaism and Christianity (Collins 1979).

Two results of the study of the genre merit special notice. First, apocalypses are not concerned only with cosmic eschatology of the kind familiar from the books of Daniel and Revelation. They are also, even primarily, revelations of heavenly mysteries (see also Rowland 1982). Much of the study of apocalyptic literature in the last decades of the twentieth century has been concerned with ascents to heaven and descents to the netherworld, and with the continuities between this literature and later Jewish mysticism (Himmelfarb 1983, 1993). Second, the genre is not peculiar to Judaism and Christianity, but has parallels throughout the Graeco-Roman world. (For the wider cultural context, see Hellholm 1983; Collins 1998b.) The relationship between Jewish and Persian apocalypticism is especially intriguing, but remains obscure, in large part because of the difficulty of dating the Persian sources.

A perennial question, of basic importance to Jewish studies, concerns the relation of the apocalyptic literature to the law of Moses. The oldest parts of the Enoch literature do not refer to Moses at all. Enoch, after all, was supposed to have lived before the Flood, so overt reference to Moses would be anachronistic. The authors of the Enoch literature were evidently acquainted with the Torah of Moses and allude to it at many points. These allusions usually concern narratives (e.g. the story of Adam and Eve, or the 'sons of God' in Genesis 6) rather than legal material. There is nothing to suggest that these authors rejected the Torah. But the distinctive wisdom that they impart is something over and above the revelation of Moses, and was allegedly derived by Enoch from the tablets of heaven long before the revelation at Sinai (Nickelsburg 2001; Bedenbender 2000).

One strand of scholarship on ancient Judaism has held that the covenantal theology of the rabbis was normative throughout the later Second Temple period, and was presupposed in the apocalyptic literature. George Foot Moore, in his great description of normative Judaism, integrated the apocalypses into his synthesis (Moore 1927, repr. 1971). More recently, E. P. Sanders has argued that apocalyptic literature such as 1 Enoch fits the pattern of 'covenantal nomism', with the single exception of 4 Ezra, which Sanders viewed as atypically legalistic (Sanders 1977). More recently still, Mark Elliott has made a similar argument that the primacy of the Mosaic covenant is presupposed in all the Second Temple literature (Elliott 2000; Elliott does not recognize apocalyptic literature as a distinct category). In contrast, the Italian scholar Paolo Sacchi and his students (especially Gabriele Boccaccini) distinguish Enochic Judaism as a distinct movement in the Hellenistic period (Sacchi 1997; Boccaccini 1998). The formative ideas of this movement concerned the explanation of the origin of evil, in accordance with the myth of the Fallen Angels in 1 Enoch 6–11. Enochic Judaism was the parent movement of the Dead Sea sect, but it effected a rapprochement with Mosaic Judaism, as can be seen in the Dead Sea scrolls. Other scholars are less sanguine about attempts to reconstruct a movement of Enochic Judaism. Nonetheless, George Nickelsburg has written of Enochic wisdom in its early phases as an alternative to Mosaic religion (Nickelsburg 1998). This does not mean that it was anti-Mosaic, but that it reflects a kind of Judaism in which the idea of covenant and the law of Moses were not central categories.

What is true of the Enoch literature, however, is not necessarily true of all the Pseudepigrapha, or even of all apocalyptic literature. The book of Jubilees is closely related to the Enoch literature by its interest in the myth of the fallen angels and in the solar (364-day) calendar, which is also found in the Astronomical Book of Enoch (1 Enoch 72–82). Jubilees can be viewed as an example of the quasi-genre 'rewritten bible', or biblical paraphrase, and is a gold-mine for the study of early biblical interpretation (Kugel 1998 *passim*). Jubilees is also an apocalypse, in the sense that it is a revelation given to Moses by an angel. But the recipient is none other than Moses, and the content is a paraphrase of the book of Genesis. Moreover, this paraphrase is informed throughout by a keen interest in halachic issues. One of the objectives of the book is to show that even the patriarchs before Moses actually observed the laws that were only later revealed explicitly in the Torah. Jubilees, then, represents a form of Judaism that was very much centered on the Torah and the covenant. Nonetheless, even here something is added to the traditional Torah. The angel draws on heavenly tablets that contain the division of the years from creation to the day when heaven and earth are renewed.

The relationship between apocalyptic literature and the Mosaic Torah is illustrated most vividly in 4 Ezra (= 2 Esdras 3–14), which dates from the end of the first century CE, after the fall of Jerusalem. 4 Ezra and the closely related apocalypse of 2 (Syriac) Baruch is greatly preoccupied with the Torah and with the apparent failure of the covenant. In this respect, it is closer to Jubilees than to 1 Enoch, although it does not have as strong an interest as Jubilees in halachic issues. At the end of the book (chap. 14), Ezra is commissioned to replace the books of the law that have been burned. He is given a fiery liquid to drink, and inspired to dictate the books to five men who write them down in characters that they do not know. The dictation lasts for forty days. In all ninety-four books are written. Of these twenty-four are made public so that the worthy and unworthy may read them. But the seventy others are kept secret, in order that they may be given to the wise among the people. Moses too, had been told many wondrous things over and above what was contained in the public Torah, including the secrets of the times and knowledge of the end. According to 4 Ezra, the extra or hidden books contain 'the spring of understanding, the fountain of wisdom, and the river of knowledge'. 4 Ezra is not in any way critical of the Torah or opposed to it. But it claims to have further revelation, which discloses the larger context within which the Torah must be understood. This claim of higher revelation is one of the essential characteristics of apocalyptic literature. In contrast, rabbinic Judaism affirmed the Deuteronomic principle that the essential revelation was not in heaven, 'that you should say, "Who will go up to heaven for us, and get it for us so that we may hear it and observe it?"' but was readily at hand on earth (Deut. 30: 11–14).

Of course there is also much conventional Jewish piety to be found in the Pseudepigrapha (see e.g. the Psalms of Solomon, or the Biblical Antiquities of Pseudo-Philo). The most distinctive contribution of the Pseudepigrapha to the understanding of Judaism in the Second Temple period, however, lies in the prominence of the apocalyptic literature. While this period was known primarily from the Apocrypha, the dominant genres seemed to be wisdom and narrative, with increasing influence of the Torah. This picture was altered significantly by the recovery of the Pseudepigrapha.

THE DEAD SEA SCROLLS

Much new light has been shed on the literature of Second Temple Judaism by the discovery of the Dead Sea scrolls, beginning in 1947. The scrolls were found in proximity to a ruined settlement at Khirbet Qumran, south of Jericho. Cave 4, where the greatest number of scrolls was discovered, is merely a stone's throw from the settlement. It is commonly assumed that the scrolls constituted the library of a sectarian community that lived at Qumran, most probably a settlement of the Essene sect. There are some vociferous dissenters from this view, who hold that the scrolls originated in Jerusalem and had no connection with the settlement (Golb 1995). Whatever their relation to the site of Qumran, however, two things can be said with some confidence about the corpus of scrolls. First, it includes a range of literature, which was not all composed in a single sectarian community. This literature includes the biblical texts, which were obviously not sectarian, but also books such as Enoch and Jubilees that evidently enjoyed wider circulation. (The corpus includes fragments of some 800 texts and more than 100 distinct compositions, not including the biblical books.) If this was a sectarian library, it included writings that had originated outside the sect. Second, the scrolls cannot be taken as a random sampling of Second Temple literature. On the one hand, they include a disproportionately large number of explicitly sectarian books, including rule-books for sectarian communities. On the other hand, some well-known Second Temple literature is conspicuous by its absence. This includes 1 Maccabees, the propagandistic history of the Hasmonean house, and such books as the Psalms of Solomon and Judith, which have often been suspected of Pharisaic ideology. Nothing in the Dead Sea scrolls can be identified as Pharisaic, and only one text (4Q448, the Prayer for King Jonathan) can be read as supportive of the Hasmoneans. The corpus of the scrolls, then, is not narrowly sectarian, in the sense of containing only explicitly sectarian literature, but it is nonetheless selective, and excludes some literature for ideological reasons.

The Study of the Scrolls

The study of the scrolls can be divided into three phases. The first lasted from the early 1950s to the Arab–Israeli war of 1967. The second lasted until all the scrolls became available to all qualified scholars in 1991. The first phase saw the publication of the major, well-preserved sectarian scrolls from Cave 1, and some important pieces from the other caves. Some of these texts were not only previously unknown but represented literary genres hitherto unattested in ancient Judaism, such as the *serek*, or rule-book, and the *pesher*, or commentary. Much of the early research, however, was concerned with introductory questions such as the identification of the sectarian community and its history. A classic summing-up of the scholarship of this period can be found in Cross 1995.

For the first twenty years after the discovery in 1947 study of the scrolls was dominated by Christian scholars (with some notable exceptions). During this period most of the scrolls were under Jordanian control, and there were no Jewish scholars on the official international editorial team. Christian scholars, naturally enough, were especially interested in those aspects of the scrolls that illuminated the origin of Christianity, such as messianic expectation or the possible practice of baptism at Qumran. Other important issues included the significance of the scrolls for the history of the biblical text and for the formation of the canon. As regards the history of the text, the scrolls provide ample evidence of the antiquity of the Masoretic text (MT) that forms the basis of the Hebrew Bible. But some Hebrew manuscripts found at Qumran agree with the Greek Septuagint (LXX) against the MT, and others preserve a form of the text that is related to the Samaritan tradition. F. M. Cross formulated an influential theory that there were three local forms of the text, which developed in Babylon, Egypt, and Palestine respectively (Cross 1995: 121–42). The controversy regarding the canon centered on the Psalms Scroll from Cave 11, which contains psalms in an order different from the traditional Psalter and also includes additional psalms. The editor, J. A. Sanders, argued that the scroll shows that the canon was not yet finalized (Sanders 1965). Other scholars have countered that the Psalms Scroll was not a biblical manuscript but a liturgical collection (e.g. Talmon 1989: 244–72). It is doubtful, however, whether such a distinction can be maintained in this period. The point is that psalms were arranged differently in different manuscripts. A definitive order and number had not yet been established (Flint 1997). Moreover, there is no indication in the scrolls that a book such as Proverbs was more authoritative than Jubilees, for example. The Torah, Prophets, and Psalms were evidently authoritative at Qumran, but beyond these there was no distinction between canonical and non-canonical writings.

A new phase of scholarship was ushered in by the Arab–Israeli war in 1967. One of the by-products of the war was the appropriation of the Temple Scroll by Yigael Yadin, and its subsequent publication (Yadin 1977, 1983). This is a rewriting of biblical laws, and its interest is primarily in halachic issues. Its publication aroused new interest in the aspects of the scrolls that were continuous with rabbinic rather than with Christian interests. Even more revolutionary was the disclosure in 1984 of the so-called Halachic Letter, 4QMMT (Qimron and Strugnell 1985; cf. id. 1994). This document (which is a manifesto rather than a letter) is apparently addressed to a leader of Israel, and it outlines the reasons for the separation of a sectarian group (presumably the Dead Sea sect) from the rest of Judaism. These reasons were entirely halachic in nature, involving disagreements on the calendar and on various purity laws. It was now evident that halachic concerns were of quite fundamental interest in the Dead Sea scrolls. The positions taken on these issues in the scrolls were typically at odds with the Pharisaic halacha found later in the rabbinic writings. On some points it was in agreement with that of the Sadducees. But the scrolls showed beyond any doubt that these issues were being debated already in the first century BCE, and possibly earlier. The tradition recorded in the Mishnah and the Talmud, then, had its roots already in pre-Christian times.

Christian scholarship in the early period of research on the scrolls has often been accused of distorting this literature by exaggerating its similarity with Christianity and ignoring its halachic interests (Schiffman 1994). This charge has some justification. 4QMMT was known already in the mid-1950s, when it was classified as a 'proto-Mishnaic' text, but its significance only became apparent thirty years later when Jewish scholars were included in the research. But the aspects of the scrolls that had been highlighted by the Christian scholars were also there. Messianic expectation is prominent in many texts. The community described in the Community Rule has a quasi-monastic character, and anticipates later Christian monasticism in remarkable ways. Neither the Dead Sea scrolls nor Second Temple Judaism in general were simply an early form of rabbinic Judaism. This was also the soil from which early Christianity sprang, and the continuities with both traditions must be appreciated. In the context of Jewish studies, however, the centrality of halachic issues in the sectarian scrolls is extremely significant.

The third phase in the study of the scrolls began when the texts were made generally available in the early 1990s. As editor-in-chief, Emanuel Tov greatly expanded the editorial team and achieved an impressively rapid rate of publication. The fragmentary scrolls published over the following decade threw new light on all aspects of the study of ancient Judaism. Up-to-date summaries of the full range of scholarship on the scrolls are available in the volumes edited by Flint and Vander-Kam (1998–9) and Schiffman and VanderKam (2000). Here we will comment only on a few of the more controversial issues.

The Torah and the Prophets

The Dead Sea scrolls testify massively to the pervasive authority and influence of the Mosaic Torah in the Hellenistic and early Roman period. As noted earlier, there is some variation in the forms of the text that are preserved. Recent scholarship has questioned whether the variety can be adequately explained by Cross's theory of local texts (Tov 1992: 116–17). It is also now clear that the majority of the textual witnesses are close to the MT, although there were other text forms in circulation.

Many of the writings found at Qumran can be described as para-biblical, because they are generated by rewriting parts of the Torah and the Prophets. The Genesis Apocryphon is a colourful example of expansionistic biblical paraphrase, analogous to the book of Jubilees but quite different in its emphases. In other cases, however, it is difficult to know whether the text is intended as an interpretation of the biblical text or as an interpretation. The Temple Scroll reinterprets the legal traditions of Leviticus and Deuteronomy by presenting them in rewritten form in the guise of a revelation to Moses. In this way the writer's interpretation of the biblical laws is invested with the authority of the revelation at Sinai. Some scholars have argued that this scroll was intended as the most authoritative formulation of the Torah for the sect at the end of days (Wacholder 1983; Wise 1990: 184). It is more likely, however, to be a composition analogous to Jubilees, which was not intended to replace the biblical text but to be a guide to its interpretation.

A different kind of problem arises in the interpretation of the pesharim, or biblical commentaries, which are the most distinctive form of biblical interpretation in the Dead Sea scrolls. These date from the first century BCE, and are the oldest extant formal biblical commentaries. (A quite separate tradition of allegorical interpretation was developing in Alexandria at about the same time.) They are based on texts that were understood as prophetic, including the Psalms. They proceed on the assumption that all prophecy was addressed to the time of the commentator, which was viewed as the end of the age, but that the prophets themselves were unaware of this reference. Typically, the prophecies were interpreted with respect to events in the history of the sect or to events that were still to come in the end-time. Early scholarship on the scrolls mined these commentaries in an attempt to reconstruct the history of the sect (Cross 1995: 88–120). More recent scholarship has tended to view the pesharim rather as exegetical documents, and to focus on their understanding of the biblical text (Brooke 1994). These approaches, however, are not necessarily incompatible, as the texts were evidently interpreted in light of the history of the community.

In addition to the pesharim and the biblical paraphrases, still other forms of biblical interpretation are found in the scrolls (see Bernstein in Schiffman and VanderKam 2000: i. 377–83). The so-called Pesher on Genesis (4Q252) is especially interesting, as it combines a paraphrase of the Flood story with a pesher-style interpretation of the blessings of Jacob. The full significance of the scrolls for the history of biblical interpretation is difficult to judge because of the fragmentary character of many of the texts. This is an area where study can continue profitably for many years.

Since so many writings from Qumran are evidently dependent on biblical texts, there is a strong temptation to assume derivation from biblical prototypes, even when this is not necessarily the case. Perhaps the most egregious example of this tendency concerns the text known as 'proto-Esther' (4Q550; Milik 1992). This is a very fragmentary Aramaic story which resembles that of Esther insofar as it is set at the Persian court. It has scarcely anything else in common with the biblical book, despite attempts to find in it the name of Haman. This text is neither an adaptation of the book of Esther, nor a source for it. It is simply another Aramaic story of similar genre. We do not know how many such stories may have circulated in antiquity. There are fragments of prophetic or apocalyptic texts that mention the name of Daniel. Here again there is no clear evidence that they depend on the biblical book. They are simply other compositions in the name of Daniel, which may be quite close to biblical Daniel in time of composition. A different kind of relationship to a biblical text is illustrated by the Prayer of Nabonidus (4QprNab). Scholars have long recognized that the story of Nebuchadnezzar's madness in Daniel 4 was based on traditions about another Babylonian king, Nabonidus, who spent several years in Teima, in the Arabian desert. The Prayer of Nabonidus mentions the names of both the king and Teima, and tells how the king was smitten by a disease and how a Jewish exorcist played some part in his cure. We cannot be sure that this text was the specific source on which the author of Daniel 4 drew, but at least it illustrates the underlying tradition. In all these cases, however, understanding is complicated by the fragmentary nature of the texts. Much depends on how the lacunae are restored. J. T. Milik restored the 'proto-Esther' text so as to maximize its affinities with the biblical Esther (e.g. he restored a reference to Haman). F. M. Cross restored a comparison to a beast in 4QPrNab, with a view to explaining the transformation of the king into a beast in Daniel 4 (Cross 1984). No mention of a beast is preserved in the extant fragments of the text. Such restorations, however ingenious, must be considered hazardous.

Apocrypha and Pseudepigrapha at Qumran

These fragments of pseudo-Daniel, the tale from the Persian court, and 4QprNab are all samples of an extensive corpus of Aramaic literature found at Qumran (see Dimant 1994; Flint in Flint and VanderKam 1999: 24–66). The most important texts in this corpus are undoubtedly the fragments of 1 Enoch. All parts of that composite work except the Similitudes (1 Enoch 37–71) have been found among the scrolls. Some fragments are dated by paleography to the middle of the second century BCE. The Qumran finds, then, have removed any doubt that may have existed about the antiquity or Jewish authenticity of the Enoch literature.

Another important Aramaic text contains fragments of an Aramaic Levi apocryphon. This text is clearly related to the Testament of Levi in the Testaments of the Twelve Patriarchs. In this case, however, the discovery at Qumran has not resolved the debate over the Jewish or Christian origin of the Testaments. The extant fragments are not in the form of a Testament, and the current consensus is that they represent a source of the Greek Testaments. The origin of the latter remains in dispute.

Apocalyptic literature figured prominently in the corpus of Pseudepigrapha that was known before the discovery of the Dead Sea scrolls. The discovery of the Aramaic Enoch fragments gave an important impetus to the recent study of the genre. The scrolls, however, have not enlarged our corpus of Jewish apocalypses by very much. In part, the problem here lies in the fragmentary nature of the texts. The beginnings and endings are often lost, and so it is impossible to determine literary genre in many instances. Possible apocalypses found at Qumran include the 'Visions of Amram' (which envisions opposing, dualistic, angelic-demonic powers, the so-called 'Aramaic Apocalypse' (4Q246, 'the Son of God text'), the New Jerusalem text (a vision in the tradition of Ezekiel 40–8), and a 'four kingdoms' prophecy, where the four kingdoms are symbolized by four trees (4Q552–3). If all of these texts were composed as apocalypses they would represent a significant enlargement of the corpus. All are very fragmentary, however, and so their significance remains uncertain.

Two other points should be noted about the corpus of Aramaic literature found at Qumran. First, none of these texts contains any clear reference to community structures, and so they are not thought to be products of the Qumran sect. Rather, they are part of the wider literature preserved by the sect, but probably not peculiar to it. Second, with the exception of para-biblical texts such as the Genesis Apocryphon and the Levi Apocryphon, these texts are not especially Torah-centred. Some, such as the tales from the Persian court and the Prayer of Nabonidus, are not concerned with the Torah at all. Despite the prominence, even dominance, of the Torah in sectarian compositions, the scrolls add significantly to our knowledge of Jewish literature that was neither para-biblical nor Torah-centred in the Second Temple period. Significantly, the apocalyptic writing from the second century BCE that is most extensively concerned with the Torah and halachic issues, the Book of Jubilees, is found in Hebrew rather than in Aramaic.

The scrolls also expand significantly our corpus of non-biblical Hebrew literature. Several wisdom texts were found at Qumran, in addition to the biblical books and fragments of Ben Sira. The most extensive of these (4QInstruction, see Strugnell, Harrington, and Elgvin 1999) consists largely of traditional wisdom advice on family matters and the like, but also refers frequently to 'the mystery that is to be', which evidently concerns God's plan for the world, past, present, and future. The category of 'mystery' was hitherto characteristic of apocalyptic rather than sapiential literature. 4QInstruction is also the first Hebrew wisdom text to endorse the hope for reward and punishment in the hereafter. It contains several allusions to passages in the Torah, and evidently regards it as a source of wisdom. Yet it never thematizes the Torah in the manner of Ben Sira, or suggests that wisdom should be identified with the law of Moses. That identification is found, however, in another wisdom text from Qumran, 4Q525 (4QBeatitudes). A kind of wisdom teaching similar to 4QInstruction is found in 4QMysteries. These texts throw important light on the development of Hebrew wisdom after Ben Sira, and the expansion of the range of traditions on which the wisdom writers drew. Since these texts have only been published in the last years of the twentieth century, their study is still in its infancy.

The Distinctively Sectarian Literature

The most distinctive literature in the Dead Sea scrolls has no parallels in the Apocrypha or Pseudepigrapha. This includes rule-books (the Community Rule, the Damascus Rule, the Messianic Rule, the War Rule). The Community Rule and Damascus Rule are designed to regulate the lives of communities, and have important parallels in Greek rules for private organizations (Weinfeld 1986), although they also show the influence of traditional Jewish covenantal patterns. The War Rule also bears some analogy to Greek military manuals (Duhaime 1988), but is also dependent on priestly Pentateuchal traditions about the Israelite camp in the wilderness. Other distinctively sectarian literature that we have already noted includes the biblical commentaries or pesharim and the thanksgiving hymns, or hodayot.

The place of the distinctively sectarian literature in the study of Judaism is controversial in some respects. This literature was not preserved by the rabbis, and was presumably rejected for ideological reasons. The sectarian literature has many clear points of contact with apocalyptic literature. The books of Enoch and Daniel were preserved in multiple copies at Qumran, and as we have seen there was also a more extensive literature that was apocalyptic in a broad sense of the word. The Qumran settlement has been dubbed 'an apocalyptic community' with considerable justification (Cross 1995; Collins 1997c). The sectarian scrolls share key elements of the apocalyptic world-view. They attribute great influence on human affairs to angelic and demonic spirits, and they expect both a final judgement at the end of history and the reward and punishment of individuals after death. Yet the sectarian writers do not appear to have used the literary genre apocalypse. In part this choice may reflect the great authority attributed to the Torah of Moses at Qumran. It may also reflect the status of the Teacher of Righteousness as the supreme interpreter and mediator of divine revelation for the community. What need had the sectarians of revelations in the name of Enoch or Daniel when everything was revealed to them by their own Teacher?

The affinities of the sectarian scrolls with apocalyptic literature are evident in the War Rule and in the Instruction on the Two Spirits in the Community Rule. These were among the first Dead Sea scrolls to be published, and to a great degree they formed a lasting impression of the kind of community that produced these scrolls. In contrast, halachic concerns were not so prominent in these documents, although they receive a great deal of attention in the Damascus Document, which had been recovered from the Cairo Genizah at the end of the nineteenth century and which was also found in multiple copies at Qumran. It is now clear that halachic interests were central in the scrolls, and that this form of Judaism found no tension between apocalypticism and devotion to the Torah. It still claimed to enjoy a special revelation, but this lay in the inspired interpretation of the Torah, and was not an alternative to it.

DIASPORA JUDAISM

A quite different form of Second Temple Judaism is attested in the literature written in Greek in the Hellenistic diaspora, primarily in Egypt. Much of this literature is known to us only from excerpts and summaries made by the Roman freedman Alexander Polyhistor, who wrote before the middle of the first century BCE. Alexander's work was cited at length by the Church Father Eusebius in his *Praeparatio Evangelica*. Some fragments are also preserved by Clement of Alexandria and by Josephus (for texts and translations of these fragments, see Holladay 1983–96). Other Hellenistic Jewish writings were preserved more fully, including the voluminous works of Philo of Alexandria. All of these works owe their preservation to the interest of Christians. Only in rare cases, however, is the Jewish origin of the material in doubt. The most controversial case is that of the romance of Joseph and Aseneth (Kraemer 1998). This text is known from Christian manuscripts of the Byzantine period, and some scholars have suspected that it is a Christian composition. There are formulaic references to the bread of life and the cup of immortality, and Aseneth has an encounter with a man from heaven, who gives her to eat from a honeycomb, which is the food of angels and gives immortality. All of this brings to mind the Christian Eucharist. Yet the basic problem around which the story revolves is distinctively Jewish: the problem of intermarriage between a Jew and an idolatrous Egyptian. While the story may have been embellished by Christians in the course of transmission, there can be little doubt that it originated in the Jewish diaspora.

The first and most foundational literary work of the Hellenistic diaspora was the translation of the Bible into Greek. The Torah had been translated by the middle of the third century BCE. The Prophets and Writings followed gradually, down to the early first century BCE. The claim of the Letter of Aristeas that this translation was done at the request of the Ptolemy has little credibility. It was presumably intended to meet the needs of Jewish communities in Egypt. There has been a long-standing debate as to whether, or how far, the translators engaged in deliberate reinterpretation of the biblical text. The evidence of the Dead Sea scrolls lends support to the view that they were generally faithful to the text that lay before them, insofar as they understood it. The Septuagint, then, provided the great common ground that united Jews in the diaspora with their compatriots in Judea.

One of the primary emphases of recent scholarship on Second Temple literature has been the appreciation of the generative role of biblical interpretation across the spectrum of Judaism in this period (Kugel 1998). We have noted how many of the texts found at Qumran can be described as para-biblical, in the sense that they are generated in some way by the biblical text. This is also true of the Greek writings of the diaspora. Many of the works excerpted by Alexander Polyhistor were rewritings of the Torah in various forms. These range from faithful chronicles that attempt to resolve problems in the biblical text (Demetrius), to fanciful romance (Artapanus, who credited Moses with founding the Egyptian animal cults). Some are cast in distinctively Greek forms, such as epic poetry (Philo the Epic Poet) or tragedy (Ezekiel, on the Exodus). All of these works can be read as exercises in biblical interpretation, but there are also other influences at work. In view of the fanciful character of Artapanus' account, we may wonder whether his work was based on the biblical text at all. He was evidently aware of the main lines of the biblical tradition, but it is difficult to know in what form he was acquainted with them. Some Jewish Hellenistic authors, such as Eupolemus, who probably lived in Jerusalem, were more faithful to the biblical prototype, but others attempted to correlate the early biblical story with Greek mythology (so 'Pseudo-Eupolemus', a fragment attributed to Eupolemus which may have been composed by a Samaritan).

Alexandrian Judaism also developed a tradition of formal biblical interpretation. In the second century BCE Aristobulus wrote a work which he dedicated to Ptolemy, seeking to refute interpretations of the Torah that would make it seem crude or unsophisticated. Anthropomorphic expressions, such as references to the hands or feet of God, must be interpreted allegorically, to refer to spiritual realities. Allegorical interpretation had been developed by Greek scholars in Alexandria to deal with the scandalous behaviour of the gods in Homer. In Aristobulus it has an apologetic function, and this is also the case in the Letter of Aristeas. Aristobulus claimed that Judaism was a philosophical school, and that Plato had borrowed from Moses. In the first century CE, however, Philo of Alexandria wrote an extensive corpus of commentaries on the Torah, informed consistently by a form of Platonic philosophy. Philo does not appear to have had any significant knowledge of Hebrew, but he preserves some exegetical traditions that are paralleled in Hebrew sources. The degree to which Jewish writers in the Hellenistic diaspora were acquainted with exegetical traditions from the land of Israel remains an intriguing question that has not been fully explored.

The greatest figure in Hellenistic Jewish literature is undoubtedly Philo of Alexandria. In the middle of the twentieth century controversy had centered on the thesis of E. R. Goodenough (1935), that Philo's work reflected a Jewish mystery religion. This thesis has long been abandoned, although scholars recognize a mystical dimension in Philo's Platonic philosophy (Winston 1985). The great alternative to Goodenough's interpretation was provided by Wolfson (1947), who emphasized the philosophical aspect of Philo's work and his affinities with rabbinic Judaism. Recent work on Philo has focused more on clarifying his philosophical background in Middle Platonism (Runia 1986) and on exploring his use of Jewish exegetical traditions (Tobin 1983; Borgen 1997).

The corpus of Hellenistic Jewish literature also included several works that made only incidental use of the Torah. Several of these were attributed to pagan authors. The Letter of Aristeas was ostensibly written by one Greek to another in praise of Judaism. The Sibylline Oracles were put in the mouth of the ancient sibyl, and mingled praise of Judaism with denunciations of other peoples, especially the Romans. The Sayings of Pseudo-Phocylides represent an especially interesting case of Jewish pseudepigraphy, as they contain no explicit reference to Judaism, and are only recognized as Jewish because of correspondences with biblical laws. Scholars have disagreed as to whether such a composition was intended primarily to reinforce the Torah, by presenting it in the name of a Greek teacher (van der Horst 1990), or to inculcate ethical monotheism regardless of its Jewish associations (Collins 2000: 168–74).

Apologetic Literature?

In contrast to the Apocrypha and Pseudepigrapha, the Greek literature of the diaspora attracted the attention of Jewish scholars already in the nineteenth century. The Wissenschaft des Judentums movement found in Jewish reception of Hellenistic culture in ancient Alexandria an apt analogy for their own encounter with European culture in Germany (see Shavit 1997: 306–36). The primary interest here was in the history and political status of Alexandrian Jewry, and this interest continued to dominate the study of diaspora Judaism in the twentieth century (e.g. Tcherikover 1999). But Jewish scholars also contributed some fundamental studies of the literature, notably Freudenthal's study of the fragmentary historical works preserved by Alexander Polyhistor (Freudenthal 1874–5) and Friedländer's study of the apologetic literature (Friedländer 1903). The philosophical work of Philo commanded a lion's share of the attention, culminating in the classic work of Wolfson (1947). The analogy between ancient and modern diasporas still plays a heuristic role in recent scholarship, as Erich Gruen cheerfully admits (Gruen 1998: p. ix).

Older scholarship regarded virtually all Graeco-Jewish literature as either apologetic or missionary, on the assumption that it was intended primarily for Gentile readers. That assumption was debunked by Victor Tcherikover in a famous article in 1956. It is now agreed that there was no organized Jewish mission to the Gentiles in the Hellenistic Diaspora (Goodman 1994). Whether the literature has an apologetic purpose remains in dispute. Erich Gruen (1998) has emphasized its self-confident character, and argued that it should be viewed as the self-expression of Jews who were fully at home in the Hellenistic world. Yet the frequency with which praise of Judaism is put on the lips of fictitious Gentile characters shows that the authors felt a need for Gentile approval and respect. Much of this literature can be read as an attempt to forestall or respond to Gentile criticism, by showing that Judaism deserved the respect of right-thinking Greeks.

Much of the recent literature on diaspora Judaism has focused on the question of Jewish identity, and the tension between Jewish tradition and Hellenistic culture

(Feldman 1993; Barclay 1996; Gruen 1998; Collins 2000). The authors of this literature were certainly at home in the Hellenistic world, in the sense that Greek was their language and they were most comfortable with Greek forms of expression. There were always some points of tension, however. Chief of these was the omnipresent worship of pagan deities, and the importance of that worship in civic life. The Jews also objected consistently to some Gentile practices, such as abortion, the exposure of infants, and homosexuality. The literature from the diaspora witnesses to an attempt to appropriate Hellenistic culture in a selective way. Jews could embrace Greek literary forms, rhetoric, and philosophy, but they refused to compromise in matters of religious worship or ethical practices. Many of the Jewish texts include sharp polemics against the religious practices of the Gentiles, Greek and Roman as well as the reviled Egyptians (see e.g. the Sibylline Oracles, the Wisdom of Solomon, Joseph and Aseneth, but also Philo). This has sometimes been taken to reflect antagonism towards Hellenistic culture (Barclay 1996: 181–228). But all of these texts are written in Greek and are themselves expressions of a thoroughly Hellenized Judaism. Diaspora Jews, in short, attempted to distinguish between religion and culture in a way that had no precedent in the pagan world. They affirmed all aspects of Hellenistic culture except those that required idolatry or were offensive on ethical grounds.

In sharp contrast to the Dead Sea scrolls, the Hellenistic Jewish writings display minimal interest in halachic issues and avoid controversy over matters of purity. When the laws of *kashrut* are discussed in the Letter of Aristeas, it is only to explain them allegorically and give them a spiritual meaning. Gentile writers who comment on Judaism in this period typically focus on the distinctive practices of Jews— observance of the sabbath, abstinence from pork, refusal to worship the gods of the city, reluctance to mingle with Gentiles (see Stern 1974–84). The Jewish literature, in contrast, emphasizes those things that Jews and Gentiles had in common. Aristobulus and the Letter of Aristeas suggested that Zeus and the God of Israel were one and the same. The Jewish writers in particular sought to make common cause with Greek philosophers, who were often critical of polytheistic mythology and even shared the ethical concerns of the Jews on some occasions. We should not assume that halachic issues and ritual practices were not of concern to the authors of this literature. Philo, at least, insisted on the literal observance of the law as well as on its symbolic significance, and recent scholarship has tended to emphasize the distinctively Jewish character of most of these texts. The primary concern of this literature, however, is to show that Judaism was a tradition worthy of respect in the Hellenistic world, and to downplay its strangeness. It may be that this literature is representative only of the upper classes of Egyptian Judaism. We know that Philo belonged to a very wealthy family. Whether the lower classes shared the cosmopolitan aspirations of this literature we do not know.

The apologetic character of the Hellenistic Jewish literature of the diaspora is also in evidence in the writings of Josephus, a native of Jerusalem who wrote in Rome after the failure of the Jewish revolt. Josephus is our main source for the history of Judaism in this period, and modern scholarship has mined him repeatedly (and critically) as a historical source, especially for the war against Rome, but also for religious movements in Judaism, such as the Pharisees. Studies of his writings as literature have been of two kinds. On the one hand, the *Antiquities* has been studied as an example of biblical interpretation. L. H. Feldman has written most copiously on this subject (Feldman 1998 a and b). On the other hand, there have been important studies of his technique and *Tendenz* as an historian. In his account of the Jewish War, the *Tendenz* is political: Josephus lays the blame on the rebels and exculpates his Roman patrons. But Josephus has been shown to have modelled his works on those of Greek historians, Polybius in the *War* and Dionysius of Halicarnassus in the *Antiquities* (Lindner 1972; Attridge 1976). He also reflects the common rhetorical tendency of Hellenistic historiography to appeal to the reader's emotions. He stands in a Hellenistic tradition of didactic, rhetorical historiography, which he adapts for defence and praise of the Jewish people. Josephus also composed an explicitly apologetic work, *Against Apion*, which is our major source for the polemics between Greeks and Jews around the turn of the era.

CONCLUSION

The story of scholarship on Second Temple Judaism in modern times is a story of retrieval. None of this literature was preserved by rabbinic Judaism, except for scattered verses of Ben Sira. The Greek literature of the diaspora may not have been accessible to the rabbis, and much of it perished in the demise of the Jewish community in Egypt. Much of the apocalyptic literature, and of the distinctive material in the Dead Sea scrolls, was rejected for ideological reasons. The rejection of sectarian literature facilitated the unity of Judaism after the revolts, and may well have contributed to the survival of the religious tradition. From the viewpoint of modern scholarship, however, the loss of the literature of Second Temple Judaism was an impoverishment. The recovery of this literature over the last two centuries has been a remarkable contribution to modern Jewish studies.

It should be clear from the preceding account that modern scholarship on Second Temple literature has been primarily interested in religious history. (There is also a significant body of scholarship on political and social history that falls outside the scope of this essay.) This is also true of biblical studies, and reflects the fact that most scholars approach this literature with religious rather than aesthetic interests. In recent years, however, there has been a considerable amount of purely literary criticism of biblical texts, while there has been very little literary study of the post-biblical Second Temple literature. There have, of course, been exceptions. As recent examples, one might mention Lawrence Wills's study of the Jewish novel (Wills 1995), F. J. Murphy's attempt to discuss the *Biblical Antiquities* of Pseudo-Philo as narrative (Murphy 1993) or Carol Newsom's analysis of the rhetoric of some Qumran texts (Newsom 1990). Feminist criticism in this period has been social rather than literary, but again there are notable exceptions; see, for example, the literary study of Jubilees by Halpern-Amaru (Halpern-Amaru 1999) or the essays in Levine (1991).

Various explanations for this situation might be proposed, although none are very compelling. Recent work on the Dead Sea scrolls has been preoccupied with the editing of texts and philological considerations. In the case of the Pseudepigrapha too, the production of texts and commentaries is still a major undertaking. Literary studies may come later. To some degree, the relative lack of literary studies might be taken as a reflection of the nature of the material. There are few examples of great narrative or great poetry in these corpora. Nonetheless, there are some very interesting narratives (the Genesis Apocryphon, the Testament of Abraham) that have received very little attention, from a specifically literary perspective, while the poetry of the hodayoth surely deserves more extensive analysis than it has hitherto received. In fact, however, the literary appeal of this material has been overshadowed by its importance for the history of religion, whether it is taken to illustrate the soil from which Christianity grew, or to support the counter-claims for the antiquity of Judaism as the rabbis understood it. It is also true that this material remains to a great degree in the shadow of the Bible. Most people who teach Second Temple literature still make their primary living by teaching the Bible, especially in Christian contexts. The Dead Sea scrolls are increasingly taught in the context of rabbinic Judaism. Hellenistic Judaism is often studied under the rubric of ancient history. It is still the case that relatively few scholars have the literature between the bible and the Mishnah as their primary focus.

Be that as it may, the achievements of Second Temple scholarship hitherto are very substantial. The primary achievement has surely been the publication and philological explanation of the texts. If scholars of the next generation want to explore new methodologies, they have now a solid textual basis on which to do this.

SUGGESTED READING

For the primary texts, in translation, see Charlesworth (1983/1985) and Vermes (1997). The most comprehensive introduction to this literature can be found in Schürer (1973–87). A less technical introduction is provided by Nickelsburg (1981). See now also Alexander (2001).

On the Apocrypha see Harrington (1999); on the apocalyptic literature, Collins (1998a); on the Dead Sea scrolls, Schiffmann (1994); on the Hellenistic Jewish literature, Collins (2000).

BIBLIOGRAPHY

ALEXANDER, P. S. 2001. 'Essay with Commentary on Post-Biblical Jewish Literature.' In *The Oxford Bible Commentary*. J. Barton and J. Muddiman eds. Oxford.

ATTRIDGE, H. W. 1976. *The Interpretation of Biblical History in the Antiquitates Judaicae of Flavius Josephus*. Missoula, Mont.

AVERY-PECK, A. J., NEUSNER, J., and CHILTON, B 2001. *Judaism in Late Antiquity. Part 5. Volume 1. The Judaism of Qumran: A Systematic Reading of the Dead Sea Scrolls*. Leiden.

BARCLAY, J. M. G. 1996 *Jews in the Mediterranean Diaspora from Alexander to Trajan (323 BCE–117 CE)*. Edinburgh.

BARTON, J. 1986. *Oracles of God. Perceptions of Ancient Prophecy in Israel After the Exile*. Oxford.

BEDENBENDER, A. 2000. *Der Gott der Welt tritt auf den Sinai. Entstehung, Entwicklung und Funktionsweise der frühjüdischen Apokalyptik*. Berlin.

BOCCACCINI, G. 1998. *Beyond the Essene Hypothesis: The Parting of the Ways between Qumran and Enochic Judaism*. Grand Rapids, Mich.

BORGEN, P. 1997. *Philo of Alexandria: An Exegete For His Time*. Leiden.

BROOKE, G. J. 1994. 'The Pesharim and the Origins of the Dead Sea Scrolls.' In *Methods of Investigation of the Dead Sea Scrolls and the Khirbet Qumran Site*. 339–53. M. O. Wise *et al.* eds. New York.

CHARLES, R. H. 1913. *The Apocrypha and Pseudepigrapha of the Old Testament*. 2 vols. Oxford.

CHARLESWORTH, J. H. 1983/1985. *The Old Testament Pseudepigrapha*. 2 vols. New York.

COLLINS, J. J. ed. 1979. *Apocalypse: The Morphology of a Genre*. Semeia 14. Chico, Cal.

—— 1997a. *Seers, Sibyls and Sages in Hellenistic-Roman Judaism*. Leiden.

—— 1997b. *Jewish Wisdom in the Hellenistic Age*. The Old Testament Library. Louisville, Ky.

—— 1997c. *Apocalypticism in the Dead Sea Scrolls*. London.

—— 1998a. *The Apocalyptic Imagination*. 2nd edn. Grand Rapids, Mich.

—— ed. 1998b. *The Encyclopedia of Apocalypticism. Vol. 1. The Roots of Apocalypticism in Judaism and Christianity*. New York.

—— 2000. *Between Athens and Jerusalem: Jewish Identity in the Hellenistic Diaspora*. 2nd edn. Grand Rapids, Mich.

CROSS, F. M. 1984. 'Fragments of the Prayer of Nabonidus.' *Israel Exploration Journal* 34: 260–4.

—— 1995. *The Ancient Library of Qumran*. 3rd edn. Sheffield.

—— 1998. *From Epic to Canon: History and Literature in Ancient Israel*. Baltimore.

DIMANT, D. 1994. 'Apocalyptic Texts at Qumran.' In *The Community of the Renewed Covenant*. 175–91. E. Ulrich and J. VanderKam eds. Notre Dame, Ind.

DUHAIME, J. 1988. 'The War Scroll from Qumran and the Greco-Roman Tactical Treatises.' *Revue de Qumran* 13: 133–51.

EFRON, J. 1987. *Studies on the Hasmonean Period*. Leiden.

ELLIOTT, M. 2000. *Survivors of Israel*. Grand Rapids, Mich.

FELDMAN, L. H. 1993. *Jew and Gentile in the Ancient World*. Princeton.

—— 1998a. *Josephus's Interpretation of the Bible*. Berkeley.

—— 1998b. *Studies in Josephus' Rewritten Bible*. Leiden.

FLINT, P. W. 1997. *Dead Sea Psalms Scrolls and the Book of Psalms*. Leiden.

FLINT, P. W. and VANDERKAM, J. C. eds. 1998–9. *The Dead Sea Scrolls After Fifty Years*. 2 vols. Leiden.

FREUDENTHAL, J. 1874–5. *Alexander Polyhistor und die von ihm erhaltenen Reste jüdischer und samaritanischer Geschichtswerke*. Hellenistische Studien 1–2. Breslau.

FRIEDLÄNDER, M. 1903. *Geschichte der jüdischen Apologetik*. Zurich.

GOLB, N. 1995. *Who Wrote the Dead Sea Scrolls? The Search for the Secret of Qumran*. New York.

GOODENOUGH, E. R. 1935. *By Light, Light. The Mystic Gospel of Hellenistic Judaism*. New Haven.

GOODMAN, M. D. 1994. *Mission and Conversion: Proselytizing in the Religious History of the Roman Empire*. Oxford.

GRUEN, E. 1998. *Heritage and Hellenism: The Reinvention of Jewish Tradition*. Berkeley.

HALPERN-AMARU, B. 1999. *The Empowerment of Women in the Book of Jubilees*. Leiden.

HARLOW, D. C. 1996. *The Greek Apocalypse of Baruch (3 Baruch) in Hellenistic Judaism and Early Christianity*. Leiden.

HARRINGTON, D. J. 1999. *Invitation to the Apocrypha*. Grand Rapids, Mich.

HELLHOLM, D. ed. 1983. *Apocalypticism in the Mediterranean World and the Near East*. Tübingen.

HIMMELFARB, M. 1983. *Tours of Hell: An Apocalyptic Form in Jewish and Christian Literature*. Philadelphia.

—— 1993. *Ascent to Heaven in Jewish and Christian Apocalypses*. New York.

HOLLADAY, C. R. 1983–96. *Fragments from Hellenistic Jewish Authors*. 4 vols. Atlanta, Ga.

HORST, P. W. VAN DER 1990. *Essays on the Jewish World of Early Christianity*. Göttingen.

JONGE, M. DE. 1953. *The Testaments of the Twelve Patriarchs: A Study of their Text, Composition and Origin*. Assen.

—— 2000. 'The Testaments of the Twelve Patriarchs and Related Qumran Fragments.' In *For a Later Generation. The Transformation of Tradition in Israel, Early Judaism and Early Christianity*. R. A. Argall, B. A. Bow, and R. A. Werline eds. Harrisburg, Pa.

KAUTZSCH, E. J. 1900. *Die Apokryphen und Pseudepigraphen des Alten Testaments*. Tübingen.

KRAEMER, R. S. 1998. *When Aseneth met Joseph*. New York.

KUGEL, J. L. 1998. *Traditions of the Bible*. Cambridge, Mass.

LEVINE, A.-J. ed. 1991. *'Women like This.' New Perspectives on Jewish Women in the Greco-Roman World*. Atlanta, Ga.

LINDER, H. 1972. *Die Geschichtsauffassung des Flavius Josephus im Bellum Judaicum*. Leiden.

MILIK, J. T. 1976. *The Books of Enoch*. Oxford.

—— 1992. 'Les Modèles Araméens du Livre d'Esther dans la Grotte 4 de Qumrân.' *RevQ* 15: 321–99.

MOORE, G. F. 1971 (1927). *Judaism in the First Centuries of the Christian Era*. 2 vols. New York.

MURPHY, F. J. 1993. *Pseudo-Philo: Re-Writing the Bible*. New York.

NEWMAN, C. C., DAVILA, J. R., and LEWIS, G. S. eds. 1999. *The Jewish Roots of Christological Monotheism*. Leiden.

NEWSOM, C. A. 1990. 'Kenneth Burke Meets the Teacher of Righteousness: Rhetorical Strategies in the Hodayot and Serek ha-Yahad.' In *Of Scribes and Scrolls*. 121–31. H. W. Attridge, J. J. Collins, and T. H. Tobin ed. Lanham, Md.

NICKELSBURG. G. W. E. 1981. *Jewish Literature Between the Bible and the Mishna*. Philadelphia.

—— 1998. 'Enochic Wisdom: An alternative to the Mosaic Torah?' In *Hesed ve-emet: Studies in Honor of Ernest S. Frerichs*. J. Magness and S. Gitin eds. Brown Judaic Studies 10. Atlanta, 4a.

—— 2001. *1 Enoch. 1. A Commentary on the Book of 1 Enoch chapters 1–36; 81–108*. Hermeneia. Minneapolis.

QIMRON, E. and STRUGNELL, J. 1985. 'An Unpublished Halakhic Letter from Qumran.' In *Biblical Archaeology Today: Proceedings of the International Congress on Biblical Archaeology, Jerusalem, April 1984*. 400–7. J. Amitai ed. Jerusalem.

—— —— 1994. *Qumran Cave 4, V: Miqṣat Maʿaśē Ha-Torah. Discoveries in the Judaean Desert* 10; Oxford.

RAD, G. VON. 1965. *Theologie des Alten Testaments*. 4th edn. Munich.

ROWLAND, C. 1982. *The Open Heaven: A Study of Apocalyptic in Judaism and Early Christianity*. New York.

ROWLEY, H. H. 1944. *The Relevance of Apocalyptic*. London.

RUNIA, D. T. 1986. *Philo of Alexandria and the Timaeus of Plato*. Leiden.

SACCHI, P. 1997. *Jewish Apocalyptic and its History*. Sheffield.

SANDERS, E. P. 1977. *Paul and Palestinian Judaism*. Philadelphia.

SANDERS, J. A. 1965. *The Psalms Scroll of Qumran Cave 11 (11QPsᵃ). Discoveries in the Judaean Desert* 4. Oxford.

SATRAN, D. 1995. *Biblical Prophets in Byzantine Palestine: Reassessing the Lives of the Prophets*. Leiden.

SCHIFFMAN, L. H. 1994. *Reclaiming the Dead Sea Scrolls*. Philadelphia and Jerusalem.

—— and VANDERKAM, J. C. ed. 2000. *The Encyclopedia of the Dead Sea Scrolls*. 2 vols. Oxford and New York.

SCHÜRER, E. 1973–87. *The History of the Jewish People in the Age of Jesus Christ*. Rev. and ed. G. Vermes, F. Millar, and M. Goodman. 3 vols. Edinburgh.

SHAVIT, Y. 1997. *Athens in Jerusalem: Classical Antiquity and Hellenism in the Making of the Modern Secular Jew*. London.

STERN, M. 1974–84. *Greek and Latin Authors on Jews and Judaism*. 3 vols. Jerusalem.

STONE, M. E. ed. 1984. *Jewish Writings of the Second Temple Period. Compendia Rerum Iudaicarum ad Novum Testamentum* 2/2. Philadelphia.

STRUGNELL, J., HARRINGTON, D., and ELGVIN, T. 1999. *Qumran Cave 4. XXIV. Sapiential Texts, Part 2. 4QInstruction (Mûsār lᵉMēvîn): 4Q415ff. Discoveries in the Judaean Desert* 34. Oxford.

SUNDBERG, A. C. 1964. *The Old Testament of the Early Church*. Cambridge, Mass.

TALMON, S. 1989. *The World of Qumran from Within*. Jerusalem.

TCHERIKOVER, V. 1956. 'Jewish Apologetic Literature Reconsidered'. *Eos* 48: 169–93.

—— 1999. *Hellenistic Civilization and the Jews*. Peabody, Mass. (Reprint from 1959).

TOBIN, T. H. 1983. *The Creation of Man: Philo and the History of Interpretation*. Washington, DC.

TOV, E. 1992. *Textual Criticism of the Hebrew Bible*. Minneapolis.

WACHOLDER, B. Z. 1983. *The Dawn of Qumran: The Sectarian Torah and the Teacher of Righteousness*. Cincinnati.

Weinfeld, M. 1986. *The Organizational Pattern and the Penal Code of the Qumran Sect.* Göttingen.

Winston, D. 1985. *Logos and Mystical Philosophy in Philo of Alexandria.* Cincinnati.

Wills, L. M. 1995. *The Jewish Novel in the Ancient World.* Ithaca, NY.

Wise, M. O. 1990. *A Critical Study of the Temple Scroll from Qumran Cave 11.* Chicago.

Wolfson, H. A. 1947. *Philo: Foundations of Religious Philosophy in Judaism, Christianity and Islam.* Cambridge, Mass.

Yadin, Y. 1977 *Megillat ha-Miqdash.* 3 vols. Jerusalem.

——1983. *The Temple Scroll.* 3 vols. Jerusalem. (Revised English edn.)

CHAPTER 5

....

HISTORIOGRAPHY ON THE JEWS IN THE 'TALMUDIC PERIOD' (70–640 CE)

....

SETH SCHWARTZ[1]

INTRODUCTION: HISTORY OF THE JEWS IN THE TALMUD PERIOD

....

FEW scholars nowadays would attempt a narrative history of the Jews between the destruction of the Second Temple (70 CE) and the Arab conquest of Palestine (c.640 CE), for reasons which will be explored later in this essay. Nevertheless, on some issues there is broad if not universal consensus. After the destruction, Palestine was made into a standard Roman province in a way which at least curtailed and perhaps abrogated the Jews' traditional, if partial, autonomy. The tax of two drachmas per annum once paid to the Jerusalem Temple was now paid to the Roman state and used to rebuild the temple of Capitoline Jupiter in Rome. Nevertheless, the Jews rebelled again, with disastrous results. The Diaspora Revolt (115–17 CE) seems to have ended in the decimation or destruction of the Jewish settlements in Egypt,

[1] I would like to thank Marina Rustow, who has read and tremendously improved this chapter.

Libya, and several other places, while the Bar Kokhba Revolt (132–5) brought an end to the Jews' hopes for the restoration of Jerusalem and the Temple and, more tangibly, to Jewish settlement in the district of Judaea.

A much reduced Jewish population was now concentrated in Galilee, and of diaspora communities, the most important in the Roman Empire were now in Asia Minor and Italy. By far the largest diaspora communities, though, were situated in central Mesopotamia, under Parthian and later Sassanian (neo-Persian) rule. Though the Babylonian Talmud leaves little doubt about the ever greater importance and distinctiveness of these communities, it provides little readily useful historical information, even about the fourth through sixth centuries, when the Talmud largely took form.

In Palestine, the period after Bar Kokhba is also rather obscure. We can, though, say something about the gradual coalescence of a rabbinic movement—probably consisting originally of the scattered remnants of the priests, scribes, and Pharisees of the Second Temple period—under the leadership of a dynast eventually called a 'patriarch' or, in Hebrew, *nasi*. While the rabbis probably enjoyed some prestige as arbitrators, legal experts, and preachers, they had for several centuries no state support and must have found it difficult to compete for legal and religious authority and cultural prestige with local Greek cities and other mediators of imperial power.

This may have begun to change when the Roman Empire gradually became Christian, in the course of the fourth century. The patriarchate had probably begun its rise *c.*200 CE, in the administration of Rabbi Judah I, but acquired its highest rank and greatest authority only under the Christian emperors, in the late fourth century, when the patriarchs were more powerful and enjoyed higher rank in the Constantinopolitan senate than the governors of Palestine. The growing power of the patriarchs may explain why their office was abolished around 425. In the same period, rabbis and similar Jewish religious officials first acquired limited jurisdiction over the Jews, and the local Jewish community was for the first time since the destruction of the Temple recognized as a licit corporation.

Gradually, though, theologically motivated hostility, encouraged by some bishops and monastics, came to influence imperial attitudes. The effects of this shift were not immediately or everywhere apparent. In both Palestine and the diaspora, archaeology demonstrates not only the Jews' relative prosperity in the fifth and sixth centuries, but also the emergence of a new religious culture, characterized by the construction of elaborately decorated synagogues even in small settlements, and by the introduction of such new literary forms as the *piyyut*, the midrash collection, and even the Talmud. At the same time, perhaps especially in the eastern part of the Roman Empire (the Western Empire fell in 476), pressure on the Jews probably increased dramatically in the course of the sixth century. When first the Persians (in 614) and then the Arabs (in 634) invaded Syria and Palestine, surprisingly few people, even among the Christians, offered any resistance; but some Jews actively joined the invading forces.

HISTORIOGRAPHY

The historiography of the past sixty years on the Jews in the 'Talmud period' can be divided into two very broad tendencies, which may be designated Israeli and non-Israeli. Some of the characteristics that seem retrospectively definitive of 'Israeli' scholarship—especially a tendency toward a highly positivistic or, to borrow an expression from C. E. Hayes, 'naively historicizing' approach to rabbinic literature—in fact were widely shared before *c.*1970. But Israeli and earlier Zionist scholarship had a set of often quite self-conscious concerns which went far beyond a preference for positivistic reading of rabbinic literature and which served to distinguish it from non-Zionist scholarship. Most essentially, Zionist and Israeli scholarship was far more concerned with history than its diaspora counterparts. This was of course implicit in its nationalist project—on the common romantic assumption that only nations truly had histories (whereas religions, for example, had textual canons and evolving theologies: Myers 1995: 5–6). Furthermore, Israeli and non-Israeli scholarship have generally been founded on quite distinct social and cultural-historical assumptions. These differences have prevailed for most of the twentieth century and continue to be important today, and so constitute the primary topic of this essay.[2]

ZIONIST AND ISRAELI SCHOLARSHIP: DINUR AND KAUFMANN

The predecessors of the Zionists in the Wissenschaft des Judentums movement had laboured to generate a specifically historical consciousness among their acculturating Jewish supporters and readers (Schorsch 1994: 177–204; Roemer 2000). Like other romantics, they wished to discover and collect lost or neglected documents and monuments, and make sense of them contextually, primarily through comparative philology.[3] Though this endeavour yielded several pioneering pieces of historiography, there is no question that, especially for the period under consideration, the main concern of these scholars was not history but textual scholarship. The simple and compelling reason for this was that their work served primarily a

---

[2] Jacob Neusner published a monograph-length article on this topic (Neusner 1990) including, notwithstanding its title, a crudely polemical section on Israeli scholarship (pp. 83–104).

[3] On this chrestomathic zeal shared by the Wissenschaftler and the Zionists, see Bartal (1997 and 2000).

religious and communal need: they wished to demonstrate to the German and Austro-Hungarian authorities that Judaism was not contemptible, so the Jews merited emancipation, and to the Jews that Jewish tradition itself validated the introduction of religious reforms. The most effective way to prove these points was through contextualized reading of texts (Schorsch 1994: 177–204).

Accordingly, one of the most remarkable and problematic features of Heinrich Graetz's history was his view that with the destruction of the Second Temple the Jews no longer even had a proper history, or at most, had a surpassingly odd one:

> If you wish to sketch a clear, adequate picture of this period [70–1780 CE], you can do so in the form of a diptych. On one side, Judah enslaved, his walking-stick in his hand, his pilgrim's bundle on his back, his gloomy features turned to heaven, encircled by prison-walls, the implements of martyrdom, and the glowing iron of the brand. On the other side, the same figure with a thinker's earnestness visible on his luminous brow, the demeanour of a research-scholar in his radiant face,[4] in a classroom, filled with a vast library in all the languages of man and touching on all branches of divine and human science: the appearance of a slave with the pride of a thinker.[5]

Similarly, in his introduction to what Graetz himself called the 'talmudische Zeit', he observes: 'At the beginning of this period, one can still discern the striving to restore yet again a lost political life. This striving generated clashes, uprisings, wars and new defeats. But soon the political movement retreated, only to leave in its wake full scope for purely spiritual activity.'

At first, mainstream Zionist historical thought accepted Graetz's view that Jewish national self-determination and so a specifically national and political Jewish history came to an end more or less in 70 CE (Myers 1988). But Ben Zion Dinur argued forcefully in the introduction to the first volume of *Yisrael Ba-Golah*, published in 1926, that the 'Diaspora period' began not in 70, as had been universally thought, but around 640, with the Arab conquest of Palestine.[6] 'It would be easy enough to demonstrate that the true "exile" (of the nation as a historical-communal entity, not of its individual members) begins only from the moment that the Land of Israel ceases to be a Jewish land'—a quality which has both a political and a demographic dimension. For Dinur, Palestine's loss of its Jewish character was a centuries-long process. Though the political and demographic elements of this process were not synchronous, the Arab conquest seemed a serviceable, if admittedly rather artificial, boundary line (Dinur 1958: 5–7; 1969: 3–6).

Rejected, in this scheme, is Graetz's periodization by book—in which even the amoraic *sof hora'ah* (literally, 'the end of instruction', probably meaning the end of

---

[4] This hint at the identification of the traditional Torah scholar with the modern academic may be due to the influence of Zacharias Frankel (Schorsch 1994: 191).

[5] Graetz (1893: 1)—from the introduction to history from 70 to 1780 (my translation). Rhetorical introductory material of this sort was systematically omitted from the English translation.

[6] For criticism of a division of Jewish history into pre-exilic and exilic periods, see Biale (1986: 10–33). On Dinur, see Myers (1995: 129–50).

original and authoritative amoraic legal teaching, traditionally dated to *c*.500), for example, constitutes a meaningful historical boundary marker—replaced by politics, demography, and land tenure, the real stuff of history. The history of the Jews is here primarily a national history, and the history of the Jewish nation in turn remains primarily the history of a land, as long as the land remained Jewish, even if more Jews lived outside Palestine than in it.

In the 1920s, as later, there were other voices in the Zionist yishuv. One of the most compelling belonged to Yehezkel Kaufmann, who in his *Golah Ve-Nekhar* (published 1929–32) approached the problem of the endurance of Jewish nationhood in the absence of political sovereignty with an intellectual rigour and concentrated theoretical sophistication reminiscent of the best German sociology of the period (Kaufmann had immigrated from Berlin in 1928), but in short supply in Zionist scholarship outside the works of Gershom Scholem.[7] Kaufmann was little interested, at least in this book, in questions of periodization or territory, and was mainly concerned to investigate the role of religion in the formation and maintenance of a distinctive Jewish group, even in the absence of the material conditions which were normally (and certainly by most Zionists) regarded as essential for national existence. Perhaps unsurprisingly, given what must have seemed to some of his readers to be Kaufmann's devaluing of the national element in Judaism, *Golah Ve-Nekhar* had little detectable influence on the Zionist historiography of the Talmud period (but see below), whereas his ultra-romantic and extremely problematic *Toledot Ha-Emunah Ha-Yisre'elit* (published 1937–56) shaped Jewish biblical scholarship both in Israel and elsewhere.[8]

ALON AND URBACH

In fact, the work of Gedalyah Alon (1901, or in some accounts, 1902–50) and his followers, which eventually emerged as the mainstream of Israeli scholarship, can be viewed as a detailed elaboration of Dinur's basic ideas about the character of Jewish national life after the Destruction. Thus, the introduction to Alon's lecture notes,

[7] In fact Max Weber seems to me an obvious influence both on Kaufmann's style and on the substance of his work, yet Kaufmann failed to mention him—an omission paralleled by his failure in his biblical scholarship to engage with post-Wellhausenian developments in the field (though the parallel is imperfect since unacknowledged influence is not the same as obliviousness); Silberstein (1982), in what is otherwise a helpful essay, mentions but fails to explain Kaufmann's silence about Weber; on his biblical scholarship, see Geller (1985).

[8] There are surely institutional, not only ideological, reasons for Dinur's greater influence: he began teaching at the Hebrew University much earlier than Kaufmann (1936, as opposed to 1948), and taught in the Department of Jewish History, whereas Kaufmann taught Bible: see *Encyclopedia Judaica*, sub vv.

published in English in 1980 as *The Jews in their Land in the Talmudic Age*,[9] is basically a paraphrase of the first chapter of *Yisrael Ba-Golah*, with a few additions which will be mentioned below.

Alon's *Mehkarim*, containing articles and reviews published between 1934 and Alon's death, in addition to a few pieces he left unpublished, provides evidence of real distinction (Alon 1957; 1977). Alon's approach was shared by such rabbinically trained contemporaries as Saul Lieberman, Ephraim Elimelech Urbach, Louis Finkelstein, and many others in the 1930s, 1940s, and 1950s, and was little changed from that used by scholars of the previous generation, including Adolph Büchler (e.g. Büchler 1906)—whom Alon especially admired—Victor Aptowitzer, Louis Ginzberg (esp. Ginzberg 1909–38), and Samuel Krauss (Krauss 1948).[10] This work proceeded by using the history of halachah and somewhat more tentatively that of rabbinic biblical exegesis, in addition to 'historical' tales in the Talmud and midrashim, subjected to careful comparative analysis intended to aid in the extraction of the stories' historical kernel, in a fairly direct way to reconstruct political, social, and economic history. Alon was indubitably one of the best practitioners of this method, and the most historically sophisticated. In his eulogy of Alon, the great medievalist Yitzhak Baer reported Alon's ambition to be the Mommsen of Jewish history (Theodor Mommsen was a pioneering historian of Roman law, upon which he relied heavily for his reconstruction of Roman political and social history).[11] But what really distinguished him from his colleagues was his flexibility and eclecticism in interpreting rabbinic sources, on full display in his long critique of Finkelstein (1936) (Alon 1957: 181–227). Although Alon often sought to explain halachah against a background of political and social change, he acknowledged that not all halachic change could be accounted for in this way, that rabbinic law and exegesis had its own dynamics of development, literary context, and so on. Similarly, though Alon may have slightly misread, or over-read, Lieberman's argument about the diffusion and significance of Graeco-Roman culture in Palestine, and was deeply convinced a priori of the Jews' ingrained tendency to cultural self-enclosure,[12] the views he set out in response to Lieberman (wealthy Palestinian Jews were not all highly literate in Greek, rural common folk may have had little knowledge of the language, political and social pressures pushed the Jews in opposite cultural directions

---

[9] Originally published 1952–61 in Tel Aviv, by the Kibbutz Ha-Me'uhad.

[10] In my view this is undeniable, notwithstanding his students' insistence on his methodological innovation—amounting to his preference for hard-headed historical interpretations over 'soft' theological ones (see below), and his conviction that the 'historical kernel' of rabbinic stories may be recovered through comparison of alternate versions, and the adducing of non-rabbinic parallels. But neither concern was novel—though Alon perhaps applied them more systematically, and more effectively, than most.

[11] Yitzhak Baer's eulogy of Alon was printed as the preface to Alon (1959).

[12] Note the remarkable argument a fortiori in Alon 1957: 275–7 (a review of Lieberman 1942) that since most Palestinian pagans were ignorant of Greek, Jews certainly were even more so.

simultaneously) reflect a nuanced and attractively complex grasp of the sorts of cultural changes produced by the imposition of direct Roman rule, and their limitations.[13]

Alon's extant works convey a fiercely combative nationalism—a commitment which shaped both the surface and the deep structure of his work. Sometimes his nationalism worked to the advantage of his account. Most importantly, it predisposed him to prefer hard-headed political explanations for historical developments, and eschew theology and homiletics. For example, in some historiography written by Jews it is possible to detect a surprising strain of sentimentality about the Roman Empire.[14] By contrast, Alon regarded the Romans as essentially hostile to the Jews and their national/religious aims, and all too willing to act on their hostility. Admittedly, some of the details are imaginary (e.g. the notorious description of Yavneh as practically a prison camp—Alon 1957, 219–51). It could even be argued that in sharing the widespread belief in a golden age of Roman–Jewish relations under the Severan emperors Alon did not go far enough—unlike his friend Baer, who in an iconoclastic, brilliant, possibly wrong but wrongly neglected article first published in 1956 argued that before 313 CE the Romans scarcely distinguished Jews from Christians in legal terms: both were technically illicit, occasionally persecuted, usually tolerated by default (Baer 1956, 1961).[15] Certainly there was never any Severan golden age. In any case, Alon's view of the Romans as aggressively expansionist and strongly prone to violence may have seemed unusual or parochial even as late as the 1940s, but certainly resonates with the historiographical mainstream on Roman imperialism since the 1970s.

The other chief manifestations of Alon's nationalism are more troublesome; they pervade all his writings as fundamental presuppositions, have been unselfconsciously adopted by his followers, and have never been subjected to systematic criticism.[16] They can be distilled into three main components, intertwined and overlapping in Alon's writing, but roughly separable for heuristic purposes: (1) the Jews were always a (single) nation; (2) their nationhood had essentially a religious character (here one can speculate about the influence of Kaufmann); (3) as a result—that is, either because of their religious exclusivism or because of their profound devotion to their own nationhood, or some combination—they were unusually united internally, and unusually impervious to the cultural

---

[13] Lieberman eventually conceded some of Alon's points without ever mentioning him or his review (Lieberman 1963; 1974: 216–34).

[14] For further discussion of this issue, see Schwartz (2001b: 335–40). On Saul Lieberman's role in this, see below, though Lieberman himself shared Alon's hostility to the Romans and in his Hebrew writing normally referred to the Roman Empire as the *malkhut resha* or *malkhut zadon*—i.e. 'the wicked kingdom'!

[15] On the Romans as 'tolerant by default', see Garnsey (1984).

[16] Unlike Alon's methods of 'reading' so as to extract historical kernels from talmudic anecdotes—criticism of which was a cornerstone of the Neusnerian revolution.

influence of their conquerors—and indeed manifested throughout antiquity a strong tendency to political opposition (this is one of Alon's additions to Dinur's analysis).

The first of these premisses was of course a cornerstone of Zionist historiography. The conviction that the Jews have always been a nation is not a priori inconsistent with a high level of analytic sophistication, and, as already noted, Alon did occasionally introduce a certain complexity into his writing—sometimes acknowledging in passing that there was a variety of responses to Roman rule, that some Jews collaborated, even that many submitted to Roman authority whether or not they were conscious of acting as collaborators. Yet his Zionist commitment undoubtedly dominated his understanding of the past. Surely even the casual twenty-first-century reader of his work in Hebrew cannot fail to notice how often the word 'ummah (nation) is repeated, and how often the 'ummah is described as acting as a unit. The Jews are often (but not always) presented as unanimous in their cultural and political resistance to Rome, and in their support for rabbis and patriarchs and their obedience to their laws. Closely related to this is the tendency, which Alon shared with many of his contemporaries, to speak in terms of Jewish national and local institutions: the patriarchs and rabbis had quasi-constitutional authority (granted them at least initially by tradition and by the consensus of 'the nation', not by Rome), as did the Sanhedrin and the lower rabbinic courts and the institutions which comprised the local Jewish communities. To be sure, rabbinic literature itself often speaks of institutions, of the constitutional rights and authority enjoyed by rabbis and others. But as Alon knew very well, it most often does so in prescriptive texts, whereas rabbinic anecdotes and maʿasiyot (accounts of legal cases), which are at least ostensibly descriptive, often create a very different impression.[17] Alon's description of Palestinian Jewish life in institutional terms thus constituted a conscious choice, which requires some explanation.

A hint at one part of the explanation is provided by Baer's observation that Alon aspired to be the Jewish Mommsen—that is, that he wished to provide a firm constitutional-historical foundation for the history of the ancient Jewish polity, as Mommsen did for the Roman state. But Alon was not simply imitating Mommsen. His institutional history approach was above all a corollary of his nationalism. Institutions, after all, may be regarded as the form taken by customary asymmetrical social relations in the absence of resistance: in a society characterized by an unusually high level of internal unity, power would never need to be accumulated or exercised. Institutional prerogatives were all that was necessary to keep the society functioning in a stable way—in fact, they were the embodiment of social

---

[17] See classically Chajes's comparison of rabbinic prescriptions about how courts should operate with reports of ma'asiyot in the talmudim (Chajes 1899), and Alon's 'refutation' (Alon 1977: 382–6).

stability. This same factor also explains Alon's general failure to distinguish between prescriptive and descriptive texts: in so stable and united a society institutional prescription was likely to be translated directly into social action. Thus, the conception of Jewish history in institutional terms was closely associated with a nationalist (not necessarily only a Zionist) historiography.

As already suggested, Alon came to dominate the history of the Talmud period. Though he never produced a synthetic account of the subject,[18] and always remained in some sense an exegete of the Talmud, it is clear that he was—in self-conception, in the opinion of his students, and I would venture to say objectively—far more exclusively a historian than such peers as Lieberman and Urbach. Not unrelated to this is the fact that his work—though he and his students regarded it as purely 'scientific'—was shaped in matters large and small by an ardent commitment to Zionism, a scholarly preference which was not in fact shared by all his Hebrew University colleagues (Myers 1995: 7). His nationalism predisposed him to view talmudic history as essentially political, and to resist homiletics and, on the whole, religious idealization of the rabbis. One can imagine that his mastery of rabbinics combined with his devotion to a materialist view of causation (tempered by a near mystical conviction of the special power of Jewish nationhood throughout history), the information that he struggled with the conflict between Torah study/traditional religious commitment and science, and furthermore, the fact that he had some sort of military (guerrilla?) career in addition to his university lectureship (Dzimitrowski 1950–1: 311), all made him an exceptionally appealing figure in Jerusalem in the 1930s and 1940s, especially to what we may call modernizing yeshiva students. By this I mean young men of intellectual inclinations from highly traditional backgrounds for whom modernizing, in the context of inter-war Poland or Palestine, involved attraction to secular education and/or revolutionary political movements.

Before discussing Alon's influence in the second half of the twentieth century, it will be instructive to pause briefly to contrast him with E. E. Urbach—a slightly younger contemporary who lived until 1991, taught for many decades in the Talmud Department of the Hebrew University, and wrote extensively and influentially on rabbinic history (though unlike Alon, Urbach also worked extensively on medieval and modern rabbinics, and on purely textual and theological issues). Also unlike Alon, Urbach never established a school, despite having been institutionally better situated to do so, if only by virtue of his longevity.

---

[18] *The Jews in Their Land* was written by his students—who obviously sensed the need for a synthetic book and had a strong enough sense of *pietas* to think that their transcriptions of Alon's university lectures would serve the purpose better than anything they could have written themselves. Later on, Safrai participated in a team project which may have been intended to replace the earlier work. See below.

E. E. URBACH[19]

As already suggested, Urbach's differences with Alon were not essentially methodological. He, too, concentrated on the history of halachah, which he thought was
readily translatable into Jewish history *tout court*. He, too, assumed that the Jews
were, at least in the Talmud period, unusually united, and adopted an institutional
history approach. Nevertheless, he differed from Alon in important ways. Unlike
Alon, he often started his essays with historical, rather than exegetical, questions,
and indeed often seemed more *au courant* with contemporary historiographical
trends than Alon. He thus wrote articles on the sorts of especially social historical
issues which also engaged Roman historians and medievalists in the middle of the
twentieth century—slavery, charity, class structure.[20] Though in retrospect these
articles seem rather old-fashioned in their reluctance to introduce change, or even
much chronological specificity at all, into their arguments, and did not completely
avoid an apologetic and theological tone, they remain important, if only as collections of sources, accompanied by often still helpful explication. Alon had died
before archaeological exploration reached its peak in Israel, so he never devoted
much attention to archaeology, but Urbach occasionally made productive use of
recent discoveries. His most enduringly important article on an ancient topic, in
fact, defines to this day the mainstream of Israeli scholarship on a fundamental
historical problem raised by archaeology: how could late antique Jews make such
widespread use of figurative art, even in the decoration of synagogues, and even art
iconographically little changed from its Roman pagan sources, as archaeology
demonstrates they did (Urbach 1959)? Urbach, rejecting the view of Erwin
R. Goodenough (see below), argued that the rabbis did not prohibit figurative art
as unambiguously as has often been claimed—in fact, when compared to Christian
contemporaries like Tertullian, they were markedly lenient even about idols, out of
pastoral concern for the Jews' economic welfare. And by the time pagan iconography was used in synagogues it had lost its religious meaning and so was purely
decorative. The Jews' use of figurative art is thus fully consistent with their enduring
and profound devotion to the rabbis and rabbinic law, *pace* Goodenough. This view,
shared by the influential Israeli archaeologist and art historian Michael Avi-Yonah
(see Avi-Yonah 1981), still prevails in Israel.

Urbach's disagreement with Alon emerges most clearly in his review of the first
volume of 'Alon's' posthumous *History* (Urbach 1953). Much of the review is taken
up with detailed arguments about the historical interpretation of individual rab-

---

[19]   The most extensive account of Urbach's career and scholarship is Assaf (1993). Urbach's extensive
organizational activities included chairing the Hebrew University Talmud Department and Institute of
Jewish Studies, and, for twenty years, the World Union of Jewish Studies.

[20]   Some of these essays have appeared in English in Urbach (1999), which also contains, on pp.
xi–xvii, a brief account in English of Urbach's life. On charity, see Urbach (1951).

binic anecdotes and laws—a fact which demonstrates Urbach's methodological proximity to Alon. For example, where Alon plausibly detected factional division among the rabbis of the immediate post-Destruction period as they vied for dominance, Urbach saw them as united by the pastoral need to guide the Jews through crisis. Even this detail, though, hints at deeper differences between the two scholars. In brief, where Alon saw the rabbis as essentially political figures—with more or less realistic political concerns—continuous with the Jewish authorities of the Second Temple period, Urbach saw them in idealized Graetzian terms, as essentially religious figures, anticipatory of medieval rabbis. One may suggest the following formulation: while Alon idealized the Jewish nation, Urbach idealized the Jewish religion. Urbach, furthermore, advocated the Wissenschaft view that the 'Diaspora period' begins in 70, since the rabbis had at their disposal only the power afforded by moral suasion, as was the case throughout their subsequent history, though Urbach's Jewish masses were nearly as rabbinically oriented as Alon's. Indeed, Urbach seems to have been no less convinced a Zionist than Alon, but in his writing Urbach was less radical, endeavouring to reconcile Zionism with European liberal humanism, and with a Central European variety of liberal religious traditionalism.[21] It is thus above all in tone or mood that Urbach and Alon differed—with Urbach representing a Wissenschaft-oriented, theologically and apologetically inclined, in some sense 'soft', European/diasporic scholarship, while Alon embodied a tough, materialist, apparently intellectually rigorous, Zionist future. In the mid-twentieth century Urbach's work seemed all too continuous with a disastrously compromised diasporic Jewish past.

ISRAELI SCHOLARSHIP, 1950–1990

Much of the agenda of Israeli historiography of the Talmud period after 1950 remained that set by Alon, though enriched in ways I will presently describe. It may be said, though, that a fair amount of this scholarship has been decidedly epigonic in character, by which I mean that some of Alon's hypotheses achieved a sort of canonical status and in the process lost their original subtlety. So, for example, though Alon was mainly interested in rabbinic courts, he acknowledged

---

[21] On Urbach's self-conscious continuity with jüdische Wissenschaft, see J. Sussmann in Assaf (1993: 12–3). Urbach has not been without followers. His student, the polymathic Jerusalem professor Moshe David Herr, retains much of Urbach's breadth and tone, but has written relatively little. Herr's students, most prominently Oded Ir-Shai and Hillel Newman, have carved out an important niche for themselves in the crucial but little-studied field of the treatment of the Jews in the writing of the Church Fathers.

that many Palestinian Jews had powerful reasons to bring their legal cases to Roman courts, city councils, and the like. Alon's followers seem to have absorbed his account's rabbinocentrism, but not the qualifications, and so produced ever-more rigidly rabbinocentric accounts. Certainly, the fundamental assumptions of Alon's work—concerning the nationhood of the post-Destruction Jews, and their cultural resistance to Roman rule—were never challenged, and underwent the same process of rigidification.

Furthermore, the field absorbed only with difficulty the implications of the masses of new material—mainly archaeological—that came to light in the generation after Alon's death. For example, Alon paid little attention to the Later Roman Empire and so in effect left a 300-year long piece of the Talmud period available for his successors to work on, a stroke of luck since many or even most of the new archaeological discoveries in Israel were of Late Antique material (fourth through seventh centuries). But an examination of the most noteworthy Israeli publication concerning the period (Baras 1982–4),[22] one that can be fairly regarded as a collective work of the Jerusalem mainstream—in fact the only attempt at a synthesis aside from Avi-Yonah's textbook (originally published in 1946 as *Biyemei Roma U-Vyzantion,* and frequently reprinted)—reveals an interesting pattern. The authors for almost everything down to the fourth century are members of the Alon school (except for Lee Levine, whose work combines Israeli and diasporic features), whereas the post-Constantinian chapters are by classicists, and others. There was thus some give in the system, primarily because archaeology was regarded as a separate field from history, and because the literary sources available for the fifth and sixth centuries (given the difficulty of subjecting midrashim and the early *piyyut* to the sort of historicist reading the Alon school felt confident about using on the Tosefta and the Palestinian Talmud)[23] tended to be written in Greek or Latin and so were best left to classicists, patristics scholars, and experts in Roman law. However, the fundamental assumptions even of this larger and looser group of scholars about 'inner' Jewish history, as a history of the continuity of Jewish nationhood and rabbinic authority, remained those of Alon. This is true also of Avi Yonah's influential work.

[22] The second volume, written entirely by Yoram Tsafrir, is a fundamentally important, and still highly valuable, archaeological survey. Despite the title, the first volume concerns mainly the Jews, though there are brief chapters on christianization and the Samaritans, and somewhat longer chapters on non-ethnically specific issues like administration and population size. Remarkably, there is no separate treatment of pagans, for several centuries after 135 certainly the largest element of the Palestinian population.

[23] The dominant scholars of midrash in Israel have been the late Joseph Heinemann—a form critic who was mainly interested in reconstructing the internal history of exegetical, as well as liturgical, traditions (Heinemann 1974), and Yonah Fraenkel, an unreconstructed 'new critic', who regards historical context as irrelevant to the interpretation of talmudic and midrashic narrative and exegesis (Fraenkel 1991; younger scholars, most of them trained by the above, have been less rigorously formalist). Israeli *piyyut* scholars—there are only a few non-Israeli *piyyut* scholars—have tended to combine formalism and historicism.

Even within the rabbinic-historical mainstream, a tendency developed to explore new topics. Alon himself, for instance, had contributed a few entries to Samuel Klein's *Sefer Hayishuv*, but historical geography, following Klein's model and extending it by focusing also on problems of administrative history (following Avi-Yonah 1962; Abel 1933–8; Alt 1959; and others), now became a major concern. More interesting, in my opinion, was the Alon school's gradual production of a full-blown economic and social history—topics Alon himself had hardly discussed. Though I do not believe that the producers of this work all consciously set out to fill in the gaps left by Alon in order to produce a comprehensive, coherent, from-the-ground-up account of Jewish life in post-Destruction Palestine, this is in effect precisely what they did. But they did so in a way which accentuates the most problematic elements of Alon's method, and bespeaks their growing intellectual involution and deep isolation from the historical mainstream. In particular, the Israeli economic and social history constitutes a strong expression of Jewish exceptionalism, as I will presently explain. To be sure, this has been a feature of much Jewish historiography—in fact, of national histories in general (Endelman 1997: 10–3). But here it assumed a remarkable, and remarkably explicit, form.

FELIKS, SPERBER, Z. SAFRAI

The senior figure in this project was Yehudah Feliks (b. 1922), trained academically in Talmud and botany and for many years lecturer in and professor of Talmud and 'Land of Israel Studies' at Bar Ilan and Tel Aviv Universities. The bulk of Feliks's work has been exegetical and lexicographical, and has contributed importantly to the understanding of rabbinic agricultural law. But Feliks's dissertation, twice published with revisions and expansions and often summarized in articles and encyclopaedia entries, concerned Jewish agriculture in the Talmud period (Feliks 1990).[24]

Here is part of the introduction to one of these summaries, which gives a good idea of much of this work:[25]

... In our days, the question naturally arises: How could this small land, mostly stones and wilderness, sustain a population which at some periods reached 2–3 million, the vast majority of which subsisted on agriculture? Among the answers that have been given is

---

[24] Feliks's career is described in Y. Friedman *et al.* (1997: 7–9); a bibliography appears on pp. 11–14. Feliks published almost all his work in Hebrew, but a very brief summary of his dissertation appeared in English as 'Agriculture', *Encyclopedia Judaica*, ii. 381–98.

[25] A very similar passage appears in *Encyclopedia Judaica*, ii. 396–7.

that climatic changes which have occurred, in the direction of dryness and reduced precipi-
tation, allow the supposition that land available for agricultural exploitation was once more
extensive... [But this is not the case.] Nevertheless, it is clear that serious changes have
occurred in the agricultural landscape of the country. The stony modern landscape characteristic of extensive areas in the mountainous regions of the Mediterranean climatic zone
differs from that of the biblical period, and certainly from that of the Mishnah and Talmud
periods. In the past, these areas were farmed intensively by means of terraces, but with the
abandonment of the land by the Hebrew [sic] farmers at the end of the fourth century, the
terraces were gradually destroyed; the soil then eroded and stones surfaced.

In general it may be said that the Land of Israel sustained its many inhabitants through the
diligence of farmers who enjoyed a rather high cultural level thanks to their intensive work
on the land, and to their powerful ties to the land—their ancestral heritage. As to the Hebrew
farmer, he did not stagnate, and his heart was open to new agricultural technologies. These
factors helped the Hebrew farmer achieve exceedingly high yields, achieved again in this
country only in our own times. (Baras *et al.* 1982–4: i. 419–41)

In sum, Jewish farmers, as a result of their 'ancestral heritage' and 'high cultural
level', were unusually devoted to their land (this echoes the importance of land
tenure for Dinur and Alon), which they farmed intensively and in technically
innovative ways—so that the land produced exceptionally high yields and could
support a surprisingly large population. Elsewhere Feliks argued from rabbinic texts
that wheat yields ranged from 22.5:1 in bad years to 45:1 or more in good years,
yields in fact not equalled until modern, disease-resistant strains of wheat and
chemical fertilizers were introduced in Palestine-Israel in the 1940s and 1950s
(Broshi 1986: 50–1). Feliks was clearly anxious about this suggestion. Furthermore,
he struggled to explain away a perfectly good, ostensibly Palestinian, talmudic legal
tradition which seemed to state that wheat yields ranged between 3.75:1 and 7.5:1
(which is in line with estimates for dry-farming yields common among Roman
economic historians), since other rabbinic, plus a few biblical and New Testament,
texts seemed to imply much higher yields. Despite his own sense of the plausible,
Feliks clearly had a strong a priori interest in adopting the high figures given in
idealizing biblical and aggadic texts, and dimly implied in the halachic texts he
analysed.

Feliks did not pursue the immense social, economic, political, and cultural
implications of such high grain yields, except to note their gross demographic
impact, and to infer from them the precocious sophistication and Zionist interests
of the ancient Jewish farmers. The rest of his work consisted of discussion of plants
and agricultural practices mentioned in the Mishnah and Talmud. Feliks believed,
in my view incorrectly, that the results of this investigation simply constituted a
description of ancient Jewish agriculture, which he believed was different from
ancient 'gentile' agriculture. What he actually demonstrated was that the farming
practices described in the Mishnah were fairly typical of dry farming in the Roman
eastern Mediterranean. It remained for his successors to work out the implications
of Feliks's work.

Daniel Sperber's first two books, which are our main concern here, emerged from a rather different academic tradition (Sperber 1974—acknowledging the inspiration and help of Michael Crawford and Richard Duncan-Jones; Sperber 1978). Both were based on his dissertation at University College, London, and demonstrate his immersion in the work of Roman social and economic historians of 1950s, 1960s, and 1970s. Furthermore, Sperber seems to have regarded himself as a follower of Lieberman much more than Alon. Like his model, he was especially interested in using classical sources and Roman history to interpret difficult rabbinic texts. As a writer, he was rhetorically much 'cooler' than the followers of Alon; there is no Zionist preaching, and no description of the rabbinic past in utopian terms. What he shared with his Israeli colleagues (his books were published after his immigration to Israel in 1968 and his hiring as a lecturer in Talmud at Bar Ilan) was a tendency to highly positivistic, though not wholly uncritical, reading of rabbinic, especially halachic, sources (at a time when such an approach could no longer be taken for granted). Furthermore, the thesis of his books was unmistakably inspired by Alon. In brief, Sperber wished to argue that the decline of the Jewish population in Palestine—their abandonment of agriculture, growing economic hardship, and eventual departure—was mainly the consequence of the 'crisis of the third century',[26] and the sporadic bouts of inflation which affected the Roman economy through the middle of the fourth. Sperber thereby accepted the hypothesis of a steep decline beginning *c*.300, but implicitly and interestingly diminished Christianity's role in this decline.

Sperber's books are different from his earlier work in one important respect. In the earlier work he summarily rejected Feliks's crop yields as 'completely impossible' and 'patently absurd' (Sperber 1970: 11, n. 3).[27] In the books, however, he accepted Feliks's yields but oddly failed to integrate their implications into a description of the Palestinian agrarian economy which was otherwise as primitivizing as K. D. White's, Ramsay MacMullen's, Richard Duncan-Jones's, and Peter Garnsey's view of the Roman Imperial economy in general. Thus, the final chapter of *The Land* contains a realistic account of how the small size of the average farm plot in the Palestinian interior inhibited the introduction of innovative technologies common elsewhere in the Roman world, excluded the possibility of agricultural self-sufficiency, and interfered with the development of farmers' emotional bonds to their land. In sum, Sperber's view of Palestinian Jewish agrarian life was precisely the opposite of Feliks's, leaving the high yields of the first, second, and early third centuries unexplained.

If Sperber's work remained poised incoherently between 'Loxbridge' and Jerusalem, between Finleyite primitivism and Zionist utopianism, his younger colleague Ze'ev Safrai eventually produced an integrated and coherent social and economic

---

[26] This is the name generally given to the period, beginning in 235, of extreme political instability, constant warfare, and concomitantly, the debasement of coinage and high rates of inflation.

[27] I assume this reflects the view proposed in his dissertation, which I have not been able to see.

history of Jewish Palestine in the Talmud period. To be sure, to reach this conclusion one must ignore a number of problems in his work. Somehow, it seems easier to excuse the common Israeli scholarly practice of writing of Palestine/Eretz Israel but referring only to that country's Jewish inhabitants in a book written in 1950 or 1960 than in one published in 1994.[28] The same is true of the ardent and increasingly embattled rabbinocentrism of the account. Add to this the pervasive inaccuracy of citation, the common failure to comprehend the economic-historical models utilized or rejected, the elementarily unsound maximalist interpretation of rabbinic texts (so that, for example, every Galilean village is said to have had all the commercial and religious institutions scattered rabbinic sources ascribe to individual villages), and one begins to sense that one is witnessing a historiographical style in its terminal decadence. And yet, for all its flaws, Safrai's work cannot be ignored.

Safrai began by accepting the grain yields proposed by Feliks (1994: 108–10)—and was one of the first to grasp and explore their implications. For Safrai, these yields fuelled a modern-sounding economic system: Palestinian agriculture in the Roman and Byzantine periods was characterized not by the widespread cultivation of the wheat and barley needed for subsistence, as it had been in the Second Temple period, but rather by a tendency to regional specialization. Thus, Galilee produced olives, Judaea grapes, the Jordan Valley dates and balsam, and so on. Such a system necessitated a strong orientation toward trade, both within the province and between Palestine and its neighbours, which was thus an extremely important factor in the Palestinian economy. Dependence on trade rather than subsistence agriculture also allowed for a population growth far more massive than could be predicted on the basis of the carrying capacity of the land (as Feliks had already suggested). Hence Safrai hypothesized high population density, which meant for the Jews primarily settlement in a large number of big villages, called *'arim* in rabbinic literature, with populations ranging from 100 to 1,000 families.[29] These villages were not only home to farmers but also, because of their advanced, trade-fuelled economics, sustained a wide range of specialized artisans; so the Jewish villages were not economically dependent on (and not influenced culturally by) the neighbouring pagan, Christian, or mixed cities (Safrai 1994: 21–49). Each had authorized political institutions (the *tovei ha'ir*, *parnasim*, *hazanim*, etc.), partly controlled by the patriarchs and/or Sanhedrin and partly by an assembly of the village citizenry, which operated in accordance with halachah and local custom (pp. 46–8). Every village had a school attended by all the local boys, staffed by both primary (Bible)

---

[28] Safrai's most important work of socio-economic history (Safrai 1994) concerns only the rural Jewish population, excluding from his account even the mainly Jewish cities of Tiberias, Sepphoris, and Lydda.

[29] Safrai provided more detail in 'Godel HaUkhlusiyah Be-Eretz Yisrael Bi-Tequfah Haromit-Byzantit' (Friedman *et al.* 1997: 277–306)—proposing an average nuclear family size of 3.5 to 3.8, a population density in settled areas of 140–60 people per dunam, and a population of 2–2.5 million in cis-Jordanian Palestine, with at least 500,000 in rural Galilee.

and secondary (Mishnah) teachers (*soferim* and *meshanim*—even though in rabbinic sources these are invariably regarded as two functions served by a single individual). Every village also had a system of charity distribution (p. 50), a local militia to guard against brigands (p. 52), needless to say a synagogue, which housed the schools and had rooms for visitors (pp. 53–4), a public bath-house, and a rudimentary court system (p. 54); they also contained committees which supervised markets and other aspects of trade in accordance with Jewish law (pp. 55–60). In Safrai's account, then, all the elements of Alon's vision of Jewish life in the Talmud period, its national-religious utopian features greatly exaggerated, are incorporated into a coherent socio-economic history.

Safrai's predecessors tended to acknowledge their ideological commitments, while insisting on their complete scientific objectivity, but Safrai generally avoided the nationalistic rhetoric of his predecessors. He even rejected Feliks's Jewish exceptionalism, acknowledging that Palestine was poorer and less developed than parts of Roman North Africa or Italy—a position which would logically require Safrai to posit wheat yields higher than 35 : 1 for most of the Roman Empire and so to reject completely the work of all ancient economic and social historians of the twentieth century (hinted at on pp. 109, 10, and 436–7)!

Given the low and declining level of interest in the history of the Talmud period outside Israel, reflected in the failure even of *The Economy of Roman Palestine*, published only in English, to attract much serious attention, the main challenges to the views of Feliks *et al.* have come from Israeli archaeologists, especially Magen Broshi and Israel Finkelstein.[30] Both used hypotheses standard among classical and Near Eastern archaeologists to calculate the carrying capacity of the land, population density in settled areas and the population size of parts (Finkelstein) or all (Broshi) of the country. Both started from the assumption that in most premodern periods the economy of Palestine was dominated by subsistence agriculture, and that wheat yields were normally a conventional 5 : 1 or so. But neither has explored the implications of these for the broader history of the Jews in ancient Palestine.

Non-Israeli Scholarship

History has been far less a concern for scholars of the Talmud period outside Israel; likewise, their interests, motivations, and ideological commitments have generally—certainly in the second half of the twentieth century—been far more diffuse.

[30] Some of Broshi's more recent work is cited above. For Finkelstein, see his 1989 and 1990 articles, and with Broshi (1992).

Most scholars who have written about the post-Destruction period have been Jewish, but certainly not all of them. Two of the most influential were, respectively, a Presbyterian minister (George Foot Moore) and a lapsed fundamentalist Methodist (Erwin Ramsdell Goodenough) (see Smith 1971; 1967: 63; Sandmel 1968). Nevertheless, I think it would be safe to generalize that until very recently most scholars in the field were, as social and cultural types, not terribly different from their Israeli colleagues. (One thing that changed in the 1980s and 1990s was the revival of German, now mainly non-Jewish, rabbinic and related scholarship.) Certainly this is true of the first generation of American scholars, who were drawn from the same yeshivot and central European seminaries and universities as the Israelis. Saul Lieberman and Gedalyah Alon were roughly contemporaries at Slobodka and as graduate students in Jerusalem, and though Lieberman's American followers received his work in ways that marked them off sharply from Alon's Israeli followers, Lieberman's personal and academic interests were always primarily Israel-oriented. He regarded the Jerusalem scholars as his main colleagues, had close connections in the Israeli government and especially in the Mizrahi/National Religious Party, and played a role in the foundation of Bar-Ilan University.[31]

But many of the scholars of the next generation, too, resembled the 'modernizing yeshivah students' who dominated the field throughout the twentieth century in Palestine/Israel—in that all were struggling (perhaps explicitly in life, and implicitly, even unconsciously, in their scholarship) to balance the conflicting claims of a normative religious tradition and a set of modern, individualistic, political/cultural affiliations. But the differences are striking. Little American, British, or German scholarship is at all Zionist in orientation, which is not unsurprising given the institutional importance of Zionism in American and British Jewish life, and its alleged ideological centrality, at least for a time, among American and British Jews. One reason for this is that the most Zionistically inclined immigrated to Israel, and in fact in the 1970s and following decades many practitioners of Jewish studies in Israel were American and British immigrants, one of whom has been discussed above. But for those who remained, it is religious liberalism which seems the main influence, especially on Americans, though again its influence is far more diffuse and implicit in American scholarship than Zionism in Israeli scholarship, mainly because religious liberalism almost by definition requires a less intense and totalizing commitment than political radicalism.

---

[31] Lieberman papers at JTS, box #16. These papers also reveal some of the tensions created for Lieberman's Israeli connections by the fact that he taught at the Jewish Theological Seminary, a non-Orthodox rabbinical school.

LIEBERMAN AND GOODENOUGH

Lieberman's main work, on Palestinian rabbinic texts, has been discussed elsewhere in this volume, and his collections and scattered articles most relevant to my topic have been mentioned above. But they, and especially their reception, deserve separate notice here.[32] In brief, as has already been suggested, Lieberman was mainly concerned in this work to explain difficult passages, especially in the Palestinian Talmud and midrashim, by drawing on his considerable knowledge of classical and patristic literature, Greek papyrology and epigraphy, Roman history, and so on. Much of this exegetical work amounted to little more than brief lexicographical or text-critical notes, but on several occasions generated substantial, and still valuable, historical essays.[33] Still other pieces, published as *Greek in Jewish Palestine* and *Hellenism in Jewish Palestine*, cohered by apparently demonstrating the broad if not always deep influence of Graeco-Roman culture on the rabbis and their Palestinian Jewish contemporaries.[34] Some readers saw past the episodic character of Lieberman's work and read it as an innovative, if very partial and impressionistic, account of Roman provincial life from within; *Greek in Jewish Palestine* inspired Hans Yohanan Lewy (1904–45), a German-born classicist who taught at the Hebrew University from 1933, to imagine Lieberman as, potentially, the Rostovtzeff of the Jews—who would exploit the vast and presumably reliable rabbinic literature to produce a full social and cultural history of the Jews under Roman rule.[35] Many readers sensed that Lieberman was arguing, again indirectly and episodically, about rabbinic and general Jewish integration in a world dominated by Greek culture.

[32] It may be noted parenthetically here that although no discrete 'Lieberman school', comparable to the Alon school, ever developed, Lieberman too was the beneficiary of a kind of exaggerated *pietas*, slightly different from that displayed toward Alon. Lieberman's students and colleagues often talked (and talk) and wrote about him—not always ironically—in language drawn from eastern European rabbinic convention; a not quite full list of obituaries of and essays about Lieberman is provided by T. Preschel in Friedman (1993: 1–2), followed by a bibliography of Lieberman's work.

[33] Most importantly, Lieberman (1939–44, 1944, 1946). Though Lieberman wrote the overwhelming majority of his work in Hebrew, the historical pieces were all published in English.

[34] For some examples of the critical reception of these books—ranging from dazzlement to admiration mixed with scepticism—see especially the comments of Henri Grégoire quoted by Urbach (1984: 14–5), and Lewy (1944–5). On Alon's reaction, see above.

[35] Mikhail Ivanovich Rostovtzeff (1870–1950) was Professor of Ancient History first at St Petersburg and later at Yale, who wrote pioneering social and economic histories of the Hellenistic world and the Roman Empire. Lewy may have been consciously but implicitly comparing Lieberman and Alon, the Jewish Mommsen. Though Lewy was presumably familiar with it, few classicists outside Israel could read Alon's work, which only started to be translated into English in the 1970s. I suspect that even in translation it is too hermetic to be accessible or attractive to non-Judaists.

Lieberman proved influential in several different circles. His influence was unquestionably strongest among academic talmudists and rabbinists, who are not my concern here. Connected to these, but also in opposition to them to some extent, are a small group of postmodernist, or postmodernistically inclined scholars, in existence only since about 1990, orbiting around Daniel Boyarin—a zealous though paradoxical follower of Lieberman. These scholars will be briefly discussed below. Lieberman's influence among other scholars of ancient Judaism was more subtle and needs to be considered together with other factors. In brief, he contributed, not necessarily intentionally, to the coalescence of a liberal scholarship on the ancient Jews. In this account, the Jews did not react to the Destruction with political resistance and cultural self-enclosure, but eventually with creative engagement with the majority culture—which in this account was often abstracted from its association with the violent imperialism of an expansionist state—in a way which enriched the Jews' group identity. This view was consistent with and informed by a specifically American historiography (articulated by Salo Baron, who shared students with Lieberman) which called attention to the beneficial aspects of the experience of the Jews under foreign domination. The other main architect of the liberal mainstream of non-Israeli ancient Judaic scholarship was Erwin R. Goodenough.

Goodenough (1893–1965) was a New Testament scholar by training, and for the first part of his career as Professor of History at Yale University, an authority on the works of Philo of Alexandria. He had few students and none at all who are directly relevant to this account, but he had a tremendous influence on the field, in part because of the sheer mass and notoriety of his most important work, *Jewish Symbols in the Greco-Roman Period* (1953–67), but mainly because part of his argument in this work, mediated through Morton Smith, became one of the foundations of the work of Jacob Neusner.

In brief, Goodenough began by collecting all identifiably Jewish iconographic remains (and some material regarded only by Goodenough as Jewish) discovered by archaeologists. His method of interpreting this material involved distinguishing two levels of meaning. The more basic Goodenough called the art's 'value', that is, its religious/emotive content, which he regarded as universal, and so recoverable by introspection, among other things. The more superficial level of the symbols' meaning Goodenough called its 'interpretation'—that is, the stories the makers and viewers of the art told about it, which were culturally specific and can be reconstructed provided we know which body of literature to use to do so. (So, for example, the depiction of Greek gods on the mosaic pavements of ancient synagogues does not mean that the Jews attached religious importance to those gods— this latter is part of the art's 'interpretation', undoubtedly altered by the Jews in the act of borrowing; rather, the Jews used the images for their not specifically Greek or pagan 'values'.) Goodenough argued that, by its very existence, the art, which included many figurative elements, often borrowed quite directly from Graeco-

Roman pagan sources, demonstrated that most Jews, both in Palestine and in the diaspora, rejected rabbinic authority—since the rabbis opposed such art as a violation of the Second Commandment. More basically, there is nothing in rabbinic literature to prepare us for the type of religiosity implied by the art. For in Goodenough's view, none of it, not even rosettes and geometric designs, was merely decorative. It was all profoundly meaningful as a component of a mystical, deeply Hellenized, type of Jewish religiosity which received its most articulate formulation in the works of Philo of Alexandria.

Elements of Goodenough's argument were almost universally criticized. Few scholars accepted his Jungian approach to the interpretation of the ancient Jewish art, in all its cheerful subjectivity. It certainly seemed counter-intuitive to ascribe religious significance to geometric designs, and few were convinced of the utility of Philo's treatises in making sense of any of the art. It was also powerfully argued, primarily by Urbach, as noted above, that rabbinic attitudes toward figurative art were far more complex and ambivalent than Goodenough, who had little knowledge of rabbinics, thought. Nevertheless, some scholars were convinced that the material collected by Goodenough demonstrated the diffusion of a not easily reconstructed type of Jewish religiosity very different from that advocated by the rabbis—even if the makers and viewers of the art were not necessarily hostile to rabbinic Judaism, as opposed to ignorant of or apathetic toward it. Such scholars, of whom Morton Smith was the most eloquent, were convinced that for all its flaws Goodenough's work was revolutionary, and would require a complete revision of ancient Judaic scholarship (Smith 1967).[36]

As scholars, Goodenough and Lieberman were utterly different. Lieberman regarded the rabbis as essentially the leadership of the Jews after the Destruction, religiously conservative in most respects but at the same time culturally 'Hellenized'. Goodenough regarded mainstream Judaism as profoundly Hellenized, to the point of being essentially a peculiar type of Graeco-Roman mystery religion; his rabbis rejected Hellenism and so were historically marginal until some time near the end of antiquity. But elements of these views could be yoked together to produce a single image of an ancient Judaism thoroughly and creatively engaged with the 'Hellenistic' culture of the Roman East, yet maintaining some sense of distinctiveness.[37]

---

[36] After remarking that Goodenough had failed to demonstrate the existence of an Empire-wide anti-rabbinic mystical Judaism, Smith wrote (1967: 66): '*Soit.* Columbus failed, too. But his failure revealed a new world, and so did Goodenough's... The extent and importance of the Jewish iconic material was unrealized before Goodenough's collection of it. Informed opinions of ancient Judaism can never, henceforth, be the same as they were before he published. So long as the subject is studied and the history of the study is preserved, his work will mark an epoch.'

[37] Here we may mention, aside from the scholars to be discussed in the next sections, Judah Goldin, in various essays (Goldin 1988); Gerson Cohen, whose main concerns lay elsewhere; the books of Henry Fischel, which push Lieberman's Hellenized rabbis to an extreme (e.g. Fischel 1977); and the rather neglected work of the art historians Joseph Gutmann (e.g. Gutmann 1973, among much else) and Bernard Goldman (Goldman 1966), to name only the most conspicuous.

SMITH AND NEUSNER

The first scholar to try to reconcile the visions of Lieberman and Goodenough was probably Jacob Neusner, in a very early essay on Goodenough's *Jewish Symbols* (Neusner 1963). In fact, Neusner was probably the most enthusiastic serious reviewer of Goodenough, and though he continued to subscribe to Lieberman's views about the Hellenism of the rabbis, this notion eventually became much less central to his system than Goodenough's hypothesis of rabbinic marginality.

The other main influence on Neusner was Morton Smith (1915–91). Like Goodenough, Smith was originally a New Testament scholar from a Protestant background who lapsed into atheism. The only systematic work Smith ever wrote on rabbinic literature was his Ph.D. dissertation (Hebrew University, 1945)[38] published in English in 1951, which devoted a chapter (pp. 142–51) to the argument that the several documents of rabbinic literature posed a 'synoptic problem' (that is, they feature slightly different versions of the same basic material) very similar to that posed by the Gospels. It should thus be possible to apply to rabbinic literature some of the same sort of analysis scholars had long used on the New Testament, Smith implied. This thesis was highly eccentric in the context of the Talmud scholarship of the mid-twentieth century, and it is surely no accident that Smith wrote his dissertation in the classics department under the unlikely supervision of Moshe (Max) Schwabe, an authority on Late Imperial Greek literature. Though Smith subsequently became close to Lieberman, as far as I am aware he had little or no contact with Jerusalem rabbinists or Jewish historians.

What was novel about Smith's suggestion was the supposition that rabbinic texts could be approached as texts, literary artefacts, shaped by the interests, including the self-interest, of their authors/compilers, and so having like all artefacts a real but complex relation to the social realities which shaped them, as opposed to unedited or barely edited repositories of authoritative 'traditions' with little or no reality as texts but of undoubted historicity. Though Smith later wrote several articles on rabbinic and other post-Destruction Jewish topics, the main focus of his work was the Hebrew Bible and associated history, the New Testament, and ancient magic. I suspect that he was reluctant to explore rabbinics further because he feared he would never have the requisite expertise. In any case, Smith's programme was eventually, and gradually, taken up by Neusner.

As a rabbinical student at the Jewish Theological Seminary, Neusner had studied with Lieberman, and he subsequently completed a Ph.D. at Columbia under the supervision of Baron and Smith. His dissertation, *A Life of Yohanan Ben Zakkai*

---

[38] Smith, a student at Harvard Divinity School, won a travelling fellowship to visit Palestine in 1940 and was stranded there during the Second World War, and so finished his degree in Jerusalem.

(1962), begins with an explanation of why he eschewed the sceptical, Bultmann-esque, project (surely urged on him by Smith) of analysing the rabbinic traditions about Yohanan not only to retrieve their historical core but also to reconstruct the concerns of their tradents and the biases of the rabbinic documents' editors, and produced instead what was in most respects a conventional Wissenschaft-style rabbinic biography. Over the next decade Neusner continued to write rabbinic history in the positivist style, resulting in the massive *History of the Jews in Babylonia* (1965–70), but by 1970 had completely revised his work on Rabban Yohanan ben Zakkai in line with Smith's ideas, and quickly followed this with the much longer *Rabbinic Traditions About the Pharisees Before 70* (1971), and *Eliezer ben Hyrcanus* (1973), which utilized the same method. In the introduction to the first of these books, (1970: p. xi), Neusner wrote:

Here my task is critically to study and analyse th[e] sources [on Yohanan], to try to locate the origins of different parts of them, to see how the whole structure grew. My purpose is thus not to produce a connected history of the man and his time, but to offer systematic observations on the tradition about him and through it, on the development of a sample body of talmudic literature... In my *Life*, I described the content, and now turn to the formation, of the tradition.

I do not suppose we can come to a final and positive assessment of the historicity of various stories and sayings. We surely cannot declare a narrative to be historically reliable simply because it contains no improbabilities... We must not confuse verisimilitude with authenticity.

The result was revolutionary. In fact, the few reviewers of Neusner's book, though mainly sympathetic, had little sense of its importance.[39] The immediate effect of Neusner's work was to introduce methodological self-consciousness into a field previously marked by its relative rarity; to generate a high level of scepticism about the task of extracting historical information from rabbinic laws and anecdotes; and to shift attention from the content of the traditions to the historical factors affecting their transmission. For those who accepted Neusner's work, it was now impossible to write rabbinic biographies, and the hypothesis of the rabbis' political, social, and cultural marginality now became widespread, if with a certain ambivalence and confusion, detectable even in Neusner's own work. It was now possible to speak of a distinctive 'rabbinic' Judaism (though the term had long been current, especially in German scholarship), just one element in a landscape populated by diverse

---

[39] Jongeling (1971)—positive but brief; Wacholder (1972)—incoherent, admiring but dismissive; Roberts (1975: a review of Neusner 1973; the earlier book was not noticed)—mainly sympathetic, but with a mild case of polite anti-Judaism, wondering why Neusner wasted so much time on discussion of rabbinic legal minutiae; Jackson (1973: review of Neusner 1970 and 1971 not reviewed in the journal). Jackson alone grasped the significance of Neusner's work. Morton Smith published what was essentially a promotional piece in 1972, recapitulated by Neusner himself in 1973: ii. 437–58.

'Judaisms'. Neusner thus produced an account which appealed to a post-war American and European environment in which hierarchy and orthodoxy were questioned, variety, change, and creativity (an important corollary of Neusner's view in the 1980s and 1990s that each successive rabbinic document was utterly different from its predecessors) celebrated. On the other hand, Neusner's work cast doubt on the entire oeuvre of the Zionist and Israeli historians, which had always assumed the historicity of rabbinic documents and their utility in reconstructing the history of the Jews in general, not just that of a marginal Jewish subculture, and was largely ignored by them. But it proved incapable of providing a historical account to replace the one now discredited, and in general seems to have contributed to the decline of 'talmudic history' outside Israel, and to the rise of a 'history of religions' approach.[40]

Neusner's extensive early work is absolutely dwarfed by his voluminous writing of the 1980s and 1990s, by the end of which he had published over 800 books and many hundreds of articles (over 300 are listed in RAMBI, the Hebrew University's bibliography of articles in Jewish studies, but I suspect this list is far from complete and in any case excludes reviews). In this period Neusner emerged as an exceptionally problematic figure in the field, whose increasingly rare flashes of brilliance were lost in a firestorm of vituperation, repetition, and general unreadability.[41] But his work of the 1970s was influential far outside his circle of students,[42] and though there are signs of a gathering reaction, the main conclusions of his early work—especially concerning the textuality of the rabbinic texts, the need for methodological self-consciousness, the futility of writing rabbinic biography or of any straightforwardly positivist reading of rabbinic texts—have become part of the non-Israeli scholarly *koine*, and are in little immediate danger of being displaced.

[40] Notwithstanding the rather half-hearted defence of the topic by Neusner's student David Goodblatt, then teaching at the University of Haifa and serving, like Lee Levine, as a sort of bridge between Israel and the United States (Goodblatt 1980). By this time Neusner had demonstratively renounced history in favour of the phenomenology of religious systems (Judaisms), which he counter-intuitively thought were effectively identical with individual textual corpora—hence the series of books on 'the Judaism' of the Mishnah, the Yerushalmi, and so on. Goodblatt remained a (rather sceptical) talmudic historian even after his return to the United States.

[41] Not to mention some staggering wrong-headedness; for example (in addition to the example given in the last note) the contention, highly consequential in Neusner's work, that the rabbis were philosophers, already found in Neusner (1981). This was a dominant theme in some of his later works and led to many futile books, e.g. on the rabbis' 'economics', and on the question of why they never developed a 'science' (for in their taxonomic zeal the rabbis were more like Aristotle than Plato. But not every taxonomist is an Aristotelian).

[42] Who included Robert Goldenberg (see e.g. Goldenberg 1998), Baruch Bokser (see Bokser 1986; Bokser died in 1989), in addition to David Goodblatt, to list only those who were most successful at moving beyond Neusner's agenda.

ARCHAEOLOGY

For practical reasons, archaeology was never as important in American or European Jewish studies as it is in Israel, yet there were some important developments in the 1960s, 1970s, and 1980s. In America, Eric Meyers and his associates and students provided important material foundations for the increasingly normative liberal historiography on the ancient Jews. In his technical archaeological work, Meyers insistently rejected an old-fashioned version of classical and Near Eastern (or 'biblical') archaeology of which the main goal was allegedly to discover either grand structures, or material which could be connected to canonical literary texts, preferably by confirming their truth. Instead, Meyers claimed to embrace a context-oriented archaeology which was mainly concerned to contribute to the reconstruction of ancient societies, especially those members of them unattested in the literary sources—for example, poor villagers. In his synthetic writing, though, Meyers used archaeology to argue for Jewish acculturation in Late Antique Palestine, and, less convincingly, for the peaceful coexistence of Jews and their neighbours (which is in fact unproveable from archaeological remains). For him, Late Antique Palestine was a liberal Jewish utopia, just as it was a national religious utopia for Ze'ev Safrai.

Much more importantly, Meyers was also among those advocating the new chronology of the Palestinian synagogues, first suggested by the Franciscan excavators of Kefar Nahum (Capernaum). In brief, in the 1960s archaeologists lifted the floor of the supposedly second-century synagogue of Kefar Nahum and found thousands of low-denomination coins of the fourth and early fifth centuries. This led them to challenge the traditional dating of 'Galilean style' synagogues (characterized by decorated façades, simple interiors, gabled, three-part entryways, and so on) to the second and third centuries, which in turn has provoked a re-examination of the stratigraphy of other 'early' synagogues, and led to the conclusion that they were actually built in the fourth century or even much later, and to a growing scepticism about the utility of architectural style in dating ancient synagogues. The implications of this redating are actually revolutionary, but are just now starting to be considered (Schwartz 2001a).[43]

---

[43] Levine (2000) accepts the new chronology, but it has had no effect on his presentation of the material.

SCHÄFER, COHEN, GOODMAN

Peter Schäfer, of Berlin and Princeton, Shaye Cohen, now of Harvard, and Martin Goodman, of Oxford, who all began their careers in the 1970s, exemplify the impact of Neusner's early work far outside the circle of his students, in widely scattered academic precincts. None can strictly be called a follower of Neusner, but all learned from him lessons about the importance of tradition-history in the evaluation of rabbinic texts, scepticism about the texts' historicity, and, at the very least, agnosticism about the social and political position of the rabbis in post-Destruction Palestine. All have also striven, to a greater or lesser extent, to free themselves from the sort of internalist Jewish history practised by their Israeli colleagues, in an effort to understand Jewish history as a component of the history of the Roman Empire—an inheritance less from Neusner than from Lieberman and Smith, and in Goodman's case probably from Arnaldo Momigliano and Fergus Millar.

Schäfer, in his historically oriented work (his textual work will not be considered here), is the most methodologically rigorous and consistent of the three. In brief, in his longer works, especially in the 1970s and 1980s, he tended to proceed by beginning with a historical question, then gathering and setting out, in chronological order and divided by corpus, the relevant texts and other material. This technique permitted detailed and compelling analysis of how certain sorts of historical traditions grew, with no connection to the events they purported to describe: a good example is his study of the rabbinic tradition of a religious persecution associated with the Bar Kokhba Revolt (Schäfer 1990). This study showed that the tradition, barely present in the Mishnah, grew more detailed and important as it passed chronologically through the rabbinic corpora. In general, Schäfer's sceptical positivism (as we may call it) proved a much more effective tool for dislodging accreted speculative reconstruction than for constructing new accounts. In the case of the Bar Kokhba Revolt, Schäfer's proposed explanation—it was connected to an internal struggle between Jewish 'Hellenizers' or collaborationists, and separatists—in my view has much more merit than has generally been allowed, but has convinced few (Schäfer 1981). Here again, I think he was hindered by his theoretical constraints, which made it practically impossible to make a strong positive case of any sort. As Schäfer's interests broadened in the 1980s and 1990s, to take in hekhalot texts, magic, and the seemingly inexhaustible question of the extent of the rabbis' integration in the cultural world of the Roman East—he was less completely dominated by his sceptical positivism, but one still has a sense in his work of excessive restraint—to be sure, an admirable characteristic in a self-indulgent world, but one which seems to inhibit him from complete execution of the historian's task.

Shaye Cohen, like Neusner, studied with Lieberman at the Jewish Theological Seminary, where he subsequently taught, and completed his Ph.D. at Columbia under the direction of Smith (in 1975), and in 1991 succeeded Neusner at Brown. Cohen produced a substantial corpus of work, especially in the 1980s, about Jewish identity in antiquity and the related topics of conversion, mixed marriage, circumcision, and personal status. Here he has been especially concerned to discover the earliest attestations of practices, discoveries enabled by rigorously precise collection and analysis of literary material, and is not unwilling to speculate about why certain practices (e.g. conversion rituals) changed, or why words changed meaning or mentalities shifted, at certain times (Cohen 1999). Cohen, like Schäfer, is thus a sceptical positivist, who works on the assumption that history can be reconstructed provided the sources are analysed carefully enough. Cohen's argument that Judaism changed from ethnicity to religion has dominated discussion of the subject (though in a recent revision of this argument, Cohen has softened the problematic binary opposition somewhat), even among people who disagree with his dating of the shift to the Hasmonean period. His account of Yavneh and the coalescence of rabbinic Judaism after 70, as not the rise of an orthodoxy, but precisely the rejection of sectarianism and the embrace of pluralism, has become the standard view outside Israel, notwithstanding its sentimentality and its all-too-obvious appeal to Jewish religious liberalism (Cohen 1984). Nevertheless I would argue that, like Schäfer and for the same reasons, Cohen is much better at dismantling arguments than at constructing them. For both, history boils down to appropriately sceptical methods of reading; the use of models adapted from social theory, sociology, and social anthropology, which has the potential to resolve the tensions implicit in sceptical positivism, is quite self-consciously excluded.[44]

Goodman is something of an outlier in this group. His primary training at Oxford was in classics and Roman history, not rabbinics, and he is unquestionably a historian rather than a textual scholar—one of the few in this field outside Israel. Furthermore, underlying much of his work is the theoretical question of the exemplarity of the Jews as a subject people of the Roman East—a question, some might argue, properly of Roman rather than Jewish history. Nevertheless, Goodman's first book, written in dissertation form fewer than ten years after the publication of *Development of a Legend*, constitutes what was probably the first, and is also in my view still one of the most successful attempts yet to use a Neusnerian approach to rabbinic texts to construct a positive, if necessarily hypothetical,

---

[44] Presumably models are rejected because of their alleged reductionism and determinism. Certainly models have often been used poorly by ancient Judaists, among others, but it is also possible to use them with discernment and flexibility—not as reified structures into which to force the 'evidence', but as ways of subtly and carefully probing it, asking illuminating questions, and so on. For an exemplary use of social-theoretical models in a work of ancient Judaic scholarship, see Baumgarten (1997); cf. Marcus (1996).

account of an important period of post-Destruction Jewish history (Goodman 1983: esp. 3–16). Goodman was not precisely unique in the range of his knowledge, whether viewed as a Jewish or as a Roman historian, but he was and has remained unusually up to date in both fields and unusually engaged in their internal issues and debates. I would suggest also that his methodological eclecticism and his willingness to consider all remains as evidence, his recognition that he is writing about a society that is likely to have been recognizably human, have allowed him to circumvent the methodological impasse discussed above.

Britain is unquestionably outside the mainstream of rabbinic-oriented scholarship, and it seems to me unlikely that it has the potential to turn into a subsidiary centre, as Germany has with the help of Schäfer. Goodman's work has thus been received as if it were to some extent peripheral to the concerns of the American and Israeli centres, though it has served the important purpose of introducing classicists and Roman historians to Jewish history and rabbinics. Nevertheless, Goodman's work in fact addresses concerns of the mainstream, and for the most part does so more compellingly and with more sophistication than most Israeli and American scholars seem willing to appreciate.

The 1990s and Beyond

I would suggest that a generational shift is beginning to coalesce. In America and Europe this shift takes the form of a reaction against Goodenough- and Lieberman-influenced integrationism and Neusnerian scepticism and phenomenology, and in Israel, of a reaction against reflexively Zionist naive historicism. A feature of this shift is a growing interest, influenced by developments in classics and ancient history, in seeing the Jewish experience in Christian late antiquity (c.300–650) as meaningfully different from that in the pagan Roman Empire. However, I have the impression (which could be falsified statistically, though with difficulty) that the numerical balance in Jewish studies in general is shifting away from the study of antiquity and the middle ages and toward modernity, for reasons which may have little to do with the inner intellectual dynamics of the field.

To be sure, the fact that this change is just beginning to take shape implies that the 1990s, and following, were characterized by significant continuity with the previous decades. As of the time of this writing (2001), Israeli figures like Shmuel Safrai are still publishing, while slightly younger scholars like Aharon Oppenheimer, Lee Levine, Daniel Sperber, Isaiah Gafni (e.g. Gafni 1990), Ze'ev Safrai, and Joshua Schwartz (e.g. Schwartz 1986), who all started publishing between the late 1960s and *c.*1980, are still in their prime, as are Peter Schäfer, Shaye Cohen, Martin Goodman, David Goodblatt, and Eric Meyers outside Israel. And several younger scholars continue to work along the same lines. Efrat Habas-Rubin and, to some extent, Steven Fine, for example, continue to write maximalist and positivistic rabbinic history in the classic Israeli style (e.g. Fine 1998), while several younger students of Neusner and of Schäfer still embrace sceptical positivism—for example, Martin Jacobs's important, *echt*-Schäferian book on the patriarchate (Jacobs 1995). In the same sorts of circles, the by-now traditional cultural-historical hypotheses—in Israel, of the Jews' cultural self-enclosure, and outside Israel, of their productive integration—are still in place, though, as already suggested, without the nationalist rhetoric or the normalizing excesses.

Some of the change now detectable is evolutionary: Catherine Hezser's work, for example, retains an orientation toward sceptical positivism absorbed from both Cohen and Schäfer. But her utilization of network theory in her fundamentally important 1997 book on the social history of the rabbinic movement, which argues against the work of Lee Levine that the Palestinian rabbis for most of their ancient history constituted not an institutionalized class but a loosely agglomerated group, integrated mainly by informal social contacts, and interested in promoting their own legal authority by establishing relations of social dependency with other Jews, marks in my opinion a significant methodological advance (Hezser 1997; cf. Levine 1989).

A similar combination of a sceptical approach to literary sources, a desire to understand whether and how the Jews continued to function as a group under Roman rule and in what ways their experience was typical for Roman subjects and citizens in general, and an openness to experimentation with models, characterizes the work of Hayim Lapin. Like Goodman, Lapin is unusually engaged in and knowledgeable about issues in Roman history, and has recently been making productive use of post-colonial theory in his work. His dissertation was a sophisticated attempt to contextualize a body of rabbinic economic law, and his shorter works have been characterized by keen intelligence and a concentrated and profound theoretical awareness, if also by a certain tortuousness and over-elaborateness of exposition (Lapin 1995, 1999).

In Israel, too, there are signs of a gradual loosening of old constraints—most often achieved by scholars working outside the rabbinic mainstream. For example, since the late 1980s Hannah Cotton, an Oxford-trained Greek papyrologist teaching in the Classics Department of the Hebrew University, has been working on scattered collections of Greek, mainly legal, documents discovered in the Judaean desert in a way which has increasingly led her to challenge her colleagues' assumption that rabbinic law was normative for post-Destruction Jews (Cotton and Yardeni 1997; Cotton 1993, 1998).

Probably the most significant work of the 1990s by a young Israeli scholar is Hillel Newman's 1997 Hebrew University dissertation, written under the supervision of

M. D. Herr, *Jerome and the Jews*. Though this work features no innovations in method and continues to subscribe, though in a greatly attenuated way, to an Alon-derived rabbinocentrism, it is so thorough, comprehensive, careful, and untendentious a work that it must be regarded as one of the most important contributions to the field in recent years, and will also be a fundamental contribution to Jerome studies, if it is translated from Hebrew.

An interesting development of recent years affecting both the United States and Israel is the emergence of a group of scholars strongly influenced by postmodern literary theory. As already suggested, this group has coalesced around Daniel Boyarin, who for the first part of his career, in the 1970s and 1980s, was more or less a conventional talmudic philologist, working in Jerusalem. A drastic change in his work can be dated to 1990, with the publication of a theoretical work on midrash which has been discussed elsewhere in this volume (chapter 6). Since then Boyarin has been not only remarkably productive, but also remarkably broad in his interests and in his willingness to master new corpora of material. He has also become increasingly engaged in the 'new historicism'—a rather diffuse literary-theoretical orientation which claims, as Boyarin himself describes it, that '... all texts [*sic*] are by definition equally credible; for the object of research is the motives of the construction of the narrative itself which is taken to attest to the political context of its telling or retelling rather than to the context of the content of the narrative. All texts inscribe the social practices within which they originate ...' Most relevant here is his work, still in progress, on the relation of Judaism and Christianity in antiquity, arguing in brief that the construction of a significant discursive (and social?) separation between the two entities was primarily the work of rabbis and Church Fathers of the fourth centuries (Boyarin 1999). Boyarin has also been a champion of gender studies, a field not completely neglected in ancient Jewish studies, but not previously pursued with much theoretical sophistication (Boyarin 1993).

Of all scholars of ancient Judaism working today, Boyarin is probably the most productively engaged with the intellectual concerns of the wider academy, in addition to having mastered all the tools traditionally valued by academic rabbinists and their ilk. It is of course impossible to predict what sort of impact he will have inside the field of ancient Judaism. He has certainly attracted highly talented students and associates in both America and Israel—Christine Hayes (Hayes 1997), Charlotte Fonrobert (Fonrobert 2000), Joshua Levinson (Levinson 1996), and Galit Hasan-Rokem (Hasan-Rokem 2000) may be mentioned as especially accomplished/promising—but like Neusner before him, has also generated opposition (expressed, like the opposition to Neusner, initially as obliviousness). At very least, though, Boyarin and his associates will certainly have a conspicuous place in a scholarly landscape which seems to me (perhaps only because we do not yet have the advantage of hindsight) increasingly fragmented.

APPENDIX: THE BABYLONIAN DIASPORA

The very extensive scholarship on the Babylonian Talmud has been surveyed elsewhere in this volume. There exist in addition small and problematic corpora of scholarship on 'rabbinic culture' and the history of the Jews in Babylonia which merit brief discussion here. The reason why this scholarship is problematic is that so little is known about late Parthian and Sassanian Babylonia—in sharp contrast to the Roman Empire in the same period—and there is furthermore next to no extra-talmudic information about the Jews. So, given the impossibility of extracting a continuous, or an episodic but detailed, history from the talmudic text itself, and the difficulty of even speculating usefully about the existence of a rabbinic group sufficiently integrated and discrete to have had its own 'culture', the argument could surely be made for maintaining a tactful silence about Babylonian Jewry before the Islamic period. Nevertheless, the best of this scholarship is interesting and provocative, and possesses a certain heuristic value as an aid to the interpretation of talmudic and gaonic texts. Anyway, extra-talmudic information, though very scarce indeed, is not wholly lacking, and the Talmud itself may not be as resistant to historical interpretation as the most determined sceptics insist, though it remains true that even the most basic historical questions elude solution.

The most comprehensive history of the Jews of Parthian and Sassanian Babylonia has been mentioned above (Neusner 1965–70)—it is characterized by a positivistic approach to the Babylonian Talmud, but also by an attempt to retrieve whatever non-rabbinic sources may be relevant to Jewish history, and also by an engagement with general historiography on the Parthian and Sassanian Empires. Subsequent work has had a narrower scope, focusing on the exilarchate (the Babylonian counterpart of the patriarchate) and on questions of inner-rabbinic history (Beer 1976), or on questions of Jewish communal organization, and relations between the rabbis and the Jewish communities (Gafni 1990; Kalmin 1999). Also noteworthy is an attempt—rather half-hearted, given its acknowledged neglect of Syriac and Graeco-Roman sources, but still useful—to produce a gazetteer of Jewish Babylonia, along the lines of S. Klein's *Sefer Ha-Yishuv* for Palestine (Oppenheimer 1983). Furthermore, very many talmudists have glancingly attended to historical problems raised by the Talmud—but mainly as a way of explaining texts, rather than history (e.g. Friedman 1993, 1998).

Attention to 'rabbinic culture' has been a growth industry in the 1990s. This work acknowledges that the Talmud cannot be used to reconstruct Jewish culture *tout court* (as still attempted, e.g., by Stern 1994), and instead regards it as a primary ethnographic source for the partial recovery of a distinctive Jewish subculture. The best of this work (e.g. Boyarin 1993; Satlow 1995; Rubenstein 1999; Jaffee 1992, 1997) has produced real results. But, given enduring questions about the nature of the

Talmud, the character and date of its redaction, and so on, it remains appropriate to wonder whether these results may legitimately be reified into a historical account, or must remain purely hermeneutical constructs, useful because they permit better understanding of difficult texts, while telling us rather little about the actual rabbis of Late Antique Babylonia.

SUGGESTED READING

As has been suggested, there is no single work which covers the post-Destruction period in an adequate way, but there are some synthetic works which may be diffidently recommended. For Palestine, in addition to Alon (1957 and 1977); Avi-Yonah (1962 and 1981); Baras *et al.* (1982–4); Goodman (1983); Levine (1989 and 2000); and Schwartz (2001a), Cohen (1987), and Schäfer (1995), provide reliable introductions, especially for the earlier part of the period. For Babylonia, Neusner (1965–70) and Gafni (1990) may be recommended.

BIBLIOGRAPHY

ABEL, F. M. 1933–8. *Geographie de la Palestine*. 2 Vols. Paris.

ALON, G. 1957. *Mehkarim Be-Toledot Yisrael Bi-Tekufat Bayit Sheni, Uvi-Tekufat HaMishnah Veha-Talmud*. E. Z. Melamed and S. Safrai eds. 2 vols. Tel Aviv.

—— 1959. *Toldot Hayehudim Be-Eretz Yisrael Bi-Equfat HaMishnah VehaTalmud*. Jerusalem.

—— 1977. *Jews and Judaism in the Classical World*. Trans. I. Abrahams. Jerusalem.

ALT, A. 1959. *Kleine Schriften zur Geschichte des Volkes Israel*. 3 vols. Munich.

ASSAF, D. ed. 1993. *E. E. Urbach: A Bio-Bibliography*. Supplement to Jewish Studies, Forum of the World Union of Jewish Studies, 1. Jerusalem.

AVI-YONAH, M. 1962. *Historical Geography of Palestine*. Jerusalem.

—— 1981. *Art in Ancient Palestine*. Jerusalem.

BAER, Y. 1956. 'Israel, the Christian Church, and the Roman Empire from the Days of Septimius Severus to the "Edict of Toleration" of 313.' *Zion* 21: 1–49. Published in expanded form in English in *Scripta Hierosolymitana* 7 (1961): 79–149.

BARAS, Z., SAFRAI, S., TSAFRIR, Y., and STERN, M. eds. 1982–4. *Eretz Israel from the Destruction of the Second Temple to the Muslim Conquest*. 2 vols. Jerusalem.

BARTAL, I. 1997. 'The In-gathering of Traditions: Zionism's Anthology Projects.' *Prooftexts* 17: 77–93.

—— 2000. 'The Kinnus Project: Wissenschaft des Judentums and the Fashioning of a "National Culture" in Palestine.' In *Transmitting Jewish Traditions: Orality, Textuality, and Cultural Diffusion*. 310–23. Y. Elman and I. Gershoni eds. New Haven.

BAUMGARTEN, A. I. 1997. *The Flourishing of Jewish Sects in the Maccabean Era: An Interpretation*. Leiden.

BEER, M. 1976. *The Babylonian Exilarchate in the Arsacid and Sassanian Periods*. Tel Aviv.

BIALE, D. 1986. *Power and Powerlessness in Jewish History*. New York.

BOKSER, B. 1986. *The Origins of the Seder: The Passover Rite and Early Rabbinic Judaism.* Berkeley.

BOYARIN, D. 1993. *Carnal Israel: Reading Sex in Talmudic Culture.* Berkeley.

——1999. *Dying for God: Martyrdom and the Making of Christianity and Judaism.* Berkeley.

BROSHI, M. 1986. 'Demographic Changes in Ancient Eretz Israel: Methodology and Estimates.' In *Man and Land in Eretz Israel in Antiquity.* 50–1. A. Kasher, U. Rappaport, and A. Oppenheimer eds. Jerusalem.

BÜCHLER, A. 1906. *Der galiläische Am HaAres des zweiten Jahrhunderts: Beiträge zur inneren Geschichte des palästinischen Judentums in den ersten zwei Jahrhunderten.* Vienna.

CHAJES, H. P. 1899. 'Les juges juifs en Palestine de l'an 70 à l'an 500.' *Revue des etudes Juives* 39: 39–52.

COHEN, S. J. D. 1984. 'The Significance of Yavneh: Pharisees, Rabbis, and the End of Sectarianism.' *Hebrew Union College Annual* 55: 27–53.

——1987. *From the Maccabees to the Mishnah.* Philadelphia.

——1999. *The Beginnings of Jewishness.* Berkeley.

COTTON, H. 1993. 'The Guardianship of Jesus Son of Babatha: Roman Law and Local Law in the Province of Arabia.' *Journal of Roman Studies* 83: 94–108.

——1998. 'The Rabbis and the Documents.' *Jews in a Graeco-Roman World.* 167–79. M. Goodman ed. Oxford.

——and YARDENI, A. eds. 1997. *Hebrew, Aramaic, and Greek Documentary Texts from Nahal Hever and Other Sites.* DJD 27. Oxford.

DINUR, B. Z. 1958. *Yisrael Ba-Golah.* Vol 1. Tel Aviv.

——1969. *Israel and the Diaspora.* Philadelphia.

DZIMITROWSKI, H. Z. (later Dimitrowski) 1950–1. 'Gedalyah Alon z'l.' *Kiryat Sefer* 26: 310–14.

ENDELMAN, T. 1997. 'Introduction: Comparing Jewish Societies.' In *Comparing Jewish Societies.* 1–21. T. Endelman ed. Ann Arbor, Mich.

FELIKS, Y. 1990. 'HaHaqlaut Be-Eretz Yisrael Bi-Tequfat HaMishnah VehaTalmud.' Unpublished diss. Hebrew University (1960). Published in 1963, and in an expanded version: *HaHaqlaut Be-Eretz Yisrael Bi-Yemei HaMiqra, HaMishnah VehaTalmud.* Jerusalem.

FINE, S. 1998. *This Holy Place: On the Sanctity of the Synagogue during the Greco-Roman Period.* Notre Dame, Ind.

FINKELSTEIN, L. 1936. *Akiba: Scholar, Saint and Martyr.* New York.

FINKELSTEIN, I. 1989. 'The Land of Ephraim Survey 1980–1987: Preliminary Report.' Tel Aviv 15–6: 117–83.

——1990. 'A Few Notes on Demographic Data from Recent Generations and Ethnoarchaeology.' *Palestine Exploration Quarterly* 122: 47–52.

——and BROSHI, M. 1992. 'The Population of Palestine in Iron Age 11.' *Bulletin of the American Schools of Oriental Research* 287: 47–60.

FISCHEL, H. 1977. *Essays in Greco-Roman and Related Talmudic Literature.* New York.

FONROBERT, C. 2000. *Menstrual Purity: Rabbinic and Christian Reconstructions of Biblical Gender.* Stanford.

FRAENKEL, Y. 1991. *Darkhei HaAggadah VehaMidrash.* Jerusalem.

FRIEDMAN, S. ed. 1993. *Saul Lieberman Memorial Volume.* New York–Jerusalem.

——1998. 'In Search of the Historical Ben Derosai.' *Sidra* 14: 77–91.

FRIEDMAN, Y., SAFRAI, Z., and SCHWARTZ, J. eds. 1997. *Hikrei Eretz: Studies in the History of the Land of Israel in Honor of Professor Yehudah Feliks*. Ramat-Gan.

GAFNI, I. 1990. *The Jews of Babylonia in the Talmudic Era*. Jerusalem.

GARNSEY, P. 1984. 'Religious Toleration in Classical Antiquity.' In *Persecution and Toleration. Studies in Church History* 21: 1–27. W. J. Sheils ed. Oxford.

GELLER, S. 1985. 'Wellhausen and Kaufmann.' *Midstream* 31.10: 39–48.

GINZBERG, L. 1909–38. *The Legends of the Jews*. 7 Vols. Philadelphia.

GOLDENBERG, R. 1998. *The Nations that Know Thee Not: Jewish Attitudes Towards Other Religions*. New York.

GOLDIN, J. 1988. *Studies in Midrash and Related Literature*. Philadelphia.

GOLDMAN, B. 1966. *The Sacred Portal: A Primary Symbol in Ancient Jewish Art*. Detroit.

GOODBLATT, D. 1980. 'Towards the Rehabilitation of Talmudic History.' *History of Judaism: The Next Ten Years*. 31–44. B. Bokser, ed. Chico, Cal.

GOODMAN, M. D. 1983. *State and Society in Roman Galilee, A.D. 132–212*. Totowa, NJ.

GRAETZ, H. 1893. *Geschichte der Juden*. Vol. 4. 3rd edn. Leipzig.

GUTMANN, J. 1973. *The Dura-Europus Synagogue: A Reevaluation*. Missoula.

HASAN-ROKEM, G. 2000. *The Web of Life: Folklore and Midrash in Rabbinic Literature*. Stanford.

HAYES, C. 1997. *Between the Babylonian and Palestinian Talmuds*. New York.

HEINEMANN, J. 1974. *Aggadah and its Development*. Jerusalem.

HEZSER, C. 1997. *The Social Structure of the Rabbinic Movement in Roman Palestine*. Tübingen.

JACKSON, B. J. 1973. Review of Neusner 1970, *JJS* 24: 185–7.

JACOBS, M. 1995. *Die Institution des Jüdischen Patriarchen*. Tübingen.

JAFFEE, M. 1992. 'How Much Orality in Oral Torah?' *Shofar* 10: 53–72.

—— 1997. 'A Rabbinnic Ontology of the Written and Spoken Word.' *Journal of the American Academy of Religion* 65: 525–49.

JONGELING, B. 1971. Review of Neusner 1970, *JSJ* 2: 89–90.

KALMIN, R. 1999. *The Sage in Jewish Society of Late Antiquity*. New York.

KRAUSS, S. 1948. *Paras VeRomi BaTalmud UvaMidrashim*. Jerusalem.

LAPIN, H. 1995. *Early Rabbinic Civil Law and the Social History of Roman Galilee: A Study of Mishnah Tractate Bava Mesia*. Atlanta, Ga.

—— 1999. 'Palestinian Inscriptions and Jewish Ethnicity in Late Antiquity.' *Galilee through the Centuries: Confluence of Cultures*. 239–67. E. Meyers ed. Winona Lake, Ind.

LEVINE, L. 1989. *The Rabbinic Class in Roman Palestine in Late Antiquity*. Jerusalem.

—— 2000. *The Ancient Synagogue: The First Thousand Years*. New Haven.

LEVINSON, J. 1996. 'The Tragedy of Romance: A Case of Literary Exile.' *HTR* 89: 227–44.

LEWY, H. Y. 1944–5. 'Derakhim Hadashot Be-Heqer HaHellenizm HaYehudi.' *Zion* 10: 197–200.

LIEBERMAN, S. 1939–44. 'The Martyrs of Caesarea.' AIPHOS 7: 395–446.

—— 1942. *Greek in Jewish Palestine*. New York.

—— 1944. 'Roman Legal Institutions in Early Rabbinics and in the Acta Martyrum.' *JQR* 35: 1–57.

—— 1946. 'Palestine in the Third and Fourth Centuries.' *JQR* 37: 31–54.

—— 1963. 'How Much Greek in Jewish Palestine?' *Biblical and Other Studies*. 123–41. A. Altmann ed. Cambridge, Mass.

—— 1974. *Texts and Studies*. New York.

MARCUS, I. 1996. *Rituals of Childhood: Jewish Culture and Acculturation in the Middle Ages.* New Haven.

MYERS, D. N. 1988. 'History as Ideology: The Case of Ben Zion Dinur, Zionist Historian Par Excellence.' *Modern Judaism* 8: 167–93.

—— 1995. *Re-Inventing the Jewish Past: European Jewish Intellectuals and the Return to History.* Oxford.

NEUSNER, J. 1963. 'Notes on Goodenough's Jewish Symbols.' *Conservative Judaism* 17: 77–92.

—— 1965–70. *History of the Jews in Babylonia.* Leiden.

—— 1970. *Development of a Legend: Studies on the Traditions concerning Yohanah ben Zakkai.* Leiden.

—— 1971. *Rabbinic Traditions about the Pharisees before 70.* 3 vols. Leiden.

—— 1973. *Eliezer ben Hyrcanus.* Leiden.

—— 1981. *Judaism: The Evidence of the Mishnah.* Chicago.

—— 1990. 'The American Contribution to Scholarship on Rabbinic Judaism.' In *Approaches to Ancient Judaism,* NS 2: 57–184. J. Neusner ed. Atlanta, Ga.

OPPENHEIMER, A. 1983. *Babylonia Judaica in the Talmudic Period.* Beihefte zum *Tübinger Atlas des vorderen Orients* 47. Wiesbaden.

ROBERTS, B. J. 1975. Review of Neusner 1973, *Journal of Theological Studies* 26: 180–2.

ROEMER, N. 2000. 'The Historicizing of Judaism in 19th-Century Germany: Scholarly Discipline and Popular Historical Culture.' Unpublished diss., Columbia University.

RUBENSTEIN, J. 1999. *Talmudic Stories: Narrative Art, Composition, Culture.* Baltimore.

SAFRAI, Z. 1994. *The Economy of Roman Palestine.* London.

SANDMEL, S. 1968. 'An Appreciation.' In *Religions in Antiquity: Essays in Memory of Erwin Ramsdell Goodenough.* 3–17. J. Neusner ed. Leiden.

SATLOW, M. 1995. *Tasting the Dish: Rabbinic Rhetorics of Sexuality.* Atlanta, Ga.

SCHÄFER, P. 1981. *Der Bar Kokhba Aufstand: Studien zum zweiten jüdischen Krieg gegen Rom.* Tübingen.

—— 1990. 'Hadrian's Policy in Judaea and the Bar Kokhba Revolt: A Reassessment.' *A Tribute to Geza Vermes: Essays on Jewish and Christian Literature and History.* 281–303. P. R. Davies and R. T. White eds. Sheffield.

—— 1995. *The History of the Jews in Antiquity.* Luxembourg.

SCHORSCH, I. 1994. *From Text to Context: The Turn to History in Modern Judaism.* Hanover, NH.

SCHWARTZ, J. 1986. *Jewish Settlement in Judaea from the Bar Kokhba Revolt to the Arab Conquest.* Jerusalem.

SCHWARTZ, S. 2001a. *Imperialism and Jewish Society, 200 B.C.E. to 640 C.E.* Princeton.

—— 2001b. 'The Rabbi in Aphrodite's Bath: Palestinian Society and Jewish Identity in the High Roman Empire.' *Being Greek Under Rome: Cultural Identity, the Second Sophistic, and the Development of Empire.* 335–61. S. Goldhill ed. Cambridge.

SILBERSTEIN, L. 1982. 'Historical Sociology and Ideology: A Prolegomenon to Yehezkel Kaufmann's Golah Vnekhar.' In *Essays in Modern Jewish History: A Tribute to Ben Halpern.* 173–95. F. Malino and F. Cohen Albert eds. London and Toronto.

SMITH, M. 1951. *Tannaitic Parallels to the Gospels.* JBL monograph series 6. Philadelphia.

—— 1967. 'Goodenough's Jewish Symbols in Retrospect.' In *JBL* 86: 53–68.

—— 1971. 'George Foot Moore.' In *Encyclopedia Judaica* xii. 294.

SPERBER, D. 1970. 'Costs of Living in Roman Palestine.' *Journal of the Economic and Social History of the Orient* 13: 1–15.

Sperber, D. 1974. *Roman Palestine, 200–400, Money and Prices.* Ramat-Gan.

—— 1978. *Roman Palestine, 200–400, the Land: Crisis and Change in Agrarian Society as Reflected in Rabbinic Sources.* Ramat-Gan.

Stern, S. 1994. *Jewish Identity in Early Rabbinic Writings.* Leiden.

Urbach, E. E. 1951. 'Megamot Datiot Ve-Hevratiot Be-Torat HaTzedaqah shel Hazal.' *Zion* 16: 1–27.

—— 1953. 'HaYehudim Be-Artzam Bi-Tequfat HaTannaim.' *Behinot* 4: 61–71.

—— 1959. 'The Rabbinical Laws of Idolatry in the Second and Third Centuries in the Light of Archaeological and Historical Facts.' *Israel Exploration Journal* 9: 149–65, 229–45.

—— 1984. 'Shaul Lieberman U-terumato Li-khlal Mada'ei Ha-yahadut.' *Lezikhro shel Shaul Lieberman* (no editor). Jerusalem.

—— 1999. *Collected Writings in Jewish Studies.* Ed. M. D. Herr and R. Brody. Jerusalem.

Wacholder, B. Z. 1972. Review of Neusner 1970, *JBL* 91: 123–4.

CHAPTER 6

CLASSICAL RABBINIC LITERATURE

CATHERINE HEZSER

CLASSICAL rabbinic literature comprises all those ancient Jewish literary compilations which transmit the traditions of tannaitic (70–200 CE) and amoraic (third-to
fifth-century CE) rabbis in Palestine and Babylonia: the Mishnah, the Tosefta, the
Palestinian and the Babylonian Talmuds (also called the Yerushalmi and the Bavli),
and various midrashim.[1] The dating of each of these collections often remains
uncertain and is disputed amongst scholars (see esp. Stemberger 1996). Some works,
such as the Babylonian Talmud and some late midrashim, seem to have been edited
in post-amoraic, that is, in gaonic or early medieval times. Whereas the Mishnah,
the Tosefta, and the tannaitic midrashim are written in Mishnaic Hebrew, the
Palestinian and the Babylonian Talmuds and the amoraic midrashim contain
both Hebrew and Aramaic traditions, with the Aramaic portions usually being
considered later than the Hebrew ones. The rabbinic editors of all of these works

---

[1] For more information on individual works of rabbinic literature see Stemberger 1996. In this
chapter the following abbreviations will be used: M. = Mishnah; T. = Tosefta; y. or PT = Palestinian
Talmud; b. or BT = Babylonian Talmud; ARN = Avot de Rabbi Nathan (A = version A, B – version B);
Gen. R. = Midrash Genesis Rabbah; Ex. R. = Midrash Exodus Rabbah; Lev. R. = Midrash Leviticus
Rabbah; Deut. R. = Midrash Deuteronomy Rabbah; Pes. R. = Pesiqta Rabbati; PRK = Pesiqta de Rav
Kahana; Tanh. = Midrash Tanhuma; Tanh. B. = S. Buber edn. of Midrash Tanhuma. For the abbrevi-
ations of Mishnah, Tosefta, and Talmud tractates see the list in Stemberger 1996.

remain anonymous, that is, they never identify themselves to the reader. Accordingly, rabbinic literature must be seen as a collective rather than an authorial literature, transmitting a wide variety of partly divergent and contradictory views and teachings rather than providing a linear systematic outline of a particular individual's point of view.

The critical study of rabbinic literature began in the nineteenth century with the so-called Wissenschaft des Judentums (Science of Judaism), whose representatives began to apply to rabbinic texts historical and philological methods which were also used in other fields of the humanities. Subsequently, the study of rabbinic texts left the narrowly defined religious realm of the *yeshivot* (orthodox institutions of Talmud study) and entered the secular domain of scientific study.[2] This move would eventually lead to a much broader spectrum of students of rabbinic texts: rabbinic texts were no longer studied by the *yeshiva bokher* (male yeshiva student) only, but also by culturally assimilated Jews (such as the representatives of the Science of Judaism), students of early Christianity, and classicists, whether male or female.[3]

The secularization of the study of rabbinic texts naturally went hand in hand with a change in the questions asked and the issues examined. Traditional scholars from the gaonim to the maskilim were primarily concerned with the halachic (legal) meaning of the texts and focused on the (by then) authoritative Babylonian tradition, neglecting the Palestinian Talmud and the midrashim. If the latter were commented on at all, they were usually interpreted on the basis of the Bavli rather than being understood in the context of their own time and place. Modern critical study of rabbinic literature, on the other hand, considers the Palestinian works of equal importance to the Bavli, and views all rabbinic documents in their own terms. The traditional explanation of particular terms and phrases and the search for the texts' halachic meaning has been supplemented by broader literary and historical concerns, such as the formal structure, literary genre, development, and historical reliability of the texts.

Although the critical study of rabbinic literature is still in its infancy, it has experienced a number of significant advances during the last decades and years. The availability of critical editions and synoptic versions of a number of rabbinic documents enables scholars increasingly to base their research on informed text-critical judgements. The traditional use of rabbinic texts as historical sources has given way to a more careful and critical analysis of the transmission history, literary development, and ideological functions of the texts. If form-critical approaches

---

[2] This change took place despite the fact that Jewish studies did not enter the university canon at that time. The Hochschule für die Wissenschaft des Judentums in Berlin was independent of both the university and the orthodox rabbinate.

[3] This last point needs to be emphasized, since until recently the scholarly study of rabbinic literature remained a specifically male occupation. Significant contributions to the study of rabbinic literature written by women have only appeared since the 1980s.

which isolate, identify, and compare the small units behind the redactional layers are combined with redaction criticism, the ways in which the editors of the respective documents reworked and compiled their material can be determined. The application of methods and theories from related fields such as literary theory allows us to see the texts from a new perspective. Furthermore, the Graeco-Roman context in which the rabbinic tradents and editors lived and in which the texts were formed and transmitted has come to be considered an essential background for a proper understanding of the texts. The diversity of contemporary approaches necessarily increases the number of controversial issues and debates in the field. But it also makes rabbinic texts more accessible to, and relevant for, a larger and more variegated readership than traditional Talmudic scholarship did.

TEXT-CRITICISM AND EDITIONS

The first task of all scholarship into rabbinic literature is the analysis of the textual evidence which should not be confused with the search for an 'Urtext'. Studies of ancient book-publication practices have shown that the search for an 'Urtext' of many ancient literary works is doomed to fail: with its publication, the author or editor released a finished text from his or her responsibility (van Groningen 1963). The result was that the text would be recopied many times, in forms which were beyond the author's or editor's control. This form of publication would lead to the circulation of variant scribal copies of a text, which were nevertheless considered copies of one and the same 'finished' literary work. The existence of variant manuscript versions and recensions is not a convincing argument against an intentional and carefully planned 'final' redaction of rabbinic works (against Schäfer 1986: 144 and Becker 1999: 2–6). As Milikowsky has stressed, 'the question of redactional variation should not be identified with the question of redactional identity' (Milikowsky 1988: 204). Variant manuscript versions are the necessary outcome of the medieval transmission history of the text and should be examined in their respective chronological and geographical contexts. Analysis of the redactional processes and the nature and form of the pre-redactional material available to the editors is an entirely different issue, which may be discussed in connection with text-critical issues but should not be confused with them (see also Bokser 1990: 80–5).

The analysis of the textual evidence of rabbinic texts requires the easy accessibility of manuscript variants. Scholars nowadays generally agree about two basic models for the proper presentation of rabbinic texts: editions based on the 'best' manuscript, with collations of variant readings from other manuscripts and printed editions listed at the bottom of the page, or manuscript synopses accompanied by the evaluation of manuscript variants by families. To date, such editions and synopses are available for a few rabbinic documents or individual tractates of documents only.

Chanoch Albeck's edition of the Mishnah (1952–9, with various reprints) merely provides the vocalized text of the first printed edition, and attempts to create a critical edition based on variant readings are still incomplete.[4] Similarly incomplete is Saul Lieberman's critical edition of the Tosefta (1955–88, repr. 1992–), based on the Vienna manuscript with variant readings from other manuscripts, Genizah fragments, and the first printed edition. It comprises the first three orders and the Bavot tractates of the fourth order of the Tosefta only. For the remainder of the text one has to depend on the Zuckermandel edition (1880–1/1882, repr. with supplements, 1993), the only complete edition of the text, which is, however, based on the inferior Erfurt manuscript up to T. Zeb. 5 : 5. For the order of Toharot in the Tosefta, Rengstorf's critical edition (1967) is preferable to Zuckermandel.

The manuscript synopsis of the Talmud Yerushalmi, edited by Peter Schäfer and Hans-Jürgen Becker (1991–8), is now almost complete, with the last volume (order Moed) due to come out in 2002. The synopsis presents the text of the Leiden manuscript of the Yerushalmi, which is the only complete manuscript of the text, together with the texts of the first printed editions (Venice, Constantinople, Amsterdam) and other available manuscript versions (Venice, Escorial, Sirillo).[5] The synoptic presentation of the manuscripts provides scholars with an easily accessible text base for the comparison of textual variants. The actual text-critical work, that is, the estimation of the significance and value of the respective readings and of the relationship between them, is left to the individual scholar him- or herself. As far as the Bavot-tractates are concerned, significant differences exist between the Leiden and the Escorial manuscript versions of the text. The critical edition of the Escorial manuscript edited by Rosenthal (1983) provides a good basis for comparisons of the two texts.

For the Babylonian Talmud, a joint Israeli–German project under the guidance of Sh. Friedman, M. Glatzer, and P. Schäfer has set itself the task of creating a typology of the entire textual evidence available. The goal of the project is to evaluate the Talmud's textual transmission with the help of codicology, palaeography, and textual criticism, and to create a *stemma codicum* as the preliminary basis of a future

---

[4] The Mishnah edition project of the Institute for the Complete Israeli Talmud covers order Zeraim only (Sacks 1972, 1975). The Giessener Mishnah project (1912–35, 1956–) seems to have come to a temporary end with the death of its editors Karl Heinrich Rengstorf, Rudolf Meyer, and Leonhard Rost. Hopefully the approach of the later volumes of this project, to take the Kaufmann MS with the oldest complete text of the Mishnah as the base text and supplementing it by a critical apparatus with variant readings, will eventually be continued.

[5] The Yerushalmi synopsis does not contain the extant Geniza fragments of the Yerushalmi, which will appear in a separate volume edited by Yaakov Sussmann (for an earlier collection see Ginzberg 1909).

text-critical edition of the Bavli. To date, only one chapter of a Bavli tractate, namely b. B.M. ch. 6, has been published in the form of a text-critical edition (Friedman 1996), which constitutes the basis of the editor's commentary (Friedman 1990). In the introduction to his text edition (Friedman 1996: 25–55), Friedman suggests the division of the early textual witnesses of b. B.M. ch. 6 into two families or recensions, one more conservative and the other more creative, both of which seem to derive from an earlier but no-longer extant written text. He also traces the development of the two recensions through the works of the gaonim and medieval commentators on the Bavli. As editor-in-chief of the Scholarly Edition of the Babylonian Talmud produced by the Israeli Society for the Interpretation of the Talmud, Friedman's approach will in the future also be applied to other tractates and orders of the Bavli. His methodology constitutes a further necessary step beyond the mere presentation of manuscript variants in the form of a critical or synoptic edition.

For ARN, Schechter's synoptic edition of ARN A and ARN B (1887, repr. 1997) is available.[6] As far as the Midrashim are concerned, some good text editions exist, such as Theodor/Albeck's edition of Gen. R. (2nd edn. 1965, repr. 1996), which takes the British Museum manuscript as its base text and lists variants from other manuscripts in the apparatus.[7] Other text-critical Midrash editions are Margulies's edition of Lev. R. (1953–60, repr. 1993), Finkelstein's edition of Sifra on Leviticus (1983–90), and Mandelbaum's edition of PRK (1962, reprinted 1987), all of which also include the relevant Genizah material, as well as Ulmer's most recent synoptic edition of Pes. R. (1997–9). Shinan's edition of Ex. R., based on a Jerusalem manuscript, covers the first part of the document only (Shinan 1984). Less useful than the editions just mentioned are those based on the first printed text, such as Horovitz/Rabin's edition of Mekhilta de R. Yishmael (1931, 2nd edn. 1970), or on an eclectic text taken from various manuscripts, such as Lauterbach's edition of the Mekhilta (1933–5), Finkelstein's edition of Sifre Deuteronomy (1939), and Horovitz's edition of Sifre Numbers (1917, 2nd edn. 1966). For many midrashim, either no scholarly editions exist at all or the ones which exist are methodologically deficient. To create such critical editions or synoptic presentations of the textual evidence is clearly an important task that should be undertaken in the near future.

The creation of scholarly text editions must be followed by text-critical investigations into the relationship and significance of the variants. One important step into this direction has already been undertaken by Shamma Friedman in his work on b. B.M. ch. 6, as pointed out above (Friedman 1996). Manuscripts need to be differentiated by family, and quotations in early medieval witnesses to the text have to be compared with the extant manuscript versions. Only then will it be possible to

---

[6] In Göttingen Hans-Jürgen Becker is currently preparing a facsimile edition of the Genizah fragments of ARN, combined with a redaction-critical analysis of the textual evidence.

[7] The Genizah fragments to Gen. R. and MS Vat. 60 are not included in this apparatus, but published separately by Sokoloff (1982).

assess the complex textual history of rabbinic works, to identify different post-redactional recensions of a text, and to determine the specific ways in which texts were transmitted and at the same time transformed within their respective communities.

Future research into the textual transmission of rabbinic documents should also take studies of ancient and medieval scribal practices into account. The question whether specific textual variants can be considered scribal errors, corrections, or intentional changes, and whether intentional scribal changes were the result of blurred boundaries between scribes and authors/editors, can only be answered on the basis of new insights into the roles and functions of literary scribes in ancient and medieval society.

INTRODUCTIONS AND COMMENTARIES

The first scholarly introduction to the Mishnah was written by J. N. Epstein (1948, 2nd edn. 1964), and is still unsurpassed in its depth and scope.[8] Epstein's main focus is the development of the Mishnah, from the time of the pre-Mishnah collections to the Talmudic period, and the Mishnah's textual transmission in Talmudic and post-Talmudic times. This development is dealt with exhaustively, and serves to underline his theory that a single, fixed Mishnah text never existed, neither at the time of its 'author' Rabbi Yehudah ha-Nasi (also known simply as 'Rabbi') nor afterwards. Epstein assumes that Rabbi himself produced several Mishnah collections, based on divergent tannaitic sources, and that collections made by other rabbis were circulating at the same time. Some rabbis would use and transmit these other collections and base their interpretations on them.

In fact, every 'academy' may have had its own Mishnah collection. If this is correct, it would not be striking that different versions of Mishnaic rules appear in the Palestinian and Babylonian Talmuds, and even in different tractates of one and the same Talmud. Amoraic statements which seem to contradict the Mishnah may respond to no longer identifiable versions in recensions or collections which were eventually lost. Epstein considerably refined source criticism and research into the transmission history of the Mishnah, but he never stated his methodology, never summarized his thesis, and never questioned the traditional belief that Rabbi was the 'author' of the Mishnah. These deficiencies, as well as the sheer bulk of his writing and exhaustive quotation of examples, make Epstein's introduction difficult to use for anyone but specialist Talmudic scholars. All scholarship on the Mishnah

[8] A good description and critical assessment of Epstein's work is provided by Bokser (1973: 13–55).

has to take Epstein's argumentation into account, but one may ask whether such detailed quotation and analysis of variants and emendations should be included in an introductory work.

Albeck's introduction to the Mishnah (1971) is less complex and detailed, but also less critical. Albeck assumes, for example, that in cases of halachic uncertainty, where divergent halachic views existed, the high court decided which opinion should be accepted. Like Epstein, he reckons with various stages in the development of the Mishnah, and with Mishnah collections of different schools. But he is less explicit with regard to the variety of versions still circulating at and after Rabbi's time. Despite the possibility of later additions, Albeck considers Rabbi to have been the final editor of the Mishnah, who collected and arranged the *mishnayot* but did not change or harmonize his sources. His version was allegedly accepted by everyone immediately (see ibid. 160 f.).

Both Epstein and Albeck also wrote introductions to amoraic literature, but Albeck's work (a second part was announced but never published) deals with the Babylonian Talmud only (Albeck 1969). Again, his approach is traditional and consists of explaining terms, describing the academies in Babylonia in which the redaction is believed to have taken place, and discussing earlier theories concerning the sources and processes of the redaction. The first and second part of Epstein's *Introduction to Amoraitic Literature* (1962) basically consist of an introduction to selected Bavli tractates with notes and explanations to selected passages. The introduction to the Yerushalmi in the third part of the book is more systematic, beginning with a discussion of the place and time of the redaction and moving on to problematic issues such as the existence of parallel sugyot, the relationship of the Bavot tractates to the rest of the Yerushalmi, the relationship of the Yerushalmi to Gen. R. and the Bavli, and Babylonian traditions and sugyot in PT.

Epstein's introduction to the Yerushalmi was preceded by that of Z. Frankel (1870), which is still the only introduction devoted to the Palestinian Talmud exclusively. As an introduction to the historical background, language, style, and editing processes of the Yerushalmi it is still unsurpassed. Unfortunately the discussion of basic introductory issues is rather short in comparison to the extensive explanation of certain recurrent technical terms and phrases and the alphabetical list of amoraim mentioned in the Yerushalmi which constitute the main part of the book.

Although these scholarly introductions are all interested in the sources and development of the respective rabbinic documents, they hardly leave the traditional halachic realm to investigate the literary structure and the historical value and context of the transmitted material. In their extensive discussion of technical terms, emendations, and corrections they can be considered tools which help the Talmudic scholar understand particular passages rather than systematic and methodological introductions into the study of the documents as such. While the modern bibliographical guides to the Yerushalmi by Bokser and to the Bavli by

Goodblatt (both in Neusner 1981), the discussion of the manuscript evidence of the Mishnah, Tosefta, Bavli, and Yerushalmi by Michael Krupp (in Safrai 1987), and the introduction to the Talmud and midrashim by Stemberger (2nd edn. 1996) all help the uninitiated student in gaining access to rabbinic works, a methodological introduction to the study of rabbinic literature, which would cover text-critical, form-critical, and redaction-critical issues in a systematic way and provide examples of how to approach rabbinic texts, is still a desideratum. What is needed is an introduction to the various methodological approaches and debated issues in rabbinic scholarship, as well as introductions to particular documents which are more systematic and user-friendly than Epstein's and Frankel's works and present an up-to-date discussion of various aspects of the texts.

The chapters on the PT and BT by Bokser and Goodblatt in Neusner (1981) and the respective articles in Safrai (1987) provide good references to and descriptions of traditional commentaries on the Talmuds. Amongst the first scholarly commentaries on rabbinic works, Saul Lieberman's multi-volume but unfinished commentary on the Tosefta (10 vols., 1955–88) stands out. Lieberman created a running commentary to the text of the Tosefta, with reference to parallel *baraitot* (tannaitic traditions not included in the Mishnah) in the Yerushalmi and Bavli and quotations in medieval commentaries as well as explanations of Greek and Latin loanwords and other difficult terms and phrases. As such Lieberman's work can be considered a tool helpful to anyone trying to understand particular *baraitot*, but not to those who are interested in broader halachic, literary, transmission-historical, and redaction-critical issues. Lieberman's commentary on the Talmud Yerushalmi (2nd edn. 1995), modelled after his commentary on the Tosefta, consists of one volume only, covering tractates Shabbat, Erubin, and Pesachim. This similarly 'technical' commentary provides short explanations of certain terms and phrases and references to parallels in other documents, but hardly anything more.

A much more detailed commentary on the Yerushalmi was undertaken but also never completed by L. Ginzberg (4 vols., 1941–61). It covers y. Ber. 1–5 only. As the subtitle, 'A Study of the Development of the Halakhah and Haggadah in Palestine and Babylonia', already indicates, Ginzberg's aim was to provide a running commentary to each tractate and chapter which traces the development of the halachic issues discussed within rabbinic literary works, medieval authorities, and the extant manuscripts and Genizah fragments. Ginzberg pays close attention to the style and terminology of the Yerushalmi, but his tradition-historical arguments and conclusions are sometimes questionable and presented in an unsystematic way. (See also Bokser in Neusner 1981: ii. 248.) Both Lieberman's and Ginzberg's main concern was proper halachic understanding. They are therefore useful for traditional rabbinic scholarship, but fail to address issues relevant to the modern historical-critical study of the texts.

Amongst the more recent commentaries on the Babylonian Talmud, the ones by Halivni (1968 ff.) and Friedman (1990) are most noteworthy. None of them has yet been completed. Halivni's approach can be called tradition- and redaction-historical: he examines the types of sources which were used by the Bavli editors and the ways in which these editors integrated their source material into the larger whole. One of his major questions is whether and to what extent the anonymous (*stam*) portions differ from the earlier amoraic layers of the Talmud. Halivni does not deal with redaction-critical issues on a broader and more general scale. These issues are only discussed by him in connection with individual Talmudic passages. No conclusions for the redaction-history of the Bavli as a whole are drawn on the basis of these exegetical observations and hypotheses. Although Halivni's source-critical commentary goes beyond Lieberman's and Ginzberg's commentaries in its tradition-historical approach, it resembles these commentaries in being aimed at the traditional Talmudic scholar concerned with the halachic meaning of the text.

The most comprehensive commentary on the Bavli ever undertaken has recently been provided by Friedman (1990), in a 400-page volume which covers b. B.M. 6 only. The commentary is based on the already-mentioned text edition by the same author (Friedman 1996) and the textual variants indicated therein. It proceeds from one *sugya* to the next and focuses on the understanding of the *sugya* as a whole rather than explaining every individual term and phrase separately. Another advantage over Lieberman's and Ginzberg's approaches is the close attention which Friedman pays to the literary-historical development of the text. He distinguishes between various levels within the Bavli, identified as *baraita*, *memra*, and *talmud*. Comparisons with parallels in other rabbinic documents reveal the ways in which the Bavli editors reworked traditions and/or supplemented traditions by secondary additions. But parallels also indicate the relatively stable form of the traditions before their inclusion into the respective documents. Friedman's commentary is not limited to literary-historical issues but also elucidates the legal and economic background and context of the topics discussed in the Talmud text. Since the socio-economic situation was subject to both chronological and geographical changes, Babylonian sages may not have properly understood a Palestinian text and/or they may have adapted it to the circumstances of their own time and place. It is therefore necessary to analyse the realia behind each individual level of a tradition's transmission and reception history, up to the time of the medieval commentaries. In its discussion of realia in connection with literary- and transmission-historical problems, its attention to textual variants and to the literary structure of each *sugya*, as well as its detailed analysis of the understanding of the texts by the later gaonim and rishonim (i.e. medieval commentators), Friedman's commentary provides a model for the writing of modern scholarly commentaries to rabbinic works.

FORM-ANALYTICAL AND
FORM-HISTORICAL APPROACHES

Form-critical approaches which analyse the forms, literary functions, and 'Sitz im Leben' of the traditions incorporated into larger literary works have been employed by classicists and biblical scholars for centuries. To date, no comprehensive form history of rabbinic literature exist and only some of the forms in which rabbinic teachings are transmitted have been studied by scholars on an individual basis. (On form-critical approaches to rabbinic literature see also Saldarini 1977, Bokser 1980, and Stemberger 1996:49–53, and the literature referred to there.)

Only some of the earlier studies concerned with formal aspects of rabbinic texts can be mentioned here. Abraham Weiss (1962) already distinguished between different amoraic literary forms and considered the *memra* and *sugya* the main building-blocks of the Talmud. In his study of aggadah Joseph Heinemann (1974) compared different versions of traditions and investigated the possible settings that might have led to the creation and modification of aggadic narratives. In his earlier works Heinemann had applied form-criticism to prayer texts (Heinemann 1964; see also id. 1977) and proems in midrashim (id. 1971). Henry A. Fischel's studies examine the relationship between rabbinic and Graeco-Roman stylistic and rhetorical forms (see Fischel 1968, 1973, 1977), and Yonah Fraenkel's works similarly deal with the forms and rhetorical elements employed in aggadic narratives (see Fraenkel 1981 and 1991).

While all of these studies investigate formal aspects of rabbinic literature, none of them makes consistent use of the form-critical methodology applied to biblical and classical texts. The first scholar who applied this methodology to rabbinic texts was Jacob Neusner. In his study of the traditions about the Pharisees, Neusner (1971) acknowledged the influence of form-criticism but noted that the categories developed on the basis of biblical texts might not fit rabbinic literature. He also distances himself from the form-historical approach, maintaining that the recovery of earlier forms of rabbinic traditions behind the current redactional layer of the documents is not possible anymore. Accordingly, the purpose of synoptic comparisons of variant versions of traditions is not to detect the 'original form' of a tradition but 'to follow the history of sayings, stories, and biographical details through several documents' (ibid. 189).

Neusner's own categorization of the material is, however, also open to objection. Since he does not distinguish between tradition and redaction, he lists redactional introductory formulas alongside traditional stories. His refusal to trace the transmission history of a tradition and to seek to determine editorial changes and additions runs the risk that his form-critical analysis may seem superficial. It is reasonable to assume that the traditions incorporated into rabbinic documents underwent a number of stages of transmission and that the editors consciously reworked and adapted earlier material to the respective literary contexts. If that is the case, one cannot simply dismiss the question of transmissional and redactional changes, even if the 'original' form of a tradition is irrecoverable.

Another form-analytical approach dismissing form-historical questions and adapting the use of formal categories developed on the basis of other types of literature is that of Arnold Goldberg (see the collected articles in Goldberg 1999). In a programmatic article (in Goldberg 1999: 50–79, originally published in 1977), he suggests that one should approach rabbinic texts inductively, by describing and cataloguing their recurrent literary patterns and by determining these patterns' or forms' function within their larger literary contexts. Like Neusner, Goldberg believes that earlier forms and earlier 'Sitze im Leben' (functions) of the traditions are irrecoverable, that one can only discern their 'Sitz in der Literatur' (literary purpose). Goldberg applied his form-analytical methodology to a number of smaller literary forms, such as the *mashal* (parable) and *maaseh* (story), as well as to larger formal units such as 'the form midrash', consisting of a Scriptural quotation (called *lemma*) and its commentary (which can comprise other forms, such as the *mashal* and *maaseh*), and the various forms of rabbinic homilies (see also Lenhard 1998, below). Both Neusner's and Goldberg's approaches can basically be seen as synchronic analyses of the component parts of the surface structure of rabbinic texts (on Goldberg's approach, see also Schäfer 1986: 144 f.).

Previous research on rabbinic parables had mostly been carried out by New Testament scholars interested in the form for comparative reasons. Paul Fiebig, who was one of the earliest scholars to deal with rabbinic parables, openly disparages them as inferior to those attributed to Jesus on both stylistic and moral-ethical grounds (see Fiebig 1904 and 1912).

Later scholars tried to view rabbinic parables on their own terms before comparing them with the parables of the New Testament. They also distanced themselves from Fiebig's judgemental remarks concerning the literary and theological value of the respective traditions. The first to be mentioned in this regard is David Flusser. Flusser's study of the nature of rabbinic parables (Flusser 1981) set the parameters for all further scholarly study of the form. Unfortunately, the second part of his book was announced but never published, so that his work remains incomplete. Flusser wrote parts of his book in Luzern, and his approach influenced Clemens Thoma and his collaborators (see Thoma and Lauer 1986 and 1991, Thoma and Ernst 1996), who undertook an edition of all rabbinic parables found in a particular midrash (such as PRK, Gen. R., and Ex. R.) In these editions the rabbinic parables are translated and explained, with reference to existing parallels elsewhere in rabbinic literature and in the New Testament. The comparative approach is also applied in Dschulnigg's study of the parables of PRK (Dschulnigg 1988, based on Thoma and Lauer) and in Hezser's comparison between the parable of the workers in the vineyard (Matt. 20: 1–15) and similar rabbinic parables about workers and wages (Hezser 1990).

David Stern (1981 and 1991) is mainly concerned with the ways in which parables are used within the larger literary genre of midrash. He differentiates between the rhetorical function of the *mashal* (parable) and the exegetical function of the *nimshal* (application) in this regard. The addition of the *nimshal* is seen as an expression of the midrashizing transformation of the parable. While parables were originally transmitted orally, Stern believes that their original oral setting or 'Sitz im Leben' cannot be reconstructed anymore. The *nimshal* compensates for the missing original setting. But the actual relationship between *mashal* and *nimshal* remains unclear.

Probably the most studied rabbinic literary form to date is the rabbinic story. Whereas rabbinic narratives have traditionally been taken at face value and used as historical sources, providing information on particular rabbis and events (see e.g. Herr 1971, Safrai 1971), Neusner (1980 and 1987a) has stressed the literary nature and ideological function of rabbinic tales (see also Gafni 1982). The sage story serves as a medium conveying a message, namely various aspects of the particularly rabbinic world view and way of life (see Neusner 1992). Six of the most famous sage stories transmitted in the Babylonian Talmud have recently been analysed by Jeffrey L. Rubenstein (1999). Rubenstein shows that these Bavli stories are sophisticatedly constructed narratives in whose formulation the anonymous editors of the Bavli played a significant role. In their present form the stories elucidate the values of the stammaim and the culture of the Babylonian rabbinic academy.

One particular type of 'sage story' is the so-called *chreia*, *apophthegma*, or pronouncement story (see Hezser 1993: 288–91; 1996 and the literature cited therein). This originally Hellenistic literary form consists of a narrative setting which leads to a climactic ending in the form of a striking 'pronouncement' or action attributed to the main protagonist. Such stories were told about Hellenistic philosophers of almost all philosophical schools, and they appear in the gospels and in later monastic collections (such as the *Apophthegmata Patrum*) as well. The *chreia* seems to have been a formidable means of propagating the world-view and life-style of marginal figures with circles of followers, such as scholars, saints, and philosophers, and seems to have been transmitted by these sages' students. They juxtapose the teachers' wisdom and exemplary behaviour with the values and practices of mainstream society. The stories had both an ethical and an epideictic function: they elevated the reputation of the teacher and transmitted his teachings to later generations.

A specifically halachic story form is the case story or *maaseh* (see Goldberg 1999). The entire form of the case story is very concise and can be considered an abstraction of a formerly more detailed case report. The main interest of the transmitters and editors were the case decisions at the stories' end. Case stories in the Bavot-tractates of the Bavli have been studied by Segal (1990), and those in the Bavot-tractates of the Yerushalmi by Hezser (1993). Precedents and legal rulings are also the most frequently used literary forms in which Roman legal traditions were transmitted in antiquity (see Hezser 1998: 583 ff.). They seem to have had their 'Sitz im Leben' in rabbis' and Roman legal experts' practice of giving legal advice.

Besides the smaller literary forms of the parable, story, and legal rule, a few larger forms which occasionally incorporate one or the other smaller form have been investigated by scholars as well. One of them is the enumeration of scriptural examples. Towner (1973) has traced the tradition-history of the respective midrashic pericopes and catalogued the lists according to their respective functions in the midrashic contexts.

Another larger rabbinic form which has received scholarly attention is the rabbinic homily. Abraham Marmorstein has pointed to similarities between some types of rabbinic homilies and the Stoic-Cynic *diatribe* (Marmorstein 1929). In one type of *diatribe* dialogues between two parties are introduced by the third party of the speaker or writer, who remains in the background. Marmorstein points to fictional and anonymously presented midrashic dialogues between God and Israel or biblical personages as examples of this form. A study of the rabbinic homily resulting from Arnold Goldberg's research project on the topic has recently been presented by Doris Lenhard (1998). The rabbinic homily is described as an ideal-typical macro-form which contains various smaller micro-forms, the so-called 'compositional forms', which allegedly appear in the homily according to a fixed order. The second part of Lenhard's work consists of an 'Index of Rabbinic Homilies', that is, a formal description of rabbinic homilies found in Lev. R., PRK, Pes. R., Tanh., Tanh. B., and Deut. R. Like Goldberg's, Lenhard's work is limited to the description and categorization of the rabbinic form. She neither deals with pre-redactional developments nor with redactional additions or revisions, since in Goldberg's approach rabbinic documents are merely seen as secondary compilations of homilies without any plan or character of their own.

The form-analytical approach as practised by Goldberg and Neusner is too limited to be very useful on its own. It should be combined with form-historical, tradition-historical, and redaction-historical approaches to do justice to the centuries-long process of transmitting rabbinic traditions and to the complex and multi-level redactional work of ancient editors. Furthermore, a merely descriptive approach, which focuses on the surface structure of the documents only and refuses to ask questions which go beyond the literary text, discourages a historical-critical investigation of rabbinic texts and makes historical enquiries difficult. The investigation of the possible 'Sitz im Leben' or social-ideological function of specific literary forms and of the ways in which traditions were changed according to the varying interests of their transmitters and editors and adapted to the different circumstances of another time and place should not be dismissed, despite the necessarily hypothetical nature of any conclusions that can be reached. It is to be hoped that a comprehensive form history of rabbinic literature will be written in the not-so-distant future. It would constitute an invaluable tool to all students of rabbinic texts.

REDACTION CRITICISM AND THE COMPARISON OF DOCUMENTS

Redaction history, that is, the examination of the ways in which the editors of particular rabbinic documents incorporated, adapted, changed, supplemented, explained, and harmonized the traditional material which they received, presupposes that the rabbinic editors were more than mere compilers who combined and juxtaposed the received traditions without adding anything on their own. The approach presupposes the existence of a redactional programme, even if it may have been limited to the formal 'orchestration' of the material, to use Baruch M. Bokser's terms. Redaction critics thus assume that a circle of editors consciously collected, selected, arranged, and reworked material, and that these editors are responsible for the basic arrangement of the material which is available to us today.

Redaction history also distinguishes between the 'final' redaction and later scribal changes introduced during the centuries-long process of recopying. Once a text was released ancient authors and editors had no more control over its contents. Since no copyright laws existed, the circulating copies of a text would hardly be identical. The notion of an 'original' text was unknown to the ancients. Each scribal copy constituted a distinct version of the text, but all of these versions were seen as exemplars of one and the same literary work. The standard distinction between the redactional work and later scribal changes and additions should be maintained, even if it is impossible to reconstruct with certainty the 'original' version of a text (on this issue see Schäfer 1986, Milikowsky 1988, and Schäfer's rejoinder 1989; see also Becker 1999, below).

A number of redaction-critical approaches which take the diachronic development of the texts into account have been written with regard to the Bavli. While Neusner maintained that the composition of the Bavli happened at a particular time and was carried out according to a formal and ideological 'plan and program' (Neusner 1991a: 460 f; 1991b: 4), other scholars have argued that the Bavli developed over a longer period and that the incorporated material underwent several stages of redaction. Some of them, such as J. N. Epstein (1962: 12), merely repeat the traditional theory, developed by the gaonim in the Middle Ages, according to which Ravina and Rav Ashi constituted the 'end of *horaʾah*', followed by two intermediate generations and finally by the saboraim who allegedly 'sealed' the Talmud, but the enigmatic talmudic terminology does not allow for such wide-ranging historical conclusions (see Goodblatt in Neusner 1981: 312). Apart from these dubious phrases, there is no internal evidence supporting the theory that representatives of the last amoraic generation in the fifth century CE edited the

Bavli. The editing of the Bavli must therefore be attributed to a later period of time (that is, the time of the anonymous editors, the so-called 'stammaim').

Accordingly, later scholars commonly distinguish between two layers of the Talmud, the *gemara*, which is considered roughly to equal the amoraic material until the 'end of *horaʾah*', and the later *talmud*, that is, the anonymous additions, revisions, and harmonizations of the amoraic sources (see Halivni 1968 ff.). The role of the post-Rav Ashi amoraim and their relation to the stammaim has been examined by Halivni's student Richard Kalmin (1985). Kalmin has shown that a strict distinction between the two is not possible and that boundaries between them were blurred. It seems that some of the named amoraim of the time after Rav Ashi participated in the anonymous redaction of the Talmud (see also idem 1989). Another student of Halivni, David Kraemer (1984), has pointed to stylistic characteristics of the successive generations of Babylonian amoraim: whereas the earlier amoraim's statements are often apodictive, the later amoraim seem to have preferred the argumentative form and provided explanations for earlier material. They seem to have foreshadowed the later anonymous editors' work in this regard. Altogether, the theory that the Bavli was edited during 'stammaitic' times, that is, between the fifth and seventh centuries CE, has generally been accepted in scholarly circles today (see also Lightstone 1994).

In the case of the Yerushalmi, the traditional theory that (with the exception of the earlier Bavot-tractates) it was edited in Tiberias in the late fourth to early fifth centuries CE (see Frankel 1870, repr. 1967), is still commonly believed to be valid. Connected with the assumption of a fourth-/fifth-century redaction is the belief that the Yerushalmi was left unfinished, since it lacks *gemara* on the last two orders of the Mishnah (with the exception of Niddah). To explain this alleged unfinishedness scholars have developed the so-called 'persecution theory'. According to this theory the redaction of the Yerushalmi should be seen as a reaction to the persecution of Palestinian Jews under the Christian emperors at the end of the fourth century CE (see e.g. Ginzberg 1955: 27). Since the editors had little time for deliberation, they had to work hastily. Therefore they could not compile a Talmud on the last two orders and had to keep their own contributions very limited.

The assumption that the Yerushalmi is incomplete is obviously based on its comparison with the Bavli, that is, on its lack of a similarly broad discursive framework attributed to the *stam*. The Yerushalmi is measured according to the Bavli, then, of which it is considered to be a preliminary draft, but this assumption fails to treat the Yerushalmi on its own terms. The differences between the Yerushalmi's and Bavli's anonymous layers can rather be explained by reference to the large time difference (probably at least 200 years) between their redactions. In addition, if the commonly held belief that Palestinian Jews suffered religious persecutions in the fourth century is to be rejected (see Lieberman 1946–7), then 'at this point, we . . . do not have an adequate explanation why y. was compiled when it was' (Bokser in Neusner 1981: ii. 197).

Although no direct evidence on the time or period in which the Yerushalmi was edited exists, there are also no convincing reasons to dismiss the assumption that most tractates were edited by the generations after the amoraim last mentioned in the text, that is, between the end of the fourth and the beginning of the fifth centuries CE. As to the reasons for the compilation, the codification of the (albeit later) *Corpus Iuris Civilis* under the reign of Justinian may serve as an analogy. The compilation of such legal collections was initiated by circles of legal scholars and motivated by antiquarian and classicizing objectives: the collections were meant to preserve traditions which had accumulated over centuries, to make them available to and accessible by scholars of one's own and future generations. As such, the creation of the Yerushalmi may be seen in the context of other restorative endeavours which formed part of the so-called 'Byzantine renaissance' (see Hezser 1998: 636).

Lieberman (1931) argued that the Bavot-tractates of the Yerushalmi were edited earlier than the rest of the Yerushalmi. In comparison with the other tractates, their anonymous redactional portions are much more limited in quantity and scope. He dated this earlier redaction to the middle of the fourth century and located it in Caesarea rather than Tiberias. References to Caesarean sages, the alleged Caesarean 'local color', and the prevalence of Greek and Latin loan-words were adduced as arguments in favour of this assumption. The likelihood of an earlier date of the Bavot-tractates has been confirmed by Gerd Wewers (1984) as a result of his redaction-critical comparison between passages in the Bavot-tracates and their parallels elsewhere in the Yerushalmi, but the arguments in favour of a Caesarean redaction presented by Lieberman are not decisive, as Hezser (1993) has shown. Loan-words appear in other Yerushalmi tractates and in midrashim as well. Most traditions in the Bavot-tractates are attributed to non-Caesarean rabbis. The textile industry and seafaring mentioned in the Bavot-tractates, which allegedly constitute the 'local color', are also to be found at a number of other places. Whether the Bavot-tractates were edited in Caesarea can therefore neither be proven nor excluded. Although an urban centre seems likely, an exact identification of the place where this earlier redaction of parts of the Yerushalmi took place must ultimately remain an open (and probably unanswerable) question.

The particular nature of the redaction of specific rabbinic documents is also elucidated by comparisons between documents. The comparison between the Palestinian and Babylonian Talmuds obviously occupies a particularly important place in this regard. The title of Neusner's seven-volume comparison of the surface structure of selected Yerushalmi and Bavli tractates, *The Bavli's Unique Voice* (1993), already indicates the purpose of the enterprise. In these volumes Neusner tries to show that the Bavli does not build and expand upon the Yerushalmi text but constitutes an independent and entirely unique approach to the issues and sources at hand. As the only intersection between the Yerushalmi and the Bavli Neusner identifies their quotation from and reference to Scripture and Mishnah. He maintains, however, that when the Bavli speaks for itself, these shared intertexts are of little significance. In the end Neusner concludes that the Talmuds do not so much differ in form as in their respective 'intellectual program', but what these distinctive intellectual programmes consist of is never specified (see also Neusner 1986a).

To determine the formal and intellectual differences between the two Talmuds one would have to work diachronically, comparing the tradition-historical and redactional development of individual traditions, combinations of traditions, and entire *sugyot*, a task which goes beyond Neusner's phenomenological-descriptive approach. Such a detailed study has been undertaken by Christine Hayes (1997). On the basis of a text- and source-critical examination of selected halachic passages from tractate Avodah Zara of the Babylonian Talmud Hayes tries to determine whether halachic divergencies are based on internal literary and/or redactional differences between the Talmuds or external cultural and/or historical differences between Palestine and Babylonia. As one would expect, a combination of both causes seems to have been the case. Obviously the examination has to be extended to other Bavli tractates to determine whether the conclusions can be generalized.

Another important project of comparison between rabbinic documents is the one carried out by Hans-Jürgen Becker (1999). The many parallels between the Talmud Yerushalmi and Gen. R. have already occupied scholars in the past. These scholars have usually tried to determine which document was dependent on the other, that is, used the other one (or an earlier redactional stage of it) as a source (see the survey of earlier scholarship in Becker 1999: 8–15). Becker argues against such direct-dependency theories, since they cannot account for the complex and variegated relationships between the texts. Despite the many similarities, no mutual interdependence is recognizable. The editors of the Yerushalmi cannot be assumed to have known the Gen. R. version or vice versa. 'Therefore' one can not speak of a parallel text's primary literary place or origin in one document and adaptation by the other. Becker suggests that the parallels are rather due to the fluid transmission history of the texts both before and after their inclusion into the larger literary works. Various versions of a text seem to have circulated individually or in collections, as commentaries on or unrelated to a particular Mishnah passage or scriptural verse, before they were eventually included in the Yerushalmi and Gen. R. The comparison between parallels is thus able to go beyond the surface structure of the documents and to elucidate the complex transmission history of the text.

Besides the Talmuds, the Mishnah is especially prone to warrant comparisons with other documents. For obvious reasons, the foremost task is to determine the relationship between the Mishnah and the Tosefta. Traditionally, the Tosefta was seen as a dependent expansion and commentary on the Mishnah and/or a collection of independent *baraitot*. Alberdina Houtman (1996), who has undertaken a detailed synoptic comparison of small textual units from tractates Berakhot and Sheviʾit, shows that such a broad generalizing conclusion is no longer valid. The detailed analysis of the texts indicates that on the level of individual textual units various types of relationships exist between the Mishnah and Tosefta, and that sometimes the Toseftan halachot may have been more 'authentic', serving as the Mishnah's source, rather than vice versa. She suggests that the enterprise of collecting a Tosefta should be seen as a reaction to attempts (by other rabbinic circles) to create a prototype of the Mishnah. Clearly, more comparative work is necessary to confirm (or dismiss) this theory.

A similar, though more limited, tradition-historical comparative approach has been applied to the Mishnah and Sifra by Ronen Reichman (1998). Based on the comparison between twenty parallel texts, Reichman argues that the Mishnah texts are the result of a redactional adaptation of Sifra prototypes, that is, that the Mishnah is directly dependent on Sifra. Like Houtman, Reichman reaches a conclusion which stands in diametric opposition to the traditional view which, in this case, holds that Sifra was edited later than the Mishnah and dependent on it.

The main problem underlying all of these comparative studies is how to determine and demonstrate literary interdependence amongst individual traditions or even entire documents. The common assumption is that shorter versions precede longer ones, which are considered to be expansions. The studies mentioned show that such a criterion is not always appropriate, that shorter versions may as well be summaries and abbreviations of more lengthy prior texts. The relation between the textual differences, expansions, and changes on the one hand and the respective literary context and editorial framework on the other may provide supporting evidence in determining whether the former can be attributed to the editors or must be considered traditional. But clear-cut conclusions can never be reached in this regard. Due to such uncertainties, the diachronic tradition-historical approach can reach hypothetical conclusions only, whose usefulness and validity depends on the persuasiveness of the argumentation. Although the reservations against such an approach which are, for example, expressed by Jacob Neusner, are understandable, the approach should not be abandoned but seen as an important supplement to redaction-critical methodologies. Neither the mere analysis of the literary structure of the documents nor the mere comparison between individual traditions and units can, on their own, yield significant conclusions about the procedures and world-views of the editors of the respective documents. Such conclusions can only be reached if the two approaches are combined to supplement and reinforce each other. It seems that a lot of work still needs to be done in this regard, not only as far as the Mishnah, Tosefta, Yerushalmi, and Bavli are concerned, but for the midrashim as well.

Rabbinic Literature and Postmodern Literary Theory

Certain issues discussed in postmodern literary criticism, such as intertextuality, indeterminacy, intersubjectivity, authorship, and the identification of the intended reader, provide new perspectives from which rabbinic literature can be examined. Until now such topics have been investigated in connection with rabbinic midrash only, but one can assume that these approaches will advance the study of other rabbinic documents as well.

The issue of intertextuality has been disputed amongst scholars in connection with the so-called 'synoptic problem'. Neusner (1986b and 1987b) has maintained that synoptic comparisons between rabbinic texts are only useful if a synoptic relationship between these documents can be established, that is, if mutual dependencies similar to the ones amongst the Gospels exist. He defines intertextuality as the relationship of one document to another rather than the relationship between individual traditions or literary units within these documents. As already pointed out above, his focus is on the uniqueness of individual documents rather than on shared traits or materials. That 'all rabbinic documents relate synoptically to all others' (1987: 12) is considered self-evident and not worthy of further investigation, but a direct dependence of one document on another cannot be established. Due to this lack of genealogical connections between rabbinic works, a synoptic comparison between them is allegedly useless.

According to Morton Smith (1988), Neusner's position is based on a misunderstanding of the word 'synoptic': 'The term implies *nothing* about their source relations, either to each other or to any supposed common source' (ibid. 111). Therefore rabbinic documents need not be directly dependent on each other to make synoptic comparisons useful. The creation of a synopsis 'neither requires nor *per se* proves any theory of source relations' (ibid. 112). It merely means seeing texts together in order to determine—and, as a next step, explain—similarities and differences between them. Morton Smith' positive view of the usefulness of synoptic comparisons has been accepted by most scholars.

Daniel Boyarin (1990a) goes one step further in defining the terms 'intertextuality' and 'intertext' on the basis of postmodern literary theories. The intertext of rabbinic midrash is provided (a) by the biblical canon itself and (b) by the ideological intertextual code of rabbinic culture at large. Accordingly, midrash is described as 'a dialogue with the biblical text conditioned and allowed by that ideology' (ibid. 17). The intertextuality of rabbinic midrash consists of the ways in which it 'preserves the signifying practices of a culture precisely by transforming them' (ibid. 25). Defined in this way, intertextuality has both 'disruptive' and 'reconstructive' features. Boyarin's broader cultural definition of intertextuality (in comparison with the merely literary focus on synoptic parallels suggested by Morton Smith) is particularly useful for rabbinic collections, which represent a multiplicity of voices rather than the world-view of one particular author or editor.

Similarly, William Cutler (1990) has suggested that one should not limit the context or intertext of rabbinic texts to the literary dimension, but that one should examine the historical, political, social, and ideological contexts as well. This approach to intertextuality 'suggests that one must understand all of the forces at play in a historical period so that we may fully understand every aspect of the text' (ibid. 109). The surrounding Graeco-Roman cultural context becomes extremely significant in this regard. It is part of the 'discursive space' in which rabbinic documents developed, irrespective of direct influences and dependencies. In fact the influence question and the positivistic search for 'sources' and 'origins' becomes irrelevant and inappropriate against the background of this broader meaning of intertextuality. Whether a text was actually influenced by any specific other text can never be ascertained. It is much more interesting and important to focus on Graeco-Roman culture at large as the intertext of particular rabbinic texts in order to understand the cultural choices the authors, transmitters, and editors made. The main question must be, then, how the 'discursive space' of Roman Palestine is represented in rabbinic documents. An important step into this direction of inquiry has been made by the contributors to the volumes *The Talmud Yerushalmi and Graeco-Roman Culture* (Schäfer 1998 and Schäfer and Hezser 2000, with a third volume forthcoming in 2002), who examine a variety of thematic issues without sharing a single methodological approach.

Another aspect of rabbinic texts which has been emphasized by postmodern literary critics is the plurality of meanings and interpretations which they transmit. The discussion has mainly focused on whether the term 'indeterminacy' is an adequate description of this pluralism of views. Susan A. Handelman (1982), who viewed rabbinic literature against the background of Derrida's writings, has argued that in rabbinic works different interpretations of Scripture and different views on a variety of issues are juxtaposed and considered equally valid. For the rabbis, the process of study and discussion rather than the fixation and systematization of their teachings was most relevant. There was also no central authority which censored the multiplicity of teachings: 'The Rabbis enunciated, judged, and analyzed—but in an ongoing communal process that disseminated authority' (ibid. 50).

Handelman's assumptions have been criticized by David Stern and William Scott Green. According to Stern (1988), the multiple interpretations in midrash have little to do with Handelman's concept of indeterminacy. He maintains that for the rabbis the Torah was not an open text which allowed for an unlimited variety of interpretations. One should rather speak of a 'unified and univocal reading of Scripture rather than a truly polysemous one' (ibid. 139). Similarly, William Scott Green (1987) has criticized the notion of indeterminacy. He even speaks of a closed halachic system instead: rabbinic interpretations of Scripture 'operated within a limited conceptual sphere and a narrow thematic range' (ibid. 162). Therefore 'it is doubtful that rabbis ascribed "endless multiple meanings" to Scripture' (ibid. 163). However, Stern's and Green's arguments against Handelman's emphasis on rabbinic pluralism are not very convincing. Though all rabbis will have shared certain fundamental convictions about the Torah and its application to daily life, within this framework of agreements multiple ways of dealing with the concrete details of Torah interpretation and practice could be expressed (see also Ulmer 1994: 354; Boyarin 1990b). There was no higher authority which dismissed some teachings and approved of others, except for the choices made by the final editors of rabbinic documents.

Questions of authorship and readership of rabbinic documents have also been inspired by modern literary theories. In contrast to the large majority of Graeco-Roman and early Christian writings, rabbinic texts are transmitted anonymously and their authors/editors are unidentifiable. They are not the product of individual authorial intentions but the creations of different sets of scholars who chose not to identify themselves. Rabbinic works are intersubjective in that they contain a variety of opinions on almost all of the issues addressed, rather than presenting the opinion of one author in a clear-cut and systematic way. These collective works were apparently meant to open up further discussion of issues rather than to bring closure by offering one solution only. The possibility 'to determine the intentions of authors of various documents, that given documents bear a single univocal meaning' must therefore be dismissed (see Eilberg-Schwartz 1987: 195).

This last aspect of rabbinic works, namely their ability to open up further discussion, leads to the question of the intended readership. It is obvious that the reader is required to make meaning of the texts him- or herself (see ibid. 197). Therefore David Kraemer has stressed that the understanding of rabbinic *gemara* requires 'extraordinary intellectual capabilities' (Kraemer 1993: 129). In all likelihood the intended reader of rabbinic texts was the male rabbinic scholar, or the more or less advanced student of rabbis, who was able to make sense of unstated assumptions, allusions, and gaps. This reader is invited to participate in the critical enquiry initiated by the texts, to challenge previous views and interpretations rather than to agree with authoritative traditions of the past (see ibid. 132–3). His task was to develop received traditions, to transform them, and adapt them to the particular circumstances of his own time and place.

Suggested Reading

For previous surveys on the 'status quaestionis' of research into rabbinic literature, see Bokser (1983 and 1990), Schäfer (1986), and Stemberger (2000). Good introductions to particular rabbinic documents are to be found in Neusner ed. (1981–2 vols.: Mishnah, Midrash, Palestinian, and Babylonian Talmud), Neusner (1994), and Stemberger

(1996—revised edn.: all rabbinic documents). Safrai ed. (1987) provides introductions to the historical background of rabbinic literature, the concepts of Oral Torah and halachah, and particular rabbinic documents (Mishnah, Tosefta, Palestinian and Babylonian Talmud), but from a traditional rather than critical point of view. In this volume the sections on the manuscript evidence of the respective documents, written by Michael Krupp, are especially useful. For a collection of articles, all written by former students of Neusner, which critically assess earlier approaches to the Mishnah, see Neusner (1973).

BIBLIOGRAPHY

ALBECK, CH. ed. 1952–9. *Shishah Sidre Mishnah (The Six Orders of the Mishnah)*. Jerusalem and Tel Aviv. Repr. 1988.

—— 1969. *Introduction to the Talmud, Bavli and Yerushalmi* [Hebrew]. Part 1. Tel Aviv.

—— 1971. *Einführung in die Mishnah*. Berlin and New York.

BECKER, H.-J. 1999. *Die grossen rabbinischen Sammelwerke Palästinas. Zur literarischen Genese von Talmud Yerushalmi and Midrash Bereshit Rabba*. TSAJ 70. Tübingen.

BOKSER, B. M. 1973. 'Jacob N. Epstein's *Introduction to the Text of the Mishnah*', and 'Jacob N. Epstein on the Formation of the Mishnah'. In *The Modern Study of the Mishnah*. 13–36, 37–55. J. Neusner ed. Leiden.

—— 1980. 'Talmudic Form-Criticism'. *JJS* 31: 46–60.

—— 1983. 'Recent Developments in the Study of Judaism, 70–200 C.E.'. *Second Century* 3: 1–68.

—— 1990. 'Talmudic Studies'. In *The State of Jewish Studies*. 121–33 and 225–7. S. J. D. Cohen and E. I. Greenstein eds. Detroit.

BOYARIN, D. 1990a. *Intertextuality and the Reading of Midrash*. Bloomington and Indianapolis.

—— 1990b. 'Inner-Biblical Ambiguity, Intertextuality and the Dialectic of Midrash: The Waters of Marah'. *Prooftexts* 10: 29–48.

CUTLER, W. 1990. 'Citing and Translating a Context. The Talmud in its "Postmodern" Setting.' *Ju* 39: 104–111.

DSCHULNIGG, P. 1988. *Rabbinische Gleichnisse und das Neue Testament. Die Gleichnisse der PesK im Vergleich mit den Gleichnissen Jesu und dem Neuen Testament*. Bern, Frankfurt, New York, and Paris.

EILBERG-SCHWARTZ, H. 1987. 'When the Reader Is In the Write.' *Prooftexts* 7: 194–205.

EPSTEIN, J. N. 1948. *Introduction to the Text of the Mishnah* [Hebrew]. 2 vols. Jerusalem. 2nd edn. Jerusalem 1964.

—— 1962. *Introduction to Amoraitic Literature: Babylonian Talmud and Yerushalmi* [Hebrew]. Jerusalem.

FIEBIG, P. 1904. *Altjüdische Gleichnisse und die Gleichnisse Jesu*. Tübingen and Leipzig.

—— 1912. *Die Gleichnisreden Jesu im Lichte der rabbinischen Gleichnisse des neutestamentlichen Zeitalters*. Tübingen.

FINKELSTEIN, L. ed. 1939. *Siphre ad Deuteronomium. H.S. Horovitzii schedis usus cum variis lectionibus et adnotationibus eddidit*. Berlin. Repr. New York, 1969.

FINKELSTEIN, L. ed. 1983–90. *Sifra on Leviticus. According to Vatican Manuscript Assemani 66 with variants from the other manuscripts, Genizah fragments, early editions and quotations by medieval authorities and with references to parallel passages and commentaries.* 4 vols. New York.

FISCHEL, H. 1968. 'Studies in Cynicism and the Ancient Near East: The Transformation of a *Chria.*' In *Religions in Antiquity: Essays in Memory of Erwin Ramsdell Goodenough.* 372–411. J. Neusner ed. Leiden.

——1973. *Rabbinic Literature and Greco-Roman Philosophy: A Study of Epicurea and Rhetorica in Early Midrashic Writings.* Leiden.

——ed. 1977. *Essays in Greco-Roman and Related Talmudic Literature.* New York.

FLUSSER, D. 1981. *Die rabbinischen Gleichnisse und der Gleichniserzähler Jesus. Part 1: Das Wesen der Gleichnisse.* Bern, Frankfurt, and Las Vegas.

FRAADE, S. D. 1991. *From Tradition to Commentary: Torah and Its Interpretation in the Midrash Sifre to Deuteronomy.* Albany, NY.

FRAENKEL, Y. 1981. *Studies in the Spiritual World of the Aggadic Story* [Hebrew]. Tel Aviv.

——1991. *Ways of the Aggadah and the Midrash* [Hebrew]. Masada.

FRANKEL, Z. 1870. *Einleitung in den Jerusalemischen Talmud* [Hebrew]. Breslau. Repr. 1967.

FRIEDMAN, S. H. ed. 1990/1996. *Talmud Arukh. BT BAVA MEZIA VI. Critical Edition with Comprehensive Commentary.* New York and Jerusalem.

GAFNI, I. 1982. 'Court-Tales in the Babylonian Talmud: Literary Formations and Historical Projections' [Hebrew]. *PAAJR* 49: 23–40.

GINZBERG, L. ed. 1909. *Yerushalmi Fragments From the Genizah.* New York.

——1941–61. *A Commentary On the Palestinian Talmud: A Study of the Development of the Halakhah and Haggadah in Palestine and Babylonia* [Hebrew]. 4 vols. New York.

——1955. *On Jewish Law and Lore.* Philadelphia.

GOLDBERG, A. 1999. *Rabbinische Texte als Gegenstand der Auslegung. Gesammelte Studien I and II.*, ed. Margarete Schlüter and Peter Schäfer. 2 vols. *TSAJ* 73. Tübingen.

GREEN, W. S. 1987. 'Romancing the Tome: Rabbinic Hermeneutics and the Theory of Literatue.' *Semeia* 40: 147–68.

GRONINGEN, B. A. VAN 1963. 'ΕΚΔΟΣΙΣ.' *Mnemosyne* S.4 16: 1–17.

HALIVNI, D. WEISS 1968 ff. *Sources and Traditions: A Source-Critical Commentary on the Talmud* [Hebrew]. Tel Aviv.

HANDELMAN, S. A. 1982. *The Slaughters of Moses: The Emergence of Rabbinic Interpretation in Modern Literary Theory.* Albany, NY.

HARTMAN, G. H. and BUDICK, S. eds. *Midrash and Literature.* New Haven and London.

HAUPTMAN, J. 1988. *Development of the Talmudic Sugya: Relationship Between Tannaitic and Amoraic Sources.* Lanham, Md.

HAYES, CH. E. 1997. *Between the Babylonian and Palestinian Talmuds: Accounting For Halakhic Differences in Selected Sugyot from Tractate Avodah Zarah.* New York and Oxford.

HEINEMANN, J. 1964. *Prayer in the Period of the Tannaim and the Amoraim* [Hebrew]. Jerusalem.

——1971. 'The Proem in the Aggadic Midrashim—A Form-Critical Study.' *SH* 22: 100–22.

——1974. *Aggadah and its Development* [Hebrew]. Jerusalem.

——1977. *Prayer in the Talmud.* Berlin and New York.

HERR, M. D. 1971. 'The Historical Significance of the Dialogues Between Jewish Sages and Roman Dignitaries.' *SH* 22: 123–50.

HEZSER, C. 1990. *Lohnmetaphorik und Arbeitswelt. Das Gleichnis von den Arbeitern im Weinberg im Rahmen rabbinischer Lohngleichnisse. NTOA* 15. Fribourg und Göttingen.

HEZSER, C. 1993. *Form, Function, and Historical Significance of the Rabbinic Story in Yerush-almi Neziqin. TSAJ* 37. Tübingen.

—— 1996. 'Die Verwendung der hellenistischen Gattung Chrie im frühen Christentum und Judentum.' *JSJ* 27: 371–439.

—— 1998. 'The Codification of Legal Knowledge in Late Antiquity: The Talmud Yerushalmi and Roman Law Codes.' In P. Schäfer ed. *The Talmud Yerushalmi and Graeco-Roman Culture. Vol. 1: 581–641. TSAJ* 71. Tübingen.

HOFFMAN, L. A. *Covenant of Blood: Circumcision and Gender in Rabbinic Judaism.* Chicago and London.

HOROVITZ, H. S. ed. 1917. *Siphre d'be Rab. Fasciculus primus: Siphre ad Numeros adjecto Siphre Zutta.* Leipzig. 2nd edn. Jerusalem 1966.

—— and RABIN, I. A. eds. 1931. *Mechilta d'Rabbi Ishmael. Cum variis lectionibus et adnota-tionibus.* Frankfurt. 2nd edn. Jerusalem 1970.

HOUTMAN, A. 1996. *Mishnah and Tosefta: A Synoptic Comparison of the Tractates Berakhot and Shebiit. TSAJ* 59. Tübingen.

KALMIN, R. L. 1985. 'The Post-Rav Ashi Amoraim: Transition or Continuity? A Study of the Role of the Final Generations of Amoraim in the Redaction of the Talmud.' Unpublished Ph.D. thesis, Jewish Theological Seminary, New York.

—— 1989. *The Redaction of the Babylonian Talmud: Amoraic or Saboraic?* Cincinnati.

KRAEMER, D. C. 1984. 'Stylistic Characteristics of Amoraic Literature.' Unpublished Ph.D. thesis, Jewish Theological Seminary, New York.

—— 1990. *The Mind of the Talmud: An Intellectual History of the Bavli.* New York and Oxford.

—— 1993. 'The Intended Reader As a Key to Interpreting the Bavli.' *Prooftexts* 13: 125–40.

—— 1995. *Responses to Suffering in Classical Rabbinic Literature.* New York and Oxford.

—— 1996. *Reading the Rabbis: The Talmud As Literature.* Oxford.

LAUTERBACH, J. Z. ed. 1933–5. *Mekhilta de Rabbi Ishmael: A Critical Edition on the Basis of the MSS and Early Editions With an English Translation, Introduction and Notes.* 3 vols. Philadelphia.

LENHARD, D. 1998. *Die rabbinische Homilie. Ein formanalytischer Index. FJS* 10. Frankfurt.

LIEBERMAN, S. 1931. *The Talmud of Caesarea* [Hebrew]. Jerusalem.

—— 1946–7. 'Palestine in the Third and Fourth Centuries.' *JQR* 36: 329–70 and 37: 31–54.

—— ed. 1955–88. *The Tosefta: The Orders of Zeraim, Moed, Nashim and Nezikin.* New York. Repr. 1992 ff.

—— 1955–88. *Tosefta Kifshuta* [Hebrew]. 10 vols. New York.

—— 1995. *Hayerushalmi Kifshuto: A Commentary Based on Manuscripts of the Yerushalmi and Works of the Rishonim and Midrashim in Mss. and Rare Editions* [Hebrew]. Part 1, Vol.1: *Shabbat, 'Erubin, Pesahim.* 2nd edn. New York and Jerusalem.

LIGHTSTONE, J. N. 1994. *The Rhetoric of the Babylonian Talmud, Its Social Meaning and Context.* Waterloo, Ont.

MANDELBAUM, B. ed. 1962. *Pesikta de Rav Kahana: According to an Oxford Manuscript, With Variants from all Known Manuscripts and Genizoth Fragments and Parallel Passages, With Commentary and Introduction.* 2 vols. New York. Repr. New York 1987.

MARMORSTEIN, A. 1929. 'The Background of the Haggadah.' *HUCA* 6: 183–204.

MARGULIES, M. ed. 1953–60. *Midrash Wayyikra Rabbah: A Critical Edition Based on Manu-scripts and Geniza Fragments. With Variants and Notes.* 5 vols. Jerusalem. Repr. in 2 vols., New York and Jerusalem 1993.

MILIKOWSKY, C. H. 1988. 'The Status Quaestionis of Research into Rabbinic Literature.' *JJS* 38: 201–11.

NEUSNER, J. 1971. *Rabbinic Traditions about the Pharisees before 70*. 3 vols. Leiden.

—— ed. 1973. *The Modern Study of the Mishnah*. Leiden.

—— ed. 1981. *The Study of Ancient Judaism*. 2 vols. New York.

—— 1986a. *Comparative Midrash: The Plan and Program of Genesis and Leviticus Rabbah*. Brown Judaic Studies 111. Atlanta, Ga.

—— 1986b. 'The Synoptic Problem in Rabbinic Literature: The Cases of the Mishnah, Tosepta, Sipra, and Leviticus Rabbah.' *JBL* 105: 499–507.

—— 1987a. 'Sage, Story, and History: The Medium and the Message in the Fathers According to Rabbi Nathan.' *Hebrew Studies* 28: 79–111.

—— 1987b. *Canon and Connection: Intertextuality in Judaism*. Lanham, New York, and London.

—— 1991a. *The Bavli's One Voice: Types and Forms of Analytical Discourse and Their Fixed Order of Appearance*. Atlanta, Ga.

—— 1991b. *The Rules of Composition of the Talmud of Babylonia: The Cogency of the Bavli's Composition*. Atlanta, Ga.

—— 1992. *Judaism and Story: The Evidence of the Fathers According to Rabbi Nathan*. Chicago.

—— 1993. *The Bavli's Unique Voice: A Systematic Comparison of the Talmud of Babylonia and the Talmud of the Land of Israel*. 7 vols. Atlanta, Ga.

—— 1994. *Introduction to Rabbinic Literature*. New York.

REICHMAN, R. 1998. *Mishnah and Sifra. Ein literarkritischer Vergleich paralleler Überlieferungen*. TSAJ 68. Tübingen.

RENGSTORF, K. H. ed. 1967. *Rabbinische Texte. Erste Reihe: Die Tosefta. Seder VI: Toharot*. Stuttgart.

ROSENTHAL, E. S. ed. 1983. *Yerushalmi Neziqin: Edited From the Escorial Manuscript with an Introduction by E. S. Rosenthal, Introduction and Commentary by S. Lieberman*. Jerusalem.

RUBENSTEIN, J. L. 1999. *Talmudic Stories: Narrative Art, Composition, and Culture*. Baltimore and London.

SACKS, N. ed. 1972. *The Mishnah. Vol. 1: Order Zeraim I*. Jerusalem.

—— ed. 1975. *The Mishnah. Vol. 2: Order Zeraim II*. Jerusalem.

SAFRAI, S. H. 1971. 'Tales of the Sages in the Palestinian Tradition and the Babylonian Talmud.' *SH* 22: 209–32.

—— ed. 1987. *The Literature of the Sages: First Part: Oral Torah, Halakhah, Mishna, Tosefta, Talmud, External Tractates*. CRINT II.3. Assen/Maastricht and Philadelphia.

SALDARINI, A. 1977. '"Form-Criticism" of Rabbinic Literature.' *JBL* 96: 257–74.

SCHÄFER, P. 1986. 'Research into Rabbinic Literature: An Attempt to Define the Status Quaestionis.' *JJS* 37: 139–52.

—— 1989. 'Once Again the Status Quaestionis of Research into Rabbinic Literature: An Answer to Chaim Milikowsky.' *JJS* 40: 89–94.

—— ed. 1998. *The Talmud Yerushalmi and Graeco-Roman Culture. Vol. 1*. Tübingen.

—— and BECKER, H.-J. eds. 1991–8. *Synopse zum Talmud Yerushalmi*. 5 vols. Tübingen.

—— and HEZSER, C. eds. 2000. *The Talmud Yerushalmi and Graeco-Roman Culture. Vol. 2*. Tübingen.

SCHECHTER, S. ed. 1887. *Avoth de-Rabbi Nathan.* Vienna. Reprinted 'With References to Parallels in the two Versions and to the Addenda in the Schechter edition', New York and Jerusalem, 1997.

SEGAL, E. L. 1990. *Case Citation in the Babylonian Talmud: The Evidence of Tractate Neziqin.* Atlanta, Ga.

SHINAN, A. ed. 1984. *Midrash Shemot Rabbah: Chapters I-XIV.* Tel Aviv.

SMITH, M. 1988. 'The Synoptic Problem in Rabbinic Literature: A Correction.' *JBL* 107: 111–12.

SOKOLOFF, M. ed. 1982. *The Geniza Fragments of Bereshit Rabba.* Jerusalem.

STEMBERGER, G. 1996. *Introduction to Talmud and Midrash.* 2nd edn. Edinburgh.

—— 2000. 'Talmud und Rabbinische Literatur.' In *Wissenschaft vom Judentum. Annäherungen nach dem Holocaust.* 121–33 and 225–7. M. Brenner and S. Rohrbacher eds. Göttingen.

STERN, D. 1981. 'Rhetoric and Midrash: The Case of the Mashal.' *Prooftexts* 1: 261–80.

—— 1991. *Parables in Midrash: Narrative and Exegesis in Rabbinic Literature.* Cambridge, Mass.

—— 1988. 'Midrash and Indeterminacy.' *Critical Inquiry* 5: 132–61.

THEODOR, J. and ALBECK, CH. eds. 1965. *Midrash Bereshit Rabbah: Critical Edition with Notes and Commentary.* 3 vols. 2nd edn. Jerusalem. Repr. 1996.

THOMA, C. and LAUER, S. 1986. *Die Gleichnisse der Rabbinen. Erster Teil: Pesiqta de Rav Kahana (PesK).* Bern, Frankfurt, and New York.

—— —— 1991. *Die Gleichnisse der Rabbinen. Zweiter Teil: Bereschit Rabba 1–63.* Bern, Frankfurt, and New York.

—— and ERNST, H. 1996. *Die Gleichnisse der Rabbinen. Dritter Teil: BerR 63–100/ShemR 1–22.* Bern, Berlin, and Frankfurt.

TOWNER, W. S. 1973. *The Rabbinic 'Enumeration of Scriptural Examples': A Study of a Rabbinic Pattern of Discourse With Special Reference to Mekhilta D'R. Ishmael.* Leiden.

ULMER, R. 1994. 'Postmoderne rabbinische Hermeneutik.' *ZRG* 46: 352–65.

—— ed. 1997–9. *Pesiqta Rabbati: A Synoptic Edition of Pesiqta Rabbati Based on All Extant Manuscripts and the Edition Princeps.* 2 vols. South Florida Studies in the History of Judaism. Atlanta, Ga.

VISOTZKY, B. L. 1995. *Fathers of the World: Essays in Rabbinic and Patristic Literatures.* WUNT 80. Tübingen.

WEISS, A. 1962. *Studies in the Literature of the Amoraim* [Hebrew]. New York.

WEWERS, G. A. 1984. *Probleme der Bavot-Traktate. Ein redaktionskritischer und theologischer Beitrag zum Talmud Yerushalmi.* Tübingen.

ZUCKERMANDEL, M. S. ed. 1880/1. *Tosephta.* Pasewalk. Suppl. Trier 1882. Repr. 1993.

CHAPTER 7

THE NARRATIVES OF MEDIEVAL JEWISH HISTORY

JOSEPH DAN

THE BOOK OF TEARS

IT is surprising to realize that no historian of Judaism wrote a history of the Middle Ages in Jewish history. The comprehensive histories of this period are included in general works in which the Middle Ages could not be avoided: Heinrich Graetz, Shlomo Dubnow, Salo Baron, Ben Zion Dinur, and Ben Sasson in the Hebrew University series. The biblical period, the Second Commonwealth, the Talmudic period, as well as modern times, were subjects to which scholars dedicated detailed historical works—but not to the Middle Ages. This, in itself, is an indication that this period was not regarded as an equal one, and that its historical study is plagued by prejudices and negative narratives. It is even difficult to find collections of papers, Festschrifts, and symposia dedicated to the Middle Ages as such.[1]

A partial explanation may be found in an exception. Between 1923 and 1926 a Jewish historian, Shlomo Bernfeld, wrote in Charlottenburg, Berlin, a three-volume

---

[1] An exception is Bonfil *et al.* 1989. Ben Sasson was one of the few dedicated medievalists among Jewish historians. F. Y. Baer, his teacher, concentrated his efforts in his last years on the study of the roots of the relationship between Judaism and Christianity in antiquity; see below, n. 14.

historical work, consisting mainly of an anthology of sources, entitled *Sefer ha-Demaot*, 'The Book of Tears'. The first two chapters are dedicated to the Hasmonean period and the rebellions against Rome in antiquity. The third chapter deals with the persecutions of the Jews in the Islamic world, and the rest of the work—nearly a thousand pages—is a collection of historical and literary descriptions of the persecutions of the Jews in Christian countries up to the eighteenth century. In the Introduction the author explains that he had hoped that his work would be a record of a past which will never return, yet the upsurge of anti-Semitism which he witnessed around him seemed to indicate that the end had not yet arrived, and who could know what misfortunes awaited the Jewish people in the future. These volumes present a history of the Middle Ages up to the 'Age of Reason', which the author hoped would be the beginning of a new age in which the fate of the Jews would be different, yet this hope, he states in the end of his work, seems to have been unfounded.[2]

Bernfeld's work is focused in one aspect of history, though he perceives it as the dominant one in the long period covered by his volumes. In other works two aspects are added: *Galut*, exile, and the lack of sovereignty, individual and national. These three main characteristics of the Jewish Middle Ages are negative ones, and emphasize the passive nature of Jewish history in this period. When these elements are placed in the centre of the description of these centuries, periodization follows: the Middle Ages begin when Jewish passivity and lack of sovereignty become manifest, and they end when there seems to be a chance of individual and/or national equal rights being won, a change which will bring persecutions to an end. This is the basic prejudice (or narrative) which serves as a basis for the reluctance to deal with the Middle Ages as a preferred subject of historical study.

The prejudicial nature of the term 'Middle Ages' in European and world history has been recognized long ago; it expresses the wish to leap directly from the glory of classical antiquity to the awakening of the human spirit, dormant for over a thousand years, to the Renaissance and the Age of Reason. It is surprising how persistent this concept is, after being proven irrelevant and erroneous again and again. The term itself is a negative one, indicating that there is no positive characteristic which can be applied to these centuries. It is not surprising, therefore, that a similar phenomenon is found in Jewish historiography, and that the Middle Ages are portrayed as a time that nobody wants to be too involved in. The images and ideas associated with this period are intuitively regarded as those that should be rejected and forgotten; no redeeming values can be gleaned from the study of this period.[3] The world in which the historian lives can benefit from adapting norms which are opposed to those which dominated medieval times. This attitude clearly

<hr/>

[2] See his Introduction to the last volume. The Introduction is signed and dated: 'Berlin, Charlottenburg 1925' (Bernfeld 1924–6.)

[3] An exception may be the description of the struggle to establish an autonomous, somewhat independent structure of the Jewish community (*kehilah*), which is described as a heroic effort of

denotes the presence of potent narratives which tend to marginalize the medieval world.

In this chapter a few such narratives will be examined: the way narratives shape the chronological boundaries of the Middle Ages; their consequences concerning the examination of the relationships between Jews and non-Jews in the medieval world; and the place of history of ideas in the descriptions of the Middle Ages.

PERIODIZATION

In 1913 the poet Zalman Schneur published an apocalyptic poem, *Yemey ha-Beynayim Mitkarvim*, 'The Middle Ages Are Approaching' (written when he was studying medicine in Germany), in which he gave an eloquent and powerful expression to the premonition that a new wave of persecutions and massacres awaited European Jewry. It was often quoted between the two world wars by Zionist activists, and later served as a proof that Zionism was aware of the approaching Holocaust. Most of the poem is dedicated to detailed, horrible descriptions of torture and murder, which characterized, so the poet postulated, the Middle Ages. Indeed, in historical perspective the phrase *yemey ha-beynayim* ('the Middle Ages') in this poem is equivalent to the term Holocaust as used decades later. The medieval period is clearly portrayed as one in which Jews were tortured and massacred; by implication, other periods do not include this phenomenon in a dominant way. A period of intense persecutions should be labelled *yemey ha-beynayim*, disregarding its chronological place.[4]

Schneur the poet expressed an attitude similar to that of the historian Shloms Bernfeld. Another variation, which shaped the structure of a major historiographical work of the twentieth century, is presented in the multi-volume study and presentation of sources written by Ben Zion Dinur (Dinaburg), a professor of modern Jewish history at the Hebrew University of Jerusalem and an active member of the Israeli Labour party, who served also as the minister of education in the Israeli government. This work is divided into early volumes called *Yisrael be-Arzo* ('Israel in its Homeland'), followed by ten volumes of *Yisrael ba-Golah* ('Israel in Exile'). Most of the work is dedicated to the medieval period; Dinur's position is that

self-preservation and the maintaining of individual and communal dignity: see e.g. Baer (1950). This study, and other influential articles, were collected and published in the second volume of Baer (1985).

[4] Contemporary Hebrew uses the term *yemey ha-beynayim* or *heshkat yemey ha-beynayirn* in a somewhat different way: to denote the age in which ignorance and religious fanaticism are dominant. Contemporary ultra-Orthodox rabbis are portrayed as representing medieval or 'dark ages' norms of intolerance and bigotry within Judaism.

persecutions and horrors are the unavoidable results of exile, of the loss of national sovereignty. As long as the people live in exile they will be subject to persecutions. The new age, the redemption from the sequence of massacres and suffering, is the establishment of Jewish independence in the nation's old-new homeland, Israel. Dinur was undoubtedly the most eloquent voice of Zionist historiography in the twentieth century.[5]

These two narratives, in fact, do not suggest a date at which the Middle Ages ended and Modern Times began. The end of the medieval period was or will be reached when persecutions end (according to Berenfeld and Schneur) or when exile comes to an end (according to Dinur). The situation is not much clearer among the many historians, who may be described as mainstream of Jewish historiography, who view the transition from the Middle Ages to Modern Times in Jewish history as associated with the process of the emancipation of the individual Jews in Europe.

It has been almost universally accepted among twentieth-century historians that the Jewish Middle Ages began with the conquests of the Muslims in the beginning of the seventh century. It is obvious that the European dating of the beginning of this period with the collapse of the western Roman Empire was meaningless from the point of view of Jewish history. The fact that the legitimate Roman dynasties ceased to govern the city did not affect Judaism; most Jews at that time lived in the Byzantine and Persian empires. The rise of Islam, on the other hand, united the vast majority of Jewry under the rule of one empire, and had a great impact on the legal, economic, cultural, and religious status of almost all Jews. Should this principle— the impact of an event on the majority of Jews—serve also to denote the end of the Middle Ages?

Gershom Scholem suggested that such an event was the messianic awakening of 1666, led by Shabbatai Zvi and his prophet, Nathan of Gaza. This movement engulfed almost all Jewry; it started in the heart of the Ottoman Empire, but swiftly spread east and west and established itself within a few months from the Nether-lands to Poland, from Yemen to Morocco, with great centres in Italy and Syria. It was an unparalleled universal Jewish event, carried by a prophetic-messianic message that the old order of exile had crumbled and the era of redemption had dawned. The ensuing crisis that summer, when news of Shabbatai Zevi's conversion to Islam spread among believers, did not bring an end to the movement but rather created a paradoxical new religion within Judaism, in many cases working under cover: groups of secret Sabbatians operated for 150 years—until the early nineteenth century—in almost every Jewish community in the world. According to Scholem, this upheaval eroded the basis of old Jewish institutions and values, casting doubt

---

[5] Dinur's complete dedication to Zionist historiography did not impair the scholarly value of his studies. The volumes of *Yisrael ba-Golah* are still a most meaningful contribution to the study of the Jewish Middle Ages. Dinur surveyed thousands of sources and collected and presented them in a critical, accurate, historical manner.

on the principles which had directed Jewish life for centuries, and opened the gates of the Jewish ghettos from within, enabling the new ideas and concepts of Europe to enter and change Jewish life.[6] The modern period did not start, according to this thesis, as a result of transformations in Europe nor as a result of the new attitude of Christian states towards the Jews, following the French Revolution. The new era began when Jews were ready to pay attention to voices from the outside, because of a great crisis which had occurred within Jewish culture and which made the continuation of separate and isolated Jewish existence impossible. In the conclusion of his easy 'Redemption Through Sin', Scholem wrote:

The leaders of the 'School of Mendelssohn', who were neither Sabbatians themselves, of course, nor under the influence of mysticism at all, to say nothing of mystical heresy, found ready recruits for their cause in Sabbatian circles, where the world of rabbinic Judaism had already been completely destroyed from within, quite independently of the efforts of secularist criticism. Those who had survived the ruin were now open to any alternative or wind of change; and so, their 'mad visions' behind them, they turned their energies and hidden desires for a more positive life to assimilation and the Haskalah, two forces that accomplished without paradoxes, indeed without religion at all, what they, the members of 'the accursed sect', had earnestly striven for in a stormy contention with truth, carried on in the half light, of a faith pregnant with paradoxes.[7]

These sentences—written by Scholem, who was 40 years old at the time (1937), in a Jerusalem which was beginning to sense the approaching tragedy that was about to engulf Europe—constituted as radical a heresy as could be imagined. This thesis destroyed the basic values which supported the Zionist narrative and the cherished historical understanding of the Middle Ages and Modern Times. If accepted, Jewish modernity did not arise from values of rationalism, humanism, and enlightenment which conquered Europe and opened its gates to the outcast Jews chained by medieval culture; rather, it was the result of an implosion of rabbinic culture which self-destructed through its adherence to mysticism and messianism. Jews did not choose modernity; they were driven to it by their kabbalistic aspirations, which proved too paradoxical to bear.

Scholem's views on this subject were almost completely ignored. His historical thesis concerning the link between Sabbatianism and enlightenment was emphatic-

---

[6] Scholem only ever expressed this view briefly and did not elaborate or present any detailed proof for it. When the World Congress of Jewish Studies was about to convene in Jerusalem in 1981, Scholem was invited to deliver the keynote address. He chose the subject of the impact of Sabbatianism on the Jewish enlightenment and modernity. However, several weeks before the Congress, he apologized that he was physically incapable of delivering the lecture; a few months later he died. As far as I know, no notes of this lecture or anything else related to this subject were found in his papers.

[7] Scholem (1971: 141). A few years later, in a lecture delivered in 1938 on Sabbatianism, Scholem complained: 'Yet in the whole of Jewish historical literature you will find no reference to this highly important relation between the mystical heretics and the representatives of the new rationalism. It is as though this spiritual and often even ancestral relationship was regarded as something to be ashamed of' (ibid. 301). He then goes on to present what he regarded as the intense link between the Sabbatian heretical underground and the establishment of the Jewish reform movement (ibid. 304).

ally rejected.[8] There was no real debate concerning the question of whether the turning-point between the Middle Ages and Modern Times should be sought in internal or external processes.[9] Viewing these phenomena after several decades, it seems to me that the reason for the unease and discomfort surrounding this debate was the concept of the Jewish Middle Ages: should that period be regarded as an abyss, a patch of darkness covering a millennium of Jewish life, which was ended when the great light of enlightenment, freedom, and emancipation vanquished it? Or was that culture a dynamic one, which brought forth the new era from its own womb, through its internal contradictions, aspirations, and paradoxes, marginalizing the impact of the great positive processes occurring in Christian Europe? One might say that Scholem's thesis was 'too Jewish' for historians dedicated to integrating Jewish history into European history to accept.[10]

CULTURE SHINING IN THE DARKNESS

The gloom of exile, persecutions, and massacres which dominated the 'historical proper' study of the Jewish Middle Ages may have been the cause of another meaningful characteristic of the study of the period: the independence—indeed, the separation—of the study of Jewish culture in that period from the matrix of Jewish history in general. Unlike the historian, scholars studying Jewish creativity could point, with great pride, to the achievements of Jewish writers throughout the Middle Ages. A scholar studying the *Guide of the Perplexed* of Maimonides need not feel inferior to anyone studying any aspect of medieval philosophy, Islamic or Christian.[11]

A scholar of Jewish mysticism studying the *Zohar* does not feel inferior to any student of mysticism working on any similar Christian or Islamic work. The history

---

[8] The detailed discussion and rejection of this thesis was presented recently in a monograph by Shmuel Werses (Werses 1988); but the views expressed in this work were dominant among Jerusalem historians since the 1940s.

[9] One of the reasons for this, on the personal level, was the gulf separating historians of the Jewish people from the scholars studying Jewish thought, spirituality, and mysticism, headed by Scholem. He was regarded by some of his Jerusalem colleagues as an intruder in the field of history; he should study kabbalistic texts and leave history to historians.

[10] A detailed analysis of the problem of periodization is found in Herr (1989).

[11] Some things are very difficult to measure, but I believe it can be postulated that Maimonides serves as a focus for more studies—books and articles—than any single figure in Jewish history, biblical, talmudic, medieval, or modern. Scholars, for a variety of reasons, feel comfortable when writing on Maimonides; his stature is undisputed, respect towards him is universal, his relevance to modernity is axiomatic.

of Hebrew medieval poetry, both religious (*piyyut*) and secular, is satisfying and rewarding. Israel Davidson proudly presented his extensive index of Hebrew poetry as testimony to the wealth of Jewish poetic creativity (Davidson 1925–33; and see also Schirman's four-volume anthology of Hebrew poetry in Spain and Provence: Schirman 1954). Writing monographs on Jewish scientists who contributed to European culture, like Gersonides (Ralbag, Rabbi Levi ben Gerson), can be done without any apologies for the unique Jewish fate. Study of the great figures of Jewish halachists, who shaped Jewish religious life during this period, can be a demonstration of spiritual depth, compassion, and religious tenacity. Thus, the poverty of Jewish historiography concerning general Jewish history of the period is balanced by a wealth of works describing and analysing Jewish cultural creativity throughout the same time.

There is, however, a price to pay when monographs on Jewish culture are written without having, parallel to them, comprehensive works of history. It can be argued that even the best studies of Jewish medieval culture are flawed by the absence of a sense of history, of being integrated within a larger cultural-historical context. It is impossible to write scholarly monographs on Jewish philosophy without referring to Arabic philosophy (especially as many of the works were written originally in Arabic), or about Hebrew poetry or grammar outside the frameworks derived from Arabic literature and language by which they were moulded. Yet it seems that most scholarly works of this kind are marked by the lack of a sense of history, both of internal Jewish history and of related phenomena in European history. Important works like E. E. Urbach's *Ba'aley ha-Tosafot*,[12] a survey of halachic schools in France and Germany in the High Middle Ages, makes almost no reference to the surrounding European culture, and it deals with the Jewish works without attempting to demonstrate historical development. Even a masterpiece like Gershom Scholem's history of the early kabbalah (Scholem 1948), whose author cannot be suspected of disregarding historical methodology, makes only a few references to the European culture of the time, and presents no systematic attempt to integrate the emergence of the kabbalah with larger processes in Jewish medieval culture.

EXTERNAL INFLUENCE

One of the most distinctive characteristics of the study of the Jewish Middle Ages in the last three generations is the preoccupation with the problem of 'external influence' on Jewish culture, a term most often relating to 'Christian influence'.

---

[12] The recent works on similar subjects by Avraham Grossman represent a marked improvement in this field, presenting a keen historical awareness (see Grossman 1981 and 1990).

The most important landmark in this scholarly debate may be found in an article by Y. F. Baer, the dean of medieval Jewish historians at the Hebrew University, written in 1939 about the *Sefer Hasidim*, 'The Book of the Pious', which was regarded as the ethic and religious manifesto of the Ashkenazi Hasidic movement in the Rhineland in the late twelfth and early thirteenth centuries.[13] Baer assumed that the Ashkenazi Hasidim knew Latin and were familiar with spiritual developments in the Catholic Church and the monastic movements, and associated the religious trends which he discovered in *Sefer Hasidim* with the Franciscan and Dominican awakening in Christianity. The article expresses in clear terms what can be found in many other studies by Baer concerning Jewish medieval history and culture: the most meaningful phenomena which developed within Judaism should be understood as a result of the inspiration, influence, and spiritual climate prevailing among the surrounding European—especially religious Christian—culture. Medieval Judaism cannot be studied as an isolated subject; it should be viewed as an offshoot of European culture as a whole. The direction of spiritual currents is always from the outside towards Jewish society; it is difficult to find in Baer's work examples of the opposite direction, Jews influencing their non-Jewish surroundings. This attitude was adopted by Baer's disciples and their disciples in Israel, the United States, and Europe. Jewish medieval historians today may be regarded as exemplifying the 'third generation' of Baer's teachings.[14]

There is no doubt that a thousand years of Jewish life in Europe cannot be understood without a detailed analysis of the interrelationship between the handful of Jews in large cities and the surrounding society and culture. There cannot be a valid study of any chapter in Jewish history without taking this interrelationship into account as a major component of any historical occurrence. Yet this is not the subject discussed here. The question which should be analysed in great detail in any review of twentieth-century historiography of the Jews in the Middle Ages is the attribution of value terms to the historical study of this subject. The impact of Christian culture on Judaism cannot be doubted. What should be, though, is the attitude attributing positive or negative value to this impact. It is my suggestion, presented here for further debate, that Jewish historiography of the Middle Ages zigzagged in the twentieth century between the concept that external influence on Judaism is a shameful transgression to be ignored or marginalized, and the concept

---

[13] Baer (1938: 1–50). At about the same time Gershom Scholem, a close friend of Baer's, wrote the chapter on this movement which was included as the third chapter in *Major Trends in Jewish Mysticism* (1941: 80–118).

[14] Baer's last years were dedicated to a quest for this connection in Late Antiquity, in the relationship between Second Commonwealth and Talmudic-period Judaism and the Hellenistic, and later Christian, ancient culture. Baer (1955) presented what he regarded as the close connections between Jewish and Greek culture. There followed a series of detailed studies, which were collected in a large volume of studies (Vol. I of Baer 1985). These theses by Baer were received mostly by embarrassed silence, and a few scattered voices of opposition. His articles were published in *Zion*, the journal which he founded and edited, and his disciples treated him with great respect—but totally ignored or rejected his views.

according to which everything of any meaning or value in Judaism in this period is the result of the impact of the tense relationship between Jews and Christians in medieval Europe.[15] Some scholars, leaning towards the first kind of attitude, tried to portray Jewish life as autonomous, and saw the only meaningful contact in the massacres and persecutions,[16] while other scholars tend to regard any article which does not bring forward an example of Christian influence on Judaism as meaningless and unimportant. These two conflicting attitudes have a common denominator: they express apologetics rather than historical study. On the one hand, Christian influence denigrates and cheapens the noble independence of Jewish culture, and should be ignored or explained as unimportant and meaningless. On the other hand, Jewish history derives its dignity from its continuous contacts with European history (even if it is a confrontation or conflict), and an absence of such a connection deprives Jewish history of any importance.

The dramatic change in the sociology of Jewish historiography should be taken into account in this context. Since the second half of the twentieth century most scholars in the field of Jewish history (and other disciplines as well) work in the framework of general universities, and they lecture and publish for a mixed audience which includes Jews and non-Jews. They struggle to be integrated in the general society of historians, which is dominated by Christian scholars, especially where the Middle Ages is concerned. This audience seems to them to be interested in points of contact between Jewish and European history, while studies dealing with specifically Jewish subjects are regarded as marginal. It may happen that a Jewish historian feels pressured to demonstrate that he is a master not only of Jewish subjects but also of history in general, mainly Christian. This is true not only of historians working in general institutions of higher learning in America and Europe, but also of Israeli scholars, who travel and lecture abroad and occasionally serve as visiting professors in foreign institutions. While this integration of Jewish and European history is most welcome and a very satisfying development, if it leads to an apologetical attitude it has grievous dangers.

---

[15] I cannot explain the reasons why such complexity of attitudes is relatively absent from the study of the relationship between Jewish and Islamic cultures in the Middle Ages, in Eastern countries and in Spain. The fact that Jewish poetry, grammar, philosophy, science, and other disciplines were completely integrated within Arabic civilization, and that Arabic was the main language of cultural expression (including halachah—even Rav Saadia's Jewish prayer-book was written in Arabic), is not regarded as a problem which should be praised or hidden. One of the possible reasons is that the acceptance of Arabic culture was not regarded as having religious significance, while every contact with Christianity was conceived of as religiously dangerous—or rewarding.

[16] This attitude includes also the tendency to relegate anything which is unpleasant (for the scholars) in Jewish medieval culture to Christian influence. In December 1966 I gave a lecture in the meeting of the American Academy for Jewish Research in New York, discussing the development of a Hebrew narrative describing the marriage between a Jew and a female demon. After the lecture Professor Saul Lieberman took me aside and asked me—or, actually, told me—'This is not our story, it was derived from the Christians, right?'

It should be taken into account that in several cases attempts to view Jewish medieval cultural phenomena as a result of Christian influence have failed. One example is the case of *Sefer Hasidim*, mentioned above. Y. Baer's detailed presentation of this school of Jewish pietists as closely similar to Christian monastic movements did not bear fruit. The scholars of the Kalonymus family in the Rhineland who produced this book did not know Latin, and upon close examination by several scholars, no details which confirm Baer's thesis have been found.[17] Similarly, the attempt to explain the appearance of the kabbalah in Provence in the beginning of the thirteenth century as a result of the impact of the **Catharist** 'gnostic' heresy which dominated the regions where the early kabbalists lived, failed to show any connections between the terminology and basic concepts, as well as the general world-view, of the two religious phenomena.[18] Of course, failure in one case cannot serve as a prediction concerning the success of another. Each case should be studied on its own terms, because the two generalizations are undoubtedly valid: Jews were influenced by Christians, and Jews did have an autonomous culture independent of the social and religious impact of the surrounding people. As both of these principles are correct, every particular case could be proven as representing one or the other, and only the immediate, relevant details can serve as evidence to its belonging to the first or the second category. The historian should be careful not to attach any value judgement to one or the other. Nothing becomes better or worse because it reflects Christian influence, or because it is proven to be an autonomous, internal development. The only question to be asked—a very difficult one—is that of whether the facts are right or wrong. There is no place for any value judgement which expresses an apologetic attitude.[19]

While in some cases the question of 'Christian influence' is still problematic in Jewish historiography, there has been a marked improvement in the treatment of texts and historical critical attitude towards sources. The debate concerning the validity of the testimonies concerning the persecutions of the Jews during the early Crusades is an example of meaningful historical reflection and analysis (see Marcus

---

[17] It is impossible to prove a negative; there is no way to show that 'there was no external influence'. Yet the numerous studies of *Sefer Hasidim* in the last half-century by Haym Soloveitchik, Ivan Marcus, Israel Ta-Shema, and myself have not used Baer's thesis and did not find it helpful to the understanding of the phenomenon.

[18] See e.g. Shahar (1971).

[19] A few years ago an excited debate followed the presentation of a thesis concerning the relationship between Jewish martyrdom (*kidush hashem*) and the blood libel, by Professor Israel Jacob Yuval of the department of Jewish History at the Hebrew University, in an article in *Zion* (1993). The editors of this journal then dedicated a double issue to the discussion, and many other scholars participated in it. Recently Professor Yuval published a volume of studies on that and other subjects, including a thesis concerning the reliance of the Jewish Passover Seder ceremony on anti-Christian polemical motives (see Yuval 2000). Any serious discussion of an important historical problem is legitimate. It is to be deplored that value terms and value judgements did intrude into the presentation and discussion of this complex problem.

1982; Chazan 1987; and Berger 1997). Another example is the critical analysis of the *Sefer Hasidim*: this work was regarded until recently as a collective expression of the spiritual development of Jewish ethics in the Middle Ages, which was expressed in a meaningful pietistic movement or sect within which the unique characteristics of Jewish-German culture took actual historical shape. It has been proven, however, that the texts are not what they seem, that much material in the traditional *Sefer Hasidim* (printed in Bologna in 1538) is not Ashkenazi at all; the principal author of the work, Rabbi Judah ben Samuel the Pious, was a lonely, controversial preacher whose ideas were never accepted even by his closest disciples, and no such movement ever existed outside of his dreams and ambitions (see Dan 1998: pp. lxxiii-lxxvi). The same attitude is evident in other central subjects concerning Jewish medieval political, social, and cultural developments in that period. The intense interest in the position of women in Jewish society has an impact on the study of medieval texts in general, bringing seemingly marginal phenomena to the forefront of historical analysis.[20]

The vast panorama of new studies of many aspects of Jewish medieval history represents meaningful advances in the understanding of the history of the Jews in the Middle Ages. Yet it seems that this great effort and its impressive achievements remain out of focus. There is no comprehensive framework; there is no agreement concerning the chronological boundaries of medieval times in Jewish history. We do not have a contemporary, up-to-date comprehensive history of the period. The process of diffusion, in which the history of the Jews in Spain is a separate subject, is treated as independent of that of the Jews in France and Germany, and the various aspects of Jewish medieval culture—religion, ritual, literature, law, ethics, mysticism—are presented often as isolated from other subjects and the general development of Jewish society. The debate concerning the complex relationship between the Jews and their surrounding society lacks precision and focus, and is sometimes plagued with ideological agendas and value judgments. It is to be hoped that the energy and vigour dedicated today to the detailed study of particular phenomena will be directed in the future also towards a comprehensive understanding of this fascinating period.

SUGGESTED READING

Useful introductory discussions of the nature of medieval Jewish history can be found in Baer (1985), Bonfil *et al.* (1989), and Berger (1997).

---

[20] Grossman (2001, including a detailed bibliography: 509–34); Eliav-Feldon and Hen (2001); Baskin (1998 and 1995). A penetrating, comprehensive study of the ideological concepts deciding the role of women in Judaism was presented recently by Rachel Elior (Elior 2000).

BIBLIOGRAPHY

BAER, Y. 1950. 'The Foundations of the Jewish Community Organization in the Middle Ages.' [Hebrew.] *Zion* 15: 1–41.

—— 1955. *Yisrael ba-Amim* (Israel Among the Nations). Jerusalem.

—— 1985. *Studies of the History of the Jewish People.* Jerusalem.

BASKIN, J. R. 1995. 'Images of Women in Sefer Hasidim.' In *Mysticism, Magic and Kabbalah in Ashkenazi Judaism.* 93–105. J. Dan and K. Groezinger eds. Berlin and New York.

—— 1998. 'Jewish Women in the Middle Ages.' In *Jewish Women in Historical Perspective.* 101–27. J. R. Baskin ed. Detroit.

BERGER, D. 1997. *From Crusades to Blood Libels to Expulsions: Some New Approaches to Medieval Antisemitism.* Second Annual Lecture of the Victor J. Selmanowitz Chair of Jewish History. New York.

BERNFELD, S. 1924–6. *Sefer ha-Demaot* (Book of Tears). 3 vols. Berlin.

BONFIL, R., BEN SASSON, M., and HACKER, Y. eds. 1989. *Studies of the Middle Ages Dedicated to the Memory of Hayim Hillel ben Sasson.* Jerusalem.

CHAZAN, R. 1987. *European Jewry and the First Crusade.* Berkeley. Ga.

DAN, J. 1998. *Jewish Mysticism.* Northvale, NJ.

DAVIDSON, I. 1925–33. *Otzar ha-Shirah veha-Piyyut.* New York.

ELIAV-FELDON, M. and HEN, Y. eds. 2001. *Women, Children and the Elderly: Esssays in Honour of Shulamit Shahar.* Jerusalem.

ELIOR, R. 2000. 'Absent Present.' *Alpayim* 20: 214–71.

GROSSMAN, A. 1981. *The Early Rabbinic Authorities in Ashkenaz.* Jerusalem.

—— 1990. *The Early Rabbinic Authorities in France.* Jerusalem.

—— 2001. *Hasidot u-Mordot: Jewish Women in the Middle Ages.* Jerusalem.

HERR, M. D. 1989. 'The Meaning of the Term "Middle Ages" in Jewish History.' In Bonfil *et al.* (1989): 83–98.

MARCUS, I. G. 1982. 'From Politics to Martyrdom: Shifting Paradigms in the Hebrew Narratives of the 1096 Crusade Riots.' *Prooftexts* 2: 40–52.

SCHIRMAN, C. 1954 (1960). *The Hebrew Poetry in Spain and Provence.* 4 vols. Jerusalem and Tel Aviv.

SCHOLEM, G. 1941. *Major Trends in Jewish Mysticism.* Jerusalem.

—— 1948. *Reshit ha-Kabbala.* Jerusalem and Tel Aviv.

—— 1962. Repr. 2002. *Ursprung und Anfänge der Kabbala.* Berlin.

—— 1971. *The Messianic Idea in Judaism and Other Essays on Jewish Sprituality.* New York.

SHAHAR, S. 1971. 'Catharism and the Beginnings of the Kabbalah in Languedoc: Elements Common to the Catharic Scriptures and the Book *Bahir.*' *Tarbiz* 40: 483–507.

URBACH, E. E. 1955 (1972). *Ba'aley ha-Tosafot.* Jerusalem.

WERBLOWSKY, R. Y. ZWI. ed. 1987. *Origins of the Kabbalah.* Princeton.

WERSES, S. 1988. *Enlightenment and Sabbatianism: The History of a Struggle* [Hebrew]. Jerusalem.

YUVAL, I. J. 1993. 'Vengeance and Damnation, Blood and Defamation: From Jewish Martyrdom to Blood Libel Accusations.' [Hebrew] *Zion* 58: 33–90.

—— 2000. '*Two Nations in Your Womb*': Perceptions of Jews and Christians. Tel Aviv.

CHAPTER 8

MEDIEVAL JEWRY IN CHRISTENDOM

RAM BEN-SHALOM

RESEARCH over the past quarter-century in the disciplines of history and 'Jewish studies' has dramatically increased our understanding of how the centres of Jewish life in Christian Europe developed during the Middle Ages. This does not mean, however, that the older scholarship—that produced by the Wissenschaft des Judentums or the historiography written between the nineteenth and the mid-twentieth centuries—have lost their relevance. These include studies tracing the history of the Jews over a chronological range of epic proportions, from biblical times up to the modern age, as well as monographs of a more narrow focus (e.g. Graetz 1893–8; Dubnov 1933; Güdemann 1897–9; Agus 1969; Baron 1958–83; Baer 1966). An exhaustive bibliographical essay was published in the 1970s that surveyed the historical literature written up to that point about the Jews of the Christian Middle Ages (Marcus 1976). The present survey will highlight the more recent developments in the field and will not address all those areas and subjects of scholarly interest. Consequently, those readers seeking a more extensive treatment of a specific subject should refer to this essay's bibliography, where they will find references to older works which themselves contain further leads to additional studies. Moreover, fairly complete surveys of the literature and the state of scholarship regarding both Ashkenaz (Germany) and Sepharad (the Iberian Peninsula) are to be found in sundry books and journals published in the past decade (in Germany: Toch 1998; in Spain: Carrete Parrondo 1992a; Assis and Ibánez-Sperber 1998–2000; Ladero Quesada 1999).

The present survey begins in the early Middle Ages, and specifically addresses questions concerning the economic and political situation of Jewry in Western Europe. The period of the high Middle Ages follows, with a focus on developments in community life and the character of Jewish society. I will then discuss Jewish foundation myths that were born in the twelfth century in an attempt to explain and interpret the social and cultural changes of the time. The nature of the interaction and the form of discourse that characterized the medieval relations between a (Christian) majority and a (Jewish) minority culture will be the next subject of discussion. It begins with an examination of the legal status of the Jews in Western Europe and the Byzantine Empire—a status that guaranteed the existence of the Jews as a religious minority in Christian society—and continues with an account of far-reaching changes that occurred in Western Christendom that led to the persecution and marginalization of the Jews and a renewal of accusations of ritual murder and blood libel.

Another expression, or arena, of Jewish–Christian discourse was religious debate, through which each side shaped its relations both with the other and with itself. This essay will focus on several aspects of this discourse: how Christianity was viewed in Jewish halachic and polemical literature; the symbolic and ritual assimilation of Christian cultural values; and the matrix of representations that mutually influenced both the majority and the minority sides of this relationship. A separate discussion of Jewish life in Spain will follow, since, for a significant segment of the period under study, Spain was under Muslim rule. In many respects, the Jewish life that developed in Spain from the end of the twelfth century was fundamentally different from that which grew up in northern Europe. On the other hand, the experience of persecution and expulsions that traumatized northern European Jewry in the fourteenth century did not bypass the Jews in Spain. Indeed, persecution and expulsion almost emptied Western Europe of a Jewish presence by the end of the fifteenth century. They certainly caused a general eastward shift in the centre of Jewish existence, toward the eastern Mediterranean and the Ottoman Empire. Nevertheless, Judaism survived in the Iberian Peninsula, later emerging in other countries as well (such as France, Holland, Germany, England, and Italy) during the sixteenth and seventeenth centuries as converso communities. The conversos are the final subject of this survey. They were a provocative presence in Iberian and Western European society, and stimulated the birth of several modern tendencies within Jewish society.

THE EARLY MIDDLE AGES

Jews began to settle in Western Europe during the reign of the Roman Empire. Until the Middle Ages, however, information about them is scarce. We do not know, for instance, if Jewish settlement there was continuous, in the same way as it was in southern Italy under Roman-Byzantine rule up through the eleventh century. According to one view on the question, centres of Jewish life grew and flourished in Germany and France during the early medieval period, particularly once Emperor Charlemagne (768–814) and his successors began to encourage Jewish migration from Italy and Spain into the Frankish kingdom. This they did by granting the Jews certain privileges, including formal authorization of their settlement, guarantees of their life and livelihood, a right to self-government, and Jewish autonomous management of their religious affairs. The Jews were even exempted from paying custom duties and were granted the right to travel freely, the aim being that they would play a role in local and international trade and in the feudal economy (Grossman 1981: 1–18).

A contending version of events posits that there was no ongoing Jewish existence to speak of in Germany during the Carolingian period. At the very most, a minute number of Jewish merchants were to be found in the region, but next to nothing is known about their place of residence or the length of their stay. According to this view, Jewish settlement only commenced in the first years of the tenth century at the very earliest, though it was certainly under way by the middle of the century (Toch 1997). There once existed a scholarly consensus pertaining to Jewish control of international trade and a Jewish monopoly of trade and finances, a presence that presumably lasted from the Carolingian period until the end of the eleventh century (e.g. Agus 1969). Today many historians have vastly scaled back the estimation of the extent of this Jewish trade, while also emphasizing that the Jews were not the only ones to be active in this pursuit. Jewish movement into moneylending at interest in northern Germany and northern France cannot, consequently, be explained as the result of prohibitions on Jewish trading in the Mediterranean, but rather as a response to urban and economic change occurring between the twelfth and the early fourteenth centuries in those regions of Jewish settlement (Toch 2001). In addition to commercial pursuits, Jews were known to have also become owners of large estates, even keeping Christians in their service. The presumption once prevailed, too, that Jews wielded tangible political power and not inconsiderable influence over monarchs and the aristocracy in the early Middle Ages (Blumenkranz 1960; Zuckerman 1972; Bachrach 1977). These views seem to have had no empirical basis. For while the legal status and social standing of the Jews were formally established and defined, their political clout was limited. The Church's attacks on Jews in the ninth century was usually provoked by close social contact between Jews and Christians rather than by excessive Jewish political power (Stow 1992: 43–54).

There are other revisions of older scholarly assumptions that are worthy of mention. In the past, anti-Jewish legislation and persecution in Visigoth Spain were considered to be the result of the conversion of the king, Recared (586–601), from Arianic Christianity to Catholicism (Baer 1966: i. 19; Albert 1976; Rabello 1983: 81–2). Today that view has been challenged, and the indifference of Visigoth Catholics to canon law and papal directives concerning the Jews has been emphasized instead. It has also become apparent that there is no basis in the sources for claims that religious persecution in Spain was brought on by Jewish missionary activity or a Jewish conspiracy against the authorities. On the other hand, some consider the anti-Jewish laws to be the outcome of both the considerable Byzantine political and religious influence in the Iberian peninsula and the close 'national' relationship that existed between the monarchy and the Church in Spain (Roth 1994: 7–40). This has been the context for studies concerning the question of the political loyalty of the Jews. In the past, scholars emphasized the assistance offered by Spanish Jews to the Muslim invasion of 711 (Rabello 1983: 79–80). Others reject that view, pointing to the support on the part of the Visigoth aristocracy for the Jews (Stow 1992: 53). At a later date, in the twelfth and thirteenth centuries, figures in the Spanish Church fabricated tales of purported Jewish conspiracies and Jewish betrayal of Visigoth cities and their delivery into the hands of the Muslims. These allegations have no basis in reality. At the same time, there is no reason to doubt the credibility of Muslim chronicles that testify to Jewish support for the Muslim forces, depicting Jews as serving as garrison troops in the conquered Christian cities (Ashtor 1977: i. 9–15; Roth 1994: 73–5).

The Development of Jewish Communities and Jewish Society

The process of urbanization that took place in northern Europe after the eleventh century spurred the growth of Jewish communities. In the Rhine valley in Germany (Ashkenaz) an important centre of religious study and Jewish literary activity emerged. Its scholars even began to issue halachic rulings departing both from Babylonian precedents and from halachic tradition in the Land of Israel (Grossman 1981). This Ashkenazic centre of learning drew students from northern France and from points as distant as Provence and Spain. The centre of Torah study in France, for a long time a satellite of German and Provençal scholarship, emerged in its own right with the arrival in Troyes of Solomon Bar Isaac (Rashi, 1040–1105), who had received his training in the academic centres of Mainz and Worms. By the end of the eleventh century the Jewish communities in northern France had become the most important centres of Jewish spiritual life in Christian Europe. They did not, however, in contrast to received opinion, constitute a direct extension of Ashkenazic practice. French Jewish activity was characterized by its openness and receptivity toward surrounding non-Jewish society and by its social and intellectual connection to the 'twelfth-century Renaissance' (Grossman 1995). This Jewish 'renaissance' found additional expressions in regular intellectual intercourse with Christian theologians (for instance, the monks of Saint Victor), in an ongoing dialogue between Jews and Christians over issues of biblical interpretation (Grabois 1975; Kamin 1991), and in the adoption of dialectical approaches to the study of the Talmud in the spirit of the new cathedral schools (Kanarfogel 1992: 66–85). Research has underscored, in particular, the differences in education and scholarship practiced in northern France and Ashkenaz on the one hand, and in Spain and Provence on the other. While in the latter countries the yeshivas functioned as public institutions (as did elementary schools as well), in northern Europe they were identified with the scholar who stood at their head, who received no funds or a wage from the community, nor was excused from paying taxes (Kanarfogel: 1992). In addition, sections of the Jewish legalistic elite in northern France and Germany, those known as 'ba'alei ha-tosafot', were steeped in mystical and magical practices that until then had been confined to circles of the 'hasidei Ashkenaz' (Kanarfogel 2000). The hasidei Ashkenaz have also become the subject of scholarly re-evaluation, which includes studies of their social structures and the historical forces that shaped their community. At least two levels of pietistic ideology are to be found at work here. One is that of R. Judah the Pietist; the second that of his student, R. Eleazar of Worms. One cannot explain Ashkenazic hasidism only as a twelfth-century phenomenon, or only in terms of its Christian influences, or as the result of persecution and notions of martyrology, or as a reaction to the practices of the 'ba'alei ha-tosaphot'. Consequently, there is need to examine as well the influence of ancient Jewish sources, such as the Heikhalot literature, on hasidic life (Marcus 1981, 1986; Schäfer 1990).

Aspects of Jewish social and family life have also become subjects of recent scholarly attention. These include, for example, community regulations concerning family practices (Grossman 1988) and the loosening of Ashkenazic family structure in the fifteenth century, manifested, for instance, in a climbing divorce rate (Yuval 1983); socialization by means of education and ritual practice towards the ideal of *kiddush hashem* (Jewish martyrdom) (Goldin 1997, 2002); the role of women in the community and the general standing of women in Jewish society and the family (Baskin 1998: 108–27); the status of widows and the type of economic activity they engaged in (Tallan 1991, 1992); the social standing of deviants (persons with deformities, lepers, idiots, and the insane) (Shoham-Steiner 2000). Other subjects, including sexuality and the erotic, attitudes towards birth, and rites of death, have been studied in the wider contexts of Jewish life in

Western Europe generally and in comparison to Christian society (Biale 1992; Cohen 1989; Horowitz 1995; Nirenberg 1996: 127–65). Similar comparative projects have focused on women and the family, community practices, and religious life. This research reveals an improvement in the condition and status of women that began in Ashkenaz in the thirteenth century. It has also identified a consequent reaction that redefined woman's image from pious and pure to arrogant and rebellious. Expressions of violence directed toward women have also been studied (Grossman 2001). The place of women in society has also found a place in the scholarship about Jews in Italy. Historians have, in addition, asked new questions about youth culture in Jewish society (Bonfil 1994; Weinstein 1998; Adelman 1998). A similar research agenda characterizes studies of Jewish life in Spain and Provence that have analysed family life, marriage, concubines, and sexual conduct (Assis 1988, 1997: 255–78), the status of women, women's image, and attitudes towards women (Levine-Melammed 1988, 1999; Dishon 1994; Barkai 1995a), widowhood (Emery 1987), and crime, violence, and murder (Assis 1985; Cohen 1981; Lourie 1988a, 1988b). It would appear that these new fields will continue to attract scholarly attention in the future.

Studies of Provençal Jewry (which includes those Jews who settled throughout southern France) until the thirteenth century principally rest on rabbinic writings and, in part, on Latin documents and chronicles. The numerous local archives to be found throughout the region have been the source of many recent studies, some concerning the thirteenth century but most devoted to the fourteenth and fifteenth centuries. Questions about Jewish communal autonomy, community institutions, the development of centres of learning, the Exilarch dynasty, taxation, the Jewish economy, moneylending at interest, social conflicts, scientific activity, riots during the Black Death epidemic, Christian–Jewish relations, commercial connections with northern Africa, and persecutions and expulsions have all been the focus of study (Vicaire 1977; Kriegel 1979; Iancu 1981; Stouff 1991). Topographic research has focused on Jewish neighbourhoods in the cities of Provence. Community institutions have been the specific subject of detailed study (Iancu-Agou 1974), while monographs devoted to several of the more important individual communities and based on archival materials of social and economic significance have appeared (Shatzmiller 1973b; Stouff 1980; Coulet 1980). Some scholars have even examined the relationship between the Jews of Provence and the Papal Inquisition during its early period in the 1230s, when the Inquisition was directed against Maimonides' work *Guide of the Perplexed* (Cohen 1982: 44–50). Inquisition activity then continuously escalated, from the publication of the Pope's *Turbato corde* in 1267 (Shatzmiller 1973a; Kriegel 1977) until the tightening of control over Jewish communities in the early fourteenth century, during the reign of the inquisitor Bernard Gui (Yerushalmi 1970), and the Jewish conversions to Christianity of the Shephards' Crusade (1320), in the period of the inquisitor Jacques Fournier (Pales-Gobilliard 1977). Some of the repentant converts found refuge in the Crown of Aragon. This development led to an increase in the Papal Inquisition in Aragon (Assis 1983; 1987). The possibility of a connection between Jews and Cathars has also been investigated in the context of the persecution of heretics, together with the connection between the campaigns against the Albigensians and the Jews (Shatzmiller 1989).

MYTHS

A subject attracting considerable recent scholarly interest has been Jewish myths concerning foundational narratives and cultural changes. Some studies address the shift of the centres of Torah study from the Islamic East to the European West. Others compare the symbolism and typology of Jewish myths to those found in contemporary Christian mythology. This direction has opened up numerous new interpretative possibilities. Thus, for example, the Ahima'atz Scroll is no longer only considered to be a genealogical record of an important family in southern Italy, but a transitional tale (*translatio scientiae*) giving expression, on the one hand, to the transplanting of educational and cultural institutions from the Babylonian academies to southern Italy, and on the other hand, to the shift from the cultural influence of the Holy Land to that of Babylon, all the while also generating an independent cultural system that maintained elements of the ancient tradition of the Land of Israel (Bonfil 1989). Comparing the legend of Charlemagne with Christian chronicles reveals a variety of traditions that influenced the Jewish Exilarch in Narbonne ('The King of the Jews') that enjoyed outright ownership of landed property (*allodium*). The relationship of the Jews of Provence to the Jewish centre in Babylon and to the House of David is also exposed. The revisions that the myth underwent from the twelfth century—when the hero and founder of the dynasty is depicted as a Babylonian scholar belonging to the House of David—to the thirteenth century—when he has metamorphasized into a fearless Jewish warrior in the court of Charlemagne—have also been studied for the first time. These legends were intended to justify Jewish ownership of agricultural estates in Narbonne and the economic power and spiritual authority of the Exilarch family (Grabois 1967, 1991). The 'legend of Rabbi Meshulam (ben Kalonymus)', in contrast, functioned as a foundation myth for Ashkenazic Jewry. It depicts the emergence of a new centre for Torah study in Mainz that replaced the fading East (Babylon). It underlines both the importance of traditional Babylonian authority and the cohering, independent nature of Jewish life and leadership in Ashkenaz. Analogous to the legend of Rabbi Meshulam was a sephardic foundation myth known as 'the legend of the four captives'. It told of Moses ben Hanoch, a scholar from southern Italy (the successor of Babylon), who founded the academy (*beit hamidrash)* in Cordoba in the tenth century. At the same time, comparison of these Ashkenazic and Sephardic legends also reveals the difference between these two Jewish centres. Sephardic Jewry perceived itself to be a novel phenomenon, lacking a local provenance and thus in need of legitimation as the spiritual heir to Babylon. Ashkenazic Jewry, in contrast, sought to secure Babylonian recognition of its halachic independence, or even superiority (Zfatman 1993). Historians have shown how Jewish foundation myths in Italy, Ashkenaz, Provence, and Spain served as the basis for political claims both within Jewish society and in its external contacts with Christians (Shatzmiller 1985). At the same time, the need to address the folkloristic, or literary, nature of these texts has also been recently advocated, and such inquiries will certainly influence, if not change, the historical picture (Yassif 1999).

THE LAW

It is most difficult to compose a singular narrative of Jewish history in the Christian world. During the Middle Ages regions of the Byzantine Empire were significantly different from those new countries emerging in Western Europe, in what had once been the Carolingian Empire. The Roman legal tradition, which included specific rules and regulations concerning the Jews, did not lose its relevance during Byzantine rule. Roman law remained important in Western Europe as well. Catholicism preserved much Roman legislation. In fact, from the beginning of the fourth century Roman laws were a contributing factor to the medieval Church's stand vis-à-vis the Jews. In light of this situation, a basic understanding of the legal status of the Jews and of Judaism in Roman, pagan, and Christian law between the second and sixth centuries is a requirement for studying the Jewish position in medieval law (Linder 1987). In the fourth century the Christianizing Roman Empire adopted the pagan tradition of tolerance towards Judaism. Some scholars reject the widespread conviction that the Christian conversion of the Emperor Constantine the Great and the policies of his immediate successors effected a dramatic change in the standing of the Jews. Alongside a certain exacerbation in the Jewish policies of Constantine that was the result of strong Christian influences, the legal practices of his reign also manifested positive elements regarding the Jews (Linder 1974). In opposition to claims that Constantine effected no deviations from the constitutional practices of his predecessors (Cohen 1976), others view the legislation he promulgated as marking a shift in the status of the Jews (Simonsohn 1991: 6–7). It has also been recently discovered that the prohibition on Jewish entry into Jerusalem, formerly thought to be the initiative of Constantine, was actually prompted by the Church in

Jerusalem and the local representatives of the Roman government, and not by the emperor. The earlier role assigned to Constantine can be traced to a hagiographic literature that had developed around the figure of the emperor, which flourished in Byzantium during the ninth century (Ir-Shai 1995). The claims by scholars that Constantine's conversion caused a shift in policy towards the Jews from enlightened tolerance to zealous persecution, a shift that supposedly laid the foundation for the persecution of the Jews in Europe for the next several hundred years, has no basis in the historical record. It has rested, rather, solely on myths concerning 'Constantine, the first Christian emperor' that informed his image as the 'enemy of Judaism' (Linder 1974, 1976).

Alongside anti-Jewish elements, a more tolerant Roman legal tradition survived that found expression in the legal corpus of the Byzantine emperors. Nevertheless, the most noteworthy aspect of these laws was probably their divergence from the traditional definition of the Jews as *Iudaei*, together with their consistent use of negative expressions such as 'superstition', 'impiety', 'absence of faith' (sacrilege), 'plague', 'contamination', and 'stupidity' in characterizing the Jews. This reflected a fundamental change in the perceptions of the imperial chancellory, from recognition of the Jews as a special group to a definition of Judaism as a religion or cult analogous to pagan faiths and heresies and thus a candidate for legal prohibition or restriction. In assuming the Jews to be enemies of the Roman Empire, the possibility even arose, starting in the fifth century, of repudiating a Jew's citizenship and passing discriminatory legislation against him. Two distinct and even contradictory views seemed to have coexisted in the chancellory: on the one hand there developed a systematic persecution of the Jews as a formally defined public; on the other, the traditional legal defence of the Jews' special status was not forgotten (Linder 1987).

This was the constitutional context for the development of 'Jewish laws' in the Christian world between the sixth and the twelfth centuries: from the disintegration of the Roman Empire until the development of centralized government and the codification of canon law. A geographic distinction should be made between those areas under Byzantine rule and Western Europe, and between secular and Church law. In addition, a secondary division is to be discerned at the level of the state, between Merovingian law, Carolingian law, Visigoth law, and late imperial law. Within the Church we find ecumenical councils, provincial or national councils (in Gaul and Spain), and canonical compilations (Linder 1997). In thus recognizing the great plethora of sources and variety of practice, a far more ambitious synthetic treatment of the legal status of Jews and Judaism becomes possible, together with a geographic analysis of actual legislation and a close study of and comparison between secular and religious legality.

Byzantine legislation was the direct continuation of legal praxis in Christianized Rome, and it integrated secular and Church law. Byzantine Jewish life, from the Persian conquest of the Holy Land and the Islamic conquests of the seventh century until the fourth Christian Crusade of 1204, has received only scant scholarly attention in recent years. Our knowledge of this field continues to rely on older studies (Baron 1958–83; Starr 1939; Sharf 1971). Official Byzantine practice vis-à-vis the Jews rested on the legal codes of Theodosius II (408–50) and Justinian (527–65). There were four instances, however, between the seventh and tenth centuries, when these codes were ignored and forced conversions were carried out by imperial edict. These instances of religious persecution have been assigned sundry historical explanations. It would seem that the primary cause for violating the official trad-ition of according the Jews a certain, albeit inferior, status is to be found in external circumstances. The forced conversions (practised against other religious minorities as well during these years, such as the Paulicians) can be understood as an attempt on the part of the imperial leadership to effect national unity by imposing religious unanimity. This policy unfolded against the backdrop of a struggle against external enemies: Muslims and Slavs. The Church more consistently respected the letter and the spirit of the law than did the emperors, however. Thus, for instance, following the persecutions by Leo III (721–2), the Seventh Ecumenical Council of 787 repudiated forced religious conversion (Ankori 1977, 1984: 93–156; Constan-telos 1977).

The Fourth Crusade (1204) resulted in the division of the Byzantine Empire into discrete Latin principalities. This did not bring about any catalytic change in the social and cultural life of Byzantine Jewry, however. If anything, an improvement in their condition might have taken place. This was traceable to the influence of the empire of the Palaeologues, which expanded after the liberation of Constantinople in 1261 and skilfully mobilized its Jews in order to counterbalance the economic pressures emanating from Venice and Genoa. This trend continued up until the Ottoman conquest of Constantinople in 1453 (Bowman 1985: 98).

The last group of 'Jewish Laws' relevant to our discussion are six collections of documents culled from Church archives (principally from the Vatican) that shed light on papal policy toward the Jews and Judaism between 492 and 1555. These documents include a conclusive topical survey of their content (Simonsohn 1991). The starting-point for this survey that addresses Jewish existence in Christendom begins with Augustine's (354–430) doctrine of testimony (*Testimonium*). That doctrine represented a growing recognition of the Jews as the carriers of the Bible, corroborating the basis of Christology, and recognition of their presence in the Christian world as playing a crucial historical role in Christianity. This doctrine took shape as part of an Augustinian hermeneutics in regards to both the Old and New Testaments. It was not, as thought in the past, a result of concrete contact with the Jews. The Augustinian doctrine generated an image of the Jew as a living fossil, bound by the dead letter of his law, blind to the correct interpretation of the Bible, and trapped in the rituals of the Scripture. This type of Jew never actually existed. It certainly diverged fundamentally from those living Jews who were to be found throughout the Roman Empire. But this figure had decisive implications for the

Christian view of Jews and Judaism. It legitimized the Jewish presence in Christen-dom, even if that was one of servitude and dispersal. It also channelled Christian anti-Jewish polemics toward an interpretation of the Old Testament, directing it to a Christian and pagan audience rather than to the Jews. Lastly, this image of the Jew anchored a general Christian indifference towards post-biblical Judaism (Cohen 1999a: 23–71).

A Persecuting Society

Some historians argue that the Christian world began to adopt anti-Jewish violence and persecution as early as the early eleventh century, a result of apocalyptic hopes and fears (Landes 1996). More common opinion, however, identifies the twelfth century as the crucial divide. Christian society, and in particular the educated stratum of administration (the *literati*), redefined its categories of social deviants (lepers, heretics, and Jews) and worked to systematically banish them to the margins of society. Some historians locate the source of this process in the aspiration of this intelligentsia to enhance its social standing. As such, any examination of the changing relationship of Christianity toward the Jews from the twelfth century must be viewed through the prism of a more general process which marginalized the deviant elements of society and transformed them into true 'out-groups' (Moor 1987). Europe came into increased contact in this period with the surrounding non-Christian world. Acquaintance with Islam, which only grew after the *Reconquista* in Spain and the Crusades to the East, expanded the Christian discourse with non-believers. The 'hermeneutic Jew'—that is, the Jew as a construction of Christian thought—consequently ceased to function as a unique 'other'. This multiplicity of 'others' undermined the Jew's Augustinian status (a preferred one in several aspects), and quickened his exile to the social margins. The Jew was now assigned any number of negative traits, either real or imagined, that he shared with additional groups (Muslims, lepers, and heretics), and that included the ambition to destroy Christianity from within (Cohen 1999a: 156–65).

Two factors emerged at this time as dominant in overturning the Church's traditional tolerance: these were the rationalization of the anti-Jewish polemic and the 'discovery' of a post-biblical Jewish literature (Funkenstein 1993: 172–201). The twelfth-century renaissance witnessed the rise of new interpretive practices within Christianity that assigned a rational explanation to every constituent elem-ent in nature and religion. Contemporaries began to assume that all persons were imbued with logic. It thus followed that, since Christianity was a rational religion, everyone should be a Christian. Those who were not—who rejected the fundamental presumptions of a rational Christian faith—were not, therefore, entirely human. Such a view marginalized the Jews even further. Descriptions of the Jews began to appear in certain Christian sources which depicted them as subhuman animals, and associated them with the demonic and satanic spheres of existence. This expulsion of the Jews from the rational world provoked a new interest on the part of medieval scholars in post-biblical Jewish texts. The Talmud was now identified as the principal source of evil (Abulafia 1996).

It is important to note that this rationalization of faith contained dangers for Christianity as well. Doubts arose concerning a number of traditional dogmas and sacraments. Should one accept, for instance, the literal claim that in the course of the rite of the Eucharist the bread and wine were indeed transformed into the flesh and blood of Jesus? Such implicit challenges to Christian truths provoked a repression of the new rationality during the course of the twelfth century designed to reinforce the traditional dogmas. This reaction within Christianity might very well have contributed to the movement away from the older form of anti-Jewish thought and the Augustinian image of the Jew, shifting it towards an irrational anti-Semitism, characterized by dehumanization and accusations of ritual murder, blood libel, and desecration of the host. The Jews represented the antithesis of Church dogma, and the Christian sense of guilt and confusion about the emerging scepticism vis-à-vis their own beliefs and sacraments found an outlet in the new figure of the Jew. This psychological process strengthened the Christian religious consciousness as it was being challenged by the threat of rational thought (Langmuir 1990a: 275–305).

The growing popularity of the demonic image of the Jew and the Jew's identification with witchcraft and magic (Bonfil 1988) reached a climax in 1321 when a group of Jews (and lepers) were accused of poisoning wells in France. Similar accusations were also made during the days of the Black Death in 1348. Historians have connected these events to the witch-hunts of the second half of the fourteenth century (Ginzburg 1989). It is interesting to note, however, that, in spite of this new demonic image, there were relatively few instances in which the Inquisition actually accused Jews of practicing witchcraft (Foa 1996).

The new currents of thought characteristic of the twelfth century begat an anti-Talmudic ideology within the Church. This, in turn, led to the institution of public debates between Christians and Jews in the thirteenth century. These debates resembled, and functioned as, show trials designed to delegitimize the Jewish Talmud. They resulted in public burnings of Jewish texts and aggressive missionary activity on the part of Christians. For the first time the Church began to intervene directly, forcing its views onto internal religious Jewish questions. The leading proponents of this practice in the thirteenth century were the mendicant orders, who enjoyed the consistent co-operation of both popes and secular rulers (Cohen 1982). Despite some scholarly reservations (e.g. Berger 1997a: 9–12; Foa 1996), it seems that this assault on the Talmud and rabbinic literature as heretical works was integral to the new image of the Jew, who was differentiated from the biblical, or

Augustinian, figure. The identification of Judaism as a heresy that had strayed from its original biblical path and, as a result, had sacrificed its standing in the Christian world, was consistent with the unprecedented missionary efforts now being made by the Church within Jewish communities. Once Judaism was denied a legitimate place it had to either be Christianized or expelled. This activity was also accompanied by an aggressive programme of searching the Talmudic literature for proofs of Christological truths. The aim was to use the Jews' own conceptual language and rabbinic tradition (and authority) in order to convince them of the need to embrace Christian baptism. That polemical interest in Talmudic texts did not contradict the simultaneous efforts to define Judaism as a heresy. Rather, it signalled a tactical change in pursuing the same goal (Cohen 1999a; Shatzmiller 1994a; Chazan 1989; 1992). The missionary programme often received monarchical support. Even those rulers such as James II, king of Aragon, who were considered to be defenders of the Jews, and in whose courts numerous Jews were to be found filling official positions, encouraged mendicant efforts, sought to improve the status of Jewish converts to Christianity, and even extended support to (a moderate) Inquisition directed against those Jews accused of blasphemy and against converts who had returned to their Jewish faith. However, the Inquisition that at first targeted specific individuals soon incited a more general attempt to destroy whole Jewish communities who were accused of harbouring such individuals and of practicing heresy (Assis 1997a: 52–63).

In seeking an explanation for the deterioration in the situation and status of the Jews in this period, there is no longer any need to choose between an emphasis on the growing nationalism in Western European countries and an emphasis on the religious unity of the Church, or between theories about the cohering power of monarchies versus theories on the decline of the Church (Berger 1997a: 11–12). The fact is, mendicant influence within royal courts did not necessarily attest to monarchical weakness, but rather, to a genuine acceptance of a new worldview and its integration within the older tradition of legal defence of the Jews. Mendicant ideology influenced members of the governing bodies of the cities. Some historians view this ideology as an overly extreme expression of urban public opinion, which had for a long time controlled its violent anti-Jewish impulses. Among those mendicants most active against the Jews in the fifteenth century, the Franciscans (and in particular the Observants) stand out. They actively supported a demonization of the Jew and took an active role in blood libels (Bonfil 1994; Ben-Shalom 1998).

The twelfth and thirteenth centuries were thus a turning-point in the history of Jewish life in Western Europe. This same period witnessed an escalating confrontation between Christianity and Islam. The Crusades and the Spanish *Reconquista* were manifestations of the latter. It was once commonly assumed that the First Crusade (1096–9) constituted a traumatic break in Christian–Jewish relations: organized attacks by crusaders (and the accompanying mob) resulted in the destruction of Jewish communities and the death of numerous Jews in the region of the River Rhine. Many of these Ashkenazic Jews chose a martyr's death of *kiddush hashem*, even slaying their own families—their wives and children—in order to avoid forced conversion to Christianity. The sense among the Jews was that their existence in the Christian world had become a tenuous one. Moreover, these persecutions were seen to have effected a dramatic change in the economic life and the legal status of the Jews. This view has recently been exposed as wrong. Although several important communities in Ashkenaz were indeed destroyed during the pogroms of 1096, most were not attacked. Likewise, Jewish demographic and economic development continued unabated in the years that followed. The cultural decline discernable among German Jewry (Grossman 1981: 435–9) was accompanied by a cultural flowering in French Jewish communities, an indication of the transmission of the centre of Jewish life from Germany to France. The destruction of Jewish communities in 1096 was, consequently, a local event that did not fundamentally alter the general condition of European Jewry. Tellingly, the events of 1096 found no substantial place in the Jewish historical consciousness of the Middle Ages (Chazan 1987; Schwarzfuchs 1989).

The Hebrew chronicles that recorded the events of 1096 and gave expression to a form of Jewish martyrology were almost unknown until their publication in the second half of the nineteenth century. Since then, scholars have sought to understand the nature and judge the empirical credibility of these chronicles. Some have uncritically accepted the authenticity of the accounts contained in them. Others reject the very possibility of a historical reconstruction of events based on these essentially literary work (Marcus 1982, 1990). Yet still there are those who have attempted to distinguish between the historical and the fictional elements of the chronicles, and to critically recapture events in light of that distinction (Chazan 1987, 1991). Meanwhile, others emphasize the value of the chronicles in providing insight into the nature of the society and culture of the generation in the twelfth century that had survived the trauma (converts and their descendents). As such, the martyrological narrative is an authentic expression of the experience of conversion and the subsequent guilt of the survivors, as well as a telling testimony to the integration of Christian motifs and symbols into Jewish discourse (Cohen 1994, 1999b; 2001).

BLOOD LIBELS

The chronicles of 1096 (*Tatnu*)—the chilling depictions of martyrdom that included the ritual slaughter of children, together with the chronicles' anxious expectation of messianic retribution directed against the gentiles—also serve as the textual basis for drawing a connection between the Jewish sanctification of God through martyrdom (the practice of *kiddush hashem*) and the Christian accusations of blood libel directed against the Jews. Previous explanations of the blood-libel tradition had identified its appearance in the twelfth century (at Norwich, in 1144) and its rapid spread throughout Christendom as the most recent incarnation of a much older narrative. However, twelfth-century sources that incorporate the blood libel, and those medieval circles that subscribed to it, make no reference to the ancient accusations by pagan writers concerning cannibalistic rituals purportedly practised in the Temple. Nor do they refer at all to the incident at Inmestar, Syria, in 415 when Jews were accused of crucifying a Christian child during Purim festivities (Langmuir 1984; 1990b: 214; Limor 1993–8: v. 7–170). Some historians have traced the source of the blood libel to the Jewish custom of hanging the figure of Haman in effigy at Purim (Roth 1933; Horowitz 1994a; Mentgen 1994). Others identify Christian society's own neglect of its children as a source of the blood libel. The Christians' supposed sense of guilt subsequently provoked them to transfer their feelings of inadequacy onto the Jewish minority, which was generally far more attentive to its children (Schultz 1986). That view which points to a parallel, or relationship of some kind, between Christian blood libels and Jewish traditions of martyrdom—and the Ashekenazic ritual of revenge—relies primarily on the close chronological incidence of the phenomena. This coincidence is also informed by an analogy that can be made between the distortions in the Christian interpretation of the Jewish blood ritual common during periods of pogroms and the interpretation of their own blood ritual by Jews of the post-1096 generations.

Martyrology and ritual murder are both associated with human sacrifice. In the former (*kiddush hashem*), the Jews sacrifice their children in what is considered to be a sublime act of spiritual transcendence. In the latter (the blood libel), the Jews murder a Christian child in what is viewed as a detestable act representative of their murderous, satanic nature. As such, blood libel is revealed to be a perverted echo of Christian perceptions of the Jewish blood ritual, which is itself connected to the eschatological notion of Jewish vengeance against Christians (Yuval 1994, 2000: 151–218).

This explanation has provoked numerous reservations amongst scholars. These touch upon, for instance, the idea of the 'converted redemption' that was to take place among Ashkenazic Jewry together with the anticipated messianic revenge (Grossman 1994); the emphasis on the spread of the blood libel in Germany during the second half of the thirteenth century rather than the twelfth century (Breur 1994); the absence in the Christian sources from the twelfth century of any recognition of Jewish notions of 'eschatological vengeance' and of the martyrological sacrifice of children in order to hasten the revenge (Berger 1997a: 18–22); and an alternative reading of the chronicles of 1096 that underplays the eschatological aspect of Jewish responses during the pogrom and emphasizes such other features as finding hiding-places and shelters (Chazan 1997: 74–7).

In addition to historical debate over the sources of the blood libel, scholarly attention has also been recently focused on the libel of host desecration, whose initial appearance in Europe coincided with the doctrine of transubstantiation and elevation of the ritual of the Eucharist into the central sacrament of Catholicism. The Paris libel of 1290 no longer seems to be the source of this host-desecration libel, in other words, but its earliest manifestation. It is also noteworthy that, in contrast to the blood libel, libels concerning host desecration vanished after the Reformation (Rubin 1999). However, until that happened this second form of libel had resulted in the wholesale destruction of Jewish communities in Europe, serving as the cause of pogroms and expulsions (Lotter 1988).

The Reformation's critique of the doctrines and practices of the late medieval Church (including 'human fabrications' of Roman doctrines and rituals) is what undermined the traditional place of ritual murder in Christian discourse. Elite and popular views of the phenomenon began to part ways. Criminal investigations of ritual murder accusations merged into prosecutions for child murders as the religious, magical, and sacrificial elements became less prominent (Po-chia Hsia 1988).

THE JEWISH–CHRISTIAN POLEMIC

There existed a long tradition of 'anti-Jewish' polemics (*Adversus Iudaeos*) whose beginning can be dated with the Church Fathers themselves and whose development can be traced in the writings of Church figures in the European Middle Ages. A catalogue of these Christian polemics written against Judaism points to a typology that distinguishes between an older style, that paid particular attention to interpretations of the biblical text, and newer forms of argumentation that were characterized by rational systems of thought and focused on the Talmud and post- biblical Jewish literature as key texts. Even within this 'new polemic', whose origins are evidenced in the twelfth century and whose development can be traced over the course of the thirteenth century, it is possible to discern two distinct trends: one directed against the Talmud, whose main effort was in exposing the heretical distortions characteristic of Talmudic legend and revealing the existence of anti-Christian Jewish writings; and one actually immersed in Talmudic texts that, since Petrus Alfonsi in the early twelfth century and continuing with Alanus ab Insulis in the second half of the century, and especially accelerating after the Barcelona disputation (1263), sought to uncover Christological proofs contained within the Talmud itself (Funkenstein 1971, 1991: 82–102; Cohen 1999a: 216–8). These distinctions, or typologies, of polemic have been developed by scholars in their discussion and debates over the origins of the new style of polemic: what were its goals and who constituted the groups and institutions that embraced them (Cohen 1982: 19–32; 1999: 313–89; Chazan 1989)?

Jewish polemical literature only began to appear in Europe in the twelfth century. Its works are revealing of a system of religious argumentation principally derived from a long-standing Jewish anti-Christian literary tradition practised in Muslim countries (Lasker 1993; Lasker and Stroumsa 1996: i. 13–35). This Jewish anti-Christian polemic was characterized by four separate modes, each one evocative of the new Christian tactics, if not actually adopting the forms of the latter in an attempt to turn the tables on Christianity (Cohen 1992).

In addition to the aggressive mendicant-order polemic practised against the Jews, a pattern of private religious debates developed in this period that was of a far more tolerant character. These polemics reflected the open, cosmopolitan culture of the Mediterranean commercial world (Limor 1991, 1994). Scholars have also given expression to the popular nature of the polemical genre itself, which was evidenced, for instance, in the debates held amongst female conversos in the towns and villages of Castile and Aragon (as documented in the files of the Inquisition) (Gutwirth 1996). Even within the category of the 'new polemic' one can discern a range of nuances. As one historian has recently claimed, as zealous a Christian missionary as Ramon Llull was far more attentive to the literary works of medieval Jewry than to the conventional hermeneutic stereotype of the Jew in the same period (Hames 2000).

THE ATTITUDE TOWARDS CHRISTIANITY

Jewish perceptions of the Christian world constitute another subject of scholarly controversy. The chronicles of 1096 contained passionate invective directed at Christianity and Christians (Abulafia 1985). A number of polemical works, the product principally of Ashkenazic pens, similarly targeted Christianity and its belief system (Berger 1979: 12–3, 44; 1986; Rosental 1970: 28). But while Jewish perceptions of the surrounding culture were based on the religious differences between Jews and Christians, they were no less informed by commonalities: a shared economic life and continuous social intercourse. These themes were already explored in an older, limited scholarship that was principally focused on Ashkenazic Jewry. A gap was revealed to have existed between the halachic directives of Ashkenazic culture and the actual nature (the *minhag*) of Jewish–Christian relations. The Jews apparently ignored most of these formal legal principles, whose tendency was to separate them from their Christian neighbours during the latters' holidays and rituals. As a result, the Tosaphists pursued an interpretive practice that, in certain cases, excluded the Christians from Talmudic generalizations concerning pagan worship (*avoda zara*). Such views, in fact, contained the seeds of tolerance towards Christians, finding mature expression in the halachic thought of Menachem Hameiri (who resided in Perpignan and died in 1315). Hameiri assigned Christianity a positive religious standing and transformed this view into a halachic principle adaptable to all times and places. Hameiri belonged to a group of rationalists influenced by the Greek-Arabic philosophical tradition that had reached Spain, and was also a halachic scholar belonging to the Ashkenazic school. The concept of 'nations bounded by the ways of the law' favoured—indeed established—by Hameiri in order to grant Christianity a positive standing came from outside of the world of halacha; its origins were in philosophical and theological thought (Katz 1953, 1977: 35–45, 116–28).

The historical controversy ignited by the discovery of Hameiri's tolerant approach (Urbach 1980; Katz 1984: 307–10) seems meanwhile to have died down. Scholars today are increasingly aware, and accepting, of the originality and importance of his system of thought (Blidstein 1990; Halbertal 1994), one characteristic of a larger group of Jewish scholars in Provence and Spain whose intellectual positions were analogous to similarly oriented Christian circles (Shatzmiller 1977; Gutwirth 1985a), and whose views adumbrated the beginnings of religious tolerance within Judaism (Berger 1992). Additional expressions of close social contact between Jews and Christians are being continuously discovered by careful research in the archives, for instance, in studies carried out on the cities in Italy (Toaff 1996) and in Hungary (Brend 2001: 225–37). On the other hand, other groups, and in particular the kabbalists, clung to negative images of Christianity and even developed a demonic, satanic image of Christianity, perhaps as a mirror response to the ongoing Christian demonization of the Jew (Idel 1981).

SYMBOLS, RITUALS, AND IMAGES

The social intercourse between the Jewish minority and the surrounding majority Christian culture generated considerable tension and conflict. However, numerous recent studies have shown that the Jews also adapted to Christian society, even making patterns of Christian culture their own. Jewish literature is revealing of a simultaneous dynamic of attraction and repulsion on the part of the Jews in their relations to the fundamentals of Christian life. Thus, for example, the desecration of the cross is presented by some as no less than an expression of the Jews' own desire for the cross (to be contrasted to earlier interpretations which did not even recognize the possibility of such behaviour) (Horowitz 2001a). The induction ceremony for Jewish children on their first day of school, which included licking letters and biblical passages smeared with honey and receiving the physical tutelage of the teacher, was comparable to (and revealed a conceptual internalization of) the celebration of Christian Mass and Christian representations of corporeal intimacy between Madonna and child (Marcus 1996). Moreover, development of a ceremonial language for the Jewish Passover reveals a relation to Christian practice. The surrounding Christian culture influenced the Jews of Ashkenaz to give the name 'Great Sabbath' to that sabbath which fell a week prior to Passover, and the day was assigned a liturgical status comparable to Palm Sunday. Likewise, the ceremony in which the *afikoman*—a piece of unleavened bread ritually set aside during the Seder service on Passover eve and holy in the eyes of Ashkenazic Jewry—is consumed acquired messianic significance and assumed a form reminiscent of Christian communion (Yuval 2000: 219–66). Studies comparing Christian imagery and Ashkenazic ritual and typology of Ashkenazic narratives point to a strong pull on the Jews from Christian culture, not to mention a considerable degree of concern on the part of Jewish circles provoked by this attraction (Marcus 1995).

A similar dynamic of internalization of cultural symbols is evidenced in Christian Spain and Provence as well. This can be seen, for instance, in the inclusion of Christian ideas in the *Zohar* (Libes 1983). The new attitude (particularly on the part of early kabbalistic circles) towards the intentions of individuals during sexual intercourse between husband and wife (Cohen 1997), an asceticism inspired by spiritual developments within Christianity (Saperstein 1992), the unqualified admiration of Spanish Jewry for the monarchy (Assis 1992), together with a growing awareness amongst Christians of Jewish ritual, Jewish leaders, and the texts and cultural values of Spanish Jewry (existing alongside the satanic typology of the Jew)—all were reflected in the vernacular literature of fifteenth-century Spain (Gutwirth 1984, 1992: 57–62). Similar cultural and mental patterns found expression amongst Italian Jewry during the Renaissance. This does not necessarily point to any tendency towards assimilation, but rather to the simple fact that the Jews were of this same world (Bonfil 1994). This growing social integration, developing alongside their new separation from Christian society, was clearly to be seen in the realm of appearance. A study of dress habits of the time shows that Jews and Christians belonged to the same social and cultural universe, and shared the same sartorial taste. At the same time, starting in the thirteenth century, dress also became a means of separating the Jew out (by means of a specific sign sewn onto the clothing or, in Germany, adoption of a pointed hat for Jews to wear). The simultaneous elimination and creation of boundaries between Jew and Christian was also manifest in the literary sphere, for instance in the widely read *Roman of Alexander* and in the legends of King Arthur (Limor 1993–7: ii. 219–72; iv. 301–49).

The figure of the Jew in the Christian imagination was later accompanied by images of Jewish cowardice or of the feminine traits of the Jewish male, images that often stood in stark contrast to the violent reality of Jewish life (Horowitz 2001b). A similar disparity between image and reality is discernable in the iconography of the Jew, who was depicted by Christian painting as an eastern Muslim adorned in a long beard (at a time when most Jews preferred to shave their beards, in the style of their Christian neighbours) (Horowitz 1994b), or in the form of the Jewish moneylender (who was not necessarily a hated figure) (Shatzmiller 1990). At the same time, an image of the Jew as the keeper of ancient knowledge—which accordingly granted legitimacy to Christian tradition and identity (in particular in connection to holy places in the Holy Land and religious relics)—deepened in the Christian consciousness. Some Christian traditions presented a complex image of the Jew as 'sitting on the fence' and adopting Christian traits and practices (Limor 1996). This discourse even gave birth to a moral rhetoric on the mutual exemplary qualities of the 'other', such as, for instance, Christian celebrations of 'Jewish learning' or Jewish views on Christian loyalty to Church ritual. While this rhetoric was intended as a moral and social self-critique by each side, it no doubt had a positive impact on the image of the Christian in Jewish eyes and vice versa (Saperstein 1986a).

SPAIN—SOCIETY AND CULTURE

The Jews of thirteenth-century Iberia (living in Aragon, Navarre, Castile, and Portugal) filled important economic and bureaucratic roles in service to the local monarchy and aristocracy. As a result of the migration of Spanish Jews from Muslim to Christian regions that was accompanied by a process of cultural transplantation, Jewish courtier life in Christian Spain was characterized by several aspects of Muslim court practice (Septimus 1982).

The economic and cultural disparity between rich and poor that increased over the second half of the thirteenth century incited political confrontations within the Jewish communities and resulted in tax reforms and changes in the community leadership (most of which were of limited duration) (Assis 1997a: 237–41). The communities themselves did not present a singular policy in their attitude and relations with the Jewish courtier, who in many instances broke off any connection with internal Jewish matters, being as he was a full participant in the political struggles of aristocratic Spanish society. In the past, historians sought to analyse the courtiers as a single class and emphasize a continuity of practice from the earlier period of Muslim rule, known as the 'Golden Age' of Spanish Jewry.

One manifestation of the purported continuity of Jewish culture over time was found in the Hebrew medical corpus, which was translated from Arabic. This body of medical knowledge allowed Jewish physicians to become conversant in the healing sciences and up-to-date regarding scientific innovations in both the Muslim and Christian worlds. This, in turn, explained their high standing in the royal courts of Castile and Aragon and in the urban centres of south-western Europe (Barkai 1995b, 1998: 6–37; Assis 1996; Tavares 1982–4; Shatzmiller 1994b; Iancu-Agou 1980).

Recent scholarship has defined the kingdoms situated in the Iberian Peninsula as distinct political entities. This is part of an attempt to analyse the specific character of each court, region, or city. Such studies have encompassed an impressively wide range of subjects, including demographic themes, the professions and the economy of the Jews, the practice of moneylending at interest, Jewish property, community leadership, intercommunity relations, the Jewish residential quarter, religious life, education, family life, culinary practices, marriage, death, synagogue practices, pogroms, conversions, and expulsions (Gutwirth 1989; Assis 1997a, b; Hinojosa Montalvo 1993; Motis Doldar 1996; Gampel 1989; Assis and Magdalena 1990; Leroy 1985; Carrasco Perez 1993, 1994–9; Castaño 1997; Tavares 1992; Lipiner 1997). The policies pursued by the local leadership of the community, the community's economy, and the system of regional tax-collection (the *collecta*) have been examined in light of the attempts (isolated attempts, that were not always successful) to establish a communal umbrella organization embracing the different communities in each kingdom (Gutwirth 1986; Assis 1997a: 179–96). In a departure from previous scholarly orthodoxy that posited a Jewish 'aristocratic' elite dominated by the courtier classes, who were supposed to have dictated its general cultural orientation, recent studies have described the rise of a Jewish bourgeoisie with a distinct agenda of its own that wielded considerable public influence (Gutwirth 1998). In addition, significant aspects of Jewish popular culture are also new subjects of historical research (Lourie 1995).

The interest of Jewish courtiers in philosophical subjects was to be found at the centre of a scholarly debate over the existence of an Averroistic group in Spain and the extent of its influence on the religious conversions of the fourteenth and fifteenth centuries. Some have argued that Jewish Averroism (a blend of radical philosophy, scepticism, astrology, and magic) was the cause of a decline in community discipline, the practice of tradition, and structures of belief that had traditionally bolstered Jewish resistance to Christian missionary efforts (Baer 1966: ii. 253–77). Others reject this interpretation, claiming that, save for the allegations of Jewish opponents, there is no historical evidence supporting the conclusion that Averroism undermined or weakened Jewish religious life. Likewise, and most importantly, there is no literary testimony to the existence of an Averroistic Judaism. The crisis of faith that overtook Spanish Jewry was, in contrast, a crisis of a mystical and ascetic nature that coincided with and attached itself to the dominant Christian trend of the time. In fact, the rising popularity of mysticism and Kabbalah—and not radical rationalism—is what facilitated religious conversion (Ben-Sasson 1984: 232–8). At the same time, however, a radical philosophical (Averroistic) corpus was recently uncovered in the writings of the Jewish Neoplatonic circle in Spain. It points to the conclusion that the critique of Jewish Averroism was directed towards a specific group of philosophers. Here there is evidence of Jewish critics assailing those who had formulated a theoretical basis for disregarding the commandments (Schwartz 1996). The discovery of such radical thinkers does not entirely prove that a connection existed between Averroism and the mass religious conversions of the fifteenth century. In fact, no single cause can explain the phenomenon of the conversos. Another recent interpretation of the conversion issue attributes significant influence to a rising anti-Talmudic sentiment amongst the Jews themselves that was reflective of a general opposition to rabbinic authority (Gutwirth 1993).

Other traits of the courtier class have also been examined, as have leading figures in these circles which, it would appear, did not constitute a homogeneous public (Beinart 1994: 385–480; Lawee 2001). Mapping their political and social location in contemporary Christian Spanish society also makes it possible to extrapolate the political tendencies of the courtier class within Jewish society, as well as the critique directed against them (Gutwirth 1989).

What underlay this philosophical Averroism was Maimonides' work, *Guide of the Perplexed*. It constituted the foundation for Jewish philosophy in Spain and Provence (Berger 1997b). Alongside these Aristotelian tendencies, one also finds a Neoplatonic style of thought based on the biblical interpretations of Abraham ibn Ezra (Schwartz 1996). Philosophy's popularity among the Jews provoked a series of intense social debates in Spain and southern France in the thirteenth and early fourteenth centuries, climaxing in 1305 when the Rashba (ibn Adret), the most prominent leader of Spanish Jewry at the time, issued a prohibition on philosophical studies for anyone younger than 25, and banned completely a group of radical philosophers. These steps did not, however, achieve their desired effect. In fact, philosophical activity flourished in the following years, and it is quite possible that the attempts to repress it had the opposite results. Yet by the early fourteenth century the *Guide of the Perplexed* was no longer the focus of opposition, as it had achieved legitimate standing even in the eyes of its foes. Now, rather, controversy was focused on radical allegoric philosophy which, in contrast to the past, was no longer just studied by small numbers of learned groups but circulated widely by means of travelling preachers moving between the communities of Provence and Spain (Ben-Shalom 1996, 2000a; Berger 1997b: 85–108). The quick retreat by Rashba—who claimed that the initial prohibition on the work of Maimonides had only been local (that is, restricted to Barcelona)—together with the expulsion of the Jews from France (1306), brought an end to this social-political controversy. One interesting explanation for this capitulation pointed to the political situation in southern France, where the king of France, Philip the Fair, laboured intensively to establish his juridical authority (Saperstein 1986b). Another explanation emphasized Rashba's fear that the Christian establishment (both the Church and the secular authorities, and especially aggressive Inquisitors) would find additional justification for accusing the Jews of heresy (Ben-Shalom 2000a). The manner in which allegoric philosophy was spread by travelling preachers opens a relatively new field for research into the history of communications in the medieval world, and specifically in Jewish society. Avenues of communication included, for instance, messengers (both Jews and Christians), the mails, various types of correspondence, the issue of language itself, and questions of time and space (Grossman 1995; Goldin 1996; Ben-Shalom 1996; Debenedetti Stow 1996; Saperstein 1989).

Pogroms in the Fourteenth Century

It is generally agreed that the foundations of Jewish communal life in Spain began to collapse in the fourteenth century, a process that found expression in the first violent pogroms directed against the Jewish public in Spain, in the Shepherds' Crusade, and in accusations of well-poisoning (1320–1), the Black Death (1348), civil war in Castile (1366–9), and the pogroms of 1391 (Baer 1966: ii. 1–169). At the same time, we must acknowledge that violence against minorities and marginal groups such as heretics, lepers, women, Jews, and Muslims was a permanent, everyday aspect of life in the Middle Ages. According to one view, the first half of the fourteenth century witnessed the birth of an irrational fear of minorities, who were accused of conspiring to destroy Christendom (Ginzburg 1991). However, in contrast to earlier scholarly perceptions that emphasized the *longue durée* of Christian anti-Semitism (e.g. N. Cohn 1975), the new research shows that violence was an integral element of the social status quo. It constituted an opportunity to vent social pressures and mark the boundaries between majority and minority, centre and periphery (Nirenberg 1996: 200–30).

One estimate posits that a third of Spanish Jewry was murdered during the 1391 pogrom, while another third converted (Beinart 1992a). Scholars have recently begun to put forward more modest figures in calculating the death and destruction that overtook the Jewish communities in the province of Andalusia, along the eastern coast, and in Catalonia, which were far harder hit than Aragon and central and northern Castile (Mitre Fernández 1994: 50–4; Blazquez Miguel 1988: 27). Meanwhile, in contrast to depictions of a precipitous decline in the social and spiritual condition of Spanish Jewry in the fifteenth century, some historians view this same period as one of continuity and ongoing intellectual and cultural creativity, together with growing stability in the spheres of self-government and economic life (Gutwirth 1992). It was once also common to compare the martyrological response to external threats on the part of the Jews of Germany and France to the religious conversions undertaken by Spanish Jews who found themselves in the same circumstances. Today it is clear that martyrology and conversion coexisted in both centres of Jewish culture. The roots of Spanish Jewish martyrology are to be found in the Christian ethos dominant in Spain in the fourteenth century (Ben-Shalom 2000b).

Expulsions and Ghettos

By the middle of the sixteenth century few Jews were left in Western Europe. Those who still lived there were to be found in the cities of Germany and Italy. This was the result of a process lasting 200 years in which the Jews had been expelled from the continent's emerging nation-states. In 1290 the Jews were forced out of England. In 1306 they were expelled from France, an act accompanied by additional expulsions during the course of the fourteenth century, leading to the final expulsion in 1394. In 1492 the Jews were thrown out of Spain and in 1500–1 they were expelled from the County of Provence, which had been annexed to the French crown. In Germany the Jews were forced out of numerous cities during the fifteenth century. Similarly, starting in the second half of the same century, scores of Jewish communities in Italy underwent the same experience. The phenomenon of expulsion is recognized today as a Western European cultural trait. While principally directed against the Jews, this was not exclusively the case. France expelled moneylenders, Lombardians, and Cahorsins (usurers from Cahors) (1268, 1311) and Spain expelled the Moriscos (Muslims forced to convert to Christianity) in 1609. In all these instances, the expelling authority was secular while its justifications spoke of the need to protect Christian faith and social mores. Some view the expulsions as a transition phenomenon within European society, away from more extreme forms of persecution, such as pogroms and massacres (Kedar 1996).

One cannot isolate a single, central cause for the expulsions that would be equally applicable to each and every instance. In England the Jews were expelled as part of an ongoing constitutional crisis over the rights and privileges of the crown, the Church, and the aristocracy. In France no such single explanation is available, and we must point instead to a variety of motives, such as the desire for riches and the lust for Jewish property, stabilization of the currency, attempts to address the problem of moneylending at interest that provoked social tensions among the lower classes, mobilization of the populace on behalf of the political agenda of the monarchy, a carefully chosen act designed to demonstrate to the country's barons the paramount status of the crown, together with the crown's commitment to national unity and to eradicating religious and moral perversions (Stow 1992: 281–308; Kohn 1988: 251–75; Iancu 1981; Stacy 1993; Jordan 1989). A number of causes have been proposed for the expulsion from Spain (Castile and Aragon). Some emphasize the profits of the 'Catholic kings'. Others point to the pressure applied by the urban oligarchy in Castile, under the control of conversos who were anxious to save themselves from the Inquisition. Still others identify the success of the Spanish feudal aristocracy in resisting a challenge from a capitalist commercial class associated in the public imagination with the Jews. Popular demands to expel the Jews, particularly from the lower classes, have also been noted.

Some suggest that this was the climax of a historical process that contained two contradictory tendencies: protection of the Jews as a source of income for the royal treasury, that also sought to restrain Jewish influence over the conversos, on the one hand; and the programme of the Inquisition for rooting out the Jewish population from the kingdom, on the other. Ultimately, the most convincing explanation of these events is based on the view of the expulsion of the Jews as resulting from the pressures of the Inquisition and from religious motivations (that find direct expression in the actual edict ordering the expulsion). For its part, the Spanish crown took advantage of these events to advance its agenda of national centralization and bring about the unification of Castile and Aragon into a single kingdom practising a single faith. In addition, Ferdinand and Isabella were now able to present themselves as religious heroes, which strengthened their public standing against opponents of the crown (Kriegel 1978; Orfali and Motis Doldar 1991; Beinart 1994; Kamen 1997: 16–27). In general, Western Europe's expulsion of the Jews rested on two central developments. These were a vision of a redeemed Christian society that would reinforce its spiritual borders while banishing from them the imaginary forces of evil, and a growing tendency on the part of secular rulers to view the spiritual condition of their subjects as an integral aspect of their governing mandate (Kedar 1996).

In addition to expulsions, the Jews were also pushed into ghettos as a result of papal initiative in the sixteenth century. These ghettos, in fact, eventually became the symbol of anti-Jewish prejudice. However, establishment of even the first ghetto, in Venice in 1516—which, unlike its successors, did not originate in papal action—did not signal a deterioration in the condition of the Jews. The Venice ghetto, rather, was a compromise, one that discontinued Venice's traditional Jewish policy of total banishment. In the long run as well, the European ghettos did not signify a deterioration in conditions but constituted a new middle ground between integration and expulsion: acceptance of the Jew as an isolated element within society, without surrendering missionary hopes to Christianize him, but not at any price (Bonfil 1994). On the one hand, the ghetto expressed the Jews' foreignness; on the other, the ghetto made a place for the Jew in the city, and thus can be understood as an unambiguous recognition of the Jew as a permanent fixture of urban life in Europe. Such permanence effected a reorganization of community life, even encouraging greater awareness on the part of the Jews of the wider geographic and cultural context of their lives (Weinstein 2000).

THE CONVERSOS

The 1391 pogrom in Spain resulted in a new social phenomenon, the conversos (*anusim*). Several additional waves of voluntary converts joined their ranks in the fifteenth century. In Portugal, in contrast, events developed differently. After the edict expelling the Jews was published (1497), the king, Manuel I, decided to decree their forced conversion. This is the source of the distinction between converso society in Spain and in Portugal. The former coexisted for a century alongside a Jewish community that offered both support for the conversos' clandestine practice of Judaism, while, at the same time reminding them of their 'otherness' vis-à-vis both Jews and Christians, and so also undermining their hidden Jewish identity. In Portugal, on the other hand, there were no Jews to interfere with the conversos' Jewish identity, which was even perceived to be the correct form of Judaism. (Yerushalmi 1981: 1–21; 1998; Tavares 1992). However, a conversos problem did arise in Portugal at the end of the fifteenth century, with the arrival of conversos from Spain. That migration even sparked a bishop's inquisition (Tavares 1997).

Beginnings of the public debate in Iberian culture over the conversos problem are to be found in the Sentence-Statute, promulgated by Pedro Sarmiento in Toledo in 1449, that contained expressions of racial hatred and discriminatory legislation resting on notions of 'blood purity' (*Estatutos de limpieza de sangre*). From that point on, theologians and politicians in Spain could not avoid addressing the issue and debating the extent of the danger presented by the conversos (Orfali 1996). Studies clearly show that the efforts to drive conversos out of public positions were anchored in ancient Visigoth law (Albert 1982). Until the integration of racial ('blood purity') policies within the Habsburg legal codes in 1516, they stood outside of the law of the state and were spread through the cities and institutions of Castile by local initiative undertaken by various corporations (Edwards 1999). Differences in Spanish and Portuguese practice have also been examined, as have the respective duration of the laws' enforcement (Bethencourt 1995: 303–4). Meanwhile, the baseless allegation (Castro 1971) about Jewish racial views based on the Scriptures that was purportedly introduced into Spanish society by the conversos, and that constituted the roots of the 'blood purity' laws in the mid-fifteenth century, has been rejected (Netanyahu 1997: 1–42). Clearly, the growing importance of lineage in Spanish society in the fifteenth century, among both Christians and Jews, was a result of the predicament caused for both sides after 1391 by the conversos (Gutwirth 1985b).

Historiographical differences regarding the conversos problem and the Iberian Inquisition have been the subject of study in the past, emphasis being placed on respective Hispanic and Jewish perspectives. The former sees the conversos as unique to the region and ignores other, wider aspects of the phenomenon, such as their return to the Jewish fold in the Low Countries and in the Spanish Jewish communities throughout the Mediterranean, not to mention the mission of conversos society in the New World. Jewish historiography, on the other hand, has generally ignored the conversos as an element assimilating into Iberian society and contributing to the spiritual and cultural development of sixteenth- and seventeenth-century Spain (Kaplan 1988). Recent studies tend to distinguish between conversos living in different kingdoms in Spain, particularly Castile and Aragon (Carrete Parrondo 1992b), and Portugal (Tavares 1982–4). In addition to the historiographical issues, an attempt was also made to frame a general historical and typological description of the problem, and present a synthetic explanation of the religious experience of the conversos and an inventory of their religious and cultural practice (Gitliz 1996).

And so, scholarship has heatedly debated the character of converso life and that of the *anusim* (forced converts), particularly in regards to their Judaism. On the one hand, some historians claim that the vast majority sought to preserve their Judaism. They consequently emphasize the existence of an ongoing relationship between the Jewish communities in Spain and the *anusim* (and conversos), in spite of the growing rupture between the two societies during the fifteenth century (Baer 1996: ii. 246; Ben-Sasson 1984: 208–20). An opposing historical view contends that, even in the first post-1391 generation of *anusim*, many sought to break their ties with Judaism and move significantly closer to Christianity. This trend only grew over the following generations, and by the middle of the fifteenth century a majority of the *anusim* and conversos could be counted as adamantly loyal Christians. According to this version of events, the Inquisition did not seek to root out Jewish heresy from *anusim* society, but to destroy that society and exorcise it from the Spanish nation. The motivations were social and racial. That is why the Inquisition invented the fiction of a Jewish heresy. Explicit manifestations of Judaism among conversos at the end of the fifteenth century and over the following century are explained as a separate phenomenon, a renewed interest on the part of the *anusim* in their Jewish roots that arose once the aggressiveness of the Spanish Inquisition convinced them that they had no real place in the Christian world. In other words, the conversos did not have a Jewish identity that rested on secretly maintained religious practices or on carefully concealed Jewish customs nurtured over scores of years (Netanyahu 1999, 1995, 1997: 156–182; Roth 1995: 114–16).

Some even went so far as to argue that the majority of conversos in sixteenth-century Portugal also aspired to live like good Christians. The first post-conversion generation (1497) was already integrated in Portuguese society. The Inquisition, in fact, sought to root out this new bourgeoisie that had appeared in Portugal in the guise of 'new Christians' (Saraiva 1985, 2001). In order to support this conclusion historians have had to challenge the reliability of the Inquisition's files. The confessions of those subject to interrogation are considered to be inauthentic. They are read as reflections of the methodical racial thinking of their interrogators, who, by means of torture, substituted their own thinking in these confessions. Nevertheless, a number of recent studies have revealed the considerable value these files offer to scholars investigating medieval society. We should be sceptical, then, about so roundly disqualifying them as a source on the lives of the conversos (Kaplan 1988; Gitliz 1996). In addition, Inquisition files provide a broader social picture in general than that derived from more orthodox historical sources, namely the literary production of the educated strata (Meyuhas Ginio 1993: 139). Critical examination of the files of the Spanish Inquisition shows that the Jews and conversos did not constitute a singular social group, united in a common faith in opposition to the 'old Christians' (which is how they were often romantically portrayed in the past). On the other hand, an extended web of contacts and connections between the two groups, resting on familial, social, and economic relationships, was certainly at work. One should also distinguish between the different generations of conversos. Some historians define the post-1391 generations of *anusim* as a distinct group that was well integrated into traditional Christian society and which viewed the Jews and newer waves of conversos from the time of the expulsion in a most negative light (Carrete Parrondo 1992b: 19–31, 93–5). It has also been recently argued that the accusations brought before the Inquisition concerning a lapse back to Judaism were not always motivated by fears of heresy, but by economic competition between families or by political interests (Contreras 1992).

Studies have described the Spanish Jewish diaspora in Western Europe—former *anusim* communities that had migrated out of the Iberian Peninsula—as a setting for modernity's penetration of the Jewish world, whose expression included Enlightenment and assimilation. Return to their Judaism actually provoked an acute crisis of identity amongst some *anusim*, for they now found themselves firmly outside both the Jewish and the Christian worlds. As rationalists who subscribed to an ethos of philosophy, logic, and science that they had imbibed in Catholic universities, they now developed a rational critique of the Bible and refused to recognize the intricacies of Jewish law. The renewed contact between the rabbinic establishment and the descendents of Iberian Jewry generated, on the one hand, a new spiritual and cultural dimension that some identify as the roots of Spinozan secularism, and on the other, a rebirth of Jewish spirituality that became incorporated in additional internal trends within Judaism such as the Sabbatian movement (Yerushalmi 1981; Kaplan 1989; Révah 1995; Popkin 1979, 1992; Ruderman 1991: 196–9; Swetschinski 2000; Barnai 2000; 39–51). It should be emphasized, however, that, despite the transformations that overtook the Spanish Jewish diaspora in the sixteenth and seventeenth centuries, and despite the appearance of a critical approach to the halacha (Fishman 1997), the notion of change itself as a positive value in its own right was still absent. In terms of its self-consciousness, this was still a traditional community seeking to adapt to the challenges of modernity (Kaplan 1991).

SUGGESTED READING

Limor (1993–8), has written a series of textbooks that present a comprehensive review of most of the spheres of contact between Jews and Christians in western Europe. A broad, up-to-date view of Jewish life in various western European countries, albeit focusing principally on Germany and France, is to be found in Stow (1992). Those interested in pursuing questions concerning the relations of the Church and its sundry institutions towards the Jews should see Simonshon (1991); Cohen (1982, 1999); Chazan (1989, 1992). An interesting comparative perspective on Jewish life in Christian and Muslim societies, respectively, is provided by M. R. Cohen (1994). A most useful work supplying basic information on the history of the Jews in Spain and the richness of Jewish culture in the Iberian Peninsula and in the Spanish Jewish diaspora is Beinart (1992[b]; 1998) On the history of the *anusim* (conversos) in Spain, Portugal, and the Low Countries see Kaplan (1994); Meyuhas Ginio (1999); Gitliz (1996).

BIBLIOGRAPHY

ABULAFIA, A. S. 1985. 'Invectives Against Christianity in the Hebrew Chronicles of the First Crusade.' In *Crusade and Settlement*. 62–72. P. W. Edbury ed. Cardiff.

—— 1996. 'Twelfth-Century Renaissance Theology and the Jews.' In *From Witness to Witchcraft: Jews and Judaism in Medieval Christian Thought*. 125–39. J. Cohen ed. Wiesbaden.

ADELMAN, H. 1998. 'Italian Jewish Women.' In *Jewish Women in Historical Perspective*. 150–168. J. R. Baskin ed. Detroit.

AGUS, I. A. 1969. *The Heroic Age of Franco-German Jewry: The Jews of Germany and France of the 10th and 11th Centuries: The Pioneers and Builders of Town-Life, Town-Government and Institutions*. New York.

ALBERT, B. 1976. 'Un nouvel examen de la politique anti-juive wisigothique.' *REJ* 135: 3–29.

—— 1982. 'The 65th Canon of the IVth Council of Toledo (633) in Christian Legislation and its Interpretation in the "Converso" Polemics in XVth Century Spain.' *Proceedings of the World Congress of Jewish Studies* 8: 43–8. Jerusalem.

ANKORI, Z. 1977. 'Greek Orthodox Jewish Relations in Historical Perspective—The Jewish View.' *Greek Orthodox Theological Review* 22: 17–57.

ANKORI, Z. 1984. *Encounter in History: Jews and Christian Greeks in Their Relation Through the Ages* [Hebrew]. Tel Aviv.

ASHTOR, E. 1977. *The Jews of Muslim Spain* [Hebrew]. Jerusalem. = *The Jews of Moslem Spain*. Philadelphia.

ASSIS, Y. T. 1983. 'Juifs de France réfugiés en Aragon (XIIIᵉ–XIVᵉ, siècles)', *REJ* 142: 209–27.

—— 1985. 'Crime and Violence in Jewish Society in Spain (XIII–XIVth Centuries).' [Hebrew]. *Zion* 50: 221–40.

—— 1987. 'The Papal Inquisition and Aragonese Jewry in the Early Fourteenth Century', *Mediaeval Studies*, 49: 391–410.

—— 1988. 'Sexual Behaviour in Medieval Hispano- Jewish Society.' In *Jewish History: Essays in Honor of Chimen Abramsky*. 25–59. A. Rapoport-Albert and S. J. Zipperstein eds. London.

—— 1992. 'Jewish Attitudes to Christian Power in Medieval Spain.' *Sefarad* 52: 291–304.

—— 1996. 'Jewish Physicians and Medicine in Medieval Spain.' In *Medicine and Medical Ethics in Medieval and Early Modern Spain: An Intercultural Approach*. 33–49. S. S. Kottek and L. García-Ballester eds. Jerusalem.

—— 1997a. *The Golden Age of Aragonese Jewry: Communities and Society in the Crown of Aragon, 1213–1327*. London.

—— 1997b. *Jewish Economy in the Medieval Crown of Aragon, 1213–1327: Money and Power*. Leiden, and Cologne. New York.

—— and IBÁÑEZ-SPERBER eds. 1998–2000. *Hispania Judaica Bulletin*. Jerusalem.

—— and MAGDALENA, R. 1990. *The Jews of Navarre in the Late Middle Ages* [Hebrew]. Jerusalem.

BACHRACH, B. S. 1977. *Early Medieval Jewish Policy in Western Europe*. Minneapolis.

BAER, Y. 1966. *A History of the Jews in Christian Spain*. Vols. 1–2. Philadelphia.

BARKAI, R. 1995a. 'Greek Medical Traditions and Their Influence on Medieval Perception of Woman.' In *A Glimpse into the Lives of Women in Jewish Societies* [Hebrew]. Y. Azmon ed. Jerusalem.

—— 1995b. 'Between East and West: A Jewish Doctor from Spain.' *Mediterranean Historical Review* 10: 49–63.

—— 1998. *A History of Jewish Gynaecological Texts in the Middle Ages*. Leiden, Boston, and Cologne.

BARNAI, J. 2000. *Sabbateanism—Social Perspectives*. [Hebrew]. Jerusalem.

BARON S. W. 1958–83. *A Social and Religious History of the Jews*. Vols. 1–18. New York and London.

BASKIN, J. R. 1998. 'Jewish Women in the Middle Ages.' In *Jewish Women in Historical Perspective*. 101–27. J. R. Baskin ed. Detroit.

BEINART, H. 1992a. 'The Great Conversion: The Problem of the Anusim and their Fate in the Fifteenth Century.' [Hebrew]. In *The Heritage of Spain*. 280–308. H. Beinart ed. Jerusalem.

—— 1992b. ed. *Moreshet Sepharad: The Sephardi legacy*. Jerusalem.

—— 1994. *The Expulsion of the Jews from Spain* [Hebrew]. Jerusalem.

—— 1998. *Chapters in Judeo-Spanish History* [Hebrew]. 2 vols. Jerusalem.

BEN-SHALOM, R. 1996. 'Communication and Propaganda Between Provence and Spain: The Controversy Over Extreme Allegorization (1303–1306).' In *Communication in the Jewish Diaspora: The Pre-Modern World*. 171–225. S. Menache ed. Leiden.

—— 1998. 'The Blood Libel in Arles and the Franciscan Mission in Avignon in 1453: Paris Manuscript, Héb. 631.' [Hebrew]. *Zion* 63: 391–408.

—— 2000a. 'The Ban Placed By the Community of Barcelona on the Study of Philosophy and Allegorical Preaching—A New Study.' *REJ* 159: 387–404.

—— 2000b. 'Kidush ha-Shem and Jewish Martyrology in Aragon and Castile in 1391: Between Spain and Ashkenaz.' [Hebrew]. *Tarbiz* 70: 227–82.

BEN-SASSON, H. H. 1984. *Continuity and Variety: Essays Selected by J. R. Hacker.* [Hebrew]. Tel Aviv.

BERGER, D. 1979. *The Jewish–Christian Debate in the High Middle Ages: A Critical Edition of the Nizzahon Vetus with an Introduction, Translation, and Commentary.* Philadelphia.

—— 1986. 'Mission to the Jews and Jewish- Christian Contacts in the Polemical Literature of the High Middle Ages.' *The American Historical Review* 91: 576–91.

—— 1992. 'Christians, Gentiles, and the Talmud: A Fourteenth-Century Jewish Response to the Attack on Rabbinic Judaism', *Religionsgespräche im Mittelalter*, 115–30 B. Lewis and F. Niewöhner, eds. Wiesbaden.

—— 1997a. 'From Crusades to Blood Libels to Expulsions: Some New Approaches to Medieval Antisemitism.' *Second Annual Lecture of the Victor J. Selmanowitz Chair of Jewish History.* New York and Jerusalem.

—— 1997b. *Judaism's Encounter with Other Cultures: Rejection or Integration?* 60–141. J. J. Schacter ed. Northvale, NJ and Jerusalem.

BETHENCOURT, F. 1995. *História das Inquisições. Portugal, Espanha e Itália, séculos XV–XIX.* São Paulo.

BIALE, D. 1992. *Eros and the Jews.* New York.

BLAZQUEZ MIGUEL, J. 1988. *Inquisicion y Criptojudaismo.* Madrid.

BLIDSTEIN, G. 1990. 'Maimonides and Me'iri on the Legitimacy of Non-Judaic Religion.' In *Scholars and Scolarship: The Interaction Between Judaism and Other Cultures—The Bernard Revel Graduate School Conference Volume.* 27–35. L. Landman ed. New York.

BLUMENKRANZ, B. 1960. *Juifs et Chrétiens dans le monde occidental, 430–1096.* Paris.

BONFIL, R. 1988. 'The Devil and the Jews in the Christian Consciousness of the Middle Ages.' [Hebrew] *Antisemitism Through the Ages.* 91–8. S. Almog ed. Jerusalem.

—— 1989. 'Myth, Rhetoric, History? A Study in the Chronicle of Ahima'az.' In *Culture and Society in Medieval Jewry: Studies Dedicated to the Memory of Haim Hillel Ben-Sasson.* 99–135. M. Ben-Sasson *et al.* eds. Jerusalem.

—— 1994. *Jewish Life in Renaissance Italy.* Berkeley.

BOWMAN, S. B. 1985. *The Jews of Byzantium: 1204–1453.* Alabama.

BREND, N. 2001. *At the Gate of Christendom: Jews, Muslims and 'Pagans' in Medieval Hungary, c.1000–c.1300.* Cambridge.

BREUR, M. 1994. 'The Historian's Imagination and Historical Truth.' [Hebrew]. *Zion* 59: 317–24.

CARRASCO PÉREZ, J. 1993. *Sinagoga y Mercado: Estudios y textos sobre los Judíos en el reino de Navarra.* Pampelona.

—— et al. 1994–9. *Navarra Judaica—Documentos para la historia de los judíos en el reino de Navarra.* 7 vols. Pampelona.

CARRETE PARRONDO, C. 1992a. 'Les juifs dans l'Espagne médiévale. État bibliographique (1965–1991).' In *Minorités religieuses dans l'Espagne médiévale.* 103–30. P. R. Baduel ed. Aix-en-Provence.

—— 1992b. *El Judaísmo español y la Inquisición.* Madrid.

CASTAÑO, J. 1997. 'Social Networks in a Castilian Jewish Aljama and the Court Jews in the Fifteenth Century: A Preliminary Survey (Madrid 1440–1475).' *La España Medieval* 20: 379–92.

CASTRO, A. 1971. *The Spaniards.* Berkeley.

CHAZAN, R. 1987. *European Jewry and the First Crusade.* Los Angeles and London.

—— 1989. *Daggers of Faith: Thirteenth-Century Christian Missionizing and Jewish Response.* Berkeley.

—— 1991. 'The Facticity of Medieval Narration: A Case Study of the Hebrew First Crusade Narrative.' *AJS Review* 16: 31–56.

—— 1992. *Barcelona and Beyond: The Disputation of 1263 and Its Aftermath.* Berkeley.

—— 1997. *Medieval Stereotypes and Modern Antisemitism.* Berkeley, Los Angeles, and London.

COHEN, A. 1981. 'Jewish Criminals in France at the End of the Fourteenth Century.' [Hebrew]. *Zion* 46: 146–54.

COHEN, J. 1976. 'Roman Imperial Policy Toward the Jews From Constantine until the End of the Palestinian Patriarchate (ca. 429).' *Byzantine Studies* 3: 1–29.

—— 1982. *The Friars and the Jews: The Evolution of Medieval Anti-Judaism.* Ithaca, NY and London.

—— 1989. *'Be Fertile and Increase, Fill the Earth and Master It': The Ancient and Medieval Career of a Biblical Text.* Ithaca, NY and London.

—— 1992. 'Towards a Functional Classification of Jewish Anti-Christian Polemic in the High Middle Ages.' In *Religionsgespräche im Mittelalter.* 93–114. B. Lewis and F. Niewöhner eds. Wiesbaden.

—— 1994. 'The "Persecutions of 1096"—From Martyrdom to Martyrology: The Sociocultural Context of the Hebrew Crusade Chronicles.' [Hebrew]. *Zion* 59: 167–208.

—— 1997. 'Sexuality and Intentionality in Rabbinic Thought of the Twelfth and Thirteenth Centuries.' [Hebrew]. *Te'uda,* 4: 155–72.

—— 1999a. *Living Letters of the Law: Ideas of the Jew in Medieval Christianity.* Berkeley.

—— 1999b. 'The Hebrew Crusade Chronicles in their Christian Cultural Context.' In *Juden und Christen zur Zeit der Kreuzzüge.* 17–30. A. Haverkamp ed. Sigmaringen.

—— 2001. 'From History to Historiography: The Study of the Persecutions and Constructions of their Meaning.' [Hebrew]. In *Facing the Cross: The Persecutions of 1096 in History and Historiography.* 16–31. Y. T. Assis *et al.* eds. Jerusalem.

COHEN, M. R. 1994. *Under Crescent and Cross. The Jews in the Middle Ages.* Princeton.

COHN, N. 1975. *Europe's Inner Demons: An Inquiry Inspired by the Great Witch-Hunt.* London.

CONSTANTELOS, D. 1977. 'Greek Orthodox Jewish Relations in Historical Perspective.' *Greek Orthodox Theological Review* 22: 6–16.

CONTRERAS J. 1992. *Sotos contra Riquelmes: Regidores, inquisidores y criptojudíos.* Madrid.

COULET, N. 1980. 'Autour d'un quinzain des métiers de la communauté juive d'Aix en 1437.' In *Minorités techniques et métiers, Actes de la table ronde du Groupement d'Intéret Scientifique, Sciences Humaines sur l'Aire Méditerranéenne, Abbaye de Sénanque, Octobre 1978.* 79–104. Aix-en-Provence.

DEBENEDETTI STOW, S. 1996 'A Judeo-Italian Version of Selected Passages From Cecco d'Ascoli's Acerba.' In *Communication in the Jewish Diaspora: The Pre-Modern World.* 283–311. S. Menache ed. Leiden, New York, and Cologne.

DISHON, J. 1994. 'Images of Women in Medieval Hebrew Literature.' In *Women of the Word: Jewish Women and Jewish Writing.* 35–49. J. R. Baskin ed. Detroit.

DUBNOV, S. 1933. *A History of the Jews.* [Hebrew]. Vols. 4–5. Tel Aviv.

EDWARDS, J. 1999. 'The Beginnings of a Scientific Theory of Race? Spain, 1450–1600.' In *From Iberia to Diaspora: Studies in Sephardic History and Culture*. 179–96. Y. K. Stillman and N. A. Stillman. Leiden, Boston, and Cologne.

EMERY, R. 1987. 'Les Veuves juives de Perpignan.' *Provence historique* 37: 559–69.

FISHMAN, T. 1997. *Shaking the Pillars of Exile: 'Voice of a Fool', an Early Modern Jewish Critique of Rabbinic Culture*. Stanford.

FOA, A. 1996. 'The Witch and the Jew: Two Alikes that Were Not the Same.' In *From Witness to Witchcraft: Jews and Judaism in Medieval Christian Thought*. 361–74. J. Cohen ed. Wiesbaden.

FUNKENSTEIN, A. 1971. 'Basic Types of Christian Anti-Jewish Polemics in the Later Middle Ages.' *Viator* 2: 372–82.

—— 1991. *Image and Historical Consciousness within Judaism and Its Cultural Environment* [Hebrew]. Tel Aviv.

—— 1993. *Perceptions of Jewish History*. Berkeley.

GAMPEL, B. 1989. *The Last Jews on Iberian Soil*. Los Angeles.

GINZBURG, C. 1989. *Ecstasies: Deciphering the Witches' Sabbath*. London.

GITLIZ, D. M. 1996. *Secrecy and Deceit: The Religion of the Crypto-Jews*. Philadelphia and Jerusalem.

GOLDIN, S. 1996 '"Companies of Disciples" and "Companies of Colleagues": Communication in Jewish Intellectual Circles.' In *Communication in the Jewish Diaspora: The Pre-Modern World*. 127–39. S. Menache ed. Leiden, New York, and Cologne.

—— 1997. *Uniqueness and Togetherness: The Enigma of the Survival of the Jews in the Middle Ages*. [Hebrew]. Tel Aviv.

—— 2002. *The Ways of Jewish Martyrdom* [Hebrew]. Tel Aviv.

GRABOIS, A. 1967. 'The Legendary Image of Charlemagne as Reflected in the Hebrew Sources of the Middle Ages' [Hebrew]. *Tarbiz*: 22–58.

—— 1975. 'The *Hebraica Veritas* and Jewish–Christian Intellectual Relations in the Twelfth Century.' *Speculum* 50: 613–34.

—— 1991. 'The *Nesiim* of Narbonne—On the Image and Nature of Jewish Leadership in Southern France in the Middle Ages.' [Hebrew]. *Michael* 12: 43–66.

GRAETZ, Z. 1893–8. *The History of the Jews: Translated into Hebrew with Supplements and Notes by S. P. Rabbinowitz and Notes by A. A. Harcabi* [Hebrew]. 3–6. Warsaw.

GROSSMAN, A. 1981. *The Early Sages of Ashkenaz: Their Lives, Leadership and Works (900–1096)* [Hebrew]. Jerusalem.

—— 1988. 'The Historical Background to the Ordinances on Family Affairs Attributed to Rabbenu Gershom Me'or ha-Golah (The Light of the Exile).' In *Jewish History: Essays in Honor of Chimen Abramsky*. 3–23. A. Rapoport-Albert and S. J. Zipperstein eds. London.

—— 1994. '"Redemption by Conversion" in the Teachings of Early Ashkenazi Sages.' [Hebrew]. *Zion* 59: 325–342.

—— 1995. *The Early Sages of France: Their Lives, Leadership and Works* [Hebrew]. Jerusalem.

—— 1996. 'Communications among Jewish Centers During the Tenth to the Twelfth Centuries'. In *Communication in the Jewish Diaspora*, 107–26. ed. S. Menashe. Leiden.

—— 2001. *Pious and Rebellious: Jewish Women in Medieval Europe* [Hebrew]. Jerusalem.

GÜDEMANN, M. 1897–9. *Torah and Life in the Medieval West* [Hebrew]. Vols. 1–3 Warsaw.

GUTWIRTH, E. 1984. 'The Jews in 15th Century Castilian Chronicles.' *JQR* 74: 379–96

GUTWIRTH, E. 1985a. 'Actitudes judías hacia los Cristianos en la España del siglo XV: Ideario de los traductores del latín.' In *Actas del II Congreso internacional Encuentro de las tres culturas*. 189–96. Toledo.

——1985b. 'Lineage in XVth C. Hispano-Jewish Thought.' *Miscelanea de estudios arabes y hebraicos* 34: 85–91.

——1986. 'Tendencies Towards Centralization in Fifteenth Century Castilian Jewish Communities.' [Hebrew]. *Te'uda* 4: 231–246.

——1989. 'Abraham Seneor: Social Tensions and the Court-Jew.' *Michael* 11: 169–229.

——1992. 'Towards Expulsion: 1391–1492.' In *Spain and the Jews: The Sephardi Experience, 1492 and After*. 51–73. E. Kedourie ed. London.

——1993. 'Conversions to Christianity Amongst Fifteenth-Century Spanish Jews: An Alternative Explanation.' In *Shlomo Simonshon Jubilee Volume: Studies on the History of the Jews in the Middle Ages and Renaissance Period*. 97–121. D. Carpi *et al*. eds. Tel Aviv.

——1996. 'Gender, History and the Judeo–Christian Polemic.' In '*Contra Judaeos*.' 257–78. O. Limor and G. G. Stroumsa eds. Tübingen.

——1998. 'Widows, Artisans, and the *Issues of Life*: Hispano-Jewish Bourgeois Ideology.' In *In Iberia and Beyond: Hispanic Jews Between Cultures*. 143–73. B. D. Cooperman ed. Newark and London.

HALBERTAL, M. 1994. 'Rabbi Menachem Hameiri: Between Torah and Philosophy.' [Hebrew]. *Tarbiz* 63: 63–118.

HAMES, H. J. 2000 *The Art of Conversion: Christianity and Kabbalah in the Thirteenth Century*. Leiden, Boston, and Cologne.

HINOJOSA MONTALVO, J. 1993. *The Jews of the Kingdom of Valencia: From Persecution to Expulsion, 1391–1492*. Jerusalem.

HOROWITZ, E. 1994a. ' "And It Was Reversed": Jews and their Enemies in the Festivities of Purim.' [Hebrew]. *Zion* 59: 129–68.

——1994b. 'On the Significance of the Beard in Jewish Communities in the East and Europe in the Middle Ages and Early Modern Times.' [Hebrew]. *Pe'amim* 59: 124–48.

——1995. 'The Jews and the Moment of Death in Medieval and Modern Times.' *Judaism* 44: 271–81.

——2001a. 'Medieval Jews Face the Cross.' In *Facing the Cross: The Persecutions of 1096 in History and Historiography* [Hebrew]. 118–40. Y. T. Assis *et al*. eds. Jerusalem.

——2001b. 'A "Dangerous Encounter": Thomas Coryate and the Swaggering Jews of Venice.' *JJS* 52: 341–53.

IANCU-AGOU, D. 1974. 'Topographie des quartiers juifs en Provence médiévale.' *REJ* 133: 11–156.

——1980. 'Une strate mince et influence: les médecins juifs aixois a la fin du XVe siècle (1480–1500), activités économiques et état social.' In *Minorités techniques et métiers, actes de la table ronde du Groupement d'Intéret Scientifique, Sciences Humaines sur l'Aire Méditerranéenne, Abbaye de Sénanque, Octobre 1978*. 105–24. Aix-en-Provence.

——1981. *Les Juifs en Provence, 1475–1501. De l'insertion à l'expulsion*. Marseilles.

——1998. *Être Juif en Provence: au temps du roi René*. Paris.

IDEL, M. 1981. 'The Attitude Towards Christianity in the Book of Hameshiv.' [Hebrew]. *Zion* 46: 77–91.

IR-SHAI, O. 1995. 'The Prohibition Issued by Constantine the Great on Jewish Entrance to Jerusalem: Between History and Hagiography.' [Hebrew]. *Zion* 60: 129–78.

JORDAN, W. C. 1989. *The French Monarchy and the Jews: From Philip Augustus to the Last Capetions*. Philadelphia.

KAMEN, H. 1997. *The Spanish Inquisition: A Historical Revision*. London.

KAMIN, S. 1991. *Jews and Christians Interpret the Bible*. Jerusalem.

KANARFOGEL, E. 1992. *Jewish Education and Society in the High Middle Ages*. Detroit.

—— 2000. *'Peering Through the Lattices'. Mystical, Magical and Pietistic Dimensions in the Tosafist Period*. Detroit.

KAPLAN, Y. 1988. 'The Problem of the Anusim and the "New Christians" in Historical Research of the Last Generation.' In *Studies in Historiography: Collected Essays* [Hebrew]. 117–44. M. Zimmerman *et al.* eds. Jerusalem.

KAPLAN, J. 1989. *From Christianity to Judaism: The Story of Isaac Orobio de Castro*. Oxford.

—— 1991. 'The Path of Western Sephardi Jewry to Modernity.' [Hebrew]. *Pe'amim* 48: 85–103.

—— 1994. *The Western Sephardi: Diaspora*. [Hebrew]. Tel Aviv.

KATZ, J. 1953. 'Religious Tolerance in the Method of Rabbi Menachem Hameiri in Halacha and Philosophy.' [Hebrew]. *Zion* 18: 15–30.

—— 1977. *Between Jews and Gentiles* [Hebrew]. 2nd edn. Jerusalem. = Katz, J. 1961. *Exclusiveness and Tolerance: Studies in Jewish–Gentile Relations in Medieval and Modern Times*. London.

—— 1984. *Halacha and Kabbala: Studies in the History of the Religion of Israel, its Divisions and its Social Contexts* [Hebrew]. Jerusalem.

KEDAR, B. Z. 1996. 'Expulsion as a Problem in World History.' [Hebrew]. *Alpayim* 13: 9–22.

KOHN, R. 1988. *Les Juifs de la France du Nord dans la seconde moitié du XIVe siècle*. Paris.

KRIEGEL, M. 1977. 'Prémarranisme et inquisition dans la Provence des XIIIe et XIVe siècles.' *Provence Historique* 27: 313–23.

—— 1978. 'La Prise d'une decision: l'expulsion des Juifs d'Espagne en 1492.' *Revue Historique* 260: 49–90.

—— 1979. *Les Juifs à la fin du moyen âge dans l'Europe méditerranéenne*. Paris.

LADERO QUESADA, M. A. 1999. 'Grupos marginales. In *La Historia Medieval en España. Un balance historiográfico (1968–1998)* 505–33. Pamplona.

LANDES, R. 1996. 'The Massacres of 1010: On the Origins of Popular Violence in Western Europe.' In *From Witness to Witchcraft: Jews and Judaism in Medieval Christian Thought*. 79–112. J. Cohen ed. Wiesbaden.

LANGMUIR, G. 1984. 'Thomas of Monmouth: Detector of Ritual Murder.' *Speculum* 59: 209–36.

—— 1990a. *History, Religion and Antisemitism*. Berkeley.

—— 1990b. *Toward a Definition of Antisemitism*. Berkeley.

LASKER, D. J. 1993. 'Judeo–Christian Polemics and Their Origins in Muslim Countries.' [Hebrew]. *Pe'amim* 57: 4–16.

—— and STROUMSA, S. 1996. *The Polemic of Nestor the Priest: Qiṣṣat Mujādalat al-Usquf and Sefer Nestor Ha-Komer*. Jerusalem.

LAWEE, E. 2001. *Isaac Abarbanel's Stance Toward Tradition*. Albany, NY.

LEROY, B. 1985. *The Jews of Navarre in the Late Middle Ages*. Jerusalem.

LEVINE-MELAMMED, R. 1998. 'Sephardi Women in the Medieval and Early Modern Periods.' In *Jewish Women in Historical Perspective*. 128–149. J. R. Baskin ed. Detroit.

LEVINE-MELAMMED, R. 1999. *Heretics or Daughters of Israel? The Crypto-Jewish Women of Castile*. New York and Oxford.

LIBES, J. 1983. 'Christian Influences on the Book of the Zohar.' [Hebrew]. *Jerusalem Studies in Jewish Thought* 2/1: 43–74.

LIMOR, O. 1991. 'Missionary Merchants: Three Medieval Anti-Jewish Works from Genoa.' *Journal of Medieval History* 17: 35–51.

—— 1993–8. *Jews and Christians in Western Europe: Encounter Between Cultures in the Middle Ages and the Renaissance* [Hebrew]. Vols. 1–5. Tel Aviv.

—— 1994. *Die Disputation zu Ceuta (1179) und die Disputation zu Mallorca (1286): Zwei antijüdische Schriften aus dem mittelalterlichen Genua*. MGH, Quellen zur Geistesgeschichte des Mittelalters. Munich.

—— 1996. 'Christian Holiness, Jewish Authority.' [Hebrew]. *Katedra* 80: 31–62.

LINDER, A. 1974. 'Roman Rule and the Jews in the Time of Constantine.' [Hebrew]. *Tarbiz* 44: 95–143.

—— 1976. 'Ecclesia and Synagoga in the Medieval Myth of Constantine the Great.' *Revue belge de philologie et d'histoire* 54: 1019–60.

—— 1987. *The Jews in Roman Imperial Legislation*. Detroit.

—— 1997. *The Jews in the Legal Sources of the Early Middle Ages*. Detroit.

LIPINER, E. 1997. *Two Portuguese Exiles in Castile: Dom David Negro and Dom Isaac Abravanel*. Hispania Judaica 10. Jerusalem.

LOTTER, F. 1988. 'Hostienfrevelvorwurf und Blutwunderfälschung bei den Judenverfolgungen von 1298 ("Rintfleisch") und 1336–1338 ("Armeleder").' *Fälschungen im Mittelalter*. MGH Schriften 33. 5: 533–83

LOURIE, E. 1988a. 'Complicidad Criminal: Un aspecto insolito de convivencia judeo-cristiana.' In *Actas del III congreso internacional encuentro de las tres culturas*. 933–108. C. Carrete Parrondo ed. Toledo.

—— 1988b. 'Mafiosi and Malsines: Violence, Fear and Faction in the Jewish Aljamas of Valencia in the Fourteenth Century.' In *Actas del IV congreso internacional encuentro de las tres culturas*. 69–102. C. Carrete Parrondo ed. Toledo.

—— 1995. 'Cultic Dancing and Courtly Love: Jews and Popular Culture in Fourteenth Century Aragon and Valencia.' In *Cross Cultural Convergence in the Crusader Period: Essays Presented to Aryeh Grabois on His Sixty-Fifth Birthday*. 151–82. M. Goodich *et al.* eds. New York.

MARCUS, I. G. 1976. 'The Jews in Western Europe: Fourth to Sixteenth Century.' In *Bibliographical Essays in Medieval Jewish Studies*. 17–105. L. V. Berman ed. New York.

—— 1981. *Piety and Society: The Jewish Pietists of Medieval Germany*. Leiden.

—— 1982. 'From Politics to Martyrdom: Shifting Paradigms in the Hebrew Narratives of the 1096 Crusade Riots.' *Prooftexts* 2: 40–52.

—— 1986. 'Hierarchies, Religious Boundaries and Jewish Spirituality in Medieval Germany.' *JH* 1/2: 7–26.

—— 1990. 'History, Story and Collective Memory: Narrativity in Early Ashkenazic Culture.' *Prooftexts* 10: 365–88.

—— 1995. 'Jews and Christians Imaging the Other in Medieval Europe.' *Prooftexts* 15: 209–26.

—— 1996. *Rituals of Childhood: Jewish Acculturation in Medieval Europe*. New Haven.

MENTGEN, G. 1994. 'The Origins of the Blood Libel.' [Hebrew]. *Zion* 59: 343–49.

MEYUHAS GINIO, A. 1993. 'Self-Perception and Images of the Judeoconversos in Fifteenth-Century Spain and Portugal.' *Tel Aviver Jahrbuch für deutsche Geschichte* 22: 127–52.

——1999. *Anusim and 'New Christians' in Spain* [Hebrew]. Tel Aviv.

MITRE FERNÁNDEZ, E. 1994. *Los Judios de Castilla en tiempo de Enrique III. El pogrom de 1391*. Valladolid.

MOOR, R. I. 1987. *The Formation of a Persecuting Society: Power and Deviance in Western Europe, 950–1250*. Oxford.

MOTIS DOLDAR, M. A. 1996. 'Poblacíon, urbanismo y estructura política de las aljamas judías de Aragón en el siglo XV.' *Hispania* 56: 113–64.

NETANYAHU, B. 1995. *The Origins of the Inquisition*. New York.

——1997. *Toward the Inquisition: Essays on Jewish and Converso History in Late Medieval Spain*. Ithaca, NY and London.

——1999. *The Marranos of Spain. From the Late 14th to the Early 16th Century According to Contemporary Hebrew Sources*. 3rd edn. Ithaca, NY and London.

NIRENBERG, D. 1996. *Communities of Violence: Persecution of Minorities in the Middle Ages*. Princeton.

ORFALI, M. 1996. 'Jews and Conversos in Fifteenth-Century Spain: Christian Apologia and Polemic.' In *From Witness to Witchcraft: Jews and Judaism in Medieval Christian Thought*. 337–60. J. Cohen ed. Wiesbaden.

—— and MOTIS DOLDAR, M. A. 1991. 'An Examination of the Texts of the General Edict of the Expulsion.' [Hebrew]. *Peʿamim* 46/7: 148–68.

PALES-GOBILLIARD, A. 1977. 'L'Inquisition et les Juifs: le cas de Jacques Fournier.' In *Juifs et Judaïsme de Languedoc* = *Cahiers de Fanjeaux* 12: 97–114. B. Blumenkranz et M. H. Vicaire eds. Toulouse.

PO-CHIA HSIA, R. 1988. *The Myth of Ritual Murder. Jews and Magic in Reformation Germany*. New Haven and London.

POPKIN, R. H. 1979. *The History of Scepticism from Erasmus to Spinoza*. Berkeley, Los Angeles, and London.

——1992. 'Jewish Christians and Christian Jews in Spain, 1492 and After.' *Judaism* 41: 248–67.

RABELLO, A. M. 1983. *The Jews in Visigothic Spain in the Light of the Legislation* [Hebrew]. Jerusalem.

REVÁH, I. S. 1995. *Des Marranes a Spinoza*. H. Mechoulan *et al*. eds. Paris.

ROMANO, D. 1992. 'The Contribution of Spanish Jewry to the Sciences.' In *The Heritage of Spain* [Hebrew]. 190–206. H. Beinart ed. Jerusalem.

ROSENTAL, J. ed. 1970. *The Book of Joseph the Zealous of Rabbi Joseph bar Nathan Oficial* [Hebrew]. Jerusalem.

ROTH, C. 1933. 'The Feast of Purim and the Origins of the Blood Libel.' *Speculum* 8: 520–6.

ROTH, N. 1994. *Jews, Visigoths and Muslims in Medieval Spain: Cooperation and Conflict*. Leiden, New York, and Cologne.

——1995. *Conversos, Inquisition, and the Expulsion of the Jews from Spain*. Madison, Wisc. and London.

RUBIN, M. 1999. *Gentile Tales: The Narrative Assault on Late Medieval Jews*. New Haven and London.

RUDERMAN, D. B. 1991. 'Hope Against Hope: Jewish and Christian Messianic Expectations in the Late Middle Ages.' In *Exile and Diaspora: Studies in the History of the Jewish People Presented to Professor Haim Beinart*. 185–202. A. Mirsky *et al.* eds. Jerusalem.

SAPERSTEIN, M. 1986a. 'Christians and Jews—Some Positive Images.' *HTR* 79: 236–46.

——1986b. 'The Conflict over the Rashba's Herem on Philosophical Study: A Political Perspective.' *JH* 1: 27–38.

——1989. *Jewish Preaching, 1200–1800: An Anthology*. New Haven and London.

——1992. 'Christians and Christianity in the Sermons of Jacob Anatoli.' *JH* 6/2 (The Frank Talmage Memorial Volume, II): 225–42.

SARAIVA, A. J. 1985. *Inquisição e Cristão Novos*. Lisbon.

——2001. *The Marrano Factory: The Portuguese Inquisition and its New Christians, 1536–1765*. Translated, Revised and Augmented by H. P. Salomon and I. S. D. Sasoon. Leiden.

SCHÄFER, P. 1990. 'The Ideal of Piety of the Ashkenazi Hasidim and Its Roots in Jewish Tradition.' *JH* 4/2: 9–23.

SCHULTZ, M. 1986. 'The Blood Libel—A Motif in the History of Childhood.' In *Proceedings of the World Congress of Jewish Studies* 9: 55–60; *Journal of Psychohistory* 14: 1–24.

SCHWARTZ, D. 1996. *The Philosophy of a Fourteenth Century Jewish Neoplatonic Circle* [Hebrew]. Jerusalem.

SCHWARZFUCHS, S. 1989. 'The Place of the Crusades in Jewish History.' In *Culture and Society in Medieval Jewry: Studies Dedicated to the Memory of Haim Hillel Ben-Sasson* [Hebrew]. 251–67. M. Ben Sasson *et al.* eds. Jerusalem.

SEPTIMUS, B. 1982. *Hispano-Jewish Culture in Transition*. Cambridge, Mass. and London.

SHAMIR, Y. 1981. 'The Legends Used in the Polemic of Rabbi Moses Ha-Kohen of Tordesillas' [Hebrew]. *Proceedings of the World Congress of Jewish Studies* 7: 43–52. Jerusalem.

SHARF, A. 1971. *Byzantine Jewry From Justinian To the Fourth Crusade*. London.

——1995. *Jews and Other Minorities in Byzantium*. Jerusalem.

SHATZMILLER, J. 1973a. 'L'Inquisition et les Juifs de Provence au XIIIᵉ siècle.' *Provence Historique* 23: 326–35.

——1973b. *Recherches sur la communauté juive de Manosque au moyen âge, 1241–1329*. Paris.

——1977. 'Contacts et échanges entre savants juifs et chrétiens à Montpellier vers 1300.' *Cahiers de Fanjeaux* 12: 337–44.

——1985. 'Politics and the Myth of Origins: The Case of the Medieval Jews.' In *Les Juifs au regard de l'histoire. Mélanges en l'honneur de Bernard Blumenkranz*. 49–61. G. Dahan ed. Paris.

——1989. 'The Albigensian Heresy as Reflected in the Eyes of Contemporary Jewry.' In *Culture and Society in Medieval Jewry: Studies Dedicated to the Memory of Haim Hillel Ben-Sasson* [Hebrew]. 333–52. M. Ben-Sasson *et al.* eds. Jerusalem.

——1990. *Shylock Reconsidered: Jews, Moneylending, and Medieval Society*. Berkeley.

——1994a. *La Deuxième Controverse de Paris. Un chapitre dans la polémique entre Chrétiens et Juifs au moyen âge*. Paris.

——1994b. *Jews, Medicine, and Medieval Society*. Berkeley and Los Angeles.

SHOHAM-STEINER, E. 2000. '"The Left (Hand) Repels while the Right Draws Near": The Involuntary Deviants in "Sefer Hasidim".' In *Being Different: Minorities, Aliens and Outsiders in History* [Hebrew]. 93–132. S. Volkov ed. Jerusalem.

SIMONSOHN, S. 1991. *The Apostolic See and the Jews: History*. Toronto.

STACY, R. 1993. 'English Jewry in the Thirteenth Century and the Problem of the Expulsion.' In *Expulsion and Return: English Jewry over the Ages* [Hebrew]. 9–25. D. Katz and Y. Kaplan eds. Jerusalem.

STARR, J. 1939. *The Jews in the Byzantine Empire: 641–1204*. New York.

STOUFF, L. 1980. 'Activités et professions dans une communauté juive de Provence au bas moyen-âge, la Juiverie d'Arles 1400–1450.' In *Minorités techniques et métiers, actes de la table ronde du Groupement d'Intéret Scientifique, Sciences Humaines sur l'Aire Méditerranéenne, Abbaye de Sénanque, Octobre 1978*. 57–77. Aix-en-Provence.

——1991. 'Chrétiens et Juifs dans l'Arles du bas moyen âge: Leurs relations.' In *Les Sociétés urbaines en France méridionale et en péninsule ibérique au moyen âge, actes du colloque Pau, 21–23 septembre 1988*. 519–37. Paris.

STOW, K. R. 1992. *Alienated Minority: The Jews of Medieval Latin Europe*. Cambridge, Mass. and London.

SWETSCHINSKI, D. M. 2000. *Reluctant Cosmopolitans: The Portuguese Jews of Seventeenth-Century Amsterdam*. London.

TALLAN, C. 1991. 'Medieval Jewish Widows: Their Control of Resources.' *JH* 5: 63–74.

——1992. 'Opportunities for Medieval Northern-European Jewish Widows in the Public and Domestic Spheres.' In *Upon My Husband's Death*. L. Mirrer ed. Ann Arbor, Mich.

TAVARES, M. J. P. F. 1982–4. *Os judeus em Portugal no século XV*. Vols. 1–2. Lisbon.

——1987. *Judaísmo e inquisição. Estudos*. Lisbon.

——1992. *Los judios en Portugal*. Madrid.

——1997. 'Expulsion or Integration? The Portuguese Jewish Problem.' In *Crisis and Creativity in the Sephardic World: 1391–1648*. 95–103. B. R. Gampel ed. New York.

TOAFF, A. 1996. *Love, Work and Death: Jewish Life in Medieval Umbria*. London.

TOCH, M. 1997. 'The Formation of a Diaspora: The Settlement of Jews in the Medieval German Reich.' *Aschkenas* 7: 55–78.

——1998. *Die Juden im Mittelalterlichen Reich*. Munich.

——2001. 'The Economic Activities of German Jews in the 10th to 12th Centuries: Between Historiography and History.' In *Facing the Cross: The Persecutions of 1096 in History and Historiography* [Hebrew]. 32–54. Y. T. Assis *et al.* eds. Jerusalem.

URBACH, A. A. 1980. 'The Tolerant Method of Rabbi Menachem Hameiri: Its Origin and Limits.' In *Chapters in the History of Jewish Society in the Middle Ages and Modern Era, Dedicated to Professor Jacob Katz on his Seventy-Fifth Birthday By His Students and Friends* [Hebrew]. 34–44. I. Etkes and J. Shalmon eds. Jerusalem.

VICAIRE, M. H. ed. 1977. *Juifs et Judaïsme de Languedoc = Cahiers de Fanjeaux* 12. Toulouse.

WEINSTEIN, R. 1998. 'Rituel du mariage et culture des jeunes dans la Société Judéo-Italienne des 16ᵉ–17ᵉ siécles.' *Annales. Histoire Sciences Sociales* 53: 455–79.

——2000. ' "Segragatos non autem eiectos" (segregated yet not Ejected): Jews and Christians in Italian Cities During the Catholic Reformation.' In *Being Different: Minorities, Aliens and Outsiders in History* [Hebrew]. 93–132. S. Volkov ed. Jerusalem.

YASSIF, E. 1999. 'Legends and History: Historians Read Hebrew Legends of the Middle Ages.' [Hebrew]. *Zion* 64: 187–220.

YERUSHALMI, Y. H. 1970. 'The Inquisition and the Jews of France in the Time of Bernard Gui.' *HTR* 63: 317–76.

——1981. *From Spanish Court to Italian Ghetto: Isaac Cardoso: A Study in Seventeenth-Century Marranism and Jewish Apologetics*. 2nd edn. Seattle and London.

YERUSHALMI, Y. H. 1998. *Sefardica: Essais sur l'histoire des Juifs, des Marranes et des Nouveaux-Chrétiens d'origine Hispano-Portugaise.* Paris.

YUVAL, I. J. 1983. 'Edicts [*takanot*] against the Rise of Divorce in Germany in the Fifteenth Century.' [Hebrew]. *Zion* 48: 177–215.

—— 1994. ' "The Lord Will Take Vengeance for His Temple"—Historia sine ira et studio.' [Hebrew]. *Zion* 59: 351–414.

YUVAL, I. J. 2000. *'Two Nations in your Womb': Perceptions of Jews and Christians* [Hebrew]. Tel Aviv.

ZFATMAN, S. 1993. *The Jewish Tale in the Middle Ages: Between Ashkenaz and Sepharad* [Hebrew]. Jerusalem.

ZUCKERMAN, A. 1972. *A Jewish Princedom in Feudal France, 768–900.* New York.

CHAPTER 9

MEDIEVAL JEWRY IN THE WORLD OF ISLAM

MARK R. COHEN

ISLAM arose in the seventh century in Arabia through the preaching of the prophet Muhammad (d. 632). At the time, the overwhelming majority of world Jewry lived either in the Zoroastrian Persian empire, what is today modern Iran and Iraq (which the Jews called Babylonia), or under Christian Byzantine rule, in Greece, Asia Minor, Syria, Palestine, Egypt, North Africa, and Italy. A small settlement inhabited the non-Byzantine regions of North Africa and Visigothic Spain. Northern Latin Europe hardly knew any Jewish presence. On the other hand, Jews had dwelt in Arabia for several centuries prior to the rise of Islam. When, following Muhammad's death, the new Muslim religion united the Persian and Byzantine empires through conquest, adding Spain to its empire at the beginning of the eighth century, the overwhelming majority of world Jewry found itself living under Islamic rule. From their zones of concentration in Babylonia and Palestine in late antiquity, Jews migrated westward within the Islamic domains, thickening existing settlements in the Mediterranean and founding new ones. Sizeable Jewish communities grew in cities like Qayrawan in Tunisia, Fez in Morocco, Cordova in Muslim Spain, and Alexandria and Old Cairo in Egypt, where the twelfth-century Spanish Jewish traveller, Benjamin of Tudela, found 3,000 and 7,000 Jews, respectively. Though population figures other than Benjamin's are hard to come by, it can be safely asserted that the majority of Eastern (Islamic) over Western (Christian) Jewry continued at least until the twelfth century (Baron 1952–83: iii. 113–14, who estimates a global Jewish population of 2 million at that time).

Nineteenth-century Jewish historians of the 'Wissenschaft des Judentums' school painted the experience of medieval Jewry in the world of Islam in idyllic, almost mythic terms and in stark contrast to the sorrowful, oppressive, persecutory history of Jews living in medieval Christendom. The Jews of Arab lands, particularly those in Muslim Spain, were thought to have lived in a 'Golden Age', even an 'interfaith utopia', the opposite of the 'lachrymose' European Jewish past (the term 'lachry-mose' in this context is attributed to Salo W. Baron in an essay of 1928: (Baron 1928). This antinomy served the political agenda of the Wissenschaft des Judentums historians. Though promised emancipation and full political and cultural integra-tion into society following the French Revolution, Jewish academics had continued to experience discrimination, including exclusion from university teaching pos-itions. By the second half of the nineteenth century this prejudice took the new form of racial and political anti-Semitism. The interfaith utopia, or better, the myth of an interfaith utopia in Spain and under Islam in general, challenged supposedly enlightened European Christians to live up to the promise of emancipation and grant the Jews rights and privileges that were at least as 'liberal' as the 'tolerant' treatment Jews enjoyed under the rule of medieval Muslims.[1]

This rosy comparison between the 'Golden Age' under Islam and the era of persecution under Christendom, sketched against the background of the political agenda of nineteenth-century Central European Jewish intellectuals, was carried forth into the twentieth century, reinforced by the brutal Nazi persecution of the Jews culminating in the Holocaust. On the other hand, the Arab–Jewish dispute over Palestine generated a fresh political issue which impacted on the historiog-raphy of medieval Jewry in the world of Islam. Opposing sides in the conflict exploited or revised the 'myth of the interfaith utopia' with their own political purposes in mind. Arabs, as well as non-Arab supporters of Arab nationalism, waved the flag of Jewish–Muslim harmony in the past and, directly or by implica-tion, blamed contemporary Zionism for Arab hostility in the present. Eliminate the so-called Zionist threat, even do away with the Jewish State, the argument went, and Jews and Arabs would return to the halcyon days of tolerant interfaith relations as in the Golden Age, with Jews living peacefully in Palestine under Arab-Muslim rule.

In response, many Zionist writers replaced the Golden Age theory with what I have called, interchangeably, 'the counter-myth of Islamic persecution' or 'the neo-

---

[1] For an idyllic, twentieth-century exposition of the 'Golden Age' in Muslim Spain, see Ashtor (1973–84), a translation of the Hebrew original of 1960–66. Gerber (1992) surveys the Muslim period and the Reconquista era.

lachrymose conception of Jewish-Arab history'. Revisionists claimed that Jewish life under Islam, beginning with the time of the Prophet Muhammad, was marked by hardship and persecution almost as bitter as the brutalizing ordeal of Jewish life under Christendom. By implication, Arab anti-Semitism was not a new story, but rather an ancient pathology, not likely to go away even if Israel were to make major political concessions for peace to the emergent Palestinian nation (Cohen 1994: chap. 1, which reviews literature on both sides of these arguments).

JUDAISM AND ISLAM

Even before the conflict over Palestine, the concept of a 'Muslim-Jewish interfaith utopia' was reflected in the debate over Islamic origins. Did the Prophet Muhammad take his inspiration from Judaism? The pioneering word on this was said in the nineteenth century by a German-Jewish student, Abraham Geiger, later to become one of the founders of Reform Judaism. His prize essay of 1833, in answer to the question 'What did Muhammad take from Judaism?', identified terms, concepts, and stories in the Qur'an that, in his opinion, could only have derived from Judaism (Geiger 1898). Other Jews have followed in his train (for an extreme case see Katsh 1954). Still others, mostly Christians, have favoured Christianity in the search for the major influence on Muhammad (e.g. Bell 1926). Pious Muslims reject all outside influences, accepting literally the Qur'an's claim of direct divine revelation (see additional bibliography in Cohen 1995).

There is little dispute that in its origins Islam owed much to the influence of Judaism, or that developed Islam bears substantial similarities to rabbinic Judaism (strict monotheism; reliance upon a divinely revealed scripture that must be 'interpreted' by experts; daily prayer; certain fasts; and dietary laws, to name a few). Moreover, there is little disagreement that mature Islam influenced Judaism in reverse. The 'symbiosis' of Islam and Judaism, a concept formulated by S. D. Goitein to replace the older 'interfaith utopia' (Goitein 1955), constitutes one of the leitmotifs of the contemporary study of Jewish history in the medieval Islamic world (Wasserstrom 1995; Bernard Lewis (1984) has rephrased it as 'the Judeo-Islamic tradition'). It explains much of the interplay between Jews and Arabs and between Judaism and Islam, which most scholars recognize to be the earmark of Jewish history in its Islamic phase. (Some important observations about the relationship between Judaism and Islam are found in Lazarus-Yafeh 1981.)

The Cairo Genizah:
The Premier Source for Jewish Life
in the World of Islam

The same S. D. Goitein is associated with the most important discovery that has been made in research on the history of Jews in the world of Islam in the twentieth century and beyond: the Cairo Genizah (Reif 2000). This premier source of information has deepened our understanding, not of an 'interfaith utopia', but of the economic, social, political, and cultural embeddedness of the Jews in medieval Islamic society.

An ancient Jewish taboo, having roots in the Mishnah and the Talmud, prohibits the destruction of pieces of sacred writing—in theory, fragments of the Bible containing God's name, but in practice anything copied or printed in the Hebrew script. These papers must be buried in a genizah (the word *genizah* means both 'burial place' and the act of 'burying'). Normally, a genizah is located in a cemetery. Every Jewish community in the Middle Ages had a genizah, and burial of worn pages from Hebrew books is still practised by traditional Jews around the world today.

The Cairo Genizah, however, was unique. For various reasons (not fully understood to this day) (Cohen and Stillman 1985), it was situated inside the synagogue, the so-called Ben Ezra Synagogue in Fuṣṭāṭ (Old Cairo), a structure that dates back to the Middle Ages and possibly even to pre-Islamic times (Lambert 1994). The atypical nature of the Cairo Genizah had two fortunate consequences: first, the contents were concentrated in one space and easily accessible, once discovered; and second, because Egypt has a very arid climate the pages buried there had stood the test of centuries, without mouldering, so that, even when a page is torn or riddled with holes, the ink can be read today almost as clearly as when it was copied, in some cases as long as a thousand years ago.

Discovered at the end of the nineteenth century, the contents of the Cairo Genizah were dispersed among more than twenty-five libraries and private collections, from Cincinnati, Ohio, to St Petersburg, Russia. They contain upwards of 210,000 fragments of handwritten text (many fragments assigned a single shelfmark have multiple pages, considerably expanding the total number of pages to around three-quarters of a million). The vast majority are leaves from books, such as medieval Hebrew poetry, rabbinic fragments, midrashic and halachic texts, philosophical works, magical and mystical texts, and liturgical fragments (usually, pages from prayer books). These remains contain pages from many unknown works, vastly expanding our knowledge of Jewish culture in the medieval Islamic world. The Genizah even contains fragments of Arab belles-lettres and Islamic religious texts, such as pages from the Qur'an transcribed into Hebrew letters. These finds in themselves provide evidence of the Jewish–Islamic 'symbiosis' and of the cultural embeddednes of the Jews in Arab-Muslim society of the Middle Ages. Moreover, the very concept of 'genizah', it has been shown by Joseph Sadan with particular reference to fragments of the Qurʾan, was shared by Muslims, another case of cultural similarity that informed the historical interplay between Judaism and Islam (Sadan 1986; Cohen forthcoming).

Quite surprisingly, the Cairo Genizah also encompasses a wide variety of individual documents from everyday life, many of which we would call 'secular'. They date mostly from the eleventh to thirteenth centuries and include letters, court records, marriage contracts, deeds of divorce, wills, business documents and accounts, and lists of recipients of charity and of gifts for charitable purposes. These fragments, which Goitein called 'historical documents' to distinguish them from the literary fragments mentioned above, constitute perhaps 5 per cent of the Genizah as a whole (Goitein 1967–93: i. 9–16). Most of them are written in Judaeo-Arabic, that is, Arabic in Hebrew characters and displaying grammatical and syntactic features differentiating it from the classical Arabic of the Qurʾan and all other medieval Arabic writings. Some of the Genizah fragments are official documents, such as petitions to be submitted to Muslim authorities, and are hence written in Arabic script (Khan 1993).

The historical documents from the Genizah have revealed aspects of economic, social, and family life, as well as of material culture and the mentality of the individual, that were previously completely unknown. They also confirm that the so-called 'classical' Genizah period (eleventh to thirteenth centuries) was one of relative security (Stillman 1979: 40, calls this period 'The Best Years'), especially compared to the high Middle Ages in the Ashkenazic lands of northern Europe. Furthermore, Goitein's many publications argued persuasively that the Genizah civilization constituted a more-or-less unified 'Mediterranean Society' of Jews, Muslims, and Christians, making the Genizah an important source for general Islamic social and economic history (Goitein 1967–93). This claim is now recognized in the general Islamic field, including among Arab scholars (Udovitch 1970; Constable 1994; Khalilieh 1998; Rabie 1972; El-Hawary 1994).

TOLERANT ISLAM? THE LEGAL STATUS OF THE JEWS

The myth of the interfaith utopia stemmed from and at the same time contributed to a sympathetic Jewish view of Islam as a tolerant religion, quite different from the negative attitude toward Islam 'exposed' in Edward Said's *Orientalism* (Said 1978;

Lewis 1968; Kramer 1999). But constructing Jewish history around the idea of Islamic tolerance fails to take into consideration an important fact. Tolerance, at least as we know it in the West since the time of John Locke, was not considered a virtue in medieval monotheistic societies. Exclusive by nature, monotheists declare all others (including other monotheists) to be infidels. If medieval Christianity 'tolerated' Judaism, that is, permitted Jews to live and practise their religion, it was because Christians believed (especially since the time of St Augustine, 354–430; see below) that God wished Jews to be preserved as witnesses to Christian triumphalism. If medieval Islam treated Jews better than did Christianity, it was for a variety of reasons that will become clear in the course of this essay. (This is the subject of Cohen 1994, some of the argument of which recurs here.) The historian, however, must not expect to find principled tolerance. Rather, he should search for historical factors that mitigated natural *in*tolerance. This, rather than 'interfaith utopia', better serves the contextual representation of the past and permits the observer to see, and explain, acts of Islamic oppression that did occur, without exaggerating them selectively into a 'countermyth of Islamic persecution', as recent revisionism has done (e.g. Bat Ye'or 1985).

In recent decades there has been considerable discussion, on both sides of the larger debate, around the issue of Muhammad's own 'policy' toward the Jews of Medina (e.g. Gil 1974; Arafat 1976; Ahmad 1979; Rubin 1985; Kister 1986). Regardless of where the 'truth' about Muhammad and the Jews lies, it is well accepted that Jews (and Christians) in the world of Islam benefited from legal toleration as 'protected people' (*ahl al-dhimma*), a status awarded to the so-called People of the Book (*ahl al-kitāb*), who had received a scripture revealed by God (Fattal 1958). As one of two, sometimes three or more *dhimmī* groups (Islam assimilated Persian Zoroastrians and Indian Hindus into the *dhimmī* category), Jews were not singled out for special consideration. This meant that the natural Islamic (monotheistic) discrimination against infidels was diffused. No special law for the Jews developed in Islam, as it did in Christendom, where by the high Middle Ages Jews were considered 'serfs of the royal chamber', the special 'property' of monarchs or barons or towns. Sometimes the Church asserted exclusive power over the Jews, invoking an old patristic doctrine about the 'perpetual servitude of the Jews'.

Islamic legal prescriptions governing Jewish life were embodied mostly in the so-called 'Pact of 'Umar', itself incorporated into the Islamic holy law (the *sharī'a*) (Tritton 1930; Cohen 1999; Kallfelz 1995). As such, these regulations were preserved, with stability, over time, and rarely given to arbitrary deviations. The law of the *dhimma* included restrictions that originally seem, Albrecht Noth has argued, to have been meant more to protect the fragile identity of the minority of conquering Muslims than to oppress the infidel (Noth 1987). But with the passage of time, certainly by the end of the first Islamic century, these came to be discriminatory in a negative sense. Non-Muslims could not erect new houses of worship nor repair old ones; they had to observe their religious rites indoors and quietly, so as not to insult the superiority of Islam; they could not take Arabic honorific names (Abū ʿImrān, for instance); they were required to dress in distinctive garb, notably with a belt called the *zunnār*; they could not own captive slaves designated for Muslims; they had to show loyalty to Muslims; they could not sell pork or alcoholic beverages in Muslim quarters (since these were forbidden in Islam). In return for observance of these restrictions, and also for payment of an annual poll tax (*jizya*), *dhimmīs* were granted freedom of religion, protection by the state for their persons and property, and also communal autonomy—the freedom to live according to their ancestral religious laws. *Dhimmīs* were also forbidden from holding public office, but this expressed itself mainly as a restriction directed at their Muslim employers and as the object of complaints poised at complicit Arab rulers who violated the proper hierarchy underlying the *dhimma* system (on Jews in public office, see Fischel 1937).

With the exception of the fiscally important poll tax, the sources at our disposal indicate that, especially during the classical centuries (seventh to thirteenth), the restrictive laws of the *dhimma*, including the ban on office-holding, were enforced irregularly and sporadically. Moreover, moves to make the laws more severe, or to enforce their provisions when thought to have been violated, generally had to pass the juristic reasoning and on-scene investigation of Muslim religious scholars. Loyal to divinely inspired text, Muslim jurists and judges (like Jewish halachic scholars) were more likely to stick to tradition and to exercise due process of law than to expand, arbitrarily, the humiliating laws of the *dhimma*. When the 'mad' Egyptian Caliph al-Ḥākim ran amuck, persecuting Christians and Jews in the first two decades of the eleventh century (one of the few serious persecutions affecting Jews), Muslims themselves realized that his excesses outrageously violated the Pact of ʿUmar, 'the stipulations which al-Ḥākim "added" to the ʿUmariyyan ones', in the words of a medieval Arab historian (Cohen 1994: 74). Or, much later on, during generally more difficult times, a move in the eighteenth century to force Jews in Yemen to collect excrement from private homes provoked a spirited debate between Sunni and Shiʿi scholars that swirled around religious texts and religious arguments (Haykel forthcoming).

From the earliest period of Islam, Jews and Christians encountered little opposition when constructing new synagogues and churches, even in the newly founded Muslim garrison towns, where this was especially forbidden. Moreover, as Islam spread and Jews migrated to far-reaching parts of the empire, they established or enlarged communities and erected new houses of worship without opposition. When questions arose, Islamic jurists generally accepted testimony about the old age of buildings as sufficient excuse to exempt them from destruction or confiscation. Repairs were condoned when they met a juridical requirement that previously existing ('old') materials be employed for the refurbishment (Perlmann 1975; Ward 1989).

Unlike Christianity, Judaism is not a religion of outdoor spectacle, so Jews were far less affected by the restriction on public display of religious practice than their

Oriental Christian neighbours. An exception was funeral processions, which took Jews outside and were sometimes vulnerable to Muslim mob attacks (Mann 1920–2: i. 30–2).

Jews assumed Arabic honorific names—Abū ʿImrān is the by-name of Moses Maimonides—and, as the Genizah shows (Goitein 1967–93: iv. 194), and as sources describing repeated renewal of the dress regulations attest, Jews and other *dhimmīs* usually dressed like everybody else. Jews held slaves, mainly household domestics, but also as financial agents, and both Jews and, in greater numbers, Christians continued to hold government posts long after Arabs mastered the art of bureaucracy, and even during the late Middle Ages, when anti-*dhimmī* sentiment increased (Perlmann 1942).

JEWS IN THE ECONOMY OF ISLAM

There is little scholarly disagreement that the economic position of the Jews under medieval Islam was more favourable than that of their brethren in the West. However, while it is generally understood how the problematic economic role of the Jews of Christendom—as stigmatized, alien, long-distance traders in predominantly agrarian and sedentary Barbarian Europe, and later on as despised money-lenders—contributed to Jewish difficulties (Baron 1952–83: iv. chap. 22 and xii. *passim*), it has not been fully appreciated how the improved economic status of the Jews of Islam contributed to their relative security.

Recent research challenging the thesis of Jewish predominance in commerce (especially the slave trade) in early medieval Europe (Toch 2000), if upheld, will still not affect the crucial contrast with the Muslim world, where the Jewish economic role supported rather than undermined Jewish security. Attempts to find economic causes for Muslim 'anti-Semitism' in the Middle Ages, reminiscent of the European case, have not been convincing (Grossman 1988). This is because, unlike their co-religionists in Latin Christendom, the Jews of Islam were well integrated into the economic fabric of society at large (Goitein 1967–93: i; Cohen 1994: chap. 5). The relative absence of economic discrimination, especially during the classical centuries, makes a vivid impression, demanding explanation.

To begin with, Islamic scripture and traditions favour commercial activity, and this positive attitude carried over into Islamic law as it gradually took shape during the early centuries following the rise of the new religion. The compatibility of Islamic law and theology with profitable economic activity both resulted from and contributed to what S. D. Goitein called 'the rise of the Near Eastern bourgeoisie in early Islamic times' (Goitein 1957). This occurred centuries before its counterpart in Europe. The brisk and enterprising trade of early Islam resulted in large measure from the rapid creation of a vast, unified empire with great resources and a huge demand for goods. By the ninth century the Islamic world—innately an urban civilization—was reaping the benefits of flourishing trade and employing sophisticated instruments of credit for converting capital into profit that the medieval West did not acquire until the high Middle Ages.

For the largely urban Jews, the significance of Islam's positive attitude to both urban life and trade cannot be overstated. It gave them, by association, more status and a higher degree of integration than they could achieve in northern Europe, where the prejudice against merchants, and against the towns in which they lived, relegated the urbanized Jewish trader to the status of an alien, marginal character.

For other important reasons, too, itinerant Jewish merchants in the Islamic orbit were spared the stigma of 'otherness' suffered by Jews in Europe. They were indigenous to the Near East—not immigrants, as in the Latin West—and largely indistinguishable physically from their Arab-Muslim neighbours (originally, one of the main reasons behind the dress regulations and other symbols of separation in Islamic *dhimmī* law). Furthermore, their geographical movement was part and parcel of a general phenomenon in which Muslim (and Oriental Christian) merchants moved goods and themselves over vast distances in search of financial gain, often in partnership with Jews.

The traversibility of boundaries between Jew and non-Jew in daily economic affairs echoes throughout Jewish sources for our period. The relatively relaxed ambience of interfaith relations in the Islamic marketplace created trust and forged bonds which diminished the ever-present religious disdain for Jews as members of an infidel religion.

While our main source, the Cairo Genizah, probably gives disproportionate weight to Jewish merchants because it is they, more than others, who wrote letters filled with or soliciting information needed to conduct business affairs with a minimum of uncertainy or risk (Goitein 1973), the Jews exhibited broad economic diversification, and this, too, made them less 'other' and hence more secure. At least in the classical centuries (seventh to twelfth), and to a certain extent even later, commercial and trade guilds like the ones that excluded Jews in Europe, did not exist. Artisans of all sorts appear everywhere in the Genizah, highly skilled (and reasonably well paid) and working poor alike. Jews were involved in dyeing, metalwork, weaving, bread-baking, wine-making, manufacture of glass vessels, tailoring, tanning, production of cheese, sugar manufacture, and silkwork. Where financially possible, Jews owned agricultural land, and many raised crops in the arable Egyptian countryside. Jews also owned and worked orchards and date-groves.

This variegated economic profile, much more diverse and much more widespread than even Bernhard Blumenkranz claims for early medieval Jewry in the

Latin West (Blumenkranz 1960), militated against the social abuse that Jews in Christian lands had to endure, in part on account of their identification with a limited and problematic set of occupations. Even in moneylending, Jews in the orbit of medieval Islam were not singled out prejudicially. They were as likely to be debtors of other Jews as of Muslims. The theme of the malevolent Jewish money-lender was not absent from Arabic literature, but nowhere did it carry the religious animus so characteristic of religious writings in the medieval Christian world; nor, as in Europe, did it underlie the occasional popular Muslim outbursts or atrocities against Jews. Those usually occurred where Jews attained unacceptable degrees of power in Muslim society, in violation of the laws of the *dhimma*.

Cultural Embeddedness

The nature and extent of the embeddedness of medieval Jewry in Arabic/Islamic culture has undergone the least amount of challenge in scholarly literature, even by partisans of the 'neo-lachrymose conception of Jewish-Arab history'. Scholars have assimilated and even extended S. D. Goitein's formulation regarding 'symbiosis'. Steven M. Wasserstrom, for instance, has discussed Jewish-Shiʿite symbiosis in the early Islamic period, stretching Goitein's concept to encompass the domain of 'marginal elites comprised of semi-erudite intellectuals' (Wasserstrom 1995; quotation from 212–13).

The embeddedness begins with language. In the Fertile Crescent prior to the Arab conquest Jews spoke Aramaic, the lingua franca of that region. In those parts of Persia where Aramaic was not prevalent, they spoke Persian. They spoke Greek in Hellenistic Egypt and other parts of the Roman world, and Arabic in the Arabian Peninsula. Everywhere, Hebrew remained a literary language, reserved especially for ritual texts, though Aramaic, the spoken tongue in the yeshivot of Palestine and Babylonia, appears as the language of the two Talmuds and of the early Aramaic midrashim.

So it is in part natural that Arabic assumed the role of the new Jewish vernacular in the lands conquered by the Arabs beginning in the middle of the seventh century (except in the Iranian provinces, where even converts to Islam retained their Persian tongue). What is not naturally understood is that the Arabic spoken and written by the Jews, especially as reflected in manuscripts of the Cairo Genizah, teaches much about the Arabic of medieval Muslims and, in turn, about the embeddedness of the Jews in Arab culture.

Like Muslims, Jews spoke a colloquial version of Arabic, which scholars call 'Neo-Arabic', differentiating it from 'classical Arabic'. The latter, the language of pre-

Islamic Bedouin poetry and of the Qurʾan, became the model for all Arabic writing (Versteegh 1997). Since the Jews (the same is true of the Oriental Christians) did not revere the language of the Qurʾan, they allowed features of the colloquial dialect to creep into their writings, especially their casual letters. For this reason medieval Judaeo-Arabic is an important witness for medieval colloquial Arabic in general, supplementing in an important way the evidence of modern Arabic dialects (Blau 1999).

The most telling feature of the Jewish adoption of Arabic, which attests vigorously to Jewish cultural embeddedness in the Islamic world, is that the Jews not only spoke Arabic, but also used it for nearly every type of writing, even religious works that in the past had been composed in either Hebrew or Aramaic. Many factors contributed to the nearly wholesale Jewish adoption of Arabic. The language itself is similar to Hebrew, which made Judaeo-Arabic transcription easy. It also facilitated an easy glide between languages. This intertwining of tongues (and thus of cultures) can be seen not only in the occasional appearance in Judaeo-Arabic Genizah letters of a Hebrew word in the middle of a sentence, but also in the sudden shift, for no apparent reason, from Hebrew to Arabic characters for a word or brief phrase. Moreover, some subjects simply could not be easily expressed in Hebrew or Aramaic, especially philosophy and the sciences, including medicine, which had no Hebrew or Aramaic vocabularies, whereas those did exist in Arabic, the language of religious and secular high culture, alike. By the tenth century, therefore, as the writings of the great head of the Babylonian yeshiva of Sura, Saadya Gaon (d. 942), prove, Arabic had become the dominant language, written as well as spoken, of the Jews living in the orbit of Islam. Indeed, it was Saadya, and the anti-rabbinic sect of the Karaites that arose in the early Islamic period in Iran and Iraq, who made it so.

A particularly revealing sign of Jewish linguistic acculturation is the translation of holy texts. Even before Saadya, Jews had tried their hand at making an Arabic version of the Bible, as we know from fragments preserved in the Cairo Genizah (Blau 1992). Saadya himself produced a complete translation of the Torah, as well as an Arabic commentary on the text. His translation quickly attained canonical status, and to this day it is printed alongside the Hebrew original and the older, Aramaic translation of the Pentateuch by Yemenite Jews, and read by them in the synagogue. Saadya also compiled the first Arabic prayer book (following earlier efforts in Hebrew/Aramaic), in which the rubrics and commentary (not the actual prayers) and a long introduction were cast in the vernacular Arabic of the Jews (Reif 1993: 185–9). This siddur was already in use in the late tenth century in Saddya's home country of Egypt (Cohen and Somekh 1989–90).

Saadya is also responsible for pioneering Jewish religious philosophy in Arabic. By the middle of the ninth century Muslims had access in Arabic translation to the major part of the 'Greek sciences' (in addition to works from India and Persia). The process had begun a century earlier, thanks to the efforts mainly of Christian translators. Christians had sustained the study of Greek philosophy as the hand-maiden of religion in Byzantine and Sassanian monasteries during late antiquity. Saadya adopted the prevailing Graeco-Arabic philosophic theology of his time, the Mu'tazilite Kalām, 'dialectic'), which sought to 'rationalize' seemingly irrational aspects of holy scripture (like anthropomorphisms) and show that religion was compatible with reason. Saadya's work, entitled *Kitāb al-amanāt wa'l-i'tiqadāt* ('The Book of Beliefs and Convictions'), set a precedent for all of Jewish-Islamic religious philosophy (English translation, Rosenblatt 1948). Saadya was followed by a galaxy of great Jewish thinkers, ranging from the Neoplatonist Solomon ibn Gabirol in eleventh-century Spain, to the illustrious Spanish-Jewish Aristotelian, Maimonides (d. 1204), who spent most of his career in Egypt, to the latter's son, Abraham (d. 1237), who, though trained in Aristotelian philosophy in his father's house, cultivated (along with many Jewish judges and other colleagues in Egypt) a Jewish form of Sufism (Sirat 1985).

Philosophy was studied by Jews, Muslims, and Christians in interdenominational settings, where the particularities of each religion hardly made a difference. In fact, Jews—the elite of course—participated in this as well as other intellectual endeavours as near-equals with Muslims in what has long been been called 'the Renaissance of Islam' in the tenth century. In the words of Joel Kraemer, '[c]osmopolitanism, tolerance, reason, and friendship made possible the convocation of these societies [of learning], devoted to a common pursuit of the truth and preservation of ancient wisdom, by surmounting particular religious ties in favor of a shared human experience' (Kraemer 1986: 55–60; quotation from 60).

This world of shared intellectual discourse could exist because, in origin and content, much of it was neither Islamic nor Jewish nor Christian: it was Greek. Moreover, Arabic was not just the language of the dominant, and hostile, majority religion, but also the linguistic medium of mathematics, logic, and medicine, subjects that we would call (and they felt were) secular.

As the Greek–Arabic paidaeia encompassed medicine, Jewish philosophers in the Arab orbit functioned also as physicians. Medicine was an interdenominational profession, and Jews both studied with and served the sick in hospitals alongside Muslim (and Christian) physicians. They merited honourable mention in many a Muslim biographical dictionary of great doctors. Maimonides and his son Abraham are but two particularly illustrious examples (Meyerhof 1938).

Cultural embeddedness found expression also in the formal study of Hebrew. Muslims began to analyse the grammar of Arabic as soon as they realized that neophytes to Islam needed assistance in acquiring the new language. Lexicons also proved necessary. Initially devised to help poets, they were arranged in the order of final letters, for rhyming. Qur'anic commentary also flourished. Jews followed suit, again beginning with Saadya Gaon, by applying themselves to the linguistic study of Hebrew (Dotan 1997). This entailed, among other things, figuring out the root structure of the language. It took some trial and error (as well as vigorous debate) before the triliteral stem of Hebrew words was 'discovered'. Hebrew dictionaries were also compiled for the first time, mimicking Arabic lexicography.

The Arabic text of the Qur'an was originally written with consonants only. Again, for the benefit of converts, a vowel system was invented (adapting symbols from Syriac) for the holy book. The Hebrew text of the Bible was similarly consonantal and vowel-less. Jews in Babylonia and in Palestine, working separately, and probably inspired by the example of Muslims with the Qur'an, devised marks to indicate vowels and also cantillation signs. The system that prevailed was the one perfected in Tiberias, Palestine, in the eighth or ninth century, by mostly anonymous *ba'alei masorah*, 'masters of the tradition' (of reading and chanting the biblical text) (Dotan 1967). It became canonized as the 'Masoretic' text, the one in use universally by Jews today. Doubtless animated by the Muslim example, too, the study of biblical Hebrew motivated a new kind of biblical commentary, in which presentation of the literal meanings of words, based on the new grammar and lexicography, took its place next to the traditional midrashic method and often displaced it.

An old theory in Jewish scholarship argues that it was the Karaites who pioneered Hebrew linguistic, exegetical, and masoretic studies, and, more than the Arabic environment, stimulated the Rabbanite majority in the same direction (Pinsker 1860; Dotan 1977). A more recent and more subtle version of the 'Karaites as originators' theory, consistent with cultural embeddedness, argues the case for Karaite openness to Arabic literary models before the Rabbanites, precisely because, as a dissident sect, they lacked the inhibitions against innovation that still marked Rabbinic culture at that time (Drory 2000: 151–5; more on this theory, with abundant examples, in Drory 1988). The issue of cultural embeddedness in the Islamic world underlies some of the discussion of the very origins of the Karaite movement, a problem still not fully resolved, as well as the so-called 'scripturalism' of the early propagators of the sect (Cook 1987; Ben-Shammai 1992). Some point to the influence of Islamic Shi'ism, particularly as the Jewish messianic precursors of Karaism arose in the Persian environment, where Shi'ism, the major sectarian opposition group to orthodox Islam, itself first flourished (Friedlaender 1910–13). Iranian (Zoroastrian) trends of asceticism appearing in early Karaism contribute another dimension to the theory of external influences. A provocative but tendentious Marxist interpretation privileges the explanation of class struggle between rich and poor over the influence of Islamic ideas or even diachronic factors within Judaism (Mahler 1949). It nonetheless helped stimulate another, more sophisticated social-historical study of early Karaism and its spread to Byzantium (Ankori 1959). Seeking diachronic influences on the rise of Karaism, some scholars have pointed to the anti-rabbinism of the Graeco-Roman period, particularly the Sadducees, and postulated that an ancient, 'underground' opposition to the Oral Law resurfaced in the early Islamic period (Geiger 1911: 260 ff.). Other approaches favouring diachronic explanations contend that remnants of the ancient Dead Sea sectarians in the early

Islamic period formed one of the dissident elements influencing early Karaism (Wieder 1962; Erder 1994); or, contrarily, that the Karaites were strongly influenced in their law by the halachah of Philo, who lived in first-century Alexandria (Revel 1911–13). Trying to nail down the connection between the Karaites and ancient sectarianism, it has also been proposed that nascent Jewish sectarian groups of the early Islamic period simply discovered ancient texts like those found among the Dead Sea scrolls (themselves permeated with trends paralleling Iranian Zoroastrian doctrines), and co-ordinated their religious beliefs, and political opposition to the Geonim, with these literary forerunners (Ankori: 20–1). Whatever the case, in the tenth century Karaism reached a 'Golden Age' of Hebrew language study and attendant Bible commentaries, of legal treatises, of anti-rabbinic polemic, and other genres of literary creativity, which owed much to the culture of Arabic and Islam in which Jews were so deeply embedded (Nemoy 1952). With the new access to the horde of Karaite manuscripts in the St Petersburg Firkovitch collection, and especially their rehabilitation as authentic, scholarship stands poised at the beginning of a significant re-evaluation of Karaite intellectual history.

Jewish law, the domain of the rabbis, was itself not immune to synchronic influences. Politics in the Islamic world set the stage. The rapid unification of the former Byzantine and Persian empires under Islamic rule, and the centralization of the Islamic empire in Iraq in the mid-eighth century, afforded the opportunity for the Babylonian Geonim and their yeshivot to assert the pre-eminence of their Talmud over the rival one compiled in Palestine (Brody 1998). In fact, so successful were the Babylonians in overshadowing their Palestinian rivals that the Palestinian yeshiva only came into the full light of history, along with rich detail about Jewish life in Islamic Palestine, as a result of twentieth-century discoveries in the Cairo Genizah (Mann 1920–22; Gil 1983, 1992).

In achieving Babylonian supremacy, the scholars of the yeshivot of Islamic Iraq emulated Muslim legal scholars, especially as the most important Islamic legal activity took place in that very region. It began with responsa (*teshuvot*), answers by rabbinic masters to questions, usually on Jewish law, but sometimes concerning linguistic difficulties in the Bible. The phenomenon of responsa, like the *ius respondendi* in Roman law, seems to have existed in Talmudic times, but it blossomed under Islam and helped the Babylonian Geonim to extend their sway across the Islamic world as far as Muslim Spain. The *fatwā* parallel (the word means 'responsum')—whereby Islamic legal scholars answered questions about Islamic holy law—may actually have been influenced by the Jewish example. Both the *fatwā* and the Jewish *teshuvah* continue until this very day, serving as a reminder of the Jewish–Islamic symbiosis of former times.

Other forms of Jewish legal creativity that flourished in the world of Islam similarly recall the mutuality of the two religions. For instance, in the early centuries of Islam, as Islamic legal material accumulated, lawyers seeking to bring this material under control embarked upon a process of winnowing and codification.

The winnowing was achieved by the 'traditionalists' and the codification by the *fuqahā*. The traditionalists assembled *ḥadīths*, both according to chains of trans-mission, which had to be 'checked' for accuracy, as well as by subject. Codes of special subjects were compiled for judges.

Islamic codification inspired the Geonim to recodify Jewish law (the last code, the Mishnah, had been completed around the year 200 CE) (Baron 1952–83: vi. 75–107). Especially after they began to be compiled in Arabic, the very structure and language of these codes followed Islamic models. Many of the subject headings of Islamic law were assimilated, while the system of organization (employing taxonomies based on Graeco-Arabic logic) was itself Islamic. What is most astonishing is that even some of the particularities of Islamic law seem to have found their way into Geonic codes (Libson 1991). The 'summa' of Jewish codes compiled in the medieval Islamic world, Maimonides' *Mishneh Torah*, though composed in Hebrew, appears to contain some echoes of Islamic jurisprudence as well (Libson 1990), while its rational organization and occasional philosophic digressions certainly betray the influence of the Arabic environment (Twersky 1980).

The most well-known example of Jewish cultural embeddedness under medieval Islam is Hebrew poetry, whose conscious debt to Arabic and Arabic prosody was fully recognized by the poets themselves (Scheindlin 1986, 1991). The older Hebrew poetry, originating in late antiquity in Palestine, was composed in a form of rabbinic Hebrew having many (often purposeful) difficult linguistic features. Entirely reli-gious and meant for use in the synagogue, it was heavily infused with allusions to talmudic and midrashic themes, including mystical concepts current during the talmudic age. This genre, called *piyyuṭ*, was later conveyed to Italy and thence to northern Europe, and formed the basis of medieval Ashkenazic poetry (Spiegel 1960).

In the Arab world, Jews developed a radically new form of verse, modelled on Arabic. This began in Islamic Iraq and from there spread as far as Muslim Spain, where it reached its zenith. This poetry had rhyme (the older *piyyuṭ* used rhyme syllables, so this was not completely new), as well as metre. The metre was quantita-tive, based on the length of syllables. Jews mimicked Arabic metrics, devising a somewhat artificial method to make Hebrew conform to Arabic scansion. Rather than the rabbinic Hebrew of the older liturgical poetry, Hebrew poets of the Arab world wrote exclusively in biblical Hebrew, following the Arabic model of using the language of the Qur'an. This also allowed poets to artfully exploit biblical allusions. Special types of Arabic poems, like the *qaṣīda* (ode), were given Hebrew counter-parts. Perhaps most revealing of Jewish acculturation, entirely secular themes, such as love, wine, women, young men, nature, even war, found a new home in Hebrew poetic garb. The poets did not abandon religious poetry for the synagogue, though they used biblical Hebrew even here, and incorporated many philosophical and ascetic notions adopted from Islamic philosophy and mysticism (Menocal, Schein-dlin, and Sells 2000).

Hebrew poetry composed in the medieval Islamic world represents a cultural embeddedness that even the revisionist historiography does not deny. Dispute centres, rather, around the *degree* to which the poets identified with their Arab environment. Some scholars believe that the poets, who were often also rationalistic philosophers, were thoroughly 'Arabized', even secret sceptics about the superiority of Judaism. But many of the poets discussed their literary product self-consciously, and even expressed compunctions about the Arabized enterprise (Brann 1991). Another view portrays the authors of secular poetry as living a 'Judeo-Arabic duality', blending as much as possible rabbinic Judaism with Arabic-Islamic culture (Scheindlin 1991: 3–12). A compromise position takes them as unconflicted, enjoying Arabic 'secular' styles in their leisure moments, without being plagued by feelings of disharmony with their Judaism (G. D. Cohen 1967: 286).

INTERRELIGIOUS POLEMICS

The issue of Jewish cultural embeddedness in the Islamic world has given rise to some argumentative discussion of the question of Muslim–Jewish interreligious polemics.[2] Compared to the scope and quantity of Christian–Jewish disputation (public and private) in the Middle Ages, Islam and Judaism seem on the face of things to have adopted a relatively aloof posture toward one another. To be sure, the Qur'an, its commentaries, as well as the *ḥadīth* literature, contain numerous hostile utterances about the Jews (also about the Christians). And formal polemical treatises (some, however, directed at *dhimmīs* as a group) are not wanting. Revisionists of the myth of the interfaith utopia would like to see anti-Jewish utterances in early Islamic literature as formative features of an abiding Islamic anti-Judaism (Ben-Shammai 1988), and Jewish relative silence in response as a sign of fear. This relatively new emphasis on early Islamic hostility toward the Jews appears to stem from an attempt to find deep genetic and endemic roots in classical Islam for modern Arab anti-Semitism. A recent study of Qur'anic ethics by a Muslim scholar seeks to demonstrate, to Muslims who think otherwise, too, that the foundation text of Islam contains the seeds of tolerance and pluralism, and this includes its teachings about Jews and Christians (Sachedina 2001). Most scholars concede, in fact, that Arab anti-Semitism in the modern world arose relatively recently, in the nineteenth century, against the backdrop of conflicting Jewish and Arab nationalisms, and was imported into the Arab world primarily by nationalistically minded

---

[2] For a select bibliography on the subject and related issues see Perlmann (1996) and also the articles published in the same volume, ed. Hava Lazarus-Yafeh (1996).

Christian Arabs (and only subsequently was it 'Islamized') (Ma'oz 1976: 5–23; Stillman 1975: 198).

The revisionist approach to medieval Islamic–Jewish polemics, while understandable given the conflict raging between Judaism and Islam today, entails some distortion of the past. Classical Islamic hostility toward Judaism, even with its occasional loud outbursts of Jew-hatred and anti-Jewish violence, is fundamentally different from the implicit model: medieval Christian anti-Semitism. In Christianity, the Jewish Bible, the 'Old Testament' (in Christian parlance), constitutes an essential part of Christian faith. Christologically understood, it prefigures the coming of Jesus and other Christian beliefs. The argument between Jews and Christians began with the Bible and continued to foster heated Christian opposition to Judaism (and vigorous Jewish response) throughout the Middle Ages.

For Islam, by way of contrast, the text of the Jewish Bible (likewise, the Christian Gospels) is taken to be a corruption of divine revelation, which the Qur'an restored to its pristine form. Islam does not depend upon the Hebrew Bible to attest to its own truth. Some of the basic beliefs and practices of Judaism evoke less hostile responses in Muslims than in Christians. Christianity, for instance, has never been able to sit by calmly with the fact that Jews rejected Jesus, let alone with the fact that Jews maintain stubbornly that the Messiah is yet to come. Islam—at least orthodox (Sunni) Islam—is less hostile toward Judaism than is Christianity, in part because it is less messianic than the latter. Jewish monotheism, furthermore, is less repugnant to Islam than the Christian form, with its 'idolatrous' (in Muslim eyes) Trinity. Some Jewish practices are certainly deficient in Muslim eyes, though many of them were originally imitated, then rejected, by Muhammad. Others, like the dietary laws and the idea of a halachah, took hold.

As mentioned above, Christianity 'tolerated' Judaism in the Middle Ages thanks largely to the so-called 'doctrine of witness' of St Augustine. According to this, Christians need the Jews—in a petrified form, as they know them from the Bible—to 'testify' to their own triumph, to preserve the authentic text of the Old Testament, and, at their conversion at the time of the Second Coming, to testify finally to the truth of Christianity. When, in the twelfth and thirteenth centuries, Christians 'discovered' the Talmud for the first time, they (or some of them) realized that contemporaneous Jews were very different from the Jews of St Augustine's time. They were under the sway of rabbis, who, they opined, hid the truth of Christ from them with their midrashim on holy writ. Christians began to question whether the Jews still merited the protection guaranteed by the witness doctrine (J. Cohen 1982, 1999). This coincided with the period of intensified anti-Semitism, forced conversions, persecutions, and, ultimately, expulsion of the Jews from most of Latin Europe.

Islam, by way of contrast, needs no doctrine of witness for its own self-identity. Further, it cares little about the fact that Jews live by the Talmud and the rule of rabbis. After all, Islam too has a 'holy law', the *sharī'a*, which means the same and has the same function as Jewish halachah, as well as *'ulamā'*, similar to the rabbis, who interpret and adjudicate that law. Jews are 'tolerated' in the midst of Islam because they once received a divine book, and their physical and religious security is assured for that and for practical reasons: their annual poll-tax payment. Only when they violated their assent to the code of restrictions codifying their religious inferiority, especially by rising to high positions in government and evading the policy of humiliation (even if with the tacit approval of Muslim rulers), could they—legally—be made to suffer oppression and even persecution.

The Community

Jewish sources, especially those originating in the Genizah, depict the autonomous Jewish community under medieval Islam in finer detail than any other Jewish community in pre-modern times. Research on this aspect of Jewish life still continues, but much has already been learned and, not surprisingly, older conceptions have come in for revision. The debate revolves around whether external, synchronic (mainly Islamic) or internal, diachronic (mainly Jewish) forces prevailed in determining the character of Jewish self-government (Cohen 1997).

Prior to the systematic and comprehensive study of the historical documents of the Genizah by Goitein, scholars depicted the Jewish community of the Islamic world in terms of centralization and autocracy. This conformed with the contours of Muslim government, in which the central caliphate controlled the periphery from Baghdad and prevented local, urban autonomy from emerging. Favouring synchronic influences, a parallel was drawn with the Jewish exilarchate and the two yeshivot of Sura and Pumbedita in Babylonia, which, beginning with the Abbasid period, held sway over Jewish communities throughout the Islamic world and seemingly prevented local Jewish communities from exercising self-rule.

Early Genizah studies began to uncover local Jewish communal leaders in Egypt and Palestine with obscure titles and unclear functions. Nonetheless, the first book-length study of the Genizah documents, by Jacob Mann (1920–22), maintained the dominance of the central authority of the yeshivot of Babylonia. Furthermore, giving weight to external forces, Mann also concluded that Egyptian Jewry developed its own, independent central authority in the person of the Nagid, who was appointed by the Fatimid caliph to counter the influence of the Babylonian exilarch, an appointee of his Abbasid rival in Baghdad.

A powerful and influential statement of the theory of Babylonian centralization found expression in an article published in Hebrew by the Israeli historian Yitzhak

Baer (1950). Baer argued, diachronically, that the centralistic regime of the Jewish community of the Geonic period continued and consolidated the hierocratic organization of the Nesi'ut in pre-Islamic Palestine. An autonomous, 'democratic', local Jewish community, reviving the stifled, local Jewish community of Palestine during the Second Commonwealth, (re)emerged into the full light of day only in northern Europe, where mutual influences of Jewish community and budding Christian commune interacted between the tenth and twelfth centuries. Flickers of localism cropped up here and there in the Islamic world, such as in the distant Jewish commercial centre of Islamic Qayrawan, as early as the late ninth century, or among the Karaites. But local autonomy was essentially a *European*, not a Middle Eastern Jewish phenomenon, Baer insisted. Signs of territorial Jewish autonomy appeared in Muslim Spain, associated with the title of Nagid, but the structure of the fundamental unit of Jewish communal life, the local community, was still enveloped in Baer's time in a fog of undefined titles of functionaries in the Genizah, whose role in society were far from understood.

It remained for Goitein to unravel the mysteries of the Genizah and propose a revision of the dominant thesis, as regards Egypt in the first instance, but also other parts of the Islamic world (his various studies were brought together and expanded in Goitein 1967–93: ii). Arguing diachronically, he claimed that, at the time of the Arab conquest, the Palestinian yeshivah continued its role of leadership in lands of the late antique Byzantine empire. Later, in the tenth century, the yeshivah attained the recognition of the Fatimid caliphate of Egypt (969–1171) as central authority over the Jews—in spite of the greater learning of the Babylonian academies. Palestinian authority was eclipsed in the latter third of the eleventh century as a result of both internal and external factors. The Nagidate, in Arabic called the 'headship of the Jews', assumed the yeshivah's authority at that time. In one sense, these clarifications reinforced the theory of centralization, though Goitein drew an important distinction between 'ecumenical' institutions, his adjective (borrowed from Christian Church organization) for the yeshivot and the exilarchate, and their 'territorial' counterparts, the Nagidates of Egypt, Spain, Qayrawan, and the Yemen.

More dramatic was Goitein's uncovering, based on a clearer understanding of the titles and functions appearing in the Genizah documents, of an organized local Jewish community in Egypt and elsewhere around the Mediterranean, coexisting with the centralistic or 'ecumenical' institutions of Babylonia and Palestine. His argument underwent challenge by Eliyahu Ashtor (1965), who, inclined to favour synchronic, that is, external forces, in Jewish history, maintained that the Jewish community was essentially autocratic, like Muslim government. The present writer's more recent study (Cohen 1980) reinforces Goitein's thesis about the origins of the office of head of the Jews from new perspectives, arguing for the interaction of both external and internal forces in this political development. In a sophisticated elaboration of Baer's tentative suggestion about Qayrawan, Menahem Ben-Sasson

(1996) claims to have found the origins of the medieval, local Jewish community in that North African city, two centuries earlier than the period unveiled by the documents of the Genizah. However, there is no reason to believe that local communal life did not exist in Egypt earlier than the eleventh century just because Genizah documents from that period have hardly survived. Elinoar Bareket's (1999) work on Jewish leadership in Egypt in the first half of the eleventh century refines and deepens Goitein's work, though her challenge (1998 and 2000; also 1999), following the lead of Shulamit Sela (1994 and 1998), to the Goitein–Cohen thesis about the origins of the headship of the Jews has not found acceptance among other scholars of the period.

More work on the Jewish community in the world of Islam will have to be undertaken to answer the question, prominent in the debate so far, whether in organization and function the community owed more to diachronic forces, reaching back into Jewish late antiquity, or to synchronic influences, product of the surrounding Islamic environment. The answer may be difficult to reach, since few relevant Jewish sources exist between the codification of the Baylonian Talmud (fifth century) and the Islamic era, especially the 'classical Genizah period' of the eleventh–thirteenth centuries. Nonetheless, in some ways the informalism of Jewish communal organization in the Genizah period, less corporate from a legal standpoint than the Jewish community of Christian Europe (where the Christian commune seems to have had some influence on Jewish communal life), seems in many ways similar to the less corporate and more informal organization of the Muslim town in which the Jewish community was situated.

THE FUTURE

Future research on medieval Jewry in the world of Islam will do well to keep its sights on the interaction of synchronic and diachronic forces in all areas of investigation. It should also abandon the abuses of history for contemporary political purposes embodied in the 'myth of the interfaith utopia' and the 'counter-myth of Islamic persecution'. Like any other period of diaspora Jewish history, even more so given the extent of Jewish embeddedness in the society and culture of Islam, study of Jewish life under medieval Islam should be based on a profound knowledge of the Arabic-Islamic context. This should hopefully lead to more integration of Jewish and general Islamic history, done well so far by some scholars, the most recent being the team of literary experts who contributed chapters to the meritorious *Literature of al-Andalus*, part of the Cambridge History of Arabic Literature. By devoting more time and energy to the Cairo Genizah and to Judaeo-Arabic, students of Islamic social and economic history and of the history of the Arabic language will enrich their own work, while at the same time illustrating further how much Jews were embedded in the civilization of medieval Islam.

Mining nuggets of knowledge from the Genizah documents requires the training of talented research students to carry on the work of Goitein and his students and followers. Computerization will facilitate research on the Genizah historical documents. One undertaking, the Princeton Geniza Project (1986–), is creating a full-text, searchable database of transcriptions of historical documents from the Genizah, hopefully to be linked some day with digitized images of the actual manuscripts housed in libraries around the world. Other projects, including systematic cataloguing of the Genizah collections of various libraries as well as a 'union catalogue' of the entire Genizah, will further the aims of this field.[3] Finally, it is to be hoped that more attention in the universities (I include denominational Jewish institutions and also universities in Israel) will be paid to the era surveyed here, the Arab period of medieval Jewish history, the fountainhead of the more popular field of 'Sephardic studies', which emphasizes the Ottoman period in the East as well as Jewish life in Christian Spain and the diffusion of Sefardim throughout the Mediterranean and northern Europe in the wake of the expulsion of the Jews from Catholic Spain in 1492.

SUGGESTED READING

The following suggestions are given for the benefit of newcomers to the subject. Bernard Lewis (1984) offers an excellent introduction to the subject of Jewry under Islam, carrying the story down to early modern times. Norman Stillman (1979) has both a useful introductory essay on the Middle Ages and a selection of primary sources in translation. Mark Cohen (1994) presents a comparative study of Muslim–Jewish and Christian–Jewish relations in the Middle Ages. The one-volume abridgment (Goitein-Lassner 1999) summarizes two of the five volumes of the original, five-volume masterpiece, and can be read as an entrée into this work, but there is no substitute for the real thing (Goitein 1967–93). For the Jews of Palestine, a history almost exclusively reconstructed from Genizah documents, see the narrative, historical volume of the monumental three-volume work by Moshe Gil (1983). The second and third volumes contain over 600 edited Genizah documents; the narrative introductory volume is available in English (Gil 1992). On the Jews of Babylonia and particularly the role of the rabbinic elite in the creation of medieval Jewish culture, Brody (1998) is recommended. Gil's mammoth four-volume opus on the Jews of Babylonia (Gil 1997), containing over 800 edited documents (including a large corpus of merchants' letters), will serve the purposes of the Hebrew reader alone, until an English version of this too appears. Gerber

---

[3] A union catalogue is being prepared by the Friedberg Genizah Project .

(1992) provides a handy overview of the Jews in Muslim and later Christian Spain. Cohen (1980) is a case-study of the most important institution of leadership in the Jewish community of Egypt, while Ben-Sasson (1996) encompasses the history of a key community in North Africa from its beginnings to its end in the middle of the eleventh century. The essays in Menocal, Scheindlin, and Sells (2000) portray Jewish belles-lettres, properly, as a subset of Andalusi Arab literature. Scheindlin (1986 and 1991) offer representative examples of Hebrew secular and relgious poetry from Spain, in translation. Finally, reading selectively in the relevant volumes of Baron (1952–83) can serve the beginner well if one knows that the discussions of medieval Jewry in the world of Islam before 1200 are spread among volumes 3, 4, 5, 6, 7, 8, and that the era 1200–1650 is covered in volumes 17 and 18 (the last deals with the Ottoman period). It is also important to be aware that the section on 'economic transformations' in volume 4 was written before the major publications about the Genizah by Goitein and his students and followers, and that many advances in knowledge about Jewish culture in the Arab world have been made since Baron's summaries in volumes 5–8. The annotated bibliography (Cohen 1995) contains a guide to additional readings on the entire subject of medieval Jewry in the world of Islam.

BIBLIOGRAPHY

AHMAD, B. 1979. *Muhammad and the Jews: A Re-examination.* New Delhi.

ANKORI, Z. 1959. *Karaites in Byzantium: The Formative Years, 970–1100.* New York.

ARAFAT, W. N. 1976. 'New Light on the Story of Banu Qurayza and the Jews of Medina.' *Journal of the Royal Asiatic Society of Great Britain and Ireland.* 100–7.

ASHTOR, E. 1965. 'Some Features of the Jewish Communities in Medieval Egypt.' [Hebrew]. *Zion* 30: 61–78, 128–57.

—— 1973–84. *The Jews of Moslem Spain.* Trans. Aaron Klein and Jenny Machlowitz Klein. 3 vols. Philadelphia. The Hebrew original appeared in 1960–6.

BAER, Y. 1950. 'The Origins and the Organization of the Jewish Community in the Middle Ages.' [Hebrew]. *Zion* 15: 1–41.

BAREKET, E. 1998. '*Rais al-Yahud* in Egypt under the Fatimids: A Reconstruction' [Hebrew]. *Zmanim* 64: 34–43.

—— 1999. *Fustat on the Nile: The Jewish Elite in Medieval Egypt.* Leiden. The Hebrew original appeared in Jerusalem in 1995.

—— 2000. '*Rais al-Yahud* in Islamic Countries: A Double Reflection.' [Hebrew]. *Dvarim* 3: 35–48.

BARON, S. W. 1928. 'Ghetto and Emancipation: Shall We Revise the Traditional View?' *Menorah Journal* 14: 515–26. Repr. in *The Menorah Treasury.* 50–63. Leo W. Schwarz ed. Philadelphia. 1964.

—— 1952–83. *A Social and Religious History of the Jews.* 2nd edn. 18 vols. New York and Philadelphia.

BAT YE'OR. 1985. *The Dhimmi: Jews and Christians under Islam.* Rutherford, NJ. The French original appeared in 1980.

BELL, R. 1926. *The Origin of Islam in its Christian Environment.* London.

BEN-SASSON, M. 1996. *Ṣemiḥat ha-qehillah ha-yehudit be-arṣot ha-Islam (The Emergence of the Local Jewish Community in the Muslim World: Qayrawan, 800–1057).* Jerusalem.

BEN-SHAMMAI, H. 1988. 'Jew-Hatred in the Islamic Tradition and the Koranic Exegesis.' In *Antisemitism through the Ages.* 161–9. Shmuel Almog ed. and Nathan H. Reisner trans. Oxford. The Hebrew original appeared in Jerusalem, 1980.

—— 1992. 'The Karaite Controversy: Scripture and Tradition in Early Karaism.' In *Religionsgespräche im Mittelalter.* 11–26. Bernard Lewis and Friedrich Niewöhner eds. Wiesbaden.

BLAU, J. 1992. 'On a Fragment of the Oldest Judaeo-Arabic Bible Translation Extant.' In *Genizah Research after Ninety Years: The Case of Judaeo-Arabic.* 31–9. Joshua Blau and Stefan C. Reif eds. Cambridge.

—— 1999. *The Emergence and Linguistic Background of Judaeo-Arabic: A Study of the Origins of Neo-Arabic and Middle Arabic.* 3rd edn. Jerusalem.

BLUMENKRANZ, B. 1960. *Juifs et chrétiens dans le monde occidental, 430–1096.* Paris.

BRANN, R. 1991. *Compunctious Poet: Cultural Ambiguity and Hebrew Poetry in Muslim Spain.* Baltimore.

BRODY, R. 1998. *The Geonim of Babylonia and the Shaping of Medieval Jewish Culture.* New Haven.

COHEN, G. D. ed. and trans. 1967. *Sefer ha-Qabbalah,* by Abraham ibn Daud. Philadelphia.

COHEN, J. 1982. *The Friars and the Jews: A Study of the Development of Medieval Anti-Judaism.* Ithaca, NY.

—— 1999. *Living Letters of the Law: Ideas of the Jew in Medieval Christianity.* Berkeley, Los Angeles, and London.

COHEN, M. R. 1994. *Under Crescent and Cross: The Jews in the Middle Ages.* Princeton.

—— 1995. 'The Jews under Islam from the Rise of Islam to Sabbatai Zevi: A Bibliographical Essay.' In *Sephardic Studies in the University.* 43–119. Jane S. Gerber ed. Madison, NJ.

—— 1997. 'Jewish Communal Organization in Medieval Egypt: Research, Results and Prospects.' In *Studies in Muslim–Jewish Relations: Judaeo-Arabic Studies.* 73–86. Norman Golb ed. Amsterdam.

—— 1999. 'What was the Pact of 'Umar: A Literary-Historical Study.' *Jerusalem Studies in Arabic and Islam* 23: 100–57.

—— forthcoming. 'Jewish and Islamic Life in the Middle Ages: Through the Window of the Cairo Geniza.' In a volume of essays on Jewish–Muslim creative coexistence in the Middle Ages. Ed. Joseph Montville.

—— and SOMEKH, SASSON 1989–90. 'In the Court of Ya'qub ibn Killis: A Fragment from the Cairo Genizah.' *JQR,* 80: 293–314.

—— and STILLMAN, Y. K. 1985. 'The Cairo Geniza and the Custom of Geniza among Oriental Jewry: An Historical and Ethnographic Study.' [Hebrew]. *Pe'amim* 24: 3–35.

CONSTABLE, O. R. 1994. *Trade and Traders in Muslim Spain: The Commercial Realignment of the Iberian Peninsula.* Cambridge.

COOK, M. 1987. ''Anan and Islam: The Origins of Karaite Scripturalism.' *Jerusalem Studies in Arabic and Islam* 9: 161–82.

DOTAN, A. 1967. *Diqduqei ha-te'amim of Aharon b. Moshe ben Asher.* Jerusalem.

—— 1977. *Ben Asher's Creed A Study of the History of the Controversy.* Missoula, Mont.

—— 1997. *Or rishon be-hokhmat ha-lashon (The Dawn of Linguistics: The Book of Elegance of the Language of the Hebrews by Saadia Gaon.)* 2 vols. Jerusalem.

DRORY, R. 1988. *Reshit ha-magga'im shel ha-sifrut ha-yehudit 'im ha-sifrut ha-'aravit ba-me'ah ha-'asirit (The Emergence of Jewish–Arabic Literary Contacts at the Beginning of the Tenth Century).* Tel Aviv.

DRORY, R. 2000. *Models and Contacts: Arabic Literature and its Impact on Medieval Jewish Culture*. London.

ERDER, Y. 1994. 'The Karaites' Sadducee Complex.' *Israel Oriental Studies* 14: 195–226.

FATTAL, A. 1958. *Le Statut légal de non-Musulmans en pays d'Islam*. Beirut.

FISCHEL, W. J. 1937. *The Jews in the Economic and Political Life of Medieval Islam*. London. Repr. New York 1969.

FRIEDLANDER, I. 1910–13. 'Jewish-Arabic Studies.' *JQR* 1: 183–215; 2: 481–516; 3: 235–300.

GEIGER, A. 1898. *Judaism and Islam*. Madras. English trans. of *Was hat Muhammad aus den Judenthume ausgenommen*. 1833.

—— 1911. *Judaism and its History*. Trans. Charles Newburgh. New York. The German original appeared in 1864–71.

GERBER, J. S. 1992. *The Jews of Spain : A History of the Sephardic Experience*. New York.

GIL, M. 1974. 'The Constitution of Medina: A Reconsideration.' *Israel Oriental Studies* 4: 44–66.

—— 1983. *Ereṣ yisrael ba-tequfah ha-muslimit ha-rishonah (Palestine During the First Muslim Period (634–1099))*. 3 vols. Tel Aviv.

—— 1992. *A History of Palestine, 634–1099*. 1983. Trans. Ethel Broido. Cambridge and New York. Trans. of vol. 1 of Gil 1983 .

—— 1997. *Be-malkhut yishmael bi-tequfat ha-geʾonim. (In the Kingdom of Ishmael)*. [Tel Aviv] and Jerusalem.

GOITEIN, S. D. 1955. *Jews and Arabs: Their Contacts through the Ages*. New York.

—— 1957. 'The Rise of the Near Eastern Bourgeoisie in Early Islamic Times'. *Journal of World History* 3: 583–604; repr. in Goitein's *Studies in Islamic History and Institutions*. Leiden 1966: 217–41.

—— 1967–93. *A Mediterranean Society: The Jewish Communities of the Arab World as Portrayed in the Documents of the Cairo Geniza*. 5 vols. plus index volume prepared by Paula Sanders. Berkeley, Los Angeles and London.

—— 1973. *Letters of Medieval Jewish Traders, Translated From the Arabic*. Princeton.

—— and LASSNER, J. 1999. *A Mediterranean Society: An Abridgment in One Volume*. Berkeley, Los Angeles, and London.

GROSSMAN, A. 1988. 'The Economic and Social Background of Hostile Attitudes toward the Jews in the Ninth and Tenth Century Muslim Caliphate.' In *Antisemitism Through the Ages*. Shmuel Almog ed. and Nathan H. Reisner transl. Oxford and New York. 171–87. The Hebrew original appeared in Jerusalem in 1980.

EL-HAWARY, M. 1994. *Mufradāt ṭibiyya min al-geniza al-qāhiriyya (Medical Vocabulary from the Cairo Genizah)*. Cairo.

HAYKEL, B. 1994. forthcoming. 'Monopolizing a Precious Commodity Through Humiliation: Muslim Debates About Expulsion, Sanitation and Jews in 18th Century Yemen.' Unpublished paper, forthcoming as an article or part of a book.

KALLFELZ, W. 1995. *Nichtmuslimische Untertanen im Islam: Grundlage, Ideologie und Praxis der Politik frühislamischer Herrscher gegenüber ihren nichtmuslimischen Untertanen mit besonderem Blick auf die Dynastie der Abbasiden, 749–1248*. Wiesbaden.

KATSH, A. 1954. *Judaism in Islam: Biblical and Talmudic Backgrounds of the Koran and its Commentaries: Sura II and III*. New York.

KHALILIEH, H. S. 1998. *Islamic Maritime Law: An Introduction*. Leiden.

KHAN, G. 1993 *Arabic Legal and Administrative Documents in the Cambridge Genizah Collections*. Cambridge.

KISTER, M. J. 1986. 'The Massacre of the Banū Qurayẓa: A Re-examination of the Evidence.' *Jeruslem Studies in Arabic and Islam* 8: 61–96.

KRAEMER, J. L. 1986. *Humanism in the Renaissance of Islam: The Cultural Revival During the Buyid Age.* Leiden.

KRAMER, M. ed. 1999. *The Jewish Discovery of Islam: Studies in Honor of Bernard Lewis.* Tel Aviv.

LAMBERT, P. ed. 1994. *Fortifications and the Synagogue: The Fortress of Babylon and the Ben Ezra Synagogue in Cairo.* London.

LAZARUS-YAFEH, H. 1981. 'Judaism and Islam: Some Aspects of Mutual Cultural Influences.' In *Some Religious Aspects of Islam.* Leiden.

—— ed. 1996. *Sofrim muslemim ʿal yehudim ve-yahadut (Muslim Authors on Jews and Judaism: The Jews among their Muslim Neighbours).* Jerusalem.

LEWIS, B. 1968. 'The Pro-Islamic Jews.' *Judaism* 17: 391–404.

—— 1984. *The Jews of Islam.* Princeton.

LIBSON, G. 1990. 'Parallels between Maimonides and Islamic Law.' In *The Thought of Moses Maimonides: Philosophical and Legal Studies.* 209–48. Ira Robinson ed. Lewiston, Ky.

—— 1991. 'Islamic Influence on Medieval Jewish Law? Sefer Ha-ʿarevuth ("Book of Surety") of Rav Shmuel ben Hofni Gaon and Its Relationship to Islamic Law.' *Studia Islamica* 73: 5–23.

MAHLER, R. 1949. *Ha-Qaraʾim (Karaites: A Medieval Jewish Movement for Deliverance).* Trans. from the Yiddish by Ephraim Shemueli. Merhavya.

MANN, J. 1920–2. *The Jews in Egypt and in Palestine under the Fāṭimid Caliphs.* 2 vols. [London]. Repr. New York 1970.

MAʿOZ, M. 1976. *The Image of the Jew in Official Arab Literatrure and Communications Media.* Jerusalem.

MENOCAL, M. R., SCHEINDLIN, R. P., and SELLS, M. eds. 2000. *The Literature of Al-Andalus.* Cambridge and New York.

MEYERHOF, M. 1938. 'Medieval Jewish Physicians in the Near East, From Arabic Sources.' *Isis* 28: 432–60. Repr. in *Studies in Medieval Arabic Medicine,* ed. P. Johnstone. London 1984.

NEMOY, L. 1952. *A Karaite Anthology: Excerpts from the Early Literature.* New Haven.

NOTH, A. 1987. 'Abgrenzungsprobleme zwischen Muslimen und Nicht-Muslimen: Die "Bedingungen ʿUmars (aš-šurūṭ al-ʾumariyya)" unter einem anderen Aspekt gelesen.' *Jerusalem Studies in Arabic and Islam* 9: 290–315.

PERLMANN, M. 1942. 'Notes on Anti-Christian Propaganda in the Mamluk Empire.' *Bulletin of the School of Oriental and African Studies* 10: 843–61.

—— ed. and trans. 1975. *Shaykh Damanhuri on the Churches of Cairo (1739).* Berkeley and Los Angeles.

—— 1996. 'Selected Bibliography of Medieval Muslim-Jewish Polemics and Related Topics.' In *Sofrim muslemim ʿal yehudim ve-yahadut (Muslim Authors on Jews and Judaism: The Jews among their Muslim Neighbours).* 155–60. Hava Lazarus-Yafeh ed. Jerusalem.

PINSKER, S. 1860. *Lickute Kadmoniot: Zur Geschichte des Karaismus und der karäischen Literatur.* Vienna.

Princeton Geniza Project 1986– . URL: www.princeton.edu/~geniza.

RABIE, H. 1972. *The Financial System of Egypt, A. H. 564–741/A.D. 1169–1341.* London.

REIF, S. C. 1993. *Judaism and Hebrew Prayer: New Perspectives on Jewish Liturgical History.* Cambridge.

REIF, S. C. 2000. *A Jewish Archive from Old Cairo: The History of Cambridge University's Genizah Collection.* Raymond, Surrey.

REVEL, B. 1911–13. 'An Inquiry into the Sources of Karaite Halakah.' *JQR* 2: 517–54; 3: 337–96.

ROSENBLATT, S. trans. 1948. *The Book of Beliefs and Opinions,* by Saadya Gaon. New Haven.

RUBIN, U. 1985. 'The "Constitution of Medina": Some Notes.' *Studia Islamica* 62: 5–23.

SACHEDINA, A. 2001. *The Islamic Roots of Democratic Pluralism.* Oxford.

SADAN, J. 1986. 'Genizah and Genizah-Like Practices in Islamic and Jewish Traditions.' *Bibliotheca Orientalis* 43, no. 1/2: 36–58.

SAID, E. 1978. *Orientalism.* New York.

SCHEINDLIN, R. P. 1986. *Wine, Women and Death: Medieval Hebrew Poems on the Good Life.* Philadelphia.

——1991. *The Gazelle: Medieval Hebrew Poems on God, Israel, and the Soul.* Philadelphia.

SELA, S. 1994. 'The Head of the Rabbanite, Karaite and Samaritan Jews: On the History of a Title.' *Bulletin of the School of Oriental and African Studies* 57: 255–67.

——1998. 'The Headship of the Jews in the Fāṭimid Empire in Karaite Hands' [Hebrew]. In *Mas'at Moshe: Studies in Jewish and Islamic Culture Presented to Moshe Gil.* 256–81. Ezra Fleischer, Mordechai A. Friedman, and Joel A. Kraemer eds. Jerusalem and Tel Aviv.

SIRAT, C. 1985. *A History of Jewish Philosophy in the Middle Ages.* Cambridge and Paris.

SPIEGEL, S. 1960. 'On Medieval Hebrew Poetry.' In *The Jews: Their History, Culture, and Religion.* 3rd edn., i. 854–92. Louis Finkelstein ed. New York. Repr. in *The Jewish Expression.* 174–216. Judah Goldin ed. New York 1970.

STILLMAN, N. A. 1975. 'New Attitudes Toward the Jew in the Arab World.' *Jewish Social Studies* 37: 197–204.

——1979. *The Jews of Arab Lands: A History and Source Book.* Philadelphia.

TOCH, M. 2000. 'Jews and Commerce: Modern Fancies and Medieval Realities.' In *Il ruolo economico delle minoranze in Europa. Secc. XIII–XVIII (Atti della XXXI Settimana di Studi, Istituto Francesco Datini, Prato).* 43–58. Simonetta Cavaciocchi ed. Florence.

TRITTON, A. S. 1930. *The Caliphs and their Non-Muslim Subjects: A Critical Study of the Covenant of 'Umar.* London. Repr. [London] 1970.

TWERSKY, I. 1980. *Introduction to the Code of Maimonides (Mishneh Torah).* New Haven and London.

UDOVITCH, A. L. 1970. *Partnership and Profit in Medieval Islam.* Princeton.

VERSTEEGH, K. 1997. *The Arabic Language.* Edinburgh.

WARD, S. 1989. 'Taqī al-Dīn al-Subkī on Construction, Continuance, and Repair of Churches and Synagogues in Islamic Law.' In *Studies in Islamic and Judaic Traditions.* 169–88. William S. Brinner and Steven Ricks eds. Atlanta, Ga.

WASSERSTROM, S. M. 1995. *Between Muslim and Jew: The Problem of Symbiosis Under Early Islam.* Princeton.

WIEDER, N. 1962. *The Judean Scrolls and Karaism.* London.

CHAPTER 10

RABBINIC LITERATURE IN THE MIDDLE AGES: 1000–1492

ISRAEL TA-SHMA[1]

DESPITE its title, this essay does not deal with the full range of rabbinic literature, but is limited to what rabbis wrote in their capacities as rabbis and in the context of performing their rabbinic functions: in other words—halachic literature in all its aspects—talmudic commentary, books of legal decisions, responsa, halachic monographs, works on prayer and liturgy, the holidays, and customs. Maimonides, for example, arguably the greatest rabbi of all time, wrote the *Mishneh Torah*, the most famous code of Jewish law, as well as the equally renowned *Guide of the Perplexed*. The latter, however, deals with philosophy and therefore does not concern us here. Books of kabbalah and poetry, even if they were written by rabbis of the first rank, will not be dealt with here, although from time to time we will mention these areas as well as others, such as biblical exegesis, which also incorporate halachic material.

According to a fairly reliable estimate, the number of books written in the area of halachah exceeds the number of books written in all the other areas of Jewish studies

---

[1] Translated from the Hebrew by Barry D. Walfish.

combined. Based on the extant literature, this is undoubtedly the case. It is impossible to estimate their total number, but the number of volumes on library shelves today, which comes close to representing a complete collection of what exists, reaches several thousand. Among these are over a thousand volumes of commentaries on the Talmud, some of which were composed as series encompassing many tractates. Some of these series were written in several editions or went through several parallel recensions. A unique characteristic of this halachic literature, which sets it apart from other areas of creativity, is that a large part of it, perhaps even all of it, has not become outdated, so that it continues to serve the rabbinic scholars in yeshivot then as now with the same remarkable degree of vitality. The other areas of rabbinic creativity, as with other areas of medieval scholarship in general, serve only students and scholars of medieval culture, with some notable classic exceptions, such as the commentaries of Rashi and Nahmanides on the Torah, the *Kuzari* of Judah ha-Levi and some of his poems, and the Zohar. The comments of the Tosafists on the Talmud and the talmudic novellae of Nahmanides, his students, and the students of their students, are an essential component of the curriculum of yeshivot to this day, and the active discussion of their words occupies most of the students' time. This fact has important implications for the state of research, since many rabbinic institutions and yeshivot, in Israel and the diaspora, invest tremendous effort in organizing, classifying, locating, photographing, editing, and distributing the vast halachic literature which is found in manuscripts in libraries all over the world, for the benefit of their many students and the advancement of the level of rabbinic scholarship. This flurry of publication activity has made available to scholars a great deal of source material, contributed tremendously to the advancement of scientific research, and aroused interest in such research among the members of the yeshivah community. A similar process has not happened in any other area of rabbinic scholarship, except, to a much smaller extent, in the field of kabbalah. Worthy of special mention is Machon Yerushalayim, under the direction of Rabbi Yosef Buksboim, which has been active in Jerusalem for some thirty years, publishing from manuscript rabbinic works of unprecedented quality and quantity from all periods, in new, critical, corrected editions, with proper introductions. The work of this institution provides the necessary foundation for the building of a contemporary rabbinic research library. In the United States, similar work is being carried out by the younger Ofek Institute under the direction of Rabbi Avraham Shoshana, which publishes fewer volumes, but whose scientific standards are more rigorous. A unique scientific project dedicated entirely to the publication of sources from manuscript in all areas of Jewish creativity, including much medieval halachic material, is Mekize Nirdamim (founded 1864), the oldest scientific body of its kind, which has been steadily active from the time of its founding until today, publishing many important rabbinic texts. For a list of all its publications until the year 1964, see Mekize Nirdamim (1964).

This corpus of medieval rabbinic texts, which is today witnessing a renaissance, constitutes the basis of what is called *mishpat ʿivri* (Jewish law). This complex and glorious legal edifice, embedded in hundreds of volumes of responsa, concentrating especially on economics, trade, and society, was an important expression of the autonomy of the Jewish community in the Middle Ages and a demonstration of the intellectual prowess of its leaders. This autonomy enabled the Jewish community to exist apart from the surrounding hostile Gentile environment until the modern period, and the multi-faceted legal system which it established constitutes today the foundation for the demand, heard in many circles, for the renewal of the Jewish legal system in the re-established Jewish polity. This is further proof of the timeliness of this literature.

It is possible to describe this literature according to four different categories: geography, chronology, content, and literary genre. The following description will relate to content and literary genre, while taking note of geographical and chronological divisions. The books have reached us in the main from European countries—Germany, France, Spain, Italy, and Provence—but also from Morocco, Egypt, Syria, Iraq, and Yemen. Rabbinic literature began to be produced in all the European regions more or less at the same time—the beginning of the eleventh century. The books written in Christian Europe were all without exception written in Hebrew, while the rabbinic literature written in Islamic countries was written partly in Hebrew and partly in Judeo-Arabic (an Arabic dialect written in Hebrew script).

FRANCO-GERMANY

The lands of Germany (-Bohemia) and France will be dealt with here as a single geographic framework, while bearing in mind the fact that this integrated, unified conception is controversial. This region has been the subject of comprehensive, exacting, in-depth research in the second half of the twentieth century, based on the foundation laid by some of the important scholars of the first half of the century. B. M. Lewin was the first to discover in the Cairo Genizah the remains of the halachic literature of the early scholars of Palestine, and to point out the surprising connection between this literature and the beginnings of halachic literature in Ashkenaz. His work was continued by Mordecai Margulies, and especially by J. N. Epstein, whose dozens of pioneering studies of medieval rabbinic literature, characterized by familiarity with and control of the literature, along with a clear historical approach, complete faithfulness to the ancient texts, and absolute scholarly reliability, set a very high standard for future research. His essays have been recently gathered in a three-volume edition (Epstein 1984–91). Avigdor Aptowitzer, in his book *Introduction to the Book of Ravyah* (Aptowitzer 1938), collected, researched, and analysed for the first time a great deal of historical material which was scattered in many literary sources, in print and in manuscript, and thus was able to trace in broad outline the biographies of many rabbinic scholars from the eleventh to the thirteenth centuries. Based on this work, E. E. Urbach made a monumental pioneering effort to establish the Tosafist school in its historical context, concentrating on the biographies and activities of dozens of central Tosafist figures, their learning methods, student–teacher relations, and attitudes to their surroundings. He also explained the order of the editing of the various editions of the Tosafot to the entire Talmud, tractate by tractate. This monumental work appeared in two major editions (Urbach 1955, 1981), the second one fuller, with several new chapters. In addition, Urbach published an edition of *Arugat ha-bosem* (The Spice Garden) of the *piyyut* commentator Abraham ben Azriel of Bohemia, and in the full-volume introduction to the work he described at great length the history of *piyyut* exegesis in Ashkenaz, France, and Bohemia (the only locales that produced this type of literature, which occupied many of their scholars). This introductory volume (Urbach 1961) also made an important contribution to knowledge of the biographies and activities of rabbinic figures in Ashkenaz in the twelfth and thirteenth centuries.

In his book Urbach combined Germany and France as a single historical-cultural unit. This view is controversial and open to criticism from several aspects, as was well formulated by Yaacov Sussmann in his bio-bibliographical survey of the works and research methodology of Urbach (Sussmann 1998: 24–5). Despite the great affinity between the two cultures—especially in comparison with Jewish culture in the Spanish milieu—it is important to make certain clear distinctions between the two regions. It is not a coincidence that Tosafist literature is primarily a French phenomenon, while the Ashkenazic Pietist movement is almost completely absent from France. The resulting opposing influences on the 'unity' of this common movement, mainly with regard to questions concerning the proper attitude to tradition versus innovation, were stressed in the works of Ta-Shma and Grossman which will be cited below.

An important historical link in the history of rabbinic literature in this field—which separated it into its two regions—was forged by Avraham Grossman in his two books, *The Early Sages of Germany* (Grossman 1981) and *The Early Sages of France* (Grossman 1995). The book on Germany deals with the generation of the teachers of Rashi, that is, the end of the tenth century and the entire eleventh century, while the book on France continues the description into the twelfth century. These books drew upon vast amounts of material in print and manuscript, placing it all in a general historical context. In this research, Grossman availed himself of the material collected by Simcha Emanuel, who dedicated many years to the study of Hebrew manuscripts, as is mentioned in the introduction to his second book. Grossman's books, especially the one on Ashkenaz, did for the eleventh century what Urbach did for the twelfth and thirteenth centuries, and like the latter, Grossman excels in integrating a significant amount of original rabbinic material with material of purely historical interest.

A different aspect of rabbinic culture is examined in Ta-Shma (1992a), which provides a detailed analysis of the nature of custom in Ashkenaz as a unique religious and cultural phenomenon in the eleventh century, the connections between Ashkenazic custom and early Palestinian halachah, and the 'Babylonian' revolution that occurred there in the transition from a Palestinian orientation to a Babylonian one, which depends on the Babylonian tradition and the teachings of the Geonim. In the wake of this revolution, the early Palestinian halachah was elevated and became 'sanctified' custom, pushing aside normative halachah. Ashkenazic halachah held out as 'custom' for many generations, even against the simplicity of Babylonian *sugyot*, all the while making various efforts to harmonize them. Ta-Shma's *Ritual, Custom, and Reality in Franco-Germany, 1000–1350* (1996) describes the various historical conceptions which pervade the study of the 'development of the halachah' in the Middle Ages in general and in the twelfth century in particular, in the light of various studies in parallel fields, such as the twelfth-century renaissance and the penetration of Roman law into France and Provence in this period. Ta-Shma's third book (1999–2002), describes the exegetical activity of the scholars of Ashkenaz and France, from the teachers of Rashi until the end of the fourteenth century, while comparing their methods with the parallel learning experience that developed in France during the eleventh–fourteenth centuries in the seminaries attached to the monasteries and the universities which were being created at that time. In these books the difference between France and Germany in relation to every one of the topics in question is stressed, while emphasizing the French character of the Tosafist phenomenon which paralleled the development of the pre-university and university curricula, which were limited also to France at that time and were totally absent from the cultural scene in Germany.

The key figure in the distinction between the cultural areas of Germany and France is Rabbi Jacob Tam, who more than any other French scholar reflects in his personality and erudition the nature and scope of the Tosafist revolution that took place in France in the first part of the twelfth century. A comprehensive study of his life, creativity, students, and his circle is the primary desideratum in this area, and this is being supplied by Rami Reiner, first in his MA thesis at the Hebrew University and now in his doctorate. In his research, Mr Reiner is availing himself of the results of a comprehensive search in printed editions and many manuscripts for the responsa of Rabbeinu Tam (and incidentally of Rashbam and Rabbi Isaac the Elder and other contemporary Tosafists). This research, supported by the Fund for Basic Research of the Israel Academy of Sciences, has brought to light more than 200 responsa which had not been included in the *Sefer ha-Yashar* of Rabbeinu Tam, some of which were completely unknown until now. There is a plan to publish a critical edition of this rich and important material.

It should be pointed out that the early scholars of Ashkenaz, until Meir of Rothenburg in the second half of the thirteenth century, did not collect their responsa themselves, and so we do not possess any original collections of responsa for any of these early scholars; what we possess are later collections, some gathered by later medieval scholars, but most collected by scholars and savants of the nineteenth and twentieth centuries, who worked from what was known in their time. Today it is possible to improve most of the existing editions. A legal index of all the material in the printed editions of the responsa of the medieval scholars of Ashkenaz, France, and Italy has recently been published (Lifshitz and Shohetman 1997). Meir of Rothenburg was the first scholar of Ashkenaz to preserve his responsa, which numbered in the thousands. His students continued to gather this material, resulting in the creation of many early, partially overlapping collections. A complete concordance of his responsa—which are the key to knowing the rabbinic literature in Germany in the transitional generation from the Tosafists to the fourteenth century—has been compiled by Simcha Emanuel at the beginning of the above-mentioned index. In addition, Emanuel has published a series of articles devoted to the systematic classification of this variegated literature according to its various components. Another important contribution of Emanuel was his doctoral thesis on lost books from the time of the Tosafists (Emanuel 1993), in which he recorded all the extant testimonies concerning the existence of such books, in an attempt to identify them and identify their remains in manuscripts and various secondary quotations.

Important research has also been carried out on the German rabbinic literature of the fourteenth and fifteenth centuries, but this has been partial in scope and does not provide a complete picture. Israel Yuval, in his book *Sages in their Generations* (1988), described a long line of rabbinic figures of secondary personal and communal stature, thereby providing a description—not common in scholarly literature—of the rabbinic and social milieu which characterized Germany in the period of decline following the Black Plague. Yuval made use of civil records which were preserved in German city archives (from the fourteenth century on), comparing them with original rabbinic material preserved in Jewish sources. This resulted in interesting biographical portraits which, when combined, provide a fascinating general historical picture. It has long been accepted that in the fourteenth and fifteenth centuries the intellectual level of the rabbinic elite in Germany declined drastically, that scholarly creativity and the ability to wrestle with the demands of renewed life which was typical of the Tosafist period ceased, and that this period is characterized by submissive dedication to the chains of tradition. Y. Dinari attempted to demonstrate, in his book *The Scholars of Ashkenaz in the Late Middle Ages* (1984), that this position is exaggerated and that it is possible to detect an evolution of the halachah in these generations as well, though at a reduced rate.

SPAIN

Rabbinic literature in Spain is divided into two distinct periods: the Muslim period, with centres in Lucena and Cordoba, which ended in 1141; and the Christian period, with centres in Toledo, Gerona, and Barcelona. The Muslim period is subdivided, from a halachic perspective, into two sections: (1) until R. Samuel ha-Nagid, that is, until the beginning of the eleventh century; and (2) from this time until the destruction of the communities there and the closing of the main yeshivah in Lucena in 1141. The Christian period opens at the beginning of the thirteenth century with the halachic activity of R. Meir Abulafia. From 1140 to 1200 there is a lacuna in the area of rabbinic literature, which resulted from the destruction of the communities in the south and their migration northward in the period of the Reconquista.

The first part of the Muslim period is integrally connected with the activity of the Babylonian geonim, mainly through the mediation of the Torah-study centre in Kairouan, North Africa, and it is impossible to speak of independent, original rabbinic scholarship in Spain until the beginning of the eleventh century. The beginning of this independence dates to the settlement of two foreigners, apparently from southern Italy, Rabbi Moses and his son Rabbi Hanokh, who were active there at the turn of the eleventh century. The classic study of this subject is Gerson Cohen's annotated edition of the *Book of the Tradition* by Abraham Ibn Daud (Cohen 1967). The small amount of material which deals with the earlier period is to be found in the responsa of the geonim and their literature, and this was compiled and studied by scholars who dealt with the geonic period and its literature. The rabbinic material known at the time was utilized by Eliyahu Ashtor in the excellent notes to the first volume of his book, *The Jews of Moslem Spain* (Ashtor 1973–84). Ashtor was of the opinion that the local level of learning was very high at this early period. Ta-Shma (1974) critiques this opinion.

Beginning with R. Samuel ha-Nagid, the student of the above-mentioned R. Hanokh, the amount of original rabbinic material written in Spain and its yeshivot steadily increases. R. Samuel himself, already in his youth in 1015, twenty-five years before the death of R. Hai Gaon, when the latter was at the peak of his power and renown, took independent critical stances vis-à-vis geonic scholarship. The study of this period is still in its infancy; worthy of mention are the introduction of Mordecai Margulies to the book *Hilkhot ha-Nagid* (Margulies 1962) and the comprehensive seventy-five-page article by Sheraga Abramson about Samuel ha-Nagid and his place in the chain of halachic tradition in eleventh century Spain (Abramson 1987). In his article Abramson published new Genizah material, and he took issue with most of the assumptions and conclusions of Margulies

Concerning Isaac Ibn Ghiyyat and his commentary on the Talmud, see Ta-Shma (1982), which includes full bibliographic citations.

Isaac Alfasi, the linchpin of the Spanish halachic tradition in the eleventh century, lived most of his life in North Africa, but served as the head of the central yeshivah in Lucena, Spain, during his last twenty-five years. Despite all that has been written about him, including the excellent series of articles by Israel Francus which appeared in *Sinai* in recent years and especially the book of I. Schepansky, *Rabbeinu Efrayim, Student-Colleague of the Rif* (1976), we still lack the essential material for writing his biography and describing the many aspects of his halachic struggles with his colleagues. This material is buried in the pages of the Cairo Genizah and will certainly be uncovered in the future. The lack of a comprehensive work on Alfasi makes it impossible to attain a deep understanding of the trends in Spanish rabbinic literature in the second half of the eleventh century. David Sklare's recent article 'R. David b. Seʿadyah Alger and his work Al-Hawi' (1998) sheds much light on some important rabbinic scholars who were active in Spain in the second half of the eleventh century. Ta-Shma (1999–2002: pt. 1, chap. 5) discusses at length eleventh-century Spanish talmudic commentaries.

A great deal of information on Spanish halachic literature, most of which has been lost, can be garnered from ancient book-lists found in the Cairo Genizah. More than half of these lists have been published, mostly by Nehemia Allony, who has also produced an index of the contents of 100 such lists, which is to be published in the near future. Abramson went to great lengths to demonstrate that the Spanish sages, who were famous for their glorious poetry and their linguistic capabilities, and not necessarily as rabbinic scholars, were also well versed in Talmud and halachah. His many studies on this topic include his book, *From the Mouths of Linguists* (1988: 195–243), his edition of *Ben Mishlei* by Samuel ha-Nagid (1947), and his article 'The Words of the Sages in the Wisdom of the Nagid' (1952). Abramson has published more than any other modern scholar in the area of rabbinic and Hebrew literature in Muslim Spain. A full bibliography of his writings has been prepared by A. Choueka (Choueka 1997).

We turn now to Christian Spain. Yitzhak Baer's monumental study on the Jews in Christian Spain (Baer 1961) concentrated on the political, economic, and social aspects of the lives of Spanish Jewry. In doing so, he paid considerable attention to the areas of philosophy and kabbalah, because of the social impact of these intellectual trends, but he completely ignored rabbinic creativity and Torah study in the yeshivot. On this point, see Ta-Shma, 'Halachah, Kabbalah and Philosophy in Christian Spain' (1992–4). In actual fact, the rabbinic literature created in the yeshivot of Christian Spain constitutes one of the primary accomplishments of Spanish Jewry, in both quantity and quality. The work of Meir ha-Levi Abulafia, as well as his central position in the spiritual and social life of the Jewish community, were skillfully described by Bernard Septimus (1982). For his talmudic exegesis, see Ta-Shma (1999–2002).

Concerning Jonah Gerondi, the central rabbinic figure in Spain after Abulafia, see Ta-Shma (1988), and for his talmudic exegesis, Ta-Shma (1999b–2002). The latter also describes the exegetical work of Nahmanides, Rashba (Solomon ibn Adret), and their students, and includes all relevant bibliography. No adequate complete biography of Nahmanides exists, because of a lack of source material. The known material was collected by Charles B. Chavel in his book *Ramban* (Chavel 1960). There is more information on Rashba, which has been gathered in the introductions to his commentaries on the various talmudic tractates published by Mossad Harav Kook and Oraita. Rashba is the greatest and most comprehensive respondent in all of rabbinic literature, and his responsa number well over 3,000. Until now eight collections of his responsa have been published, some larger, some smaller, and there is much partial overlap between two or more of the collections. A significant number of responsa are still found only in manuscript form. A new ten-volume edition, including unpublished material from many manuscripts, was published in Jerusalem (1990) by Masozet Israel publishing house. Another rich collection has been published lately in Jerusalem by Machon Yerushalayim. Hayyim Zalman Dimitrovsky has been working for many years on a comprehensive edition of all the material, including all the necessary introductions and indexes, which should appear in the near future. In the meantime, an edition of the well-known collection of letters entitled *Minhat kena'ot* (Offering of Jealousy), which deals with the Maimonidean controversy, and a collection of letters by Rashba on biblical matters have appeared under Dimitrovsky's editorship (Dimitrovsky 1990). As for the Ritba (Yom-Tov ben Abraham ibn al-Ishbili), who also commented extensively on the Talmud, all of the relevant material has been collected and properly analysed in the introductions to the various editions of his commentaries on the Talmud published by Mossad Harav Kook. On the nature of his commentary, see also Ta-Shma (1999–2002).

A central problem in this area is the extent of the penetration of the Franco-German culture into Spain and the influence of this culture on the life-style and practices of Spanish Jewry from the thirteenth century on. The influence of the French Tosafists is recognizable, beginning with the exegetical activity of Nahmanides, and the Ashkenazic influence on Jonah Gerondi and his students, in the spirit of German Pietism, is very recognizable. Ashkenazi influence is also recognizable on the Zohar, which was composed in Spain in the last third of the thirteenth century. Ta-Shma (1999) deals extensively with this topic, as does Ta-Shma (1995 and 2001c).

NORTH AFRICA

The production of rabbinic literature in North Africa ends in 1057, with the destruction of Kairouan, and begins again only towards the end of the fourteenth century. In the beginning it was connected with the teachings of the Babylonian Geonim, and there was intensive correspondence between the two centres for a long time. The material connected with this early period was collected, in the main, by Genizah researchers, especially Sheraga Abramson in his book *In the Centres and the Diasporas in the Geonic Period* (Abramson 1965), and M. Ben-Sasson (1996: chaps. 3–4). The chief and almost sole work from this early period to have reached us is *Sefer Halachot gedolot—Aspamya* which reflects a North African reworking of R. Simeon Kayyara of Baghdad's *Halachot gedolot*, with additional material. The two most important scholars in the first half of the eleventh century are Rabbeinu Nissim b. Jacob and R. Hananel b. Hushiel. R. Nissim was the son of a local rabbinic family, who headed a central yeshivah in Kairouan and maintained an intensive correspondence with Rav Sherira and Rav Hai Gaon, his son; R. Hananel came with his father from southern Italy, settled in Kairouan, and also headed a yeshivah in that city. The rabbinic activity of R. Nissim Gaon was summarized in great detail in Abramson's monumental work (1965). A great deal of material on R. Hananel was gathered in Abramson (1994/5). A critical edition of R. Hananel's commentaries on most of the tractates of the Talmud, completed by Genizah fragments, edited by a team of editors headed by David Metzger, has recently appeared (Hananel 1989). Concerning Isaac Alfasi, see above in the section on Spain. I. Schepansky (1976) has written on R. Ephraim of Kale Hamad. On these scholars and others see the comprehensive survey in Hirschberg (1974–81: 298–361 [chap. 6: Spiritual Life]).

One of the difficult unsolved questions concerning the history of rabbinic literature in this region, is the question of the possible—but still not adequately proven—connections between early North African Jewry and the Palestinian halachic tradition, and the possibility—which seems likely but is also unproven—that R. Hananel, whose family originated in southern Italy, was responsible for the spread of the Talmud Yerushalmi and its study in these areas, while at the same time widening the gap between it and the Babylonian school which had been dominant until his arrival there. On these questions and what was written about them, and about the Pirkoi ben Baboi affair and its consequences, and on the question of the place of composition of the *Sefer Metivot*, which juxtaposed Babylonian and Palestinian *sugyot*, see Ben-Sasson (1996). In his opinion, there is no evidence to support familiarity with the Talmud Yerushalmi and its study among North African Jewry, or the influence of Palestinian halachah and tradition on this community before the eleventh century.

ITALY

We have little information concerning rabbinic literature in Italy in the tenth century and what we have is not very clear. Some of the evidence was gathered by M. Margulies (1972) and by B. Klar in his edition of *Megillat Ahima'az* (Scroll of Ahima'az) (Klar 1944). New material was gathered by Ta-Shma in the preface to M. B. Lerner's edition of an early commentary on Leviticus Rabbah (Ta-Shma 1995b: 1–16). The first extant rabbinic work written in Italy is the *'Arukh* of Nathan ben Jehiel, head of the yeshivah in Rome, and a scion of the family of yeshivah heads there who lived and flourished in the second half of the eleventh century. The multi-volume critical edition of Alexander Kohut (*Nathan ben Jehiel*, 1878–92), despite its wealth of content, introduction, and indexes, is inadequate today, because the editor did not have at his disposal the wealth of manuscript material from the Cairo Genizah and from the European Genizah (see below) that has since come to light. This situation is most recognizable in the internal alphabetical organization of the book, its division into entries, and in the significance of these for the linguistic message of the book and the implications with regard to content. Professor Abramson published a wealth of material concerning this book in his book *On the Study of the Arukh* (1973/4) (which includes an index) and his article (1984: 193–222).

Whatever is known about the rabbinic scholar R. Shelomoh min ha-Yatom, who was active in the middle of the twelfth century, is summarized in Ta-Shma (1999–2002: i. 223–4).

The greatest Italian scholar of the Middle Ages was Isaiah of Trani (Rid), who was active in the late twelfth to early thirteenth centuries. He produced several recensions of his Talmud commentary and many other halachic works. A comprehensive monograph on him has been produced by Ta-Shma and will be published in the near future. A brief summary of the monograph appears in Ta-Shma (1999–2002: i. 174–86). The latter work also includes a summary of everything known about Judah ben Benjamin Anau (ibid. i. 187). The central halachic figure in Italy in the generation after Isaiah of Trani is Zedekiah ben Abraham, author of the primary halachic work of Italian Jewry, *Shibbolei ha-leket*, which was edited in a full edition by S. Buber in 1887 and in a partial one by S. K. Mirsky in 1966, both with important introductions. Various editions of the book exist in print and in manuscripts and their identities were studied by Ta-Shma (1994). The grandson of Isaiah of Trani is Elijah the Second of Trani. What is known about him was summarized in Ta-Shma (1999–2002: i. 188–9). The last medieval Italian scholar is Judah Romano, whose works have been hardly studied. But see the lengthy article by Ta-Shma (2001b) and Bonfil (1994).

PROVENCE

....

Rabbinic literature first appears in Provence at the beginning of the eleventh century and flourishes in the twelfth and thirteenth centuries. The early history of this literature was first surveyed by B. Z. Benedict in a series of articles which were published in the 1940s and 1950s in *Tarbiz* and were later assembled in book form (Benedict 1985). Benedict is of the opinion that, although we have no traces of the teachings of Provençal scholars of the eleventh century, there did exist a well-developed study methodology, which remained oral since it was not the custom to record it. A more advanced study was carried out by Isadore Twersky in a series of articles, especially the comprehensive article on the culture of Provençal Jewry (Twersky 1968), and in his pioneering book on Abraham ben David (Rabad) of Posquières, the author of critical glosses on Maimonides' *Mishneh Torah* (Twersky 1962). Despite the serious errors in this book, which were pointed out by Haym Soloveitchik (1991), this is an important pioneering work which served as a model for subsequent works in the field. Further research was carried out by Ta-Shma in a series of studies which appeared in various fora and were gathered in book form under the title *Rabbi Zerahyah, Author of the Maor and his Circle* (Ta-Shma 1992). This book presents for the first time an accurate chronology for the understanding of the sequence of events in Provence in the twelfth century, and refutes Benedict's hypothesis concerning the eleventh-century presence in that region of a school of Torah study. The book surveys the Torah-study landscape in Provence in the twelfth century, and analyses the conflicting influences on its rabbinic culture which stemmed from its location between France to the north (Tosafists) and Spain to the south (school of Alfasi and his successors), and the opposing schools and personal tensions that were created as a result.

Concerning Judah al-Bargeloni (of Barcelona), the most influential rabbinic figure in terms of Torah study and teaching (and to a large extent the study of philosophy as well) in Provence in the generation after Alfasi, nothing has been written except for the introduction by Hanokh and Shalom Albeck to their edition of *Sefer ha-Eshkol* (1938). Our knowledge concerning rabbinic life in Provence in the twelfth century was limited because of the disappearance in the Soviet Union of one of the most important manuscripts related to the subject, the collection of responsa of R. Abraham b. Isaac of Narbonne. Recently the manuscript has resurfaced, and small sections of it have begun to be published (Emanuel 1995; Hurvitz 1995). On the story of the disappearance of this manuscript, its importance, and its reappearance, see the introduction to Emanuel's edition and see also Emanuel (1990). When the publication of the entire manuscript is completed it will be possible to give a more accurate portrayal of Provençal rabbinic literature in the twelfth century.

There are no similar studies for thirteenth-century Provence, but Moshe Halbertal's book, *Between Torah and Wisdom* (2000) is worthy of special mention. It describes in depth the special tendency among Provençal scholars of the thirteenth century to combine Torah study with the study of philosophy, following the example of Maimonides who combined in his personality both conflicting disciplines and elevated both to new heights. The book pays special attention to R. Menahem ha-Meiri, the greatest Provençal scholar of the second half of the thirteenth century, whose religious and secular inclinations were closer to the above-mentioned Maimonidean ideal than those of any other Provençal scholar. His famously tolerant attitude towards the Gentiles, which has been studied in the past because of its deep historic significance, is subjected to a fresh comprehensive analysis in this book, which also includes a rich bibliography of relevant material.

Oriental Countries

Scholarly research in this area is very limited. A great deal of Genizah material pertaining to Maimonides and his son Abraham has been analysed and published by Mordechai A. Friedman in various fora. The easiest access to this material is through a suitable computer program (see next section). A variety of rabbinic literature from the Genizah related to the circle of Maimonides' students and his household has been published by Elazar Hurvitz (Hurvitz 1995) and S. Emanuel (Emanuel 1995). See also the introduction by Ta-Shma to the commentary of R. Judah Almadari to Tractate Hullin (Ta-Shma 1993). Rabbi Yosef Kafih published a great deal of material pertaining to the sages of Yemen throughout his career in various fora. A complete list of his publications is about to appear in a memorial volume in his honour. The scholar Yosef Tobi has also published important work in this field.

Published Research Tools

This essay deals with published material only. A great deal of help can be obtained from powerful computer programs which store vast amounts of halachic material, which can be searched for desired words and phrases. These are commercial databases, which are very valuable study tools, and which are frequently updated. Bibliographic databases which document current research are especially important; through them one can obtain up-to-date lists of the publications of active scholars.

This essay is focused only on conventional printed study aids and not on electronic material, but for access to the electronic material see *http://library.brandeis.edu/judaica/judelectronic.html*; *http://jewishhistory.huji.ac.il/Syllabi/syllab.html*; and *http://www.lib.umd.edu/ETC/JEWST451.html*.

The chief sources of knowledge of medieval rabbinic literature are the major libraries of the cities of Europe, which have preserved thousands of Hebrew manuscripts from the Middle Ages, a substantial part of them halachic. Today the microfilms of the majority of known Hebrew manuscripts from all over the world are stored in the Institute for Microfilmed Hebrew Manuscripts at the Jewish National and University Library in Jerusalem. More than half of these have been professionally catalogued by the staff of the Institute. The rest are listed with the help of the printed catalogues of the various libraries which house the collections, to the extent that these exist. A complete alphabetical listing of all the collections of Hebrew manuscripts in the world, both public and private, including bibliographical information, can be found in Richler (1994). In addition the book includes information on the present location of various historic collections. Particular mention should be made of the catalogues of several large libraries in Europe which were rechecked by the staff of the Institute and published in new editions which demonstrate the identifying ability of the Institute's staff and the excellent research tools which they have at their disposal. A large volume, containing thousands of supplementary entries and corrections to the catalogue of the Bodleian Library in Oxford, and including complete bibliographic citations to recent research scholarly literature, was published in Oxford in 1994 under the direction of Malachi Beit-Arié. A similar volume for the Biblioteca Palatina in Parma has been completed and recently been published (Parma, 2001), and work on the collection of the Vatican Library is in progress. Especially important is the catalogue of Genizah fragments of the Jacques Mosseri Collection which was edited by the Institute staff (Mosseri 1990). The collection itself is not available to the public and only films of the material are housed in the Institute. The catalogue includes excellent indexes. Another important contribution of the Institute is its publication *From the Archives of the Institute of Microfilmed Hebrew Manuscripts*, which includes seventy-five short articles by Institute staff and some users which describe new literary discoveries, mostly medieval, which were revealed in the course of work at the Institute. The book is well indexed and includes a lot of information not available elsewhere.

Another research aid found at the Institute is the collection called the European Genizah which includes photographs of thousands of Hebrew manuscripts which were torn out—mainly during the fourteenth and fifteenth centuries—and used as binding material for Christian books in monasteries and city archives and libraries. For a description see David and Tabori (1998). Unlike films of other Hebrew manuscripts, which can usually be seen in their home libraries, the fragments of the European Genizah can be seen and studied only at the Institute. It should also be mentioned that the Jewish National and University Library itself possesses one of the largest collections of Hebrew manuscripts in the world, numbering some 10,000 items. Its internal catalogue has never been prepared for publication and therefore is hardly used at all by scholars of Jewish studies.

Neil Danzig (1997) has prepared a modern, detailed, well-indexed catalogue of the halachic and midrashic Genizah fragments found in the E. N. Adler collection at the Jewish Theological Seminary of America.

Another important research tool is *Sarei ha-Elef*, in its second, corrected edition (Kasher and Mandelbaum 1978). This book lists all the works of the geonim and medieval rabbis available in print in all subject areas, divided into seven main categories. The following categories are relevant to our topic: (4) Introductions, Principles, and Commentaries on the Mishnah and Talmud; (5) Responsa; (6) Literature of *poskim* (decisors); and (7) Others. The book includes detailed indexes, and a section of corrections and additions which include important comments which were sent to the editors by various readers. An important supplement to this work was published by Mandelbaum 1981.

Between the years 1981 and 1987 there appeared the five volumes of the indexing project of the responsa of the sages of North Africa and Spain. These indexes were published by the Institute of Jewish Law of the Hebrew University Law School under the editorship of Professor Menachem Elon (Elon 1981–7). The project includes a two-volume detailed legal index, a two-volume historical index, divided into well-defined sections, and an index of sources, from the Bible to the last of the cited books. The latest volume of this project—a legal index of the responsa of the scholars of France, Germany, and Italy—appeared in 1997 under the editorship of B. Lifshitz and E. Shohetman. These indexes are complete and very detailed and are of inestimable value for the study of the halachic literature of the medieval rabbinic scholars (*rishonim*, early decisors). They include a concordance to the responsa of Solomon ibn Adret and Meir of Rothenburg, the printed editions of whose works are compositionally problematic.

Haym Soloveitchik's book *Responsa As a Historical Source* (1990) is a valuable methodological work, which demonstrates in great detail how one is to use ancient texts and how to avoid many errors which stem from insufficient familiarity with the special literary nature of the material.

A complete classified bibliography of all the material in Jewish studies which appears in the major scientific journals and religious periodicals in the world in all the major languages, appears annually in the periodical *Bibliography of Articles in Jewish Studies* (Rambi), edited by Bityah Ben-Shammai. This publication has a special section devoted to halachah and religious literature. Quite complete lists of doctoral dissertations in Jewish studies and related fields at Israeli universities appear in the annual *Jewish Studies*, published by the World Union of Jewish Studies. Dissertations on halachic topics are included in the sections 'Talmud' and 'Jewish History', among others. A list of medieval halachic scholars accompanied by 'essential necessary information' including a list of each scholar's halachic works, edited in chronological order and by geographical region, was published by Yitzhak Shailat (1998). A unique work is *Otsar ha-gedolim Alufei Ya'akov* by Naftali Ya'akov Hakohen (1967). This work lists rabbinic figures of all generations, mainly from the Middle Ages, in a non-systematic alphabetical order. Each entry includes a great deal of information, but without citation of sources. In essence this book is a collection of slips of paper that the author compiled over his lengthy life-span. These were published as they were, without any editing or revision of the text. Certain entries should be combined, others should be split. In general, it is almost impossible to verify the information given. Nevertheless, the book includes a great deal of information and can be helpful if used with caution.

Medieval talmudic exegesis is described in full, by region and in chronological order, in Ta-Shma (1999–2002). The first volume covers the period 1000–1200, the second 1200–1400. A third volume, which is in press, will also include a chapter on oriental scholars. The book is based on some 150 detailed articles on the subject published by the author, which are consistently referred to along with other literature. The primary methodologies in use by contemporary scholars were summarized in Ta-Shma (1996: 23–35).

Studies of prayer and custom deal with many topics pertaining to medieval rabbinic literature. The scores of essays by Naphtali Wieder on the history of the liturgy deal mainly with early Ashkenazic liturgy, as it appears in *Mahzor Vitry, Sefer ha-Pardes, Sefer ha-Manhig*, and others, in comparison with the versions in Palestinian Genizah fragments and contrasting them with Babylonian usage. His studies have recent been gathered in a two-volume set (Wieder 1999). Ezra Fleischer's book *Prayer and Palestinian Prayer Customs From the Genizah* (Fleischer 1988) is devoted to the study of ancient Palestinian liturgy as it is being revealed in the fragments of the Cairo Genizah, but because of the close connections between Ashkenazic liturgy and Palestinian tradition this book serves as a primary resource for the study of Ashkenazic liturgy. Ta-Shma (1992a) offers an analysis of Ashkenazic custom as a cultural-religious phenomenon, illustrated by detailed examples. Other books in this area are Zimmer (1996) and Gartner (1995). A variegated collection of sources and studies on customs with some bibliography is provided in Sperber (1989–98). Ta-Shma (1995a; rev. edn. 2001c) is devoted to the study of the Ashkenazic influence on the customs and some of the halachot found in the *Zohar* and the historical significance of this phenomenon. A comprehensive bibliography of all the research material in Hebrew and other languages pertaining to prayer and customs and related topics can be found in Tabory (1993).

Several journals devote relatively large amounts of space to medieval rabbinic literature. *Tarbiz*, published by the Institute of Jewish Studies at the Hebrew University, heads the list, but it lacks an index after volume 30 (1960). *Kovez 'al yad*, published by Mekize Nirdamim, the oldest academic publisher in Israel, appears almost annually, publishing new texts in medieval rabbinic literature that have never seen the light of day. It too lacks an index. Much benefit can be derived from the index to the first hundred volumes of *Sinai* which appeared at the end of the the jubilee volume celebrating the hundredth anniversary of the founding of the journal (1987). This index, unlike indexes to other journals, devotes a special section to Maimonides and other medieval rabbis (pp. 195, 202), which makes it easier to access the many articles on these subjects published in this important journal.

Especially important are the individual bibliographies of scholars which have been published, in most cases in their Festschriften or memorial volumes. There is no comprehensive listing of the contents of these volumes for the last few decades. For works published before 1970, one can consult Shunami (1965, 1975) or Berlin (1971). In this case, the most efficient method of searching is through computer programs which deal with this subject-matter, such as *http://jnul.huji. ac.il/rambi.*

Research Desiderata

Rashi and His Circle

Despite the vast amount of research carried out on Rashi, there is still no comprehensive biography of this great medieval sage, which would also deal with his students and family. Without such a work, we cannot properly understand the stages in the transition from the generation of Rashi's teachers—which has already been properly researched (and any added information that reaches us, will be only incidental)—to the generation of Rabbeinu Tam and the Tosafist revolution connected to him, a subject which has also been well researched. An understanding of the generations of Rashi and his students could attenuate the sense of revolution which one gets from studying the Tosafist period, and would create an intellectual continuum between the periods.

Tosafists

Although the Tosafist period has been well researched, the biblical commentaries of the Tosafists have hardly been studied at all. There is a large body of literature, as large or larger than the commentaries of the Tosafists on the Talmud, a small portion of which has been published and most of which is still only in manuscript form. A partial beginning has been made by R. Jacob Gelis, who published extensive sections from 200 manuscripts under the title *Tosafot ha-Shalem*. So far ten volumes have been published covering Genesis and Exodus (Gelis 1982). There is a lot of historical and general cultural information buried in these works, but a great deal of effort needs to be invested in extracting it.

Piyyut Exegesis

Urbach's introduction to *ʿArugat ha-bosem* laid the foundations for the study of *piyyut* exegesis, and recently Professor A. Grossman has invested a great deal of energy in continuing this work. There is much material in manuscript, only a small part of which has been properly exploited until now. It is difficult to exaggerate the importance of continuing the research in this area.

Byzantium

The study of rabbinic literature in Greece, or to be more accurate, in Byzantine areas, has yet to begin. General historical chapters are to be found in the works of historians who dealt with the history of the Jews in these areas, but there exists no study of the rabbinic literature of Byzantine Jewry. For a comprehensive survey of all the material written concerning the historical-cultural connection between the Jews of Byzantium and Ashkenaz until the fifteenth century, see Ta-Shma (2001a). Dov Schwartz (2002) has written a good introductory article on the philosophy and religious thought of Byzantine Jews in the Middle Ages.

Spain in the Fifteenth Century

Our knowledge in this area is very limited, and is drawn mainly from information derived from the literature of the first generation of Spanish exiles. This information offers far from an accurate picture of reality, especially since the chroniclers of this generation were all students of R. Isaac Aboab and Y. De Leon, from the school of R. Isaac Canpanton, and they tended to drop from their lists the names of scholars of other schools of thought, especially those who opposed Canpanton. For a preliminary attempt at studying this area, see Ta-Shma (1999). This is a case of dozens of scholars and authors who have been forgotten because of the above-mentioned censorship, and careful research promises to uncover an almost completely new area of study.

The Orient

The study of rabbinic literature in the Orient (Egypt, Syria, Palestine, Iraq, and Yemen) has been totally neglected. A vast amount of Genizah material is awaiting scholarly redemption. One should mention, however, the comprehensive, detailed, fundamental work of Professor M. A. Friedman, which has enriched our knowledge of Maimonides and his son Abraham, as well as the work of E. Hurvitz and R. Abraham Shoshana, who have published Genizah material related to scholars from the circle close to Maimonides, his students, and family members who studied with him. However, many other scholars were active in these areas. Cf. Ta-Shma (1993).

SUGGESTED READING

Readers of English should certainly consult Elon (1994) and Urbach (1996). Additional reading on the Babylonian yeshivot of the early Middle Ages might now begin with Brody (1998). The most important of medieval Jewish law-codes is the subject of Twersky (1980). Nonetheless, even a cursory glance at the reference list for this essay will reveal that the most rudimentary research requires a good reading knowledge of Hebrew. Basic studies of particular varieties of rabbinic literature include: Ta-Shma (1999–2002), Urbach (1986), Fleischer (1975), and Soloveitchik (1990). Important studies of various 'schools' of rabbinic jurists include: Grossman (1995 and 2001), Dinari (1984), and Yuval (1988). Several significant studies treat 'minhag' or custom in medieval and early modern Jewish law: Sperber (1989–98), Ta-Shma (1996), and Zimmer (1996).

BIBLIOGRAPHY

ABRAMSON, S. ed. 1947. *Samuel ha-Nagid. Ben Mishlei* [Hebrew]. Tel Aviv.
—— 1952. 'Divrei Hazal be-shirat ha-Nagid.' In *Divrei ha-Kongres ha-rishon le-madaʿei ha-Yahadut*. 274–8. Jerusalem.
—— 1965. *Ba-merkazim uva-tefutsot bi-tekufat ha-geonim*. Jerusalem.
—— 1973/4. *Le-heker he-ʿAruch: arbaʿah perakim le-heker he-ʿAruch le-Rabi Natan ben Yehiʾel.* Jerusalem.
—— 1984. 'Sefer ha-ʿAruch le-R. Natan b. R. Yehiʾel mi-Roma.' *Sinai* 95: 27–42.
—— 1987. 'Mi-torato shel Rav Shemuʾel ha-Nagid mi-Sefarad.' *Sinai* 100: 7–73.
—— 1988. *Mi-pi baʿalei leshonot*. Jerusalem.
—— ed. 1994/5. *Hananel ben Hushiel. Peirush Rabbeinu Hananel la-Talmud*. Jerusalem.
ALBECK, S. and ALBECK, H. eds. 1934/5. *Abraham ben Isaac, of Narbonne. Sefer ha-Eshkol*. Jerusalem. Repr. Jerusalem 1983/4.
APTOWITZER, V. 1938. *Mavo le-Sefer Ravyah*. Jerusalem.
ASHTOR, E. 1973–84 *The Jews of Moslem Spain*. 3 vols. Philadelphia.
BAER, Y. 1961. *A History of the Jews in Christian Spain*. Philadelphia.

BEN-SASSON, M. 1996. *Zemihat ha-kehilah ha-yehudit be-artsot ha-Islam: Kairouan 800–1057.* Jerusalem.

BENEDIKT, B. Z. 1985. *Merkaz ha-Torah be-Provans.* Jerusalem.

BERLIN, C. 1971. *Index to Festschriften in Jewish Studies.* Cambridge, Mass.

Biblioteca Palatina 2001. *Hebrew Manuscripts in the Biblioteca Palatina in Parma: Catalogue.* B. Richler ed. Jerusalem.

Bodleian Library 1994. *Catalogue of the Hebrew Manuscripts of the Bodleian Library: Supplement of Addenda and Corrigenda to vol. 1* (A. Neubauer's Catalogue). Compiled under the direction of Malachi Beit-Arié. R. A. May ed. Oxford.

BONFIL, R. 1994. *Be-maṛʾah kesufah: hayyei ha-Yehudim be-Italyah bi-yemei ha-Renesans* [Hebrew translation of Italian original]. Jerusalem.

BRODY, R. 1998. *The Geonim of Babylonia and the Shaping of Medieval Jewish Culture.* New Haven.

CHAVEL, C. B. 1960. *Ramban: His Life and Teachings.* New York.

CHOUEKA, A. 1997. 'Kitvei Sheraga Abramson zal—reshimah bibliyografit.' In *Le-zikhro shel Sheraga Abramson: devarim she-neʾemru bi-melot sheloshim le-moto.* 26–66. Jerusalem.

COHEN, G. 1967. *Abraham Ibn Daud. Book of Tradition (Sefer ha-qabbalah).* Ed. and trans. G. D. Cohen. Philadelphia.

DANZIG, N. 1997. *Katalog shel seridei halachah u-midrash mi-genizat Kahir be-osef E. N. Adler shebe-sifriyat Bet ha-midrash le-rabanim be-Amerikah.* New York.

DAVID, A. and TABORY, J. eds. 1998. *ha-Genizah ha-Italkit.* Jerusalem.

DIMITROVSKY, H. Z. ed. (Adret, Solomon ben Abraham). 1990. *Teshuvot ha-Rashba; ve-zoraf lahen Sefer Minhat kenaʾot le-R. Abba Mari de-Lunel.* Jerusalem.

DINARI, Y. 1984. *Hachmei Ashkenaz be-shilhei yemei ha-beinayim: darcheihem ve-chitveihem ba-halachah.* Jerusalem.

ELON, M. ed. 1981–7 *Mafteah ha-sheʾelot veha-teshuvot shel hachmei Sefarad u-Zefon Afrikah.* 5 vols. Jerusalem.

——1994. *Jewish Law: History, Sources, Principles.* Trans. from the Hebrew by B. Auerbach and M. J. Sykes. 4 vols. Philadelphia.

EMANUEL, S. 1990. 'Ketav-yad Moskvah 566—teʾur rishoni.' *Kiryat Sefer* 63: 301–6.

——1993. 'Sifrei halachah avudim shel Baʿalei ha-Tosafot.' Unpublished Ph.D diss., Hebrew University of Jerusalem.

——ed. 1995. *Teshuvot ha-geʾonim ha-hadashot.* Jerusalem.

EPSTEIN, J. N. 1983–91. *Mehkarim be-sifrut ha-Talmud uvi-leshonot shemiyot.* 3 vols. Jerusalem.

FLEISCHER, E. 1975. *Shirat-ha-kodesh ha-ʿivrit bi-yeme-ha benayim.* Jerusalem.

——1988. *Tefilah u-minhagei tefilah erez-yisreʾeliyim bi-tekufat ha-Genizah.* Jerusalem.

GARTNER, Y. 1995. *Gilgulei minhag be-ʿolam ha-halachah.* Jerusalem.

GELIS, Y. 1982. *Tosafot ha-shalem: ozar peirushei Baʿalei ha-Tosafot ʿal Torah, Neviʾim u-Chetuvim.* Jerusalem.

GROSSMAN, A. 1981. *Hachmei Ashkenaz ha-rishonim.* Jerusalem.

——1995. *Hachmei Tsarefat ha-rishonim.* Jerusalem.

——2001. *Hachmei Ashkenaz ha-rishonim.* 3rd edn. Jerusalem.

HALBERTAL, M. 2000. *Bein Torah le-hochmah: Rabbi Menahem ha-Meʾiri uvaʿalei ha-halachah ha-Maimoniyim be-Provans.* Jerusalem.

HAKOHEN, N. Y. 1967. *Otsar ha-gedolim Alufei Yaʿakov.* 10 vols. Haifa.

HANANEL BEN HUSHIEL. 1989. *Peirushei Rabbeinu Hanan'el ben Hushi'el la-Talmud.* D. Metzger ed. Jerusalem. 1989–94 (7 vols. to date).

HIRSCHBERG, H. Z. 1974–81. *A History of the Jews in North Africa.* 2nd rev. edn. 2 vols. Leiden.

HURVITZ, E. ed. 1995. *Teshuvot ha-ge'onim 'im teshuvot u-fesakim me-hachmei Provintsyah.* New York.

KASHER, M. and MANDELBAUM, Y. D. 1978. *Sarei ha-elef.* Jerusalem.

KLAR, B. ed. 1944. *Ahimaaz ben Paltiel. Megilat Ahima'az.* Jerusalem.

LIFSHITZ, B. and SHOHETMAN, E. eds. 1997. *Mafteah ha-she'elot veha-teshuvot shel hachmei Ashkenaz, Zarefat, ve-Italyah.* Vol. 1. Jerusalem.

MANDELBAUM, Y. D. 1981. 'Hosafot le-Sefer 'Sarei ha-Elef.' *Noam* 23: 244–313.

MARGULIES, M. (Samuel, ha-Nagid) ed. 1962. *Hilchot ha-Nagid.* Jerusalem.

—— ed. 1972. *Halachot Ketsuvot.* Jerusalem.

Mekize Nirdamim, 1964. *Hevrat Mekize Nirdamim.* Jerusalem.

Mosseri Catalogue 1990 *Katalog shel osef Z'ak Mozeri = Catalogue of the Jacques Mosseri Collection.* Jerusalem.

Reshimat Ma'amarim Be-mada'ei ha-Yahadut = *Index to Articles in Jewish Studies.* Jerusalem 1966–49 vols. to date. Now available online.

RICHLER, B. 1994. *Guide to Hebrew Manuscript Collections.* Jerusalem.

SCHEPANSKY, I. 1976. *Rabbeinu Efrayim: talmid haver shel ha-Rif.* Jerusalem.

SCHWARTZ, D. 2002, forthcoming. 'Rationalism and Astral Magic in Jewish Thought in Late Medieval Byzantium.' *Aleph* 2.

SHAILAT, I. 1998. *'Al ha-rishonim: sefer 'ezer le-toledot ha-rishonim ve-hibbureihem ha-hilchatiyim.* Ma'aleh Adumim.

SHUNAMI, S. 1965. *Bibliography of Jewish Bibliographies.* 2nd edn. Jerusalem.

—— 1975. *Bibliography of Jewish Bibliographies.* Supplement to 2nd edn. 1965. Jerusalem.

SKLARE, D. 1998. 'R. David ben Se'adyah Alger ve-hibburo al-Hawi.' In *Mifgashim ba-tarbut ha-'Arvit ha-Yehudit shel yemei ha-beinayim: divrei ha-Ve'idah ha-revi'it shel ha-Hevrah le-heker ha-tarbut ha-'Arvit ha-Yehudit shel yemei ha-beinayim.* 103–23. J. Blau *et al.* eds. *Te'udah* 14. Tel Aviv.

SOLOVEITCHIK, H. 1990. *She'elot u-teshuvot ke-makor histori.* Jerusalem.

—— 1991. 'History of Halakhah: Methodological Issues: A Review Essay of I. Twersky's 'Rabad of Posquières.' [1962, rev. edn. 1980].' *Jewish History* 5/1: 75–124.

SPERBER, D. 1989–98. *Minhagei Yisrael: Mekorot ve-toledot.* Jerusalem. 6 vols. to date (1998).

SUSSMAN, Y. 1998. 'Mif'alo ha-mada'i shel Profesor Efrayim Elimelekh Urbakh.' In *Efrayim Elimelekh Urbakh: biyo-bibliyografyah mehqarit.* 7–116. D. Assaf ed. Musaf Mada'ei ha-yahadut 1. Jerusalem: World Union of Jewish Studies, 1993.

TA-SHMA, I. M. 1974. 'Shipput 'ivri u-mishpat 'ivri ba-me'ot ha-11–12 bi-Sefarad (li-yedi'at mazzav limmud ha-Torah 'al-pi sh.u-t. ha-Rif.' *Shenaton ha-mishpat ha-'ivri* 1: 353–72.

—— 1982. 'Mi-peirushav shel ha-Rav Yizhak Ibn Giyat le-masekhet Bava mezi'a.' *Kovez 'al yad* 10: 57–72.

—— 1988. 'Hasidut Ashkenaz bi-Sefarad: Rabbeinu Yonah Gerondi—ha-ish u-fo'olo.' In *Galut ahar golah: mehkarim be-toledot Yisra'el muggashim le-Profesor Hayim Bainart li-melot lo shiv'im shanah.* 165–94. Jerusalem.

—— 1992a. *Minhag Ashkenaz ha-kadmon.* Jerusalem.

TA-SHMA, I. M. 1992b. *Rabbi Zerahyah ha-Levi ba'al ha-Ma'or u-venei hugo: le-toledot ha-sifrut ha-rabbanit be-Provans*. Jerusalem.

——1992–4. 'Halachah, kabbalah, u-filosofyah bi-Sefarad ha-Nozrit.' In *Shenaton ha-mishpat ha-'ivri*. 18–19: 479–495.

——1993. 'Shitotav shel Rabbi Yehudah al-Madari 'al ha-Rif.' In *Yehudah Almadari. Perush Shehitat Hullin rabbati*. Jerusalem.

——1994. 'Sefer 'Shibbolei ha-leket' u-chefilav.' *Italia* 11: 39–52.

——1995a. *ha-Nigleh sheba-nistar: le-heker sheki'ei ha-halachah be-sefer ha-Zohar*. Tel Aviv.

——1995b. 'Petah davar.' In *Peirush kadum le-Midrash Va-yikra rabbah*. M. B. Lerner ed. Jerusalem.

——1996. *Halachah, minhag u-metsi'ut be-Ashkenaz: 1000–1350*. Jerusalem.

——1999–2002. *Ha-Sifrut ha-parshanit la-Talmud be-Eiropah uvi-Tsefon Afrikah: korot, ishim ve-shitot*. 3 vols. 1–2. Jerusalem.

——1999. 'Li-yedi'at mazzav limmud ha-Torah bi-Sefarad ba-me'ah ha-15.' In *Dor geirush Sefarad: kovez ma'amarim*. 47–62. Y. T. Assis and Y. Kaplan eds. Jerusalem.

——2001a. 'Le-toledot ha-kesharim ha-tarbutiyyim bein Yehudei Bizantyon ve-Ashkenaz.' In *Me'ah she'arim: 'iyyunim be-'olamam ha-ruhani shel Yisra'el bi-yemei ha-beinayim le-zecher Yizhak Tverski*. 61–70. E. Fleischer *et al.* eds. Jerusalem.

——2001b. 'The Acceptance of Maimonides' Mishneh Torah in Italy.' *Italia* 13–15: 79–90.

——2001c. *ha-Nigleh sheba-nistar: le-heker sheki'ei ha-halachah be-sefer ha-Zohar*. Expanded edn. Tel Aviv.

TABORY, J. 1993. *Reshimat ma'amarim be-'inyenei tefilah u-mo'adim. Kiryat Sefer*, supplement to vol. 64. Jerusalem.

TWERSKY, I. 1962. *Rabad of Posquières: A Twelfth-Century Talmudist*. Cambridge, Mass.

——1968. 'Aspects of the Social and Cultural History of Provençal Jewry.' *Journal of World History* 11: 185–207.

——1980. *Introduction to the Code of Maimonides (Mishneh Torah)*. New Haven.

URBACH, E. E. 1955. *Ba'alei ha-tosafot*. Jerusalem.

——1961. *Mavo le-Sefer 'Arugat ha-bosem*. Jerusalem.

——1980. *Ba'alei ha-tosafot*. 4th edn. Jerusalem.

——1986. *Ba'ale ha-Tosafot: Toledotehem, hiburehem, shitatam*. 5th edn. 2 vols. Jerusalem.

——1996. *The Halakhah: Its Sources and Development*. Trans. from the Hebrew by R. Posner. Tel Aviv.

YUVAL, I. J. 1988. *Hachamim be-doram: ha-manhigut ha-ruhanit shel Yehudei Germanyah be-shilhei yemei ha-beinayim*. Jerusalem.

WIEDER, N. 1999. *Hitgabbeshut ha-tefilah ba-Mizrah uva-Ma'arav*. Jerusalem.

ZIMMER, E. 1996. *'Olam ke-minhago noheg*. Jerusalem.

CHAPTER 11

THE STUDY OF HEBREW LITERATURE OF THE MIDDLE AGES: MAJOR TRENDS AND GOALS

TOVA ROSEN

ELI YASSIF

INTRODUCTORY SURVEY

OUR survey aims at a critical examination of *modern research* on medieval Hebrew literature. However, for the sake of the non-specialist, we would like to offer here a most general outline of medieval Hebrew literature itself. Our definition of 'medieval Hebrew literature' excludes writing in Jewish languages other than Hebrew, and singles out 'literature' from other types of non-literary Hebrew writing. The variety of literary types included in our survey ranges from liturgical and secular poetry to artistic storytelling and folk literature.

When does medieval Hebrew literature begin? Rather than trying to pinpoint a beginning (or beginnings, since each literary type has its own, sometimes vague, historical beginning), it will prove more fruitful to employ here a genealogical approach. Both early liturgical poetry (known as *piyyut*) and the medieval Hebrew story are rooted in the soil of the Talmudic period. Liturgical poetry, believed now to have emerged at the end of the Talmudic period (around 500) in Byzantine Palestine, was the earliest literary genre of medieval Hebrew literature.[1] And although heavily absorbed in the mentality and language of contemporary midrash, piyyut had carved its own independent forms. The beginnings of medieval Hebrew storytelling were even more deeply connected to the narrative traditions of the Talmud. However, the constitutive moment of the birth of piyyut and narrative as distinct medieval genres had to do with their separation from the encyclopedic, all-embracing nature of the Talmud. Unlike the Talmud, in which all branches of knowledge and creativity were contained in one and the same composition, and were subjected to the rabbis' holistic approach to learning, medieval literature is characterized by the separation and independence of its genres. Hence, the beginning of medieval Hebrew literature coincides with the emergence, each in its due time, of independent compositions dedicated to liturgy, poetry, storytelling, philosophy, religious law (halacha), biblical commentary, linguistics, mysticism, and historiography. The first separate compositions of Hebrew prose appeared in the Jewish communities of the East—Iraq, Iran, and Palestine—and were certainly affected by earlier and similar developments in Arabic culture.

From here on we shall follow the separate paths of evolution of the different genres and sub-genres of poetry and prose.

Medieval Hebrew Poetry

The inception of piyyut is intimately linked to the development and customs of Jewish prayer. The basic assumption is that *piyyutim* could not have emerged in the synagogue prior to a relative maturation and crystallization of the prayers themselves. The first *paytanim* (liturgical poets) were cantors who offered their communities a poetic alternative to the standard prayers. The intricate structures of the paytanic compositions correspond to the complex compositions of the prayers themselves. The vast number of extant early piyyutim (most of them discovered last century in the Cairo Genizah) testifies to the great need for a constantly renewed repertory. Their sophisticated formal arrangements (rhyme, acrostics, sound devices), their enigmatic language (often incorporated with midrashic allusions), and their use of Hebrew neologisms, indicate the intellectual and aesthetic demands

---

[1] i.e., some century-and-a-half before the Muslim conquest of Palestine. According to the now widely accepted definition of historian Hayyim Ben Sasson, the Jewish Middle Ages began with the Muslim conquests in the seventh century and ended with the turbulence in the Jewish world in the wake of the Sabbatian movement in the seventeenth century.

of their audiences. Some common features between Jewish and Christian liturgy promoted the assumption that they either influenced each other, or at least developed along analogous lines.

After reaching its peak (roughly between the mid-sixth century CE and the second half of the eighth) in Palestine, piyyut shifted to centres in the diaspora; to eastern communities (Syria, Egypt, North Africa, and especially Iraq) and to Central Europe (Italy, from where it spread later to Germany and southern France, constituting the Ashkenazic School).

Secular poetry does not enter the scene until the tenth century. Its most renowned practitioners were the Hebrew poets of the Andalusian Golden Age. However, of critical importance to the understanding of the growth of secular poetry in Spain are cultural developments which took place in Iraqi Jewry during the tenth century. The Babylonian leader Saadia Gaon (an innovative *paytan* in his own right), initiated a revolutionary project for Jewish writing which yielded far-reaching results in all spheres of Jewish learning (grammar, philosophy, poetics and more). His project involved, among other things, the remodelling of Jewish writing upon literary models adopted from Arabic culture. Following Arabic puristic ideals, his treatise on poetry (indeed, the first Hebrew *poetics*) required that Hebrew poetry be written in pure biblical Hebrew. Although Saadia referred mainly to piyyut, his poetic vision affected mainly secular poetry. And despite modest sporadic attempts at secular poetry in the Jewish East, Saadia's ideal materialized in the farthest West of the Jewish world—in Muslim Spain.

The agent of change was Saadia's student, the poet and grammarian Dunash ben Labrat, who emigrated to Cordoba in the middle of the tenth century, at the call of the Jewish courtier Hasday Ibn Shaprut. Dunash's 'invention'—to scan Hebrew poetry in Arabic metres—despite the opposition it aroused, can be considered as the founding moment of the Hebrew-Andalusian school of poetry. This courageous move paved the way for other poetic developments, namely, the adoption of the Arabic rhyme system, Arabic verse forms, thematic genres, rhetoric, and poetic tenets. The revival of 'pure' biblical Hebrew as a poetic language—often seen as a manifestation of renewed national awareness—was itself modelled upon the puristic linguistic ideals cultivated by Arabic poets and linguists.

From Dunash on, Hebrew poetry in Spain thrived in the ambience of the Spanish-Jewish arabicized elite of courtiers and rabbis, and took on the characteristics of Arabic courtly poetry. Professional Hebrew poets, involved in the circles of the Jewish courtiers serving the Andalusian rulers, wrote, like their Arabic peers, poems of love and wine, friendship and praise, lament and complaint (and, in the case of Samuel ha-Nagid, the vizier of Granada, even war poems), reflecting the interests and moods of their social circle. From the echelons of these courtiers-rabbis-poets came also the Spanish liturgists. Major poets (like Solomon Ibn Gabirol, Moses Ibn Ezra, Judah ha-Levi, and Abraham Ibn Ezra), as well as lesser-known writers, were also most prolific in liturgy. Spanish liturgical poetry is divided between a conservative trend preserving features of the Old Eastern piyyut, and an innovative trend introducing to Jewish religious poetry Arabic formal features, as well as certain philosophical and ascetic influences from Arabic poetry and thought.

Migrations of Hebrew authors out of Spain spread the achievements of the prestigious Andalusian school to other Jewish communities who were to become the heirs of the Andalusian centre. Judah ha-Levi left Spain for Egypt in 1140. In the same year Abraham Ibn Ezra left for North Africa and Italy, and later wandered also in Provence and France. Alharizi voyaged in Iraq, Syria, and Egypt around the first quarter of the thirteenth century. Their visits affected the productivity of both secular and religious poetry in these eastern centres, with each centre gradually developing its own local style.

Following the migration of Jews from Muslim to Christian Spain (during the Berber invasions and the first Christian reconquest in the second half of the twelfth century), a second Jewish-Spanish school evolved in Castille and Catalonia (and in Provence), and continued to exist until the Expulsion of the Jews in 1492. Though generally adhering to the prosody, genres, and themes of their predecessors, the poets of the new school seem to differ from the Andalusians in several ways. First, there is a marked decrease in creativity in the field of religious poetry. This occurs parallel to, and perhaps also due to, the increase in Kabbalistic activity. Secondly, a new secular genre is introduced in this period—artistic narratives in rhymed prose. The most famous variant of rhymed prose is the Hebrew *maqama*, modelled upon the Arabic genre. In translating narrative compilations (especially from the Arabic), and in incorporating motifs culled from Jewish and Arabic folk-tales as well as from contemporary Romance literatures, these rhymed Hebrew narratives constitute an interesting locus of intercultural contacts. The development of artistic Hebrew narratives participates in and contributes to a new revival of the Hebrew language. The puristic biblical style so idealized in Andalusian poetry gives way to a more versatile Hebrew, infused with mishnaic, talmudic, and medieval layers, used not only in narratives but also in translations and original works of a speculative nature.

The waves of refugees spreading north and south after the 1492 Expulsion joined the existing literary centres around the Mediterranean. A revival of a new trend of poetry, imbued with a Kabbalistic air, is characteristic of the poetry written from the sixteenth century on. Its effects were especially felt in North Africa, Turkey, and even in remote Yemen. Religious poetry continued to be written by Jews in the East until the beginning of the twentieth century. Though it exceeds by far the bounds of the definition 'medieval', this later poetry is medieval in spirit, theme, and form, and is thus being studied by scholars of medieval poetry.

Ashkenazic piyyut ceased to be a productive school much earlier. It is accepted that the invention of printing in the sixteenth century, which brought about the standardization of Ashkenazic rite, blocked new piyyutim from entering the prayer book. Of all poetic schools, it was the Ashkenazic which remained most loyal to the tradition of the ancient piyyut, and which thus, also, became the most isolated. Only minimal influence of the Spanish school may be discerned (since the thirteenth century). It is especially notable for its lamentations reflecting the distress of German Jews during the Crusades.

The first stage of the Italian school, beginning around 800 as a follower of the Palestinian piyyut, is considered as belonging to the Ashkenazic school, from which it departed in the late twelfth century. During the thirteenth century it was under the poetic influence of the Andalusian school. Since the beginning of the fourteenth century it combined Andalusian poetics with influences from contemporary Italian literature, adopting the themes and forms of Renaissance, Baroque, and Classicist trends. Italian Jewish authors produced secular and religious poetry, narratives, plays, and so on. The Italian school persisted until the nineteenth century, with its last phase being parallel to the birth of modern Hebrew literature of the Enlightenment.

The Hebrew Story in the Middle Ages

In the Middle Ages the Hebrew story was, especially in its beginning, under the strong influence of the previous period: the haggadic story in the Talmud and midrash. The development of the Hebrew story in the Middle Ages was long and complicated, as it drew from the rich narrative world of rabbinic sources in the domain of genres, thematic diversity, literary style, and complex function. This dependence can be seen in the fact that many medieval compositions were still called 'midrash', and that a high percentage of the stories were adapted from the Talmud and midrashim and were not medieval in origin.

The first Hebrew composition we know of, from the eighth or ninth century, in which typical medieval characteristics can be observed, is the 'Midrash of the Ten Commandments'. Its author, as well as its readers, saw in it a continuation of midrashic literature. It is built around the biblical verses and their midrashic interpretation, and includes in the course of its discussion some narrative illustrations to support it. It is possible to see in each of the ten chapters of this composition a separate 'midrash', based upon one of the ten commandments. Here, however, lies the main difference. The midrashic-ethical component in this composition is very limited, and readers are meant to feel that this part is not important, and that the author is simply paying his debt to his cultural and religious norms (so that his composition will be legitimized), before rushing on to get to the stories, which receive the main artistic emphasis. While the midrashic sections of the composition are borrowed from talmudic literature, most stories are new and unknown previously in Jewish literature, and are long and developed narratives. The 'Midrash of the Ten Commandments' is a typical example of the process of 'continuation and change' marking the emergence of Hebrew prose in the Middle Ages. In accord with this process, most Hebrew narratives appear not in independent narrative composition like the 'Midrash of the Ten Commandments', but in commentaries, historical books, moralistic treatises, travel itineraries, or hagiographical accounts of holy men. However, the literary uniqueness of the period lies in its courageous departure from the literary norms of the previous period.

The genre of the 'rewritten biblical story' is the main component of midrashic literature, and continues to be created extensively in the Middle Ages. However, when a biblical story is retold in this period, it appears not in the context of a homily, as in the midrashim, but as an independent prose narrative which has torn itself free from the bounds of the biblical verse. Such compositions are 'Midrash Vayosha', 'The Chronicles of Moses', 'Ma'aseh Avraham', and especially 'Sefer ha-Yashar', written at the end of the Middle Ages. Each of these, like many other compositions uses the biblical story as a nucleus for a new, developed, and independent fictive narrative, whose world and style is that of the Middle Ages.

The next important prose genre in this period is the collection of stories. These compositions, from the beginning of the Middle Ages, bring together different stories from various sources and treating different topics. They express, maybe more than any other literary genre of the time, the emergence of Hebrew prose as a unique creation. Examples are: 'The Alphabet of Ben Sira', where a framework narrative includes outstanding subversive stories; 'An Elegant Composition Concerning Relief after Adversity' by Rabbi Nissim of Kairuan, composed in the eleventh century as a moralistic work, but focusing on the stories, not the mores; 'Sefer ha Ma'asim', from twelfth-century France, constructed according to the literary patterns of European *exempla* literature; and, most important, 'Sefer Hasidim'—the basic document of the German Pietists of the thirteenth century. Though it was not intended to be a literary composition, its author, Rabbi Judah the Pious, included about 400 original stories, thus creating one of the most interesting narrative compositions of the Middle Ages.

Another important genre of Hebrew prose is the historical narrative. Although generally the tendency was to consider this genre as belonging to historiographical writing, it is clear today that most of the compositions in this genre are fictional, stylized creations, not historical 'documents'. First and foremost among these compositions is 'Sefer Jossipon', the tenth-century Italian story of the Second Temple. It is based on the historical narrative of Flavius Josephus, but it selects portions from his book, adds to the narrative rabbinic and medieval material, and creates a 'historical novel' typical of the Middle Ages. Another historiographical work, the eleventh-century 'Megilat Ahima'az' from southern Italy, is a saga of the Ahima'az family over 300 years. Its author, Ahima'az ben Paltiel, collected family traditions and committed them to writing in a highly stylized Hebrew, and in rhyme. It is thus the first rhymed prose in the Hebrew literature of the Middle Ages. Another historical narrative is 'Sefer ha-Zichronot' (the Book of Memory), from early fourteenth-century Germany. It tells the history of the Jewish people from the creation of the world to the end of days—the messianic period—and thus belongs to a popular historiographical genre of the period—the universal history. Another important characteristic of this work is that it is a collection of dozens of full or fragmentary medieval compositions which the author of 'Sefer ha-Zichronot' considered to be 'authentic documents', and which he organized and framed as a part of Jewish historical memory. In the later Middle Ages one of the refugees from Spain, Gedalya Ibn Yahya, wrote 'Shalshelet ha-Kabbalah', one of the most controversial historical books of the time. Gedalya presented here the intellectual history of the Torah sages from the beginning to his own days. When he described the history of the great sages of the Middle Ages—Rashi, Maimonides, Nahmanides, and others—he incorporated dozens of legends he had heard and read, and so became one of the most important contributors to Jewish hagiographical writing in the later Middle Ages.

Another popular genre of the time was the bestiary and fable. Medieval people were fascinated with the origin, character, and behaviour of animals, and even more with their resemblance to human beings. In the Hebrew prose of the time, the earlier bestiaries were created in the East—the 'Alphabet of Ben Sira' and 'Igeret Ba'alei Hayyim'. Fables also appeared in the context of other works, as in the talmudic commentaries of Rav Hai Gaon of Iraq and Rashi in France. However, the peak of this genre in Jewish culture was 'Mishlei Shu'alim' (Fox Fables) by the thirteenth-century French author Rabbi Berechia ha-Nakdan—one of the largest, most sophisticated collections of fables in European literature.

THE STUDY OF HEBREW LITERATURE

Like literature itself, the study of literature cannot be detached from historical and cultural contexts. In this essay we wish to outline the development of the modern scholarship of medieval Hebrew literature (starting from its widely acknowledged beginnings in the Wissenschaft des Judentums movement of the early nineteenth century) in three main contexts:

1. The context of its internal development, based on its own goals, necessities, and achievements.
2. The context of contemporaneous developments in the general discipline of literary criticism. To what extent does the scholarship of medieval Hebrew literature correspond to trends and currents that have been prevalent in literary criticism and research in other languages in general, and in the study of medieval

literatures in particular; and to what extent does it share the aesthetic assumptions and intellectual views accepted in the general field?

3. The context of modern Jewish history. The scholarship of medieval Hebrew literature has developed concurrently with certain historical processes (the struggle of Western European Jews for cultural recognition; the attempt to establish a new cultural centre for the Jewish people in Palestine in the beginning of the twentieth century; the establishment of the State of Israel; relationships between Israel and the diaspora; tensions between religious and secular Jews; the Israeli-Arab conflict, etc.). We must ask, then, whether and how such 'external' historical contexts have affected currents and trends in the development of the research, and whether and how different scholars have attempted, explicitly or implicitly, to participate in and shape cultural life.

Our review of the principal currents in the study of medieval Hebrew literature is divided into two sections: the study of medieval Hebrew poetry, and that of the medieval Hebrew prose. With the exception of a few scholars who have tackled both forms (particularly in the early phases of the research), the study of medieval Hebrew prose and poetry has developed into two distinct, separate disciplines. As in the study of non-Jewish medieval literatures, this may be due to such external factors as the perceived elitism of poetry, as opposed to the more 'popular' and 'folkloristic' qualities of medieval prose, or to internal factors, including the considerable differences in forms of aesthetic expression, target audiences, and social functions. Although medieval literatures—Jewish, Christian-European, and Arabic alike—do include hybrid-forms like the *maqamas* and the romance, which explicitly tread the line between poetry and prose (and have been studied as such), the existence of such hybrid genres should not blur the reality of two distinct disciplines in the study of medieval literature—hence the bifurcated structure of this essay.

MEDIEVAL HEBREW POETRY

Modern scholarship of medieval Hebrew poetry has had two constitutive moments: whereas the first—the Wissenschaft des Judentums enterprise of the mid-nineteenth century—gave the field its impetus and *raison d'être*, the second—the discovery of the Cairo Genizah at the end of that century—transformed the study of medieval Hebrew poetry by supplying it with a vast abundance of research material (which is yet to be exhausted) and making possible a new array of syntheses and conclusions.

The latter half of the nineteenth century constituted the first chapter in the history of this academic field. The great figures of the Wissenschaft des Judentums (Zunz, Steinschneider, Luzzatto) placed the research of Hebrew literature—and of Hebrew poetry in particular—at the core of their scholarly agenda. Leopold Zunz's research aims, as formulated in his 1818 programme for the Wissenschaft des Judentums, were emblematic of the emancipatory apologetics of this agenda: since actively religious Jewish life, and the literature produced under its wing, have come to an end, they should henceforth be scrutinized using scientific tools; the Science of Judaism should devote itself to the study of Hebrew literature, in which the unique character of Judaism has been preserved; such an endeavour would not only stimulate intellectual vigour and fill a spiritual void in modern Judaism, but would also raise a contribution to general humanistic studies, thus helping to promote equal rights for the Jews. For Zunz, not the Talmud and the Kabbalah, but rather the midrash and the piyyut—those two literary genres whose primary locus of vitality ('Sitz im Leben') was the synagogue—were the forms most representative of the Jewish genius. Zunz's three great works on the piyyut brought medieval liturgy to the centre of Jewish scholarship. Whereas the first of these volumes (1855) was devoted to the penitential piyyutim, the second (1859) included *kerovot* by numerous paytanim (liturgical poets), and examined the role of the piyyutim in Jewish life. Zunz's third great book (1865) was a pioneering attempt to lay down a systematic, chronological bio-bibliography of hundreds of poets and thousands of piyyutim, from the beginnings of the genre to the sixteenth century.[2]

Preceding Zunz's great works on the piyyut were pioneering attempts by other scholars, of whom we shall at this point mention Franz Delitzsch, a Protestant missionary associated with the Wissenschaft des Judentums scholars whose volume on post-biblical Jewish poetry appeared already in 1836. Parallel to Zunz, Moritz Steinschneider had published his *Jewish Literature* (1857), which in addition to liturgical poetry examined also a variety of Jewish writings (including non-liturgical poetry and speculative prose). Of interest for us are his chapters on the poetry of Muslim Spain (where he laid the foundation for scrutinizing it vis-à-vis the contemporaneous Arabic literature) and the rhymed prose of Jewish writers from Christian Spain and Provence (which he discussed against the background of Spain's Christian literature). Among his other bibliographical endeavours, Steinschneider edited the catalogues of Hebrew manuscripts in five major European libraries (including Leiden, Berlin and Oxford's Bodleian Library), where his

---

[2] Our overview wishes to highlight trends and achievements in the field in the latter half of the twentieth century, especially in recent decades. For information on the development of research in the more distant past and for bibliographical references, the reader is thus referred to previous, more or less comprehensive surveys about the state of the art. On the Wissenschaft des Judentums research, see Davidson (1930) and Schirmann (1970). Schirmann (1942) focuses primarily on the study of Spanish poetry between the two world wars. Schirmann (1967) and Pagis (1979) include short historical surveys, but they focus mainly on methodological difficulties, lacunas, and future tasks.

uncovering of hidden literary treasures earned him the justified title 'the Father of Jewish Bibliography'.

Another great contributor to the bibliographical and textological research in this field was the Italian scholar Samuel David Luzzatto (ShaDaL), who indexed, identified, described, published, and commented on hundreds of piyyutim. His introduction to *Mahzor Benei Roma* (1856) is a thorough examination of the history of the piyyut. Although Luzzatto had close links with the German Wissenschaft des Judentums scholars, he was a traditionalist who did not share their views on emancipation and on reform in Judaism. Because of his ideas concerning national and cultural revival, several modern critics (Bialik and Rawnitzky 1924, Schirmann 1942) have preferred Luzzatto to scholars like Zunz, to whom Judaism was in the process of being 'lowered to its grave'. Luzzatto, in contrast, stressed Judaism's vitality and originality and emphasized the role of the Hebrew language and literature in cultivating the Jewish spirit: treating these as a living literary tradition, thought Luzzatto, would reinforce the commitment of Jews to Judaism. Luzzatto's profound identification with the national ideology of Judah ha-Levi, whose poems he published (Luzzatto, 1840; 1864), contributed considerably to ha-Levi being perceived not just as Spain's greatest Jewish poet, but also as a pre-Zionist national and cultural icon.

The products of the Wissenschaft des Judentums research fluctuated between two poles: on the one hand, ambitious, wide-ranging projects which, although based on the incomplete research materials available at the time, aimed at a bibliographical and historical mapping of all post-biblical Jewish literature; and on the other, sporadic publications of poems discovered in prayer books and manuscripts. Already in the early decades of the nineteenth century, and increasingly so in later decades, various scholars began publishing a myriad of single piyyutim (an effort soon to include secular poems as well) in the major periodicals of the Wissenschaft des Judentums, as well as in more obscure journals associated with the Jewish Enlightenment movement (the Haskalah), in jubilee volumes and in self-published pamphlets. *Hevrat Meqizei Nirdamim* (literally translated, 'Society for the Awakeners of the Asleep')—a society dedicated to the publication of significant Hebrew manuscripts—was established in 1862, with Luzzatto among its founders. Those publications, which were for the most part sporadic and fragmentary (and at times even amateurish and sloppy), were harshly criticized by later scholars. Bialik (1924), to quote just one such critic, castigated the 'miserable work' of the Wissenschaft scholars, calling it 'an insipid and negligent collection of bits and pieces' (an accusation from which he excused Luzzatto, however). Most attempts by late nineteenth-century scholars to publish complete *diwan*s, especially by Spanish-Hebrew poets, also resulted in deficient, incomplete products. However, deeply flawed as such efforts were from the perspective of later critics—due either to methodological difficulties or to the limited available knowledge—they incontrovertibly laid the indispensable bibliographical and paleographical foundations for the discipline.

The main difficulty facing the early generations of scholars was the physical condition of the material that was to serve as the empirical foundation of their research. The majority of the poetic material (both liturgical and secular) resembled an archipelago submerged underwater. The initial task was to discover the lost islands of that archipelago, combine the visible segments, and deduce whatever remained hidden. This undertaking was somewhat simpler regarding the liturgical material, which was partially preserved (albeit in altered versions after years of incessant modification) in prayer books that were still in use in the nineteenth century. It was much more difficult regarding the secular poems, which had sunk into oblivion and only gradually began to surface in obscure collections. The fragmentation of the material, its dispersal in libraries, archives, and private collections, as well as the sometimes damaged condition of the manuscripts, all contributed to the difficulty. There were cases where pages containing different parts of the same poem would be discovered in different places by different scholars, over a span of several decades. The evolution of the field has thus been intertwined with the continuous (and still ongoing) discovery and mapping of the research material itself. *The Thesaurus of Medieval Hebrew Poetry*, edited by Israel Davidson and published in New York between 1924 and 1938, supplied scholars with a significant bibliographical tool. The work was incomplete, however—even at the time of its initial publication—since it only listed already-published poems. Only a small appendix catalogued a small part of the then extant manuscripts. The *Thesaurus* included roughly 36,000 poems, listed alphabetically by their first words. Each entry cited the editions in which the poems had been published, and included references to earlier indices by previous scholars (Zunz, Luzzatto, Landshuth) who had begun indexing the material.

These material difficulties, which were only exacerbated following the discovery of the Genizah (see below), held back the research agenda considerably. For decades scholars were weighed down by the feeling that any attempt to recapitulate the available knowledge on a poet, school, or era, would inevitably remain incomplete and tentative. In the absence of catalogues and additional bibliographical tools, even the publication of critical editions based on a maximal number of extant manuscript versions was deemed a goal hard to achieve.[3] And in the absence of standard editions, scholars were discouraged from attempting to write extensive histories or monographs, not to mention explications, interpretations or literary analyses.

---

[3] Nevertheless, quite a number of editions (not all of them complete) were published during the last century, of which will be mentioned here: Yellin (1932–7); Brody (1938); Jarden, (1956); Mirsky (1961); Mirsky (1977); Jarden (1966–83); Pagis (1967); Jarden (1973–6); Brody and Schirmann (1974); Levin (1976–80); Schmeltzer (1979); Jarden (1980–6); David (1982); David (1987); Bar Tikva (1986). Important bodies of work that still await publication in standard editions include the liturgical poems of Moses Ibn Ezra and the secular poems of Abraham Ibn Ezra. The absence of such editions is also felt in the field of rhymed prose. Other editions are mentioned throughout the essay. Also see n. 30, on editions of liturgical poets based on the findings of the Genizah.

The story of two editions—one deficient, the other a success, both edited by Heinrich Brody, a scholar who focused on textual criticism—will illustrate the aforementioned difficulties. The *Dîwân Jehudah ha-Levi*, on which Brody laboured for decades (1894–1930), was a flawed edition marred by numerous textual mistakes and by the erroneous inclusion of poems by other poets. It was also far from including ha-Levi's complete oeuvre. Additional manuscripts—which included versions different from the ones already published, as well as hitherto-unknown poems by ha-Levi—continued to surface gradually (first in the Cambridge collection of the Genizah, and lately in the Genizah collection at the Library of St Petersburg) while the edition was being prepared and after it was published. Even today, nearly a century after Brody's effort, there is still no authorized edition of Judah ha-Levi's work. The absence of such an edition has been, and will continue to be, an obstacle toward the completion of any creditable study of ha-Levi's poetry.

Brody's three-volume edition (1935) of Moses Ibn Ezra's secular poems is regarded, in contrast, as a masterpiece of scholarship. His work on the edition began at the end of the nineteenth century, met with numerous difficulties and setbacks, and remained unfinished when he died at 1942. The delay turned out for the better, however, since in the meantime the important MS Schocken 37, which includes copies of numerous diwans by Andalusian poets (including Ibn Ezra), was discovered. Brody himself died while working on the second volume, and the work was completed by other scholars from the Schocken Institute (see below), including Zulay, Schirmann, and Habermann. The Ginzburg manuscript from Moscow was discovered after Brody's death, and the 'new' poems included in it were published in the third volume of the edition, which was completed by Dan Pagis in 1970 (around the same time he was working on his dissertation). It would not be far from the truth to contend that this outstanding critical edition, assembled by the great aforementioned scholars, also helped yield Pagis's own masterful literary study on Moses Ibn Ezra (Pagis 1970, see below).

The emergence of a scholar of Brody's stature, after a period of mediocrity and stagnation (1870–90), greatly encouraged the study of medieval Hebrew poetry. More than any other scholar, Brody emblematized the giant leap in the evolution of the field between the end of the nineteenth century and the early decades of the twentieth. Another revolutionary event—whose full significance and consequences regarding Jewish studies in general, and the study of Hebrew poetry in particular, were difficult to envisage at the time—was the unearthing of the Cairo Genizah in 1896. Among the myriads of documents brought to Cambridge by Solomon Schechter (roughly 100,000 fragments, according to his own estimate), pages of poetry were second only to biblical fragments. Other assortments of Genizah fragments were scattered earlier in various libraries around the world. Additional unopened boxes of documents brought by Schechter were discovered in various Cambridge storerooms at the end of the 1950s; these included yet more poetic treasures, which were catalogued as the 'new series' (T.S.–N.S.) and outnumbered the old one.

I. Davidson was the first scholar who, by publishing his *Mahzor Iannai* (1919), drew attention to the revolutionary potential of the Genizah. Nevertheless, the study of the liturgical poetry of the Genizah began in earnest only in 1930, with the establishment of the Research Institute for Hebrew Poetry in Berlin (founded by S. Z. Schocken). The Institute's aim was to assemble all the important manuscripts (or photocopies thereof) scattered around the world, and by the 1940s it had managed to collect no less than 25,000 photocopied pages. In their joint activity, the scholars gathered in the Institute realized Bialik's concept of *kinnus* or 'ingathering' (see below). In retrospect, the two main foci of research in the twentieth-century history of the discipline—the study of secular Andalusian-Hebrew poetry on the one hand, and the study of the Genizah and the liturgical poetry on the other—were already becoming distinct through the Institute's activity. The divergence—and to some extent even antagonism—that began developing between these two major trends would only intensify toward the end of the twentieth century (see below). Heinrich Brody, who was the Institute's first director, and the young Jefim Schirmann who worked with him, concentrated their efforts on the Spanish poetry. At the same time, other scholars—among them Menahem Zulay—began cataloguing the liturgical poetry of the Genizah and were laying the foundations for the systematical research of the piyyut by publishing single piyyutim, critical editions, and studies. Important works on Spanish Hebrew poetry (Brody, Schirmann), on ancient Eastern *piyyut* (Zulay), and on the liturgical poetry of Ashkenaz (Habermann) were published by the Institute's publishing house and appeared in its periodical *Yediʿot ha-Machon le-Heqer ha-Shira ha-ʿIvrit*, seven volumes of which were issued in Berlin and Jerusalem between 1933 and 1958.

From the 1920s, Jewish studies became entangled with the ideological aims of the Zionist cultural revival. With the founding of the Institute for Jewish Studies at the Hebrew University in Jerusalem (1925), the field's centre of gravity shifted from the diaspora to mandatory Palestine, and the Wissenschaft des Judentums became 'Jewish studies'. Also contributing to this development was the relocation of the Schocken Institute from Berlin to Jerusalem in 1934. In his essay surveying the state of the art between the two world wars, Schirmann (1942) explicitly connects the 'impetus for the study of Spanish poetry... [with] the Zionist idea as broadly construed and... [with] its partial realization following the Balfour Declaration'. The most obvious representative of this trend—the engagement of academic research in the service of national ideology—was no other than national poet H. N. Bialik. In the introduction to his edition of Ibn Gabirol's poems (1924), Bialik announced the centrality of Spanish Hebrew poetry to the modern enterprise of the Jewish revival. In insisting that only this chapter of Jewish creativity in the diaspora can fill 'the empty void between the poetry of the Bible and that of our own time', Bialik in fact issued an astoundingly harsh verdict on almost 2,000 years of

Jewish literature. Demanding that the poetry of Spain be read as a living body of literature—and not as research material for scholars—Bialik condemned the Wissenschaft des Judentums scholars for their 'diasporic' and 'Western' mentality, which in his view left them 'without an audience, without a national language, without a central, overarching idea, entrenched in foreign tongues'. Their studies he called 'a desolate valley strewn with dry bones... and filled with ruins'. Bialik thus harnessed contemporary research to the urgent task of what he termed the *kinnus*— the ingathering, anthologizing, and popularizing of treasures from the Jewish past. To further this goal he founded in Odessa the *Dvir* publishing house (which he later moved to Berlin and Tel Aviv), in which—together with Rawnitzki—he edited and published *Sefer ha-Aggada* (see below), and the poems of Solomon Ibn Gabirol.[4]

The 'obvious' manner in which the Hebrew poetry of the Spanish period was linked to the Zionist reconstruction of Jewish culture may be explained in various ways. Although the secular Hebrew poetry of Spain was not 'secular' in the modern sense of the word—written as it was by religious authors, and functioning in the context of a religious culture—its most representative students and scholars tended to emphasize (perhaps overemphasize) its 'secular' aspects and the 'universal' values (beauty, humour, passion, hedonism—or alternatively, pessimism) which it shared with other literatures. The Spanish Jews, as apparently portrayed in these poems, were described as being 'at home' in Gentile culture (while also retaining their ties with their ancient tradition), and as possessing a wider spectrum of human interests and dispositions than their 'exilic' counterparts. In other words, they seemed more 'normal', more eligible to serve as role-models for the 'new Jew'. The precedent of the revival of the Hebrew language in Spain contributed undoubtedly as well to the 'Zionization' of the Spanish poetry. Biographical details concerning Spain's Jewish poets were appropriated by the new national narrative. Judah ha-Levi, who in the nineteenth century was considered a 'Romantic' poet, was subjected (already in the early days of Zionism) to this ideological transformation, and was made to become the 'first Zionist *aliyya*-maker'. Similarly, Samuel ha-Nagid was later portrayed as a prototypical courageous Jewish warrior.[5]

Concurrently with (though certainly independently of) the Zionization of Spanish Hebrew poetry, there was voiced the call to study Arabic poetry as its comparative background. The first scholar who devoted himself to the systematic

---

[4] Despite Bialik's subtle intuition in determining the version of the text and in the commentary, this edition does not meet the rigorous criteria of philological research (Schirmann 1942). Bialik's prestige contributed to the popularity of the Spanish poets and to the inclusion of Jewish poetry from Spain in high-school curricula. (Schirmann himself contributed to this effort by publishing small booklets of poems by Ibn Gabirol and ha-Levi for high-school students.)

[5] On Judah ha-Levi's nineteenth century revival, see S. Werses (1990). Samuel ha-Nagid remained unknown to scholars until 1924, when D. S. Sassoon publicized the fact that a manuscript of the diwan had been in his possession. The diwan was published in 1934, and was followed two years later by Schirmann's great essay on ha-Nagid's war poems (1936, repr. in Schirmann 1979). Samuel ha-Nagid, military leader of Granada, is the protagonist of a nationalistic children's poem by Nathan Altermann (1963).

comparison of Arabic and Hebrew poetry was David Yellin, who was familiar with both poetries on a first-hand basis, and who in 1926 became the first lecturer of medieval literature in the Hebrew University. His 1941 book was the first detailed and systematic inquiry of its type into stylistics, poetics, and rhetoric. Yellin drew upon Moses Ibn Ezra's book on poetics[6]—the only theoretical essay on poetry written (in Arabic) by a Jewish Andalusian poet—and demonstrated how Ibn Ezra drew his ideas from Arabic books of rhetoric.[7] Yellin's book is a survey of rhetorical devices organized taxonomically, with each trope and figure explained separately and illustrated using analogous Hebrew and Arabic examples. Yellin, who was also the first to coin Hebrew terms for rhetorical concepts in Arabic, immersed himself in medieval Arabic poetics, which he considered to be an indispensable key for understanding and enjoying the contemporary Hebrew poetry. In his introduction to Yellin's book, Brody noted that familiarity with the Arabic poetics is essential to an understanding of the Hebrew poetry. Schirmann (1942), on the other hand, had reservations regarding the scholastic nature of Arabic poetics, leading him to claim that it can in no way contribute to the enjoyment of the Western reader and should be subjected 'to all due criticism'. An inconspicuous tension between scholars of European versus those of oriental origin here comes to the fore.[8] (It is not accidental perhaps that Schirmann, who by that time had spent only a few years in Palestine, chose to interpret this aesthetic opposition as one between Western and Eastern tastes, rather than between medieval and modern ones.) Schirmann (1967) still regarded Yellin's method as a hindrance to proper literary criticism: 'an antiquated "Poetics" held sway amongst us ... which has not as yet entirely disappeared from the work of our literary critics.' In his own writings Schirmann seldom compared the Hebrew texts with their Arabic counterparts, referring only to an Arabic 'influence' and 'atmosphere' apparent in the Hebrew poems. One scholar who did indeed subject Yellin to 'all due criticism' was Dan Pagis, who—in his introduction to the second edition of Yellin's book (1970)—criticized Yellin for his treatment of isolated figures without relating to their contexts and relations to each other.

---

[6] Translated into Hebrew twice: by Halper (1924) and Halkin (1976).

[7] Similarly, in his excellent edition of the *Diwan Todros Abulafia* (1932–7), Yellin's commentary pointed to Abulafia's close affinity to Arabic poetics.

[8] Yellin was born in Jerusalem to a mother of Iraqi origin. The first-hand, ongoing familiarity of Eastern Jews with Spain's secular Jewish poets (whose diwans they copied continuously), as well as with Arabic literature, yielded several scholars. Preceding Yellin was Saul Abdullah Yosef, a Baghdad-born merchant who lived in Hong Kong, where he closely followed the publications of nineteenth-century scholars and regularly sent corrections of his own to the journals in which they appeared. In reaction to Brody's *Diwan Jehudah ha-Levi*, Yosef published his own interpretative work (*Givat Shaul*), in which he cited Arabic verses corresponding to the Hebrew ones. Because of his Arabic education, Yosef considered himself a more competent commentator than his Western counterparts. The Arabic context of Spain's Hebrew literature had been noted earlier by Steinschneider, and even Luzzatto sensed intuitively that Hebrew rhetoric has its origin in Arabic poetry. In the introduction to his book, Yosef Tobi (2000) surveys the history of the Hebrew/Arabic comparative scholarship. More on this topic below.

Pagis did admit that acquaintance with the Arabic poetics was indispensable, but blamed Yellin for ignoring the poets' broader poetic considerations, their views on poetic originality, and the relation between rhetoric, subject-matter, and poetic genres—topics to which later works by Pagis (1970) and Levin (1980, 1995) would be devoted (see below).

Yellin's successor at the Hebrew University was Brody's greatest student, Jefim Schirmann—who, as the foremost scholar of medieval and Renaissance-era Hebrew poetry, determined to a great extent the shape and character of the field in the twentieth century. Schirmann consolidated the instruction of the subject at the Hebrew University, and from amongst his students emerged some of the discipline's greatest scholars in the latter half of the century. The most widely influential of his numerous publications[9] was *Hebrew Poetry in Spain and Provence* (1st edn. 1957, 2nd edn. 1960). This four-volume anthology, compiled according to criteria of both historical representation and aesthetic merit, was acknowledged immediately upon its publication as the accepted canon of Hebrew masterpieces written in Spain over a period of 550 years. Bialik's call—expressed in his concept of the *kinnus*—for the propagation of scholarly knowledge throughout the wider circles of the learned public (without a dilution of academic standards) found its most perfect realization in this anthology, whose large circulation and accessible nature helped establish the study and instruction of Spain's Hebrew poetry as the main axis and centre of gravity of the medieval field. In addition to the major poets of Al-Andalus, the anthology provided the general public with a first glance into the works of countless 'minor' poets. It also represented poets who wrote in Christian Spain before the Expulsion, and compiled important pieces of rhymed prose. In his separate intro-ductions to the selected texts of each poet, Schirmann clarified historical and biographical matters, related the works and their authors to various literary trad-itions, and took first steps at setting principles of aesthetic judgement. These introductions served as embryonic seeds for Schirmann's great historical opus, which was published posthumously.

Already in a 1965 lecture before the Israeli Academy of Sciences (Schirmann 1967)—or even earlier, in fact, in an essay from 1942—Schirmann lamented the lack of a broad, systematic monograph on the poetry of Spain: 'The time has not yet come to describe the history of Hebrew literature from a new viewpoint. We are still

---

[9] Schirmann's works span the entire range of Hebrew poetry from the early Middle Ages to the Renaissance. In addition to the poetry of Spain and Provence, which occupied the centre of his work, Schirmann devoted his scholarly attention to the Hebrew poetry and drama and the Jewish music of Italy. He also wrote on ancient liturgical poetry and authored a few essays on Ashkenaz and Yemen. In addition, he published poems from manuscripts in critical editions (Schirmann 1965; 1974), edited anthologies for schools, wrote monographic essays, and so forth. Also of note is his bibliographical project of annual indices of editions, as well as of books and articles on medieval literature, published continuously in the periodical *Kiryat Sefer* from 1950 to 1978. For *An Accumulated Index* of his annual lists, see Schirmann (1989). For a list of Schirmann's own studies (up to 1970), see 'Abramson and Mirsky' (1970: 413–27).

far from completing the bibliographical and historical part of our work, which is the foundation on which we can build.' Schirmann himself did not get around to writing such a monograph until the final years of his life. Drafts found in his legacy and based on his lectures at the Hebrew University were the source for two large volumes published in recent years, *The History of Hebrew Poetry in Muslim Spain* (Schirmann and Fleischer 1996) and *The History of Hebrew Poetry in Christian Spain and Southern France* (Schirmann and Fleischer 1997). Both volumes were edited by Schirmann's student Ezra Fleischer, at that time already one of the foremost scholars in the field, who completed some missing sections and added detailed bibliographical notes in order to bring the work up to date. Thanks to Fleischer's generous supplements, this book will no doubt continue to serve as a comprehensive introduction and a useful and accessible textbook for many years to come. The volumes are organized according to the same biographical-historical method Schirmann employed in his aforementioned anthology. The major poets are discussed in extensive monographic chapters, which survey their historic and biographic backgrounds, topical subject-matter, and formal and thematic innovations (as well as their non-literary writings, if any). Smaller chapters on minor poets are woven into the chronological presentation. The second volume devotes additional chapters to the later poetry of Christian Spain and Provence, with a special emphasis on rhymed prose.

The dated literary approach of these volumes should not be ignored, however.[10] Although they were published at the very end of the twentieth century—a quarter of a century after the ground-breaking work of Schirmann's students (see below) and approximately fifteen years after the great scholar himself passed away (1981)—they represent a previous phase in the history of the discipline. In fact, they embody the philological bearings characteristic of orientalist studies in the German universities of the early twentieth century, as well as the biographical inclination prevailing then in literary research. In the absence of solid biographical facts about the medieval poets—and based on the romantic assumption that 'poetry is biography', with no consideration of the fictional dimension—Schirmann drew biographical conclusions from the texts themselves. Furthermore, the eclectic internal structure of the chapters prevents any treatment of synchronic phenomena (e.g. generic typology or the use of figurative language) or description of the development of these literary phenomena in diachronic cross-sections (e.g. the evolution of each thematic type, the genealogy of forms, fluctuation of conventions and literary tastes, linguistic and formal developments, background for innovations, and so on). The first volume devotes separate sub-chapters to the secular and liturgical poems of each poet. This poses a twofold difficulty: on the one hand, the focus on individual poets prevents the author from delineating the discrete evolutionary paths of these two very distinct poetries; on the other hand, the individual chapters do not coalesce into

---

[10] Scheindlin (1999) discusses this extensively in his review-essay on these books.

integrative monographs. The bookshelves of Hebrew literature still await holistic monographs (of the type extant in other literatures) that would cross-cut between interpretations of single texts, observations on literary style, biographical facts, individual psychology, and general socio-cultural considerations. The mental phenomenon that produced bodies of work as diverse and imbued with contradictions as Ibn Gabirol's or Judah ha-Levi's still remains a challenge. Schirmann's second volume also contains separate chapters on individual poets, and, with the exception of a few sporadic remarks, lacks a comprehensive discussion of socio-cultural contexts or of the significant literary changes that occurred in this school of poetry following its migration from Al-Andalus to Christian territories.

The significant academic revisions that changed the face of the discipline were made in particular by two of Schirmann's disciples, Dan Pagis and Ezra Fleischer, who began their work at the end of the 1960s. As much as Pagis and Fleischer were Schirmann's successors, however, they also diverged from the path laid out by their revered teacher. Whereas Pagis devoted his efforts to the secular poetry, Fleischer dedicated himself to the liturgical corpus. This clear division of labour underscored the perceived separation between these two fields—which, owing perhaps to the prominence of Spain in Schirmann's work, had not been so stark before. Pagis's and Fleischer's two respective seminal books on the liturgical (Fleischer 1975) and the secular poetry (Pagis 1976) open with similar statements that justify the demarcation of distinct histories and poetics for each field. Both scholars wished to provide a comprehensive portrayal of the different centres and schools, Spain being just one of them. Furthermore, both shared the fundamental assumption that the history of poetry is not one with 'the lives of the poets'. Employing formalistic methods that had begun to take root in literary research in Israel at the end of the 1960s, Pagis and Fleischer turned their attention from the authors to the texts, and from a general historiographic approach to the inner evolution and deep structures of the literary phenomena. Henceforth, our review of research trends in the last thirty years will be divided into separate discussions of secular and liturgical poetry.

In the study of secular poetry, the following directions and trends have emerged in recent decades: (1) historical-literary research: surveys of centres and schools; (2) comparative research (against the background of Arabic and Romance literatures); (3) studies with emphasis on aesthetics, poetics, and rhetoric; and (4) application of contemporary theories (New Criticism, formalism, structuralism, post-structuralism, cognitive theories, feminism). Needless to say, any clear-cut distinction between the aforementioned trends is artificial, since more than one direction of research can often be discerned in the work of a single scholar.

The crossroads at which the scholarship of medieval poetry found itself in the 1960s was identified in a 1967 essay by Schirmann, in which he lamented not only the absence of a comprehensive history (see above), but also the lack of tools for 'the analysis of a poem as a literary, artistic creation'. He also suggested the relative backwardness of the Hebrew field in this respect, in comparison with advance in the scholarship of other medieval literatures: 'For a number of years now, there has been an upheaval in literary research in Europe and successful attempts have been made to bridge the generations to apply new methods of examining the literary writings of old. Let us hope that we shall arrive at a similar change in the field of Hebrew literature.'[11]

It was Dan Pagis who took up the challenge of applying newer theories to the field. In the introduction to his book on Moses Ibn Ezra, *Secular Poetry and Poetic Theory* (1970)—which may be considered a post-Schirmannic manifesto—Pagis forged and legitimized the use of modern theoretical and methodical tools for the study of medieval Hebrew poetry. Like Schirmann before him, Pagis rejected Yellin's relativist approach—according to which an ancient poetry may only be comprehended in relation to its own explicit poetics. In Pagis's opinion, when a work of art is judged solely by the standards of its own era, it may force on the modern reader criteria that differ from his or her own insights and tastes. On the other hand, Pagis remained faithful to Schirmann's caveat that the 'transfer of foreign concepts' should 'proceed carefully and with circumspection'. He rejected previous attempts by modern Hebrew literary critic Eddy Zemach (1962) to offer readers New Criticism-style close readings of secular (and liturgical) medieval poems. Whereas in the United States and Europe New Criticism was already superseded in literary research by formalism and structuralism, in the study of Hebrew literature Zemach's interpretations were considered a bold innovation. For the first time, medieval Hebrew poems were presented as works of art bearing aesthetic values. Pagis, however, opposed Zemach's ahistorical attitude, which in his opinion ignored medieval poetics and mentalities.[12]

In Pagis's view, modern readers could be brought closer to the ancient texts through what he called a 'perspectivist' approach, combining an acquaintance with medieval poetics and other classical poetics with modern theories of poetry. Only such a combination would enable the modern critic to elucidate the relation

[11] In this context, a short but seminal essay by Joseph Weiss (1952) should not go without mention. In his explication of the relation between 'Courtly Culture and Courtly Poetry', in which he demonstrated how poetry and language served not only to reflect courtly reality but to shape it as well, Weiss attempted, for the first time in the history of this field, to utilize methods from the 'sociology of culture' and free the research from its fixation on the then current philological-textological and biographical methods.

[12] See also Pagis (1979). Zemach's interpretations nevertheless had a decisive influence on the teaching of this poetry in Israeli universities and high schools, as well as on its appeal for modern Israeli poets. In a way, one could say that the wide acceptance of this poetry among teachers and students fulfilled Bialik's demand to 'remove the poetry of Spain from ... [the realm of] scientific research and bring it to the public domain of current literature ... [in order to] let it imbue contemporary literature with its scent' (Bialik and Rawnitzky 1924). For additional interpretations of single poems see Rosen-Moked and Zemach (1983) and Scheindlin (1986). Tzur (1987) uses his interpretations of medieval poems for illustrating cognitive theories of reading. Although he calls his approach 'perspectivist', it is entirely ahistoric.

between conventions and single poems, and between form, content, and style. Pagis's book is the finest demonstration of this method, confronting the explicit poetic views articulated in Ibn Ezra's theoretical essay on poetics with the poetic assumptions and aesthetic criteria implicit in Ibn Ezra's own poetic praxis, and using modern tools to examine both. Pagis also distinguished between descriptive poetics and aesthetic judgement. Rather than attempting to bring the medieval poetry closer to contemporary modern tastes, he tried to enhance our understanding of its otherness and exoticism.

In this book—which in the years following its publication had a profound influence on the approach of other scholars of medieval poetry—Pagis concentrated on the poetry of Moses Ibn Ezra, whom he considered to be the most characteristic representative of classic Andalusian poetry. In describing the morphology of the different genres and their rhetorical and figurative forms, Pagis applied structuralist methods and created a critical foundation that enabled him (as well as other scholars) to portray and evaluate the poetry of the entire school.[13]

Pagis's second book, *Change and Tradition* (1976), represents yet another phase in the study of genres and their consideration from a historic perspective. It was the first attempt since the general introductions of the Wissenschaft des Judentums to portray the history of this poetry in broad strokes. (Schirmann's two great historical volumes, it should be remembered, were published roughly twenty years *after* Pagis's book.) Unlike Schirmann's chronological-monographic approach, Pagis's is a historical poetics investigating the evolution of the literary phenomena themselves. Thus Pagis follows the evolution of genres, their prosody, morphology, thematic, rhetoric, and so on, as well as the development of modes of representation, poetry's perception of itself, fluctuations in literary tastes, social changes and their effect on authors and audiences, the developmental dynamics of the Hebrew language vis-à-vis the poetry, contacts with other literatures and cultures, and so forth. These are shown to be a dynamic chain of traditions and innovations, continuities and ruptures, reactions and interactions. Here, as in his book published in English (1991) and in the collected essays (1993) published after his premature death, Pagis offers an expansive thesis that argues for a dynamic historical continuity through transformations and modifications, extending from mid-tenth-century Spain to the beginnings of the Haskalah poetry.

In addition to his exposition of the various types of poetry in Spain and Italy, Pagis made an important contribution to the study of the rhymed prose genres that evolved in Christian Spain (and crossed to Italy as well), and discussed their literary pluralism and social functions.[14] Pagis's refusal to consider the maqama a 'pure' genre whose 'rules' should dictate the evaluation of other, more hybrid forms of

[13] Rosen-Moked (1985) utilized similar structuralist tools in her analysis of the Hebrew *muwashshah* genre.

[14] Matti Huss, Pagis's student, has devoted his research to rhymed prose, examining its immanent poetics as well as its relation to contemporary narratology. See Huss (1994, 2001). Raymond Scheindlin

prose, captures his literary approach in a nutshell. Pagis similarly rejected normative rhetoric as a sole aesthetic standard. He opposed the employment of the Andalusian tradition as a set of criteria for the evaluation of other poetic schools, and in the focus on generic 'conventions' he saw a restrictive method. His repeated plea to consider literary reality in all its plurality, hybridity, and dynamism is part of his important legacy. (See also Pagis 1979.)

The chapters in *Change and Tradition* that discuss the two Latin-Romance centres of Hebrew poetry—Christian Spain and Italy—were the first general expositions of these two schools. (Schirmann (1997), who, as already mentioned, devoted an entire volume to the poetry of Christian Spain, did not include in it a general introduction or overview.) For the first time, the Hebrew literature of Christian Spain was presented as an independent school bearing its own characteristics. Unlike previous scholars, Pagis did not portray this school as an inferior, epigonic sequel to the poetry of Muslim Spain, but as a departure to a new poetics. Schirmann's and Pagis's works on Christian Spain still require completion, elaboration, and summation. The conjecture (expressed repeatedly by both scholars, and by others as well) that, starting from the thirteenth century, Hebrew poetry and rhymed prose interacted with Romance literatures (Provençal, Catalonian, and Castillian) has been heretofore explored in a few isolated studies, with merely tentative conclusions (Doron 1989; Scheindlin 1994; Sáenz-Badillos 1996). A more precise and general picture is yet to be drawn, and the field awaits comparative studies by scholars well versed in Hebrew and Romance languages. We can only assume that such a contribution would come from contemporary Spain, which hosts an active centre of research in the field of medieval Hebrew poetry. Unlike its Israeli and American counterparts, the Spanish research community includes many non-Jewish scholars, who view medieval Hebrew culture as an integral layer in Spain's multilingual and multicultural history.[15]

Pagis's book also includes the first—and so far the only—general exposition of the secular Italian poetry, whose origins can be traced to the early Spanish influence of the thirteenth century, and whose branches extend to the nineteenth century.[16]

---

and Judith Dishon have also published studies in this field. Tova Rosen (Rosen 2000a; 2000b) discussed works written in rhymed prose from a feminist perspective.

[15] Several journals (*Al-Andalus*, *Sefarad*, and others) devoted to the history and culture of Jews and Arabs in Spain have been active in Spain for decades. Conferences on Spain's three cultures have been held regularly in recent years. *Poesía Estrófica* (Corriente and Sáenz-Badillos 1991) is the result of a conference devoted to strophic poetry in the three cultures. The view that Hebrew poetry is one component of Spain's multicultural mélange received its first explicit articulation in S. M. Stern's studies on the *muwashshah* (Stern 1974). Spain's most active and prolific scholar of Hebrew poetry at present is Angel Sáenz-Badillos. Among his many publications we shall mention here only his critical editions of the grammatical essays of Dunash, Menahem, and the disciples of Menahem, and his bilingual (Hebrew–Spanish) editions of poems by ha-Nagid and ha-Levi.

[16] See also Pagis's writings on Italy in his books from 1991 and 1993. Schirmann, who did not include the poetry of Italy in his historical volumes, did devote many studies to it (see Schirmann 1979, as well

Pagis laid emphasis on the new metrical, formal, and thematic syntheses between Jewish-Arabic elements and the dominant Italian influence, and demonstrated how Italy's Hebrew writers subsequently developed independent styles removed from the Spanish models. Pagis's work on Italy continued in his 1986 book dedicated to a unique genre of complex poetic and graphic riddles, common among Jewish Italian authors until the nineteenth century. Another contribution to the study of Italy was made by Pagis's student, Dvora Bregman, especially in her studies on the Hebrew sonnet in Italy (1985; 1986). The Italian school of poetry (whose origins as a centre of piyyut date back to the ninth century[17]) lasted roughly a millennium, during which it underwent numerous changes and transformations that are yet to be comprehensively examined.

While Schirmann and Pagis viewed Hebrew poetry in a European context, other scholars continued in Yellin's footsteps by examining Hebrew poetry vis-à-vis its Arabic counterpart. This trend has grown and evolved in recent decades—perhaps also due to the realization that the Hebrew–Arabic literary synthesis created in Al-Andalus was part of an entire Jewish–Arab cultural space that existed in the East (and which also included writing in Judaeo-Arabic).

The most comprehensive work of comparative criticism after Yellin was done by Israel Levin, who focused exclusively on the poetry of Spain. In his essays, which he began publishing in the 1960s, and in the three volumes of his *The Embroidered Coat* (1995), Levin devised a consistent method for examining the relation between the Hebrew genres of Andalusian secular poetry and their Arabic models. Unlike Yellin and Ratzaby, Levin did not make atomistic comparisons, but rather generated a systematic thematic typology of entire genres (praise, bravado, love, wine, meditative and moralistic poetry, and so on),[18] in which the Hebrew types are examined for their proximity to (and sometimes divergence from) their Arabic models. Although Levin aimed for a synchronic-normative exposition of the genres, his method allowed him sometimes to underscore the different personal styles of individual poets within the generic conventions.[19] Several chapters also include mini-anthologies of Arabic (particularly Jahilic and Abassid) poetry translated into

---

as his bibliography in Abramson and Mirsky). Already in 1934 Schirmann published an anthology of Italian poetry as well as the first Hebrew play written in Italy.

[17] See also the chapter on Italian piyyut in Fleischer (1975).

[18] A similar path was taken by the Dutch scholar Arie Schippers (1994). Yellin's disciple, Nehemia Allony, continued his mentor's comparative method, but in several of his essays discussed also the more fundamental question of how Hebrew poets confronted Arabic poetry, drew upon it, and competed against it (Allony 1991). Dozens of essays by Yehuda Ratzaby, a Yemen-born scholar versed in Arabic poetry, are comparative lists of Hebrew and Arabic motifs. For a bibliography of Ratzaby's essays, see Dishon and Hazan (1991).

[19] Levin's other works include monographs on Samuel ha-Nagid (1967) and Abraham Ibn Ezra (1970), and a book on the mysticism of Ibn Gabirol (1986). He also edited a critical edition of Abraham Ibn Ezra's liturgical poems (1976–80). In several essays he noted echoes of medieval poetry in the work of modern poets. For a bibliography of his writings, see Rosen and Tzur.

Hebrew. On many occasions, Levin stresses the process of 'Hebraization' and 'Judaization' of these poems. When describing the thematic genres, Levin also discusses the cultural mentality they convey (courtly hedonism in the wine poetry; Sufi, ascetic and *adab* views in the moralistic poetry, and so on). Also stressed in Levin's work are the relations between liturgical and secular poetry (e.g. Levin 1971).

Another scholar bringing his Arabic scholarship to the study of Hebrew literature is Raymond Scheindlin, whose first work (1974) had an Arab-Andalusian poet (Al-Mu'tamid) for its subject. In his books on secular Hebrew poetry (*Wine, Women and Death*, 1986) and the liturgical Hebrew poetry of Al-Andalus (*The Gazelle*, 1991), Scheindlin combined his profound knowledge of both literatures with refined literary taste and keen interpretative skills. His excellent English translations of selected poems in these two volumes,[20] and his interpretations, which combine close readings with a familiarity with the poets' mental and cultural worlds, have contributed greatly to the proliferation of medieval poetry in Western universities.[21] Characteristic of Scheindlin (as well as of Levin) is the holistic literary approach to liturgical and secular poetry (in this respect, see his monograph on Moses Ibn Ezra, in Menocal *et al.* 2000).

Another scholar who stresses the indispensability of intimate acquaintance of the modern critic with medieval Arabic poetry and thought is Yosef Tobi. In his book *Proximity and Distance* (2000), he insists that Hebrew poetry must be compared not just generally to Arabic poetry but specifically to its temporally and geographically close Andalusian counterpart (a demand that he himself was only partially able to fulfill). Like Levin, he emphasizes the 'influence' of Arabic literature on Hebrew poetry and the 'assimilation' and 'imitation' of Arabic forms and conventions by Hebrew poets; unlike his predecessor, though, he is more drastic in stressing the Jewish character of that poetry. He draws attention to literary motifs and conceptual elements from Arabic culture that were *rejected* by the Jews, yet gives this rejection a rather simplistic religious explanation; in his view, the Hebrew poets embraced 'foreign' themes only when these did not conflict with their own Jewish world-view. Studies by Brann and Drory, which offer more intricate theoretical explanations for such rejection mechanisms, are not taken into consideration in Toby's discussion of the problem.

[20] Also noteworthy is the fairly extensive selection of medieval Hebrew poetry that appeared in the bilingual anthology *The Penguin Book of Hebrew Verse*, translated by T. Carmi (1981).

[21] The United States has been a prominent centre for the study of Hebrew poetry throughout the twentieth century. The first medievalist stronghold in the United States was founded by Solomon Schechter, discoverer of the Genizah, who in 1902 was appointed Provost of the Jewish Theological Seminary in New York. Schechter moved parts of the Genizah collection from Cambridge to the JTS and published selections from it. Also active in New York in the beginning of the twentieth century was Israel Davidson. Shalom Spiegel arrived at the Seminary in 1929. His studies on the liturgical poems of ha-Qallir were not published, but he became known for his outstanding study on Ashkenazi liturgical poetry (1967). The Institute for Medieval Hebrew Literature in the JTS in New York is named after him and is currently headed by his disciple, R. Scheindlin. Another scholar active in the United States today is Ross Brann (below).

Another Hebraist-Arabist, Ross Brann, uses deconstructive methods to examine the Hebrew poets' own perceptions of their poetry. In his 1991 book Brann shows how these poets adopted the negative ('poetry is untruth') or ambivalent ('poetry is beautiful in spite of its untruth') attitudes toward poetry prevalent in the Arabic poetics and poetry. He examines how they appropriated the topos of *The Compunctious Poet* (the title of his book), looks for the specificity of that topos in its Hebrew renditions, and discusses its different uses by different Hebrew poets. He also points to the poets' own ambivalence regarding the Arabic element in their poetry. In exposing the intricate and organic manner in which a minority culture becomes enchanted with the dominant culture and appropriates its values—while at the same time continuing to fence itself off from it and struggle for its uniqueness, using methods borrowed from the dominant culture itself—Brann presents here an elaborate alternative to mechanistic (or impressionistic) theories of 'influence'. Owen and Brann's 1997 study is another elaboration on questions of cultural interaction, contact, and conflict—this time involving the three cultures of Muslim Spain. The volume *Al-Andalus* (Menocal *et al.* 2000), from the *Cambridge History of Arabic Literature* series includes chapters on Hebrew literature (by Brann, Scheindlin, Drory, and Rosen), as an integral part of the cultural history of Muslim Spain.

Taking a similar approach are Rina Drory's studies on intercultural contacts (1988; 2000). Adopting formalist-functionalist theories, Drory substitutes the obsolete notion of 'influence' with the more useful term 'interference', and with the view of literature as a function of socio-cultural relations. Unlike others who strive to prove the 'Judaization' of Arabic culture, Drory's chapters on Saadia, Dunash, Moses Ibn Ezra, and Alharizi investigate the Arabicization of Jewish culture and the role of the dominant Arabic literature in the reconstitution of Jewish literature between the tenth and thirteenth centuries. Drory is not interested in the migration of themes or ideas from one literature to another, nor is she busy source-hunting. Rather, she asks: under what cultural conditions does a group (in this case a minority group) borrow literary models, linguistic practices, and textual functions from another (majority) group? And how do the adopted elements then function in their new social or literary environment? What are the mechanisms of selection or rejection?

In recent years—after such literary aspects finally received due attention—historiographic questions seem to have returned to the forefront of the research agenda, albeit in a more complex and intricate manner. These questions involve the history and development of the different literary centres, the contacts between them, and their divergence from one another, as well as an evaluation of their contribution. Also involved are various scholarly interests, which touch on present-day controversial issues as the Arab–Jewish 'symbiosis' or the secular–religious synthesis. New studies—in particular, the considerable progress in the study of the Genizah and piyyut in the last three decades—have shed new light on these questions. Is the scholarship of Spain indeed, as Schirmann claimed, 'a field in its own right', and is it still justified to consider Spain the focal point of the discipline?

Did the secular poetry of Al-Andalus emerge *ex nihilo*, as various scholars previously claimed? Can the literary centres that developed in Christian Spain, Provence, Italy, and the Muslim East, starting from the thirteenth century, be construed as branches of an original Spanish centre, or did they function as independent centres with their own distinct histories (which also happened to include contacts with Muslim Spain)? Should the poetry of Spain be discussed in the context of European centres of Hebrew poetry, or in the context of Hebrew poetry written in the Muslim world? And, finally, how do new findings in the liturgical field help shed light on the secular poetry?

Re-evaluations concerning the place of Spain have emerged from several directions. Scheindlin (1999) asserts that Schirmann—in his anthology and later in the two *History* volumes—founded a historiographic tradition which placed the poetry of Al-Andalus in a Western European context. (Pagis, who followed in Schirmann's footsteps, stretched the geographic canvas to include Italy, and the historic one to include the beginnings of Haskalah poetry in the early eighteenth century.) In Scheindlin's (1999) view, however, the use of the modern term 'Spain' to designate a single geographic-cultural unit ignores the Eastern context in which the poetry of Al-Andalus should be considered. The Jewish poets of Al-Andalus did not perceive themselves as progenitors of 'Hebrew Spanish poetry', but as the culmination of a literary development that began in the East. The innovations of the Andalusian Golden Age were facilitated by the much earlier Arabicization of Jewish culture in Iraq at the end of the Gaonic period (Drory 1988); the Andalusian style began spreading to the Maghreb, Egypt, Iraq, and other locales well before the expulsion of the Jews from Spain; many works by poets from Spain were discovered in the Genizah, and entire Andalusian-style diwans were written in the East. All the above—in addition to the persistence of the Andalusian style (albeit in modified forms) in all Mediterranean countries (and even in Yemen) long after the Expulsion and until the twentieth century—support, according to Scheindlin, the construal of the Andalusian centre as a Western branch of an Eastern Jewish world, and of the Eastern centres of poetry that followed it as its legitimate successors, no less (and perhaps more) than their European counterparts.[22]

The greatest twentieth-century scholar of Hebrew liturgical poetry, Ezra Fleischer, has also focused primarily on the East. Adding the religious–secular opposition to the Eastern–Western one, Fleischer suggests that Spain be seen as an anomalous 'secular' branch of a religious Jewish world. In his view, Spanish poetry is a unique chapter in the history of this world, the product of a 'non-traditional Jewish society' with a ' "secular" worldview'. Yet, from the panoramic perspective of the history of Jewish creativity, Spain is merely 'a chapter, not a new

[22] The eastern poetry, both before and after the Golden Age, has not been sufficiently studied. Yahalom and Be'eri have published works on Hebrew poetry in the Ottoman Empire after the Expulsion from Spain. Ratzaby and Tobi have studied and published selections from the Hebrew poetry of Yemen, Ephraim Hazan from the poetry of North African Jews.

beginning' (Fleischer 1998). Spain's diminished importance in Fleischer's eyes corresponds with the smaller role he ascribes to the Arabic element in its poetry. In his opinion, the 'mental turn' that occurred in Spain (and was reflected in its poetry) 'did not stem from the contact with the Arabic poetry' of Al-Andalus, but originated ever earlier in the East (ibid.). By calling this culture 'secular' (the inverted commas are Fleischer's), he certainly does not intend to claim it was anti-religious; what he presumably means is that the Jewish–Arab symbiosis affected not only aspects of everyday life, and not only the non-liturgical poetry, but also religious thought and culture. This symbiosis was, in Fleischer's view, 'alien' to traditional Judaism and therefore 'unauthentic' (an expression he uses frequently). 'The Arab–Jewish symbiosis was an utter mirage' (Schirmann–Fleischer 1997: 92)—and the evidence, according to Fleischer, is its collapse at the end of the Golden Age. Fleischer bases this dialectical interpretation of the Spanish poetry—as both a continuation and a revolution—on the findings of the Genizah, which reveal the sheer wealth of the liturgical poetry, as well as its longevity and the extent of its expansion, and thus, in Fleischer's view, counterbalance the distorted enchantment of many a modern scholar with the aestheticism and secularity of the Spanish poetry. Thanks to the Genizah, writes Fleischer, 'the secular Hebrew poetry of Spain has been assimilated in the grand expanse of our ancient poetry and has become an authentic part of it' (Fleischer 1998). Fleischer's conclusions thus seem to indicate another swing of the pendulum. Whereas early scholars (Zunz, Luzzatto, and others) sought to establish piyyut as the focus of research—only to have Bialik and Schirmann stress the centrality of Spain—Fleischer has now restored emphasis on the liturgical poetry.

The diminution of Spain's dominance in Fleischer's eyes is demonstrated in the relatively short chapter on liturgical Spanish poetry in his *Hebrew Liturgical Poetry in the Middle Ages* (1975). This seminal work offers the first systematic exposition of liturgical poetry since the great studies of the mid-nineteenth century. Introducing a new historical account of over a thousand years of Hebrew liturgical poetry, the book describes the different eras and centres in the development of this poetry, from its fifth-century origins in Palestine, through its extensions in Iraq, to its various European branches in Spain, Italy, and Germany. However, unlike the great works of the Wissenschaft des Judentums, Fleischer's book is not a chronological listing of poems and poets but a historical poetics that attempts to examine the liturgical genres, their genesis their ritual functions, their typical structures, prosodies, rhetoric, and the dynamic transformations they underwent in different generations and schools. The gist of Fleischer's innovative thesis on the genesis of this poetry is as following: (1) the monumental compositional structures of the ancient liturgical genres correspond to the sequence of the different sections in the prayer cycle;[23] (2)

---

[23] For instance, the *Kerova*, *Kedushta*, and *Shiv'ata* genres correspond to the 'Amida prayer, whereas the composition of the *Yotzer* genre correspond to the blessings of the *Shema'*.

starting from the fourth century, these genres developed from the praxis of prayer in Palestinian synagogues; (3) the first liturgical poets or *paytanim* were cantors who performed their liturgical pieces as alternatives to the established prayer forms used by the public. Fleischer's structural-genealogical approach and his attention to poetic elements (rhyme, strophic patterns, ornamentation, etc.) allow him to periodize the formal development of the genres, based on which he provides his chronology of ancient liturgical poetry in Palestine and in the Eastern and European schools that followed. In his second book (1984) Fleischer focuses on the characteristics of *Yotzer*-type compositions through different eras.

All this would not have been possible if not for the Genizah. 'The Genizah was a constitutive element of primal importance in the study of this poetry; not only did it complement what had already been known, it also provided the foundations for the field' (Fleischer, 1989). The scarce material available to nineteenth-century scholars consisted of texts from (mostly European) prayer books, which had been abridged and muddled by later copyists. The vast (and more authentic) material of the Genizah had already been subjected to the scrutiny of earlier scholars (the most important of whom was Menahem Zulay) during the first seventy-five years of the twentieth century.[24] However, the scholarly edifice erected by Fleischer was entirely new. In his books and numerous articles[25] Fleischer has not only contributed myriads of new syntheses and conclusions, but also introduced revolutionary changes to the approaches and perceptions prevalent in the field.

The work of modern scholars investigating the liturgical poetry of the Genizah may be likened to that of an archeologist, who unearths concealed items in order to reconstruct an entire lost culture on their basis. The sorting, listing,[26] paleographic deciphering, and attempted dating of manuscripts and poems, their description based on formal criteria, the combination of fragments to form complete works, the preparation of critical editions, and so on—all of these still constitute a work in progress. Teams of tireless scholars have been labouring on this colossal task for years, first in the Schocken Institute, then as part of the Project for the Research of Poetry and Piyyut, founded in 1967 by the Israeli Academy for Arts and Sciences and headed since its inception by Ezra Fleischer.[27] This foundational work helped

---

[24] Schechter (on his publications from the *piyyutim* of the Genizah, see Fleischer 1998, n. 7); Davidson (ibid., n. 8, and also Davidson 1919); Spiegel (1939); Zulay (Fleischer 1998, nn. 10, 11, 12, 20; also Zulay 1964, 1995). Also noteworthy are Genizah scholars Alexander Scheiber from Budapest and Arie (Lev) Wilsker from Leningrad.

[25] For a list of Fleischer's books and nearly 200 articles, see Elitzur-Be'eri (1994).

[26] So far, the Piyyut Project has recorded close to 60,000 whole poems and fragments (thus doubling the amount of material that had been included in Davidson's *Thesaurus*). Additional materials from the Genizah that had not been available to Western scholars have been recently discovered in the St Petersburg Library (Leningrad).

[27] This institute emerged in 1950 from The Institute of Microfilmed Hebrew Manuscripts in Jerusalem, whose activity was supported by David Ben-Gurion, and which so far has microfilmed 90% of all known Hebrew manuscripts from collections around the world.

complete and correct jumbled texts, provide additional information on known poets, unearth countless works by newly discovered ones, and generate monumental, surprisingly complex compositions—based on which scholars have been able to pinpoint styles, reconstruct schools and eras, and shed new light on the entire history of piyyut. Pioneering contributions to the stylistically based periodization of different eras in the history of liturgical poetry were made by Zulay (see Zulay 1964),[28] whose conclusions were later elaborated and perfected by Fleischer's structurally based periodization.

Space does not allow a complete exposition of the entire inventory of places, eras, and individuals illuminated by the Genizah. Hence, we shall only mention a few of the Genizah's general and specific contributions to the study of medieval poetry and piyyut. First of all, the Genizah unearthed 600-years' worth of pre-Andalusian liturgical poetry. The first edition of Yannai's piyyutim (Davidson 1919) not only brought to light a great poet, but also drew scholarly attention to the vast potential of the Genizah. Gradually, more ancient paytanim were discovered—some previously unknown, some the true value of whose work was revealed for the first time.[29] The Genizah refuted the earlier assumption that Babylonian Jews did not write piyyutim. This theory was based on the explicit rejection of the Palestinian piyyut by Babylonian rabbinical authorities. The Genizah, however, provided scholars with liturgical works composed in Iraq during the Gaonic period.[30] According to Fleischer, the meteoric rise of Spain could not have been fully comprehended, had the Genizah not revealed the full extent of the stagnation of the late Eastern piyyut (ninth to eleventh centuries) and the innovations of Saʿadia Gaon, which led to those of the Andalusian poets. The Geniza also included surprising material on pre-Andalusian secular poetry, refuting the view that the secular Andalusian school emerged *ex nihilo* (Fleischer 1998: 264). New material was also discovered about the first Andalusian poets of the tenth century[31] and the first Italian paytanim of the ninth century (ibid. 263). No current edition of Andalusian diwans can be imagined without using the remains of such diwans as the ones found in the Genizah (Yahalom 1999). Andalusian poems from the Genizah were published by Schirmann (1965). Also unearthed in the Genizah were documents (some autographic) con-

---

[28] For a philological study on the language of the ancient *piyyut*, see Yahalom (1985). On the relation between the payetaic rhetoric and the language of the Midrash, see Mirsky (1969).

[29] A partial edition of Yannai's work was edited by Zulay (1938). A critical edition was published by Z. M. Rabinovitz (1985–7). Other poets whose work was salvaged from the Genizah include Josef Ibn Avitur (an unpublished dissertation by Fleischer), The Anonymous (Fleischer 1974), Rav Saʿadia Gaon (Zulay 1964 and Y. Tobi, an unpublished dissertation), Shimʿon bar Megas (Yahalom 1984), and a series of paytanim edited by S. Elizur: Elʿazar birabbi Qillar (1988), Yehuda birabbi Binyamin (1988), Yehoshua bar Khalafa (1994), and Yosef ha-Levi ben Khalfon (1994). Elizur has also contributed to the scholarship on one of the greatest paytanim, Elʿazar birabbi Qillar, whose full work remains unpublished. Additional editions of other paytanim still await publication.

[30] Tova Beʾeri is about to publish a new edition of piyyutim by Baghdadi poet Yosef Albaradani (also see Beʾeri 1999).

[31] Fleischer's articles on this topic are listed in Fleischer 1998, n. 30.

cerning the life of Judah ha-Levi, making him the most extensively biographically documented poet (see also Fleischer in Rosen and Tzur 1994). New poems by ha-Levi were discovered as well. The Genizah also included many works by Eastern poets and paytanim, contemporaries of the Genizah itself. Yosef Yahalom has written about the role of this poetry in Eastern society starting from the twelfth century, as it is reflected in the poems themselves.

In addition to the abundant poetic material provided by the Genizah or to any literary and historical conclusions drawn from it, the Genizah provides insight into the social world and *mentalité* of the poets and their audiences in Palestine between the fourth and eighth centuries (Fleischer 1999). The sheer quantity of the piyyutim implies their widespread dissemination, which probably reached the common population as well. The complex poetic practices implicit in the piyyutim (structure, prosody, rhetoric, ornamentation) indicate the high aesthetic demands of their audiences—suggesting that despite the absence of a formal poetics, piyyut was not just a devotional form but an art form as well. The neologistic language and the learned references to midrashim indicate a high level of literacy. Fleischer also maintains that the poems' strophic structures and use of refrains are suggestive of the choral music of the ancient synagogues.

A different approach is prevalent in Yosef Yahalom's discussion of the relation between *Poetry and Society* (the title of his 1999 book). Unlike Fleischer, who bases his examination of poetry's place in society and the nature of its audience on the *poetic* qualities of the works, Yahalom chooses to interpret the ancient piyyutim as historical documents reflecting the real world (customs, beliefs, language, material culture, etc.) in which the poets and their audiences lived.

In conclusion, much progress seems to have been made in the last few decades, especially in the field of liturgical poetry, where new editions have been published and new syntheses have been introduced based on the study of Genizah. The scholars of piyyut are no longer satisfied with philological and historical research, but also explore historical poetics and discuss the piyyutim as literary works. In the study of secular poetry, on the other hand, relatively little progress has been made since Pagis's breakthrough in the 1970s. In contrast with much of the contemporary research on other medieval European literatures, where the newest modern and postmodern critical approaches are applied, most scholars of medieval Hebrew literature remain faithful to approaches that were new three decades ago. True, the material problems that encumbered the field from its inception still exist. Important critical editions are yet to be published. Some literary centres, schools, genres, and intercultural interactions (which have been mentioned throughout this article) have not been sufficiently studied. Also, from a technological and bibliographical perspective, the study of Hebrew literature lags behind that of other medieval literatures, where all the literary material is available on CD-Rom and research-facilitating concordances have been published. But even beyond such material difficulties, the theoretical questions which preoccupy current literary criticism—discourse and reality, fictionality, theories of reading, ethnicity, power structures, gender relations, sexuality, and others—have hardly been explored in our field.[32] It seems to be time for a new breakthrough of the type made by Pagis—one that would bridge the thirty-forty-year gap that exists between the study of medieval Hebrew poetry and the current approaches prevalent in the general field of literary research and criticism.

MEDIEVAL HEBREW NARRATIVE

The term 'medieval Hebrew narrative' is a relatively new one. Whereas medieval Hebrew poetry was acknowledged even by early scholars as a unique and distinct cultural field, one of great importance to the world of Jewish letters, no such recognition was awarded to its prosaic counterpart. While some scholars regarded medieval Hebrew prose as a direct, uninterrupted continuation of the prose litera-ture of the preceding era—the midrashim—others defined it as 'late Midrash', with unique characteristics distinguishing it from the 'classic' midrashim. Both ap-proaches, however, regarded the narrative prose literature of the Middle Ages as belonging to a body of 'midrashic' texts typified by certain historiographic, exegetic, moral, and mystical characteristics, and did not consider it an autonomous body of work, as they did the contemporaneous Hebrew poetry.

The work of the two major scholars of ancient Hebrew literature in the first half of the nineteenth century was emblematic of this attitude, and constituted one of the reasons for its emergence. Leopold Zunz's masterly book on the subject, published in Berlin in 1832,[33] was written on two different levels and with two different aims in mind: one scholarly, delineating the historical-philological foundations for the study of the midrashim, the other polemical and apologetic, seeking to establish the rituals prevalent in the Central European synagogues of his time as a continu-ation of the Jewish liturgy of the Talmud and midrash period. For both of these reasons, Zunz considered it a task of utmost importance to establish the historical continuity of the different midrashic works. Indeed, the entire history of the midrash—from such ancient midrashim as *The Fathers According to Rabi Nathan* and *Midrash Genesis Raba*, to later medieval compositions such as *Midrash Vayisaʾu* and *The Chronicles of Moses*—was presented in his book as one continuous se-

---

[32] With the exception of the aforementioned studies by Brann and Drory. For a gender-oriented investigation of medievel Hebrew literature, see Rosen (2002).

[33] On the historical and biographical background of this book and the evolution of the second edition, on which Chanoch Albeck's Hebrew translation (Jerusalem, 1946) was based, see Glatzer (1988).

quence. Although Zunz was well aware of the temporal gap between the different midrashic works—in fact, he was the first to point out these gaps, and insisted on their consideration when discussing the midrashim—he did not consider it important to date the different compositions or to periodize different genres as belonging to distinct eras.[34] Zunz did mention differences between 'ancient Midrash' and 'later developments in the Aggadah', or between 'the first and the second rabbinical periods'; these, however, were merely general distinctions, used by Zunz in order to differentiate earlier works from later ones, and especially in order to demonstrate that the midrash—as both a textual tradition and a social practice—enjoyed a never-disrupted historic continuity. The inclusion in one chapter of *Midrash Temurah*, dating from the thirteenth century, alongside such ancient midrashim as *The Fathers According to Rabi Nathan* and *Tana debei Eliyahu*, or of *The Scroll of Fasting* (*Megillat Taʿanit*)—one of the earliest texts of Rabbinic literature—alongside such typical medieval narrative texts as *The Itinerary of Eldad the Danite*, *Midrash of the Ten Commandments*, *Midrash Vayisaʿu*, *The Chronicles of Moses*, and *The Book of Jossipon*,[35] is indicative of Zunz's perception of continuity, which despite its failure to discern the distinct and unique character of medieval Hebrew prose continued to have a profound influence on the study of Hebrew literature in the following generations.

When the Hebrew translation of Zunz's book was published in 1946 (and later in additional editions), the elaborate task of updating his findings and conclusions was undertaken by the most prominent scholar of ancient Hebrew literature at that time, Chanoch Albeck. Albeck's updated version of Zunz's book is still considered to be the most authoritative work on the times, character, and evolution of the midrashic literature, and for many years served as the basic textbook for generations of students and scholars of the Aggadic literature. Albeck's additions, which constitute an important scholarly apparatus in their own right, survey the literature written on the topic until the 1950s and delineate the main parameters for future research on the Aggadic literature. But rather than criticizing or qualifying Zunz's conclusions regarding the continuity between the medieval compositions and the Aggadic literature of the Rabbinic period, Albeck reinforces them by adding medieval works unknown to Zunz, providing numerous references to manuscripts and first editions, and offering additional comments that present the Aggadic literature as a cohesive body of work, with no distinction from later medieval works. Needless to say, this agreement between two such authoritative figures as Zunz and Albeck—who represent two different eras in the history of the discipline and mark its transition from Europe to Israel—has had a decisive effect on the almost total overlooking of medieval Hebrew prose in the study of Hebrew literature.

[34] For a summary of this topic, see Niehoff (1995).
[35] pp. 51–67: all references to the Hebrew edition (see n. 33 above).

The second major scholar who contributed considerably to the acceptance of this misconception of medieval Hebrew prose was Moritz Steinschneider, whose monumental work *Jewish Literature*—originally written as an encyclopedic entry—was published in book-form in 1850 (and translated into English in 1857).[36] The book was deeply influenced by Zunz's opus, and although its emphases were different— for instance, in examining Jewish literature in other languages and discussing the influence of foreign cultures, especially the Arabic, on Jewish authors—Steinschneider made no new distinctions regarding medieval Jewish prose. He, too, considered medieval Aggadic literature to be a natural continuation of Rabbinic literature, and in the medieval midrashim he saw no formal or thematic novelty that would justify their construal as harbingers of a new literary era. Even in his series of lectures on medieval Jewish literature, given between 1859 and 1897 in the theological seminary he headed in Berlin (Steinschneider 1938)[37]—in which he distinguished between different types of works on national, geographical, religious, political, cultural, linguistic, scientific, and philosophical topics—prose was not discussed as an independent field worthy of research in its own right, but was simply mentioned in the context of the above topical fields.

Although Zunz and Steinschneider, through their decisive influence on the development of Judaic studies, helped establish medieval Hebrew prose as an important field worthy of discovery, publication, and research, their approach hindered almost completely any attempt to study this form as a literary expression of medieval Jewish creativity, the way its poetic counterpart was studied. Thus, the great philological task of discovering works in manuscript libraries and publishing them—either as single texts or in critical editions compiling all extant versions of the same work—became the focus of research in the generations of scholars following Zunz and Steinschneider.

Single texts were published throughout this period in various journals and periodicals—among them Steinschneider's bibliographically orientated *Hebräische Bibliographie* and the main journal of Judaic studies, the *Monatschrift für Geschichte und Wissenschaft des Judentums*—as well as in dozens of other publications. One publishing project devoted mostly to medieval Hebrew prose was Adolph Jellinek's monumental series of pamphlets (the first of which was published in 1853), in which he published what he called 'small midrashim' (*kleine Midraschim*), taken mostly from manuscripts but also from rare first printed editions. Jellinek edited six such compilations, the last of which was published in 1877. Hundreds of texts, accompanied by short introductions about their history and versions, were published in these pamphlets over a quarter of a century (Niehoff 1998: 119–28).

Jellinek's own use of the term 'small midrashim' to denote works of medieval Hebrew narrative prose reinforced the views of his predecessors. The word 'small'

---

[36] On the book and its background, see Marx (1947: 147–9).
[37] On this series of lectures, see ibid. (139–41).

here indicates the limited scope of these compositions, which, unlike the 'classic' midrashim, usually embraced no more than a few pages. Jellinek, however, also used the term in order to denote their post-Rabbinic medieval origins. Jellinek's fourth pamphlet, for example, included the following texts: *Midrash Aggadat Bereshit, Rabbi Simeon bar Yohai's Prayer, Agadat Shamhazai* and *Azael, Life of Enoch, Midrash of the Ten Exiles, Midrash 'In the Eighth Day', Midrash of Goliath the Philistine, Tales* (*ma'asiyot*) and *Parables of Solomon*. Only three of these works may be classified as midrashim—and even they differ essentially from the ancient midrashim and have typically medieval literary characteristics. The other six are clear cases of narrative texts—new thematically as well as in their narrative structure—which in no way 'continue' the midrashic literature.

Jellinek's pamphlets, which have been compiled and republished in three new editions, were among the most important works enabling modern scholars to examine medieval Hebrew prose from a broader, more comprehensive perspective. Jellinek's project drew attention, even if inadvertently, to the impressive scope of medieval Hebrew prose, its incorporation of numerous spiritual and social facets of medieval Jewish life, and its diverse and significant literary qualities. Jellinek's work was the basis for Y. D. Eisenstein's epigonic edition, distributed in his ultra-orthodox encyclopedic project *Otzar Yisrael* (Eisenstein 1915), which apparently enjoyed an even wider circulation than that of the original work. This edition included most of the texts published in Jellinek's pamphlets, organized alphabetically and accompanied by additional versions of the same compositions that were compiled from various sources. Eisenstein, too, classified these texts as 'small midrashim' and attributed their significance to their supposed continuation of ancient midrashic literature.

Also influential, though hardly flawless, was Louis Ginzberg's monumental *The Legends of the Jews* (Ginzberg 1909–38), which presented—in a paraphrased English translation—the expanded biblical narrative as rewritten through the ages, from the literature of the Second Temple era to seventeenth- and eighteenth-century folklore. *The Legends of the Jews* includes such medieval tales and legends as *The Chronicles of Moses, Alphabeth of Ben-Sira, Midrash of the Ten Commandments, Midrash Vayosha, Midrash Vayisa'u* (or the *Wars of Jacob's Sons*), and many others—presented almost in their entirety and accompanied by detailed comparative notes which contribute considerably to our understanding of them. The approach implicit in Ginzberg's work was ambiguous. On the one hand, by placing these texts directly after the ancient midrashim in each chapter, it portrayed the medieval narratives as lacking any historical distinction: thus, for example, paragraphs from the medieval *Chronicles of Moses* immediately follow the *Midrash on Exodus* (*Shemot Raba*), as if they belonged to the same period and were characterized by the same creative approach. On the other hand, Ginzberg's comparative notes draw attention to the folkloristic nature of the medieval texts, the remarkable development of their narratives, and the considerable difference between them and the ancient midrashim. This view is also manifest in Ginzberg's important essays on the subject.[38] Ginzberg's work became not only one of the pillars for the comparative study of Aggadic literature in the twentieth century, but also the most popular and influential Western anthology of Jewish legends, making medieval Hebrew prose the subject of unprecedented interest and scholarly attention.

The origins of this development can be traced to a trend that preceded *The Legends of the Jews*, yet stemmed from a similar methodical background—the definition of medieval Hebrew prose as part of the period's Jewish folk culture, that is, as folk literature. Folklorist Moses Gaster, who published two comprehensive volumes of medieval prose—a collection of stories (Gaster 1924) and a translated anthology (Gaster 1899)—was among the first scholars to make this transition. Gaster had the lamentable habit of dating the texts he discovered and published to impossibly early periods—perhaps in order to magnify the importance of his discoveries. For instance, he claimed that the collection of stories he labelled *The Exempla of the Rabbis* pre-dated the Talmud and the Midrash and was in fact the original source for the stories included in them—whereas in reality it could not possibly pre-date the thirteenth or fourteenth centuries. It is, nonetheless, a medieval anthology of great importance, in which not only the repertoire of medieval oral and written prose finds expression, but also the history of Hebrew prose in general (Dan 1976: 492–8; Alexander 1993: 793–805). A similar treatment was given to *The Chronicles of Jerahme'el*, one of the most important and comprehensive anthologies of Hebrew prose. Although Gaster published just part of the work—the first section, which revolves around the expanded biblical narrative—and in English translation only, his effort has contributed much to our acquaintance with medieval Hebrew prose. Again, Gaster dated the work to the sixth century—although the text itself includes the explicit statement that it is the combined effort of the eleventh/twelfth-century Italian poet and scholar Jerahme'el Ben Shlomo and the fourteenth-century German author Elazar ben Asher ha-Levi.

Gaster also published dozens of texts in his numerous articles, later compiled in the third volume (the appendix volume) of his collected essays (Gaster 1928)—an important resource on the different types of medieval Hebrew prose. Gaster's significant work was not limited to his publishing efforts, but included commentary as well. His comprehensive introduction and comparative notes to *The Exempla of the Rabbis* are among the most important contributions to the scholarship of medieval Hebrew narrative literature. Through his comparisons of Hebrew stories and their analogues in European and Arabic folk literatures, Gaster highlighted the contacts between medieval Hebrew prose and the host cultures in which it operated. As we shall see, this relation to European and Eastern literatures is one of the defining characteristics of the Hebrew prose of the period. Gaster also stressed the

---

[38] L. Ginzberg, 'Jewish Folklore: East and West' (a lecture given in 1938), in Ginzberg (1955): 61–73; Ginzberg (1960): 220–50; Heller (1933–4): 51–66; 165–90, 281–307, 393–418; (1934–5): 29–52.

complex relationships between written and oral forms of medieval Hebrew prose. Although he pointed out the oral characteristics of the stories, he traced their widespread dissemination to the circulation of popular booklets and pamphlets (which he found in manuscripts)—and later of first printed editions—which introduced these stories into the repertoire of Hebrew literature toward the end of the Middle Ages. The texts published in the third volume of Gaster's collected essays were often included as appendices to research articles that had been previously published in various publications—especially ones devoted to international folk-lore. In these articles, Gaster situated the medieval Hebrew texts in the more general context of narrative literature, identified character types common to other litera-tures (e.g. 'the child-stealing witch'), and discussed various theoretical questions, among them the relation between oral and written versions of the same stories, as well as the Indo-European hypothesis—a frequently discussed theory at the time, which regarded Indian folk-tales as the origin of European folk literature. Like Ginzberg after him, Gaster regarded the Hebrew folklore of the Middle Ages as strong evidence in support of this hypothesis—particularly in light of the Jews' unique position between East and West.[39] Thus, although seemingly inadvertently, Gaster helped to define some of the chief parameters for the study of medieval Hebrew prose in the following generations.

It seems, however, that the greatest contributor to the changing status of medieval Hebrew prose was one who did not consider himself a typical scholar. Although M. J. Berdyczewski (Bin Gorion) did not use the term 'medieval Hebrew prose', his great anthology *Mimekor Yisrael* (Bin Gorion 1938) was compiled with the clear intention of presenting the Hebrew prose literature of the period in its full diversity and distinctiveness. As with many other 'revolutions' in the cultural sphere, the main (though certainly not sole) motivation for his work came from his critical reaction to yet another effort—Bialik and Ravnitzky's *Sefer ha-Aggadah* ('The Book of Legends': Bialik and Ravnitzky 1992)—which already then was considered the canonical anthology of Hebrew legends. Berdyczewski's explicit criticism of their work touched on two central issues: 'In our opinion, any book that compiles the words of the ancients and wishes to provide us with original selections from their literature, must to some extent point out temporal and generational differences, and should not—if it is to fulfill its aims in full and not in approximation—mix everything in one pot' (Berdyczewski (1956): ii. 249). In other words, Berdyczewski protested against the aforementioned tendency to ignore the autonomy and ori-ginary thrust of the medieval stories and present them merely as 'midrashim'. Berdyczewski also criticized Bialik and Ravnitzky for including in their anthology much non-narrative material—midrashic homilies and Rabbinic sayings—and ignoring the all-important narrative distinctiveness of the Aggadah vis-à-vis the

---

[39] This thesis appears in an important essay that for some reason was not included in *Texts and Studies* (Gaster 1886–7).

Halakha. Berdyczewski's main point of criticism, however, concerned what he considered to be the conservative character of *Sefer ha-Aggadah*—its emphasis on normative values, on accepted Jewish morality, on the rational—which ignored other elements responsible for magical, erotic, and sensual literature. The main thrust of this literature was to be found in medieval prose, which Berdyczewski wished to salvage from its obscurity by highlighting what *Sefer ha-Aggadah* tried to conceal and suppress.

Mimekor Yisrael is indeed a vast collection of stories compiled from every possible source: first printed editions, scholarly publications, halakhic documents, medieval exegetic texts, historical writings, moralistic works, and philosophical compositions. The book represents an almost complete array of narrative genres: expanded biblical stories and exempla, historical legends, stories of magic and sorcery, animal fables, travel stories, mystical parables, and didactical moralistic tales.[40] Berdyczewski's aims were cultural rather than scholarly: in his view, *Sefer ha-Aggadah* was only a partial and selective representation of ancient Jewish literature. In *Mimekor Yisrael* he saw the means for a more complete and faithful portrayal of medieval Hebrew literature, underscoring aspects of Jewish culture that previous scholars had tended to conceal and efface. (See Dan Ben-Amos in Bin Gorion 1990: pp. xxiii–xliv.)

Joseph Dan's *The Hebrew Story in the Middle Ages* (1974) was probably the first work in the study of Hebrew literature devoted exclusively to prose, and also the first to use that term in relation to its subject-matter. The book's basic premise is that the medieval Hebrew story is essentially different from the Hebrew prose that preceded it, mainly because of its literary autonomy and liberation from the chains of historic, halakhic, and theological contexts. This autonomy was responsible for the evolution of new narrative themes and forms and for a growth in narrative complexity. The chapters of the book are eclectic, dealing with different phases in the history of medieval narrative literature, including the narrative literature of the German Pietists, narrative elements in Jewish philosophy and the Kabbalah, and stories by Renaissance-period Italian Jews. Also discussed are such topics and genres as biblical stories in the Middle Ages, the myth of the Messiah and the legends Isaac Luria (the Ari), as well as single stories ('The Tale of the Jerusalemite', 'The tale of King Arthur', 'The Legend of Joseph dela Reina') and collections of tales (*Alphabet of Ben Sira, Tales of Sendebar, Midrash of the Ten Commandments*). There is a certain contradiction between the book's basic assumption regarding the autonomy of medieval prose literature, and the supposition, expressed throughout the book, that most medieval Hebrew stories were not written independently, but rather emerged as part of certain exegetic, historical, moralistic, and mystical

---

[40] The work was published after Berdyczewski's death by his son, Emanuel bin Gorion, in 6 volumes between 1938 and 1945. An updated edition was published in 1965. Selections from the book were published during Berdyczewski's lifetime in a German translation (1913–27). Also published was a complete English translation (1990).

contexts and practices. The main causes for the evolution of the Hebrew prose literature of the period may be related to factors other than the literary autonomy of this form—the influence of European and Arabic literatures, changes in the leisure culture of the Jews, their search for new expressions for their everyday life, and other socio-historical factors. At any rate, Dan's work paved the way toward the acceptance of medieval Hebrew prose as an independent field of study and research.

Three main trends that have considerably changed the study of medieval texts emerged in the last half of the twentieth century. The first of these is the 'historiographic trend'. The interest of historians in the Jewish tales of the Middle Ages is obvious. Since many events have no existing documentation, historians have to resort to such literary texts, which are often fictional and supernatural in content and nature. The use of such tales for historical research ranges from the pole of naive positivistic treatment to that of total rejection: while some scholars have regarded the texts as representing factual occurrences, others have categorically refused to consider them as significant historical documents. Such conflicting approaches are prevalent in biographies about medieval authors, very little documentation of whom remains outside their own writings. Typical in this respect are studies on the life of Rabbi Shlomo Yitzhaki (Rashi). While some biographers have resorted to the many known tales on Rashi's life (for instance, that Rashi's father was a wealthy trader of precious stones; that Rashi travelled extensively from community to community to spread his writings, and so on) in order to write certain sections of his biography, other scholars—prominent among them Zunz—completely rejected the historical significance of these stories, denouncing their promulgators as ignorant distributors of lies (see Yassif 1993: 492).

This approach did not change until the 1960s, when seminal works by G. D. Cohen and A. Graboïs were published. In his study of 'The Story of Four Captives,' from *Sefer ha Kabbalah* (*The Book of Tradition*) by Andalusian author Abraham ibn Daoud (Cohen 1960–1: 51–131; cf. also Cohen 1967), Cohen contends that this tale on the dissemination of the Torah among Jewish communities throughout the Mediterranean—by Eastern scholars who were captured by pirates—should be read as a document of cultural rather than factual significance. The story indicates the changing attitudes of Spanish Jews toward the authority of the important Eastern centres of Torah scholarship, and toward their own place in the contemporary Jewish world. Thus, as a historian taking advantage of literary tools, Cohen uses his precise and detailed analysis of the tale to point out the mental (rather than external) processes that occurred in a particular historical period—the principal surviving evidence for which can be found in the literary material. A similar approach characterizes Graboïs's study on Jewish stories about Charlemagne (Graboïs 1967: 22–58). Sharing Cohen's view, Graboïs insists that such stories cannot be taken to represent any factual events related to the conquests of Charlemagne and the founding of his kingdom, in which Jews may have been involved; they do, however, attest to attempts made by Jews hundreds of years later—at the time the stories were written—to receive legitimization from Christian authorities and secure their property rights and political status. In this case, the textual analysis of a work of prose exposes the ways in which such texts can express mental attitudes and serve as exclusive means for the communication of communal anxieties and desires.

This trend, which continued well into the 1970s, was carried on by Ivan Marcus's studies on the chronicles of the 1096 Crusade Riots. Before Marcus, the historical content of the chronicles—published in critical annotated editions by Neubauer and Stern (1892) and Habermann (1971)—had hardly been disputed. No one considered treating the chronicles themselves as 'tales' or narrative works of prose. Marcus drew attention to their literary style, to the residues of older, mostly midrashic traditions in the plot, and to the fact that the voice of later generations—and not the ones involved in the depicted events—is represented in the chronicles. Marcus's literary analysis of the texts led him to the conclusion that the chronicles were a cultural construct, through which later communities wished to express their identity and anxieties (Marcus 1982: 40–52; 1999: 37–48). Historian Robert Chazan, who insisted on the importance of the chronicles not just as cultural constructs but as historical documents as well, started a major polemic with his harsh criticism of Marcus's approach (Chazan 1991: 31–56). The historical significance of medieval narrative prose—and in particular the legitimacy of literary (stylistic, structural, comparative) analysis as part of the historical discussion—lies at the centre of this controversy and its various offshoots.

The most comprehensive—and perhaps most important—narrative prose compositions of the Middle Ages are historiographic works, which recount Jewish history in the Second Temple era, the Rabbinic period, and the Middle Ages in extensive, complex, and detailed narratives. Like the 'independent' tales discussed above, these compositions pose a similar dilemma for scholars. On the one hand, they are the major historiographical works provided by the Jewish culture of the period; on the other, they deviate enormously from currently accepted norms of historiographic writing, and should therefore be treated as works of narrative prose rather than historiography—or in modern terms, as something resembling a historical novel. These literary and folkloristic aspects of the historiographical Hebrew writing of the Middle Ages are highlighted in S. W. Baron's monumental historical opus, *A Social and Religious History of the Jews*. Baron regarded these texts not as historiographical achievements, but as expressions of the period's imaginative and creative thrust, reflective of what he calls 'the historical folklore' of medieval Jews (Baron 1958: vi. 152–233, vii. 135–215).

Perhaps the most distinctive example of such a text is *The Chain of Tradition* by sixteenth-century author Gedalya ibn Yihya. The book documents the generations of scholars from the Rabbinic era to ibn Yihya's own period, on the basis of both written and oral evidence. In addition, the work is strewn with dozens of hagiographic stories about such great medieval scholars as Rashi, Maimonides, Rabbi Abraham ibn Ezra, Rabbi Moshe ben Nahman, and others. Most describe the supernatural miracles performed by their protagonists and reflect medieval Jewish folklore. Nevertheless, *The Chain of Tradition* is presented by its author not as a folkloristic collection of tales but as a historiographic work. Its inclusion of fabulous narratives and factual inaccuracies aroused the rage of historically sensitive Jewish scholars, who dubbed it 'The Chain of Lies'. Modern scholars commend it, however, for its seminal significance in the evolution of the Jewish hagiographic literature starting from the sixteenth century, and also for its revelation of a cultural phenomenon—the adulation and worship of holy figures in medieval Jewish culture—that may have remained little-known if not for ibn Yihya's book (Dan 1986: 77–86; Yassif 1999: 322–31). It is lamentable that, to this day, no authorized and reliable critical edition of this important book is available—one that would examine ibn Yihya's original work and distinguish it from the supplements and modifications added to his widespread book in later generations.

Other medieval narrative-historiographic works *have* been published in laudable critical editions. First to be mentioned is the *Chronicle of Ahima'az* ben Paltiel, also known as *Megilat Ahima'az*. This historical chronicle, which dates from 1054, is exceptional for several reasons. First, it remained unknown to Jewish scholars until the middle of the nineteenth century, when its manuscript was discovered by Adolph Neubauer, librarian of Hebrew manuscripts at the Bodleian library, in the cathedral of Toledo. Secondly, it is the most narrow and specific historical chronicle available to us—the story of one family from the Apulia region of Southern Italy, which lived there for three centuries before the writing of the chronicle by one of its members, Ahima'az ben Paltiel. The *Chronicle* is unique from a literary perspective as well—it is written entirely in rhyme, a rare phenomenon in the Jewish historiography of the period. A first edition of the text, based on the manuscript, was hastily published by Neubauer shortly after his discovery. A more creditable edition of the work was published by Benjamin Klar in 1944. Klar's exemplary edition is annotated, vocalized, and systematically edited, with a detailed critical epilogue that examines the work in the literary and historic context of Jewish culture in Southern Italy during the first millennium. Also of great scholarly importance is the collection of *piyyutim* appended to the text, which indicates that the protagonists of the *Chronicle* were poets whose liturgical poems reached numerous communities. The events depicted in the *Chronicle* (which, as already mentioned, remained unknown until modern times) are alluded to in various *piyyutim*, as well as in historical and literary documents whose historic context and significance can only be understood now, after the publishing of this work. Thanks to its historic and literary importance, the *Chronicle of Ahima'az* has been studied by several other scholars, including Yassif, who examines the work's literary structure and its relation to contemporaneous Jewish and Christian folk literatures, and Bonfil, who in his seminal work discusses the system of mythical symbols on which one of the stories in the *Chronicle* is based, and explores its historical significance (Yassif 1984b: 18–42; Bonfil 1989: 99–136)

Another historiographical work that has long been regarded as a literary text is *Shevet Yehuda* by Solomon ibn Verga (1554), which describes the violent actions taken against the Jews of Spain in the few generations preceding their final expulsion. The text, which advances from minor disasters and tragedies to the cataclysmic calamity of the Expulsion, presents these events dramatically through a narrative re-enactment of the relationships within the Jewish communities and between the Jews and the Christian rulers of Spain. Some of the stories are meticulously structured and presented in a highly sophisticated and accomplished Hebrew style. Several scholars have called the stories of *Shevet Yehuda* 'novelistic' and emphasized their deep affinity to contemporary Italian and Spanish novels (see Baer 1923; Yerushalmi 1976; Abramsky 1985). Many other stories are short and concise, and centre on supernatural occurrences: the salvation of a community from a blood libel, a supernatural assault on Christian rulers, Jewish mystics and holy men using their supernatural powers for the benefit of their communities. All of these are typical folk-tales handed down to the author—according to his own claims—from the oral traditions of different communities. As such, they divulge the topical interests and character of the folk literature of the Jewish communities in Spain before the Expulsion (Loeb 1892: 1–29; Yassif 1999: 298–301). Rather than focusing on its significance as a historical document, the studies of *Shevet Yehuda* have stressed the aesthetic qualities of the work and the emphasis laid by its author on literary style no less than on informative content.

The most important achievement in the research and publication of medieval historiographic prose is David Flusser's edition of *The Book of Jossipon*. For hundreds of years—from the eleventh century to early modern times—this tenth-century text was for European Jews the authoritative history of the Second Temple period. It was considered the Hebrew substitute for the historical works of Flavius Josephus, and was even thought to be the 'original' book written by Josephus in Hebrew for his own people. The text's many different manuscripts and printed editions—as well as its relation to Josephus' work and unique status in the historical memory of the Jews—made the publication of a critical edition an extremely important, yet difficult and intricate task. The commentary and alternative versions accompanying the text are a masterwork of precision and attention to detail. Flusser paid particular attention to the differences between *The Book of Jossipon* and Josephus' historical narrative, and elucidated them in thousands of notes and explanations (Flusser 1978–80). These comments are of utmost importance to the study of medieval Hebrew prose: they reveal the differences in historical outlook and narrative methods between the ancient world and the Middle Ages, and disclose the uniqueness of the Hebrew prose of the latter period. Flusser's second volume (most of which is devoted to his studies on *The Book of Jossipon*) includes two chapters of essential relevance to the study of Hebrew prose. The first, 'The Literary

Project of the Author of the Book of Jossipon,' examines the differences between Josephus and Jossipon, the latter's use of other sources, both Jewish and European, and his methods as a historian-narrator. In the second chapter, 'The Book of Jossipon as a Work of Art', Flusser analyses the unique style of the author (which in his view belongs to the contemporaneous Italian tradition of 'sublime prose'), the text's structural approach, and the psychological residues that influenced the author's historical interpretation and narrative considerations. It is indisputable that Flusser's edition of *The Book of Jossipon* is among the finest critical editions of any medieval historiographic text—Jewish or otherwise—and offers a unique contribution to the study of the narrative prose of the period.

Another historiographic work of direct relevance to *The Book of Jossipon* is *The Book of Memory* (also known as the *Chronicles of Jerahme'el*), the last 'layer' of which was written around the year 1300 in Germany. The manuscript, which travelled extensively before being purchased in 1898 by the Bodleian Library, was well known even before it reached Oxford, and sections of it had been studied earlier. *The Book of Memory* includes an entire copied version—one of the earliest and most reliable ones—of *The Book of Jossipon*, which Flusser used extensively in his edition. This work is unique for combining two literary-historiographic genres of great import-ance: universal history—the chronicles of man from the Creation to the historian's own time (or to the coming of the Messiah)—a historiographic genre that was popular in Central Europe precisely at the time of El'azar ben Asher ha-Levi, author of *The Book of Memory*; and the literary anthology, which collected complete texts as well as fragments in single volumes. The author of *The Book of Memory* offers a chronicle of the Jewish people, from the creation of the world to the coming of the Messiah, by copying historical, midrashic, and narrative texts (in part or in full) and presenting them in chronological order—purportedly without any rewriting or adaptation of the authentic documents. Hundreds of texts, representing various genres and generations of medieval Hebrew prose, are thus copied and compiled according to El'azar's unique structural and historical approach. Interestingly, the literary basis for *The Book of Memory* is an older text, probably from the eleventh or beginning of the twelfth century, written by the Italian Jewish scholar and poet Jerahme'el ben Solomon. Thus, the text's two main strata represent two distinct phases in the evolution of medieval Hebrew prose—the first, which has its origin in eleventh-century Italy, is closer in spirit to *The Book of Jossipon*, whereas the second, from fourteenth-century Germany, marks later development in the Hebrew prose of Northern and Central Europe. A partial English translation of *The Book of Memory* was published at the very end of the nineteenth century (Gaster 1899). The complete critical edition, with alternate versions, parallel texts, annotation and a comprehen-sive introduction examining the work's narrative structure and artistic qualities, has been recently published (Yassif 2001).

The second trend in the study of medieval Hebrew prose focuses on relations between Hebrew prose and other cultures and literatures—particularly those of the

Christian-European and Muslim-Arabic world. In contrast with the aforementioned tendency to regard medieval Hebrew prose as a continuation of the earlier Jewish literature of the Talmud and the Midrash, most of the scholars taking the second approach tend to examine the Jewish literature in the context of its creation, stressing the relationships between the Jews and the highly developed dominant majority-cultures in which they lived. Historically, the comparative approach to the study of Hebrew prose developed concurrently with the rival 'isolationist' approach. Emblematic of the former was the pioneering work (1880–88) of Moritz Güdemann—Chief Rabbi of Vienna toward the end of the nineteenth century—which led to one of the major breakthroughs in this direction. The main goal of Güdemann's work was to demonstrate the similarity and interdependence of Jewish life and culture in Western Europe and the life and culture of the Christian majority. Güdemann drew attention to similarities in educational systems, customs, biblical exegesis, folk beliefs, and literature, insisting that the evolution of medieval Hebrew prose cannot be comprehended without its examination vis-à-vis other Western European literatures. From this perspective he discussed, for instance, the tale of the Jewish Pope, which was directly linked to ideological and political controversies in the Christian world. He also discussed magical tales that had emerged in both cultures, as well as many of the stories that appeared in the books of the German Pietists (especially in *Sefer Hasidim*) and were closely related to the European exempla literature. The fact that the Christian exempla literature, which encompassed thousands of oral homilies and dozens of written collections of exempla, blossomed in Germany in the thirteenth century, at precisely the time when *Sefer Hasidim* was written, indicates the close relation between the two literatures. The similarities between the Christian exempla texts and the stories that appear in *Sefer Hasidim* indeed call for a close scrutiny of this relationship. Güdemann's monumental work soon paved the way for studies by other scholars who related the medieval Hebrew stories to their counterparts in the rich European literature of the period (see e.g. Dan 1971: 18–27; Yassif 1988: 217–56). Among these were Moses Gaster, whose numerous works have already been mentioned, and Israel Lévi—founder, editor, and frequent contributor to the journal *Revue des Études Juives*—who discovered the European sources for many Jewish folktales (Scheiber 1980: 19–37). Lévi published an important Hebrew edition of the *Romance of Alexander the Great*, based on the prevalent medieval Hebrew version (Lévi 1887), and studied the enigmatic origins of various narrative texts, as well as the changes in their social significance and role.

A more current contribution to the comparative approach is the series 'Between Jews and Christians' published by the Open University of Israel and edited by Ora Limor. The series examines the complex relationship between the two cultures on several different levels, one of which involves 'representations of the past', that is, the literary expressions of this relationship. Ora Limor and Yisrael Yuval (1997), who wrote the volume on this topic, offer three models for the literary relation between the two cultures. The first of these is 'the shared representation', in which Jews and Christians adopt the same text (the example here is the *Romance of Alexander the Great*) and regard it as a common expression of both cultures' view of the past and of their cultural origins. The second model is 'the parallel representation', in which each culture generates 'parallel' narrative texts, clearly related to each other, yet modified to express the different interests and mentalities of each culture. The examples offered for this model are the stories on Titus and the mosquito, the departure of Rabbi Yohanan ben Zakkai from Jerusalem, the killing of infants (in the New Testament and in the biblical story of Moses in Egypt), and the blood libels. All have different Jewish and Christian versions, whose discrepancy points to the distinct interests and views of each culture. The third model is that of 'the opposed representation', in which one culture generates a narrative diametrically opposed to the super-narrative of the other. The most obvious example is *The Chronicles of Jesus* (*Sefer Toldot Yeshu*), which retells the story of Jesus from a Jewish perspective. This text offers a critical and irreverent alternative to the fundamental Christian myth, with a narrative structure that closely follows the Christian one, while at the same time subverting it and undermining its basic assumptions.

Studies dealing with Islamic culture pose different questions and challenges. Here, the starting-point for many studies is the classic question *What did Muhammad Take from Judaism?* (the title of a book by Abraham Geiger[41])—the assumption that the fundamentals of Islamic literature are derived from Jewish culture, especially from the Hebrew tales that infiltrated Islamic culture via the Jewish tribes of the Arabian peninsula. The possible influence of the medieval Jewish Aggadic literature on Islamic culture is not relevant to our present discussion, unless we assume—as many studies have—that Islamic sources preserve traces of such Jewish stories as the magical tale of the Queen of Sheba, the stories of Abraham, or the tales of King Solomon, for which no other evidence has survived. But here, of course, we must ask whether these stories are of Jewish origin at all—whether they did not in fact emerge independently in Islamic tradition, and only then crossed to Jewish culture. Such questions of historical precedence, which in the late nineteenth and early twentieth centuries were at the forefront of the research in this field, seem now more like polemical squabbles than research problems of essential importance.

Nevertheless, such studies have drawn attention to the fact that much medieval Hebrew prose has its origin in Islamic culture, or in the intensive contacts between Judaism and Islam throughout the Middle Ages. The genre where this influence was particularly felt seems to have been the biblical tales. Both cultures, Jewish and Islamic, acknowledged the primacy and sacredness of the Bible. In fact, the forefathers of the Hebrew nation were regarded in Islamic culture as prophets, who both preceded and heralded the appearance of Muhammad. It should not surprise us, then, that expanded biblical stories enjoyed widespread circulation in Islamic

---

[41] 'Was hat Mohammed aus dem Judenthume aufgenommen?' was Geiger's doctoral dissertation.

culture as part of the genre of 'prophetic stories' (*kisas al'anbiya*). The significance of this genre to our understanding of the contemporaneous Jewish culture lies in our ability to reconstruct lost ancient Jewish tales on the basis of their Muslim counterparts. On the other hand, the Islamic 'prophetic stories' were also an endless source of material for Jewish storytellers, who identified in these tales their own consecrated biblical figures, and adopted them with certain necessary modifications. Several classic studies discuss the biblical and post-biblical residues in the Qur'an and in exegetic Islamic literature. Among these are works by Weil (1846), Speyer (1931), Schwarzbaum (1982), and Rubin (1999), which offer general and comprehensive expositions of the similarities between the biblical narrative and the Qur'an, and studies by Salzberger (1907) and Seymor (1924), which focus on specific figures—particularly King Solomon, who was a central protagonist in the stories and legends of both cultures.

Whereas such early studies focused on comparative aspects, which in the early decades of the twentieth century received the majority of scholarly attention, later studies have dealt with questions of more essential significance. Aviva Schussman's doctoral dissertation (1981) discusses the religious and social contexts in which the literatures of both cultures evolved, the similarities and relation between rabbinic exegetical methods and the narrative characteristics of the 'prophetic stories', the modification of Hebrew biblical tales by Muslim storytellers, and the adaptation and alteration of Islamic traditions in Jewish culture. The changing approaches of late-twentieth-century research are demonstrated in two works that discuss the novella of the Queen of Sheba. An important volume of essays edited by Pritchard (1974) includes several essential studies that examine references to the Queen of Sheba in the Bible, in Islamic, Jewish, and Christian traditions, and in Ethiopian culture. These comparative studies provide the full array of sources from all the relevant cultures, but are predominantly informative, and for the most part discuss questions of similarity and influence. Another recent work (Lassner 1993) examines significant Jewish and Islamic texts about the encounter between King Solomon and the Queen of Sheba from a more fundamental perspective, which manages to transcend the merely comparative approach. In Lassner's view, this encounter represents not only a confrontation between two rulers, but also one between a man and a woman. Both cultures model their respective narratives of this encounter on their perceptions of gender relations and male–female distinctions. The analysis and comparative discussion of the different versions shed light not only on the texts themselves, but also on the different images employed by each culture to represent gender and power relations. Such matters could not have been tackled by scholars in the first half of the twentieth century; the changes in the interpretation of narrative texts, so evident in the later studies, clearly illustrate the changing interests and perspectives in the study of medieval Hebrew prose in the last quarter of the century.

The third trend in the research of medieval Hebrew prose is the folkloristic approach. The basic assumptions underlying this approach may be regarded as one of the main reasons for the failure of medieval Hebrew prose to assume its proper place in modern scholarship. From a typical nineteenth-century viewpoint, medieval prose was classified, both explicitly and implicitly, as folk literature rather than belletristic, as the kind of literature that appealed to the lower, uneducated classes of Jewish society, and was characterized by a magical and fantastical world-view—an utter abomination for nineteenth-century Judaic scholars. Although such assumptions were never well founded, they had a considerable effect on the scholarly agenda. Indeed, with the exception of one known case—a collection of stories by one of the greatest rabbinic authorities of the eleventh century, Rabbi Nissim of Kairouan (Brinner 1977)—the vast majority of medieval Hebrew prose was not written by great scholars. On the contrary, some of the greatest medieval Jewish scholars were known for their hostility toward these stories, which they regarded as vain works of mere sensual pleasure (see e.g. Yassif 1988–9: 887–905; Elbaum 2000). This literature enjoyed widespread popularity across broad sectors of the Jewish population—and not necessarily the most learned and educated ones. Medieval prose was typified by a simple, functional narrative style characteristic of folk literature, which paid little attention to artistic ornamentation. In addition, the bulk of Hebrew prose of the period was anonymous—its authors did not deem it necessary to add their names to it, and thus remained unknown. This is, of course, typical of the fundamental anonymity and the communal—rather than individual—nature of folk literature. All of these significant traits of medieval Hebrew prose were identified by scholars early on; but whereas early scholarship regarded them as shortcomings and as a legitimate reason for ignoring these narrative works, the recent folkloristic approach views them as the forte of this literature.

From among the dozens of studies taking this approach—either intentionally or inadvertently via their conclusions—a few of the more deliberate and methodical ones shall be mentioned. Haim Schwarzbaum's excellent work on the fables of Berechiah ha-Nakdan (1979) is emblematic of this approach. Schwarzbaum was one of the most important scholars of comparative folklore. His earlier work on the stories of the convert Petrus Alphonsi—one of Spain's most important Christian theologians in the turn of the eleventh century, and a founder of the novelistic genre in European literature—won international recognition thanks to its great erudition and foundational contribution to any later study of European folk prose (Schwarzbaum 1989: 239–358). Schwarzbaum's study of Berechiah ha-Nakdan—a Hebrew fabulist who lived in France, probably in the thirteenth century—examines in meticulous detail each of Berechiah's 119 parables, using the folkloristic approach prevalent in the first half of the twentieth century. Schwarzbaum compared Berechiah's version of each parable with all the corresponding variants, starting from the ancient Near East and going through every known culture (including ones from East Asia). He discussed the evolution of each fable and its modifications in every culture, focusing in particular on the role of Hebrew parables in the fable-literatures of the Middle Ages. In this respect, Schwarzbaum's work is not only the greatest

contribution to the study of Hebrew parables in medieval times, but also a significant contribution to the comparative study of parable literature in general. Like
many other comparative folklorists, Schwarzbaum ignored fundamental questions
such as social contexts, literary structures, and symbolic language of the fables,
opting to focus on the comparative aspect, which he considered to be of paramount
importance. Nevertheless, modern scholarship of Jewish fable-literature cannot be
imagined without his essential and fundamental contribution.

A combination of a philological study—a critical edition of a medieval text based
on extant manuscripts—with the folkloristic approach is offered by Yassif's edition
of one of the boldest narrative texts in the entire medieval Hebrew literature—the
Alphabet of Ben Sira—which dates from the ninth or tenth century (Yassif 1984a).
This edition, which is based on all the extant manuscripts, examines the narrative
structure of the text as a frame-story, and offers a detailed folkloristic comparison
between the stories included in this work and folk Arabic-Persian traditions from
the same period. The comparative study shows that the Hebrew prose of the late
Gaonic period was an integral part of the folk culture of the region, and that the Jews
utilized these narrative traditions in a functional, intricate, and fascinating manner
that had a substantial influence on later development of Jewish prose in the East and
in Europe.

The comparative aspect is central to Zfatman's work (1993), albeit from a more
historical and linguistic perspective. Zfatman wishes to examine the relationship
between medieval Hebrew and Yiddish prose through the prism of one central story.
Her discussion of the story's different versions is adorned, however, by her flexible
and versatile use of different folkloristic methods, including comparative, structural, and contextual research. She highlights the complex generic transition, from
the legend ('aggadah')—the constitutive narrative on which the Jewish community
attempts to base its legal status in a certain locale—to the fairy tale ('ma'asiya'), on
which the community later relies in order to determine its social boundaries and
norms. Zfatman employs her intricate folkloristic analysis in order to understand
the society in which these stories were told and the mental undertones experienced
by Jewish communities in the process of transition between early and late medieval
times—processes which found their chief expression in folktales rather than in
official, historical, or halakhic documents.

Another distinctive folkloristic study that applies advanced methods of folkloristic research is Tamar Alexander's work (Alexander-Frizer 1991) on the stories of *Sefer
Hasidim* (dating from thirteenth-century Germany). Alexander examines three
narrative models on which the stories of *Sefer Hasidim* are based: the traditional
pattern, the adaptive pattern, and the unique pattern. Although this study—like the
last two aforementioned works—is based on a comparative analysis of different
versions, it employs a contextual-functional method of research, which starts from a
detailed scrutiny of the contexts in which each story appears: the immediate
context—the story's location in the full text, and the broader context—the story's

place in the belief system of the German Pietists. Although Alexander's study discusses only four of the hundreds of stories included in *Sefer Hasidim*, it demonstrates how a detailed examination of the different contexts in which a story appears may serve as an important tool for deciphering its meaning and conceptual significance. The three models she suggests for examining the relationship between the stories and their real historical and ideological backgrounds should be the starting-point for any future examination of folktales within an ideological context.

In the fifth chapter of his 1999 book, Yassif attempts to classify medieval Hebrew prose according to generic principles, and finds that the Jewish folktales of the Middle Ages fall into the following genres: (1) the expanded biblical story, which is a distinctive cursor of internal Jewish tradition and a continuation of the talmudic-midrashic tale or *Aggadah*; (2) the exempla story, which served as a narrative tool for observing social norms, securing the stability of religious institutions and ensuring the cultural cohesiveness of the Jewish community; (3) the historical tale, which was the principal means for shaping the collective memory of the Jews, in Eastern and European communities alike. The historical tales, however, exposed individual and communal tensions and anxieties that could not find expression in any 'proper' historical document, but only in the semi-fictional narratives of the historical tale; (4) hagiography, which—since the adulation of saints and holy figures did not exist, to the best of our knowledge, in the rabbinic era—constituted an important innovation in medieval Jewish culture. Although the infiltration of hagiography into Jewish culture, especially in the late medieval period, was undoubtedly affected by the Christian hagiolatry, these stories did fulfill internal Jewish societal needs; (5) novellas and gender stories, which shed light on another side of contemporary Jewish life—folk culture's treatment of family life and the complex representations of women (some of which were derived from ancient Jewish traditions, others from later medieval developments); and (6) stories of magic and demonology, which were one of the most popular and widespread narrative genres in the two dominant cultures of the period. The Jewish tales of magic do not just attest to Jewish 'superstitions', however, but are primarily an expression of the tense confrontation between Jews and Gentiles, and as such can shed light on the gruelling existential problems that preoccupied the Jews in that period.

The attempt made in the aforementioned essay to define the language of medieval Hebrew prose through generic classification, enables us to locate the main spheres of contact between the narrative works and the existential, spiritual, and psychological reality of the period, and helps us to realize that, regardless of its folk origins, this literature can shed light on dark—yet highly important—corners in medieval Jewish culture.

The trend discernible in recent studies combines the classic philological study of manuscripts—which are virtually the only authentic documents that remain from medieval Jewish culture—with literary and folkloristic research. This trend, which employs structural, functional, and contextual research methods in order to shed light on the deep structures of the narrative texts, is the direction in which the study of medieval prose should proceed in the future. By combining studies on medieval prose with work by historians, students of folk culture, psychologists, and anthropologists who discuss the same subject-matter from different perspectives, these rich and fascinating texts will assume their proper place in our understanding of Jewish life and culture in the Middle Ages.

SUGGESTED READING ON MEDIEVAL HEBREW POETRY

For introductory reading on medieval Hebrew poetry English readers are referred to the following items in the bibliography: Brann (1990), Scheindlin (1986 and 1991), and to articles by Brann, Drory, Rosen, and Scheindlin in the Al-Andalus volume (Menocal *et al.* (2000)). These, however, cover only the Hebrew poetry, secular and religious, written in Spain. For secular literature (poetry and rhymed narratives) in Spain as well as in Renaissance Italy see Pagis (1991) and Pagis (1976, in Hebrew). For a comprehensive survey of liturgical poetry in its Eastern as well as its European centres throughout the Middle Ages, see Fleischer (1975, in Hebrew).

SUGGESTED READING ON MEDIEVAL HEBREW NARRATIVE

On the general theme of Jewish culture and literary creativity in the Middle Ages, the best introductory-comprehensive survey is still Baron (1958). Two important collections of texts translated into English are: Gaster (1928, texts and studies), and Bin Gorion (1990). On the midrashic background of medieval Hebrew narrative, see the classical Zunz (1832 and 1946, in German and Hebrew). The first comprehensive surveys of story collections and specific stories in medieval Jewish culture are Dan (1974, in Hebrew), and Yassif (1999). *Encyclopedia Judaica* (Jerusalem, 1973), although not updated, has good scattered information on specific books, authors, and themes of the Hebrew narrative in the Middle Ages, in English.

BIBLIOGRAPHY

ABRAMSKY, J. D. 1985. 'On the Essence and Content of Shevet Yehudah.' In *On the Paths of the Eternal Jew* [Hebrew]. Tel Aviv.

ABRAMSON, S. and MIRSKY, A. eds. 1970. *Hayyim (Jefim) Schirmann Jubilee Volume* [Hebrew]. Jerusalem.

ALEXANDER, P. S. 1993. 'Gaster's Exempla of the Rabbis: A Reappraisal.' In Gabrielle Sed-Rajna (ed.), *Rashi 1040–1990*. Paris.

ALEXANDER-FRIZER, T. 1991. *The Pious Sinner: Ethics and Aesthetics in the Medieval Hasidic Narrative*. Tübingen.

ALLONY, N. 1991. *Studies in Medieval Philology and Literature; Collected Papers, IV Hebrew Medieval Poetry* [Hebrew]. Y. Tobi ed. Jerusalem.

ALTERMANN, N. 1963. *Sefer ha-Tevah ha-Mezameret*. Tel Aviv. 1963.

BAER, I. 1923. *Untersuchungen ueber Quellen und Komposition des Schebet Jehuda*. Berlin.

BARON, S. 1958. *A Social and Religious History of the Jews*. vols. VI and VII. New York.

BAR TIKVA, B. 1986. *Liturgical Poems by Yitzhak Hasniri*. Ramat Gan.

BE'ERI, T. 1999. 'Hebrew Poetry in Babylonia During the Tenth and Eleventh Centuries as Portrayed in Geniza Manuscripts.' [Hebrew.] *Té'uda* 15: 23–36.

BERDYCZEWSKI, M. J. 1913–27. *Der Born Judas und die Sagen der Juden*. Leipzig.

—— 1956. *The Writings of M. J. Bin Gorion (Berdyczewski)*. Tel Aviv.

BIALIK, H. N. and RAVNITZKI, Y. H. eds. 1924. *The Poems of Solomon Ibn Gabirol*. Berlin.

—— —— 1992. *The Book of Legend (Sefer ha-Aggadah)*. Trans. W. G. Braude. New York.

BIN GORION, M. J. 1938. *Mimekor Yisrael* [Hebrew]. Tel Aviv.

—— 1990. *Mimekor Yisrael—Classical Jewish Folktales*. Prepared by Dan Ben-Amos. Blomington and Indianapolis.

BONFIL, R. 1989. 'Myth, Rhetoric, History: A Study in the Chronicle of Ahima'az.' In *Culture and Society in Medieval Jewry: Studies Dedicated to the Memory of Haim Hillel Ben-Sasson*. Jerusalem.

BRANN, R. 1990. *The Compunctious Poet: Cultural Ambiguity and Hebrew Poetry in Muslim Spain*. Baltimore.

—— and OWEN, D. eds. 1997. *Languages of Power in Islamic Spain*. Bethesda, Md.

BREGMAN, D. 1985. *The Golden Way: The Hebrew Sonnet During the Renaissance and the Baroque* [Hebrew]. Jerusalem.

—— 1988. *A Bundle of Gold: Hebrew Sonnets from the Renaissance and the Baroque* [Hebrew]. Jerusalem.

BRINNER, W. M. 1977. *Nissim Ben Jacob ibn Shahin, An Elegant Composition Concerning Relief after Adversity*. Trans. from the Arabic. New Haven and London.

BRODY, H. ed. 1894–1920. *Dîwân des Abu-l-Hasân Jehuda ha-Levi*. Vols. 1–4. Berlin.

—— ed. 1935–78 *Moses Ibn Ezra: Secular Poems*. vol 1 1935, Berlin; vol. 2 1942, Jerusalem; Vol. 3 D. Pagis ed., 1978, Jerusalem.

—— 1938. 'Meshulam DaPierra'. *Yedi'ot*. 4: 1–117.

—— and SCHIRMANN, J. 1974. *Ibn Gabirol: Secular Poems*. Jerusalem.

CHAZAN, R. 1991. 'The Facticity of Medieval Narrative: A Case Study of the Hebrew First Crusade Narratives.' *AJS Review*, 16: 31–56.

COHEN, G. D. 1960–1 'The Story of the Four Captives.' *Proceedings of the American Academy for Jewish Research* 29: 55–131.

—— 1967. *The Book of Tradition: Sefer ha-Qabbalah by Abraham ibn Daud*. London.

CORRIENTE, F. and SÁENZ-BADILLOS, A. eds. 1991. *Poesia Estrófica Árabe y Hebrea y sus Paralelos Romances*. Madrid.

DAN, J. 1971. 'Rabbi Judah the Pious and Caesarius of Heisterbach—Common Motifs in Their Stories.' *SH* 22: 18–27.

—— 1974. *The Hebrew Story in the Middle Ages* [Hebrew]. Jerusalem.

—— 1976. 'Ms. 8°3182 of the National Library.' *Kiryat Sefer* 51: 492–98 [Hebrew].

—— 1986. 'Hagiographic Literature: East and West.' *Pe'amim* 26: 77–86 [Hebrew].

DAVID, Y. 1982. *Joseph Ibn Zaddik*. New York.

DAVID, Y. 1987. *Isaac Ibn Ghiyyat*. Jerusalem.

DAVIDSON, I. 1919. *Mahzor Iannai*. New York.

DAVIDSON, I. 1924–33. *Thesaurus of Medieval Hebrew Poetry*. Vols. 1–4. New York. Supplement in *Hebrew Union College Annual* (1937–8), 12–13: 715–823. Repr. edn. (with introduction by J. Schirmann), New York, 1970.

—— 1930. 'The Study of Mediaeval Hebrew Poetry in the Nineteenth Century.' *Proceedings of the American Academy for Jewish Research* 1: 33–48.

DELITZSCH, F. 1836. *Zur Geschichte der jüdischen Poesie*. Leipzig.

DISHON, J. and HAZAN, E. eds. 1991. *Studies in Hebrew Literature and Yemenite Culture: Jubilee Volume Presented to Yehuda Ratzaby* [Hebrew]. Ramat Gan.

DORON, A. 1989. *Todros Ha-Levi Abulafia* [Hebrew]. Tel Aviv.

DRORY, R. 1988 *The Emergence of Jewish Arabic Literary Contacts at the Beginning of the Tenth Century* [Hebrew]. Tel Aviv.

—— 2000. *Models and Contacts: Arabic Literature and Its Impact on Medieval Jewish Culture*. Leiden.

EISENSTEIN, J. D. 1915. *Ozar Midrashim* [Hebrew]. New York.

ELBAUM, J. 2000. *Medieval Perspectives on Aggadah and Midrash* [Hebrew]. Jerusalem.

ELIZUR, S. *et al.* eds.1994. 'E. Fleischer's List of Publications.' Prepared by T. Beeri and S. Ben-Ari. In *Knesset Ezra: Studies Presented to Ezra Fleischer* [Hebrew]. Jerusalem.

FLEISCHER, E. 1975. *Hebrew Liturgical Poetry in the Middle Ages* [Hebrew]. Jerusalem.

—— 1984. *The Yozer: Its Emergence and Development* [Hebrew]. Jerusalem.

—— 1988. 'Perspectives on Our Early Poetry After 100 Years of Studying the Cairo Geniza.' *Madaʿe ha-yahadut* [Hebrew]. 38: 253–65.

—— 1999. 'The Cultural Profile of Eastern Jewry in the Early Middle Ages As Reflected by the Payetanic Texts of the Geniza.' [Hebrew]. *Teʿuda* 15: 1–22.

FLUSSER, D. 1978–80. *The Josippon* [Hebrew]. Ed. with an Introduction, Commentary, and Notes. Jerusalem.

FRIEDMAN, M. A. ed. 1999. *A Volume Dedicated to a Century of Geniza Research*. [Hebrew]. *Teʿuda* 15.

GASTER, M. 1886–7. 'Jewish Folklore in the Middle Ages', *Jewish Chronicle* 31 Dec. 1886, 7 and 21 Jan. 1887.

—— 1899. *The Chronicles of Jerahmeʾel*. London.

—— 1924. *The Exempla of the Rabbis*. London.

—— 1928. *Texts and Studies*. London.

GEIGER, A. 1833. *Was hat Mohammed aus dem Judenthum aufgenommen?* Bonn.

GINZBERG, L. 1909–38. *The Legends of the Jews*. 7 vols. New York.

—— 1955. *On Jewish Law and Lore*. Philadelphia.

—— 1960. 'Fragmentary Haggadot.' In *Halakha and Aggadah* [Hebrew]. Tel Aviv, pp. 220–50.

GLATZER, N. N. 1988. *Leopold Zunz: The Man, His Life and Creation*. [Hebrew] Jerusalem.

GRABOÏS, A. 1967. 'Representations of Charlemagne in Medieval Hebrew Sources.' *Tarbiz* 36: 22–58 [Hebrew].

GÜDEMANN, M. 1880–8. *Geschichte des Erziehungswesens und der Kultur der abendländischen Juden während des Mittelalters*. 3 vols. Berlin.

HABERMANN, A. M. 1946. *Sefer Gezerot Ashkenaz ve-Tzarfat* [Hebrew]. Jerusalem.

HALKIN, A. S. (tr.) 1976. *Sefer ha-Iyyunim ve-ha-Diyyunim (kitab al-muhadara wa-l-mudhakara) by Moses Ibn Ezra* [Arabic and Hebrew]. Jerusalem.

HALPER, B. Z. (tr.) 1924. *Sefer Shirat Israel (kitab al-muhadara wa-l-mudhakara) by Moses Ibn Ezra*. [Hebrew]. Leipzig.

HAZAN, E. 1986. *The Poetics of the Sephardi Piyyut* [Hebrew]. Jerusalem.

—— 1995. *Hebrew Poetry in North Africa* [Hebrew]. Jerusalem.

HELLER, B. 1933–4. 'Ginzberg's Legends of the Jews.' *JQR* 24: 51–66, 165–90, 281–307, 393–418.

—— 1934–5. 'Ginzberg's Legends of the Jews.' *JQR* 25: 29–52.

HUSS, M. 1994. 'Allegory and Fiction: Problems in the Determination of the Allegorical Mode in the Hebrew Rhymed Narrative in Spain.' [Hebrew]. In T. Rosen and R. Tzur (eds.), *Israel Levin Jubilee Volume* 1. Tel Aviv, pp. 95–126.

—— 2001. 'It Never Happened Nor Did It Ever Exist: The Status of Fiction in the Hebrew Maqama.' [Hebrew]. *Jerusalem Studies in Hebrew Literature* 18: 57–104.

JARDEN, D. 1956. *Mahberot Immanuel*. Jerusalem.

—— 1966–83. *Samuel ha-Nagid*. Vols. 1–3. Jerusalem.

—— 1973–6. *Secular and Liturgical Poetry of Solomon Ibn Gabirol*. Vols. 1–4. Jerusalem.

—— 1980–6. *The Liturgical Poetry of Judah ha-Levi*. Vols. 1–4. Jerusalem.

JELLINEK, A. 1853–77. *Bet ha-Midrasch: Sammlung kleinen Midraschim . . . aus der ältern jüdischen Literature* [Hebrew]. Leipzig.

KLAR, B. 1944. *Megilat Ahimaaz: The Chronicle of Ahimaaz, With a Collection of Poems From Byzantine Southern Italy and Additions* [Hebrew]. Jerusalem.

LASSNER, J. 1993. *Demonizing the Queen of Sheba: Boundaries of Gender and Culture in Postbiblical Judaism and Medieval Islam*. Chicago and London.

LÉVI, I. 1887. *Le Roman d'Alexandre*. Paris.

LEVIN, I. 1963. *Samuel Hanagid: His Life and Poetry* [Hebrew]. Tel Aviv.

—— 1970. *Abraham Ibn Ezra: His Life and Poetry* [Hebrew]. Tel Aviv.

—— 1971. '"I Sought the One Whom My Soul Loveth": A Study on the Influence of Erotic Secular Poetry on Hebrew Religious Poetry.' [Hebrew]. *Hasifrut* 3/1: 116–49.

—— 1976–80. *Abraham Ibn Ezra: Religious Poems*. Tel Aviv.

—— 1986. *Mystical Trends in the Poetry of Solomon Ibn Gabirol* [Hebrew]. Lod.

—— 1995. *The Embroidered Coat: The Genres of Hebrew Secular Poetry in Spain* [Hebrew]. Vols. 1–3. Tel Aviv. (Vol. 1, 1st edn. 1980.)

LIMOR, O. and YUVAL, I. 1997. *Jews and Christians in Western Europe: Encounters between Cultures in the Middle Ages and the Renaissance* [Hebrew]. Tel-Aviv.

LOEB, I. 1892. 'Le Folk Lore Juif dans la chronique du Schébet Iehuda d'Ibn Verga.' *REJ* 24: 1–29.

LUZZATTO, S. D. 1840. *Betulat bat Yehuda*. Prague.

—— 1856. *Mabo le-Mahzor Benei Roma*. reprinted by D. Goldschmidt. Tel Aviv. 1966.

—— 1864. *Diwan Yehuda ha-Levi*. Lyck.

MARCUS, I. 1982. 'From Politics to Martyrdom: Shifting Paradigms in Hebrew Narratives of the 1096 Crusade Riots.' *Prooftexts* 2 : 40–52.

—— 1999. 'The Representation of Reality in the Narratives of 1096.' *JH* 13: 37–48.

MARX, A. 1947. *Essays in Jewish Biography*. Philadelphia.

MENOCAL, M. R., SCHEINDLIN, R. P., and SELLS, M. 2000. *The Literature of Al-Andalus*. Cambridge.

MIRSKY, A. 1961. *Itzhak Ibn Khalfun*. Jerusalem.

—— 1969. *The Origins of Form of Early Hebrew Piyyut* [Hebrew]. Jerusalem. (2nd. edn. 1985.)

—— 1977. *Yose ben Yose*. Jerusalem.

NEUBAUER, A. and STERN, M. 1892. *Hebräische Berichte über Judenverfolgungen während der Kreuzzüge*. Berlin.

NIEHOFF, M. R. 1995. 'Zunz's Treatment of the Aggadah as an Expression of Jewish Spirituality.' [Hebrew]. In *Tarbiz* 64: 423–60.

NIEHOFF, M. R. 1998. 'Jellinek's Approach to Aggadah.' *JS* 38: 119–28.

PAGIS, D. 1967. *Levi Ibn al-Tabban.* Jerusalem.

—— 1970. *Secular Poetry and Poetic Theory: Moses Ibn Ezra and His Contemporaries* [Hebrew]. Jerusalem.

—— 1976. *Change and Tradition in the Secular Poetry: Spain and Italy* [Hebrew]. Jerusalem.

—— 1979. 'Trends in the Study of Medieval Hebrew Literature.' *AJS Review* 4: 125–41.

—— 1986. *A Secret Sealed: Hebrew Baroque Emblem Riddles from Italy and Holland.* Jerusalem.

—— 1991. *Hebrew Poetry of the Middle Ages and the Renaissance.* Berkeley.

PAGIS, D. (ed. E. Fleischer) 1993. *Poetry Aptly Explained: Studies and Essays on Medieval Hebrew Poetry* [Hebrew]. Jerusalem.

PRITCHARD, J. B. ed. 1974. *Solomon and Sheba.* London.

RABINOVITZ, Z. M. 1985–7. *The Liturgical Poems of Rabbi Yannai According to the Triennial Cycle of the Pentateuch and the Holidays.* 2 vols. Tel Aviv.

ROSEN, T. 2000a.

ROSEN, T. 2003. *Unveiling Eve: Reading Gender in Medieval Hebrew Literature.* Philadelphia.

—— and TZUR, R. 1994. *Israel Levin Jubilee Volume: Studies in Hebrew Literature* I [Hebrew].Tel Aviv.

ROSEN-MOKED, T. 1985. *The Hebrew Girdle Poem (Muwashshah) in the Middle Ages* [Hebrew]. Haifa.

—— and ZEMACH, E. M. 1983. *A Sophisticated Work: Close Readings in Samuel Ha-Nagid* [Hebrew]. Jerusalem.

RUBIN, U. 1999. *Between Bible and Qurʾan.* Princeton.

SÁENZ-BADILLOS, A. 1996. 'Hebrew Invective Poetry: The Debate between Todros Abulafia and Phinehas Halevi.' *Prooftexts* 16: 49–73.

SALZBERGER, G. 1907. *Die Salomo-Sage in der semitischen Sagenkunde.* Berlin.

SCHEIBER, A. 1980. 'Le Folklore Juif dans la Revue des Éudes Juives.' *REJ* 139: 19–37.

SCHEINDLIN, R. P. 1986. *Wine, Women and Death: Medieval Hebrew Poems on the Good Life.* Philadelphia.

—— 1991. *The Gazelle: Medieval Hebrew Poems on God, Israel and the Soul.* Philadelphia.

—— 1994. 'The Love Stories of Jacob ben Eleazar: Between Arabic and Romance.' *Proceedings of the Eleventh World Congress of Jewish Studies.* Division C/ 3: 16–20. Jerusalem.

—— 1999. Review-essay on Schirmann–Fleischer (1996) and Schirmann–Fleischer (1997). [Hebrew]. *Zion* 64: 384–400.

—— 2000. *Moses Ibn Ezra.* In Menocal *et al.* 2000: 252–64.

SCHIPPERS, A. 1994. *Spanish Hebrew Poetry and the Arabic Literary Tradition: Arabic Themes in Hebrew Andalusian Poetry.* Leiden.

SCHIRMANN, J. 1934. *Anthologie der Hebraischen Dichtung in Italien.* Berlin.

—— 1942. 'The Research on Spanish Hebrew Poetry (1919–1939).' In *Sedarim, Measef Sofre Eretz Israel* [Hebrew]. 475–81. Tel Aviv.

—— 1960. *Hebrew Poetry in Spain and Provence,* Vols. 1–4 [Hebrew]. Jerusalem and Tel Aviv. (1st edn. 1957.)

—— 1965 ed. *New Hebrew Poems From the Genizah* [Hebrew]. Jerusalem.

—— 1967. 'Problems in the Study of Post-Biblical Hebrew Poetry.' In *The Israel Academy of Science and Humanities Proceedings* 11/12. Jerusalem.

—— 1970. 'Introduction' to 2nd edition of Davidson (1924–33).

—— 1979. *Studies in the History of Hebrew Poetry and Drama.* [Hebrew]. Vols. 1–2 Jerusalem.

—— 1989. *J. Schirmann's Bibliography of Studies in Hebrew Mediaeval Poetry 1948–1978: Accumulative Index.* Compiled and ed. by E. Adler, G. Davidson, A. Kehath, and P. Ziv. Beer Sheva.

—— 1996 (ed., supplemented, and annotated by E. FLEISCHER). *The History of Hebrew Poetry in Muslim Spain* [Hebrew]. Jerusalem.

—— 1997 (ed., supplemented, and annotated by E. FLEISCHER). *The History of Hebrew Poetry in Christian Spain and Southern France* [Hebrew]. Jerusalem.

—— and BRODY, H. eds. 1974. *Solomon Ibn Gabirol: Secular Poems* [Hebrew]. Jerusalem.

SCHMELTZER, M. 1979. *Isaac ibn Ezra.* New York

SCHUSSMAN, A. 1981. *Stories of the Prophets in Muslim Tradition* [Hebrew]. Jerusalem.

SCHWARZBAUM, H. 1979. *The Mishlei Shuʿalim (Fox Fables) of Rabbi Berechiah ha-Nakdan.* Kiron.

—— 1982. *Biblical and Extra-Biblical Legends in Islamic Folk Literature.*

—— 1989. 'International Folklore Motifs in Petrus Alphonsi's "Disciplina Clericalis".' In *Jewish Folklore Between East and West,* ed. E. Yassif. Beer Sheva, pp. 239–358.

SEYMOR, ST. J. 1924. *Tales of King Solomon.* London.

SPEYER, H. 1931 *Die Biblischen Erzählungen im Qoran.*

SPIEGEL, S. 1939. *Yediʿot* 5: 269–91.

—— 1967. *The Last Trial.* Philadelphia.

STEINSCHNEIDER, M. 1857. *Jewish Literature from the Eighth to the Eighteenth Century.* London.

—— 1938. *Allgemeine Einleitung in die Jüdische Literatur des Mittelalters.* Jerusalem.

STERN, S. M. 1974. *Hispano-Arabic Strophic Poetry: Studies.* Ed. L. P. Harvey. Oxford.

TOBI, Y. 2000. *Proximity and Distance: Medieval Arabic and Hebrew Poetry* [Hebrew]. Haifa.

TZUR, R. 1987. *Mediaeval Hebrew Poetry in a Double Perspective: The Versatile Reader and Hebrew Poetry in Spain: Papers in Cognitive Poetics* [Hebrew]. Tel Aviv.

WEIL, G. 1846. *Biblical Legends of the Mussulmans.* New York.

WEISS, J. 1952. 'Courtly Culture and Courtly Poetry.' [Hebrew]. *Proceedings of the World Congress of Jewish Studies* 1/3: 96–403.

WERSES, S. 1990. 'Judah ha-Levi in the Mirror of the Nineteenth Century.' In *Trends and Forms in the Literature of Enlightenment* [Hebrew]. Jerusalem.

YAHALOM, J. 1985. *Poetic Language in the Early Piyyut* [Hebrew]. Jerusalem.

—— 1999. 'Remains of the Collected Poetry of Jewish Andalusian Poets in the Cairo Geniza.' [Hebrew]. *Teʿuda* 15: 37–46.

—— 1999. *Poetry and Society in Jewish Galilee of Late Antiquity.* Tel Aviv.

—— 2001. *Judaeo-Arabic Poetics: Fragments of a Lost Treatise by Elazar ben Jacob of Baghdad* [Hebrew]. Jerusalem.

YASSIF, E. 1984a. *The Tales of Ben-Sira in the Middle Ages* [Hebrew]. Jerusalem.

—— 1984b. 'Studies in the Narrative Art of Megilat Ahimaʿaz.' [Hebrew]. *Jerusalem Studies in Hebrew Literature* 4: 18–42.

YASSIF, E. 1988. 'The Exemplary Story in Sefer Hasidim.' [Hebrew]. *Tarbiz* 57: 217–56.

—— 1988–9. 'Leisure and Generosity: Theory and Practice in the Emergence of the Hebrew Tale at the Close of the Middle Ages.' [Hebrew]. *Kiryat Sefer* 62: 887–906.

—— 1993. 'Rashi Legends and Medieval Folk Culture.' In *Rashi 1040–1990.* G. Sed-Rajna ed. Paris, pp. 483–92.

—— 1999. *The Hebrew Folktale: History, Genre, Meaning.* Trans. J. S. Teitelbaum. Blooming-ton and Indianapolis.

YASSIF, E. 2001. *The Book of Memory, That Is The Chronicles of Jerahmeʾel. A Critical Edition* [Hebrew]. Tel Aviv.

Yediʿot 1933–58 *Yediʿot ha-Machon le-Heqer ha-Shira ha-ʿIvrit. Proceedings of the Schocken Institute.* 7 vols. Berlin–Jerusalem.

YELLIN, D. ed. 1932–7. *Gan ha-Meshalim ve-ha-Hidoth: Diwan of Don Tadros Abu-l-afia.* [Hebrew]. Jerusalem.

——1941. *Introduction to the Hebrew Poetry of the Spanish Period* [Hebrew]. Jerusalem. (2nd edn. 1972.)

YERUSHALMI, Y. H. 1976. *The Lisbon Massacre of 1506 and the Royal Image in the Shebet Yehuda.* Cincinnati.

ZEMACH, E. 1962. *Ke-shoresh etz: New Readings of Eleven Secular Poems by Solomon Ibn Gabirol* [Hebrew]. Jerusalem.

ZFATMAN, S. 1993. *Between Ashkenaz and Sefarad: The Jewish Tale in the Middle Ages* [Hebrew]. Jerusalem.

ZULAY, A. 1938. *Piyyute Yannai* [Hebrew]. Berlin.

——1964. *The Liturgical Poetry of Saadia Gaon and His School* [Hebrew]. Jerusalem.

——1995. (Ed. E. Hazan.) *Eretz Israel and Its Poetry: Studies in Piyyutim from the Cairo Geniza* [Hebrew]. Jerusalem.

ZUNZ, L. 1832. *Die Gottesdienstlichen Vorträge der Juden, historisch Entwickelt.* Berlin.

——1855. *Die synagogale Poesie des Mittelalters.* Berlin.

——1859. *Die Ritus des synagogalen Gottesdienstes.* Berlin.

——1865. *Literaturgeschichte der synagogalen Poesie.* Berlin.

——1946. *Hadrashot be-Yisrael ve-Hishtalshelutan ha-Historit* [Hebrew]. Trans. M. A. Zack and completed by Ch. Albeck. Jerusalem.

CHAPTER 12

··

MEDIEVAL KARAISM

··

MEIRA POLLIACK

I. OVERVIEW AND *DESIDERATA*

KARAISM is best defined as a Jewish religious movement of a scripturalist and messianic nature, which crystallized in the second half of the ninth century in the areas of Persia–Iraq and Palestine.[1] It has continued to exist during medieval and modern times, until the present day. Throughout these periods it underwent various transformations and resurgent cycles of creativity: its major geographical centres gradually shifted from the Middle East to Turkey, the Crimea, and Eastern Europe; its ethos and creed were adapted and redefined; its languages and literatures diversified and grew. Indeed, in some places and eras its mere definition as a Jewish movement was challenged, whether from within Karaite circles or from without them.[2]

These inner-diversities in self-definition and religious practice sometimes appear to be more adequately expressed by the notion of 'Karaisms' (as some would have it, similarly to the notion of 'Judaisms'). The past millenium, nevertheless, has witnessed an overriding consistency in the Karaite upholding of a scripturalist ethos and in its posing as an alternative form (or even ideal) of Jewish identity. This ethos has been essential to the movement's long-standing vitality and unrivalled position as an alternative voice within pre-modern Judaism. For these reasons, Karaism should be regarded, in my view, as an integral part of Judaism, its history and

---

[1] On current debates concerning the origins of Karaism, see further below. On the inadequacy of the term 'sect' as often applied to Karaism, see Olszowy-Schlanger (1998: 5–8), Khan (2000: 3).

[2] For current views on Karaite self-definition in Eastern Europe, see e.g. Harviainen (1992: 53–9).

literature, or as one of its manifestations. In the same vein, the full integration of Karaite studies into the wider discipline (and sub-disciplines) of Jewish studies is a major *desideratum* for future research.

In popular Jewish circles, and in the wider academic discipline of Jewish Studies, Karaism has often been viewed as an isolated phenomenon. Beyond the polemic reactions it aroused over the centuries, its literature has not been given its due place as authentic, innovative, or interesting in its own right. Any fruitful bearing it may have had on Jewish history or thought was mostly dismissed. To a certain extent this position has been couched in the antagonistic mindset of medieval rabbinic sources in which Karaism was generally portrayed as the 'enemy from within', adjoining Israel's outside foes in undermining the validity of Jewish tradition and threatening it with disintegration and collapse.[3]

Considering the tendentious nature of its history of research, it is not unexpected that in the framework of this volume 'Medieval Karaism' is discussed as a separate title from 'Medieval Judaism' and assigned to a different author. This is partly a factual reflection of the state of uninformed disposition between both fields of research, though partly, no doubt, an attempt to give each of them their fair due. In the past decade, nevertheless, there has occurred a paradigmatic shift in the research of Karaism, which is beginning to break down some of the artificial barriers constructed between it and the fields of Jewish studies.

This is a slow yet distinctive process: as more Karaite sources are being recovered or re-analysed as expressions of an authentic and creative religious movement, so their relationship with other Jewish sources and their value for the study of Jewish history and literature are being recognized (Frank 2001a: 3–4).

In the following I shall try to contribute to this desired objective by charting out significant new directions in the research of medieval Karaism. The general outlook which underlies my perception of Karaism, as proposed in this article, is that it was dependent on mainstream intellectual traditions of medieval Judaism to an extent much deeper than previously recognized. More precisely, the discussion will be delimited to the period of nascent Karaism in the areas of Persia–Iraq (ninth century) and the 'Golden Age' of Judaeo-Arabic literary activity, which took place mainly in Palestine (tenth–eleventh centuries). This age was abruptly ended by the Crusaders' conquest of Jerusalem in 1099, after which the community transferred to Egypt, its major new centre, while its literature dispersed to Byzantium and Spain (Gil 1983: 632–7).

It should not be overlooked, however, that other heights of Karaite creativity in the latter medieval and pre-modern eras, in the regions of Byzantium, the Ottoman

---

[3] See e.g. the famous rebuke of Naṭronai ben Hilai, Gaon of Sura (853–61), damning ʿAnan ben David, the grandfather of Daniel, who 'instituted an evil and iniquitous Talmud of his own' (Gil 1999: 72 and *passim*). On the possible reasons for the marginal status of Karaism in Jewish Studies see Lasker (2000). On the effect of the rabbinic polemic stance towards Karaism on its overall estimation, see esp. Olszowy-Schlanger (1998: 5–8).

Empire, and Eastern Europe, are also coming under renewed scrutiny. The latter field, especially, is witnessing a revival of interest and research analogous to that concerned with the 'Golden Age'.[4] Though these periods lie beyond the scope of our discussion, they highlight another *desideratum* for future research: the writing of a Karaite history, that will demonstrate its diachronic dimension over continents, cultures, and generations.

The welcomed flowering of Karaite research thus poses a demanding dual challenge for Jewish studies as a whole, which may only be met as a collective scholarly endeavour. Its objective is, on the one hand, the integration of Karaism into the synchronic study of Judaism, according to its different historical periods, geographical centres, and literary genres, and on the other, the recording of the rich history of Karaism, as a continuous religious stream. In my view, both tasks converge with the primary aim of Jewish studies in our 'post-ideological' era, namely, the deeper understanding and accurate description of the complex oeuvre produced by the Jewish people throughout their distinctive history.

The discussion is structured as follows: new developments and breakthroughs in research are highlighted, with specific emphasis on the state of *manuscript sources*, and the fields of Karaite *history* and *hermeneutics* (II). In light of the above, I shall attempt to redefine the major impetus behind the Karaite movement (III). The conclusions will review the issues that have been raised and outline the major paradigmatic shift in the current understanding of Karaism (IV).

II. New Directions of Research

Many seminal works have appeared over the past decade, reflecting new directions of research into the history of medieval Karaism and its major fields of learning and literature, including Hebrew grammar, Bible translation, exegesis, prayer, halachah and philosophy. These have broken new ground and yielded novel insights whose detailed account lies beyond the scope of this essay.

In this context, two main areas of research will be highlighted in which the debate has been significantly intensified and enriched, in my view, enabling us to better understand the nature of medieval Karaism, its motives and interests. The first is the area of Karaite history, in particular the question of its origins. The second area

---

[4] Apart from Ankori's seminal work (1959), the Karaites of Byzantium have been the focus of several recent studies, which have also refocused on contemporary Karaite communities in Eastern Europe (Frank 2001a: 5, 12; Ahiezer and Shapira 1991). On the Karaites in Israel and their personal status, see e.g. Corinaldi (1996).

concerns Karaite hermeneutics, in other words, the Karaite approach to the Hebrew Bible and its learning, which was based on the interrelated disciplines of biblical grammar, translation, and exegesis.

Manuscript Sources

Before enlarging on these issues, it should be pointed out that the process of redefining medieval Karaism has been largely enabled by the recent recovery of a wide range of Karaite manuscripts. These are known as the Firkovitch collections, housed in the National Library of Russia in St Petersburg and in the Russian Academy of Sciences (St Petersburg and Moscow branches). Even though obtained in the nineteenth century, the manuscripts have only become fully available to international scholarship since the collapse of the Soviet Union. In the past few years they have all been photographed, re-catalogued, and made easily accessible by the Institute of Microfilmed Hebrew Manuscripts at the National and University Library in Jerusalem (Sklare 1997: 7–10).

The collections include some 16,000 Karaite manuscripts (many of which contain scores or hundreds of leaves, while others are more fragmentary) which mostly date from the tenth to the twelfth centuries. They are written in Hebrew, Arabic, and Judaeo-Arabic, and cover a wide range of intellectual and religious interests typical of medieval Judaeo-Arabic culture at large (Frank 2001a: 4). The manuscripts appear to have originated from libraries or *genizoth* of Karaite synagogues (or cemeteries) in Old Cairo, and possibly elsewhere in the Middle East (Ben-Sasson 1991: 47–67; Beit-Arié 1991: 33–46). They were acquired by the nineteenth-century Karaite scholar bibliophile, Abraham Firkovitch (1787–1874), who collected them during his tours of the Middle East, and especially in his last grand tour (1863–5) of Jerusalem and Cairo (Harviainen 1996: 25–37).

The Firkovitch material is gradually being integrated into the study of earlier known Judaeo-Arabic Karaite sources. These include manuscripts in Western collections which were also obtained during the latter half of the nineteenth-century, often from the same venues (Hoerning 1899),[5] or extracts from medieval Karaite works that were printed by the Karaites themselves or by scholars of Wissenschaft des Judentums (i.e. Pinsker 1860).[6]

---

[5] Such as the 'Karaitica' collections (mostly in the possession of the British Library in London and the Bibliothéque Nationale in Paris), and some Karaite sources in the collections of the Cairo Genizah (mostly in the possession of Cambridge University Library).

[6] Some Judaeo-Arabic sources were already translated into Hebrew by the Byzantine Karaites. The Hebrew works of the later Byzantine phase (such as those of Aaron ben Elijah and Aaron ben Jospeh) were published by the Karaite press in Gozlow in the mid-nineteenth century and onwards (Frank 2001a: 17–19). A comprehensive bibliography of scholarship by and about the Karaites is currently being prepared by Barry D. Walfish.

The Cairo Genizah, which was situated in the Ben-Ezra Rabbanite Synagogue that served the Palestinian community of Fusṭāt (Old Cairo), has also absorbed some distinctively Karaite sources. Some may have been transferred there from Karaite synagogues and burial grounds, while others reached it via Karaite individuals who became attached to the Rabbanite community, either through marriage or other family or commercial ties (Khan 1990: 1–2). These sources may also have served as reading materials in cases of Rabbanites who had a keen interest in Karaite views.[7] Although the Cairo Genizah sources have generally been studied since the late nineteenth century, they still yield important insights in respect of the Karaites, as in other fields, as shall be further illustrated below (*History*, section C).

All of these materials may now be studied, analysed, and put into context within a wider framework. The editing, research, or reappraisal of Karaite literature, whether in print or in manuscript collections, is thus taking place against a fuller background of newly recovered sources, all of which contribute to the process of redefinition of Karaism and Karaite studies.

Due to the complexity of manuscript data, and the abstruseness and magnitude of the medieval Karaite oeuvre, the majority of the great Judaeo-Arabic compositions still remain unedited and unpublished; decades of collective scholarly effort will be needed in order to bring their treasures to light. Until this task is accomplished, it will be difficult to achieve a comprehensive and balanced view of medieval Karaism, nor for that matter, of the Jewish Middle Ages.

The following account of the fields of *history* and *hermeneutics* has been ventured in consideration of this handbook's objective in providing a snapshot, however ephemeral, of the state of current research and its desired directions. Considering the dynamic nature of Karaite studies at the present and their state of flux, my attempt at a general perspective and leading conclusions is bound to be tentative and its conclusions will change over time, with each discovery and analysis of a new Karaite manuscript.

History

Since the late nineteenth century historians of Judaism and Islam have tried to explain Karaism in the light of comparable scripturalist trends in the history of religion. These manifest a common desire to reinstate the revelational text as the sole basis of religious practice, and reject the concept of 'received tradition' as a complementary source of religious authority.

Two modes of explanation have traditionally been pursued in the discussion of Karaism in light of comparative religious phenomena. The one (A) traces its major

---

[7] The latter possibility has been somewhat overlooked. The mutual interest amongst these groups is also reflected in the Rabbanite sources found in the Firkovitch collections.

impetus to Second Temple scripturalist trends (such as the Sadducees or Qumra-nites), intrinsic to Judaism; while the other (B) identifies this impetus as external to Judaism, borrowed or grafted onto it from Islamic models of scripturalism (such as early Shiʿism). In either explanation, the major motivation underlying Karaism and its driving force are generally sought in factors, not necessarily mutually exclusive, which lie outside the 'mainstream' of medieval rabbinic thought, in other words, outside the intellectual traditions of the major Gaonic centres. The paradigmatic shift in the understanding of Karaism as a phenomenon integral to medieval Judaism is mainly served by Moshe Gil's recent theories concerning its origins (C).

A. Regarding the Jewish milieu of influence, Abraham Geiger (1911: 260–9) was among the first to seek connections between Karaite halachah and ideology and the Sadducee rejection of the oral tradition of the Pharisees as well as their halachah, as reported in classical rabbinic sources.[8] These attempts intensified once the Judaeo-Arabic work, *Kitāb al-ʾanwār wal-marāqib* by the tenth-century Karaite historian-philosopher Abū Yaʿqūb Yūsuf al-Qirqisānī, became more widely known during the twentieth century. In it he surveys the dissenting groups that preceded Karaism, mentioning amongst them the Sadducees and a certain sect of the caves.[9]

With Solomon Schechter's publication (1910) of a medieval copy of the Damascus Document found in the Cairo Genizah, which he dated correctly to the Second Temple period, the first element of Qumran literature became integrated into the discussion. Once the Dead Sea scrolls were fully discovered, and this text re-emerged in its corpus, it became the single source of physical evidence on which to hinge the claim of Karaite indebtedness to Qumranic circles of antiquity, known for their anti-Pharisaic ideology. Accordingly, though the medieval copy of this document was found in the repository of the Rabbanite Ben-Ezra synagogue, it is possible that it reached there via Karaite connections (see above). No evidence, however, of Karaite ownership has been preserved in this document or concerning it. Some consider that at a certain stage of its history the document was transferred to the Ben Ezra genizah from the genizah of one of the Karaite synagogues in the city, or that Schechter may have uncovered some of his material independently from Karaite genizoth. The content of these genizoth, however, as has been revealed in recent years, does not support this assumption, since no copies of sectarian or Qumranic documents have been identified amongst the Firkovitch manuscripts. The linkage between the medieval Karaites and the Damascus Document thus remains a dubious point.

The study of Karaite and Qumranic parallels was also boosted by the indirect evidence provided in a report by the Nestorian Catholicus of Baghdad, Timotheos,

[8]   These attempts were pre-dated, to a certain extent, by the tendency to name the Karaites 'ṣedoqim' in medieval rabbinic sources (see e.g. Abraham Ibn Ezra's introduction to the Torah, known as *ha-shiṭṭah ha-ʾaheret* (Ibn Ezra 1874: p. 2 of Appendix).

[9]   See Qirqisānī, ʾAnwār (Nemoy edn., vol. 1, sects. 6–14, 3–80 and esp. pp. 11–12, 42). The survey has also been translated and discussed by Nemoy (1930) and Chiesa and Lockwood (1985).

written around 815 (Barun 1901). In it he recounts that a Jewish scholar with whom he was acquainted mentioned the chance discovery 'ten years ago' of books in a cave near Jerico (much in the same way that they were discovered in 1947). He tells of the excitement these aroused amongst the Jews of Jerusalem, who flocked to the region and found there 'biblical books and other books in Hebrew script'. Since the Karaites inaugurated a movement of return to Palestine in around 880 CE, this testimony, though describing an event that occurred almost a century earlier, has been widely cited in support of the theory of Karaite pre-discovery of Qumranic texts.[10]

It is against this background that Naphtali Wieder published several articles (1956/7; 1958) culminating in his influential book *The Judean Scrolls and Karaism* (1962). In it he introduced a new dimension, intended to endorse 'the complete consensus of scholarly opinion, *viz.* that a close kinship exists between the people of Qumran-Damascus and the Karaites' (p. v). This dimension included a detailed comparative study of the interpretive literatures of the Qumranites and the early Karaites, with regard to their general approach and terminology, in which Wieder perceived what he termed a common 'prognostic' orientation which was applied by both groups in their study of prophetic texts. In other words, they read them as if they contained some form of prior knowledge ('prognosis') concerning the actual history of their schisms. Wieder also concluded that the Karaites adopted from Qumranic sources certain terms and self-designations, such as *maskilim, shavey pesha'* (all of which, nevertheless, are derived from biblical sources), as well as the specific interpretive technique of the *pesher,* namely, the non-literal and often messianic actualizations of the biblical text.[11] His conclusions have often been recited as an established fact in the general argumentation for Qumranic influence upon the Karaites (Erder 1987: 67; 1994: 203; 1999: 313; Drory 1988: 106–10; Gil 1999: 93). Of late (Polliack 2001), I have attempted a detailed critique of Wieder's hermeneutic theory concerning the Karaite adoption of the *pesher* model and Qumranic terminology (see further below, *Hermeneutics*).

Few historians today accept the idea of 'genetic' continuity between the Karaites and the Qumranites as espoused by Wieder, in that live 'remnants of the Qumranites formed one of the dissident elements that went into the formation of the Karaite sect' (1962: 254). The more arguable opinion, intensively propounded by

[10] It is known that Timotheos requested to see these texts, yet it is not clear whether they ever reached Iraq. This shattering discovery is not mentioned or hinted in any way in medieval Jewish (including Karaite) sources. For a pointed debate over its significance see Erder versus Ben-Shammai (1987: 59, 73); Gil (1999: 93).

[11] See Wieder (1956/7: 101; 1962: 199, and the detailed comparative discussion there on pp. 53–94). His general view is well captured in the following statement from his preface (1962: p. vi): 'Just as their scriptural kinsmen at Qumran-Damascus have found the history of their own time and sect mirrored in Scripture, so the Karaites firmly believed that contemporary events...the rise of their own movement, its mission and destinies, its suffering and ultimate triumph in the messianic era were forecast by the prophets and portrayed in the biblical records. Their conviction of the legitimacy and cogency of this method may be gauged form the fact that many *pesher* interpretations became part and parcel of the intellectual equipment of the Karaite propagandists.'

Erder in recent years, is that the Karaites were 'non-organically' dependent on Qumranic literature, which though suppressed, was in some way rediscovered by them upon their return to Palestine. The burden of proof has mainly been sought by Erder in the field of comparative Qumranic and Karaite halachah, namely, in their non-normative interpretations and conclusions concerning biblical law and religious practice.[12] In my view, the results of this research remain as yet inconclusive, largely because the halachic argumentation and conclusions common to both literatures may reflect analogous scripturalist motivations in the interpretation of biblical law, a long-standing feature of Jewish interpretive history, without necessarily attesting a chain of historical influence.

B. Amongst those who sought in Islam the major impetus for Karaism, Heinrich Graetz (1895: 166) was the first to highlight the analogy between Karaite rejection of Oral Law (*Torah she-be-ʿal-pe*) and the synchronic rejection of tradition (the *Sunna*) in heterodox Islam. It has been pointed out, nevertheless, that the Shiʿites did not contest the institution of received tradition traced back to the Prophet Muḥammad, as much as they cast doubt, as the followers of ʿAlī, on the legitimacy of the Companions and Caliphs as the bearers of this tradition (Friedlander 1910–13). In a key article, Michael Cook (1987) has tried to focus on scripturalist attestations in eighth-century heterodox Islamic sources, mostly Muʿtazilite or Kharijite, in demonstrating the existence of scripturalist models in Islam which pre-dated Karaism and may have furnished its major argumentation. Daniel Lasker (1989a) has surveyed the arguments concerning various aspects and degrees of influence with regard to Karaite borrowing of Islamic interpretive methodology (such as the four principle methods of Islamic jurisprudence), as well as religious customs (such as prayer rituals).[13]

The Islamic context of Karaism, on the other hand, has not been properly integrated into the discussions of Judaists which focus on Karaism's diachronic dimension as an anti-traditionalist Jewish trend. At most, Islam has been credited as a historical catalyst in the medieval re-emergence of this trend, which also found expression in the Judaeo-Persian messianic movements of the eighth century that pre-dated Karaism, and were partially absorbed into it during the ninth century.[14] From the second half of the tenth century Islamic theology (notably Muʿtazilite

---

[12] On Karaite–Qumranic analogies concerning laws of purity, incest, Sabbath, and calendar, some of which are also related with regard to Jewish sectarians active mainly in Persia during the eighth–ninth centuries (including Abū ʿīsā al-ʾIṣfhānī and Mīshawayh al-ʿUkbarī), see Erder (1992, 1994, 1996, 1997a-b, 1998). The field of comparative Karaite and sectarian Jewish halachah was pioneered by Geiger (1911: 260–9) and followed by Revel (1911–13) and Paul (1969).

[13] For more recent reappraisals which generally de-emphasize the Islamic 'nature' of Karaism and highlight its independent features and the complexity of its relation to heterodox Islam, see Ben-Shammai (1992, 1993a), Astren (2002), and Polliack (2002a). On the Karaites as depicted in medieval Muslim historiography, see Wasserstrom (1985) and Adang (2002).

[14] On these movements see n. 16 below.

kalām) is seen to have had a formative effect on Karaism, as it did on Rabbanite literature. The Arabic elements in both religious orientations are thus explained as reflecting medieval Judaism's general debt to Islam, while Karaism is vaguely classified as more Islamic 'in origin', in a somewhat generalizing and blurred fashion.

No wide-scale attempt, however, has been made to encompass and integrate both the comparative Jewish and Islamic phenomena into a comprehensive history of Karaism, which still remains a major *desideratum* for future research.

C. In concluding this survey of historical approaches to Karaism, Moshe Gil's theory is addressed in detail, since it represents a novel direction in the explanation of Karaism as a composite Jewish movement whose origins may be placed more firmly within the Gaonic Jewish milieu. As shall be shown, this direction accords with other phenomena which have recently come to our attention in the study of Karaite literature (see below, *Hermeneutics*), which reposition Karaism, moving it from the margins to the centre of medieval Jewish intellectual history.

On the basis of new sources, mainly from the Cairo Genizah, Moshe Gil has convincingly established the conglomerate nature of early Karaism, and the fact of its consolidation in the mid-ninth century, and not in the mid-eighth century as was traditionally held.[15] This was the result of an uneasy coalition between two distinctive forces: one came from the heart of Babylonian establishment—the 'house' or descendants of the exilarch (*rosh golah*) ʿAnan ben David. The other came from the adherents of various dissenting Jewish groups, which had a common history of messianic sectarianism, active in the Muslim world (especially in Persia), during the seventh–ninth centuries.[16] The latter force was represented by Benjamin al-Nihāwendī and Daniel al-Qūmisī, the true founders of the Karaite movement. It was they who joined up with ʿAnan ben David's great-grandson, also named ʿAnan, thus forging the movement around the mid-ninth century (Gil 1999: 99–100).

ʿAnan ben David (son of Ḥisdai son of Busṭenai, the first exilarch to be appointed by the Muslims) lived in the reign of the Chalif al-Manṣūr (754–75). He appears to have been denied the exilarchate in favour of a member of another branch of the same family,[17] yet he cannot be credited with the founding the Karaite schism.

---

[15] Various discussions of this topic may be found in Gil (1983: 632–7; 1992: 782–90; 1997: 652–60). For the most recent detailed synthesis of his work on early Karaism see Gil (1999: 71–101), and cf. the rich referencing to earlier discussions by Pinsker, Harakavy, Zucker, and Nemoy provided in the notes and bibliography.

[16] Their leaders are described in Jewish and Muslim historiography, including, Abū ʿīsā al-ʾIṣfahānī and his pupil Yudgān (active in the reign of the Chalif ʿAbd al-Mālik: 685–705), Mīshawayh al-ʿUkbarī and Abū ʿImrān Mūsā al-Zaʿafrānī al-Tiflīsī (active in the ninth century). Further on their tenets and possible connection to nascent Karaism, see Gil (1999: 91–100); Erder (1996: 162–99; 1997b: 187–201).

[17] Namely, David ben Yehudah, a descendant of ʾIddai, Ḥisdai's brother. The story of ʿAnan ben David's imprisonment is explained as containing a historical core that relates to his great-grandchild, also named ʿAnan, son of Daniel (see Gil 1999: 82). The accusation of Naṭronai Gaon (see n. 3 above) reflects his anti-sectarian sentiments, more relevant to the period of Daniel, ʿAnan's grandson (ibid. 72–3).

Although his book of precepts expresses non-orthodox positions in its halachic conclusions, its methodology and argumentation have long since been recognized as talmudic (Harkavy 1903: pp. xi–xii; Poznanski 1902–3: 179–81; Nemoy 1952: 8–9; Ben-Shammai 1993b). It is more likely that his non-normative stance, not uncommon in the history of Jewish halachic debate, was appropriated by later generations as a means of deepening the historicity of the Karaite–Rabbanite rift (Gil 1999: 71–84).[18]

The historical evidence points rather to ʿAnan's grandson, Daniel (son of Saul), as standing at the centre of a major controversy over the post of the Babylonian exilarchate. He was ousted from this position during the reign of the Chalif al-Maʾmūn (813–33), sometime around the years 820–25. He is still reported, however, to have had strong following amongst the Babylonian Yeshivot, especially Sura, until the mid-ninth century.[19] It was Daniel's son, also named ʿAnan (the great-grand-child of ʿAnan ben David), who appears to have moved firmly into the Karaite camp, joining forces, as stated earlier, with Benjamin al-Nihāwendī in the second half of the ninth century.[20]

This 'unholy' coalition provides the most plausible explanation, in my view, for the inner tension that we find in early Karaite literature, particularly in al-Qūmisī's criticism of ʿAnan ben David (Polliack 1997: 28), and the general distinction between 'Ananism' and 'Karaism' common to Jewish and Muslim heresiographical sources (Wasserstrom 1985: 35–79).

Moreover, Gil's most recent innovation concerns the Palestinian branch of ʿAnan ben David's family, descendant from his other grandchild, Josiah. They, namely, his great-grandchildren Ṣemaḥ and Jehoshafaṭ, continued to function as heads of the Palestinian Yeshivah well into the last quarter of the ninth century, whence their position was undermined by Aharon ben Moshe, head of the Meir Gaon family. It is possible that Benjamin al-Nihāwendī studied in his youth under Josiah, in the Palestinian Yeshivah, a matter which further facilitated the union of the Karaites with the embittered house of ʿAnan (Gil 1999: 87, 95, 97).

Gil's basic claim is that as long as ʿAnan's family had control over both positions of power in the Jewish world—the Babylonian Exilarchate and the Gaonite of the Palestinian Yeshivah—the traditional hegemony of Palestine in determining the Jewish calendar (and possibly other aspects of Jewish law) was respected. The

---

[18] Or, possibly, as a means of consolidating the coalition with ʿAnan's descendants. The fact that in some tenth-century Karaite sources ʿAnan ben David is conceived as the precursor of the movement (see Yefet's commentary on Zechariah in following) and some of his positions are clearly adopted and developed, should be taken into account, nevertheless, in tracing the Karaites' intellectual history. Cf. Polliack (1997: 23–4); Olszowy-Schlanger (1998: 11–12); Khan (2000: 2).

[19] See Gil (1999: 79–81). The same Daniel figures in several independent sources as the main instigator of Karaism, whereas the references to ʿAnan ben David mainly reflect the general antagonism towards his house, and the Babylonian branch of his descendants.

[20] The latter was the first to use the term *beney miqra* (see Gil 1999: 82, 88, 97). On this term see further below.

ousting of this family disturbed the delicate balance, and reaccentuated the ancient fissure between the Babylonian and Palestinian centres, each with its long-standing and separate traditions. This process culminated in the famous dispute over the calendar in the days of Meir Gaon, in which Saadiah sided with the Babylonians, and the Palestinian lead was curtailed (Gil 1999: 91).

The implications of this historical analysis have not yet been fully realized nor integrated into the research of early Karaite literature. They already point, neverthe-less, to important new directions. First, they firmly demonstrate that the emergence of Karaism cannot be explained as the result of a personal grievance on the part of a rejected member of the Babylonian Jewish 'aristocracy'. Rather, Karaism grew out of the deeper political and intellectual unrest, characteristic of the Jewish world in the ninth century. Secondly, at least one of its major components was deeply rooted in the traditions of Jewish intellectual establishment, and even more so in the compe-tition over hegemony between its two centres of Babylonia and Palestine.

This competition represented, in my view, the clash between two different interpretive traditions. At its core lay the ancient and perpetual questions of who has the right to determine the meaning of the Bible in general, and its legal texts in particular, and which interpretations should dominate. It is into this clash that we should look further, in future research, when trying to establish in greater detail the origins of Karaism and the nature of its literature.

Hermeneutics

The formative role of the Judaeo-Persian constituent in nascent Karaism, repre-sented by founding figures such as al-Nihāwendī and al-Qūmisī, has not only been highlighted in recent historical discussions of the movement's origins. It has also provided a new focus for research on Karaite biblical study, which was largely conducted through the interrelated disciplines of grammar, translation, and exe-gesis.

The turning-point in the formation of the Karaite exegetical discipline is found in the works of Daniel al-Qūmisī, a native of the district of Qūmis in the province of Tabaristān. He headed a Karaite return-movement to Palestine in around 880 (Ben-Shammai 1991: 267–8; Gil 1992: 784–7). In comparison with the works of ʿAnan and Nihāwendī, the surviving commentaries of al-Qūmisī have been seen to reflect a shift from books on legal percepts (sifrey miṣwot) to independent exegetical writing (Mann 1935: 8–18; Zucker 1959: 168–83; Ben-Shammai 1986: 43–6). Since ʿAnan's work need not necessarily be regarded as distinctively Karaite, al-Qūmisī's writings are more likely to have set the independent tone for Karaite exegesis at large as distinctive from typical modes of rabbinic interpretation.

In terms of their structure and methodology, al-Qūmisī's commentaries are unprecedented in medieval Jewish literature. Written in Hebrew, with some Arabic glosses, they inherently follow the biblical text, verse by verse, interpreting it as a cohesive literary unit (Zucker 1959: 182, 203; Ben-Shammai 1986: 45–6; Drory 1988: 105). This approach was uncommon in midrashic literature: its language was predominantly Aramaic and its interpretive methodology generally tended to atomize and decontextualize biblical verses, phrases, and even words. The verse-by-verse structure of the halachic and aggadic midrashim is often superimposed on them by their literary editors, as an external redactional principle, not one deeply inherent to the ancient sages' reading of the Bible nor to their interpretive methods.

Al-Qūmisī's methodological innovations were axiomatic: his commentaries implement an overall linguistic-contextual approach to Scripture, characterized by lexicographical and grammatical notes, semantic explications, analysis of the meaning of a word, phrase, or verse according to its immediate and wider contexts, an awareness of thematic units, and general remarks on the literary structure and coherence of the biblical text (Polliack 1997: 26–36). They also demonstrate the beginning of a historical orientation in biblical interpretation, which binds the meaning of a verse to the reconstructed realities of biblical time and place (Polliack 2001: 286–291). In all these, al-Qūmisī laid the foundations for the work of the later Karaite exegetes of the Jerusalem school, such as Yefet ben ʿEli, who further developed the literary-historical approach to the Hebrew Bible.

To a certain extent, the only precursor to al-Qūmisī's linguistic-contextual conception may be found in the rabbinic interpretive orientation known as *peshaṭ* (Polliack 1999: 300–3). This orientation, however, is only vaguely attested in rabbinic sources as focusing on the 'literal' or 'plain' meaning of the biblical text. It was overpowered by the attractions of decontextualized, homiletical forms of biblical interpretation (*midrash/derash*), which constitute the dominant orientation of rabbinic tradition, at least in the major sources of the Talmudim and midrashim which have come down to us (Halivni 1991: 3–88; Stern 1997: 15–38).

Theoretical works in the field of hermeneutics generally teach us, however, that 'literal' and 'non-literal' orientations tend to exist side by side in the history of our understanding of texts (Szondi 1995: 5–13). They tend not to develop diachronically, eventually replacing one another, but rather synchronically, in dialectical reaction to one another. In the long textual history of Bible exegesis, these two orientations constitute major interpretive streams that are active simultaneously. While in certain periods literal readings (philological, grammatical, contextual) are more dominant, in others they become dormant or marginal, while non-literal readings (allegorical, homiletic, spiritual, didactic, messianic) become the preferred mode of relating to Scripture.

None of these orientations, however—and more importantly, none of the conceptions that underlie them—ever totally disappear. This is because both of them derive from the same impulse, which is to overcome or sublate the linguistic and historical gap between the reader-interpreter of the sanctified text and its original 'author' or time of writing (ibid. 8). Ideological, socio-political, as well as religious

and psychological circumstances naturally determine the amount of tension between these literal and non-literal readings, not only within different schools and
historical periods of biblical interpretation, but also within the work of the same
school or individual commentator.

The difference between the two modes lies in the contrary procedures which they
apply in solving the problem of the ageing of the biblical text (ibid. 4–5, 8–9).
Grammatical modes of interpretation (generally subsumed under the 'literal'
orientation) reflect the desire to maintain the identity of that which was once
meant. They therefore focus on the conceptual world of the text, striving, as
much as possible, to establish what its words actually say. They preserve the text's
original entity or 'meaning' by accompanying its original linguistic signs, which
have become historically alien, with new expressions in the form of literal translation, glosses, or wider explanations.

By contrast, allegorical modes of interpretation (which are subsumed under
'non-literal' orientation), express the desire to break away from the immediate
contextual sense, and point to a meaning beyond it. They tend to replace the
original linguistic sign by giving it a new meaning which is derived from the
conceptual world of the interpreter. This orientation, however, does not necessarily
undermine the literal sense, since it is based on the conception of Scripture's
manifold textual meaning. This was, in fact, the underlying conception of Jewish
exegesis since rabbinic times. Midrash was not meant to replace the plain meaning
of the Bible but to suggest other (essentially endless) possibilities of meaning, all of
which were viewed as manifestations of its omni-significance, the 'seventy facets of
the Torah'.[21]

In al-Qūmisī's works, and in those of the Jerusalem Karaites, the literal orientation became the dominant one. Their primary innovation lies in the systematic
application of modes of grammatical interpretation to the Hebrew Bible, whose
extent and sophistication is unattested in rabbinic sources. In my view, the main
stimulus behind this paradigmatic shift was not inspired by external models,
adopted by the Karaites from Arabic literature (Drory 1988: 110–23).[22] Rather, it
was provided by inner-Jewish, mainly rabbinic models (such as the *peshaṭ* orientation) which the Karaites adapted to their scripturalist ethos. More precisely, the
Karaites' exclusion of extra-biblical homiletical methods of interpretation typical of

---

[21] On this conception see in Halivni (1991), Stern (1997), Heinemann (1970: 11–14), and the rabbinic
sources quoted in Polliack (1999: 310).

[22] Drory's seminal work (1988) offered the first detailed analysis of the Karaite literal orientation in
biblical exegesis. Moreover, her conclusions concerning the extent of the Karaite adoption of Arabic
modes are complex. In her view, it mainly occurred on the levels of interpretive conception, structure,
and terminology. The exegetical content, however, and some of the methods, grew out of internal
Karaite ideology and polemical needs, especially out of the negation of rabbinic literary models and
their total abandonment (p. 120). In my view, the Karaite conception of literal interpretation was
grounded in Jewish sources, and did not exclude, in theory nor in practice, the use of rabbinic models,
provided these could be adapted to Karaite needs (see further below).

oral tradition, and their refocusing on the self-contained text of the Hebrew Bible, largely facilitated this shifting of trends.

Notwithstanding their scripturalist ethos, it is known that the Karaites did not reject all elements of rabbinic tradition. After all, an important constituent of their movement came from the heart of rabbinic establishment (see the discussion in *History* above), and they all appear well educated or knowledgeable in rabbinic sources (Tirosh-Becker 1998: 382). When these offered conceptions, methodologies, or interpretations which appeared to the Karaites as logically sound or contextually based, they were quite capable of adopting and developing them even further, as an intellectual source for their own reasoning and argumentation. Accordingly, the literal orientation in Karaite exegesis may have been nurtured by elements of the *peshaṭ* trend and certain contextual methods (*middot*) of rabbinic exegesis (Polliack 1999: 302–3; Khan 2000: 3–4, 25). These elements were familiar to the Karaites, either through their immediate knowledge of rabbinic literature, or through their association with professional scholarly circles engrosed in the textual study of the Hebrew Bible.[23]

In the same vein it should be recognized that the non-literal orientation which permeated midrashic literature was not altogether circumvented by the early Karaites, but was also partially adopted and adapted to their purposes. This orientation, which derives the meaning of the biblical text from the conceptual world of the commentator, is manifested in the Karaites' conscious tendency to 'actualize' Scripture. In other words, certain books, passages, or verses are interpreted as pointing to contemporary events of their time, mostly to the history of the Karaite schism, its role, and its destiny.

Such interpretations generally favoured poetic texts which were prone to non-literal or allegorical interpretation in the history of Jewish exegesis (such as Canticles, Psalms). They especially preferred the prophetic genre (i.e. classical prophetic literature as well as prophetic passages throughout the Bible at large), whose prognostic dimension was a long-standing notion of ancient Jewish and rabbinic sources. In these, the prophets were conceived as imparting an eternally divine message, whose relevance is atemporal, in that it may be realized beyond the specific limitations of historical time and place, over and over again, throughout history (see, for instance, Babylonian Talmud, Megillah 14a). In effect, this was yet another manifestation of Scripture's omni-significance in rabbinic thought.

Non-literal (allegorizing, symbolic, and messianic) forms of reading were commonly used in rabbinic midrash as a means of actualizing Scripture and highlighting its contemporary socio-political or didactic relevance to the audience of the time. It is not surprising, therefore, that the Karaites, in wishing to accentuate their place in history, relied on this familiar mode of Jewish interpretation by applying the prognostic dimension of prophecy to their own movement. In this manner they

---

[23]   See further below and cf. Khan (2000: 20, 25).

were able to represent their messianic and scripturalist vocations as possible real-
izations of the biblical text, adopting the same orientation and symbolic language
which was amply available to them in 'mainstream' Jewish exegesis, and with which
they were instinctively familiar.[24]

I have argued in detail elsewhere (Polliack 2001) that the attempt to identify
this 'actualizing' trend in Karaite exegesis with the type of '*pesher*' exegesis attested
in Qumranic literature is essentially mistaken.[25] In terms of their conceptual
framework, methodology, and terminology such 'actualizations' exhibit no features which are distinctively unique to the Qumran *pesher*. The only undisputed
element these literatures have in common is an underlying non-literal orientation
in the reading of prophetic literature, and the accentuation of its prognostic
dimension, features which the Qumran *pesher* itself is likely to have borrowed
from ancient midrash (Polliack 2001: 277–8). This orientation, as well as the
scripturalist-messianic mindset and biblically derived terminology attested in the
literature of both groups, may convincingly be explained as phenomenological
parallels, common enough in the history of religions. In my view, they cannot
serve as the basic proof for the influence of Qumranic literature upon the Karaites,
nor as a valid argument in the establishment of a wider historical theory concerning
possible connections between the Karaites and the Qumran sectaries (see above,
History).

Moreover, the attempt to view early Karaite exegesis in the light of Qumranic
sources has sometimes contributed to the skewed understanding of Karaism as a
'marginal', 'Jewish sect'. Recent studies help confirm, however, that the Karaite
tendency to actualize Scripture grew out of a natural familiarity with rabbinic
midrash, and shared the same underlying impulse in highlighting the Bible's
contemporary relevance. The Karaites had no need to look outside rabbinic literature in order to find precedents for their non-literal (messianic or didactic) interpretations, whether in clandestine Jewish circles, or for that matter in non-Jewish
circles. The various models offered by midrash were familiar and near to hand.

In this, as in other aspects of their exegetical work, the Karaites continued pre-
Islamic Jewish modes of biblical study that are also attested in 'mainstream' rabbinic
Judaism. At the same time, they adapted them to their specific needs, and were
further inclined to develop, perfect, and enhance them, in accordance with various
factors, such as their scripturalist disposition, strong linguistic background and
education, and their growing exposure to Arabic thought and literature.

---

[24] Further on the Karaite acceptance of the rabbinic understanding of the Bible's omni-significance
and multiplicity of meaning, see Ben-Shammai (1992: 15); Polliack (1999: 310).

[25] This hypothesis was first introduced by Wieder (see above). Drory's use of the term 'pesher
model' in designating the non-literal orientation of early Karaite exegesis (1988: 106–10) contributed to
the confusion. In effect, it relied on Wieder's assumptions, and on her overall theory that in overthrow-
ing the conventions of Jewish literature the Karaites had to look outside mainstream rabbinic literature,
to 'unoccupied' genres, which they found in sectarian Jewish sources or in Arabic literature.

An example of such a development, already attested in al-Qūmisī's Hebrew commentary on the Minor Prophets,[26] is the functional differentiation between literal and non-literal modes of interpretation which the Karaites administered within their exegetical works. Unlike the ancient rabbis, they were openly conscious of their hermeneutic, and called the attention of their readers to it. They did so by designating certain interpretations as *ta'wīl* (= non-literal) and others as *tafsīr* (= literal), or by other means that highlighted the transition from one manner of reading the biblical text to the other.[27] This functional division reflects the Karaites' developed literary-historical consciousness, as well as the influence of Arabic hermeneutic theory and terminology. The latter was essential to the creation of an exegetical language in which they could adequately express their understanding of Scripture. In essence, however, it was derived from inner-Jewish sources.

Various new studies corroborate, from different angles, the significant extent to which the early Karaites were indebted to pre-Islamic Jewish (rabbinic) traditions and their continuing dialogue with their Hebraic and Aramaic elements. The Karaites' knowledge and use of mishnaic Hebrew (Maman 1991; Olszowy-Schlanger 1996) and their extensive quotations from halachic and aggadic midrashim, some of which later became obsolete, have been widely established (Tirsoh-Becker 1991, 1993, 1998). Karaite legal documents have been shown to derive from Babylonian halachic traditions, despite their Hebraic formulations (Olszowy-Schlanger 1998: 1–14 and *passim*).

Unique practices of transcribing the biblical text into Arabic characters were motivated by the wish to preserve the accurate reading tradition of the biblical text, especially in cases where contemporary reading traditions were at variance with the Tiberian Masoretic text (Khan 1990: 20; 1992). The Karaite tradition of Arabic Bible translation preserved and continued literal modes, typical of early, pre-Saadianic, Judaeo-Arabic renderings of the Hebrew Bible. These did not result from a simple or conservative imitative impulse, but were adapted to the Karaites' ethos of biblical study, reflecting their wish to arrive at the accurate presentation of the language of the biblical text, and hence at a correct understanding of its meaning (Polliack 1997: 280).

Most recently, the Karaite approach to the study of Hebrew grammar has been thoroughly analysed and put into context in two major works on Karaite linguistics (Khan 2000, 2001a). In these it has been firmly established that the early Karaite tradition of Hebrew grammar, which formed the basis for Karaite biblical study at large, originated in the East, mainly in the Karaite grammatical schools that were already well developed in Iran during the ninth century.

This tradition is mainly embedded in the grammatical commentary on the Hebrew Bible, known as the *Diqdūq* of the Karaite grammarian, Abū Yaʿqūb Yūsuf

---

[26] See e.g. his commentary on Hosea 2: 8 (Markon 1957: 3), discussed in Polliack (2001: 290–1).

[27] Regarding al-Qūmisī, cf. Polliack (2001) Regarding Yefet, see further below.

ibn Nūḥ, who lived in Jerusalem in the second half of the tenth century. Earlier sources in which it is reflected include Judaeo-Persian grammatical commentaries, fragments of which have been preserved in the Cairo Genizah, and certain grammatical terms employed in the commentaries of Daniel al-Qūmisī. This evidence concords with tenth-century Karaite sources which identify the city of Iṣfahān as a major Jewish centre for the study of biblical grammar and exegesis. It appears that this tradition was transferred to Palestine by Karaite scholars who emigrated there from the regions of Iran and Iraq (Khan 2000: 10–11, 13–14). It is therefore possible that the Persian component in early Karaism was not only responsible for its revolutionary messianic spirit but also for its particular emphasis on a linguistic-contextual approach to the biblical text. The interdependency of the disciplines of grammar and textual exegesis is a distinctive characteristic of all the above-mentioned sources.

Khan identifies two major traits that distinguish the early Karaite grammatical tradition. First, it had a clear hermeneutic function, in that its purpose was the application of grammatical analysis in order to elucidate the precise meaning of the biblical text, and not the analysis of Hebrew language per se. The Karaite concern with linguistic form arose from the conviction that there was a direct link between form and meaning (ibid. 12, 17–21, 132–3). Secondly, it relied on technical Hebrew terms and hermeneutic principles which are attested in rabbinic and masoretic sources, pre-dating the tenth century.[28] In particular, it applied the Hebrew term *diqduq* in the sense that it has in masoretic and rabbinic sources, as 'investigating the fine points of Scripture' (ibid. 14–15).[29] The name *baʿaley miqra* (which later came to be identified with the Karaites) is used in rabbinic sources as an epithet for the Masoretes. It may also refer to scholars who are professionally occupied with the fine textual study of the Hebrew Bible, as opposed to the study of the Mishnah and Gemara. All these factors suggest that 'the grammatical activity denoted by the term *diqduq* in the early Karaite tradition was closely associated with the work of the Masoretes' (ibid. 19, 20–1, 25).[30]

The implication of Khan's analysis is that the early Karaite grammatical tradition was not originally isolated from mainstream Judaism. Rather, it became distinct from the tradition followed by the Rabbanites only during the tenth century.[31]

---

[28] See e.g. the tem *leshon yaḥid* (= 'singular'), *leshon ʿavar* (=past), and other such terms which are also found in the Masoretic list known as *diqduqe miqra*.

[29] The Arabicized form *al-diqdūqiyyūnā* designated those responsible for such careful investigation.

[30] Other Hebrew elements found in the early Karaite grammatical texts, which correspond to Masoretic terminology, were taken over from Arabic grammatical thought, or borrowed from the Hellenistic and Syriac traditions which served as a common source of influence on both Arabic and Jewish grammar. This leads to the conclusion that: 'many of the Hebrew terms have their origin in the early Islamic period (7th–8th centuries) when the Near East was a melting pot of ideas' (Khan 2000: 24).

[31] On the differences between the early tradition and the work of later Karaite grammarians of the eleventh century, such as Abū Faraj Harūn, who were more deeply affected by the the Arabic grammatical tradition (especially that of the Baṣran school), see Khan (1997; 2000: 8, 22); Basal (1997).

Moreover, Karaite biblical study at large, and its grammatical emphasis in particular, grew out of a deep association with the professional bearers of the textually orientated stream of rabbinic literature (*peshaṭ*), which emphasized the disciplined analysis of the Bible's structure (ibid. 24–5).

A major point that still needs to be clarified is whether, historically, the Karaites actually emanated from circles of scholars whose expertise was in Scripture (*miqra*) rather than in rabbinic homiletics (*mishnah, talmud, midrash*), or whether they re-established the *peshaṭ* orientation and further developed it through intellectual dialogue with literary Jewish traditions. The answer may, possibly, lie in the middle. More importantly, the historical context which enabled the admixture between the grammarians of Persia and Iraq, the Masoretic scholars of Palestine and Iraq, and the House of ʿAnan needs to be properly addressed with regard to Karaism's early intellectual history. How were the early grammatical traditions integrated or synthesized, for instance, with the traditions of the Masoretes? Was this done by way of counter-reaction to Babylonian-centred rabbinic traditions of biblical study? Was the literal orientation, only sporadically attested in the *peshaṭ* stream of rabbinic tradition, the main source of the Karaite approach to Scripture? Or rather, was it deliberately adopted and developed later by the Karaite grammatical school as a way of integrating their ʿAnanite Gaonic brethren more firmly into the Karaite scripturalist ethos?

These and many other fascinating questions will undoubtedly be addressed as research progresses and further critical editions of major Karaite works are made available.

III. REDEFINING THE MAJOR IMPETUS BEHIND KARAISM

As noted above (*History*), Karaism has often been conceived as the Jewish variation on the theme of *sola scriptura*, namely, as an anti-traditionalist, scripturalist movement, akin to other such movements in the history of religion. This contextualization nonetheless blurs the idiosyncratic feature of Karaite scripturalism: its rejection of the exclusive authority of the rabbinic sages, as canonized in the Mishnah and Talmud, in defining the meaning of the Hebrew Bible. In other words, the Karaites did not promulgate a total dismissal of the actual traditions or methods of biblical interpretation as embodied in the corpus of Oral Law. In general, their scripturalist ideology encouraged a linguistic-contextual (or 'literal') orientation in the study of the Bible and its exegesis, rather than a non-contextual (or 'non-literal') orientation, typical of rabbinic midrash. The latter orientation was applied, nevertheless, by the Karaites in their allegorizing or actualizing readings of certain texts. In effect, the Karaites engaged in the study of rabbinic sources not only for polemical purposes, but also because they acknowledged their interpretive function, namely, they accepted their hermeneutic value as a repository of potential explanations of the biblical text.

The canonization of the Babylonian Talmud and the definitive status it acquired during the sixth–seventh centuries had come to undermine the flexible function of live interpretation in biblical study, which was so essential to Jewish religious life and social stability. Once a certain tradition, however polyphonic, was sanctified and made exclusive, the long-standing Jewish unease with interpretive authority as such, which had already erupted in the late Second Temple period, causing Judaism to splinter, was reawakened and further accentuated.

Maimonides may already have hinted that the final canonization of rabbinic tradition, in other words, its transference from a flexible oral mode to a fixed written mode in the late talmudic period, was one of the causes of the Karaite schism.[32] This explanation better accounts, in my view, for the movement's *raison d'être* than its typical casting in the light of the polarization between 'written Torah' and 'oral Torah' as the utter rejection of the latter.

The debate over interpretive authority appears to have been the core motivation behind the Karaite rift. Karaism, in this light, represents the medieval manifestation of one of the most persistent and deep-set cruxes of Jewish thought and identity, namely: what is considered the correct interpretation of the Hebrew Bible, and who is invested with the authority to interpret it?

Different derivations have been proposed for the names *kara'im*, *beney miqra*, or *ba'aley miqra*, which do not appear before the ninth century. The most plausible explanation, nonetheless, is the most obvious, in that they derive from the Karaites' general affinity with the Hebrew Bible (*miqra'*), and their mastership of its text.[33] In my view, these self-appellations served to underline the Karaites' general scriptural orientation, in conceiving of *miqra*, as a self-contained text, which should be studied independently from the rabbinic corpus, and not as commensurate with it, as it had come to be viewed over the centuries.

In sum: the Karaites attempted to redefine the Jewish canon and reform Jewish religious practice by reviving the unhindered, direct, and individual study of the Hebrew Bible, and by rejecting the interpretive authority of oral tradition, as codified in the Mishnah, Talmud, and midrashim. A balanced expression of their 'credo' is reflected in the commentary on Zechariah 5: 7–8, by the Karaite exegete

---

[32] See *Guide of the Perplexed*, beginning of chap. 71. Also cf. Leibovitch (1979: 15–18).

[33] For further suggestions, see Nemoy (1952: p. xvii); Gil (1992: 784; 1999: 97); Erder (1994: 198–202). As rightly emphasized by Khan (2000: 3), the missionary and sectarian explanations of the name are 'based on too great an emphasis on their [i.e. the Karaites'] supposed religio-political division from mainstream Judaism'.

Yefet ben ʿEli, who lived in Jerusalem during the second half of the tenth century. Yefet offers an allegorical reading of the prophet's vision of a wicked woman who is thrust into the *ʾephah* (= a container), which is then sealed by a leaden weight and carried to the land of Shinʿar, where its house will be built. The wicked woman entombed alive in the *ʾephah* is interpreted as a complex symbol for rabbinic Judaism and its destiny:[34]

And he [= the prophet] said: 'This is wickedness' [Zech. 5: 8] and he compared it [= the *ʾephah*] to a wicked woman in order to demonstrate that they [= the Rabbanites] are sinners before God, for they composed these [talmudic] books, and compelled the nation to believe in them and to act according to them, and condemned to death those who disagreed with them. They did not say: 'so we reason and so it occurred to us and search yourselves O Israel as we have searched.' Had they done so, they would have been saved from the condemnation of the Lord of the Universe. For this is what ʿAnan did, who said: 'search diligently in the Torah and do not rely on my opinion' and Benjamin said in concluding his words: 'I Benjamin am one of thousands and scores of thousands and am not a prophet [nor a] son of a prophet' etc. So all the Karaite scholars used this method and established what appeared to them as the truth and encouraged people to search [= for themselves], so much that a man is entitled to disagree with his father and the father will not say to him: 'why have you disagreed with me?' and a student with his Rabbi. This is why God forgave them when error befell some of their opinions, and they were absolved because they opened the eyes of men and brought them out of darkness into light.

Yefet's commentary is the earliest documented source of the often-quoted saying attributed to the figure whom the Karaites (as well as some Muslim and Rabbanite sources) credit with the founding of their movement in the mid-eighth century, the exilarch ʿAnan ben David. Current study (see *History* (C) above) suggests it was rather ʿAnan's great-grandson, the second ʿAnan, who together with Benjamin al-Nihāwendī forged the Karaite schism, around a century later, in the mid-ninth century. Hence the proverb: 'search diligently in Scripture and do not rely on my opinion', in its half-Aramaic half-Hebrew formulation, is likely to have been projected onto earlier times.[35] More significant than its historicity is the question of the proverb's meaning. A key to this puzzle, at least in Yefet's understanding, is provided by the proximate quote from Benjamin (al-Nihāwendī), which emphasizes his status as one of a multitude of men: 'I am no prophet [nor a] son of a prophet' (adapting Amos 7: 14).

Scholars have tended to analyse these sayings as detached from each other and their immediate context in Yefet's commentary (which indeed may not have been

---

[34] For the Arabic text see MS Or.2401 fol.174a–175b of the British Library (IMHM mic. no. 6065). The English translation is my own. Further on this text (and its manuscript sources) see also Ben-Shammai (1992: 15–16; 1993a: 320–27); Polliack (1999: 303–8). On Yefet's actualization method in interpreting this passage (described by him by the Arabic rhetorical term *taʾwīl*), see the above discussion (*Hermeneutics*).

[35] On the proverb's mixed language and historicity, see references in n. 34.

their original context). Hence they have been understood as expressions of the Karaite rejection of the 'chain of Oral Law', through which the ancient rabbis traced their authority back to Moses (Mishnah, Avot 1: 1 and *passim*). Allusions to this 'hereditary chain' are not absent from Yefet's above-cited commentary. A closer reading of the passage in its entirety, however, shows that Yefet clearly understood these sayings as repudiations of the 'books' in which the interpretive tradition of the rabbis became fixed and invested with heavenly (and hence exclusive and overriding) authority. In the continuation of the above-quoted passage, he says so explicitly: 'They [= the Rabbanites] sealed the Mishnah and Talmud and did not leave a path for those who came after them to set down not even a single letter.'

The sayings reflect, therefore, the Karaite self-perception and historical consciousness, as it was consolidated during the tenth century. They are quoted in support of Yefet's overall rebuke of the 'sealing' of the live, inquisitive, and open tradition in the interpretation of the Hebrew Bible, and its replacement with what he sees as a fixed, transmitted tradition, whose 'house' (i.e. establishment) was installed in Babylonia.

The Karaites perceived themselves, accordingly, as the Jews who continue the pure and ancient quest for the unhindered study of the Hebrew Bible, in which mistakes are inevitable and form part of the process of learning. They were indeed troubled by the possibility that their interpretations of biblical law might also be mistaken, and their prayers and commentaries express an acute awareness of the possibility of error. This was partly due to their developed exegetical consciousness, which grasped the open-ended nature of the process of translation and interpretation (Polliack 1996, 1998). Partly, it was the result of their natural recoiling from the mere audacity of challenging Oral Law, that long-established interpretive tradition which for centuries was placed on equal standing with Scripture.

In the sphere of religious experience, breaking codes by which they had been raised and had come to internalize must have had a deeply disturbing effect on the early Karaites. The time required for the proper revision of Written Law meant that they could not replace the old interpretations with new ones at a satisfactory pace. With regard to the legal corpus of the Bible, this presented an existential problem which left them in a state of limbo: not beholden to the accepted norms, yet at the same time not fully committed to new ones. The Karaites' justification in their own eyes, however, was that they began the inevitable process of revision, which would break a millenium of interpretive deadlock and eventually lead the nation back to the right path.

They understood this process, however, as one of trial and error, and demanded candidness in this respect, partly in reaction to what they perceived as rabbinic conceit in espousing the heavenly (and 'free of mistakes') derivation of Oral Law. The concern that they might be committing error in their study of the Law and Scripture at large is evident in many of their works, including the above-quoted commentary, but it finds poignant expression in Yefet's Introduction to his commentary on Deuteronomy:[36]

And we ask of Him, whose mention is exulted, that he forgive the errors and mistakes which may transpire, and that he absolve us from any admonition, for he knows our intention, for we do not intend to be at variance with Him, but we seek the truth. [He knows] that we are interpreting the words of the [Karaite] scholars, may God have mercy on them,[37] and may he establish them, for they opened the eyes of the people of Exile who dwell in darkness, that in which we are now, and taught them, and instructed them, and directed them away from transgression, on which they were set, to the way of the truth and to the law of the Lord of the Universe.

Yefet emphasizes his indebtedness to the work of earlier generations of Karaite scholars (al-'ulamā', al-shuyūkh). This is not only a conventional expression of modesty. It also reflects his consciousness of his place within a wider community of interpreters, whose inspiration may be sought in pre-rabbinic times, all of whom partake in a collective historical effort to reach the true understanding of God's commandments.

Rabbinic Judaism had long since cast herself in the role of 'turn it [i.e the Torah] over, and over again' (M.Avot 5: 19), in order to uncover its endless meanings. In their emphasis on 'searching diligently in the Torah' the Karaites wished to cast themselves in similar light, and re-adapt this role to their needs.[38] Accordingly, the special merit of the Karaite quest for true meaning was presented as an alternative model of non-elitist, egalitarian, and individualistic inquiry into Scripture. Moreover, this was the model preferred by the Ancients, the Psalmists and Prophets, such as Amos. It derived from the intellectual and spiritual qualities of the scholar rather than from inherited ties of family and class. It was only through such forms of biblical study that Israel could be liberated from an erroneous, self-serving interpretive tradition and reach its salvation.

This last aspect clearly reflects the Karaite opposition to the spiritual authority and political leadership of medieval rabbinic establishment, as institutionalized in the roles of the gaon (head of a major yeshiva) and rosh golah (the exilarch, community leader). As shown earlier, this opposition was partly due to the ongoing political struggles of the house of 'Anan, whose grandchildren and great-grandchildren, in Babylonia and in Palestine, were barred from such positions by the late ninth century. It also formed part of the wider struggle for hegemony between these two centres of the Jewish world and amongst them.

The ideology that bolstered this opposition, nonetheless, was two-fold. Primarily, it was directed against the Geonims' upholding of their status as the legitimate heirs

---

[36] See MS B369, fols. 15–16 of the Institute of Oriental Studies of the Russian Academy of Sciences (IMHM mic. no. 53542). The English translation is my own.

[37] This blessing refers to them as deceased.

[38] Further on the comparison between these proverbs, see Ben-Shammai (1992: 15); Polliack (1999: 310).

of the ancient sages, the bearers of the 'chain of Oral Law', and so reinforcing and continuing what the Karaites perceived as a mistaken tradition in the interpretation of biblical law. In early Karaite sources the verse, 'and their fear of me is a commandment of men learnt by rote' (Isaiah 29: 12), is already applied (amongst other verses) as a designation of this false tradition, one which is effected by men and passed on orally, in mindless verbal recitation, as they saw it, with no actual basis in Word of God.[39]

On a secondary level this ideology was also directed against the social and educational elitism of Gaonic establishment, wherein high-level accomplishment in Oral Law was generally kept within closed family circles of distinguished lineage, often excluding the outsider from positions of power within the community. The statement attributed to Benjamin al-Nihāwendī (see above), 'I am not a prophet [nor a] son of a prophet' (adapting Amos 7: 14), is best interpreted in this light. Benjamin is casting himself (and the Karaites) in the role of the true Prophet Amos, whose cutting words are directed against the status-conscious Priest of Bet-El, Amaziah, a prefiguration of rabbinic establishment. His quest for God's truth is explained as non-dependent on membership of a prophetic guild (beney-ha-nevi'im) nor on the assertion of his father's name. In other words, it is not self-centred or self-serving, but derives from his inner vocation, as one called by God 'from behind the sheep' to administer his true Word.[40]

Benjamin, similar to another ninth-century founding figure, Daniel al-Qūmisī, came from Judaeo-Persian stock. The far-flung Persian communities did not have direct access to positions of power in the Jewish world and were generally subjugated to the Babylonian centre. This may partly explain their role as nesting-grounds for Jewish messianic and sectarian activity throughout the eighth and ninth centuries (see above, History). Recent research, however, has highlighted their long-standing intellectual traditions, particularly in the linguistic study of the Hebrew Bible (see above, Hermeneutics). Considering this complex background, Benjamin's frustration with the rabbinic elite may have been no less considerable than the antagonism felt by the ousted descendants from the House of 'Anan.[41]

Karaite ideology clearly exaggerated the historical position of the Rabbanites, who were certainly not as detached from Scripture nor as elitist as the Karaites would have it at the time. This combination served to accentuate the Karaite political agenda, which was meant to appeal to various dissatisfied or repressed

[39] See e.g. al-Qūmisī's commentary on Hosea 3: 4 (Markon 1957: 5).

[40] Both senses, of generic association and father–son relationship—are reflected by the Hebrew term ben-navi'. The saying also suggests that all Bible interpretation, after the prophetic period, may be prone to mistakes, in contrast to the rabbinic claim that the sages inherited their 'non-mistaken' oral interpretations from the Prophets, in the chain of Oral Law (Mishnah Avot 1 and passim): see Polliack (1999: 307–8).

[41] Even more so if we accept the possibility that he studied in his youth with 'Anan's grandchild, Josiah, who is likely to have held the position of the Gaon of the Palestinian Yeshivah (Gil 1999: 95).

circles within the Jewish world. It was also influenced by parallel intellectual trends in the Islamic world.

It would be wrong, nevertheless, to interpret this agenda, with its strong focus on the need for change and reform, as perpetrated by self-driven and self-serving agitators from within the Jewish world, or as grafted onto Judaism from the Islamic world. Like all complex and enduring historical movements, Karaism was essentially responding to the truth of its time, to what it perceived as its endemic social and spiritual ills. The movement of return to Palestine, and the establishment of a spiritual and intellectual centre therein, was part of this response.

In its formative stages, Karaism may certainly be regarded as part of a wider messianic trend in Jewish history, and a type of 'messianic nationalism' may be added to the list of its earliest characteristics. The Jerusalem Karaites, to which Yefet belonged, called themselves by symbolic, scripturally derived designations, such as 'returnees from sin' (*shavey pesha'*), 'roses' (*shoshanim*), and 'mourners of Zion' (*'aveley ṣiyyon*), thus reflecting their self-perception as a pioneering community with a rectifying role in Jewish history.[42]

In this 'Golden Age' the Karaites produced major works in the fields of Hebrew grammar, Bible translation, exegesis, law, and philosophy.[43] Many of the Jerusalem 'returnees' had originated from Persia (Daniel al-Qūmisī). Others had roots in Iraq (Yefet ben 'Elī al-Baṣrī, Abū Faraj Harūn), where the great Karaite philosopher, exegete, and historian Abū Yūsuf Ya'qūb al-Qirqisānī, continued his work throughout the tenth century. As has been shown, the Jerusalem Karaites developed fields of learning that were already well established amongst the Karaites of Persia and Iraq in the ninth century, and they invariably refer to their forerunners as 'our teachers' or 'the teachers of the exile'. These and all other Karaites who remained outside the Holy Land represented the 'buds' of early Spring, while the Karaite settlers saw themselves as the 'roses', a distinguished pioneering group amongst their brethren, who fulfilled Karaite ideology on a day-to-day basis.[44]

In the view of the 'returnees from sin', the misleading interpretive tradition embodied in Oral Law was the primary cause for Israel's existence in what was considered a state of perpetual mistake, which in religious terms amounted to a condition of sin. This state of existence also explained the extension of Exile and its

[42] On the negation of exile in the messianic doctrine of the Jerusalem Karaites and aspects of their life-style, cf. Erder (1997). On their self-perception, liturgy, and exegesis see Frank (1995; 2001b: 1–17). On my qualms concerning Wieder's attribution of these biblically derived appellations to Qumranic influences, see above (*Hermeneutics*).

[43] On these first four areas see our discussion above (*Hermeneutics*). On al-Qirqisānī and the Karaite philosophical ouevre, see e.g. Nemoy (1952: 42–68); Vajda (1971, 1985); Ben-Shammai (1977).

[44] See Polliack (2001: 281–2) and the further references provided therein.

various forms of deprivation as experienced by the Jewish people. The emergence of the Karaite movement was conceived as a sign of the end of Exile precisely because its scripturalist orientation was seen to address the major cause behind Exile, namely, the misinterpretation of biblical law.

The role of the Karaites was thus portrayed in messianic language as fulfilling the destiny of Jewish history. Spiritually, they were redressing its state of sin; physically, they were moving back to the Land of Israel, and therein leading an ascetic life-style, as further underlined in Yefet's introduction to his commentary on Exodus:[45]

For Exile is like darkness and the shadow-of-death and men walk in it like the blind . . . At the end of exile, however, there awakened a people who fixed their intention upon the Lord of the Universe, and they did not seek knowledge for the purpose of [political] leadership in this world, rather, their quest was to attain the truths and to comply with him in all their might . . . When the Lord of the Universe perceived their intention he opened their eyes and showed them the way to most of the truths, and they wrote books and taught pupils.

In summary: the Karaites reopened the fundamental and menacing question of the right interpretation of biblical law, a question which persistently lies at the heart of Jewish self-definition and inner controversy, from the post-biblical era to this very day. By doing so, they thought they could gradually rectify the Jews' existence in a state of mistake, and thus enable and hasten the end of Exile. The nature of Karaism as an authentic Jewish movement, which represents an inner-Jewish response to this long-standing crux of Jewish thought, is made evident in this rectifying messianic hope, amply expressed in the works of Yefet and other Jerusalem Karaites. The rise of Islam and the arabization of the Jews may well have contributed to the surfacing or accentuation of this hope, yet these were external factors, while the driving force lay deeply within Jewish historical consciousness and literature.

It is difficult to establish the accurate numerical and proportional force of the Karaites amongst the Jews of the medieval Islamic world (who in themselves constituted the absolute majority of the Jewish people at that time). Their profound intellectual force, however, is gradually being recognized and, in my opinion, lies beyond doubt. The Karaite challenge went to the heart of medieval Jewish identity and certainly contributed to many aspects of Jewish thought and literature, particularly in the fields of philosophy, linguistics, and exegesis. These contributions had a transforming and enduring effect on medieval Judaeo-Arabic culture, and subsequently they helped shape the development of medieval Jewish thought as a whole.

---

[45] MS 0054, fols. 4–5, of the National Library of Russia (IMHM mic. no. 53814). The English translation is my own.

IV. CONCLUSIONS: THE PARADIGMATIC SHIFT IN THE STUDY OF KARAISM

Since the late nineteenth century historians of Judaism and Islam have tried to explain Karaism in the light of comparable scripturalist trends in the history of religion. These reflect a common desire to reinstate the revelational text as the sole basis of religious practice, and reject the concept of 'tradition' as a complementary source of religious authority.

Two separate modes of explanation have traditionally been pursued in the light of comparative religious phenomena, though they are by no means mutually exclusive. One identifies the major motivation underlying Karaism as intrinsic to Judaism, drawn from earlier scripturalist models (such as the Sadducees or Qumranites), and the other identifies it as external to Judaism, borrowed or grafted onto it from heterodox Islamic models. In either explanation, the major impetus behind Karaism and its driving force are generally sought in factors which lie outside the 'mainstream' of medieval rabbinic thought, that is, outside the rabbinic intellectual tradition (see *History*, above).

In the Jewish milieu, Karaism was explained as deriving from live remnants or literary sources identified with suppressed Jewish circles of Late Antiquity. The rise of Islam was credited with sparking off these dormant subterranean trends, some of which also found expression in the Judaeo-Persian sectarian-messianic movements of the eighth century that pre-dated Karaism, and were partially absorbed into it during the ninth century. Eventually, Islam lent its theological language to tenth-century Karaite and Rabbanite literatures, exerting a formative influence on both.

In the Islamic milieu, various aspects and degrees of influence have been discussed. Scripturalist heterodox Islam was seen to provide the essential impetus behind Karaism, which otherwise would not have appeared on the historical horizon of medieval Judaism, and various arguments were made concerning Karaism's dependency on Islamic concepts and methodology. Some even held that all 'new' content brought to Judaism via Karaism was Islamic in origin, hence its depiction as a form of 'Islamic Judaism'.[46]

The above-charted modes of explanation still persist in current discussions of Karaism, yet a paradigmatic shift may be distinguished in the past decade concerning our understanding of its relationship to medieval Judaism at large. New historical and literary data are enabling us to review Karaism as yet another manifestation of mainstream medieval Jewish thought. In other words, the overrid-

---

[46] See Lasker (1989a: 34). The latter depiction makes much of common Karaite and Islamic customs, such as visual moon observation in determining the calendar, aspects of synagogue architecture, and worship (prostration, and the removal of shoes). Not all of these, however, are fully substantiated by Karaite practice or historical sources: see Lasker (1989a: 30–5).

ing explanations for the motivation behind Karaism and the nature of its literature are gradually being sought within the rabbinic milieu. They are being explained, hence, as an integral part of the unique historical circumstances and learning traditions that prevailed in the major Jewish centres of learning in Persia, Iraq, and Palestine.

Karaism is thus coming into its own, not as a 'sect' drawing its life-blood from clandestine trends or foreign soil,[47] but as an authentic medieval Jewish religious movement which gave expression to fundamental and long-standing traditions of Jewish thought, learning practices, and religious experience. This understanding does not preclude the possibility that elements of ancient Jewish sectarianism or earlier messianic movements had submerged within Karaism, nor the possible role that heterodox Islam played in its formation. As with other complex historical movements, Karaism too was forged by different (and even conflicting) forces.

The significance of this paradigmatic shift is that it enables the concurrence of literary and historical data into a lucid explanation of early Karaism and its intellectual roots. Accordingly, the Karaites' approach to the Hebrew Bible and its language is made clearer against the background of continuous Jewish traditions in the study of the Hebrew Bible that pre-dated the schism of the Jews under Islam. The Karaites did not simply preserve or rehash these traditions, as some would suggest; rather, they continued to adapt and develop them, by means of their dialectical engagement with rabbinic literature and according to their deep-felt literal orientation in the study of the Hebrew Bible.

Despite their scripturalist ethos, nevertheless, they were not at odds with rabbinic interpretation as such, nor with its methodology, rather, they treated it as a stepping-stone for their own insights and innovations. Their adoption of the Arabic language and the encounter with its literature during the latter half of the tenth century introduced new categories of thought and terminology, in which they could perfect their innovations. Nevertheless, the Karaites still remained focused on their Judaic intellectual heritage, as contained in post-biblical literature, with which they were deeply familiar.

The Karaites' literal orientation in biblical interpretation has often been misconstrued as a total rejection of rabbinic interpretive tradition. In fact, as I have tried to show, the Karaites objected to the exclusive authority attributed to this tradition, especially through the canonization of the Mishnah and Talmud, not so much to its content. They valued some of its aspects as legitimate expressions of the ongoing inter-generational pursuit of the Bible's true meaning, and as part of their wider interpretive heritage.

The complexity of the Karaite movement is not only reflected in its early social and geographical admixture between the Babylonian–Palestinian branches of the

---

[47] Cf. the well-argued objections to the application of this term and its implications in Olszowy-Schlanger (1998: 5–8) and Khan (2000: 3–4).

house of ʿAnan and the Judaeo-Persian messianic-scripturalists. It is also attested in the conglomerate nature of the various intellectual traditions that characterized each of its centres: the grammatical traditions in the study of the Hebrew Bible, which originated in Persia; the study of the biblical text and its vocalization traditions, which formed the professional interest of the Masoretic schools in Palestine and Iraq; certain hermeneutic principles (mainly contextual and analogical), which occupied the students of midrashic and talmudic literature in the Babylonian and Palestinian Yeshivoth. All of these traditions were undoubtedly central to mainstream medieval Jewish thought long before the schism had erupted.

The Karaites were responsible for the special fusion of these intellectual traditions and their further development and enhancement as part of their underlying scripturalist ethos and literal orientation in Bible interpretation. The manner in which this was achieved will undoubtedly form the subject of many future studies. In my view, these traditions came together most successfully in the literary-historical approach to the Bible, innovated by the medieval Karaites. Many of the later developments in the medieval *peshaṭ* tradition, including those by Abraham Ibn Ezra or David Kimḥi, are essentially beholden to the insights and methodologies initially developed in the Judaeo-Arabic works of Yefet ben ʿEli and other Karaite commentators of the tenth and eleventh centuries. In consideration of present studies and in anticipation of future research, one may postulate that the development of literary-historical Bible exegesis was Karaism's major contribution to Jewish medieval thought.

SUGGESTED READING

Major excerpts from medieval Judaeo-Arabic and Hebrew Karaite sources were published in the invaluable works of nineteenth-century pioneers of Karaite studies, such as Pinsker (1860), Poznanski (1902–3, 1908), and Harakvy (1903). The best English anthology of early Karaite literature is still that edited by Nemoy (1952). Its fine selection reflects some major Karaite fields of interest, though with a clear tendency towards halachic and polemic texts. Its introduction and excerpts naturally do not provide insight into major new editions and paradigmatic shifts that have occurred in the past half-century, especially in the fields of Karaite linguistics, translation, exegesis, and philosophy. Discussions of new works and editions pertaining to the above-mentioned literary fields are mainly concentrated in our review of *Hermeneutics*, above. To these may be added the freshly published collection of articles (Khan 2001b). Major works pertaining to Karaite origins are mostly listed under *History* above. Detailed bibliographical surveys, however, may be found in the updates by Lasker (1989b, 2000) and Frank (2001a), and in the eagerly awaited comprehensive bibliography of scholarship by and about the Karaites, prepared by Walfish (2002 forthcoming). The lacuna in reliable handbooks on Karaism, which echoes the absence of novel anthologies, is only partially addressed by various encyclopedic surveys, mostly devoted to major Karaite figures, such as Schur (1992, 1995). This situation will hopefully be improved by the volume of updated studies on Karaite Judaism edited by Polliack (2002b forthcoming).

BIBLIOGRAPHY

AHIEZER, G. and SHAPIRA, D. 2001. 'Karaites in Lithuania and in Volhynia-Galicia until the Eighteenth Century' [Hebrew]. Pe'amin 89: 19–60.

ADANG, C. 2002 (forthcoming). 'The Karaites As Portrayed in Medieval Islamic Sources.' In M. Polliack ed. (2002b).

ANKORI, Z. 1959. Karaites in Byzantium, The Formative Years 970–1100. New York.

ASTREN, F. D. 1993. 'History, Historicization, and Historical Claims in Karaite Jewish Literature.' Unpublished doctoral diss. University of California, Berkeley.

ASTREN, F. D. 2002 (forthcoming). 'Islamic Contexts of Karaism', in Polliack (2002b).

BARUN, O. 1901. 'Ein Brief des Katholikos Timotheos I über Biblische Studien des 9. Jahrhunderts.' Oriens Christianus 1: 299–313.

BASAL, N. 1997. 'Excerpts From the Abridgment (al-Mukhtasar) of al-Kitāb al-Kāfī by Abū Farag Harūn in Arabic Script.' Israel Oriental Studies 17: 197–225.

BEIT-ARIÉ, M. 1991. 'Hebrew Manuscript Collections in Leningrad.' [Hebrew]. Jewish Studies 31: 33–46.

BEN-SASSON, M. 1991. 'Firkovitch's Second Colletion: Remarks on Historical and Halakhic Materials.' [Hebrew]. Jewish Studies 31: 47–67.

BEN-SHAMMAI, H. 1977. 'The Doctrines of religious Thought of Abū Yūsuf al-Qirqisānī and Yefet ben 'Elī.' Vols. 1–2. [Hebrew]. Unpublished doctoral diss., Hebrew University of Jerusalem.

—— 1985. 'Studies in Karaite Atomism.' Jerusalem Studies in Arabic and Islam 6: 243–298.

—— 1986. 'Karaite Exegetes and their Rabbanite Environment.' [Hebrew]. In Proceedings of the Ninth World Congress of Jewish Studies. 43–58. Jerusalem.

—— 1987. 'Some Methodological Notes Concerning the Relationship Between Karaites and Ancient Jewish Sects.' [Hebrew]. Cathedra 42: 69–84.

—— 1991. 'Fragments of Daniel al-Qumīsī's Commentary on the Book of Daniel.' Henoch 60: 371–404.

—— 1992. 'The Karaite Controversy: Scripture and Tradition in Early Karaism.' In Religionsgespräche im Mittlealter. 11–26. B. Lewis and F. Niewöhner eds. Wiesbaden.

—— 1993a. 'Return To Scriptures in Ancient and Medieval Jewish Sectarianism and in Early Islam.' In Les Retours aux écritures: fondamentalismes présents et passés. 319–39. E. Patlagean and A. Le Boulluec eds. Louvain and Paris.

—— 1993b. 'Between 'Ananites and Karaites; Observations on Early Medieval Jewish Sectarianism.' In Studies in Muslim-Jewish Relations. 19–29. R. L. Nettler ed. I, Chur.

—— et al. eds. 2000. Judaeo-Arabic Manuscripts in the Firkovitch Collections, Yefet ben 'Elī al-Basrī, Commentary on Genesis: A Sample Catalogue [Hebrew]. Jerusalem.

CHIESA, B. and LOCKWOOD, W. 1985. Ya'aqūb al-Qirqisānī on Jewish Sects and Christianity. Frankfurt am Main.

COOK, M. 1987. ''Anan and Islam: The Origins of Karaite Scripturalism.' Jerusalem Studies in Arabic and Islam 9: 161–82.

CORINALDI, M. 1996. 'Karaite Halakhah.' In An Introduction to the History and Sources of Jewish Law. 251–69. N. S. Hecht et al. eds. Oxford.

DRORY, R. 1988. The Emergence of Jewish–Arabic Literary Contacts at the Beginning of the Tenth Century [Hebrew]. Tel Aviv.

ERDER, Y. 1987. 'When did the Karaites First Encounter Apocryphic Literature Akin to the Dead Sea Scrolls.' [Hebrew]. *Cathedra* 44: 53–68.

—— 1992. 'The First Date in Megillat Taʿanit in Light of the Karaite Commentary on the Tabernacle Dedication.' *JQR* 82: 362–83.

—— 1994. 'The Karaite Sadducee Dilemma.' *Israel Oriental Studies* 14: 195–226.

—— 1996. 'The Doctrine of Abū ʿIsā al-Isfahānī and its Sources.' *Jerusalem Studies in Arabic and Islam* 20: 162–99.

—— 1997a. 'The Negation of Exile in the Messianic Doctrine of the Karaite Mourners of Zion.' *HUCA* 68: 109–40.

—— 1997b. 'The Observance of the Commandments in the Diaspora on the Eve of the Redemption in the Doctrine of the Karaite Mourners of Zion.' *Henoch* 19: 176–202.

—— 1998. 'Remnants of Qumranic Lore in Two Laws of the Karaite Benjamin al-Nihāwandī Concerning Desired Meat.' [Hebrew]. *Zion* 63: 5–38.

—— 1999. 'The Attitude of the Karaite Yefet ben ʿEli to Moral Issues in Light of his Interpretation of Exodus 3: 21–22.' [Hebrew]. *Sefunot* 22: 313–33.

FRANK, D. 1995. 'The *Shoshanim* of Tenth-Century Jerusalem: Karaite Exegesis, Prayer and Communal Identity.' In *The Jews of Medieval Islam: Community, Society and Identity.* 199–245. D. Frank ed. Leiden.

—— 2001a. 'The Study of Medieval Karaism.' In *Hebrew Scholarship and the Medieval World: Studies in Honour of Raphael Loewe.* 3–22. N. De Lange ed. Cambridge.

—— 2001b. 'Karaite Exegesis.' In *Hebrew Bible/Old Testament: The History of Its interpretation.* Vol. I/2: 110–128. M. Saebo ed. Göttingen.

FRIEDLANDER, I. 1910–13. 'Jewish Arabic Studies.' *JQR* NS 1 (1910–11): 183–215; 2 (1911–12): 481–517; 3 (1912–13): 235–300.

GEIGER, A. 1911. *Judaism and its History.* New York. English trans. of *Judentum und seine Geschichte.* Breslau 1910.

GIL, M. 1983. *Palestine During the First Muslim Period (634–1099)* [Hebrew]. Vol. I. Tel Aviv.

—— 1992. *A History of Palestine, 634–1099.* Trans. E. Broido. Cambridge.

—— 1997. *In the Kingdom of Ishmael* [Hebrew]. Vol. I. Tel Aviv.

—— 1999. 'Karaite Antiquities.' [Hebrew]. In *A Century of Geniza Research (Teʿuda 15).* 71–107. M. A. Friedman ed. Tel Aviv.

GRAETZ, H. 1895. *Geschichte der Juden.* Vol V. Leipzig.

HALIVNI, D. W. 1991. *Peshat and Derash: Plain and Applied Meaning in Rabbinic Exegesis.* New York.

HARKAVY, A. 1903. *Studien und Mittheilungen* [Hebrew]. Vol. VIII. St Petersburg.

HARVIAINEN, T. 1992. 'The Karaites of Lithuania at the Present Time and the Pronunciation Tradition of Hebrew Among Them: A Preliminary Survey.' In *Proceedings of the Ninth International Congress of the International Organization For Masoretic Studies.* 53–69. A. Dotan ed. Atlanta, Ga.

—— 1996. 'The Cairo Genizot and Other Sources of the Second Firkovitch Collection in St. Petersburg.' In *Proceedings of the Twelfth International Congress of the International Organization For Masoretic Studies.* 25–36. J. Revell ed. Atlanta, Ga.

HEINEMANN, J. 1970. *Darkhey ha-aggadah.* Jerusalem.

HOERNING, R. 1899. *Six Karaite Manuscripts of Portions of the Hebrew Bible in Arabic Characters.* London.

IBN EZRA, A. 1874. 'Introduction to the Torah (shiṭṭah ʾaheret).' In *Ibn Ezra Literature: Hebrew Appendix to the Essays and Writings of Abraham Ibn Ezra*. iv. 1–9. M. Friedlander ed. London.

KHAN, G. 1990. *Karaite Bible Manuscripts from the Cairo Genizah*. Cambridge.

——1992. 'The Medieval Karaite Transcriptions of Hebrew into Arabic Script.' *Israel Oriental Studies* 12: 157–76.

——1997. 'Abu al-Faraj Harun and the Early Karaite Grammatical Tradition.' *JJS* 48: 314–34.

——2000. *The Early Karaite Tradition of Hebrew Grammatical Thought, Including a Critical Edition, Translation and Analysis of the Diqduq of Abu Yaʿqub Yusuf ibn Nuh on the Hagiographia*. Leiden.

——2001a. *Early Karaite Grammatical Texts*. Masoretic Studies 9. Atlanta, Ga.

——ed. 2001b *Exegesis and Grammar in Medieval Karaite Texts*. Journal of Semitic Studies Supplement 13. Oxford.

LASKER, D. J. 1989a. 'Islamic Influences on Karaite Origins.' In *Studies in Islamic Origins and Judaic Traditions*. ii. 23–47. W. M. Brinner and S. D. Ricks eds. Atlanta, Ga.

——1989b. 'Karaites, Developments 1970–1988.' In *Encyclopedia Judaica Yearbook 1988–89*. 855–7.

——2000. 'Karaism and Jewish Studies.' [Hebrew]. In *Jewish Culture in Muslim Lands and Cairo Geniza Studies*. No. 1: 1–29. M. Friedman ed. Tel Aviv.

LEIBOVITCH, I. 1979. *Siḥot ʿal pirqey ʾavot we-ʿal ha-rambam*. Jerusalem.

MAIMONIDES 1972. *Dalālah al-ḥāʾirīn (Guide of the Perplexed)*. J. Qafih ed. Jerusalem.

MAMAN, A. 1991. 'Karaites and Mishnaic Hebrew: Quotations and Usage.' [Hebrew]. *Leshoneneu* 55: 221–68.

MANN, J. 1935. *Texts and Studies in Jewish History and Literature*. Vol II: *Karaitica*. Philadelphia.

MARKON, I. D. 1957. *pitron sheneym ʿasar, perush literey ʿasar ḥibro daniel al-qūmisī* (Daniel al-Qumisi's commentary on the Minor Prophets). Jerusalem.

NEMOY, L. 1930. 'Al-Qirqisānī's Account of the Jewish Sects and Christianity.' *Hebrew Union College Annual* 7: 317–97.

——1947. "Anan ben David: A Re-Appraisal of the Historical Data.' In *Semitic Studies in Memory of Immanuel Low*. 239–48. A. Scheiber ed. Budapest.

——1952. *Karaite Anthology: Excerpts from the Early Literature*. New Haven.

OLSZOWY-SCHLANGER, J. 1996. 'Karaite Linguistics: The Renaissance of the Hebrew Language Among Early Karaite Jews, and Contemporary Linguistic Theories.' *Beiträge zur Geschichte der Sprachwissenschaft* 7: 81–100.

——1998. *Karaite Marriage Documents from the Cairo Geniza: Legal Tradition and Community Life in Medieval Egypt and Palestine*. Leiden.

PAUL, A. 1969. *Écrits de Qumran et sectes juives aux premiers siècles de l'Islam: recherches sur l'origine du Qaraisme*. Paris.

PINSKER S. 1860. *Lickute Kadmoniot. Zur Geschichte des Karaismus und der karäischen Literatur* [Hebrew]. Vienna.

POLLIACK, M. 1996. 'Medieval Karaite Views on Translating the Hebrew Bible into Arabic.' *JJS* 47: 64–84.

——1997. *The Karaite Tradition of Arabic Bible Translation: A Linguistic and Exegetical Study of Karaite Translations of the Pentateuch From the Tenth to the Eleventh Centuries*. Leiden.

POLLIACK, M. 1998. 'Medieval Karaite Methods of Translating Biblical Narrative into Arabic.' *Vetus testamentum* 48: 375–398.

—— 1999. 'The Emergence of Karaite Bible Exegesis.' [Hebrew]. *Sefunot* 22: 299–311.

—— 2001. 'On the Question of the Pesher's Influence on Karaite Exegesis.' [Hebrew]. In *Fifty Years of Dead Sea Scrolls Research*. 275–294. Jerusalem.

—— 2002a forthcoming. 'Rethinking Karaism: Between Judaism and Islam.' In *Jews of Islam* (provisional title). D. Wasserstein ed. Leiden.

—— ed. 2002b forthcoming. *Karaite Judaism: Guide to the History and Literary Sources of Medieval and Modern Karaism*. Leiden.

POZNANSKI, S. 1902–3. "Anan et ses écrits.' In *Revue des Études Juives* 44: 161–87; 45: 50–69, 176–203.

—— 1908. *The Karaite Literary Opponents of Saadia Gaon*. London. Repr. from *JQR* (1906–8) 18–20.

—— 1939–1945. *Qirqisānī, 'Anwār. Abū Yūsuf Ya'qūb al-Qirqisānī. Kitāb al-'anwār wal-marāqib: The Book of Lights and Watchtowers*). L. Nemoy ed. Vols. I–II. New York.

REVEL, B. 1911–13. 'Inquiry Into the Sources of Karaite Halakah.' *JQR* NS 2: 517–44; 3: 337–96.

—— 1913. *The Karaite Halakhah and its Relation to Sadducean, Samaritan and Philonic Halakhah*. Philadelphia. Repr. in *Karaite Studies*. P. Birnbaum ed. New York 1971.

SCHECHTER, S. 1910. *Fragments of a Zadokite Work*. Cambridge.

SCHUR, N. 1992. *History of the Karaites*. Frankfurt am Main.

—— 1995. *The Karaite Encyclopedia*. Frankfurt am Main.

SKLARE, D. 1997. *Judaeo-Arabic Manuscripts in the Firkovitch Collections: The Works of Yusuf al-Basir. A Sample Catalogue. Texts and Studies* [Hebrew]. Jerusalem.

STERN, D. 1997. *Midrash and Theory: Ancient Jewish Exegesis and Contemporary Literary Studies* 15–38. Evanston, Ill.

SZONDI, P. 1995. *Introduction to Literary Hermeneutics*. 5–13. Cambridge.

VAJDA, G. 1971. *Deux commentaires karäites sur l'Ecclésiaste*. Leiden.

—— 1985. *Al-Kitāb al-Muhtāwī de Yūsuf al-Baṣīr*. Leiden.

WALFISH, B. D. 2002 forthcoming. *Bibliography of Scholarship By and About Karaites* (Provisional title). Jerusalem.

WASSERSTROM, S. M. 1985. 'Species of Misbelief: A History of Muslim Heresiography of the Jews.' Unpublished doctoral diss., University of Toronto.

WIEDER, N. 1956/7. 'The Qumran Sectaries and the Karaites.' *JQR* 47: 97–113.

—— 1958. 'The Dead Sea Scrolls Type of Biblical Exegesis Among the Karaites.' In *Between East and West: Essays Dedicated to the Memory of Bela Horovitz*. 75–106. A. Altman ed. Oxford and London.

—— 1962. *Judean Scrolls and Karaism*. London.

TIROSH-BECKER, O. 1991. 'Preliminary Studies in Rabbinic Quotations Embedded in the Pentateuch Commentaries of the Karaite Scholar Yeshu'ah Ben Yehudah.' [Hebrew]. *Massorot* 5–6: 313–40.

—— 1993. 'A Linguistic Study of Mishnaic Quotations Embedded in Yeshu'ah ben Yehudah's Commentary on Leviticus.' [Hebrew]. *Massorot* 7: 145–86.

—— 1998. 'Linguistic Study of a Rabbinic Quotation Embedded in a Karaite Commentary on Exodus.' In *Studies in Mishnaic Hebrew*. 380–407. M. Bar-Asher ed. Jerusalem.

ZUCKER, M. 1959. *Rav Saadya Gaon's Translation of the Torah: Exegesis, Halakha, and Polemics in R. Saadya's Translation of the Pentateuch* [Hebrew]. New York.

CHAPTER 13

SEPHARDI AND MIDDLE EASTERN JEWRIES SINCE 1492

SARAH ABREVAYA STEIN*

THE SEPHARDIC MYSTIQUE/ THE SEPHARDIC MISTAKE

THE last time a volume surveying the field of Jewish studies was published, in 1990, Sephardi and Middle Eastern Jewries did not command an essay of their own (S. Cohen and Greenstein 1990). Indeed, in that volume, entitled *The State of Jewish Studies*, Sephardi and Middle Eastern Jewries were by and large absented from discussion of Jewish history, literature, philosophy, art, and scholarship in the early modern and modern periods. Sephardi history, it was implied, ended with the Expulsion from Spain, though this event, too, was referenced only in passing: in order, according to contributor Ivan G. Marcus, that readers not be 'unduly influenced by the Sephardic Mystique and its claim that the Spanish-Jewish experience is central and supremely significant in Jewish History' (116).

* Thanks to Aron Rodrigue, Joel Beinin, Rebecca Stein, and participants in Stanford University's Jewish Studies colloquium for comments on an earlier draft of this essay.

The notion of the 'Sephardic Mystique' was introduced by Ismar Schorsch (Schorsch 1985) and quickly appropriated by others (J. Gerber 1985, Marcus 1985). This myth had its origins in nineteenth-century Wissenschaft des Judentums scholarship, where it took root in the writings of Heinrich Graetz, Moritz Güdemann, and Leopold Zunz, among others. These historians, supporters of Jewish acculturation and integration in the Western European society of their day, sought historical models that they and their Jewish contemporaries might emulate. They found one such archetype in the so-called 'Golden Age' of Islamic Spain, a period stretching from the ninth to the eleventh century in which an Islamic–Jewish symbiosis—unparalleled in the lands of Christian Europe—was understood to have been achieved.

The allure of the Golden Age of Spain, labelled the 'Sephardic Mystique' by Schorsch, persisted into the twentieth century (despite a trenchant critique by Salo Baron that called for an alternative to the 'lachrymose' view of Ashkenazi history that was promulgated by the narrative of the Sephardic Mystique: Baron 1928). The glorified view of a medieval Islamic–Jewish symbiosis was not countered until the 1960s, when popular and scholarly writers began to espouse what Mark Cohen has trenchantly labelled the 'neo-lachrymose conception of Jewish–Arab History' (M. R. Cohen 1986, 1991, 1994). According to this view, the achievements of the Golden Age were realized only by a narrow elite and, for the vast majority of Jews living under the rule of Islam, life was consistently gloomy, marked by anti-Semitism, disenfranchisement, and persecution. This new view of Islamic–Jewish history has permeated both popular and scholarly sources, among them Martin Gilbert's cartographic survey of Jewish life in the lands of Islam (1976) and the popularized studies of Egyptian Jewish history penned by Bat-Ye'or (the pseudonym of Giselle Littmann: Bat Ye'or 1971, 1974). (An extended discussion of the 'neo-lachrymose conception of Jewish–Arab History' by Cohen and a critical response by Norman Stillman may be found in the journal *Tikkun*—M. R. Cohen 1991; Stillman 1991. See also Beinin 1998: 14–19.)

Cohen's musings contribute to a new generation of scholarship, much of it focusing on the medieval period (1994; see also Chapter 8 in this volume), that aspires to reconsider the history of Jews living under the rule of Islam without falling prey either to the Sephardic Mystique or to the 'neo-lachrymose conception of Jewish–Arab History'. This pursuit of equipoise is shared by scholars of early modern and modern Jewish history as well: but arguably scholars of these later periods have been prone to slightly different kinds of exaggeration. Rather than celebrating a 'Sephardic Mystique', we have mourned its loss, committing, in its stead, what might be called 'the Sephardic Mistake'. We have assumed that in the aftermath of the Golden Age of Spain, in the aftermath of expulsion and the Sabbatian crises, Sephardi culture became monolithic, static, tangential to the larger Jewish world, and of little interest to the scholar of Jewish studies. Thus the otherwise judicious Lucy Dawidowicz could claim in a lecture of 1990 that, while the Ashkenazim met their forced exodus from the Rhineland with 'optimism and confidence' that fuelled 'the Golden Era of Ashkenazi Jewry', 'the Sephardi rabbis in the sixteenth century responded to the expulsion from Spain in the same way the rabbis had reacted after the destruction of the Second Temple: they turned their backs on history...' (Dawidowicz 1992: 13–14). Perhaps even more startling, scholars in the field of Sephardi studies, too, echo this sentiment.

Statements like these may help to explain the context in which *The State of Jewish Studies* was published. As Jane Gerber argued in her introduction to *Sephardic Studies in the University* (1995), as recently as seven years ago there was little indication that scholarship on modern Sephardi and Middle Eastern Jewries, though already quite extensive, was permeating the field of Jewish studies as a whole. In this regard, the content of *The State of Jewish Studies* was but one sign of an overall trend. Other measures of this problem surfaced—and continue to surface—elsewhere: in undergraduate surveys of Jewish History, culture, or society, in which non-European Sephardi and Middle Eastern Jewish culture is rarely represented; in scholarship in which 'Jewish' is equated with 'Ashkenazi' or 'European'; in the persistent lack of comparative scholarship in the field of Jewish studies; in professional meetings for practitioners of Jewish studies, during which presentations on Sephardic or Middle Eastern Jewish culture tend to be confined to a few ethnically delineated panels; and, finally, in the self-concept of scholars of non-Ashkenazi Jewries, many of whom chose to affiliate with Middle East studies rather than (and not in addition to) Jewish studies.

Relative to trends such as these, the choice to include an essay on this topic in this volume represents a rather profound paradigm shift. It signals that the study of early modern and modern Sephardi and Middle Eastern Jewries—and, by extension, these Jewries in and of themselves—are dynamic and relevant to scholars of Jewish studies. And it suggests that the field of Sephardic and Mizrahi studies—and perhaps Jewish studies too—has matured and grown. Strikingly, in recent years the field(s) of Sephardi and Middle Eastern Jewish studies have begun to root themselves in the university; academic programmes devoted to the study of these Jewries are now situated at the Hebrew University, Jerusalem, the Sorbonne, Stanford University, the University of California, Los Angeles, and the University of Washington, Seattle, among other locations; new faculty positions in the field are being advertised annually; scholars in the field have created a 'Sephardic Studies Caucus', complete with a website featuring syllabi and *curricula vitae* (http://www.princeton.edu/~rsimon/ssc.htm); and, perhaps more exciting still, a new wave of doctoral candidates are being trained in Israel, the United States, and Europe. Despite these significant achievements, certain challenges still confront the student of Sephardi and Middle Eastern Jewries, be she a specialist in the subject or in another field of Jewish studies. In the pages that remain, four such challenges will be delineated.

First, our conceptual language and categories still need to be challenged and rethought: what is to be gained—and what to be lost—by grouping Sephardi and Middle Eastern Jewries into one historical category: and ought we to discriminate between them? Second, while recent scholarship has challenged the 'Sephardic Mystique' and the 'neo-lachrymose view of Jewish–Arab History', there are other influential teleologies that warrant reconsideration, among them the teleologies of Westernization, modernization, and Zionism, all of which assume a Eurocentric perspective. Third, there remain numerous important gaps in our knowledge of Sephardi and Mizrahi culture and history, including social history, women's and gender history, comparative and inter-ethnic history. And finally, while scholars should note with satisfaction that scholarship on non-Ashkenazim is entering the canon of early modern and modern Jewish studies, we must recognize that inclusion is only half the battle: facing us still is the task of using this scholarship to reconsider pre-existing assumptions about Jewish culture and to construct, in their stead, more inclusive theories about Jewish identity, culture, and practice.

SEPHARDI AND MIDDLE EASTERN JEWRIES DISCRIMINATED

'Sephardi' and 'Middle Eastern' are slippery terms, and their coupling is problematic. As a historical term, 'Sephardi' describes the Jewish descendents of the practising Jews and *conversos* who fled or were expelled from the Iberian peninsula in the fourteenth, fifteenth, and sixteenth centuries in the wake of Christian reconquest, growing Judeo-phobia, and the Inquisition. In exile from *Sepharad* (Hebrew for 'Spain'), these Jews found new homes in the Ottoman and Dutch empires, in Western Europe, the Americas, and the Middle East, where they tended to remain discrete ethnic communities, remaining in most cases culturally distinct from both the Jewish and non-Jewish communities they joined in their new homes.

Even before the forcible creation of the Sephardi diaspora, Iberian Jewish culture was internally diverse; in the wake of the expulsions from Spain and Portugal, this diversity multiplied further still. Sephardi culture inevitably fused with the local, regional, and transnational cultures with which Jews came into contact, such that, in the course of a few generations, Sephardim varied from region to region, speaking different languages, developing independent culinary and sartorial traditions, engaging in distinct vocational pursuits, and, in general, affiliating with the cities, towns, empires, or regions in which they lived: even as they continued to self-identify as Jews and as Sephardim, be it publicly or in hiding. Thus the *conversos* of early modern Amsterdam (Bodian 1997) and the Sephardim of south-western France (Malino 1978), south-eastern Europe (Benbassa and Rodrigue 2000), Spanish America (Barantan 1993; Uchmany 1993), and Surinam (R. Cohen 1982, 1991) had, by the sixteenth century, begun to differ from one another in meaningful and lasting ways.

All this diversification notwithstanding, beginning in the fifteenth century and extending at least until the late nineteenth, it was possible to speak of a 'Sephardi world order' that extended across the Mediterranean basin and into the Middle East, Northern Europe, and the Americas (Schroeter 1994). Despite the fact that they had become divided by political boundaries, language, and religious and cultural practice, Sephardim remained linked by the flow of capital, bodies, and ideas, and by the power of self-representation and memory. Because these bonds transcended the borders of nation states, empires, regions, and continents, and because they endured for over five centuries, they are not easily characterized. A sense of the complexity of the cultural and material relationships that sustained the Sephardi diaspora is perhaps captured best in a number of edited volumes which bring together the expertise of a large numbers of scholars (Abitbol *et al.* 1997; Beinart 1992; Gampel 1997; Ginio 1992; Goldberg 1996; Kedourie 1992; Stillman and Stillman 1999; Stillman and Zucker 1993). A wide-reaching study of the Sephardi diaspora has also been written by Jane Gerber (1994), while Esther Benbassa and Aron Rodrigue have co-written an exhaustive study of Sephardi life in Turkey and the Balkans, a region they call the 'Eastern Sephardi heartland' (2000: p. xix); both are appropriate for use in the classroom as well as by specialists in the field. For the beginner, impressionistic accounts of Sephardi culture are offered by Mair José Benardete (1982) and Paloma Diaz-Mas (1993).

Like Sephardi and Ashkenazi Jewries, the Jewries of the Middle East have always been an internally diverse group, divided by language and religious and social practice, as by the borders of polities. But while the Sephardi and Ashkenazi diasporas emerged in the late medieval period, Jews had remained in various regions of the Middle East for millennia. The Jews of Persia thus developed (culturally, materially, and socially) quite independently from the Jews of Yemen, while these Jewries differed from the Musta'rabim (or Judeo-Arabic) communities that stretched across North Africa and through Syria, Iraq, Palestine, and Egypt.

Within these three 'cultural zones' Jewish culture was by no means homogenous. An argument could be made that Moroccan Jewry was its own 'Jewish cultural area' due, in part, to Morocco's long history as an independent kingdom (Deshen and Zenner 1996: 7). Further, though the majority of Sephardim who settled in North Africa in the wake of the expulsions from Spain were absorbed into the majority and pre-existing Musta'rabim communities, some settled in distinct coastal communities, retaining a Judeo-Spanish dialect known as *haketia* (Chouraqui 1968). The Jews of Central Asia, meanwhile, had historical roots in Persia, but their cultures and languages nonetheless differed from the Jews who lived within the borders of Persia or Iran, and these differences ossified over time (Fischel 1950, 1953; Loeb 1977, 1982).

Given the diversity of Middle Eastern Jewries, synthesizing their histories is no minor task. The most up-to-date and influential attempts at this project have been conducted—in very different fashions—by Bernard Lewis (1984) and Norman Stillman (1979, 1984). Lewis's *The Jews of Islam* maintains a breathless focus that encompasses one millennium and an enormous geographic range (see also the contributions to Ettinger 1981). As the title of this work might suggest, Lewis's monograph privileges the way in which Islamic law and high politics regarded and managed Jewish subjects. In the process, his work by and large ignores intracommunal dynamics and the finely grained texture of local Jewish cultures. In contrast, Stillman's two-volume work (*The Jews of Arab Lands* and *The Jews of Arab Lands in Modern Times*) presents not only historical essays, but also a collection of documents written primarily by Jews in the Arab Middle East (a region, it should be specified, that excludes the European territories of the Ottoman Empire, and thus the Sephardi heartland). In contrast to Lewis, Stillman encourages us to assume the perspective of Jewish subjects rather than that of the Islamic leadership.

Despite these differences, Lewis's and Stillman's influential monographs have a number of significant features in common. Both present Middle East Jewries as largely reactive populations, accommodating first Islamic law and society and, in time, the growing influence of the West. Neither offers a vivid picture of Jewish social or economic history, and neither attends to the presence of Jewish women. Despite these and other shortcomings, both are valuable sources for use by scholars and in the classroom, because they provide comprehensive overviews of their subject-matter while remaining accessible to undergraduates. Somewhat more outdated—but nonetheless valuable—are the historical surveys by Hayyim J. Cohen (1975) and H. Z. Hirschberg (1969), and Raphael Patai's anthropological study of Middle East Jewry (1971). A number of edited works, some with an anthropological focus, have also greatly contributed to our ability to understand Middle Eastern Jewish culture in relational terms, although nearly all of these focus exclusively on the nineteenth and twentieth centuries (M. R. Cohen and Udovitch 1989; Goldberg 1996; Deshen and Zenner 1982, 1996).

One may emphasize the historical differences that distinguished Sephardim from Middle Eastern Jewries, and Middle Eastern Jewries from one another: but one may also speak (as does Lewis) of the things these Jewries had in common, including the rule of Islam, which undoubtedly facilitated transnational economic, legal, and social practices. Arguably, however, it was not so much the rise or rule of Islam that linked Sephardi and Middle Eastern Jewries to one another (or, indeed, caused them to be linked in the minds of scholars), as it was events born of the nineteenth and early twentieth centuries: the emancipation of some of Europe's Jewries, the forces of colonialism and orientalism, the emergence of the social sciences, of Western European Jewish philanthropy and of Zionism, the creation and construction of the

state of Israel, and the gradual dissolution of the vast majority of Jewish communities in the Middle East, North Africa, and south-eastern Europe. These forces
brought the Jews of Western Europe—and the first generation of scholars of Jewish
studies—into physical and conceptual contact with the Jews of the Middle East,
North Africa, and south-eastern Europe (and, one might add, with the Jews of
Eastern Europe as well) on an unprecedented scale, catalyzing, in the process, new
vectors of contact between Sephardi and Middle Eastern Jewries. The Jewish world
was changing both physically and metaphysically, and with it was developing the
way in which scholars would image the past.

If the conceptual and historical intertwining of Sephardi and Middle Eastern
Jewries had roots in the late nineteenth and early twentieth centuries, it has
continued to be nurtured in recent years. Contemporary Middle Eastern politics,
intellectual debates born of the American academy, and the production of history
and myth about Israel, the Holocaust, and the Jewish past have perpetuated this
fusion and invested it with new meanings. These are among the forces that have led
scholars to intertwine the history of Sephardi and Middle Eastern Jewries, in ways
which alternately discriminate against these Jewries and allow us to study them in a
more discriminating manner.

SEPHARDI AND MIDDLE EASTERN
JEWRIES AND DISCRIMINATION

Let us turn, then, to the factors that have encouraged scholars to view the history of
Sephardi and Middle Eastern Jewries in concert. There is, first, the uneven story
of Jewish emancipation. Daniel Schroeter has argued that 'until the emancipation of
Western Jewry, the Mediterranean and the North Atlantic were still part of the same
Sephardi network' (1994: 86–7), while, in the wake of the emancipation in France,
the Western Sephardim were compelled to identify with the nation in which they
lived, and not as members of a corporate body with links in the Mediterranean
world (see also Malino 1978). If emancipation encouraged France's Sephardim to
feel French, the chequered history of similar decrees in North Africa, the
Middle East, and the Ottoman Empire made the Jews in these regions seem—at
least to their Jewish peers in Western Europe—acutely disenfranchised. Arguably
this dichotomy was exaggerated from the start, a sign of the naiveté of liberalism
and the complexity of life on the ground. After all, while in Western Europe political
emancipation tended to precede social emancipation, in the lands of Islam the
status of the *dhimmi*—even in the absence of political emancipation—conferred on

non-Muslims a certain degree of social emancipation (Birnbaum and Katznelson 1995).

More than emancipation, it was colonialism that encouraged Western European Jews to reconceptualize their co-religionists to the east. With the semi-imperial relationship developing between the Ottoman Empire and Western Europe, with the Napoleonic invasion and three-year occupation of Egypt and the French colonialization of Algeria, the Jews of Western Europe began to envision the Jews of the Middle East, North Africa, and Mediterranean not as partners in commercial or intellectual exchange, but as 'Orientals' in need of protection and 'regeneration' (Berkowitz 1989). A spark was provided by the notorious Damascus Affair of 1840, during which Jews in Damascus were blamed for the disappearance of a Capucin friar. This modern-day blood libel stimulated widespread concern among the Franco-and Anglo-Jewish elites, prompting widespread debate and political intervention (Frankel 1997). In the wake of the affair (and in the aftermath of successful diplomatic intervention), the Franco-Jewish elite formed the Alliance Israélite Universelle (AIU), an organization designed to educate and thus 'regenerate' Levantine Jewry, thereby facilitating their integration into the majority society. By the first decade of the twentieth century the AIU's reach extended from Iran to Morocco and across Turkey and the Balkans: by the eve of the First World War over 40,000 Sephardi and Middle Eastern Jewish girls and boys were attending Alliance schools, receiving instruction in French and being trained to model themselves on the image of the French Jewish bourgeoisie (Rodrigue 1990: p. xix. See also Benbassa 1991, 1996; A. Cohen 1986; Laskier 1983; Netzer 1974; Schwarzfuchs 1981; Tsur 1996; Yehuda 1996).

There is little doubt that the schools of the AIU made available secular learning to Jewish students—and professional positions to Jewish adults, many of whom were women—who might otherwise have been denied these opportunities: the schools of the AIU were, we must remember, initiated at the behest of local elites, and more often than not operated with the approval of local rabbinical leadership (Rodrigue 1990; Stillman 1996; Yehuda 1996; and Zohar, 1986, 1988, 1993). (The complexities of these relationships can be introduced to students with the aid of an evocative collection of primary documents assembled and edited by Aron Rodrigue (1993).) At the same time, the work of the AIU was but a sign that the Jewries of North Africa, the Middle East, and the Ottoman Empire were increasingly dependent upon their Western European Jewish peers. With the AIU a new generation of Jewish colonialist philanthropy was born (Benbassa 1996, Schroeter 1984), and with it came new understandings of Jews' relationships to one another that persist to this day.

Western European Jews were not the only ones concerned with broadening the rights of non-Muslims living under Islamic rule. A decade-and-a-half after the French conquest of Algeria in 1830, a French ordinance announced the reorganization of the Algerian Jewish community into a *consistoire* system based on the French model. In 1870 the French granted citizenship to the Jews of Algeria; not coincidentally, the driving force behind this act was Isaac Adolphe Crémieux, the minister of justice, a founding leader of the AIU and the man after whom the so-called 'Crémieux Decree' was named (Ansky 1950; Chouraqui 1968; Hirschberg 1974–81; Schwarzfuchs 1981; Stillman 1991). The granting of French citizenship to the Jews of Algeria created many opportunities but also came with certain costs, not least of which was the denuding of Algerian Jews' status as Arab Jews. The repercussions of this became particularly apparent during the war for independence, by which time Jews had been branded agents of the colonial regime.

A slightly less dramatic version of these events unfolded in the Ottoman Empire. Beginning in the 1830s, the Ottoman leadership approved the first in a series of reforms known collectively as the Tanzimat Reforms. Adopted under pressure from Western European countries, the Tanzimat Reforms lacked both popular support and the means of implementation. And, rather than facilitating Jews' (and other non-Muslims') integration into Ottoman society, as did the emancipation of Jews in Western and Central Europe, these reforms actually lessened the rights of Jews and other non-Muslims, transforming them, as Aron Rodrigue and others have argued, from a 'millet' vested with special privileges and rights, to a disenfranchised and disassociated 'minority' (Braude 1982; Karpat 1982; Kayali 1997; Makdisi 2000; Rodrigue 1995). This was a sign that the logic of the Western European nation state was uneasily grafted onto the multi-ethnic, multiconfessional, and multilingual context of the Ottoman Empire, which had arguably developed more (as well as less) appropriate means of ensuring its subjects' coexistence. For Western European Jewry, however, the Tanzimat Reforms were further proof that the Jews of the Empire were disadvantaged and disenfranchised.

As colonialism was remapping the Middle East and North Africa, then, it was also remapping the Jewish world in subtle ways. Once composed of multiple and overlapping networks of Jewries, this world was now understood to be conceptually divided in half, conforming to polarities invented by colonial discourse and policy: the polarities of Occident–Orient, West–East, benevolent–needy, and modern–backward. Significantly, these categories were not based in logic, geography, or history. The Jews of Eastern Europe, after all, were branded *Ostjuden* (Eastern Jews or Orientals) though they, like many Western European Jews, had roots in *Ashkenaz* (the German Rhineland). (See e.g. the contributions to Frankel 1984.) Further, at the turn of the twentieth century Levantine Jewish centres like Alexandria and Salonika were far more cosmopolitan than were many of the centres of Jewish life in France, Germany, or Britain. Finally, as memoirs and autobiographies from this and later periods attest, even members of the Sephardi, Middle Eastern, or North African Jewish elite who were educated in a French cultural milieu could never, in the eyes of their French peers, shed their 'Oriental' origins (Benbassa and Rodrigue 1998; Memmi 1992; Sciaky 1946).

These dynamics would be reiterated within Zionist discourse and by the processes of state-building. Until recently, research on the Sephardi, North African, and

Middle Eastern Jewries' relationship to the Zionist movement and State of Israel has been driven by a Zionist teleology: that is, it has perceived Israel and Zionism as having liberated Sephardi, Middle Eastern, and North African Jewries from cultural stagnation, political impotence, and virulent anti-Semitism. To make these arguments, scholars have concentrated a great deal of attention on uncovering long histories of indigenous Zionism (much of it spiritual or messianic); on tracing the enthusiastic reception of turn-of-the-century European Zionist delegates and literature; on fathoming the growing popularity of cultural and territorial Zionism in the decades that followed; and on exploring the rising tide of Arab nationalism which, it was argued, drove Jews to Jewish nationalism, and, in time, to *aliyah* (emigration to Israel). (See e.g. the various contributions under the heading 'Islamic Lands' in Abitbol 1981; Davis 1980; Laskier 1992a; Klorman 1993; Meir 1993; Shulewitz 1999; Stillman 1984; Yehuda 1981, 1986.)

In recent years, however, we have seen the emergence of a new generation of scholarship which offers alternatives to this hitherto-inviolable narrative. We have learned that the appearance of Zionist literature and delegates in the Middle East, North Africa, and the Ottoman interior were received with scepticism and hostility as well as enthusiasm. Many Sephardi and Middle Eastern Jews, it appears, were inclined towards political sentiments other than Zionism: towards Sephardism (Benbassa and Rodrigue 2000: 143–150), communism (Beinin 1998), various forms of pan-ethnic socialism (Lockman 1986), Alliancist and anti-Zionist politics (Benbassa 1993, 1995; Laskier 1983; Nahum 1997; Rodrigue 1980; Stein forthcoming 2003), Ottomanism (Campos forthcoming; Stein forthcoming; see also the contribution by Ilber Ortayli in Levy 1994), and even national patriotism (Memmi 1962; Shiblak 1986). Recent scholarship has also allowed us to appreciate that the Zionism formulated in a turn-of-the-century Western, Central, and East European landscape was little concerned with the needs or desires of Sephardi and Middle Eastern Jewries, despite rhetorical gestures of inclusivity; indeed, the Zionist pioneers of the late nineteenth and early twentieth centuries were more inclined to see non-Ashkenazim as potential labourers than co-architects of a Jewish state (Massad 1996; Shafir 1989; E. Shohat 1997, 1999). Beginning in the first decades of the twentieth century, Jewish state-builders (and, eventually, the state itself) began encouraging the emigration of Jews from the countries of the Arab Middle East, culminating in dramatic airlifts that, it turns out, did not always have the support of the émigrés themselves (Shiblak 1986). Simultaneously, Israel's MAPAI and Labor governments were funnelling Jewish immigrants from the Arab Middle East into development towns or into border neighbourhoods previously inhabited by Palestinian Arabs, offering them inadequate housing and educational facilities, and depriving them of the opportunities offered their Ashkenazi peers. In the process, families were separated, communities divided, and a clear class divide and division of labour was created and maintained (Chetrit 2000; Cohen-Almagor 1995; Giladi 1990; Massad 1996; Shiblak 1986; E. Shohat 1997, 1999; Smooha 1978; Swirski 1989; Weingrod 1985).

If Zionist philosophy and Israeli policy were turning non-Ashkenazi Jews into an Israeli underclass, they were also succeeding in amalgamating these Jewries into one ethnic and conceptual category. In Israeli official and popular parlance, these Jewries were called 'edot ha-mizrah' (Orientals) or 'binei edot hamizrah' (descendents of Oriental ethnicity), and, in time, simply 'Mizrahim' (Eastern/Oriental). (The ironic inversion of this, perhaps, is that contemporary Israeli parlance uncannily labels a certain class of Ashkenazim 'Anglos': the only context, one imagines, where Jews are considered English natives.) These terms for Sephardi, Middle Eastern, and North African Jews, it has been argued, strips Sephardi Jews of their European heritage, posits Jewishness and Arabness as antonyms, and has the ironic effect of denying Middle Eastern Jews' identity as indigenous North Africans and Middle Easterners (Alcalay 1993; E. Shohat 1999). Discursive and practical attempts to appropriate Sephardi and Middle Eastern Jewries within Israel and within an Ashkenazi-derived Jewish historical consciousness have had profound implications: among them the political conservativism of Mizrahim in Israel and the complex view of modernity that surfaces in their narratives (see e.g. the contributions to Alcalay 1996).

In recent decades the history of Sephardi and Middle Eastern Jewries' confluence has taken an unexpected turn. Since the 1970s, and with increasing precision in the 1990s, Jewish activists and academics have begun 'reclaiming' the term 'Mizrahi', using it to describe not only Middle Eastern Jewries, but all Jews of non-Ashkenazi descent (Alcalay 1996; Cohen-Almagor 1995; Giladi 1990; Massad 1996; E. Shohat 1999; Swirski 1989). Tellingly, this scholarship also uses the term 'Mizrahi' as a synonym for 'Arab Jews' and occasionally as synonyms for 'Sephardi' (E. Shohat 1997), despite the fact that, historically, many Sephardim lived not in the Arab Middle East but in the European regions of the Ottoman Empire. As this suggests, to date, the burgeoning field of Mizrahi studies has been oriented away from historical research and towards sociological, anthropological, and literary studies. Complicating matters still further is the fact that a number of scholars of Sephardi and Middle Eastern Jewries (most of whom operate in the American academy) perform the opposite inversion: employing the terms 'Sephardi' and 'Sephardi studies' as conceptual umbrellas that encompass all Jews who lived under the rule of Islam (J. Gerber 1995; E. Shohat 1998; Stillman and Zucker 1993). If scholars of 'Mizrahi studies' are seeking to celebrate the Middle Easternness of their subjects, scholars of 'Sephardi studies' who use the term 'Sephardi' in this broad sense seem to be straining to reassert the Europeanness of their subjects, divorcing them, in the process, from thorny Middle East politics.

The Jews of Islam, Middle East Jews, Mediterranean Jews, Levantine Jews, Oriental Jews, Maghrebi Jews, Musta'rabim, Sephardim, Mizrahim: which of these terms should be employed—and which rejected—by the scholar of Jewish studies? Arguably, there is no single answer to this question: instead, the terminology we employ must reflect our intellectual trajectories. Scholars interested in Jews' experience of Islamic law and society will continue to find value in the category 'the Jews of Islam', while those concerned with considering Jews' contribution to regional cultural practices will certainly not find the study of North African, Mediterranean, and Middle Eastern Jewries to be exhausted. Those interested in how nineteenth-and twentieth-century Jews in the Ottoman Empire, North Africa, and the Middle East encountered and evaluated the expansionist policies of Western Europe (and, perhaps, the colonialist philanthropy of Western European Jewry), will find compelling reasons to study Sephardi and Middle Eastern Jewries in concert, while other scholars will be more interested in studying relationships between Jews and non-Jews, or in transcending ethnicity altogether (recent scholarship, for example, has examined the culture of work in Salonika: Ginio 1998).

This is not to suggest that each of these terms or approaches will be equally compelling to all readers. It is, for example, difficult to imagine an intellectual justification for resuscitating the term 'Oriental'. On the other hand, there is no reason to reject approaches or framing devices that have yet to be explored or imagined, particularly as the field of Sephardi and Middle Eastern Jewish studies is young and still quite small. Instead, what is called for at this juncture is an elaboration of the protean historical and cultural identities listed above, and the theoretical and empirical research that will allow us to understand each more deeply and critically. Research such as this will in the end allow scholars to look beyond the nineteenth and twentieth centuries and to look at these centuries with new eyes; and this, in turn, will allow us to decentre events and trends that pivot around Western Europe, Western European Jews, and the *Wissenschaftlich* imagination that continues to define the canon of Jewish studies. If this range of approaches catalyses historical and historiographic debate, the field will be richer for it. Perhaps our most pressing task, then, is to grapple with Sephardi and Middle Eastern Jewries as discriminating historical actors: actors who experienced but also changed the worlds around them.

DISCRIMINATING SEPHARDI AND MIDDLE EASTERN JEWRIES

What dimensions of Sephardi and Middle Eastern Jewish studies are well developed, and in what directions must the field continue to expand? One may profitably begin with 1492, a date of great import to the Sephardi world but of little relevance to most Jews of the Middle East.

It is to the study of Ottoman Empire that the greatest quantity of scholarship on Sephardim has been devoted. The presence of Jews in the Ottoman lands long preceded their expulsion from the Iberian Peninsula. Some Jewish communities remained through the transition from Byzantine to Ottoman rule (Bowman 1985; Epstein 1980); others came in the wake of expulsions from Hungary and France in the late fourteenth century (Marcus 1951). When Jews began fleeing the Iberian Peninsula *en masse*, the Ottoman Empire was entering its most expansionist period: by the sixteenth century its rule would extend to most of the Middle East and North Africa, and thus encompassed most Sephardi and Middle Eastern Jewries.

Ottoman Jews were always an internally diverse group, encompassing Romaniots (Greek Jews), Italian Jews, Ashkenazim from Germany and Eastern Europe, Karaites (a sect that rejects the Talmud as a basis for Jewish law: Beinin 1998; Danon 1924–5), Musta'rabim (Arabic-speaking Jews), and Maghrebi Jews, as well as Sephardim and *conversos* from the Iberian Peninsula. Given the dizzying variety of Ottoman Jewries, it is perhaps for the best that no single work has attempted to offer a thorough synthesis of Ottoman Jewish history. The student of Ottoman Jewry must, as a result, piece together this history based on a wide array of sources. There are, to begin with, a number of fine surveys of Ottoman Jewish history that focus exclusively on European Turkey and the Ottoman-controlled Balkans. Of these, the most recent and thorough is by Aron Rodrigue and Esther Benbassa (2000). (See also the contributions to Galante 1985; J. Gerber 1982; Levy 1992; Shaw 1991; and Weiker 1992. Two earlier studies also remain informative: Franco 1897 and Rosanes 1930–45.) As was mentioned above, Bernard Lewis's study of Jewish life under Islamic rule (1984) encompasses the history of Ottoman rule, but, focusing as it does on the legal and religious place of Jews in Islamic society, offers little in the way of a detailed cultural history. Norman Stillman's two-volume study of Jewish life in the Arab Middle East (1979 and 1984), meanwhile, while offering a vivid picture of Jewish life in the Arab provinces of the empire, does not reach into the Sephardic heartland of southeastern Europe (see also H. Cohen 1973; Hirschberg 1969; Patai 1971).

Studies of the empire's Sephardim are more voluminous than are studies of its Middle Eastern Jewries. The creation of Sephardi communities and leadership in the empire has received a fair amount of scholarly attention (see the various contributions to Barnai 1992a; Bornstein-Makovetsky 1989; Braude and Lewis 1982; Epstein 1980, 1982; Hacker 1984, 1992; Rodrigue 1992; A. Shohat 1981, 1997). Certainly we know more about the ways in which Sephardim adjusted to their new homes than we know about Middle Eastern Jewries' adjustment to Ottoman leadership (it has been suggested, by Stillman and others, that Ottoman rule was less oppressive than that of the Mamelukes in Egypt and Syria or the Safavid Persians in Iraq: but whether or not these transitions catalysed perceptible cultural and social changes remains unclear (Stillman 1979: 87)).

Careful attention has also been accorded Jews' contributions to the early modern Ottoman and Middle Eastern economy. Thus Ottoman Jews' involvement in the production and distribution of textiles (Braude 1979, 1992; Panova 1976; Rozen 1988; A. Shohat 1971), banking and financiering (Bashan 1989; H. Gerber 1985, 1986), and medicine (Galante 1985; Heyd 1963) have all been closely examined, though the day-to-day experience of work remains somewhat more elusive. (Studies of Jews' role in the Ottoman economy may also be found in Benbassa and Rodrigue 2000; H. Gerber 1978, 1982; Goffman 1994; and Emmanuel 1935. See also the contributions to Rozen 1996a).

Our knowledge of early modern Ottoman Jewries, however, remains curtailed by three important factors. First and most importantly, this field remains quite small. Early modern Ottoman Jewish social history has been little explored, in large part because so much scholarship has focused on emerging elites. Thus we still have a rather blurry picture of the lives of the uneducated and the poor: conditions which were the norm rather than the exception for most Ottoman subjects, Jews among them. Similarly, there is little to no scholarship on the experience of early modern Jewish women (Lamdan 1996), families, or children. A number of studies that explore particular urban settings, it should be noted, do greatly helped to enrich our sense of quotidian Jewish culture in the early modern Ottoman setting: among them are studies of Izmir (Smyrna) (Barnai 1982a, 1982b, 1992b, 1997; Goffman 1990, 1999), Istanbul (Galante 1985; Heyd 1953), Salonika (Emmanuel 1935; Ginio 1998; Hacker 1978; Néhama 1935–78), Bursa (H. Gerber 1980), Jerusalem (A. Cohen 1984; A. Cohen and Pikali 1993; Rozen 1984), Aleppo (Zenner 2000), Safed (Avitsur 1962; see also the bibliographic survey on Safed in Ben-Menahem 1962), and Fez (J. Gerber 1980). (See also a number of essays in Levy 1994.)

The second limitation is that most of the scholarship on the early modern period tends to consult exclusively Jewish *or* Ottoman sources: and, accordingly, focuses either on internal cultural dynamics or on the juridical and religious place of Jews in Ottoman and Islamic law. Thus, although we have a rather vivid picture of the way in which Jews were imagined and discussed by Ottoman and Islamic law (see the essays by Braude, Hacker, Kunt, and Karpat in Braude and Lewis 1982; A. Cohen 1994; A. Cohen and Pikali 1993; Lewis 1984; Masters 2001), and a sense of how Jews, including the rabbinical elite pictured the world around them (Goldman 1970; Lehmann 2001; Shmuelevits 1984; Stillman 1979 and 1984, we still lack a syncretic picture of early modern Jewish life in the Ottoman lands. (Bernard Lewis (1984) has discussed the impact of these trends as well.)

Finally, the field could benefit greatly from further debate about the chronological frame of early modern Sephardi and Middle Eastern Jewish history. We might consider the conceptual hazards of commencing this period with the expulsions from Spain, an event that had little impact on many of the Jews of the Middle East. We greatly need to reconsider the assumption that the late seventeenth through nineteenth centuries—the long aftermath of the Sabbatian crises—were periods of cultural stasis. We ought, in addition, to join scholars of Ottoman studies in rethinking the notion of an unstoppable and all-encompassing 'decline' that weakened the Ottoman economy, military, and state in the eighteenth and nineteenth centuries (Aksan 1999; Barkey 1994; Doumani 1995).

Lastly, it would behove us to continue to explore the event that is often viewed as the culmination of the early modern period: the Sabbatian crises. Undoubtedly, the rise and fall of the pseudo-messiah Shabbatai Sevi in the late seventeenth century has commanded more attention than any other episode in early modern Ottoman history. Gershom Scholem's account of Shabbatai Sevi (1973) and the movement he spawned remains the single most important study of this affair. In Scholem's view, the rise of Sabbatianism was born of trauma sustained from the expulsion from Spain two centuries earlier. Recent scholarship has assumed a somewhat different approach, arguing that Sabbatianism was catalysed by internal evolutions within Kabbalist thought (Idel 1988, 1992a). A study of the nuances of this debate is more suited to other chapters in this volume e.g. 9; for the moment, however, a more general assessment is warranted. Strikingly, what Scholem and Idel have in common is that they identify dynamics internal to Jewish history and culture as the principal catalysts of—and, perhaps, the lasting impact of—Sabbatianism. In the process, the rise of Shabbatai Sevi's influence (and by extension, early modern Ottoman Jewish society as a whole) has been uprooted from the context in which it was spawned. In the process, there has been little enquiry into the ways in which Sabbatianism may have reflected messianic trends in the Islamic world or economic and social conditions in the Ottoman Empire. This act of historical disassociation has had the additional effect of elevating the importance of events in Christian Europe (in this case, the expulsion from Spain) at the expense of events in Islamic Europe or the Middle East, despite the fact that such scholarship ostensibly focuses on an episode that unfolded in the very heart of the Ottoman Empire and rippled throughout the Jewish and Islamic worlds.

In all of these regards, scholarship on the Sabbatian crises—and on early modern Ottoman Jewry as a whole—shares certain limitations with scholarship on the modern period. Much of the scholarship on modern Ottoman Jewish history has focused on ways in which Ottoman Jewries responded to events that were motivated by or took place in Western Europe: among them the growing importance of the Atlantic economy and the so-called 'peripheralization' of the Ottoman; the semi-imperial relationship the empire assumed relative to Western Europe; the adoption of centralizing reforms inspired by (and adopted under pressure from) the nation states of Western Europe; and the rise of Franco-and Anglo-Jewish philanthropy (see the contributions to Braude and Lewis 1982; Goldberg 1996; Levy 1994; and Rodrigue 1992. See also Benbassa 1993; Chouraqui 1968; Laskier 1983; Levy 1992; Rodrigue 1990; Schwarzfuchs 1981; Shaw 1981; Zohar 1986, 1988, 1993). As a result, scholarship on modern Ottoman Jewish history—like scholarship on the Ottoman Empire as a whole—continues to pivot around the processes of Westernization and modernization.

As abstract processes, Westernization and modernization did catalyse tremendous change. But the tendency to focus exhaustively upon them—and, indeed, to uphold the categories unproblematically—has a number of potentially dangerous consequences. First, it allows non-specialists (and many specialists in the field) to continue to perceive Ottoman Jewry as compradors and 'agents' of Western Europe: a misleading assessment that strips Ottoman Jews of their place within the indigenous Ottoman social and economic fabric. Second, focusing upon links between Ottoman Jews and the Jews and nation states of Western Europe tends to inhibit the exploration of material, cultural, and quotidian relationships that developed between Jews and non-Jews, and between Jews in disparate regions of the empire or beyond (Stein forthcoming). In consequence, scholarship that compares and integrates the study of Jews and other *millets* (Braude and Lewis 1982; Masters 2001; Ginio 1998; Schroeter 1989; Zenner 1982b; see also the contributions to Landau 1988 and Levy 1994) is particularly valuable, and further research on the historical experience of multi-ethnicity is much needed. Third, the modernization paradigm tends to render overly stark the divide beyond the worlds of the religious and the worlds of the secular which were arguably far more intertwined in the Middle Eastern, North African, and south-eastern European contexts than they were in Western, Central, or Eastern Europe (Stillman 1996). Finally, as many other scholars have argued, theories of Westernization and modernization threaten to strip historical subjects of agency, and contexts of their specificity.

Such critiques of modernization theory have by now become formulaic. Perhaps more worrying still, the proposed antidote to modernization theory—an approach that completely disentangles the European and non-European landscapes, seeking, in the process, to view non-Europeans 'on their own terms'—threatens to prove as artificial as the approach it seeks to replace. What is called for, instead, are re-evaluations of Jewish modernities that take seriously the imbalanced power relations that permeated the Jewish world while remaining attentive both to the complex divisions that internally fissured Sephardim, Mizrahim, and Ashkenazim *and* to the cultural, political, and intellectual vectors that linked these Jewries one to another.

As in study of the early modern history, in the field of modern Ottoman Jewish history there remain significant scholarly holes. We know very little about Jewish migratory patterns prior to the twentieth century (Karpat 1989; McCarthy 1983; Shaw 1979; see also the contributions by Karpat and McCarthy in Levy 1994), or about Ottoman Jewish material cultures (Juhasz 1990; Mann 1997; Rozen 1994; see also the contributions by Juhasz and Mann in Levy 1994). Scholars have only just begun to study the experiences of Jewish women under the rule of the Ottoman Empire (Benbassa 1991; Levy 1987; Rodrigue 1990, 1993; Simon 1992, 2000, 1994), and much more work is warranted on the historical role of gender among Ottoman Jewries (Zenner 1982c; Zohar 1996). Though there has been a great deal of investigation of Ottoman Jews' burgeoning economic relations to Western Europe in the nineteenth and twentieth centuries (see above), precious little attention has been paid to Jews' involvement in highly localized economies (and much of this has focused on the exceptional case of Salonika (Quartaert 1996; see also the contributions to Veinstein 1992)). Finally, there is a continued need to grapple with the complexity of Ottoman Jewish culture in the eighteenth century: a period that has been assumed to be defined by a cultural stasis that arose in the wake of the Sabbatian affair (for a novel approach to this time, see Lehmann 2001).

Scholarship on European Turkey and the Ottoman-controlled Balkans has tended to be more extensive than scholarship on the Arab provinces that were more or less annexed by the Ottoman Empire. Much of the research that has been conducted on Jewish life in the Middle East and North Africa has focused on the late nineteenth and twentieth centuries, with coverage of the Ottoman period relegated to introductory chapters. The study of Jewish life in Ottoman-controlled Palestine is, for obvious reasons, more well developed than is the study of Jewish life in other of the Arab provinces (Ben-Zvi 1955, 1960; A. Cohen 1984; Campos forthcoming; Gaon 1928–38; Glass and Kark 1991; Heyd 1960; Lewis 1978. In addition, a number of works bring together primary sources on the topic, among them: A. Cohen 1976; Heyd 1960; Ish-Shalom 1965; Yaari 1971, 1976). Scholars can also benefit from explorations of Ottoman-controlled Egypt (see the contributions to Landau 1988. See also Bat Ye'or 1971; Beinin 1998; Landau 1969; Laskier 1992a; Krämer 1989), Syria (Sutton 1988; Zenner 1982a, b, c; Zohar 1986, 1990), Iraq (Avishur 1982; Deshen 1996; Kedourie 1971, 1989; Rejwan 1996; Yehuda 1984, 1996), and the Arab provinces as a whole (Masters 2001).

The study of North African Jewries (encompassing periods of Ottoman and European rule) has largely been pioneered by anthropologists and, partly as a result, relatively few studies of North African Jewries have assumed a temporally or regionally wide-reaching focus, though anthropological works are among the most historically minded sources on the region (the most wide-reaching include Chouraqui 1968; Goldberg 1990; Hirschberg 1974–81; Laskier 1994; Schroeter 1988). Due to extensive ethnographic fieldwork conducted in and after the 1960s, we have a vivid sense of Jewish life in Tripolitania, Tunisia, Algeria, and Morocco (De Felice 1985; Epstein 1968; Geertz et al. 1979; Goldberg 1972, 1980, 1990, 1994; Shokeid 1982; Stillman 1988; Tessler 1981; Udovitch and Valensi 1984; see also the contributions to Deshen and Zenner 1982; Simon 1992, 2000; Stillman 1999). Other research allows us to consider North African Jewish life through the eyes of the intellectual elite or the religious leadership (Bar-Asher 1981; Epstein 1968; Goldberg 1992; Hirschberg 1969; Manor 1982), local maskilim (Chetrit 1990, 1991; Laskier 1983; Tsur 1996; Zohar 1986, 1988, 1990, 1993), and political activists (Abitbol 1980, 1981; Yehuda 1981, 1986; see also the contributions to Davis 1980).

Given their long and rich histories, the Jews of Persia and Central Asia have received far too little attention, and unfortunately tend to be depicted as hailing from 'exotic places' (Blady 2000) and 'remote corners of the world' (Cowen 1971). Studies of Iranian Jewry include a few wide-reaching surveys, the most extensive of which have been written by Walter Fischel (Fischel 1950, 1980; see also Soroudi 1981). In addition, a number of sources offer an intimate picture of life in particular Jewish communities in Iran (Fischel 1953; Loeb 1977, 1982), among them the community of the forced converts, the Jadid al-Islam (Patai 1997). The influence of the Alliance (A. Cohen 1986; Netzer 1974) and Zionism (Netzer 1980) on the Jews of Iran have received limited attention, as has the story of anti-Semitism in the region (Netzer 1979, 1980; these topics and others are also touched upon by the contributors to Shaked 1982). Sadly we know very little about intellectual or rabbinical culture in the Persian setting (Moreen 1987), about interactions between Jews and non-Jews in the region that were not marred by violence (Shaked 1982), or about cultural or commercial ties that may have linked Persian Jews to the Jews of the Arab Middle East or Central Asia. The Jews of Central Asia have also largely been ignored. One may turn to a number of rather general studies of the Jews of Afghanistan (Robinson 1953), Kurdistan (Brauer 1993; Epstein 1982; Feitelson 1982), and Georgia (Arbel and Magel 1992). No such general work has been conducted on the Jews of Bukhara, however, though some focused research explores their experience of Soviet rule (Zand 1979, 1988). Georgian Jews' experience under Russian and Soviet rule has also received some attention (Altshuler 1975, 1990).

The story of Sephardi, North African, and Middle Eastern Jewries, complex from the outset, would become infinitely more intricate as the borders of the Ottoman Empire began to retract, the colonial borders of Italy, France, and Britain to expand, and as new nation states were created in the Balkans, Turkey, the Middle East, and North Africa. What superficial (and practical) commonalities the Ottoman system imposed on its Jewish subjects were now jettisoned: in their place were erected a myriad of legal and educational systems, social and linguistic norms, and state-sponsored demographic transformations (including ethnic purges and population exchanges). As the twentieth century unfolded, Sephardi and Middle Eastern Jewries served in warring armies and governments and embraced (or, as was often the case, submitted to) processes of nation-building. These new conditions created both opportunities and constraints: produced new emotional and political affinities and attenuated others. Scholars of Ottoman Jewish history have interpreted the era of state-building in a variety of ways. Some scholars, for example, have celebrated the transformation of Ottoman Jewish subjects into Turkish citizens (Levi 1992a,b; Shaw 1991; Weiker 1992), while others have argued that in the Turkish and Balkan settings the crumbling of empire was accompanied by an overall decline in Jews' rights and opportunities (Rodrigue 1995). Neither of these arguments, however, are generalizable. The Jewries of North Africa, the Middle East, and south-eastern Europe did not respond to decolonization or state-building in the same way; indeed, within each of these regions Jews debated how best to accommodate, promote, or thwart the changes these transitions wrought.

To date, we have only the most impressionistic sense of these debates. There exists an almost complete dearth of scholarship devoted to exploring Jewish involvement or reactions to the processes of decolonization and state-building: the literature that exists focuses on Turkey and the Balkans (Bali 1999; Benbassa and Rodrigue 2000; Shaw 1991; Weiker 1992) and Egypt (Beinin 1998; Krämer 1989). The absence of further work on this subject is not accidental: it reflects the overriding assumption that Jews were not only alienated from, but were victims of Arab, Turkish, and Balkan nationalism; Jews, it is assumed, were affected by state-building but neither contributed nor reacted to it. While this assumption strains credulity, scholarship on Sephardi and Middle Eastern Jewish life in the twentieth century tends, accordingly, to focus on the growing appeal of Zionism (see above) and anti-Semitism (Laskier 1992a; Lewis 1986; Stillman 1984; and see above): forces that sought, in their own ways, to disassociate Jews from the countries in which they lived. This is not to say that anti-Semitism and Zionism were not features of the twentieth-century Middle Eastern, North African, or south-east European Jewish landscape, but rather that there are other contours of this landscape that demand attention as well—that may, indeed, alter our understanding of the centrality of these forces. We might, for example, consider the ways that Jews contributed to and shaped Egyptian politics (Beinin 1998), Middle Eastern food (Roden 1994), or a North African sense of self (Bahloul 1994).

Tragically, the length of time in which Jews could make these contributions differed dramatically. The Sephardi heartland of south-eastern Europe was all but decimated in the Holocaust, during which 87 per cent of certain communities perished (this percentage is attributed to the Jews of Greece, who as a whole suffered the highest percentage of loss of any Jewish community: Carpi 1984; Gutman 1990; Mazower 1993; Molho and Néhama 1948; see also Chapter 17 of this volume). In the Arab Middle East (Abramski-Bligh 1986), in Turkey (Bali 1999; Levi 1992; Shaw 1993), and in North Africa (Laskier 1992b), Jewish communities survived the war largely intact. Even before the war, however, Jewish emigration from these regions (as from south-eastern Europe) was on the rise: in the 1950s and 1960s, as tensions rose between Israel and the countries of the Arab Middle East, it would become the norm (Beinin 1998; DellaPergola 1988; Gat 1997; Giladi 1990; Goldberg 1971; Hirschberg 1974–81; Kazzaz 1991; Miller 1996; Schwarzfuchs 1981; Shulewitz 1999; see also the useful graph and table in Goldberg 1997: 327–8. For a survey of Jewish migration in and emigration from Turkey and the Balkans, see Rodrigue and Benbassa 2000: 159–91). By the last decades of the twentieth century most Sephardi and Middle East Jewries lived not in North Africa, the Arab Middle East, Turkey, or the Balkans, but in Israel, France, the United States, Canada, and Latin America.

Sephardi life in the Americas long preceded the arrival of Jews from the Middle East: and, for that matter, the arrival of most Ashkenazim from Europe. As has already been noted, there exists a fairly rich literature about early modern Sephardi life in the Dutch, Spanish, and British colonies of the New World (see above):

scholarship on the modern period, however, remains thinner. Recent scholarship has fortunately dispelled the caricature of the aloof Sephardic 'grandees' of New York that has governed scholarly and lay imaginations since the 1970s (Birmingham 1971). Instead, it has offered a sense of the diversity of Sephardic life across geographic, class, and cultural lines in the United States and Canada (Adatto 1939; Angel 1974, 1982; Ben-Ur 1998a, b, 2001; Papo 1987; Stampfer 1987; see also the literary contributions to Matza 1997), and in Latin America (Avni 1991; DellaPergola 1987; Elkin 1980; Lesser 1992; Mirelman 1990; see also the contributions to M. A. Cohen 1993).

In recent years there has also been a surprising proliferation of writings (scholarly and popular) about more contemporary Sephardi and Mizrahi culture. This includes a growing number of literary and memoiristic works (the latter a genre historically lacking from the Sephardi and Middle Eastern Jewish cultural worlds (Rodrigue and Benbassa 1998: p. ix)); among them are the following sources (Aciman 1994; Alhadeff 1997; Benezra 1996; Burla 1968; Canetti 1979; Courtine-Denamy 2001; Kastoryano 1993; Kattan 1980; R. A. Levy 1987; S. Lévy 2000; Matalon 1998; Memmi 1992; Perera 1995; Sciaky 1946; and the contributions to Matza 1997 and Alcalay 1997. In addition, scholarly research has expanded our sense of contemporary Sephardi and Middle Eastern Jewish culture as it is experienced in, among other places, France (Bahloul 1996a, 1994, 1996a, b), Israel (Cohen-Almagor 1995; Deshen and Shokeid 1974; Giladi 1990; Goldberg 1972; Massad 1996; Shiblak 1986; E. Shohat 1997, 1999; Swirski 1989), and the United States (Beinin 1998; Papo 1987; Sutton 1979, 1988; Zenner 2000; see also the general survey by Sitton 1985). This research has allowed us to appreciate that, in certain contexts, Sephardi, Middle Eastern, and North African Jewish culture was reconstituted and dynamized in the twentieth century.

WHITHER SEPHARDI AND MIZRAHI STUDIES?

This chapter has navigated through a complex and substantial area of scholarly literature that in recent years has come to define a prominent sub-field of Jewish studies. The purview of this scholarship is enormously sophisticated. It is interdisciplinary and transnational in scope, and it spans a staggering geographic, cultural, and temporal terrain. If the umbra of scholars of Sephardi, Middle Eastern, and North African Jewries is expansive, however, the penumbra of their scholarship does not yet spread as widely as it should.

To be sure, certain themes and moments in the histories of Sephardi, Middle Eastern, and North African Jewries have captured the imagination of the larger field of Jewish studies. The expulsion from Spain, the Sabbatian crises, the rise of anti-Semitism in the Arab world, the migration of Jews from the lands of Islam to the state of Israel: all of these are accepted as chapters in the history of early modern and modern Jewries. But students of Jewish studies—students of Sephardi and Middle Eastern Jewish studies among them—must be taught that there is more to these Jewries' stories. Sephardi, Middle Eastern, and North African Jews circulated in rich and diverse cultural worlds, developed deep and abiding relationships with non-Jews, helped shape local, regional, and national cultures and politics. New scholarship is required to reveal the full richness and historical implications of these phenomena.

Expanding the field of Sephardi and Middle Eastern Jewish studies is, however, only half the challenge. More difficult still is the task of transforming the chronologies, teleologies, and vocabularies that define the core of early modern and modern Jewish studies, such that the experience of non-European Jewries is understood to be neither exceptional, reactive, nor tangential. For this to be accomplished, scholars of Sephardi and Middle Eastern Jewries must transform our understanding of certain concepts that have proven critical to the field of Jewish studies (and, for that matter, Ottoman and Middle Eastern studies) as a whole. Tradition and modernity, the Jewish and the non-Jewish, the philanthropist and the disadvantaged, the indigenous and the interloper: these polarities must be dismantled and reconstructed in a way that accounts for the perspectives and histories of Sephardi and Middle Eastern Jewries.

At the same time, scholars of Jewish studies who operate outside this sub-field must resist normalizing the history and culture of European Jewries. What is required is not simply a more accommodating or nuanced understanding of Sephardi and Middle Eastern Jewries, though this, of course, is desirable as well. Instead, what is needed is a debunking of the stark division between Ashkenazim, Sephardim, and Mizrahim—divisions that invite monolithic readings of the Islamic world and of Europe as well. This new departure provides an opportunity to examine local contexts with a more finely tuned eye and to inhabit transregional landscapes we have not yet begun to imagine.

There are practical and political reasons to call for a field of Sephardic studies, Mizrahi studies, or even Sephardi and Mizrahi studies. These ought not be ignored; indeed, it may well be intellectually and institutionally useful for scholars to operate within such parameters. Ultimately, however, categories such as these threaten to perpetuate structures and assumptions that may be better dismantled. The fine thing about scholarly labour is that one tends to gain rather than lose from multiple intellectual alliances, which is all the more reason why scholars of Jewish studies may look upon the growing field of Sephardi and Middle Eastern Jewish studies with enthusiasm and interest.

SUGGESTED READING

Readers interested in an introduction to Jewish life under the rule of Islam during the period in question may consult Bernard Lewis (1984), though they should be cognizant that this work reproduces many stereotypes about Muslim and Jewish relations in the modern period. Norman Stillman's two-volume work on the Jews of the Arab Middle East is probably the most accessible survey of this region (1979, 1984), as is André Chouraqui (1968) and H. Z. Hirschberg (1974–81), on North Africa. A historical survey of the Sephardic diaspora from the expulsion from the Iberian Peninsula to the present day is presented by Jane Gerber (1992): a more detailed but nonetheless wide-reaching study of the Judeo-Spanish community by Esther Benbassa and Aron Rodrigue is also recommended (2000). An introduction to the themes that have preoccupied scholars of early modern and modern Sephardi, Middle Eastern, and North African Jewries are found in the large number of edited volumes that have been referred to in the course of this chapter (among them: Beinart 1992b and c; Deshen and Zenner 1996; Goldberg 1996). Other useful bibliographic essays in the field have been written by Robert Attal (1973; and with Y. Tobi 1980), Hayim Cohen (1976), and Mark Cohen (1995).

BIBLIOGRAPHY

ABITBOL, M. 1980. 'North Africa'. In *Zionism in Transition*. 197–210. M. Davis ed. New York.
——1981. 'Zionist Activity in the Maghreb.' *Jerusalem Quarterly* 21: 64–5.
——HASAN-ROKEM, G., and ASSIS, Y.-T. eds. 1997. *Hispano-Jewish Civilization After 1492.* Jerusalem.
ABRAMSKI-BLIGH, I. 1986. 'The Jews of Syria and Lebanon under Vichy Rule.' [Hebrew.] *Pe'amim* 28: 131–57.
ACIMAN, A. 1994. *Out of Egypt: A Memoir.* New York.
ADATTO, A. 1939. 'Sephardim and the Seattle Sephardic Community.' Unpublished MA thesis, University of Washington, Seattle.
AHRONI, R. 1986. *Yemenite Jewry.* Bloomington, Ind.
AKSAN, V. 1999. 'Locating the Ottomans Among Early Modern Empires.' *Journal of Early Modern History* 3/2: 103–34.
ALCALAY, A. 1993. *After Jews and Arabs. Remaking Levantine Culture.* Minneapolis.
——ed. 1996. *Keys to the Garden, New Israeli Writing.* San Francisco.
——1999. *Memories of Our Future: Selected Essays 1982–1999.* San Francisco.
ALHADEV, G. 1997. *The Sun at Midday: Tales of a Mediterranean Family.* New York.
ALTABÉ, D. F., ATAY, E., and KATZ, I. J. eds. 1996. *Studies on Turkish-Jewish History: Political and Social Relations, Literature, and Linguistics.* New York.
ALTSHULER, M. 1975. 'Georgian Jewish Culture Under the Soviet Regime.' *Soviet Jewish Affairs* 5/2: 21–40.
——1990. *The Jews of the Eastern Caucasus: The History of Mountain Jews from the Beginning of the Nineteenth Century* [Hebrew]. Jerusalem.
ANGEL, M. 1974. *The Sephardim of the United States: An Exploratory Study.* New York.
——1978. *The Jews of Rhodes: The History of a Sephardic Community.* New York.
——1982. *La America: The Sephardic Experience in the United States.* Philadelphia.

ANSKY, M. 1950. *Les Juifs d'Algérie du Décret Crémieux a la liberàtion.* Paris.

ARBEL, R. and MAGEL, L. 1992. *In the Land of the Golden Fleece: The Jews of Georgia: History and Culture.* Tel Aviv.

ATIAS, M., SCHOLEM, G., and BEN-ZVI, Y. 1948. *The Poems and Praises of the Sabbateans* [Hebrew]. Tel Aviv.

ATTAL, R. 1973. *Les Juifs d'afrique du nord: bibliographie.* Jerusalem.

—— and TOBI, Y. 1980. 'Oriental and North-African Jewry: An Annotated Bibliography 1974–1976.' [Hebrew]. *Sefunot.* 1: 401–95.

AVISHUR, Y. 1982. *Studies on History and Culture of Iraqi Jewry.* Or Yehuda.

AVITSUR, S. 1962. 'Safed—Center of the Manufacture of Woven Woolens in the Fifteenth Century.' [Hebrew]. *Sefunot* 6: 41–69.

AVNI, H. 1991. *Argentina and the Jews.* Tuscaloosa.

BAHLOUL, J. 1994. 'The Sephardic Jew as Mediterranean: A View from Kinship and Gender.' *Journal of Mediterranean Studies* 4/2: 197–207.

——1996a. 'The Sephardi Family and the Challenge of Assimilation: Family Ritual and Ethnic Reproduction.' In *Sephardi and Middle Eastern Jewries: History and Culture in the Modern Era.* 312–24. H. E. Goldberg ed. Bloomington, Ind.

——1996b. *The Architecture of Memory: A Jewish-Muslim Household in Colonial Algeria, 1937–1962.* Cambridge.

BALI, R. N. 1999. *An Adventure of Turkification (1923–1945): Turkish Jews During the Republican Period* [Turkish]. Iletisim, Istanbul.

BAR-ASHER, S. 1981. 'The Jews in North Africa and Egypt.' In *History of the Jews in the Islamic Countries* [Hebrew]. 119–98. S. Ettinger ed. Jerusalem.

BARKEY, K. 1994. *Bandits and Bureaucrats: The Ottoman Route to State Centralization.* Ithaca, NY.

BARNAI, Y. 1982a. 'The Origins of the Jewish Community in Smyrna in the Ottoman Period.' [Hebrew]. *Peʿamim* 12: 47–58.

——1982b. 'Congregations in Smyrna in the Seventeenth Century.' *Pe'amim* 48: 66–84.

——1988. ' "Blood Libels" in the Ottoman Empire of the Fifteenth to Nineteenth Centuries.' In *Antisemitism through the Ages.* 189–94. S. Almog ed. Oxford.

——1990. 'On the History of the Jews in the Ottoman Empire.' In *Sephardi Jews in the Ottoman Empire: Aspects of Material Culture.* 18–35. E. Juhasz ed. Jerusalem.

——1992a. 'Messianism and Leadership: The Sabbatean Movement and the Leadership of the Jewish Communities in the Ottoman Empire.' In *Ottoman and Turkish Jewry.* 170–4. A. Rodrigue ed. Bloomington, Ind.

——1992b. 'The Sabbatean Movement in Smyrna: The Social Background.' In *Jewish Sects, Religious Movements, and Political Parties.* 113–22. M. Mor ed. Omaha, Nebr.

——1993. 'Christian Messianism and the Portuguese Marranos: The Emergence of Sabbateanism in Smyrna.' *JH* 7: 119–26.

——1997. 'Prototypes of Leadership in a Sephardic Community: Smyrna in the Seventeenth Century.' In *Crisis and Continuity in the Sephardic World, 1391–1648.* 146–64. B. R. Gampel ed. New York.

BARANTAN, M. G. 1993. 'Cryptojews in Rio de la Plata in the Seventeenth Century.' In *New Horizons in Sephardic Studies.* 137–47. Y. Stillman and G. K. Zucker eds. Albany, NY.

BARON, S. W. 1928. 'Ghetto and Emancipation.' *Menorah Journal.* 14/6: 515–26.

BASHAN, E. 1989. 'Jewish Moneylending in Constantinople and Smyrna During the 17th and 18th Centuries as Reflected in the British Levant Company's Archives.' In *The*

Mediterranean and the Jews: Banking, Finance and International Trade. 57–73. A. Toaff and S. Schwarzfuchs eds. Ramat-Gan.

BAT-YE′OR [pseudonym of Giselle Littmann] 1971. *Les Juifs en Egypte: aperçu sur 3000 ans d'histoire.* Geneva.

—— 1974. *The Jews of Egypt* [Hebrew]. Tel Aviv.

—— 1985. *The Dhimmi: Jews and Christians under Islam.* Rutherford, NJ.

—— 1971. 'The *Converso* Community in Fifteenth Century Spain.' In *The Sephardi Heritage.* 425–57. R. D. Barnett ed. New York.

—— 1992a. 'The Conversos and their Fate.' In *Spain and the Jews: The Sephardi Experience 1492 and After.* 92–122. London.

—— 1992b. 'The Great Conversion and the Converso Problem.' In *Moreshet Sepharad: The Sephardi Legacy.* 346–82. Jerusalem.

—— 1992c. *Moreshet Sepharad: The Sephardi Legacy.* Jerusalem.

—— and GUILADI, Y. 1981. *Conversos on Trial.* Jerusalem.

BEININ, J. 1998. *The Dispersion of Egyptian Jewry: Culture, Politics, and the Formation of a Modern Diaspora.* Berkeley.

BEJARANO, M. 1996. 'L'Integration des Sephardes en Amerique Latine: Le cas des communautes de Buenos Aires et la Havane.' In *Memoires Juives D'Espagne et du Portugal.* 207–19. E. Benbassa ed. Jerusalem.

BEKSELMAN, M. 1995. 'The Development of Economic Activity of Bukharan Jews in Central Asia at the Turn of the 20th Century.' *Shvut.* 1–2 /17–18: 63–79.

BENARDETE, M. J. 1982. *Hispanic Culture and Character of the Sephardic Jews.* New York.

BENAYAHU, M. 1971–7. 'The Sabbatean Movement in Greece.' *Sefunot (Book of Greek Jewry)* 4/14: 79–108.

BENBASSA, E. 1991. 'L'Education feminine en Orient: L'école de Filles de l'Alliance Israélite Universelle à Galata, Istanbul (1879–1912).' *Histoire, Economie, et Société.* 4: 529–59.

—— 1993. *Une diaspora sepharade en transition.* Paris.

—— 1995. *Haim Nahum: A Sephardic Chief Rabbi in Politics, 1892–1923.* Tuscaloosa.

—— 1996. 'Modernization of Eastern Sephardi Communities.' In *Sephardi and Middle Eastern Jewries, History and Culture in the Modern Era.* 89–99. H. E. Goldberg ed. Bloomington, Ind.

—— and RODRIGUE, A. 1998. *A Sephardi Life in Southeastern Europe: The Autobiography and Journal of Gabriel Arié, 1863–1939.* Seattle.

—— —— 2000. *Sephardi Jewry, A History of the Judeo-Spanish Community, 14th–20th Centuries.* Berkeley.

BENEZRA, N. M. 1996. *Une enfance juive a Istanbul (1911–1929).* Istanbul.

BEN-MENAHEM, N. 1962. 'A Bibliography of Publications on Safed.' [Hebrew]. *Sefer Zefatt* 6: 475–503. I. Ben-Zvi and M. Benayahu eds. Jerusalem.

BEN-UR, A. 1998a. *Where Diasporas Met: Sephardic and Ashkenazic Jews in the City of New York, a Study in Intra-ethnic Relations, 1880–1950.* Brandeis University.

—— 1998b. 'The Ladino (Judeo-Spanish) Press in the United States, 1910–1948.' In *Multilingual America: Transnationalism, Ethnicity, and the Languages of American Literature.* 64–77. W. Sollors ed. New York.

—— 2001. 'The Exceptional and the Mundane: A Biographical Portrait of Rebecca Machado Phillips, 1746–1831.' In *Women and American Judaism: Historical Perspectives.* 46–80. J. D. Sarna and P. Nadell eds. Waltham, Md.

BEN-ZVI, I. 1955. *The Land of Israel under Ottoman Rule: Four Centuries of History.* Jerusalem.

—— 1957. *The Exiled and the Redeemed.* Philadelphia.

—— 1960. 'Eretz Yisrael under Ottoman Rule, 1517–1917.' In *The Jews: Their History, Culture and Religion.* 602–89. L. Finkelstein ed. New York.

BERKOWITZ, J. R. 1989. *The Shaping of Jewish Identity in Nineteenth-Century France.* Detroit.

BIRMINGHAM, S. 1971. *The Grandees: America's Sephardic Elite.* New York.

BIRNBAUM, P. and KATZNELSON, I. eds. 1995. *Paths of Emancipation : Jews, States, and Citizenship.* Princeton.

BLADY, K. 2000. *Jewish Communities in Exotic Places.* Northvale, N.J.

BODIAN, M. 1997. *Hebrews of the Portuguese Nation: Conversos and Community in Early Modern Amsterdam.* Bloomington, Ind.

BONFIL, R. 1988. 'Change in the Cultural Patterns of a Jewish Society in Crisis: Italian Jewry at the Close of the Twentieth Century.' *JH* 3/2: 11–30.

—— 1989. *Rabbis and Jewish Communities in Renaissance Italy.* Oxford.

BORNSTEIN-MAKOVETSKY, L. 1989. 'Structure, Organisation, and Spiritual Life of the Sephardi Communities in the Ottoman Empire from the Sixteenth the Eighteenth Centuries.' In *The Sephardi Heritage: The Western Sephardim.* 314–48. R. D. Barnett and W. M. Schwab eds. Grendon, Northants.

BOWMAN, S. 1985. *The Jews of Byzantium, 1204–1453.* Tuscaloosa.

—— 1986. 'Jews in Wartime Greece.' *Jewish Social Studies* 48: 45–62.

BRAUDE, B. 1982. 'Foundation Myths of the *Millet* System.' In *Christians and Jews in the Ottoman Empire: The Functioning of a Plural Society.* In Braude and Lewis (1982): i. 69–88.

—— 1992. 'The Rise and Fall of Salonica Woolens, 1500–1650: Technology Transfer and Western Competition.' In *Jews, Christians, and Muslims in the Mediterranean World After 1492.* 216–36. A. M. Ginio ed. London.

—— and LEWIS, B. eds. 1982. *Christians and Jews in the Ottoman Empire: The Functioning of a Plural Society.* New York.

BRAUER, E. 1993. *The Jews of Kurdistan.* Detroit.

BUNIS, D. 1981. *Sephardic Studies.* New York.

—— 1999. *Voices from Jewish Salonika: Selections from the Judezmo Satirical Series Tio Ezrá I Su Mujer Benuta and Tio Bohor I Su Mujer Djamila.* Jerusalem.

BURLA, Y. 1968. *In Darkness Striving.* Jerusalem.

CAMPOS, M. forthcoming. 'A "Shared Homeland" and its Boundaries: Late Ottoman Palestine Between Imperial Commitment and Communal Identification, 1908–1914.' Unpublished Ph.D. diss., Stanford University.

CANETTI, E. 1979. *The Tongue Set Free: Remembrance of a European Childhood.* New York.

CARPI, D. 1977. 'The Rescue of Jews in the Italian Zones of Occupied Croatia.' In *Rescue Attempts during the Holocaust: Proceedings of the Second Yad Vashem International Historical Conference.* 465–525. I. Gutman and E. Zuroff eds. Jerusalem.

—— 1984. 'The Jews of Greece During the Holocaust (1941–1943).' In *In the Past and Today: Annual Lectures on Greek Jewry (1977–1983)* [Hebrew]. 196–7. Z. Ankori ed. Tel Aviv.

CHETRIT, J. 1990. 'Hebrew National Modernity against French Modernity: The Hebrew Haskalah in North Africa at the End of the Nineteenth Century.' [Hebrew]. *Miqqedem Umiyyam* 3: 129–168.

CHETRIT, J. 1991. 'The Movement of Hebrew Haskalah in Morocco at the End of the Nineteenth Century and its Contribution to the Zionist Awakening.' In *Recherches sur la culture des Juifs d'Afrique du Nord.* 313–331. I. Ben-Ami ed. Jerusalem.

CHETRIT, S. S. 2000. 'Mizrahi Politics in Israel: Between Integration and Alternative.' *Journal of Palestine Studies.* 29/4: 51–65.

CHOURAQUI, A. N. 1968. *Between East and West: A History of the Jews of North Africa.* Philadelphia.

COHEN, A. 1976. *Ottoman Documents on the Jewish Community of Jerusalem in the Sixteenth Century* [Hebrew]. Jerusalem.

——1984. *Jewish Life under Islam: Jerusalem in the Sixteenth Century.* Cambridge, Mass.

——1986. 'Iranian Jewry and the Educational Endeavors of the Alliance Israélite Universelle.' *Jewish Social Studies* 48/2: 15–44.

——1994. *A World Within: Jewish Life as Reflected in Muslim Court Documents from the Sijill of Jerusalem (XVIth Century).* Philadelphia.

—— and LEWIS, B. 1978. *Population and Revenue in the Towns of Palestine in the Sixteenth Century.* Princeton.

—— and PIKALI, E. 1993. *Jews in the Moslem Religious Court: Society, economy, and communal organization in the XVIth century* [Hebrew]. Jerusalem.

COHEN, H. 1976. *Oriental and African Jews in the Middle East, 1800–1971: An Annotated Bibliography* [Hebrew]. Jerusalem.

——1973. *The Jews of the Middle East 1860–1972.* New York.

COHEN, M. 1995. 'The Jews under Islam: From the Rise of Islam to Sabbatai Zevi: A Bibliographic Essay.' In *Sephardic Studies in the University.* 43–119. J. Gerber ed. Madison, Wisc.

COHEN, M. R. 1986. 'Islam and the Jews: Myth, Counter-Myth, History.' *Jerusalem Quarterly* 38: 125–37.

——1991. 'The Neo-Lachrymose Conception of Jewish-Arab History.' *Tikkun* 6: 55–60.

——1994. *Under Crescent and Cross.* Princeton.

—— and PECK, A. J. eds. 1993. *Sephardim in the Americas: Studies in Culture and History.* Tuscaloosa.

—— and UDOVITCH, A. L. eds. 1989. *Jews Among Arabs: Contacts and Boundaries.* Princeton.

COHEN, R. ed. 1982. *The Jewish Nation in Surinam: Historical Essays.* Amsterdam.

——1991. *Jews in Another Environment: Surinam in the Second Half of the Eighteenth Century.* Leiden.

COHEN, S. J. D. and GREENSTEIN, E. L. 1990. *The State of Jewish Studies.* Detroit.

COHEN-ALMAGOR, R. 1995. 'Cultural Pluralism and the Israeli Nation-Building Ideology.' *International Journal of Middle East Studies* 27/4: 461–84.

COURTINE-DENAMY, S. 2001 *La Maison de Jacob.* Paris.

COWEN, I. 1971. *Jews in Remote Corners of the World.* Englewood Cliffs, NJ.

DANON, A. 1924–5. 'The Karaites in European Turkey: Contributions to their History Based Chiefly on Unpublished Documents.' *Jewish Quarterly Review* 15: 325–7.

DAVIS, M. ed. 1980. *Zionism in Transition.* New York.

DAWIDOWICZ, L. S. 1992. *What Is the Use of Jewish History?* New York.

DEFELICE, R. 1985. *Jews in an Arab Land: Libya, 1835–1970.* Austin, Tex.

DELLAPERGOLA, S. 1987. 'Demographic Trends of Latin American Jewry.' In *The Jewish Presence in Latin American.* 85–134. J. L. Elkin and G. W. Merkx eds. Boston.

DESHEN, S. 1982. 'The Social Structure of Southern Tunisian Jewry in the Early 20th Century.' In Deshen and Zenner (1982): 123–36.

—— 1996. 'Baghdad Jewry in Late Ottoman Times: The Emergence of Social Classes and Secularization.' In Deshen and Zenner (1996): 187–96.

—— and SHOKEID, M. 1974. *The Predicament of Homecoming, Culture and Social Life of North African Immigrants in Israel.* Ithaca, NY and London.

—— and ZENNER, W. P. eds. 1982. *Jewish Societies in the Middle East: Community, Culture and Authority.* Lanham, Md., New York, and London.

—— —— eds. 1996. *Jews Among Muslims: Communities in the Precolonial Middle East.* London.

DIAZ-MAS, P. 1993. *Los sefardies: historia, lengua, y cultura.* Barcelona.

DOUMANI, B. 1995. *Rediscovering Palestine.* Berkeley.

DUMONT, P. 1980. 'La Structure sociale de la communauté juive de Salonique à la fin du dix-neuvième siècle.' *Revue Historique* 263: 351–410.

—— 1982. 'Jewish Communities in Turkey During the Last Decades of the Nineteenth Century in Light of the Archives of the Alliance Israélite Universelle.' In Braude and Lewis eds. (1982): i. 209–42.

ELKIN, J. L. 1980. *The Jews of the Latin American Republics.* Chapel Hill, NC.

EMMANUEL, I. S. 1936. *Histoire des Israélites de Salonique.* Paris.

EPSTEIN, I. 1968. *The Responsa of Rabbi Simon b. Zemah Duran as a Source of the History of the Jews in North Africa.* New York.

EPSTEIN, M. A. 1980. *The Ottoman Jewish Communities and Their Role in the Fifteenth and Sixteenth Centuries.* Freiburg.

—— 1982. 'The Leadership of the Ottoman Jews in the Fifteenth and Sixteenth Centuries.' In Braude and Lewis eds. (1982): i. 89–100.

EPSTEIN, S. 1982. 'The Jews of Kurdistan.' *Ariel* 51: 65–78.

ERAQI-KLORMAN, B.-Z. 2001. 'The Forced Conversion of Jewish Orphans in Yemen.' *International Journal of Middle East Studies* 33/1: 23–47.

ETTINGER, S. ed. 1981. *History of the Jews in the Islamic Countries.* Jerusalem.

FABER, E. 1992. *A Time For Planting: The First Migration, 1654–1820.* Baltimore.

FAUR, J. 1992. *In the Shadow Of History.* New York.

FEITELSON, D. 1982. 'Aspects of the Social Life of Kurdish Jews.' In *Jewish Societies in the Middle East: Community, Culture and Authority.* 251–72. S. Deshen and W. P. Zenner eds. Lanham, Md., New York, and London.

FISCHEL, W. J. 1950. 'The Jews of Persia: 1795–1940.' *Jewish Social Studies* 12: 119–60.

—— 1953. 'Isfahan: The Story of a Jewish Community in Persia.' *Jewish Social Studies Publication* 5: 111–28.

—— 1980. 'The Jews in Medieval Iran (16th-18th Centuries): Political, Economic, and Communal Aspects.' [Hebrew]. *Pe'amim* 6: 5–32.

FRANCO, M. 1897 (reissued 1973). *Essai sur l'histoire des Israélites de l'Empire Ottoman depuis les origines jusqu'à nos jours.* New York.

FRANKEL, J. 1984. 'Symposium: "*Ostjuden* in Central and Western Europe: The East European Jew and German Jewish Identity".' *Studies in Contemporary Jewry* 1–200. Bloomington, Ind.

—— 1997. *The Damascus Affair: 'Ritual Murder,' Politics, and the Jews in 1840.* Cambridge.

FREIDENREICH, H. P. 1979. *The Jews of Yugoslavia: A Quest for Community.* Philadelphia.

GALANTE, A. 1985. *Histoire des Juifs de Turquie.* Istanbul.

GAMPEL, B. R. ed. 1997. *Crisis and Creativity in the Sephardic World.* New York.

GAON, M. D. 1928–38. *The Jews of the East in Palesine: Past and Present* [Hebrew]. Jerusalem.

GAT, M. 1997. *The Jewish Exodus from Iraq, 1948–1951.* London.

GEERTZ, C., GEERTZ, H., and ROSEN, L. 1979. *Meaning and Order in Moroccan Society: Three Essays in Cultural Analysis.* Cambridge.

GENOT-BISMUTH, J. 1993. 'The Universita Degli Hebrei and the Nationi of the Venice Ghetto (1516–1630): A Reconsideratio of Some Presuppositions of Contemporary Jewish Historiography.' In *New Horizons in Sephardic Studies.* 15–36. Y. Stillman and G. K. Zucker eds. Albany, NY.

GERBER, H. 1978. 'Enterprise and International Commerce in the Economic Activity of the Jews in the 16th–17th Centuries.' [Hebrew]. *Zion* 43: 38–67.

—— 1980. 'Jews in the Economic Life of the Anatolian City of Bursa in the Seventeenth Century.' [Hebrew]. *Sefunot* 16: 235–72.

—— 1982. *The Jews of the Ottoman Empire in the Sixteenth and Seventeenth Centuries: Economy and Society* [Hebrew]. Jerusalem.

—— 1985. 'Jews and Moneylending in the Ottoman Empire.' *JQR* 72: 100–18.

—— 1986. 'Jewish Tax Farmers in the Ottoman Empire in the 16th and 17th Centuries.' *Journal of Turkish Studies* 19: 143–54.

GERBER, J. S. 1980. *Jewish Society in Fez 1450–1700.* Leiden.

—— 1985. 'Reconsiderations of Sephardic History: The Origin of the Image of the Golden Age of Muslim-Jewish Relations.' *The Solomon Goldman Lectures.* N. Stampfer ed. Chicago.

—— 1992. *The Jews of Spain: A History of the Sephardic Experience.* New York.

—— 1995. *Sephardic Studies in the University.* Madison, Wisc.

GILADI, G. N. 1990. *Discord in Zion.* London.

GILBERT, M. 1976. *The Jews of Arab Lands: Their History in Maps.* London.

GINIO, A. M. ed. 1992. *Jews, Christians, and Muslims in the Mediterranean World After 1492.* London.

GINIO, E. 1998. 'Marginal People in the Ottoman City: The Case of Salonica During the Eighteenth Century.' Unpublished Ph.D. diss., the Hebrew University of Jerusalem.

GLASS, J. B. and KARK, R. 1991. *Sephardi Entrepreneurs in Eretz Israel: The Amzalak Family 1816–1918.* Jerusalem.

GLICK, T. F. 1997. 'On Converso and Marrano Ethnicity.' Gampel (1997): 59–76.

GOFFMAN, D. 1990. *Izmir and the Levantine World.* Seattle.

—— 1996. 'Jews in Early Modern Ottoman Commerce.' In Rozen (1996a): 49–72.

—— 1999. 'Izmir: From Village to Colonial Port City.' In *The Ottoman City Between East and West.* 79–134. D. G. Edhem Eldem and B. Masters eds., Cambridge.

GOITEIN, S. D. 1953. 'Jewish Education in Yemen as an Archetype of Traditional Jewish Education.' In *Between Past and Future: Essays and Studies on Aspects of Immigrant Absorption in Israel.* 109–46. C. Frankenstein ed. Jerusalem.

—— 1955. *Jews and Arabs: Their Contact Through the Ages.* New York.

—— 1969– . *A Mediterranean Society: The Jewish Communities of the Arab World as Portrayed in the Documents of the Cairo Geniza.* 6 vols. Berkeley.

GOLDBERG, H. 1971. 'Ecological and Demographic Aspects of Rural Tripolitanian Jewry, 1853–1959.' *International Journal of Middle East Studies* 2: 209–26.

—— 1972. *Cave Dwellers and Citrus Growers: A Jewish Community in Libya and Israel.* Cambridge.

—— 1980. *The Book of Mordechai: A Study of the Jews of Libya*. Philadelphia.

—— 1990. *Jewish Life in Muslim Libya: Rivals and Relatives*. Chicago.

—— 1993. 'Religious Responses Among North African Jews in the Nineteenth and Twentieth Century.' In *The Uses of Tradition, Jewish Continuity in the Modern Era*. 119–44. J. Wertheimer ed. New York and Jerusalem.

—— 1994. 'Jerba and Tripoli: A Comparative Analysis of Two Jewish Communities in the Maghrib.' *Journal of Mediterranean Studies* 4/2: 278–99.

—— 1996. 'The *Maskil* and the *Mequbbal*, Mordecai Ha-Cohen and the Grave of Rabbi Shim'on Lavi in Tripoli.' In Goldberg ed. (1996): 168–89.

—— ed. 1996. *Sephardi and Middle Eastern Jewries: History and Culture in the Modern Era*. Bloomington, Ind.

GOLDMAN, I. M. 1970. *The Life and Times of Rabbi David Ibn Abi Zimra: A Social, Economic and Cultural Study of Jewish Life in the Ottoman Empire in the 15th and 16th Centuries as Reflected in the Responsa of RDBZ*. New York.

GOLDNER, Y. W. 1996. 'Jewish Merchants in Ragusa as Intermediaries Between East and West in the Sixteenth and Seventeenth Centuries.' In Rozen (1996a): 73–192.

GUERSHON, I. 1996. 'The Foundation of Hispano-Jewish Associations in Morocco. Contrasting Portraits of Tangier and Tetuan.' In Goldberg (1996): 181–9.

GUTMAN, I. ed. 1990. *Encyclopedia of the Holocaust*. London.

HACKER, J. 1978. *The Jewish Society of Salonika in the Fifteenth and Sixteenth Centuries: A Chapter in the History of Jewish Society in the Ottoman Empire*. Jerusalem.

—— 1982. 'Ottoman Policy toward the Jews and Jewish Attitudes Toward the Ottomans During the Fifteenth Century.' In Braude and Lewis (1982): 117–26.

—— 1984. 'The Chief Rabbinate in the Ottoman Empire in the Fifteenth-Sixteenth Centuries.' [Hebrew]. *Zion* 49/3: 225–63.

—— 1992. 'The *Sürgün* System and Jewish Society in the Ottoman Empire During the Fifteenth to Seventeenth Centuries.' In Rodrigue ed. (1992): 1–65.

HEYD, U. 1953. 'The Jewish Communities of Istanbul in the Seventeenth Century.' [Hebrew]. *Oriens* 6/2: 299–314.

—— 1960. *Ottoman Documents on Palestine 1552–1615: A Study of the Firman According to the Mühimme Defteri*. Oxford.

—— 1963. 'Moses Hamon, Chief Jewish Physician to Sultan Suleyman the Magnificent.' *Oriens* 16: 152–70.

HIRSHBERG, H. Z. 1969. 'The Oriental Jewish Communities.' In *Religion in the Middle East: Three Religions in Concord and Conflict*. 119–225. A. J. Arberrgy ed. Cambridge.

—— 1974–81. *A History of the Jews in North Africa*. Leiden.

IDEL, M. 1988. *Kabbalah: New Perspectives*. New Haven.

—— 1992a. 'Religion, Thought, and Attitutes: the Impact of the Expulsion on the Jews.' In Kedourie ed. (1992): 123–39.

—— 1992b. 'Spanish Kabbalah After the Expulsion.' In Beinart (1992c): 166–78.

—— 1993. '"One from a Town, Two from a Clan": The Diffusion of Lurianic Kabbala and Sabbateanism: A Re-Examination.' *JH* 7: 79–104.

INALCIK, H. 1989. 'Jews in the Ottoman Economy and Finances, 1450–1500.' In *Essays in Honor of Bernard Lewis*. 513–14. C. E. Bosworth, C. Issawi, R. Savory, and A. L. Udovitch eds. Princeton.

ISH-SHALOM, M. 1965. *Christian Travels in the Holy Land: Descriptions and Sources on the History of the Jews in Palestine*. Tel Aviv.

ISRAEL, J. 1984. 'The Changing Role of the Dutch Sephardim in International Trade, 1595–1715.' *Dutch Jewish History* 44–9.

——— 1990. *Empires and entrepôts: The Dutch, the Spanish monarchy, and the Jews, 1585–1713.* London.

JUHASZ, E. ed. 1990. *Sephardi Jews in the Ottoman Empire: Aspects of Material Culture.* Jerusalem.

KAPLAN, Y. 1997. 'The Self-Definition of the Sephardic Jews of Western Europe and Their Relation to the Alien and the Stranger.' In Gampel (1997): 119–20.

KARPAT, K. 1982. '*Millets* and Nationality: The Roots of the Incongruity of Nation and State in the Post-Ottoman Era.' In Braude and Lewis (1982): 141–69.

——— 1989. 'The Migratory Movements of Jews in the Ottoman Empire.' [Hebrew]. *Cathedra* 51/78–92.

KASTORYANO, L. 1993. *Quand l'innocence avait un sens: chronique d'une famille juive d'Istanbul d'entre les deux-guerres.* Istanbul.

KATTAN, N. 1980. *Farewell, Babylon.* New York.

KAYALI, H. 1997. *Arabs and Young Turks: Ottomanism, Arabism and Islamism in the Ottoman Empire, 1908–1918.* Berkeley.

KAZZAZ, N. 1991. *The Jews in Iraq in the Twentieth Century.* Jerusalem.

KEDOURIE, E. 1971. 'Jews of Baghdad in 1910.' *Middle East Studies* 7: 355–61.

——— 1989. 'The Break Between Muslims and Jews in Iraq.' In Cohen and Udovitch (1989): 21–64.

——— ed. 1992. *Spain and the Jews: The Sephardi Experience 1492 and After.* London.

KLORMAN, B.-Z. E. 1993. *The Jews of Yemen in the Nineteenth Century: A Portrait of a Messianic Community.* Leiden.

KRAEMER, J. L. 1992. 'Spanish Ladies from the Cairo Geniza.' In Ginio ed. (1992): 237–67.

KRÄMER, G. 1989. *The Jews in Modern Egypt, 1914–1952.* Seattle.

KUNT, I. M. 1982. 'Transformation of Zimmi into Askeri.' In Braude and Lewis (1982): 55–68.

LAMDAN, R. 1996. 'Female Slaves in the Jewish Society of Palestine, Syria and Egypt in the Sixteenth Century.' In Rozen (1996a): 355–72.

LANDAU, J. 1969. *Jews in Nineteenth-Century Egypt.* New York and London.

——— ed. 1988. *The Jews of Ottoman Egypt* [Hebrew]. Jerusalem.

LASKIER, M. M. 1983. *The Alliance Israélite Universelle and the Jewish Communities of Morocco: 1862–1962.* Albany, NY.

——— 1989. 'Jewish Emigration from Morocco to Israel: Government Policies and the Position of International Jewish Organizations, 1949–1956.' *Middle Eastern Studies* 25: 323–62.

——— 1992a. *The Jews of Egypt, 1920–1970: In the Midst of Zionism, Anti-Semitism and the Middle East Conflict.* New York.

——— 1992b. *The Jews of the Maghrib in the Shadow of Vichy and the Swastika* [Hebrew]. Tel Aviv.

——— 1994. *North African Jewry in the Twentieth Century: The Jews of Morocco, Tunisia and Algeria.* New York.

LEBEL, J. 1986. 'The Extermination of the Jews of Yugoslavia: The Communities of Macedonia, Pirot, and Kossovo.' [Hebrew]. *Pe'amim* 27: 67–74.

LEHMANN, M. 2001. 'Judeo-Spanish Musar Literature and the Transformation of Ottoman-Sephardic Society (Eighteenth Through Nineteenth Centuries).' Unpublished Ph.D. diss. Freie Universität, Berlin.

LESSER, J. 1992. 'From Pedlars to Proprietors: Lebanese, Syrian and Jewish Immigrants in Brazil.' In *The Lebanese in the World*. A. Hourani and N. Shehadi eds. London.

LEVI, A. 1992a. *Jews in the Turkish Republic: Their Legal and Political Situation* [Turkish]. Istanbul.

——1992b. *The Sephardim in the Ottoman Empire*. Princeton.

——ed. 1994. *The Jews of the Ottoman Empire*. Princeton.

LEVY, R. A. 1987. *I Remember Rhodes...* New York.

LÉVY, S. 2000. *Salonique à la fin du XIXᵉ siècle*. Istanbul.

LEWIS, B. 1984. *The Jews of Islam*. Princeton.

——1986. *Semites and Anti-Semites: An Inquiry into Conflict and Prejudice*. New York.

LIEBMAN, S. 1974. *The Inquisitors and the Jews in the New World*. Coral Gables, Fla.

——1982. *New World Jewry, 1493–1825: Requiem for the Forgotten*. New York.

LOCKMAN, Z. 1986. *Comrades and Enemies: Arab and Jewish Workers in Palestine, 1906–1948*. Berkeley.

LOEB, L. D. 1977. *Outcaste: Jewish Life in Southern Iran*. London.

——1982. 'Prestige and Piety in the Iranian Synagogue.' In Deshen and Zenner (1982): 285–310.

MCCARTHY, J. 1983. *Muslims and Minorities: The Population of Ottoman Anatolia and the End of the Empire*. New York.

MAKDISI, U. 2000. *The Culture of Sectarianism: Community, History, and Violence in Nineteenth-Century Lebanon*. Berkeley.

MALINO, F. 1978. *The Sephardic Jews of Bordeaux: Assimilation and Emancipation in Revolutionary and Napoleonic France*. Tuscaloosa and London.

MANN, V. B. 1997. 'Sephardic Ceremonial Art: Continuity in the Diaspora.' In Gampel (1997): 282–300.

MANOR, D. 1982. *Kabbale et ethnique au Maroc: la voie de Rabbi Jacob Abihatsira*. Jerusalem.

MARCUS, I. G. 1985. 'Beyond the Sephardic Mystique.' *Orim: A Jewish Journal at Yale* 1/1: 35–53.

MARCUS, S. 1951. 'Contribution to the History of Jews of Adrianople.' [Hebrew]. *Sinai* 29/7–8: 10–11.

MASSAD, J. 1996. 'Zionism's Internal Others: Israel and the Oriental Jews.' *Journal of Palestine Studies* 25/4: 53–68.

MASTERS, B. 2001. *Christians and Jews in the Ottoman Arab World: The Roots of Sectarianism*. Cambridge.

MATALON, R. 1998. *The One Facing Us: A Novel*. New York.

MATKOVSKI, A. 1959. 'The Destruction of Macedonian Jewry in 1943.' *Yad Vashem Studies* 3: 203–58.

——1982. *A History of the Jews in Macedonia*. Skopje.

MATZA, D. ed. 1997. *Sephardic American Voices: Two Hundred Years of a Literary Legacy*. Hanover, NH.

MAZOWER, M. 1993. *Inside Hitler's Greece: The Experience of Occupation*. New Haven.

MEIR, E. 1993. *The Zionist Movement and the Jews of Iraq, 1941–1950*. Tel Aviv.

MELAMMED, R. L. 1999. *Heretics or Daughters of Israel? The Crypto-Jewish Women of Castile*. Oxford.

MEMMI, A. 1962. *Portrait of a Jew*. New York.

——1992 (originally published in 1955). *The Pillar of Salt*. Boston.

MENASHRI, D. 1991. 'The Jews of Iran: Between the Shah and Khomeini.' In *Anti-Semitism in Times of Crisis*. 353–71. S. L. Gilman and S. T. Katz eds. New York.

MEYERS, A. R. 1982. 'Patronage and Protection: The Status of Jews in Precolonial Morocco.' In Deshen and Zenner (1982): 85–104.

MÉZAN, S. 1925. *Les Juifs espagnols en Bulgarie*. Sofia.

MILLER, S. G. 1996. 'Kippur on the Amazon. Jewish Emigration from Northern Morocco in the Late Nineteenth Century.' In Goldberg ed. (1996): 190–209.

MIRELMAN, V. 1990. *Jewish Buenos Aires, 1880–1930*. Detroit.

MOLHO, M. and NÉHAMA, J. eds. 1948. *In Memoriam: Hommage aux victimes juives des Nazis en Gréce*. Salonika.

MOREEN, V. B. 1987. *Iranian Jewry's Hour of Peril and Heroism: A Study of Babai Ibn Luf's Chronicle (1617–1662)*. New York and Jerusalem.

NAHUM, H. 1997. *Juifs de Smyrne, XIXe–XIXe siècle*. Paris.

NÉHAMA, J. 1935–78. *Histoire des Israélites de Salonique*. Paris and Thessaloniki.

NETANYAHU, B. 1966. *The Marranos of Spain from the Late Fourteenth to the Early Sixteenth Century*. New York.

NETZER, A. 1974. *The Jews of Persia and the Alliance in the Late Nineteenth Century: Some Aspects*. Jerusalem.

—— 1979. 'Problems of Cultural, Social and Political Integration of Iranian Jews.' [Hebrew]. *Gesher* 96–7: 69–83.

—— 1980. 'Iran.' In Davis (1980): 225–32.

—— 1980. 'The Persecution of Iranian Jewry in the 17th Century.' [Hebrew]. *Pe'amim* 6: 32–56.

NINI, Y. 1991. *The Jews of Yemen, 1800–1914*. Chur.

PANOVA, S. 1976. 'The Development of the Textile Industry in the Balkan Countries and the Role of the Jewish Population in the XVIth–XVIIth Centuries.' *Annual* 11: 123–40.

PAPO, J. 1987. *Sephardim in Twentieth Century America: In Search of Unity*. San José, Calif.

PATAI, R. 1986. *The Seed of Abraham: Jews and Arabs in Contact and Conflict*. Salt Lake City.

—— 1997. *Jadid al-Islam: The Jewish 'New Muslims' of Meshhed*. Detroit.

PERERA, V. 1995. *The Cross and the Pear Tree: A Sephardic Journey*. Berkeley.

QUARTAERT, D. 1996. 'The Industrial Working Class of Salonika, 1850–1912.' In Rozen (1986a): 311–32.

RAVID, B. 1989. 'An Autobiographical Memorandum by Daniel Rodriga, *Inventore* of the *Scala* of Spalato.' In *The Mediterranean and the Jews: Banking, Finance and International Trade*. 189–213. A. Toaff and S. Schwarzfuchs eds. Ramat Gan.

—— 1992. 'A Tale of Three Cities and their Raison d'État: Venice, Livorno, and the Competition for Jewish Merchants in the Sixteenth Century.' In Ginio (1992): 138–62.

REJWAN, N. 1986. *The Jews of Iraq: 3000 Years of History and Culture*. Boulder, Col.

ROBINSON, N. 1953. *Persia, Afghanistan, and Their Jewish Communities*. New York.

RODEN, C. 1994. 'Jewish Food in the Middle East.' In *Culinary Cultures of the Middle East*. 153–8. S. Zubaida ed. London.

RODRIGUE, A. 1990. *French Jews, Turkish Jews: The Alliance Israélite Universelle and the Politics of Jewish Schooling in Turkey, 1860–1925*. Bloomington, Ind.

—— 1992. *Guide to the Ladino Materials in Harvard College Library*. Cambridge, Mass.

—— ed. 1992. *Ottoman and Turkish Jewry: Community and Leadership*. Bloomington, Ind.

—— 1993. *Images of Sephardi and Eastern Jewries in Transition, the Teachers of the Alliance Israélite Universelle, 1860–1939*. Seattle.

—— 1995. 'From *Millet* to Minority: Turkish Jewry.' In *Paths of Emancipation: Jews, States, and Citizenship.* 238–61. P. B. Katznelson ed. Princeton.

—— 1996. 'Eastern Sephardi Jewry and New Nation-States in the Balkans in the Nineteenth and Twentieth Centuries.' In Goldberg ed. (1996): 81–9.

ROSANES, S. 1930–45. *History of the Jews of Turkey and the Middle East* [Hebrew]. Jerusalem.

ROTH, C. 1946. *The History of the Jews in Italy.* Philadelphia.

—— 1959. *The Jews in the Renaissance.* Philadelphia.

—— 1977. *Doña Gracia of the House of Nasi.* Philadelphia.

ROTH, N. 1995. *Conversos, Inquisition, and the Expulsion of the Jews from Spain.* Madison, Wisc.

ROZEN, M. 1984. *The Jewish Community of Jerusalem in the Seventeenth Century* [Hebrew]. Tel Aviv.

—— 1985. 'The Livornese Jewish Merchants in Tunis and the Commerce with Marseilles at the End of the Seventeenth Century.' [Hebrew]. *Michael* 9: 87–129.

—— 1988. 'Contest and Rivalry in Mediterranean Maritime Commerce in the First Half of the Eighteenth Century: The Jews of Salonika and the European Presence.' *Revue des Études Juives* 147: 309–52.

—— 1994. *Hasköy Cemetery: Typology of Stones.* Tel Aviv and Philadelphia.

—— ed. 1996a. *The Days of the Crescent: Chapters in the History of the Jews in the Ottoman Empire* [Hebrew]. Tel Aviv.

—— 1996b. 'The Corvée of Operating the Mines in Siderokapisi and Its Impact on the Jewish Society of Salonika in the Sixteenth Century.' In Rozen (1996a): 13–38.

RUDERMAN, D. B. 1981. *The World of a Renaissance Jew: The Life and Thought of Abraham Farissol.* Cincinnati.

SCHECHTER, S. 1945. 'Safed in the Sixteenth Century: A City of Legists and Mystics.' In *Studies in Judaism.* 202–306. Philadelphia.

SCHORSCH, I. 1989. 'The Myth of Sephardic Sypremacy.' *Leo Baeck Institute Year Book* 47/66: 47–66.

SCHROETER, D. 1984. 'Anglo-Jewry and Essaouira (Mogador) 1860–1900: The Social Implications of Philanthropy.' *Transactions of the Jewish Historical Society of England* 28: 60–88.

—— 1988. *Merchants of Essaouira: Urban Society and Imperialism in Southwestern Morocco, 1844–1886.* Cambridge.

—— 1989. 'Trade as a Mediator in Muslim-Jewish Relations: Southwestern Morocco in the Nineteenth Century.' In Cohen and Udovitch (1989): 113–40.

—— 1994. 'Orientalism and the Jews of the Mediterranean.' *Journal of Mediterranean Studies* 4/2: 183–96.

SCHWARZFUCHS, S. 1981. *Les Juifs d'Algérie et la France (1830–1855).* Jerusalem.

SCIAKY, L. 1946. *Farewell to Ottoman Salonica.* Repr. 2000. New York.

SEGRE, R. 1992. 'Sephardic Settlements in Sixteenth-Century Italy: A Historical and Geographical Survey.' In Ginio (1992): 112–37.

—— 1997. 'Sephardic Refugees in Ferrara: Two Notable Families.' In Gampel (1997): 164–86.

SEROUSSI, E. 1992. 'Between the Eastern and Western Mediterranean: Sephardic Music After the Expulsion from Spain and Portugal.' In Ginio (1992): 198–206.

SHAWR, G. 1989. *Land, Labour, and the Origins of the Israeli–Palestinian Conflict, 1882–1904.* Cambridge.

SHAKED, S. ed. 1982. *Irano-Judaica: Studies Relating to Jewish Contacts With Persian Culture Throughout the Ages.* Jerusalem.

SHAW, S. 1979. 'The Population of Istanbul in the Nineteenth Century.' In *Türk Tarih Dergisi* 32: 403–314.

—— 1991. *The Jews of the Ottoman Empire and the Turkish Republic.* New York.

—— 1993. *Turkey and the Holocaust: Turkey's Role in Rescuing Turkish and European Jewry.* New York.

SHELAH, M. ed. 1990. *History of the Holocaust: Yugoslavia* [Hebrew]. Jerusalem.

SHENHAV, Y. 1999. 'The Jews of Iraq, Zionist Ideology, and the Property of the Palestinian Refugees of 1948: An Anomaly of National Accounting.' *International Journal of Middle East Studies* 4/31: 605–30.

SHIBLAK, A. 1986. *The Lure of Zion: The Case of the Iraqi Jews.* London.

SHMUELEVITZ, A. 1984. *The Jews of the Ottoman Empire in the Late Fifteenth and the Sixteenth Centuries: Administrative, Economic, Legal and Social Relations as Reflected in the Responsa.* Leiden.

SHOHAT, A. 1971–8. 'The King's Cloth in Salonika.' *Sefunot* 12: 169–88.

—— 1981. 'Notes on the Communal Organisation of the Jews in the Ottoman Empire in the Sixteenth Century.' *Miqqedem Umiyyam* 1: 133–7.

SHOHAT, E. 1988. 'Sephardim in Israel: Zionism From the Standpoint of its Jewish Victims.' *Social Text* 19–20: 1–35.

—— 1997. 'Sephardim in Israel: Zionism From the Standpoint of its Jewish Victims.' In *Dangerous Liasons, Gender, Nation, and Postcolonial Perspectives.* 39–68. A. McClintock, A. Mufti, and E. Shohat eds. Minneapolis.

—— 1999. 'The Invention of the Mizrahim.' *Journal of Palestine Studies* 29/1: 5–20.

SHOKEID, M. 1982. 'Jewish Existence in a Berber Environment.' In Deshen and Zenner (1982): 105–22.

SHOLEM, G. 1973. *Shabbatai Sevi: The Mystical Messiah.* Princeton.

SHULEWITZ, M. H. ed. 1999. *The Forgotten Millions: The Modern Jewish Exodus from Arab Lands.* London.

SIMON, R. 1992. *Change Within Tradition Among Jewish Women in Libya.* Seattle.

—— 2000. 'Between the Family and the Outside World: Jewish Girls in the Modern Middle East and North Africa.' In *Jewish Social Studies* 7 /1: 81–108.

SIMONSOHN, S. 1977. *History of the Jews in the Duchy of Mantua.* Jerusalem.

SITTON, D. 1985. *Sephardi Communities Today.* Jerusalem.

SMOOHA, S. 1978. *Israel: Pluralism and Conflict.* Berkeley.

SOROUDI, S. 1981. 'The Jews in Islamic Iran.' *Jewish Quarterly* 21: 99–114.

STAMPFER, J. ed. 1987. *The Sephardim: A Cultural Journey from Spain to the Pacific Coast.* Portland, Dreg.

STEIN, S. 2000. 'Creating a Taste For News: Historicizing Judeo-Spanish Periodicals of the Ottoman Empire.' *Jewish History* 14/1: 9–28.

—— 2003 forthcoming. *Making Jews Modern: Yiddish and Ladino Newspapers of the Russian and Ottoman Empires.* Bloomington, Ind.

STILLMAN, N. A. 1979. *The Jews of Arab Lands: A History and Sourcebook.* Philadelphia.

—— 1984. *The Jews of Arab Lands in Modern Times.* Philadelphia.

—— 1986. 'Antisemitism in the Contemporary Arab World.' In *Antisemitism in the Contemporary World.* 70–85. M. Curtis ed. Boulder, Col.

—— 1988. *The Language and Culture of the Jews of Sefrou, Morocco: An Ethnolinguistic Study.* Manchester.

—— 1991. 'Reply to Mark Cohen.' *Tikkun* 6: 60–4.

—— 1996. *Sephardi Religious Responses to Modernity.* London.

STILLMAN, Y. and ZUCKER, G. K. eds. 1993. *New Horizons in Sephardic Studies.* Albany, NY.

—— and STILLMAN, N. A. eds. 1999. *From Iberia to Diaspora: Studies in Sephardic History and Culture.* Leiden, Boston, and Cologne.

SUTTON, J. A. D. 1979. *Magic Carpet: Aleppo in Flatbush, the Story of a Unique Ethnic Jewish Community.* New York.

—— 1988. *Aleppo Chronicles: The Story of the Unique Sephardeem of the Ancient Near East— In Their Own Words.* New York.

SWIRSKI, S. 1989. *Israel the Oriental Majority.* London.

TESSLER, M. 1981. 'Ethnic Change and Nonassimilation Minority Status: The Case of Jews in Tunisia and Morocco and Arabs in Israel.' In *Ethnic Change.* 154–97. S. C. Keyes ed. Seattle.

TIETZE, A. and YAHALOM, J. 1995. *Ottoman Melodies, Hebrew Hymns: A 16th Century Cross-Cultural Adventure.* Budapest.

TOBI, Y., BAR-ASHER, S., and BARNAI, J. 1981. *The Jews of the Middle East* [Hebrew]. Jerusalem.

TSUR, Y. 1994. 'Jewish "Sectional Societies" in France and Algeria on the Eve of the Colonial Encounter.' *Journal of Mediterranean Studies* 4: 163–77.

—— 1996. 'Haskalah in a Sectional Colonial Society Mahdia (Tunisia) 1884.' In Goldberg ed. (1996): 146–67.

UCHMANY, E. A. 1993. 'The Periodization of the History of the New Christians and Crypto-Jews in Spanish America.' In Stillman and Zucker (1993): 109–36.

UDOVITCH, A. and VALENSI, L. 1984. *The Last Arab Jews: The Communities of Jerba Tunisia.* Chur.

VEINSTEIN, G. ed. 1992. *Salonique, 1850–1918: La 'ville des Juifs' et le reveil des Balkans.* Paris.

VITAL, D. 1982. *Zionism: The Formative Years.* Oxford.

WEIKER, W. F. 1992. *Ottomans, Turks, and the Jewish Polity.* New York and London.

WEINGROD, A. ed. 1985. *Studies in Israeli Ethnicity: After the Ingathering.* New York.

YAARI, A. 1971. *Letters from the Land of Israel* [Hebrew]. Ramat-Gan.

—— 1976. *Travel Accounts of the Land of Israel* [Hebrew]. Ramat-Gan.

YAHIL, L. 1990. *The Holocaust: The Fate of European Jewry.* Oxford.

YEHUDA, Z. 1981. *Organized Zionism in Morocco: 1900–1948.* Jerusalem.

—— 1982. 'On a Jewish Community in Iraq in an Era of Change: The Jewish Community of Hilla.' [Hebrew]. *Studies in the History and Culture of Iraqi Jewry.* 83–120.

—— 1984. 'The Social Ties between Jews and Muslims in Baghdad at the End of the Nineteenth Century According to Local Jewish Sources.' *Umma ve-toldoteha* 2: 55–64.

—— 1986. 'Moroccan Jewry and the Zionist Organization in the Years 1900–1948.' [Hebrew]. *Zion* 51: 341–7.

—— 1996. 'Iraqi Jewry and Cultural Change in the Educational Activity of the Alliance Israélite Universelle.' In Goldberg ed. (1996): 134–45.

YERUSHALMI, Y. H. 1981. *From Spanish Court to Italian Ghetto: Isaac Cardoso: A Study in Seventeenth-Century Marranism and Jewish Apologetics.* Seattle.

YERUSHALMI, Y. H. 1982. 'Between Amsterdam and New Amsterdam: The Place of Curacao and the Caribbean in Early Modern Jewish History.' *American Jewish History* 2: 172–93.

—— 1989. *Zakhor: Jewish History and Jewish Memory.* New York.

ZAND, M. 1979. 'Bukharan Jewish Culture Under Soviet Rule.' *Soviet Jewish Affairs* 9/2: 15–24.

—— 1988. 'Bukharin Jewry and the Russian Conquest of Central Asia.' *Pe'amim* 35: 47–83.

ZENNER, W. P. 1982a. 'Jews in Late Ottoman Syria: External Relations.' In Deshen and Zenner (1982): 155–209.

—— 1982b. 'Syrian Jews and their Non-Jewish Neighbors in Late Ottoman Times.' In Deshen and Zenner (1982): 161–72.

—— 1982c. 'Jews in Late Ottoman Syria: Community, Family and Religion.' In Deshen and Zenner (1982): 187–209.

—— 2000. *A Global Community: The Jews From Aleppo, Syria.* Detroit.

ZOHAR, Z. 1986. 'Halakhic Responses of Syrian and Egyptian Rabbinical Authorities to Social and Technological Change.' *Studies in Contemporary Judaism* 2: 18–51.

—— 1988. 'New Horizons: A Major Nineteenth-Century Baghdadi Posek's Heightened Awareness of Socio-Cultural Variety and Change.' [Hebrew]. *Pe'amim* 36: 89–107.

—— 1990. 'Jewish Communities in Syria 1880–1918: Demography, Economics and Communal Institutions in the Late Ottoman Period.' [Hebrew]. *Pe'amim* 44: 80–109.

—— 1993. *Tradition and Change* [Hebrew]. Jerusalem.

—— 1996. 'Traditional Flexibility and Modern Strictness: Two Halakhic Positions on Women's Suffrage.' In Goldberg ed. (1996): 134–45.

ZORATTINI, P. C. I. 1993. 'Sephardic Settlement in Ferrara under the House of Este.' In Stillman and Zucker (1993): 5–14.

CHAPTER 14

EUROPEAN JEWRY IN THE EARLY MODERN PERIOD: 1492–1750

ELISHEVA CARLEBACH

CONCEPTIONS OF THE EARLY MODERN PERIOD IN JEWISH HISTORIOGRAPHY

CLASSICAL Jewish historiography depicted a sharp break between medieval and modern patterns, the movements of transformation seeming to emerge virtually *ex nihilo*. The transition in Heinrich Graetz's masterful history exemplifies that approach. 'While the tumult continued in the Jewish camp between the two rabbis and their followers over the matter of the amulets . . . signs of new times emerged in Europe: the Jewish sage Moses Mendelssohn and the Gentile sage Ephraim Lessing entered into a bond of mutual friendship' (1913: viii. 526–7; similarly Grayzel 1968: 468–9). With some exceptions, most grand histories of the Jewish people did not see the early modern period as a discrete age of transition worthy of study in its own right (see e.g. the collection Ben-Sasson and Ettinger 1971). Historians of the founding generations, such as Graetz, viewed the medieval period as an unrelieved continuum of cultural isolation, Gentile persecution, and religious obscurantism. Muslim Spain (see Halkin 1956: 215–63) and Renaissance Italy (see Roth 1959) stood as exceptions to this bleak picture, ideal images of the cultural benefits that accrued to societies that granted Jews a modicum of political or cultural freedom. In this conception of Jewish history, modernity began abruptly, with Moses Mendelssohn and the Haskalah ending medieval cultural isolation, the French Revolution and acts of legal emancipation reversing political liabilities, and movements of religious reform modernizing Judaism (Meyer 1975). In European historiography, pioneering works such as Burckhardt (1958), Hazard (1953), Febvre (1982), and Davis (1975) staked claims for certain early modern societies or circles as being worthy of study because they possessed the unique characteristics of an age of transition, with all its inherent paradoxes.

Gradually, historians of the Jews accepted the period roughly between the sixteenth and late eighteenth centuries as a distinct historical unit that possessed unique characteristics, neither fully medieval nor yet bearing the hallmarks of the modern. Several themes that transcend geographical and national boundaries dominate the historiography of this period. One ubiquitous question is that of Jewish insularity versus integration into the majority society. Was the early modern period primarily one of medieval isolation, or were Jews slowly opening their culture and way of life to outside influences which ultimately eroded the hold of traditional patterns completely? Did different Jewish populations experience drastically different processes of modernization, or can overarching patterns be discerned that cross political boundaries? Did Sephardic and Ashkenazic Jews in Western Europe lead parallel but separate Jewish lives, or were there numerous points of contact and even influence? What was the influence of the growing availability of inexpensive printed materials on Jewish social and intellectual life, and on the relationship between Jews and the newly emerging Christian denominations?

In Jewish historiography, Katz (1961a, 1961b, 1973) wrote the most influential works establishing the early modern period in Western and Central Europe as one deserving its own modes of enquiry. He devoted three books to investigating the nature of Ashkenazic Jewish society in early modern western and central Europe. His *Tradition and Crisis* (1961) was the first work to consider the social-historical characteristics of Ashkenazic society in this age of transition. He viewed all of Ashkenazic Jewry as one historical unit; Sephardic Jews play no role in this narrative. In *Exclusiveness and Tolerance*, Katz emphatically and repeatedly characterized the period as one of cultural insularity. Change in the mid-eighteenth century came, in his view, only as a result of immanent crises of traditional Jewish authority, Haskalah in the West and Hasidism in Eastern Europe. Shohet's (1960) nearly contemporaneous survey differed from Katz's in its emphasis on the process of incipient disintegration of traditional modes of Jewish thought and relationship to Christian society. Shohet identified rabbinic interest in non-rabbinic subjects such as mathematics, sciences, and current events, the rise in the number of conversions out of Judaism, and the use of European vernaculars among Jews, *inter alia*, as signs that the Haskalah did not emerge suddenly but as the result of a gradual but steadily growing openess to non- Jewish culture and society. More recently, Feiner (1988) and Sorkin (2000) have argued for a proto-Haskalah in the late seventeenth and early eighteenth centuries, citing a considerable number of figures whose interests were subsequently idealized by the maskilim in Western Europe. Still, these individuals did not view their lives and works within the framework of a movement with articulated goals for the transformation of Jewish society. Ruderman (1995) posited that early modern European Jewish society contained many different circles, both among Sephardim and Ashkenazim, which maintained many avenues of intellectual exchange, keeping abreast of the latest philosophical discussions, scientific trends, and medical discoveries of their times. University-trained physicians, educated former marranos, and rabbis experimenting in the physical sciences, transmitted their knowledge of developments in European scientific and intellectual discourse into Jewish society. In an extremely useful survey, Israel (1985) viewed the period as one in which mercantilist politics dominated European states. This practical economic orientation pushed German states to admit Jews as subjects, reversing centuries of exclusion. The 'Court Jews', invited at the behest of the states, travelled widely in non-Jewish circles, with fewer constraints than most other Jews, becoming models and agents of change within the Jewish communities they called home. They emerged from both Sephardic and Ashkenazic milieus, providing numerous points of contact with Christian society.

THE ITALIAN RENAISSANCE

Cecil Roth's *The Jews in the Renaissance* (1959) introduced Jewish historians to the riches of Jewish life in this multifaceted world. His work provided the standard perspective on the subject for decades. Roth introduced his book as a 'study of the interaction of two societies and two cultures at one of the seminal periods of the world's history'. In the course of painting a colourful picture of Jewish life in Italy during the Renaissance, Roth argued that the Jews made seminal contributions to Renaissance culture, laying the foundations for the entire period in their role as translators and intermediaries who transmitted the Greek masterpieces through the Arabic and into the European world. In addition to their contributions to Renaissance culture, Roth highlighted the many instances in which Renaissance culture influenced Jews to breach the boundaries of their traditional pursuits to participate in cultural activities associated with the Renaissance. Roth's presentation of this historical moment was influenced by the tradition of Jewish historians seeking usable models of creative interaction with non-Jewish society from the Jewish past. His idealization of the Renaissance serves as a very useful springboard for an examination of terms such as symbiosis, acculturation, and assimilation with regard to Jewish–Christian interactions.

While many other works examine Italian Jewry and the Renaissance from various angles, perhaps the most serious and overarching response to Roth's rather idealistic picture was Bonfil (1994). Rejecting both the idea of a symbiosis between two equally strong cultures and those historians who tended to see the story of Italian Jewry as another chapter in the lachrymose history of Jewish suffering at the hands of hostile others, Bonfil viewed the life of Jews within the milieu of early modern Italian society as the life of a minority affirming and defining its difference within the majority culture. His approach does not attempt to view the two as mutually influential, as they are unequal and different by definition. Both Jewish and Christian society underwent dynamic changes during this period, but these transformations do not mean that either effaced its essential Jewish or Christian characteristics. Ravid (1988, 1992, 2001), on various aspects of Venetian Jewry, Toaff (1998) on the Jews of Umbria, and Stow (2001) exemplify the diverse contributions to the seemingly inexhaustible history of this fascinating Jewry by historians working from multidisciplinary perspectives. The translation and essays in (M. R. Cohen 1988) and analysis of the profound contradictions within the oeuvre of Leone Modena (Fishman 1997), especially as expressed in the sceptical treatise *Kol Sakhal* (Voice of a Fool) and its place within the intellectual framework of Modena's other works, represent the paradoxes and extremes of this society in transition. Adelman (1993, 2001) has drawn especially useful pictures of Jewish women in Renaissance Italy, and Ruderman (1995) provides eloquent evidence that the standard 'Renaissance' periodization does not apply to the internal life of Italy's Jews. They continued to develop their scientific curiosity and intellectual virtuosity long after the conventional deadline of the Counter-Reformation as the end of the period of cross-fertilization passed.

INTELLECTUAL HISTORY

Jewish intellectual history in the early modern period is characterized by increasingly successful attempts to cross traditional disciplinary boundaries. Intellectual fields that can be described as primarily indigenous, such as kabbalah and halacha, and those whose roots lie in the western intellectual tradition, such as philosophy and science, had various points of conjunction both within the Jewish world and beyond it. None of these strands can be strictly separated: Jews possessed a long tradition of confronting and absorbing the classical philosophical texts and traditions of the West; kabbalistic influence played an increasingly strong role in halachic discourse, while many attempts to synthesize kabbalah and philosophy resulted in the confluence of discourses long considered to be opposites, as exemplified in the thinkers analyzed by Idel (1992).

Since the publication of Scholem's first works, study of kabbalah has emerged as one of the more vital branches of Jewish studies, characterized a generation ago by scholars such as Isaiah Tishby and Meir Benayahu, who published many foundational texts and worked primarily in Israel. Idel (1988) authored one of the most profound reformulations of past historiographical assumptions. Building on the undisputed magisterial work of Scholem, Idel reimagined kabbalah as a theurgic system which differs greatly from the purely philosophical kabbalah of Scholem. Contemporary kabbalah scholarship is practised in centres of Judaic scholarship the world over, and includes the work of Eliot Wolfson and Daniel Matt in the United States, Peter Schaefer in Berlin, Charles Mopsik in France, and in Israel, Moshe Idel and Yehudah Liebes. Collectively, these scholars have reshaped the contours of Jewish intellectual history, with particular impact on the early modern period, when new centres of kabbalistic creativity and new forms of synthesis between kabbalah and other disciplines such as philosophy and halacha emerged.

Several milieus provided particularly fertile soil for the cross-currents of ideas. Renaissance Italian humanists such as Pico della Mirandola and his Florentine circle gave impetus to Christian Hebraist studies, and particularly to Christian study of kabbalah. That circle influenced German humanists such as Johannes Reuchlin in their defence of Hebrew and Jewish books as valuable tools for Christian scholars (Reuchlin 1993; cf. esp. Intro. by Idel and pp.v–xxix). In the years between the sixteenth and the eighteenth centuries, German Hebraists continued to expand the field, arguably laying the groundwork for the modern scientific study of Judaism, albeit in works always biased by a Christian perspective. The list of notable contributions to this genre includes the works of the Buxtorfs of Basel (Burnett 1996), Johann Jakob Schudt, Johannes Wagenseil, Georg Bodenschatz, and Johann Andreas Eisenmenger, to cite just a few (Carlebach 2001: 170–221). Within Italian Jewry, intellectual biographies such as that of David Messer Leon (Tirosh-Rothschild 1991), Abraham Farissol (Ruderman 1981), and the recent magisterial edition of Azariah de Rossi's *Meor Eynaim* (Weinberg 2000) have added depth to the picture of a Jewish mentality that traversed other intellectual domains with relative ease.

THE JEWS OF CENTRAL EUROPE IN THE EARLY MODERN PERIOD

The best scholarship on central European Jewry through the eighteenth century is heavily weighted toward the Jews of German lands, with the notable exception of Rudolfine Prague during its sixteenth century Renaissance, and Putík (2000) for the seventeenth. Histories of Jews in Hungary and the rest of Bohemia and Moravia in this period remain a desideratum. For German Jewry, however, the picture is different. Originally the surveys of Moritz Güdemann and parochial local histories served as the sole guides to a Jewry severely diminished after the fourteenth-century plague. Recent scholarship, however, has constructed a much clearer picture of German Jews in late medieval and early modern times. Their population configuration changed utterly because of the expulsions from large cities in the late fifteenth and early sixteenth centuries. With the exception of a few large urban ghettoes, notably in Frankfurt am Main, Worms, and Prague, Jews lived scattered in small groups over vast territories, often in small clusters of several Jewish families within a Christian milieu. Several distinctive cultural and intellectual patterns emerge from this condition. Yuval (1988) has drawn a detailed picture of the patterns of rabbinic spiritual leadership in the fourteenth through sixteenth centuries, illuminating the way the rabbinate adjusted to a territorial rather than primarily urban jurisdiction, and how rabbinic leadership evolved within families and classes, a testimony to the continued vitality of committed Jewish life under duress. Dinari (1984) provides an intellectual rabbinic history, emphasizing the distinctive directions of halacha in early modern German lands, its uniquely strong relationship to *minhag*, and the enduring imprint that this period left on the history of halacha. Zimmer (1999) has drawn a picture of the lively individual rabbis who served German communities in the sixteenth and seventeenth centuries, their outreach to the Jews of the country-side, their internal disputes, and their enormous pride in preserving *minhag Ashkenaz* intact.

Several pioneering studies have broken down the barriers between the German historiographical tradition of nostalgic local histories (*Heimatsgeschichte*) and the tendency for German-Jewish historians to write local histories of Jewish communities which paralleled but often did not intersect with the congruent German-Christian histories. While scholars have long published accounts based on *pinkasei kehillah* and charters granted to Jews to define the terms of their settlement (e.g. Baer 1922), full social histories of Jewish life, especially in the rural setting, have just begun to be written. In the past decade social-historical analyses such as those of Rohrbacher (1995), Ullman (1999), and Ulbrich (1999) have illuminated in fine detail the degree to which the lives of Jews in small rural settlements of early modern German lands were interwoven in the economic and social worlds they inhabited.

These works use gender as one of the categories of analysis, allowing us for the first time to see in detail the proportion of women within the population at all age levels, their relationship to their Christian neighbours, and their economic roles. By giving us detailed statistics, such as the number of Jewish families living in each dwelling, a sense of the spatial and residence arrangements emerges. Weissler (1998) illuminates new aspects of the spiritual life of Ashkenazic women in her extensive study of the *techina* literature. Her innovative construction of an internal rhythm of family and personal events that marked the contours of daily life for Jewish women constitutes a pioneering application of gender categories to sources that have long been known and used by scholars, but never to this effect. While not a conventional history in any sense, Weissler's work opens new possibilities for rewriting the history of early modern Ashkenaz in a way that is more inclusive of the lives of Jewish women.

THE SEPHARDIC DIASPORA IN WESTERN EUROPE

The expulsion of the Jews from Spain in 1492 and from Portugal in 1497 had a profound impact on the life of Western European Jews, even beyond that on Iberian Jewry itself. Most settlement by Jews in western Europe in lands from which Jews had been expelled for centuries began with the trickle of marrano Jews seeking refuge, sometimes decades or even centuries after the original expulsions. Jewish life in England, in the Dutch provinces, in southern France, in parts of Italy, in German lands and even farther east, had its early modern foundations with the arrival of the 'men of the Portuguese nation' (Kaplan 1994; Sorkin 1999).

The resettlement of former marranos, primarily of Portuguese origin, in Western Europe constitutes one of the dramatic narratives of Jewish rebirth in early modern Western Europe. While the largest number of Spanish and Portuguese exiles headed for the Ottoman Empire, where they reconstituted Jewish communities uprooted by the expulsions of 1492 and 1497, others escaped from the Iberian Inquisition to Western European cities. There, they emerged from under the mask of Catholicism. Marranos who migrated to Bordeaux, Bayonne, and St-Jean-de-Luz in southern France slowly adopted the structure of a Jewish community as they gradually shed their Catholic outward appearance. They formed the most acculturated Jewish community in early modern France, and played a visible and vital role in the debate over Jewish emancipation in eighteenth-century France. (Malino 1978). The marranos who settled in Elizabethan England laid the foundations for the first Jewish community in London since the medieval expulsion of the Jews (Endelman 1979; Shapiro 1996).

The small core of refugees who settled in Antwerp ultimately migrated to Amsterdam, which soon grew to be the most influential of all former marrano settlements. They played a leading role in the Dutch economy and its commercial success, at the same time as they served as a model for smaller communities such as those in London and Hamburg, even some in the New World. This community enjoyed remarkable success in its project to educate marranos into Jewish learning and community, producing dozens of Jewish texts in Spanish and Portuguese for the edification of former marranos. The greatest testimony to the success of this literature is its eventual obsolescence: the defences of and introductions to Judaism had done such a fine job of educating the newcomers, that they no longer needed translations of Jewish lore and law into Spanish and Portuguese. Bodian (1997) and Swetschinski (2000) provide a sophisticated analysis of the different strands of identity, Jewish, Iberian, and Dutch, that intermingled to create a renewed Sephardic identity in Western Europe.

Several outstanding figures within this community have become vehicles for scholarly exploration of the complex social, intellectual, and spiritual struggles and contributions of former marranos. The most renowned of these figures, Menasseh ben Israel, a rabbi and scholar steeped in biblical and rabbinic learning as well as philosophical and Christian theological works, enjoyed a scholarly reputation far beyond the Jewish community. Kaplan, Mechoulan, and Popkin (1989) exemplifies recent scholarship that presents a fuller context for understanding the achievement and personality of Menasseh. Two significant Jewish apologists, physicians and philosophers in their own right, Isaac Cardoso and Isaac Orobio de Castro, are subjects of illuminating studies. Yerushalmi's (1971) pioneering exploration of Cardoso's life bridged both halves of the marrano trajectory, beginning with the truncated Jewish identity formed in Portugal and Spain, the education of a physician, flight from the Inquisition, and then his new life in the Venetian ghetto, where his embracing of Judaism led him to become a passionate apologist for the Jewish faith and a loyal traditionalist within the community. Kaplan's study of Orobio (1989) provides a similarly complex picture of a passionate defender of traditional Jewish faith, of marrano origin, who took on detractors of Judaism from within the community, such as Spinoza, and from without, as in his dialogue with Philip von Limborch.

The philosopher Baruch/Benedict Spinoza has inspired generations of scholars to try to sort out the marrano element in Spinoza's sceptical pantheism, a path pioneered by Gebhardt and continued by Revah. They drew fertile lines from the heretical thinking of former marranos Uriel da Costa and Juan de Prado to that of Spinoza. Yovel (1988), and more recently Nadler (1999) summarized much of that scholarship in comprehensive discussions considering whether Spinoza was the first secular Jew and marranism a pathway to Jewish modernity. Recent scholarship continues to tease out from sources as disparate as Inquisitorial dossiers to communal archives the tormented path of Iberia's Jews as they emerged into the freedom and confusion of early modern Europe and paved new and innovative paths to Jewish identity.

Applying gender as a category of analysis to marrano sources has also begun to yield tantalizing fruits. In a pattern that emerges from Melammed's (1999) analysis of the Inquisitorial testimonies of marrana women, the women consciously shaped their homes into bastions of crypto-Jewish identity and subversion of the Catholic faith. Coerced by Church and Inquisition to abandon all external trappings of the Jewish faith, marranas kept Jewish traditions and identity alive by teaching their daughters the domestic observances they identified as central to Jewish tradition. They hoped to be 'saved' by observing the Law of Moses, an unconscious adaptation of the Christian idea of salvation to their Jewish world-view. Kramer's (1994) suggestive article on the considerable role of Jewish women in the weaving industry that sustained the cultural efflorescence of sixteenth-century Safed confirms that, while social history of Jews throughout the early modern world is still very much in its infancy, future studies will not be able to construct a picture of Jewish life that does not include the lives of Jewish women.

MESSIANISM

No single event has reverberated as strongly through Jewish historiography of the early modern period as the messianic movement of Sabbatai Zevi. The historiography of the movement drew scholarly attention to several issues in Jewish messianism (Goldish 2000–1). The first is the pervasiveness of messianism in early modern Jewish life, both in terms of the sheer number of messianic figures as well as in the scope and enthusiasm of their audiences. Asher Lemlein, David Reubeni, and Shelomo Molkho appeared in the first half of the sixteenth century, and each generated enthusiastic responses among large numbers of Jews (Silver 1927: 110–50; Lenowitz 1998: 99–147). Sabbatai Zevi's movement erupted into the public eye in 1665, continuing to generate confusion, along with all manner of epigones, at least through to the death of Eva Frank. Scholarship has focused both on the messianic personalities and on the social, geographical, and ideological configurations of their respective movements.

The figures of Molkho and Zevi highlight the role of marranism and religious ambiguity in Jewish consciousness in the early modern period. Molkho, born a *converso*, died a martyr's death, while Sabbatai Zevi, born to a Romaniot Jewish family of Izmir, rejected martyrdom in favor of apostasy. In both cases, the fluidity of their identities struck a responsive chord among the many Jews who had themselves experienced the trauma of dual identity (Yerushalmi 1971: 303–6).

The distant and proximate factors that combined to produce enthusiastic messianism formed another subject for heated historiographical debate. In the nineteenth century the historian Graetz assigned messianism to the range of negative, irrational phenomena, along with mysticism and superstition, which resulted from Jewish cultural insularity (Graetz 1913: vii. 297–307; viii. 232). Scholem (1973) sought to link the movement to the much earlier trauma of the expulsions from Iberia, and the mythical response they generated in the kabbalistic teachings of Isaac Luria. Barnai (2000) linked the rise of the movement to the chronologically closer Chmielnicki uprisings in Poland of 1648/9, and its rapid spread to the mobility and networking of the Sabbatian emissaries. Idel (1993) refuted Scholem's emphasis on the mystical intellectual framework by proving that Lurianic Kabbalah did not become widely known until after the rise of Sabbatai's movement. While kabbalistic concepts were used by Nathan of Gaza, Abraham Cardoso, and other interpreters of Sabbatai's mission, they cannot be assigned a causal role.

The Sabbatian movement fuelled some of the most dramatic controversies in the early modern Jewish world, such as those between Nehemiah Hayon and Hakham Zevi, Moses Hayim Luzzatto and Moses Hagiz, and Jacob Emden and Jonathan Eybeschuetz (Carlebach 1990). Several generations of rabbis devoted a significant portion of their careers to combating Sabbatian practices and ideas, from Jacob Sasportas, a seventeenth-century contemporary of the movement (Tishby 1954), to David Fleckeles, who published a work against the Frankist movement in 1800 (Fleckeles 1800). The fear of a similar spiritual debacle motivated the strong early opposition to Beshtian Hasidism and shaped the rabbinic response to innovation in the century to follow. Many aspects of the movement remain to be thoroughly explored, from local contexts such as the Turkish and Polish, to the continued exploration of Sabbatian influence on the Jewish–Christian polemic, its internal growth as a sect, and the lasting influences of its ideas and customs on Jewish tradition.

SUGGESTED READING

Two works offer sweeping assessments of early modern European Jewry. Katz (1961b) uses internal Jewish sources to paint an idealized, somewhat static picture of the mindset of Ashkenazic Jews on the threshold of modernity. Israel (1985) covers the same period with a far different emphasis on new economic policies that led to the resettlement of Jews, and the gradual engagement of both Ashkenazic and Sephardic Jews in European economic, intellectual, and scientific activities. Bodian (1997) analyses the constitution of new forms of Sephardic Jewish community and identity in Western Europe, while Yerushalmi (1971) and Kaplan (1989) eloquently depict the marrano odyssey from Iberian persecution to professing

Judaism. Ruderman (1995) offers a fresh look at the long-term impact of Renaissance humanism on Jewish learning in Italy. Scholem's (1973) magisterial survey of the Sabbatian movement that swept through European Jewry in the seventeenth century remains a classic for its overwhelming scholarship and insight into this astonishing chapter of Jewish history.

BIBLIOGRAPHY

ADELMAN, H. E. 1993. 'The Educational and Literary Activities of Jewish Women in Italy During the Renaissance and the Catholic Restoration.' *Shlomo Simonsohn Jubilee Volume* 9–23. Tel Aviv.

—— 2001. 'Jewish Women and Family Life, Inside and Outside the Ghetto.' *The Jews of Early Modern Venice.* 143–65. Robert Davis ed. Baltimore.

BARNAI, J. 2000. *Sabbateanism: Social Perspectives.* [Hebrew]. Jerusalem.

BAER, F. 1922. *Das Protokollbuch der Landjudenschaft des Herzogtums Kleve.* Stuttgart.

BEN-SASSON, H. H. and ETTINGER, S. eds. 1971. *Jewish Society Through the Ages.* New York.

BODIAN, M. 1997. *Hebrews of the Portuguese Nation: Conversos and Community in Early Modern Amsterdam.* Bloomington, Ind.

BONFIL, R. 1994. *Jewish Life in Renaissance Italy.* Trans. Anthony Oldcorn. Berkeley.

BURCKHARDT, J. 1958. *The Civilization of the Renaissance in Italy.* New York.

BURNETT, S. G. 1996. *From Christian Hebraism to Jewish Studies: Johannes Buxtorf (1564– 1629) and Hebrew Learning in the Seventeenth Century.* Leiden, New York, and Cologne.

CARLEBACH, E. 1990. *The Pursuit of Heresy: Rabbi Moses Hagiz and the Sabbatian Controversies.* New York and London.

—— 2001. *Divided Souls: Converts from Judaism in Germany, 1500–1750.* New Haven and London.

COHEN, M. R. trans. and ed. 1988. *The Autobiography of a Seventeenth-Century Rabbi: Leon Modena's Life of Judah.* Princeton.

DAVIS, N. Z. 1975. *Society and Culture in Early Modern France: Eight Essays.* Stanford.

DINARI, Y. A. 1984. *The Rabbis of Germany and Austria at the Close of the Middle Ages: Their Conceptions and Halakha Writing.* Jerusalem.

ENDELMAN, T. 1979. *The Jews of Georgian England, 1714–1830: Tradition and Change in a Liberal Society.* Philadelphia.

FEBVRE, L. 1982. *The Problem of Unbelief in the Sixteenth Century: The Religion of Rabelais.* Trans. Beatrice Gottlieb. Cambridge, Mass.

FEINER, S. 1988. 'Hahaskalah ha-muqdemet be Yahadut ha-me'ah ha-shemonah esreh.' *Tarbiz* 67: 189–240.

FISHMAN, T. 1997. *Shaking the Pillars of Exile: 'Voice of a Fool,' as Early Modern Jewish Critique of Rabbinic Culture.* Stanford.

FLECKELES, D. 1800. *Ahavat David.* Prague.

GOLDISH, M. 2000–1. 'New Approaches to Jewish Messianism.' *AJS Review* 25/1: 71–83.

GRAETZ, H. 1913. *Divrei Yemei Yisrael.* Trans. (into Hebrew) S. P. Rabinovitch. Warsaw.

GRAYZEL, S. 1968. *A History of the Jews.* New York.

HALKIN, A. S. 1956. 'The Judeo-Islamic Age.' In *Great Ages and Ideas of the Jewish People.* L. Schwarz ed. New York.

HAZARD, P. 1953. *The European Mind, 1680–1715.* London.

IDEL, M. 1988. *Kabbalah: New Perspectives.* New Haven.

—— 1992. 'The Magical and Neoplatonic Interpretations of the Kabbalah in the Renaissance.' In *Essential Papers on Jewish Culture in Renaissance and Baroque Italy.* 107–69. D. Ruderman ed. New York.

—— 1993.'One from a Town, Two from a Clan: The Diffusion of Lurianic Kabbalah and Sabbateanism: A Re-examination.' *Jewish History* 7: 79–104.

ISRAEL, J. 1985. *European Jewry in the Age of Mercantilism, 1550–1750.* Oxford.

KAPLAN, Y. 1994. *Ha-Pezura ha-Sefaradit ha-Ma'aravit.* Tel Aviv.

—— 1989. *From Christianity to Judaism: The Story of Isaac Orobio de Castro.* Trans. R. Loewe. Oxford and New York.

—— MECHOULAN, H., and POPKIN, R. H. eds. 1989. *Menasseh ben Israel and his World.* Leiden, New York, and Cologne.

KATZ, J. 1961a. *Exclusiveness and Tolerance.* London.

—— 1961b. *Tradition and Crisis: Jewish Society at the End of the Middle Ages.* New York.

—— 1973. *Out of the Ghetto: The Social Background of Jewish Emancipation, 1770–1870.* Cambridge, Mass.

KRAMER, J. L. 1992. 'Spanish Ladies from the Cairo Geniza.' In *Jews, Christians, and Muslims in the Mediterranean World After 1492.* Alisa Meyuhas Ginio ed. London.

LENOWITZ, H. 1998. *The Jewish Messiahs: From the Galilee to Crown Heights.* Oxford.

MALINO, F. 1978. *The Sephardic Jews of Bordeaux.* Alabama.

MELAMMED, R. L. 1999. *Heretics or Daughters of Israel? The Crypto-Jewish Women of Castile.* New York and Oxford.

MEYER, M. 1975. 'Where Does the Modern Period in Jewish History Begin?' *Judaism* 24: 329–38.

NADLER, S. 1999. *Spinoza: A Life.* Cambridge.

PUTIK, A. 2000. 'The Prague Jewish Community in the Late 17th and Early 18th Centuries.' *Judaica Bohemia* 35: 4–140.

RAVID, B. C. I. 1988. 'The Establishment of the Ghetto Nuovissimo of Venice.' In *Yehudim be-Italya.* 35–54. H. Beinart ed. Jerusalem.

—— 1992. 'From Yellow to Red: On the Distinguishing Headcovering of the Jews of Venice.' *Jewish History* 6 (1–2): 179–210.

—— 2001. 'The Forced Baptism of Jewish Minors in Early-Modern Venice.' *Italia* 13–15: 259–301.

REUCHLIN, J. 1993. *On the Art of the Kabbalah.* Trans. Martin and Sarah Goodman. Intro. G. Lloyd Jones and Moshe Idel. Lincoln and London.

ROHRBACHER, S. 1995. 'Medinat Schwaben: Jüdisches Leben in einer süddeutschen Landschaft in der Frühneuzeit.' In *Judengemeinden in Schwaben im Kontext des Alten Reiches.* 80–109. R. Kiessling ed. Berlin.

ROTH, C. 1959. *The Jews in the Renaissance.* Philadelphia.

RUDERMAN, D. B. 1995. *Jewish Thought and Scientific Discovery in Early Modern Europe.* New Haven and London.

SCHOLEM, G. 1973. *Sabbatai Sevi: The Mystical Messiah, 1626–1676.* Princeton.

SHAPIRO, J. 1996. *Shakespeare and the Jews.* New York and London.

SHOHET, A. 1960. *Im hilufe tekufot: reshit ha-Haskalah be-Yahadut Germanyah.* Jerusalem.

SILVER, A. H. 1927. *A History of Messianic Speculation in Israel.* Repr. 1978. New York.

SORKIN, D. 1999. 'The Port Jew: Notes Toward a Social Type.' *JJS* 50: 87–97.

—— 2000. *The Berlin Haskalah and German Religious Thought.* London.

STOW, K. 2001. *Theater of Acculturation: The Roman Ghetto in the 16th Century.* Seattle and London.

SWETSCHINSKI, D. 2000. *Reluctant Cosmopolitans: The Portuguese Jews of Seventeenth Century Amsterdam.* London.

TIROSH-ROTHSCHILD, H. 1991. *Between Worlds: The Life and Thought of Rabbi David ben Judah Messer Leon.* Albany, NY.

TISHBY, I. 1954. Intro. to Jacob Sasportas, *Tzitzat Novel Tzvi.* Jerusalem.

TOAFF, A. 1988. *Love Work and Death: Jewish Life in Medieval Umbria.* Trans. J. Landry. London and Portland, Oreg.

ULBRICH, C. 1999. *Shulamit und Margarete. Macht, Geschlecht und Religion in einer ländlichen Gesellschaft des 18. Jahrhunderts.* Vienna, Cologne, and Weimar.

ULLMANN, S. 1999. *Nachbarschaft und Konkurrenz: Juden und Christen in Dörfern der Markgrafschaft Burgau, 1650–1750.* Göttingen.

WEINBERG, J. 2000 trans. *Azariah de' Rossi, The Light of the Eyes.* New Haven and London.

WEISSLER, C. 1998. *Voices of the Matriarchs: Listening to the Prayers of Early Modern Jewish Women.* Boston.

YERUSHALMI, Y. H. 1971. *From Spanish Court to Italian Ghetto: A Study in Seventeenth-Century Marranism and Jewish Apologetics.* New York and London.

YOVEL, Y. 1989. *Spinoza and Other Heretics.* 2 vols. Princeton.

YUVAL, I. 1988. *Scholars in their Time: The Religious Leadership of German Jewry in the Late Middle Ages* [Hebrew]. Jerusalem.

ZIMMER, E. 1999. *The Fiery Embers of the Scholars: The Trials and Tribulations of German Rabbis in the Sixteenth and Seventeenth Centuries* [Hebrew]. Jerusalem.

CHAPTER 15

WESTERN AND CENTRAL EUROPEAN JEWRY IN THE MODERN PERIOD: 1750–1933

DAVID RECHTER

For many years, historical writing about the Jewish experience in modern western and central Europe was guided by the twin lodestars of emancipation and assimilation. Historians focused either on the transformations of Jewish society that accompanied the achievement—or the aspiration to achieve—one or both of these, or on the response this engendered in society at large. While this is still for the most part true, there has been a substantial broadening and deepening of the definitions, contours, and content of these concepts. This is not merely new wine in old bottles; rather, new questions have been asked, new angles of vision developed, new methodologies introduced, and a more variegated and diverse picture of Jewish society has emerged as a consequence. To take just one example, the notion of 'assimilation' has by and large given way to 'acculturation', a concept that allows for greater flexibility in accounting for the manifold ways in which Jews adapted to the challenges and demands of modern Europe. These developments are also evidence that modern Jewish historiography has been receptive to the transforming effects of postmodernism—whether for good or ill—and the attendant decline of a master narrative.

According to the standard model of Jewish history, the approximately half-million Jews in western and central European lands around the middle of the eighteenth century were a distinct group with a distinct place in a hierarchical society. The definition of Jews was not problematic, nor was it especially difficult to explain their functions and status in society. Some 200 years later, by the beginning of the 1930s, almost none of this was true. The over two-and-a-half million Jews in these areas were now equal citizens of their respective states, generally acculturated and comfortable members of German, French, Dutch, Czech, or Austrian society, or well on their way to becoming so. In short, the foundations and conditions of Jewish life had been transformed in every imaginable way, part of a similarly wholesale transformation of European societies, and the very notion of Jewish separateness was becoming an anachronism. If emancipated and acculturated, Jews nonetheless in many ways remained a recognizable group, whether by choice or circumstance. Partly this was a matter of self-definition, partly it was imposed from without. Their success notwithstanding, the door of acceptance for Jews was only 'half-open' (Lowenstein et al. 1997: chap. 6), the Jewish Question was still unresolved, and anti-Semitism was by no means a spent force. And while most felt these to be remnants of the past rather than a serious threat to the present or future—an entirely defensible position until the Second World War—they were to be proved horribly mistaken by the Holocaust. A standard model perforce oversimplifies, and this is no exception. It does, though, usefully provide the outlines of the story as commonly told. As already noted, in essence this story remains the reigning paradigm for the study of the Jewish experience in modern central and western Europe.

It is not, however, the whole story, nor should it be thought that it is a uniform one. Quite the contrary. The historiographical direction of this field has been increasingly to stress that diversity and difference lie at the heart of Jewish history in modern Europe. This is nicely encapsulated in the title given to a new edition of a volume that in 1990 was called *From East and West: Jews in a Changing Europe, 1750–1870*; in 1998 it reappeared as *Profiles in Diversity: Jews in a Changing Europe* (Malino and Sorkin 1990, 1998). In 1978 Jacob Katz, a senior figure of an older generation of historians, could write that '[E]mancipation, in its wider sense, occurred more or less simultaneously. It can also be said to have followed a similar, if not identical, course' (Katz 1973: 3). By 1987, when Katz edited a volume of essays called *Toward Modernity*, the contributors stressed instead that there was in fact no single European Jewish model, but rather many models (Katz 1987). Or, as the title to yet another such volume put it, there was not so much one single path of emancipation as there were *Paths of Emancipation* (Birnbaum and Katznelson 1995). While the historiographical consensus has thus moved significantly, the larger context—the centrality of emancipation—remains in place. That diversity and difference now take pride of place is unsurprising when we consider that the Jews were to be found in every European society. This is the history of an archetypal European minority, and in western and central Europe Jews were everywhere a minority and nowhere a majority. Even if we take diversity and difference as a given, we can nonetheless find threads that connect the experience of the Jews across political and cultural divides and borders. Despite the myriad ways in which Jews conceived of themselves and were conceived of by others, and despite the obvious lack of a uniform or common modern European Jewish experience, there were still some identifiable common experiences—for example, the push towards integration into the surrounding society, into the brave new world of modern Europe—that helped to define and shape the Jews and their history.

Defining the Jews and shaping their history were by no means simple tasks. This brings us directly to what is perhaps the dominant historiographical theme in this field, that of identity. Identity plays a role in modern Jewish historiography some-what akin to the intangible and invisible ether that was thought to permeate the universe in pre-relativity science, exerting an indeterminate influence on all matter. In recent decades historians of European Jewry have placed identity, both individual and collective, at the heart of their work; this is reflected in the all-pervasive historiographical themes of emancipation and acculturation, along with their by-products and ripple effects (Haskalah, religious reform, anti-Semitism, Zionism, to name but a few of the more well-known). One is hard pressed to find a book in this field that does not in some fashion address the issue of identity, whether in its title (Penslar 2001; Rozenblit 2001; Koltun-Fromm 2001; Hart 2000; Pickus 1999; Brenner and Penslar 1998; Meyer 1990; Berkovitz 1989) or in its argument. A good example of the latter is a recent history of medicine and German Jewry, where we find the following: 'Medicine and its culture have had a significant impact on the creation of modern Jewish identity' (Efron 2001: 4). Such a focus is not exclusively the domain of the modern era. As Amos Funkenstein, in writing about the entirety of Jewish history, remarked: 'Few cultures are as preoccupied with their own identity and distinction as the Jewish' (Funkenstein 1993: 1). This can apply to historians as much as to their subjects. Combining history, historiography, and self-reflection, a number of studies have explored the ways in which scholarship and scholars themselves have been instrumental in the forging of Jewish identities (Myers 1995; Schorsch 1994; Funkenstein 1993; Yerushalmi 1982).

That identity should be a leitmotif derives in large part from what is now a strongly entrenched approach that treats Jewish history as the history of a distinct and distinguishable minority, and as a universal minority at that (at least in pre-Second World War Europe). In this regard, the Jewish experience lacks nothing in terms of contemporary relevance and historical importance. One of the most influential new ideas in this field in the past two decades reflects this tendency to view Jewish history through a minority prism: the notion that, unbeknownst to themselves, German Jews by the middle of the nineteenth century formed a 'sub-culture', that they were distinct from other Germans by dint of their demography, cultural preferences, ideological strivings, and relationship with the state (Sorkin 1987). This sub-culture, defined as a 'minority group use of the majority culture...in large measure composed of elements of the majority culture, [yet]... nevertheless identifiably distinct' (Sorkin 1992: 178), was held together by a secular ideology of emancipation, by Jewishness rather than Judaism; it 'offered a distinct political outlook...a view of history [and]...a notion of German Jewry as a community' (ibid. 189). A similar perspective on Jews as a distinctive minority is evident in recent works on the Jews of, for example, Königsberg (Kaliningrad), Breslau (Wrocław), Germany, Habsburg Austria, and, in a different context, England (Schüler-Springorum 1996; Van Rahden 2000; Gotzmann, et al. 2001; Kieval 2000; Rozenblit 2001; Dubin 1999; Feldman 1994).

A minority group in any given society expends a great deal of time, thought, and energy trying to establish where, how, and indeed if it fits into the broader society. The Jews were exemplary in this respect. What did it mean to be Jewish in a modern society? Were the Jews a religious group only—'Germans of the Mosaic Faith', in a standard phrase of the time? Or were they this and more? A 'community of fate', as another popular western and central European definition of the late nineteenth century put it? An ethnic group? A people? A fully fledged secular nationality? Or a combination of some or all of these? For its part, the majority society asked similar questions from a different perspective. Could and should the Jews be accommodated as Jews into a nation state? How much should be demanded of them in terms of change and adaptation to majority mores and culture? From the Enlightenment to the Holocaust, these issues touched the lives of Jews across western and central Europe, giving rise to what came to be known, in a drastic but serviceable compression, as the Jewish Question. In reductionist and inelegant form, this can be stated as: What should be the place of the Jews in modern Europe?

It is in the form of the Jewish Question—and its concomitant, anti-Semitism—that those with an interest in the history of modern Europe most often encounter the Jews. Indeed, it is one of the principal reasons why students of modern European history ought to be interested in, and know at least something about, European Jews and their experiences. The emergence of the Jews from their separate and contained existence of pre-Enlightenment times—out of the ghetto, in shorthand—led them to become a lightning-rod for much of the opposition to the ill-understood and much-feared forces of modernization, forces that were quite naturally perceived by many as a threat to their traditions and way of life. In *fin-de-siècle* France, we have the Dreyfus affair; in Imperial Germany, the respected conservative historian Heinrich von Treitschke summoned up a storm with his pithy formulation: 'The Jews are our misfortune'—just one emblematic moment in a more than century-long German debate about the role of Jews in German society; in the Dual Monarchy of Austria-Hungary the Viennese Mayor Karl Lueger, leader of an avowedly anti-Semitic political party that enjoyed great popularity in the late nineteenth and early twentieth centuries, habitually referred to Budapest as Judapest; and at the same time, the anti-Jewish medieval blood libel was revived across central Europe with no small measure of success. Such a list could be extended indefinitely.

It should, then, come as no surprise that the Jewish Question and anti-Semitism remain central concerns of this field, not least because in terms of historical memory and popular perception the Holocaust casts such a long shadow over much of what preceded it. This shadow notwithstanding, the teleology of popular perception—that is, that anti-Semitism led inexorably to its logical conclusion in the Holocaust—has been belied by studies of anti-Semitism in different contexts that reveal its many forms. Just as the notion of emancipation has been broken down to reveal a variety of emancipations, or a variety of emancipation processes, so too anti-Semitism has lost its monolithic aspect, and we now have many anti-Semitisms, or many and varied forms of anti-Semitism (Winock 1998; Lindemann 1997; Felsenstein 1995; Harris 1994; Pauley 1992; Almog 1990; Reinharz 1987; Katz 1980). While there naturally is a relationship between anti-Semitism and the Holocaust, it is not one of inevitable progression from the former to the latter. There are few, if any, straight lines to be drawn in history. Similarly, an earlier historiographical correlate of this approach, the so-called 'lachrymose' version of Jewish history (Schorsch 1994: 376–88), the idea that Jewish history is a vale of tears and a litany of persecutions, has been largely laid to rest by a substantial body of scholarship that has focused, to draw a crude contrast, on the success rather than the failure of emancipation (Endelman 1991). Not entirely laid to rest, however. A monumental recent survey of European Jewish history, written in traditional Zionist mould, describes late-nineteenth-century German Jewry as suffering from 'a creeping socio-psychological malaise', and comments that its experience showed an 'underlying pattern of decline' which was 'inexorable' and 'irreversible'. (The condition of Russian and Polish Jewry is likewise described as 'implacably deteriorating'.) In brief, this view maintains the conviction that the post-Enlightenment period for the Jews was one of permanent and slow-burning crisis, and that the Jews in modern Europe remained 'what they had always been . . . an anomalous and peculiar people for whom no fully acceptable and secure place could be made available either in theory or in practice' (Vital 1999: 316–17, 509, 643–6, 756).

Jewish attempts to deal with the Jewish Question and anti-Semitism were the motor for the development of modern forms of Jewish political ideologies and movements. As a field of historical research, modern Jewish politics was created and elaborated in the past two to three decades (Biale 1994, 1986; Schorsch 1994: 118–32; Mendelsohn 1993; Lederhendler 1989; Frankel 1981). An earlier view, of considerable longevity, held that there was no significant political dimension to Jewish society; that as a dispersed and powerless minority Jews had no real politics. Historians of modern Jewish politics have charted the emergence and growth of new forms of Jewish politics from the mid-to-late nineteenth century. They have argued that the prevailing orthodoxy conceived too narrowly of politics as a matter of governments, states, armies, and power, and that lack of Jewish political power ought not to be confused with lack of Jewish politics or political activity. Like so much else in Jewish history, this new politics took its cues and models from the surrounding societies, adapting them along the way. Thus, the development of liberalism, nationalism, socialism, and communism saw the parallel flowering of Jewish versions of these ideologies.

While the bulk of work in this field focuses on the Jewish political heartlands of eastern Europe and the Russian Empire, it also touches upon western and central Europe (Green 1998, 1986; Hyman 1992; Frankel 1992). If in eastern Europe Jewish political culture in its dominant forms was autonomous, a politics of the masses (or striving to be so), often democratic and often demanding a full-time commitment, in western and central Europe a different model held sway. Here Jewish politics was typically part-time and oligarchic, not so much mass politics as group-interest politics. In the east, secular nationalism, radicalism, and anti-nationalist Orthodoxy battled for hegemony, while liberalism was a minority pursuit. In the west we find a mirror image: Jewish liberalism was ascendant, eclipsing autonomous Jewish nationalism, radicalism, and Orthodoxy. That the Jews were a definable group was a given for Jewish liberals. This, though, was the lowest common denominator, and no agreement existed as to what sort of group the Jews were, and how, therefore, they ought to present themselves politically. In a word, we are back to identity.

Studies have been made of the Alliance Israélite Universelle in France, the first of the great cosmopolitan Jewish political lobbying organizations (Graetz 1996), of the Centralverein, the largest liberal German Jewish organization of the late nineteenth and early twentieth centuries (Matthäus 1988; Friesel 1986; Ragins 1980; Reinharz 1975; Schorsch 1972), and of its Austrian counterpart, the Austrian Israelite Union (Wistrich 1989; Toury 1988, 1985). The Austrian Empire, with its multinational population, intensely ethnicized polity, and uneasy amalgam of eastern and western modes of Jewish politics, has attracted greater notice than elsewhere in this region, giving rise to studies of Austrian and Viennese Jewish politics (Rechter 2001; Freidenreich 1991; Budischowsky 1990; Weitzmann 1987; Palmon 1985), Zionist youth movements (Jensen 1995), Galician Jewish socialism and nationalism (Kuhn 2001; Everett 1982), Marxist Zionism (Unger 2001), and Prague liberalism (G. Cohen, 1986). This trend shows no sign of slackening, with, for example, work currently underway on biographies of prominent political figures, on Czech and Galician Jewish nationalism, and on Jewish autonomy in the empire. Much still remains to be done in other areas. The premier Jewish political movement, Zionism, continues to be the subject of thorough examination (Wendehorst forthcoming; Lavsky 1996; Shimoni 1995; Kornberg 1993; Berkowitz 1993; Abitbol 1989; Gaisbauer 1988; Eloni 1987; S. Cohen 1982), but other movements, such as the Anglo-Jewish Association, the Jewish Territorial Organization, and the Jewish Colonization

Association, have received little systematic attention to date. As expressions of a once-broad and viable Jewish political culture, all deserve more extensive treatment.

The divide between east and west in modern Jewish politics reflects another notable theme of the past few decades in this field, the notion of geography as destiny. It needs to be said that the linking of central and western Europe in this chapter is rather uncommon. The reigning historiographical division is east and west, with 'East-Central Europe' also frequently invoked, and 'Central Europe' a much-discussed and much-abused concept in its own right (Mendelsohn 1983; Katzburg 1990). These are broad descriptive categories rather than tools of analysis, but for our purposes they do transcend the merely geographic. European Jewish history in the post-Enlightenment era is often divided for convenience along a loosely drawn east–west axis, a divide that is at one and the same time part and parcel of broader historiographical trends and a product of the Jewish situation. Jews in western and northern Europe were quicker to acculturate and modernize, were less obviously different from those among whom and with whom they lived, and there were fewer of them, both in absolute terms and relative to the rest of society. Jewish eastern Europe is commonly cast as a foil lacking the modern attributes of the west, with less acculturation and integration, slower and less modernization, stronger Orthodoxy, and teeming masses rapidly increasing their numbers: in short, an almost complete Jewish society in and of itself, in contrast to an ethnic or religious group forming an integral part of the wider society.

This comes with a caveat: these are definitions that we do not need to pursue too vigorously, as doing so will only serve to drop us into a bottomless pit of uncertainties and contingencies. We should be careful not to overload these categories with too heavy a burden of explanation, nor to demand too great a degree of precision. They are useful, although somewhat unrefined and imprecise, distinctions that underlie much historiography in this field, and as such they can assist in making sense of what can be a bewilderingly complex picture. European Jewry, as should have become clear by now, was simultaneously a collective of some sort unto itself and a part of many other collectives. The boundaries between east and west were not always clear, nor is it plain what constitutes 'central'. For our purposes, central can be taken to mean the Jews of the Habsburg Empire, which managed to incorporate Jewish east and west in a single, if unwieldy and fractious, whole. Large-scale migration from east to west was a consistent feature of much of this period, so a mingling of the two was a defining characteristic of Jewish society in central and western Europe; the consequent tension and conflict arising from the ceaseless 'East meets West' has been a significant historiographical theme for some time already (Wertheimer 1987; Maurer 1986; Aschheim 1982). In any event, the east–west divide is undergoing modification, as further explorations of various cities, regions, and communities give rise to different perspectives and as angles of vision on modernity and its constituents shift (on which see below). In addition, the continuing attention to Habsburg Jewry has also contributed to a blurring of boundaries (Rozenblit

2001; Rechter 2001; Kieval 2000, 1988; Katz 1998; Patai 1996; Wrobel 1994; Silber 1992; Löwenheim 1991; Beller 1989; McCagg 1989; Wistrich 1989; Oxaal *et al.* 1987; Palmon 1985).

The overarching framework for much of what has been discussed above—the core issue of identity, the minority perspective, the still-regnant emancipation paradigm, the Jewish Question, the east–west divide—is the search for the modern. In other words, the many and various ways in which European Jews became modern is now a staple of historical discourse and can be said to characterize the historiography in this field. But here again we need to be careful with our terminology. The very idea of modernity, and a Jewish variant thereof, has itself been the subject of exhaustive discussion. As a historian of the American Revolution has written: 'Making modernity their grail gives historians a strong incentive to discover telltale signs of its emergence' (Rakove 2001: 32). While it is possible to ponder this at considerable length and with considerable sophistication (Meyer 1975), it is equally possible— and more practical for our purposes—to take a prosaic, common-sense approach. Most historians work on the assumption that they can recognize European modernity in the broadest sense when they see it; modernization often functions as a catch-all phrase, implicitly conveying a series of large-scale forces that worked to transform western (and sometimes central) European societies. We can pinpoint three such forces that directly affect the Jews of these regions, beginning in the century or so leading up to our mid-eighteenth-century starting-point: Enlightenment, mercantilism/early capitalism, and absolutism and the strengthening of centralized authority. All of these continue to receive intensive attention from historians (Penslar 2001; Ruderman 2000; Sorkin 2000; Dubin 1999; Israel 1997).

A whole host of related developments came into play as indirect outgrowths of these major forces: industrialization, urbanization, secularization, increasing religious tolerance (or at least moves towards this), social and economic mobility— many of which can be subsumed under the banner of liberalism, a political, social, and cultural ideology that seemed for much of the nineteenth century to promise a brighter and more civilized future for all. Jews enthusiastically hitched their wagons to the forward march of liberalism, and were well recompensed for so doing, as it was under the liberal aegis that Jews were promised civic and legal equality and its supposed correlate, integration into modern society. In sum: the aspiration to, and partial achievement of, emancipation and integration—in a word, modernity— remains omnipresent in the historical treatment of the Jewish experience in this period. And to reiterate what has already been made clear, this was the furthest thing imaginable from a straight line: not the smooth rise and rise of Jewish modernity, of integration and acculturation, but rather an endlessly complex process of back and forth, success and failure, mutual accommodation and rejection.

The history of German Jewry has traditionally been the case study par excellence of the difficulties involved in this process, and if many other cases are by now well documented, German Jewry's experience is still the subject of an industry of research. A recent multi-authored four-volume historical synthesis bears witness to this. Its titles, too, tell us much about the continuing vitality of the reigning paradigm: *Tradition and Enlightenment; Emancipation and Acculturation; Integration in Dispute; Renewal and Destruction* (Breuer and Graetz 1996; Brenner *et al.* 1997; Lowenstein *et al.* 1997; Barkai and Mendes-Flohr 1998). But Germanocentrism, the once-powerful notion that Germany could be used as a model for the development of other Jewish societies, is a thing of the past, eroded in recent decades by a marked tendency to look further afield, both geographically and conceptually. This broadening of horizons is also a function of enlarging the views of what constitutes Jewish modernity, and on the nature of the historical processes that led to it. It should be noted, though, that the old dispensation has not entirely disappeared. German Jewry has recently been described, for example, as 'in some ways the most advanced of the western communities, in many eyes the most important' (Vital 1999: 311). But this attitude is now notable for being the exception rather than the rule.

A good case study of how the field has developed, in terms of becoming increasingly complex and sophisticated in its examination of historical processes, is research on the Haskalah, the Jewish Enlightenment movement, where many of the themes and developments discussed above are evident. The dominant tenor of Haskalah scholarship for the past century-and-a-half has been the relationship of the Haskalah to Jewish modernization, investigating 'whether it was cause or effect, syndrome or symptom' (Feiner and Sorkin 2001: 2). Until a few decades ago it was taken as axiomatic that the Haskalah, initiated in the latter decades of the eighteenth century and dominated by paradigmatically modern German Jews, launched European Jewry into a modernizing transformation. Now, though, the Haskalah is being both dethroned and deconstructed. In the same fashion that the grand and rather monolithic historiographical edifices of emancipation and anti-Semitism fractured to give way to more varied and subtle readings, so too the new wave of determinedly historicist Haskalah history wishes to 'restore to the Haskalah ambiguity and equivocality, detail and texture' (ibid. 2–3). What is involved here is both rethinking and fine tuning. It has been suggested, for example, that we need to differentiate between an early and late Haskalah, each of which manifested distinctive but related intellectual, religious, and ideological tendencies (ibid. Sorkin 2000). Further, the economic and medical analyses of Haskalah writers have been examined and mined both for what they say about late-eighteenth-and early-nineteenth-century Jewish society and for their role in the apparently ubiquitous quest for the modern (Efron 2001; Penslar 2001).

Complementary to this rethinking, the notion of the Haskalah as the 'big bang' of Jewish modernization is being questioned as different strands of modernization are scrutinized—religious, intellectual, secular, political, cultural, economic—in different regions. More than twenty years ago, for example, the methodology of social history was brought to bear as a counterpoint to the prevailing duopoly of the history-of-ideas and Haskalah-focused Germanocentrism. The traditional view subscribed to the trickle-down theory, positing that ideas made history and that intellectual and social elites initiated the processes of historical change. These assumptions were challenged by work on Anglo-Jewry, where an almost unsung modernity of a different hue needed no Haskalah to set it in motion. This work included a strong focus on non-elite Jewish society, on the poor, the pickpockets, and the pugilists as exemplars of an unarticulated and unforced modernity, a world apart from idea-driven intellectuals and merchant savants (Endelman 1979, 1990). Recently, building on this idea but tweaking it, the notion of an identifiably English form of Haskalah has been cautiously raised, staking out a middle ground and arguing that both approaches—historical change from above, historical change from below—are part-right, part-wrong (Ruderman 2000). An entirely typical example, it should be said, of the way in which historiographical debates proceed.

Similarly important in widening the scope of the search for the modern has been work on Sephardi Jews, descendants of the expulsions and migrations from the Iberian peninsula that began in the late fifteenth century. The economically and socially successful Jews of sixteenth-and seventeenth-century Amsterdam, for example, have been depicted as an acculturated and cultivated minority, their lifestyle and status providing something of a foretaste of what was to become possible only in the nineteenth century for their Ashkenazi counterparts, but with fewer (although some) of the anxieties and dilemmas posed by the later Jewish Question (Kaplan 2001; Bodian 1997). In the same vein, studies of Italian Jewry and of the Sephardim of seventeenth-and eighteenth-century England and France have stressed their readiness to engage with cultural, intellectual, and social influences and values of the surrounding society. This was a reciprocal accommodation: the Sephardi Jewish embrace of these non-Jewish societies was met with a relative willingness on the part of the hosts to open their doors to these particular Jews on terms considerably less onerous than those later expected of much of German and central European Jewry (Dubin 1999; Bonfil 1994; Endelman 1990; Malino 1978). The elaboration of these fast-track and seemingly less angst-ridden processes of Sephardi modernization has further contributed to the historiographical decentring of Germany and the German Haskalah (Kaplan 2000). Although Sephardi Jews became an increasingly outnumbered minority in much of western and central Europe during the nineteenth century, a result of continuing eastern European Jewish immigration, their significance as an ideal type or role model for Jewish modernity should not be underestimated (Schorsch 1994: 71–92).

A related, and potentially significant, development with regard to moving the German model of modernization from centre-stage is the recently minted concept of 'Port Jews'. The Port Jew has been proposed as a 'social type' to complement two classic modernizing agents in central Europe: the seventeenth-and eighteenth-century Court Jews, who provided a range of invaluable financial, military, and supply services to the ruling courts in central Europe while at the same time acting as representatives of Jewish communities there, and the late eighteenth-and early nineteenth-century Enlighteners (commonly known as maskilim). Port Jews were 'merchant Jews of sephardi or, to a lesser extent, Italian extraction who settled in the port cities of the Mediterranean, the Atlantic seaboard and the New World'. In these societies, which put a premium on commerce, the Jews founded settlements 'that were constituted not as autonomous communities subject to special Jewry laws but as merchant corporations (Trieste, Bordeaux) or voluntary religious associations (London, Amsterdam). These communities often enjoyed extensive privileges... and some were among the first to attain the rights characteristic of emancipation.' And, once more, the question of identity appears inseparable from the question of modernity: 'The port Jew can... be said to represent a... particular path to modernity... [S]ome port Jews pioneered a new form of identity in which Judaism was comprised not of religious practice or belief but a form of ethnic loyalty manifest in solidarity with a community' (Sorkin 1999: 88–9, 96–7; Dubin 1999). Moreover, the geographical spread of Port Jews suggests that investigation of their experiences can also help to further the shift away from the restrictive bipolarity of the east–west paradigm discussed above.

Playing a role both in the pursuit of the modern and in the move away from the German-centred perspective is Jewish historiography's version of the English channel, that is, the divide between Anglo-Jewish history and that of the continent. In recent decades an older, apologetic and celebratory Anglo-Jewish historiography has been superseded by a more critical approach that draws on themes familiar to historians of continental European Jewry (emancipation—or in the Anglo-Jewish context, the non-issue of emancipation—acculturation and integration, the Jews as a distinctive minority or otherwise, anti-Semitism and the existence of a Jewish Question) in its discussion of the markedly different British context. This has engendered a heated debate, an Anglo-Jewish *Historikerstreit* that focuses not on the adoption of different methodologies or perspectives such as social or ethnic history, about which there is little disagreement, but on the issues raised, the questions asked, and the far-reaching conclusions drawn. Put differently, to what degree is it relevant and useful to examine Anglo-Jewish history using the analytical categories and definitions that have become normative in the study of the history of the Jews of western and central Europe? Are we comparing like with like? (Endelman 1999, 1979; Rubinstein 1996; Stansky 1995; Feldman 1994; Cesarani 1990.)

One aspect of this debate can also be construed as an alternative, or expanded, perspective to the east–west axis. The claim has been made that Anglophone Jewry deserves more attention as a coherent and self-conscious entity, and that the Jews of the United States, Great Britain, and the present and former Commonwealth countries have led the way in terms of Jewish integration and acculturation. Unlike anywhere on the continent, so this argument runs, the new Jewish world (and Britain) knew no Jewish Question, the issue of the Jewish presence often being subsumed into the larger matter of mass immigration. Consequently, Jews suffered from less—and less intense—anti-Semitism and were more secure and successful than anywhere in Europe. Furthermore, the demographic balance of power in the Jewish world had already markedly shifted away from Europe before the Second World War (Rubinstein 1996). This view uses as its primary reference point Anglophone pluralist liberal democracy, detaching Anglo-Jewry from its European context in favour of a link to American and other Anglophone Jewries (and quite clearly audible here are echoes of other debates about Britain's relationships with Europe and the United States). Clearly, there are limits to the degree of possible detachment, especially given the large migration from eastern Europe into all these countries from the late nineteenth century. Yet this perspective does provide an intriguing potential modification to the influential continental east–west model, as well as furnishing further material for thought about the differing roads to, and versions of, Jewish modernity.

These varying perspectives would seem to indicate that (like identity) modernity, in the minds of historians at least, 'has a nasty habit of emerging all the time' (Rakove 2001: 33). The 'Jewish doctor', for example, has recently been described as 'a harbinger of modernity... Jewish physicians played an important role in... the modernization and secularization of German Jewry' (Efron 2001: 265–6). So too nineteenth-century Jewish political economists have been tapped for service, portrayed as instrumental in the Jewish 'project of reconceptualization... the move among Jews to a secular historical self-understanding' (Penslar 2001: 7). The reverse side of the coin is that the conspicuous absence of modernity has also been widely noted. Urban and rural divergences are of particular importance in this context. Studies of non-urban Jewries have made it clear that in many parts of western and central Europe what we think of as pre-modern Jewish society (i.e. mostly unacculturated, organized in corporate, tight-knit, self-contained communal structures, dominant Orthodoxy) remained a substantial force to be reckoned with in the modern period (Hyman 1991; Lowenstein 1976). Rural Jews, enmeshed in the surrounding society and economy as peddlers, traders, and dealers in agricultural products, were not merely pockets of resistance to an unstoppable modernizing tide, but formed an integral part of the Jewish landscape until well into the nineteenth century. Even in quintessentially modern and urban Amsterdam, by consensus one of the first sites of Jewish modernity, the new and the old coexisted. For much of the modern period the city was home to a very large, very poor, and largely unacculturated Jewish community (Sonnenberg-Stern 2000).

The discrete yet interconnected lives of the modern and not-so-modern have also been uncovered and explored in recent work on the various forms of Judaism that flourished right up until the Second World War (Katz 1998; Schorsch 1994; Breuer 1992; Ellenson 1990; Meyer 1988). The continuing salience of religion in modern Europe is a weighty theme of general historiography that, like so many others, has been taken up in Jewish historiography too, although here there remains much work still to be done. The fragmentation of the comparatively cohesive and unitary pre-Enlightenment Jewish community into denominations with differing religious ideologies and praxis signified a sea-change for Jewish society. Nonetheless, religion continued to play a key role in shoring up Jewish identity in the face of the challenges to both Judaism and Jewishness posed by the depredations of assimilation and the inroads of acculturation and secularism. The very possibility of separating Judaism and Jewishness, and the knotty and ambivalent relationship that developed between the two poles of this Jewish duality, were of course themselves signs of modernity, functions of increasing choice for Jews. Once more, identity, diversity, and difference are the keynotes. Emancipation and modernity still loom large as the backdrop, but studies of the rural, the poor, the Orthodox, and the religious modernizers have helped shape an image of Jewish society that incorporates a wealth of variety and heterogeneity.

Difference and diversity return us to our starting-point. If we can define certain basic continuities in the thematic direction of this field, along with some fundamental solidities in its overall conceptual architecture, it should also be clear that continuity and solidity by no means imply intellectual stagnation. There is, naturally, room for new directions as well as expansion of existing agendas. An attempt to combine these has been made in recent comparative work that aims to discern both what separates the various Jewish experiences and what connects them. Studies of this sort have tried to elucidate like and unlike on different levels, within nation states, across national and regional boundaries, and even on the broadest, pan-European level, endeavouring to see the history of each Jewish society 'as a distinctive instance of a larger set of historical processes' (Birnbaum and Katznelson 1995: 17). For all the problems involved in acquiring familiarity with diverse societies, languages, cultures, and their historiographies, such an approach would seem particularly well suited to the history of a Europe-wide minority (Wyrwa forthcoming; Liedtke and Wenderhorst 1999; Brenner *et al.* 1999; Liedtke 1998; Endelman 1997).

The numerous studies of Jewish communities of various cities, regions, and states that have appeared in the past two decades have a great deal to contribute in this regard, not only for what they tell us about the individual cases in question but also because they provide the necessary building-blocks for comparison. Given that Jews lived in so many parts of western and central Europe, it would appear safe to assume that more of the same is on the way. Galicia, for example, awaits comprehensive treatment, although it is a moot point whether this should be classified as 'central' rather than 'eastern' European Jewry (or perhaps both). Hungary, too, falls into this ambiguous category, and it too deserves more attention. More generally, some obvious gaps remain, although no attempt can be made here to be comprehensive. The revolutions of 1848, a series of events of the greatest historical magnitude that bulk imposingly large in general historiography, have been sorely neglected (Grab and Schoeps 1983; Mosse *et al.* 1981). Gender, which has received a degree of attention (Frankel 2000; Hyman 1995; Baskin 1991; Kaplan 1991), could attract more. The genre of biography is underdeveloped (although see Koltun-Fromm 2001; Stanislawski 2001; Brämer 2000; Malino 1996; Kornberg 1993), while the varieties of religious Judaism have not yet been adequately investigated in depth. The First World War, a subject intensively examined in general historiography, has only lately begun to draw serious attention (Rozenblit 2001; Rechter 2001; Levene 1992; Frankel 1988; Mosse and Paucker 1971). In short, there is no lack of possible material.

The cosmopolitan nature of the field's subject-matter finds an echo in the distribution of its institutional strongholds. North America and Israel remain the chief power centres, with a recent notable infusion of vitality coming from Germany and, to a lesser extent, Austria, where a new generation of researchers has entered the field in strength. This last group can now be said to constitute a third pillar of the Jewish historiographical establishment (with an additional buttress provided by historians in Great Britain), and it should come as no surprise that these German and Austrian historians concentrate for the most part on the history of the Jews in Germany and other German-speaking regions. Notwithstanding the obvious complications and baggage involved in pursuing Jewish historical research in post-Holocaust Germany and Austria, their work is clearly animated by the assumption that this is, after all, part of their own history. The first post-Soviet decade has also seen the emergence of a new generation of central European scholars released from the straitjacket of Marxist historical dictates and eager to explore the Jewish component of their own national histories, a trend only likely to grow.

Anything more than the most generalized prescription as to future directions would be foolhardy. The continuing integration of the subject into the broader field of modern European history is much to be desired, and in fact seems likely. It is a truism, that nevertheless bears repeating, that Jewish historiography needs to be part of general historical enquiry rather than at its margins. While some of the concerns of Jewish history are *sui generis*, the current methodologies and the overall shape of the field faithfully reflect its intellectual contexts. The very lack—or at least the decline—of a normative or master narrative testifies to this, as does the prominence of specialized disciplines, such as gender history, the history of medicine and science, or economic history, that intersect with the discipline of Jewish history, playing a part both in constructing it and locating it in wider fields of historical enquiry. This has been aptly characterized as the 'normalization' of Jewish historical scholarship, a sign of its 'integration [that word again] into the secular academy' (Endelman 1999: p. xii). Normalization and integration were of course among the primary impulses at work in the early nineteenth-century Wissenschaft des Judentums movement, the scholarly investigation of the Jewish past. In this sense, the field has demonstrated considerable continuity for nearly two centuries, and there seems every reason to believe that the aspiration to intellectual (and institutional) normalization, and the desire to maintain what has already been achieved in this regard, will remain powerful forces in the foreseeable future.

SUGGESTED READING

The volumes by Breuer and Graetz (1996), Brenner *et al.* (1997), and Lowenstein *et al* (1998), all of which offer both survey and analysis, are a good place to get acquainted with recent work in this field. Mendelsohn (1993) is a concise masterpiece, thought-provoking and eminently readable. Both Birnbaum and Katznelson (1995) and Frankel and Zipperstein (1992) provide a breadth and depth of coverage of the important themes. The documents collected in Mendes-Flohr and Reinharz (1995) bring many of these themes to life, while Friesel (1990) is a good guide to geography and history.

BIBLIOGRAPHY

ABITBOL, M. 1989. *Les Deux Terres Promises: les juifs de France et la sionisme, 1897–1945.* Paris.

ALMOG, S. 1990. *Nationalism and Antisemitism in Modern Europe 1815–1945.* Oxford.

ASCHHEIM, S. E. 1982. *Brothers and Strangers: The East European Jew in German and German Jewish Consciousness 1800–1923.* Madison, Wisc.

BARKAI, A. and MENDES-FLOHR, P. 1998. *Renewal and Destruction, 1918–45.* Vol. 4 of *German-Jewish History in Modern Times.* M. A. Meyer ed. New York.

BASKIN, J. R. ed. 1991. *Jewish Women in Historical Perspective.* Detroit.

BELLER, S. 1989. *Vienna and the Jews, 1867–1938: A Cultural History.* Cambridge.

BERKOVITZ, J. R. 1989. *The Shaping of Jewish Identity in Nineteenth-Century France.* Detroit.

BERKOWITZ, M. 1993. *Zionist Culture and West European Jewry Before the First World War.* Cambridge.

BIALE, D. 1986. *Power and Powerlessness in Jewish History.* New York.

—— 1994. 'Modern Jewish Ideologies and the Historiography of Jewish Politics.' In *Studies in Contemporary Jewry* 10: 3–16. J. Frankel ed. New York.

BIRNBAUM, P. and KATZNELSON, I. eds. 1995. *Paths of Emancipation: Jews, States, and Citizenship.* Princeton.

BODIAN, M. 1997. *Hebrews of the Portuguese Nation: Conversos and Community in Early Modern Amsterdam.* Bloomington, Ind.

BONFIL, R. 1994. *Jewish Life in Renaissance Italy.* Berkeley.

BRÄMER, A. 2000. *Rabbiner Zacharias Frankel: Wissenschaft des Judentums und konservative Reform im 19. Jahrhundert.* Hildesheim.

BRENNER M. and PENSLAR, D. J. eds. 1998. *In Search of Jewish Community: Jewish Identities in Germany and Austria 1918–1933.* Bloomington, Ind.

—— JERSCH-WENZEL, S., and MEYER, M. A. 1997. *Emancipation and Acculturation 1780–1871.* Vol. 2 of *German-Jewish History in Modern Times.* M. A. Meyer ed. New York.

—— LIEDTKE, R., and RECHTER, D. eds. 1999. *Two Nations: British and German Jews in Comparative Perspective.* Tübingen.

BREUER, M. 1992. *Modernity Within Tradition: The Social History of Orthodox Jewry in Imperial Germany.* New York.

—— and GRAETZ, M. 1996. *Tradition and Enlightenment 1600–1780.* Vol. 1 of *German-Jewish History in Modern Times.* M. A. Meyer ed. New York.

BUDISCHOWSKY, J. 1990. 'Assimilation, Zionismus und Orthodoxie in Österreich 1918–1938: Jüdisch-politische Organisationen in der Ersten Republik.' Unpublished Ph.D. diss., University of Vienna.

CARON, V. 1988. *Between France and Germany: The Jews of Alsace-Lorraine, 1871–1918.* Stanford.

CESARANI, D. ed. 1990. *The Making of Modern Anglo-Jewry.* Oxford.

COHEN, G. 1986. 'Jews in German Liberal Politics: Prague, 1880–1914.' *Jewish History* 1: 55–74.

COHEN. S. A. 1982. *English Zionists and British Jews.* Princeton.

DUBIN, L. 1999. *The Port Jews of Habsburg Trieste: Absolutist Politics and Enlightenment Culture.* Stanford.

EFRON, J. M. 2001. *Medicine and the German Jews: A History.* New Haven.

ELLENSON, D. 1990. *Rabbi Esriel Hildesheimer and the Creation of a Modern Jewish Orthodoxy.* Tuscaloosa.

ELONI, Y. 1987. *Zionismus in Deutschland: Von den Anfängen bis 1914.* Gerlingen.

ENDELMAN, T. M. 1979. *The Jews of Georgian England, 1714–1830.* Philadelphia.

—— 1990. *Radical Assimilation in English Jewish History, 1656–1945.* Bloomington, Ind.

—— 1991. 'The Legitimization of the Diaspora Experience in Recent Jewish Historiography.' *Modern Judaism* 11: 195–209.

—— ed. 1997. *Comparing Jewish Societies.* Ann Arbor, Mich.

—— 1999. *The Jews of Georgian England, 1714–1830.* Ann Arbor Paperbacks Edition. Ann Arbor, Mich.

EVERETT, L. P. 1982. 'The Rise of Jewish National Politics in Galicia, 1905–1907.' In *Nation-building and the Politics of Nationalism: Essays on Austrian Galicia.* 149–77. A. S. Markovits and F. E. Sysyn eds. Cambridge, Mass.

FEINER, S. and SORKIN, D. eds. 2001. *New Perspectives on the Haskalah.* London.

FELDMAN, D. 1994. *Englishmen and Jews: Social Relations and Political Culture 1840–1914.* London.

FELSENSTEIN, F. 1995. *Anti-Semitic Stereotypes: A Paradigm of Otherness in English Popular Culture, 1660–1830.* Baltimore.

FRANKEL, J. 1981. *Prophecy and Politics: Socialism, Nationalism, and the Russian Jews, 1862–1917.* Cambridge.

—— ed. 1988. *The Jews and the European Crisis 1914–1921.* Studies in Contemporary Jewry, 4. New York.

—— 1992. 'Modern Jewish Politics East and West (1840–1939): Utopia, Myth, Reality.' In *The Quest for Utopia: Jewish Political Ideas and Institutions Throughout the Ages.* 81–103. Z. Gitelman ed. Armonk, NY.

—— ed. 2000. *Jews and Gender: The Challenge to Hierarchy.* Studies in Contemporary Jewry, 16. New York.

—— and ZIPPERSTEIN, S. J. eds. 1992. *Assimilation and Community: The Jews in Nineteenth-Century Europe.* Cambridge.

FREIDENREICH, H. P. 1991. *Jewish Politics in Vienna 1918–1938.* Bloomington, Ind.

FRIESEL, E. 1986. 'The Political and Ideological Development of the Centralverein before 1914.' *Leo Baeck Institute Year Book* 31: 121–46.

—— 1990. *Atlas of Modern Jewish History.* New York.

FUNKENSTEIN, A. 1993. *Perceptions of Jewish History.* Berkeley.

GAISBAUER, A. 1988. *Davidstern und Doppeladler.* Vienna.

GOTZMANN, A., LIEDTKE, R., and VAN RAHDEN, T. eds. 2001. *Juden, Bürger, Deutsche: Zur Geschichte von Vielfalt und Differenz 1800–1933*. Tübingen.

GRAB, W. and SCHOEPS, J. H. 1983. *Juden im Vormärz und in der Revolution von 1848*. Stuttgart.

GRAETZ, M. 1996. *The Jews in Nineteenth-Century France: From the French Revolution to the Alliance Israélite Universelle*. Stanford.

GREEN, N. 1986. *The Pletzl of Paris: Jewish Immigrant Workers in the Belle Epoque*. New York.

—— 1998. ed. *Jewish Workers in the Modern Diaspora*. Berkeley.

HARRIS, J. 1994. *The People Speak! Anti-Semitism and Emancipation in Nineteenth-Century Bavaria*. Ann Arbor, Mich.

HART, M. B. 2000. *Social Science and the Politics of Modern Jewish Identity*. Stanford.

HYMAN, P. 1991. *The Emancipation of the Jews of Alsace: Acculturation and Tradition in the Nineteenth Century*. New Haven.

—— 1992. 'Was there a "Jewish Politics" in Western and Central Europe?' In *The Quest for Utopia: Jewish Political Ideas and Institutions Throughout the Ages*. 105–17. Z. Gitelman ed. Armonk, NY.

—— 1995. *Gender and Assimilation in Modern Jewish History: The Roles and Representation of Women*. Seattle.

ISRAEL, J. 1997. *European Jewry in the Age of Mercantilism*. 3rd edn. New York.

JENSEN, A. 1995. *Sei Stark und mutig! Chasak we' emaz! 40 Jahre jüdische Jugend in Österreich am Beispiel der Bewegung 'Haschomer Hazair' 1903 bis 1943*. Vienna.

KAPLAN, M. 1991. *The Making of the Jewish Middle Class: Women, Family, and Identity in Imperial Germany*. New York.

KAPLAN, Y. 2000. *An Alternative Path to Modernity: The Sephardic Diaspora in Modern Europe*. Leiden.

—— 2001. 'Gente Politíca: The Portuguese Jews of Amsterdam vis-à-vis Dutch Society.' In *Dutch Jews as Perceived by Themselves and as Perceived by Others*. C. Brasz and Y. Kaplan eds. Leiden.

KATZ, J. 1973. *Out of the Ghetto: The Social Background of Jewish Emancipation, 1780–1870*. Cambridge, Mass.

—— 1980. *From Prejudice to Destruction: Anti-Semitism, 1700–1933*. Cambridge, Mass.

—— ed. 1987. *Toward Modernity: The European Jewish Model*. New Brunswick.

—— 1998. *A House Divided: Orthodoxy and Schism in Nineteenth-Century Central European Jewry*. Hanover, NH.

KATZBURG, N. 1990. 'Central European Jewry Between East and West'. In *A Social and Economic History of Central European Jewry*. 33–46. Y. Don and V. Karady. eds. New Brunswick.

KIEVAL, H. J. 1988. *The Making of Czech Jewry: National Conflict and Jewish Society in Bohemia 1870–1918*. New York.

—— 2000. *Languages of Community: The Jewish Experience in the Czech Lands*. Berkeley.

KOLTUN-FROMM, K. 2001. *Moses Hess and Modern Jewish Identity*. Bloomington, Ind.

KORNBERG, J. 1993. *Theodor Herzl: From Assimilation to Zionism*. Bloomington, Ind.

KUHN, R. 2001. 'The Jewish Social Democratic Party of Galicia and the Bund.' In *Jewish Politics in Eastern Europe: The Bund at 100*. J. Jacobs ed. Basingstoke.

LAVSKY, H. 1996. *Before Catastrophe: The Distinctive Path of German Zionism*. Detroit.

LEDERHENDLER, E. 1989. *The Road to Modern Jewish Politics*. New York.

LEVENE, M. 1992. *War, Jews, and the New Europe: The Diplomacy of Lucien Wolf 1914–1919*. Oxford.

LIEDTKE, R. 1998. *Jewish Welfare in Hamburg and Manchester, c.1850–1914*. Oxford.

—— and WENDEHORST, S. eds. 1999. *The Emancipation of Catholics, Jews and Protestants: Minorities and the Nation State in Nineteenth-Century Europe*. Manchester.

LINDEMANN, A. S. 1997. *Esau's Tears: Modern Anti-Semitism and the Rise of the Jews*. Cambridge.

LÖWENHEIM, A. 1991. 'The Leadership of the Neolog Jewish Congregation of Pest in the Years 1914–1919: Its Status and Activity in the Jewish Community.' [Hebrew]. Unpublished Ph.D. diss., Hebrew University of Jerusalem.

LOWENSTEIN, S. M. 1976. 'The Pace of Modernization of German Jewry in the Nineteenth Century.' *Leo Baeck Institute Year Book* 21: 41–56.

——1994. *The Berlin Jewish Community: Enlightenment, Family and Crisis, 1770–1830*. New York.

—— MENDES-FLOHR, P., PULZER, P., and RICHARZ, M. 1997. *Integration in Dispute 1871–1918*. Vol. 3 of *German-Jewish History in Modern Times*. M. A. Meyer ed. New York.

McCAGG, W. O. 1989. *A History of Habsburg Jews 1670–1918*. Bloomington, Ind.

MAGNUS, S. 1997. *Jewish Emancipation in a German City: Cologne, 1798–1871*. Stanford.

MALINO, F. 1978. *The Sephardic Jews of Bordeaux: Assimilation and Emancipation in Revolutionary and Napoleonic France*. Tuscaloosa.

——1996. *A Jew in the French Revolution: The Life of Zalkind Hourwitz*. Oxford.

—— and SORKIN, D. eds. 1990. *From East and West: Jews in a Changing Europe, 1750–1870*. Oxford.

—— —— eds. 1998. *Profiles in Diversity: Jews in a Changing Europe*. Detroit.

MATTHÄUS, J. 1988. 'Deutschtum and Judentum under Fire: The Impact of the First World War on the Strategies of the Centralverein and the Zionistische Vereinigung.' *Leo Baeck Institute Year Book* 33: 129–47.

MAURER, T. 1986. *Ostjuden in Deutschland 1918–1933*. Hamburg.

MENDELSOHN, E. 1983. *The Jews of East Central Europe Between the World Wars*. Bloomington, Ind.

——1993. *On Modern Jewish Politics*. New York.

—— ed. 1999. *People of the City: Jews and the Urban Challenge*. Studies in Contemporary Jewry, 15. New York.

MENDES-FLOHR, P. and REINHARZ, J. eds. 1995. *The Jew in the Modern World: A Documentary History*. 2nd edn. New York.

MEYER, M. A. 1975. 'When Does the Modern Period of Jewish History Begin?' *Judaism* 24: 329–38.

——1988. *Response to Modernity: A History of the Reform Movement in Judaism*. New York.

——1990. *Jewish Identity in the Modern World*. Seattle.

MOSSE, W. E. and PAUCKER, A. eds. *Deutsches Judentum in Krieg und Revolution 1916–1923*. Tübingen.

——, and RÜRUP, R. eds. 1981. *Revolution and Evolution: 1848 in German-Jewish History*. Tübingen.

MYERS, D. N. 1995. *Re-Inventing the Jewish Past: European Jewish Intellectuals and the Zionist Return to History*. New York.

OXAAL, I., POLLAK, M., and BOTZ, G. eds. 1987. *Jews, Antisemitism and Culture in Vienna*. London.

PALMON, A. 1985. 'The Jewish Community of Vienna Between the Two World Wars, 1918–1938.' [Hebrew]. Unpublished Ph.D. diss., Hebrew University of Jerusalem.

PATAI, R. 1996. *The Jews of Hungary*. Detroit.

PAULEY. B. F. 1992. *From Prejudice to Persecution: A History of Austrian Anti-Semitism*. Chapel Hill, NC.

PENSLAR, D. J. 2001. *Shylock's Children: Economics and Jewish Identity in Modern Europe*. Berkeley.

PICKUS, K. 1999. *Constructing Modern Identities: Jewish University Students in Germany, 1815–1914*. Detroit.

PULZER, P. 1992. *Jews and the German State: The Political History of a Minority, 1848–1933*. Oxford.

RAGINS, S. 1980. *Jewish Responses to Anti-Semitism in Germany, 1870–1914: A Study in the History of Ideas*. Cincinnati.

RAKOVE, J. 2001. 'Drink Hard, Pray Hard and Simply Vanish.' *London Review of Books*, 5 Apr.: 32–3.

RECHTER, D. 2001. *The Jews of Vienna and the First World War*. London.

REINHARZ, J. 1975. *Fatherland or Promised Land: The Dilemma of the German Jew, 1893–1914*. Ann Arbor, Mich.

—— ed. 1987. *Living With Antisemitism: Modern Jewish Responses*. Hanover, NH.

ROZENBLIT, M. L. 2001. *Reconstructing A National Identity: The Jews of Habsburg Austria during World War I*. New York.

RUBINSTEIN, W. D. 1996. *A History of the Jews in the English-Speaking World: Great Britain*. Basingstoke.

RUDERMAN, D. B. 2000. *Jewish Enlightenment in an English Key: Anglo-Jewry's Construction of Modern Jewish Thought*. Princeton.

SCHORSCH, I. 1972. *Jewish Reactions to German Anti-Semitism, 1870–1914*. New York.

—— 1994. *From Text to Context: The Turn to History in Modern Judaism*. Hanover, NH.

SCHÜLER-SPRINGORUM, S. 1996. *Die jüdische Minderheit in Königsberg/Preussen, 1871–1945*. Göttingen.

SHIMONI, G. 1995. *The Zionist Ideology*. Hanover, NH.

SILBER. M. ed. 1992. *Jews in the Hungarian Economy 1760–1945*. Jerusalem.

SONNENBERG-STERN, K. 2000. *Emancipation and Poverty: The Ashkenazi Jews of Amsterdam, 1796–1850*. Basingstoke.

SORKIN, D. 1987. *The Transformation of German Jewry, 1780–1840*. New York.

—— 1992. 'The Impact of Emancipation on German Jewry: A Reconsideration.' In *Assimilation and Community: The Jews in Nineteenth-Century Europe*. 177–99. J. Frankel and S. J. Zipperstein eds. Cambridge.

—— 1999. 'The Port Jew: Notes Towards a Social Type.' *JJS*, 50/1: 87–97.

—— 2000. *The Berlin Haskalah and German Religious Thought: Orphans of Knowledge*. London.

STANISLAWSKI, M. 2001. *Zionism and the Fin de Siècle: Cosmopolitanism and Nationalism from Nordau to Jabotinsky*. Berkeley.

STANSKY, P. 1995. 'Anglo-Jew or English/British: Some Dilemmas of Anglo-Jewish History.' *Jewish Social Studies*, 2/1 (NS): 159–78.

TOURY, J. 1985. 'Troubled Beginnings: The Emergence of the Österreichisch-Israelitische Union.' *Leo Baeck Institute Year Book* 30: 457–75.

——1988. 'Years of Strife: The Contest of the Österreichisch-Israelitische Union for the Leadership of Austrian Jewry.' *Leo Baeck Institute Year Book* 33: 179–99.

UNGER, S. 2001. *Poale Zion in the Austrian Empire, 1904–1914* [Hebrew]. Tel Aviv.

VAN RAHDEN, T. 2000. *Juden und andere Breslauer: Die Beziehungen zwischen Juden, Protestanten und Katholiken in einer deutschen Grossstadt von 1860 bis 1925.* Göttingen.

VITAL, D. 1999. *A People Apart: The Jews in Europe 1789–1939.* Oxford.

WEITZMANN, W. R. 1987. 'The Politics of the Viennese Jewish Community, 1890–1914.' In *Jews, Antisemitism and Culture in Vienna.* 121–51. I. Oxaal, M. Pollak, and G. Botz eds. London.

WENDEHORST, S. forthcoming. *British Jewry, Zionism and the Jewish State, 1936–56.* Oxford.

WERTHEIMER, J. 1987. *Unwelcome Strangers: East European Jews in Imperial Germany.* New York.

WINOCK, M. 1998. *Nationalism, Anti-Semitism and Fascism in France.* Stanford.

WISTRICH, R. S. 1989. *The Jews of Vienna in the Age of Franz Joseph.* Oxford.

WROBEL, P. 1994. 'The Jews of Galicia under Austrian-Polish Rule, 1869–1918.' *Austrian History Yearbook* 25: 97–138.

WYRWA, U. forthcoming. *Von der Aufklärung zur Emanzipation: Jüdische Erfahrungen im preußisch-toskanischen Vergleich.* Tübingen.

YERUSHALMI, Y. 1982. *Zakhor: Jewish History and Jewish Memory.* Seattle.

CHAPTER 16

EASTERN EUROPEAN JEWRY IN THE MODERN PERIOD: 1750–1939

MICHAEL STANISLAWSKI

The Jewish communities of Russia, Poland, Ukraine, Lithuania, and Latvia constituted by far the largest Jewry in the world before the Holocaust. But because of a combination of factors specific to this part of the world—tsarist autocracy, Soviet repression, the vicissitudes of Jewish life in inter-war Poland, Lithuania, and Latvia, and the murder of most native Judaic scholars in the Second World War—the scholarly study of East European Jewry has lagged behind that of Western European, and particularly German, Jewry. Even before the Holocaust, the two greatest obstacles to the scholarly study of East European Jewish history and culture were both an objective and a subjective one: first, the inaccessibility of archival documents located in the Soviet Union; and second, the pervasive power of both popular and ideologized representations of East European Jewry. Already in the early years of the twentieth century there had emerged a double-edged stereotype of East European Jewry in the modern period: on the one hand, a nostalgic, reverent, romanticized image of an idyllic 'shtetl' existence—a society marked by blissful, integrated, seamless spirituality; on the other hand, this idyll was said to be engulfed in a perpetual battle for its very existence, a never-ending fight with a dastardly external enemy always either threatening or engaging in physical violence. In other words, over the blissful idyll there hovered an omnipresent cloud of pogrom that erupted regularly and steadily, until it overtook that idyll and destroyed it, in the inexorable descent of doom.

In fact, the tension between objective description and retroactive romanticization is itself centuries-old in Eastern European Jewish history. In the late seventeenth century Nathan Hannover, the most important Jewish chronicler of the devastation wreaked on Polish Jewry during the Chmielnicki Uprising of 1648, added a fascinating appendix to his account, lionizing the purity and righteousness of the communities that were destroyed. This canonization of pre-1648 Polish-Jewish society has long been criticized by professional historians as historically inaccurate, effacing the complexity and multifaceted reality of a vibrant and diverse Jewry in the sixteenth and seventeenth centuries. Similarly, after the First World War and the destruction of the life and culture of much of East European Jewry in that conflict, the Russian and Ukrainian Civil Wars, and the Soviet–Polish war, novelists, short-story writers, and sermonizers updated Hannover by immortalizing the 'world of the shtetl'—'A World That Is No More' (*a velt voz is nishto mer*), in the evocative words of the great Yiddish writer I. J. Singer. These literary re-creations were often stylistically brilliant and psychologically compelling, but they were utterly ahistorical, and their influence on the 'collective memory' of East European Jewry was vast and incalculable. Moreover, that collective memory was dramatically conditioned by the emigration of almost 5 million East European Jews to the West and to Israel in the years 1882–1924, (and then in the two major post-Second World War waves of emigration, 1945–68, and 1968–present.) Finally, in the wake of the destruction of East European Jewry in the Holocaust, it became exceedingly difficult to paint a picture of that society that did not suffer from an excess of reverence or an excess of hindsight. Indeed, to some it has seemed inappropriate—even blasphemous—to object to either side of the stereotypical view of East European Jewry, to attempt to redress popular oversimplification by means of a detached search for truth.

Over the last several decades a small group of professional historians, literary scholars, and social scientists in North America, Israel, Western Europe, and most recently in the former Soviet Union and Eastern Europe itself, has attempted to dislodge these stereotypes, to study East European Jewish history and culture without lenses tinted by nostalgia or horror, personal or familial loyalty, or political and religious commitment, not to speak of the dangers of hindsight—that is, of judging pre-Second World War Jewries through knowledge gained after their destruction but unknowable to them. This scholarly enterprise has pointed out the diversity and internal fissures of East European Jewry, and the utter ahistoricity of the concept of 'handwriting on the wall', legible only in retrospect. Within the rarefied world of the academy this attempt has been modestly successful, but the study of East European Jewry remains hampered by the multilingual complexity of that culture and by the small number of women and men willing to dedicate their lives to its scholarly reconstruction. Suffice it to say that the audience for works on the destruction of East European Jewry still far outpaces the audience for works on the history and culture of that community before its end. But the current moment holds much promise, since libraries, archives, and private collections long inaccessible to scholars of Russian, Polish, Ukrainian, and Baltic Jewries are now open, and more and more material about this fascinating civilization is coming to light with each passing day.

A CAPSULE HISTORY OF EAST EUROPEAN JEWISH SCHOLARSHIP

In order to understand the state of the field today, one must first attempt a brief (and necessarily highly selective) history of pre-Second World World scholarship on modern East European Jewry. As is well known, Wissenschaft des Judentums arrived in Eastern Europe only in the last decades of the nineteenth century, particularly among the group of scholars centred around Simon Dubnov in St Petersburg, with offshoots in Vilna, Warsaw, and Odessa. In many ways these scholars were participants in or heirs to the Haskalah movement, and indeed their ties to the Haskalah organization the 'Society for the Promotion of Enlightenment Among Russian Jewry' were intense and long-lived. With this affiliation came several crucial biases which would characterize much of Eastern European Jewish scholarship until the 1970s: a dedicated opposition to the tsarist regime, and demand for its replacement by a liberal or socialist state which would grant equal rights to the Jews and other minorities; a concomitant commitment to Jewish nationalism, of either the 'autonomist', Zionist, or Bundist variety, or in the case of Soviet-Jewish scholarship, to Bolshevik ideology on the Jews; and a virtually axiomatic derogation of traditional Judaism as an oppressive legacy to be superseded by progressive, Enlightenment-or Marxist-based Jewishness. The only exception to this neglect of traditional Jewish society was Hasidism, which could be mined as a source of populist, socialist, or neo-Romantic folk wisdom or as a font of populist resistance to the rabbinic establishment. Closely connected with this latter trend was the early and sustained popularity of folkloristic research, soon joined by attempts at sociological and economic research, also marked by a populist, and often nationalist as well as Marxist, agenda. At the same time, if somewhat paradoxically, Wissenschaft and nationalist scholarly influence began slowly to infiltrate into traditional Jewish society in Eastern Europe, and there emerged a small but interesting traditionalist scholarly movement that would grown in inter-war Poland (and then develop along unusual lines in post-Second World War America and Israel.)

Certainly the most influential products of this first, pre-First World War phase of scholarship on East European Jewish history and culture were the works of Simon Dubnov (1860–1941). His *World History of the Jewish People* was first issued in Russian and then in a reworked, ten-volume German edition (Dubnow 1925–30). There is an excellent Hebrew translation of this work (Dubnow 1964/5). Only two parts of this work have been rendered into English: the most famous and most useful is the three-volume history of the Jews in Russia and Poland, first published by the Jewish Publication Society in Philadelphia from 1916 to 1920 and recently republished (Dubnow 1975). In this classic text, Dubnov's unsurpassed master narrative is grand in scope and in nationalist, anti-tsarist fervour, and should be used with this in mind. An English translation of other parts of the *World History* (Dubnow 1967–73) is utterly unreliable. Among Dubnov's other remarkable historical works are his history of Hasidism, originally written in Hebrew as *Toledot hahasidut* (Dubnow 1930–2), still not translated into English, though available both in Yiddish and in German editions. Dubnov was also instrumental in the compilation of the first-rate Russian-Jewish encyclopaedia, *Evreiskaia entsiklopediia* (1906–13), which is still the best reference work in any language on pre-1914 East European Jewry. Among the most useful early productions of Russian-Jewish scholarship are: Iulii Gessen's more detached political history of Russian Jewry (Gessen 1925) and S. M. Ginzburg and P. S. Marek's authoritative collection of Yiddish folksongs (Ginzburg and Marek 1901). In addition, there is an interesting Russian-language collaborative history of the Jews focusing on East European Jewry, with fundamental information on Polish-Jewish history, edited by Majer Balaban (Balaban 1914). Finally, there is an excellent bibliography of all works on Russian Jewry published in Russian before 1892 (*Sistematicheskii ukazatel'* 1892). A prime example of the intersection between Haskalah, Wissenschaft, and traditionalist scholarship is the most extensive attempt at a history of halachah to date, Chaim Tchernowitz's *Toledot ha-poskim*, written in Russia but only published in the New World (Tchernowitz 1946–7).

For several years after the Russian Revolution, scholarship on the Jews progressed in the Bolshevik-run state, albeit under increasingly tense political constraints. Most interesting are the volumes of the periodical of the St Petersburg Historical-Ethnographic Society entitled *Evreiskaia starina*, which continued to appear intermittently until 1930 and included valuable materials from previously closed tsarist archives. One of the editors of this journal, Saul Ginzburg, emigrated to the United States, where his highly valuable works were published in Yiddish under the title *Historishe verk*. At the same time, the literary scholar Israel Zinberg continued to write his invaluable history of Jewish literature, first published in Yiddish in 1930–7 (Zinberg 1972–8). As Stalinism progressed, works on Jewish themes were more and more subjected to political censorship, a process well documented in Alfred Abraham Greenbaum's study (Greenbaum 1978). Perhaps ironically, some of the most innovative works were published under the auspices of the Academy of Sciences of the USSR—including the Ukrainian journal *Zbirnyk prats' Akademiia nauk URSR, Evreis'ka istovyko-arkheografichna komisiia* (Zbirnyk 1928–9).

Quite a different situation obtained in inter-war Poland, where Jewish scholarship faced little if any political constraints, but where increasingly limited access to university education and declining material conditions hampered progress in Judaic Wissenschaft. Of highest importance are the many works of Majer Balaban, the dean of Polish-Jewry history (on him, see Biderman and Balaban 1976). Of primary importance is Balaban's bibliography on the history of Polish Jewry (Balaban 1939) and his many monographs on the history of the Jews in Galicia, for example, his history of the Jews in Krakow and Kazimierz (Balaban 1931) and his path-breaking history of the Reform synagogue of Lwow (Balaban 1937). Other noted Jewish scholars active in inter-war Warsaw included the social and economic historian Ignacy Schipper, whose history of Jewish trade in Poland (Schipper 1937) is still of great utility, and the works of the young Emanuel Ringelblum, whose study of Jews in the Kosciuszko rebellion showed great promise (Ringelblum 1938).

In 1925 the YIVO Institute for Jewish research was founded in Vilna and became the centre of a dedicated group of Yiddishist historians, literary scholars, and social scientists. Of fundamental importance is YIVO's *Historishe shriftn* (YIVO 1929–39), *Filologishe shriftn* (YIVO 1926–9), and *Shriftn far psikhologye un pedagogik* (YIVO 1933–40). YIVO's influence spread far beyond Vilna, as witnessed by the publication of its Lodz branch, *Lodzsher visnshaftlekhe shriftn* (Lodzsher 1938). To gauge the nature of YIVO's highly engaged Yiddishist scholarship, see Max Weinreich (1935) and Dawidowicz (1989). Parallel to this expansion of secular Jewish scholarship in inter-war Poland was the proliferation of traditional Jewish scholarship; for one example of Orthodox Jewish historiography see the works of Isaac Lewin (Lewin 1932) and the relevant sections of Salo Wittmayer Baron's *Bibliography of Jewish Social Studies, 1938–1939* (Baron 1941).

At the same time, of course, scholarship on East European Jewry was produced by academics in Western Europe, the Palestinian Yishuv, and America. The Berlin branch of the YIVO Institute produced a series of very important volumes, including *Shriftn far ekonomik un statistik* (YIVO 1928–32), edited by the most important sociologist of the Jews in this period, Jacob Lestchinsky; and I. M. Cherikover issued a vital study of the pogroms in Ukraine in the Civil War period (Cherikover 1923). But the most influential writings by far on East European Jewry emanating from inter-war Germany were the works on Hasidim by Martin Buber, whose neo-Romantic retellings of the stories of Hasidic masters were world-famous and contributed mightily to the stereotypical rendering of East European Jewish society.

In Palestine, the so-called 'Jerusalem School' centred around the Hebrew University of Jerusalem included several important scholars of East European Jewry, including Ben-Zion Dinaburg, later Dinur, and Yosef Klausner. Both these scholars brought an intense Zionist commitment to their scholarly work; as a result, although highly influential in their time, by the late twentieth century their scholarly

writings were largely dismissed as overwhelmed by their ideological fervour. Nonetheless, Klausner's *Historiah shel ha-sifrut ha-ivrit ha-hadashah* (Klausner 1930–50)
is still highly useful for its bibliographical and biographical data. Of course, the
works of Gershom Scholem touching upon East European Jewish history, and
particularly Hasidism, were of crucial importance and remain highly influential,
if always controversial. In the United States, émigré historians worked largely
outside the academic establishment, and increasingly under the auspices of the
New York branch, and then headquarters, of the YIVO Institute. Among these
scholars was Jacob Shatzky, the author of the three-volume history of the Jews of
Warsaw (Shatzky 1947–53), and I. M. Cherikover, the editor of the two-volume
history of the Jewish Labor Movement (Cherikover 1943–5). Finally, the dean of
American Jewish historians, Salo Wittmayer Baron, dealt to some degree with East
European Jewish developments in the first edition of his *Social and Religious History
of the Jews* (Baron 1937). Only one of Baron's students, Isaac Levitats, wrote a
dissertation which was published as a separate book (Levitats 1943). Of a far
different order was a work by a Polish-trained scholar temporarily in the United
States, Raphael Mahler's Marxist-Zionist account of the struggle between Hasidism
and Haskalah in Galicia in the first half of the nineteenth century (Mahler 1942).
Although based on a remarkable database and thorough knowledge of the subject,
Mahler's highly tendentious analysis makes for painful reading today.

The end of the Second World War in 1945 marked the demise of East European
Jewish scholarship *in situ.* Soviet scholars were essentially forbidden to work on
matters Jewish, and this prohibition—and the corollary closing of archives—con-
tinued until the last years of the Gorbachev era. In Poland, a Jewish Historical
Institute was established in Warsaw, but its focus was almost exclusively on the
Holocaust, and its staff was dramatically affected by the vagaries of Stalinism and
post-Stalinism in communist Poland, including a purge of its personnel in the anti-
Jewish government actions in 1968. The lone unaffiliated Jewish historian to remain
active was Artur Eisenbach, whose many works on nineteenth-century Polish-
Jewish history are absolutely crucial to the study of that subject: most successful
was his study of the struggle for the emancipation of Polish Jewry (Eisenbach 1972);
less so was his later history of that emancipation (Eisenbach 1991).

But through the decades of the 1950s and 1960s, by far the most active centre of
research and writing on East European Jewish history and culture was the Hebrew
University of Jerusalem. The most influential historian of the period was Shmuel
Ettinger, who unfortunately did not publish much; his lectures on modern Jewish
history as a whole, including that of Eastern Europe, were published in Hebrew and
then in English in the collaborative volume edited by his colleague H. H. Ben-Sasson
(Ben-Sasson 1976), and his massive research into Russian anti-Semitism in Ettinger
(1978). Less famous but to some degree more productive was Israel Halperin, who
edited a collaborative history of Polish Jewry (Halperin 1948–53), and published a
collected volume of essential studies (Halperin 1968). A crucial new voice in East

European Jewish scholarship was that of Chone Shmeruk, who moved from the study of history to that of Yiddish literature, and whose early works included the editing of the first collection of Soviet-Yiddish poetry and prose (Shmeruk 1964). At Tel Aviv University, important work was done on the Jewish labour movements and especially socialist Zionism by Moshe Minc and Moshe Mishkinsky. Finally, although at first sidelined by the Hebrew University establishment, the masterful historian Jacob Katz gradually came to prominence both at home and abroad, and his *Tradition and Crisis*, first published in Hebrew in 1958 and in English in 1961, set the study of East European, and particularly traditional, Jewish history and culture on a new track, informed by German sociological methodology.

In the United States, the 1950s and early 1960s marked a not especially fruitful period for scholarship on East European Jewish history and society. The circle around YIVO, now with its headquarters in New York, continued to produce important works of scholarship, but with little connection to the outside academic world, except in the realm of Holocaust research. Émigré scholars continued to publish (e.g. Schwartz 1951, and Aronson *et al.* 1960). In 1964 Salo Baron contributed the best up-to-date history of Russian Jewry to that time (Baron 1964), although this volume did not live up to Baron's usually meticulous level of scholarship. It is still useful and far superior to Louis Greenberg's utterly lachrymose and unscholarly *The Jews in Russia* (Greenberg 1951). Far more innovative and still highly useful was Lucy Dawidowicz's compilation of autobiographical and memoirist accounts (Dawidowicz 1967). By far the most influential work of the period, however, was *Life Is with People* (Zborowski and Herzog 1952), a quasi-anthropological, highly ahistorical, and methodologically perverse attempt to portray East European Jewish society; on this effort, see Barbara Kirshenblatt-Gimblett's introduction to the new 1995 Schocken edition.

Thus, by the mid-1960s there was a solid corpus of scholarly work on Eastern European Jewish history and culture, built upon the foundations established by Dubnov, Balaban, and others before the Second World War, and continued mostly at the Hebrew University in Jerusalem and at YIVO in New York. But it is crucial to note that every major scholar mentioned so far in this survey was born in Eastern Europe, learned its many languages from birth as if by osmosis, and was intimately involved both in the tragedy of the Holocaust and in the internecine battles of Jewish political and cultural warfare in Eastern Europe. Against this backdrop it is not at all surprising to note that the scholarship produced up to this point was without exception heavily influenced by overt nationalist, Zionist, and to some extent Marxian biases. It did not seem likely that a new generation of scholars, not born in Eastern Europe itself, would work these fields in the coming years. On the contrary, however, the next several decades witnessed a substantial reawakening and revitalization of scholarship on East European Jewish history and culture. First, the Hebrew University proved fertile ground for the support of research into this field, not only on the part of its own graduates but also of those of Western universities where the first expansion of Jewish studies was taking place. An interesting moment was reached when two young historians, Ezra Mendelson and Jonathan Frankel, trained in Russian and Jewish History in the United States and Britain, came to Jerusalem to teach Eastern European Jewish history outside the framework of the Jewish History Department. Their dissertations were published as *Class Struggle in the Pale: The Formative Years of the Jewish Workers' Movement in Tsarist Russia* (Mendelson 1970), and *Prophecy and Politics: Socialism, Nationalism, and the Russian Jews, 1862–1917* (Frankel 1981). These scholars' unusual institutional location betokened a radical, if gradual and at first unnoticed, departure from both the Haskalah-based East European and the heavily ideological Jerusalem School, a phenomenon one could call the 'normalization' of the field, ironically to borrow a word from the Zionist lexicon. That is, the new cohorts of scholars of East European Jewry, whether in Israel, the United States, or in Western Europe, were self-consciously committed to a more 'detached' or even 'objective' presentation of the history and culture of East European Jewish history on a par not only with the study of other Jewish communities, but more importantly perhaps, of European history and social science as a whole. Thus, whatever their personal politics, they wrote history not as committed activists, Zionists, or socialists, but solely as professional historians. This had, of course, been the dream and to some extent the self-assessment of previous historians as well, but their historical situation did not make such detachment possible. In sharp contrast, the historians coming of professional age in the 1960s and 1970s did not have the same historical, material, and to some extent life-and-death struggles to contend with, and therefore could operate in a more 'value-neutral' environment. Moreover, the expansion of Jewish studies in American and, to a lesser extent, British universities provided a vital new context to engage in less internally over-determined Judaic scholarship. Thus, for example, in addition to works in history, the first text informed by American political science theory and practice was Zvi Gitelman's groundbreaking study of Soviet Jewish policy and the Evsektsiia (Gitelman 1972). At the same time, at Columbia University in New York there developed the most important programme in Yiddish studies in the Western world, first guided by the great linguist Uriel Weinreich and then by his successor Marvin Herzog. Under Uriel Weinreich and his father, Max Weinreich at YIVO, there studied a group of innovative scholars of Yiddish literature and culture, including Dan Miron and Ruth Wisse. Miron's dissertation was published as *A Traveler Disguised: A Study in the Rise of Modern Yiddish Fiction in the Nineteenth Century* (Miron 1973), and Wisse's as *The Schlemiel as Modern Hero* (Wisse 1971).

Very soon a generational shift transformed the very heart of the Jerusalem School, the Jewish History Department at the Hebrew University, where doctoral students managed to combine the methodological and research interests of the otherwise irreconcilable Ettinger and Katz. Thus, Israel Bartal wrote a highly original doctoral dissertation entitled 'Ha-lo-yehudim ve-hevratam be-sifrut ivrit ve-yidish be-mizrah eropah ben ha-shanim 1856–1914' (Non-Jews and their Society in Hebrew and

Yiddish Literatures in Eastern Europe, 1856–1914) (Bartal 1980), still awaiting translation into English, and Immanuel Etkes broke entirely new ground in his thesis on Rabbi Yisrael Salanter and the Musar movement, completed in 1974, first published in Hebrew in 1982, and in 1993 in English as *Rabbi Israel Salanter and the Mussar Movement: Seeking the Torah of Truth* (Etkes 1993). This latter work betokened an entirely new trend in East European Jewish scholarship—serious work on traditional Jewish society, untouched either by Zionist or Marxist polemics or by apologetic Orthodoxy. This was yet another aspect of the 'normalization' of East European Jewish scholarly discourse, and owed most to the influence of Etkes's mentor Jacob Katz, who pioneered the scholarly study of Orthodoxy as a whole.

At the same time, the YIVO Institute in New York witnessed a renaissance that ultimately proved to be short-lived but led to the support of a cohort of young scholars at American Universities whose dissertations were later published (e.g. Stanislawski 1983; Zipperstein 1985; Klier 1986; Orbach 1980) and to work on Polish-Jewish history under the tutelage of the émigré historian Lucjan Dobroszycki. Other scholars, not previously active in Jewish studies, began to work on Jewish topics: for example, Henry Jack Tobias (Tobias 1972) joined the earlier Bernard K. Johnpoll (Johnpoll 1967). Moreover, the appearance of revisionist studies on Russian Jewry by three leading American historians of Russia who never before had focused specifically on the Jews—Richard Pipes's article on Catherine II and the Jews (Pipes 1975); a series of articles by Hans Rogger (later collected in Rogger 1986); and by Arcadius Kahan (Kahan 1986)—reinforced the emerging trend of North American-born scholars of East European Jewish history and culture entering the American academic mainstream, at the same time as a new generation of Israeli-born academics were transforming the study of Russian, Polish, and Ukrainian Jewry in Jerusalem and soon at the other universities in Israel. In due course this new cohort of scholars would themselves become the sponsors of graduate research and doctoral dissertations in the United States, Israel, and Britain.

Perhaps the most far-reaching, and certainly the most controversial, innovation to emerge in this period was the claim by several scholars that the long-held assumption of tsarist governmental complicity in the pogroms of 1881–2 had to be revised or rejected altogether. In a groundbreaking work, I. Michael Aronson studied anew the published accounts of the pogroms and came to the conclusion that they were unplanned, sporadic explosions of dislocated workers and had no authorization from the authorities, who on the contrary tried to quell these disorders but were unable to do so. Aronson—who unfortunately later left the academic world—later expanded upon this account (in Aronson 1990), and his view was extended to the early twentieth century in a dissertation at the University of Michigan by Shlomo Lambroza (Lambroza 1981). This fundamental revisionist tack led to a collaborative volume edited by Lambroza and Klier (1992). Soon, an entire book arguing essentially this point would be dedicated to the most infamous pogrom of the late tsarist period, that in Kishinev in 1903 (Judge 1992).

In due course, the most innovative works produced by the new cohort of scholars, both in the United States and in Israel, were on the cultural and ideological history of East European Jewry in the modern period (as well as on pre-Partition Polish Jewry and on Hasidism, covered in other chapters in this volume). Not surprisingly, scholars came to see the importance of revisiting the Haskalah and the Zionist movement, and there appeared, *inter alia*, works by Mendelson (1981), Shapira (1984), Stanislawski (1988), Lederhendler (1989), and Zipperstein (1993). A parallel development was the re-emergence, in Israel, Western Europe, and North America, of interest of Jews in modern Poland: in 1973 Tel Aviv University began to publish an excellent journal on Polish-Jewish history, entitled *Gal-Ed*, and in England in 1986 the Institute for Polish-Jewish Studies launched the important journal *Polin*. In the latter year a peculiar but highly useful bibliography on Polish-Jewish history was published by George J. Lenski and Halina T. Lerski (Lenski and Lerski 1986). Soon a fascinating book was published in collaboration between the Israeli scholar Israel Bartal and the Canadian scholar Magdalena Opalski (Bartal and Opalski 1992). Of the many works to appear in the mid- and late 1990s that dealt with modern East European Jewish history and culture, perhaps the most noteworthy was that by Feiner (1995), which thoroughly revised the study of the Haskalah's attitude to Jewish history.

THE FIELD TODAY

Despite this flourishing of publications on Jewish history in modern Eastern Europe, as noted in the introductory section, this field remains beset by several fundamental problems, the most prevalent of which is the nearly absolute failure of the scholarly enterprise to affect popular perceptions of East European Jewish history, which remain mired in the lachrymose/romanticized stereotypes discussed above. To a small extent the most recent rise of near-professional and professional interest in Jewish genealogy has begun to lessen the popular resistance to the scholarly enterprise, as genealogists discover more and more records of Jewish history in Eastern Europe and become aware of the fascinating complexities of that society.

On the scholarly front several major lacunae remain, which can be broken down into a variety of categories:

(1) *Geographical*: for reasons which are not entirely clear, the vast bulk of the scholarship on modern East European Jewish history has focused on the Jews of the Pale of Settlement. The other Jewish communities of late-eighteenth- and nineteenth-century, and pre-First World War East European Jewry have received far less attention. Mention has already been made of Artur Eisenbach's important works on the Jews of Congress Poland, but these concerned only a small part of

the history of that fascinating community. Since Balaban's day there has been little if any serious scholarly investigation of the Jews of Galicia, the southern Polish province annexed by Austria from the late eighteenth century to the First World War (with the small and problematic exception of Mahler's history of the clash between Hasidism and the Haskalah in Galicia noted above). Ezra Mendelson did some pioneering work on Galician-Jewish history (reflected in Mendelson 1983), but unfortunately his lead has not been followed with sustained monographical research, though several dissertations are now being written on aspects of Orthodox society in Galicia, and Mendelson himself is completing a biography of the important Galician-Jewish artist Maurycy Gottlieb. Similarly, the Jewish community of the north-west provinces of Poland annexed by Prussia has received very little scholarly attention (for now there is only the useful (but preliminary) Hagen 1980).

(2) *Demographic and Social History*: perhaps the most glaring lack in the historiography of East European Jewry in the modern period is the absence of sustained demographic or social histories of Jewish communities throughout the length and breadth of Eastern Europe, of the order of the two excellent such studies on the pre-Partition period (Hundert 1992 and Rosman 1990). Until and unless many more such studies are researched and written, on the basis of now available archival material, much of what we think we know about the essential social, economic, and demographic history of East European Jews remains highly tentative. Recently some important studies on this front have appeared in Polish (e.g. Zalewska 1996).

(3) *Gender and Women's History*: obvious but crucial to note is that the works listed heretofore have focused almost exclusively on males and on the historical experience and representations of East European Jewish men. Three pioneering works exploring the gender dynamics of East European Jewry (Hyman 1995, Balin 2000, and Freeze 2001) are but the beginning of scholarship into this crucial topic. Of great importance is Ada Rapoport-Albert's absolutely path-breaking study (Rapoport-Albert 1988).

(4) *New Views on 'Assimilation', and 'Assimilated Jews'*: one of the corollaries of the highly ideologized nature of scholarship on East European Jewish history is the broad acceptance of the terms 'assimilation,' and 'assimilationism', to denote the world-view of Jews who did not share in the ideologies of modern Jewish nationalism or who tried to create a Jewish culture in the Russian and Polish (and to a far lesser extent, Ukrainian) languages (on this phenomenon see Mendelson 1993 and Stanislawski 2001). The most important works on Russian-Jewish culture are by Nakhimovsky (1992), Safran (2000), and an unpublished dissertation by Olga Litvak (Litvak 1999). Alas, comparable monographs on the potentially even more fascinating Polish-Jewish culture and society have not yet appeared (Heller 1977 is useful but conceptually outdated; unfortunately, Guterman 1993 is conceptually muddled).

(5) *Traditional and Non-Traditional Jewish Society in Eastern Europe*: as noted above, one of the most important trends in contemporary scholarship on East European Jewish history is the new-found interest in traditional Jewry and Judaism in the modern period, beyond the vital studies on Hasidism. The early work of Immanuel Etkes of the Hebrew University has already been highlighted in this regard; see also his study of Lithuanian learned circles in Jerusalem (Etkes 1991). On non-Hasidic Jewry see also Nadler (1997) and Shapiro (1999). It is not in the least to slight these works to remark that they represent but the tip of the iceberg of the work that must be done to understand traditional Jewish society and intellectual life, in all its permutations and manifestations, in the modern period. In contrast, there is no extant work whatsoever on non-traditional Judaism in modern Eastern Europe, a much smaller but historically pregnant topic last critically studied in 1937 by Majer Balaban (for now see the vital information in Meyer 1988).

(6) *Memoirs, Autobiographies, and Memorial Volumes*: there is a vast literature of memoirs and autobiographies written by East European Jews in the last century-and-a-half, and a parallel library of memorial volumes commemorating Jewish communities in Eastern Europe, known in Yiddish as 'yizker bikher', and usually published by associations of survivors. These genres are of fundamental importance both as source materials and as repositories of collective memory, but there has been little sustained scholarly analysis of the ways in which these materials can be used as resources for the analytic reconstruction of East European Jewish history in the modern period, particularly against the backdrop of the enormous amount of recent literary scholarship on autobiographical writing and the substantial academic analysis of collective memory and popular historiography. For a bibliography of the memorial books, see the appendix by Zachary M. Baker (Baker 1998).

(7) *Scholarship* in situ: after the fall of communism, scholarship on the modern history of Eastern European Jewry began slowly to emerge once more in Russia, Poland, the Ukraine, and Lithuania. To date, the most successful such enterprises are the various Jewish research institutes (often called 'universities' in local parlance), in Moscow, St Petersburg, and Vilnius, as well as the Jewish Historical Institute in Warsaw and at the Jagiellonian University in Krakow. While important materials and studies have begun to be published in these and other centres, no major monographs have as yet appeared, largely due to the necessity of training an entirely new generation of scholars in the methodologies of Western critical scholarship as well as Wissenschaft des Judentums, not to speak of the basics of Judaism as well as Hebrew and Yiddish. Impressive efforts have been made in this direction, however, and the future looks promising, if modest.

CONCLUSION

In sum, as of this writing, the study of the modern history of East European Jews is not a field (like some others surveyed in this volume) riven at present by deep conceptual or ideological divides or abiding scholarly or methodological controversies. The past debates on this score between Israeli and diaspora Jewish scholarship have all but disappeared, as has even more dramatically the attempt at a Marxist version of *juedische Wissenschaft*. While the major works of the founders of the field from Simon Dubnov on ought still to be celebrated, and more importantly, still studied, and as we note the recent impressive resurgence of interest in the history and culture of East European Jewry in the modern age, the work before us is still vast and largely undone. In the end, as at the beginning, the crucial challenge to the field is not to succumb to the lachrymose and romanticized stereotypes of Jewish life in Eastern Europe, at the same time as we find the will, the personnel, and the resources to continue to explore the history of this largest Jewry in the world before the Holocaust.

SUGGESTED READING

For the study of Eastern European Jewry in the modern period, one is advised to begin by consulting the following works: Dubnow (1975), Stanislawski (1983), Mendelsohn (1983), and Baron (1964).

BIBLIOGRAPHY

ARONSON, G., HERTS, Y. S., et al. 1960. *Di geshikhte fun bund*. New York.

ARONSON, I. M. 1990. *Troubled Waters: The Origins of the 1881 Anti-Jewish Pogroms in Russia*. Pittsburgh.

BACON, G. 1996. *The Politics of Tradition: Agudat Yisrael in Poland, 1916–1939*. Jerusalem.

BAKER, Z. M. 1998 *Appendix to From a Ruined Garden: The Memorial Books of Polish Jewry*. Ed. and trans. by J. Kugelmass and J. Boyarin. 2nd expanded edn. Bloomington, Ind.

BALABAN, M. 1914. *Istoriia evreiskago naroda*. Moskva.

—— 1931. *Histoja Zydow w Krakowie i na Kazimierzu, 1304–1868*. Cracow.

—— 1937. *Historia Lwowskiej synagogi postepowej*. Lwow.

—— 1939. *Bibliografia historii Zydow w Polsce i w krajach osciennych za lata 1900–1930*. Warsaw.

BALIN, C. 2000. *To Reveal our Hearts: Jewish Women Writers in Tsarist Russia*. Cincinnati.

BARON, S. W. 1937. *Social and Religious History of the Jews*. 3 vols. New York.

—— 1941. *Bibliography of Jewish Social Studies, 1938–1939*. New York.

—— 1964. *The Russian Jew Under Tsars and Soviets*. New York.

BARTAL, I. 1980. 'Ha-lo-yehudim ve-hevratam be-sifrut ivrit ve-yidish be-mizrah eropah ben ha-shanim 1856–1914.' Unpublished diss., Hebrew University.

—— and OPALSKI, M. 1992. *Poles and Jews: A Failed Brotherhood.* Hanover, NH.

BEN-SASSON, H. H. 1976. *History of the Jewish People.* Cambridge, Mass.

BIDERMAN, I. and BALABAN, M. 1976. *Historian of Polish Jewry.* New York.

CHERIKOVER, I. M. 1923. *Antisemitism i pogromy na Ukrainiie 1917–1918 gg.* Berlin.

—— 1943–5. *Geshikhte fun der yidisher arbeter-bavegung in di fareynikte shtatn.* New York.

DAWIDOWICZ, L. 1967. *The Golden Tradition: Jewish Life and Thought in Eastern Europe.* New York. Repr. 1996.

—— 1989. *From that Place and Time: A Memoir, 1938–1947.* New York.

DOBROSZYCKI, L. and KIRSHENBLATT-GIMBLETT, B. 1977. *Image Before My Eyes: A Photographic History of Jewish Life in Poland, 1864–1939.* New York. Repr. 1995.

DUBNOW, S. 1925–30. *Weltgeschichte des Jürischen Volkes, von seinen Uranfangen bis zur Gegenwart.* Berlin.

—— 1930–32. *Toledot ha-hasidut.* 3 vols. Tel Aviv.

—— 1964–5. *Divre yeme am olam: toldot am Yisrael mi-yeme kedem ad dor aharon.* Tel Aviv.

—— 1967–73 *History of the Jews.* 5 vols. South Brunswick, NJ.

—— 1975. *History of the Jews in Russia and Poland.* New York.

EISENBACH, A. 1972. *Kwestia rownouprawnienia Zydow w Krolestwie Polskim.* Warsaw.

—— 1991. *Emancypacia Zydow na ziemiach polskich 1785–1870 na tle Europejskim.* Trans. into English as *The Emancipation of the Jews in Poland, 1780–1870.* Oxford.

ETKES, I. 1991. *Lita bi-yerushalayim: ha-ilit ha-lamdanit be-lita u-khehilat ha-perushim bi-yerushalayim le-or igrot u-khetavim shel R. Shemuel mi-Kelm.* Jerusalem.

—— 1993. *Rabbi Israel Salanter and the Mussar movement: Seeking the Torah of Truth.* Philadelphia.

ETTINGER, S. 1978. *Ha-Antishemiyut ba-et haḥadashah: pirke meḥkar veʿiyun.* Tel Aviv.

FEINER, S. 1995. *Haskalah ve-historyah: toldoteha shel hakarat-avar yehudit modernit.* Jerusalem.

FRANKEL, J. 1981. *Prophecy and Politics: Socialism, Nationalism, and the Russian Jews, 1862–1917.* Cambridge.

FREEZE, C. 2001. *Jewish Marriage and Divorce in Imperial Russia.* Hanover, N. H.

GESSEN, I. 1925–7. *Istoriia evreiskogo naroda v Rossii.* 2 vols. Leningrad.

GINZBURG, S. M. and MAREK, P. S. 1901. *Evreiskiia narodnyia pesni v Rossii.* St Petersburg.

GITELMAN, Z. 1972. *Jewish Nationality and Soviet Politics: The Jewish Sections of the CPSU, 1917–1930.* Princeton.

GREENBAUM, A. A. 1978. *Jewish Scholarship and Scholarly Institutions in Soviet Russia, 1918–1953.* Jerusalem.

GREENBERG, L. 1951. *The Jews in Russia.* 2 vols. New Haven.

GUTERMAN, A. 1993. *Me-Hitbolelut li-leʾumiyut: Perakim be-toledot bet ha-keneset ha-gadol ha-sinagogah be-Varshah 1806–1943.* Jerusalem.

HAGEN, W. 1980. *Germans, Poles, and Jews: The Nationality Conflict in the Prussian East.* Chicago.

HALPERIN, I. 1948–53. *Bet yisrael be-polin: mi-yamim rishonim ve-ad li-yemot ha-hurban.* 2 vols. Jerusalem.

—— 1968. *Yehudim ve-Yahadut be-Mizrah Eropah: Mehkarim be-toledotehem.* Jerusalem.

HELLER, C. S. 1977. *On the Edge of Destruction: Jews of Poland Between the Two World Wars.* New York.

HUNDERT, G. 1992. *The Jews in a Polish Private Town: The Case of Opatow in the Eighteenth Century.* Baltimore.

HYMAN, P. 1995. *Gender and Assimilation in Modern Jewish History: The Roles and Representation of Women.* Seattle.

JOHNPOLL, B. K. 1967. *The Politics of Futility: The General Jewish Workers Bund of Poland, 1917–1943.* Ithaca, NY.

JUDGE, E. 1992. *Easter in Kishinev: Anatomy of a Pogrom.* New York.

KAHAN, A. 1986. *Essays in Jewish Social and Eonomic History.* Chicago.

KLAUSNER, Y. 1930–50. *Historiah shel ha-sifrut ha-ivrit ha-hadashah.* 6 vols. Jerusalem.

KLIER, J. 1986. *Russia Gathers Her Jews: The Origins of the 'Jewish Question' in Russia, 1772–1825.* DeKalb, Ill.

LAMBROZA, SH. 1981. 'The Pogrom Movement in Tsarist Russia, 1903–06.' Unpublished diss., University of Michigan.

—— and KLIER, J. 1992. *Pogroms: Anti-Jewish Violence in Modern Russian History.* New York.

LEDERHENDLER, E. 1989. *The Road to Modern Jewish Politics: Political Tradition and Political Reconstruction in the Jewish community of Tsarist Russia.* New York.

LENSKI, G. and LERSKI, H. 1986. *Jewish–Polish Coexistence, 1772–1939: A Topical Bibliography.* New York.

LEVITATS, I. 1943. *The Jewish Community in Russia, 1772–1844.* New York.

LEWIN, I. 1932. *Klatwa zydowska na Litwie w XVII i XVIII wieku.* Lwow.

LITVAK, O. 1999. 'The Literary Response to Conscription: Individuality and Authority in the Russian-Jewish Enlightenment.' Unpublished diss., Columbia University.

Lodzsher visnshaftlekhe shriftn. 1938. Lodz.

MAHLER, R. 1942. *Der kamf tsvishn haskole un khsides in galitsye in der ershter helft fun nayntsntn yorhundert.* New York. English edn. *Hasidism and the Jewish Enlightenment: Their Confrontation in Galicia and Poland in the First Half of the Nineteenth Century.* Philadelphia 1985.

MENDELSON, E. 1970. *Class Struggle in the Pale: The Formative Years of the Jewish Workers' Movement in Tsarist Russia.* Cambridge.

—— 1981. *Zionism in Poland: The Formative Years, 1915–1926.* New Haven.

—— 1983. *The Jews of East Central Europe Between the World Wars.* Bloomington, Ind.

—— 1993. *On Modern Jewish Politics.* New York.

MEYER, M. A. 1988. *Response to Modernity: A History of the Reform Movement in Judaism.* New York.

MIRON, D. 1973. *A Traveler Disguised: A Study in the Rise of Modern Yiddish Fiction in the Nineteenth Century.* New York. Repr. with a foreword by K. Frieden 1996.

NADLER, A. 1997. *The Faith of the Mithnagdim: Rabbinic Responses to Hasidic Rapture.* Baltimore.

NAKHIMOVSKY, A. 1992. *Russian-Jewish Literature and Identity: Jabotinsky, Babel, Grossman, Galich, Roziner, Markish.* Baltimore.

ORBACH, A. 1980. *New Voices of Russian Jewry: A Study of the Russian-Jewish Press of Odessa in the Era of the Great Reforms, 1860–1871.* Leiden.

PIPES, R. 1975. 'Catherine II and the Jews: The Origins of the Pale of Settlement.' *Soviet Jewish Affairs* 5: 3–20.

RAPOPORT-ALBERT, A. 1988. 'On Women in Hasidism: S. A. Horodecky and the Maid of Ludmir Tradition.' In *Jewish History: Essays in Honour of Chimen Abramsky.* A. Rapoport-Albert and S. J. Zipperstein eds. London.

EASTERN EUROPEAN JEWRY   411

RINGELBLUM, E. 1938. *Zydzi w powstaniu kosciuszkowskiem*. Warsaw.

ROGGER, H. 1986. *Jewish Policies and Right-Wing Politics in Imperial Russia*. Berkeley.

ROSMAN, M. 1990. *The Lords' Jews: Magnate-Jewish Relations in the Polish-Lithuanian Commonwealth during the Eighteenth Century*. Cambridge, Mass.

SAFRAN, G. 2000. *Rewriting the Jew: Assimilation Narratives in the Russian Empire*. Stanford.

SCHIPPER, I. 1937. *Dzieje handlu zydowskiego na zierniach polskich*. Warsaw.

SCHWARTZ, S. M. 1951. *The Jews in the Soviet Union*. Syracuse, NY.

SHAPIRA, A. 1984. *Berl: The Biography of a Socialist Zionist, 1887–1944*. Cambridge.

SHAPIRO, M. 1999. *Between the Yeshiva World and Modern Orthodoxy: The Life and Works of Rabbi Jehiel Jacob Weinberg, 1884–1966*. London.

SHATZKY, J. 1947–53. *Geshikhte fun yidn in varshe*. New York.

Sistematicheskii ukazatel' literatury o evreiakh na russkom iazyke. 1892. St Petersburg.

SHMERUK, C. 1964. *A shpial oyf a shteyn: antologye: poene un proze*. Tel Aviv.

STANISLAWSKI, M. 1988. *For Whom Do I Toil? Judah Leib Gordon and the Crisis of Russian Jewry*. New York.

——1983. *Tsar Nicholas I and the Jews: The Transformation of Jewish Society in Russia, 1825–1855*. Philadelphia.

——2001. *Zionism and the Fin-de-Siècle: Cosmopolitanism and Nationalism from Nordau to Jabotins*. Berkeley.

TCHERNOWITZ, C. 1946–7. *Toledot ha-Poskim*. New York.

TOBIAS, H. J. 1972. *The Jewish Bund in Russia from its Origins to 1905*. Stanford.

TSINBERG, Y. 1930–7. *Di geshikhte fun der literatur bay yidn*. 8 Vols. in 10. Vilna.

WEINREICH, M. 1935. *Der veg tsu undzer yungt: yesoydes, metodn, problemen fun yidishe yung-forshung*. Vilna.

WISSE, R. 1971. *The Schlemiel as Modern Hero*. Chicago.

YIVO 1926–9. *Filologishe shriftn*. Vilna.

——1928–32. *Shriftn far ekonomik un statistik*. Berlin.

——1929–39. *Historishe shriftn*. Warsaw and Paris.

——1933–40. *Shriftn far psikhologye un pedagogik*. Vilna.

ZALEWSKA, G. 1996. *Ludnosc gydowska w Warszawie w okresie miedzywojennym*. Warsaw.

Zbirnyk prats' Akademiia nauk URSR, Evreis'ka istoryko-arkheografichna komisiia. 2 vols. 1928–9. Kiev.

ZBOROWSKI, M. and HERZOG, E. 1952. *Life Is With People: The Culture of the Shtetl*. New York.

ZINBERG, I. 1972–8. *A History of Jewish Literature*. Trans. and ed. B. Martin. Cleveland.

ZIPPERSTEIN, S. 1985. *The Jews of Odessa*. Stanford.

——1993. *Elusive Prophet: Ahad Haam and the Origins of Zionism*. Berkeley.

CHAPTER 17

THE HOLOCAUST

SAUL FRIEDLÄNDER[1]

NOTWITHSTANDING almost six decades of scholarship and a fast-swelling stream of publications—a recent estimate mentions approximately 20,000 studies (Pohl 2000)—the historiography of the Holocaust still remains divided in its initial and traditional clusters: the history of the perpetrators, that of the bystanders, that of the victims (Marrus 1987; Hilberg 1992). As research progresses, the dividing-line between the first and the second category becomes increasingly porous; yet the division remains valid in general terms (and useful for the sake of a systematic presentation) in view of the essential differences between these categories and the difficulty in establishing a framework that would encompass such an unusually complex and vast array of events and agents.

Most of the historical publications about the Holocaust deal with the perpetrators (the Germans and their collaborators) and their anti-Jewish policies and measures in the Reich and throughout occupied Europe; at times, they comprise succinct comments about the reactions of the surrounding world and of the Jewish victims (Hilberg 1961). Explicitly or implicitly, their argument is that the impact of the surrounding world (the 'bystanders') on German policies was limited, that of the victims, nil. Thus the history of Nazi policies and measures often tends to be considered as equivalent to the history of the Holocaust as such.

The second cluster of monographs examines the attitudes and initiatives of the bystanders, of local authorities in occupied countries, of the European populations (including German society), the churches, the neutral countries, and the Allies, in the face of the unfolding events. The third historiographical cluster deals with the

---

[1] I wish to thank Dr Orna Kenan of UCLA for her considerable help in editing this text.

life and death of the victims, mostly by countries, cities, areas, ghettos, and camps, or in terms of specific reactions to Nazi initiatives: resistance, accommodation, inertia. Here, as a symmetrical opposite to the studies about the perpetrators, one sometimes finds schematic presentations of Nazi policies and the reactions of the surrounding world (Dawidowicz 1975).

Writing the history of the Holocaust, it should be stressed, has encountered some unusual obstacles. Until the early 1970s the 'Final Solution' was hardly mentioned in German historical scholarship about the Nazi era (Herbert and Groehler 1992). An obvious reason for this long silence was the active involvement of some of the most important historians of post-war Germany in the propaganda and the policies of the Nazi regime, including Nazi policy regarding the Jews (Schulze and Oexle, 1999). The more general reason for this state of things was the widespread repression of the immediate past that characterized German society for several decades after the war (Frei 1999). There were notable exceptions to this reticence, but they were few and far between (Scheffler 1961; Kolb 1962; Genschel 1966; Krausnick 1965; Jäckel 1969; Adam 1972).

The change was hesitant and slow, notwithstanding the wide echo of the Eichmann trial in Jerusalem in 1961 and of the Auschwitz trials in Frankfurt in 1965. The most comprehensive history of *The German Dictatorship*, published in 1969 by the liberal historian Karl-Dietrich Bracher, included seven pages about the murder of the European Jews out of approximately 600 pages (Bracher 1969). At the same time left-wing historians, mainly in West Germany, were attempting to interpret Nazism as a variety of fascism, an interpretation that had little relevance for the study of the Holocaust. The first full-length study about the crimes of the Wehrmacht, including its crimes against the Jews, was published only in the late 1970s (Streit 1978); further large-scale German publications about the criminal behaviour of the army had to wait until the mid-1990s (Heer 1995).

The NBC mini-series *Holocaust*, screened in the Bundesrepublik in 1979, was a major turning-point in terms of public interest, and a steep rise in scholarly publications about the extermination of the Jews of Europe followed. Public debates and controversies induced in part by the symbolic dates '1983' (fifty years from Hitler's accession to power) and '1985' (forty years from the end of the war) followed; they reached their peak in the so-called 'historians' controversy' of 1986/7 about the comparability or exceptionality of the 'Final Solution' and about the 'apologetic' tendencies resurfacing in West Germany in regard to the Nazi period (Diner 1987; Maier 1988; Baldwin 1990). From the mid-1980s German historiography of Nazi anti-Jewish policies and of the regime's extermination campaigns grew rapidly, and many of the studies that will later be dealt with were written, from the early 1990s on, by a new generation of German historians.

Avoidance of the subject for several decades after the end of the war was not limited to Germany. Until the early 1980s very little had been published about

French collaboration in the persecution and deportation of its Jews: it was left to foreign historians to break the taboo (Marrus and Paxton 1983). Polish historiography about the collaboration of Poles with the Germans in the persecution and, possibly, the extermination of the Jews is merely starting, six decades after the events (Gross 2001). Full historical investigation of the relations between Switzerland and the Third Reich, particularly in regard to the Jews, started only in the mid-1990s (The Independent Commission of Experts 2002). In the communist world, any historical research on the subject was strictly regulated and very heavily restricted. It should be added that, at least during the first three decades after the war, none of the most prominent American or British historians of contemporary Germany, Nazism, or the World War (Alan Bullock, Hugh Trevor-Roper, A. J. P. Taylor, Gordon Craig) dealt with the Holocaust, or even alluded to it in more than a few words.

Implicitly, in the West, the Holocaust and its history were considered as a subject to be written by Jews and for Jews. A considerable number of memoirs, diaries, memorial books, and other testimonies about the fate of Jewish communities and individuals was published in the immediate post-war years and during the 1950s, mainly in Hebrew, Yiddish, and various East European languages. This vast production cannot be considered as history in the strict sense of the term, but it often includes details of substantial historical importance (Kugelmass and Boyarin 1983).

The difficulties faced by Jewish historians were formidable: balancing scientific distance with emotional involvement and the urge to commemorate the victims. Initially, many of the researchers involved were not trained professional historians (Poliakov 1951; Reitlinger 1953; Adler 1955; Billig 1955; Poliakov and Wulf 1959). Nonetheless, it was then that Jewish scholars produced some outstanding works, possibly unmatched to this day (Hilberg 1961; Trunk 1972). As for the most prominent Jewish members of the international historians' guild who were dealing with modern Germany or had temporarily turned to its history during the post-war period (Lewis Namier, Felix Gilbert, Hans Rosenberg, Hans Rothfels), like their non-Jewish peers, they refrained from addressing the extermination of the Jews at any length, if at all (Friedländer 1993). Even the Leo Baeck Institute, established in 1954 for researching the history of German Jewry, avoided dealing with the Nazi period until 1985.

In this essay I shall focus primarily upon major issues in each of the separate historiographical areas indicated above, and upon ongoing controversies. In the conclusion I shall suggest some new directions for research and interpretation.

NAZI ANTI-JEWISH POLICIES
AND MEASURES

The historiography of the perpetrators deals either with the general historical context of the events or with concrete policy initiatives and their implementation, the structure of relevant institutions and agencies, even with the careers of some main individuals. From the outset, historians had access to an unusual wealth of documents, mainly from the archives seized by the Western Allies and returned to Germany in the early 1960s. From 1989 on the archives of the ex-Soviet Union and other former European communist countries also became widely accessible. Moreover, the post-war trials and the prosecution of Nazi criminals, which went on until the end of the last century, further produced vast amounts of testimony and new archival material. Important collections of documents were published throughout this entire period; only some of the more accessible and diversified collections will be listed here (Jüdisches Historisches Institut 1961; Hilberg 1971; Dawidowicz 1976; Adler *et al.* 1979; Arad *et al.* 1981; Mendelsohn 1982; Pätzold 1984; Longerich 1989; Friedlander and Milton 1990–5; Noakes and Pridham 2001). Indications are available in various guides and handbooks, although they are often linguistically limited (Niewyk and Nicosia 2000). Methodological studies regarding sources of Holocaust research are still at their beginning (Hilberg 2002).

At the level of the general historical context, monocausal interpretations have not been missing. These interpretations have ranged from the identification of the Nazi anti-Jewish extermination campaign with Hitler's anti-Bolshevik crusade (Mayer 1988) to the specific impact of a particular 'German ideology' (Mosse 1964), from the massive influence of biological-racial and eugenic theories on the exterminatory policies of the 'Racial State' (Burleigh and Wippermann 1991) to attempts at demonstrating the singularity of the Holocaust as the result of a cumulative, age-long anti-Semitic tradition (Katz 1980).

In very schematic terms, these interpretations cover a gamut of arguments, from the most general socio-political phenomena that downplay the particular anti-Jewish character of Nazi policies to the singular anti-Jewish aspect of the events. The most frequently used generalizing conceptual framework is modernity, with its two major offshoots: totalitarianism and racial-biological thinking. The core argument linking Nazism and modernity can be summed up as follows: the origins of Nazism are not seen as an irrational trend in Western history, hostile to the forward march of reason and modern scientific thinking. On the contrary, Nazism and its crimes are seen as the result of the ever-expanding control of instrumental rationality over society, and the elimination of difference in a utopian quest for an all-encompassing, homogeneous racial community. This basic argument was partly alluded to in a very complex way in Adorno and Horkheimer's *Dialectic of*

Enlightenment (Adorno and Horkheimer 1975); it was diversely reworked by histor-ians and sociologists such as Detlev Peukert and Zygmunt Bauman (Bauman 1989; Peukert 1993). As we shall see further, a spate of recent studies about Nazi extermin-ations has reinforced the notion of the 'pitiless instrumental rationality' of Nazism as inherent to modernity (Aly and Heim 1991). The cost–benefit calculations, applied in these studies to the mass murder of human beings, do not seem unre-lated, in the authors' view, to the rationality of modern capitalism.

An emphasis on totalitarianism necessarily derives from the general framework of modernity (as totalitarian rule can be enforced only by way of modern propaganda, surveillance techniques, and also by systematically organized terror and, eventually, mass murder). In its most accepted version, this approach stresses the similarity between Stalinist and Nazi mass annihilations (Laqueur 1994; Burleigh 2000). In a more militant—some would say 'apologetic'—version, the historiographical mes-sage is, directly or indirectly, that of the primacy of the Gulag over 'Auschwitz', of 'Bolshevik' killings as the trigger and model for the Nazi 'response' (Nolte 1987; Courtois *et al.* 1997). Criticism of the comparison betwen Nazism and Stalinism is no less widespread than the support of it (Kershaw 1994; Gleason 1995).

A major difficulty in defining Nazism and its exterminatory policies as an aspect of totalitarianism stems from the fact that the Third Reich was a hybrid political and social system. On the one hand, the similarities between the Nazi and Soviet regimes are obvious. On the other hand, many of the terror and extermination policies of the Third Reich were no less determined by 'German' aspects rooted in German history and sharing little in common with any Soviet or other national equivalent. Hannah Arendt attempted to integrate these specific German historical developments in *The Origins of Totalitarianism*; yet her highly original and pioneering study was some-what idiosyncratic in this respect (Arendt 1951). Moreover, neither the Soviet nor any other modern regime ever set up killing centres for the systematic and total extermination of millions of human beings, of an entire human group, nor was physical extermination an integral part of the communist creed, whereas it was built into the Nazi world-view (Kershaw and Lewin 1997).

Racial-biological thinking is but another facet of modernity. The development of 'scientific' racism in the nineteenth century, and of eugenics and racial anthropol-ogy at the turn of the twentieth century, with the added ingredient of Social Darwinism, indeed led to the heart of Nazi ideology. Combined with anti-Semitism, racial-biological thinking thus seems to point conclusively to the intellectual origins of the 'Final Solution' (Mosse 1978; Proctor 1988; Schmuhl 1987). This interpretation is widely accepted and, undoubtedly, demands to be integrated into the ideological background of Nazi persecution of the carriers of hereditary diseases (Bock 1986), the extermination of the mentally ill (Klee 1983; Friedlander 1995; Burleigh 1994), the Sinti and Roma (Zimmermann 1996; Lewy 2000), the 'asocials' (Ayass 1995), and the homosexuals (Peukert 1982, 1987; Jellonek 1990), as well as the Jews. The Nazi plans regarding the Slav populations of the East, mainly the notorious 'Generalplan Ost', aiming at the decimation of millions of inhabitants of Eastern Europe and the Soviet Union, fall within this same category of racial-biological ideology (Rössler and Schleiermacher 1993).

The 'war against the Jews', however, carried, in Hitler's mind and in the world-view of the Party hard core, a further element, possibly a decisive one: the Jews were not only a race which, like the other 'diseased' groups, polluted the Aryan racial pool or, like the Slavs, were an 'inferior' population that could be terrorized and decimated at will; they also presented a mortal danger for the Aryan race, as they strove to achieve the control of Germany and, ultimately, world domination (Cohn 1967). The struggle against the Jews was a matter of life and death; victory meant salvation, defeat—the perdition of Germany and of Aryan humanity (Friedländer 1997). The origins of Hitler's own anti-Jewish obsession are anything but clear. Whether the Vienna period was determinant is increasingly uncertain, given recent findings on young Hitler's manifold relations with Jews in the Austrian capital (Hamann 1999). It seems more probable that Hitler's anti-Jewish hatred stemmed from Germany's defeat and the influence of his Munich post-war environment, mainly that of his ideological mentor Dietrich Eckart (Mosse 1964; Fest 1974; Friedländer 1997; Kershaw 1999).

According to the approaches centred essentially on the anti-Jewish factor, the 'Final Solution' was, above all, the result of the cumulative growth of an age-long hatred of the Jews. This approach usually underlines the continuity between the religious roots of traditional Christian anti-Judaism and modern racial anti-Semitism in Western society (Poliakov 1965–85; Katz 1980). In a different guise, modern anti-Semitism is linked to a specific course of German history (*Sonderweg*), characterized by a tradition of German anti-liberalism and the growth of a *völkisch* (nationalist-racist-anti-Semitic) ideology throughout the nineteenth and early twentieth centuries (Stern 1961; Mosse 1964, 1978). The most extreme version of this 'Sonderweg' interpretation has centred on the existence of a specifically German 'eliminationist' anti-Jewish hatred to which Nazism offered the longed-for outlet (Goldhagen 1996).

Whereas modernity and totalitarianism—and even racial-biological thinking—are too vague, an exclusive emphasis on the age-long role of anti-Semitism is too reductive. First, it does not sufficiently stress the considerable difference between various forms of anti-Semitism, from Hitler's apocalyptic interpretation of the struggle against the Jews to that of the party theoreticians of race, or the traditional religious and socio-economic anti-Jewish hostility shared by most segments of the German and European population. Second, the approach that stresses the specificity of German anti-Semitism does not thoroughly enough question the continuity between the pre-1914 German anti-Jewish tradition and the virulent anti-Semitism born of the war and the defeat (Volkov 1989). Finally, the sole emphasis upon anti-Semitism disregards the complex interaction between anti-

Jewish ideology, racial-biological thinking in more general terms, economic exploit-ation, and various 'pragmatic' Nazi goals.

The introduction of a variety of elements into the overall historical picture allows for more complex, less monolithic interpretations. It allows one to take into account the decisive role of Hitler, but also the constant interaction between the Nazi leader on the one hand, the party, state agencies, and German society on the other. Such an approach implies the *convergence of distinct historical developments*, each pointing to some aspects of the events, that resists a reduction to monocausal interpretations and overly simple conceptual frameworks (Friedländer 1997).

Most of the historical work about the perpetrators belongs to a more limited level of inquiry. It addresses concrete Nazi policies and decisions, the dynamics of radicalization of the regime, the internal 'logic' of the system, and the main insti-tutions, groups, and even individuals actively involved in the anti-Jewish policies and the 'Final Solution'.

At this narrower level of analysis, considerable progress has been made during the last decade or so, due in particular to the already mentioned availability in Eastern Europe of vast collections of German documents, mostly inaccessible to Western researchers before the collapse of the communist regimes. Some of the new docu-ments, mainly found in the Moscow Special Archives, are of major significance. Thus, the discovery and publication of Heinrich Himmler's *Dienstkalender* (ap-pointments diary) has, as we shall see further on, led to new interpretations regarding the decision to launch the total extermination of European Jewry (Witte *et al.* 1999).

The complete publication of the Goebbels diaries (Fröhlich 1987–2001), of Hitler's speeches for the 1926–33 period (Vollnhals *et al.* 1992–8), as a complement to the collected speeches covering the other periods of the Nazi leader's career (Domarus 1962–3; Jäckel and Kuhn 1980), as well as the considerable monographic work on different aspects of Nazi racial policies (eugenics, sterilization, and eutha-nasia), allow for a better contextualization of the anti-Jewish policies of the 1930s and of Hitler's role in their elaboration.

The anti-Jewish legislation (Walk 1991) and the evolution of the economic anti-Jewish drive of the 1930s have also been thoroughly interpreted (Genschel 1966; Barkai 1989; Hayes 1994; Bajohr 1998), as has been the daily life of the Jews of Germany under Nazi rule (Paucker 1986; Benz 1988; Gruner 1997; Kaplan 1998). The publication of new archival material on the history of the Reich Representation of the Jews in Germany during the pre-war years has added further insight regarding Jewish reactions to the constant stream of Nazi orders and measures (Kulka 1997).

Thus the interaction of local authorities and party leadership in the micro- and macro-management of the persecutions during the pre-war period is by now extensively documented (Schleunes 1970; Adam 1972; Friedländer 1997), as are the reactions of the Jewish community. Even previously well-known issues, such as the elaboration and impact of the policies regarding 'mixed breeds' before the passage of the Nuremberg Racial Laws of 1935 and afterwards (Lösener 1961; Adam 1972), are now thoroughly researched (Noakes 1989; Meyer 1999). The same can be said about the precise unfolding of the November 1938 pogrom—particularly Hitler's role in it (Döscher 1988; Kershaw 2000; Kley 2000). The main progress and the major debates in the historiography of the Holocaust relate to the war period.

Whereas until the pogrom of 1938 the elaboration and implementation of the anti-Jewish measures was largely in the hands of the state bureaucracy, after that date the role of party agencies became predominant. Formally, Hitler appointed Göring as co-ordinator of Jewish affairs, but the power wielded by the supreme SS chief Heinrich Himmler, and by his second-in-command, the head of the Security Police (Sicherheitspolizei or Sipo) and of the SS secret service (Sicherheitsdienst or SD), Reinhard Heydrich, over Jewish matters grew rapidly (Wildt 1995, 2002). The 'Main Office for the Security of the Reich' (Reichssicherheitshauptamt or RSHA), created in September 1939 and placed under Heydrich's command, established a single agency including the SD, the Gestapo (Secret State Police) (Paul and Mallmann 2000), and the Kripo (Criminal Police). At first in charge of the dwindling emigration of Jews from the Reich and of the deportations and 'resettlement' operations, then of the murder operations of the 'Einsatzgruppen' on Soviet territory, the RSHA became the hub of the extermination programme and of its implementation (Wildt 2002).

Within the RSHA itself, the Jewish section IV B4 under Adolf Eichmann and its agents in various countries, 'Eichmann's men', have been systematically studied (Safrian 1993; Steur 1997; Lozowick 2000). From the ranks of the RSHA came most of the commanders of the 'mobile killing units of the Security Police and the SD', the Einsatzgruppen (Krausnick and Wilhelm 1981; Ogorreck 1996; Klein 1997; Wildt 2002). Alongside the RSHA, several other SS agencies were central to the anti-Jewish campaign . The SS Economic Administration Main Office (SS Wirtschaftsverwaltungs-Hauptamt or WVHA), set up in 1942 under the command of Oswald Pohl, was in charge of the concentration camps and of the entire SS economy (Naasner 1998; Schulte 2001). The Higher SS and Police Leaders (Höhere SS und Polizeiführer or HSSPF) were Himmler's personal delegates in the occupied countries, East and West: they were responsible, among other tasks, for the co-ordination of the activities of the SS units and the co-operation in all anti-Jewish measures of other Nazi agencies, as well as local authorities (Birn 1986).

Most historians would agree that there were no precise Nazi plans for the extermination of the Jews until after the attack on the Soviet Union. However, there were projects of territorial 'resettlements'. After the failure of some earlier attempts, massive deportations took place during the winter of 1939/40 from the western annexed part of Poland (Warthegau) into the non-annexed, directly German ruled General Government, in October 1940 from the Reich into non-occupied France, and in February 1941 from Vienna into the General Government.

Soon, however, the Nazis abandoned the idea of 'resettling' all European Jews in the Lublin area of the General Government (Safrian 1993). From the spring to the fall of 1940 a new territorial plan, the 'Madagascar plan', was actively pursued, as a result of the defeat of France (Jansen 1997; Brechtken 1998). Then, once the decision to attack the Soviet Union was taken in December 1940, Nazi planners and Hitler himself set their eyes on the Russian Far North as the appropriate territory for herding together the Jewish population of Europe and ensuring its ultimate extinction (Longerich 1998; Aly 2000).

Policies regarding the fate of the Jews confined in the ghettos of former Poland changed several times, moving from planned 'attrition' to planned 'productivization' (Browning 1992; Musial 1999). In both cases, however, the forced-labour camps and labour battalions were often deadly, and life in the ghettos was one of chronic epidemics, starvation, and soaring mortality rates, at least until some eight months before the deportations, at which time the situation was somewhat stabilized in the major ghettos (Yahil 1990; Browning 1992).

Mass murder started in occupied Soviet territories after the German attack against the Soviet Union on 22 June 1941 (Hilberg 1961; Krausnick and Wilhelm 1981; Klee et al. 1991; Ogorreck 1996; Klein 1997). At first it targeted mostly Jewish men, but by early August 1941 it spread, in stages, to the entire Jewish population.

The recognition in the 1990s of a much wider involvement of police and Wehrmacht units in the killings in the Eastern territories and in the Balkans than was previously suspected, led to a major change of perspective regarding the perpetrators. It became clear that the ideologically motivated Einsatzgruppen, were only a part of a much wider network of killing units (Breitman 1991; Browning 1993; Manoschek 1995; Goldhagen 1996; Heer et al. 2000). These well-established findings ignited a fierce debate. Was this widespread murderous participation of individuals and units with limited ideological motivation the result of general psychological and sociological traits applicable to 'ordinary men' of any background (Browning 1993), or should this—often eager—participation be linked to a specific brand of Jew-hatred common among 'ordinary Germans' (Goldhagen 1996)? It was during these months of rapidly expanding killing operations on Soviet territory that, sometime during the second half of 1941, the decision to exterminate all the Jews of Europe was taken.

The immediate genesis of the 'Final Solution' remains the object of conflicting interpretations. Some historians still argue that the decision to exterminate all the Jews of Europe pre-dated the 22 June 1941 attack on the Soviet Union (Breitman 1991; Friedlander 1995). Others contend that this decision was taken by Hitler soon after the beginning of the campaign, during the period of 'euphoria' in the wake of the early successes, and that it found its expression in Göring's letter to Heydrich of 31 July 1941 ordering him to make the necessary preparations for the 'final solution of the Jewish question in Europe'. According to that same interpretation, a second order launching the implementation of the 'Final Solution' was given in October of

1941 (Browning 1985, 2000). Other historians, avoiding the two-stage order, argue that the decision to start the general extermination must have been taken sometime in late September 1941 and that the implementation began shortly afterwards, in October (Burrin 1994). In any case, according to the last two approaches the implementation of the 'Final Solution' started in October 1941. It is during that month that the construction of the Belzec extermination camp—possibly that of Sobibor—began, and that the search for an extermination site near Lodz was ordered (it became the Chelmno extermination site); also in October Gestapo Chief Heinrich Müller forbade any further emigration of Jews from the continent, 'in view of the forthcoming Final Solution' (Browning 1985; 2000; Burrin 1994).

The order for the 'Final Solution' has also been linked to the United States' entry into the war, in other words, to the transformation of the European war into the 'world war' which, as Hitler had 'prophesied' in his Reichstag speech of 30 January 1939, would lead to 'the extermination of the Jewish race in Europe' (Hartog 1997; Gerlach 1998a). This interpretation seems bolstered by a close sequence of events: on 4 December the Russians counter-attacked in front of Moscow; on 7 December the Japanese attacked Pearl Harbor, and on 11 December Hitler declared war on the United States. On 12 December, according to Goebbels's diary, Hitler addressed the Gauleiters and declared that, now the war had become total, the Jews, its initiators, would have to pay with their lives. A few days later, on 18 December according to Himmler's appointments' diary, the SS chief met with Hitler and wrote down: 'Jewish question/eradicate as partisans' (in the original a vertical line divided the two parts of the entry; its significance is not clear) (Gerlach 1998a). The reference to 'partisans' is clearly a way of describing an enemy lurking behind the lines, an internal foe who, just as in 1917/18, would stab Germany in the back if given the chance.

Some historians believe that the decisive order was issued only in the spring of 1942 (Longerich 1998); finally, others remain doubtful about the existence of any precise order given at the highest level; they consider the total extermination of the Jews as an outcome of the cumulative effects of local initiatives and of an unfolding process following its own dynamics (Broszat 1977; Mommsen 1991).

The debates about the genesis of the 'Final Solution' carry some further historiographical implications. For some fifteen years a distinction between two sets of interpretations of the decision-making process in the Nazi system persisted (Mason 1981; Friedländer 1984). The 'functionalists', on the one hand, argued that Nazi decision-making was anarchic and not determined by long-range plans nor by Hitler's ideologic tenets; neither was it subject, in fact, to central decisions imposed by Hitler himself. Rather, the decisions were the outcome of haphazard circumstances and of an ongoing internal competition between various party chieftains and party or state agencies, creating thereby a process of 'cumulative radicalization' that led to most extreme results such as the 'Final Solution' (Broszat 1977; Mommsen 1991). On the other hand, 'intentionalists' put the emphasis on the impact of ideology, on long-term planning, and the centrality of Hitler's decisions (Jäckel 1969; Dawidowicz 1975; Fleming 1984).

The documents now at our disposal clearly indicate Hitler's direct and crucial intervention in the process leading to the 'Final Solution', first in September 1941, when the Nazi leader suddenly reversed his previous stance and decided on the immediate deportation of the Jews from the Reich to the ghettos in the East (Adler 1974; Witte 1995), then, in October and November, when he alluded with increasing frequency to the extermination of the Jews, and finally, in December of that year, in his speech to the Gauleiters on the 12th, and in his order to Himmler on the 18th. This direct intervention remains identifiable in the spring of 1942 (Longerich 1998). Yet the intentionalists may not have sufficiently taken into account the regional or institutional goals pursued by party appointees or by various agencies in the murderous initiatives taken in the East, as was shown in the studies previously mentioned. Moreover, in the overall extermination process, the internal 'logic' of the system of necessity played a role. Thus, it is a constant interaction of central decisions and local initiatives that seems best to represent the way policies developed in Nazi Germany generally, and with regard to the Jews in particular.

More specifically, even if the decision to launch the total extermination of European Jewry was taken in the fall of 1941 (late September or October), and even after Heydrich outlined the main aspects of the 'Final Solution' at the Wannsee Conference of 20 January 1942 (Pätzold and Schwarz 1992; Scheffler and Grabitz 1995; Klein 1995; Gerlach 1998a; Roseman 2002), the implementation of the murder programme developed in stages until the late spring of 1942 (Longerich 1998). Only in June 1942 did Himmler set a definitive schedule for the completion of the operation: the European Jews were to be exterminated *within one year* (Smith and Peterson 1974); in mid-July the SS Chief ordered that the entire Jewish population of the General Government be exterminated by the end of the year (Jüdisches Historisches Institut 1960). At the same time the mass deportations started from all over the continent to the extermination camps (Hilberg 1961; Adler 1974; Klarsfeld 1983–5; Moore 1997; Longerich 1998). Successive decisions were thus taken over a period of some eight months, which, step by step, widened the scope of the annihilation and shortened the time-span for its implementation. In conclusion, the launching of the 'Final Solution' was unquestionably decided by Hitler and organized, implemented, and monitored by Himmler, Heydrich, and the related individuals, agencies, and auxiliaries throughout occupied Europe.

Apart from the mass murder operations of the mobile killing units on ex-Soviet territory, the main instruments of the 'Final Solution' were the extermination camps and their gas chambers. They became the latest—and entirely new—addition to the concentration camp system. The concentration camps, established at the very beginning of the regime, became a single organization from 1934 onwards. The network grew from seven main camps in the pre-war Reich to hundreds of main and satellite camps all over occupied Europe at the height of the war. The inmates were first and foremost political opponents, then 'asocials' (in Nazi parlance), followed by members of religious sects, homosexuals, and also Jews (mainly after November 1938). From the end of 1941 the setting up of the extermination sites and camps started.

The camp system in general has been thoroughly investigated, both historically and sociologically (Sofsky 1997; Herbert *et al.* 1998; Frei *et al* 2000); Auschwitz in particular, apart from the publication of the autobiography of its first commandant and the documentation relating to the trial of some of its major perpetrators (Broszat 1958; Adler *et al.* 1979; Paskuly 1992), has been the object of several major studies (Pressac 1989; Piper 1993; Gutman and Berenbaum 1994; Dwork and Jan Van Pelt 1996; Frei *et al.* 2000), and so have several other camps, such as Dachau (Steinbacher, 1993), Mauthausen (Horowitz 1990) and Theresienstadt (Adler 1960; Karny *et al.* 1992), Sobibor (Schelvis 1998). However, the earliest extermination sites, Chelmno in the Warthegau and the so-called 'Aktion Reinhard' camps in the General Government (Belzec, Sobibor, Majdanek, and Treblinka), in which around 2 million Jews were murdered, are less thoroughly researched, as much of their archives were destroyed by the Nazis and as very few of their inmates survived. The construction, organization, and basic functioning of these camps are nonetheless known from some contemporary documents, from testimonies presented during the post-war judicial proceedings (Hilberg 1961; Scheffler and Arndt 1976; Rückerl 1977; Arad 1987), and from at least one lengthy series of in-depth interviews with a former camp commander (Sereny 1974).

All the extermination camps were located in the General Government with the exception of Auschwitz, built next to the town of that name in East Upper Silesia, a territory annexed to the Reich. These camps became 'operational' in the first half of 1942, and the use, for the killings, of carbon monoxide, produced by static diesel engines—instead of the gas vans used in the Soviet Union and mainly in Chelmno (Beer 1987)—was replaced, in due time, by a more effective killing agent, Zyklon B gas (Kogon *et al.* 1993; Arad 1987; Czech 1989; Pressac 1989; Steinbacher 2000).

Simultaneously, the killings further east continued by way of huge-scale massacres. The detailed history of these killings is now well known area by area, throughout the whole period of German occupation (Pohl 1996, 2000; Benz *et al.* 1998; Sandkühler 1996; Gerlach 1999; Dieckmann 2000). On 2 November 1944, after the extermination of most of Hungarian Jewry (Braham 1981; Gerlach and Aly 2002) and as defeat was approaching, Himmler gave the order to put an end to the killings. The order was not obeyed, and the Jewish inmates of the camps about to be liberated were often marched within the shrinking territories controlled by the Germans in what came to be known as the 'death marches', throughout the winter of 1944/5 (Krakowsky 1984; Goldhagen 1997).

Various hypotheses about the functional advantages that the Germans expected from the extermination of the Jews (the settlement of ethnic Germans, economic-demographic plans for a reorganization of the continent, improved food supply for the Wehrmacht and the Reich) have been presented over the last years. Whether convincing or not, these arguments have introduced new elements into the historiographical debate (Aly 2000; Gerlach 1999). In these studies the mass murder of the Jews appears as the result of the already mentioned cost–benefit calculations, the quintessential aspect of modernity. In this approach, the extermination of the Jews is not interpreted as an aim, in and of itself, but as the outcome of other—often pragmatic—overriding Nazi goals. Such an interpretation represents the full 'historicization of National Socialism'—and thus of the Holocaust: a 'non-moralistic', empirical approach. Whatever the validity of the arguments for the 'historicization of National Socialism' may be in abstract terms (Broszat 1990; Broszat and Friedländer 1990), the conclusions drawn from these studies about the nature of the 'Final Solution' are difficult to sustain, when the anti-Jewish policies are considered on the scale of the entire continent. What does the resettlement of ethnic Germans in former Poland or the food supply for the Wehrmacht on the Eastern Front have to do with the extermination of the Jews of Holland, Norway, Saloniki, or the island of Rhodes?

The total number of Jewish victims is difficult to assess: in the population census of some countries Jews were not identified as such, relevant documents were destroyed, national borders shifted, and Jews fled from one area to another. By early 1943 the chief statistician of the SS, Richard Korherr, reported to Himmler and Hitler that over 3 million Jews had been exterminated. Post-war inquiries resulted in estimates ranging from 5.1 to possibly about 6.2 million Jewish victims (Hilberg 1989; Benz 1991).

THE BYSTANDERS

As mentioned at the outset, the dividing-line between perpetrators and bystanders is steadily shifting. It shifts mainly in one direction: from bystander to perpetrator. In other words, as research progresses, wider groups previously deemed as passive are identified as active participants in the persecution and extermination process. The focus in this section will be on new categories of bystander/perpetrators, on old/new questions regarding the essentially passive authorities, institutions, and populations in occupied Europe, on the Allies, the neutrals, and the churches.

Above and beyond the identification of vast numbers of 'ordinary men' as occasional or professional killers, considerable new information has been gathered about the involvement of wide groups of direct collaborators and auxiliaries of the Nazis. The participation of Lithuanians, Latvians, Bielorussians, Ukrainians, Romanians, Croats, Slovaks, Hungarians, and Poles in different phases of the persecutions and the exterminations is increasingly well documented (Braham 1981; Steinberg 1990; Ezergailis 1996; Pohl 1996; Sandkühler 1996; Cesarani 1997; Benz *et al.* 1998; Gerlach 1999; Dieckmann 2000; Dean 2000; Ioanid 2000; Gross 2001). New documents on local collaboration have been discovered in the West (Klarsfeld 1983–5; Grynberg 1991; Moore 1997; Michman 1998). Among other recent finds, the lists of Jews residing in France, established by the French police after June 1940 (*le fichier juif*) and made available to the Germans, were discovered in the archives of the Ministère des Anciens Combattants in Paris, in the 1990s (Rémond 1996).

The shifting line separating bystanders and perpetrators, as well as the discovery of a vast new category of institutions deeply involved in the anti-Jewish measures, has recently become apparent in the economic domain, particularly in regard to the scope and procedures of the continent-wide takeover of Jewish property and assets, in the wake of the persecution, deportation, and murder of its owners.

Beyond ongoing study on German industry, slave labour and the Holocaust (Hayes 1996), research in the late 1990s uncovered the 'aryanization' operations of large European financial institutions, such as the Dresdner Bank and the Deutsche Bank (Bähr 1999; James 2001). It also brought to light the gold transactions of the Reichsbank with the Swiss National Bank, among others. These transactions involved gold stolen by the Germans from central banks in occupied countries but also from the victims in the camps (including gold teeth extracted from corpses), all of it smelted into ingots by the German Degussa Company and transferred to the Reichsbank (Independent Commission of Experts 2002). Research on the policies of major insurance companies in regard to their Jewish clients who became victims of the extermination has been partly published (Feldman 2001), and is partly still ongoing. Several recent publications also deal with art looted from Jews throughout occupied Europe (Petropoulos 1996; Feliciano 1997; Heuss 2000).

Whatever went on in the Reich and in occupied Europe at the top of the economic pyramid also proliferated at its bottom. Hundreds of thousands of Germans and other Europeans pounced on any profit to be made from the elimination of the Jewish population: businesses and homes were distributed to deserving *Volksgenossen* or collaborators (Botz 1975); furniture, rugs, clothes, and other personal belongings were sold at dirt-cheap prices at 'Jew markets' in major German cities (Bajohr 1997, 2001), or taken over by local authorities and populations. At all levels, a bond of greed may have reinforced the desire for a definitive disappearance of the victims.

If we turn from the economic domain to the response of various national authorities to German demands or orders regarding their Jews, the establishment of common denominators at the level of the continent becomes extremely difficult, although some comparative attempts were made (R. Cohen 1987; Blom 1989). Some allies of Nazi Germany, particularly the Italians, protected the Jews in their home country and in areas they occupied (Croatia, the south-east of France), not only against local initiatives but against the Germans themselves (Michaelis 1978; Steinberg 1990; Carpi 1994). The Bulgarians and the Hungarians delivered foreign Jews but attempted to protect their own (successfully in the first case, unsuccessfully in the second, after the Germans occupied Hungary in March 1944) (Chary 1972; Braham 1981; Cesarani 1997). Finland refused to deliver its Jews; Vichy France eagerly helped in the arrest and deportation of foreign Jews but became laggard when the turn of French Jews arrived (Klarsfeld 1983; Marrus and Paxton 1983). The Slovaks demanded the deportation of their Jews, then stalled and later collaborated again (Bauer 1994; Rothkirchen 1998); at first the Romanians eagerly participated in the mass murders, but from 1942 on they became increasingly reticent regarding German demands for the deportation of their Jews, as they sensed the turn of the military tide (Ioanid 2000).

In view of these differences, the impact of various degrees of local anti-Semitism becomes a central issue. The answer is paradoxical: in some occupied or satellite countries with a high degree of popular and elite anti-Semitism, an important proportion of the Jewish community escaped (Romania, France), while in countries in which anti-Semitism was relatively weak, most of the Jewish population perished (Holland) (Moore 1997). Hence, in this area, attempts at comparative studies (Fein 1979) have to take a wider variety of factors into account.

The attitudes of the governments and authorities of the neutral and Allied countries to the Jews attempting to flee the Reich or German-occupied Europe are essentially known by now. The Swiss policy regarding Jewish refugees was notoriously harsh since 1938, and in August 1942, at the peak of the deportations from Western Europe, the Bern government ordered the complete closure of the country's border to Jews. Notwithstanding some public protests and brief wavering, the federal and cantonal authorities did not change their basic policy until late 1943 and 1944. Approximately 20,000 Jews were refused entry into Switzerland or were driven back after having crossed the border (Independent Commission of Experts 2002).

The refugee policies of other neutral countries and of the Allies can only be mentioned here. In 1942 the Swedes changed their formerly very restrictive policy, probably under the impact of the deportations from Norway (Levine 1996). Spain and Portugal allowed a massive transit of refugees through their territories during the entire war (Avni 1982; Wyman 1984). From the spring of 1939 Great Britain almost entirely closed the doors of Palestine to Jewish immigration, out of fear of Arab reactions in an increasingly tense international situation. Illegal Jewish immigration started. At first it was encouraged by the Germans in their eagerness to get rid of the Jews by any means (Ofer 1990; Bauer 1994). From the spring of 1941, however, the RSHA stopped its support and the entire enterprise tapered off. By that time the illegal immigrants caught by the British were deported to Mauritius or Eritrea, notwithstanding major tragedies such as the sinking of the *Patria* and later of the *Struma*, with hundreds of refugees on board (Wasserstein 1988; London 2000). The policy of the British dominions can be summed up in the notorious sentence of a Canadian official: 'None is too many' (Abella and Troper 1982).

From the beginning of the war in Europe, and particularly after the defeat of France, the United States did not even fill the already very restrictive national quotas imposed on Jewish immigration (the quotas were applied by countries and only indirectly targeted Jews). The American consular services, acting on instructions from above, accumulated administrative obstacles, mainly, it seems, due to the fear of possible infiltration by foreign agents (Breitman and Kraut 1987). There was little that organized American Jewry could or dared to do to fight for a change of attitude (Feingold 1995; Ne'eman Arad 2000). In this atmosphere the Bermuda Conference on refugees, convened by the United States and Great Britain in 1943, was as much of a charade as the Evian Conference of 1938 (Wyman 1984). Only in 1944, with the establishment of the War Refugee Board, did American policy show some first signs of change (ibid.).

The heterogeneous bystanders' domain further includes some highly controversial issues that have been repeatedly scrutinized over the last two decades. The response of the leadership of the Jewish community in Palestine to information about the extermination in Europe has been considered as slow by some scholars (Porat 1990), entirely inadequate by others (Gelber 1979; Segev 1993); such criticism has also been decidedly rejected (Teveth 1996). The dilatory policies of the Allied powers in regard to various rescue plans, their refusal to bomb Auschwitz (Gilbert 1981; Neufeld and Berenbaum 2000), the hiding of information about the extermination operations reaching London and Washington (Breitman 1998), can now be better researched as a result of the ongoing declassification of vast numbers of official documents.

The attitudes and decisions of the Christian churches during the Nazi period were crucial, due to their massive influence on the populations throughout the continent. The record of both the Protestant and the Catholic churches in Germany is particularly well researched, also in regard to the anti-Jewish policies of the regime (Lewy 1964; Scholder 1977; Kulka and Mendes-Flohr 1987; Röhm and Thierfelder 1990–5; Gerlach 1993; Siegele-Wenschkewitz 1994; Bergen 1996; Gailus 2001). All in all, the record is one of tentative help to converted Jews, little more. Directly related research on the attitude of the Vatican to the Holocaust has stalled. After publishing a selective choice of its own documents (*Actes et Documents* 1965–81), the Vatican steadfastly refuses to give access to its archives, as was made clear, once more, in July 2001 to a joint Jewish–Catholic historians commission. This adamant stand, and ever-recurring rumours about a possible beatification of the wartime Pope, Pius XII, have fuelled a controversy that already started in the 1960s; the stream of publications remains unabated (Morley 1980; Cornwell 2000; Miccoli 2000; Phayer 2000;

Zucotti 2000). The non-availability of the Vatican archives has blocked any major advance in our knowledge regarding the attitude of Pope Pius XII to the persecution and extermination of the Jews, including the deportation of the Jews of Rome from 'under his own windows'. It should be mentioned, however, that the Pope's non-intervention left much latitude to bishops throughout the continent. Some of them, mainly in Eastern Europe and in the Balkans, saw in the German policies a welcome 'liberation' from the Jews. In Western Europe many bishops remained faithful to traditional Christian anti-Jewish attitudes and, at the outset at least, favoured limiting 'Jewish influence' in their countries and supported the anti-Jewish legislation. Later, a small minority, mainly in Western-occupied Europe, protested and even beseeched the Pope to intervene (after the deportations started), to no avail (Delpech 1982; Kulka and Mendes-Flohr 1987; Phayer 2000).

At all levels, the attitude of the bystanders gets much of its historical significance from what was or was not known about the fate of the Jews. The difference established by Walter Laqueur between 'knowledge' and 'understanding' remains theoretically of the essence (Laqueur 1980). Yet the information received at diverse stages was abundant, in Germany, throughout the continent, and beyond. In Germany it was probably not repressed to escape guilt or unbearable choices, as some historians have argued (Bankier 1992), but rather understood and mostly met with passivity, indifference, and, widely enough, a measure of support often stemming from traditional anti-Semitism (Gellately 1990, 2001; Johnson 1999; Bankier 2000), even among opponents of the regime (Gerlach 1995; Korenke 1999; Mommsen 2000).

In concrete terms, information about the massacre of Jews on Soviet territory became widespread very soon after the onset of the killings, in the summer and fall of 1941 (Breitman 1998; Bourgeois 1998; Sebastian 2000). Rumours about total extermination and about the existence of extermination camps spread more haphazardly, but we know that the Allies (Laqueur 1980; Gilbert 1981; Laqueur and Breitman 1986; Breitman 1998), the governments-in-exile (Engel 1987, 1993), the neutrals (Independent Commission of Experts 2002) the Vatican (Friedländer 1966, 1969; Phayer 2000), and the International Committee of the Red Cross (Favez 1999) were well informed in the early summer of 1942, possibly even before. London and Washington publicly confirmed the veracity of the information in the fall of that same year (Wasserstein 1988; Wyman 1984). That being said, the debate about what was known and understood, by whom, and when, is not about to cease, as understanding the events and abstaining from ongoing protest or active rescue initiatives (Gutman and Zuroff 1977) is at the core of the issue of historical responsibility.

THE VICTIMS

In the common perception of the Holocaust, even among the small group of survivors who participated in Jewish armed resistance in the ghettos, the camps, or the wider reaches of occupied Europe, the millions of Jews who perished are often considered as totally passive victims, as 'sheep led to slaughter'.

Yet as the years go by, it becomes increasingly clear that Jewish existence under Nazi domination was by no means exclusively a process of passive suffering and submission, with spurts of armed revolt in some rare cases. First, it should be recalled again that, from the beginning of the war to late 1941, the aim of the Germans was probably not to exterminate the Jews then and there, but rather to hound and persecute them in the most diverse ways. Thus, any steps taken by the victims as individuals or communities to impede, deflect, or slow down these German measures, or to further their own material and spiritual existence under these conditions, were part of an ongoing and complex confrontation with their persecutors (Gutman 1982; Kwiet and Eschwege 1984; Dobroszycki 1984; Loewy and Schoenberner 1990).

Even during the phase which followed, that of extermination, we discover constant initiatives by Jews in each area, in each country, to escape their murderers and save what could be saved by all possible means, from hiding, to bribes, to armed resistance. Simultaneously, in the still surviving ghettos and collective hiding-places, various political and cultural activities continued. The historical importance of this behaviour cannot be measured by its ultimate outcome but by its very existence.

In France, Slovakia, Hungary, and Romania, as well as in Italy and in the areas under Italian occupation, Jewish initiatives throughout those years also engaged local authorities at various levels. In France, for example, the heads of French Jewish organizations negotiated with Vichy officials and tried to win their protection against various German measures, particularly against the German decision to set up a central organization for all the Jews in France (French and foreign alike). And, as the representatives of French Jewry negotiated with Petain's administration, they also tried to distance themselves from the foreign Jews living in their midst (R. Cohen 1987; J. Adler 1987; Poznanski 1994). In Slovakia, the attempts of a group of Jewish personalities to buy Jewish lives by bribing SS delegates and local officials and, further, to expand this plan to the whole of occupied Europe, went on for over two years and possibly delayed the local deportations for a while. This plan has become known in considerable detail, although interpretations of it differ (Bauer 1994).

Some of the most important debates of the 1960s and 1970s about the attitudes of the 'Jewish Councils' (Hilberg 1961; Arendt 1963; Robinson 1965) and the nature and scope of Jewish resistance have come to some measure of informed resolution. The considerable differences in attitudes from one council to the other, as well as the vast array of modes of resistance, are now generally accepted (Trunk 1972; Gutman and Haft 1979). The immense variety of Jewish life in occupied Europe and in the Reich, as well as the immediate aftermath of the Holocaust, are reflected in the diversity of new studies, only minimally alluded to in this section. Over decades, for example, a vast historical literature which cannot be listed here has dealt with Jewish armed resistance. New research on the subject allows more detailed assessments of its manifold aspects (Tec 1993; Kagan and Cohen 1998; Porat 2000), but the emphasis on armed resistance seems to be diminishing in the history of the Holocaust.

Recent historiography about the victims remains focused in great part on full-scale communities, institutions, and political movements (Loewy and Schoenberner 1990; Poznanski 1994; Cohen and Cochavi 1995; Gruner 1997; Moore 1997; Kermish 1979–97; Schwarzfuchs 1998). Over the last few years, however, research has turned increasingly to the fate of individuals, to the individual life and death of Jews in Nazi-occupied Europe. In this domain, local studies and the growing importance of everyday history had been bolstered over the decades by the publication of highly important diaries, as, for example, that of the Chairman of the Warsaw Judenrat, Adam Czerniakow (Czerniakow 1979), of the joint employee and secret historian of the Warsaw Ghetto and of Polish Jewry, Emmanuel Ringelblum (Ringelblum 1958), of the Warsaw Hebrew School director, Chaim Kaplan (Kaplan 1965), and a large number of other such testimonies in Eastern and Western Europe, among which, obviously, is the diary of Anne Frank (Frank 1997). More than 300 such diaries had been published by 1999 and over eighty have been translated into English (Rozett 2001). Over the last two decades new collective chronicles and personal memoirs have been uncovered or, mainly, translated into widely read languages: the diary of a leading member of the French UGIF (Union Generale des Israelites de France) Raymond-Raoul Lambert, the part memoir, part diary of a member of the Ottwock Jewish police, Calel Perechodnik; the diary of Warsaw schoolteacher and administrator, Abraham Lewin; that of the Dresden professor, Victor Klemperer; of the Bucharest writer, Mihail Sebastian; of the Warsaw Bund official, Hermann Kruk (Dobroszycki 1984; Lambert 1985; Lewin 1989, Perechodnik 1996; Klemperer 1998/9; Sebastian 2000; Kruk 2002). The study of the victims' diaries is becoming a domain of its own (Heer 1997; Patterson 1999; Shapiro 1999; Kassow 1999).

The historical importance of the victims' diaries has been mostly unquestioned; not so, however, that of the survivors' memoirs or depositions. Some historians have remained highly sceptical regarding the utilization of these reminiscences (Hilberg 1988, 2002). An important argument was and is that, in their memoirs, the survivors were in fact often telling an 'identical' story, patterned by some kind of common collective memory, repeating some topoi from one text to the other. One could add that the memoirs of Jews who were involved in the 'politics' of the Councils, in the Zionist youth movements, or in Jewish political parties in Eastern or Western Europe were sometimes self-serving and apologetic. Moreover, the memory of some survivors is not always precise, due in part to the very nature of the events. But these objections are even more valid regarding the memoirs of the perpetrators. The answer may simply be that a critical analysis should be equally stringent and equally valid for all such texts.

CONCLUDING REMARKS

From the 1980s onward, and mainly in the 1990s, the Holocaust has become one of the events of twentieth-century history most frequently referred to in public debates, the media, and educational programmes throughout the Western world. It is debated and written about by theologians, philosophers, and legal scholars among others; it has become a vast literary domain; its influence on the arts is considerable. In history, essays and comments on the historiography of the Holocaust are growing in number (Friedländer 1993; Bartov 1996, Bauer 2001). The social and psychological reasons for this sudden and massive growth in interest and the dynamics of collective memory and memorialization have been differently assessed (Young 1993; Hartman 1994; Reichel 1995; Herf 1997; Wiedmer 1999; Assmann and Frevert 1999). Whatever the explanations may be, the view that sees this expansion as the result of political manipulation, initiated mainly by American Jewish organizations for political purposes, is based more on conspiracy theory than on evidence. Nonetheless, the sudden public interest in the Holocaust and the wide coverage of anything related to it have occasionally led to the seeping of sensationalism into historical research. The proliferation of large-scale, semi-scholarly conferences and of simplified teaching curricula also carry the danger of trivialization.

In the same context, one cannot avoid a reference to 'negationism', according to which the Holocaust never took place, or alternatively, gas chambers never existed, the number of Jews murdered by the Nazis was minimal, and Hitler was unaware of the systematic extermination of the Jews until 1943. The negationists' campaign started soon after the end of the war, and grew in shrillness with the growing interest in the Holocaust itself. This endeavour, whatever its individual or social-political origins, represents a system inaccessible to argumentation or documentary proof (Vidal-Naquet 1987; Lipstadt 1993). Negationism had and has no identifiable impact on the course of historiography, except for some retorts to David Irving's theses or to those of some French negationists (Broszat 1977; Fleming 1984; Pressac 1989), and the recourse to the expertise of historians in various judicial proceedings, most recently in David Irving's London court case (Evans 2001).

In terms of historiography per se, it could be useful, in concluding this essay, to make some suggestions regarding the history of the victims, comparative studies, and an integrated history of the Holocaust.

The history of the victims has to overcome its relative insularity, due mainly to the fact that it is rarely dealt with by historians of non-Jewish background. The reasons for such reticence are understandable but should, at this stage, be overcome: non-Jewish historians should be able to research Jewish life and death in the ghettos and the camps, and to examine the politics of Jewish organizations or parties, East and West. In short, this domain has to be opened to the same critical inquiry as the other 'clusters'. Issues belonging both to the history of the victims and to that of the bystanders could be investigated in common. For example, the argument often brought up in Eastern Europe to explain the anti-Jewish violence of the local populations, once the Germans marched in, is that Jews, in vast numbers, collaborated with the communist authorities, particularly with the NKVD, in the countries and areas occupied by the Soviet Union between 1939 and 1941. Although this issue has been repeatedly studied (Davies and Polonsky 1991; Levin 1995), common research efforts could lead to further insights.

The second issue that demands close attention is that of comparative studies. Before addressing my main point, let me stress again that comparisons at the level of political systems, such as totalitarianism, are important even if yet inconclusive. One should also consider, at the same level of inquiry, comparing Nazi exterminations with various other genocidal phenomena (Armenia, Cambodia, Rwanda, East Timor, Bosnia). Few systematic studies have followed this approach (Horowitz 1976; Kuper 1982; Rummel 1996); in general, research tends to focus on the specific cases of genocide, and comparison remains perfunctory.

Within the framework of the history of the Holocaust itself, it was mentioned above that the considerable differences from one area and country to the other make it difficult to establish continent-wide common denominators regarding the attitudes and behaviour of the bystanders (Fein 1979). But this difficulty does not mean that further comparative work is not necessary or possible. In his magisterial comparative history of the Jewish Councils, Isaiah Trunk did not formulate any overarching conclusions; yet the sheer comparison of various domains of activity, of the internal organization, of the personality of members of the Councils, offers an essential foundation for the general assessment of similarities and differences (Trunk 1972). The same systematic inquiries can (and should) be made regarding Christian religious responses to the fate of the Jews, elite and popular anti-Semitism in different countries during the extermination years, various modes of economic exploitation and robbery of the victims, and responses of anti-Nazi clandestine organizations and resistance movements to the deportations, among a vast number of possible issues.

Comparative studies would be a first step towards what seems to be the essential next stage of Holocaust historiography: an increasingly integrated historical representation of this past. Assembling information and studies about essential topics in encyclopedias (Gutman *et al.* 1990; Laqueur 2001), in collective volumes (Friedlander and Milton 1980; Bauer and Rotenstreich 1981; Cesarani 1994; Bartov 2000), in textbooks (Bauer 1982; Yahil 1990; Benz 1999; Wistrich 2002), and in readers (Noakes and Pridham 2001) have, at times, achieved valuable results. Juxtaposition, however, is not identical with integration. Schematically put, integration is called for by the increase of sub-specialization in this domain and growing awareness of complexity regarding attitudes and behaviour: the shift of borderlines between the first two clusters and the extension of that 'grey zone' of ambiguous attitudes, roles, and modes of behaviour so subtly described by Primo Levi (Levi 1988). Integration would also highlight the simultaneity of events and allow thereby a better understanding of the full scope of the Holocaust.

Essentially, however, an integrated history implies the constant presence of the history of the victims, as a collectivity, but also as individuals, within the general historical representation of this past. Some years ago the Berkeley historian Thomas Laqueur wrote a highly perceptive critique of what he called the 'business as usual' historiography of the Holocaust, one that 'fails to confront both the particular moral breakdown these events imply and the subjective terror that they inspired' (Laqueur 1997). Only the integration of individual fate in the general narration could eventually enable the historian to overcome the dichotomy between the unfathomable abstraction of the millions who perished and the tragedy of individual life and death in the time of extermination.

SUGGESTED READING

Michael Burleigh's *The Third Reich* (2000) is one of the most recent histories of Nazi Germany that puts a major emphasis on the persecution of the Jews in the 1930s and on the Holocaust. It may be the best available overall introduction to the subject. German historiography on Nazi extermination policies in the East, mainly written by German historians in the late 1990s, is best presented in a volume of studies edited by Ulrich Herbert (2000). A small fragment of the world of the victims and of the bystanders is powerfully illuminated in the two volumes of Victor Klemperer's diaries of the years 1933–45 (1998/9). Finally, Bob Moore's monograph on Nazi policies and the fate of the Jews of Holland (1997) offers a complex and compelling picture of the fate of a Jewish community in Western Europe.

BIBLIOGRAPHY

ABELLA, I. and TROPER, H. 1982. *None is Too Many: Canada and the Jews of Europe, 1933–1948*. New York.

Actes et documents du Saint Siège relatifs à la Seconde Guerre Mondiale. 1965–1981. Vatican City.

ADAM, U. D. 1972. *Judenpolitik im Dritten Reich*. Düsseldorf.

ADLER, H. G. 1960. *Theresienstadt, 1941–1945: Das Antlitz einer Zwangsgemeinschaft*. Tübingen.

——1974. *Der Verwaltete Mensch. Studien zur Deportation der Juden aus Deutschland*. Tübingen.

——LANGBEIN, H. and LINGENS-REINER, E. eds. 1979. *Auschwitz: Zeugnisse u. Berichte*. Cologne.

ADLER, J. 1987. *The Jews of Paris and the Final Solution: Communal Response and Internal Conflicts 1940–1944*. New York.

ADORNO, T. W. and HORKHEIMER, M. 1975. *Dialectic of Enlightenment*. New York.

ALY, G. 2000. *'Final Solution': Nazi Population Policy and the Murder of the European Jews*. London.

——and HEIM, S. 1991. *Vordenker der Vernichtung. Auschwitz und die deutschen Pläne für eine neue europäische Ordnung*. Hamburg.

ARAD, I. 1987. *Belzec, Sobibor, Treblinka: The Operation Reinhardt Death Camps*. Bloomington, Ind.

——GUTTMAN, Y., and MARGALIOTH, A. eds. 1981. *Documents on the Holocaust: Selected Sources on the Destruction of the Jews of Germany, Austria, Poland and the Soviet Union*. Jerusalem.

ARENDT, H. 1951. *The Origins of Totalitarianism*. New York.

——1963. *Eichmann in Jerusalem: A Report on the Banality of Evil*. New York.

ASSMANN, A. and FREVERT, U. 1999. *Geschichtsvergessenheit, Geschichtsversessenheit. Vom Umgang mit deutschen Vergangenheiten nach 1945*. Stuttgart.

AVNI, H. 1982. *Spain, the Jews, and Franco*. Philadelphia.

AYASS, W. 1995. *'Asoziale' im Nationalsozialismus*. Stuttgart.

BÄHR, J. 1999. *Der Goldhandel der Dresdner Bank im Zweiten Weltkrieg*. Leipzig.

BAJOHR, F. 1997. *'Arisierung' in Hamburg. Die Verdrängung der jüdischen Unternehmer 1933–1945*. Hamburg.

——2001. *Parvenüs und Profiteure. Korruption in der NS Zeit*. Frankfurt.

BALDWIN, P. ed. 1990. *Reworking the Past: Hitler, the Holocaust and the Historians' Debate*. Boston.

BANKIER, D. 1992. *The Germans and the Final Solution: Public Opinion Under Nazism*. Oxford.

——ed. 2000. *Probing the Depth of German Antisemitism: German Society and the Persecution of the Jews, 1933–1941*. New York.

BARKAI, A. 1989. *From Boycott to Annihilation: The Economic Struggle of the German Jews, 1933–1943*. Hanover, NH.

BARTOV, O. 1992. *Hitler's Army: Soldiers, Nazis and War in the Third Reich*. New York.

——1996. *Murder in Our Midst: The Holocaust, Industrial Killing, and Representation*. New York.

—— 2000. *The Holocaust: Origins, Implementation, Aftermath.* London.

BAUER, Y. 1982. *A History of the Holocaust.* New York.

—— 1994. *Jews for Sale? Nazi–Jewish Negotiations 1933–1945.* New Haven.

—— 2001. *Rethinking the Holocaust.* New Haven.

—— and ROTENSTREICH, N. eds. 1981. *The Holocaust as Historical Experience: Essays and a Discussion.* New York.

BAUMAN, Z. 1989. *Modernity and the Holocaust.* Cambridge.

BEER, M. 1987. 'Die Entwicklung der Gaswagen beim Mord an den Juden.' *Vierteljahrshefte für Zeitgeschichte* 35: 403–17.

BENZ, W. ed. 1988. *Die Juden in Deutschland, 1933–1945: Leben unter Nazionalsozialistischer Herrschaft.* Munich.

—— ed. 1991. *Dimension des Völkermords.* Munich.

—— *et al.* eds. 1998. *Einsatz im 'Reichskommissariat Ostland'. Dokumente zum Völkermord in Baltikum und Weissrussland, 1941–44.* Berlin.

—— 1999. *The Holocaust.* New York.

BERGEN, D. L. 1996. *Twisted Cross: The German Christian Movement in the Third Reich.* Chapel Hill, NC.

BILLIG, J. 1955. *Le Commissariat général aux questions juives, 1941–1944.* Paris.

BLOM, J. C. H. 1989. 'The Persecution of the Jews in the Netherlands in a Comparative International Perspective.' *Dutch Jewish History*, 2.

BOCK, G. 1986. *Zwangssterilisation im Nationalsozialismus. Studien zur Rassenpolitik und Frauenpolitik.* Opladen.

BOTZ, G. 1975. *Wohnungspolitik und Judendeportation in Wien 1938 bis 1945. Zur Funktion des Antisemitismus als Ersatz nationalsozialistischer Sozialpolitik.* Vienna.

BOURGEOIS, D. 1998. *Business helvétique et Troisième Reich.* Lausanne.

BRACHER, K.-D. 1969. *Die Deutsche Diktatur.* Cologne.

BRAHAM, R. L. 1981. *The Politics of Genocide: The Holocaust in Hungary.* 2 vols. New York.

BRECHTKEN, M. 1998. *'Madagaskar für die Juden': Antisemitische Idee und politische Praxis, 1895–1945.* Munich.

BREITMAN, R. 1991. *The Architect of Genocide: Himmler and the Final Solution.* New York.

—— 1998. *Official Secrets: What the Nazis Planned, What the British and Americans Knew.* New York.

—— and KRAUT, A. M. 1987. *American Refugee Policy and European Jewry 1933–1945.* Bloomington, Ind.

BROSZAT, M. ed. 1958. *Rudolf Höss. Kommandant in Auschwitz.* Stuttgart.

—— 1977. 'Hitler und die Genesis der Endlösung. Aus Anlass der Thesen von David Irving.' In *Vierteljahrshefte für Zeitgeschichte* 25.

—— 1990. 'A Plea for the Historicization of National Socialism.' In *Reworking the Past: Hitler, the Holocaust and the Historians' Debate.* P. Baldwin ed. Boston.

—— and FRIEDLÄNDER, S. 1990. 'A Controversy about the Historicization of National Socialism.' In *Reworking the Past: Hitler, the Holocaust and the Historians' Debate.* P. Baldwin ed. Boston.

BROWNING, C. R. 1985. *Fateful Months: Essays on the Emergence of the Final Solution.* New York.

—— 1992. *The Path to Genocide: Essays on the Launching of the Final Solution.* Cambridge.

—— 1993. *Ordinary Men: Reserve Police Battalion 101 and the Final Solution in Poland.* New York.

BROWNING, C. R. 2000. *Nazi Policy, Jewish Workers, German Killers.* Cambridge.

BURLEIGH, M. 1994. *Death and Deliverance: 'Euthanasia' in Germany, 1900–1945.* Cambridge.

—— 2000. *The Third Reich: A New History.* New York.

—— and WIPPERMANN, W. 1991. *The Racial State: Germany 1933–1945.* Cambridge.

BURRIN, P. 1994. *Hitler and the Jews: The Genesis of the Holocaust.* London.

CARPI, D. 1994. *Between Mussolini and Hitler: The Jews and the Italian Authorities in France and Tunisia.* Hanover, NJ.

CESARANI, D. ed. 1994. *The Final Solution: Origins and Implementation.* London.

—— ed. 1997. *Genocide and Rescue: The Holocaust in Hungary 1944.* Oxford.

CHARY, F. 1972. *The Bulgarian Jews and the Final Solution, 1940–1944.* Pittsburgh.

COHEN, A. 1987. 'Pétain, Horthy, Antonescu and the Jews, 1942–1944: Toward a Comparative View.' *Yad Vashem Studies* 18: 163–98.

—— and COCHAVI, J. eds. 1995. *Zionist Youth Movements During the Shoah.* New York.

COHEN, R. 1987. *The Burden of Conscience: French Jewry's Response to the Holocaust.* Bloomington, Ind.

COHN, N. 1967. *Warrant for Genocide: The Myth of the Jewish World Conspiracy and the Protocols of the Elders of Zion.* London.

CORNWELL, J. 1999. *Hitler's Pope: The Secret History of Pius XII.* New York.

COURTOIS, S. *et al.* 1997. *Le Livre noir du communisme. Crimes, terreur et répression.* Paris.

CZECH, D. 1989. *Kalendarium der Ereignisse im Konzentrationslager Auschwitz Birkenau. 1939–1945.* Reinbek.

CZERNIAKOW, A. 1979. *The Warsaw Diary of Adam Czerniakow: Prelude to Doom.* R. Hilberg, S. Staron, and J. Kermisz eds. New York.

DAVIES, N. and POLONSKY, A. eds. 1991. *Jews in Eastern Poland and the USSR, 1939–1946.* New York.

DAWIDOWICZ, L. S. 1975. *The War against the Jews 1933–1945.* London.

—— ed. 1976. *Holocaust Reader.* New York.

DEAN, M. 2000. *Collaboration in the Holocaust: Crimes of the Local Police in Bielorussia and Ukraine, 1941–1944.* London.

DELPECH, F. 1982. 'Les Églises et la persecution raciale.' In *Églises et Chrétiens dans la IIe Guerre mondiale.* Lyon.

DIECKMANN, C. 2000. 'The War and the Killing of the Lithuanian Jews.' In Herbert (2000): 240–76.

DINER, D. ed. 1987. *Ist der Nationalsozialismus Geschichte?* Frankfurt.

DOBROSZYCKI, L. ed. 1984. *The Chronicle of the Lódz Ghetto 1941–1944.* New Haven.

DOMARUS, M. ed. 1962–3. *Hitler. Reden und Proklamationen, 1932–1945.* Vol. 1: *Triumph (1932–1938).* Vol. 2: *Untergang (1939–1945).* Neustadt a. d. Aisch.

DÖSCHER, H.-J. 1988. *'Reichskristallnacht.' Die November Pogrome 1938.* Frankfurt am Main.

DWORK, D. and JAN VAN PELT, R. 1996. *Auschwitz: 1270 to the Present.* New York.

ENGEL, D. 1987. *The Polish Government-in-Exile and the Jews, 1939–1943.* Chapel Hill, NC.

—— 1993. *Facing a Holocaust: The Polish Government-in-Exile and the Jews, 1943–1945.* Chapel Hill, NC.

EVANS, R. J. 2001. *Lying About Hitler: History, Holocaust, and the David Irving Trial.* New York.

EZERGAILIS, A. 1996. *The Holocaust in Latvia 1941–1944. The Missing Center.* Riga.

FAVEZ, J.-C. 1999. *The Red Cross and the Holocaust*. Cambridge.

FEIN, H. 1979. *Accounting for Genocide*. New York.

FEINGOLD, H. L. 1995. *Bearing Witness: How America and Its Jews Responded to the Holocaust*. Syracuse, NY.

FELDMAN, G. D. 2001. *Die Allianz und die Deutsche Versicherungswirtschaft, 1933–1945*. Munich.

FELICIANO, H. 1997. *The Lost Museum: The Nazi Conspiracy to Steal the World's Greatest Works of Art*. New York.

FEST, J. C. 1974. *Hitler*. New York.

FLEMING, G. 1984. *Hitler and the 'Final Solution'*. Berkeley.

FRANK, A. 1997. *The Diary of a Young Girl: The Definitive Edition*. O. H. Frank and M. Pressler eds. New York.

FREI, N. 1999. *Vergangenheitspolitik. Die Anfänge der Bundesrepublik und die NS-Vergangenheit*. Munich.

—— . et al. eds. 2000. *Ausbeutung, Vernichtung, Öffentlichkeit. Neue Studien zur Nationalsozialistischen Lagerpolitik*. Munich.

——, STEINBACHER, S. and WAGNER, B. eds. 2000. *Standort-und Kommandanturbefehle des Konzentrationslagers Auschwitz 1940–1945*. Munich.

FRIEDLANDER, H. 1995. *The Origins of Nazi Genocide: From Euthanasia to the Final Solution*. Chapel Hill, NC.

—— and MILTON, S. eds. 1980. *The Holocaust: Ideology, Bureaucracy and Genocide*. Milwood, NY.

—— eds. 1990–5. *Archives of the Holocaust: An International Collection of Selected Documents*. 22 vols. New York.

FRIEDLÄNDER, S. 1966. *Pius XII and the Third Reich: A Documentation*. New York.

—— 1969. *Kurt Gerstein: The Ambiguity of Good*. New York.

—— 1984. 'From Antisemitism to Extermination: A Historiographical Study of Nazi Policies Towards the Jews.' *Yad Vashem Studies* 16: 1–50.

—— ed. 1992. *Probing the Limits of Representation: Nazism and the 'Final Solution'*. Cambridge, Mass.

—— 1993. 'Trauma, Transference and "Working Through" in Writing the History of the Shoah.' In *History, Memory and the Extermination of the Jews of Europe*. Bloomington, Ind.

—— 1997. *Nazi Germany and the Jews*. Vol. 1: *The Years of Persecution 1933–1939*. New York.

FRÖHLICH, E. ed. 1987–2001. *Joseph Goebbels, Die Tagebücher von Joseph Goebbels. Sämtliche Fragmente*. Munich.

GAILUS, M. 2001. *Protestantismus und Nationalsozialismus*. Cologne.

GELBER, Y. 1979. 'Zionist Policy and the Fate of European Jewry (1939–1942)'. *Yad Vashem Studies* 13: 133–67.

GELLATELY, R. 1990. *The Gestapo and German Society*. Oxford.

—— 2001. *Backing Hitler*. Oxford.

GENSCHEL, H. 1966. *Die Verdrängung der Juden aus der Wirtschaft im Dritten Reich*. Göttingen.

GERLACH, C. 1995. 'Männer des 20. Juli und der Krieg gegen die Sowjetunion'. In Hannes Heer and Klaus Naumann (eds.), *Vernichtungskrieg*. Frankfurt.

—— 1998a. 'The Wannsee Conference, the Fate of German Jews and Hitler's Decision in Principle to Exterminate all European Jews.' *Journal of Modern History*. 70/4.

GERLACH, C. 1998b. *Krieg, Ernährung, Völkermord. Forschungen zur deutschen Vernichtungspolitik im Zweiten Weltkrieg*. Hamburg.

—— 1999. *Kalkulierte Morde: Die Deutsche Wirtschafts-und-Vernichtungspolitik in Weissrussland, 1941 bis 1944*. Hamburg.

——. and ALY, G. 2002. *Das Lezte Kapitel: Realpolitik, Ideologie und der Mord an den ungarischen Juden, 1944/45*. Stuttgart.

GERLACH, W. 1993. *Als die Zeugen Schwiegen. Bekennende Kirche und die Juden*. Berlin.

GILBERT, M. 1981. *Auschwitz and the Allies*. London.

GLEASON, A. 1995. *Totalitarianism: An Inner History of the Cold War*. Oxford.

GOLDHAGEN, D. J. 1996. *Hitler's Willing Executioners: Ordinary Germans and the Holocaust*. New York.

GRUNER, W. 1997. *Der Geschlossene Arbeitseinsatz deutscher Juden: Zur Zwangsarbeit als Element der Verfolgung, 1938–1943*. Berlin.

GROSS, J. T. 2001. *Neighbors: The Destruction of the Jewish Community in Jedwabne, Poland*. Princeton.

GRYNBERG, A. 1991. *Les Camps de la honte*. Paris.

GUTMAN, Y. and ZUROV, E. eds. 1977. *Rescue Attempts During the Holocaust*. Jerusalem.

—— 1982. *The Jews of Warsaw: Ghetto, Underground, Revolt*. Bloomington, Ind.

—— and HAFT, C. eds. 1979. *Patterns of Jewish Leadership in Nazi Europe, 1933–1945*. Jerusalem.

—— *et al.* eds. 1990. *Encyclopedia of the Holocaust*. 4 vols. New York.

—— and BERENBAUM, M. eds. 1994. *Anatomy of the Auschwitz Death Camp*. Bloomington, Ind.

HAMANN, B. 1999. *Hitler's Vienna: A Dictator's Apprenticeship*. New York.

HARTMAN G. H. ed. 1994. *Holocaust Remembrance. The Shapes of Memory*. Cambridge, Mass.

HARTOG, L. J. 1997. *Der Befehl zum Judenmord: Hitler, Amerika und die Juden*. Bodenheim.

HAYES, P. 1994. 'Big Business and "Aryanization" in Germany, 1933–39.' *Jahrbuch für Antisemitismusforschung* 3: 254–81.

——. 1996. 'IG Farben und der IG Farben Prozess'. In Fritz Bauer Institut (ed.), *Auschwitz. Geschichte. Rezeption und Wirkung*. Frankfurt.

HEER, H. ed. 1997. *Im Herzen der Finsternis: Victor Klemperer als Chronist der NS-Zeit*. Berlin.

—— *et al.* eds. 2000. *War of Extermination: The German Military in World War II*. New York.

HERBERT, U. ed. 2000. *National Socialist Extermination Policies: Contemporary German Perspectives and Controversies*. New York.

—— and GROEHLER, O. 1992. *Zweierlei Bewältigung. Vier Beiträge über den Umgang mit der NS-Vergangenheit in den beiden deutschen Staaten*. Hamburg.

—— ORTH, K. and DIECKMANN, K. C. eds. 1998. *Die Nationalsozialistischen Konzentrationlager*. 2 vols. Göttingen.

HERF, J. 1997. *Divided Memory: The Nazi Past in the Two Germanies*. Cambridge, Mass.

HEUSS, A. 2000. *Kunst-und Kulturgutraub. Eine vergleichende Studie zur Besatzungspolitik der Nationalsozialisten in Frankreich und der Sowjetunion*. Heidelberg.

HILBERG, R. 1961. *The Destruction of the European Jews*. Chicago.

—— ed. 1971. *Documents of Destruction*. Chicago.

—— 1988. 'I Was Not There.' In *Writing and the Holocaust*. Berel Lang ed. New York.

—— 1989. 'The Statistic.' In *Unanswered Questions: Nazi Germany and the Genocide of the Jews*. François Furet ed. New York.

—— 1992. *Perpetrators, Victims, Bystanders: The Jewish Catastrophe 1933–1945*. New York.

—— 2002. *Sources of Holocaust Research: An Analysis*. Chicago.

HOROWITZ, I. 1976. *Genocide: State Power and Mass Murder*. New Brunswick, NJ.

HORWITZ, G. J. 1990. *In the Shadow of Death: Living Outside the Gates of Mauthausen*. New York.

HÖSS, R. 1992. *Death Dealer: The Memoir of the SS Kommandant at Auschwitz*. Buffalo.

Independent Commission of Experts, Switzerland, National Socialism and the Second World War 2002. *Final Report*. Zurich.

IOANID, R. 2000. *The Holocaust in Romania: The Destruction of Jews and Gypsies Under the Antonescu Regime 1940–1944*. Chicago.

JÄCKEL, E. 1969. *Hitlers Weltanschauung. Entwurf einer Herrschaft*. Tübingen.

——. and KUHN, A. eds. 1980. *Hitler, Sämtliche Aufzeichnungen: 1905–1924*. Stuttgart.

—— and ROHWER, J. eds. 1985. *Der Mord an den Juden im Zweiten Weltkrieg. Entschlussbildung und Verwirklichung*. Stuttgart.

JAMES, H. 2001. *The Deutsche Bank and the Nazi Economic War Against the Jews: The Expropriation of Jewish-Owned Property*. New York.

JANSEN, H. 1997. *Der Madagaskar Plan: die beabsichtigte Deportation der europäischen Juden nach Madagaskar*. Munich.

JELLONEK, B. 1990. *Homosexuelle unter dem Hakenkreuz*. Paderborn.

JOHNSON, E. A. 1999. *Nazi Terror: The Gestapo, Jews and Ordinary Germans*. New York.

Jüdisches Historisches Institut Warschau ed. 1960. *Faschismus-Getto-Massenmord: Dokumentation über Ausrottung und Widerstand der Juden in Polen während des zweiten Weltkrieges*. Berlin.

KAGAN, J. and COHEN, D. 1998. *Surviving the Holocaust With the Russian Jewish Partisans*. London.

KAPLAN, C. A. 1965. *Scroll of Agony: The Warsaw Diary of Chaim A. Kaplan*. A. I. Katsch ed. New York.

KAPLAN, M. A. 1998. *Between Dignity and Despair: Jewish Life in Nazi Germany*. New York.

KARNY, M., BLODIG, V., and KARNA, M. eds. 1992. *Theresienstadt in der Endlösung*. Prague.

KASSOW, S. D. 1999. 'Vilna and Warsaw, Two Ghetto Diaries: Herman Kruk and Emanuel Ringelblum'. In Robert Moses Shapiro (ed.), *Holocaust Chronicles*. Hoboken, NJ.

KATZ, J. 1980. *From Prejudice to Destruction: Antisemitism, 1700–1933*. Cambridge.

KERMISH, J. ed. 1979–97. *The Jewish Underground Press in Warsaw*. 6 vols. Jerusalem. [Hebrew].

KERSHAW, I. 1994. 'Totalitarianism Revisited: Nazism and Stalinism in Comparative Perspective.' *Tel Aviver Jahrbuch für Deutsche Geschichte* 23: 23–40.

—— 1999/2000. *Hitler*. Vol. 1: *1889–1936: Hubris*. Vol. 2: *1936–1945: Nemesis*. London.

—— and LEWIN, M. eds. 1997. *Stalinism and Nazism: Dictatorships in Comparison*, Cambridge.

KLARSFELD, S. 1983/5. *Vichy—Auschwitz. Le rôle de Vichy dans la solution finale de la question juive en France*. Vol. 1: *1942*. Vol. 2: *1943–1944*. Paris.

KLEE, E. 1983. *'Euthanasie' im NS-Staat*. Frankfurt am Main.

—— et al. eds. 1991. *'The Good Old Days': The Holocaust as Seen By the Perpetrators and Bystanders*. New York.

KLEIN, P. ed. 1997. *Die Einsatzgruppen in der besetzten Sowjetunion*. Berlin.

—— ed. 1995. *Die Wannsee-Konferenz vom 20 Januar 1942.Analyse und Dokumentation*. Berlin.

KLEMPERER, V. 1998/9. *I Will Bear Witness: A Diary of the Nazi Years*. 2 vols. New York.

KLEY, S. 2000. 'Hitler and the Pogrom of November 9/10, 1938.' *Yad Vashem Studies* 28: 87–112.

KOGON, E. *et al*. eds. 1993. *Nazi Mass Murder: A Documentary History of the Use of Poison Gas*. New Haven.

KOLB, E. 1962. *Bergen-Belsen: Geschichte des 'Aufenthaltslager' 1943–1945*. Hannover.

KORENKE, T. 1999. *Der Widerstand und die Juden*. Essen.

KRAKOWSKI, S. 1984. 'The Death Marches in the Period of the Evacuation of the Camps.' In *The Nazi Concentration Camps*. Y. Gutman and A. Saf eds. Jerusalem.

KRAUSNICK, H. 1965. 'Judenvefolgung.' In *Anatomie des SS-Staates*. Hans Buchheim *et al*. 2 vols. Olten.

—— and WILHELM, H.-W. 1981. *Die Truppe des Weltanschauungskrieges. Die Einsatzgruppen der Sicherheitspolizei und des SD, 1938–1942*. Stuttgart.

KRUK, H. 2002. *The Last Days of the Jerusalem of Lithuania: Chronicles from the Vilna Ghetto and the Camps, 1939–1944*. ed. B. Harshar. New Haven.

KUGELMASS, J. and BOYARIN, J. eds. 1983. *From a Ruined Garden: The Memorial Books of Polish Jewry*. New York.

KULKA, O. D. 1997. *Deutsches Judentum unter dem Nationalsozialismus. Dokumente zur Geschichte der Reichsvertretung der deutschen Juden, 1933–1939*. Tübingen.

—— and MENDES-FLOHR, P. eds. 1987. *Judaism and Christianity Under the Impact of National Socialism*. Jerusalem.

KUPER, L. 1982. *Genocide: Its Political Use in the Twentieth Century*. New Haven.

KWIET, K. and ESCHWEGE, H. 1984. *Selbstbehauptung und Widerstand. Deutsche Juden im Kampf um Existenz und Menschenwürde, 1933–1945*. Hamburg.

LAMBERT, R.-R. 1985. *Carnet d'un Témoin, 1940–1943*. Ed. Richard Cohen. Paris.

LAQUEUR, T. 1997. 'The Sound of Voices Intoning Names.' *London Review of Books*. 5 June.

LAQUEUR, W. 1980. *The Terrible Secret: An Investigation into the Suppression of Information about Hitler's 'Final Solution'*. London.

—— 1994. *The Dream that Failed: Reflections on the Soviet Union*. New York.

—— and Baumel, J. eds. 2001. *The Holocaust Encyclopedia*. New Haven.

—— and BREITMANN, R. 1986. *Breaking the Silence*. New York.

LEVI, PRIMO, 1988. *The Drowned and the Saved*. New York.

LEVIN, D. 1995. *The Lesser of Two Evils: Eastern European Jewry under Soviet Rule*. Philadelphia.

LEVINE, P. A. 1996. *From Indifference to Activism: Swedish Diplomacy and the Holocaust 1938–1944*. Stockholm.

LEWIN, A. 1989. *A Cup of Tears: A Diary of the Warsaw Ghetto*. Ed. Antony Polonsky. New York.

LEWY, G. 1964. *The Catholic Church and Nazi Germany*. New York.

—— 2000. *The Nazi Persecution of the Gypsies*. New York.

LIPSTADT, D. 1993. *Denying the Holocaust: The Growing Assault on Truth and Memory*. New York.

LOEWY, H. and SCHOENBERNER, G. eds. 1990. *'Unser einziger Weg ist Arbeit.' Das Ghetto in Lodz, 1940–1944*. Frankfurt am Main and Vienna.

LONDON, L. 2000. *Whitehall and the Jews 1933–1948. British Immigration Policy, Jewish Refugees and the Holocaust.* Cambridge.

LONGERICH, P. 1989. *Die Ermordung der europäischen Juden. Eine umfassende Dokumentation des Holocaust 1941–1945.* Munich.

—— 1998. *Politik der Vernichtung. Eine Gesamtdarstellung der nationalsozialistischen Judenverfolgung.* Munich.

LÖSENER, B. 1961. 'Als Rassereferent im Reichsministerium des Innern'. *Vierteljahrshefte für Zeitgeschichte* 9: 264–313.

LOZOWICK, Y. 2000. *Hitlers Bürokraten: Eichmann, seine willigen Vollstrecker und die Banalität des Bösen.* Zurich.

MAIER, C. 1988. *The Unmasterable Past: History, Holocaust and German Nationalism.* Cambridge, Mass.

MANOSCHEK, W. 1995. 'Serbien ist Judenfrei': Besatzungspolitik und Judenvernichtung in Serbien, 1941/42.* Munich.

MARRUS, M. 1987. *The Holocaust in History.* Hanover, NH.

—— and PAXTON, R. O. 1983. *Vichy France and the Jews.* New York.

MASON, T. 1981. 'Intention and Explanation: A Current Controversy about the Interpretation of National Socialism.' In *Der 'Führerstaat': Mythos und Realität.* G. Hirschfeld and L. Kettenacker eds. Stuttgart.

MAYER, A. 1988. *Why Did the Heavens Not Darken? The 'Final Solution' in History.* New York.

MENDELSOHN, J. ed. 1982. *The Holocaust: Selected Documents.* 18 vols. New York.

MEYER, B. 1999. 'Judische Mischlinge', Rassenpolitik und Verfolgungserfahrung, 1933–1945.* Hamburg.

MICCOLI, G. 2000. *I dilemmi e i silenzi di Pio XII.* Milan.

MICHMAN, D. ed. 1998. *Belgium and the Holocaust.* Jerusalem.

MOMMSEN, H. 1991. 'The Realization of the Unthinkable: The Final Solution of the Jewish Question.' In *From Weimar to Auschwitz.* Princeton.

—— 2000. 'Der Widerstand gegen Hitler und die Nationalsozialistische Judenverfolgung.' In *Alternative zu Hitler.* Munich.

—— 2002. *Auschwitz, 17 Juli, 1942. Der Weg zur europäischen 'Endlösung der Judenfrage'.* Munich.

MOORE, B. 1997. *Victims and Survivors: The Nazi Persecution of the Jews in the Netherlands, 1940–1945.* London.

MORLEY, J. F. 1980. *Vatican Diplomacy and the Jews, during the Holocaust, 1939–43.* New York.

MOSSE, G. L. 1964. *The Crisis of German Ideology: Intellectual Origins of the Third Reich.* New York.

—— 1978. *Toward the Final Solution: A History of European Racism.* London.

MUSIAL, B. 1999. *Deutsche Zivilverwaltung und Judenverfolgung im Generalgouvernement.* Wiesbaden.

NAASNER, W. ed. 1998. *SS-Wirtschaft und SS Verwaltung.* Düsseldorf.

NE'EMAN ARAD. G. 2000. *America, its Jews, and the Rise of Nazism.* Bloomington, Ind.

NEUFELD, M. J. and BERENBAUM, M. eds. 2000. *The Bombing of Auschwitz.* New York.

NIEWYK, D. and NICOSIA, F. 2000. *The Columbia Guide to the Holocaust.* New York.

NOAKES, J. 1989. 'The Development of Nazi Policies Towards the German-Jewish "Mischlinge" 1933–1945.' *Leo Baeck Institute Yearbook* 34: 291–354.

NOAKES, J. and PRIDHAM, G. eds. 2001. *Nazism, 1919–1945.* 4 vols. Vol.3: *Foreign Policy, War and Racial Extermination: A Documentary Reader.* Exeter.

NOLTE, E. 1987. *Der europäische Bürgerkrieg 1917–1945. Nationalsozialismus und Bolschewismus.* Berlin.

OFER, D. 1990. *Escaping the Holocaust: Illegal Immigration into the Land of Israel, 1939–1944.* New York.

OGORRECK, R. 1996. *Die Einzatsgruppen und die Genesis der Endlösung.* Berlin.

PÄTZOLD, K. 1984. *Verfolgung, Vertreibung, Vernichtung: Dokumente des faschistischen Antisemitismus, 1933 bis 1942.* Frankfurt am Main.

——and SCHWARZ, E. 1992. *Tagesordnung: Judenmord. Die Wannsee-Konferenz am 20. Januar 1942. Eine Dokumentation zur Organisation der 'Endlösung'.* Berlin.

PATTERSON, D. 1999. *Along the Edge of Annihilation: The Collapse and Recovery of Life in the Holocaust Diary.* Seattle.

PAUCKER, A. ed. 1986. *Die Juden im Nationalsozialistischen Deutschland, 1933–45.* Tübingen.

PAUL, G. and MALLMANN, K.-M. eds. 2000. *Die Gestapo im Zweiten Weltkrieg.* Darmstadt.

PERECHODNIK, C. 1996. *Am I a Murderer? Testament of a Jewish Ghetto Policeman.* Boulder, Col.

PETROPOULOS, J. 1996. *Art as Politics in the Third Reich.* Chapel Hill, NC.

PEUKERT, D. K. 1982. *Volksgenossen und Gemeinschaftsfremde. Anpassung, Ausmerze und Aufbegehren unter dem Nationalsozialismus.* Cologne.

——1987. *Inside Nazi Germany: Conformity, Opposition and Racism in Everyday Life.* New Haven.

——1993. 'The Genesis of the Final Solution from the Spirit of Science.' In *Reevaluating the Third Reich.* T. Childers and J. Caplan eds. New York.

PHAYER, M. 2000. *The Catholic Church and the Holocaust, 1930–1965.* Bloomington, Ind.

PIPER, F. 1993. *Die Zahl der Opfer von Auschwitz.* Oswiecim.

POHL, D. 1996. *Nationalsozialistische Judenverfolgung in Ostgalizien 1941–1944. Organisation und Durchführung eines staatlichen Massenverbrechens.* Munich.

——2000. 'Die Ermordung der europäischen Juden. Neue Erkenntnisse der historischen Forschung.' In *NS-Diktatur, DDR, Bundesrepublik.* T. Bauer *et al.* eds. Neuried.

——2000. 'Schauplatz Ukraine: Der Massermord un den Juden im Militärverwaltungsgebiet und im Reichskommissariat, 1941–1943'. In Norbert Frei *et al.* (eds.), *Ausbeutung, Vernichtung, Öffentlichkeit. Neue Studien zur Nationalsozialistischen Lagerpolitik.* Munich.

POLIAKOV, L. 1951. *Bréviaire de la haine,* Paris: Calmann-Lévy.

——1965–85. *The History of Antisemitism.* 4 vols. New York.

——and Wulf, J. 1959. *Le IIIe Reich et les Juifs.* Paris.

PORAT, D. 1990. *The Blue and the Yellow Star of David: The Zionist Leadership in Palestine and the Holocaust, 1939–1945.* Cambridge, Mass.

——2000. *Beyond the Reaches of Our Souls. The Life and Time of Abba Kovner* [Hebrew]. Tel Aviv.

POZNANSKI, R. 1994. *Être juif en France pendant la Seconde Guerre mondiale.* Paris.

PRESSAC, J.-C. 1989. *Auschwitz: Technique and Operation of the Gas Chambers.* New York.

PROCTOR, R. N. 1988. *Racial Hygiene: Medicine under the Nazis.* Cambridge, Mass.

REICHEL, P. 1995. *Politik mit der Erinnerung.* Munich.

REITLINGER, G. 1953. *The Final Solution: The Attempt to Exterminate the Jews of Europe, 1939–1945.* London.

RÉMOND, R. 1996. *Le 'fichier juif'. Rapport de la commission présidée par René Rémond au Premier ministre.* Paris.

RINGELBLUM, E. 1958. *Notes from the Warsaw Ghetto: The Journal of Emmanuel Ringelblum.* J. Sloan, ed. New York.

ROBINSON, J. 1965. *And the Crooked Shall be Made Straight: The Eichmann Trial, Jewish Catastrophe and Hannah Arendt's Narrative.* Philadelphia.

RÖHM, E. and THIERFELDER, J. 1990–5. *Juden, Christen, Deutsche (1933–1945).* 5 vols. Stüttgart.

ROSEMAN, M. 2002. *The Villa, the Lake, the Meeting: Wannsee and the Final Solution.* London.

RÖSSLER, M. and SCHLEIERMACHER, S. eds. 1993. *Der 'Generalplan Ost'. Hauptlinien der nationalsozialistischen Planungs-und Vernichtungspolitik.* Berlin.

ROTHKIRCHEN, L. 1998. 'The Situation of the Jews in Slovakia Between 1939 and 1945.' *Jahrbuch für Antisemitismusforschung* 7: 46–70.

ROZETT, R. 2001. 'Bibiliographical Essay.' In *The Holocaust Encyclopedia.* W. Laqueur and J. Baumel, eds. New Haven.

RÜCKERL, A. ed. 1977. *Nationalsozialistische Vernichtungslager im Spiegel deutscher Strafprozesse. Belzec, Sobibor, Treblinka, Chelmno.* Munich.

RUMMEL, R. 1996. *Death By Government.* New Brunswick, NJ.

SAFRIAN, H. 1993. *Die Eichmann-Männer.* Vienna.

SANDKÜHLER, T. 1996. *'Endlösung' in Galizien. Der Judenmord in Ostpolen und die Rettungsinitiativen von Berthold Beitz 1941–1944.* Bonn.

SCHEFFLER, W. 1961. *Judenverfolgung im Dritten Reich 1933 bis 1945.* Frankfurt am Main.

——. and ARNDT, I. 1976. 'Organisierter Massenmord an Juden in national-sozialistischen Vernichtungslagern'. *Vierteljahrshefte für Zeitgeschichte* 24/2: 105–35.

——and GRABITZ, H. 1995. 'Die Wannsee-Konferenz. Ihre historische Bedeutung in der Geschichte des Nationalsozialistischen Völkermords.' *Acta Universitatis Wratislaviensis.* N1715. Wrocław.

SCHELVIS, J. 1998. *Vernichtungslager Sobibor.* Berlin.

SCHLEUNES, K. A. 1970. *The Twisted Road to Auschwitz: Nazi Policy Toward German Jews, 1933–1939.* Urbana, Ill.

SCHMUHL, H.-W. 1987. *Rassenhygiene, Nationalsozialismus, Euthanasie. Von der Verhütung zur Vernichtung 'lebensunwerten Lebens' 1890–1945.* Göttingen.

SCHOLDER, K. 1977. *Die Kirchen und das Dritte Reich.* Vol. 1. Frankfurt am Main.

SCHULTE, J. E. 2001. *Zwangsarbeit und Vernichtung. Das Wirtschaftsimperium der SS.* Paderborn.

SCHULZE, W. and OEXLE, O. G. eds. 1999. *Deutsche Historiker im Nationalsozialismus,* Frankfurt.

SCHWARZFUCHS, S. 1998. *Aux Prises avec Vichy. Histoire politique des Juifs de France (1940–1944).* Paris.

SEBASTIAN, M. 2000. *Journal 1935–1944: The Fascist Years.* Chicago.

SEGEV, T. 1993. *The Seventh Million: The Israelis and the Holocaust.* New York.

SERENY, G. 1974. *Into that Darkness: From Mercy Killing to Mass Murder.* London.

SHAPIRO, R. M. ed. 1999. *Individualizing the Holocaust Through Diaries and Other Contemporaneous Personal Accounts.* Hoboken, NJ.

SIEGELE-WENSCHKEWITZ, L. ed. 1994. *Christliches Anti-Judaismus und Antisemitismus: Theologische und Kirchliche Programme Deutscher Christen.* Frankfurt.

SMITH, B. F., and PETERSON, A. F. eds. 1974. *Heinrich Himmler, Geheimreden 1933 bis 1945 und andere Ansprachen*. Frankfurt am Main.

SOFSKY, W. 1997. *The Order of Terror: The Concentration Camp*. Princeton.

SPEER, A. 1970. *Inside the Third Reich*. New York.

STEINBACHER, S. 1994. *Dachau*, Frankfurt.

—— 2000. *'Musterstadt' Auschwitz. Germanisierungspolitik und Judenmord in Ostoberschlesien*. Munich.

STEINBERG, J. 1990. *All or Nothing: The Axis and the Holocaust 1941–1943*. London.

STERN, F. 1961. *The Politics of Cultural Despair: A Study in the Rise of the Germanic Ideology*. Berkeley.

STEUR, C. 1997. *Theodor Dannecker: Ein Funktionär der Endlösung*. Tübingen.

STREIT, C. 1978. *Keine Kameraden. Die Wehrmacht und die sowjetischen Kriegsgefangenen 1941–1945*. Stuttgart.

TEC, N. 1993. *Defiance: The Bielski Partisans*. New York.

TEVETH, S. 1996. *Ben Gurion and the Holocaust*. New York.

TRUNK, I. 1972. *Judenrat: The Jewish Councils in Eastern Europe under Nazi Occupation*. New York.

VIDAL-NAQUET, P. 1987. *Les Assassins de la mémoire: 'Un Eichmann de papier' et autres essais sur le révisionnisme*. Paris.

VOLLNHALS, C. *et al*. eds. 1992–8. *Adolf Hitler, Reden, Schriften, Anordnungen (1925–1933)*. 6 vols. Munich.

VOLKOV, S. 1989. 'The Written Matter and the Spoken Word: On the Gap Between Pre-1914 and Nazi Antisemitism.' In *Unanswered Questions: Nazi Germany and the Genocide of the Jews*. F. Furet ed. New York.

WAGNER, B. C. 2000. *IG Auschwitz. Zwangsarbeit und Vernichtung von Häftlingen des Lagers Monowitz 1941–1945*. Munich.

WALK J. ed. 1981. *Das Sonderrecht für die Juden im NS-Staat*. Heidelberg.

WASSERSTEIN, B. 1988. *Britain and the Jews of Europe, 1939–1945* Oxford.

WIEDMER, C. 1999. *The Claims of Memory: Representations of the Holocaust in Contemporary Germany and France*. Ithaca, NY.

WILDT, M. 1995. *Die Judenpolitik des SD, 1935–1937*. Munich.

—— 2002. *Generation des Unbedingten. Das Führungskorps des Reichssicherheitshauptamtes*. Hamburg.

WISTRICH, R. S. 2001. *Hitler and the Holocaust*. London.

WITTE, P. 1995. 'Two Decisions Concerning the "Final Solution to the Jewish Question": Deportations to Lodz and the Mass Murder in Chelmno.' *Holocaust and Genocide Studies* 9/3: 318–45.

—— *et al*. eds. 1999. *Heinrich, Himmler, Der Dienstkalender Heinrich Himmlers 1941/42*, Hamburg.

WYMAN, D. S. 1984. *The Abandonment of the Jews: America and the Holocaust 1941–1945*, New York.

YAHIL, L. 1990. *The Holocaust*. New York.

YOUNG, J. E. 1993. *The Texture of Memory: Holocaust, Memorials and Meaning*. New Haven.

ZIMMERMANN, M. 1996. *Rassenutopie und Genozid: Die Nationalsozialistische 'Lösung der Zigeunerfrage'*. Hamburg.

ZUCCOTTI, S. 2001. *Under His Very Windows: The Vatican and the Holocaust in Italy*. New Haven.

CHAPTER 18

SETTLEMENT AND STATE IN ERETZ ISRAEL

S. ILAN TROEN

WHILE Zionist ideology has long been part of the rubric of Jewish history, the study of its realization through the social, cultural, and political history of the Yishuv and Israel has been relatively neglected. The Jews of Eretz Israel ('the Land of Israel') numbered less than half of 1 per cent of world Jewry at the beginning of the twentieth century. Israel now accounts for about 40 per cent and is approaching parity with the United States. Forecasts indicate that it is likely to become the largest Jewish community in history within a generation. This remarkable development explains why the study of modern Israel, from the early settlements at the end of the nineteenth century through the current dilemmas facing the Jewish state, is becoming a new and vital area of study both within Israel and abroad.

Of course, Israel has not been entirely outside the realm of academic interest. The Arab–Israeli conflict has long been a staple of courses dealing with the Middle East and with international relations. The case of Israel is often included in sociological and anthropological curricula dealing with modernization and immigration. The kibbutz, too, has attracted the interest of students of utopianism and communal experimentation. However, Israeli history and society has only recently become a discrete topic or field of study within the humanities and social sciences, and included in university curricula, even in Israel.

Change began in Israel in the early 1990s, when various collections of courses under the title of 'Israel Studies' were organized as a modest subset within the BA degree. The first BA programme with departmental status was approved at the end of that decade by Israel's Council on Higher Education for Ben-Gurion University of the Negev. Others are likely to follow. At the same time, less extensive initiatives have been undertaken outside Israel to establish lectureships, chairs, and even centres for the study of Israel at a growing number of universities, including Emory, Rutgers, Brandeis, Indiana, American University, the Jewish Theological Seminary, the Oxford Centre for Hebrew and Jewish Studies, and the School for African and Oriental Studies at the University of London. The study of Israel is increasingly valued as a distinct subject that is at once associated with Jewish studies and with long-established interests in the social sciences. These twin locations suggest a creative synergy through multidisciplinary approaches that will shape how scholarship on Israel may develop.

The growing interest is visible also outside the curriculum. Over the last decade new journals have appeared in English, especially *Israel Studies*, published by Indiana University Press, and *Israel Affairs*, published in London by Frank Cass. Both operate with multidisciplinary editorial boards composed of scholars from the United States, Israel, and Britain. There are also new journals oriented towards particular disciplines such as sociology and history. At the same time, established publications in Jewish studies devote increasing space to articles dealing with Israel. Moreover, academic publishers offer a greater number of monographs, whether originally written in English or translated from Hebrew. The largest list is the State University of New York's Series on Israel Studies, initiated in 1988 and edited by Russell Stone, with about sixty books in print. There are, of course, journals and other outlets for monographs in Hebrew. This efflorescence of English-language publications for foreign and even Israeli scholars indicates the heightened status and recognition of the field. Interest in this developing field is also manifest in the activity of the Association of Israel Studies, a professional organization with a strong bias towards the social sciences, and anchored in the United States but with strong representation in Israel and to a lesser extent in Europe.

BEGINNINGS OF RESEARCH

The basis for Zionist and Israeli social sciences was set during the British Mandate, when the Jewish Agency extensively engaged experts in community development and economics. The arrival of Dr Arthur Ruppin to head the Eretz-Israel office of the World Zionist Organization in 1907 foreshadowed this policy and its consequences for scholarship. In addition to a doctorate in law, he earned a second doctorate in sociology. Particularly, the latter served him well as he systematically contributed to a scientific basis for advancing Zionist colonization. In this capacity he conducted the first modern census in Palestine and appointed experts to identify and solve development problems. By the 1930s there were departments for research in the Jewish Agency and a network of official and unofficial publications producing data and analysis.

S. N. Eisenstadt, founder of the Department of Sociology at the Hebrew University, David Horowitz, the first Director of the Bank of Israel, and Alfred Bonné, Ruppin's successor at the Jewish Agency and the first Dean of Social Sciences at the Hebrew University, are but a few of the practitioner/scholars who began their careers by planning for colonization and by gathering data for the international battle over public opinion. The literature they produced remains an essential beginning for students of Israeli society and history. It contains data, defines problems, and provides a historical perspective on how that generation of founders viewed Palestine and on what they hoped to accomplish. Their work is uncritical of the Zionist claim to Palestine, and it directly confronts those who question its legitimacy or would hinder its realization (Troen 1989).

The conflict over Palestine stimulated the creation of an international literature on Jewish and Arab Palestine. While it was largely devoted to the questions of historical and legal rights to the country, it also incorporated fundamental research on Palestine's economic absorptive capacity. Two crucial multi-volume items in this literature are still useful for re-creating the economic, social, political, and institutional history of the Yishuv and of Palestine as a whole. They are the products of teams of foreign researchers who conducted their work with the support of foreign, non-Zionist sources: Robert Nathan, Oscar Gass, and Daniel Creamer (Nathan *et al.* 1946; ESCO 1947). These volumes were at the centre of the deliberations of international bodies, including the United Nations, over the future of the country. The cumulative work of researchers inside and outside the country led Chaim Weizmann to claim in a December 1945 letter to United States President Harry Truman that 'Palestine, for its size, is probably the most investigated country in the world'.

POPULAR HISTORY AND TEXTS

Academic historians played little role in creating a history of the Yishuv. Instead, both before and after the establishment of Israel, they focused on the history of ideology and party politics, with an emphasis on ideological debates. This emphasis may reflect a deeply ingrained attachment to ideas characteristic of an earlier stage of the Zionist movement. Theodor Herzl concluded *Altneuland* (1902) with the injunction that dreams could be turned into realities: 'Wenn Ihr wollt, ist es kein Märchen' (If you will it, it is no legend). Ideas and ideological debate were crucial in the Zionist experience, for they informed adherents on what they ought to do to create new realities. The centrality of ideas is highlighted in works by academic historians both in Israel and abroad. For example, Arthur Hertzberg's widely read classic, that has recently been updated, is entitled *The Zionist Idea: A Historical Analysis and Reader* (Hertzberg 1997). Ben Halpern contributed another model study in *The Idea of the Jewish State* (Halpern 1961). Even Halpern's posthumous volume (2000), co-authored with Jehuda Reinharz, is significantly oriented towards ideological issues. Walter Lacquer (1976), Shlomo Avineri (1981), David Vital (1975), and Gideon Shimoni (Shimoni 1985), scholars who have worked in Israel and the diaspora, have contributed large and detailed studies on Zionist history, with a strong emphasis on ideology. Similarly, Israel Kolatt (1964), Yosef Gorny (1973), and Anita Shapira (1977), writing on the Labour movement, place social and political phenomena firmly within an ideological context.

Despite the proliferation of studies on ideology, there is a relative paucity of general histories written by university scholars. Instead, the history of Israel has attracted considerable attention from journalists and popular writers as well as academics with primary interests elsewhere. A good example is Martin Gilbert, whose *Israel: A History* offers a political and military chronicle that is nevertheless derivative of the work of others rather than the product of original research. His study is also typical of a genre of popular publications that deal primarily with politics and wars (Gilbert 1998).

Few general histories have been undertaken by academics who have deep and specialized knowledge of the subject and who have actually culled archives and other primary documentation. An early and extremely valuable text is by Noah Lucas (1974). In addition to discussions of ideology, it provides valuable analysis on institutional development, Israeli politics, social and economic issues, and the Arab–Israel conflict. Lucas's study concludes with the 1967 Six-Day War and has not been updated. It is also regrettably out of print, except in China, where it has recently been translated and become the text though which that substantial portion of humanity can learn about Israel.

The most comprehensive and current text is Howard M. Sachar (2000). It first appeared in 1976 and has been revised and expanded, currently carrying the story through the Oslo Accords of 1993. This account has grown to more than 1,100 pages and is as thorough a text as one might want. In addition to attention paid to the continuing conflict with Arabs and related diplomatic and military affairs, it also examines cultural and social issues. Nevertheless, Israel's social and cultural history remains to be synthesized by historians. More than a generation of scholarship has greatly broadened our knowledge in this area. It may also be that social history, broadly defined, may be of greater interest to someone living in Israel. Sachar, like Gilbert and Lucas, has had extensive experience and connections with the country, but he has made his home abroad. Scholars looking at Israel from the outside and writing in English may be expected to focus their story differently from those who experience Israel primarily through Hebrew and from the inside.

BIOGRAPHY

Wherever one resides, both laymen and scholars have access to a wide variety of essential non-academic literature. Much is in the form of biography that, in the tradition of Carlyle, celebrates the lives of heroes. Israeli historiography is also replete with self-promoting autobiography. *Trial and Error: The Autobiography of Chaim Weizmann* is an early and well-remembered example of this genre (Weizmann 1949). Generations of founders, and political and military figures, from David Ben-Gurion to Menachem Begin, Golda Meir, Abba Eban, Moshe Dayan, Shimon Peres, and Yitzhak Rabin, have themselves penned or have had ghost-written historical accounts in which their role is abundantly, if not excessively, portrayed (Ben-Gurion 1972; Begin 1977; Meir 1975; Eban 1977; Dayan 1976; Peres 1999; Rabin 1979). Others within the military and diplomatic service, including Chaim Herzog and Gideon Rafael, have authored biographical/historical accounts (Herzog 1996; Rafael 1981). Presumably Ehud Barak, a Chief of Staff and then Prime Minister, immediately engaged in writing his memoirs on leaving office. An interesting variation is Benjamin Netanyahu, whose large volume on a very broad canvass reflects his perception of the challenges and struggles Jews have confronted throughout history (Netanyahu 1993). While obviously not an actual actor in these historic episodes, Netanyahu apprises the reader of how events should be interpreted and even how he would have acted had he been there.

Taking up the pen has become the secular Zionist variation of the ancient Jewish commandment wherein kings were enjoined to become scribes as a necessary part of assuming office. The writings of and on Ben-Gurion are probably the prime example of this phenomenon. His diaries, as well as his essays, statements, and reflections, often collected in government yearbooks or other official publication, were later reissued as separate volumes or refashioned and edited by in-house intellectuals and writers. Similarly, Michael Bar-Zohar wrote a biography that drew on public and private documentation as well as personal contact (Bar-Zohar 1967). More recently, after Ben-Gurion's death, the former *Ha'aretz* journalist Shabtai Teveth produced an important and well-researched volume that benefited from privileged access to documentation, some of which had yet to be publicly released (Teveth 1987). The place and contribution of Ben-Gurion is also assured by an Act of the Knesset that created an archives and a research centre to study him and his times. While the Ben-Gurion Research Center is affiliated with Ben-Gurion University, it is also connected to disciples still active in public affairs who continue to monitor the institute's operations.

While few national leaders have enjoyed such public largesse, Israel has a multitude of archives dedicated to individuals, movements, and institutions. Similarly, institutions associated with Zalmon Shazar and Yitzhak Ben-Zvi, both former Presidents as well as dedicated amateur historians, were established with state support to promote the 'legacy' (*moresheth*) of their namesakes as well as their interest in Zionist history. The same obtains for Yad Jabotinsky that supports the study of Revionist Zionism, and institutions in the names of Begin and of Rabin that further their *moresheth*. A list of national historical institutes that are designed to represent groups and institutions would include several that further the study of different branches of the kibbutz movement, centres for the study of Zionism, the Histadrut, the illegal immigration during the Mandate, the heritage of Iraqi Jewry and other immigrant groups, the Israel Defence Forces and its various branches, and so on. Such institutions have assembled their own archives and they support scholarship through publication programmes, museums, public commemorations, and prize competitions for essays by senior scholars, and university or even high-school students. However academic this effort may be, it is necessarily partial to the interests of particular groups dedicated to placing their perspective firmly in the public square.

EARLY DESCRIPTIONS

Interpreting the experience of building the Yishuv has been intrinsic to Zionist activity since its beginnings. Alter Droyanov and Shulamit Laskov collected in seven volumes the *takanot* and *britot* (articles of incorporation and covenants) that the Lovers of Zion and other Zionist groups generated through 1890 alone (Droyanov and Laskov 1982–93). These were more than merely formal documents for organizing new societies. Framed in public assemblies by groups of Jews throughout Europe and in the lands of their migration in North America and elsewhere, they are outlines of the societies the emigrants intended to create. Anchored in both biblical tradition and contemporary social theory, they provided a mandate and justification for the Zionist enterprise and the means for achieving it. As such they established the ideological and practical foundations for what was to become the state of Israel. It is interesting to note that although these documents are usually expressed in terms that derive from Jewish religious tradition, religious and secular Jews drew upon the same sources.

Imbued with a historical sensibility that fused the past with the future, the actual pioneers portrayed themselves as participants or at least witnesses to an event of meta-historical significance: the long-promised Return to Zion and the Ingathering of the Exiles. This may explain why keeping a diary was so widespread. Ben-Gurion's diary is the most extensive and important of these for reconstructing Israeli history from the Second Aliyah through the second decade of the state. Reading this enormous treasure-trove one senses in the painstaking recording of even apparently minute and banal events that, perhaps like the Puritans, who were also inveterate recorders of daily events, Ben-Gurion believed that Providence or History, if not an ever-watchful God, was looking over his shoulder. Ben-Gurion shared the diary with colleagues in the leadership of the Zionist institutions, thereby disseminating not only details on the affairs of the Zionist movement but his interpretation of events (Ben-Gurion 1983).

Diaries were but one instrument of establishing a public record. The Kressel Collection at the Oxford Centre for Hebrew and Jewish Studies has an excellent archive of ubiquitous popular histories in published volumes, pamphlets, and newspaper clippings. Celebrations of the founding and the development of settlements were expressed in Jubilee volumes that rarely waited for the fiftieth anniversary. Rather, they were organized even at the fifth and certainly at the tenth, twentieth, twenty-fifth, and subsequent anniversaries. Moreover, these publications, rich in source material for today's historians, early developed a set form. They begin with an historical and physical description of the site on which the settlement was established—a kind of natural history of the locale—and then proceed to its settlement by the ancient Hebrews. The Jewish connection with the land is elaborated as much as biblical, rabbinic, and archaeological sources permit. There is a decided decline in information following the destruction of the Second Temple, and virtually nothing further is recorded during the long period of Muslim conquest and control. The narrative quickly picks up with the coming of the first Zionist pioneers, whether they settled in the 1880s or 1950s. It is here that the pages multiply with stories of individuals and events. The dominant theme is the progress and travails of making the desert bloom and conquering the environment through productive labour. Toward the end of the volume there are pictures of founders and, poignantly, also of those who died in the struggle to secure their achievements. In essence, this is the 'hegemonic narrative' that present-day critical scholars find wanting and open to censure. Arabs are not part of this history and, as occurs in the textbooks for Israeli children, the history of Jews in Eretz Israel is central. The course of Jewish history flows without reference to the experience in the diaspora, with its 'lachrymose' heritage. While Ben-Zion Dinur, an influential historian of the Hebrew University since the 1930s and Minister of Education in the early 1950s, gave

theoretical and institutional expression to this historiosophical position, his research and policies in fact reflected what had already been popularly established in
Zionist society (Myers 1995).

ACADEMIC BIOGRAPHY

Critical historical studies of individuals and Zionist society developed later outside
public and academic history. Academic biography, for example, is a relatively new
phenomenon. Jehuda Reinharz's outstanding volumes on Chaim Weizmann (1985),
Anita Shapira's on Berl Katznelson (1984), Gabriel Sheffer on Moshe Sharett (1996),
Yaacov Shavit on Vladimir Jabotinsky (1988), and Pnina Lahav on Simon Agranat
(1997) are examples of a new trend that has recently taken hold. This growing genre
now extends to men and women in diverse fields, from generals to citizens. Some
important figures in the Yishuv and state await attention. None may be more central
than Levi Eshkol (Shkolnik), who was a major figure in Zionist settlement and
Labour politics and who emerged as Ben-Gurion's successor. As such, he was at the
helm during the 1967 war, one of the defining moments in Israeli history.

The relatively late interest of academics in writing biography reveals a bias in the
way the Zionist story has been told. In the mid-1980s I made a survey of doctoral
dissertations under way at Israeli institutions and discovered that there were
virtually no graduate students writing biography. This was surprising for one
familiar with American and British historiography, where legions of students
work on presidents and prime ministers as well as leading public figures in politics,
the arts, and industry. Instead, most students in Israeli history departments were
writing on institutions, political parties, and events. Moreover, few dealt with topics
beyond independence. This bias may have two sources.

First, Zionist academic historiography tended to celebrate the collective rather
than the individual as decisive in the grand drama of the Return to Zion. The
underlying and unspoken assumption is that Destiny, Providence, or some other
transcendent force has interacted with the Jewish people in the conduct of history. It
may also be that class or nation have been seen as the central forces in historical
development. In this kind of narrative, too, the individual is less significant, just as
in the Haggadah the role of Moses, certainly a key actor, is excluded from the record.
Recently this avoidance of biography has been mitigated due to readily accessible
and extensive documentation that has become available and a new public sensibility
that privileges the individual over the collective.

Second, a traditional, narrow interpretation of a 'scientific' method requires that
history be written from documents, preferably official ones located in archives. Since

Israeli law requires at least thirty years for release of government records, it was argued that post-independence history could only be written beginning in the 1980s at the earliest. As a consequence, historians in Israel mostly ignored a host of issues germane to understanding their own society. In this vacuum, scholars in anthropology, sociology, geography, economics, political science, and international relations have created the historical account. Given this context, the study of Israel is likely to continue as a multidisciplinary endeavour. Historians will need to be familiar with the work of colleagues across the academy, and social scientists will have to take account of an incipient revolution in the scope and depth of historical research.

SOCIAL-SCIENCE ROOTS OF ACADEMIC SCHOLARSHIP

As we have seen, academic historians, practising a discipline defined in Israel as rooted in the humanities, must read fundamental texts composed primarily by sociologists, political scientists, and others working in the social sciences. A prime example is the writings of Eisenstadt, the father of Israeli sociology. From his early work on, his research entails historical accounts of the development of Jewish society in Palestine and the early years of the state (Eisenstadt 1954 and 1967). On such a central historical problem as whether the creation of Israel marks a break or constitutes continuity with the Yishuv, the best place to begin is still the joint publication of the political scientist Dan Horowitz and the sociologist Moshe Lissak (1978). Haim Barkai (1977) and Nahum Gross (1988) researched significant economic issues, such as the changing economy of the kibbutz and the economy of the Yishuv. They and their successor, Jacob Metzer (1998) are located in the Department of Economics of the Hebrew University. Only recently have students trained in Jewish history embarked on an investigation of these topics (Karlinsky 2000).

IMMIGRATION HISTORY

Similarly, the study of immigration, once a preserve of social scientists, has become an active field for this generation of historians. Moreover, if the historiography had previously treated aliyah only as a heroic act, with agents of the Zionist movement as heroes, recent scholarship has adopted a critical perspective that emphasizes the role and plight of the immigrants. Tom Segev, a journalist with a doctorate in history who writes for *Ha'aretz*, produced a popular book with extensive footnotes (Segev 1986) that signalled the change. Segev criticizes the then standard version of the massive ingathering of European survivors from the Holocaust and immigrants from Arab lands of the Middle East. In his narrative, politicians and officials are depicted as victimizers of impotent and trusting newcomers. Immigrants are viewed by the establishment as instruments to achieve national goals, and treated with a lack of sensitivity rooted in ethnic or religious prejudice. In so doing, Segev translated into scholarship what many Oriental Jewish immigrants and their children had expressed at the polls in 1977 in overturning the Labour party for the Likud.

Radical or revisionist sociologists and anthropologists prepared the way for this reappraisal. During the mid-1950s students of Eisenstadt's seminar on Israeli sociology at the Hebrew University were enlisted in graduate seminars and by grants to document and assist in the historical moment of national revival. In the view of a later generation of social scientists, removed by some thirty and forty years from these events, Eisenstadt's students were accomplices to social injustice and their work is therefore suspect, if not deserving of censure.

Such a view misrepresents what these scholars and those of the next generation created. Eisenstadt's young researchers, such as Moshe Shokeid (1971), Alex Weingrod (1966), Shlomo Deshen (Deshen and Shokeid 1974), and Emanuel Marx (1976) in fact produced a rich anthropological and sociological literature, rooted in case studies of villages and development towns in the Galilee and the Negev. They sympathetically depicted the plight and dilemmas of immigrants, often from their perspective, and did not merely support the establishment view that, in order to be transformed into Israelis, immigrants needed to abandon or lessen their connection to their traditional cultures.

Among the themes that emerge from their work is the 'social gap' between European and Oriental Jewry. Measuring inequalities among Israeli Jews became a prime academic concern. Sammy Smooha (1978) advanced the discussion to this new direction. Shlomo Swirsky (1981) deepened the analysis of inequalities. By the 1990s Uri Ram, a sociologist deeply influenced by Swirsky, brought together this new sociological literature in a book that was both a review and a call for new directions (Ram 1995).

The substance of this work, as well as the tone of the rhetoric, were deeply disturbing to those nurtured in traditional Zionist ideology, particularly of the Labour movement with its language replete with the promise of equality. The critics dealing with the obvious disparities in Israeli society laid the charges of hypocrisy and lust for power—'hegemony'—against Ashkenazi founders and their followers. Such criticism, which attempted a fresh and dispassionate re-evaluation of Israeli society, had its own biases, embedded in borrowed paradigms generated in the historical experience of other cultures, primarily the United States.

A historical literature that would re-examine the history of immigration was clearly needed to move the discussion forward. An earlier generation had focused on the founders of the Second and Third Aliyah as immigrants, particularly those associated with the Labour movement. However there had been no detailed examination of the period of massive immigration after independence. The history of Israeli immigration has begun to develop in this direction. It is still very much engaged in identifying heroes and villains enmeshed in opposing sides in what continues to be generally conceived as a heroic enterprise. Moreover, it is common for writers to have some personal knowledge or connection with the events they study, so that scientific scholarship is melded and enriched with what children and grandchildren have learned from family history. Thus Hanna Yablonka, the daughter of survivors from Czechoslovakia who rebuilt their lives in Israel, produced the first serious historical account of the absorption of Holocaust survivors into Israeli society (Yablonka 1999). Historical monographs are not yet available on particular groups from Northern Africa, Yemen, and throughout the Middle East. However, based on the articles that are being published in journals or specialized, edited books, they should soon be in evidence (Ofer 1996).

NEW JEWS AND NEW SOCIETIES

The history of immigration and other topics of developing Zionist society are perhaps inevitably suffused with contending conceptions of the 'New Jew'. In common with other national movements throughout Europe, divergent streams within Zionism postulated variations of a modern version of the new society and the individuals required to build and inhabit it. Such formulations involved imagining distinctive communities, whether secular or religious, bourgeois or socialist. Their common characteristic is an emphasis on the needs of the nation. In this context, the attributes of individuals became blurred, and the nature and needs of the nation were foregrounded.

The kibbutz and the kibbutznik were the most celebrated example of this phenomenon because they appeared to herald the most dramatic deviation from traditional Jewish society. The kibbutz represented a secular revolution against traditional Jewish religious culture, and was described in the appealing language of universal socialism imagining utopian communities. At the same time, it was committed to fulfilling goals and needs of a specific people. Zeev Sternhell (1998) has ably captured the particularistic characteristics of Labour Zionism in general, and demonstrates how it privileged nationalism over socialism. Sternhell's strident criticism seems to single out Zionism for its pragmatic attachment to socialism, as though it differed from European socialist movements in privileging the nation over class. In the context of European socialism the kibbutz was unexceptional, nor was it unusual to imagine that its social order could be constructed to address immediate and existential problems that Jews confronted as a people. The massive and comprehensive work by Henry Near (1992) details the issues and the ways in which contending conceptions of collective goals were addressed.

The reputation of the kibbutz has undergone substantial decline since the publication of Martin Buber's *Paths in Utopia* (Buber 1949). Buber expresses unequivocal admiration for the kibbutz movement at its apogee, idealizing it as 'the experiment that has not failed'. At a time of disillusionment with European totalitarianism of the right and the left, the ideal of a small democratic society of virtuous young Jewish men and women was a compelling alternative, even to the liberal democracies of Western Europe and the United States. At present the kibbutz appears as a problematic society, perhaps on the verge of dissolution, in the face of changes in Israeli society. The kibbutz movement has taken the lead in analysis with a view to correcting itself. Eliezer Ben-Rafael's *Crisis and Transformation* (1997) is a consequence of an exhaustive process of self-examination.

The kibbutz, as the ultimate paradigm of the Zionist social revolution, has become the foil for critiques of contemporary Israeli society. Yaron Ezrahi (1997) is an excellent example from a flood of recent writing critical of collective norms in Israel, espousing their replacement with an explicitly American-inspired individualism. Conscious imitation of what is defined as the American model can be found in many academic disciplines, including 'critical' sociology, 'revisionist' history, and 'postmodern' and 'deconstructionist' critiques; in recent decisions in Israeli courts; in literature, theatre, and film; in the movement to privatize government- or Histadrut-controlled companies and institutions; and in the Americanization of the political system through the direct election of the prime minister, the head of Israel's representative government. It is in this climate that Ezrahi attacks formerly sacred principles: 'The primacy and the omnipresence of the community in the kibbutz and in the larger Israeli society seem to have inhibited the growth of individualism and the culture of the self, two aspects of democratic life that have been essential for the formation of assertive, competent, critical, and largely independent citizens in other Western countries'. (Ezrahi 1997: 36). A convenient source of both critical literature and rejoinders is found in the 'Zionist Dialectics' section of *Israel Studies*. One essential response is by Eliezer Schweid. He is critical of the quest for individual liberty and private gratification at the expense of social solidarity and responsibility, and locates it primarily in an imitation of the American experience after the Second World War, particularly the 1960s. American 'post-modernism' became the model for Israeli 'post-Zionism' (Schweid 1996).

As with all other settlements, the physical design of the kibbutz was a reflection of social and political intentions. Emmanuel Yalan's *The Design of Agricultural Settlements* (1975) is a veritable text on how rural communities mirror distinctive social systems. The classic historical and sociological study is by Dov Weintraub, Moshe Lissak, and Yael Azmon (1969). More than 600 of these villages were constructed across the countryside from the 1880s through the first decade of the state. In examining this enormous effort, it should be remembered that the kibbutz was but one option. With more than 3,000 items listed in an authoritative bibliography of the kibbutz, attention to this form of settlement masks the variety of Zionist settlement.

The unromantic reality has been that most Jews had middle-class aspirations and lived in cities, even as in the diaspora. At no time did more than 20 per cent engage in agriculture. The more established Zionist society has become, the more it has approximated advanced Western societies where more than 95 per cent of people are employed in industry, commerce, and occupations beyond agriculture. It is remarkable, therefore, that the urban frontiers imagined by Zionist pioneers and planners and the cities they produced are largely *terra incognita*. There is no direct correlation between the number of people who settled in a place and the literature historians and chroniclers have generated about it. Erik Cohen (1970) suggests how deeply the bias against the town is embedded in Zionist thought.

Despite attention to agrarian and communitarian ideals, the centrality of the urban and capitalistic side of Zionism is clearly articulated in Herzl's *Altneuland*. This popular tract reflects attitudes and realities that have yet to find their way into scholarship. The hero of Herzl's utopian novel is a highly literate engineer, and most of the other characters are readily identifiable as members of Herzl's own circle of Central European Jews. As Amos Elon has observed, *Altneuland* 'resembles a contemporary Viennese melodrama' and the novel's atmosphere is suffused with the dreams of Hugo von Hofmannsthal's poetry and the mood of Gustav Mahler's music (Elon 1975: 348). The characters' conversation is permeated with the social and political ideas that informed the planning of the new society. Drawn from a large fund of reform thought, these ideas were no doubt familiar and congenial to educated, urban, Jewish bourgeois readers and captured the imaginations of the mass of Zionist enthusiasts in the towns of Eastern Europe. Indeed, Herzl's utopia was meant to be inhabited by settlers intent on incorporating the best of what they admired in European urban culture. This is, in fact, what happened. That is, Tel Aviv's early pioneers built an opera house and established a symphony orchestra and a host of other familiar institutions in the sand dunes. While the kibbutz began to spread across the countryside during the British Mandate, the coast was developed with two major European-style cities, Tel Aviv and Haifa, but their development has not been chronicled in the kind of history familiar in western historiography. The interest in Tel Aviv is only now beginning. A start has been made in a project headed by Yaacov Shavit of Tel Aviv University. I have also given considerable attention to urban pioneering as distinct from the rural counterpart (Troen 2002). It is to be hoped that emerging research will delineate what was genuinely original in the achievements of modern builders of Zion and what they retained from their past.

ZIONIST ARCHETYPES

Zionist society apparently did produce a new and distinctive Jewish personality. The emergence of the term 'sabra' by the end of the 1930s bespeaks a perception that a new brand of Jewish youth sprang from the cities and villages of Palestine. Two essential studies, written with the tools of sociology and anthropology and with a clear historical perspective, chart the recognition that the children of European Jews were being transformed in Palestine: Tamar Katriel (1986) and Oz Almog (2000). By the end of the 1930s a fully fledged modern Hebrew-based culture had taken root in a society that was fast approaching half a million. With a Hebrew-language school system, youth movements, a host of cultural institutions and a vibrant national literature in Hebrew, the elements were in place for implementing the Zionist *Bildung*.

As Anita Shapira demonstrates (1992), theorists like Ahad Ha-Am, Berdichevsky, and Brenner gave much thought to shaping the values of Jewish youth as they observed the initial attempts to build settlements. Indeed, Rachel Elboim-Dror's essential studies on the history of Zionist educational thought reveal how widespread and intensive was the discourse in the early colonies (Elboim-Dror 1986 and 1993). An important consequence of these debates was the creation of a new curriculum as in Jewish history, geography and studies of the 'homeland' (Firer 1985; Bar-Gal 1993 and 1999). Indeed, debates over the curriculum are a prism through which to view the conflict and even disillusionment that ensued when the grand visions of Zionist theory confronted the realities of implementation. More study should be carried out on the heated debates that lead to the replacement of the Talmud with the Bible as the central subject in the education of Jews, and the elimination of the *siddur*, the most widely and regularly read book in Jewish history, from the curriculum in secular schools after independence.

An important part of this history could focus on the disappointment of the founders with the realities they themselves produced. Beginning with Achad Ha-Am's comments on the curriculum at the Herzlyia gymnasium prior to the First World War, to the 1932 public 'trial of youth' by the Hebrew writers' union in Tel Aviv, to the institution of a curriculum of 'Jewish Consciousness' in secular schools in the mid-1950s and to the 1994 Shenhar Report from the Ministry of Education, successive generations of intellectuals, educators, and citizens have expressed alarm at what the children of Zion were becoming (Shenhar *et al.* 1994). They have tried, with limited success, to provide Jewish children in an avowedly secular Jewish state with a secular 'Jewish' education. Immigrants and native-born became loyal citizens, Zionists committed to the new society and deeply rooted in the land. But increasingly they did not see themselves as responsible members of the Jewish people in the diaspora, nor did they maintain ties to a common culture which they no longer shared. Successive generations of Israeli educators have tried to square this circle. They have sought to engender loyalty to a newly defined national culture rooted in a specific locale without severing connections to a culture based in religion, without geographic borders, and extending across millennia. This inherent contradiction is a rich subject that still demands attention. An exploration of this issue should include Amos Elon (1971), although he focuses on what underlay the different political perspectives of the generations rather than their broader value systems.

Education of the new Israelis also took place outside the formal environment of schools. An extraordinarily creative and still growing literature examines 'myths', 'representations', social customs, and ceremonies, and uncovers the ways Israelis have been shaped by a multitude of public rituals (Azaryahu 1995). An outstanding example of this approach is by Yael Zerubavel (1995). Zerubavel distinguishes between what really happened and what people say happened, or between history and memory. Examining events, such as the Roman siege of Masada and Trumpeldor's death in the defence of Tel-Hai, that have become central to the national culture, she demonstrates how changing interpretations are linked to the evolution of society and its internal conflicts. This intellectual exercise can readily suggest that the invention and changing of myths may be a form of conscious exploitation for political purposes. Thus the history of culture can be used to investigate political purposes and the manipulation of public behaviour by ambitious interests (Ben-Yehuda 1995).

Such a view is implicit in the pioneering study by two scholars from Bar-Ilan University, Charles Liebman and Eliezer Don-Yehiya (1983), that contributed to opening new lines of research. Drawing on the work of American social scientist Clifford Geertz, they applied the concept of 'civil religion' to Israeli society and demonstrated how Ben-Gurion and the state's new leadership utilized traditional religious culture for building a modern, secular state. Their analysis is inherently critical, for they suggest that civil religion is less authentic than the original and, in its artificiality is likely to fade, leaving a growing vacuum in Israeli society. While their perception is open to dispute, methodologically they demonstrate how manifestations of public culture reflect underlying values and intentions.

In recent years scholars have built on this precedent while also incorporating the teachings of Jacques Derrida's literary theory and Michel Foucault's power-related analyses to examine the language, symbols, meanings, and purposes of a wide variety of phenomena. These include public ceremonies on Independence Day; memorial services for fallen soldiers; Holocaust memorials; ceremonies in schools; the significance of public monuments, such as Mount Herzl and its rituals; ethnic festivals, such as the Moroccan post-Pesach celebration of Maimuna; the 'march of the living', visits by high-school students to concentration camps in Poland; pilgrimages to religious shrines of North African and East European rabbis; the rise and decline of popular archaeology; and how public remembrances of Rabin's assassination are constructed. Throughout lurk revisionist or postmodernist suspicions that behind any history is a mere narrative, manufactured for the advantage of a particular group.

CRITICISM AND REVISIONISM

Politics and ideology have always played an important role in the writing of Israeli history. There has been both celebration and criticism with the balance between the two having undergone a significant change in recent years. At present there are scholars who blame conscious decisions of policy-makers for contemporary crises. This scholarship is also prescriptive, suggesting that the errors of the past may be corrected. Seen in this way, the study of history becomes an exercise for the benefit of contemporary politics. Before proceeding to examine this movement, it is well to observe alternatives taken by critical scholarship.

Re-examination of Israeli society is widespread, and is not the preserve of revisionists. An important example is Dan Horowitz and Moshe Lissak's book (1989), the last collaborative work by the senior scholars. The book was completed just before the outbreak of the first *intifada* of 1988, and at the same time (as we shall see) that Benny Morris declared a revisionist agenda for a new generation (Morris 1988).

Horowitz and Lissak found paradox and contradiction in a society from which too much was expected. Zionist utopianism raised prospects of a felicitous, just, and integrated society that was not realized and probably unattainable. Most of the shortcomings revolve around the problems of 'cleavage'. In fact, they identify multiple cleavages: between Arabs and Jews; between religious and secular; between ethnic groups, and especially across the Oriental and European fault-lines; between new immigrants and established groups; and between classes. Rather than the healthy and whole society envisioned by Zionist founders, they describe one racked by social and political fragmentation and conflict. Despite their recourse to the dry and terminologically dense language of social science, there is something fundamentally humanistic in their analysis. Paradox, irony, contradiction, unexpected consequences, and human failing are attributed to Israeli society, even as they have been to others. The Israeli case is but an acute version of what may be found elsewhere.

Of all the cleavages that have attracted the attention of revisionists, Arab–Jewish relations have generated the most strident and extreme criticism. As has often been the case, sociologists are in the forefront. They compare Zionist settlement with models of European colonialism in North America, Northern and Southern Africa, and Australia. According to this analysis, Zionists created but another settler society. They had no special rights to the country, and their arrival and subsequent expansion wronged the inhabitants. Baruch Kimmerling pioneered the comparative perspective and highlighted the economically irrational decision of Zionist authorities to pay Jews higher wages in preference to cheaper Arab labour (Kimmerling 1982 and 1983). This issue came to maturity in the work of Gershon Shafir (1989). After examining the initial period in the organization of the prototype kibbutz, Degania, prior to the First World War, Shafir faults settlers and their supporters in the Zionist establishment for devising a means of efficient but exclusive Jewish colonization. Despite the small numbers in the kibbutz movement, it was in Degania that Shafir locates the roots of what Horowitz and Lissak term the 'dual economy' and 'dual society' that came to characterize the Yishuv. Labour Zionist pioneers of the Second Aliyah, who played a disproportionately large role in establishing Israel, championed the separation that is the cause of the long-standing conflict between Arabs and Jews.

Shafir's argument does not examine the conflict between Jews and Arabs in the larger context of Ottoman policies that discriminated against Jews, and overlooks the demand for ethnic, cultural, and religious differentiation inherent in the nationalisms sought by all of Palestine's inhabitants and neighbours in the region. For Shafir, economic interest is what drives human behaviour. It is not without irony that he prefers the settlement practices of the First Aliyah, when the use of Arab labourers inhibited the growth of Jewish settlements and would likely have ended the dream of a Jewish state. His analysis prescribes the transformation of Israel into a denationalized state on an American model, or 'a state of all its citizens' rather than a 'Jewish state'. Shafir's critique implicitly opposes Israel's Law of Return that encourages Jewish immigration that is, by definition, at the expense of Arabs and others. Thus, the failure to achieve harmony and justice is the fault of Jews who insist on maintaining a state in which their culture dominates. Typically, as in much revisionist literature, Arabs are viewed as hapless victims rather than equal participants in a conflict.

The War of Independence is another founding moment in which revisionists locate an 'original sin'. This event has become and is likely to remain a contentious subject for this generation of scholarship, if not longer. It is revealing in the *Zeitgeist* of Israeli society at the end of the 1980s, that the work of three historians on this war—Benny Morris, Ilan Pappé, and Avi Shlaim—coincided with Shafir's publication. Benny Morris trumpeted their collective research as heralding a 'new historiography' (Morris 1988; Furstenberg 1997). Shafir agreed. A self-critical society had come to maturity in reaction to the wrongful extension of control beyond the 1948 armistice lines into Arab territories after 1967, and to the 1982 incursion into Lebanon. Due to the availability of new documents under Israel's Archives Law, scholars of the new generation could re-examine the past in search of explanations of these policies. Thus political protest is explicitly linked to scientific scholarship.

In his 1987 publication Morris refutes the idea that Arabs fled the emerging state only because their leaders advised them to, or because they themselves elected to do so. In a careful reconstruction of the stages of their flight, he documents occasions when expulsion was carried out and identifies the moment when a decision not to permit their return became policy. Morris thus demonstrates that force was used to determine the country's demography. This finding has been extended to support the argument that Zionism engaged in the 'conquest' of Arabs lands. In subsequent work Morris is intent on detailing the history of the idea of population 'transfer' in Zionist thought and action (Morris 1994). Although Morris does not identify with all the ways his work has been interpreted, his scholarship has been used to diminish Israel's moral basis and legitimacy.

Shlaim and Pappé have concentrated on negotiations between Israel and its Arab neighbours. Shlaim argues in his 1988 work that Israel's leaders conspired with Abdullah to prevent the formation of the Palestinian state that was to have been established following partition. That is, in moral terms Israel is blameworthy for denying the just claims of Palestine's Arabs. Pappé faults Israel in the armistice negotiations after the war and for the subsequent hostile relationships between the antagonists (Pappé 1988, 1992). In these and in subsequent works, all three scholars contribute to reversing the 'myth' that Israel was born in a struggle of the 'few against the many', the weak against the strong, and that it is the wronged party in the dispute. In the most recent retrospective, Eugene Rogan and Avi Shlaim elevate Israel into a significantly superior power, even as the Arab side is exposed for its relative weakness, discord within and among its armies, and other shortcomings (Rogan and Shlaim 2001). This reading of the period would surprise many Israelis who lived through it. Ben-Gurion's diaries and a mass of public testimony document anxiety over failure and the large loss of life, in a conflict that was not only a formal war between armies but a civil conflict, fought often at close range (Ben-Gurion 1983; Lorch 1968).

Other revisionist scholarship has come to similar conclusions for subsequent wars. These critical perspectives, in which Israel is held responsible for unnecessary regional conflict, have been compared to American revisionist scholarship of the Cold War which depicts the United States as an aggressor, insensitive to the understandable needs and claims of the other side. This perspective is in marked contrast to such traditional analyses as Nadav Safran (1978) or Chaim Herzog (1982), wherein Israel is a beleaguered state responding to aggression or engaging in pre-emptive strikes.

The scholarship of Morris, Shlaim, and Pappé is constantly challenged (Gelber 2001). The most thorough and damaging criticism has come from the London-based scholar Efraim Karsh (2000). In his book Karsh undermines confidence in the essential and fundamental claim that revisionist findings are based on new and objective research. In an exacting pursuit of the documentation indicated in quotations and footnotes, he reveals systematic distortions in the way new information has been excised from its context and re-presented as 'new evidence'. Contemporary readers of current Israeli scholarship now have before them a growing library of claims and counter- claims. There are useful aids for negotiating this contested ground (Silberstein 1999; Ginossar and Bareli 1996).

At the time of writing this chapter there are reports in the Israeli press that revisionism and post-Zionism are in decline. It is not clear that this is so. If it is, it may be related to the success of the counter-attack, to the ultimately small number of revisionists, and to a time of conflict and bloodletting that mutes criticism and induces patriotism. My sense is that such reports are premature. Even prior to the First World War, there was a tradition of self-criticism regarding the relationship with Palestine's Arabs. Doubts about the wisdom and justice of policies will probably remain, because friction with Arab neighbours is unlikely to subside and explanations for the century-old conflict will continue to be sought. However much the Arab side will be held responsible, it is likely that Israeli scholars will seek to identify Israel's share in the continuing conflict.

There is at least one issue identified with the revisionist camp that does appear to have been resolved, due to diligent and imaginative searching of archives. It concerns the role of the Yishuv, especially its leadership, during the Holocaust. Just as the question of why Jews did not 'do more' to save their brethren has aggravated scholars of American Jewry in recent years, so too the question has occasioned a bitter debate concerning the morality and probity of the Yishuv's leadership. The attack was lead by Tom Segev (1993) and supported in part by other scholars, notably Dina Porat (1990) and Idith Zartal (1998). They claim that the leadership was insensitive to the needs of Holocaust victims and survivors, and viewed them as secondary to the immediate and pragmatic issues facing the Yishuv. Life continued as normal in the cafés of Tel-Aviv during the war, and politicians viewed survivors only in terms of their public-relations uses and recruitment value after its end. There have been several responses, including that by Shabtai Teveth (1987). Teveth's work draws in significant measure on the extraordinarily comprehensive research conducted by Tuvia Friling, then responsible for the Ben-Gurion Archives. Using this resource and others in Israel and abroad, Friling describes a plethora of rescue plans. Apparently the need for secrecy was so great that the paper trail has inevitably proven elusive. It is now clear that few actions could be carried out and even fewer were successful. The Yishuv failed in its rescue attempts, as did Jewish communities elsewhere, but not for want of trying (Friling 2000).

ISRAEL AS A JEWISH STATE

Throughout this essay I have repeatedly touched on research related directly and indirectly to the Jewishness of Israel. The enduring interest in this topic has lead to efforts to measure the Jewishness of Israelis. Beginning with Simon Herman (1971), through Charles S. Liebman and Elihu Katz (1997), there is a sociological tradition of survey work used for qualitative assessments. These studies invariably produce at least some surprising results, such the unexpectedly high percentage of Israelis who fast on Yom Kippur, keep a kosher home, light candles, and so on. Given the secular ideology of Israel's founders, and the avowedly secular content and orientation of Israeli schools, as discussed above, their findings are interpreted by some as evidence of the continued existence of Jewish culture, even if the traditional awe and obedience to halachah has been eroded. The content and transmission of Jewish culture has also occupied those who probe the issue in philosophical terms. A recent collection of the correspondence between Ben-Gurion and nearly fifty intellectuals after the establishment of the state illuminates the diversity of opinion on the topic (Ben-Rafael 2001). A thoughtful and insightful analysis of the controversy with Ben-Gurion that grew out of these exchanges is found in Michael Keren (1983). Yoram Hazony, the director of the Shalem Institute, a right-wing think-tank, has caused a stir in Israel and the diaspora with a powerful critique of what he sees as the attrition of Jewish values, including a commitment to an independent Jewish state on its historic, promised land (2000). Hazony claims that the greatest challenge facing Israel is internal disintegration stemming from a loss of identity, rather than the Arab threat. According to Hazony, this crisis is a consequence of the teachings of a group of, largely German-born, intellectuals who led the Hebrew University from the 1920s through until at least the 1950s. The greatest onus is placed on Martin Buber, who argued for a bi-national state, that is, a state whose Jewish character was willingly compromised. Hazony's polemic has many flaws, particularly misinterpretations of Buber and even Herzl and Ben-Gurion, as well as an exaggerated assessment of the influence of university intellectuals. However, his thesis that there has been a loss of Jewish identity does resonate among some sections of the public. His work serves as the basis for a campaign of right-wing intellectuals and politicians, with the authority of the current rightist Minister of Education, to give increased attention to Jewish history in the curriculum and to ensure that textbooks manifest greater sympathy for the Jewish perspective.

In contrast to Hazony's negative assessment of the power and influence of Judaism and Jewish practices in Israeli life, a more positive view has emanated from scholars at Bar-Ilan University since the 1980s. Daniel Elazar and colleagues in political science have consistently argued for the pre-eminence of Jewish roots in the formation and operation of Israeli society, and its political culture in particular. In a variety of studies Elazar develops the notion of 'covenant' as it is first expressed in the biblical period and evolves in Jewish communities through the centuries and throughout the diaspora until the present (Elazar 1989). Alan Dowty, a political scientist and historian at Notre Dame University, has built on this perception (Dowty 1998); this extended essay demonstrates the significant role of Jewish culture among the many forces and traditions that have shaped and continue to influence Israeli politics and society.

A useful way of addressing the Jewishness of Israel is to compare it with other Jewish communities, particularly the American. This exercise produces contradictory results. Boas Evron (1995) argues that Israel cannot be both a territorial state that includes a sizeable minority of non-Jews and remain a democratic one if it continues to identify with diaspora Jewry. Choosing democracy, he urges cutting Israel loose from its traditional religious and universal moorings and socializing its citizens to a secular and localized identity. In this way the post-emancipation quest for normality among Jews can be achieved. In Zion, they can again become a Middle Eastern people, as they were in the past. On the other hand, Jews living abroad generally express their Jewishness within a religious culture, and they can readily create their own forms of association and identity in the democratic societies of the west. Evron sees this split as already occurring, and as a desirable outcome of Jewish history. This thesis originated in the 1940s among the Canaanites, an intellectually powerful group that has had far greater impact than the numbers of formal adherents would suggest (Diamond 1996; Shavit 1987). The reality is that, despite the enormous evidence for the Jewish character of Israelis and their state, there is a strong counter-tendency.

Other students of Israeli and American Jews find growing differences amidst shared values and behaviour. Charles Liebman and Stephen Cohen (1990) reflect on this perception in their study of religious behaviour in the two cultures. However, most Jews in both of these societies have powerful secular tendencies and express their Jewish identity outside the synagogue and traditional rituals. The first examination to systematically explore the behaviour and values of secular Jewishness is an edited volume by Deborah Dash Moore and myself (Moore and Troen 2001). The essays in the volume indicate that many Israeli and American Jews share a common kinship and history deriving from Europe, particularly its eastern portions. However, secularized Jews in both societies now establish identities in significantly different ways. As a minority within a powerful host culture, American Jews continue to negotiate their Jewish selves in a host society whose language, literature, and traditions have been significantly different than their own. Jews in Israel have engaged in recovering their own language and culture within an autonomous and sovereign society and without reference to the cultures that surround them. Distinctive social and political ecologies make for differences that can be readily measured in political behaviour and are reflected in literature, the arts, attitudes towards the shared European past, and even towards the Holocaust. However, unlike Evron, who posits separation, we find that solidarity based on a sense of belonging to a world Jewish community continues together with this diversity.

The impact of the lack of restrictions occasioned by autonomy for Jews in Israel, together with the inhibitory effect of a hostile environment on interactions with proximate other cultures, is certain to be part of the agenda of those who study Israeli society. Within this area, the development of ultra- orthodoxy into a politically powerful and discrete segment in Israeli society commands the greatest attention. Perhaps the weakest part of European Jewry in terms of losses and material resources at the end of the Second World War, haredi communities that emigrated to Israel enjoyed the protection of the state for their reorganization and regeneration despite explicit and avowed opposition to Zionism. Dependence on a secular Jewish state and estrangement from its culture have produced a history of tension and conflict. It is interesting that the leading scholar on ultra-orthodoxy, Menachem Friedman, had hoped to write his dissertation on this topic while a graduate student at the Hebrew University in the 1970s. That proved impossible as a student in history, so his historical reconstruction and analysis are presented through sociology (Friedman 1991). He finds that the continued growth of haredi communities may be countered by the dominant secularity of Israeli society and their inability to sustain themselves economically, despite massive transfers of funds from the government. Within this rubric, the strategies of accommodation adopted by the various communities require definition and explanation, as does an analysis of tensions between the groups within this sector. Such a literature is emerging among a new generation of scholars, including historians.

Ultimately, the study of haredi communities in Israel reminds us that many of the challenges Jews have faced since emancipation are still not resolved and continue to arouse controversy. Zionism was and remains but one of the many responses to the opportunities and threats of the contemporary world. The diversity and fragmentation within Israel indicate that responding to modernity, even within and through a Jewish state, will continue to engage scholars through at least the current generation.

SUGGESTED READING

The issues presented in this essay are many and diverse but, undoubtedly, there will be readers who feel that one or several topics have been neglected or too lightly treated. Also, the references are primarily to readings in English, despite an enormous literature in Hebrew. Beyond the items cited in this text, the most important place to inaugurate further study is through bibliographies and journals. An excellent introduction to articles and books in Hebrew and other languages is through RAMBI (Reshimat Maamarim be-Madaei ha-Yahadut), the Index of Articles on Jewish Studies managed by the Hebrew University and accessible through its website: http://sites.huji.ac.il/jnul/rambi. A second website that focuses on social issues in contemporary Israel is managed by the Henrietta Szold Institute through http://www.szold.org.il. There are essential and established journals, pre-eminently *Cathedra. Teoria uVikoret* is essential for critical perspectives grounded in contemporary methodologies. *Iyunim Be-Tekumat Israel* is a relative newcomer that, with only eleven volumes, has emerged as an extraordinarily valuable venue for new scholarship in the humanities and social sciences, as well as debates over agendas for future research. In English, *Israel Studies* accomplishes the same (http://www.iupjournals.org/israel/). It also attracts scholars outside Israel on the range of issues that engage students of Israeli society and, by design, presents differing and opposing perspectives.

BIBLIOGRAPHY

ALMOG, O, 2000. *The Sabra: The Creation of the New Jew.* Berkeley.

AVINERI, S. 1981. *The Making of Modern Zionism: Intellectual Origins of the Jewish State.* New York.

AZARYAHU, M. 1995. *Pulhane Medinah : Hagigot Ha-Atsmaut ve-Hantsahat ha-Noflim, 1948–1956.* Sede-Boker.

BAR-GAL, Y. 1983. *Moledet ve-ge'ografyah be-me'ah shenot hinukh Tsiyoni.* Tel Aviv.

—— 1999. *Sochnut taamula Eretz Israel; ha-Keren ha-Kayemeth le-Israel 1924–1947.* Jerusalem.

BAR-ZOHAR, M. 1967. *The Armed Prophet: A Biography of Ben-Gurion.* London.

BARKAI, H. 1977. *Growth Patterns of the Kibbutz Economy.* Amsterdam.

—— 1990. *Yeme be-reshit shel ha-meshek ha-Yisreeli.* Jerusalem.

BEGIN, M. 1977. *The Revolt.* New York.

BEN-GURION, D. 1954. *Rebirth and Destiny of Israel.* M. Nurock ed. and trans. New York.

—— 1965. *Ben-Gurion Looks Back in Talks with Moshe Pearlman.* New York.

—— 1972. *Israel: A Personal History.* New York.

—— 1983. *Yoman Ha-Milhamah; Milhemeth Ha-Atzmaut, 5708–5709.* G. Rivlin and E. Orren eds. 3 vols. Tel Aviv.

BEN-RAFAEL, E. 1997. *Crisis and Transformation: The Kibbutz at Century's End.* Albany, NY.

—— 2001. *Jewish Identities: Fifty Intellectuals Answer Ben-Gurion.* Beer-Sheva.

BEN-YEHUDA, N. 1995. *The Masada Myth: Collective Memory and Mythmaking in Israel.* Madison, Wisc.

BONNÉ, A. 1943. *The Economic Development of the Middle East: An Outline of Planned Reconstruction After the War.* Jerusalem.

BUBER, M. 1949. *Paths in Utopia.* Trans. R. F. C. Hull. London.

COHEN, E. 1970. *The City in Zionist Ideology.* Jerusalem.

DAYAN, M. 1976. *The Story of My Life: Moshe Dayan.* London.

DESHEN, S. and SHOKEID, M. 1974. *The Predicament of Homecoming: Cultural and Social Life of North African Immigrants in Israel.* Ithaca, NY.

DIAMOND, J. S. 1986. *Homeland or Holyland?: The 'Canaanite' Critique of Israel.* Bloomington, Ind.

DOWTY, A. 1998. *The Jewish State: A Century Later.* Berkeley.

DROYANOV, A. and LASKOV, S. 1982–93. *Ketavim le-Toledot Hibat Tsion ve-Yishuv Eretz-Israel.* 7 vols. Tel Aviv.

EBAN, A. 1977. *Abba Eban: An Autobiography.* New York.

EISENSTADT, S. N. 1954. *The Absorption of Immigrants.* London.

—— 1967. *Israel Society.* London.

ELBOIM-DROR, R. 1986. *Ha-Hinukh ha-Ivri be-Erets Yisrael.* Jerusalem.

—— 1993. *Ha-Mahar shel ha-Etmol.* 2 vols. Jerusalem.

ELON, A. 1975. *Herzl.* New York.

—— 1971. *The Israelis: Founders and Sons.* New York.

ESCO Foundation for Palestine, 1947. *Palestine: A Study of Jewish, Arab, and British Policies.* New Haven.

EVRON, B. 1995. *Jewish State or Israeli Nation.* Bloomington, Ind.

ELAZAR, D. 1989. *People and Polity: The Organizational Dynamics of World Jewry.* Detroit.

EZRAHI, Y. 1997. *Rubber Bullets: Power and Conscience in Modern Israel.* New York.

FIRER, R. 1985. *Sochenim shel ha-Hinuch ha-Zioni.* Haifa.

FRIEDMAN, M. 1991. *Ha-Hevrah ha-Haredit: Mekorot, Megamot ve-Tahalikhim.* Jerusalem.

FRILING, T. 2000. *Hets ba-Arafel: David Ben-Gurion, Hanhagat ha-Yishuv ve-Nisyonot Hatsalah ba-Shoah.* Beer-Sheva.

FURSTENBERG, R. 1997. *Post-Zionim: The Challenge to Israel.* New York.

GELBER, Y. 2001. *Palestine, 1948: War, Escape and the Emergence of the Palestinian Refugee Problem.* Brighton and Portland, Oreg.

GILBERT, M. 1988. *Israel A History.* London.

GINOSSAR, P. and BARELI, A. eds. 1996. *Tsiyonut: Pulmus ben Zemanenu: Gishot Mehkariyot ve-Ideologiyot.* Sede Boker.

GORNY, Y. 1973. *Achdut ha-Avodah 1919–1930: ha- Yesodot ha-raayoniyim ve-haShita ha-Medinit.* Tel Aviv.

GROSS, N. 1988. *Laying the Foundations of Israel's Economic System 1948–1951.* Jerusalem.

HALPERN, B. 1961. *The Idea of the Jewish State.* Cambridge, Mass.

—— and REINHARZ, J. 2000. *Zionism and the Creation of a New Society.* Hanover, NH.

HAZONY, Y. 2000. *The Jewish State: The Struggle for Israel's Soul.* New York.

HERMAN, S. 1971. *Israelis and Jews: The Continuity of an Identity.* New York.

HERTZBERG, A. 1997. *The Zionist Idea: A Historical Analysis and Reader.* Philadelphia.

HERZOG, C. 1982. *The Arab–Israeli Wars: War and Peace in the Middle East.* New York.

—— 1996. *Living History: A Memoir.* New York.

HOROWITZ, D. and HINDEN, R. 1938. *Economic Survey of Palestine: With Special Reference to the Years 1936 and 1937.* Tel Aviv.

—— and LISSAK, M. 1978. *The Origins of the Israeli Polity.* Chicago.

—— —— 1989. *Trouble in Utopia: The Overburdened Polity of Israel.* Albany, NY.

KARLINSKY, N. 2000. *Perihat he-Hadar : Yazamut Peratit ba-Yishuv, 1890–1939.* Jerusalem.

KARSH, E. 2000. *Frabricating Israeli History: The 'New' Historians.* London.

KATRIEL, T. 1986. *Talking Straight: Dugri Speech in Israeli Sabra Culture.* New York.

KEREN, M. 1983. *Ben-Gurion and the Intellectuals: Power, Knowledge, and Charisma.* DeKalb, Ill.

KIMMERLING, B. 1982. *Zionism and Economy.* Cambridge, Mass.

—— 1983. *Zionism and Territory: The Socio-Territorial Dimension of Zionist Politics.* Berkeley.

KOLATT, I. 1964. *Ideologyah u-Metsiut bi-Tenuat ha-Avodah be-Erets Yisrael 1905–1919.* Jerusalem.

LAHAV, P. 1997. *Judgement in Jerusalem: Chief Justice Simon Agranat and the Zionist Century.* Berkeley.

LAQUEUR, W. 1976. *A History of Zionism.* New York.

LIEBMAN, C. and DON-YEHIYA, D. 1983. *Civil Religion in Israel: Traditional Judaism and Political Culture in the Jewish State.* Berkeley.

—— and COHEN, S. 1990. *Two Worlds of Judaism: The Israeli and the American Experiences.* New Haven.

LIEBMAN, C. S. and KATZ, E. eds. 1977. *The Jewishness of Israelis: Responses to the Guttman Report.* Albany, NY.

LORCH, N. 1968. *The Edge of the Sword: Israel's War of Independence, 1947–1949.* Foreword by S. L. A. Marshall. Epilogue by Yigael Yadin. Jerusalem.

LUCAS, N. 1974. *The History of Modern Israel.* London.

MARX, E. 1976. *The Social Context of Violent Behaviour: A Social Anthropological Study in an Israeli Immigrant Town.* Boston.

MEIR, G. 1975. *My Life by Golda Meir.* New York.

METZER, J. 1998. *The Divided Economy of Mandatory Palestine.* Cambridge.

MOORE, D. D. and TROEN, S. I. 2001. *Divergent Jewish Cultures: Israel and America.* New Haven.

MORRIS, B. 1987. *The Birth of the Palestinian Refugee Problem, 1947–1949.* Cambridge.

—— 1988. 'The New Historiography: Israel Confronts Its Past.' *Tikkun* 4: 19–23, 99–102.

—— 1994. *1948 and After: Israel and the Palestinians.* Oxford.

MYERS, D. N. 1995. *Re-inventing the Jewish Past: European Jewish Intellectuals and the Zionist Return to History.* New York.

NATHAN, R., GASS, O., and CREAMER, D. 1946. *Palestine: Problem and Promise. An Economic Study.* Washington, DC.

NEAR, H. 1992. *The Kibbutz Movement: A History.* Oxford.

NETANYAHU, B. 1993. *A Place Among the Nations: Israel and the World Order* New York.

OFER, D. 1996. *Ben Olim le-Vatikim: Yisrael ba-Aliyah ha-Gedolah, 1948–1953.* Jerusalem.

PAPPÉ, I. 1992. *The Making of the Arab–Israeli Conflict: 1947–1951.* London.

—— 1988. *Britain and the Arab–Israeli conflict, 1948–1951.* New York.

PERES, S. ed. 1999. *Battling For Peace: Memoirs.* By David Landau. London.

PORAT, D. 1990. *The Blue and the Yellow Star of David: The Zionist Leadership in Palestine and the Holocaust, 1939–1945.* Cambridge, Mass.

RABIN, Y. 1979. *The Rabin Memoirs.* Boston.

RAFAEL, G. 1981. *Destination Peace: Three Decades of Israeli Foreign Policy.* London.

RAM, U. 1995. *The Changing Agenda of Israeli Sociology: Theory, Ideology and Identity.* Albany, NY.

REINHARZ, J. 1985. *Chaim Weizmann: The Making of a Zionist Leader.* New York.

ROGAN, E. and SHLAIM, A. eds. 2001. *The War for Palestine; Rewriting the History of 1948.* Cambridge.

SACHAR, H. M. 2000. *A History of Israel From the Rise of Zionism to Our Time.* New York.

SAFRAN, N. 1978. *Israel: Embattled Ally.* Cambridge, Mass.

SCHWEID, E. 1996. '"Beyond" All That—Modernism, Zionism, Judaism.' *Israel Studies* 1/1: 224–46.

SEGEV, T. 1986. *1949: The First Israelis.* New York.

—— 1993. *The Seventh Million: The Israelis and the Holocaust.* New York.

SHAFIR, G. 1989. *Land, Labor and the Origins of the Israeli–Palestinian Conflict, 1882–1914.* Cambridge.

SHAPIRA, A. 1977. *Ha-Maavak ha-Nichzav: Avodah Ivrit, 1929–1939.* Tel Aviv.

—— 1984. *Berl: The Biography of a Socialist Zionist.* Cambridge.

—— 1992. *Land and Power: The Zionist Resort to Force, 1881–1948.* Oxford.

—— 1995. 'Politics and Collective Memory: The Debate Over the New Historians in Israel.' *History and Memory* 7: 11–40.

SHAVIT, Y. 1987. *The New Hebrew Nation: A Study in Israeli History and Fantasy.* London.

—— 1988. *Jabotinsky and the Revisionist Movement, 1925–1948.* London.

SHEFFER, G. 1996. *Moshe Sharett: Biography of a Political Moderate.* New York.

SHENHAR, A. *et al.* 1994. *A People and the World: Jewish Culture in a Changing World* [Hebrew]. Jerusalem.

SHIMONI, G. 1995. *The Zionist Ideology.* Hanover, NH.

SHLAIM, A. 1988. *Collusion Across the Jordan: King Abdullah, the Zionist Movement, and the Partition of Palestine.* Oxford.

SHOKEID, M. 1971. *The Dual Heritage: Immigrants From the Atlas Mountains in an Israeli Village.* Manchester.

SILBERSTEIN, L. J. 1999. *The Postzionism Debates: Knowledge and Power in Israeli Culture.* New York.

SMOOHA, S. 1978. *Israel: Pluralism and Conflict,* Berkeley.

SWIRSKI, S. 1981. *Lo Neheshalim ela Menuhshalim : Mizrahim ve-Ashkenazim be-Yisrael: Nituah Sotsyologi ve-Sihotim Peilim u-Feilot.* Haifa.

STERNHELL, Z. 1998. *The Founding Myths of Israel: Nationalism, Socialism, and the Making of the Jewish State.* Trans. David Maisel. Princeton.

TEVETH, S. 1987. *Ben-Gurion: The Burning Ground, 1886–1948.* Boston.

TROEN, S. I. 1989. 'Calculating the "Economic Absorptive Capacity" of Palestine: A Study of the Political Uses of Scientific Research.' *Contemporary Jewry* 10/2: 19–38.

—— 2002. *Imagining Zion: Dreams, Designs and Realities in a Century of Jewish Settlement.* New Haven.

VITAL, D. 1975. *The Origins of Zionism.* Oxford.

WEINGROD, A. 1966. *Reluctant Pioneers: Village Development in Israel.* Port Washington, NY.

WEINTRAUB, D., LISSAK, M., and AZMAN, Y. 1969. *Moshava, Kibbutz and Moshav: Patterns of Jewish Rural Settlement and Development in Palestine.* Ithaca, NY.

WEIZMANN, C. 1949. *Trial and Error: The Autobiography of Chaim Weizmann.* New York.

YABLONKA, H. 1999. *Survivors of the Holocaust: Israel After the War.* New York.

YALAN, E. 1975. *The Design of Agricultural Settlements: Technological Aspects of Rural Community Development.* Haifa.

ZARTAL, E. 1998. *From Catastrophe to Power: Holocaust Survivors and the Emergence of Israel.* Berkeley.

ZERUBAVEL, Y. 1995. *Recovered Roots: Memory and the Making of the Israeli National Tradition.* Chicago.

CHAPTER 19

AMERICAN JEWISH HISTORY

HASIA DINER

AMERICAN Jewish history as a field of scholarly inquiry takes as its subject-matter the experience of Jews in the United States and places it within the context of both modern Jewish history and the history of the United States. Its practitioners see their intellectual project as inextricably connected to both histories. Therefore they see themselves as integral members of two scholarly communities, identifying with modern Jewish historians and with American historians.

At the beginning of the twenty-first century the enterprise of American Jewish history—the scholars themselves, the journals, the books, courses, and conferences—enjoys a condition of robust health. Its health is not just a matter of access to resources, particularly teaching positions in American colleges and universities which have been earmarked for the study of the American Jewish experience, but it also concerns issues of scholarly quality and visibility.

Those who write and teach American Jewish history hold doctorates from American universities and are trained in the same way as their colleagues in other specialties. Of equal importance, they are asking sophisticated and subtle questions about cultural identity and social relationships. They pay mindful attention to the profound duality which runs through American Jewish history, manifested in the multiple ways in which their subjects—American Jews—defined for themselves modes of religious and communal behaviour which they hoped would fit the demands of both their Jewish and American communities. American Jewish historians write with deep understanding about the complexities of labels, such as

'American' and 'Jewish', and communicate to their readers and students the many negotiations that American Jews engaged in as they functioned simultaneously as Jews and Americans at various points in the past.

They recognize the historical contingency of the phenomena they study. How Jews defined public places for themselves and their faith tradition in the eighteenth century, for example, differed dramatically from the ways Jews behaved in the middle of the twentieth century. American Jewish historians recognize that America changed and so did the Jews, and they therefore place a great deal of emphasis on the political, economic, and cultural shifts which took place in the larger and overlapping worlds occupied by American Jews. They participate fully in the intellectual developments that have taken place within American history and as such, by the start of the twenty-first century, like their Americanist colleagues, explore the fluidity of racial categories, the shifting boundaries of gender relationships, and intersections of class, age, and generational position as they seek to explore various aspects of Jewish life in the American past. At the same time that American historians have committed themselves to placing America in a global context, so too Jewish historians are looking—again—at American Jews' connections to and relationships with their co-religionists around the world.

The intellectual and professional vigour evident at the end of the twentieth century represents a new stage in the development of the field. American Jewish history went through a lengthy and complicated process before achieving its current status. Well into the 1950s, American Jewish history was considered an intellectual backwater of Jewish historical scholarship, and within the world of American historians it barely existed at all.

The origins of this professionalized and energetic thrust in the scholarship on the history of American Jews owes its origins to two interrelated contexts, the traumatic events of the Second World War, and the changed nature of American society, particularly—although not exclusively—educational reforms, ushered in during the post-war era of the Cold War and through the 1950s. By the end of the Second World War the American Jewish community had become the largest concentration of Jews in the world. It was also the wealthiest, most powerful, and freest. It replaced in many significant ways the previous centre, eastern Europe, most of whose Jews had been physically destroyed in the war, while those who remained, lived under Stalinist rule, unable to engage in the open exchange of ideas and in the untrammelled search for information about the past which historical scholarship requires.

It was in the context of this tectonic shift in world Jewry that scholars of modern Jewish history turned to the United States to make up for the losses visited upon the Jewish people. Some of the most eloquent calls for the serious study of American Jewish history took as their starting-point the awesome responsibilities shouldered now by America's Jews. Salo Baron, speaking before the Synagogue Council of America on 12 October, 1942 to mark the 450th anniversary of Columbus's 'discovery of America', took note of the moment: 'The middle of the Second

World War', he commented, 'does not seem to be an appropriate time for celebrations.... The fate of the Jewish people is being decided now for generations to come.' But he went on to link the patriotic moment with the need for the writing of American Jewish history: 'If such celebrations . . . are to have any meaning at all they ought to give us pause to consider the great historic experiences of the past and to help us derive from them a lesson and perhaps comfort in our present perplexities' (Baron 1971: 15–16). Eight years later he gave the keynote address at the American Jewish Historical Society's annual meeting. Although the Society had been in existence since 1892, Baron's was the first strident and systematic assessment of the state of the field to be heard within its walls, as well as the most specific blueprint as to how American Jewish history could serve 'a religious group which has a deep emotional stake in its very survival' (ibid. 73).

This charge by Baron placed upon American Jews and the historians among them a responsibility towards their people as an 'eternal' and world-wide collectivity. He charged American Jews to write their history in order to serve the needs of the Jewish people.

Behind Baron's call for the writing of American Jewish history lay another project. Baron was the first scholar in the United States with a position in an American university—Columbia—to identify Jewish history as a field of academic inquiry. He argued, both in speeches and articles and directly in the vast compendium of books which he wrote, that all of Jewish historical writing needed to be seen as much more than an endless series of studies of persecutions, what he labelled the 'lachrymose' view of the Jewish past. Similarly, he argued rhetorically and in his scholarly writing that Jewish life itself was a fit subject for scholarship. How Jews functioned politically, economically, and socially was as worthy a subject of scholarly inquiry, according to Baron, as was the production of religious texts by rabbis in the past, the other main thrust of Jewish historical writing.

In his call for American Jewish history Baron recognized that it provided the perfect laboratory for his ideal vision of Jewish history. He understood how different American Jewish history had been from European Jewish history, and that it was *the* setting in which to study the Jews in their full lived context. America had, after all, produced few, if any, Judaic scholars, at least in terms of individuals whose writings added to the corpus of authoritative Judaic texts. The United States had produced no martyrs either. Therefore if he wanted Jewish history as a whole to move away from tears and exegesis to studies of family life, material culture, trade patterns, occupations, and involvement with political parties, then America, not Germany, Poland, Russia, and all the other diaspora settings, where an abundance of suffering and histories of rabbinical scholarship complicated the search for Jewish social history, offered a place to study the Jewish past in its fullest social context.

America might have been the best setting for conducting Jewish history research, but Baron seriously doubted if those who were already studying the American Jewish past were actually up to the task. What he surveyed, during the 1940s and

1950s when he was most involved in calling for American Jewish history, was basically a handful of dedicated amateurs committed to uncovering documents and placing them in archives. The works in American Jewish history which Baron found wanting and which made him wonder if a solid corpus of scholarship would ever come into being tended to be highly defensive, and indeed the defence of the Jews at home and abroad had been the basic motivation for the founding of the American Jewish Historical Society in 1892. The two functions were linked. By finding documents which demonstrated the early history of the Jews in the United States, their presence on American shores before national independence, and their role in the creation of the nation, American Jewish communal leaders felt that they could buttress Jewish claims to a place in America at the end of the nineteenth century and into the early decades of the twentieth.[1]

The articles which appeared in the journal of the American Jewish Historical Society and the books which were published tended to follow this twinned purpose. Such pieces as Herbert Friedenwald, 'Some Newspaper Advertisements of the Eighteenth Century', or Simon Wolf, 'The American Jew as Soldier and Patriot', were cut from the same cloth. Jews had been in America since its earliest days. They had contributed to the growth of its economy and had participated in creating its democratic infrastructure. All charges of the Jews' foreignness, parasitism, and lack of loyalty, these defender-historians asserted, should be discounted in the face of the documents being collected and the articles and books being written. All the writers of these articles were Jewish communal activists who laboured for Jewish causes in numerous settings, and the writing of this kind of history provided them, they hoped, with one more weapon in their arsenal of defence.[2]

This kind of historical writing Baron found unsatisfying. He wanted to see full-time, university-trained scholars, equipped not *just* with a zeal for the Jewish people, but with the tools of the academy as well, to define the history of American Jews.

A formidable barrier to the actualizing of Baron's vision was the fact that history as a profession remained remarkably closed to Jews. It functioned very much as a Gentile, indeed Protestant, preserve. Like English literature, another academic stronghold of an older elite, the field of American history considered itself responsible for preserving the legacy of the nation's founders. Those best equipped to act as gate-keepers were, naturally, scholars who shared the values and outlook (as well as religion, ethnicity, gender, and race) of those who had written America's key documents and who had built its institutions. Until the end of the Second World

---

[1] Gurock (1993–4: 155–270) is the single best analysis of the history of the journal *American Jewish History*, the American Jewish Historical Society as an academic body, and the field of American Jewish History. See also Gurock (1983) for a thorough history of the field and a rich bibliography as of the early 1980s.

[2] For two examples of this genre, so typical of the first half of the twentieth century, see Friedenwald (1897) and Wolf (1895).

War it had been possible for those who guarded the gates to effectively keep out those whose ancestors had not been present at the nation's birth and who subscribed to religious traditions quite far removed from America's white Protestant founders. Historian Peter Novick has ably shown how calls for 'objectivity' by the luminaries in the field masked mighty efforts to keep out Jews and others of 'foreign' background who did not conform to the historians' ideal of those most likely to effectively protect the American legacy (Novick 1988).

But the tide turned by the end of the Second World War. Anti-discrimination legislation in many northern and western states (and finally, by 1964, on the federal level), the passage of the GI Bill, and a growing American revulsion for the cruder forms of exclusion worked to open doors to the masses of American Jews, the young women and men whose parents had been immigrants, and who came of age during and after the Second World War. Carl Bridenbaugh, a president of the American Historical Association and a scholar of the colonial era, saw this new trend and he lamented. In his 1962 presidential address to the AHA he mourned that, 'today we must face the discouraging prospect that we all, teachers and pupils alike, have lost much of what...earlier generations possessed, the priceless asset of a shared heritage'. If Bridenbaugh thought that his reference to 'shared heritage' might be too subtle to fully convey his point, he went on. He complained, 'many of the younger practitioners of our craft, and those who are still apprentices, are products of lower middle-class or foreign origins, and their emotions not infrequently get in the way of historical reconstructions' (Levine 1993: 15).

In this historical context American Jewish history began to coalesce in both the context of American and modern Jewish history. One of Baron's strategies to redress the paucity of scholarly work in the field was to begin training a generation of graduate students who would conduct the kinds of research that he thought necessary. Hyman B. Grinstein was Baron's first doctoral student at Columbia. Grinstein's dissertation on early New York Jewry was published as *The Rise of the Jewish Community of New York* in 1945. It not only brought together a vast amount of empirical data on social, political, religious, and economic activities of New York Jews for two centuries following 1654, and showed how they changed over time, but he demonstrated the impact of the American environment on New York Jews up to the beginning of the Civil War (Grinstein 1945).

Grinstein's book was definitely encyclopedic in its scope, but fitted well into an clearly defined and academically acceptable genre within American historical scholarship, the urban biography. Other than the fact that he studied Jews, little differentiated Grinstein's work from other contemporary works like Bessie Louise Pierce's history of Chicago, Bayard Still's history of Milwaukee, Blake McKelvey's four-volume history of Rochester, or Constance McLaughlin Green's history of Washington, DC, in two volumes. Like Grinstein's book, the historians adopted a decidedly positivist tone. Life in these cities basically got better over time as institutions became more democratic and government more responsive. To prove their point, they unearthed massive amounts of empirical data on the history of their chosen cities (Pierce 1937; Still 1948; McKelvey 1945, 1949, 1956, 1961; McLaughlin Green 1962–3).

In the wake of Grinstein's history of New York a whole spate of American Jewish urban biographies followed, although not necessarily because of his work. Studies of the Jews of Chicago, Charleston, South Carolina, and Philadelphia were published by Jewish publishing houses, the first by Bloch and the other two by the Jewish Publication Society of America, which had also brought out Grinstein's book (Gutstein 1953; Reznikoff and Engelman 1950; Wolf II and Whiteman 1957). Similarly, in 1953 the Jewish Theological Seminary established its American Jewish History Center which went on, with the financial support of the various communities themselves, to commission even more studies of this kind. Out of this effort came books on the Jews of Buffalo, Milwaukee, Cleveland, and Los Angeles. These books also bore the imprimatur of the Jewish Publication Society (with the exception of the Cleveland and Los Angeles books, which came out well after the Center had folded and the enterprise had been shelved).

By coincidence, less than a decade after the war's end and the revelation of its tragic dimensions, American Jews marked the tercentenary of the Jewish presence in that territory which in 1776 became the United States. In 1954, deep into the Cold War, they celebrated in a variety of venues and in a number of public ways the experience of the small group of Jews who landed in New Amsterdam in September 1654. The twenty-three Jews who disembarked in the Dutch colony, which soon changed hands and became a British colony, had come from Brazil. In the main Sephardim, they carried family and community memories which disposed them to fear the Portuguese who had just wrested Recife from the relatively tolerant Dutch. Dreading the persecutions of the past and the introduction of the office of the Inquisition, they set sail and ended up in the Netherlands' chief North American colony. Despite the objections of the governor-general of New Amsterdam, Peter Stuyvesant, the Jews remained on Manhattan island. They adjusted well when the city and colony changed names and became New York, and the refugee Jews planted there the seeds for what would become American Jewry.

Coming as it did immediately after the Second World War and during the Cold War, this tale of the first Jews of North America took on a mythic cast. It had all the elements of an epic, almost biblical, tale of a Jewish flight from destruction and ultimate redemption in a land of promise. The details highlighted during the festivities focused on both the Jews' perseverance in the face of hostility and on the benign atmosphere of America which ultimately prevailed.[3] It allowed the American Jewish past to be understood as an 'adventure in freedom' (Handlin 1954a). It made it possible for Jews to think about their history in the

---

[3] For an analysis of the tercentenary and its cultural and political underpinnings, see Goren (1999: 195–203).

context of American exceptionalism and to be able to proclaim that 'America is different'.[4]

The tercentenary, like the war so shortly before it, stimulated communal thinking about history. It was indeed upon the occasion of this tercentenary that Moses Rischin, a doctoral candidate at Harvard University, compiled *An Inventory of American Jewish History*, a compendium of observations as to what had already been written, what resources existed to make it possible to write more, and which topics ought to engage the attention of scholars. Rischin's answer to the first question was simply: not very much of a worthwhile quality. Succinctly he stated, 'very little that is useful has been done'. American Jewish history as it stood at the moment of the tercentenary had been 'left to the amateur, the antiquarian, the necrologist and the undaunted sentimentalist'. The slim volume went on to make a powerful case for the existence of vast amount of primary material that existed in great profusion for any scholar who would ask the 'proper questions'. That primary material could then be used to analyse the social, political, cultural, and economic history of American Jews. Rischin sketched out a research agenda which anticipated the turn of the American historical profession to the study of social and cultural phenomenon in nearly prophetic terms (Rischin 1954: 1).

The *Inventory* was graced with an introduction by Rischin's mentor, Oscar Handlin, who played a pivotal role in this transitional moment in American Jewish historiography, despite the fact that it was not that work at all which gained him prestige in the profession. Handlin was the author of *Boston's Immigrants*, a pathbreaking study of Irish immigrants. It was upon this work and its analysis of the economic and social barriers to Irish integration that Handlin launched his scholarly career, and with it he secured his position at Harvard. His *magnum opus, The Uprooted*, won him not only a Pulitzer Prize but a key place in American historiography, in that generations of scholars have dedicated themselves since its publication to chipping away at its basic premise. *The Uprooted* was Handlin's statement about *the* immigrant experience which he posited as *the* American experience. Notably, it had nothing to say about Jews as immigrants, and its basic premise was that the paradigmatic immigrant was a peasant. The contours of the great migrations which he portrayed conformed not one bit to the experiences of Jews as immigrants or as new Americans seeking to cope with a new home (Handlin 1951).

But Handlin also developed a kind of side career as an American Jewish historian. He wrote an important article for the *American Jewish Yearbook*, an annual

---

[4] In the 1950s in particular the theme of 'American exceptionalism' commanded a great deal of scholarly interest. In the context of the concept of the 'national character', scholars interested in a variety of aspects of American history and culture focused on the idea that the United States possessed a singular and exceptional way of life. For example, Hartz (1955) attributed the essence of America to the absence of a feudal past, while Pierson and others focused on Americans' high levels of physical mobility which allowed them the chance to always 'start over'. See Pierson (1973). See also in the context of American Jews, Rosenberg (1964).

publication of the American Jewish Committee, on the history of Jewish immigration to the United States in 1948, as well as an article for *Publications of the American Jewish Historical Society* in 1951, which had been his address to the Society. In 1948 *Commentary*, a magazine also sponsored by the AJC, convened a two-day conference for twenty-eight scholars, which took as its point of departure the widely assumed low state of American Jewish history as a field, and as its mission, how to upgrade it. Three months before the conference Handlin had written an article for *Commentary* on 'Our Unknown American Jewish Ancestors'. Reflecting the rhetoric which prevailed at the conference, Handlin's article charged that American Jews 'lived in abysmal ignorance of the real history of American Jewry. What passes now for history is an accumulation of details of little consequence, only slightly related either to the real problems of the present or to the real people of the past' (Gurock 1993–4: 202). One of the conference's charges was to sponsor a 'systematic survey of the needs and opportunities for research in American Jewish history'. Not surprisingly, then, Handlin in writing the Foreword to Rischin's *Inventory*—which was that survey—accentuated the 'widespread neglect' of the American Jewish past, the 'disregard . . . of valuable material', and deplored a body of writings which 'were usually overlaid with an apologetic tone, with filiopietism, and with excessive zeal to demonstrate the contributions of particular groups of ancestors to American history' (Handlin 1954b: p. vii).

Handlin and Rischin, unlike Baron, basically pushed the small number of practitioners of American Jewish history to think of themselves as part of the world of professional American historians. Handlin and the others who attended the *Commentary* meeting believed that the most important function of an energized and professionalized cadre of American Jewish historians would be to 'bring the specialists in Jewish history working in close enough contact with other American historians to be aware of the main developments in the larger field' (Handlin 1949).

It is noteworthy, although not surprising, that those who worked most assiduously to bring American Jewish history into line with American history thought of the latter as synonymous with the national, or indeed the universal, within the American context. It would have been impossible for Handlin or Rischin to see, let alone assert, that American historians were in the main writing the equally filiopietistic history of a small, thin strata of the elite, and claiming for their subjects the entirety of the American experience. From the point of view of those historians like Handlin and Rischin, who were the children of immigrants and were among a vanguard of Jews who had embarked upon careers teaching American history within the academy, American historical scholarship represented the apogee of objective analysis. They never took note of the fact that American history was, in the 1950s and before, the history of well-off white men, overwhelmingly Protestant and of British derivation. New England, more than any other region, was defined as the heartland of American democracy and the seedbed of its political institutions. The overwhelming tendency of American historians had, in fact, been to write 'ethnic history', although they would have never admitted that was what it was. The historians whose work Rischin and Handlin hoped that rising American Jewish scholars would emulate were in fact studying their own group and were searching for their own, parochial roots in America.

The historical writing against which Handlin and his student measured the pre-1950s corpus of American Jewish historical scholarship not only had taken one small swathe of American life and generalized from it about all that was worthy of study in the American past, but it was also overwhelmingly political in focus. American historians concerned themselves with the origins and inner workings of governmental institutions. Treaties, legislatures, and political parties counted in American history. Ironically, Rischin in his *Inventory* called for a new and more sophisticated American Jewish historical scholarship of the future that was actually vastly broader and strikingly more innovative than anything that American historians were writing in 1954. By suggesting that the field would be enriched if historians studied 'Mass Leisure and Mass Sports', 'the evolution of the family, the role of women, reading habits, eating habits, sources of social prestige and emulation', he actually anticipated not only the social-history revolution of the 1960s and 1970s—always attributed to E. P. Thompson's 1963 *The Making of the English Working Class*—but also the paradigm of cultural history which arose by the late 1980s as a frame of analysis which explored meaning and the historic complexities of identity (Thompson 1966).

Despite the subtle difference in focus between Baron, who addressed the deficiencies of American Jewish history vis-à-vis European and modern Jewish history, and Handlin, who fretted over it in relationship to American history, the two came together in September 1954—the exact month of the tercentenary—in Peekskill, New York, at a symposium organized by the American Jewish Historical Society. Jointly they envisioned an end to 'parochialism and fragmentation', and the beginning of an era in which American Jewish history would be 'part of the larger scheme of American history as well as world Jewish history' (Davis and Meyer 1957: 141–2).

The event that most dramatically marked the turning-point in the field and the beginning of a serious professionalized American Jewish history was the 1962 publication of Moses Rischin's *The Promised City*, derived from his dissertation. It was not just that it took as its subject-matter the east European Jewish enclave in New York, its work patterns, its union organizing, its theatre, and its journalism, that made it notable. It was the fact that *The Promised City* defined an analytic problem and turned to archival and other primary sources to answer it. Its purpose was not to uncover *everything* about New York Jews or *everything* about the immigrants from Russia and Poland who flocked there in the last decades of the nineteenth century. Rather, the book posed a conceptual problem—how did a group of immigrants 'torn from the villages of Eastern Europe' go about the process of 'becoming modern Americans'—and then organized the data to provide an answer (Rischin 1962).

Rischin's innovative book planted the seeds which began to bear fruit in the 1970s. In less than ten years after the publication of *The Promised City*, Leonard Dinnerstein, with a doctorate from Columbia University, published *The Leo Frank Case* (Dinnerstein 1968), while his classmate Arthur Goren's *New York Jews and the Quest for Community* appeared in 1970 (Goren 1970). That same year Henry Feingold, with a doctorate from New York University, saw to completion the release of *The Politics of Rescue: The Roosevelt Administration and the Holocaust, 1938–1945* (Feingold 1970). Taken as a group, these three books, all published by prestigious university presses, challenged both the patriotic tone of the tercentenary and the consensus school of American historical scholarship. All three presumed a basic dissonance between American expectations and Jewish interests, and saw conflicts within the Jewish community as a key factor in shaping behaviour.

The next decade saw even more in the way of American Jewish historical writing which firmly planted it into the soil of social history, and which asked challenging questions about Jews, their relationship to American society, and their relationships with other Americans. In 1977 Thomas Kessner brought American Jewish history into the world of comparative mobility studies by looking at Jews and Italians in New York City during the peak immigration decades and, using quantitative methods, asked questions about differences, similarities, and their causations (Kessner 1977). That same year Hasia Diner asked, in *In the Almost Promised Land* (Diner 1977), how American Jews in the early twentieth century made sense of issues of race, racism, and the plight of African Americans. Both books clearly articulated the position that one cannot understand American Jewish history without understanding the nature of American diversity. The next few years witnessed the publication of Jeffrey Gurock's, *When Harlem Was Jewish* (Gurock 1979), and Deborah Dash Moore's *At Home in America* (Moore 1981), both of which situated American—New York City—Jewish history into urban history, a burgeoning sub-field of the decade. Jonathan Sarna's biography of Mordecai Noah, published in 1980 situated the diplomat-playwright-Jewish communal activist-newspaper publisher in the evolving structures of Jacksonian America and in the world-wide Jewish politics of the early nineteenth century (Sarna 1980).

From that point on it is pointless to mention all of the books published in the very fertile field of American Jewish history, books which not only fit the dominant paradigms in American history, but which in fact pioneered in them. Indeed, so fertile were the decades of the 1970s and 1980s that by the late 1980s the American Jewish Historical Society decided that the time had come to commission a kind of 'state-of-the-art' set of books which would, in five volumes, synthesize American Jewish history as it was reflected in the vast outpouring of books and articles of the past forty years.

In 1992, exactly 100 years after the founding of the American Jewish Historical Society, the series The Jewish People in America was published by Johns Hopkins University Press, under the general editorship of Henry Feingold. While each book was different and reflected the particular interests and proclivities of its author, as a totality they demonstrated the strength of the social-history paradigm upon American Jewish history. Each volume paid a great deal of attention to work and business, to family patterns and the impact of migration on social formation. Each book attempted to situate Jews in a complex web of relationships with both their non-Jewish American neighbours and with the Jewish people around the world. Each treated the religious lives of American Jews as a reflection of their negotiation with American conditions, and each took seriously leisure, popular culture, and social life as indicators of identity (Faber 1992; Diner 1992; Sorin 1992; Feingold 1992; Shapiro 1992).

It is obviously impossible to list, let alone discuss, all of the significant books in American Jewish history that have been produced in the four decades since Rischin's *Promised City*. In the intervening years American Jewish historians have opened up the systematic study of immigration from Europe and the internal Jewish migration within America (see e.g. Soyer 1997 and Moore 1994). They explore patterns of work, the Jewish labour movement, and other forms of economic support within Jewish communities (Markowitz 1993 and Wenger 1996). They have taken Jewish community life as a major focus of their attention, and have looked at the impact of local conditions upon those communities. They have explored the idea of the Jewish community as a living political organism, whose structure took its form from both Jewish concerns and American realities (Svonkin 1997 and Dollinger 2000). Since the late 1970s no subject has been as transformative of the field than women's history, and many works have examined the changing roles of women and men within American Jewry and the ways in which they have constructed each other. Jews as industrial workers and schoolteachers, as rabbis—both male and female—and as students, criminals, civil-rights activists, and architects of American liberalism represent just some of the issues which have engaged—and continue to engage—American Jewish historians (Ashton 1997; Antler 1997; Wenger 1988; Nadell 1998; additionally, for an anthology of original articles that span the field of American Jewish women's history, see Nadell and Sarna 2001).

Historians of the American Jewish history, by the beginning of the twenty-first century, have moved, in step with their colleagues in American history, towards an embrace of cultural studies. Riv-Ellen Prell, a trained anthropologist, produced an important book, *Fighting to Become Americans: Jews, Gender, and the Anxiety of Assimilation*, in 1999. In this book she took image and self-image seriously as causative factors in the internal history of American Jews. Like many cultural historians of this era, she argued from the present, and read back into the past a series of concerns as salient forces in Jewish adaptation to America (Prell 1999). Likewise, Hasia Diner's *Hungering For America: Italian, Irish, and Jewish Foodways in the Age of Migration* (2002) not only joined a growing number of works on the history of food as a serious element in social and cultural history, but made it clear that American Jewish history needed a comparative context.

Latin American Jewish history and Canadian Jewish history have paralleled the developments in American Jewish history, although their size, by definition, does not approach that of the United States 'behemoth'. For a long time Latin American Jewish history functioned primarily as community history, and the studies of individual Jewish communities—in Cuba, Argentina, and Brazil, for example— existed somewhat independent of the histories of the countries in which they lived. The only exception to this somewhat disembodied history of Jews in these places involved the various histories of anti-Semitism. To understand the history of anti-Semitism had to involve studies of the larger society. Since historians asked questions about the sources of anti-Jewish behaviour and rhetoric, they were forced to look at the various elements within the social structure, the nature of the press, religion, politics, and the like, in these countries (Elkin 1998). Canadian Jewish history fits this model as well. It focused on the Jewish community, the growth of its institutions and its formative events, and considered the larger Canadian context only in as much as that context helped situate anti-Semitism (Abella and Troper 1998; Speisman 1982).

The trends which characterize the contemporary scene in American Jewish historical studies can be seen in the related fields of Canadian and Latin American Jewish history as well, and in recent years Latin Americanists and Canadianists have begun to think in more complicated categories about Jewish history. They have begun to ask questions about Jews as just one element in a number of complex and complicated societies. They have indeed begun to move away from asking how Jews differed from other Argentines, Cubans, or Canadians, and rather to probe how Jews functioned in countries which had numerous minority groups within their borders. Jeffrey Lesser's *Negotiating National Identity* posited the Jewish experience in the heart of Brazil's many ethnic groups, all involved in negotiating identities. Gerald Tulchinsky has done the same for Canada (Lesser 1999; Tulchinsky 1992).

It is noteworthy that the field of American Jewish history which has evolved has been the locus of very little controversy. No great historiographical debates have torn it apart into rival camps. The study of Zionism and the Left have led to few disputes, despite the possibilities for argumentation raised by those controversial subjects. While some American Jewish historians have been more interested, for example, in making women's history an integral part of the whole than others, none have objected to the imperative to study gender in order to provide a full and accurate picture of how Jews have lived in America. Some of the younger scholars of the 1990s have pushed for a more nuanced readings of 'classic' American Jewish texts, but most in the field, including the more established and traditional-minded of their colleagues, themselves work on the assumption that different groups within a community will see a phenomenon differently and according to their own concerns, thus making room for the deconstructionist mode of analysis.

If American Jewish historians have lagged behind at all in terms of being willing to think in fresh ways, it may be in their continued adherence to the master narrative inherited from the past. In the worn and relatively uninterrogated retelling of Jewish and American Jewish history, the immigration to America was rigidly divided into 'German' and 'Eastern European' (almost always capitalized and therefore understood as a reified entity) eras. The two immigrant streams, the conventional thinking runs, differed dramatically from each other in terms of the nature of the migration, patterns of settlement in America, and attitudes the immigrants had towards their Jewishness and vis-à-vis the degree to which they embraced the modern, western world. Because of those vast differences, the two groups met each other in America as enemies. American Jewish historians have strayed little from the pogrom narrative as the explanation for the exodus from eastern Europe and from the romance of the pre-modern 'shtetl' as the place the immigrants left.

Despite this continued reliance by most American Jewish historians on a core interpretation which is being chipped away at by some, the field continues to grow and develop in new and innovative ways[5]. As a field, it has been remarkable open to the contribution and participation of scholars who do not actually define themselves as American Jewish historians. The reception of two books in particular can demonstrate this openness. Susan Glenn came out of labour history and women's history. She had never participated in the conferences or other activities of American Jewish history, and she had in fact no training in Jewish history at all. But her 1990 book, *Daughters of the Shtetl*, now occupies a canonical position in the field. It is cited by all scholars who work in late nineteenth- and early twentieth-century American Jewish history. It appears on the required reading lists for graduate students in American Jewish history as a key text. Anyone who studies the history of Jewish women knows and takes seriously Glenn's book, despite the author's distance from the field as an organized scholarly entity (Glenn 1991). Likewise, historical sociologist Ewa Morawaska wrote her first book on patterns of life among Slavic immigrants to Johnstown, Pennsylvania. After completing that study Morawska turned her attention to the east European Jews who also lived in that steel and coal-mining town. Her book, *Insecure Prosperity*, won the coveted Saul Viener Prize of the American Jewish Historical Society, recognized as such by American Jewish historians as the outstanding book of the year. Morawska was unknown to almost all of the scholars in the field until the book came out, but they recognized the importance of her contribution despite her outsider status (Morawska 1996).

Because of its openness, richness, and quality, books in the field are now sought after by some of the most prestigious presses in the United States, including such highly selective university publishers as Harvard, Princeton, Yale, California, and Johns Hopkins, which in the past had not looked to this area for their lists. American Jewish historians are now teaching in private and public institutions

---

[5] On the challenges to the standard narrative which American Jewish historians have been slow to incorporate, see Kuznets (1975), Stanislawski (1983), Diner (1992).

around the country, some occupying positions at major American institutions of higher learning.

Perhaps more importantly, the books published by American Jewish historians are now being read and discussed in great detail by their colleagues who study modern Jewish history in both the United States and Israel. America is no longer a Jewish history backwater. Indeed, scholars who focus on the histories of the older communities, Russia, Poland, France, and Germany, are increasingly now familiarizing themselves with American Jewish history as a crucial component of the world Jewish experience. Some Jewish historians with graduate training, scholarly reputations, and previous publications in European Jewish history have actually shifted over to do research on American Jewish history as well.[6] This in part reflects the recently acknowledged but long present global dimension to Jewish history.[7] It also demonstrates the depth of the research and the complexity of the questions being asked by American Jewish historians.

They no doubt also recognize that the apparatus for the study and discussion of American Jewish history is extremely solid. First, the presence of the American Jewish Historical Society in the Center for Jewish History which opened in New York in 2000 testifies to the centrality of the field in the world of Jewish studies scholarship. The American Jewish Archives in Cincinnati on the campus of Hebrew Union College continues to collect and made available to scholars rich collections, including the papers of individual, and often quite ordinary, American Jews, communal records, and newspapers. Secondly, the biannual scholars' conferences sponsored by the American Jewish Historical Society since the mid-1980s, and dedicated to presenting new research in American Jewish history, are seen as important venues for exchanging ideas. Graduate students and emerging young scholars in history, American studies, and cultural studies see these conferences as significant occasions for showcasing their work.

American Jewish history scholarship is sustained by journals as well as books and conferences. Two journals, *American Jewish History*, in continuous publication since 1892, and the more recent addition, *American Jewish Archives*, founded in 1948, present article-length studies of various aspects of American Jewish history, while the more general Jewish history journals such as *YIVO Annual*, *Jewish Social Studies*, *Jewish History*, *AJS Review*, and *Studies in Contemporary Jewry*, are likely in any issue to include essays on the American Jewish past. Clearly Jewish historians have come to define both what happened in America in the past and what is being produced now from within the field of American Jewish history as of significance. Within the

---

[6] See e.g. the amount of attention given to American Jewish history in Zipperstein (1999). The careers of Eli Lederhendler, Paula Hyman, and Jack Wertheimer also bear out the growing significance of American Jewish history. Trained in Russian, French, and German Jewish history, they are now active contributors to the enterprise of American Jewish history.

[7] Frankel (1997) is just one recent example of the absolutely necessary transnational dimension of Jewish history.

profession of Jewish history, at least as practised within the United States, it is reasonable to conclude that no specialty or sub-field could claim such intense activity and vitality.

Yet American Jewish history, despite its intellectual excellence and the recognition it has achieved in the realm of modern Jewish history, continues to be something of a stepchild within American history. With some very important exceptions, particularly among those historians who study either immigration or religion, most Americanists evince little interest in the field or respect for what it has produced[8]. Numerous Americanists write books which cry out for contextualization into American Jewish history, but ignore those calls. They indeed write books about Jews, with Jews as major and minor players, but make no effort to know the literature in American Jewish history and to see where their efforts would be enriched by that exposure.

James Goodman's *Stories of Scottsboro* offers an illustrative case of this blindness to the field of American Jewish history. In a deeply researched, complex book, Goodman set out to lay before his readers the many versions of 'what happened', starting in March 1931, when two white women accused a group of African American boys of having raped them aboard a freight train moving through northern Alabama. The ensuing Scottsboro case became a *cause célèbre* in America. Trials, including two in front of the US Supreme Court, grew out of this accusation, and the plight of the accused garnered headlines around the world. Goodman described his project as an attempt to depict a 'conflict between people with different ideas about what happened and different ideas about the causes and meaning of what happened—a story about the conflict between people with different stories of Scottsboro' (Goodman 1994: p. xii).

Why should Goodman have taken note of the scholarship in American Jewish history? In what way would cognizance of American Jewish history have made this a better and richer book? For one, the lawyer who defended the Scottsboro boys, Samuel Leibowitz, was Jewish. The Alabama prosecutor and the Alabama press made a big point that the defence was in the hands of 'the Jews' and that 'Jew money' was subverting real justice. While Goodman dealt with the anti-Jewish rhetoric which swirled around Leibowitz, he made no references whatsoever to the large body of literature on Jews in the South, and to American—particularly southern— anti-Semitism. Secondly, and perhaps most importantly, the Jewish press around the country in the 1930s, written in English and Yiddish, defined the Scottsboro case as a Jewish matter. It reported on it extensively. The Jewish publications provided extensive documentation of exactly what Goodman was looking for, that is, they too had a 'story of Scottsboro'. *Opinion*, a Jewish magazine of the 1930s, for example, went so far as to opine that it, and all American Jews (in whose name it felt it could

---

[8] For an example, see Gabaccia (1994), which is a fairly recent and important exception to the absence of interest in the experience of American Jews in the context of American history generally.

speak), took 'an especial pride in the fact that the chief counsel ... was a Jew. Both as a member of such a group and as an inheritor of his own tradition, it is inevitable that the Jew should take active and leading parts in all such struggles as that at present being waged around the Scottsboro injustice' (Diner 1977: 114). In Goodman's widely praised book, the wealth of material available on this subjects from the field of Jewish history is utterly absent.

So too Ellen Carol DuBois and Vicki L. Ruiz's heavily used anthology, *Unequal Sisters: A Multi-Cultural Reader*, found nothing from the field of American Jewish history to include when trying to document the impact of race and ethnicity on women's history. In the 1990 edition of the book they include a personal 'think piece' by the novelist Meredith Tax, who made reference to her own personal feelings of Jewishness, while the second (1994) edition included an article by Tax on the 'Uprising of the Thirty Thousand', the shirtwaist strike of 1909. The DuBois and Ruiz book, as an exemplar of multicultural historical scholarship, basically asserts that Jews did not have a culture which made them different than other Americans, and that if there was anything worth thinking about at all in this context, it was the labour organizing of the early part of the century, and even that did not deserve the attention of a historian. For all the scholarship on Jewish women by Paula Hyman, Joyce Antler, Deborah Dash Moore, Sidney Weinberg, even Susan Glenn, nothing from the field made its way into this book, which is assigned in college courses around the country (DuBois and Ruiz 1990, 1994).

Little of what has been produced in the field of American Jewish history has been highlighted in the most prestigious journals in American history, particularly the *Journal of American History*. While the *JAH* faithfully reviews most of the books published on the history of the Jews of the United States, it has rarely included articles on the subject. Of the four articles that appeared in the decade of the 1980s, only one was written by an active practitioner of American Jewish history, Jonathan Sarna. Another was written by David Gerber, a historian with only a tangential interest in the Jewish past, definitely secondary to his larger interest in American immigration and ethnic history. The other two, fine and informative articles though they were, were contributed by individuals, David Levering Lewis and Nancy McLean, who had scholarly agendas far removed from that of contributing to the store of knowledge and interpretation about the history of the Jews of the United States (Sarna 1981; Gerber 1982; Lewis 1984; McLean 1991). In the 1990s the only article to have any connection to the history of the Jews of the United States took as its subject the notorious Leopold and Loeb case and its multiple readings. But, as in the case of the Goodman book, the author made no reference to any of the published works on the history of Chicago Jewry, nor did she explore the ways in which Jews, as reflected in their publications—including Chicago Jewish newspapers and magazines—constructed the case (Fass 1993).

How can we reconcile the vigour of the field and the generally high regard which it enjoys within the ranks of Jewish historians on the one hand, with its near invisibility in American historical scholarship? By the 1990s American immigration history had generally declined in favour within the ranks of American historians, and the study of European-derived ethnicity in particular generated little excitement, except among its practitioners, who believed that there was still much more to be learned about the women and men who came to America from Italy, Ireland, Germany, Greece, Poland, and the like. Likewise, religious history had long occupied a peripheral zone in the interests of most scholars of American history, and American Jewish historians were—ironically—becoming much more concerned with the religious dimension by the 1990s and beyond.

But, perhaps at the most fundamental level, the experience of American Jews as relatively poor immigrants who achieved, with a remarkable degree of ease and speed, middle-class status does not fit the prevailing interpretive mood of American history, which focuses on the entrenched nature of privilege. That Jews, outsiders to American culture upon their arrival in the United States, were able to penetrate barriers and enter the mainstream clashes with the way historians want to see the American past. As a group who craved both economic security and respectability, their story lacks the dramatic punch of resisters and rebels to the American ethos. In an intellectual climate which validates certain kind of differences, particularly those associated with certain phenotypical characteristics, Jews seem to historians to have been too white, too affluent, too European, and too accommodating to American culture to be included in the multicultural histories being written at the beginning of the twenty-first century.

However much American Jewish historians would like to be part of the larger profession, they are in fact undeterred by the relatively cold shoulder given their work by the Americanists around them. Historians committed to researching, writing, and teaching about the American Jewish past continue to define new areas of scholarship that they deem intellectually valid. If others are less than receptive, that has been—and will continue to be—no real hindrance to the continued growth of the field.

SUGGESTED READING

The series The Jewish People in America offers the best in-depth overview of American Jewish history as of the early 1990s: Diner (1992); Faber (1992); Feingold (1992); Shapiro (1992); Sorin (1992).

BIBLIOGRAPHY

ABELLA, I. M. and TROPER, H. 1998. *None is Too Many: Canada and the Jews of Europe, 1933–1948*. Toronto.

ANTLER, J. 1997. *The Journey Home: Jewish Women and the American Century.* New York.

ASHTON, D. 1997. *Rebecca Gratz: Women and Judaism in Antebellum America.* Detroit.

BARON, S. 1971. *Steeled by Adversity: Essays and Addresses on American Jewish Life.* Philadelphia.

DAVIS, M. and MEYER, I. S. eds. 1957. *The Writing of American Jewish History.* Proceedings of the Conference of Historians Convened by the American Jewish Historical Society on the Occasion of the Three Hundredth Anniversary of the Settlement of Jews in the United States at Peekskill, New York on September 13th and 14th, 1954. *Publications of the American Jewish Historical Society* 46/3. New York.

DINER, H. R. 1977. *In the Almost Promised Land: American Jews and Blacks, 1915–1935.* Westport, Conn.

—— 1992. *A Time for Gathering: The Second Migration, 1820–1880.* Baltimore.

—— 2002. *Hungering for America: Italian, Irish, and Jewish Foodways in the Age of Migration.* Cambridge, Mass.

DINNERSTEIN, L. 1968. *The Leo Frank Case.* New York.

DOLLINGER, M. 2000. *Quest for Inclusion: Jews and Liberalism in Modern America.* Princeton.

DUBOIS, E. C. and RUIZ, V. L. 1990, 1994. *Unequal Sisters: A Multi-Cultural Reader in U.S. Women's History.* New York.

ELKIN, J. L. 1998. *The Jews of Latin America.* New York.

FABER, E. 1992. *A Time for Planting: The First Migration, 1654–1820.* Baltimore.

FASS, P. 1993. 'The Making and Remaking of an Event: The Leopold and Loeb Case in American Culture.' *Journal of American History* 80/3: 919–51.

FEINGOLD, H. 1970. *The Politics of Rescue: The Roosevelt Administration and the Holocaust, 1938–1945.* New Brunswick, NJ.

—— 1992. *A Time for Searching: Entering the Mainstream, 1920–1945.* Baltimore.

FRANKEL, J. 1997. *The Damascus Affair: 'Ritual Murder', Politics, and the Jews in 1840.* Cambridge.

FRIEDENWALD, H. 1897. 'Some Newspaper Advertisements of the Eighteenth Century.' *Publications of the American Jewish Historical Society* 6: 49–60.

GABACCIA, D. 1994. *From the Other Side: Women, Gender, and Immigrant Life in the United States, 1820–1990.* Bloomington, Ind.

GERBER, D. 1982. 'Cutting Out Shylock: Elite Anti-Semitism and the Quest for Moral Order in the Mid-Nineteenth Century American Market Place.' *Journal of American History* 693: 615–37.

GLENN, S. 1991. *Daughters of the Shtetl: Life and Labor in the Immigrant Generation.* Ithaca, NY.

GOODMAN, J. 1994. *Stories of Scottsboro.* New York.

GOREN, A. A. 1970. *New York Jews and the Quest for Community: The Kehillah Experiment, 1908–1922.* New York.

—— 1999. *The Politics and Public Culture of American Jews.* Bloomington, Ind.

GRINSTEIN, H. 1945. *The Rise of the Jewish Community of New York, 1654–1860.* Philadelphia.

GUROCK, J. S. 1979. *When Harlem Was Jewish, 1870–1930.* New York.

—— 1983. *American Jewish History: A Bibliographical Guide.* New York.

—— 1993–4. 'From Publications to American Jewish History: The Journal of the American Jewish Historical Society and the Writing of American Jewish History.' *American Jewish History* 81/2: 155–270.

GUTSTEIN, M. 1953. *Priceless Heritage: The Epic Growth of Nineteenth Century Chicago Jewry.* New York.

HANDLIN, O. 1949. 'New Paths in American Jewish History: Afterthoughts of a Conference.' *Commentary* Apr.: 388–94.

—— 1951. *The Uprooted: The Epic Story of the Great Migrations That Made the American People.* New York.

—— 1954a. *Adventures in Freedom: Three Hundred Years of Jewish Life in America.* New York.

—— 1954b. 'Foreword.' In Rischin (1954): p. vii.

HARTZ, L. 1955. *The Liberal Tradition in America: An Interpretation of American Political Thought Since the Revolution.* San Diego.

KESSNER, T. 1977. *The Golden Door: Italian and Jewish Immigrant Mobility in New York City 1880–1915.* New York.

KUZNETS, S. 1975. 'Immigration of Russian Jews to the United States: Background and Structure.' *Perspectives in American History* 9: 35–126.

LESSER, J. 1999. *Negotiating National Identity: Immigrants, Minorities, and the Struggle for Ethnicity in Brazil.* Durham.

LEVINE, L. W. 1993. *The Unpredictable Past: Explorations in American Cultural History.* New York.

LEWIS, D. L. 1984. 'Parallels and Divergences: Assimilationist Strategies of Afro-American and Jewish Elites from 1910 to the Early 1930s.' *Journal of American History* 71/3: 543–64.

MCKELVEY, B. 1945. *Rochester: The Water-Power City, 1812–1854.* Cambridge, Mass.

—— 1949. *Rochester, The Flower City, 1855–1890.* Cambridge, Mass.

—— 1956. *Rochester: The Quest for Quality, 1890–1925.* Chicago.

—— 1961. *Rochester: An Emerging Metropolis, 1925–1961.* Rochester.

MCLAUGHLIN GREEN, C. 1962–3. *Washington.* Princeton.

MCLEAN, N. 1991. 'The Leo Frank Case Reconsidered: Gender and Sexual Politics in the Making of Reactionary Populism.' *Journal of American History* 78/3: 917–48.

MARKOWITZ, R. A. 1993. *My Daughter, the Teacher: Jewish Teachers in the New York City Schools.* New Brunswick, NJ.

MOORE, D. D. 1981. *At Home in America: Second Generation New York Jews.* New York.

—— 1994. *To the Golden Cities: Pursuing the American Jewish Dream in Miami and L. A.* New York.

MORAWSKA, E. 1996. *Insecure Prosperity: Small-Town Jews in Industrial America, 1890–1940.* Princeton.

NADELL, P. 1998. *Women Who Would Be Rabbis: A History of Women's Ordination, 1889–1985.* Boston.

NADELL, P. and SARNA, J. eds. 2001. *Women and American Judaism: Historical Perspectives.* Hanover, NH.

NOVICK, P. 1988. *That Noble Dream: The 'Objectivity Question,' and the American Historic Profession.* Cambridge.

PIERCE, B. L. 1937. *A History of Chicago.* New York.

PIERSON, G. 1973. *The Moving American.* New York.

PRELL, R. E. 1999. *Fighting To Become Americans: Jews, Gender, and the Anxiety of Assimilation*. Boston.

REZNIKOFF, C. and ENGELMAN, U. Z. 1950. *The Jews of Charleston: A History of an American Jewish Community*. Philadelphia.

RISCHIN, M. 1954. *An Inventory of American Jewish History*. Cambridge, Mass.

—— 1962. *The Promised City: New York Jews, 1870–1914*. Cambridge, Mass.

ROSENBERG, S. 1964. *America Is Different: The Search for Jewish Identity*. London.

SARNA, J. 1980. *Jacksonian Jew: The Two Worlds of Mordecai Noah*. New York.

—— 1981. 'The American Jewish Response to 19th Century Christian Missions.' *Journal of American History* 681: 35–51

SHAPIRO, E. 1992. *A Time for Healing: American Jewry Since World War II*. Baltimore.

SORIN, G. 1992. *A Time for Building: The Third Migration, 1880–1920*. Baltimore.

SOYER, D. 1997. *Jewish Immigrant Associations and American Identity in New York, 1880–1939*. Cambridge, Mass.

SPEISMAN, S. A. 1982. *A Coat of Many Colours: Two Centuries of Jewish Life in Canada*. Toronto.

STANISLAWSKI, M. 1983. *Tsar Nicholas I and the Jews: The Transformation of Jewish Society in Russia, 1825–1855*. Philadelphia.

STILL, B. 1948. *Milwaukee: The History of a City*. Madison, Wisc.

SVONKIN, S. 1997. *Jews Against Prejudice: American Jews and the Fight for Civil Liberties*. New York.

THOMPSON, E. P. 1966. *The Making of the English Working Class*. New York.

TULCHINSKY, G. 1992. *Branching Out: The Transformation of the Canadian Jewish Community*. Toronto.

WEINBERG, S. S. 1988. *The World of Our Mothers: Lives of Jewish Immigrant Women*. Chapel Hill, NC.

WENGER, B. 1996. *New York Jews and the Great Depression: Uncertain Promise*. New Haven.

WOLF II, E. and WHITEMAN, M. 1957. *The History of the Jews of Philadelphia: From Colonial Times to the Age of Jackson*. Philadelphia.

WOLF, S. 1895. 'The American Jew as Soldier and Patriot.' *Publications of the American Jewish Historical Society* 3: 21–40.

ZIPPERSTEIN, S. J. 1999. *Imagining Russian Jewry: Memory, History, Identity*. Seattle.

CHAPTER 20

....

THE HEBREW LANGUAGE

....

PABLO-ISAAC HALEVI (KIRTCHUK)

THE term 'Hebrew' designates a language which, under diverse forms and in different contexts through the ages, has been the Jewish people's linguistic vehicle of cult, culture, and communication. Its early form was adopted by the first Abrahamites who became established in the country known first as Canaan, then Eretz Israel, and its contemporary form is spoken today by the 6 million inhabitants of Israel. It is also familiar to a varying extent to most Jews in the diaspora.

A form of Biblical Hebrew (BH) is attested on tablets from the fourteenth century BCE and represents the written register of the language of the Israelite tribes who later—during the eleventh century BCE—established a kingdom in the land formerly known as Canaan. Though there is no extant manuscript harking back to that period, some biblical texts are faithfully represented in the Dead Sea scrolls (DSS), many of which date from the first century BCE. Among the DSS there are also the Hebrew originals of some apocryphal books previously known only in Greek or Ethiopic translation. Ancient Hebrew is represented also by a certain amount of epigraphic and epistolary documents ranging from the fourteenth century BCE to 132–5 CE. From the beginning of that period we have the glosses from Tel El Amarna, hence from pre-Israelite Canaan, which bear a very strong resemblance to Hebrew. Fifteen centuries later we have Bar Kokhba's letters. In between we have, among others, the Gezer Calendar (tenth century BCE), about seventy ostraca from Samaria (eighth century BCE) and a hundred from Arad (seventh and beginning of the sixth century BCE), the Lakhish letters (sixth century

BCE), and the Shiloah Tunnel inscription (seventh century BCE). All of this extra-biblical material is very important since it displays words, structures, and pronunciations unknown from other sources, shedding additional light on Classical Biblical Hebrew: the written norm represented in CBH existed along with oral variants, which eventually yielded the norm of written Late Biblical Hebrew (LBH). It includes among others things, the Song of Songs and Ecclesiastes, several Psalms, and the frame story of the book of Job. LBH, in turn, had a spoken form of its own, which eventually yielded the following stage.

Indeed, from the second century BCE onwards, the written documents testify to a real change in the grammar of the language. This is the stage known as Rabbinic or Mishnaic Hebrew (MH), after the most important document written in it, the Mishnah—a collection of juridic oral debates developed and ultimately based upon the written Law, the Torah. Other documents from the same stage are legal treatises such as the Mekhilta, the Sifra, and the Sifre, as well as the midrashim, consisting of short anecdotes and commentaries, both halachic (juridic) and ʾaggadic (philosophical and literary). All of them reflect the oral language spoken between the second century BCE and the third century CE, probably descended from a colloquial variant spoken during late biblical times. A caveat exists, however, concerning the linearity of the language's evolution up to that point: this evolution is not always reflected in the documents from the corresponding period. Thus, early features may be found in late texts: bisyllabic *segolata* (thus called after the *segol* vowel in both their syllables): /mɛlɛk/ʿking', /qodɛš/ ʿ(distinction >) sanctity', /saʿar/ 'tempest' result from the resolution of the consonant cluster in final position, the stress accent remaining on the first syllable. Now the primary, monosyllabic forms /malk, qudš, saʿr/ are found in Origen's transliteration of the Hebrew Bible (third century CE), while in the Septuagint transliteration (third century BCE) one finds the later bisyllabic forms similar to those of the Tiberian vocalization.

Hebrew ceased to be spoken in the third century CE and persisted only in a written form (cf., among others, Rashi's commentaries on the Bible, eleventh century). From the third century onwards Hebrew continued to be used for juridical, intellectual, philosophical, poetic, and liturgical purposes but not for daily oral communication, save in particular circumstances when Jews from different countries had to resort to it in order to understand each other. In Muslim Spain written Hebrew acquired some new characteristics: it is Medieval Hebrew (MdH). At the turn of the twentieth century it became anew the mother tongue of an ever-increasing population, which uses it in all realms of life.

THE REVIVAL OF HEBREW

The Jewish equivalent of the Enlightenment movement in Europe is called 'Haska-lah'. It was in vogue in the eighteenth and nineteenth centuries and promoted a trend among Jews of becoming acquainted with science and the humanities as well as with traditional Jewish scholarship. Its members felt a necessity of reactivating Hebrew and endowing it with a power to express the contemporary reality and a modern *Weltanschauung*. Indeed, they felt Yiddish to be somewhat homely, senti-mental, proper to express the daily experiences of the inhabitants of the Shtetl rather than a system of cognition and communication apt to express the most elevated thoughts and the finest perceptions of Man. On the other hand, they felt alien to the European languages and their ways of conveying those thoughts and feelings. Their natural choice then fell upon Hebrew which, though not a spoken tongue for the time being, had the prestige of a great language of culture, the one which had been properly and utterly Jewish from the dawn of civilization. An archetypal figure within this movement was, from a stylistic point of view, the nineteenth-century writer Abraham Mappu, whose novels, based on biblical themes and written in a style inspired by CBH, constitute a pale image of the much more ambitious endeavour launched at the turn of 1870: the Revival of Hebrew.

This is indeed an unprecedented enterprise, which has remained unique ever since. True, Basque and Irish have been the objects of similar attempts, but the comparison does not hold. On the one hand, neither had ever ceased to be spoken altogether; on the other, both failed to become the main language of Euskadi or of Eire respectively. Hebrew, which had ceased to be a truly spoken tongue during the third century, is now the official language of Israel and its 6 million inhabitants. Many of them are functionally monolingual in Hebrew, which has become the mother tongue of the last three generations of Israeli-born Jews (the so-called *sabras*), and presumably of many more to come. In addition, it is continually adopted by the millions of Jews who do not cease to immigrate to Israel from all over the world, a factor which to a large extent accounts for the success of its revival. Indeed, the reasons for this success are basically of two orders, ideological and practical. The first is the will of the Jewish people to find anew its independence at all levels, national, cultural, and linguistic. The second determines that a group of people speaking a very large spectrum of languages, but who hardly have any of them in common, and yet desperately need and want to communicate with each other, are bound to learn the language which is, at some cultural-cum-psychological level (remote as it may be), common to them all. In the present case that language is Hebrew. Naturally, in order for the process actually to work, it was required that the language be latent in the individuals' minds, which was indeed the case: less than a century ago a vast majority of Jews were observant to varying extents, which means that they were proficient in reading and understanding Hebrew. Thus, in order to be able to speak it they only had to transform passive knowledge into active, not to acquire the language as if they were complete beginners.

The seminal figure in the Revival of Hebrew as a spoken tongue was Eliezer Ben-Yehuda (1858–1922), who began his public struggle for the cause in 1879 with the publication in the Hebrew journal *HaShaḥar* of an article entitled '*Šəʾela loḥata*', that is, 'A Burning Question', whose title was changed by the editor, Peretz Smolenskin, into '*šəʾela nikbada*', 'A Considerable Question'. Ben-Yehuda exposed there the cardinal place of language as a constituent of national identity in general, and the necessity of reactivating Hebrew in the framework of the Zionist endeavour. Once established in Jerusalem with his wife Deborah (after her death, he married her sister Hemda), Ben-Yehuda devoted himself to lexicographic and neologistic work. He raised his children solely in Hebrew, and his eldest child, Itamar Ben-Avi (1885–1943, lit. 'son of *avi*', i.e. 'son of my father', '*avi*' being also+an acronym for his father's full name) founded his own journal and pursued his father's task. It would be inappropriate to say that the renaissance of Hebrew is due to Ben-Yehuda alone, and yet it must be admitted that without his impulsion, his erudition, and his determination the process would perhaps not have been crowned with success. On the other hand, as Hagège (2000) rightly notes, had Ben-Yehuda been a professional linguist he would not have attempted such an ambitious endeavour. The revival of Hebrew is therefore a visionary's victory rather than a specialist's achievement—which is often the case with projects characterized by their grandeur. At some points in its recent history the primacy of Hebrew has been endangered, especially during the 1920s when 'the languages fight' in the country's most renowned polytechnic institute, Haifa's Technion, threatened the imposition of German as the teaching language of the institution. At the time it was not clear, either, whether Hebrew should be the training language of schoolteachers in the pedagogical institute Beth haMidrash leMorim of Jerusalem. Eventually the choice fell upon Hebrew as a result of demonstrations by both faculty and students, and the institution's name became Beth haMidrash leMorim haIvri, with the emphatic position of the adjective *ibvī*, i.e. Hebrew, reflecting the circumstances of its emergence. Later on the flux of immigrants from different areas ensured that Hebrew would be taught and spoken as the only common language for Jews whose languages were as diverse and as numerous as their native origins.

Another important figure in the process of the revival of Hebrew was philologist and linguist H. Z. Torczyner-Tur Sinai (1886–1973), who contributed valuable insights concerning the language's diachronic grammar, enhancing its development on harmonic bases, in accordance with the language's own resources and respecting its Semitic origins. Powerful personalities who played a major role in this process, either by their scientific or by their literary work, include among others intellectuals David Yelin (1864–1941) and Joseph Klausner (1874–1958), as well as poets Haiim N. Bialik (1873–1934), Samuel Y. Agnon (1888–1970), Abraham Shlonsky (1900–73), Alexander Pen (1906–72), Nathan Alterman (1910–70), Yonatan Ratosh (1908–81), and David Avidan (1934–95).

As for linguistic research of Israeli Hebrew (IH), the foremost scholar and the one who elevated Israeli Hebrew—even the term is his—to the rank of a distinct stage in the history of the language, and not merely a pale reflection of its noble ancestors, is the late Haiim B. Rosén (1922–99). Having acquired a solid foundation in classical philology, then a thorough linguistic training in Paris under Émile Benveniste, Rosén devoted his life to investigating Hebrew, mostly IH, with the methods of structural linguistics, coining linguistic terms in Hebrew and making a decisive contribution to the constitution of the conception of IH as a complete, coherent, and self-sufficient speech system, namely a specific form of Hebrew in its own right.

IH has been reactivated as a result of the will of its speakers, who decided to acquire the language and make it their children's mother tongue for generations to come. Its development, normalization, and standardization are therefore institutionally regulated. This responsibility rests upon the Academy of the Hebrew Language, which according to its status has to ensure a harmonic development of the language based on the investigation of its grammar and lexicon through its diverse sources. The Academy, founded in 1953, is the successor of Va'ad haLashon, 'The Language Committee' created by Ben-Yehuda in 1905, which fulfilled an equivalent role from its foundation in Ottoman-ruled Palestine, through the British mandate (1917–47), and during the first years of existence of the State of Israel as such (1948–53).

LINGUISTIC CHARACTERIZATION

Hebrew belongs to the Semitic language family within the Afro-Asiatic stock (cf. also Bynon 1984). According to the model based on shared innovations (Faber 2000) this family is divided into two major branches: (1) East Semitic (ES) includes Assyrian and Babylonian, both of which are known under the common term 'Akkadian', as well as Eblaite ; (2) West Semitic (WS), divided into two main sub-branches: (a) Central Semitic, including on one hand Arabic and on the other hand the North-West Semitic group, constituted of Ugaritic, Canaanite (including Hebrew), Aramaic, and Deir-Alla ; (b) South Semitic, whose western group includes

Ethiopian and Old South Arabian, and whose eastern group includes contemporary Soqotri, Mehri, Harsusi, and Jibbali.

Within the Canaanite group of North-West Semitic, in the Central-Semitic sub-branch of the WS branch, Hebrew is akin to Moabite (known above all from the tombstone of King Mesha, from the fourteenth century BCE); to Phoenician and its avatars, Punic and Neo-Punic; to Ammonite; and to the Canaanite of Tel El Amarna, considered as Proto-Hebrew. It is also close to Ugaritic, though this language does not entirely belong in the Canaanite group.

Among the characteristics which Hebrew shares with other West Semitic languages, the most striking one is suffix-conjugation for the perfect aspect (from MH onwards it encodes the past tense). As a member of the central sub-branch of WS it displays some additional properties too, such as pharyngalization as a secondary articulation—a rephonologization of Proto-Semitic (PS) postglottalization (Cantineau 1952, Martinet 1953) which we find to this day in Ethiopian; the non-geminate prefix-conjugation for the imperfect aspect (from MH onwards future tense); the within-paradigm generalization of vowels in prefix conjugation, and the generalization of /-t-/ in suffix conjugation verbs.

As a member of the Northwest Semitic division, Hebrew changes Proto-Semitic word-initial /#w-/ into /#j-/ and has a double marking of the plural on the *segolata* or nouns built on the $R_1 \epsilon R_2 \epsilon R_3$ pattern—first by vocalic quantity: the /ɛ/ of the second radical in the singular becomes /å/ in the plural; then by suffixation—/-īm#/ is added to the /R₁əR₂åR₃-/ nominal theme. A second peculiarity is the assimilation of /l/ to /q/ for the root /lqḥ/ in the imperfect aspect, and a third one is the metathesis of morphological /-t-/ and R1{R1 = sibilant} at the *hitpaṣṣēl* forms, cf./*hitsakkēl/ > /histakkēl/.

Finally, within Canaanite, Hebrew displays some shifts peculiar to this group: /ā/ > /ō/, /-tu/ > /-tī/ for the first person singular perfect, /a/ > /i/ in the first syllable of the derived intensive (/*kannis > kinnēs/) and factitive (/hik̠nīs/) stems (the so-called Law of Attrition), and finally the spread of the /-nū/ form for the suffixed accusative and genitive pronominal first person plural. All of these properties, fixed once and for all in BH, characterize the structure of Hebrew through all of its stages to this day.

TYPOLOGY

In terms of classical morphological typology *à la* Humboldt and Sapir, Hebrew is an inflecting language. Moreover, morphology is probably its most resisting structure bearing an unequivocal Semitic stamp. In terms of syntax (note that we do not use the well-known terminology of the late Joseph Greenberg (1915–2001), since it lacks coherence inasmuch as it includes a part of speech (V) along with parts of the sentence (S,O); such a confusion presupposes that all languages have only verbal predicates, which is wrong: of all languages, Semitic ones, including Hebrew, are perhaps the most famous to have nominal sentences, that is, sentences whose predicate is a not a verb but a noun, without even, in the non-marked tense, a copula ; moreover, that terminology refers explicitly to 'word-order', whereas grammatical morphemes are part and parcel of that order: therefore, it is element-order that we must refer to), BH has the verbal predicate in initial position, with the subject marker affixed to it, then a possible explicit nominal or deictic subject in second position, and finally the other verbal complements. This order is preserved in MH and MdH, whereas in IH the order of the first two components is reversed: first comes the nominal or deictic subject, then the verbal or nominal predicate. Only if the clause is subordinate or if it begins with a circumstantial complement does the BH order prevail. In all cases, the object takes the third position. Nominal sentences begin with the nominal or deictic subject, then comes the nominal or deictic predicate. This is the unmarked order, which is, however, liable to change rather freely for pragmatic purposes (focalization and topicalization, mainly). In BH the copula as such is not obligatory in nominal sentences; if it does occur, it is only for purposes of focalization of the preceding element. IH, on the other hand, uses the copula as a device to separate the subject from the predicate in nominal sentences. BH being a synthetic language, all finite verbs take a subject affix, but the bi-or tri-valent verb (Tesnière 1959) can take, in addition, a direct object suffix. Thus, /raʔi-tī/ *see, past-1sg.subj* means 'I saw', and /rəʔi-tī-hå/ *see, past-1sg.subj* 3sg.f.obj. means 'I saw her'. Hebrew conforms to Greenberg's Universals; thus, the attribute (including adjectives, subordinate clauses, and genitives) follows the noun and the preposition precedes it. In BH possession is also synthetically expressed, by a mark of the possessor suffixed to the possessum. IH, on the other hand, has no object markers on the verb in the colloquial register but does display them, to some extent, in a literary style or high register, and the possessive markers appended to the noun itself in BH are still appended, but to the particle /š ɛl/.

Another typological difference which distinguishes IH from BH and MH relates to nominal composition and prefixation. BH exhibits practically no example of nominal composition—most nouns are construed by derivation and can be expanded by means of the construct-state or of *tamyīz*. IH, on the other hand, has a number of compound nouns and a score of nominal prefixes, mostly quantitative and spatio-temporal (Kirtchuk 1997).

BH makes a clear-cut distinction between definite and indefinite nouns, correlating mostly with presence or absence of the definite article (of deictic origin) /#ha-/ prefixed to the noun. In MH there is a drastic diminution in the use of this device, the distinction being neutralized in most contexts and expressed, when absolutely necessary, by other devices, mostly a deictic demonstrative or a possessive suffix. This attrition of determination results from Aramaic influence. Aramaic, due to the freezing of the definite article /-å#/ suffixed to the noun, lost the determination opposition altogether. IH, which in this regard follows BH syntax, exhibits at present a trend similar to the one attested in MH as far as determination is concerned, once again as a result of foreign influence—this time not Aramaic but English. Thus, IH has expressions like /zəḵujjot ʾadam/ 'human rights', a construct-state where the non determination of / ʾadam/ 'man' is a calque from English, whilst normative Hebrew syntax requires /zəḵujjot ha ʾadam/ 'the rights of Man'.

A question arising from the rapid evolution of IH is whether it can still be considered a Semitic language from a typological viewpoint. The question is in itself ill-posed, since 'Semitic', 'Indo-European', and the like are, by definition, genealogical terms, and therefore no specific typological interpretation should be attached to them. Still, since Semitic languages do have a common typological core in the realms of phonology, morphology, syntax, and vocabulary, just as do other linguistic families, one can reformulate the question in appropriate typological terms and then try to answer it, provided the criteria are carefully selected and defined, and a broad variety of languages from the families under analysis are examined. Failing to do so properly may lead to the mistaken conclusion that IH belongs to a supposed Indo-European type, the Standard Average European (SAE) imagined by Benjamin Lee Whorf. IH continues to be a Semitic language, not only on a genealogical basis but on typological grounds as well (Goldenberg (1995) and Kapeliuk (2003)).

THE STUDY OF HEBREW

The Christian World, Before the Modern Era

Origen, a Greek-speaking Christian from Alexandria (186–255), is the first major biblical scholar produced by the Church. He is the author of the document known as the Hexapla, after its six synoptic columns: the Hebrew original, its Greek transliteration, three Greek translations (by Aquila, Symmachus, and Theodotion), and finally Origen's own adaptation of another Greek translation (allegedly the Septuagint) so as to match word to word the Hebrew original. The Hexapla has not survived, probably destroyed at Caesarea during the Islamic conquest in the seventh century. Yet, as his command of the language was rather dubious, it would be inaccurate to present Origen as the pioneer of *Hebraica veritas* (the character of truth attributed to the Hebrew original of the biblical text, and hence the need to study Hebrew in order to understand the Scripture properly). He is surely, though, the man who opened the way in this direction.

Jerome (348–420) was to give this quest a more scholarly character. A truly trilingual scholar, his fondness for the Latin classics was as profound as his attachment to penetrating the *Hebraica veritas* through a study in depth of Hebrew and its grammatical and lexical structures, which allowed him to express in the Vulgate, his translation into Latin, the *sensuum veritatem* of the Hebrew rather than its *verborum ordo*. Jerome was aware of the many problems of translation, both at the technical and at the theoretical level, and solved them successfully and often with elegance. Therefore he is considered not only as a great figure in Hebrew studies in the Christian world, but also as a great translator.

In the Middle Ages the tradition of Hebrew studies among Christians re-emerges in the eleventh century with Andrew of St Victor and with the re-establishment of these studies among the Cistercian monks of Monte Cassino. It was another monk of St Victor's, Hugo (1097–1141), who stated that 'the Greek text of the Bible is better than the Latin, and the Hebrew better than the Greek'. The mainstream of Christian intellectual life, however, ignored Hebrew until the fifteenth century, that is, the beginning of the Renaissance.

It is in Venice that we find the first Christian Italian to acquire a thorough knowledge of the language: Marco Lippomano (1390–1438). Florence, however, was the city in which the study of Hebrew spread and eventually entered the curriculum of the *studia humanitatis*. Thus, we have a letter from the beginning of the fifteenth century sent by Leonardo Bruni Aretino, a prestigious humanist from Florence, in which he warned Giovanni Cirignano de Lucca against the study of the language since, as he puts it 'everything worth reading in this language has already been translated into Latin, and besides, many saints did not know the first thing about Hebrew'. Which means that Cirignano did undertake its study, just as did Poggio Bracciolini (1380–1459), another Florentine, who said that he studied Hebrew in order to understand Jerome's translation of the Bible published a thousand years earlier, in 393. At the same period and in the same city lived Giannozzo Manetti (1396–1459), who learned Hebrew from two Jews, one of whom was Immanuel Abraham de San Miniato. Manetti possessed number of Hebrew books, including Maimonides' *Guide of the Perplexed* as well as commentaries by Rashi and 'Ibn Ezra on several books of the Bible. So complete was his command of the language that he was able to produce a Latin translation of the Psalms (Dröge 1992). A sign of the interest in Hebrew manifested in Florence is the curious conjecture formulated in 1546 by Giovanni Battista Gelli, according to which the Italian dialect of Tuscany is descended not from Latin but from Etruscan, which would itself be an offshoot of Hebrew and Aramaic... In Lucca the Dominican Pagninus (1470–1536) became the first Renaissance scholar to produce a Latin translation of the whole Bible from the original languages. Completed in 1518, this was published at Lyons in 1528, and was to be much used by Miles Coverdale in making his English version (1539).

From the second half of the fifteenth century to the second half of the sixteenth, Christian intellectuals in Italy displayed a threefold interest in learning Hebrew: in order to read the Bible in the original, to become acquainted with Jewish mysticism, and to gain access to the Hebrew translations of Islamic philosophy (Tamani 1992). These aims, however, called for a thorough knowledge of the language, and a better solution was found—the Hebrew versions were translated into Latin by a selected group of Jewish intellectuals working in three foci: Florence, the heart of literary and artistic life; Venice, the capital of scientific and philosophical erudition; and Padua, the centre of Aristotelian Averroism. These translators were: Elia del Medigo, Qalonymos Ben David, Abraham De Balmes (also author of *Peculium Abrae, Grammatica hebraea*, Venezia, D. Bomberg 1523), Jacob Mantino, Paolo Ricci, Vitale Nisso, and Mose Alatino. Del Medigo from Padua was one of the Hebrew teachers of the man who was to become the emblematic figure of Hebrew studies in Christian circles in Italy and all of Europe: Giovanni Pico (1463–94), count of Mirandola. He exerted a decisive influence on another intellectual who was to become a star of Hebrew studies among Christians: Johannes Reuchlin (1455–1522).

This German savant met Pico in 1490, and from then on began to study post-biblical Hebrew. Already as a student in Paris in 1473, however, Reuchlin had studied Hebrew with J. Wessel of Gansfort. He employed also the services of Obadia Ben Jacob Sforno, the renown exegete who founded a Talmudic school in Bologna. In 1508 Reuchlin wrote to a certain Abbot Leonard stressing the importance of the knowledge of Hebrew for a proper understanding of the Old Testament. As a result of his meeting with Pico, he became proficient in post-biblical language and literature and was called *trilingue miraculum*. He published several works on Kabbalah and was the leading Christian authority on Jewish mysticism. In 1506 he published *De rudimentis hebraicis*, a Hebrew grammar and dictionary in which he shows a close affinity to Qimḥis *Book of Roots*, and in 1518 *De accentibus et orthographia linguae hebraicae*. Nevertheless, Reuchlin took the precaution of justifying his great interest in Hebrew by his conviction that the study of the language among Christians should be promoted as a means of understanding better the bases of their own religion. In 1510 Reuchlin sprang to the defence of Hebrew and its literature against a campaign launched by the mendicant orders and the universities they controlled, whose aim was the destruction of all Hebrew books which, according to them, were inimical to the Christian faith. In this controversy, which lasted for a decade, Hebrew and its study appeared as symbols of humanism, the Renaissance, and the search for knowledge, while its opponents appeared as scholastic minds representing the spirit of the Middle Ages. The key figure of humanism in Central Germany, Konrad Muth, took a stand for Reuchlin and hence for the study of Hebrew. Erasmus of Rotterdam made no secret of his opposition to Hebrew studies, but held Reuchlin's personality in high esteem. It is thanks to Pico and

Reuchlin that Christians accepted Hebrew as a necessary branch of the study of divinity, and as a third language to be studied alongside Latin and Greek (Lloyd Jones 1983).

A contemporary of Pagninus was Sebastian Münster (1489–1552), professor of Hebrew at Basle, who published seventy-five works, over half of which were devoted to the study of Hebrew and other Semitic tongues. He had acquired his early knowledge of Hebrew from Konrad Pellikan (1478–1556) of Zurich, but also from the great Jewish hebraist from Lithuania, Eliahu Levitas (1468–1549), also known as Baḥur after the name of his grammatical opus *Habbaḥur*, a pun meaning both 'the lad' and 'the selected'. Münster produced a Latin translation of the Old Testament in 1535. The pioneer and chief promoter of Hebrew studies among the Swiss Reformers was Ulrich Zwingli (d. 1531), who acquired a very good command of the language. Moreover, he used the application of grammatical and philological rules to the Hebrew text to support his exegesis of its meaning—especially in his exegesis of Genesis in which he diverged from standard Christian interpretations—and took pleasure in quoting opinions of rabbis in support of his own in questions of grammar and lexicography. In a work published in 1523 Zwingli insisted on the need for Christian ministers to know Hebrew and advocated its inclusion in the syllabus of grammar schools. Zwingli was surrounded by a group of learned men, among whom was the bright Leo Jud (1482–1542). His Latin translation of the Old Testament appeared in 1543, a year after his death. Helvetic Hebraism had to wait some time for new figures with such charisma, but they did arrive in Basle within one and the same family: Johann Buxtorf (1564–1629), author of *Lexicon Hebraicum et Chaldaicum* in 1607 and of *Thesaurus Grammaticus Linguae Sanctae Hebraeae*, and his homonymous son. Another illustrious Protestant hebraist was Immanuel Tremellius (1510–80), who at the age of 31 became instructor in Hebrew at a seminary in Lucca. Having become interested in Protestant teachings, he had to flee Italy and established himself first as Hebrew teacher in Strasbourg, whence he moved to England and taught Hebrew in Cambridge for a while. On Queen Mary's accession he moved to Heidelberg, where he published some scholarly works, including a Latin translation of Targum Jonathan to the Twelve Minor Prophets, an Aramaic and Syriac grammar, and his *magnum opus*, a Latin translation of the Old Testament. The Church of Rome did not condemn any of those translations, but the authoritative version continued to be Jerome's Vulgate.

The interest in Hebrew in Protestant circles was not founded on humanistic grounds, as was the case in Italy, nor was it considered a constitutive part of a liberal education, as was the case among German humanists. Rather, it had a theological purpose, clearly formulated by Martin Luther himself. In his opinion, which had immense influence, Hebrew had to be included in the syllabus of pastors and monks for them to grasp properly the sense of the Scriptures. In this conviction he had been confirmed by his friend and collaborator Philip Melanchthon (1497–1560), nephew and disciple of Reuchlins. On his appointment as professor of Greek at Wittenberg,

Melanchthon delivered an address in which he called for the promotion of Hebrew (as well as of Greek and Latin) at the university. In 1546 and 1549 he delivered two speeches in which he pleaded for the study of Hebrew among Christians. In 1521 the Hebrew teacher in Wittenberg, Adrianus, was succeeded by Matheus Aurogallus (c.1490–1543), who produced several books on Hebrew grammar and lexicography. He was succeeded by Caspar Cruciger the elder. Another hebraist among German Reformers was Andreas Osiander, teacher of Hebrew at Nuremberg (and also the first to publish Copernicus' *De revolutionibus orbium caelestium*). In 1612 was published in Germany the *Lexicon pentaglotton* by Valentin Schindler, influential throughout the seventeenth century, which uses all the aids to Hebrew lexicography, including the comparison of Hebrew words with those of other Semitic languages and with the ancient translations.

In France, the importance of Hebrew for establishing a correct text of the Old Testament was recognized in the twelfth century by Stephen Harding, the English abbot of Cîteaux. Nicholas of Lyra (c.1270–1340), who taught in Paris, was one of the most famous hebraists of the late Middle Ages. He had an intimate knowledge not only of the biblical text in Hebrew, but also of its Jewish medieval commentators, and above all Rashi. He introduced Jewish interpretations of the Old Testament to Christian theologians on a large scale, and secured a place for it in the Reformers' thought. Eventually, the Collège de France, opened in Paris by Francis I in the first half of the sixteenth century for the promotion of humane letters, became the leading institution in Europe as far as the study of Hebrew is concerned. It boasted no less than three teachers of Hebrew: François Vatable (d. 1547), Agathias Guidacerius (1477–1540), and Paul Paradis (d. 1549). One of their immediate successors, Qanquarbre, published in 1554 *De re grammatica hebraeorum opus*. It is probably there that Jean Calvin studied Hebrew during his stay in Paris (1530–3), under the influence of his cousin Robert Olivetan, who was the first Reformer to publish a translation of the Old Testament into French. France produced another great hebraist with Richard Simon (1638–1712) who, though a conservative Catholic, practised the study of BH using the same scholarly equipment and methods as would be applied to any other ancient tongue, including philological science, textual criticism, lexicography, and grammar (McKane 1989). In 1751 a Chair of Hebrew was created at the Sorbonne by the duc d'Orleans, 'for the purpose of reviving Oriental learning in the University of Paris and explaining the Hebrew Scriptures'. In this Parisian atmosphere of intellectual freedom and cultural opportunities was educated the eighteenth-century Scottish hebraist Alexander Geddes, whose openmindedness and scholarship are reminiscent of Richard Simon's.

In 1533 Calvin fled to Basle, and continued his training there with Münster and another renowned hebraist, Simon Grynaeus. During his exile from Geneva (1538–41) Calvin spent most of his time in Strasbourg, where Hebrew was taught by Wolfgang Capito and Martin Bucer. A third hebraist present in the city at the time was Gregor Caselius. Capito published a Hebrew grammar in 1518, and Bucer a commentary on the Psalms in 1529. The city of Strasbourg adopted an educational programme designed by J. Sturm (1507–89), a graduate of the trilingual school in Louvain. In the curriculum he elaborated he put an emphasis on Greek and Latin and proposed Hebrew as an option, which eventually was chosen by many students.

Calvin provided Geneva with a school and an academy in 1559, and the first principal was Theodore Beza, an enthusiastic promoter of Hebrew, whose *Icones*, pen-portraits of famous scholars, which he dedicated in 1580 to James VI of Scotland, included six Christian hebraists: Reuchlin, Förster, (1495–1556, who published a Hebrew dictionary in 1543), Münster, Fagius, Tremellius, and Vatable (Horden). The chair of Hebrew in Calvin's academy was filled by A. Chevallier, who gave eight hours of instruction per week, five of which were devoted to Hebrew grammar. A long line of hebraists followed, and Hebrew held a prominent place in the curriculum. The academy's library also possessed important documents, including three copies of Daniel Bomberg's Rabbinic Bible edited in Venice. Eventually, the Geneva Academy drew students from many countries, and Calvinist scholars became some of the leading Christian hebraists of the seventeenth century. In 1572 its library contained as many as twenty titles in Hebrew, including four Bibles, two concordances, five dictionaries, five grammars, a Targum, a prayer book, a book of Kabbalah, and a book of commentaries. In 1584 the Chair of Hebrew in Geneva was bestowed upon the poet and theologian Antoine de la Roche Chandieu (1534–91), who even adopted two Hebrew pseudonyms: Zamariel and Sadeel. Another renown Huguenot hebraist was the poet Agrippa d'Aubigné (1552–1630), who read Hebrew, biblical and post-biblical, 'without points' (= vowel signs).

In Spain, Isidore of Seville (*c.*560–636), in his encyclopaedic work the *Etymologiae*, mediated the Hebrew scholarship of Jerome to the mediaeval Church; and the incipient knowledge of the language possessed by Bede (*c.*673–735) in Northumbria and Alcuin (735–804) from Yorkshire, comes from Isidore. In 1238, during the first period of the Reconquista, the Master-General of the Dominicans, Raymund de Peñaforte, established centres within the order for the study of Hebrew and Arabic, and encouraged Paulo Christiani (a convert from Judaism) and Raymund Martini in their studies of Jewish writings for the purposes of conversion to Christianity. It is in Alcalá de Henares, Castille, with the foundation in 1498 by Francisco Ximénez de Cisneros of the College of San Ildefonso, that the very first attempt was made towards the pattern of trilingual instruction which eventually spread around the continent. In 1508 the first professor of Hebrew, Alfonso de Zamora, was appointed. He was a recognized authority in all things Hebrew and made the university an acknowledged centre in the field. At Alcalá studied another outstanding figure of Hebrew studies in the Christian world of the Renaissance, Benito Arias Montano (1527–98). His articles on grammar and lexicography appended to the polyglot Bible whose edition he supervised prove that he was an accomplished hebraist, whose intellectual honesty led him to prefer the Bible translation of Pagninus (1470–1536) to Jerome's Vulgate.

The University of Louvain inaugurated its 'Collegium Trilingue' in 1520, under the guidance of Jerome Busleiden. The first Hebrew teacher was Matheus Adrianus, one of the first Christian scholars to draw up a systematic course of instruction in Hebrew, and Louvain must be credited with providing an example of what could be done to promote Hebraic studies (Lloyd Jones 1983).

In England, although Bede frequently discussed Hebrew terms with a confidence which gained him the reputation of being an hebraist, in addition of an expert in Greek, there is some doubt over the possibilities he had of actually learning these languages in seventh to eighth-century England. The first real teacher of Hebrew was Robert Grosseteste (1175–1253), bishop of Lincoln, although the extent of his knowledge is controversial. By the middle of the thirteenth century Roger Bacon of Oxford (c.1210–90) was advocating the study of Hebrew for other than missionary purposes, and though he had only an imperfect command of the language, he did write a Hebrew grammar. Herbert of Bosham (c.1120–90), secretary of Thomas Becket, is considered to have been proficient in Hebrew and familiar with Rashi's commentary on the Bible. Two younger contemporaries of his, Ralph Niger (c.1150–1200) and Alexander Neckam (1157–1217), show some acquaintance with the language in their scholarly works. Cambridge sees its first important hebraist with Henry de Costesy, appointed reader in 1326, who probably learned under Nicholas of Lyra in Paris and was interested in the literal meaning of Scripture. One of his successors was Richard Brinkley (1480–1518). To acquire official status, however, Hebrew studies in England had to wait until the first third of the sixteenth century, when they were promoted by Richard Fox, who founded Corpus Christi College in Oxford, and by John Fisher, founder of St John's at Cambridge, who had learned the language from Robert Wakefield, the first English hebraist worthy of the name, who had taught in some of the most famous universities on the continent: Louvain, Paris, and Tübingen. At the dissolution of the monasteries he obtained a Hebrew dictionary completed by Laurence Holbeach (d. c.1410), on the basis of work begun by a former prior, Gregory of Huntingdon (d. c.1290). In 1524 he delivered an oration in praise of Semitic studies under the title *Oratio de laudibus et utilitate trium linguarum, Arabicae, Chaldaicae et Hebraicae* ('Chaldaic' meaning Aramaic), and six years later produced his *Syntagma de hebraeorum codicum incorruptione*. In addition to promoting their study, he proved the kinship existing between the three Semitic tongues, based on morpho-semantic consider-ations, and showed how some Greek and Latin words were of Hebrew origin. The statutes of Oxford and Cambridge universities gave an important place to the study of Hebrew in the curriculum, beside that of Greek and Latin, and in 1535 Mel-anchthon's works replaced those of Duns Scotus (whose supporters opposed the teaching of Hebrew) as part of the syllabus for divinity students at both univer-sities. Two prominent figures who, from their high positions, promoted the study of the humanities in general and that of Hebrew in particular were William Warham, chancellor of Oxford and archbishop of Canterbury, and Thomas Wolsey, cardinal archbishop of York. The Catholic Church of England encouraged the study of Hebrew as a means of promoting the renewal of Christian life. Permanent Chairs of Hebrew were created at Oxford and Cambridge as a result of Henry VIII's split with the Catholic Church, which brought the universities increasingly under royal control. In 1536 an act of parliament was approved leading eventually to the creation of those Chairs, and Hebrew was taught on the pattern of the trilingual colleges at Alcalá and Louvain. Thomas More himself was aware of the importance of Hebrew and he encouraged all students of the Old and New Testaments to go *ad purissimas fontes*, that is, to the Hebrew and Greek originals. By the end of the century Hebrew was part of the curriculum in most of the incipient grammar schools (Lloyd Jones 1983).

In the Netherlands, Hebrew was included in the syllabus of theology students at the University of Leiden from its foundation in 1575, when the Chair was conferred on Johann Drusius, whose edition of Martinius' grammar was the first Hebrew book to be published in the country. Three other outstanding Dutch hebraists of the time were Thomas Erpenius (1584–1624), Sixtinus Amama (1593–1629), and Constatijn L'Empereur (1591–1648), all of whom left their mark on Hebrew studies for generations (van Rooden 1989). Incidentally, the *Compendium grammatices linguae hebraeae* of Baruch Spinoza (1632–77) appeared in the Netherlands at that period.

On the *Mayflower* there were two hebraists of competence, William Bradford and William Brewster. The Puritans of New England were avid students of the Hebrew Bible, and the most famous of their scholars, Cotton Mather, used many Hebrew words and phrases in his prolific writings. This enthusiasm led to the inclusion of the language in the curricula of the ten American colleges founded before 1776. At Harvard, where the first two presidents, Dunster and Chauncey, were scholars of Hebrew, since its foundation in 1636 all students had to study the language. A converted Jew, Judah Monis, appointed instructor of Hebrew in 1722, published a *Grammar of the Hebrew Tongue*, in 1735 in Boston, considered the first of its kind meant for instruction at an American university. Hebrew ceased to be an obligatory subject at Harvard in 1787. Yale, founded in 1701, offered Hebrew in its early years. It was later to become a centre of interest in Hebrew under the presidency of Ezra Stiles, who assumed the chair in 1777, but it was no longer a required subject after 1789. A number of Yale graduates founded Dartmouth College in 1769, where Hebrew was given special prominence until 1828 (it has been re-established in the 1980s). An indigenous North American hebraic mysticism also developed in the seventeenth and eighteenth centuries, and played an important part in folk religion, producing the Mormon beliefs in the nineteenth century.

THE MUSLIM WORLD:
FIRST CENTURIES OF THE HEGIRA

In ʾal ʾAndalus the study of Hebrew was enhanced as a reaction to both ʿarabīyya—the movement which believed in the supremacy of Arabs and Arabic over other Muslims and their tongues, and šuʿubīyya—the movement which held that all Muslims were equals but were superior to all other groups. Many Jewish authors extolled their own values, their own history, and their own culture and language. Among them we encounter Saʿadia Gaʾon (Fayyum, 882–942), who stated in the Hebrew introduction to his ʾEgron that Hebrew is the holy tongue; that it had been chosen by God from the very beginning of Creation, and therefore was prior even to Arabic; and that it is in Hebrew that the angels praise God. Saʿadia established a methodical comparison between Hebrew and Arabic, which implicitly considers Aramaic as well.

Dunaš ʾIbn Tammim (Kairouan, tenth – eleventh century) says in his commentary to Sep̄er Yeṣira that Hebrew was the tongue of Adam. Menaḥem Ben Saruq (Tortosa, 910–Córdoba, 970), in his Maḥberet, praises Hebrew as the purest and most perfect of tongues. Dunaš Ben Labraṭ (Fez, 920–Córdoba, 990), Menaḥem's adversary, says that God set Hebrew apart as excellent and superior to all other tongues. The genial poet and philosopher Shlomo ʾIbn Gabirol (Málaga, 1022–Valencia, 1058), defended similar positions. Moše ʾIbn ʿEzra (Granada, 1060–Estella, 1139) made an original point in stressing the purity and correctness of the Hebrew of Tiberias, justifying implicitly the vocalization system created in that city in the eighth century. Yehuda Halevi (Spain, 1080–Jerusalem, 1124) is one of the fiercest contenders for Hebrew's superiority, stating in his Kūzarī that it is in Hebrew that Adam designated beings and things with their adequate names. Abraham ʾIbn ʿEzra (Toledo, 1092–Rome, 1167), in his Sap̄a Beꝛura ('Pure Language'), gives etymological arguments in the same vein. Yehuda Ben Shlomo ʾalHarizi (1165–1235), in his Taḥkemonî, compares Hebrew to the Tree of Life whose leaves distilled life-giving health. Jacob Ben Elazar (Toledo, 1170–1230), in his Sep̄er HaMešalim ('Book of Parables'), thanks God for having gratified his people with Hebrew.

All of them believed Hebrew to be the first language of Humanity, but also that of the prophets and of revelation, the language of the angels, one of incomparable beauty. Hebrew was necessarily a perfect language, extremely rich in nuance and expression, capable of rendering any human feeling and experience (Alony 1995).

The most significant reaction of Jewish scholars in ʾalʾAndalus to Muslim cultural pressure was their determination to preserve their own language in the realm of poetry. According to Alony, had Jewish poets succumbed to ʿarabīyya at this point, they would have been assimilated and Hebrew would have faded away. And as poetry's alma mater is language, the Jews from ʾalʾAndalus produced some of the finest works in Hebrew grammar and lexicography. 'Grammar' in this context means mainly morpho-phonology, since for somebody familiar *with* and inspired *by* Arabic grammar, as were those Jewish authors, a language like Hebrew, which unlike Arabic has no variable nominal case endings depending on syntactic functions, is considered as being deprived of syntax.

Some of the important works produced in 'al'Andalus are, in the realm of grammar, *Seper Ṣaḥot or* 'Book of the Elegance (= Norm)' by Saʿadia Gaʾon, *Seper haRiqma* or the 'Book of Embroidery', and *Seper Hašorašīm* or the 'Book of Roots' by Yona ʾAbu ʾalWalīd Marwānî ʾIbn Janāḥ (Córdoba, 990–Zaragoza, 1050); *Seper ʾOtiyyōt haNoaḥ wᵉhaMešek* or the 'Book of the Quiescent and the Long Letters', by Yehuda Ḥayyūj (945–1000), and *Seper haMiklol* or the 'Book of Structure' (= Grammar), perhaps the most comprehensive one, by David Qimḥi, also known by his acronym Radaq (1160–1235), who had also composed his own Book of Roots. Ḥayyūj's work is wholly synchronic and not at all comparative: it consists in a theory of the Hebrew root which combines morphology and phonology and determines its triliterality. Its influence went far beyond his time and scope, and has had an impact on modern Semitic studies, on Indo-European studies, and even on general linguistics. As for Radaq's *Miklol*, it turned out to be an indispensable tool for many Christian hebraists of the Renaissance. Moše haKohen Chiquitilla or Gikitila (last part of the eleventh century) translated into Hebrew most of Ḥayyūj's grammatical works and composed one himself, dealing with nouns whose plural form is either unexpected or twofold. Yehuda Ben Balaʿam (Toledo–Seville, same period) wrote three grammatical books on BH, one dealing with homonyms, one with particles, and one with the denominative verbs. He made lexical and grammatical comparisons with Arabic. Isaac Ben Barun (Zaragoza, end of the eleventh century) is the author of the *Muʾazzana* or 'Balance' (of the similarity between Hebrew and Arabic, with references to Aramaic also). He is very methodical in making grammatical comparisons, this setting him apart from all his predecessors. His treatment of lexical items in BH includes references to Latin and Berber in addition to Arabic and Aramaic. A work which unfortunately has been almost totally lost was written by the poet and leader Samuel haNagid (993–1056): a concordance-dictionary including not only the author's own analyses but also a multitude of examples and references to his predecessors, ancient and contemporary, as well as grammatical considerations. Another book in the field of lexicography is *Gᵉbiʿa Hakesep* or the 'Silver Cup' by Josep ʾIbn Kaspi (1278–1340).

In the neighbouring area of southern France flourished a great dynasty of scholars and translators, the Tibbonides from Granada, residing in Lunel (from the eleventh to the fourteenth century.)

As for the oriental part of the Muslim world, Haʾi Gaʾon (Iraq, tenth to eleventh centuries) wrote a comprehensive dictionary of biblical Hebrew, post-biblical Hebrew, and Aramaic which reflects a theory of the root prior to the one enounced by ḥayyūj. For Haʾi Gaʾon, a root includes all the attested permutations of its consonants: thus, *k.n.s.*, *n.s.k.*, *s.k.n.*, and *n.k.s.* constitute one and the same root. This view, which is not always correct, reveals nonetheless a deeper insight than classic structural linguistics is ready to accept. Another grammarian from the same area was Abraham of Babylon, who made grammatical comparisons between Hebrew and Aramaic.

AMONG THE KARAITES

One of the principles of Karaism, according to which truth is to be sought by each individual without relying on an external authority, led to an intense study of Hebrew. Indeed, a translator exerts authority upon both the original text and the reader; therefore, everybody should read nothing else but the original, which in turn must be carefully established. The result is the Massoretic text, that is, a version of the original Hebrew Bible fixed once and for all both in its consonants and its vowels, which we owe mostly to the Karaite family of Ben Asher (Tiberias, eighth to tenth centuries). Paul Kahle (cf. Szyszman 1980) characterized their work as follows: the Karaites fixed the vocalization rules applying to the biblical text; they were considered as experts on these questions and furnished valuable works dealing with them; their text has been unanimously accepted throughout the world, both among Jews and elsewhere; they also initiated the study of Hebrew grammar, and despite their ideological markedness, the work of the Ben Ashers influenced the other 'milieux savants' as well. The *Codex Alepensis*, the most ancient manuscript of the entire Hebrew Bible, is written by Aharon Ben Moshe Ben Asher, the last known member of this illustrious dynasty of scholars.

Linguistic scholarship among the Karaites continued with such authors as Rabbi David Ben Abraham ʾalFassi (Morocco, early tenth century), whose *JāmiʿaʾalʾAlfāṭ* or 'Collection of Words' includes comparative considerations. He is one of the very first to have explored this path of linguistic research, which was made explicit by the Karaite Yehuda ʾIbn Qurayš (tenth century) in his *Risāla* or 'Letter'. Although comparative linguistics eventually reached its climax with the great German and Danish comparatists of the nineteenth century, following the pioneering work of Sir William Jones and Rasmus Rask on Germanic and other branches of Indo-European, the history of comparative linguistics ignores the insights of Alfassi and other Jews who had compared Semitic languages a whole millennium earlier. It is high time that the debt of the former to the latter be recognized.

ʿAli Ben Sulayman, also known as ʾalŠeiḵ ʾAbu ʾalḤasan ʾalQuds (*fl.* eleventh century), composed an *ʾEgron* or biblical Hebrew dictionary in Arabic, based upon the one by Levi Ben Yap̄et Halevi (*fl.* last quarter of the tenth century), itself based upon the one by Rabbi David Ben Abraham ʾalFassi. Sulayman does not accept the triliterality of the Hebrew root as established by Ḥayyūj; rather, for him, the root counts two and in some cases only one consonant. Like ʾalFassi, he displays treasures of erudition when comparing BH with Arabic and Aramaic, and even with (Talmudic and) Mishnaic Hebrew. The only extant version of ʿAli Ben Sulayman's *ʾEgron* is in St Petersburg, a manuscript written by R. Eliyyah Ben Mordᵉk̲ay Ben Yosef from Baṣra, Iraq.

In the first half of the eleventh century flourished ʾAbu ʾalFaraj Harun ʾIbn ʾalFaraj, 'the grammarian from Jerusalem', who was invested in comparative philology, both lexical and grammatical, between Hebrew and Aramaic, and as he was proficient in Arabic this language was referred to as well. This holistic approach is encoded in the Arabic name of his book, *Kitāb ʾalMuš tamil* (1027) or 'Book of the Wholeness'. Moše ʾIbn ʿEzra, when quoting him, says in Arabic *qarāʾi walāʾ rabbāni*, namely 'he is Karaite, not rabbinical'. There are manuscripts of it in St Petersburg and in the Museum of Warsaw, and some fragments are in the British Museum as well. The Bodleian Library, Oxford, possesses an abridged version by an anonymous author. Another abridged version is by ʾalFaraj himself, *Kitā b ʾalKaffi*.

The Karaite Iaʿᵃqob̲ Ben Shlomo from Russia (twelfth century) composed a grammatical treatise in order for his brethren to gain a better comprehension of God's commands and purposes. Rabbi ʾAharon Hariš̌on started a book on BH grammar and style called *Kᵉlil Yofi* or 'Splendid in Beauty', but death prevented him from finishing it and it was completed by Isaac Hatiš̌bi and printed in Constantinople. A revised edition was published by Isaac Ben Abraham Hatroki (1533–94).

The Karaite interest in Hebrew linguistics was enhanced by the position of their ideologist Iaʿᵃqob̲ ʾalQirqisāni (*fl.* 937), according to whom 'the Hebrew language is the primordial tongue in which God addressed Adam and other prophets' (Nemoy 1980).

THE MODERN ERA

With the French Revolution began an era in which religion was no longer associated with high education. As far as Hebrew is concerned, ever since the nineteenth century it has been studied by experts in Semitic philology and other fields as well as in biblical studies. The commanding figure in the field in the nineteenth century was H. F. W. Gesenius (1786–1842), author of both a Hebrew and Aramaic Lexicon of the Old Testament in 1810–12 and a grammar published in 1813. Heinrich Ewald (1803–75) published in 1838 his *Grammatik der Hebräischen Sprache des Alten Testaments*. In 1881 appeared the *Historisch-Kritisches Lehrgebaude der Hebräischen Sprache* by Eduard König (1846–1936). In Paris, at the Collège de France, Antoine Fabre d'Olivet (1767–1825) published in 1816 his *La Langue hébraïque restituée*, and in 1855 Ernest Renan (1823–92) published there his *Histoire générale et système comparé des langues sémitiques*, which did not prevent his banishment from the Collège for having called Jesus 'that extraordinary man'. Both facts are symptomatic: on one hand the philologist who, despite his Christian education, rejects the apparently indissoluble link between the study of Hebrew and faith in the dogma; on the other, the institution which finds this position difficult to accept. Even in our day the Chair at the Collège de France is common to Hebrew and Aramaic, the languages of the Hebrew Bible. Still, Renan's attitude did triumph: his compatriot Paul Joüon (1871–1940) published in 1923 his *Grammaire de l'Hébreu biblique* (translated into English, much augmented and re-edited in 1991–6, by T. Muraoka from the University of Leiden). It is a masterpiece of linguistic insight, notwithstanding Joüon's being a clergyman. The study of Hebrew as it exists presently at universities all over the world reflects Renan's scientific position rather than the theological stance of his adversaries. At North American universities the study of Hebrew is organized on seven different models (Band 1993). The first is Protestant and theologically oriented. Since it is situated in the divinity schools of the universities, Band calls it Divinity School Hebrew (DSH). Protestant sponsorship entails strong cultural implications even today, when some of those schools teach Contemporary Hebrew as well.

The second model is Semitic Philology Hebrew: in this framework, the language is taught in the major universities along with Arabic and Aramaic (and more recently with Akkadian and Ethiopic as well). This model started in the nineteenth century, its foremost figure being Gesenius, whose lexicon of BH and Aramaic was anglicized by Francis Brown, S. R. Driver, and C. A. Briggs in 1907 (*Hebrew and English Lexicon of the Old Testament*) and his Grammar by A. E. Cowley in 1910 (*Gesenius's Hebrew Grammar*; both works are appreciated in the scholarly world to this day). By the end of that century this model (SPH) was well established in Harvard, Columbia, the University of Pennsylvania, Johns Hopkins, the University of Chicago, and at Berkeley. It was, as Band puts it, a Hebrew without Jews. Nevertheless, their growing importance eventually led to important changes in this respect also.

Following the tradition of Wissenschaft des Judentums there emerged the Americanized Wissenschaft Hebrew (AWH), whose representative figures until the 1970s were the medievalist Harry Wolfson at Harvard and the modernist Salo Baron at Columbia.

The fourth model was very powerful and also very well known, and many Hebrew speakers of the senior generation today learned the language in its institutions: it is the Tarbut Ivrit Hebrew (TBH), named after the movement commonly known as

Tarbut. Born in Europe, a late offshoot of the national movements of 1848, its impact was strengthened during the First World War. Jewish immigration brought the movement to the Americas, where its members founded and staffed most of the Hebrew colleges. Tarbut also entered the general academic world: not in Divinity schools, Semitic Philology departments, or Judaic studies, but in the framework of Modern Languages departments.

With the Second World War, the Holocaust, and the creation of the State of Israel in 1948 Hebrew took a further step and became the language of an independent country, and entered the university curriculum as such. It was taught and studied according to structural linguistic methods, applied to Hebrew in Israel by Haiim Rosén (1957, 1967). The education of millions of immigrants in *Ulpanim* or Hebrew schools for adults contributed to generating an aura around the language as a special phenomenon because it has been so recently and remarkably revived. This is what Band calls Area Studies Hebrew (ASH).

The sixth model is Jewish Studies Hebrew (JSH), which offered a holistic view of the language in all its historical periods and suggested a preparation for reading Hebrew of all types and styles, as well as of writing and speaking it. Yet, since many students were admitted to courses in Jewish history and the like without being advised to learn Hebrew, this model, ideally and academically the most appropriate to university teaching, turned out to be mainly theoretical.

The last model is Israeli Hebrew (IH): instructors in American universities often come from Israel, and it is their variety of language which has become the norm in teaching Hebrew in North America and elsewhere at the present time. *Mutatis mutandis*, these models apply to the study of Hebrew in the modern era in universities all over the world.

In Israel, besides being the official teaching language in all Jewish educational institutions at all levels (at Arab institutions it is taught as first foreign language), Hebrew is studied as an independent subject at all the universities except the Technion of Haifa and the Weizmann Institute of Science at Rehovot. The other five, namely the Hebrew University of Jerusalem and the Universities of Tel Aviv, Haifa, Bar-Ilan, and Ben-Gurion University of the Negev have departments of Hebrew Language devoted to both teaching and research. All count among their faculty both linguists and philologists working on the different aspects, periods, and corpora of Hebrew: sacred; literary and colloquial; written and oral. To give a few examples, Haim Cohen of BGU is currently co-ordinating a research project on biblical Hebrew lexicography, and Shlomo Izre'el of TAU is supervising the constitution of a Corpus of Contemporary Hebrew. The Academy of Hebrew Language has some research projects of its own, the most ambitious and prestigious one being the Historical Dictionary, a CD-ROM with access through the Internet which will eventually constitute the most complete source of lexico-semantic, grammatical, and textual information on Hebrew words through the ages. In Israel there are also twenty-two colleges, most of which teach Hebrew language.

Hebrew is taught in universities throughout Europe, but not usually in departments devoted to the study of Hebrew alone (for information on Hebrew in France, see the internet sites *http://www.morim.com/nouveau.htm* and *http://www. hebreu.org*; for information on Hebrew studies in the Netherlands and Belgium, email *phbroers@wxs.nl*). In North America, Hebrew is taught in 606 colleges and universities (see the internet site *http://carla.acad.umn.edu/ictl/access/html*; some 400 of the Hebrew teachers in the USA are associated in the NAPH (National Association of Professors of Hebrew), whose internet site is *http://polyglot.iss. wisc.edu/naph/*). In Latin America, Hebrew is taught in Argentina, at the Universidad Nacional in Buenos Aires and in Córdoba; in Brazil, in São Paulo at the Universidad Nacional and at the Universidad de Campinas; and in Chile, in Santiago at the Universidad de Chile.

Suggested Reading

The history of the Hebrew language is accurately and succinctly described in Rabin (1989), by a renowned philologist of the Semitic languages (1915–96). This is a concise work containing a large amount of information and accessible to the lay person. Other very valuable books on the subject are Sáenz-Badillos (1988, English trans. 1993), from the contemporary Spanish specialist of Hebrew language and culture, and Kutscher (1982), from the great Hebrew philologist (1909–71). For the scholar interested in BH, the best grammar is by Joüon and Muraoka 1991–6. The Hebrew of the Dead Sea scrolls is best described in Qimron (1986), by its foremost expert.

The most recent and complete publication on Mishnaic Hebrew is Bar Asher (1999), by the President of the Hebrew Language Academy. Segal's Grammar of MH (1958) is still valuable. As for the contact between Hebrew and the classical languages in antiquity, few works are as instructive as Rosén (1978 and 1995). A good overall account of the Hebrew Language is the article in the *Hebrew Encyclopedia* (Rosén *et al.* 1974), which offers first-rate views on all its aspects. Concerning the revival of Hebrew, one can consult Rabin and Sivan (1980). The latter played an active part in neologistic and normative activity within the process they describe. Ben Chaim (1992) describes the fight which Hebrew and hebraists had to wage in order for the language to invest all areas of life in modern Israel. This enterprise, eventually crowned with success, was far from easy and its issue far from self-evident. Ze'ev Ben Chaim has been participating in this struggle ever since his *aliya* to Israel in the 1930s as a young Ph.D. in Semitic Philology from Berlin. President of the Hebrew Academy for many years and instigator of its Historical Dictionary project, he has the best qualifications to describe the 'language's fight', as the title of his book puts it.

Israeli Hebrew is accurately described in Rosén (1977), a masterpiece of its kind by the foremost figure of Israeli Hebrew research: even the term is his. It is an accurate presentation of the language's structures. Other works by the author intended for the scholar and the reader interested in deep linguistic insight are Rosén (1957 and 1967). Schwarzwald (2001) is the most recent publication in the field. It contains much grammatical information as well as many examples.

The typological character of Hebrew is best described by Goldenberg (1995). The illustrious Israeli expert on Semitic and general linguistics demonstrates that Hebrew remains intrinsically Semitic, not only from a genealogical point of view but typologically as well. He also shows that, had Hebrew continued to be spoken after the third century, it would probably have changed much more than it actually has done at all levels: phonology, morphology, syntax, and vocabulary.

BIBLIOGRAPHY

ALONY, N. 1995. *El Resurgimiento de la Lengua Hebrea en al-Andalus*. Madrid.

BAND, A. 1993. *From Sacred Tongue to Foreign Language: Hebrew in the American University*. In Mintz (1993a): 171–86.

BAR-ASHER, M. 1999. *L'hébreu mishnique: études linguistiques*. Leuven–Paris.

BEN CHAIM, Z. 1992. *B^{e}Milham^{e}tah shel Lashon*. Jerusalem.

BEN YEHUDAH, E. 1948. *Dictionary of the Hebrew Language, Ancient and Modern* [Hebrew]. Jerusalem.

BYNON, J. 1984. *Current Progress in Afro-Asiatic Linguistics*. Amsterdam and Philadelphia.

CANTINEAU, J. 1952. 'Le Consonantisme du sémitique.' *Semitica* 4: 79–94.

DRÖGE, CH. 1992. 'Les Débuts des études hébraïques chez les humanistes italiens.' In Zinguer (1992): 65–88.

DUBOIS, C. G. 1992. 'Posterité des langues d'Aram.' In Zinguer (1992): 129–53.

ENGAMMARE, M. 1992. 'Olivetan et les commentaires rabbiniques.' In Zinguer (1992): 27–64.

FABER, A. 2000. 'Genetic Subgrouping of the Semitic Languages.' In Hetzron (2000).

GLINERT, L. 1993. 'Hebrew from Symbol to Substance.' In Mintz (1993a): 227–50.

GOLDENBERG, G. 1995. Ha'Ibrit k^{e}lašon šemit haya'. In *HaLašon ha 'ib.ritb^{e}hit pathutah ub^{e}hithadšutah*, 148–90. Jerusalem.

GOLDMAN, SH. ed. 1993a. *Hebrew and the Bible in America: The First Two Centuries*. Hanover and London.

—— 1993b. 'Biblical Hebrew in Colonial America: The Case of Dartmouth.' In Goldman (1993a): 201–8.

HAGÈGE, CL. 1993. *The Language Builder. = Current Issues in Linguistic Theory* 94. Amsterdam and Philadelphia.

—— 2000. 'L'Hébreu de la vie à la mort, de la mort à la vie.' In *Halte à la mort des langues*. 271–341. Paris.

HERTZBERG, A. 1993. 'The New England Puritans and the Jews.' In Goldman (1993a): 105–21.

HETZRON, R. ed. 2000. *The Semitic Languages*. London and New York.

JACOBSON, D. 1993. 'Language and Culture in the Teaching of Hebrew at American Universities.' In Mintz (1993a): 209–26.

JOÜON, P. and MURAOKA, T. 1991–6. *A Grammar of Biblical Hebrew*. Rome.

KAPELIUK, A. 2003, in press. 'HaTipologia šel hašemīt hahadaša'. In *Sheva': Safot-Balshanut-Ivrit*. Beer Sheva.

KIRTCHUK, P. 1989. 'Classes de verbes en hébreu biblique et contemporain: étude morpho-syntaxique et sémantique.' *Actances* 4: 137–173. Paris.

KIRTCHUK, P. 1993. '/ ʾet/ ou ne pas / ʾet/: l'actant Y en hébreu et au-delà.' *Actances* 7: 91–113. Paris.

—— 1997. 'Renouvellement grammatical, renouvellement lexical et renouvellement conceptuel en Sémitique.' In *La Dénomination*. 37–68. Cl. Boisson and Ph. Thoiron eds. Zyon.

KUTSCHER, E. Y. 1982. *History of the Hebrew Language*. Jerusalem.

LLOYD JONES, G. 1983. *The Discovery of Hebrew in Tudor England: A Third Language*. Manchester.

MCKANE, W. 1989. *Selected Christian Hebraists*. Cambridge.

MARTINET, A. 1953. 'Remarques sur le consonantisme sémitique.' *Bulletin de la Société de Linguistique de Paris* 49: 124–65. Paris.

MINTZ, A. ed. 1993a *Hebrew in America*. Detroit.

—— 1993b. 'A Sanctuary in the Wilderness: The Beginnings of the Hebrew Movement in America in *Hatoren*.' In Mintz (1993a): 29–67.

MORAG, SH. 1995. *Meḥqarīm biL^eˇson haMiqraˊ*. Jerusalem.

NEMOY, L. 1980 [1952]. *Karaite Anthology*. New Haven and London.

POZNANSKI, S. 1908. *The Karaite Literary Opponents of Saadiah Gaon*. London.

QIMRON, E. 1986. *The Hebrew of the Dead Sea Scrolls*. Cambridge, Mass.

RABIN, H. 1989. *A Short History of the Hebrew Language*. Jerusalem.

—— and SIVAN, R. 1980. *The Revival of the Hebrew Language*. Jerusalem.

RAPHAELI, R. 1993. 'Toward Hebrew Literacy: From School to College.' In Mintz (1993a): 251–63.

ROODEN, P. T. VAN 1989. *Theology, Biblical Scholarship and Rabbinical Studies in the Seventeenth Century*. Studies in the History of Leiden University. Leiden.

ROSÉN, H. B. 1957. *Ha ʿib̲rīt ˇselanu*. Tel Aviv.

—— 1967. *Ib̲rīt Tova*. Jerusalem and Tel Aviv.

—— 1977. *Contemporary Hebrew*. The Hague.

—— 1978. *L'Hébreu et ses rapports avec le monde classique. Essai d'Evaluation culturelle*. Paris.

—— 1995. *Hebrew at the Crossroads of Cultures*. = *Orbis Supplementa*, tome 11. Leuven and Paris.

—— *et al.* 1974 'Ib̲rīt, Lašon', in *Hebrew Encyclopedia* [Hebrew]. Tel Aviv.

ROTHSCHILD, J. P. 1992. 'Quelles notions le "grand public" des lettrés chrétiens dans la France du XVIᵉ siècle eut-il de l'hébreu?' In Zinguer (1992): 172–96.

SÁENZ BADILLOS, A. 1988. *Historia de la Lengua Hebrea*. Sabadell. English trans. 1993. *History of the Hebrew Language*. Cambridge.

—— TARRAGONA BORRAS, J. 1988. *Gramáticos Hebreos de Al-Andalus*. Córdoba.

SCHWARZWALD, O. 2001. *Modern Hebrew*. Munich.

SEGAL, M. H. 1958. *Mishnaic Hebrew Grammar*. Oxford.

SOULIÉ, M. 1992. 'L'Hébreu et l'imitation des textes bibliques dans la poésie polémique protestante.' In Zinguer (1992): 105–14.

STINSON, CH. 1993. 'Northernmost Israel: England, the Old Testament and the Hebraic *Veritas* As Seen By Bede and Roger Bacon.' In Goldman (1993a): 3–13.

SZYSZMAN, S. 1980. *Le Karaisme*. Lausanne.

TAMANI, G. 1992. 'Traduzione ebraico-latine di opere filosofiche e scientifiche.' In Zinguer (1992): 105–14.

TESNIÈRE, L. 1959. *Eléments de Syntaxe Structurale*. Paris.

ZINGUER, I. ed. 1992. *L'Hébreu au temps de la Renaissance*. Leiden, New York, and Cologne.

CHAPTER 21

MODERN HEBREW LITERATURE

GLENDA ABRAMSON[1]

The assumption that Israeli Hebrew literature has a unique and trans-formative significance in Israeli culture is argued sociologically, historic-ally, theoretically and aesthetically... Almost throughout its history Israeli literature related first to the society and only then was it organized canonically. It can never be understood merely in terms of its style or technique, or in ways in which other literatures are discussed, because this places a distance between the texts and the community of which they are part. Israeli Hebrew writing bears the burden of the responsibilities of a certain history and historiography.

(Gover 1994: 7)

HEBREW literature has a rich tradition and a continuous line of development from biblical times to the present day. Even so, unlike other world literatures, it was written in a language few of its readers spoke until modern times. The Jewish vernacular was either Yiddish or other Jewish languages, and Hebrew was, on the whole, reserved for elevated use, or study. It therefore did not develop its vocabulary sufficiently to allow the creation of fiction, although some secular poetry, influenced by foreign trends, had been written from the medieval period. To write fiction in

[1] I would like to thank Professor Gershon Shaked for his valuable suggestions for the first part of this paper, and Professor Avraham Balaban and Dr Rivka Maoz for their helpful advice.

Hebrew would demand the invention of a world of the imagination without the vocabulary to describe it, using a language which for almost 2,000 years had been textual rather than spoken and colloquial. Hebrew was therefore inadequate for authentic creative expression; its nature as a holy tongue and its biblical ancestry were a bar to the exercise of the literary imagination. The religious authorities, who were the only arbiters of literary development until modern times, frowned upon the reading and writing of Hebrew for anything but a religious purpose. For this reason Hebrew fiction developed much later than the fiction of other cultures.

It was only in the eighteenth century, with the Hebrew Enlightenment, the Haskalah, that secular Hebrew literature was able to develop. Before then, Jewish intellectual activity had been confined almost exclusively to the study of the sacred Jewish texts, the Bible, the Mishnah, Midrash, the prayerbook, the Talmud, and other religious writings. The intellectual élite of the Jewish communities was drawn from the students of the all-male religious high-schools (*yeshivot*). It seems strange that modern *secular* Hebrew literature should have arisen indirectly from these pious ranks, yet these men were the most educated and learned, with a thorough knowledge of the Hebrew language. Paradoxically, perhaps, they were the first authors of modern Hebrew literature.

This literature grew in the eighteenth and nineteenth centuries mainly in the areas of Jewish settlement in Eastern Europe. After the anti-Jewish pogroms following the assassination of Tsar Alexander II in 1881, there was a large movement of Jews away from these areas to the the United States and Europe. A significant number of writers emigrated to the Jewish settlement in Palestine, the Yishuv, taking their literature with them and developing it with the rapid development of Hebrew as a spoken language. This is another of the many unusual aspects of the literature, that it grew and achieved its greatest brilliance outside its own linguistic and historical territory.

Today there are over 3 million Hebrew-speakers in Israel alone. A flourishing literature is being written there in Hebrew, composed of fiction, poetry, and drama. The growth of the Hebrew language has contributed to the viability, and therefore to the adoption, of new literary genres. Modern Hebrew literature has established a clear national identity, responsive at last to its own territorial conditions, expressed in a literary language which is finally also a vernacular. The reason why this literature is particularly interesting is that it is not the result of an organic growth over the centuries, as other literatures are. Rather, it was given its modern shape not only by its writers but also by a number of intellectuals—philosophers, cultural historians, journalists, and critics—who were concerned with its quality and function. They were able to mould the literature according to certain theoretical and ideological principles. They made sure that, from the beginning of its development, creative writing and social issues would be closely linked, as they are in the majority of developing cultures where the balance of function and aesthetics varies sharply.

Is Modern Hebrew Literature Modern?

Responding to a lecture on modern Hebrew literature, Raphael Loewe, a leading British scholar of medieval Hebrew literature, once commented that its modern incarnation is neither modern, nor Hebrew, nor literature. The main question is the meaning of the word 'modern' in relation to this literature. When we discuss 'modern' Hebrew literature we are immediately confronted with the problem of periodization. This is of critical importance, since 'modernity' signified substantial ideological changes not only in the nature of the literature but also in its function. There are many conflicting views about 'modernity', both chronological and aesthetic, culminating in a question used by the Hebrew literary scholar Barukh Kurzweill as the title of one of his works of literary criticism: modern Hebrew literature: continuity or revolution? (Kurzweill 1959, 1971). The delimitation for 'modernity' as a definition seems to be at a point when secular Hebrew literature (that is, works with a non-religious purpose) became a recognized genre. If a representative work were to be cited, it would probably be Moshe Hayim Luzatto's *Layesharim tehilla*, published in 1743 in Amsterdam, an allegorical drama of love written in Hebrew. Gershom Scholem, on the other hand, related Hebrew modernism to the period of the Sabbatian heresy in the late seventeenth century. Dov Sadan, an eminent Hebrew literary scholar, cites the three major streams of Hebrew literature, Haskalah, hassidism, and the mitnagdic movement, as constituting modern Hebrew literature (Sadan 1950: 6). Gershon Shaked begins his history of modern Hebrew literature from the 1880s (Shaked 1977). No single factor defines Hebrew modernism, mainly due to the variety of critical perceptions, of which secularism is only one. For example, despite his allegorical works, we could not attribute 'secularism' to Luzzatto, whose writing served the ideology of humanism *within* religious Judaism. Literature without a religious purpose, and in European styles, had been written before that, while the secular literature of the nineteenth and twentieth centuries rested—and still rests, in the twenty-first century—on religious modes and vocabulary. So in one sense Professor Loewe is right: modern Hebrew literature may not be 'modern', by any conventional evaluative criterion.

The Nature of Modern Hebrew Literature: Early Development

The most popular view is that modern Hebrew literature originated in the middle of the eighteenth century with the Haskalah. Because it was influenced by the German Enlightenment, the *Aufklärung*, the Haskalah found itself in almost constant conflict with traditional Jewish institutions. Most of its gains were made against religious opposition, marking one of the major dialectical processes at work within the growth of modern Hebrew literary criticism, the struggle between 'secularism' and 'religiosity', a struggle which manifested itself from the beginning of the literature's development,[2] and which continued well into the Israeli period.

The second dialectical process within the criticism developed as a result of the catastrophic situation of Russian Jewry in the nineteenth century. This led writers of the early Russian Haskalah to advocate cautious social reforms, and from that time onwards Haskalah literature set out primarily to provide a moral and social education for the backward Jewish communities of the Pale of Settlement. From the outset, therefore, the function of modern Hebrew literature was determined both by writers and scholars. In addition to being part of the Jewish society's intellectual and cultural development, creative literature would serve as a document for social development, in accordance with the utilitarian ideas of the critics (see Neiman 1983: 115). With the rise of this new genre and its mandate of intervention in society came discussions about the literature itself. Whenever 'modern' Hebrew literature is deemed to have been established, the study of Hebrew *belles lettres* as a genre began with the Haskalah.

With the advent of Zionism the tension between the need to establish a literature which would affect social processes, reflect 'universal' aesthetic and moral principles, and express the authentic nature of the Jewish nation gradually developed into an intense concern with the expression of nation and, later, nationhood in the literature. According to Timothy Brennan, 'nations are an imaginary construct that depend for their existence on an apparatus of cultural fiction in which imaginative literature plays a decisive role' (Bhabha 1990: 49). Because of the nature of its religio-nationalistic community, Jewish literature had always to be aware of the boundaries of the imagination, whereas in secularized cultures the growth of nationalism, for example, in Europe at the end of the eighteenth century, had coincided with the decline of religious modes of thought.

---

[2] For example, early satires, such as Joseph Perl's *Megalleh Temirim* and *Bohen Zaddik*, were primarily directed against the Hassidic movement. This trend persisted throughout the history of the Haskalah, to Smolenskin's negative portraits of the *baal shems*.

Scholarly Arguments About Modern Hebrew Literature

As mentioned earlier in this chapter, a number of Jewish intellectuals were responsible for guiding the developing literature according to certain criteria. What is interesting is that they did not always agree on these criteria, although generally they perceived the literature in similar ways. During the period of transition from Haskalah literature to that of the so-called 'revival' (1880 to 1920), these intellectuals, many of them writers, debated the future and the nature of Hebrew literature. They were towering figures who drew up prescriptive lists of what the literature should or should not do. At that time, with the new ideas of the nation gradually taking hold, it seemed essential for them to determine literature's direction. Writers either obeyed their *diktats* or opposed them, either adding to the growing canon or giving reason to be rejected from it. The process of the canonization of literary works was largely the responsibility of these intellectual critics, and the question of national ideology constituted a vital factor in this process. For them, the national criterion became one of the central evaluative criteria in Hebrew literary criticism and in the establishment of a modern Hebrew canon. Also, this nationalistic focus determined the nature of literary criticism, as well as its difference from that of other cultures, that is, its crucial concentration on Hebrew literature *as a whole*, rather than on individual works, unlike the situation today.

Early twentieth-century literary criticism, therefore, used these three major dialectical issues, the religious–secular divide, literary functionalism, and nationalism, as its framework for evaluation. Ahad Ha-'am, philosopher, editor, and social psychologist, and one of the most influential, if prejudiced, commentators on Hebrew literature, saw it as a medium through which the existential problems of the Jewish people could be expressed. Although not a literary scholar, or even particularly fond of creative literature, Ahad Ha-'am's evaluation of it was a paradigm of the debates taking place at the time. In his introduction to the first edition of his journal *Hashiloah* (Ahad Ha-'am 1897), he expresses his somewhat ambiguous views of the literature. On the one hand he sees it in conventionally tendentious terms as being a functional part of the development of the nation; on the other, more surprisingly, as having value without any function. Yet according to Ahad Ha-'am's programme, given the present condition of the nation, the literature should not waste its energy on images and metaphors in the face of more necessary and useful matters which demand its attention.[3]

---

[3] Ahad Ha-'am repeats the words 'use' or 'usefulness' a number of times in this discussion, particularly the literature's usefulness in extending knowledge of the nation (or the nation's knowledge of itself).

Ahad Ha-ʿam's concern is that literature should 'penetrate into the spirit of the nation' and affect its way of life. Not for him vague 'universal' values; rather, Jewish nationalism would be a means of mediating universal values, which would then become part of the specific culture. Ahad Ha-ʿam insisted that writers of Hebrew literature should confine themselves to Jewish subjects. This, too, was an idea that dominated throughout the history of Hebrew literary scholarship. Only Zionism would provide the conditions in which the national spirit could flourish. In Dov Sadan's words, 'Our hope for the literature is that with its having reached the final station, which was its first station, it expects better days than those of its wandering from nation to nation' (Sadan 1950: 20).

Like those of Ahad Ha-ʿam, the ideas of other major critics of the time are based on a complex combination of literary and ideological criteria. The lively criticism that flowed from these intellectual arbiters swung between two poles: literature related to social and national ideas, and literature as a reflection of universal values. The poet H. N. Bialik sought the fusion of the aesthetic aims of the artist 'with the traditions and ideals of the nation'. He offered what, in his opinion, was the only viable model for Hebrew literary creation, that of a synthesis of the new in literature and its historical sources, and an avoidance of Europeanization. In this way the new writing would reflect the spirit of the people without being a religious literature (Parush 1992: 137). The novelist Micah Joseph Berdyczewsky, with a more romantic and *ars poetica* approach, called for the unity of Jewish and universal ideas. He reflected a fairly common suspicion of European culture, and above all he advocated individual freedom and creativity against the stultifying demands of the religious tradition. With some prescience, Berdyczewsky and others saw that strong fidelity to the character of the nation could also limit the achievement of a work of art, and that shunning European influence was not necessarily to the literature's advantage.

The view of Y. H. Brenner, the cultural father of much of the literary scholarship to follow, was a more sophisticated and elusive amalgamation of his literary ideas and his grasp of nationhood. His emphasis on realism, which he defined very specifically, led him to view the question of literary nationalism differently from his contemporaries (see A. Zemach 1984: 76–69). He believed that in a 'good' literary work there is always a faithful expression of the problems of a nation and its society. The greatness of literature is derived from its awareness of reality 'as it is', rather than the sentimental idealization of it. A national Jewish literature is a literature that will lead to self-evaluation, the productivization of the Jewish nation, and the striving for a national culture. Indeed, a national writer, in the true sense, is a writer who expresses the concerns of the group.

Brenner rejects Ahad-Ha-ʿam's model for, in his opinion, nationalism is not expressed by its relationship to Judaism, cultural superiority, the mission of Israel, or Zionism. On the contrary, these are seen as serious obstacles to self-evaluation. He disagrees with Bialik as well, for he does not stress the importance of the historical canon, assuming that as long as writers continue to create in Hebrew and describe their Jewish lifestyles the national character of the new Hebrew culture will be safeguarded. And, as to the national–universal division, as long as this literature is faithful and therefore national in the widest possible sense of the word, so it will be more human and universal (Brenner 1972: 297).

The question of the relationship of modern Hebrew literature to biblical and other religious sources has troubled literary scholars throughout the modern period and up to the present day. From the beginning of modern literary scholarship this relationship was the critical focal point. Some critics, like Bialik, saw traditional literature as an essential component of the contemporary canon, while others were convinced that Hebrew literature had to conform as well to the European canon (see Parush 1992). Brenner was convinced that the Hebrew canon, based on the literature of the recent past and the present, constitutes the main source, perhaps the only source, for the developing Hebrew culture. 'As long as the *yishuv* preserves its exilic mentality and feeds off the tradition of diaspora culture (which is mainly unproductive) it will not be saved and its literature will not be different from the literature written in the diaspora' (Parush 1992: 296). His view would define a new literary culture almost without antecedents. All these were the largely non-aesthetic criteria by which critics either included or omitted works from the canon.

LITERARY SCHOLARSHIP IN ISRAEL

These ideas about Hebrew literature in general, together with many of the individual opinions, filtered into Israeli literature and criticism despite Israeli writers' brave but ambivalent declaration after 1948 of independence from diaspora culture and the birth of a new one. Both of those radical watersheds of cultural change, the Haskalah and the period of Israel's foundation, led to flurries of intellectual analysis and concern about the direction the changing culture would take. The three central critical issues, tradition, function, and nation, weighed as heavily upon literature in Israel as they had in the period of literary development in the diaspora. Critics turned their attention from the development of Hebrew literature in the diaspora to the nature of the literature in its native land: 'Thrown into turmoil, literary thinkers asked the basic questions once again: What was the guiding principle of Hebrew literature? What were its future prospects? What if any would be the links between ongoing Israeli literature and the literary tradition? Would this literature remain in any sense a *tsofeh leveyt yisrael*—that is, would it concern itself in any significant way with the large, worldwide Jewish ambience and with the lessons of Jewish history?' (Miron in Wirth-Nesher 1994: 104).

The pre-state writers and scholars had brought with them from Europe many of their ideas about Hebrew literature and had added others, for example, their admiration of Soviet writing and Marxist literary theories, expressed in the literature's strong commitment to social function and the collective. Critics of the time, such as David Canaani and Y. Rosenzweig, demanded that the literature present positive stereotypes in the all-important socialist collective (Shaked 1988: 191–2; Gertz 1983: 12–14). Yet literary criticism of the 1950s and early 1960s in Israel is uncertain and conflicted: on the one hand, it commends the literature for its vitality and social commitment; on the other, it condemns it for its lack of sophistication and complexity, its narrowness of vision, its Levantinism. One critical school demanded quasi-Soviet social realism, the other, a literature based on the Jewish cultural tradition. A representative journal of the 1940s and 1950s was *Yalkut hare'im*, edited by Moshe Shamir who had already achieved fame by having defined and then glorified the young *sabra* hero, one of the staples of the early founding mythology (Shamir 1951). In his introduction to the journal Shamir demands that the literature express the reality of the world in which the writers live, and that it should reflect movements, trends, and developments. Shamir's idea of reflecting the world and life 'as they are' echoes Brenner's demand for reality 'as it is' without romantic illusions, and he argues that this does not contradict the most profound idealism. Shamir is convinced that social revolution and literary revolution are inextricably tied (Shamir 1946). Ultimately, his important contribution was to ally the pioneering movement and socialist Zionism with *belles lettres*, reinforcing the goal of a literature committed to an ideological system.

One of most significant journals of the period was *Likrat*, which represented the converse not only of Shamir's ideas but of the norms of the literary centre at this time. Its support came from a group of young writers, including poets Yehuda Amichai and Natan Zach, who disliked the dominant socialist-functionalist literature and were determined to break away from the Russian-influenced literature of earlier writers and their journals. Risking the ire of the critics, *Likrat* proposed some of the qualities of modernist European writing and avoided political or ideological comment. Generally *Likrat* returned to the aesthetic ideal of literature, giving a clear answer to the questions raised by some of the earlier scholars: Hebrew literature could indeed be universal and it could be non-nationalistic.

Unlike *Likrat*, some other journals of the 1950s awarded Hebrew literature the role of reinforcing the ideals of pioneering, socialism, and Zionism. In theory at least, this literature represented the elite culture of high values. Other journals, such as *Masa, Ittim, Alef, Molad, Perakim, Akhshav*, and *Keshet*, attempted a compromise, expressing the aesthetic criterion that literature should reflect the inner rather than external world, but should not neglect 'the truth of the Hebrew present' and the fate of the nation.

SCHOOLS OF ISRAELI CRITICISM

As in the past, a number of great Israeli literary scholars became advocates of certain qualities they perceived as being crucial to the literature's development. Literary criticism in Israel was lively and controversial, with older, European-born scholars attempting to direct the literature according to the precepts of the earlier masters, while the young literature went its own way. These critics opposed anything which appeared to them to be 'nihilism' and 'existentialism', which they defined according to their own ideological lexicon. Both these rhetorical '-isms' belonged to a brand of modernism entirely rejected by these scholars of the early Israeli period[4] (see Katznelson 1961: 419). They conflated elements of modernism—for example, free verse and structure—with an abandonment not only of moral values but of all ideas (see Mikhali 1961: 438–41). They deplored modern literature's subjects derived from so-called 'low' areas of life, citing ugliness, prostitution, despair, and weakness, in fact 'naturalism', which to them represented the worst of European culture. For example, Gid'on Katznelson, whose obsession with 'nihilism' reduces the value of his criticism, indicts Israeli literature of his time as 'filth': 'The young poets...have not waged war on the kingdom of filth, on the contrary, they have joined it as allies. The price they have paid for this alliance has been high, a threefold loss: of faith, love and social idealism' (ibid.). Katznelson and his colleagues rejected Western influence, and in Mikhali's view, while 'old and new are not values in themselves', the values of the past supersede those of the present and generations should emulate their predecessors (Zemach 1959a: 227). These and similar opinions were expressed by the people who both edited and contributed to the most canonic journal of their time and ours, *Moznayim*. It is important to note that it was not only the new styles the critics detested, but also the tendency to see literature as an end in itself, the emphasis on form at the expense of content which was regarded as the result of foreign influences. The dearth of comparative literary studies in contemporary Israeli scholarship may be the legacy of this attitude.

The most extreme departure within Israel letters was that of the 'Canaanites', one of their mentors being the poet Yonatan Ratosh (1908–81), the only Israeli poet to formulate a clear charter for Israeli literature, one which entirely contradicted that of the conservative critics. The Canaanite narrative attempted to offer an alternative Israeliness which was seen as essentially pagan. Ratosh declared that because diaspora Jewish literature primarily chronicled the destruction of a lifestyle and its associated values, it was unacceptable as a national literature. He is scathing

---

[4] These include B. Y. Michali (1910–), Avraham Kariv (1900–76), Shlomo Zemach (1886–1974), Shimon Halkin (1898–1987), and Barukh Kurzweill (1907–72).

about the Jewish world: it is an old building which has to be cleared away before being replaced by a new one. 'Its very content, framework, problem and solution are remote from us...it remains extremely alien' (Ratosh, in Wirth-Nesher 1994: 91). Ratosh distinguishes this literature from a literature of nationhood. According to him, Hebrew literature must constitute the literary expression of the Hebrew *nation*, and therefore must be written by Hebrews rather than Jews.

Criticism of the 1950s and 1960s is a series of variations on basic themes: ideas of nation, language, and Jewish tradition. These views constituted the critics' aesthetic criteria (see Diamond 1983: 74 ff.). Kariv, who emphasizes the 'spirit of the people', defines modern Hebrew literature as decadent and a product of self-hatred (ibid. 74). Barukh Kurzweill's writings rest on his belief that the Jewish historical tradition is a 'timeless absolute that transcends the limitations of human history' (ibid. 31). Because his grasp of Judaism constituted his aesthetic principle, he could not reconcile himself to the direction chosen by Israeli literature (Kurzweill 1967: 258–60). He correctly understood that Israeli writers perceived Jewishness in nationalistic and not in religious terms. On the whole he rejected the majority of them as, in his opinion, revealing a shallow sense of historical time and a concomitant inability to create literary quality (see Shaked 1977: 21). There seems to be something of a contradiction between these critics' various interpretations of 'the spirit of the people', the 'Jewish soul', and 'religious literature', and their acceptance of the modern secular state of Israel.

The most important alternative vision of Hebrew literature is that of Dov Sadan (1902–89); he also considers secularism to be the distinguishing feature of much of this literature, but he is more interested in its underlying unity (Diamond 1983: 71–2). Sadan is the least tendentious of all his contemporary literary scholars, and perhaps the only one of his time who envisaged attainable solutions to the problems of Hebrew literature. An admirer of Freud, Sadan introduced the psychoanalytic approach into Hebrew literary interpretation, although in later years he became cautious about using psychoanalysis in criticism. His assessment of writers has less to do with ideology than with the inherent qualities of creative genius. Central to Sadan's world-view is his belief that the modern secular Jewish culture which broke away from traditional Judaism is only a transient ('episodic') stage in Jewish cultural history. He believed that ultimately there would be a synthesis between the Judaic sources of the culture and its modernity (Sadan 1950: 61–2).

What distinguishes this period of criticism, apart from its stubborn assaults on the chimeras of secularism and modernism, is not its interpretative aspect but its judgemental quality and function. Its fundamental criterion is not aesthetic. Hebrew criticism of the period did not generally apply the same evaluative criteria to its discussions of Hebrew literature as it did to foreign literature.

NEW TRENDS

By the middle of the 1960s a new generation of Hebrew writers, including A. B. Yehoshua, Amos Oz, and Yaakov Shabtai, members of the 'New Wave', were reflecting the contemporary modernism of post-war Europe in complex and multilayered texts that revealed personal rather than communal needs and a growing disillusionment with Zionism. In any case, in the 1960s the nature of critical scholarship was changing beyond recognition. Younger scholars, including Gershon Shaked and Dan Miron, were moving away from the Kurzweill school and earlier neo-Marxism to establish a critical school akin to the American New Critics. The concentration on function, national identification, and the incorporation of Jewish tradition was disappearing, and for a while it seemed that a more universalist and scientific literary scholarship would take their place. The intimations of this change were evident already in the 1960s. For example, the journal *Hasifrut*, founded in 1968 and edited by Benjamin Hrushovsky (Harshav), which ceased publication in 1986, was a significant but not uncontroversial development in Israeli literary scholarship, signalling a decisive departure from, and marginalization of, all previous ideologically based criticism. Within the context of European literary theory, Harshav defined a 'science of literature' for Israel as well. *Hasifrut* introduced a systematic professional approach to the study of Hebrew literature, with its own methodology and theory. In earlier times, as we have seen, foreign literature was the spectre threatening the native literature, but with *Hasifrut* Hebrew and other literature became equal objects of research and analysis, 'asking similar questions in similar systems'. The journal focused on aesthetics, linguistics, semiotics, semantics, psychology, communication, and, for the first time, Hebrew literature in a comparative context, an approach almost totally ignored by Hebrew literary criticism up to this point. In addition, *Hasifrut* adopted international methodology, insisting for the first time on the entire apparatus of scholarly presentation.

Harshav followed *Hasifrut* with an English-language journal, *Poetics Today* (1979), emanating from the Porter Institute at Tel Aviv University, also dedicated to 'the systematic science of literature', and providing a forum for research in poetics and semiotics. Unlike *Hasifrut*, *Poetics Today* decentralized Hebrew literature and, significantly, directed its research towards a global readership. Another influential journal, *Siman Keriah*, edited by Harshav's colleague Menahem Perry, used a similar but broader theoretical basis. Harshav was the founder in 1975 and first director of the Porter Institute, whose inaugural lecture, appropriately, was given by the distinguished linguist Roman Jakobson.

HEBREW LITERARY SCHOLARSHIP TODAY, IN ISRAEL AND ABROAD

While Hebrew literary criticism today is no longer driven by the agenda of establishing a nationalist Hebrew literature with a defined function within its society, a collective emphasis, and a strong regard for its religious sources, it is still somewhat inward-looking. It tends on the whole to ignore many of the most prominent theoretical trends from the United States and Europe. *Hasifrut* and *Poetics Today* have not had a lasting impact. The greatest change that has taken place in the past four decades is the institutionalization of the study of modern Hebrew literature in the academy in Israel and the United States. All of America's great universities and some of the smaller colleges have programmes in Jewish studies which include modern Hebrew literature. Comparatively little modern Hebrew literary scholarship has emerged from Europe, where the emphasis is still on pre-modern Jewish studies. Although there are courses in modern Hebrew literature in European universities, there is relatively little publication on the subject, perhaps because not every Hebrew literature course in Europe offers doctoral training. The research is diffuse, composed mainly of genre studies and monographs on individual Israeli authors. Interestingly, however, European scholars preceded their American colleagues in promoting the works of the *Mizrahi* and Israeli-Arab authors. Generally the study of Hebrew literature is in decline, not only in Israel but throughout the world. This may be a symptom of a general trend in the downgrading of the Humanities in general and of literary studies in particular.

This is not to say that there are no great Hebrew literary scholars working today. The diversity and breadth of literary scholarship owe a great deal to two of the intellectual heirs of Dov Sadan, the pre-eminent scholars Dan Miron and Gershon Shaked, who have, for many years, profoundly affected the study and teaching of Hebrew literature. There is little contemporary literary scholarship in Israel that does not owe something to either one them, if not only for the fact that most of the active younger scholars and critics are their students. Shaked and Miron are distinct in their approach to Hebrew literature. Together they give us a rounded and complete picture of its modern development, both aesthetically and sociologically. Both are literary analysts and cultural historians whose systemization of study is a response to the fragmentation of contemporary literary scholarship. In his five-volume work on Hebrew prose fiction, *Hasipporet ha'ivrit 1880–1980* (1998), which transcends the title's final date, as well as in other works, Shaked has spanned the development of modern Hebrew literature from the late nineteenth century onwards, giving us not only a broad overview of its trends and development but also setting its practitioners in their context within this development. He systematizes modern Hebrew literary history into groups and schools, genres, currents, and generations through numerous discussions of individual authors, each of whom is a hallmark for change, up to the present day.

Shaked has also scrupulously examined stylistic trends in the literature and reinforced the notion of its place in the context of world literature, something which is rarely done by members of the younger scholarly generation. The earlier critics, not only those of Brenner's generation but also his successors, wrote their criticism in the context of European literature, which they knew well because of their knowledge of European languages. This is not the case with younger Israeli scholars whose criticism is inclined to be insular except in the case of theoretical models being applied to Hebrew texts. Generally, because of its unique political and social circumstances, contemporary Hebrew literature still tends to be evaluated in isolation, as a phenomenon relating far more to the ideological, sociological, and political entity of the nation, both in theory and in practice, rather than as a literature in relation to other literatures. This cultural isolationism has perpetuated the evaluation of this literature according to criteria imposed by its own critics rather than those shared with critics of other literatures. This is reflected in present-day Hebrew literary scholarship, which seems on the whole to avoid comparative studies, a phenomenon noted by Miron and Shaked. Shaked has gone some way towards redressing this imbalance, and has fixed the literature squarely within the framework of general literary epistemology, theory, and criticism.

However, he has also examined Hebrew literature in the context of its society: 'A literary work has a social source. The materials at the disposal of writers are taken from and given by the environment. The literary work is one of the creative constructions that has a constant influence over reality from which it takes materials ... [and] reorganises them in order to illuminate them and the norms that are reflected in them from a new point of view' (Shaked 1989: 8). On the one hand Shaked writes a comprehensive and detailed history of a specific literature; on the other he writes analytical essays on the relationship between Hebrew and Jewish literatures, their societies, and their historical phenomena, for example, the Holocaust, the War of Independence, the diaspora, the ghetto, American Jewry, the Jew as persecuted and as persecutor, the exile and the native (see Shaked 1989: 8).

Dan Miron's contribution, in a perfect partnership with Shaked, has been through many works of literary history and detailed investigations into texts themselves, fiction in Yiddish and Hebrew, and Hebrew poetry. While Shaked concentrates primarily on the history and development of Hebrew fiction, a major part of Miron's contribution has been, *inter alia*, a critical examination of Hebrew poetry. In the early years of its existence Hebrew literary criticism focused on poetry, a legacy of the past. During the 1960s and 1970s, with the growth of fiction, the interest in poetry declined and it was pushed to the margins of the critical enterprise. Given his conviction that the Israeli public has become distanced from poetry, Miron has attempted to return it to prominence (Miron 1993). In fact, it is largely due to his efforts that poetry scholarship no longer lags far behind studies of fiction. Although Israel is not enjoying a period of significant poetic creativity, a great deal of poetry, both pre-state and Israeli of an earlier period, is being collected, republished, and re-evaluated. The poets Natan Alterman, U. Z. Greenberg, David Vogel, and Bialik feature regularly in conference discussions. In addition to them, Amir Gilboa, Yehuda Amichai, and Zelda have, in recent years, drawn scholarly attention, with book-length studies in the 1980s and 1990s (Bargad 1994; Abramson 1989; Arpaly 1983; Gold 1994; Bar-Yosef 1988). The impression of a lack of interest in modern Hebrew poetry and the study of it seems to be further contradicted by the establishment of journals devoted specifically to Hebrew poetry, such as *Hadarim* and *Helikon*, and by the growth of serious critical interest in a new group of 'religious' poets. Yet Miron is dubious about contemporary poetry scholarship, arguing that it offers nothing new, particularly in the study of biblical poetry and medieval secular poetry (Miron 1993: 540).

Miron makes the point that literary scholarship outside Israel has demonstrated a critical relationship to the Hebrew and Jewish literary traditions, an approach that is difficult to find in Israeli criticism (ibid. 541). He cites as an example the anthology *The Penguin Book of Hebrew Verse*, edited by T. Carmi, which includes Hebrew poetry of all periods. Miron does not overlook the flaws of this anthology, which appeared in the United States and Great Britain in 1981, its main fault being that modern Hebrew poetry constitutes only about one-tenth of the total contents of the book. In a slightly different way, or perhaps only with a different emphasis, Miron is making a similar complaint to that of earlier critics: insufficient attention has been paid by Israeli scholarship to the Hebrew literary tradition.

Miron's comments paradoxically highlight another phenomenon within Hebrew literary scholarship, the dearth of non-Israeli scholars of modern Hebrew literature. The majority of critical work naturally emanates from Israel, but it is in the United States that the multitude of Jewish studies programmes exist, with Hebrew literature largely being taught there by expatriate Israeli academics, themselves trained in Israeli universities. In a sense then, their teaching is a continuation of the teaching in Israel, so that writing about Hebrew literature and the teaching of it is still dominated by an Israeli perspective. It is natural to expect that literary studies be taught by members of the literary culture concerned, and that the particular mores and ideologies of that culture be transmitted, yet this could lead to a uniformity of perspective and style and even a form of parochialism. In the literature sections of Jewish studies conferences a large proportion of papers on literary topics is presented by Israeli scholars living either in Israel or abroad, who are also responsible for the majority of publications on modern Hebrew literature. This leads to another problem: while non-Israelis globally teaching and writing about modern Hebrew literature are in the minority, the quality of their work is entirely comparable to that of the Israeli scholars. Yet their marginalization by the Israeli academy is nowhere better reflected than in the long section on modern Hebrew literary criticism in the *Encyclopedia Judaica*. Four non-Israeli Hebrew literature scholars, David Patterson

(UK), Jacob Kabakoff (USA), David Aberbach (UK, Canada), and Michael Stanislawski (USA), are mentioned by name in the section on criticism of early modern literature, compiled by an American scholar. Despite the contribution made by such leading American scholars as Arnold Band and Robert Alter, each of whom has written seminal works of literary scholarship, and Britain's Leon Yudkin, who has produced many volumes of genre studies and criticism, and others in the United States, Britain, and Europe, writing in English, French, Italian, and German, they are not mentioned at all in the long list (compiled by an Israeli scholar) of those who have written on contemporary Hebrew literature.

The distinction between literary scholarship and criticism has blurred since the 1960s, when the demarcation between them was clearer, with fewer non-scholarly articles in the general press. Earlier literary scholars—Sadan, Halkin, Kurzweill, among many others—were critics and scholars at the same time, as indeed are Shaked and Miron themselves. Dan Miron distinguishes between criticism and scholarship (*bikoret* and *mehkar*), and argues that while the two disciplines remain completely separate there should be a beneficial link between them (Miron 1993: 540). On the other hand, Shaked finds it difficult to distinguish between the two (Shaked 1987: 79). According to Miron, criticism no longer asks basic judgemental questions about literature, such as the exact nature of any particular poet's greatness, and scholarship proceeds upon the assumption that the answers to these kind of questions have already been given. Avraham Balaban goes further by claiming that today there are no literary critics to maintain literary standards, only scholars. Indeed, a large number of reviews of Hebrew fiction and poetry are written by academics in the form of short essays. Editors of the literary supplements of the newspapers are a mixture of academics, writers, and professional critics.

With the overtaking of literary criticism by scholarship, individual readings of literature have supplanted the earlier unity of critical discourse. Both the academy and the literary journals have assumed the didactic role of the powerful literary critics of the first half of the twentieth century, who saw their function as directing Hebrew literature towards some future aesthetic and national goal. They have been succeeded by a global network of academics, in the professionalization of Hebrew literary scholarship. These scholars no longer discuss Hebrew literature as a whole but direct their attention to its component parts, authors, and works. In this sense criticism has lost something of its definition, by no longer asking questions about its identity and purpose and its relationship to other literatures. According to Arnold Band, these are the type of questions other cultural criticism has attempted to pose (Band 1991: 2).

The proliferation of Hebrew literature courses has led to a greater volume of research. An influential American scholar characterized present-day academic critical activity in this way: 'The career of most academic critics amounts to a quarrel in instalments with other professors over matters of parochial interest' (Delbanco 2001: 38). If it were not for the structures of employment at universities throughout the world and the need to publish continuously, the 'quarrel' could perhaps give way to a more substantive deliberation over fundamental literary and cultural issues. As it is, universities and their funding bodies require quantity rather than quality, with the result that Hebrew literary scholars publish close readings in profusion. However, these are valuable in themselves, particularly for a young literature still in the process of establishing a canon. Hebrew literary scholarship may be of 'parochial' interest because critics no longer see or seek a clearly defined function for the literature as a holistic entity. It seems that with its loss of function there are few theoretical considerations about its place in Israeli society. In this sense, perhaps Hebrew literary scholarship/criticism has come of age.

TOPICS IN LITERARY SCHOLARSHIP

Hebrew literary scholarship takes many forms. Interestingly, the particular theoretical approach of Harshav and *Hasifrut* is not widely reflected as a critical tool in publications by Israeli literary scholars, even though they are not unaware of its merits. Band argues that while theoretical discourse appears in the work of some Israeli critics, it is not central to their work. 'Israeli criticism rarely investigates the social implications of literary production and never problematizes the text' (Band 1991: 9). Post-structuralist and deconstructive readings of modern Hebrew literature are offered far more by American-based academics teaching Hebrew literature than by those in Israel. Feminist theory, however, has made significant inroads into the way in which Hebrew literature is read. The collapse of the patriarchal Zionist narrative has affected previously marginalized groups, including women writers. For the women of the 1990s the disappearance of the national consensus apparently made feminism seem superfluous. This should not obscure the fact that women fiction writers in Israel have, from the start, been a comparatively neglected literary group. Substantial critical biographies and narrative biographies of women writers—including Esther Raab, Amalia Kahana-Carmon, Leah Goldberg, and Yona Wallach—appeared only in the 1980s and 1990s (Ben Ezer 1998; Rattok 1986; Rübner 1980; Rattok 1994; Sarna 1993). While mainstream literature up to the 1980s did not lack either fictional representation of women or women writers, even the finest of them, such as Amalia Cahana-Carmon, Shulamit Hareven, and Ruth Almog, did not achieve the canonical status of their male counterparts, possibly because strong female critics were also in the minority and did not carry the authority of male critics. According to Nehama Ashkenasy, 'the novel, as young as it was, was already taken so to speak by the masculine voice and used for specific purposes' (Ashkenasy 1986: 28).

At the time, the structure of Israeli society, together with the difficult circumstances of its daily life, made the importation of Western feminism inappropriate. This changed at the end of the 1980s for two reasons: the sudden growth of prose fiction and drama by a new generation of women writers, and the increasing attention paid by female critics to feminist literary theory. Whether it is because of the influence of American and European gender theory or the spirit of the time, the door has been opened in Israel to a feminist re-evaluation of the idea of female 'otherness'. According to Yael Feldman, this has taken the form of a destabilization of the automatic identification of 'otherness' with 'demonization, marginalization or any other exclusionary attitudes' (Feldman 1999: 11). The postmodern framework has offered the possibility of exploring and developing Israeli feminism, based chiefly on American gender theories mediated through Israeli literary criticism. Consequently there has been a marked growth in Hebrew feminist criticism both by literary scholars in Israel, and by those in American universities who undoubtedly influence the Israeli critics.

In the 1980s Yael Feldman, Anne Golomb Hoffman, and Naomi Sokoloff, all teaching at American universities, were established as the leaders of literary feminism. Nehama Ashkenasy published *Eve's Journey*, which examines the evolution of female biblical images in Hebrew fiction from the Haskalah onwards. Esther Fuchs followed this in 1987 with *Israeli Mythogenies: Women in Cotemporary Hebrew Fiction*. Thereafter came a flood of feminist readings of Hebrew texts and discussions of issues of feminism and gender, for example, reception, the gendered significance of national symbols, and the restoration of forgotten women poets and fiction writers. More conference sessions than ever before are now being devoted to feminist issues, although they were already evident in the 1980s. A bibliography of women writers in Hebrew and Yiddish was published in the United States in 1992 (Sokoloff *et al.* 1992), and Yael Feldman's *No Room of Their Own: Gender and Nation in Israeli Women's Fiction*, the first book-length work of feminist criticism in English entirely devoted to Hebrew women writers, was published in the United States in 1999.

Postmodernism similarly suits the Israeli literary mood. Even though writers with postmodern tendencies, such as, for example, Yitzhak Oren, had appeared previously, critics either ignored them completely or placed them outside the developing canon. In 1982 the Lebanon War dealt a death-blow to the remains of the Zionist consensus in Israel, and it was precisely after this war that a new generation of writers began to be noticed. The war prepared the ground for a situation deemed with hindsight to be postmodern, where there was no longer an ideological centre, no consensus, no agreed system of norms and values, only separation and alienation among the various parts of Israeli society (see Balaban 1995). The word 'postmodern' became current in literary criticism, used to define an eclectic group of young Israeli writers with no apparent political agendas. This was reflected by the increase in sessions on Israeli postmodernism at all the major Jewish studies conferences. Avraham Balaban published a full length study on the subject (Balaban 1995), and a variety of postmodern readings and overviews appeared (Bartana 1993; Schwartz 1995). In the late 1970s and throughout the 1980s translations of international literature, including works by Marquez, Borges, Vonnegut, and others, all of which have postmodern attributes, became popular in Israel. Balaban, the foremost commentator on Israeli postmodernism, concludes that a new generation of literary editors had become interested in promoting the latest trends in world literature (Balaban 1995). This led to the publication of local 'postmodern' works, many of them almost immediately being accepted into the canon without a sufficient period of serious evaluation or hindsight. At the present time, almost anything that has been published becomes canonical.

It is impossible to chart or analyse the enormous amount of critical publication on modern Hebrew literature in Israel and abroad, but a sound indication of scholarly interests and trends is provided by the topics offered at major Jewish studies or Hebrew literature conferences and the publications emerging from them. Over the past twenty years publications of literary scholarship have mirrored the eclecticism of literary research in other cultures: monographs, critical biographies, genre studies, including the history of the Hebrew ballad, epic and idyll, fantasy, the historical novel, and the family saga. There are studies of themes, close readings of individual works of poetry and fiction, stylistic and structural analysis. The preponderance of studies still concentrate on in-depth or close reading of individual works or of a few works of the same author, often from a New Critical perspective. As already mentioned above, few papers on theory, prosody, or stylistics are presented at conferences. There are comparatively few inclusive overviews and little cultural criticism. A discernible change in recent years has been the increased interest in gender theory and post-colonial literary theory, both of which have provided a base for textual criticism. Lacking is sustained work on the sociology of fiction and poetry, and theoretical debates about the role of criticism itself.

An interesting phenomenon in Israeli criticism is the continuing preoccupation with the Bible as a source of allusion in modern Hebrew literature. In his day Kurzweill noted this phenomenon, but censured writers for the secular use made of religious sources (Kurzweill 1967: 260). The intertexts which the earlier, yeshiva-eduated authors and their readers took for granted require academic study by today's less traditionally educated scholars and students. Demands by earlier critics, such as Bialik, for a literary synthesis of modern literature and its traditional sources came about in Israeli literature in many unexpected ways, of which the manipulation of biblical and liturgical sources is the most widespread. In fact, in Israeli literature this allusive methodology has become more than a literary device, but rather a conceptual system which underlies much of the literature. The prevalence of this allusiveness, which also has complex ideological connotations, has led to the publication of a number of full-length studies (notably Ruth Karton-Blum 1999 and David Jacobson 1997) and many scholarly papers. Within this trend, there is a proliferation of papers on the fiction and poetry alluding to the *Akedah* (the Binding of Isaac as recounted in Genesis 22), with many variant readings of the same texts, too many to list.

A comparatively new phenomenon is the growth of discussions about Sephardi and Mizrahi literature. This aspect of Hebrew literature was previously ignored by mainstream critics. In the standard surveys of modern Hebrew literature, even over the past decade, few Mizrahi authors are mentioned or if they are, then only briefly. Those scholars who have begun studying this work have accused the literary establishment of discrimination, even racism. A spate of publications in Hebrew and English on this topic has drawn attention to some problematics of the literature and its criticism. For example, critical writing about Mizrahi writers is often tendentious, stressing the 'neglected minority' identity in a new form of political correctness, rather than invoking aesthetic criteria. Some prominent Mizrahi writers see much of this mainstream criticism as condescending, distorted, and racist; this view has been expressed by such writers as Sami Michael[5] and Shimon Ballas: 'It is much more convenient for this mainstream establishment to refer to my work as the work of an "oriental Jew". In other words, work that belongs to the margins beyond the mainstream . . . I think that by operating in this way, a great disservice is done not only to the state of literary criticism . . . but to the state of Hebrew literature' (Ballas, in Alkalay 1996: 69).[6]

Amalia Cahana-Carmon, a veteran Ashkenazi author, offers a sceptical view of the problem which has not been taken up by the criticism: 'We live in a time of change—the walls of the consensus have collapsed, at least for now. The pose of the outsider is "in". Attention is given, though fleetingly, only to the "margins," just because they are "margins." The more these margins are exceptional and extravagant, the more they are sought after' (Feldman 1999: 229). The critical focus on Mizrahi writers, whether or not there is justification for evaluating them as a distinct group, and the general growth of interest in Israel's oriental communities, has again led to a reappraisal of the Israeli literary canon.

REDISCOVERY OF CLASSICAL MODERN TEXTS

For a while the main topic in the study of Hebrew literature was Israeli literature. This was so predominantly during the period of national consolidation after 1948 and the establishing of a particular literary identity for the writers and for the

[5] In a lecture given at the Oxford Centre for Hebrew and Jewish Studies in Oxford, October 2000.
[6] Alkalay cites many similar opinions.

scholars themselves. In terms of research and publication, the works of classical canonical writers were to a large extent marginalized. Few wrote on U. N. Gnessin, Greenberg, or Alterman, while Bialik and Agnon remained subjects of study. In the past twenty years, however, this has changed. Dan Miron's comments about the dearth of attention to the Hebrew literary tradition has been addressed by a greater number of publications on historical topics, signifying a revival of interest in classical authors. There are reasons for this. First, 'classical' women writers such as Dvora Baron are being discussed in relation to the expanding interest in women's writing (Govrin 1988). Second, there has been a sea-change in Israeli perceptions of the diaspora. At the end of the 1970s, for a number of historical and political reasons, Israeli society began to view the diaspora as an integral part of its own history and to see Israel as a collective phenomenon incorporating all of its political and historical elements. With this accretion of Jewish history onto the Israeli perception of self, and with the evolution of messianic movements within Israel, came a new awareness of pre-Israel culture. The result has been a growth in the study of pre-Israel literary works and an altered approach to literature written in Hebrew on the yishuv by first-generation immigrants such as Alterman, Goldberg, or Greenberg.

The third reason is that, in the 1950s and 1960s, a study of these writers was to a certain extent circumscribed by the atmosphere of the time, the doctrinaire focusing on the needs and problems of the new state which much of the critical work emphasized. In our time, and in a climate of more universalized and theoretical scholarship, scholars have the freedom to read and reinterpret these works, bringing to bear on them tools and perspectives that were unavailable to their forebears. Many of these works written during the yishuv period have therefore been reinterpreted by contemporary scholars who attempt both to recover the literary tradition and to reread the literature within the framework of modern literary trends. A good example of this is the growth of feminist or postmodernist readings. It is to be hoped that this practice will reach even further back in time, to the literature of the Haskalah, which has remained the province of a single small group of dedicated scholars[7] for a number of decades. In fact feminist criticism has already begun examining the writing of women during the Haskalah period (see Cohen 1997; others in press).

One of the literary phenomena of the time is the rediscovery and canonization of writers who had fallen into obscurity, sometimes, as in the case of David Vogel, for ideological reasons. The literary journal *Mikan*, pulished by the Department of Hebrew Literature at Ben-Gurion University, has a section entitled 'Cultural Forgetfulness' in which it reprints 'forgotten' texts from earlier periods. Yet within this new move towards reinterpretation there is surprisingly little about the most neglected generation, the Israeli generation of the 1950s, the *dor ba'aretz*, although S. Yizhar, one of their greatest exponents, has received renewed critical acclaim. It is

---

[7] David Patterson (UK); Tova Cohen, Yehuda Friedlander, Moshe Pelli, Uzi Shavit (Israel).

possible that the Greenberg–Alterman generation is closer to contemporary sensibility than the collective-oriented and secular generation of the 1950s. In his overview of modern Hebrew literary criticism, Shaked singled out for praise modern criticism on the yishuv writers, and mentioned a few studies of Amos Oz and A. B. Yehoshua (Shaked 1987).

PUBLICATIONS

New literature appears in Israel not only in book form but also in journals such as *Moznayim* and in the press. Much of the most timely critical comment appears in the weekly supplements of the major newspapers, particularly *Ha'aretz*, whose weekend supplement provides an outstanding insight into the nature of literary scholarship in Israel. Written predominantly by academics, rather than by journalists or professional critics as in other countries, this criticism is immediate, incisive, and extremely influential. In Israel the literary advisers to the publishing houses are also academics still teaching at the various Israeli universities, and therefore able not only to influence the publication of new books but also, to a certain extent, to direct them to a specific readership. According to Avraham Balaban, the earlier critics, and even contemporary scholars such as Shaked and Miron, were able to influence the reception of works of fiction or poetry. In Balaban's opinion the situation has changed today, with media attention becoming more important and influential than any scholarly criticism. He argues that publishers are printing low-calibre work with an eye to the market. Whether as a result of Israeli postmodernism, or of a more realistic attitude to writing in Hebrew and an understanding of public taste, the boundaries between serious literature and commercial successes have become blurred. In order to supply the American academic market and to unite with foreign critical trends, Israeli scholars increasingly publish in English in the first instance or have their works translated.

   The diversity of modern Hebrew literary research is reflected not only in the publications issued by the impressive number of university institutes devoted to it, but also in a variety of journals, most but not all of them associated with university departments. The proliferation of university-based journals in Israel leads to a homogeneity of style and substance (much of it influenced by academic style in the United States), and rigidly controlled academic argument. This often extends to those journals entirely devoted to the study of Hebrew literature, including *Hasifrut, Bikoret ufarshanut, Mehkere yerushalayim besifrut ivrit, Siman Keriah, Moznayim, Proza, Iton 77, Sifrut Ivrit Modernit, Mikan,* and *Akhshav.* The most influential journal in English devoted in its entirety to the study of Hebrew literature is *Prooftexts*, which proceeds on predominantly thematic lines. It has also encouraged a broader, more cultural-historical scrutiny of Hebrew literature; for example, by devoting two complete issues to the study of Jewish autobiography, including Hebrew autobiography, or by devoting entire issues to individual writers. There is also the English-language *Modern Hebrew Literature*, published in Israel by the Institute for the Translation of Hebrew Literature, which provides brief comments on new fiction and poetry, in addition to offering synthetic articles on various aspects of the literature. Otherwise many journals in Israel and abroad offering interdisciplinary studies of Jewish culture, such as the *AJS Review*, *Modern Judaism*, *The Jewish Studies Quarterly*, *Alpayim*, *Yod*, *Reeh* and the *Journal of Modern Jewish Studies* accept research on modern Hebrew literature.

POLITICS AND LITERARY SCHOLARSHIP

Even after the establishment of the State of Israel, few writers withstood the challenge to engage with social reality. This response conformed not only to their own need to be viewed as part of the developing process of national establishment, but also because the tenets of Zionism had decreed that everyone become involved in the state-building process. Either as a consequence, or because this is always the case in emerging nations, many of the authors were also political spokespeople so that, despite the periodic retreat from positivistic and committed writing, literature and current events were unified in Israel. Writers and critics, both of the pre-State and Israeli communities, had an affinity with the ruling Labour leadership, later the Labour parties in Israel. During the 1970s, in particular after the rise of Likkud, one theoretical issue that preoccupied critics in Israel was the role of politics in the creation and judgement of literature. There is still some controversy about the extent to which political views are taken into account in literary evaluation. Although Israeli Hebrew literature has from the start been evaluated predominantly— although not exclusively—on literary rather than extra-literary grounds, present-day scholars fall into certain well-defined groups: first, those who tend towards post-Zionist analyses in their choice of texts, their reading of them, and in their deconstruction of early Israeli iconography and founding myths. Generally, literary works are discussed as works of art rather than ideological statements because some of the influential Israeli critics—including Haim Hever and Yitzhak Laor—belong to the same political centrist or left-of-centre political parties as do the most canonical writers. Over the years, however, there have been many instances of resentment by less left-leaning critics of the dominant scholarly hierarchy in Israel. On the other hand, there are those scholars who write and teach within more traditional ideological, and often no less politicized, frameworks. For example, a series of monographs on individual poets has been published by literary scholars from Bar-Ilan University, and many others are in press. The popular perception is that these more conservative readings are marginalized. In fact, although they might once have been outside the critical mainstream, they have become increasingly influential. Overall, it seems that literary criticism in Israel has not strayed very far from its functionalist roots.

FUTURE TRENDS

In the past, as we have seen, there were distinct trends within Hebrew literature, most of them prescribed by the critical figures of the day. The major difference between their criticism and that of the present time is that now there are few discernible trends in the nature or topics of scholarship, other than those theoretical issues already mentioned and the growth of historical scholarship. There is perhaps one trend which will become more obvious in the future. Balaban discerned a tendency towards absolute secularism in the present literary generation; in his words, 'the religious existentialism of the New Wave has given way to secular existentialism in the midst of which is a strong ontological crisis' (Balaban 1995: 47). From the start the general concentration on secular Zionism relegated religiously oriented writers and critics to the margins, even if the religious experience was never entirely absent from the modern Hebrew literary milieu. Now there is a noticeable inclination in poetry towards a metaphysical idiom, and scholars are beginning to reread earlier literature, even that of the apparently entirely secular *dor ba'aretz* generation, fiction writers such as David Shahar, and postmodernists such as Yoel Hoffman and Etgar Keret, from a metaphysical or 'transcendental' perspective. Balaban himself has debated the 'religiosity' of modern Hebrew writers (Balaban 2002: 63–83). Hana Yaoz, wife of a newly Orthodox Hebrew poet, has done pioneering work on contemporary Hebrew religious fiction (Yaoz 1983), and Ariel Hirschfield was one of the earliest critics to have noted the trend in poetry (Hirschfield 1993: 31). The study of the embedded 'religiosity' of literary texts is a fertile area for future Hebrew literary scholarship.

The question is whether the developments in literary criticism and scholarship come in response to cultural conditions at home, or are imported, primarily from the United States. The growth of multiculturalism, postmodernism, and feminism in Israel certainly may be attributed to the influence of foreign literary models, but the spirit of the time and changes within Israeli society also promote the altered parameters of literary scholarship. The decline of ideology among the intellectual mainstream and the concomitant breakdown of critical boundaries has made literary scholarship amenable to a new eclectic inclusiveness. Post-Zionist and conservative scholarship use similar critical tools: the difference between them is in the interpretation. Present-day Israeli scholarship is no longer judgemental or prescriptive; it makes few demands on literature other than aesthetic ones. It attempts to reflect the diversity of all Hebrew literary creativity in Israel without exclusion or marginalization. The 'parochial' differences of academic and critical opinion are healthy for the literature's development. At last, it seems, the situation of Hebrew literary scholarship has 'normalized'.

Suggested Reading

For a general overview of modern Hebrew fiction, see Shaked (2000) and Yudkin (1984). For a study of Israeli feminism, see Feldman (1999). For a comprehensive study of Hebrew postmodernism, see Balaban (1995). For general theory and criticism, see Gertz (1983), Alter (1988), Kronfeld (1996), and Mintz (1997).

Bibliography

ABRAMSON, G. 1989. *The Writing of Yehuda Amichai—A Thematic Approach.* New York.

AHAD HA-ʿAM (Asher Ginzburg) April 1897. *Lesheʾelat hasifrut haʿivrit.* Tel Aviv.

—— 1979. *Al parashat derakhim.* Vol. 2. Tel Aviv.

ALKALAY, A. ed. 1996. *Keys to the Garden.* San Francisco.

ALTER, R. 1988. *The Invention of Hebrew Prose.* Washington, DC.

—— 1994 *Hebrew and Modernity.* Bloomington, Ind.

ASHKENASY, N. 1986. *Eve's Journey.* Philadelphia.

ARPALY, B. 1983. *Haperakhim vehaʾagartal: shirat Yehuda Amichai.* Tel Aviv.

BALABAN, A. 1995. *Gal aher basipporet haʿivrit.* Keter.

—— 2002. 'Secularity and Religiosity in Contemporary Hebrew Litrature', *Middle Eastern Literatures,* 5.1: 63–83.

BAND, A. 1991. 'Literary Criticism in Israel.' *Modern Judaism* 11: 1–15.

BARGAD, W. 1994. *'To Write the Lips of Sleepers' The Poetry of Amir Gilboa.* Cincinnati.

BARTANA, O. 1993. *Shemonim: sifrut yisraʾelit bador haʾaharon.* Tel Aviv.

BAR-YOSEF, H. 1988. *Al shirat Zelda.* Tel Aviv.

BEN EZER, E. 1998. *Yamim shel leʿana udevash.* Tel Aviv.

BHABHA, H. ed. 1990. *Nation and Narration.* London.

BRENNER, Y. H. 1972. *Kol kitve Y. H. Brenner.* Tel Aviv.

Cohen, T. 1997. 'Inside and Outside the Culture: On the Appropriation of the "Father Language" As a Means To the Intellectual Formulation of Feminine Identity.' [Hebrew]. In *Sadan: Studies in Hebrew Literature*. Z. Shamir and H. David eds. ii. 69–110.

Delbanco, A. 2001. 'Night Vision'. In *New York Review of Books* 11 January.

Diamond, J. S. 1983. *Barukh Kurzweil and Modern Hebrew Literature*. Atlanta, Ga.

Feldman, Y. 1999. *No Room of Their Own: Gender and Nation in Israeli Women's Fiction*. Columbia.

Friedlander, Y. 1985. *Uri Zvi Greenberg: Mivhar ma'amarim al yetzirato*. Ramat Gan.

Fuchs, E. 1987. *Israeli Mythogynies: Women in Contemporary Hebrew Fiction*. New York.

Gold, N. 1994. *Not Like a Cypress: Transformations of Images and Structures in Yehuda Amichai's Poetry*. New York.

Gertz, N. 1983. *Hirbet Hiz'eh vehaboker shel maharat*. Tel Aviv.

Gover, Y. 1994. *Zionism: The Limits of Moral Discourse in Israeli Hebrew Fiction*. Minnesota.

Govrin, N. 1988. *Devora Baron: hamahatzit harishon*. Tel Aviv.

Hirshfield A. 1993. 'The Return of the Divine'. *Modern Hebrew Literature* 11: 23–5.

Jacobson, D. 1997. *Does David Still Play Before You?* Detroit.

Karton-Blum, R. 1999. *Profane Scriptures*. Jerusalem.

Katznelson, G. 1961. 'Le'an hem holekhim?' *Moznayim* 12, nos. 5–6.

Kronfeld, H. 1996. *On the Margins of Modernism: Decentering Literary Dynamics* Berkeley, Ca. and London.

Kurzweill, B. 1959, 1971. *Sifrutenu hahadasha—hemshekh o mahapekhah?* Jerusalem and Tel Aviv.

——1967. 'Al zeramim hadashim basifrut ha'ivrit hahadashah.' *Moznayim* 25, nos. 4–5: 257–65.

Mikhali, B. Y. 1961. 'He'arot bashulei sifrutenu hamodernit.' *Moznayim* 12, nos. 5–6: 438–41.

Mintz, A. ed. 1997. *The Boom in Contemporary Israeli Fiction*. Hanover, NH.

Miron, D. 1993. *Hadashot me'ezor hakotev*. Tel Aviv.

Neiman, M. 1983. *A Century of Modern Hebrew Literary Criticism 1784–1884*. New York.

Parush, I. 1992. *Kanon sifruti ve'idiologiah le'umit*. Jerusalem.

Rattock, L. 1986. *Amalia Kahana-Carmon*. Tel Aviv.

——1994. *Hakol ha'aher*. Tel Aviv.

Rübner, T. 1980. *Leah Goldberg, Monografia*. Tel Aviv.

Sadan, D. 1950. *Al sifrutenu*. Jerusalem.

Sarna, I. 1993. *Yona Wallach*. Jerusalem.

Schwartz, Y. 1995. 'Hasifrut ha'ivrit, ba'idan she'ahare.' *Efes Shetayim* 3

Shaked, G. 1977, 1988, 1993, 1998. *Hasipporet ha'ivrit 1880–1980*. Jerusalem.

——1987. *Yetsivot unimanehen: arba'ah perakim batorat hahitkablut*. Tel Aviv.

——1989. *En makom aher*. Tel Aviv.

——2000. *Modern Hebrew Fiction*. Bloomington, Ind.

Shamir, M. 1946. 'Im benei dori' in *Yalkut hare'im lasifrut hahadashah*. Vol. 3: Autumn 1946.

——Shamir, M. 1951 *Bemo yadav*. Tel Aviv.

Sokoloff, N., Lapidus Lerner, A. and Norich, A. eds. 1992. *Gender and Text in Modern Hebrew and Yiddish Literature*. New York.

Weiss, H. 2000. *Hamatkonet vehademut.* (Studies on Greenberg.) Ramat Gan.

Wirth-Nesher, H. ed. 1994. *What is Jewish Literature?* Philadelphia.

Yaoz, H. 1983. 'Sipporet yehudit kiyumit.' *Iton 77.* Tel Aviv.

Yudkin, L. 1984. *1948 and After: Aspects of Israeli Fiction.* Manchester.

Zemach, A. 1984. *Tenuʿah banekudah: Brenner vesippurav.* Tel Aviv.

Zemach, S. 1959a. *Matzevet veshalekhta.* Tel Aviv.

—— 1959b. *Shti vaʿerev.* Tel Aviv.

CHAPTER 22

YIDDISH STUDIES

CECILE E. KUZNITZ[*]

INTRODUCTION

THE notion of including Yiddish studies as a distinct discipline within the wider field of Jewish studies (itself a relatively recent construct) would have been virtually inconceivable before the First World War. By the end of the Second World War, a mere generation later, the Holocaust had devastated the Jewish communities whose language, history, and culture Yiddish studies sought to explore. A half-century after the catastrophe, Yiddish scholarship is only beginning to wrestle with its full impact. Today the field of Yiddish studies is vibrant, albeit in a form much different from that envisioned by its pioneers at the start of the previous century.

THE ROOTS OF YIDDISH STUDIES

The Yiddish language has a thousand-year history as the vernacular tongue of Ashkenazic, or European, Jewry. Originating among the Jewish communities of Germany and France, it was brought by migrants from Western to Eastern Europe,

* The author would like to thank Martin Goodman for his patience; Mikhail Krutikov for an important citation; and Zachary M. Baker, Kenneth Moss, and Tony Michels for their valuable suggestions.

starting around the thirteenth century. Like other Jewish vernaculars, it is written in the Hebrew alphabet and composed of elements drawn from Hebrew, Aramaic, and the co-territorial non-Jewish languages, in this case first Middle High German and later Slavic tongues. In traditional Jewish culture Hebrew was reserved for study and prayer while Yiddish was used for day-to-day activity. In pre-modern times Yiddish developed an extensive literature on both sacred and secular themes, but it was never employed for the most prestigious genres such as rabbinic learning.

The first scholarly interest in Yiddish began in the sixteenth century among German Christians, many of whom approached Yiddish as a curious dialect of German which could be mined for clues to the history of their own language. For some, such as Johann Buxtorf, this interest developed out of their study of Hebrew. Less benignly, German scholars such as Wilhelm Christian Justus Chrysander studied Yiddish to gain an entrée into Jewish society, whether to proselytize or to expose Jews' supposed nefarious doings. Thus, the Yiddish research of the nineteenth-century German criminologist F. C. B. Avé-Lallemant was an extension of his study of Rotwelsch, the language of the German criminal underworld. In Jewish circles, the earliest investigations of Yiddish, such as those of the Renaissance scholar and poet Elijah Levita (Elye Bokher), developed from the tradition of providing glosses in the vernacular to elucidate Hebrew texts.

A new approach to the study of Yiddish became possible in the late nineteenth century with the rise of Jewish nationalist movements in Eastern Europe. While Zionists worked towards establishing a Jewish homeland, Diaspora Nationalists advocated measures to secure Jewish rights in their countries of residence and to strengthen an autonomous Jewish culture. In their world-view, Yiddish, formerly considered unsuitable for high-cultural functions such as scholarship or belles-lettres, assumed a new importance. Diaspora Nationalists pointed to the existence of a Jewish vernacular to bolster their argument that Jews comprised a distinct national group among the peoples of Eastern Europe. While Zionists sought to revive Hebrew as a spoken tongue, most Diaspora Nationalists rallied around Yiddish as the vehicle of a modern, secular culture that could sustain Jewish life in the absence of a territorial base. Yiddish, formerly denigrated as the language of the uneducated, was now lauded for its utility in building a mass political movement and its populist associations with the *folk*, the common people.

Thus, modern Yiddish culture in general, and modern Yiddish scholarship in particular, was largely born out of a specific ideological context. Yiddish and Hebrew, which had traditionally filled complementary functions in Jewish life, were now set in a rivalry as adjuncts of competing versions of Jewish nationalism. Yiddish research was driven by the desire to prove its *yikhes* (lineage) as a tongue with a long independent history, not simply a dialect of German, as well as its suitability as a vehicle for a sophisticated modern culture. Thus, as Dovid Katz has observed, at the inception of modern Yiddish studies Yiddishists in the academic sense—that is, those who study the language—were inseparable from

Yiddishists in the ideological sense—that is, those who promote the language (Katz 1986: 32).

By the late nineteenth century Yiddishism in its ideological sense had encouraged the flourishing of Yiddish literature, press, and theatre. It was not until the first decade of the twentieth century that modern Yiddish scholarship took its first tentative steps, with the Yiddish language conference held in Czernowitz in 1908, where speakers delivered papers on the history of Yiddish in the language itself. A new era in Yiddish studies began on the eve of the First World War with the publication in 1912/3 of *Der pinkes* (The Record Book), edited by the literary critic Shmuel Niger. This ground-breaking work included studies of Yiddish linguistics, folklore, and literature as well as the history of the Yiddish press and theatre. Significantly, it was the first scholarly work written in Yiddish, thus affirming both the tongue's suitability for serious intellectual pursuits and its independence from the fields of German and Hebrew scholarship.

The most important contribution to *Der pinkes* was the essay and bibliography by Ber Borokhov, 'Di oyfgabn fun der yidishe filologye' (The Tasks of Yiddish Philology). Borokhov, who in his short life was a leading theoretician of Marxist Zionism as well as a pioneering scholar, made explicit the nationalist underpinnings of Yiddish studies. He argued that philology—the study of language, literature, and folklore—was the most important academic discipline since it was the most useful in promoting national revival. He further drew a distinction between the linguist, engaged in the disinterested pursuit of knowledge, and the philologist, committed to the nationalist goals of his people. Thus, for Borokhov Yiddish philology, and by extension all of Yiddish studies, was by definition both an academic and an ideological pursuit.

While individual scholars such as Borokhov and the linguist Noah Prylucki began working in the years before the First World War, it was not until the post-war period that the new political order in Eastern Europe made possible the creation of institutional bases for Yiddish studies. The first detailed call for a centre for Yiddish scholarship was issued in 1925 by the writer Nokhem Shtif. Shtif's plan was realized when the *Yidisher Visnshaftlekher Institut* (Yiddish Scientific Institute), known by its acronym YIVO, was established to promote research, teaching, and publishing in Yiddish on all aspects of the history and culture of Yiddish-speaking Jewry. Headquartered in Vilna (then Wilno, Poland), and led by Max Weinreich, Zalman Reisen, and later Zelig Kalmanovitch, YIVO created four sections for Philology, History, Economics-Statistics, and Psychology-Pedagogy. Thus, to Borokhov's concern with language YIVO added the historical study of Yiddish-speaking Jewry—already a topic of research in other languages (see Michael Stanislawski's contribution to this volume)—and the social-scientific investigation of contemporary Jewish problems, an area to which Weinreich devoted increasing attention in the 1930s. YIVO scholars saw their work as leading to the further development of Yiddish culture, which would in turn promote both Jewish rights and the dignity of the Yiddish-speaking masses in Eastern Europe. Thus, while it was always careful to maintain a distance from the political battles of inter-war Eastern Europe, YIVO's approach to Yiddish studies was firmly rooted in the Diaspora Nationalist programme.

While YIVO functioned as part of the flourishing of Yiddish culture in inter-war Poland, in the same years the Soviet Union also proved a favourable setting for the development of Yiddish scholarship. In the 1920s the Soviet policy of encouraging national minority cultures led to the unprecedented step of providing government sponsorship for Yiddish studies. The Ukrainian Academy of Sciences in Kiev and the Institute for White Russian Culture in Minsk both created Jewish sections which employed scholars of Yiddish and published Yiddish-language journals. This period of productivity was short-lived, however. Soviet scholarship was subject to increasingly strict censorship, so that by the 1930s it had more propaganda than research value, and the Jewish sections of the academies in Minsk and Kiev were eventually closed by Stalin. As for the emigrant communities of Yiddish-speaking Jewry, in 1927 fervent Hebraists at the Hebrew University of Jerusalem defeated a proposal to establish a position in Yiddish there. Jewish studies as a whole was only in its infancy in the United States, although one of first scholars to hold a chair in this field, Salo W. Baron of Columbia University, was himself born in Eastern Europe and treated, *inter alia*, the history of that Jewish community.

While the intellectual and institutional foundations of Yiddish studies were laid in the wake of the First World War, only two decades later the Holocaust devastated Yiddish-speaking Jewry. The geography of Yiddish studies inevitably shifted from its historic heartland in Eastern Europe to the newer centres of the United States and Israel. The YIVO Institute in Vilna was destroyed and most of its leaders perished, yet it was able to transfer its headquarters to its New York branch and continue its activity after the war. Most fortuitously, its leading intellectual light, Max Weinreich, was able to escape to New York with his young son Uriel, who was to become a prominent Yiddish linguist in his own right. By this time the centres of Soviet Yiddish scholarship and most of their staffs had already been liquidated by Stalin. In addition to these material and human losses, the Holocaust destroyed the very context in which Yiddish studies functioned. With the extermination of 90 per cent of East European Jewry, Yiddish lost its status as the vernacular of the Jewish masses. A few years later, the establishment of the State of Israel marked the triumph of Zionism and the eclipse of its rival, Diaspora Nationalism.

In the years after the Holocaust Yiddish studies has gained acceptance in the academic world, yet with many attendant ironies: the language has finally achieved respect as a subject worthy of serious study, but the reasons why that respect was first sought have become null and void. Meanwhile, the interest in Yiddish within the academy is matched by growing nostalgia but lessening literacy among a Jewish public ever more distant from its immigrant roots. First despised and then lauded as the language of the common people, Yiddish has now become largely the province of a small group of scholars, while previously elite Hebrew has become a vernacular tongue.

Yiddish studies today still grapples with the after-effects of the Holocaust; indeed, one might argue that it is only now beginning fully to come to grips with this shattering event, as the last remaining scholars raised in the pre-war period pass from the scene. A half-century later its senior figures are drawn from a generation born after the Second World War, without first-hand knowledge of the East European milieu that gave birth to the field, and its younger ranks are filled with those for whom Yiddish is not *mame-loshn* (mother tongue) but an acquired language. It is to a large extent these changed circumstances that shape the current directions of the field.

THE CHANGING GEOGRAPHY
OF YIDDISH STUDIES

A glance at the contemporary centres of Yiddish scholarship reveals both the evolving status of the field within the academy and the changing geography of the Jewish world. The effort to establish Yiddish studies as an independent discipline, which Borokhov formulated in his seminal essay and which culminated in the creation of YIVO, has had little success in post-war academia. Yet as Jewish studies as a whole has gained a foothold in secular institutions of higher learning, the study of Yiddish has slowly been welcomed into the fold. Thus, although the original vision of Yiddish studies has largely failed to be realized, the field today is an active one which enjoys an unprecedented degree of acceptance.

In the United States, New York, unsurprisingly, assumed a leading role in Yiddish studies in the post-war decades. YIVO continued its research and publication programmes, and in 1968 created the Max Weinreich Center for Advanced Jewish Studies to offer graduate-level courses to students enrolled in local universities. Yet by the 1990s the offerings of the Weinreich Center had become increasingly scanty. Today the institute continues to sponsor important publication projects, and its library and archives remain an unparalleled resource for Yiddish scholarship. Yet YIVO has largely abandoned its function of training scholars and supporting original research in the field, as well as its commitment to employing Yiddish as a living tongue.

Yiddish studies in New York has long benefited from the symbiosis between YIVO and Columbia University, which established the first university chair in Yiddish in the United States in 1953. While Max Weinreich led YIVO until his passing in 1969, his son Uriel held the Atran Chair in Yiddish Language, Literature, and Culture at Columbia until his premature death in 1967. The younger Weinreich also led the Program in Yiddish Studies, making Columbia the only institution in the United States where one could pursue a degree in that field as an independent discipline. For several decades this programme played a leading role in educating graduate students with a solid grounding in Yiddish language and culture, first with a focus on linguistics and later on modern literature as well. Yet in 1999 the directorship of Yiddish studies was reduced to a junior faculty position, throwing into doubt the role of the programme as a training-ground for future scholars. In addition to Columbia, only at Ohio State University can one obtain a degree in Yiddish studies in the United States. Thus, the field has not taken root in American universities as an academic discipline in its own right.

These developments are balanced by the more sanguine news that as Jewish studies has flourished on campuses nationwide Yiddish scholarship has also grown as part of this larger trend. An increasing number of schools offer at least introductory Yiddish language and courses on Yiddish literature in translation. Moreover, in the course of the 1990s two senior positions in Yiddish studies were established at Harvard and Indiana universities, currently held by Ruth R. Wisse and Dov-Ber Kerler respectively. American graduate studies now pursue topics related to Yiddish studies at universities such as Harvard, Stanford, the University of California at Berkeley, the University of Michigan, and the Jewish Theological Seminary of America. What these institutions have in common is that they have all developed leading programmes in Jewish studies. It is within that interdisciplinary framework that most American scholars pursue Yiddish scholarship, primarily in the fields of modern Yiddish literature and the history of Yiddish-speaking Jewry.

The integration of Yiddish scholarship into American Jewish studies programmes brings both costs and opportunities. It is encouraging that a number of junior faculty positions in Jewish studies have in recent years gone to Yiddish specialists, a sign of Yiddish's rising stock in the field as a whole. Yet most Yiddish scholars hold appointments that could in the future be filled by experts in other areas, and only a few universities in the United States can boast two faculty members with expertise in Yiddish. While creating more opportunities for undergraduates to gain an elementary exposure to Yiddish on campus, this configuration also makes advanced graduate training more difficult. There is some evidence of a 'trickle up' effect, however, where students encounter Yiddish culture at an earlier stage of their academic careers and then decide to pursue graduate study in the few locales where this is feasible. In addition, by situating Yiddish studies in this larger context, along with academic Jewish studies as a whole it becomes increasingly dependent on external funding from donors in the community. This raises a new set of concerns, as American Jews increasingly see Yiddish culture as an object of curiosity or nostalgia rather than as an essential part of Jewish civilization.

After its earlier failed attempt to institute the study of Yiddish, in 1951 the Hebrew University of Jerusalem successfully established a Yiddish chair which was assumed by the literary scholar Dov Sadan. While the denigration of Yiddish—usually classified as a 'foreign language' in the Jewish state—remained a sore point, Israel thus became the only locale in the post-war era where government funds went to support Yiddish scholarship. More recently other Israeli institutions have begun to offer courses in Yiddish. Most extensive are the activities of the Rena Costa Centre for Yiddish Studies at Bar-Ilan University; also notable are the efforts of Haifa University, home of the journal *Hulyot* (Links), the leading forum for Yiddish studies in Hebrew. The more central place of Jewish studies as a whole in Israeli academia means that several universities have multiple faculty members with specializations in Yiddish. Yet, as is the case in the United States, most of these positions were created at the initiative of external donors who agreed to provide the necessary funding.

While academic Yiddish studies in the United States originally focused on linguistics as its core discipline, following the specialization of the Weinreichs, in Israel the interests of Sadan directed the field from the start towards the study of literature. Today all periods of Yiddish literature, both pre-modern and modern, are the central focus of the field, reflecting the eclectic interests of Sadan, his successor Chone Shmeruk, and their students on the current faculty. In most cases Yiddish is studied in the larger context of Jewish literature, a classification similar to the American approach which is also in keeping with Sadan's and Shmeruk's holistic approach to the study of Jewish culture. While popular antipathy to diaspora cultures long limited interest in Yiddish among the Israeli public, this attitude is now slowly changing. Along with the recent influx of immigrants from the former Soviet Union, some with a knowledge of the language, this development may well lead to a growth of Yiddish studies on Israeli campuses in the coming decades. As of 2002, however, plans call for the Department of Yiddish at the Hebrew University— the only one of its kind in the world—to be absorbed into another academic unit and its baccalaureate program terminated. This discouraging development may mean that, as in the United States, Yiddish studies in Israel will favour breadth of exposure over depth of intensive training.

It is Germany that has the longest tradition of Yiddish scholarship, and despite— or perhaps because of—the trauma of the Holocaust, that tradition continues today. While Yiddish language courses have been offered at many German universities, it was not until 1990 that the linguist Erika Timm was appointed to the country's first chair of Yiddish at the University of Trier. In 1996 a second chair was established at Heinrich Heine University in Dusseldorf, currently held by Marion Aptroot. In recent years the field has benefited from the German fascination with all things Jewish, a result of the attempt to come to grips with the legacy of the Second World War. While this interest has led to the growth of Jewish studies in German academia, as in the past the majority of Yiddish students are drawn from among those specializing in German philology. Thus, the primary focus of the field is linguistics and Old Yiddish literature, those areas best able to shed light on Germans' native tongue. In this way, Yiddish scholarship continues in the tradition of *Germanistik* which marked its earliest phase, a counterpoint to the approach of Israeli scholars such as Shmeruk and Chava Turniansky who consider Old Yiddish literature in its Jewish context.

Improbably, in the 1990s Oxford, England, emerged as the most active centre of Yiddish scholarship. While Oxford's Bodleian Library was long famed for its Yiddish collection (see Hill 1999), the flourishing there of Yiddish research, teaching, and publishing was due to a confluence of factors. In 1978 the American-born linguist Dovid Katz joined the Oxford Centre for Hebrew and Jewish Studies at Yarnton Manor, which also employed several other scholars specializing in Yiddish, including Katz's student Dov-Ber Kerler. In 1995 Katz founded, and for a time headed the independent Oxford Institute for Yiddish Studies. His successors at the institute, Gennady Estraikh and Mikhail Krutikov, continued his work at Oxford and also introduced Yiddish courses at the School of Oriental and African Studies at the University of London. Taken together, these British institutions sponsored an impressive body of work in Yiddish linguistics and all periods of Yiddish literature, as well as fostering the active use of Yiddish in the academic setting.

Through the second half of the 1990s the Oxford Institute for Yiddish Studies functioned as an independent body devoted to Yiddish scholarship in Yiddish, thus coming closest to fulfilling the original programme of the founders of the field. As of 2002, however, this period of productivity has slowed. The institute has shut its doors and its future is in doubt, and the aforementioned courses at SOAS London have also been discontinued. The Oxford Centre for Hebrew and Jewish Studies has recently lost two Yiddishists and replaced them with only one, Joseph Sherman, to teach its Yiddish programme. Other European venues, however, may in the future compensate for any diminished activity in England. The Medem Library, which has long served as the focal point for Yiddish scholarship in France, has spearheaded a campaign to create a Yiddish Cultural Centre in Paris. Opening in October 2002, this new institution could play an important role in co-ordinating and promoting Yiddish education, research, and publishing throughout Europe.

One part of the world which may well prove an area of future growth for Yiddish studies is Eastern Europe, which has experienced a modest but significant revival of Jewish culture since the end of the Cold War. After departing Oxford, Dovid Katz established the Vilnius Yiddish Institute in the original home-town of YIVO, now the capital of independent Lithuania. Since 1991 David Fishman of the Jewish Theological Seminary has directed Project Judaica, the first programme in Jewish Studies in the former Soviet Union. Housed at the Russian State University for the Humanities in Moscow, it has already trained several dozen students in fields including Yiddish and East European Jewish history. That graduates of

Project Judaica now study and teach in Israel, the United States, and Canada confirms that this region of the world is contributing to the ranks of young Yiddish scholars, but does not bode well for the future development of Yiddish studies *in situ*.

YIDDISH AS A POST-VERNACULAR LANGUAGE

Even more than its changing geography, intellectual trends within Yiddish studies reflect the impact of the events of 1939–45 and 1948. First, the field today is coming to terms with the fact that Yiddish is now what may be termed a post-vernacular language. Once championed by Yiddishists because of its populist connotations, the Holocaust in Europe, as well as widespread assimilation in the United States, has rendered the tongue largely the province of a small circle of scholars and devotees. Yiddish scholarship in the inter-war period was intimately linked to the lives and aspirations of the Yiddish-speaking masses. Scholars today are increasingly distant from a Jewish public with a growing nostalgia for its East European roots but a rapidly diminishing base of knowledge.

The field is now facing the demise of the last figures born into the pre-war milieu of a vibrant Yiddish culture. The full impact of this loss has, in effect, been postponed a generation, as many of today's senior academics are native speakers raised in Yiddish-speaking homes by Holocaust survivors or ideologically committed Yiddishists (or both). Yet the decline of Yiddish as a vernacular tongue means that most younger scholars have had to master it as an acquired language. On the most fundamental level, this has made issues of language training and pedagogy central to the continued viability of Yiddish studies as a discipline. While an increasing number of universities offer at least introductory courses in Yiddish language, the quality of teaching and the commitment of students are often uneven. It has long been realized that students who wish to pursue serious work in Yiddish studies require more sustained instruction.

In 1968 YIVO and Columbia University jointly established the first intensive summer course in Yiddish, the Uriel Weinreich Program in Yiddish Language, Literature, and Culture. The graduates of the *zumer-program* (summer programme), as it is affectionately known, comprise a virtual who's who of the younger generation of Yiddish studies scholars in the United States and to a lesser extent abroad. Similar programmes have since been founded in Oxford, Vilna, and elsewhere. Another important, more recent, initiative is the International Research

Seminar in Yiddish Culture first organized in 1999 by Avraham Nowersztern of the Hebrew University and Beit Sholem-Aleichem in Tel Aviv. Held in alternate summers in Israel and the United States and conducted entirely in Yiddish, the seminar brings together leading Israeli and American scholars to present brief overviews of various topics in Yiddish studies. It thus enables students from around the world who have acquired basic literacy in Yiddish to meet and to improve their 'cultural literacy' through an intensive introduction to the field.

Beyond the need for increased emphasis on training in basic skills, Yiddish's post-vernacular status has brought about a shift in the emphases of the field. With the diminished numbers of native Yiddish speakers, those branches of scholarship have especially suffered which most depend on an ongoing speech community and cultural milieu. Of the four sections created by YIVO in 1925, Economic-Statistics and Psychology-Pedagogy have little counterpart in current research. YIVO scholars originally envisioned work in those fields as addressing the problems of contemporary Jewish society, and in the post-war years Max Weinreich continued to apply to American Jewish youth the methodology he developed in his study of Polish Jewish adolescents of the 1930s. Yet today few scholars of Yiddish studies are drawn from the social sciences, with exceptions such as sociolinguists (J. Fishman 2001, 1991; Isaacs and Glinert 1999; Peltz 1998) and political scientists writing on topics such as the Jewish Labor Bund (Jacobs 2001). A larger group with roots in this tradition consists of ethnographers and cultural anthropologists whose approach is often theoretically sophisticated (Boyarin 1996, 1994, 1991; Kirshenblatt-Gimblett 1996; Kliger 1992; Kugelmass 1996; Kugelmass and Boyarin 1998). Far from the empirical studies of Jewish economic distribution, demography, and education produced in the inter-war period, such work is one of the few areas where Yiddish studies may be said to be on the cutting edge of scholarship.

While the disciplines comprising philology—that is, linguistics, literature, and folklore—remain central to Yiddish scholarship, here too one can observe the impact of Yiddish's demographic decline. One tendency of recent research is to examine the products of Yiddish culture in historical perspective, rather than as artefacts of inherent interest in their own right. Put another way, in the absence of a vibrant Yiddish secular culture scholars often feel compelled to justify the value of examining a particular poem or proverb by reference to some larger context. In addition, a sense that the golden age of Jewish creativity in Yiddish has passed leads some to take a retrospective view, feeling that the time is now ripe to take stock of the achievements and shortcomings of Yiddish culture. In this vein, recent work on Yiddish folklore deals not with folksongs or stories per se but with the history of folklore collection (Biran 1997–8; Gottesman, forthcoming; Kiel 1992, 1991; Kuznitz, forthcoming), and an important linguistic study treats the history of Yiddish spelling (Schaechter 1999). Many literary critics consider poetry and prose as parts of more sweeping trends in Jewish life rather than focus on their aesthetic and formal qualities alone. Such work is thus at least as much cultural history as textual analysis (Cammy 2001; Nowersztern 1989b; Roskies 1999, 1995; Wisse 2000, 1991, 1988), although this is less true in general of Israeli literary scholarship.

This observation raises the thorny question of the relationship between Jewish history and Yiddish studies, a question which reflects the difficulty of defining the boundaries of the field as a whole. The founders of YIVO included the study of all aspects of the past of Yiddish-speaking communities in their definition of the field. Today, many would limit that designation to topics that touch directly on the production or consumption of Yiddish culture, rather than including all activities in which Yiddish-speaking Jews engage. As Yiddish scholarship has moved into the mainstream of academia, work that treats aspects of Yiddish culture is produced in the History departments of American universities (D. Fishman 1996; Kassow 1991b; Kuznitz 1998; Michels 2000; Moss 2001; Stein 1997; Shneer 2000; Soyer 1999; Veidlinger 2000). In Israel, some scholars deal with related topics in the history of Jewish politics (Mendelsohn 1993; Mintz 1995, 1993). The increasing focus on linguistic, literary, and folkloristic topics in a historical mode portends the closer intersection of these fields with history proper, as well as a growing role for historical research in all areas of Yiddish studies.

While the decline of Yiddish as a daily vernacular has had a decided impact on the direction of the field, one should also note the work of those who focus on Yiddish in the present tense. These include linguists who examine Jewish communities that continue to use Yiddish as a daily tongue or who at least have native fluency, such as Hasidim (Fader 2000; Isaacs and Glinert 1999), senior citizens of East European background (Peltz 1998), and elderly Yiddish speakers in Eastern Europe (the subject of ongoing work by Dovid Katz). Another strand of recent scholarship takes as its subject the very marginality of Yiddish in contemporary Jewish society, examining the place of the language in American Jewish culture (Shandler 2000) and the reception of the work of Isaac Bashevis Singer in English translation (Hadda 1997; Wolitz 2001). Essays surveying the current state of Yiddish in many settings may be found in the collection *Yiddish in the Contemporary World* (Estraikh and Krutikov 1999).

The post-vernacular status of Yiddish has also directed attention to areas of Yiddish culture less demanding of literacy. This accounts in part for the widespread success in the last two decades of the so-called klezmer revival, which now includes Yiddish folk, theatre, art, and liturgical music as well as klezmer properly defined, that is, traditional East European instrumental music. Klezmer music gained popularity in part as an entrée into Yiddish culture for those with little or no knowledge of the language itself. In addition to sparking new forms of Jewish artistic expression, the klezmer revival is now leading to a wave of serious research into the history of East European Jewish music. Supplementing extensive liner notes in many reissues of older recordings and albums re-creating or reinterpreting traditional idioms, there has recently appeared a wave of scholarly publications on klezmer (Slobin 2001, 2000; Slobin *et al.* 1998), and other types of East European Jewish music (Kalib 2001; Rubin 2000; Slobin 1996), as well as editions of the work of the Soviet Yiddish musicologist Moshe Beregovski (2001, 2000).

Another way to make Yiddish culture accessible is through the visual image. In addition to the valuable volumes of photographs published by YIVO on Polish (Dobroszycki and Kirshenblatt-Gimblett 1994) and Russian (Gitelman 2001) Jewry, are photo essays (Gavril 1996; Newman 1993; Weintraub 1993) and volumes devoted to the work of individual photographers (Kacyzne 1999; Vishniac 1999). Scholars have also recently turned their attention to Yiddish film (Hoberman 1991; Paskin 1999). Of several recent films on the klezmer revival, notable is *Tickle in the Heart* (1997); the best documentary treatment of East European Jewish life and culture remains *Image Before My Eyes* (1980). Finally, one should note a last result of declining Yiddish literacy, the increased effort to translate Yiddish texts, which will be discussed in detail below.

Yiddish Studies As a Post-Ideological Field

At the same time that contemporary Yiddish studies comes to terms with the language's demise as a vernacular, it is also shaped by the fading of the ideological turmoil out of which the field was born. As it emerged at the start of the twentieth century, modern Yiddish scholarship was allied with the programme of Diaspora Nationalism and thus enmeshed in the political controversies raging on the Jewish street. A century later such momentous events as the Holocaust, the establishment of the State of Israel, and the fall of the Soviet Union have overtaken such divisions. As the urgency of ideological rivalries recedes, scholars can look past the dichotomies of Yiddishists versus Zionists, pro- versus anti-communists, and *frume* (religious) versus *fraye* (secular) that for so long marked Jewish society. Only now, two generations after the events of 1939–45 and 1948, are young scholars at a sufficient remove from these once-burning debates that Yiddish studies may be said to be entering its post-ideological phase.

Since Yiddish studies as a scholarly endeavour was long identified with Yiddishism as a cultural and political movement, it was implicitly set in opposition to the Zionist promotion of the Hebrew language. With the creation of the State of Israel and the revival of Hebrew as a modern tongue, however, the so-called 'language war' has lost its relevance. The long-standing antipathy to Yiddish in Israel is beginning to fade, and the notion that Yiddishism is incompatible with support for Zionism has lost whatever validity it once had in the diaspora (in Israel, the leading figures in Yiddish scholarship were from the start committed Zionists). The academic world reflects these developments, as scholars look beyond the dichotomy of Yiddish–Hebrew to explore the interactions and intersections between the two. Some have used new theoretical frameworks such as gender studies to discover insights into the relationship between the two tongues (Seidman 1997). Others examine the work of bilingual writers (Feldman 1986; Szeintuch 2000) or the Yiddish literature produced in Israel (Chaver 2001). Another approach considers selected themes in the two literatures in tandem (Dauber 1999; Kronfeld 1996; Mann 1997; Sokoloff *et al.* 1992). The series of critical editions of literary texts published by the Hebrew University has featured the Yiddish work of well-known Hebrew authors (Agnon 1977; Bin-Gorion 1981; Grinberg 1979; Reuveni 1991; Steinberg 1986), thus assuring attention from Hebrew specialists. Finally, some recent studies of Jewish cultural history examine work in Yiddish, Hebrew, and non-Jewish languages in a comparative framework (Cohen 1995; Moss, forthcoming; Shmeruk 1989).

The fall of the Soviet Union and the end of the Cold War broke down barriers both metaphorically and literally within the Jewish world. On one level, these events made it possible to lay to rest old ideological conflicts over support for or opposition to communism. At the same time, they also made a wealth of new archival material, inaccessible for half a century, suddenly available to Western scholars. These developments have led to a wave of new research into Soviet Yiddish culture. Supplementing the classic anthology of Soviet Yiddish literature *A shpigl oyf a shteyn* (Shmeruk 1987), work has recently appeared on language planning (Estraikh 1999), publishing (Shneer 2001, 2000), theatre (Veidlinger 2000), and identity (Shternshis 2000), as well as on the Jewish Autonomous Region in Birobidzan (Kotlerman 2001; Weinberg 1998). Scholars are also examining the Yiddish press (Michels 2001), theatre (Nachshon 1998), and literature (Glaser 2000) produced by American supporters of communism. With the fading of Cold War antagonisms, the time is now ripe for a reappraisal of Soviet Yiddish scholarship, which despite its tendentiousness can yield valuable insights if read with care (Krutikov 1994; Shmeruk and Turniansky 1993).

Their many points of divergence notwithstanding, most Yiddishists, Zionists, and communists (of course, not mutually exclusive categories) shared the assumption that modern Jewish culture would be constructed on a secular basis. Thus, scholarship rooted in all of these ideologies tends to dismiss Orthodox Jews as irrelevant to the key issues of the day. With the resurgence of Orthodoxy, however, secular and religious camps are no longer so starkly opposed in Jewish life—at least in the diaspora—and the traditionalist segment of Jewish society has become the subject of increasing attention. One promising direction for future research is thus to examine points of contact between Yiddish cultural movements and Orthodox communities and individuals (Caplan, forthcoming; J. Fishman 1987). Another is to explore the vibrant phenomena of Yiddish language use and cultural production among Hasidim. Ironically, Yiddish studies has largely ignored the only demographically significant group that continues to use Yiddish as a day-to-day language, although—in a double irony—Hasidism is the only Orthodox Jewish movement which has received sustained attention from Jewish historians (see Stanislawski's article). While scholars have examined early Hasidic literature in Yiddish, only recently have they turned their attention to issues such as contemporary Hasidic Yiddish language use (Fader 2000; Isaacs and Glinert 1999). Many other aspects of Hasidic culture await similar treatment (Epstein 1998; Isaacs 1998; Mitchell 1999).

The trends I have described point to a more inclusive and multivalent picture of creativity in Yiddish, one which is not limited by ideologically imposed blinckers. It seeks to encompass many different segments of the Jewish community and to take into account the sometimes complex overlap between them. Yet it should be noted that this vision merely follows the contours mapped by the leading scholars of Yiddish studies decades ago. In his *History of the Yiddish Language* (1980), Max Weinreich left behind the secularist approach of his youth to reconceive of Ashkenazic Jewish culture as *derekh hashas* (the way of the Talmud). In Israel Dov Sadan went against the grain of Zionist scholarship to consider Hebrew and Yiddish literature in tandem, while his student Chone Shmeruk produced studies on topics ranging from Old Yiddish literature to Soviet Yiddish writing. If younger scholars pursue work that crosses ideological boundaries, they merely fulfill the agendas set forth by these pioneering figures.

As Yiddish studies grows more accepted within the academy and more distant from its roots in Diaspora Nationalism, it also becomes better suited to examine the ideological ground from which it sprang. In this vein, scholars are now considering the institutions and individuals who pioneered Yiddish scholarship (Frakes 1989; Kerler 1991; Kuznitz 2000; Trachtenberg 2001; Weiser 2001) as well as key moments in the formulation of Yiddishist cultural programmes and political agendas (Krutikov 2001, Moss, forthcoming; see also the articles collected in Kerler 1998). No longer compelled to extol the achievements of Yiddish to counter the language's traditionally low status, they are also free to explore aspects of Yiddish popular culture including literature (Kellman 2000) and theatre (Berkowitz 2002; Steinlauf 1995; Warnke 2001).

At the same time, emerging ideological concerns have brought new approaches to Yiddish studies. Some critics look askance at those attracted to Yiddish because they perceive this as consonant with their personal political or intellectual commitments, usually of a liberal stripe. Certainly, harnessing Yiddish scholarship to any set of orthodoxies—old or new—has the potential for distortion, particularly if such work is not equally driven by a solid grounding in the field. Yet in the hands of competent scholars, fresh concerns and perspectives can have an invigorating effect. To cite a notable example, feminists have brought new methodologies to the study of Yiddish texts, producing work on topics as varied as *tkhines* (Yiddish supplicatory prayers) (Weissler 1998) and modern Jewish literature (Seidman 1997; Sokoloff *et al.* 1992). They have also focused attention on the work of female writers of prose (Forman *et al.* 1994), poetry (Molodowsky 1999; Tusman 1992), and memoir (Rakowsky 2002).

While Yiddish's post-vernacularity leads some scholars to privilege historical sweep over close textual analysis, one might also argue that the decreasing weight of ideologically based agendas better allows critics to consider literary texts on their own intrinsic merit. Thus, along with the literary-historical works cited above, there have recently appeared studies of particular genres such as autobiography (Moseley 2002, 1990; Schwarz 1997; Shandler 2002), individual writers (Bechtel 1990; Kritz 1997; Norich 1991; Nowersztern 1992, 1990; Rozier 1999), and literary generations (Frieden 1995; Glau 1999). Scholars can consider literature at the same time in historical perspective and in formal terms, and the most ambitious works transcend the dichotomy of focusing on either text or context; Dan Miron's recently reissued classic *A Traveler Disguised* (Miron 1996) is at once an account of the origins of modern Yiddish literature and a critique of the traditional Yiddishist view of the writings of S. Y. Abramovitsh.

It was, of course, the Holocaust that most fundamentally transformed the field of Yiddish studies, thrusting it into its post-vernacular and post-ideological phase. While they still struggle today to assimilate the impact of the catastrophe, Yiddish scholars long ago began to make it the subject of their work. Some of the earliest studies of the Holocaust came from the ranks of YIVO affiliates, including Max Weinreich's *Hitler's Professors* (Weinreich 1999), originally published—remarkably—in 1946, and Isaiah Trunk's *Judenrat* (Trunk 1996), originally published in 1972. These appeared in a period when the topic was virtually ignored in mainstream academia. Yet many in Yiddish studies have since felt a reluctance to focus on the years of the Second World War, not wishing to overshadow the lives of Yiddish-speaking Jews with accounts of their destruction. Meanwhile, Holocaust scholars have been mostly drawn from the ranks of European historians with no knowledge of Jewish languages and thus unable to make use of the rich documentary and literary record compiled in Yiddish during and after the war. The ironic result is that while Holocaust studies now flourishes, it has little considered the perspectives of the victims themselves or the context of their experiences in the pre-war years.

Holocaust specialists have begun to recognize and rectify this imbalance, devoting more attention to Jewish responses to Nazi persecution. Yiddish scholars are also exploring Holocaust-related topics, including the activities of the Jewish Labor Bund during the war (Blatman 1996) and the life of the ghettos (D. Fishman 1996; Flam 1992; Kruk, forthcoming; Sakowska 1997; Shapiro 1999), helping to put to rest the one-dimensional view of Jews as passive victims of Nazi aggression. Despite the important work of figures such as David Roskies (1989, 1984), much also remains to be done in the field of Holocaust literature and memoir. The study of these genres is today so extensive as to constitute a field in its own right. Much of this work, however, fails to consider accounts produced in Yiddish, many of which were written during and immediately after the war. It instead relies heavily on sources composed at a greater chronological distance, in languages not native to the author, and solely by those who survived. It thus obscures crucial issues such as points of continuity between pre-war and wartime culture, the distinction between works composed close to the events they record and those at a distance of several decades, and the implications of writing for a Jewish versus a general audience. They also perpetuate the myth that survivors were silent in the aftermath of the war. Some Yiddish scholars are now addressing these questions (Norich 1998–9; Seidman 1996), contributing to both a better grounded and a more sophisticated approach to the study of Holocaust literature. A closer relationship between Yiddish studies and Holocaust scholarship has much to contribute to our understanding of the catastrophe, placing it in its Jewish context and giving long-overdue attention to the most heroic chapter of Yiddish cultural creativity.

CONTINUED IDEOLOGICAL CONFICT OVER YIDDISH'S POST-VERNACULAR STATUS

While Yiddish studies today is no longer characterized by the ideological fervour which marked the birth of field, internal debates do persist over the controversial theories of the linguist Paul Wexler (Wexler 2002, 1993) on the origins of Ashkenazic Jewry and the spelling reforms advocated by Dovid Katz (Katz 1993, 1987a). The most contentious issue, however, refers back to what I have termed Yiddish's post-vernacularity. Yiddish studies today is divided over the question of how to regard its subject: as an essentially closed chapter of Jewish history or as an ongoing culture. Those of the former opinion stress the lack of a demographically significant Yiddish-speaking community and the improbability that great works of literature will still be produced in the language. They see no reason to preserve Yiddish through deliberate effort, writing and speaking it if it is not one's mother tongue. Their opponents point out that Yiddish continues to flourish in the Hasidic world as well as among numerically tiny but dedicated groups of Yiddishists. Moreover, they add, Yiddish newspapers, journals, and books continue to publish new Yiddish writing, making it the envy of many so-called endangered languages.

Extending this debate to academic circles, some maintain that teaching and publishing in English or Hebrew is most efficient and allows work to reach a wide audience. Others counter that the training of Yiddish specialists should be sufficiently thorough to instill an active as well as a passive knowledge of the language. Furthermore, they argue, publishing in Yiddish serves a useful function by creating a forum for scholars in the United States, Israel, and Western and Eastern Europe who might otherwise share no common tongue. These divisions came to the fore in the reception of Benjamin Harshav's *The Meaning of Yiddish* (2000). Critics such as the linguist Mordkhe Schaechter took Harshav to task for describing Yiddish language and culture as essentially dead (as well as for his shortcomings in dealing with linguistic matters). For their part, Harshav's defenders complain that Schaechter's lexicographic work (Schaechter 1991, 1988) is overly prescriptive, given the limited number of secular Yiddish speakers requiring vocabulary for the latest technological innovations.

While the pursuit of Yiddish scholarship in Yiddish was central to the conception of the founders of the field, this vision has declined along with the numbers of native-born speakers and ideologically committed Yiddishists. As mentioned above, today YIVO has largely abandoned the practice of treating Yiddish as a living tongue, although it continues to publish, albeit irregularly, the journal *YIVO Bleter* (YIVO Pages). In recent years Dovid Katz and his heirs at Oxford carried on the Borokhov/YIVO tradition of teaching and publishing in Yiddish, while in the United States the graduate programmes at Columbia and the Jewish Theological Seminary have been prominent in training scholars with Yiddish fluency. In German and Israeli universities, many graduate-level classes are conducted in Yiddish. With the status of the Yiddish studies summer programmes at Oxford and Columbia currently unclear, it remains to be seen how viable the approach of *yidish oyf yidish* (Yiddish in Yiddish) will prove in the future.

These debates at first suggest that conflicts over Yiddishist ideology are alive and well. In fact, however, they are the exception that proves the rule, for scholars' views on these issues have little correlation to their methodology and choice of topics. Rather than approaching Yiddish literature in a historicist vein, Harshav pioneered the study of its formal qualities. Schaechter's lifework is marked by the commitment to treating Yiddish in the present tense, yet he has also produced a history of Yiddish spelling (Schaechter 1999). Both Avraham Nowersztern of Hebrew University and Ruth Wisse of Harvard University conduct graduate courses in Yiddish for pedagogical, not ideological, reasons. Not only Dovid Katz, the committed Yiddishist, but also Benjamin Harshav, who professes to believe that the language is dead, have recently published works of Yiddish fiction. Thus, as Yiddish creativity continues, the field is enlivened but not determined by divergent views of the future of Yiddish itself.

TRENDS IN YIDDISH PUBLISHING

One sign of the vitality of Yiddish studies is the appearance of a wave of new publications that both facilitate research in the field and make the fruits of Yiddish scholarship and culture accessible to a wider audience. In New York, YIVO has recently published important new reference works to guide users through the rich collections of its archives (Mohrer and Web 1998) and library (Baker and Weinberg 1990). In the former Soviet Union, the end of the Cold War has brought to light a wealth of material that Western scholars believed long destroyed. Surveys of repositories in the former Soviet lands, some conducted as part of Project Judaica, have revealed important new sources for Yiddish studies which scholars have only begun to explore (Kupovetskii *et al.* 1997; Sallis *et al.* 1996). In France, Yitskhok Niborski published a highly useful dictionary of the Hebrew and Aramaic component of Yiddish (Niborski 1999), while YIVO has reissued reference works such as Alexander Harkavy's *Yiddish–English–Hebrew Dictionary* (1998) and Nahum Stutchkoff's *Thesaurus of the Yiddish Language* (1991). YIVO also plans a new English edition of Weinreich's *History of the Yiddish Language* (1980); the original translation is incomplete and has long been out of print.

In some cases, important publication projects have taken decades to reach fruition. *The Biographical Dictionary of Modern Yiddish Literature*, begun in 1956, brought out its last volume in 1981 (Niger *et al.* 1956–81; see also Kagan 1986). In 1959 Uriel Weinreich began work on the *Language and Culture Atlas of Ashkenazic Jewry*, originally intended to document Yiddish dialects while fieldwork among native speakers would still be possible. Continued after Weinreich's untimely death by Marvin Herzog of Columbia University, the *Atlas* became a monumental effort to map many features of the culture of Yiddish-speaking Jews across the expanse of both Western and Eastern Europe. In 1992 this wealth of material finally began to be published (Baviskar *et al.* 1992–), and future volumes are eagerly awaited. A less happy fate has so far befallen the *Great Dictionary of the Yiddish Language* (Joffe and Mark 1961–), designed as the definitive lexicographic reference work on Yiddish in Yiddish. Four volumes (covering the letter aleph) of a projected twelve appeared between 1961 and 1980, first in New York under the editorship of Judah A. Joffe and Yudel Mark and later in Israel after Joffe's death. For two decades personal and institutional acrimonies, as well as the increasing cost of and diminished audience for scholarly publications in Yiddish, have hindered the completion of this essential tool.

Declining Yiddish literacy has also made more difficult the continued production of academic journals in Yiddish. A serious blow was the demise in 1995 of *Di goldene keyt* (The Golden Chain), published in Israel by the eminent poet Avraham Sutzkever since 1949. In the 1990s the Oxford Institute for Yiddish Studies issued a number of journals, including *Oksforder yidish* (Oxford Yiddish) (1990) and

Di pen (The Pen) (1994–8), which have since ceased publication. These gaps have only been partially filled by the founding in 2000 of *Toplpunkt* (Colon), an Israeli quarterly primarily devoted to literature. This publication is sponsored by the government-funded National Agency for Yiddish Culture, and one hopes it will prove only the first of this new body's worthwhile undertakings. In New York YIVO revived its *YIVO Bleter* in 1991, but only three issues have appeared to date, while Mordkhe Schaechter continues to edit the linguistically oriented *Afn shvel* (On the Threshold) (1941–   ). Finally, under the helm of Boris Sandler the venerable *Forverts* (Forward) (1897–   ), now a weekly, frequently publishes material of interest to the Yiddish scholar and serves as a forum for news and the occasional exchange of views for those in the field.

While the tongue's post-vernacular status has limited outlets for scholarly publishing in Yiddish, it has created new incentives for the translation of many genres of Yiddish writing. YIVO's publication in English of annotated selections from its archival collections of Yiddish folk-tales (B. Weinreich 1997) and autobiographies collected in Poland (Shandler 2002; see also Moseley 2002) and the United States (see Soyer 1999) make these important materials more widely accessible. Yiddish memoirs rendered into English (Bergner, forthcoming; Kotik 2002; Rakovsky 2002) and Hebrew (Kotik 1998) are a valuable source, as are journalistic accounts (Abramowicz 1999) and scholarly studies (Miron 2000) of East European Jewish life and culture. The appearance of Yiddish diaries and other writings of the Second World War in translation (Kruk, forthcoming) should help to correct some of the current shortcomings of Holocaust scholarship. The Jewish Historical Institute in Warsaw is now publishing parts of the Oyneg Shabes archive directed by Emanuel Ringelblum in the Warsaw ghetto, with translations of selected documents (Sakowska 1997). It is to be hoped that this project will continue and become better known outside of Poland, bringing long-overdue recognition to Ringelblum and his colleagues.

While rendering Yiddish literature into other languages has a long history, recent years have seen increased attention to translations of Yiddish poetry and prose into English (Abramovitsh 1996; Ansky 1992; Bergelson 1999; Buloff 1991; Manger 2002; Molodowsky 1999; Neugroschel 2002a, b, 2001a, b; Neugroschel and Kushner 1998; Peretz 2002; Sandrow 1999; Sholem Aleichem 2002, 1996; Shteynbarg, forthcoming; Sutzkever 1991, 1990; Tusman 1992) and Hebrew (Abramovitsh 2000, 1994, 1984), as well as to the process of translation itself (Hellerstein 2000; Rosenwald 2001). This new emphasis may be explained in part by the greater responsibility felt by the translator who knows that his or her work is the only way in which most readers will come to know a Yiddish text. A new chapter in Yiddish translation was inaugurated with the appearance of two bilingual anthologies, *American Yiddish Poetry*, edited and translated by Barbara and Benjamin Harshav (1986), and *The Penguin Book of Modern Yiddish Verse*, edited by Irving Howe, Chone Shmeruk, and Ruth Wisse (1987). Both volumes include Yiddish originals alongside high-quality English translations, acknowledging the need to address a new, dual audience: both the serious student of Yiddish who can read the original texts but lacks full fluency, and the non-specialist with an interest in Yiddish culture but no access to its original texts.

While *American Yiddish Poetry* concentrates on a limited number of modernist authors, the sweeping *Penguin Book* covers all trends of modern Yiddish verse, implicitly establishing one version of a Yiddish poetical canon. It thus reflects a view of Yiddish literature as a rapidly closing body of work on whose pantheon of great writers one may now pass critical judgement. The perceived need both to raise the standard of translation and to establish a canon of classic texts has recently led to several ambitious new publication projects. Schocken Books brought out five volumes of its Library of Yiddish Classics before discontinuing the series; now under the auspices of Yale University Press and the editorship of David Roskies, the Modern Yiddish Library has reprinted the Schocken translations (Abramovitsh 1996; Ansky 1992; Peretz 2002; Sholem Aleichem 1996; B. Weinreich 1997) and plans additional titles, some of which have begun to appear (Manger 2002; Sholem Aleichem 2002). In Israel, over the last two decades, Aryeh Aharoni has published several dozen volumes of Sholem Aleichem's work in Hebrew translation. The Sholem Aleichem Foundation of New York is laying plans to match that effort with a fifteen-volume edition of the works of its namesake in English. Finally, the Dora Teitelboim Foundation of Coral Gables, Florida, also sponsors useful translations of Yiddish literature (Goodman 2001).

As reading knowledge of Yiddish is increasingly confined to specialists, the appearance of reliable translations of Yiddish texts makes these sources available to a broad audience and allows scholars in other fields to incorporate elements of Yiddish culture into their research and teaching. In this way, translation can play an important role in bringing Yiddish scholarship into a closer and more productive relationship with other areas of Jewish studies, as well as with the wider Jewish public. While these developments can only be welcomed, one should also note a caveat. By placing too much weight on the value of translation, one can foster the mistaken impression that an acquaintance with the relatively tiny percentage of sources accessible to the non-Yiddish reader is sufficient for a grasp of Yiddish culture. Popular taste plays a role in decisions over which translations to publish, thus under- or over-representing particular authors or literary movements. Even with rising standards, many inferior translations still appear in print and few bother to evaluate the quality of these works; moreover, of course, even the most successful literary translation can rarely match the power of the original. A case in point is the Nobel prize-winner Isaac Bashevis Singer, whose reputation is primarily based on critical assessments of poor or substantially altered English versions of his Yiddish fiction. If, as some maintain, the future of Yiddish is in translation, this will be a much diminished version of a rich culture; it is the responsibility of Yiddish scholars to insist on presenting that culture in all its depth and variety.

While academic publishing faces new challenges in the twenty-first century, emerging technologies are also creating tools which can further Yiddish scholarship. Indeed, the combination of a rich documentary record with a small and widely dispersed target audience makes Yiddish studies an excellent candidate to benefit from the reduced costs and easier distribution promised by these new ventures. A prime example is the Steven Spielberg Digital Yiddish Library of the National Yiddish Book Center, which produces on-demand reprints of Yiddish titles which are otherwise available only in major research libraries or at prohibitively high cost. This pioneering project can serve as a model for other small fields whose literatures are largely out of print. Another important initiative is the Index to Yiddish Periodicals sponsored by the Yiddish Department of the Hebrew University. This on-line database, available through the Aleph network, has already indexed the contents of many major East European Yiddish newspapers and journals. It is to be hoped that a more user-friendly interface can be developed which will make this valuable tool better known and more easily accessible outside of Israel.

The internet has also proved a boon to Yiddish studies, allowing geographically distant scholars in the United States, Israel, Europe, and elsewhere to communicate easily. Founded in 1991, the listserve Mendele and its offshoot, *The Mendele Review* (http://shakti.cc.trincoll.edu/~mendele), feature material relevant to the academic as well as to the interested public. Several web-sites have been developed which take advantage of the audio-visual capabilities of the World Wide Web to present various aspects of Yiddish culture. The site of the Yiddish Radio Project (http://www.yiddishradioproject.org) includes sound files of historic radio broadcasts which can be played along with a running English translation. The German-based EYDES Project (http://www.eydes.org) is making the data of the *Language and Culture Atlas of Ashkenazic Jewry* available online, with such features as an interactive map of Yiddish dialects. A similar strategy of web-based publication could fruitfully be employed for the *Great Dictionary of the Yiddish Language*, allowing scholars to consult at least elements of this important resource until or unless a print version is realized. In this and other ways, the technologies of a new century can help both to preserve the culture of the past and to facilitate new research as Yiddish studies looks towards its future.

CONCLUSION

If Yiddish studies today little resembles the vision of its founders a century ago, this reflects at once its achievements and limitations. Two generations after the decimation of Yiddish-speaking Jewry, the ideal has faded of scholarship conducted in

Yiddish that would address issues vital to a broad Jewish public. At the same time, the limited success of independent institutions and programmes devoted to Yiddish studies can be seen as a positive sign, marking the increasing acceptance of the field in the university setting within the larger framework of Jewish studies. Growing chronological distance from the ideological debates of its birth and greater integration into the academy create the possibility of bringing fresh perspectives to the study of Yiddish culture. Yet as the number of native speakers and the forums for serious training in Yiddish studies diminish, the field must strive to maintain its integrity. Scholars will have to negotiate both these new challenges and opportunities as they bring Yiddish studies into the twenty-first century.

SUGGESTED READING

On the history and current state of Yiddish studies, see Katz (1986); Krutikov (2002); Nowersztern (1989a); Prager (1996, 1981); Roskies (1981); and many of the essays in Estraikh and Krutikov (1999). On bibliography, see Bratkowsky (1988) and Bunis and Sunshine (1994). For a sense of current work in English, review the collections by Estraikh and Krutikov (2001, 2000, 1999); Katz (1988, 1987b); Kerler (1998, 1991), the *YIVO Annual*, the most recent volume of *The Field of Yiddish* (Goldberg 1993), and relevant articles in *Prooftexts*, a journal devoted to Jewish literature. For an overview of Yiddish studies in Israel consult the journals *Di goldene keyt* and *Hulyot*; for Germany, *Jiddistik-Mitteilungen*. The contributions to *The Life and Times of Yiddish* (Landis 2000) and *Yiddish Language and Culture: Then and Now* (Greenspoon 1998) offer a good overview of the field, but are somewhat uneven.

BIBLIOGRAPHY

ABRAMOVITSH, S. Y. (Mendele Moykher Sforim) 1984. *Ha'ishon hakatan. Dos kleyne ment-shele.* Ed. and trans. S. Luria. Haifa.
—— 1994. *Ktavim be'ibam: Dos vintshfingerl* and *Fishke der krumer.* Ed. and trans. S. Luria. Haifa.
—— 1996. *Tales of Mendele the Book Peddler: Fishke the Lame and Benjamin the Third.* Eds. D. Miron and K. Frieden. Trans. T. Gorelick and H. Halkin. New York.
—— 2000. *Perek shira.* Ed. and trans. S. Luria. Haifa.
ABRAMOWICZ, H. 1999. *Profiles of a Lost World: Memoirs of East European Jewish Life Before World War II.* Eds. D. Abramowicz and J. Shandler. Trans. E. Z. Dobkin. Detroit.
AGNON, S. Y. 1977. *Yiddish Works* [Yiddish]. Ed. Dov Sadan. Jerusalem.
ANSKY, S. 1992. *The Dybbuk and Other Writings.* Ed. D. Roskies. Trans. G. Werman. New York.
BAKER, Z. M. and WEINBERG, B. H. eds. 1990. *The Yiddish Catalog and Authority File of the YIVO Library* [Yiddish]. Boston.

BARTAL, I., MENDELSOHN, E., and TURNIANSKY, C. eds. 1993. *Studies in Jewish Culture in Honor of Chone Shmeruk* [Hebrew]. Jerusalem.

BAUMGARTEN, J. 1993. *Introduction à la litérature yiddish ancienne*. Paris.

—— and BUNIS, D. eds. 1999. *Le Yiddish: langue, culture, société*. Paris.

—— ERTEL, R., NIBORSKI, I., and WIEVIORKA, A. eds. 1994. *Mille ans de cultures ashkénazes*. Paris.

BAVISKAR, V., HERZOG, M., and WEINREICH, U. eds. 1992– . *The Language and Culture Atlas of Ashkenazic Jewry*. Tübingen.

BECHTEL, D. 1990. *Der Nister's Work, 1907–1929: A Study of a Yiddish Symbolist*. Berne.

BEREGOVSKI, M. 2000. *Old Jewish Folk Music: The Collections and Writings of Moshe Beregovski*. Ed. and trans. M. Slobin. Syracuse, NY.

—— 2001. *Jewish Instrumental Folk Music: The Collections and Writings of Moshe Beregovski*. Eds. and trans. M. Slobin, R. Rothstein, and M. Alpert. Syracuse, NY.

BERGELSON, D. 1999. *Opgang/Descent*. Trans. J. Sherman. New York.

BERGNER, H. forthcoming. *In the Long Winter Nights: Memoirs of a Jewish Family in a Galician Township, 1870–1890*. Trans. J. Cammy. College Park, Md.

BERKOWITZ, J. 2002 *Shakespeare on the American Yiddish Stage*. Iowa.

—— ed. forthcoming. *The Yiddish Theatre: New Approaches*. London.

BEUKERS, M. and WAALE, R. eds. 1992. *Tracing An-Sky: Jewish Collections from the State Ethnographic Museum in St Petersburg*. Zwolle, Netherlands.

BIN-GORION, M. J. [Berdyczewski]. 1981. *Yiddish Works of a Distant Relative* [Yiddish]. Ed. S. Werses. Jerusalem.

BIRAN, R. 1997–8. 'Parashat berl verblunski, asfan folklor be-folin ben shtey milkhamot ha-olam'. *Mekhere yerushalayim be-folklor yehudi* 19–20: 239–270.

BLATMAN, D. 1996. *For Our Freedom and Yours: The Bund in Poland, 1939–1949* [Hebrew]. Jerusalem.

BOYARIN, J. 1991. *Polish Jews in Paris: The Ethnography of Memory*. Bloomington, Ind.

—— 1994. *A Storyteller's Worlds: The Education of Shlomo Noble in Europe and America*. New York.

—— 1996. *Thinking in Jewish*. Chicago.

BRATKOWSKY, J. 1988. *Yiddish Linguistics: A Multilingual Bibliography*. New York.

BULOFF, J. 1991. *From the Old Marketplace*. Trans. J. Singer. Cambridge, Mass.

BUNIS, D. and SUNSHINE, A. 1994. *Yiddish Linguistics: A Classified Bilingual Index to Yiddish Serials and Collections, 1913–1958*. New York.

CAMMY, J. 2001. 'Tsevorfene bleter: The Emergence of Yung Vilne.' *Polin* 14: 170–191.

CAPLAN, B. L. forthcoming. 'Orthodox Yiddish Literature in Interwar Poland.' Unpublished Ph.D. diss., Columbia University.

CHAVER, Y. 2001. 'Outcasts Within: Zionist Yiddish Literature in Pre-State Palestine'. *JSS* 7/2: 39–66.

COHEN, N. 1995. 'The Jewish Literary and Journalistic Center in Warsaw between 1920–1942 As Reflected by the Association of Jewish Writers and Journalists.' [Hebrew.] Unpublished Ph.D. diss., Hebrew University of Jerusalem.

DAUBER, J. 1999. 'The Usage of Classical Religious Texts by Early Modern Hebrew and Yiddish Writers of the Enlightenment'. D. Phil. thesis, University of Oxford.

DAWIDOWICZ, L. 1989. *From That Place and Time: A Memoir, 1938–1947*. New York.

—— ed. 1996. *The Golden Tradition: Jewish Life and Thought in Eastern Europe*. (2nd edn). Syracuse, NY.

DINER, H., SHANDLER, J., and WENGER, B. eds. 2000. *Remembering the Lower East Side: American Jewish Reflections*. Bloomington, Ind.

DI VEROLI, E. M. *et al.* 1996. *La Rassegna Mensile di Israel* 62/1–2. (Special issue devoted to Yiddish.)

DOBROSZYCKI, L. 1989. 'YIVO in Interwar Poland: Work in the Historical Sciences.' In *The Jews of Poland Between Two World Wars*. 494–518. Y. Gutman, E. Mendelsohn, J. Reinharz, and C. Shmeruk eds. Hanover, NH.

—— and KIRSHENBLATT-GIMBLETT, B. 1994. *Image Before My Eyes: A Photographic History of Jewish Life in Poland Before the Holocaust*. 2nd edn. New York.

EPSTEIN, S. 1998. *Daniel-shpil in the Bobover Hasidic community* [Hebrew]. Jerusalem.

ERTEL, R. 1986. *Le Shtetl: la bourgade juive de Pologne: de la tradition à la modernité*. Paris.

ESTRAIKH, G. 1999. *Soviet Yiddish: Language Planning and Linguistic Development*. Oxford.

—— and KRUTIKOV, M. eds. 1999. *Yiddish in the Contemporary World*. Oxford.

—— —— eds. 2000. *The Shtetl: Image and Reality*. Oxford.

—— —— eds. 2001. *Yiddish and the Left*. Oxford.

FADER, A. 2000. 'Gender, Morality, and Language: Socialization Practices in a Hasidic Community'. Unpublished Ph.D diss., Columbia University.

FELDMAN. Y. 1986. *Modernism and Cultural Transfer: Gabriel Preil and the Tradition of Jewish Literary Bilingualism*. Hoboken, NJ.

FISHMAN. D. 1989. 'The Politics of Yiddish in Tsarist Russia.' In *From Ancient Israel to Modern Judaism: Intellect in Quest of Understanding: Essays in Honor of Marvin Fox* iv. 155–171. J. Neusner, E. S. Frerichs, and N. M. Sarna eds.

—— 1996. *Embers Plucked From the Fire: The Rescue of Jewish Cultural Treasures in Vilna*. New York.

FISHMAN, J. ed. 1981. *Never Say Die! A Thousand Years of Yiddish in Jewish Life and Letters*. The Hague.

—— 1987. *Ideology, Society and Language: The Odyssey of Nathan Birnbaum*. Ann Arbor, Mich.

—— 1991. *Reversing Language Shift: Theoretical and Applied Foundations of Assistance to Threatened Languages*. London.

—— ed. 1999. *Handbook of Language and Ethnic Identity*. Oxford.

FLAM, G. 1992. *Singing for Survival: Songs of the Lodz Ghetto, 1940–45*. Urbana, Ill.

FORMAN, F., RAICUS, E., SWARTZ, S. S., and WOLFE, M. eds. 1994. *Found Treasures: Stories by Yiddish Women Writers*. Toronto.

FRAKES, J. 1989. *The Politics of Interpretation: Alterity and Ideology in Old Yiddish Studies*. Albany, NY.

FRIEDEN, K. 1995. *Classic Yiddish Fiction: Abramovitsh, Sholem Aleichem, and Peretz*. Albany, NY.

FROST, S. 1998. *Schooling as a Socio-Political Expression: Jewish Education in Interwar Poland*. Jerusalem.

GAVRIL, D. 1996. 'Time Travel Through Photographs: A Family History.' *YIVO Annual* 23: 295–319.

GITELMAN, Z. 2001. *A Century of Ambivalence: The Jews of Russia and the Soviet Union, 1881 to the Present*. 2nd edn. Bloomington, Ind.

GLASER, A. 2000. '*Proletpen* and its Poets: America's Literary Left'. Unpublished M.St. diss., University of Oxford.

GLAU, A. 1999. *Jewish Self-Consciousness in Transition: Yiddish Literature at the Beginning of the Twentieth Century* [German]. Wiesbaden.

GOLDBERG, D. ed. 1993. *The Field of Yiddish: Studies in Language, Folklore, and Literature.* Fifth Collection. Evanston, Ill.

—— 1996. *Yidish af yidish: gramatishe, leksishe, un shmues-materyaln farn tsveytn un dritn lernyor.* New Haven.

GOLDSMITH, E. 1997. *Modern Yiddish Culture: The Story of the Yiddish Language Movement.* 2nd edn. New York.

GOODMAN, H. ed. and trans. 2001. *The New Country: Stories from the Yiddish about Life in America.* Syracuse, NY.

GOTTESMAN, I. forthcoming. *Defining the Yiddish Nation: The Jewish Folklorists of Poland.* Detroit.

GREENSPOON, L. J. ed. 1998. *Yiddish Language and Culture: Then and Now.* Omaha.

GRINBERG, U. Z. 1979. *Collected Yiddish Works* [Yiddish]. 2 vols. Ed. C. Shmeruk. Jerusalem.

GROSSMAN, J. 2000. *The Discourse on Yiddish in Germany from the Enlightenment to the Second Empire.* Rochester, NY.

HADDA, J. 1988. *Passionate Women, Passive Men: Suicide in Yiddish Literature.* Albany, NY.

—— 1997. *Isaac Bashevis Singer: A Life.* New York.

HARKAVY, A. 1998. *Yiddish–English–Hebrew Dictionary.* Reprint edn. New York.

HARSHAV, B. 2000. *The Meaning of Yiddish.* 2nd edn. Stanford.

—— and HARSHAV, B. eds and trans. 1986. *American Yiddish Poetry: A Bilingual Anthology.* Berkeley.

HELLERSTEIN, K. 'Translating as a Feminist: Reconceiving Anna Margolin.' *Prooftexts* 20/1: 191–208.

HILL, B. S. 1999. 'Yiddish Bibliography at Oxford.' In *Report of the Oxford Centre for Hebrew and Jewish Studies, 1998–1999.* 98–132. Oxford.

HOBERMAN, J. 1991. *Bridge of Light: Yiddish Film Between Two Worlds.* New York.

HOWE, I., WISSE, R., and SHMERUK, K. eds. 1987. *The Penguin Book of Modern Yiddish Verse.* New York.

ISAACS, M. 1998. 'Yiddish "Then and Now": Creativity in Contemporary Hasidic Yiddish.' In *Yiddish Language and Culture: Then and Now.* 165–88. L. J. Greenspoon ed. Omaha.

—— and GLINERT, L. eds. 1999. *Pious Voices: Languages Among Ultra-Orthodox Jews.* Berlin.

JACOBS, J. ed. 2001. *Jewish Politics in Eastern Europe: The Bund at 100.* New York.

JACOBS, N. 1998. 'Introduction: A Field of Jewish Geography.' *Shofar* 17/1: 1–18.

JOFFE, J. and MARK, Y. eds. 1961– *Great Dictionary of the Yiddish Language* [Yiddish]. 4 vols. New York and Jerusalem.

KACYZNE, A. 1999. *Poyln: Jewish Life in the Old Country.* Ed. M. Web. New York.

KAGAN, B. 1986. *Lexicon of Yiddish Writers* [Yiddish]. New York.

KALIB, S. 2001. *The Musical Tradition of the Eastern European Synagogue, Volume 1: History and Definition.* Syracuse, NY.

KASSOW, S. 1991a. 'Community and Social Change in the Polish Shtetl, 1900–1939.' In *Jewish Settlement and Community in the Modern Western World.* 56–92. R. Dotterer, D. D. Moore, and S. M. Cohen eds. Cranbury, NJ.

—— 1991b. 'Jewish Communal Politics in Transition: The Vilna *Kehile*, 1919–1920.' *YIVO Annual* 20: 61–91.

KATZ, D. 1986. 'On Yiddish, in Yiddish, and for Yiddish: 500 Years of Yiddish Scholarship.' In *Identity and Ethos: A Festschrift for Sol Liptzin on the Occasion of His 85th Birthday.* 23–36. M. Gelber ed. New York.

—— 1987a. *Grammar of the Yiddish Language.* London.

—— ed 1987b. *Origins of the Yiddish Language.* Oxford.

—— ed. 1988. *Dialects of the Yiddish Language.* Oxford.

—— 1993. *Amended Amendments: Issues in Yiddish Stylistics* [Yiddish]. Oxford.

KELLMAN, E. 2000. 'The Newspaper Novel in the *Jewish Daily Forward*, 1900–1940: Fiction as Entertainment and Serious Literature.' Unpublished Ph.D. diss, Columbia University.

KERLER, D. ed. 1991. *History of Yiddish Studies.* Chur and Philadelphia.

—— ed. 1998. *The Politics of Yiddish.* Walnut Creek, Cal.

—— 1999. *The Origins of Modern Literary Yiddish.* New York.

KIEL, M. 1991. 'A Twice Lost Legacy: Ideology, Culture and the Pursuit of Jewish Folklore in Russia Until Stalinization (1930–1931).' Unpublished Ph.D. diss., Jewish Theological Seminary.

—— 1992. 'Vox Populi, Vox Dei: The Centrality of Peretz in Jewish Folkloristics.' *Polin* 7: 88–120.

KIRSHENBLATT-GIMBLETT, B. 1996. 'Coming of Age in the Thirties: Max Weinreich, Edward Sapir, and Jewish Social Science.' *YIVO Annual* 23: 1–103.

KLIGER, H. 1992. *Jewish Hometown Associations and Family Circles in New York: The WPA Yiddish Writers' Group Study.* Bloomington, Ind.

KOTIK, Y. 1998. *Mah she-ra'iti: zikhronotav shel Yehezkel Kotik.* Ed. and trans. D. Assaf. Tel-Aviv.

—— 2002. *A Journey to a Nineteenth-Century Shtetl: The Memoirs of Yekhezkel Kotik.* Ed. D. Assaf. Trans. M. Birnstein. Detroit.

KOTLERMAN, B. 2001. 'The Prewar Period of the Birobidzhan State Jewish Theater, 1934–1941.' *Jews in Eastern Europe* 44: 29–59.

KRITZ, O. 1997. *The Poetics of Anarchy: David Edelshtat's Revolutionary Poetry.* Frankfurt am Main and New York.

KRONFELD, C. 1996. *On the Margins of Modernism: Decentering Literary Dynamics.* Berkeley.

KRUK, H. forthcoming. *The Last Days of the Jerusalem of Lithuania: Chronicles from the Vilna Ghetto and the Camps, 1939–1944.* Ed. B. Harshav. Trans. B. Harshav. New Haven.

KRUTIKOV, M. 1994. 'Between Mysticism and Marxism; Meir Wiener as Writer, Critic, and Literary Historian.' *Jews in Eastern Europe* 25: 34–40.

—— 2001. *Yiddish Fiction and the Crisis of Modernity, 1905–1914.* Stanford.

—— 2002. 'Reading Yiddish in a Post-Modern Age: Some Trends in Literary Scholarship of the 1990s.' *Shofar* 20/3: 1–13.

KUGELMASS, J. 1996. *The Miracle of Intervale Avenue: The Story of a Jewish Congregation in the South Bronx.* 2nd edn. New York.

—— and BOYARIN, J. eds. 1998. *From a Ruined Garden: The Memorial Books of Polish Jewry.* Geographical index and bibliography by Z. Baker. 2nd edn. Bloomington, Ind.

KUPOVETSKII, M. S., STAROSTIN, E. V., and WEB, M. 1997. *Jewish Documentary Sources in Moscow Archives* [Russian]. Moscow.

KUZNITZ, C. 1998. 'On the Jewish Street: Yiddish Culture and the Urban Landscape in Interwar Vilna.' In *Yiddish Language and Culture: Then and Now.* 65–92. L. J. Greenspoon ed. Omaha.

—— 2000. 'The Origins of Yiddish Scholarship and the YIVO Institute for Jewish Research.' Unpublished Ph.D diss., Stanford University.

—— forthcoming. 'Ansky's Legacy: The Vilna Jewish Historic-Ethnographic Society and the Shaping of Modern Jewish Culture.' In *Between Two Worlds: S. Ansky at the Turn of the Century.* G. Safran and S. Zipperstein eds. Stanford.

LANDIS, J. ed. 2000. *The Life and Times of Yiddish: Studies in the Past and Present of the Language.* Flushing, NY.

LEVITA, E. 1996a. *Pariz un'viyeneh: mahadurah bikortit be-tseruf mavo, he'arot ve-nispahim* [Yiddish]. Eds. C. Shmeruk and E. Timm. Jerusalem.

—— 1996b. *Paris un Wiene: ein jiddischer Stanzenroman des 16. Jahrhunderts* [Yiddish]. Ed. E. Timm. Tübingen.

LOWENSTEIN, S. 1997. 'The Shifting Boundary Between Eastern and Western Jewry.' *JSS* 4/1: 60–78.

MANGER, I. 2002. *Selected Poetry and Prose.* Trans. and ed. L. Wolf. New Haven.

MANN, B. 1997. 'Icons and Iconoclasts: Visual Poetics in Hebrew and Yiddish Modernism'. Unpublished Ph.D diss., University of California at Berkeley.

MARTEN-FINNIS, S. 2000. 'Bundist Journalism, 1897–1907—Instruction, Exclusion, Polemic; The Relationship Between Leaders and Followers in the Light of Bundist Literary Activities.' *East European Jewish Affairs* 30/1: 39–59.

MENDELSOHN, E. 1993. *On Modern Jewish Politics.* New York.

MICHELS, T. 2000. 'Speaking to Moyshe': The Early Socialist Yiddish Press and its Readers.' *JH* 14: 51–82.

—— 2001. 'Socialism with a Jewish Face: The Origins of the Yiddish-Speaking Communist Movement in the United States, 1907–1923.' In Estraikh and Krutikov (2001): 24–55.

MICHMAN, J. and APTROOT, M. eds. 2002. *Jewish Polemics in Eighteenth-Century Amsterdam: The diskursn fun di naye un di alte kille.* Detroit.

MINCZELES, H. 1993. *Vilna, Wilno, Vilnius: La Jérusalem de Lithuanie.* Paris.

MINTZ, M. 1993. *New Times—New Tunes, Ber Borokhov, 1914–1917* [Yiddish]. Tel Aviv.

—— 1995. *Pangs of Youth, Hashomer Hazair 1911–1921* [Yiddish]. Jerusalem.

MIRON, D. 1996. *A Traveler Disguised: The Rise of Modern Yiddish Fiction in the Nineteenth Century.* 2nd edn. Syracuse, NY.

—— 2000. *The Image of the Shtetl and Other Studies of Modern Jewish Literary Imagination.* Syracuse, NY.

MITCHELL, B. 1999. 'London's "Haredi" Periodicals in Yiddish; Language, Literature and Ultra-Orthodox Ideology.' *European Judaism* 32/2: 51–66.

MOHRER, F. and WEB, M. 1998. *Guide to the YIVO Archives.* Armonk, NY.

MOLODOWSKY, K. 1999. *Paper Bridges.* Ed. and trans. K. Hellerstein. Detroit.

MOSELEY, M. 1990. 'Jewish Autobiography in Eastern Europe: The Pre-History of a Literary Genre.' Unpublished D. Phil. thesis, University of Oxford.

—— 2002. 'Life, Literature: Autobiographies of Jewish Youth in Interwar Poland.' *JSS* 7/3: 1–51.

MOSS, K. 2001. 'Jewish Culture Between Renaissance and Decadence: *Di Literarishe Monatsshriften* and Its Critical Reception.' *JSS* 8/1: 153–98.

—— forthcoming. 'A Time to Tear Down and a Time to Build Up': Recasting Jewish Culture in Eastern Europe, 1914–1921.' Unpublished Ph.D. diss., Stanford University.

NACHSHON, E. 1998. *Yiddish Proletarian Theatre: The Art and Politics of the Artef, 1925–1940.* Westport, Conn.

NEUGROSCHEL, J. ed. and trans. 2001a. *The Dybbuk and the Yiddish Imagination: A Haunted Reader*. Syracuse, NY.

—— ed. and trans. 2001b. *Great Tales of Jewish Fantasy and the Occult*. New York.

—— ed. and trans. 2002a. *No Star Too Beautiful: An Anthology of Yiddish Stories from 1382 to the Present*. New York.

—— ed. and trans. 2002b. *The Shtetl: A Creative Anthology of Jewish Life in Eastern Europe*. Woodstock, NY.

—— and KUSHNER, T. eds. and trans. 1998. *A Dybbuk and Other Tales of the Supernatural*. London.

NEWMAN, R. 1993. 'Pictures of a Trip to the Old Country.' *YIVO Annual* 21: 223–37.

NIBORSKI, Y. 1999. *Verterbukh fun loshn-koydesh-shtamike verter in yidish*. Paris.

NIGER, S., SHATZKY, J. *et al.* 1956–81. *Biographical Dictionary of Modern Yiddish Literature* [Yiddish]. New York.

NORICH, A. 1991. *The Homeless Imagination in the Fiction of Israel Joshua Singer*. Bloomington, Ind.

—— 1998–9. 'Harbe Sugyes/Puzzling Questions'; Yiddish and English Culture in America During the Holocaust.' *JSS* 5/1–2: 91–110.

NOWERSZTERN, A. 1989a. 'From the Folk to the Academics: Study and Research of Yiddish After the Holocaust.' In *Encyclopaedia Judaica Year Book 1988–1989*. 14–24. Jerusalem.

—— 1989b. 'Yung Vilne: The Political Dimension of Literature.' In *The Jews of Poland Between Two World Wars*. 385–98. Y. Gutman, E. Mendelsohn, J. Reinharz, and C. Shmeruk eds. Hanover, NH.

—— 1990. '"Who Would Have Believed that a Bronze Statue Can Weep"; The Poetry of Anna Margolin.' *Prooftexts* 10/3: 435–67.

—— 1992. 'Between Dust and Dance: Peretz's Drama and the Rise of Yiddish Modernism.' *Prooftexts* 12/1: 71–90.

PASKIN, S. ed. 1999. *When Joseph Met Molly: A Reader on Yiddish Film*. Nottingham.

PELTZ, R. 1998. *From Immigrant to Ethnic Culture: American Yiddish in South Philadelphia*. Stanford.

PERETZ, I. L. 2002. *The I. L. Peretz Reader*. 2nd edn. Ed. R. Wisse. Trans. H. Halkin *et al*. New Haven.

PRAGER, L. 1981. 'Yiddish in the University.' In Fishman (1981): 529–45.

—— 1996. 'Yiddish Studies in Israel Face the Twenty-first Century.' In Di Vevoli *et al.* (1996): 451–64.

RAKOVSKY, P. 2002. *My Life as a Radical Jewish Woman: Memoirs of a Zionist Feminist in Poland*. Ed. P. Hyman. Trans. B. Harshav. Bloomington, Ind.

REUVENI, A. 1991. *Short Stories* [Yiddish]. Ed. A. L. Pilowsky. Jerusalem.

ROBINSON, I., ANCTIL, P., and BUTOVSKY. M. eds. 1990. *An Everyday Miracle: Yiddish Culture in Montreal*. Montreal.

ROLL, W. and NEUBERG, S. eds. 1999. *Jiddische Philologie: Festschrift für Erika Timm*. Tübingen.

ROSENWALD, L. 2001. 'The Implications of a New Bergelson Translation.' *Prooftexts* 21/2: 237–47.

ROSKIES, D. 1981. 'The Emancipation of Yiddish.' *Prooftexts* 1/1: 28–42.

—— 1984. *Against the Apocalypse: Responses to Catastrophe in Modern Jewish Culture*. Cambridge, Mass.

—— 1989. *The Literature of Destruction: Jewish Responses to Catastrophe*. Philadelphia.

—— 1995. *A Bridge of Longing: The Lost Art of Yiddish Storytelling*. Cambridge, Mass.

—— 1999. *The Jewish Search for a Usable Past*. Bloomington, Ind.

ROZIER, G. 1999. *Moyshe Broderzon: un écrivain yiddish d'avant-garde*. Saint-Denis.

RUBIN, R. 2000. *Voices of a People: The Story of Yiddish Folksong*. 2nd edn. Urbana, Ill.

SAKOWSKA, R. 1997. ed. *Archiwum Ringelbluma: Konspiracyjne Archiwum Getta Warszawy*. Warsaw.

SALLIS, D., WEB, M., and EL'IASHEVICH, D. A. 1996. *Jewish Documentary Sources in Russia, Ukraine and Belarus: A Preliminary List*. New York.

SANDROW, N. 1996. *Vagabond Stars: A World History of the Yiddish Theater*. 2nd edn. Syracuse, NY.

—— ed. and trans. 1999. *God, Man and Devil: Yiddish Plays in Translation*. Syracuse, NY.

SCHAECHTER, M. 1988. *English–Yiddish Dictionary of Academic Terminology*. New York.

—— 1991. *Pregnancy, Childbirth, and Early Childhood: An English–Yiddish Dictionary*. New York.

—— 1993. *Yiddish II: An Intermediate and Advanced Textbook*. New York.

—— 1999. 'The Road to Orthographic Consistency: The History of the Standardized Yiddish Spelling.' [Yiddish.] In *The Standardized Yiddish Orthography*. 1–175. New York.

SCHWARZ, J. 1997. ' "When the Lamp of Art is Made to Shine Through Life's Foolscap": A Study of the Yiddish Literary Autobiography.' Unpublished Ph.D. diss., Columbia University.

SEIDMAN, N. 1996. 'Elie Weisel and the Scandal of Jewish Rage.' *JSS* 3/1: 1–19.

—— 1997. *A Marriage Made in Heaven: The Sexual Politics of Yiddish and Hebrew*. Berkeley.

SHANDLER, J. 2000. 'Beyond the Mother Tongue: Learning the Meaning of Yiddish in America.' *JSS* 6/3: 97–123.

—— ed. 2002. *Awakening Lives: Autobiographies of Jewish Youth in Poland Before the Holocaust*. New Haven.

SHAPIRO, R. M. ed. 1999. *Holocaust Chronicles: Individualizing the Holocaust Through Diaries and Other Contemporaneous Personal Accounts*. Hoboken, N. J.

SHMERUK, C. ed. 1987. *A shpigl oyf a shteyn: An Anthology of Poetry And Prose by Twelve Soviet Yiddish Writers* [Yiddish]. 2nd edn. Jerusalem.

—— 1988. *Yiddish Literature, Aspects of its History* [Yiddish]. Tel Aviv.

—— 1989. 'Hebrew–Yiddish-Polish: A Trilingual Jewish Culture.' In *The Jews of Poland Between Two World Wars*. 285–311. Y. Gutman, E. Mendelsohn, J. Reinharz, and C. Shmeruk eds. Hanover, NH.

—— 1992. *Historia Literatury Jidysz: Zarys*. Wrocław.

—— 1999. *Call for a Prophet: Historical and Literary Studies* [Hebrew]. Jerusalem.

—— and TURNIANSKY, C. eds. 1993. *Yiddish Literature in the Nineteenth Century: Collection of Yiddish Literary Research and Criticism in the Soviet Union* [Yiddish]. Jerusalem.

—— —— 2000. *Studies in Sholem Aleichem's Writings*. [Hebrew]. Jerusalem.

SHNEER, D. 2000. 'Making Yiddish Modern: The Creation of a Yiddish Language Establishment in the Soviet Union.' *East European Jewish Affairs* 30/2: 77–98.

—— 2001. 'A Revolution in the Making: Yiddish and the Creation of a Soviet Jewish Culture.' Unpublished Ph.D. diss., University of California at Berkeley.

SHOLEM ALEICHEM (Sholem Rabinovitsh) 1996. *Tevye the Dairyman and The Railroad Stories*. 2nd edn. Trans. H. Halkin. New York.

—— 1997. *Motl peysi dem khazns* [Yiddish]. Ed. C. Shmeruk. Jerusalem.

SHOLEM ALEICHEM 2002. *The Letters of Menakhem-Mendl and Sheyne-Sheyndl* and *Motl, Peysi the Cantor's Son*. Ed. and trans. H. Halkin. New Haven.

SHTERNSHIS, A. 2000. 'Soviet and Kosher: Jewish Cultural Identity in the Soviet Union, 1917–1941.' Unpublished D.Phil. thesis, University of Oxford.

SHTEYNBARG, E. forthcoming. *The Jewish Book of Fables*. Ed. and trans. C. Leviant. Syracuse, NY.

SIMON, B. 1993. *Jiddische Sprachgeschichte: Versuch einer neuen Grundlegung*. Frankfurt am Main.

SINGER, I. B. 1996. *Mayn tatns beys-din-shtub (hemshekhim zamlung)*. Ed. C. Shmeruk. Jerusalem.

SLOBIN, M. 1996. *Tenement Songs: The Popular Music of the Jewish Immigrants*. Urbana, Ill.

—— 2000. *Fiddler on the Move: Exploring the Klezmer World*. Oxford.

—— ed. 2001. *American Klezmer: Its Roots and Offshoots*. Berkeley.

—— et al. 1998. 'Klezmer: History and Culture: A Conference.' *Judaism* 185/47: 3–78.

SOKOLOFF, N., LERNER, A. L., and NORICH, A. 1992. *Gender and Text in Modern Hebrew and Yiddish Literature*. New York.

SOYER, D. 1997. *Jewish Immigrant Associations and American Identity in New York, 1880–1939*. Cambridge, Mass.

—— 1999. 'Documenting Immigrant Lives at an Immigrant Institution: Yivo's Autobiography Contest of 1942.' *JSS* 6/3: 218–243.

SPIEGEL, I. 1995. *Yeshayahu Shpigl: prozah sipurit migeto Lodz* [Yiddish]. Ed. Y. Szeintuch. Jerusalem.

STEIN, S. A. 1997. 'Illustrating Chicago's Jewish Left: Todros Geller and the L. M. Stein Farlag.' *JSS* 3/1: 74–110.

STEINBERG, J. 1986. *Collected Yiddish Stories* [Yiddish]. Ed. A. Komem. Jerusalem.

STEINLAUF, M. 1995. 'Fear of Purim; Y. L. Peretz and the Canonization of Yiddish Theater.' *JSS* 1/3: 44–65.

STUTCHKOFF, N. 1991. *Thesaurus of the Yiddish Language* [Yiddish]. Reprint edn. New York.

SUTZKEVER, A. 1990. *The Fiddle Rose: Poems 1970–1972*. Trans. R. Whitman. Detroit.

—— 1991. *Selected Poetry and Prose*. Ed. and trans. B. and B. Harshav. Berkeley.

SZEINTUCH, Y. 2000. *Aaron Zeitlin and Yiddish Literature in Interwar Poland* [Yiddish]. Jerusalem.

TIMM, E. 1987. *Graphische und phonische Struktur des Westjiddischen: unter besonderer Berücksichtigung der Zeit um 1600*. Tübingen.

—— 1999. *Matronymika im aschkenasischen Kulturbereich: ein Beitrag zur Mentalitäts-und Sozialgeschichte der europäischen Juden*. Tübingen.

TRACHTENBERG, B. 2001. 'Inscribing the Yiddish Past; Inter-war Explorations of Old Yiddish Texts.' In Estraikh and Krutikov (2001): 208–25.

TRUNK, I. 1996. *Judenrat: The Jewish Councils in Eastern Europe Under Nazi Occupation*. 2nd edn. Lincoln, Nebr.

TURNIANSKY, C. 1997. 'Yiddish Literature in Frankfurt am Main.' *Jüdische Kultur in Frankfurt am Main*. In K. R. Grözinger ed. 273–85. Wiesbaden.

—— 2000. 'The Events in Frankfurt am Main (1612–1616) in "Megillas Vints" and in an Unknown Yiddish "Historical" Song.' In *Schöpferische Momente des europäischen Judentums in der frühen Neuzeit*. 121–37. M. Graetz ed. Heidelberg.

—— 2001. 'Glikls Werk und die zeitgenössische jiddische Literatur.' In *Die Hamburger Kauffrau Glikl*. 68–90. M. Richarz ed. Hamburg.

TUSMAN, M. H. 1992. *With Teeth in the Earth: Selected Poems of Malka Heifetz Tussman*. Ed. and trans. M. Falk. Detroit.

VEIDLINGER, J. 2000. *The Moscow State Yiddish Theater: Jewish Culture on the Soviet Stage.* Bloomington, Ind.

VISHNIAC, R. 1999. *Children of a Vanished World*. Berkeley.

WARNKE, B. 2001. 'Reforming the New York Yiddish Theater: The Cultural Politics of Immigrant Intellectuals and the Yiddish Press, 1887–1910.' Unpublished Ph.D. diss., Columbia University.

WEINBERG, R. 1998. *Stalin's Forgotten Zion: Birobidzhan and the Making of a Soviet Jewish Homeland*. Berkeley.

WEINREICH, B. 1997. *Yiddish Folktales*. Trans. L. Wolf. 2nd edn. New York.

WEINREICH, M. 1980. *The History of the Yiddish Language*. Trans. S. Noble and J. A. Fishman Chicago.

—— 1993. *Geschichte der jiddischen Sprachforschung*. Atlanta, Ca.

—— 1999. *Hitler's Professors*. Reprint edn. New Haven.

WEINREICH, U. 1999. *College Yiddish: An Introduction to the Yiddish Language and to Jewish Life and Culture.* 6th edn. New York.

WEINTRAUB, A. 1993. 'Visiting a "Vanished World"; Photography and the Jewish Lower East Side.' *YIVO Annual* 21: 189–221.

WEISER, K. 2001. 'The Politics of Yiddish: Noyekh Prilutski and the Folkspartey in Poland, 1900–1926.' Unpublished Ph.D. diss., Columbia University.

WEISSLER, C. 1998. *Voices of the Matriarchs: Listening to the Prayers of Early Modern Jewish Women.* Boston.

WEXLER, P. ed. 1990. *Studies in Yiddish Linguistics*. Tübingen.

WEXLER, P. 1993. *The Ashkenazic Jews: A Slavo-Turkic People in Search of a Jewish Identity.* Columbus, Ohio.

—— 2002. *Two-Tiered Relexification in Yiddish: Jews, Sorbs, Khazars, and the Kiev–Polessian Dialect.* Hawthorne, NY.

WISSE, R. 1988. *A Little Love in Big Manhattan: Two Yiddish Poets.* Cambridge, Mass.

—— 1991. *I. L. Peretz and the Making of Modern Jewish Culture.* Seattle.

—— 2000. *The Modern Jewish Canon.* New York.

WOLITZ, S. ed. 2001. *The Hidden Isaac Bashevis Singer.* Austin, Tex.

ZUCKER, S. 1994. *Yiddish: An Introduction to the Language, Literature, and Culture.* Hoboken, NJ.

CHAPTER 23

JUDAEO-SPANISH STUDIES

ORA (RODRIGUE) SCHWARZWALD

INTRODUCTION

JUDAEO-SPANISH (JS) is the language used by the Jews originating from Spain. It flourished in the Ottoman Empire immediately after the expulsion from Spain and continued its existence there. Some of the expelled Jews settled in North Africa and used the JS variety known as *Ḥakitía* (*Ḥaketíya*). In the beginning of the twenty first century, JS is in the process of becoming an endangered language for lack of new native speakers.

In spite of the decreasing number of speakers, interest increases in the JS language and literature from an academic and folkloristic perspective. Several of the controversial issues will be raised in this chapter: (1) the names of the language; (2) the history of JS; (3) orthography and spelling; (4) literary genres; (5) JS dialects; (6) JS learning and activities today; (7) perspectives for further research.[1]

---

[1] The first five issues are discussed at length in the following books: Wagner (1990), Marcus (1965), Renard (1967), and Sephiha (1986). Detailed research bibliography until 1980 is listed in Bunis (1981).

1. THE NAMES OF THE LANGUAGE

Several names refer to the language: *Spanyolit* or *Espanyolit* (in Israel), *Espanyol*, *Ladino*, *Romance*, *Franco Espanyol*, *Judaeo Espanyol*, *Jidyo* or *Judyo*, *Judezmo*, *Zargon*, etc. in the Ottoman Empire communities, and either *Ḥakitía* or just *Espanyol* in North Africa. Each community used a certain name for the language, and the controversy about the appropriate name still exists among speakers and researchers.

Three names, however, are commonly used today to denote the language of the Ottoman Empire communities: *Judezmo* (meaning Judaism, too), *Ladino*, or *Judaeo-Espanyol* (Judaeo-Spanish). However, *Ladino* is used only among scholars to denote more specifically the JS mirror-image type language of liturgical translations from Hebrew, while either *Judezmo* or JS refers to the vernacular. The speakers and many researchers still call the language invariably by either name.

2. THE HISTORY OF JUDAEO-SPANISH

Weinreich (1973: 126) distinguished two periods in the development of JS: Sepharad I, before the expulsions from the Iberian Peninsula at the end of the fifteenth century, and Sepharad II, from the sixteenth century on. The expulsions caused the Sephardim to become almost exclusively a diaspora community.

Jews used Ibero-Romance in medieval Christian Spain as their main vernacular language. Apparently JS was developed at that time (Marcus 1962; Varvaro 1987; Revah 1970: 238–40; see Section 4 below). The Jews formed a religious ethno-sociological group that was different in customs and beliefs from the non-Jewish group. They used an extensive Hebrew–Aramaic fused component in their language, not only for religious terms. The linguistic similarity between *Ḥakitía* and the eastern JS communities after the expulsion cannot be explained as accidental, unless developed in medieval Spain. Some Iberian Spanish linguistic forms were adopted by the Jews and preserved in their speech while abandoned by their neighbours. Finally, they used *aljamiado*[2] texts already in Spain (Bunis 1992; Schwarzwald 1999).

Minervini (1992: 131–3) examined a variety of medieval *aljamiado* JS texts and showed that phonological, morphological, and lexical evidence proves that the Jews used the same dialectal variety as the Christians. Thus, in spite of the orthography, the Hebrew–Aramaic component, and the texts' special Jewish content, her conclu-

[2] *Aljamiado* is a Spanish text written in Hebrew characters.

sions do not support decidedly the claim that JS already existed in Sepharad I (Penny 1996: 55).

The periodization of JS after the expulsion from Spain varies among scholars. Based on historical, literary, and linguistic processes, one can distinguish between sixteenth-century JS and seventeenth to twentieth-century JS (Revah 1970: 240–2).[3] On the other hand, various linguistic considerations support the division between the sixteenth to eighteenth and the nineteenth to twentieth centuries (Bunis 1992: 404–12).

Written JS in the sixteenth century followed Iberian Spanish literary norms; however, the distance from Spain and the development of JS changed JS in both literary and linguistic aspects in later centuries. Vernacular forms entered the written language and many words and expressions from the local languages were fused with JS.

From the First World War to the present JS has been marked by a gradual shift from Hebrew spelling to Roman script and by an increase of French and Italian influence that has replaced local Turkish, Greek, and sometimes Hebrew elements by more 'Romanticized' forms.

2.1 Judaeo-Spanish: The Current State

At the turn of the twenty-first century the number of speakers of JS is gradually decreasing and the quantity of creative writing grows smaller. Harris (1994: 197–229) lists twenty-four reasons for the present status of JS, many of them related to each other. A few of the most important ones are:

- *Nationalism*: with the formation of separate nationalities in the Balkans and East Europe during the nineteenth century, the local languages became national. Greek, Turkish, and Bulgarian were adopted by the Jews, while JS became the informal, mundane family language.
- *Secularization and modernization*: the change from the religiously oriented community to a secular one caused JS to be associated with the traditional way of life. The youngsters wanted modernism and abandoned the previous way of life, including JS.
- *Education*: increasing numbers of Sephardic Jews acquired general education in non-religious institutions. The western North African Sephardic communities replaced Ḥakitía with Modern Spanish, while French replaced JS in the east Mediterranean as the culture language.
- *Prestige*: JS did not have the prestigious status of Spanish and French. JS-speakers degraded the language as unimportant.

[3] Sephiha (1979: 26; 1986) sets the year 1620 as the turning-point in formation of JS, viewing the sixteenth-century variety as a Hispanic one rather than JS.

- *Immigration*: many members of the Sephardic communities emigrated to various countries around the world for commercial, educational, and other reasons. They settled in various parts of Europe, America, South Africa, etc. In these countries they adopted the local languages, and their children gradually lost the ability to use JS.
- *Zionism*: with the rise of the Zionism in the nineteenth century, youth Zionist movements were established in the Balkans, Turkey, and North Africa. Many members of the Sephardic communities emigrated to Israel and formed JS communities. For example, a group from Greece established the village Tsur Moshe in Israel, where agriculture is their principle source of livelihood. However, the Israeli ideological pressure to speak only Hebrew in Israel caused the gradual loss of the JS among the younger generations.
- *The Holocaust*: thousands of JS-speaking Sephardic Jews, especially from Greece, were killed during the Holocaust. The few survivers settled in various contries around the world.
- *Intermarriages*: many Sephardic JS-speakers married Jews from other communities, e.g. Ashkenazi, Italian, Iraqi, etc. Communication between the married couples and their children is in the language of the country rather than JS.
- *Institutions*: since the Second World War there have been no learning institutions with JS as a primary language to help retain the language. The traditional religious school (*Ḥavra*, *Talmud Tora*) has been discontinued. The national language is taught in state schools, and JS is not studied even as a second language. Only in Amalia High School in Jerusalem has JS been taught as a third language (after Hebrew and English) since 1989.
- *Orthography*: the replacement of Hebrew orthography by Roman script was intended to make JS read more like other European languages, but it has had a negative effect. It has prevented speakers from enriching their vocabulary and grammar with the wealth of written literature in JS. A language without literature is a living language, but cannot be as affluent as a written one.
- *Ideology and unifying forces*: language is retained when its speakers consider it important, when formal institutions exist and the academy sets up an ideology to fight for its existence. The establishment of The National Authority for Ladino and its Culture in 1997 by the Government of Israel, aiming to preserve the language, has been an important step, but it seems too late and too little (see Section 6.2 below).

JS is not a native language to children anymore. The youngest native speakers are over 50 years old today; with their death, JS will cease to exist as a native language. Of the various reasons outlined above, the most significant are the attitude towards JS and what it represented, the geographical dispersion of the speakers, their assimilation in other communities, and their decrease in number after the Holocaust. Had JS been as prestigious as the other European languages in the eyes of its speakers, and had the other factors not interacted so strongly, perhaps its fate might have been different.

3. ORTHOGRAPHY AND SPELLING

From its early beginning JS has been written by Jews in Hebrew characters in the form that was later named Rashi. The Sephardic Jews named Rashi handwritten script *Solitreo*. Printed materials were written in either Rashi script or in square Hebrew letters, rarely vocalized.

The only Sephardi Jewish group that used Roman characters was the *Converso* (converted) Jews who returned to Judaism. Most *Converso* literature was written in either Spanish or Portuguese, naturally in Roman script (though some was written in Hebrew or Latin), rather than in JS. Therefore, I shall address myself to this community only when discussing Ladino translations and JS dialects.

JS developed a certain kind of conventional spelling system to represent Spanish and JS words in Hebrew characters; however, it was not always consistent. Neither were the vowels marked uniformly, especially in vocalized (punctuated) texts, nor were the diacritics marked regularly in consonants. The spelling became more regularized during the nineteenth century. Table 1 represents a sample of Spanish

Table 1. A sample of written words in JS in the sixteenth and nineteenth centuries

Spanish	JS 16th c.	JS 19th c.	Spanish	JS 16th c.	JS 19th c.
salud 'health'	שאלו~ שלו~ סאלו~ סלו	סאלו	*vino* 'wine; he came'	וינו	ב״ינו
vivir 'live'	ביוויר	ביב״יר	*beber* 'drink'	ביב״יר~ביביר	ביב״יר
chico 'small'	ג׳יקו	ג׳יקו	*justo* 'right'	ג׳וסטו~ג׳ושטו	ג׳וסטו
gente 'people'	ג׳ינטי	ג׳ינטי	*muger* 'woman'	מוג׳יר	מוז׳יר
hijo 'son'	היג׳ו (פ׳יג׳ו)	איז׳ו	*bajo* 'low'	באש׳ו~בשו~ בש׳ו~באשו	באש׳ו~באשו
llamar 'call'	לייאמאר	ייאמאר	*oir* 'hear'	אוייר (אולייר)	אוייר~אולייר
cinco 'five'	סינקו	סינקו	*siete* 'seven'	שייטי~סייטי	סייטי

words with their JS spelling in the sixteenth and the nineteenth centuries with the possible alternations.

As can be seen from the table, the spelling becomes more consistent and systematic in the nineteenth century. *Zayin* with a diacritic replaced the *Gimel* with a diacritic to represent the sound /ž/. *Gimel* with a diacritic represented /tš/ and /dž/. Initial historical /f/ or /h/ that were not pronounced in JS were ignored, *Kof* represented /k/. The combination of *Lamed* and *Yod* reflecting Spanish <*ll*> pronounced /y/ in JS, was replaced by Hebrew double *Yod*, not always consistently. *Shin* for the representation of /s/ was substituted by *Samech*. The letters *Kaf*, *Tzadi*, and *Tav* were normally used in words of Hebrew origin while *Het* could occur in Hebrew as well as in Turkish or dialectal varieties. Rarely would *Tzadi* represent Spanish <*c*> or ç, especially in early texts immediately after the expulsion from Spain. *Nun* and *Yod* represented Spanish ñ (Pascual Recuero 1988).

During the twentieth century many of the JS texts were written in Roman characters rather than Hebrew ones, and this orthographic change is controversial among scholars. In an international congress on Writing and orthography in Ladino held in Jerusalem, October 1999, there were fifteen academic lectures. Some of them described the orthography and spelling used in JS throughout its history, while others explicated the preferred way JS should be written in according to orthography and spelling used *de facto* in their own transliteration systems (e.g. Hassán 1978; Lazar 1988; Sephiha 1973; Shaul 1979–   ; and others).

Table 2 represents the various methods of transliteration used for some of the words according to the writers' viewpoints. Some claim that JS Roman script ought to represent Spanish spelling as much as possible, others are in favour of one sign for one JS phoneme, while still others opt for a combination of the Hebrew spelling represented in Roman characters with diacritics.

4. LITERARY GENRES[4]

As in any living language, one can distinguish between canonical or genuine written literature and folk (oral) literature. The former is known mainly to the learned and educated language-users, mostly men; the latter is widespread, well known to each and every member, and is widely practised by women. Both literatures are part of the cultural heritage of any speech community (Romero 1992b).

---

[4] The reader should address Refael's (1999) bibliography for the full list of catalogues regarding JS literature and its various genres.

Table 2. Examples of the various transcriptions used in various texts

JS word	Sephiha (1973)	Lazar (1988)	Shaul (1979–)	Nehama (1977)	Minervini (1992)	Perahya (1998)
ביב׳יר	ḥiuir∼ ḥibir	bivir	bivir	bivir	bivir∼ bibir	bivir
ביביר	beḇer	bever	bever	bever	bever	bever
ג׳יקו	ǧiko	chico	chiko	čiko	chico	tchiko
ג׳ינטי	ǧente	ǧente	djente	ǧente	gente	djente
איז׳ו	hiǧo	hiǰo	ijo	ižo	fijo	ijo
באשו	baxo	baxo	basho	bašo	baxo	bacho
ייאמאר	liamar	llamar	yamar	yamar	llamar	yamar
אוייר	o.ir	oir	oir	oir	oir	oir∼oyir
סינקו	çinko	çinco	sinko	sinko	çinco	sinko
קאמינו	kamino	camino	kamino	kamino	camino	kamino
כבוד	ḵhabod	kāḇōd	kavod	kavoḏ	kāvod	kavod
צדקה	tsedaka	ṣĕdāqah	sedaka	sedaka	ṣĕdāqāh	sedaka
תורה	ṭhora	tōrāh	tora	tora	Tōrah	tora
חכם	ḥakham	ḥāḵām	haham	jajam	ḥākam	haham
דאנייו	danio	daño	danyo	daño	daño	danyo

Most of the printed JS works were written by individuals in the community. The identity of the author is known in most cases. This genre includes scientific and religious literature, poetry, translations, prose literature, drama, and from the nineteenth century on, journalism. On the other hand, the creators of most Ladino translations and of folk literature—stories, songs, ballads, proverbs, idioms, riddles, etc.—are mostly unknown.

Two points should be raised here concerning the literary genres: First, reliance on sources: some of the genres continue the literary Iberian Spanish tradition, but they are later developed by the Sephardic Jews independently. Other genres are genuine JS traditions, either independent of any prior tradition or influenced by local literary genres. Secondly, Jewishness: some of the genres are Jewish in nature because of their inherent content while others are not Jewish at all. Only the use of JS, its Hebrew orthography, and the souce and target audience contribute to the Jewishness of the genre (Hassán 1982; Romero 1992a).

Sephardic Jews, like those of any other Jewish community, considered Hebrew as the language of learning, the holy language of high value. Therefore, a great amount of the literature written by Sephardic Jews was in Hebrew rather than in JS. In the following sections a distinction will be made between the JS literature before and after the expulsion from Spain. After this the following genres will be discussed: Ladino translations; rabbinical literature; press; drama; belles lettres; popular genres.

4.1 Sepharad I

Very little was preserved in JS prior to the expulsion; notable are the *Coplas de Yosef* by an anonymous writer and the *Proverbios Morales* by Sem Tob de Carrión (Ardutiel) (Díaz-Mas and Mota 1998). The *Kharjas* and *Taqanot Valladolid* (the Regulations of Valladolid) show the interactions between languages used by the Jews. The *Kharjas* are the concluding Spanish verses of a Hebrew poem (Hitchcock 1977); the combination of languages is systematic where the rhymes and the metric structure fit. The *Kharjas* probably belonged to the oral literary tradition, although they were sometimes created by well-reputed poets.

The *Taqanot Valladolid* for the communities in Castile, formulated by the Jewish Council in 1432, give additional proof of the interaction between Hebrew and Spanish (Minervini 1992: 181–255; Baer 1936: 280–97). Although written in Hebrew characters, the text is basically Spanish with a heavy inclusion of Hebrew words, not necessarily restricted to cultural religious terms.[5]

The other twenty-five *aljamiado* texts Minervini (1992) studied include instructions for conducting the Passover Seder, contracts, written oaths, declarations, medical recipes, and various agreements, most of them short or fragmentary. The instructions for conducting the Seder after the expulsion follow the pre-exilic linguistic tradition. The other short documents follow certain JS stylistic formulae, common among the Sephardim.

The women's *aljamiado Siddur* published by Lazar (1995b) is Ladino by definition because it is obviously a translation from a Hebrew text. It is identical in its linguistic features to Ladino translations published after the expulsion from Spain

Texts written by Jews in Roman script in Spain were mainly done for Christian patrons and their language is the Spanish of their era. *Sefer Tešuva* (Book for Repentance), although written in Roman script, is very Jewish in nature. This

---

[5] This short sentence demonstrates the case (Hebrew is stressed): *otro se ordenamos que cual quiere* qahal yšʷw (*Yishmerenu Ṣuro Vegoʾalo*) *de quince* baʿale batim *sean* mehuyavim *de tener entre si* melamed tinoqot hagun *que beze a sus fig'os* pasuq (more we order that each community of fifteen house-holders be required to have among themselves a respectable teacher who will teach their children Bible).

book also includes several short tractates.[6] The original translator is unknown, and according to Lazar (1993: pp. xii–xiii) it was copied from an original, the orthography of which is unclear. The aim of the book was to give the Jews 'a condensed version of religious and ethical texts otherwise not accessible to them' (ibid., p. xi). Another text was a translation of *Sefer Hakuzari* (Book of the Kuzari) by Yehudah HaLevy (Lazar 1990). Though very Jewish in nature, both *Sefer Tešuva* and *Sefer Hakuzari* were originally published in Roman script, probably by and for converted Jews.[7] The Jewishness of the texts is revealed through their contents and their linguistic nature, which supports the claim that JS did exist before the expulsion.

4.2 Sepharad II

As mentioned earlier, the Converso Jews of Spanish and Portuguese origin formed communities in Italy, Holland, Germany, England, and France. They used Ladino translations, as we shall see below, but most of their writings were in other languages.

4.2.1 *Ladino Translations*

The traditional custom of *šǝnayim miqra vǝ'ɛḥad targum* ('reading the scriptural portion of the week twice and the Targum (translation) once'), which originated in post-biblical times, continued throughout the generations with other vernacular languages (Peri 1955). Sephardic Jews used 'enladinado' ('[Hispanic]-translated') versions of liturgy, known as Ladino translations, as part of their traditional rituals. These Ladino translations have an educational value as a word-for-word transmissions of the sacred Hebrew text into the Judeo-Spanish vernacular.

This genre is famous for its inflexibility on the one hand, and for its archaic nature on the other. The Ladino translations reflect many Hebrew syntactic structures and they retain grammatical and lexical linguistic features typical of Medieval Spanish (Lazar 1964; Revah 1970; Sephiha 1973, 1979; Schwarzwald 1989; Bunis 1996).

Unfortunately, written medieval Ladino translations are non existant, except for the women's *Siddur* mentioned above. The seemingly Ladino translations in Roman script from before the expulsion are in fact free Spanish translations, made for Catholic patrons by either Jews, converted Jews, or others. The only remnant Ladino translations are those published after the expulsion from Spain, mainly in Italy and the Ottoman Empire.

---

[6] *Pirqey Aboth* (Ethics of the fathers), *Megillat 'Estēr* (translation of Esther), *'Oraḥ Ḥayyim* (Way of life; a translation of Jacob ben Asher's book), and *Midraš 'aseret ha-Dibrōt* (*Midrash* on the Ten Commandments).

[7] See Lazar (1990, 1993) for the question about the patrons of the publications. Note the introduction to the Escorial Bible IJ3 (Lazar 1995a).

Several liturgical texts were subject to many Ladino translations, each being read on special dates:

- The Bible. The Pentateuch read in weekly portions; Psalms; the five Scrolls read on special holidays; several *Haftarot* (e.g. the 9th of *Av*, *Rosh Hashanah*, *Yom Kippur*). The Bible was translated in full in Ferrara 1553, in Roman characters without the Hebrew text, whereas in the Ottoman Empire it was translated in parts since 1540 in Constantinople and Salonika, in Hebrew characters, mostly accompanied by the Hebrew biblical text (Lazar 2000).
- *Siddur* and *Maḥzor*. The daily *Siddur* and the holiday *Maḥzor* were also published in Ladino translations in full in Ferrara in 1552 in Roman script without the Hebrew text,[8] whereas in the Ottoman Empire only certain passages of the books were translated in Hebrew script, each next to the original Hebrew text. Texts are existent since the eighteenth century, though there might have been earlier versions that have been lost.[9]
- The Passover *Haggadah* was published as part of the *Maḥzor* in Ferrara and in the Ottoman communities. It was also published with the Hebrew text as separate booklets since 1609 in Italy and in the Ottoman Empire.
- *Pirke Avot* (Ethics of the Fathers) was read by Sephardic communities every Saturday between Passover and Pentecost, in weekly chapters. It also appeared in the Ferrara *Maḥzor* without the Hebrew text, whereas all the subsequent booklets and *Maḥzors* published since 1601 appeared with the Hebrew text (Schwarzwald 1989).

The difference between the Ladino translations stems primarily from the Jewish communities for whom the translations were done, namely, between the eastern expelled Jews and the western converted Jews. The Western communities published Ladino translations mainly in Roman script in Italy, Amsterdam, and London, and the translations were rather 'hispanized'. The eastern communities published them in Hebrew script in a variety of locations of the Ottoman Empire. Their translations were more Jewish in nature.[10]

The binary classification of east and west is based mainly on the following linguistic criteria, in addition to the orthographic differences mentioned above:

- Conventional JS spelling is used in the eastern Hebrew script translations, while western texts reflect Hispanic spelling of their times. Even Hebrew script texts from the west reflect this fact. For instance, nineteenth-century translations of

---

[8] The Amsterdam 1612 *Maḥzor* is an exact copy of the Ferrara 1552.

[9] Pre-exilic *Maḥzors* include only short instruction in JS. The Hebrew texts are not translated at all.

[10] North African communities did not publish any Ladino translations. They used Ottoman Empire versions for their purposes, and since the twentieth century they have used Ladino texts published mainly in Leghorn (Livorno).

Pirke Avot from Leghorn exhibit the use of *Het* for Modern Spanish *Jota*, which is represented by *Shin, Gimel,* or *Zayin* with an apostrophe in the eastern communities.

- The western translations make a more sparing use of Hebrew words within a hierarchy of usage. The western Roman-script Ladino translations consistently use only God's name ([A.] *Adonai*), proper names, and very few Jewish concepts. The western Hebrew-script Ladino translations contain some additional Hebrew words. The eastern ones, however, include the largest number of Hebrew words (Schwarzwald 1996: 61). The Roman-script conventions made the text read more like Spanish, hence the natural avoidance of Hebrew. Most Hebrew-script versions published in the west followed suit. The paucity of Hebrew words in their texts is due to the conscious intention of the translators, as expressed in some translations. The Ladino translations from the east made no such claims. Inclusion of the Hebrew words can reflect either the ancient traditional translations or the natural reflection of the spoken language.
- Different words and phrases are used consistently in both east and west (Sephiha 1973: 238 ff; Schwarzwald 1989, 1996). Also, there are systematic differences in grammatical forms, typical of JS.

Ladino translations are studied extensively by many scholars, some of them mentioned above. It seems that the translators intentionally tried to preserve the archaic nature of the text with its special calque features in order to keep the text educational and sacred. Thus, in spite of natural developments of JS, the translators adhere to old norms which make the spirit of the text archaic.

The printing of the Constantinople Pentateuch Ladino translation in Hebrew script in 1547 and the Ferrara Bible in Roman script in 1553, immediately after the expulsion, intrigued researchers.[11] These translations resemble each other more closely than they resemble any of the pre-expulsion Spanish translations. Therefore, one of the important issues researchers try to resolve is the origin of the Ladino translations. Lazar (1964, 1995a), for example, claims the Spanish translations of the Middle Ages set the foundations for the Ladino translations published after the expulsion. Wexler (1987) shows that clear tendencies in the Roman-script Ladino translations of the eighteenth century make the text more Jewish on the one hand, yet more Hispanic in nature on the other—which also assumes old pre-exilic versions as the origin for the translations. Bunis (1996) argues that Jewish oral tradition of Ladino translations had already existed in Spain and had been based on the Hebrew text itself. Based on the use of proper names in the Bible Ladino translations, Schwarzwald (2000) also claims that the post-exilic translations are independent of the Spanish pre-exilic translations. Also, a comparison of pre-exilic

---

[11] Not surprisingly, a congress has been devoted solely to the study of the Ferrara Bible (Hassán 1994).

Pirke Avot in *Sefer Teshuva* and the post-exilic ones proves that they are linguistically independent (Schwarzwald forthcoming).

4.2.2 *Rabbinical Literature*

Rabbinical literature refers to literature written by Sephardic rabbis on subjects like Jewish law, morals, education, customs, commentaries on and interpretations of various Hebrew cannonical texts, judicial matters, and Responsa literature, etc.[12]

Most of this rabbinical literature was written in Hebrew, but there were some exceptions. Moses Almosnino wrote *Sefer Hanhagat HaḤayyim: El regimiento de la vida* (The Management of Life: Salonika, 1564)[13] in (Judaeo-)Spanish in Rashi script, but his work became famous through the transliteration into Roman characters done for the benefit of Spanish readers. Other Rabbinical literature included, for instance, *Meza de la alma* (an edited translation of *Shulḥan HaPanim* by Yosef Karo: Salonika, 1568), *El deber de los corazones* (translated by Zadiq Forman from *Ḥovat Halevavot*: Constantinople, 1569), *Dinim de sheḥita i bediqa* (anonymous author: Constantinople, 1510), etc.

Various changes in the economic, political, and social situation of the Jews caused some decrease in the Hebrew education of later generations. The educated Sephardic leaders grasped the need to elevate the knowledge of the layman and started writing in JS as well. In addition to *Meam Loez* (see 4.2.2.1 below), other books were written in JS by Abraham ben Isaac Asa, Reuben ben Abraham of Shtip, Yehudah Eliezer Papo, Yehuda ben Shlomo Hai Alcalay, Shabetay ben Yaacob Vitas, and others (Yaari 1934: 28–37).

The rabbinical JS literature, either original or translated, is loaded with Hebrew words, phrases, and citations due to the contents of the treatises and their reliance on common Jewish knowledge of Hebrew words. The number of Turkish and sometimes Greek words increased during the nineteenth and twentieth centuries, as explained above in Section 2.

The Responsa literature, like the rabbinical homilies, was mainly in Hebrew, although addressed to a Sephardic audience. Occasionally, actual cases or wills would be cited within the Hebrew text even in early Responsa from the sixteenth century (e.g. in Rabbi Shmuel de Modena's [MaHaRaShDaM] Responsas).

Sermon collections were written by rabbis mostly in JS. *Vehokhiaḥ Avraham* by Abraham Palachi (Izmir, 1862), for instance, includes sermons of Bar Mizvah homilies. *Sefer Vayyiqra Moshe* by Moshe Shimon Pesah (Volos, 1891–1937) includes sermons of a Halachic nature and lamentations in Hebrew and JS.[14]

---

[12] Studies of the Sephardic rabbinical literature show that most of it was written in Hebrew (e.g. Bornstein-Makovetsky 2001).

[13] Almosnino also wrote the historical book *Crónica de los reyes otomanos* (The history of the Ottoman kings, also known as *Extremos y grandezas de Constantinopla*; Romeu Ferré 1998)

[14] Yaari (1934) and the complementary lists (mentioned in Refael 1999) give detailed descriptions of the printed material.

4.2.2.1 Meam Loez

Meam Loez, one of the most voluminous and important literary works in JS, was begun by Rabbi Jacob Khuli (1689?–1732). He gathered biblical commentaries from the classical Jewish sources: Mishnah, Gemarah, Halachic and Aggadic midrashes, ethical rules and homiletic interpretations, literary, historical, and kabbalic sources, as well as rabbinical commentaries on the Bible from all periods.

Jacob Khuli completed the commentary on Genesis (Constantinople, 1730). His commentary on Exodus, however, ended at the twenty-seventh chapter (*Teruma*), and was published posthumously in 1733. Following his guidelines the following rabbis carried on the enterprise: Isaac Magriso (end of Exodus, Leviticus, Numbers), Isaac Shemaria Argueti (Deuteronomy), Menachem Mitrani (Joshua), Isaac Abba (first Prophets; Isaiah), Rafael Isaac Meir Ben Veniste (Ruth), Hayim Shaki (Song of Songs), Nissim Aboud (Ecclesiastes), and Rafael Hiya Pontrimoli (Esther). Even their efforts failed to bring this monumental work to completion. This JS classic was eventually published in its unfinished form and ran into several editions in Constantinople, Salonika, Leghorn, Smyrna, etc. (Landau 1980; Maeso and Pascual Recuero 1964–70). Because of its educational value, the book has been translated with some adjustments and additions into Hebrew (S. Yerushalmi 1957–81), English (Kaplan 1977–97), and other languages.

The language of *Meam Loez* is JS; however, it echoes the Hebrew sources. On the one hand, 12–15 per cent of the words and phrases in the text are Hebrew; on the other, Hebrew phrases are reflected in JS expressions, and often the syntax is influenced by Hebrew word structure. Hebrew and JS terms alternate freely, e.g. **dinim** ~ *leyes* (laws), **navi** ~ *porfeta* (prophet), **sibot** ~ *kavzos* (reasons), **reshaʿim** ~ *ğente mala* (evil people).

Several studies of *Meam Loez* have examined its literary aspects (e.g. Landau 1980, 1981; Alexander 1986; and many others). The sources that the writers used have been analysed as well as its lexicon (e.g. Wiesner 1981; Romeu Ferré 2000); however, its language has not been seriously analysed. The study of the various books written by different authors at various times and locations will certainly shed light on language varieties of the Ottoman Jewry JS of the eighteenth and nineteenth centuries.

4.2.3 *Drama*

The first sephardic dramatic writers were Jews from Holland (Enríquez Gómez, Levi de Barrios), but their writing cannot be considered JS. As mentioned above, they belonged to the *Converso* communities and adopted Hispanic themes and literary norms, as well as Spanish linguistic standards.

The JS drama developed around Jewish themes in the early centuries after the expulsion. The story of Esther and the drama of Joseph and his brothers were repeated themes played around Purim in various communities, though not documented.[15] From the middle of the nineteenth century many new plays were produced. Some of these exist in print and manuscripts, while others are mentioned in various newspapers but are lost. Bunis (1995) described what was apparently the first play published in the Ottoman Empire. Other plays are described in catalogues (Yaari 1934: 57–9). Romero (1979) gives the most comprehensive description of these plays, though many of them are unattested in written form.

In addition to plays on biblical and historical subjects, like *David and Goliath*, *Deborah*, and *Yiftah*, there were other themes, either religiously oriented or entirely secular, comic, tragic, and tragicomic, for example *la famía misterioza* (The Mysterious Family, by J. Behar), *El bet din de los syelos* (The Court of Law of Heaven; translated from Polish), *El Ḥazino imažinado* (The Imaginary Invalid; translated from Moliere's *Le Malade Imaginaire*), *Los Buǧukes* (the Twins, translated from Shakespeare's *Comedy of Errors*), and so on.

Many of the plays were musicals or semi-musicals. In most cases they were performed by amateur players, children as well as adults. Occasionally they were produced and performed by members of youth movements in various cities. One of them has been scientifically edited with respect to its musical and folkloristic aspects by Alexander and Weich-Shahak (1994).

4.2.4 *Belles Lettres*

The second half of the nineteenth century marks the turning-point for secular literature as well. Biographies, books, and stories were written in JS in order to elevate the education of the common people. Some novels were written in JS on historical Jewish matters or people. Most of them were devoted to such matters as love, tragedies, fortune, and the like. The authors are known in some of the original stories, e.g. *La dǧudía salvada del konvento* (The Jewess Saved From the Convent, by Y. de Boton), *Muerta por el amor* (Dead For Love, by M. Ḥabib). In other books only the printer is mentioned, for example, *Estoria temeroza de un ižo muy presyozo* (A Scary Story About a Dear Son; Izmir 1913), *Entre dos amores* (Between Two Loves; Jerusalem 1907).

Some of the JS novels were adaptations or translations of literature written in Europe especially in English, French, German, and Russian, for example, Hugo's *Les Miserables*, Dumas's *The Count of Monte Cristo*, Dostoevsky's *The Brothers Karamazov*, as well as Hebrew: *Ahavat Zion* (*Amor de Zion*; Love of Zion, by Abraham Mapu), *Kisme Moledet* (*Sharmes de patria*; The Magic of Homeland, by Yehuda Burla). The source is specifically mentioned in some cases, but in others it is up to the researcher to trace it. This is a genre that has yet to be studied thoroughly (Romero 1993; Barquin Lopez 1995).

---

[15] Avner Perez informed me of a sixteenth-century MS from the Genizah and kept at the Jewish Theological Seminary in New York. It reflects classical prosody of Spanish texts.

It is wrong to claim that all JS literature is adapted (Hassán 1982). Much of the creative writing in JS was original and deserves research. Also, it should be recalled that Sephardic Jews kept on publishing and creating all kinds of literary genres, from science to *belles lettres* (e.g. Elias Canetti), in languages other than JS. The fact that a text is written in JS does not make it automatically imitative.

4.2.5 *Journalism*

Although Hassán (1982) considers all kinds of journalism published in JS as derivative, it is an independent creative genre. The first JS newspaper, *La esperansa* (Hope) was published in Izmir in 1842, followed four years later by *Sha'are hamizrah* (The Gates of the East). Since then hundreds of JS newspapers have been published in many cities (Gaon 1965), most of them in Salonika (since 1865) and Constantinople (since 1853), but also in Izmir, Vienna, Jerusalem, Sofia, Fili-popoli, Rusjuk, Tel Aviv, and in other smaller cities in the Ottoman Empire.

The first newspapers included only translated news from major foreign news-papers; however, the publication of *La epoka* (The Era), published in Salonika in 1875, marked the turning-point in the development of JS journalism. It included original articles on political matters as well as local news. The other newspapers followed suit and reduced the number of translated articles.

Rarely were the newspapers published on a daily basis. Most of them appeared two or three times a week or even just once weekly. Some of them were political newspapers, others were satirical-humorous, while the rest had a Zionist orienta-tion or were the voice of political-nationalist movements. The language of the newspapers varied accordingly: vernacular JS with a heavy Hebrew component was freely used in the satirical-humorous newspapers; a high stylistic variety of JS was used in the more politically oriented papers. The Hebrew component was avoided and replaced by Hispanized (French-like, Italian-like) forms in the other political newspapers.

In addition to news and editorial articles, the newspapers included stories, sometimes continued every week, songs in Hebrew and in JS, and had various sections, just as in modern journalism. Some of these stories were later published in book form.

A number of JS journals in Hebrew Rashi letters still existed at the beginning of the twentieth century in the Balkans and in Israel, but their number gradually decreased. Moreover, Hebrew letters were gradually replaced by Roman letters (see 2.1 above and 4.3 below).

4.2.5 *Popular Genres*

4.2.5.1 *Poetic Literature*

A rich poetic oral folkloristic tradition in JS existed in the Moroccan and eastern communities alike. Since the end of the nineteenth century the various oral traditions have been recorded and written down (Menéndez Pidal 1928). The poetic tradition includes varieties of forms—*romansas* (or *romances*), *coplas* (or *complas*), and *cantigas* (or *canticas*)—mostly sung. The *romansas* are ballads with six- or eight-syllable lines rhyming in the even-numbered lines. The *coplas* are poems of educational origin on assorted narrative or descriptive rather than lyric themes, written in stanzas, frequently acrostics, with various types of rhyming. The most famous *coplas* are dedicated to Jewish holidays and customs. The *cantigas* are lyric songs, especially love songs. Men used to sing many of the *coplas* on religious or Jewish-oriented themes, whereas the *romansas* and *cantigas* were usually sung by women (Díaz-Mas 1992: 105–6, 119; Menéndez Pidal 1928).[16]

These three types of poetry are very old and rooted in Spain (e.g. *Coplas de Yosef* mentioned in 4.1). Most of the *romansas* are not related to Jewish themes or to historical Jewish characters. They became Jewish because they were adopted by the Sephardic communities and collected in written form (e.g. Yona in Salonika, Cherezli in Jerusalem; see e.g. Armistead and Silverman 1971, 1982). The *coplas* are more Jewish in nature, but their poetic form was rooted in Spain (Hassán 1976).

Hispanicists were fascinated at finding the old poetic forms as a living oral tradition in JS culture, in spite of the geographical and temporal distance. The resemblance to Iberian traditions is reflected in musical as well as thematic and linguistic aspects. Many studies were dedicated to the *romansa*, most of them collections of the traditions in particular communities (Menéndez Pidal 1906–7; Benichou 1944; Attias 1961). Menéndez Pidal, in his numerous works, analysed the themes and their Hispanic roots. Specific *romansas* have been analysed systematically too (Refael 1998a; Alexander *et al.* 1994).

A careful analysis of the various oral poetic traditions reveals that many of the *romansas*, *coplas*, and *cantigas* are late innovations of the Sephardic Jews. The innovations follow two trends: adoption of local, non-Jewish traditions in the Ottoman Empire and in North Africa; and an independent innovation by creative writers on the lines of the old traditions, especially of *coplas* and *cantigas*. One finds, for instance, Zionist *coplas* (*Zionidas*), *coplas* on the Holocaust, and so on (Refael 1998b; Lévy 1989). Newspapers and other pamphlets include many new poems and ballads, and some of them carry the instruction to sing them to a specific well-known tune. Hence, *coplas* and *cantigas* are different from the *romansa* genre, because in many of them, especially the modern ones, the identity of the authors is known. *Coplas* are also written, like *cantes* (poems), and are not necessarily sung.

The language of these genres varies, depending on the contents and time of the poetry. *Romansas* of Hispanic source carry features of Old Spanish with almost no

---

[16] The classification based primarily on literary and thematic criteria does not accord with the speakers who call many of the *coplas romansas*.

markers of JS. *Romansas, coplas,* and *cantigas* on Jewish themes have definite Jewish markers, reflected by either Hebrew components, reference to Jewish tradition and customs, or phrases from Ladino translations. Late *coplas* and *cantigas* have vernacular forms with a heavy Turkish and Greek component as well.

4.2.5.2 *Proverbs*

Many of the JS proverbs can be traced back to Spain. The proverbs include Hispanic elements, and many of them are identical in form and content to the Spanish ones, which means that the expelled Sephardic Jews carried this oral tradition over and brought it with them to the diaspora.

The study of the JS proverbs still needs further depth (Lévy 1969).[17] Some proverbs of Hispanic origin seem to be kept intact, though the vocabulary may vary; for example, Spanish *cada uno sabe donde le aprieta el zapato* (everyone knows where his shoe hurts) is retained in eastern JS as *kada uno save onde le ergwele el sapato* (or *el kalsado*). The JS proverb *axare eamal veatorax vaikax korax* (someone who likes to enjoy the fruit of somebody else's efforts; Lit: after labour and effort took Korah) is based on biblical literature. The words are all Hebrew, though the proverb is non-existant in Hebrew. The idiom *ḥoxma i bina i kyošk enriva* (wisdom and knowledge (building) and a tower on top of them, i.e. great stupidity) includes the Hebrew synonyms *ḥokma* and *bina*. *Bina,* like *kyošk,* is a Turkish word for building, hence the word play of Hebrew and Turkish gives two entirely different meanings. In spite of the Hispanic tradition, there is a considerable innovations in JS proverbs.

4.2.5.3 *Miscellaneous*

As in any other living culture, other JS genres exist, for example, folk-tales, riddles, fables, jokes, and so on. Men wrote down many satirical tales, folk-tales, and riddles in JS texts, though most of them were transmitted orally through the JS community, especially by women. These genres still need investigation. Many folk-tales are being collected today, but their study is still in its beginning (Alexander-Frizer 2000 and the references therein). Bunis (1999b) studied the satirical supposed correspondence between typical folk characters, a husband and wife, as published in the press from Salonika, and his description is important from linguistic and literary point of view. The other types of these folkloristic creations need further research. The JS language in them seems to be the vernacular, modified according to topic.

---

[17] Alexander and Bentolila (2001), for instance, in their work on the *Ḥakitía* prove that with respect to Hispanic proverbs, proverbs can be classified according to four criteria—message, theme, form, and lexicon.

4.3 Current State

Current publications in JS are a result of some very staunch believers in the resilience of the language. The most prominent and well-known publication is *Aki Yerushalaim: Revista Kulturala Djudeo-Espanyola*, founded in 1979 by the editor Moshe Shaul as a supplement to the Israeli Radio broadcasting in JS. Various writers contribute to this journal, covering subjects like culture, folklore, history, and the current status of Sephardic Jews, as well as customs, old and new poems, information about new books, articles, records, conferences, and so on. In recent issues a few JS authentic texts in Rashi script or Solitreo have been reproduced, with a transliteration, by Avner Perez.

Other publications around the world focus on JS and Sephardic culture. *Shalom*, a Turkish newspaper from Istanbul, includes one page in JS by Silvio Ovadya. *Los Muestros: La Boz de los Sefardim*, published in Brussels and edited by Moïse Rahmani, is a multilingual quarterly. The articles on history, culture, language, folklore, music, and literature appear in French, English, Spanish, and JS. *La Lettre Sepharade* is a recent publication (since 2000) that appears concurrently in the United States in English, edited by Rosine Nussenblatt, and in France in French, edited by Jean Carasso. Haim Vidal Sephiha is responsible for the publications of *Vidas Largas* in Paris.

Original JS plays are produced from time to time in Israel and Turkey by amateur players. *Bustan Sefaradi* (A Sephardic Orchard), a popular Hebrew play that Yitshak Navon wrote about life in Jerusalem at the beginning of the twentieth century, includes JS songs, proverbs, and some idioms. It attracts a large audience, not necessarily of JS origin.

Margalit Matityahu and Avner Perez in Israel, Clarisse Nikoidski in France, and a few other poets write JS poetry, though most of their creative writings are in their mother tongues. Their poems have been published in bilingual editions. Their target audience is small, not only because poetry has relatively few readers but also because the number of JS readers is scarce. Israeli authors, when writing about Sephardic JS-speakers, characterize them by inserting JS sentences and phrases into their discourse.

Several discussion lists on the Internet inform about news in the Sephardic world. The oldest is SEFARAD managed by Yitshak Kerem (*ykerem@actcom.co.il*, distributed through Sefardic Electronic Archives *sefarad@shamash.org* as well). Each newsletter includes extensive lists of various related websites. Another discussion list has been established by Aviva Ben-Ur about Mizrahi and Sephardic Jews (*aben-ur@judnea.umass.edu*). Since 2001 a new site named Jewish Languages (*jewish-languages@lists.Stanford.EDU*) has been initiated by Sarah Bunin Benor in which one can find information about the study of Jewish languages in general, including JS. A very popular discussion internet list in JS is *ladinokomunita@ yahoogroups.com*.

5. JUDAEO-SPANISH DIALECTS

Hispanicists view JS as a dialect of Spanish; however, researchers of JS consider it an independent language rooted in Iberian Spanish. As in the case of any language that is spoken over a wide area, different dialects developed in JS.

Several linguistic features are common to all JS dialects and make it different from other varieties of Spanish, although certain features can be found in the vulgar varieties of Spanish in either Spain or America. A few of the features are listed here; the reader will find more details in Zamora Vicente (1967: 349–77), Bunis (1992: 414–20), Marcus (1965: 70–95), Wagner (1990(I)[= 1930]: 116–35), and others. The phonemes /š/, /dǧ/, and /ž/ were retained in JS (they changed in Spanish into /x/). The phonemes /v/ and /b/ are distinct (allophones in Spanish ([ß] and [b]). The equivalents to the Spanish letters ç and z are pronounced [s] and [z] in JS. Often historical /s/ would be pronounced [z] between vowels. Residues of the historical ç or z are rarely pronounced as an affricate [dž], e.g. *dodže* (twelve, Spanish *doce*). Historical *s* before *k* is pronounced š, e.g. *moška* (fly, Spanish *mosca*). The Spanish *swe* (spelled *sue*) is often realized in JS as [sxwe] or [sfwe], e.g. *esxweño ~ esfweño* (sleep). Metathesis occurs in many consonant clusters with *d* or *r*, e.g. *pedrer* (lose, Spanish *perder*). The vowels are not always as in Spanish, e.g. *kuzir* (sew, Spanish *coser*), *džugo* (game, Spanish *juego*).

Verbs are conjugated with some modifications. The suffixes *-i* (1st person), *-tes* (2nd person singular), and *-teš* (2nd person plural) are used in the preterit instead of *-é, -ste* and *-eis* in Spanish, e.g. *avlí, avlates, avlateš* (spoke, Spanish *hablé, hablaste, hablateis*). The verb *ser* (to be) and some other verbs have a special conjugation (Koén-Sarano 1999c). JS tense system is less elaborated than Spanish and compound verbs are frequently formed with the verb *tener* (have, own), rather than *haber* (have), e.g. *tengo havlado* (I have been talking). The Spanish *ustedes* formal polite form is absent. Although *nos* (us) and *nuestro* (our) are used in literary styles, the vernacular forms are *mos* and *muestro*, respectively. JS diminutive is *-iko/-ika* rather than Spanish *-ito/-ita*.

JS retained medieval Spanish vocabulary, e.g. *agora* (now), *avagar* (slowly), *kazal* (village), *merkar* (buy), *oganyo* (this year), etc. A considerable amount of Hebrew-Aramaic was fused and integrated into the language, e.g. *balabay/balabáya* (good householder *m/f*; Hebrew *baʿal habbayit/baʿalat habbayit*); (*gwevo*) *enxaminado* (hard-boiled [egg]; Hebrew *ḥamin* ((Sabbath) stew); *dezmazalado* (unlucky; Hebrew *mazal*, 'star, fate'); *aspan* (insolent; Hebrew *ʿaz panim*), etc. (Bunis 1993). Hebrew influence is revealed through syntactic structures as well.

As mentioned above, the Sephardic Jews carried dialectal varieties of Medieval Spanish to various locations in the Ottoman Empire and North Africa. In the beginning they formed separate communities and continued their customs and language as before. However, in time, because of the constant contacts between other JS-speakers, and because of the contact with various local languages, special JS dialects were formed in various places.

Communities are often classified among JS researchers as 'eastern' and 'western', but referring to several different groupings, as follows:

- 'Eastern' is the expelled Jewish community; 'western' is the *Converso* community.
- 'Eastern' is the Ottoman Empire Sephardic community; 'western' is the North African Sephardic community.
- 'Eastern' is the dialect in the Ottoman Empire that reflects features of east and middle Iberian Spanish; 'western' is the dialect in the Ottoman Empire that reflects west and north Iberian Spanish.

The *Converso* Sephardic communities deserve special reference. As shown in sections 3 and 4.2.1, they used Spanish conventions in their Ladino translations. As recalled, most of their writings were in Spanish and Portuguese, in Roman script, rather than in JS. Nevertheless, in the spoken vernacular they still retained a unique lexical usage of a variety of JS at the beginning of the twentieth century (Wagner 1990(II)[=1924]: 40–55). They are considered as west dialects only with regard to Ladino translations.

According to the second classification, eastern refers to Ottoman Empire JS, whereas western refers to *Ḥakitía*. *Ḥakitía* has been described by Benoliel (1977).[18] In addition to its general JS grammatical and lexical features, it is typified by extensive borrowings from Arabic, and by different lexical choices. The speakers retained the pharyngeal /ḥ/ and /ʿ/ in words of Hebrew and Arabic origin. The oral literary genres are slightly different from the eastern one, as can be seen by various studies of the *romansas* and *coplas* (see 4.2.5.1 above). Very little has been published in JS in North Africa. The book *Kerem Ḥemed* by Abraham Ankawe (Leghorn, 1869) followed the tradition of the Valladolid Statutes from Spain. Another rabbinical work is *Vayomer Yizḥak* (Leghorn, 1855) by Isaac ben Walid, and a few manuscripts were retained.

The most comprehensive studies on the various JS Ottoman Empire eastern and western dialects were conducted at the beginning of the twentieth century by Crews

---

[18] Only the most important works bearing on the various dialects will be mentioned here. See Bunis (1981: 42–8) for a more detailed bibliography.

(1935) and Wagner (1990(I)[= 1914]: 7–109; 1990(I)[= 1930]: 111–235, and more in 1990). Several other articles describe briefly the uniqueness of certain dialects with respect to specific phenomena like pronunciation, proverbs, loan-words, etc. (Bunis 1981: 42–8; 1988; Quintana 1997).

Within the Ottoman Empire researchers distinguish between groups of dialects reflecting source areas in the Iberian Peninsula—western versus eastern. Further differences are due to local influences of the vernacular languages and to natural language development. Sentence 1 below is taken from Marcus (1965: 100). Sentences 2–3 demonstrate other varieties:

1. *Il iju dil sinior vizinu cuandu mus meldo luqué lis acunticio a lus djidios in Ispania, todos musotrus yurimus fin qui mu si izieron lus ojus curiladus* (Monastir inYugoslavia, Sarayevo)
2. *El ijo del senior vizino cuando mos meldo loque les acontesio a los djidios en Espania, todos mosotros yorimos fin que mos se izieron los ojos corolados* (Turkey)
3. *El fijo del senior vizino cuando mos meldo loque les acontesio a los djidios en Espania, todos mosotros yorimos fin que mos se fizieron los ojos corolados* (Salonika)

(*Translation*: When the son of the neighbour read to us what happened to the Jews in Spain, we all cried until our eyes turned red.)

The linguistic differences between the dialects are marked by phonetic and lexical features. The examples above demonstrate some of the phonetic differences: *i* and *u* in 1, *e* and *o* in 2–3, respectively. Initial *f* in 3 is absent in 1–2. Lexical differences are not demonstrated here but are listed in the references mentioned above and others. Dictionaries do not always mark the dialectal differences, e.g. *faldukwera* in Salonika, *aldikera* or *džep* (pocket) in Turkey; *sedakero* (philanthropist) in Salonika, (beggar) in Turkey and Israel. Because of the continual migration between the various communities, dialectal study is very difficult, especially now that living JS communities hardly carry on the tradition.

6. JS Learning and Activities Today

Only a few institutions offer formal academic instruction in the language. Two universities in Israel have advanced programmes for the study of JS and its literature: Bar-Ilan University in Ramat Gan and the Hebrew University in Jerusalem. Ben-Gurion University in Beer Sheva and Tel Aviv University have a few introductory course in JS. Several JS academic programmes also exist in Paris, Hamburg,

Berlin, Tübingen, Madrid, and Barcelona. Sporadic university courses are given elsewhere in the world, depending on the availability of teachers (and students).

The first conference devoted to Judaeo-Spanish was initiated at the University of Leeds in England in 1979. So far there have been twelve academic conferences, most of them in London, covering various aspects of JS language and creativity. Misgav Yerushalayim, the Institute for Research on the Sephardic and Oriental Jewish Heritage, organizes an international conference every four years in which many papers regarding JS are presented. The Maurice Amado Chair in Sephardic Studies at the University of California in Los Angeles organizes colloquia and conferences, but the themes are historical, literary, and cultural rather than linguistic. Around 1992, the year that marked 500 years from the expulsion from Spain and the discovery of the New World, there were several international academic conferences dealing with the linguistic, historical, literary, philosophical, musical, and cultural impact of the expulsion on the Sephardic diaspora (a short list of the proceedings of some of them: Stillman and Stillman 1999; Leorenzo Sanz 1993; Benbassa 1996; Abitbol *et al.* 1997). JS is also discussed at length in some sections of congresses on Jewish studies—the World Congress on Jewish Studies in Israel, the American Jewish Association in the United States, and the European Association for Jewish Studies in Europe. Some of the section entitled 'Sephardic Studies' refer to Middle Eastern and Mediterranean Jewry altogether, rather than Jewry originating in Spain. A considerable number of sections in the recent EAJS in the 1998 congress in Toledo, Spain, were devoted to JS, organized by Romero and Hassán, the leading scholars in the study of JS literature.

6.1 JS Textbooks and Dictionaries

The growing interest in JS in recent years has led to the publication of numerous textbooks and dictionaries. The textbooks are primarily designated for university students. Four of them were published in Israel: Koén-Sarano (1999a, 1999b) and Shaul (1999) use JS Roman script, whereas Gattegno and Refael (1995, 1998) and Bunis (1999a) use Rashi script. Varol's (1998) textbook in France contains JS conversations and short texts in Roman script as well.

Two different attitudes are revealed in these textbooks: first, that JS is a language of culture, and therefore students must be exposed intensively to Rashi script in order to acquire the language and be able to read its rich literature; second, that JS is a language of communication and, as such, students should know its grammar and cultural background through whatever orthographic means available. Gattegno and Refael and Bunis base their books on the first attitude, therefore all JS examples, vocabulary, and texts are given in Rashi script. The other books all cite every JS word in Roman script. Explanations of grammatical phenomena and instructions in the exercises are given either in Hebrew in the Israeli books, or in French in Varol's. Varol's is the only book whose course is accompanied by a CD-ROM with recorded JS conversations and songs. All the books enable students to carry on a conversation in JS and to understand oral texts. Only Bunis's book, and to a lesser degree Gattegno and Refael's, enable students to read and understand real authentic JS texts from various genres.

Most of the dictionaries have been compiled and published outside the academic sphere. The compilers wrote down the JS vocabulary used by themselves and their ancestors in their particular dialects. The first and only JS dictionary written in Hebrew script was Cherezli (1899). It did not include any Hebrew words, assuming unjustifiably that any Hebrew reader would understand the JS meaning, even when it was remote from Hebrew, e.g. *ḥaver* (partner, rather than friend), *ḥenozo* (gentle, from Hebrew *ḥen*), etc.

All of the dictionaries published towards the end of the twentieth century are in Roman script. Nehama's (1977) is the most detailed JS–French dictionary, recording the Salonika tradition. Pascual Recuero (1977) is a small JS–Spanish dictionary with Spanish equivalents to JS words, especially those that are different from Modern Spanish. Words of Hebrew origin are either unlisted or incorrectly explained. Romano's (1995 [1933]) dictionary, based on his dissertation, is a multilingual dictionary reflecting the Bosnian tradition. Bendayan de Bendelac (1995) reflects the *Ḥakitía* vocabulary and is more thorough than the list in Benoliel (1977). Perahya and Perahya's (1998) dictionary is French-oriented, and can serve as a complement to Nehama's as it gives the JS equivalents to French words. The recent dictionaries by Perahya *et al.* (1997), Passy (1999), Benchimol and Koén-Sarano (1999), Bunis (1999a: 463–551), and Kohen and Kohen-Gordon (2000) are all bilingual dictionaries, where the languages of explanations vary: Turkish, English, and Hebrew.[19]

Lazar's (1999) *Ladino Reader* can supplement the above text books and dictionaries. This reader includes representative texts from the various genres from all the language periods, most of them in Roman-script transliteration in order to facilitate the availability of the texts to anyone interested in the wide range of JS literature.

6.2 Special Current Enterprises

Several important enterprises deserve special mention. The *Instituto de Estudios Sefardíes* (formerly Instituto Arias Montano) of the Consejo Superior de Investigaciones Cientificas (CSIS) in Madrid, Spain, aims to collect, preserve, and study JS language and literature. In addition to the huge collection of Ramon Menendez

---

[19] Other dictionaries are still in MS form. *Machon Maale Adumin* has them in its records.

Pidal's (1928) transcripts and catalogues, thousands of manuscripts, printed texts, newspapers, Michael Molho's library, and other material are collected there, catalogued and analysed by the Institute's chairman Iacob Hassán, by Elena Romero, and by their students.

Moshe Lazar edits the *Sephardic Classical Library*. This collection of JS classical texts is carefully edited and transcribed or copied in Roman characters. This enterprise makes rare books available to the JS researcher, copies of some of which have until now existed only in particular libraries around the world.

Amutat Sefarad (the Sepharad Association) in Israel, headed currently by Mordechai Arbel and Moshe Shaul (of *Aki Yerushalayim*), is a non-profit-making organization whose aim is the preservation of JS and its culture. Its most important executive branch is *Machon Maale Adumim* (the Maale Adumim Institute) next to Jerusalem, founded in 1994 and directed by Avner Perez. A considerable number of manuscripts, rare books, and other texts related to JS and its culture is being gathered there. With the help of Shaul's radio programme in JS and the Israeli *Phonoteca* at the Hebrew University, they have collected about 2,800 recordings of oral JS poetry and computerized them for scholarly use. In addition, they have collected over 6,000 proverbs, about 1,000 of them with authentic recordings. The Institute has published modern JS texts, and several books are about to come out, including a play from Bulgaria from 1899, *La Vinya de Navot* (Naboth's Vineyard), transcribed and translated into Hebrew, and the original *Meam Loez* to Genesis, with transliteration.

Amutat Sefarad and Machon Maale Adumim, with the help of the National Authority for Ladino and its Culture, are compiling a comprehensive dictionary, organized systematically and based on linguistic criteria. Some of these projects are done in co-operation with the Instituto de Estudios Sefardíes.

The *National Authority for Ladino and its Culture*, established in 1997, also aims at the preservation of JS and its culture. Yitshak Navon, the fifth president of Israel and a native speaker of JS, is the head of the authority and one of its sources of inspiration. In addition to supporting many of the enterprises related to JS in Israel mentioned above, the Authority gives financial support for the oral recording of native speakers and the salvation of books and manuscripts written in JS, new and old. Researchers of JS are given grants. It has also initiated a JS bibliographical project headed by Dov HaCohen, in which all JS books and manuscripts in Israel are listed systematically. With the help of the Authority, microfilm copies of the largest JS newspaper collection in the world, in the Ben Zvi Institute in Israel, are being prepared before the papers are spoiled. The Authority supports creative JS writing, and initiates domestic and international activities, for example study weekends, conferences, books exhibition, special courses for training JS teachers, concerts, and so on. And this is just a partial list of its activities.

Isaac Jerushalmi (Yerushalmi) edits *Ladino Books*. Rabbi Jerushalmi, of Cincinnati, Ohio, has collected Sephardic texts from Turkey, edited them, and transcribed and translated them into English, e.g. Yerushalmi (1989), Jerusalmi (1993), and others.

Researchers are working along these lines in other places. For lack of space they will not be mentioned here. All of these efforts are important for the protection and redemption of the JS tradition before it is gone forever.

7. PERSPECTIVES FOR FURTHER RESEARCH

The most imperative necessity today is to record the living JS native speakers in their use of the various literary genres and transcribe their language.[20] This basic data can later serve as corpus for any study of literary, linguistic, and textual analysis. It is a really urgent need, because the number of native speakers is gradually decreasing.

The second important task is to gather all existing JS documents, handwritten and printed. In spite of the detailed catalogues of JS creativity (Refael 1999), a great deal of manuscript material has not yet been collected in the above-mentioned institutes. Also, much of the printed material is not in libraries, and therefore has not yet been catalogued. These valuable documents exist either in private collections or as the personal belongings of people who do not always appreciate their value. Sometimes they are lost for various reasons. It is important to catalogue them and to produce monograph series on the variety of documents. The analysis of these data can be used for the study of vocabulary, grammatical structures, dialects, and other linguistic features. Although phonology and the lexicon have been studied quite intensively in the past, morphology, syntax, and semantics all need further investigation.

Time plays an important role in the redemption of whatever has remained of this beautiful language and rich linguistic heritage. As things now stand, it seems that only the activity of academic research will survive, long after the last JS native speaker has passed away.

SUGGESTED READING

Bunis's research bibliography is updated until 1980 (Bunis 1981). Studemund-Halevy's bibliographies are important, too (Studemund 1975, 1994a, 1994b). A general overview of

---

[20] Matilda Koén-Sarano, besides teaching JS, could be considered a one-woman enterprise. She records JS folk-tales and songs and publishes them in Roman script with their Hebrew translation in series of popular books.

the Sephardim and their language and literature can be found in Díaz-Mas (1992). A lot has been written since, e.g. rabbinical and other texts related to circumcision (Romero 1998), selected *coplas* (Romero 1988), selected *romansas* from Morocco (Weich-Shahak 1997, and the references therein). Wexler (1996) expresses a very controversial view regarding the development of JS, not accepted by most JS researchers.

BIBLIOGRAPHY

ABITBOL, M., HASAN-ROKEM, G., and ASSIS, Y. eds. 1997. *Hispano-Jewish Civilization After 1492*. Jerusalem.

ALEXANDER, T. 1986. 'The Character of Rabbi Isaac Luria in the Judeo-Spanish Story *The Converso and the Shewbread.*' [Hebrew.] *Pe'amim* 26: 87–107.

—— and WEICH-SHAHAK, S. 1994. *En este tiempo: Drama musical para Purim en Salónika*. Tel Aviv.

—— and BENTOLILA, Y. 2001. ' "Give a Jew a finger"—Intertextual Relations Between Hispanic Proverbs and Hakitic Proverbs.' [Hebrew.] *Ladinar* 2: 37–58.

—— BENABU, I., GELMAN, Y., SCHWARZWALD, O. R., and WEICH-SHAHAK, S. 1994. 'Towards a Typology of the Judeo-Spanish Folksong: Gerineldo and the Romance Model.' In *Yuval: Jewish Oral Traditions: An Interdisciplinary Approach* 6: 68–163.

ALEXANDER-FRIZER, T. 2000. *The Beloved Friend-and-a-half* [Hebrew]. Jerusalem and Beer Sheva.

ARMISTEAD, S. G. and SILVERMAN, J. H. 1971. *The Judeo-Spanish Ballad Chapbooks of Yacob Abraham Yona*. Berkeley.

—————— 1982. *En torno al romancero sefardi-hispanico y balcanico de la tradicion judeoespañola*. Madrid.

ATTIAS, M. 1961. *Romancero Sefaradi* [Hebrew]. Jerusalem.

BAER, F. 1936. *Die Juden im christlichen Spanien*. B. 2. Berlin.

BARQUÍN LOPEZ, A. 1995. *Edición y estudio de doce novelas aljamiadas sefardíes de principios del siglo XX*. Universidad del País Vasco.

BENBASSA, E. ed. 1996. *Mémoires juives d'Espagne et du Portugal*. Paris.

BENCHIMOL, M. and KOÉN-SARANO, M. 1999. *Vocabulario Djudeo-Espanyol (Ladino)–Ebreo, Ebreo–Djudeo-Espanyol (Ladino)*. Beer Sheva.

BENICHOU, P. 1944. 'Romances judeo-españolas de Marruecos.' *Revista de Filología Hispánica* 6: 36–76, 105–8, 255–79, 313–81.

BENDAYAN DE BENDELAC, A. 1995. *Diccionario del Judeoespañol de los Sefardíes del Norte de Marruecos*. Caracas.

BENOLIEL, J. 1977. *Dialecto Judeo-hispano-marroquí o hakitía*. Madrid.

BORNSTEIN-MAKOVETSKY, L. 2001. 'Halakhic and Rabbinic literature in Turkey, Greece and the Balkans, 1750–1900.' [Hebrew]. *Pe'amim* 86–7: 124–74.

BUNIS, D. M. 1981. *Sephardic Studies: A Research Bibliography*. New York.

—— 1988. 'The Dialect of the Old Yišuv Sephardic Community in Jerusalem: A Preliminary Linguistic Analysis.' In *Studies in Jewish Languages*. *1–*40. M. Bar-Asher ed. Jerusalem.

—— 1992. 'The Language of the Sephardim: A Historical Overview.' In *Moreshet Sepharad: The Sephardi Legacy*. 399–422. H. Beinart ed. Jerusalem.

—— 1993. *A Lexicon of the Hebrew and Aramaic Elements in Modern Judezmo*. Jerusalem.

BUNIS, D. M. 1995. 'Pyesa di Yaakov Avinu kun sus ijus (Bucharest, 1862): The first Judezmo play?' *REJ* 154/3–4: 387–428.

—— 1996. 'Translating From the Head and From the Heart: The Essentially Oral Nature of the Ladino Bible-Translation Tradition.' In *Hommage á Haïm Vidal Sephiha*. 337–57. W. Busse and M. C. Varol-Bornes eds. Berne.

—— 1999a. *Judezmo: An Introduction to the Language of the Sephardic Jews of the Ottoman Empire* [Hebrew]. Jerusalem.

—— 1999b. *Voices from Jewish Salonika*. Jerusalem and Thessaloniki.

CHEREZLI, S. Y. 1899. *Nuevo chiko diksyonario Judeo-Espagnol–Française*. Jerusalem.

CREWS, C. M. 1935. *Recherches sur le judeo-espagnol dans les pays balkaniques*. Paris.

DÍAZ-MAS, P. 1992. *Sephardim: The Jews from Spain*. G. K. Zucker trans. Chicago.

—— and MOTA, C. 1998. *Sem Tob de Carrión Proverbios Morales*. Madrid.

GAON, M. D. 1965. *A Bibliography of the Judeo-Spanish (Ladino) Press*. Jerusalem.

GATTEGNO, E. and REFAEL, S. 1995. *Primeros Pasos en Judeo-Español* [Hebrew]. Tel Aviv.

—— —— 1998. *Kurso Avansado i Superior en Judeo-Español (Ladino)* [Hebrew]. Tel Aviv.

HARRIS, T. K. 1994. *Death of a Language: The History of Judeo-Spanish*. Newark, NJ.

HASSÁN, I. M. 1976. 'Las Coplas de Purim.' Unpublished doctoral diss., Madrid.

—— 1978. 'Transcripción normalizada de textos judeoespañoles.' In *Estudios Sefardíes* 1: 147–150.

—— 1982. 'Visión panorámica de la literatura sefardí.' *Hispánia Judaica* 2: 25–44.

—— ed. 1994. *Introducción a la Biblia de Ferrara*. Madrid.

HITCHCOCK, R. 1977. *The Kharjas: A Critical Bibliography*. London.

JERUSALMI, I. 1993. *The Song of Songs in the Targumic Tradition*. Cincinnati.

KAPLAN, A. 1977–97. *Yalkut Meʿam Loʿez: The Torah Anthology*. New York.

KOÉN-SARANO, M. 1999a. *Kurso de Djudeo-Espanyol (Ladino) para prinsipiantes* [Hebrew]. Beer Sheva.

—— 1999b. *Kurso de Djudeo-Espanyol (Ladino) para adelantados* [Hebrew]. Beer Sheva.

—— 1999c. *Tabelas de verbos*. Jerusalem.

KOHEN, E. and KOHEN-GORDON, D. 2000. *Ladino–English/English–Ladino Concise Encyclopedic Dictionary*. New York.

LANDAU, L. 1980. 'Content and Form in the Meʿam Loʿez of Rabbi Jacob Culi.' [Hebrew.] Unpublished Ph.D diss., the Hebrew University in Jerusalem.

—— 1981. 'The Transformation of the Talmudic Story in Meʿam Loʿez.' In *Peʿamim* 7: 35–49.

LAZAR, M. 1964. 'Bible Translations in Ladino From After the Expulsion.' [Hebrew.] *Sefunot* 8: 337–75.

—— ed. 1988. *Ladino Pentateuch: Constantinople 1547*. Culver City. Ca.

—— ed. 1990. *Yehudah Halevi: Book of the Kuzari [15th c.]*. Culver City. Ca.

—— ed. 1993. *Sefer Tešubah: A Ladino Compedium of Jewish Law and Ethincs*. Culver City, Ca.

—— ed. 1995a. *Biblia Ladinada: Escorial I.j.3*. Madison, Wisc.

—— ed. 1995b. *Siddur Tefillot: A Woman's Ladino Prayer Book*. Culver City. Ca.

—— ed. 1999. *Sefarad in My Heart: A Ladino Reader*. Lancaster, Ca.

—— ed. 2000. *The Ladino Scriptures: Constantinople—Salonica [1540–1572]*, Vols. 1–2. Lancaster, Ca.

LÉVY, I. J. 1969. *Prolegomena to the Study of the 'Refranero Sefardi'*. New York.

—— 1989. *And the World Stood Silent: The Sephardic Poetry of the Holocaust*. Urbana, Ill.

LEORENZO SANZ, E. (co-ordinator) 1993. *Preyección histórica de España en sus tres culturas: America y el Mediterráneo.* Valladolid.

MAESO, D. G. and PASCUAL RECUERO, P. eds. 1964–70. *Mé'am Ló'ez: El gran comentario bíblico sefardí.* Vol. 1: *Prolegómenos*, 1964; Vol. 2: *Genesis* (I–XXV, 18), 1969; Vol. 3: *Genesis* (XXV, 18–L, 26), 1970. Madrid.

MARCUS, S. 1962. 'A-t-il existé en Espagne un dialecte judéo-espagnol.' *Sefarad* 22: 129–49.

—— 1965. *The Judeo-Spanish Language* [Hebrew]. Jerusalem.

MENÉNDEZ PIDAL, R. 1906–7. 'Catalogo del romancero judeo español.' *Cultura Española* 4: 1045–77; 5: 161–99.

—— 1928. *El Romancero Judéo-Espanol, Teorias e Investigaciones.* Madrid.

MINERVINI, L. 1992. *Testi Giudeospagnoli Medievali.* Vols. 1–2. Naples.

NEHAMA, J. 1977. *Dicctionaire du Judéo-Espagnol.* Madrid.

PASCUAL RECUERO, P. 1977. *Diccionario básico Ladino–Español.* Barcelona.

—— 1988. *Ortografia del Ladino.* Granada.

PASSY, A. M. 1999. *Sephardic Folk Dictionary English to Ladino—Ladino to English.* 6th edn. Los Angeles.

PENNY, R. 1996. 'Judeo-Spanish Varieties Before and After the Expulsion.' In *Donaire* 6: 54–8.

PERAHYA, K. and PERAHYA, E. 1998. *Dictionnaire Français Judéo-Espagnol.* Paris.

—— MERANDA, R., DANON, S., SEDAKA, R., and ZAKUTO, Ç. 1997. *Diksyonaryo/Sözlük Judeo-Espanyol–Türkçe/Türkçe–Judeo-Espanyol.* Istanbul.

PERI, H. 1955. 'Prayer in the Vernacular During the Middle Ages.' [Hebrew.] *Tarbiz* 24: 426–40.

QUINTANA, A. 1997. 'Diatopische Variation des Judenspanischen in den Balkanländern und in der Türkie.' *Judenspanisch II: Neue Romania* 19: 47–65.

REFAEL, S. 1998a. *The Knight and the Captive Lady.* [Hebrew]. Ramat Gan.

—— 1998b. 'Zionist Hymns in Judeo-Spanish Poetry.' [Hebrew]. *Pe'amim* 73: 41–59.

—— 1999. 'Trends and Goals in Catalogues and Bibliographies of Ladino Printed Books.' [Hebrew.] *Pe'amim* 81: 120–54.

RENARD, R. 1967. *Sépharad: Le monde et la langue judéo-espagnole des Séphardim.* Mons.

REVAH, I. S. 1970. 'Hispanisme et judaïsme des langues parlées et écrites par les Sefardim.' In *Actas del primer Simposio de Estudios Sefardies.* 233–41. I. M. Hassán ed. Madrid.

ROMANO, S. 1995 [1933]. *Dictionary of Spoken Judeo-Spanish/French/German.* Jerusalem.

ROMERO, E. 1979. *El teatro de los sefardíes orientales.* Vols. 1–3. Madrid.

—— 1988. *Coplas Sefardies.* Cordoba.

—— 1992a. *La creación literaria en lengua Sefardí.* Madrid.

—— 1992b. 'Literary Creation in the Sephardic Diaspora.' In *Moreshet Sepharad: The Sephardi Legacy.* 438–60. H. Beinart ed. Jerusalem.

—— 1993. 'Nuevos aspectos de la narrativa judeoespanola.' In Leorenzo Sanz (1993): iii. 175–94.

—— 1998. *El libro del buen retajer.* Madrid.

ROMEU FERRÉ, P. ed. 1998. *Moisés Almosnino Crónica de los Reyes Otomanos.* Barcelona.

—— 2000. *Las llaves del Meam Loez: Edición crítica, concordada y analítica de los Índices del Meam loez de la Tora.* Barcelona.

SCHWARZWALD (Rodrigue), O. 1989. *The Ladino Translations of Pirke Aboth* (*Eda VeLashon* 13) [Hebrew]. Jerusalem.

SCHWARZWALD (Rodrigue), O. 1996. 'Linguistic Variations Among Ladino Translations as Determined By Geographical, Temporal and Textual Factors.' *Folia Linguistica Historica* 17: 57–72.

SCHWARZWALD 1999. 'Language Choice and Language Varieties Before and After the Expulsion.' In Stillman and Stillman (1999): 399–415.

—— 2000. 'Proper Names in Ladino Translations: Origin and Jewish Identity.' [Hebrew]. *Pé'amim* 84: 66–77.

—— Forthcoming. 'A New Look at the Origin and Transmission of the Ladino Translations.' In *Bentolila Jubilee Book* [Hebrew]. D. Sivan and I. Kirtchuk eds. Beer Sheva.

SEPHIHA, H. V. 1973. *Le Ladino: Deutéronome.* Paris.

—— 1979. *Le Ladino (Judéo-Espagnol Calque).* Paris.

—— 1986. *Le Judéo-Espagnol.* Paris.

SHAUL, M. ed. 1979– . *Aki Yerushalayim: Revista Kulturala Djudeo-espanyola.* Jerusalem.

—— 1999. *Ladino (Spanyolit) for Beginners.* [Hebrew]. Maale Adumim.

STILLMAN, Y. K. and STILLMAN, N. A. eds. 1999. *From Iberia to Diaspora: Studies in Sephardic History and Culture.* Leiden.

STUDEMUND, M. 1975. *Bibliographie zum Judenspanischen.* Hamburg.

—— 1994a. *Bibliographie zur Geschichte der Juden in Hamburg.* Munich.

—— 1994b. *Die Sefarden in Hamburg.* Hamburg.

VAROL, M. C. 1998. *Manuel de Judéo-Espagnol: Langue et Culture.* Paris.

VARVARO, A. 1987. 'Il giudeo-spagnolo prima dell'espulsione del 1492.' *Medioevo Romanzo* 12: 154–72.

WAGNER, M. L. 1990. *Juden-Spanish I–II.* Stuttgart.

WEICH-SHAHAK S. 1997. *Romancero sefardí de Marruecos: Antología de tradición oral.* Madrid.

WEINREICH, M. 1973. *History of the Yiddish Language.* S. Noble trans. Chicago.

WEXLER, P. 1987. 'De-Judaicization and incipient re-Judaicization in 18th century Portuguese Ladino.' *Iberoromania* 25: 23–37.

—— 1996. *The Non-Jewish Origin of the Sephardic Jews.* New York.

WIESNER, C. 1981. *Jüdisch-Spanisches Glossar zum MEʿAM LOʿEZ des Iacob Kuli.* Hamburg.

YAARI, A, 1934. *Catalogue of Judeo-Spanish Books* [Hebrew.] Jerusalem.

YERUSHALMI, I. 1989. *Reuven Eliyahu Yisrael's Traduksyon Livre de las Poezias Ebraikas de Rosh ha-Shana I Kippur 5670 and the Six Selihoth of the 5682 Edition.* Cincinnati.

YERUSHALMI, S. 1957–81. *Yalkut Méʿam Loʿez.* 20 vols. Jerusalem.

ZAMORA VICENTE, A. 1967. *Dialectología Española.* 2nd edn. Madrid.

CHAPTER 24

JUDAEO-ARABIC
AND
JUDAEO-PERSIAN

GEOFFREY KHAN

JUDAEO-ARABIC

THE term 'Judaeo-Arabic' refers to a type of Arabic that was used by Jews and was distinct in some way from other types of Arabic. It is by no means a uniform linguistic entity. Different criteria, moreover, have been used to define it.

The Arabic language was used by Jews in Arabia before the rise of Islam. Some of the pre-Islamic Arabic poets were Jewish, the most famous of whom was al-Samawʾal ibn ʿĀdiyaʾ. The surviving written works of such Jewish poets do not exhibit anything that distinguishes them from the equivalent works of their non-Jewish contemporaries, and so are generally not referred to as Judaeo-Arabic. It is assumed that the Jewish communities in Arabia spoke Arabic as their vernacular language. Although we do not have any direct evidence of the nature of this spoken language, some scholars claim that there are indirect indications that it differed from the vernacular of the non-Jews.

After the Islamic conquests in the seventh century CE, the Arabic language gradually spread throughout the Near East. It was initially restricted to the Arab invading armies, but soon began to be used by the local population. This applied not only to converts to Islam but also to Jews and Christians who maintained their religion and traditional communal life. The Arabicization took place most rapidly in the large urban centres, where the Arab armies had settled and established centres of administration. In the pre-Islamic period the Jews of Iraq and Syria spoke Aramaic, whereas further west they used Berber or Romance as their vernacular languages. These languages were largely replaced by Arabic. The Jewish communities in rural areas were much slower in adopting the Arabic language. Although the Jews of the urban centres in Iraq appear to have become Arabic-speaking by the eighth century CE, there is evidence that the Jews in the countryside continued to speak Aramaic at least until the tenth century. Some Jewish communities living in the isolated mountainous areas of Northern Iraq never fully adopted Arabic as a vernacular, and continued to speak Aramaic down to modern times. A similar pattern applied to the spread of Arabic elsewhere in the Islamic empire.

During the first three centuries of the Islamic period the Jews in the Near East used the traditional rabbinic languages of Hebrew and Aramaic as their written language, although many of the urban communities were no doubt using Arabic as their vernacular at this period. One factor that may explain the slowness of the Jews to use Arabic as a written literary language was that the main centres of Jewish learning, such as the academies of Sura and Pumbeditha, were situated in the Iraqi countryside where Aramaic remained the spoken language for a longer period (Fenton 1990: 464). The first written records of Judaeo-Arabic are datable to the ninth century CE. These are largely private documents from Egypt that were written on papyrus. Both the writers and recipients were Jews. They were written in Hebrew script, which became one of the most conspicuous distinctive features of Judaeo-Arabic.

Arabic was not used in high-register literary texts written by Jews for a Jewish readership until the tenth century, although we have some evidence of Jews of a slightly earlier period writing scientific or astrological texts for a general readership. These literary texts that began to be produced in the tenth century were written in Hebrew script. Arabic in Hebrew script continued to be used by Jews in Arabic-speaking lands throughout the Middle Ages down to modern times. The term 'Judaeo-Arabic' is frequently used to refer to all such cases of Arabic written in Hebrew script. This is based on a descriptive linguistic criterion, namely its graphic representation, and also, by implication, one of communicative function, since anything written in Hebrew script would, one assumes, be addressed to a Jewish readership.

Judaeo-Arabic in this sense, that is, any form of Arabic written in Hebrew script, is not a linguistically uniform phenomenon. It is generally categorized into three chronological periods that correspond to three major phases in its linguistic development, viz. Early Judaeo-Arabic, Classical Judaeo-Arabic, and Late Judaeo-Arabic.

The term 'Early Judaeo-Arabic' is used to refer to the Judaeo-Arabic that is attested in the ninth century, mostly in papyri. The main linguistic feature that distinguishes this from Classical Judaeo-Arabic is the orthography with which the Arabic is represented. It is based essentially on the spelling practices used for Rabbinic Hebrew and Aramaic at that period. This is particularly noticeable in the use of vowel letters or *matres lectionis*. The scribes, moreover, wrote the Arabic phonetically, without taking into account the spelling conventions of Classical Muslim Arabic in Arabic script. The Arabic word for 'sun', الشـمس for example, was written אששמש, since it was written pronounced 'aššams with the *lām* of the definite article assimilated to the *šīn*. In Classical Judaeo-Arabic, which was used from the tenth to approximately the fifteenth centuries CE, the spelling that was used was made to correspond to the orthographic conventions of Arabic in Arabic script. The word for 'sun', therefore, was written אלשמש, corresponding to Arabic الشـمس. The vowel letters of Classical Judaeo-Arabic, furthermore, corresponded exactly to those of Classical Muslim Arabic in Arabic script. In Late Judaeo-Arabic, which began to be used roughly after the fifteenth century, scribes abandoned a rigorous imitation of the orthography of Classical Muslim Arabic and, as in the Early Judaeo-Arabic period, employed many of the conventions of spelling that were used for Rabbinic Hebrew and Aramaic.

In addition to differences in orthography in these three periods, there were also differences in grammatical structure. From the early Islamic period, and probably also before the rise of Islam, distinct types of Arabic were used for speech and writing. The spoken language included numerous dialects, whereas the written language was of an essentially standard form. The standard written language, in its classical form, is generally referred to as Classical Arabic. It is a feature of Judaeo-Arabic texts written in all three periods that they usually exhibit grammatical deviations from Classical Arabic. These deviations are due to interference from vernacular spoken dialects of Arabic. The extent to which the language deviates from Classical Arabic varies from text to text, but in general it is far more pronounced in Late Judaeo-Arabic than in Early and Classical Judaeo-Arabic. As a result of this, Late Judaeo-Arabic differs from region to region, since it reflects the local spoken dialects of the writers. Another feature of Judaeo-Arabic of all periods is the presence of Hebrew and Aramaic words in the language. These sometimes include more than purely technical terms associated with Jewish tradition. They are often adapted to the grammatical structure of Arabic, and take, for example, Arabic plural endings.

From the point of view of linguistic form, therefore, the following characteristic features of written Judaeo-Arabic can be identified:

1. it is written in Hebrew script;
2. it exhibits deviations from Classical Arabic; and
3. it contains Hebrew and Aramaic elements.

All three elements arise to a large extent from the traditional Jewish educational background of the scribes. This involved the learning of the Hebrew Bible and rabbinic texts rather than rigorous instruction in Classical Arabic grammar, with the result that the Jews felt more at home with Hebrew script than with Arabic script and that they had a less-than-perfect grasp of Classical Arabic.

From the strict point of view of descriptive linguistics, however, certain texts that were written by Jews lack some, if not all, of the aforementioned characteristic features of Judaeo-Arabic. This applies especially to some texts that were written by Jews belonging to the Karaite movement of Judaism. In the tenth to twelfth centuries the Karaites often wrote Arabic manuscripts in Arabic script. Manuscripts of this nature are often written in a relatively pure form of Classical Arabic. One of the reasons for their use of Arabic rather than Hebrew script seems to be that they did not feel themselves to be so rooted in the rabbinic literary tradition as the orthodox rabbanite Jews and were, consequently, more open to adopting literary and linguistic practices from the surrounding non-Jewish environment. These Karaite texts in Arabic script were, nevertheless, clearly addressed to a Jewish readership and their contents must be defined as Jewish. They generally include a number of technical Hebrew or Aramaic elements, usually in the form of citations from the Bible, generally also in Arabic script. The main feature that distinguishes them from Classical Muslim Arabic texts, therefore, is the Jewish subject-matter. From the point of view of linguistic form, however, it is difficult to classify their language as 'Judaeo-Arabic'. It is legitimate, however, to designate them as 'Judaeo-Arabic' from the point of view of social and communicative function, in that they are addressed to Jews on Jewish subjects, with contents that are likely to be largely incomprehensible to non-Jews.

In addition to the distinction between linguistic criteria and the criteria of communicative function in the definition of written Judaeo-Arabic, we should also make a distinction between a text in general and individual manifestations of a text in manuscripts. This distinction is relevant both when applying criteria of linguistic form and criteria of communicative function.

The application of criteria of linguistic form to identify the language of a written text as Judaeo-Arabic may apply to the text in general, in all its recorded forms in manuscripts. This would be legitimate where the manifestations of the texts in manuscripts are largely uniform. In many cases, however, it is necessary to apply the criteria to each manuscript individually. The Karaite texts that are found written in some manuscripts in Arabic script, for example, were often copied in other manuscripts in Hebrew script. It is, in fact, difficult to establish in which script they were originally written. In the Middle Ages the choice of script used in Karaite manuscripts seems to have been largely the reflection of individual preferences. One Karaite author, for example, before writing the manuscript of the final version of a work, felt obliged to send a letter to the man who commissioned the work asking whether he wished the text to be written in Arabic or Hebrew script (Khan 1993a).

The distinction between text in general and individual manuscripts is also relevant when applying the criterion of communicative function in the definition of Judaeo-Arabic. In the majority of cases, when a text is defined as 'Judaeo-Arabic' with regard to its communicative function, this applies to the text in general, in all its attestations. In a few cases the definition is not so straightforward. This applies, for example, to a number of manuscripts which contain Arabic texts written by non-Jewish authors that have been transcribed into Hebrew script. These texts were clearly written originally for either a Muslim or general readership, rather than one that was specifically Jewish. A wide range of texts were transcribed in this way, including even the Qur'an. A similar phenomenon is found in documentary material, in that Jews used to write in Hebrew script drafts and personal copies of Arabic documents that were addressed to Muslim officials, although the final version of the document that was sent to the official was written in Arabic script. In such cases the text in general cannot be defined as Judaeo-Arabic, based on the criteria of linguistic form or communicative function, but the manuscripts in Hebrew script could be identified as Judaeo-Arabic according to both of these criteria. Although the text in general was not designed for a Jewish readership, the manuscripts in Hebrew script were written specifically for Jews who felt more at home in that script. Conversely, some Arabic texts that were written by Jews originally in Hebrew script for a Jewish readership, were occasionally copied into Arabic script for a Muslim readership. One example of this is a manuscript of Maimonides' *Guide For the Perplexed* that is written entirely in Arabic script (Atay 1974). Finally, we should mention the fact that some early European presses printed Muslim Arabic texts in Hebrew characters simply because an Arabic fount was not available (Fenton 1990: 462–3). It is doubtful whether these should be defined as Judaeo-Arabic from the point of view of either linguistic form or communicative function.

Of course, the majority of texts that are defined as Judaeo-Arabic on the basis of criteria of linguistic form can also be so classified on the level of communicative function. Likewise many texts can legitimately be defined as Judaeo-Arabic in all their manuscript manifestations. It is important, however, to be aware of the necessity to make a distinction between these levels of analysis in some circumstances, since, as we have seen, these levels of analysis do not always coincide and it is in such cases that a single, monolithic definition of Judaeo-Arabic can be confusing. In a general overview of the subject, such as is being attempted here, however, it is helpful to have a 'working definition' of written Judaeo-Arabic which includes the features that are exhibited by the majority of texts, while remaining aware of the fact that stricter, more precise definitions are necessary in some cases. In the remainder of this survey, therefore, we shall adopt the working definition of written Judaeo-Arabic as *Arabic texts written in Hebrew script by Jews for a Jewish readership*.

We have presented above a classification of Judaeo-Arabic into three chronological periods according to its linguistic development. In general terms, the range and nature of the written material in Judaeo-Arabic also differed across these three periods.

As remarked, the scant material surviving in Early Judaeo-Arabic is mainly in the form of private documents on papyrus. There are also a few fragments of manuscripts of literary texts.

In the period of Classical Judaeo-Arabic, Judaeo-Arabic was used in a very wide range of texts. Many of the traditional texts of Judaism were translated into Judaeo-Arabic, including first and foremost the Hebrew Bible, but also other texts such as the Mishnah, the Talmuds, midrashim, and liturgy. Many new genres of Arabic text were adopted by the Jews from the Muslim cultural environment and adapted to Judaism. This reflected a close rapprochement between the Jews and Muslim culture in the High Middle Ages (approximately tenth–thirteenth centuries). The new genres of texts included works on biblical exegesis, grammar, systematically arranged handbooks of legal subjects, and works on theology and philosophy. Judaeo-Arabic was also used for a wide range of documentary material. Most letters were written in Judaeo-Arabic and also a large proportion of Jewish legal documents. Hebrew was still used as a learned language in letters by some Jewish intellectuals, such as the Geonim. It was also used by the leading Jewish poets in the Middle Ages, but many popular verses and songs were composed by Jews in Judaeo-Arabic.

In the Late Judaeo-Arabic period, the range of texts written in Judaeo-Arabic became more restricted. Among the factors that brought this about was that the Jewish communities enjoyed less intellectual rapprochement with the Muslim environment and that Spanish and Portuguese Jews refugees from the expulsions in the fifteenth century and their descendants came to be among the leading intellectuals in most Arabic-speaking Jewish communities in the Near East. Judaeo-Arabic became restricted largely to popular texts such as stories and songs or private letters. Another common type of Judaeo-Arabic text in this period was a literal translation of the Bible known as šarḥ. This was a word by word gloss which generally could not be understood independently of the original Hebrew source text. The medieval Judaeo-Arabic Bible translations ceased to be used in most Arabic-speaking Jewish communities and were supplanted by the šarḥ, the language of which was much closer to the local vernacular spoken dialect. It should be noted, however, that in the Jewish communities of Yemen, Classical Judaeo-Arabic texts continued to be copied and read down to modern times and the division between Classical and Late periods of Judaeo-Arabic is not so appropriate.

Judaeo-Arabic texts attracted the interest of Western scholars at an early stage in the development of the discipline of Oriental languages in European universities. Following the Reformation in the early sixteenth century, there was particular interest in texts that could elucidate the Bible, such as translations, commentaries, and treatises on Hebrew grammar. The Judaeo-Arabic version of the Pentateuch by Saadya Gaon was incorporated in the Paris Polyglot (1645) by Gabriel Sionita in Arabic transcription, and subsequently also in the Walton Polyglot (1657) by Edward Pococke. While serving as Anglican chaplain in Aleppo, Pococke acquired a large number of Judaeo-Arabic manuscripts, which are now in the possession of the Bodleian Library in Oxford. Pococke himself printed an extract from a manu-script containing Maimonides' Judaeo-Arabic commentary on the Mishnah (*Porta Mosis*, Oxford, 1655). In the eighteenth and nineteenth centuries a number of scholars studied and published Judaeo-Arabic texts from the Oxford collection. In the nineteenth century important collections of Judaeo-Arabic manuscripts were acquired in France, largely due to the efforts of Solomon Munk, who also made important contributions to Judaeo-Arabic scholarship. Important editions of Judaeo-Arabic texts from Western European collections continued to be made throughout the nineteenth century. We may mention here the work of Joseph Derenbourg who published some of the exegetical texts of Saadya Gaon and also the grammatical works of Ibn Janāḥ. Derenbourg's work is a good illustration of the nature of Judaeo-Arabic scholarship at this period. The emphasis was on the publication of texts on the basis of the available manuscripts. These editions are foundational works in the field. It should be noted, however, that some of the manuscripts used by scholars at this period were late and not reliable. Moreover, there were no fixed conventions about the editing of Judaeo-Arabic texts. Many of the editors took great liberties with their manuscript sources. They sometimes transcribed the text into Arabic script and even 'corrected' dialectal features of the text that were judged not to conform to the rules of Classical Arabic.

It should also be noted that at this period scholars were exclusively interested in texts from the classical period of Judaeo-Arabic literature. There was little interest in texts written in Late Judaeo-Arabic. This neglect of the later texts by scholars continued throughout the twentieth century. Some Late Judaeo-Arabic texts, how-ever, were printed and published in the local Arabic-speaking communities, the presses in the North Africa communities being particularly active. These included original works and translations, including Late Judaeo-Arabic renditions of some Classical Judaeo-Arabic works. Judaeo-Arabic newspapers were also published in various communities.

An important milestone in Judaeo-Arabic scholarship was the work *Die Arabische Literatur der Juden* (1902), by the indefatigable bibliographer Moritz Steinschneider (1816–1907). This was an exhaustive bibliographical record of the Judaeo-Arabic works that were known to him. His sources were mainly manuscript collections in Western Europe. It is still of importance today, although we now have access to a larger number of manuscripts.

By the end of the nineteenth century two important collections of Judaeo-Arabic manuscripts had been acquired by academic libraries that were to prove of immense importance. First was the so-called Firkovitch collection, which came into the possession of the Imperial Library in St Petersburg (now the National Library of Russia). This was divided into two parts, known as the first and the second Firkovitch collections. Of particular importance for Judaeo-Arabic studies is the second Firkovitch collection. This consists of more than 15,000 items that were acquired by the Karaite bibliophile Abraham Firkovitch (1787–1874). It includes a large number of Judaeo-Arabic manuscripts. Most of these were found by Firko-vitch in the Karaite synagogue in Cairo between the years 1863 and 1865. The other major collection was that of the Cairo Genizah. The Genizah was a repository for discarded manuscripts that was discovered in a medieval synagogue in Old Cairo (Fusṭāṭ) in the second half of the nineteenth century. This contained approxi-mately 200,000 fragments of manuscripts, most dating to between the tenth and thirteenth centuries. The majority of the fragments were brought to Cambridge by Solomon Schechter with the financial assistance of Charles Taylor, and were ac-quired by Cambridge University in 1898, forming the Taylor–Schechter Genizah collection. Some smaller collections of Genizah manuscripts were acquired by other libraries.

The contents of these two collections greatly enriched the Judaeo-Arabic material that was available to scholars at the end of the nineteenth century. The second Firkovitch collection contains a large number of Early Judaeo-Arabic manuscripts. These are often copies of texts that are not known from other sources and are not listed in Steinschneider's *Arabische Literatur der Juden*. Some of the manuscripts are copies of works that are known from manuscripts in other sources, but are older and more reliable. The Genizah collection, likewise, contains fragments of many Judaeo-Arabic texts that were not known at the end of the nineteenth century and early copies of known works. A unique feature of the Genizah, however, is its copious Judaeo-Arabic documentary material. This includes a vast array of private, official, and legal documents that allow scholars to reconstruct the everyday life of the Jewish community of Old Cairo (Fusṭāṭ) in the Middle Ages. Many of the Genizah fragments also give us an insight into forms popular culture, such as games, soothsaying, and magic, that are not known from literary texts. Furthermore the Genizah contains some material in Late Judaeo-Arabic and also a number of fragments that exhibit Early Judaeo-Arabic orthography.

Some of the Judaeo-Arabic material from the Firkovitch collections was pub-lished by Russian scholars such as A. Harkavy (1835–1919), P. Kokowzow (1861–1942), and A. Borisov (1903–42). For many years, during the communist era, it was virtually impossible for scholars from outside Russia to have free access to the collections. They were finally opened up to international scholarship in the last decade of the twentieth century. A card index of the manuscripts was made in St Petersburg, for the most part by A. Harkavy, but this is often rather vague and an accurate idea of the contents of the collection will only be possible after a systematic catalogue has been completed.

Scholarly work on the Cairo Genizah has fared better. H. Hirschfeld was one of the first scholars to study the Judaeo-Arabic material. Systematic work was begun on the Judaeo-Arabic documentary material by S. D. Goitein and his students, many of whom have themselves become leading authorities in the field. A large number of the Judaeo-Arabic Genizah documents have now been published and catalogues are available for a large part of the collection.

In addition to work on the Genizah, a number of other important contributions were made to the field of medieval Judaeo-Arabic studies in the twentieth century. These include text editions and various studies based on Judaeo-Arabic material.

For some texts we now have available a very large number of manuscripts. This often makes the preparation of an edition a complex task, particularly since the manuscripts frequently do not reflect a stable text. Works that became popular were often published in shortened versions. This abbreviation often existed in several degrees. An extreme example of this textual diversity of a single work is the collection of homilies attributed to David ben Abraham Maimuni, the grandson of Maimonides, which has been transmitted in a remarkable variety of versions (Almagor 1995).

The linguistic study of medieval Judaeo-Arabic did not receive serious attention until the twentieth century. Previously scholars who edited Judaeo-Arabic texts tended to take a pejorative view of the language and consider it to be a corrupted form of Classical Arabic, which, as remarked, they often did not hesitate to correct. This attitude is not held any longer, thanks to the work of J. Blau who, in his many publications, has studied the linguistic structure and background of medieval Judaeo-Arabic. He has shown that medieval Judaeo-Arabic should be regarded as a form of literary Arabic in its own right, and that editors of Judaeo-Arabic texts should reproduce faithfully the language as it appears in the manuscripts. In recent years texts in Early Judaeo-Arabic have been investigated by J. Blau and S. Hopkins. Late Judaeo-Arabic has been studied by B. Hary, who has examined the linguistic structure and background of texts from Egypt.

The Cairo Genizah has still not revealed all its secrets, and it remains the most important source for Judaeo-Arabic documentary material. It is the Firkovitch collection, however, that contains the greater proportion of unexplored manuscripts. The study and publication of the texts contained in this collection, many of which are unknown from other sources, will require the work of several generations of future scholars. The few Judaeo-Arabic texts from the Firkovitch Collection that have been published in recent years have already cast new light on medieval Judaism and, as more are published, the history books for that period of Judaism will have to be rewritten.

In order to be in a position to work with Judaeo-Arabic manuscripts, scholars need to have a good training in both Arabic and Hebrew. This is a qualification that is becoming increasingly rare among university students outside Israel. It is hoped that more students will be encouraged to combine the two languages by the exciting prospects of research. In 1984 an academic organization known as the Society for Judaeo-Arabic Studies was founded by N. Golb of the University of Chicago to promote the study of medieval Judaeo-Arabic language and texts. This society holds a biennial conference that brings together researchers in the field. The published papers of these conferences are a good indication of the current scope of the Judaeo-Arabic studies (first conference: N. Golb ed. 1997; second conference: *Sefunot*, N S 5,

1991; third conference: J. Blau and S. C. Reif eds. 1992; fourth conference: J. Blau ed. 1998). The membership of the society is international, though a large majority of its active members are Israeli. In England at present Judaeo-Arabic studies is concentrated at the University of Cambridge. This is the home of the famous Taylor–Schechter Genizah collection. For several decades now a research unit under the directorship of S. C. Reif has been working on this collection, and it includes several Judaeo-Arabic specialists among its staff. Various projects on Judaeo-Arabic material are also being undertaken at the Faculty of Oriental Studies in Cambridge that involve both Ph.D. and postdoctoral researchers under the supervision of G. Khan.

We have been concerned so far almost exclusively with Judaeo-Arabic in its written form. The term Judaeo-Arabic, however, is also used to refer to the spoken vernacular of Jewish communities in the Arabic-speaking world. Many of these have left their original places of residence and have now moved to the State of Israel. There are still, however, remnants of Arabic-speaking Jewish communities in some parts of the Arab world, especially in North Africa.

The spoken Judaeo-Arabic dialects generally differ in structure from dialects spoken by the neighbouring Muslim population. The Muslim dialects often exhibit a number of features that are characteristic of the Bedouin Arabic dialects, whereas Jewish dialects generally preserve features of the old urban dialects. It is not clear how far back this divergence of dialects among confessional communities can be traced. There is some evidence, however, that already in the Middle Ages differences had arisen due to distinct patterns of population movement of Jews and Muslims. Some of the Arabic dialects spoken by Iraqi Jewish communities exhibit features that appear to have arisen under the influence of Aramaic, their former spoken language. These, therefore, would presumably have always differed from the Muslim dialects, which did not have such an Aramaic substrate.

The best-studied case of divergence between communal dialects is that of Baghdad before the emigration of the Jews in the 1950s. H. Blanc, in his *Communal Dialects in Baghdad* (1964), has shown how the dialect of the Jewish population of Baghdad differed in all levels of grammar (phonology, morphology, syntax) and also vocabulary both from the dialect of the neighbouring Muslims and also from that of the Christians of the same town. In this work Blanc examines the general phenomenon of Arabic dialectal differences between religious communities.

A number of the items of vocabulary that are exclusive to the Arabic dialects of the Jewish communities are of Hebrew origin. These words have generally been adapted to the phonology and morphology of the dialect. This Hebrew component, together with the distinct features of grammatical structure, clearly justify the designation of the dialects as Judaeo-Arabic from the point of view of linguistic form. The term is also justified with regard to communicative function, since such dialects were, in principle, only used by Jews to communicate with other Jews and, indeed, were often incomprehensible to non-Jews.

As with the definition of written Judaeo-Arabic, there is not such a clear justification on the grounds of linguistic form to classify some types of Arabic spoken by Jews as being distinct from the neighbouring Muslim dialects. This applies, for example, to the Arabic dialects spoken by the Jews of Egypt before their mass emigration in the 1950s and 1960s. There are some small structural peculiarities in the dialect of the Rabbanite Egyptian Jews, but the Arabic spoken by the Karaite community of Cairo was largely identical in structure to that of Muslim Arabic. Such small differences that existed tended to be in the area of vocabulary, which included a number of Hebrew loan-words. In terms of communicative function, therefore, there would be grounds for labelling the Arabic spoken by the Karaites of Cairo as Judaeo-Arabic, but the case would be less clear purely on the grounds of linguistic form. A similar case was the Arabic dialect that was spoken by Jews in the Old City of Jerusalem in the first half of the twentieth century. This was essentially identical in structure to the Arabic of the neighbouring Muslims, and differed only in the usage of Hebrew loan-words and small divergences in intonation.

In a number of communities secret trade languages were invented in order to ensure that their speech was incomprehensible to Muslims, and indeed to anybody outside their professional circle. The Karaite goldsmiths of Cairo, for example, had such a trade argot, and other argots are recorded as having been used among the Jews of North Africa.

Work on the linguistic description of the spoken Judaeo-Arabic dialects has by no means been neglected. Several important grammatical studies on a variety of dialects were published in the twentieth century and continue to appear. The number and diversity of the Judaeo-Arabic dialects is, nevertheless, considerable, especially in North Africa, Iraq, and Yemen, and many of these have not received any attention. The description of these dialects has now become an urgent task for the future, since a large proportion of the speakers have left their original places of residence. This applies especially to the Jewish communities of Iraq and Yemen, who have almost totally emigrated. The dialects are already beginning to be forgotten by the younger generations of these communities, and are likely to disappear completely within the next few years. As with the case of written Judaeo-Arabic, work on the spoken forms of Judaeo-Arabic requires a knowledge of both Arabic and Hebrew. Since much of the field now has to be carried out in Israel, field-workers need to be fluent in Modern Hebrew in order to communicate successfully with informants.

JUDAEO-PERSIAN

'Judaeo-Persian' refers to Persian used by Jews. Like Judaeo-Arabic, Judaeo-Persian is not a uniform linguistic entity. The term is used to refer to both a written and a spoken form of language. The geographical area in which it was used extended beyond the boundaries of Iran and included Afghanistan, part of the Caucasus, and much of Central Asia.

Judaeo-Persian in its written form is represented in Hebrew script. It can be divided into an early and a classical period. The early period extends from the eighth century CE, which is the date of the most ancient texts so far know, until the fourteenth century. The texts from this early period are of considerable linguistic diversity. They are written in a form of New Persian, but not the form that was to become the standard language of Classical Persian literature. The early Judaeo-Persian texts, which originate in a variety of geographical areas, reflect different local Persian dialects. Some contain linguistic features that are characteristic of Middle Persian, but scholars generally regard their language to represent New Persian in its early stages of development. The texts are of a variety of different types, including inscriptions, private and legal documents, biblical commentaries, grammatical works, medical treatises, and texts concerning magic. A number of the texts may have been written by Persian-speaking immigrants in Palestine and Egypt. This applies especially to a corpus of early Judaeo-Persian texts written by Karaite Jews.

In the fourteenth century Judaeo-Persian works began to be written in a form of New Persian that was essentially identical to that of Classical Persian, except for its representation in Hebrew script and the usage of a number of Hebrew and Aramaic words. Even the orthography of Judaeo-Persian in this classical phase of its literature imitated that of Classical Persian, as was the case with Classical Judaeo-Arabic. It should be noted, however, that this literary rapprochement between the Jewish communities and the surrounding Muslim culture came later in Iran than in Arabic-speaking lands.

A variety of Bible translations were produced in Classical Judaeo-Persian as well as poetry, mainly on biblical themes. The Judaeo-Persian poets imitated not only the Classical Persian language, but also the traditional epic style of the classical Persian poets. Manuscripts of these poetic works often contain miniature illuminations similar to the ones that adorned the manuscripts of the works of the Muslim poets. Indeed, many of the writings of the classical Muslim Persian poets were transcribed into Hebrew script for the benefit of a Jewish readership. There are manuscripts in Hebrew script containing works by the famous poets Niẓāmī, Rūmī, Ḥāfiẓ, and others. These texts obviously cannot be classified as Judaeo-Persian literature and, as is the case with the transcription of Muslim Arabic texts into Hebrew script, one needs to make a distinction between the text in general and its manifestation in individual manuscripts. The manuscripts in Hebrew script can be described as Judaeo-Persian both with regard to their graphical form and their communicative function, in that they were intended exclusively for a Jewish readership.

A distinct phase in the development of Judaeo-Persian literature is represented by the production of numerous literary works by the Jews of Bukhara in the eighteenth century. These were written in the local Tajiki dialect of Persian and so differed linguistically from Classical Judaeo-Persian works. They include poetic compositions either on traditional Jewish themes or on the theme of local events, and also commentaries and translations of Jewish texts.

In the second half of the nineteenth century many Persian-speaking Jews from Bukhara, Turkestan, Afghanistan and Iran emigrated to Palestine. They set up a Hebrew printing press in Jerusalem and published a very wide range of literature in Judaeo-Persian. This was intended to meet the religious and literary interests of Persian-speaking Jews throughout the diaspora. Judaeo-Persian translations were made of Bible and rabbinic texts, commentaries, prayer books and poetry. A number of non-Jewish texts were also translated, including the *Arabian Nights* and Shakespeare's *Comedy of Errors*. A Hebrew press was set up also in Tehran at the beginning of the twentieth century, which produced many Judaeo-Persian works.

There are numbers of spoken dialects of Judaeo-Persian that are still the living vernacular of a number of Jewish communities, such as those of Kāshān, Hamadān, Iṣfahān, Kirmān, Shirāz, and Yazd. These exhibit numerous differences from standard Persian, which is ultimately derived from the local dialect of Khurasān. In most cases they are distinct from the dialects spoken by the Muslim population. In Bukhara the spoken language should strictly be defined as a variant form of the Iranian dialect of Tajik, though this is sometimes referred to as Judaeo-Persian. In the Caucasus the Jews spoke a variant of the Iranian dialect known as Tāt. The Persian Jews had secret languages, one of which, known as *Zargari* was used by goldsmiths.

Some of these spoken Judaeo-Persian dialects exhibit archaic features. This applies especially to the dialect of Yazd, which preserves an ergative verbal system that is characteristic of earlier Iranian. It is not clear whether the dialects reflected by the early Judaeo-Persian written texts were already distinct from those of the local Muslim population. Most of these texts are probably not direct representations of the spoken language, but are attempts at a literary style with interference from the vernacular.

As with Judaeo-Arabic, the beginnings of interest by Western scholars in Judaeo-Persian can be dated to the post-Reformation period, when there was an increasing enthusiasm for the philological study of the Bible and its versions. The Persian version of the Bible that was published in the Walton Polyglot (1657) was a transliteration in Arabic script of a Judaeo-Persian version that is attributed to Jacob ben Joseph Tavus, a Persian scholar active in Istanbul in the sixteenth century. A large number of manuscripts containing Judaeo-Persian Bible versions were collected at the beginning of the seventeenth century by the Florentine scholar Giambattista Vecchietti. By the nineteenth century European libraries had acquired many Judaeo-Persian manuscripts, which formed the basis of important publications by Western scholars. At this period, however, there was still no awareness of the full range of Judaeo-Persian literature, since the Western collections of manuscripts were still mainly restricted to Bible versions. A turning-point in Judaeo-Persian research was brought about by the acquisition of a large collection of Judaeo-Persian manuscripts in Bukhara and Persia by Elkan N. Adler in 1896–8. This contained works representing the full range of Judaeo-Persian literature, including poetry and popular narratives. The collection, which was subsequently acquired by the Jewish Theological Seminary in New York, inspired a number of scholars to make important contributions to Judaeo-Persian scholarship. Foremost among these was W. Bacher, whose numerous publications on Judaeo-Persian literature advanced the field considerably.

Scholars in the twentieth century continued to publish Judaeo-Persian texts from the classical period. By the end of the century a large number of the Judaeo-Persian Bible translations had been edited, largely as a result of the work of H. Paper. As in the case of Judaeo-Arabic, the Firkovitch collections of St Petersburg and the Cairo Genizah proved to be important sources for hitherto unknown Judaeo-Persian material. These collections contain several texts from the Early Judaeo-Persian period, which exhibit numerous dialectal features. They are small in number compared to the large quantity of Judaeo-Arabic manuscripts in these collections, but they represent a considerable addition to the extant material in Early Judaeo-Persian. Some of the Judaeo-Persian manuscripts in these collections were identified over a century ago. The majority, however, have only come to light in the last few decades, largely due to the work of S. Shaked. Some research has been done on this material, though the manuscripts have mostly remained unpublished and unstudied.

In the coming years it is the recently discovered Early Judaeo-Persian material that offers some of the most exciting prospects for research. These will prove to be of immense importance for the history of the Persian language, and need to be brought to the attention of all specialists in Iranian languages. They are also crucial historical sources which will fill many gaps in our knowledge of the socio-economic and cultural history of Persian-speaking Jews in the Middle Ages. A number of the texts were written by Karaite Jews, and these promise to cast light on the early stages of the Karaite movement, which had its origins in Iran. Also many manuscripts from the Classical Judaeo-Persian period remain unpublished. Co-operation between Judaeo-Persian specialists and scholars concerned with the edition of Muslim Persian texts is likely to be fruitful. Future editions of Persian poetry, for example, could profitably take greater account of the existence of manuscripts of poetry in Judaeo-Persian transcription. As in Judaeo-Arabic studies, however, probably the most urgent task for the future is the description of the spoken Judaeo-Persian dialects. Very few of these have been adequately described and, due to the emigration of the majority of the Persian-speaking Jews from Iran, many of them are now likely to disappear within the next few years. Unfortunately the number of young scholars coming into the field of Judaeo-Persian is even smaller than those taking up Judaeo-Arabic studies. Combined courses in Hebrew and Persian are only very rarely taken by students in European and American universities, and indeed even in Israeli universities. As with Judaeo-Arabic, one can only hope that an increasing awareness of the exciting prospects of importance research in Judaeo-Persian will attract more research students into the field.

SUGGESTED READING

Judaeo-Arabic

An introduction to Classical Judaeo-Arabic and its linguistic background is given by Blau (1999). The only systematic grammar of medieval Judaeo-Arabic is Blau (1979), which is written in Hebrew. J. Blau has compiled a dictionary of medieval Judaeo-Arabic, which has still not appeared at the time of writing. Y. Ratzaby (1985) has produced a helpful dictionary of the rare words occurring in Saadya's Bible translation. Students of Judaeo-Arabic will find Dozy (1967) useful when reading texts. A lexical study of the Judaeo-Arabic of the Genizah documents is Diem and Radenberg (1994). Chrestomathies of medieval Judaeo-Arabic literature have been published by Hirschfeld (1892) and Blau (1980). Studies of the Early Judaeo-Arabic texts have been published by Blau and Hopkins (1984, 1987). The most comprehensive introduction to Late Judaeo-Arabic is that of B. Hary (1992), which gives a general introduction to the background of post-mediaeval Judaeo-Arabic and a detailed analysis of the language of a text from Egypt.

   Good introductions to Judaeo-Arabic literature are Halkin (1960), Vajda (1978), Fenton (1990), and Polliack (1998), in which further bibliography can be found. The most comprehensive bibliographical tool for the study of Judaeo-Arabic literature remains that of M. Steinschneider (1902), much of the material of which was presented in a series of English articles (1897–1901). As remarked in the body of the article, however, this does not take into account a large number of manuscripts that are now available to scholars, especially from the Cairo Genizah and the Firkovitch collections. A general introduction to the field of Cairo Genizah studies is Reif (2000). Important tools for Genizah research have been produced by the Taylor–Schechter Genizah Research Unit at Cambridge (*http://www.lib.cam.ac.uk/Taylor -Schechter/*). Those of particular importance for students of Judaeo-Arabic are the catalogues of Baker and Polliack (2001), Khan (1993b), and Isaacs (1994), and the bibliography by Reif (1998). A general survey of the Judaeo-Arabic material in the Genizah is given by Baker (1995). Catalogues of Genizah fragments in smaller Genizah collections include Halper (1924, 1990). A brief card index of the Judaeo-Arabic material from the Firkovitch collections is available to readers in the National Library of Russia in St Petersburg. A large selection from this card index was published by Fenton (1991). The majority of the Judaeo-Arabic manuscripts as well as this card index have now been photographed and can be consulted on microfilm at the Institute of Microfilmed Hebrew Manuscripts (*http://www. sites.huji.ac.il/jnul/imhm/*) at the Jewish National and University Library in Jerusalem.

Microfilms of Judaeo-Arabic manuscripts from most other collections from around the world are held by this institute, as well as microfiche copies of the relevant published catalogues. A cataloguing project of the Judaeo-Arabic material in the Firkovitch collections is currently being undertaken in Jerusalem. Research on Judaeo-Arabic is also co-ordinated by the Ben-Zvi Institute for the Study of the Jewish Communities of the East in Jerusalem (*http:// www.folklore.org.il/benzvi.htm*), which also has a publication series. A number of rare printed editions of Judaeo-Arabic texts that may not be available in most university libraries are available at Oxford on microfiche (see *http://associnst.ox.ac.uk/ochjs/news/ archive/ hebrew.html*).

Some recent editions of medieval Judaeo-Arabic texts, many based on Firkovitch manuscripts, which are not mentioned in the aforementioned general surveys include: Vajda (1985) and Stroumsa (1989), on philosophy; Shy (1991), Goshen-Gottstein and Perez (1992), and Avishur (1995), on exegesis and biblical translation; Fenton (1981, 1987), on mysticism; and Dotan (1997), Khan (2000a, 2000b), and Basal (2001), on grammatical thought. Some recent editions of texts in Late Judaeo-Arabic include Zafrani (1980), Avishur (1987), and Chétrit (1994). Some important recent studies of Judaeo-Arabic texts on the basis of unpublished manuscript sources are Sklare (1996), Fenton (1997), and Polliack (1997). For Muslim literature transcribed into Hebrew script see Fenton (1990). Drafts of documents addressed to Muslims written in Hebrew script are found in Khan (1993b).

The classic treatment of the Genizah documentary material is Goitein (1967–88). Major editions of the Judaeo-Arabic Genizah documents include those of J. Mann (1931–5), M. Gil (1983, 1997), and M. Ben-Sasson (1991). An increasingly important resource is the website of the Princeton Genizah Project (*http://www.princeton.edu/~geniza/*), which includes editions of some Genizah documents in machine-readable form.

For a general survey of the literature on spoken Judaeo-Arabic dialects with special attention to those of North Africa, see Cohen (1978) and Bar-Asher (1996). Further literature on the subject is given by N. M. Waldman (1989: 161–6). The classical treatment of the phenomenon of communal dialectal divergence is Blanc (1964). For a general survey of the Judaeo-Arabic dialects of Iraq see Jastrow (1990a). The trade argot of the Karaite goldsmiths of Cairo is treated briefly in Khan (1995–7). Some recent major publications that are not included in the aforementioned surveys include Stillman (1988) on the dialect of the Jews of Sefrou, Jastrow (1990b) on the dialect of the Jews of ʿAqra and Arbīl, Piamenta (2000) on the dialect of Jews of Jerusalem in the first half of the twentieth century, and Heath (2001) on the dialects of the Jews of Morocco.

Judaeo-Persian

Good surveys of Judaeo-Persian literature are Fischel (1960, 1971, 1978), and Netzer (1985: 11–49). All of these have helpful bibliographies, the fullest and most up to date being that of Netzer. An up-to-date survey of Early Judaeo-Persian material from the Cairo Genizah and Firkovitch collections is Shaked (forthcoming), in which references can be found to most of Shaked's own work in this field. Shaked (2000) includes Firkovitch material in his survey of Judaeo-Persian Bible translations. An edition and study of the longest of the Firkovitch manuscripts, a commentary on Ezekiel consisting of 226 folios, is at present being carried out by T. Eilam-Gindin, one of Shaked's students. For a preliminary report see Eilam-Gindin (2000). An edition and analysis of an Early Judaeo-Persian Genizah text written by a Karaite has been published by Khan (2000b: 241–331). As with Judaeo-Arabic, the Institute of Microfilmed Hebrew Manuscripts holds microfilms of most known Judaeo-Persian manuscripts (see above for details). For miniature illuminations in Judaeo-Persian manuscripts, see Moreen (1985).

A description of the linguistic features of Judaeo-Persian is published in the aforementioned volume by G. Lazard (1968), a more concise version of which can be found in Lazard (1971). The Judaeo-Persian dialects against the background of the formation of the Persian language in general are studied by Lazard (1995). Netzer (1985:50–6) describes the orthographic practices found in Judaeo-Persian manuscripts. There is no dictionary devoted exclusively to Judaeo-Persian. Students reading texts in Early Judaeo-Persian will find it helpful to consult the Middle Persian dictionary of MacKenzie (1971). Chrestomathies of Judaeo-Persian, which will be useful for those new to the field, have been published by Asmussen (1968) and Moreen (2000). Very little work has been done on the spoken Judaeo-Persian dialects. Netzer (1985: 57 n.97) refers to most of the relevant publications. For secret languages used by the Persian-speaking Jews, see Yarshater (1977). Articles reflecting the current state of a wide range of Judaeo-Persian studies can be found in the series *Irano-Judaica*, four volumes of which have so far appeared (vol. 1, ed. S. Shaked, 1982; vols. 2–4, ed. S. Shaked and A. Netzer, 1990, 1994, 1999).

BIBLIOGRAPHY

ALMAGOR, E. 1995. *The Manuscripts of David Ha-Nagid's Homilies: A Bibliographical Study* [Hebrew]. Jerusalem.

ASMUSSEN, J. P. 1968. *Jewish-Persian Texts. Introduction, Selection and Glossary.* Wiesbaden.

ATAY, H. 1974. *Delâlet'ü l-Hairîn, Filozot Musa ibn Meymun el-Kurtubî 1135–1205.* Ankara.

AVISHUR, Y. 1987. *Women's Folk Songs in Judaeo-Arabic from Jews in Iraq* [Hebrew]. Tel Aviv.

——1995. *Oldest Translation of the Early Prophets into Judaeo-Arabic* [Hebrew]. Jerusalem.

BAKER, C. F. 1995. 'Judaeo-Arabic material in the Cambridge Genizah Collections.' *Bulletin of the School of Oriental and African Studies* 58: 445–54.

——and POLLIACK, M. 2001. *Arabic and Judaeo-Arabic Manuscripts in the Cambridge Genizah Collections.* Cambridge.

BAR-ASHER, M. 1996. 'La Recherche sur les parlers judéo-arabes modernes du Maghreb: État de la question.' *Histoire Épistémologie Langage* 18: 167–77.

BASAL, N. 2001. *Kitāb al-Nutaf by Juda Ḥayyūj: A Critical Edition* [Hebrew]. Tel Aviv.

BEN-SASSON, M. 1991. *The Jews of Sicily 825–1068: Documents and Sources* [Hebrew]. Jerusalem

BLANC, H. 1964 *Communal Dialects in Baghdad,* Cambridge, Mass.

BLAU, J. ed. 1998. *Encounters in Medieval Judaeo-Arabic Culture.* Tel Aviv.

——1979. *A Grammar of Mediaeval Judaeo-Arabic* [Hebrew]. 2nd edn. Jerusalem.

——1980. *Judaeo-Arabic Literature: Selected Texts* [Hebrew]. Jerusalem.

——1999. *The Emergence and Linguistic Background of Judaeo-Arabic.* 3rd edn. Jerusalem.

——and HOPKINS, S. 1984. 'On Early Judaeo-Arabic Orthography.' *Zeitschrift für Arabische Linguistik* 12: 9–27.

————1987. 'Judaeo-Arabic papyri—Collected, Edited, Translated and Analysed.' *Jerusalem Studies in Arabic and Islam* 9: 87–160.

BLAU, J. and REIF, S. C. eds. 1992 *Genizah Research after Ninety Years: The Case of Judaeo-Arabic.* Cambridge.

Catalogue of the Jack Mosseri Collection. Edited by the Institute of Microfilmed Hebrew Manuscripts with the Collaboration of Numerous Specialists. Jerusalem. 1990.

CHÉTRIT, J. 1994. *The Written Judeo-Arabic Poetry in North Africa.* Jerusalem.

COHEN, D. 1978. 'Judaeo-Arabic Dialects.' In *The Encyclopedia of Islam.* New edn. Vol. 7. Leiden.

DERENBOURG, J. 1880. *Opuscules et Traités d'Abou 'l-Walid Merwan Ibn Djanah.* Paris.

—— 1893–1900. *Oeuvres Complètes de R. Saadia ben Iosef al-Fayyoumi.* Paris.

DIEM, W. and RADENBERG, H.-P. 1994. *A Dictionary of the Arabic Material of S. D. Goitein's 'A Mediterranean Society'.* Wiesbaden.

DOTAN, A. 1997. *The Dawn of Hebrew Linguistics: The Book of Elegance of the Language of the Hebrews by Saadia Gaon. Introduction and Critical Edition* [Hebrew]. Jerusalem.

DOZY, R. 1967. *Supplément aux Dictionnaires Arabes.* 2 vols. 3rd edn. Leiden and Paris.

EILAM-GINDIN, T. 2000. 'The Commentary to Ezekiel in Early Judaeo-Persian.' [Hebrew.] *Pe'amim* 84: 40–54.

FENTON, P. B. 1981. *The Treatise of the Pool. Al-Maqāla al-Ḥawḍiyya Obadyah b. Abraham b. Moses Maimonides: Edited for the First Time from a Manuscript in the Bodleian Library, Oxford and Genizah Fragments with a Translation and Notes.* London.

—— (Yosef Yanun). 1987. *ʾal-Muršid ʾilā ʾal-Tafarrud w-al-Murfid ʾilā ʾal-Tajarrud: Dawid ben Yehušuʿa Maymūnī.* Jerusalem.

—— 1990. 'Judaeo-Arabic literature.' In *Religion, Learning and Science in the 'Abbasid Period.* 461–76. M. J. L. Young, J. D. Latham, and R. B. Sergeant eds. Cambridge History of Arabic Literature. Cambridge.

—— 1991. *A Handlist of Judeo-Arabic Manuscripts in Leningrad.* Jerusalem.

—— 1997. *Philosophie et exégèse dans 'Le jardin de la méthaphore' de Moïse Ibn 'Ezra, philosophe et poète andalou du XIIe siècle.* Leiden

FISCHEL, W. J. 1960. 'Israel in Iran: A Survey of Judaeo-Persian Literature'. In *The Jews, Their History, Culture and Religion.* 1149–90. L. Finkelstein ed. New York.

—— 1971. 'Judeo-Persian Literature.' In *Encyclopedia Judaica.* x. 432–9. Jerusalem.

—— 1978. 'Judaeo-Persian: Literature.' In *The Encyclopaedia of Islam* New edn. vii. 308–213. Leiden.

GIL, M. 1983 *Palestine During the First Muslim Period (634–1099).* 3 vols. Tel Aviv.

—— 1997. *In the Kingdom of Ismael: Studies in Jewish History in Islamic Lands in the Early Middle Ages.* Jerusalem.

GOITEIN, S. D. 1967–88. *A Mediterranean Society: The Jewish Communities of the Arab World as Portrayed in the Documents of the Cairo Geniza.* 5 vols. Berkeley.

GOLB, N. ed. 1997. *Judeo-Arabic Studies: Proceedings of the Founding Conference of the Society for Judaeo-Arabic Studies.* Harwood.

GOSHEN-GOTTSTEIN, M. and PEREZ, M. 1992. *R. Judah ibn Balʿam's Commentary on Isaiah* [Hebrew]. Ramat Gan.

HALKIN, A. S. 1960. 'Judaeo-Arabic Literature'. In *The Jews, Their History, Culture and Religion.* 1116–47 L. Finkelstein, ed. New York.

HALPER, B. 1924. *Descriptive Catalogue of Genizah Fragments in Philadelphia.* Philadelphia.

—— 1990. *Catalogue of the Jack Mosseri Collection.* New York.

HARY, B. H. 1992. *Multiglossia in Judeo-Arabic: With an Edition, Translation, and Grammatical Study of the Cairene Purim Scroll.* Leiden.

HEATH, J. 2001. *Jewish and Muslim Dialects of Moroccan Arabic*. Curzon.

HIRSCHFELD, H. 1892. *Arabic Chrestomathy in Hebrew Characters: With a Glossary*. London.

ISAACS, H. D. 1994. *Medical and Paramedical Manuscripts in the Cambridge Genizah Collections*. With the assistance of C. F. Baker. Cambridge.

JASTROW, O. 1990a. 'Die Arabischen Dialekte der Irakischen Juden'. In *XXIV. Deutscher Orientalistentag in Köln, 1988. Ausgewählte Vorträge*. 199–206. W. Diem and A. Falaturi. eds. Stuttgart.

—— 1990b. *Der Arabische Dialekt der Juden von ʿAqra und Arbîl*. Wiesbaden.

KHAN, G. 1993a. 'On the Question of Script in Medieval Karaite Manuscripts: New Evidence From the Genizah'. *Bulletin of the John Rylands University Library of Manchester* 75: 133–41.

—— 1993b. *Arabic Legal and Administrative Documents in the Cambridge Genizah Collections*. Cambridge.

—— 1995–7. 'A Note on the Trade Argot of the Karaite Goldsmiths of Cairo'. *Mediterranean Language Review* 9: 74–6.

—— 2000a. *The Early Karaite Tradition of Hebrew Grammatical Thought: Including a Critical Edition, Translation and Analysis of the Diqduq of ʾAbū Yaʿqūb Yūsuf ibn Nūh*. Leiden.

—— 2000b. *Early Karaite Grammatical Texts*. Atlanta, Ca.

LAZARD, G. 1968. 'La Dialectologie du judéo-persan'. *Studies in Bibliography and Booklore* 8: 77–98.

—— 1971. 'Judeo-Persian'. In *Encyclopedia Judaica*. x. 429–32. Jerusalem.

—— 1995. *La Formation de la langue persane*. Paris.

MACKENZIE, D. N. 1971. *A Concise Pahlavi Dictionary*. London.

MANN, J. 1931–5. *Texts and Studies in Jewish History and Literature*. Cincinnati. Facsimile edn. 1972. New York.

MOREEN, V. B. 1985. *Miniature Paintings in Judaeo-Persian Manuscripts*. Cincinnati.

—— 2000. *In Queen Esther's Garden: An Anthology of Judeo-Persian Literature*. New Haven.

NETZER, A. 1985. *Manuscripts of the Jews Of Persia in the Ben-Zvi Institute* [Hebrew]. Jerusalem.

NEWBY, G. D. 1971. 'Observations About an Early Judaeo-Arabic'. *JQR* 61: 541–61.

—— 1988. *A History of the Jews of Arabia from Ancient Times to Their Eclipse under Islam*. Columbia.

PIAMENTA, M. 2000. *Jewish Life in Arabic Language and Jerusalem Arabic in Communal Perspective*. Leiden.

POLLIACK, M. 1997. *The Karaite Tradition of Arabic Bible Translation: A Linguistic and Exegetical Study of Karaite Translations of the Pentateuch From the Tenth and Eleventh Centuries C.E.* Leiden.

—— 1998. 'Genres in Judaeo-Arabic literature'. The Halmos Lecture Series. Tel Aviv.

RATZABY, Y. 1985. *A Dictionary of Judaeo-Arabic in R. Saadya's Tafsir* [Hebrew]. Ramat-Gan.

REIF, S. C. 1998. *Published Material from the Cambridge Genizah Collections: A Bibliography 1896–1980*. With the assistance of P. Fenton, S. Hopkins, G. Khan, S. C. Reif, and D. Patterson. Cambridge.

—— 2000. *A Jewish Archive from Old Cairo: The History of Cambridge University's Genizah Collection*. Richmond.

SHAKED, S. 2000. 'List of Judaeo-Persian Bible translations'. [Hebrew]. *Peʿamim* 84: 12–20.

—— forthcoming. 'Early Judaeo-Persian texts, With Notes on a Commentary to Genesis'.

SHY, H. 1991. *Tanhum ha-Yerushalmi's Commentary on the Minor Prophets: A Critical Edition with an Introduction, Translated into Hebrew and Annotated.* Jerusalem.

SKLARE, D. E. 1996. *Samuel ben Hofni Gaon and His Cultural World: Texts and Studies.* Leiden.

SKOSS, S. 1958. 'Suggestions For Further Studies in Judaeo-Arabic Literature.' In *I. Goldziher Memorial.* ii. 42–9. S. Löwinger, J. Somogyi, and A. Scheiber eds. Jerusalem.

STEINSCHNEIDER, M. 1897–1901. 'An Introduction to the Arabic Literature of the Jews.' *JQR* os 9–13.

——1902. *Die Arabische Literatur der Juden.* Frankfort (repub. Hildesheim 1964, corrections by S. Poznanski, 'Zur jüdisch-arabischen Literatur', in *OLZ* 7 (1904), 257–74, 304–15, 345–59).

STILLMAN, N. 1988. *The Language and Culture of the Jews of Sefrou, Morocco: An Ethnolinguistic Study.* Louvin.

STROUMSA, S. 1989 *Dawud ibn Marwan al-Muqammiṣ's Twenty chapters ('Ishrūn maqala).* Leiden.

VAJDA, G. 1978. 'Judaeo-Arabic literature.' In *The Encyclopaedia of Islam.* New edn. vii. 303–7. Leiden.

——1985. *Al-Kitāb al-Muḥtawī de Yūsuf al-Baṣīr. Texte, Traduction et Commmentaire.* Leiden.

WALDMAN, N. M. 1989. *The Recent Study of Hebrew: A Survey of the Literature With Selected Bibliography.* Cincinnati.

YARSHATER, E. 1977. 'The Hybrid Language of the Jewish Community of Persia.' *Journal of the American Oriental Society* 97: 1–7.

ZAFRANI, H. 1980. *Études et Recherches sur la vie intellectuelle juive au Maroc de la fin du 15e au début du 20e siècle. Troisième partie: Littératures dialectales et populaires juives en occident musulman: l'écrit et l'oral.* Paris.

CHAPTER 25

OTHER DIASPORA JEWISH LITERATURES SINCE 1492

ILAN STAVANS

SINCE their expulsion from the Iberian Peninsula in 1492, the dissemination of the Jews in Europe, northern Africa, Asia, the Middle East, and the Americas has resulted not only in the production of a literature in modern Jewish languages and dialects such as Yiddish, Hebrew, Ladino, Judaeo-Italian, and Judaeo-Arabic, but also in a Jewish literature delivered in virtually every major Western tongue, from English to Russian and German, from Italian to French and Spanish. These literatures in non-Jewish languages obviously fit into their respective national canons: Jewish-Portuguese authors are part of Portuguese letters, Jewish-Polish authors part of Polish letters, and so on. This means that they are read first by the readers of their own languages, as minority figures whose work has a distinct ethnic flavour; and then, when these authors are translated, they are read by audiences worldwide more as Jews than as representatives of their specific countries. In other words, this duality that defines them—e.g. Jewish *hyphen* British—also inserts them into the transnational Jewish literary canon. And what kind of canon is this? How should one define it? What makes a book part of it?

The answer to these questions suggest that the People of the *Book* are indeed the People of the *Books*: not one but many, defined by a diversity of tongues. Books in Shakespeare's tongue and in those of Molière, Dostoevsky, and Dante. Scholarship on this tension between unity and multiplicity took a dramatic shift in the twentieth century. Before then these literatures were divided across national and linguistic lines. For the purpose of analysis, figures like Emma Lazarus and Arthur Schnitzler were seen as an American Jewish poet and an Austrian Jewish playwright respectively—that is, their citizenship defined them first, and then came their religious background. Likewise, Israel Zangwill was British, Marcel Proust was French, Heinrich Heine was German, and so on. But with the wide spread of nationalism in Europe, ideologically oriented critics (Zionists, Bundists, Yiddishists, etc.) began to conceive of ways to create a paradigm that would enable the forking paths in the myriad Jewish diasporas to be seen as part of a compact whole: Jewish letters across verbal and cultural boundaries. The interconnected study of the parallel literatures obviously called for erudite, polyglotic minds able to master various codes. Since Jews are not only prone to multilingualism but have thrived simultaneously as insiders *and* outsiders everywhere, these minds came along with useful tools of scrutiny. Obviously, no single individual was capable of the type of encyclopedic knowledge that might enable him to get a first-hand acquaintance of oeuvres in Croatian, Arabic, and Dutch. Still, the multilingual environment nurtured figures fluent in six to eight languages and cultures, sometime even more.

The rise of Comparative Literature as a discipline in academia in European, American, and Israeli universities after the Second World War solidified this intellectual effort. It opened the door to partial parallel studies of Jewish literatures in non-Jewish tongues and allowed for an expansion of the Jewish literary canon across nations and tongues. It also offered a pulpit to some of the lucid critical minds that, in the early twentieth century, were mostly men of letters employed as newspapers reporters, teachers, book editors, and foreign correspondents. Today there are Jewish studies programmes that include an expertise in literature in colleges and universities in the United States, England, across Europe, and in Israel. Undoubtedly, this institutionalization did not exist at the outset of the field. Among the precursors that threw the net wide was poet Hayyim Nachman Bialik, a fervent Zionist whose dream, nonetheless, was not only the physical relocation of the Jews to the Promised Land. He also sought their spiritual and cultural rebirth, and his anthology of rabbinical legend and lore, originally published in Odessa from 1908 to 1911, was part of that project (Bialik and Ravinsky 1992). He was helped by Yehoshua Hana Ravnitzky, another early Zionist and a founder of modern Hebrew journalism. The volume was but a part, albeit a magisterial one, of a larger project that Bialik had in mind. He called it *kinus*, the 'ingathering' of a Jewish literature that was dispersed over centuries of diaspora life. That library, much like its readers, needed to be centralized in a single, particular place, Israel, and in a single tongue, Hebrew—a centripetal canon. Another precursor, the Yiddishist literary critic Baʿal Makhshoves (Baʿal Makhshoves 1994), argued around the same time in favour of approaching diaspora Jewish literature as a bifrontal entity—bifrontal and bilingual. 'Some among us', he stated in Bukhovina in 1908, 'will not admit that our one and only literature has a double language.' He had in mind the debate between the standard Jewish languages of modernity in Europe: Yiddish and Hebrew. Does one really need to make a choice, wondered Ba'al Makhshoves. How is one to define a Jewish language? Though political manifestos? He then asked the most germane of all questions that pertained the present and future of the field: 'Does the [Jewish] writer live and breathe between two languages only? Don't our critics carry within them the spirit of the German language? And in our younger writers, who were educated in the Russian language, can't we discern the spirit of Russian? And don't we hear echoes of French among our colleagues, the Palestinian writers (Ben-Ami, Hermoni)?' He concluded by saying that Jews might have two languages and a dozen echoes from other foreign tongues... but only *one* literature.

One literature, many tongues—bright, decisive, a man of immense wisdom and *le mot juste*, Ba'al Makhshoves established the perimeters helping us to define and appreciate the modern Jewish literary tradition: one with decidedly open perimeters, open and transcendental. The creation of the State of Israel threw these methodological approaches into disarray. Zionists began to approach the 2,000-plus-year diaspora as a journey crowed by the Declaration of Independence in 1948. For them the view that Jewish novels would go on flourishing in places as remote and dissimilar as Mexico and South Africa was a sheer impossibility. They refuted the diaspora as a contradiction in terms, and declared its arts dead on arrival. On the other hand, diaspora Jewish authors and critics insisted that transnational Jewish letters had not come to their end with Zionism but, instead, would flourished alongside Israeli letters. In fact, they stressed that the time would come when Israeli fiction would cease to be Jewish and become strictly Israeli—hyper-politicized. Even if undeclared, the followers of Bialik and Ba'al Makhshoves are critics as diverse as Dov Sadan (Sadan 1963), Dan Miron (Miron 2000), Chone Shmeruk (Shmeruk 1960, 1985, 1992), Gershon Shaked (Shaked 1987, 2000), Lionel Trilling (Trilling 1950, 2001), Alfred Kazin (Kazin 1978), and Irving Howe (Howe 1976, 1990), among others. Each of these took a segment of the diaspora Jewish bookshelf shaped in a non-Jewish tongue and studied it one piece at a time. This cadre of critics embraced pairs or groups of authors that displayed an affinity toward an aspect of Jewishness, such as Stefan Zweig and Joseph Roth, and studied them in a contrasting fashion. The result is a multifaceted analysis that enabled readers to understand how different national cultures in the Jewish diaspora evolved in time and the extent to which Jewish authors were witnesses and catalysts of that evolution.

Hana Wirth-Nesher, an American on the faculty at Tel Aviv University, published in 1994 the volume *What Is Jewish Literature?* that is a compendium of sorts of the comparative analysis done since Bialik and Ba'al Makhshoves. It included pieces by Saul Bellow and Robert Alter that are useful tools to frame the principles of the field. I too have attempted to articulate the complications that these literatures present in a comparative examination in the introduction to Stavans (1998), and in various pieces in Stavans (2001b). Nevertheless, the most ambitious attempt to set standards of study of Jewish literature in Jewish and non-Jewish languages is Wisse (2000). Albert Memmi's *The Pillar of Salt* (1975) and Philip Roth's *Operation Shylock* (1993) might appear to be worlds apart, Wisse suggested in her volume, but there is an invisible thread that unites them. What is that threat made of? She did not only focus on non-Jewish languages. In fact, Yiddish and Hebrew play a predominant role in her analysis. In her pages she displayed a genuine esteem for high-quality literary art and trusted her instincts as a savvy reader. The common trait she invariably ascribed to what is a varied corpus of Jewish literature always pointed to Europe and the United States as sources of inspiration, though less so to France and Italy. Sephardic letters were excluded from her study, as well as Jewish books in Spanish, Portuguese, Arabic, and Greek.

Her contribution lies in her articulating important questions: does the Jewish author in non-Jewish languages, to be part of the transcultural tradition, need to include Jewish symbols and motifs in his oeuvre? The question sounds prescriptive, as if one could generate literature upon request. But it has another facet to it: is Jewish literature recognizable by its content? Other literary traditions, based on national and nationalist definitions, group their members by geography and language: a Norwegian writer is part of the canon by virtue of his birth and tongue, even if his work is written outside Norway. But Jewish literature, yet again, is altogether different. Kafka, for example, never uses the word 'Jews' in his fiction (although he does repeatedly in his diaries and correspondence). Does this mean he is out? One might respond to this question by pointing out that it is not the content but the sensibility that makes a book Jewish. That sensibility isn't present in J. D. Salinger's *Catcher in the Rye* (1951), but it is in Nathalia Ginzburg's Italian novels and stories, such as 'House at the Sea' (Jason 1990: 83–9). No doubt sensibility is a difficult scholarly concept to grasp. Is it tangible? How might the critic recognize and measure it? In truth, the concept calls for an even more fluid category: authenticity. A Jewish book in a non-Jewish language is either authentic or not. But who is to judge? The reader, of course. Indeed, the reader is the supreme arbiter. It is up to him and him alone to decide what titles are and are not part of the Jewish literary tradition.

Authenticity as a category brings to mind an argument by Jorge Luis Borges, the Argentine intellectual, delivered in an inspiring essay called 'The Argentine Writer and Tradition', included in his book *Labyrinths*. In it, Borges observes that the *Qur'an*, the Arabian book *par excellence*, contains no references to camels. He writes:

I believe if there were any doubt as to the authenticity of the *Koran*, this absence of camels would be sufficient to prove it is an Arabian work. It was written by Mohammed, and Mohammed, as an Arab, had no reason to know that camels were especially Arabian; for him they were part of reality, he had no reason to emphasize them; on the other hand, the first thing a falsifier, a tourist, an Arab nationalist would do is have a surfeit of camels, caravans of camels, on every page. (Borges 1962: 185)

No camels, then—no Jewish symbols, but Jewish nonetheless.

It is agreed that the birth of modern Jewish literature in non-Jewish languages took place in German. By 'modern' I mean a product of the Haskalah, the movement toward secularization that, some twenty years before the French Revolution of 1789, brought the Jews out of the ghettos in European cities and into the larger society. Ambivalence is the *sine qua non* in this literature: am I a Jew? Or am I a German? Should Jews, as they departed the closely knitted community that kept them secluded for centuries in the Middle Ages and Renaissance, convert to Christianity to be fully accepted? Should they instead remain loyal to Judaism, writing their fiction for only a small audience of fellow Jews? Describing Judaism as 'revealed legislation', and not, like Christianity, 'a revealed religion', the philosopher Moses Mendelssohn himself had anticipated this question: 'Integration [into European society] means renunciation', he once wrote. 'I'm first a German citizen and then a Jew...' In 1840 Heine, the author of 'Lorelei', indisputably his country's most popular poet since Goethe, wrote *The Rabbi of Bacherach*, a historical novel in which he defended the cause of Jewish emancipation. Emancipation for him meant total assimilation into the Gentile milieu. Strictly speaking, Heine, by then, was no longer Jewish, for some fifteen years prior, while finishing his law studies, he had converted to Christianity, 'for practical reasons', he argued, in an act meant as 'an entrance ticket [into European society]'. Within two generations his entire family, one sibling after the next, one nephew after another, would follow the same path, becoming thoroughly de-Judaized. But in Heine's case the manoeuver backfired. How could it not? A writer, after all, uses words to reflect on his identity and experience, and Heine's Jewish background was deeply resented in German literary circles. For political reasons, he was forced to spend the last twenty-five years of his life in exile, his books banned and the Prussian government even calling for his death. *The Rabbi of Bacherach* was a response to his critics, both a protest and a lamentation, but it didn't save him from expatriation. As his biographer Ernst Pawel wrote, '[Heine] lacked piety, observed no traditions, and would probably have been hard put to define his Judaism, yet his German critics were dead right when they read it into almost everything he ever wrote. The greatest German poet of his time was a Jew looking at the Germans from the outside, one reason why he saw them as clearly as he did' (Pawel 1995: 34).

Heine's foundational role is of little consequence, though. Some literary historians suggest that Solomon Maimon, a Polish thinker in Germany, ought to be credited with the landmark in Jewish literature through a non-Jewish language with the publication of his essays and autobiography, appearing in 1790 and 1793 respectively. Then again, between these dates the British author Isaac D'Israeli published his book *Curiosities in Literature* in English (D'Israeli 1824). Does that mean that the soil was first fertilized in Shakespeare's tongue, and not Goethe's? The truth is that no sooner did Europe embrace the ideas *liberté, egalité, fraternité* than a veritable downpour of Jewish authors begin to experiment with various continental tongues: English, German, French, and Italian. I shall not indulge in a discussion of the national canons in which Jews found a niche. The bibliography on Heine, D'Israeli, and other Jews in the dawn of modernity is considerable. Instead, I want to talk about divergent authors in their milieu and to list the significant scholarship they have generated—in particular, about a trio of diaspora Jewish authors in non-Jewish languages who serve as archetypes: Franz Kafka, Bruno Schulz, and Isaac Babel. Each of them wrote in a different non-Jewish tongue: German, Polish, and Russian; but they *Judaized* these languages, so to speak: they injected a Jewish sensibility into them. Babel's Russian was painstakingly economical, brief, unobtrusive, fastidious in its concision; Kafka, as Sander L. Gilman puts it, pushed German to become less naturalistic and more 'universal, transnational, and infinitely interpretable' (Gilman 1995: 72); and Schulz's Polish was elastic, suitable to accommodate his mythology. In these writers the florid excesses of Yiddish gave place to a Flaubertian dexterity, a sober finesse in which silence plays a prominent role. Intriguingly, none of these 'external' three, unlike their Yiddish counterparts, is a prolific writer; instead, their books are infrequent, sparse, as if stillness had been forced upon them—a painful, agonizing stillness.

There is no solid indication that the members of the trio knew about one other. Still, their legacy, when approached in the context of the Jewish literary tradition, does offer us astonishing compactness, a sense of unity none of them could ever have envisioned. Nor did anyone in this 'external trio' ever write in Yiddish, but their fascination with it—clearly Kafka's and Babel's—is transparent: Kafka was seduced by Yiddish theatre and felt a deep attraction to this language of 'raggedy and makeshift character' at a time, in Prague, when the 'internal trio' were being read in German translation; and throughout his adult life Babel longed for the Yiddish of his upbringing. As his second wife, A. N. Pirozhkova, states in her memoir, Babel befriended Shlomo Mikhoels, the Soviet Jewish actor whose performances in stage adaptations of Sh. Y. Abramovitsh's *The Travels of Benjamin III* and Sholem Aleichem's *Teyve the Dairyman* at the Jewish State Theatre in the USSR mesmerized him. He was said to be translating Sholem Aleichem's work into Russian when the NKVSD, Stalin's secret police, came to arrest him in 1939. Still, none of the three, Babel, Kafka, or Schulz, considered himself a 'Jewish writer', which of course doesn't mean that is the case. Indeed, their own refusal to be part of the tradition allows the scholar to reflect yet again on the ambivalence that defines it.

Silence is what Franz Kafka is about. While nowhere in his creative oeuvre does the word 'Jew' appear, it is, in fact, present everywhere, in spirit at least. (His diaries and correspondence, on the other hand, are filled with reflections about his religion and family tradition.) Kafka was born in Prague into a middle-class Jewish family. His father's figure looms large and monstrous in his upbringing, and is metamorphosed by Kafka into a phantom generating fear and anxiety. In Hermann Kafka's eyes (as seen through Franz's anxious perspective), his son was always unqualified, undeserving, unworthy. This sense of doom, intertwined with an impossible search for worthiness, permeates all of Kafka's oeuvre. Kafka's Jewishness has been scrutinized to exhaustion. Indeed, he might well be the Jewish author in a non-Jewish language who has provoked the most spilling of critical ink. Noteworthy are the studies by Walter Benjamin (Benjamin 1968), and Sander L. Gilman (Gilman 1995), among others. *The Castle* (Kafka 1941), is often read as a religious allegory, a man's search for a reclusive, abstract God; and *The Trial* (Kafka 1956) is about supernatural justice and unworthiness. This vision was clear in Kafka's approach to his fellow-Jews. In 1923, already fatally ill with tuberculosis, he spent time in the town of Müritz, at the side of a group of Eastern European Jews whom Berlin's Jews were recruiting. 'Half the days and nights the house, the woods, and the beach are filled with singing', wrote Kafka. 'I'm not happy when I'm among them, but on the threshold of happiness.' While these Jews represented his past, his present is symbolized by Gentile European society. But Kafka's view is that he belongs to neither of them. In a famous parable, with obvious Jewish overtones, he states: 'We are expelled from Paradise, but Paradise was not destroyed. In a sense our expulsion was a stroke of luck, for had we not been expelled, Paradise would have had to be destroyed.'

The loss of Paradise is at the centre of Bruno Schulz's oeuvre. In the town of Dragobicz, in central Poland, where he was born and where he died at the age of 50, he was a schoolteacher and an amateur artist. But more than anything, he was a silent, introspective man, utterly lacking in self-esteem. Schulz kept his literary endeavours private, never showing them to those around him. He had difficulty finding the right literary tone, mainly because he could not conceive of an audience for whom to write—an essential dilemma of the modern Jewish writer. The novel *The Street of Crocodiles* (Ficowski ed. 1998: 18–98), in fact, was sent to a distant addressee, a woman, poet, and doctor of philosophy who lived in Lvov, in letters Schulz wrote to her. When the book was eventually published in 1934, Schulz was overwhelmed by the positive response. Rather than relieving him, though, this response caused Schulz to feel invaded by the outside world and pressured to continue writing. This pressure frightened him. *Sanatorium Under the Sign of the Hourglass* (ibid. 99–265) followed three years later, but by then Schulz was terrified and had fallen back into silence and depression. Both volumes display a unique mythical vision: they are autobiographical, but without revealing much about the author's life. They give the impression of escapades within self-enclosed ivory towers, where Schulz works for himself, alone, away from society. One reads them as a kind of variation of biblical narrative: they are ahistorical; childhood, in them, is Paradise Lost. In fact, at the time of his death Schulz was purportedly writing a novel, 'The Messiah', in which, in the words of critic Jerzy Ficowski, 'the myth of the coming of the Messiah would symbolize a return to the happy perfection that existed at the beginning—in Schultzian terms, the return to childhood' (ibid. 12). When the Nazis took over Dragobicz, he was living, like most Jews, in the town's ghetto. This period was short, though: he was killed on 'Black Thursday' by a Nazi soldier. Aside from Ficowski, Cynthia Ozick has produced an eloquent essay on Schulz's Jewish sensibility (Ozick 1989).

Schulz was ambiguous about his Jewishness: the Jews around him made him anxious, yet he felt close to his biblical ancestors, at least to those he had invented for himself. Ambiguity is also Isaac Babel's *cri de coeur*. Born in Odessa, Ukraine, as cosmopolitan a Jewish centre as any other at the turn of the century, he had a Jewish upbringing, the topic of about a third of his stories. Inspired by Gorky, Babel joined the Red Army so as 'to experience real life in full', and was among Cossacks in the battalion led by the infamous Comrade S. M. Budyonny, commander of the First Cavalry Army in Poland. The stories published in *Red Cavalry* were written in around 1923 (Babel 2002: 129–96). They exemplify, in astonishing fashion, the tension between 'brainy' Jews and 'physical' Cossacks. In his other masterpiece, *Odessa Stories*, Babel writes of Benya Krik, a Jewish gangster in the days before the Soviet Revolution (ibid. 197–362). Here again is the tension between action and inaction. In other stories, all filled with a tacit violence and the pain of difference, he retrieved his childhood milieu by dealing with issues of Jewish identity. One of them, 'Karl-Yankl', is about a family feud that results from a baby born out of a mixed marriage, part-Russian, part-Jewish. The baby, Karl-Yankel, will grow up to be divided, ambivalent: half Karl (after Karl Marx), half Yankel (his Yiddish name). Will he ever be happy? The question is left open by Babel. Indeed, he ends the story with this line whispered by the narrator to himself: 'It's not possible that you won't be happy, Karl-Yankel. It's not possible that you won't be happier than I.' Babel's enlightened critics include Shklovsky (Shklovsky 1990) and Trilling (Trilling 2000). Babel has been particularly well served by *The Collected Works* (Babel 2002), a critical edition translated by Peter Constantine and edited by his daughter Natalie.

Kafka, Schulz, and Babel . . . Happiness is an impossible challenge for them. In his adult life, Babel endorsed the aesthetics proposed by the Soviet regime, but 'socialist realism' intimidated him. (Although, when the police came, he was said to be putting the final touches a new volume of short fiction.) Happiness, the kind deeply felt, eluded him, but it was thanks to that feeling of unhappiness, of homelessness, of being a pariah, that Babel, in his earlier period, wrote what he did. And pariahs are what the members of this 'external trio' are. This doesn't mean they reject Jewish-ness altogether; they simply go beyond a superficial understanding of it. Kafka's theological views, negative, despairing, and fatalistic as they are, are a reformulation of rabbinical Judaism. They offer him a home alone, a self-enclosed universe. Language, for him, is not a locus but a *credo*: Jews as nomadic, uncentred, muta-ble . . . but in language they find belief. Similarly, Schulz uses language as a retreat. His phantasmagorias are nightmarish visions of escape and transmutation. This nightmarish quality, which contains a sense of dislocation and confused identity, is in fact what characterizes the trio of Jewish authors in non-Jewish languages, and is a crucial component in this tradition.

The oeuvre by this trio is often read as a prophesy of doom. And indeed, the Holocaust flashes through their pages like a thunder announcing a tempest—an event of cosmic proportions establishing, in sharp lines, a *before* and an *after*: before is the vanished world of Yiddish-speaking Jews in Eastern Europe; after is the awareness of universal evil, the realization that man is indeed the sole ruler of God's creation and his force is easily mishandled. In Yiddish, the Holocaust is addressed as *Dem Dritn Khurbn*, the third destruction, after the first two that befell the Holy Temple in Jerusalem; but Yiddish will cease to be the verbal mode of addressing Jewish issues, for the Holocaust brought about its death as a living tongue. It also forced upon the Jewish writer a less dilettantish, more responsible role: he could no longer perceive himself as an imaginer and impersonator; instead, he was suddenly called to be a witness and an archivist. Surely I don't mean to imply that every post-Holocaust Jewish writer is a survivor. But the annihilation of 6 million Jews, a third of the world's Jewish population by mid-century, forced on Jewish letters a different mission: to become a record, to be turned into living memory. *Shtetl* life suddenly needed to be romanticized: the vanished world of Sholem Aleichem was more than a work of literature; it was memory come alive. From the ashes of the Holocaust emerged not only extraordinary novels, stories, and autobiographies—Danilo Kiš's *Garden, Ashes* (Kiš 1975), Anne Frank's *Diary of a Young Girl* (Frank 1952), Elie Wiesel's *Night* (Wiesel 1960), among them—but also a rereading of the overall Jewish literary tradition, for the event forced readers to take a different stand: judge literature not merely for its aesthetic value but for its moral stand as well. These conflicting elements—aesthetics and morality—always went hand-in-hand within the tradition, establishing a balance of sorts, but after 1945 the balance shifted in one direction. Suddenly, Jewish testimonial literature became ubiquitous, as if fiction needed to make room for remembrance.

The scholarship produced by critics on Jewish writers in non-Jewish languages that address the Holocaust is considerable. Lawrence Langer (1995), David Roskies (1984), and Alvin H. Rosenfeld (1980), to name a handful, have delivered insightful comparative literary studies. The Nazi destruction shifted the literary centres of Jewish culture dramatically. Europe had been the nucleus before the Second World War, even though massive migrations began carrying immigrants across the Atlantic and to Palestine; but the Nazis managed—inadvertently, of course—to open new homes for the Jews, including the establishment, in 1948, of the State of Israel; to expand the verbal possibilities, turning English and modern Hebrew into major literary vehicles; and, ultimately, to shift the tension at the core of the Jewish tradition, no longer between *maskilim* and Hasidim, or between Yiddishists and Hebraists, but between Zionists and Diasporists, and between secularists and the religious in contemporary Israel and the United States. The nineteenth century is about the rise of nationalist movements; and Zionism, in the hands of *fin de siècle* political leaders (like Theodor Herzl and Ahad Ha-am, among others) and visionaries like Eliezer Ben-Yehuda, allowed for a re-evaluation of Hebrew, not as a religious tongue but as a spoken language and a national vehicle. Language had to become an ideological artefact, a weapon to achieve normalcy; Jews had to be like all other nations of the world, and Hebrew would be their national tongue.

Russian, French, and German cultures have produced an array of studies on their respective Jewish literati; English has too, and far more fecundly. Indeed, since the late nineteenth century Shakespeare's tongue had been used as a literary vehicle by figures like Bejamin Disraeli and Israel Zangwill. But it is in America where, after a battle against Yiddish, it would become an inspired platform. The work of Jules Chametzky (2001), Howe (1976, 1990), and Andrew Furman (2000) on Jewish-American letters deserves notice. The United States had been a magnet and safe haven for European immigrants for many years—at least since around 1880—and American Yiddish was considered promiscuous and second-rate when compared to Yiddish spoken on the Old Continent. American Yiddish acquired literary stamina and moral standing with Abraham Cahan, editor of the important newspaper *the Jewish Daily Forward* and author of the classic *The Rise of David Levinsky*. This ascendance was strengthened by Yiddish theatre and vaudeville troupes, by popular music and film, and by intellectuals like those known as *Di Yunge*, an artistic group in New York in the 1920s and 1930s, led by poets Mani Leib and Moishe Leib Halpern. By the time Isaac Bashevis Singer, eventually a Nobel Prize recipient, arrived in Coney Island in 1935, a milieu conducive to Yiddish literature was well established. But it took the Holocaust on the one hand, and the rapid assimilation of Jews into American society on the other, to decimate the possibilities of Yiddish as a language of literature.

Bashevis Singer, even in spite of himself, is the transitional figure that cuts Jewish literature in pre- and post-Holocaust. Curiously, he is also a bridge between Jewish letters in Jewish and non-Jewish languages. Without a massive population of Yiddish readers, he became, in the eyes of second- and third-generation American-Jews, *yiddishkeit* ('Yiddishness') incarnated. American essayist Joseph Epstein, born in 1937 to Yiddish-speaking parents, but whose upbringing managed to delete all traces of *yiddishkeit*, put it bluntly: 'One of the things I owed him was—and remains—the important debt of helping to put me in touch with my own almost entirely lost historical past. My guess is that many of his readers were in the same condition as I, and that this was at least part of the profit we all derived from him and part, too, of the explanation for his popularity among American Jewish readers.' Not that Bashevis Singer was unprepared for the challenge. Since early on, he had perceived himself since the beginning as belonging to the Western tradition of Chekhov and Dostoevsky. Born in a small Polish town, he had begun writing well before emigrating to America, but his emigration forced him to cease writing—a result, apparently, of the magisterial presence of his older brother Israel Joshua Singer, an epic novelist responsible for the classic *The Brothers Ashkenazi* (Singer 1936). Bashevis Singer's rebirth, ironically, came from 'the other side': from English-speaking Jewish intellectuals with a Yiddish background (Saul Bellow, Isaac Rosen-feld, and others), who translated his work into English; and from Irving Howe, who championed his talents. Bashevis Singer authored many dozens of novels and stories for children and adults. From 1953, when 'Gimpel the Fool' was published in *Partisan Review* (Singer 1953), Bashevis Singer's work began to be displayed in mainstream American publications such as *Playboy, The New Yorker,* and *Esquire,* most unlikely forums, needless to say, for a Yiddish writer. But then again, Bashevis Singer is an 'unlikely' Yiddish writer, and there is no doubt that this accounts for the deep resentment the Yiddish literary community felt toward him. His favourite topics—eroticism, demons and chimeras, polygamy—made him a modernist with an obscure, even obscene side to him. His critics branded him as a traitor to the Yiddish tradition, a storyteller nurturing the thirst for sexuality and sensationalism in American readers. What is striking is how unconcerned Bashevis Singer was by these accusations. Most of his adult work, while written in Yiddish, was first published in English translation. This makes him, I suspect, an American writer, albeit one in a class of his own. Still, in his Nobel Prize acceptance speech in 1978 he made it clear that he considered the award a tribute not to him but to the language in which he wrote, a language of much suffering, homeless and without a future.

Howe used Bashevis Singer as a platform to explain Jewish life in the United States, from the ghetto of the Lower East Side in New York to suburbia. Other critics embarked on a similar quest: Janet Hadda produced a psychoanalytic biography, Ozick studied his astonishing outpouring of creativity, Wisse and her brother David Roskies analysed his contribution to Yiddish as well as global letters. As Yiddish was eclipsed, English moved to the foreground as America's 'Jewish' tongue. This verbal shift is useful in contrasting the author of 'Gimpel the Fool' with Saul Bellow, among the most renowned of English-speaking writers in the United States (even though he was born in Canada), and a Nobel laureate as well. In an interview of 1976, during his Nobel Prize trip to Stockholm, Bellow claimed he was first an American and then Jewish, and that English was his true home. That the Nobel Prize committee decided to make the award consecutively to two writers living in America is in some way puzzling, since its tactics have been to be balanced and to distribute its laurels around the globe. Yet one can explain this easily: Singer was a Jewish writer, Bellow an American one. Most Jewish-American writers of Bellow's generation and after are Americans to the core, closer to Poe, Hawthorne, James, and Hemingway than to the 'internal trio'. Prior to Bellow, a set of Jewish writers (among them Emma Lazarus, Ludwig Lewisohn, and Henry Roth) had pondered in a forceful manner issues of immigration and assimilation into the melting-pot. But Bellow stands as the colossus, an intellectual writer in whose hand the Jewish-American novel becomes a laboratory of ideas, and whose language—cosmopolitan, filled with modern angst—seems the perfect conduit for post-Holocaust Jewishness in non-Jewish languages.

And an expansive conduit, to judge by its artistic outpouring. Cynthia Ozick, a critic, author, and translator from the Yiddish, and a Jewish-American novelist and critic responsible for *Metaphor and Memory* (Ozick 1989) and other provocative volumes, once argued, near-sightedly it seems to me, that there 'are no major works of Jewish imaginative genius written in any Gentile language, sprung of any Gentile culture'. English, Ozick's language, she called a pagan tongue; but she also argues that America can become a site *ad hoc* for Jewish cultural rebirth. It has, no doubt: American-Jewish literature has moved from looking at the immigrant experience to approaching the whole world as its stage. And in this expanded compass is Philip Roth, a 'noise-maker' born in New Jersey, and, for his ambitious scope, a totemic figure moving the modern Jewish literary tradition into different territory. The best criticism on Roth, to my mind, is by Howe (1990), Ted Solotaroff (1987), and Sanford Pinsker (1975). Roth revised the work of Kafka and Schulz—*The Breast* (Roth 1972) is actually more Kafkaesque than Kafka himself. Roth's debut volume of stories, *Goodbye, Columbus* (1959), announced the central theme of his entire writing career: self-hatred. In his pen self-hatred will not only be an attack against Jewish parochialism but, most intriguingly, it will strive to create translingual, transcultural connections within Jewish letters. In *Zuckerman Unbound* (1981), particularly in the epilogue, 'The Prague Orgy', Eastern European letters found a home in the Jewish-American novel as the protagonist, Zuckerman, travels to Czechoslovakia in search of a lost manuscript. Roth's sensibility and his interest in *döppelgangers* always had a European flavour, and found expression in his role as series editor of the important Penguin Books series 'Writers from the Other Europe'. The series introduced to an English-speaking readership a wide range of Eastern European writers, many of them of Jewish descent, including Bruno Schulz and Danilo Kiš. Then came *The Counterlife* in 1986, an experimental, almost 'Eastern European' novel, partly set in Israel. And almost a decade later came Roth's masterpiece, *Operation Shylock* (1993), which in many ways revised the whole modern Jewish literary tradition. Set in America, the Middle East, and, indirectly, in Poland, this work is about the circuitous paths of modern Jewish history—about the Holocaust and its aftermath, about Zionism, about American Judaism looking to understand its place in a global world. Roth's English is agile, harmonic; it isn't a language of silence, like Kafka's German or Schulz's Polish; instead, it is a compendium, a synthesis, a *lingua franca*; Jewish themes and motifs are perfectly at home in it, and the novel seems written for both a Jewish and a non-Jewish audience.

Of the non-Jewish languages that have generated a Jewish literature, probably the least explored are Spanish and Portuguese. This is surprising given the size of the Jewish population in the Americas in 2000: a total of around half-a-million Jews, the largest concentrations to be found in Argentina and Brazil, with some 240,000 and 180,000 people respectively. The literature generated by this population is substantial. Since I myself spring from it, I will devote the next paragraphs to placing it in context and to offering scholarly leads. To do so, it is crucial that I place in context the three major waves of immigration across the Atlantic Ocean: the crypto-Jewish in the colonial period; the Askhenazic between 1880 and 1930, with additions at the time of the Second World War; and the Sephardic from parts of the former Ottoman Empire that started around 1880 and prolonged itself into the 1870s.

The scholarly examination of the Jewish literature of the colonial period in the Americas didn't begin in earnest until the late nineteenth century, in large part because the fever for independence that swept the continent from approximately 1810 to 1865 focused on breaking away from Spain, not only politically but also culturally, and the interest in aspects of intellectual and artistic life in the centuries of colonialism was minuscule. By the time books began to be published, they related primarily to history. These included José Toribio Medina's examination of the Inquisition in Peru, the Philippines, Colombia, Chile, Mexico, and Argentina, published between 1887 and 1905. In the United States and Europe similar academic studies were implemented by the American Jewish Historical Society. But they amounted to a partial, half-sketched picture. References to the literature of the era were largely restricted to encyclopedias. Martin A. Cohen of Hebrew Union College—Jewish Institute of Religion, described Jewish-Latin American studies as marked by 'imbalance' and youth. He expressed his dismay thus:

The Jewish experience in Latin America is known only fragmentarily. A number of books and a host of articles deal with various aspects of this experience, but together they tell only a fraction of the story. The rest remains embedded in rich stores of manuscripts and printed materials. Many of these are readily available, while others are difficult to reach. Some day patient scholars will distill this material into reliable monographs. (Cohen 1971b)

Perhaps the most significant historical figure in the Americas in colonial times among Jews was Luis de Carvajal de Younger, also known as El Iluminado. He left behind in the hands of his inquisitors an array of autobiographical papers that have literary value. The best scholarship done on him and his legacy is by Seymour B. Liebman and by Cohen himself. A crypto-Jew from a prominent family in Benavente, Spain, that resettled in Nueva España, as Mexico was known in colonial times, Carvajal was arrested in 1589 by the Inquisition under the suspicion of being a Judaizer, that is, a proselytizer. Such an accusation, even if untrue, usually meant a life of misery that went from bankruptcy and social ridicule to imprisonment of some length and torture. He was put on trail but somehow managed to persuade his persecutors of his innocence. But six years later he was arrested again, this time on charges of impenitent heresy, and was burnt at the stake in 1596, at the age of 30, in the most notorious of all autos-da-fé ever seen in the region. His journey from his birthplace in the Iberian peninsula to the site of his death in the Plaza del Quemadero in the Mexican capital is emblematic.

Carvajal was the nephew of Don Luis de Carvajal the Elder, a formidable *conquistador*, a pacifier of the Indies, and by most accounts a true humanitarian, whose reputation brought him an appointment by the kings as governor of the New Kingdom of León, in northern Mexico. The younger Carvajal, his sisters, and mother were brought to Mexico by their famous relative. It was that atmosphere, precisely, that propelled El Iluminado to explore his Jewish roots, acknowledged by various members of the family but kept quiet for fear of the Inquisition. The Inquisition began to function in Mexico in 1570. Some eighty years prior, Columbus had sailed across the Atlantic in search of a new way to the Indies. That, at least, is the belief. Did he also serve as a bridge between the Old World and the New at a time of distress to the Jewish people, when the Catholic Kings, in an edit of expulsion in 1492, aborted a large and mature community from the Iberian peninsula? The Holy Office had been active in Spain, and in a far more vicious manner than anything ever seen in the Americas, for at least a hundred years. The colonies were perceived by some as a place of religious tolerance, as is evident, among other places, in the literature of the time, including a handful of *comedias* by Lope de Vega and in an emblematic chapter in the second volume of *Don Quixote*.

A handful of intellectuals and historians have devoted their energy to studying the impact of the Inquisition on the literature by Jews and non-Jews of Spain, the Netherlands, Turkey, and Northern Africa, among them Américo Castro, Cecil Roth, Amador de los Ríos, Haim Beinart, Miguel de la Pinta Llorente, and Benzion Netanyau. But the vicissitudes caused by the institution on the literature of the Americas, from Brazil and Peru to Mexico and the Caribbean basin, remains a research field tested only shyly today. A handful of provocative, book-long studies, articles, and biographies, have appeared on the subject, most prominently by Alfonso Toro and by the above-mentioned Medina; but they lack scientific rigour as a result of the academic and technological tools used at the time, are filled with errors, and often fall prey to anti-Jewish sentiments. Liebman's work is far more consistent: *The Jews of New Spain: Faith, Flame, and the Inquisition* (Liebman 1970) is a historical survey that also offers invaluable insights into Carvajal's literature; prior to it, *The Enlightened: The Writings of Luis de Carvajal, el Mozo* (Liebman 1967) allowed readers to read for the first time in English translation the words of El Iluminado himself. A few years later, Martin A. Cohen released his *magnum opus, The Martyr Luis de Carvajal: A Secret Jew in Sixteenth-Century Mexico* (Cohen 1973).

A native of Philadelphia, Cohen is an ordained rabbi of Ashkenazic descent, and a former president of the American Society of Sephardic Studies. For years he was devoted to early rabbinical Judaism and Christianity, but felt attracted to the topic of *marranos* and the Inquisition after reading the work of Cecil Roth. In the early 1970s he edited a couple of volumes on the Jewish experience in Latin America, especially the colonial period; and he contributed entries to the *Encyclopedia Judaica* on such themes as crypto-Judaism. Most notably, Cohen, long before *The Martyr* was ready for the press, wrote essays on various members of the Carvajal family and translated the lengthy autobiography that El Iluminado wrote between 1591 and 1592. (His translations, published by the *American Jewish Historical Society* (reprinted in Cohen 1971b) appeared a year before those of Liebman.) This autobiography, in fact, is one, and by far the most important, of the three pillars on which Cohen based his research for the book. The second is a series of letters to his mother and sisters which Carvajal wrote during his second imprisonment. The uniqueness of these letters is a result of the oppressive atmosphere in which they were written. Prisoners were neither permitted to communicate with the outside world, nor with other prisoners. His mother and sisters were in a cell next to him. In order to reach them, Carvajal inscribed a message on the core of an alligator pear, hid it in melon, and asked a jailer to take the fruit to his relatives. Of course, his persecutors suspected the strategy but did not discourage it: El Iluminado continued to be provided with alligator pears and other fruit. The third pillar is a Last Will and Testament that Carvajal composed in the last months of his second trail. As Cohen suggests, more than a will, this was an expression of a thorough commitment to the Jewish religion of his forebears.

The second wave of Jewish immigration to the Spanish- and Portuguese-speaking Americas took place at the end of the nineteenth century and went on until the Second World War. The newcomers were Yiddish-speaking *shtetl*-and ghetto-dwellers. Their transition to the Argentine and Brazilian pampas was, to a large extent, the result of efforts by philanthropists and organizations like Baron Maurice de Hirsch and the Alliance Israelite Universelle. Scholarship of the literature produced by this population is far more substantial, although again, it did not get into its stride until after 1975, largely in the United States and Europe. A handful of panoramic literary anthologies offer a transcontinental view. These include Feierstein (1990), Stavans (1994), Sadow (1999), and Goldemberg (2000). Also, volumes of academic essays about various aspects of Jewish-Latin American literature have appeared in the last decade. These include Glickman and DiAntonio (1993) and Barr (1995). And a major reference is Lockhart (1997). But the academic analysis that is available follows strict national lines.

Argentina is the Latin country with the richest Jewish literature. In connection with the Ashkenazic influx, this started with the folkloric manifestations in agricultural communes such as Rajíl and Moisésville. The anthology by Feierstein (Feierstein 1998) offers a sample of memoirs and stories by *colonos*, as the Jewish immigrants were called. Their foundational literary figure is Alberto Gerchunoff, responsible for the early classic *The Jewish Gauchos of the Pampas* (Gerchunoff 1997), published in Spanish in 1910 as a token of appreciation to Argentina in its first centennial of independent life. In Spanish, academic accounts of Gerchunoff abound, written by Argentine scholars like Leonardo Senkman (1983) and Saúl Sosnowski (1987). An English translation of Gerchunoff's book was published in 1955, and was reissued in 1997 with a kaleidoscopic introduction that places him in the context of the Yiddish, Jewish, Spanish, and Latin American intellectual traditions. Beyond Gerchunoff's work, the trans-generational development in iterature is the subject of a study by Lindstrom (1989). Lindstrom's volume is concerned with issues of identity, political and religious life, and responses to anti-Semitism. Unfortunately, it suffers from defects that also colour the work of Senkman and Sosnowski: its pages feel parochial and hyper-nationalistic, failing to insert the fiction produced by Argentine Jews into the span of modern Jewish literature worldwide. Several anthologies follow a similar path, including Gardiol (1997).

More than half a century after his death, Gerchunoff remains emblematic. Up until very recently, Spanish resisted embracing the Jewish sensibility. This becomes clear in a sentence found in the 1974 edition of the *Encyclopedia Judaica* (vii. 434–5), in which *The Jewish Gauchos of the Pampas* is described as 'the first work of literary value to be written in Spanish by a Jew in modern times'. The astonishing implication is that roughly between 1492 and 1910, when Gerchunoff compiled his twenty-six interrelated fictional vignettes on life in the agricultural communities in South America in the late nineteenth century, creating a hymn to transculturation, not a single literary item of merit appeared in the language. Prior to their expulsion from the Iberian peninsula, Jews prayed in Hebrew and wrote in Aramaic and Latin, but mostly communicated in Ladino (i.e. *Spanioli* or Judaeo-Spanish), a hybrid blend of Castilian, Hebrew, Turkish, Arabic, and other verbal elements. This means that the only literature by Jews in Spanish before *The Jewish Gauchos* is a product of *marranos*, crypto-Jews and new Christians.

No wonder Gerchunoff is such a quixotic figure in the eyes of intellectuals and scholars: his lifelong project, to turn Spanish into a home for the Jews, to acclimatize the language not only to Hebraisms and Yiddishisms but to a *Weltanschauung* totally alien to it, went against the currents of history. In fact, he was not only a modern *littérateur*, as the *Encyclopedia Judaica* describes him, but more importantly, part of the *modernista* generation that renewed Hispanic American letters between 1885 and 1915. It did it by drawing heavily upon Parnassianism and Symbolism, and by establishing a new crystalline and harmonious Spanish syntax based on restraint and precision, a new language musically elegant and spiritedly metaphorical. Gerchunoff befriended Rubén Darío, Leopoldo Lugones, and Delmira Agustini— a Nicaraguan, an Argentine, and a Uruguayan respectively, all four of them pillars of the *modernista* revolution. But his struggle went beyond this: born into Yiddish, he appropriated Quevedo's tongue, making it his own, and dreamed of inserting Spanish-speaking Jews into the twentieth century by building a three-way bridge between Renaissance Spain, nineteenth-century Russia and Eastern Europe, and modern Hispanic America. An authentic polyglot (aside from Yiddish and Spanish, he was fluent in Italian, French, English, Portuguese, and Russian), his heroes were Spinoza and Heine, both uprooted speakers and 'alien guests', as well as Sholem Aleichem and Cervantes, whose verbal talent and florid imagination explain the two façades of Gerchunoff: his Jewish side and his Hispanic side. Not surprisingly, Miguel de Unamuno once described him as 'the cosmopolitan man of letters *sine qua non*' (Unamuno 1966: vii. 145).

By virtue of their number, Argentine Jewish authors have inspired a solid scholarship. Various motifs in the oeuvres of César Tiempo, Marcos Agunis, Marío Goloboff, Alicia Steinberg, Ricardo Feierstein, and Ana María Shúa have become the topic of articles in scholarly journals. In comparison, other countries from Latin America have generated far less academic commentary. This does not translate into a lack of intellectual interest. On the contrary, whereas the Jewish role in the colonial period remains an eclipsed terrain, the literature by Ashkenazism, from the immigrant generation onwards, has been plentiful, and in the last twenty-five years so has the scholarship that reflects on it. Brazil has been a cradle of exciting Jewish literature too. Important figures include the sisters Clarice and Elisa Lispector, Samuel Rawet, and especially the humorist Moacyr Scliar. The latter is responsible for a substantial number of novels, non-fiction volumes, and collections of studies. Examination of his oeuvre appears in individual academic articles and book reviews. His *Collected Stories* (Scliar 1999), nominated for the National Jewish Book Award in the United States, were released as part of the Jewish-Latin America series with a contextual introduction. The most important scholars of this tradition are Regina Igel and Nelson Vieira. The former published in 1996 a study of Jewish immigrant patterns in Brazil that is of considerable interest. But it is the latter who has been responsible for a careful, if at times abstruse, scrutiny of Portuguese-language Jewish letters. Among his various intellectual endeavours are an excellent edition of the stories by the 'possessed' figure Samuel Rawet (Rawet 1998) and *Jewish Voices in Brazilian Literature: A Prophetic Discourse of Alterity* (Vieira 1995), a volume that closely follows the terminology of Subaltern Studies developed by Gayatri Spivak. Authors from Peru, Mexico, Chile, Uruguay, Guatemala, and Venezuela, including Isaac Goldemberg, Ilan Stavans, Ariel Dorfman and Marjorie Agosín, Mauricio Rosencof and Teresa Porzecanski, Alcina Lubitch Domecq, and Alicia Freilich respectively, have also elicited scholarly consideration. Their work has been translated into several languages. Individual studies on them, in Spanish, English, and Hebrew, are available.

The third wave of Jewish immigration to the Americas is defined by a constituency that originated in parts of the former Ottoman Empire. It began to arrive across the Atlantic Ocean in 1880, approximately when the Ashkenazic newcomers were also disembarking, and it extended itself until the 1970s. Until recently the literary output of this community has been comparatively small, yet its sheer existence allows one to reflect on a major component of the Jewish-Latin American tradition that makes a bridge with the colonial past: the modern Sephardic voices. Arguably the most important figure in this component is the Mexican academic, poet, and novelist Angelina Muníz-Huberman. She is prolific, with dozens of titles to her credit and several doctoral dissertations and academic articles written on their overall contribution. Muníz-Huberman's oeuvre juxtaposes Spanish mysticism and Kabbalah with contemporary motifs. It is important in this essay to highlight a couple of her academic volumes: Muníz-Huberman (1989), which includes poems by Shmuel Hanagid and Yehuda Halevi, among scores of other medieval Ibero-Jewish authors; and Muníz-Huberman (1993), a somewhat derivative examination of Kabbalah based on the work of Gershom Scholem. But an author whose oeuvre is popular, and whose themes are contemporary Sephardic, is Rosa Nissán, responsible for the autobiographical novel *Like a Bride* and its sequel *Like a Mother* (Nissán 2002). These, to my knowledge, are the only fictional narratives, at least since the Second World War, to include a portion in Ladino, the so-called Judaeo-Spanish jargon with roots in the Iberian peninsula that probably date back to the thirteenth century, if not earlier.

Lionel Trilling says that 'literature is the human activity that takes the fullest and most precise account of *variousness, possibility,* complexity, and difficulty' (Trilling 1950: p. xv; my italics). I emphasize two of his nouns because, in the same piece, he added that criticism is the task of bringing awareness to that complexity and difficulty, though he forgets to insert the words 'variousness' and 'possibility'. Books speak to us because they are telescopes to sights distant, unknown regions, as well as to dangerous, inner parts of the self. It is up to the critic and scholar to articulate their value. To survey the territory, they must take risks, wander about with eyes wide open, venturing into unforeseen territory, making connections, learning different languages so as to have more tools at their disposal. If their reports are to have any value, they should not tell readers what they already know, but should open up new vistas.

Five centuries after the expulsion from Spain in 1492, and more than 200 years after the Haskalah, an abundance of fiction and poetry by Jews in non-Jewish languages around the globe is produced regularly. And a solid body of literary criticism that attempts to examine its ambivalence at the national and international levels goes hand in hand with it. This literary criticism is of two kinds: one is strictly academic, meant for the consumption of students and specialists; the other is literary, published in magazines and newspapers and destined for a larger readership. These two kinds complement each other. Of those I've mentioned in these pages, some are by authors-turned-critics and vice-versa. Trilling's view of the critic and scholar applies to them: they take risks, wander about with eyes wide open, and often venture into unforeseen territory. A large number of them are polyglots; none, though, is in control of the entire spectrum of study. This is because the field is wide open and unwieldy. The result is that some cultures are better known than others: Jewish letters in Canada, Australia, and South Africa, for instance, remain eclipsed from academic study; likewise, an awakening of Sephardic voices—in Ladino and Spanish—is felt in Mexico, Guatemala, Argentina, and the United States, but is still in need of critical attention; and in the Netherlands Jewish fiction written in Dutch about the Holocaust and its aftermath is popular, but little is known about it beyond the nation's borders. Bialik talked about *kinus,* the 'ingathering' of Jewish literature. Translation serves that role: it builds bridges and establishes connections. Indeed, more Jewish literature in non-Jewish languages, defined by variousness and possibility as it is, is translated today than ever before. This, thankfully, stimulates the output of critical analysis marked by Ba'al Makhshoves's dictum: *one literature, many tongues.*

SUGGESTED READING

The easiest way to get acquainted with the major trends and debates in trans-diasporic Jewish literature is through Yudkin (1982), Wirth-Nesher (1994), Stavans (1998, 2001b), and Wisse (2000). These works offer methodological tools for approaching the various national backgrounds comparatively. Beyond them, each national and linguistic background— French (Mendelson *et al.* 1989; Marks 1996); German (Kahn 1993); Russian (Rutberg *et al.* 2000); Italian (Hughes 1983); etc.—has its own peculiarities that are addressed in articles, monographs, and scholarly books. For those interested in the United States in particular, where an influential wing of trans-diasporic Jewish letters has evolved for over a century, I recommend Chametsky *et al.* (2001). Primary sources are presented in separate volumes in a series under the editorship of Sander L. Gilman at the University of Nebraska Press. For an understanding of Jewish letters in Latin America, see the works of Feierstein (1989), Sadow (1999), Stavans (1994, 2001b), and Vieira (1995).

BIBLIOGRAPHY

Ba'al Makhshoves (Israel Isador Elyashev) 1994. 'One Literature in Two Languages.' In *What Is Jewish Literature?* 69–77. H. Wirth-Nesher ed. New York.

Babel, I. 2002. *The Collected Works.* Trans. P. Constantine N. Babel ed. New York.

Barr, L. B. ed. 1995. *Isaac Unbound: Patriarchal Traditions in the Latin American Jewish Novel.* New York.

——and Sheinin, D. eds. 1996. *The Jewish Diaspora in Latin America: New Studies on History and Literature.* New York.

Benjamin, W. 1968. *Illuminations: Essays and Reflections.* H. Arendt ed. and intro. New York.

Bialik, C. N, and Ravinsky, Y. H. eds. 1992. *Sefer Ha-Aggadah: Legends From the Talmud and Midrash.* Trans. W. G. Braude. Intro. D. Stern. New York.

Borges, J. L. 1962. 'The Argentine Writer and Tradition.' In *Labyrinths: Selected Stories and Other Writings.* 177–85. D. A. Yates and J. E. Irby eds. New York.

Chametzky, J. *et al.* 2001. *Jewish American Literature: A Norton Anthology.* New York.

Cohen, M. A. ed. 1971a. *The Jewish Experience in Latin America: A Survey Study for the American Jewish Congress.* Waltham, Mass.

——ed. 1971b. *The Jewish Experience in Latin America: Selected Studies From the Publication of the 'American Jewish Historical Society'.* New York.

——1971c. 'The Autobiography of Luis de Carvajal, the Younger.' In Cohen (1971b): i. 201–42.

——1971d. 'The Letters and Last Will and Testament of Luis de Carvajal, the Younger.' In Cohen (1971b): i. 243–312.

COHEN, M. A. 1973, 2001. *The Martyr Luis de Carvajal: A Secret Jew in Sixteenth-Century Mexico.* Intro. I. Stavans. Albuquerque, N.Mex.

D'ISRAELI, I. 1824. *Curiosities of Literature.* London.

ELKIN, J. L. 1980, 1998. *The Jews of Latin America.* New York.

—— and MERKX, G. W. eds. 1987. *The Jewish Presence in Latin America.* Boston.

FEIERSTEIN, R. 1989. *Cien años de narratia judeoargentina: 1889–1989.* Buenos Aires.

—— 1990. *Cuentos judíos latinoamericanos.* Buenos Aires.

—— ed. 1998. *Los mejores relatos con gauchos judíos.* Buenos Aires.

FICOWSKI, J. ed. 1998. *Collected Works of Bruno Schulz.* London.

FRANK, A. 1952. *The Diary of a Young Girl.* Trans. from the Dutch by B. M. Mooyaart-Doubleday. Intro. E. Roosevelt. Garden City, NY.

FURMAN, A. 2000 *Contemporary Jewish American Writers and the Multicultural Dilemma: The Return of the Exiled.* Syracuse, NY.

GARDIOL, R. ed. 1997. *The Silver Candelabra and Other Stories: A Century of Jewish Argentine Literature.* Pittsburgh.

GERCHUNOFF, A. 1997. *The Jewish Guachos of the Pampas.* Trans. P. de Pereda. Intro. I. Stavans. Albuquerque, N.Mex.

GILMAN, S. 1995. *Franz Kafka, the Jewish Patient.* New York.

GITLITZ, D. M. 1996, 2002. *Secrecy and Deceit: The Religion of the Crypto-Jews* Intro. I. Stavans. Albuquerque, N. Mex.

GLICKMAN, N. and DIANTONIO, R. eds. 1993. *Tradition and Innovation: Reflections on Latin American Jewish Writing.* Albany, NY.

GOLDEMBERG, I. 1999. *The Fragmented Life of Don Jacobo Lerner.* Trans. R. Piccioto. Intro. I. Stavans. Albuquerque, N. Mex.

—— 2000. *El gran libro de la América judía.* San Juan, Puerto Rico.

HOWE, I. 1976. *The World of Our Fathers.* New York.

—— 1990. *Selected Writings: 1950–1990.* San Diego, Calif.

HUGHES, S. H. 1983. *Prisoners of Hope: The Silver Age of the Italian Jews, 1924–1974.* Cambridge, Mass.

JACOBS, J. 2002. *Hidden Heritage: The Legacy of the Crypto-Jews.* Berkeley and London.

JASON, K. ed. 1990. *Name and Tears and Other Stories.* Minnesota.

KAFKA, F. 1941. *The Castle.* Intro. T. Mann. Trans. from the German by E. and W. Muir. New York.

—— 1956. *The Trial.* Illus. G. Salter. Trans. from the German by E. and W. Muir. New York.

KAHN, L. 1993. *Between Two Worlds: A Cultural History of German-Jewish Writers.* Ames, Iowa.

KAZIN, A. 1978. *New York Jew.* New York.

KIŠ, D. 1975. *Garden Ashes.* Trans. W. J. Hannaher. New York.

LANGER, L. 1995. *Admitting the Holocaust: Collected Essays.* New York.

LIEBMAN, S. B. 1970. *The Jews of New Spain: Faith, Flame, and the Inquisition.* Coral Gables, Fla.

—— ed. and trans. 1967. *The Enlightened: The Writings of Luis de Carvajal, el Mozo.* Preface by A. Nevins. Coral Gables, Fla.

LINDSTROM, N. 1989. *Jewish Issues in Argentine Literature: From Gerchunoff to Szichman.* Columbia.

LOCKHART, D. B. 1997. *Jewish Writers in Latin America: A Dictionary.* New York and London.

MARKS, E. 1996. *Marrano as Metaphor: The Jewish Presence in French Writing*. New York.

MEDINA, J. T. 1887. *Historia del tribunal del Santo Oficio de la Inquisición en Lima*. 2 vols. Santiago de Chile.

——1889. *Historia del tribunal del Santo Oficio de la Inquisición en las Islas Filipinas*. Santiago de Chile.

——1890. *Historia del tribunal del Santo Oficio de la Inquisición en Chile*. 2 vols. Santiago de Chile.

——1899. *Historia del tribunal del Santo Oficio de la Inquisición de Cartagena de Indias*. Santiago de Chile.

——1899. *Historia del tribunal del Santo Oficio de la Inquisición en las provincias de la Plata*. Santiago de Chile.

——1905. *Historia del tribunal del Santo Oficio de la Inquisición en México*. Santiago de Chile.

MEMMI, A. 1975. *The Pillar of Salt*. Trans. from the French (1966) by E. Roditi. Chicago.

MENDELSOHN, E. ed. 1996. *Literary Strategies: Jewish Texts and Contexts*. New York.

MENDELSON, D. *et al*. eds. 1989. *Écrits français d'Israël de 1880 à nos jours*. Paris.

MIRON, D. 2000. *The Image of the Shtetl and Other Studies of Modern Jewish Literary Imagination*. Syracuse, NY.

MUÑÍZ-HUBERMAN, A. ed. 1989. *La lengua florida: Antología sefardí*. Mexico City.

——1993. *Las raíces y las ramas: fuentes y derivaciones de la Cábala hispanohebrea*. Mexico City.

NISSÁN, R. 2000. *'Like a Bride' and 'Like a Mother'*. Trans. D. Gerdes. Intro. I. Stavans. Albuquerque, N.Mex.

OZICK, C. 1983. *Art and Ardor*. New York.

——1989. *Metaphor and Memory: Essays*. New York.

PAWEL, E. 1995. *The Poet Dying: Heinrich Heine's Last Years in Paris*. New York.

PINSKER, S. 1975. *The Comedy that 'Hoits': An Essay on the Fiction of Philip Roth*. Columbia, Miss.

RAWET, S. 1998. *The Prophet and Other Stories*. Trans. and Intro. N. Vieira. Albuquerque, N.Mex.

ROSENFELD, A. 1980. *A Double Dying: Reflections on Holocaust Literature*. Bloomington, Ind.

ROSKIES, D. 1984. *Against the Apocalypse: Responses to Catastrophe in Modern Jewish Culture*. Cambridge, Mass.

ROTH, P. 1959. *Goodbye, Columbus and Five Short Stories*. Boston.

——1972. *The Breast*. New York.

——1981. *Zuckerman Unbound*. New York.

——1986. *The Counterlife*. New York.

——1993. *Operation Shylock: A Confession*. New York.

RUTBERG, N. I., *et al*. 2000. *Evrei i evreiskii vopros v literature sovetskogo perioda: Khronolo-gicheski-tematicheskii ukazatel literatury, izdannoi za 1917–1991 gg. na russkom iazyke*. Moscow.

SADAN, D. 1963. *Yoyvl-bukh: Tsum fuftsikstn geboyrn-tog fun Avram Sutskever*. Tel Aviv.

SADOW, S. 1999. *King David's Harp: Autobiographical Essays by Jewish Latin American Writers*. Albuquerque, N.Mex.

SALINGER, J. D. 1951. *The Catcher in the Rye*. Boston.

SCHULTZ, H. 1992. *Juden in der deutschen Literatur: Eine deutsch-jüdische Literaturgeschichte im Überblick.* Munich.

SCLIAR, M. 1999. *The Collected Stories.* Intro. I. Stavans. Albuquerque, N.Mex.

SENKMAN, L. 1983. *La identidad judía en la literatura argentina.* Buenos Aires.

SHAKED, G. 1987. *The Shadows Within: Essays on Modern Jewish Writers.* New York.

—— 2000. *Modern Hebrew Fiction.* Trans. Y. Lotan. Bloomington, Ind.

SHKOLVSKY, V. 1990. *Theory of Prose.* Intro. Gerald R. Bruns. Trans. and Intro. B. Sher. Lisle, Ill.

SHMERUK, C. 1960. *Jewish Literature in the Soviet Union During and Following the Holocaust Period.* Jerusalem.

—— 1985. *The Esterke Story in Yiddish and Polish Literature: A Case Study in the Mutual Relations of Two Cultural Traditions.* Jerusalem.

—— 1992. *Historia literatury jidysz: Zarys.* Warsaw.

SINGER, I. B. 1953. 'Gimpel the Fool.' *Partisan Review.* 20/3: 300–13. Trans. from the Yiddish by S. Bellow.

SINGER, I. J. 1936. *The Brothers Ashkenazi.* Trans. from the Yiddish by M. Samuel. New York

SOLOTAROV, T. 1987. *A Few Good Voices in My Head: Occasional Pieces on Writing, Editing, and Reading My Contemporaries.* New York.

SOSNOWSKI, S. 1987. *La orilla inminente. Escritores judíos argentinos.* Buenos Aires.

STAVANS, I. 1994. *Tropical Synagogues: Short Stories by Jewish-Latin American Writers.* New York and London.

—— 1998. *The Oxford Book of Jewish Stories.* New York and London.

—— 2001a. *On Borrowed Words: A Memoir of Language.* New York.

—— 2001b. *The Inveterate Dreamer: Essays and Conversations on Jewish Culture.* London and Lincoln.

TRILLING, L. 1950. *The Liberal Imagination: Essays on Literature and Society.* New York.

—— 2000. *The Moral Obligation To Be Intelligent: Selected Essays.* Ed. and intro. L. Wieseltier. New York.

UNAMUNO, M. 1966. *Obras Completas.* Madrid.

VIEIRA, N. 1995. *Jewish Voices in Brazilian Literature: A Prophetic Discourse of Alterity.* Gainesville, Fla.

WIESEL, E. 1960. *Night.* Foreword F. Mauriac. Trans. from the French by S. Rodway. New York.

WISSE, R. 2000. *The Modern Jewish Canon: A Journey Through Language and Culture.* New York.

WIRTH-NESHER, H. ed. 1994. *What Is Jewish Literature?* New York.

YUDKIN, L. 1982. *Jewish Writing and Identity in the Twentieth Century.* New York.

CHAPTER 26

HALACHA AND LAW

B. S. JACKSON, B. LIFSHITZ, A. GRAY, D. B. SINCLAIR[1]

1. INTRODUCTION

THE academic study of 'halacha', like its traditional study in the yeshiva, is far broader than the study of 'Jewish law' (*mishpat 'ivri*), as that term has come to be understood (see further Jackson 1980; Shilo 1982). For the halacha, in both its scope (including the whole sphere of religious observance) and concerns (spiritual as well as material), goes well beyond the scope and concerns of that section of it which has counterparts in secular, Western legal systems. For the purposes of this article, 'Jewish law' is that latter subsection of the halacha, a subsection moreover which has attracted the particular attentions of scholars trained in secular jurisprudence (though often also with a yeshiva background). As in the academic study of other legal systems, lawyers tend to have a near monopoly in offering 'dogmatic' analyses of the law—the object of which is to describe and analyse the present state of the binding law (*ius cogens*)—and, to a lesser extent, in comparative legal studies, whereas historians and philosophers, bringing to bear the insights and methodologies of their own disciplines, have made major contributions to the study of the

[1] This article has a complex authorial history. The original versions were contributed, some in rather different forms, largely as follows: Jackson, ss. 1, 3.1, 5, 6; Lifshitz, ss. 3.2, 4.1; Gray, ss. 3.3, 4.1; Sinclair, ss. 2, 4.2. They have all, however, been re-edited and sometimes supplemented by Jackson; it should not therefore be assumed that every author necessarily assents to every proposition stated herein, even within sections for which he or she provided the original text.

history and philosophy of the halacha (including its 'Jewish law' section). This article surveys trends in the field, in relation to both halacha and 'Jewish Law', in terms of the (commonly found) fourfold division—historical (s. 3), dogmatic (s. 4), comparative and philosophical (s. 5). But first (s. 2), some remarks on the history of scholarship itself.

2. HISTORY OF SCHOLARSHIP

2.1 Christian Hebraists

The academic study of Jewish law in Europe began with non-Jews such as John Selden (1584–1654), who possessed a remarkable command of biblical and rabbinic Hebrew and an outstanding collection of talmudic manuscripts. He concentrated almost exclusively on the Bible and the Talmud, his works including treatises on the Jewish law of marriage and divorce (1646) and the laws of succession (1631). His major compilation on international law (1640) also shows strong rabbinic influences. The famous German Bible scholar and author of the first textbook on the historical-critical approach to the New Testament, Johann Michaelis (1717–91), also composed a six-volume work on biblical law (1770–5) and individual studies on various aspects of Jewish criminal and family law (1768) and (1778).

2.2 In Rabbinical Circles

Mention may here be made of a significant debate within Orthodoxy regarding the hierarchy of authoritative sources in Jewish law, between R. Ezekiel Landau (1713–93, head of Bohemian Jewry) and the more traditional R. Moses Sofer (1762–1839, leader of Hungarian Orthodoxy) a generation later (see further Sinclair 1998). R. Landau adopted a fundamentally positive approach to modernity and issued a number of lenient rulings in relation to problems posed by modern economic and social conditions, including keeping Jewish-owned factories open on Sabbaths and Holy Days and shaving on the intermediate days of the Festivals. The methodology underlying these rulings is the principle that only rulings in the Talmud and its cognate literature are absolutely binding. Later material does not carry the same normative clout and may, therefore, either be ignored or modified in the light of the relevant talmudic principles and precedents. R. Landau articulated this method-ology far more clearly and applied it much more rigorously than did any of his predecessors. He applied it in numerous responsa and used it to good effect in crafting lenient responses to various aspects of modernity. Diametrically opposed to R. Landau's approach was that of R. Moses Sofer, whose highly negative approach to modernity was justified, *inter alia*, on the basis of a methodology which endowed the entire halachic tradition, including rulings based on custom and mysticism, with strong force. The combination of R. Sofer's anti-modernist ideology and his all-embracing approach meant that he was generally able to find some basis in the tradition for a negative reply to questions involving aspects of modernity, including keeping factories open on the Sabbath and shaving on the intermediate days of the Festivals. Not content with establishing a competing methodology to that of R. Landau, R. Sofer also sought to conceal the entire concept of a normative hierarchy within the halacha from the Jewish community at large on the grounds that the ability to make distinctions between different normative levels only played into the hands of Jews who wished to permit themselves transgressions of rabbinic, as opposed to biblical, laws. Against this, R. Zvi Hirsch Chajes (1805–55), who wrote extensively on halachic methodology and who, in his *Student's Guide through the Talmud*, laid the basis for the modern classification of the legal sources of Jewish law, was unable to accept R. Sofer's approach. In his view, it is necessary to preserve the normative purity of the halacha, as a value in its own right. In support of this argument he cites Maimonides, who lays great emphasis on exposing normative distinctions within the halacha to the public in order to avoid the biblical prohibition on adding to the Torah.

Even within eighteenth and nineteenth-century Orthodoxy, however, normative distinctions such as the one articulated by R. Landau between talmudic and non-talmudic elements remained potent factors in some schools of thought, provided that they were not used as a means of accommodating modern life. Rather, they served as a means of restoring pure talmudic law. A good example is the methodology used by R. Elijah, the famous Gaon of Vilna (1720–97), who insisted on separating original talmudic law from later accretions and on endowing that law with superior normative status. The process of separation was carried out first by establishing the authentic talmudic text and then analysing subsequent halachic development in the light of that text. This approach—the Lithuanian School—flourishes to this very day in the most Orthodox of circles (see Solomon 1993).

In more recent times, however, this approach has once again assumed a role vis-à-vis modernity in the form of the modern Orthodox movement. This movement stems from an attempt to shape a positive approach to modern society and technology based, *inter alia*, upon sharpening the distinction between the different normative levels of Jewish law. Its major achievements have been with respect to the expansion of the role of women in the religious sphere, the endowment of the State of Israel with religious significance, and the academic study of Judaism from an Orthodox perspective. Contemporary mainstream Orthodoxy, however, remains cautious and maintains, by and large, the 'all or nothing' approach to halacha made popular by R. Samson Raphael Hirsch (1808–88), leader of German Orthodoxy in the late nineteenth century.

It was the Conservative movement which in the twentieth century devoted most attention to the use of normative distinctions between biblical and rabbinic and talmudic and post-talmudic law, in order to further accommodation with modernity. Clearly, obtaining authentic texts of the Talmud and its cognate literature is an important element in this approach, and much of the scholarship generated by the movement's Jewish Theological Seminary was concerned, especially in the past, with the distillation of pure talmudic texts. In terms of practical halacha, the methodological basis for many of the Conservative movement's rulings, such as travelling on the Sabbath in order to attend synagogue, is the normative hierarchy of Jewish law. In this respect, it is noteworthy that the principal architect of the movement's halachic tradition was Louis Ginzberg (1873–1953), lecturer in Talmud at the Jewish Theological Seminary and first professor of halacha at the Hebrew University. He was also a great-grandnephew of the Vilna Gaon, and his illustrious ancestor's methodology is evident in his halachic approach and his scholarly writings.

2.3 In Academic Circles

As the spirit of modernity began to permeate the Jewish communities of Europe in the nineteenth century, the academic study of Jewish subjects was pursued by Jews as well as non-Jews. Eduard Gans (1798–1839), who was only able to rise above the rank of lecturer at the University of Berlin after his apostasy, published, amongst other works on Jewish law, an essay on the principles of the law of inheritance in the Bible and Talmud (1822–3). Joseph Saalschütz (1801–63), a rabbi in Koenigsberg, where he also lectured in Hebrew archaeology at the local university, published an extensive work on Jewish public and private law (1848), in which he sought to trace the evolution of biblical principles into talmudic doctrine. Samuel Mayer's study of Jewish, Athenian, and Roman law (1862–76) illustrates the importance already attached to the comparative study of ancient legal systems in this early period in the history of academic studies in Jewish law. Zacharias Frankel (1801–75) emphasized the influence of historical factors on the development of the halacha and provided the intellectual stimulus for the modern Conservative movement in the United States. He wrote on biblical and talmudic law (1846), and also laid out a scheme for studying the history of the post-talmudic responsa literature (1865)—in addition to his seminal works, in Hebrew as well as German, in the field of talmudic studies and exegesis (1859; 1870). The model of the rabbinical academic working in a rabbinical seminary rather than a regular university is repeated in the case of Moses Bloch (1815–1909), who was appointed Professor of Talmud and Codes in the newly opened Budapest Rabbinical Seminary in 1877. Bloch wrote a seven-volume work in Hebrew on rabbinic legislation in the Talmud (1879–1906); he also edited and published the Prague edition of the *responsa* of R. Meir of Rothenberg (1885, 1891) and wrote several important monographs on Jewish criminal and civil law (1879, 1890, 1893, 1901, 1904).

At the beginning of the twentieth century the academic study of Jewish law was an established subject in the field of classical studies in universities in both Europe and the United States. Its scope, however, was almost entirely confined to biblical and talmudic law, and research was generally conducted from the perspectives of philology, history, and ancient comparative law, with special emphasis on the principles of Roman law. A significant figure, exemplifying all these aspects of the European juristic tradition, was David Daube (1909–99), himself a major scholar in Roman law, whose publications and teaching in Cambridge, Aberdeen, Oxford, and Berkeley set new standards of attention to linguistic detail in the study of biblical law (1947), law in the New Testament (1956), and early rabbinic law (1992). Daube's status in Roman law (he held the Regius Chair of Civil Law in Oxford) enabled him to train a new generation of scholars who were able to follow him in introducing the study of Jewish law into the curricula of an increasing number of faculties of law in European and American universities.

A profound change took place in the way Jewish law was studied in the wake of the spread of Zionism in the first half of the twentieth century. The prospect of the eventual establishment of a sovereign Jewish state stimulated Jewish lawyers to examine the possibility of using Jewish law as the legal system of the nascent national homeland, and the emphasis shifted from classical studies to law.

Two notable examples of scholars working in this way in the first half of the twentieth century are Jacob Zuri, whose major work on talmudic law (1921–2) spanned capital crimes, family law, succession, property, obligations, penal law, procedure, public law, law of associations, law of priests, and the law of the Temple, and Asher Gulak. Prior to his arrival in Palestine, Gulak had been involved in founding the Hamishpat Haivri Society in Moscow in December, 1918, whose aims included the publication of legal treatises, journals, and books in the field of Jewish law and a comprehensive work— *Shaʿarei Hamishpat Haʿivri*—which would 'compile all of the sources contained in the Jewish legal literature of all the periods . . . in a clear and systematic order to facilitate research and study, such that, anyone may easily find in it whatever he seeks' (Elon 1994: 1588–9). The 'order' Gulak and other members of the society had in mind was that of modern jurisprudence and its legal categories. In 1936 Gulak was appointed Professor of Jewish Law at the Hebrew

University of Jerusalem. Most of the work published by Gulak and Zuri was in Hebrew and is characterized by a doctrinal rather than a philological or historical focus, in the manner typical of legal authors (though they both maintained the tradition of comparative legal studies, especially of Greek and Roman law); it includes many references to post-talmudic works such as Maimonides' *Mishneh Torah* and the *Shulhan Arukh* of R. Joseph Karo. In addition to highly acclaimed doctrinal and historical studies on the law of property (1929) and obligations (1939), Gulak was concerned with the systematic presentation of the major principles of Jewish civil law in the Talmud, and his four-volume *Yesodei Hamishpat Ha'ivri* is an attempt to organize and expound this material in a form consistent with modern juristic thought.

Already in 1922 Gulak had written that 'the free spirit of a people finds its primary expression in the legal system under which it lives' (1922: 3–4, cf. 1969: 28–34). The idea that Jewish law is a vital cultural asset of the Jewish people and an integral part of their national rejuvenation was shared by secular Zionists as well as religious ones: it was part of the cultural Zionism of Ahad Ha'am (1957: 272). The influence of the German jurist and historian Savigny, and the Historical School he founded, is evident in Gulak's references to the spirit of the people and the notion that law, like language, is a basic building-block of national cultures (cf. England 1980: 42–5). Also traceable to the influence of the Historical School is the notion that there are fundamental principles in every legal system which emerge on the basis of a historical study of legal sources. This idea had a powerful effect on later scholars and was to become the focus of a heated academic debate in the 1970s (see s. 4.2 below).

Gulak's successor at the Hebrew University was Abraham Freimann, who wrote mainly on the medieval period: amongst his writings are an important study (1918) on R. Asher ben Jechiel (the *Rosh*) and the editing of a series of important responsa collections by Maimonides and members of his family. His major work on marriage laws (1944) concentrates on post-talmudic literature. In 1947 Freimann headed a committee concerned with the preparation of Jewish law for adoption by the Jewish state as its national legal system (Elon 1994: 1612 f.), but his murder in 1948 cut short this work and dealt a serious blow to the *mishpat 'ivri* agenda in terms of the plan to base the legal system of the state on Jewish law. By the time of the establishment of the State of Israel in 1948, the shape of academic Jewish law studies in the country was quite well defined. Its salient features were the use of the methods and concepts of modern legal science rather than those of history, philology, and ancient comparative law typical of the classical European school, and the 'all-period' approach to research rather than a focus on the Bible and Talmud only.

3. HISTORICAL APPROACHES

This review of historical approaches to Jewish law is divided into the broad historical periods of halachic history.

3.1 Biblical Law

The study of biblical law is regarded by many as a specialism in itself. In some traditional circles it is excluded from the study of 'Jewish law', in the light of its close involvement with issues of biblical criticism (or, to similar effect, because traditional Jewry scholarship views the Bible exclusively through rabbinic eyes). Conversely, some critical scholars see biblical law as belonging to the world of the ancient Near East, rather than in any organic connection with later Jewish interpretation. There has, however, been a school of orthodox biblical scholarship (notably Kaufmann and his pupils) which has been willing to engage with critical biblical scholarship, and to offer academic arguments against it. Loewenstamm, for example, was willing to attempt reconstructions of the original biblical text, but saw the Rabbinic 'oral law', as found particularly in the halachic midrashim, as the best evidence of the original state of that text (1977/80). Nowadays, considerable diversity of basic approach is to be found in the study of biblical law, though most of the approaches here distinguished were richly integrated within the work of one of the principal pioneers of the study of biblical law, David Daube (1947). There is a 'legal' approach, which studies biblical 'law' primarily within the context of the other legal collections of the ancient Near East (e.g. Westbrook 1988; Otto 1988, 1991), while others seek to locate biblical law more firmly within the context of biblical literature, whether that be biblical narrative (e.g. Carmichael 1985, 1992), theology and its ritual manifestations (Milgrom 1975, 1981, 1983, 1992), or social and political history (Crüsemann 1996). The general trend away from the literary-historical approach to the Bible, seeking to identify earlier strata in the development of the text, towards a more 'holistic' or 'hermeneutic' approach, stressing the literary characteristics of the final product, is also evident in the study of biblical law (e.g. Sprinkle 1994), though the former still produces significant contributions (e.g. Schwienhorst-Schönberger 1990), and there is increasing discussion of the sociological factors (such as the divide between town and countryside) to be taken into account in theories of development within biblical law (Otto 1993/6). This trend has also served to create bridges between the study of biblical and post-biblical sources, with increasing commonalities, or coherent progression, being observed in the literary techniques deployed before and after the closure of the biblical canon. The notion of 'inner biblical exegesis' has come into vogue, from the work of Michael Fishbane (1985).

The study of biblical law today is varied in its methodologies, with interdisciplinary approaches from anthropology (e.g. Douglas 1966: ch. 3; Marshall 1993) and semiotics (Jackson 2000) interacting with the more traditional legal, literary, theological, and historical approaches. Monographs and articles are written on specific legal institutions (e.g. Chirichigno 1993, on slavery). For an overview of institutions, see Falk (1964/2001); on the general institutional and literary development of the system, see the bibliography of Welch (1991), in addition to the general tools of biblical scholarship. There is a continuing debate on the nature of the biblical legal collections (Fitzpatrick-McKinley 1999), but any attempt to appropriate them for one particular function (whether it be positive law, ethical teaching, or religious ideology) clearly depends upon strong claims regarding their literary history, as well as distancing them further from the integrated character of the halacha, as traditionally conceived and more widely acknowledged in academic approaches to later periods.

3.2 Second Commonwealth and Talmudic Law

The Second Commonwealth period of Jewish Law (Hecht *et al.* 1996: ch. 2) has generated its own issues and specialisms. The sectarian writings discovered in the caves of the Judaean desert give us a better understanding of the literature of the sages and its development, either as a whole body of legal directions or as specific rules (Schiffman 1975, 1983). The emergence of Christianity has prompted immense scholarship, not only on its Judaic roots and the problems presented by the accounts of the trial(s?) of Jesus (e.g. Cohn 1972); it also prompted the rabbis to struggle intensively with its ideas and theology by providing new emphases in both halacha and philosophy (and their interaction), as has been demonstrated by E. E. Urbach (1986) and others. Scholars have also devoted considerable attention to the chequered history of Jewish autonomy and its ultimate demise at the hands of the Romans (Piattelli 1979; Jackson 1981; Rabello 2000). The significance of the period as a bridge between biblical and rabbinic law depends in part upon how much of the tannaitic material may legitimately be read back into the Second Commonwealth period—a question addressed in particular by Falk (1972/8). Some studies of particular institutions have sought to trace the development of the law from biblical to early rabbinic times (e.g. Jackson 1972, on theft), and with it the effects of the transformation in cultural context from the world of the ancient Near East to the Hellenistic-Roman environment.

The Talmud is a collective work in which sources of different origins (tannaitic, amoraic, and saboraic) are to be found. Traditional halacha, generally speaking, seeks to unify and harmonize the sources and solve the contradictions, emphasizing particularly the last stage (that of the Saboraim). Academic research, by contrast, considers all stages to be of equal status and relevance to the last step taken by the Talmud.

It is difficult to draw a clear line between 'regular' research in talmudic literature and research into Jewish law of the talmudic period. One way of differentiating between the two is the following: if the research concentrates on the form of the text, its origins, and its variants, it should be regarded as 'regular' research; if, on the other hand, it concentrates on the substance of halachic issues, it is legal research. Some would add to this definition the requirement that the halachic topic should correspond to one recognized by real systems of positive law. Of course, a legal text can be examined from different angles—historical, linguistic, literary, and so on— and any such examination might reveal important insights about the law contained in that legal text. But there is an argument that the history of the law should itself be written by the use of legal methods—certainly if one takes the view that the Talmud was written by persons of the legal profession who used legal argumentation and legal thought. Legal logic and dogmatics which stem from the desire to achieve harmonization, actual solutions, abstraction, and so on, are all powerful factors which influence our understanding of the text at any particular historical period.

Students of Jewish law in our times have a difficult task. They have to take account of the achievements of 'regular' talmudic research (e.g. the classical works on the textual transmission and literary character of the talmudic literature and its layers, as elaborated by Y. N. Epstein, S. Lieberman, A. Weiss, Ch. Albeck, E. S. Rosenthal, D. Weiss-Halivni, and S. Y. Friedman), in order to make the best use of the optimal text. They must make use of the textual variants which are found in manuscripts, together with the fragments of deeds surviving from the Judaean desert and the Cairo Genizah (such as the pivotal research by M. A. Friedman (1980) on the *ketubah*, based on texts stemming primarily from the eleventh century). Then there are the writings from the periods of the Gaonim and Rishonim, with their original interpretations of the talmudic text. The student of talmudic law has to know the literary characteristics of the text in order to avoid deriving legal conclusions from sayings which are only rhetorical in their nature, and must be aware of both the general history of the period and that of the surrounding legal systems which might have influenced Jewish Law. The history of the period includes study of the 'legal personality' of the individual rabbis, which has generated extensive, sometimes critical, research into their sayings, as in the series of books of J. Neusner and his colleagues and others. But on top of that, scholars of talmudic law need to be educated in both law and halacha in the classical sense, in order properly to understand the give and take of the *sugyot* and make use of the commentaries and remarks of the commentators from later generations, whose sensitivity to both textual and logical discrepancies in the Talmud can be of great help to academic research in Jewish law.

Professor Menachem Elon initiated the *mishpat ʿivri* school, paying substantial but far from exclusive attention to the talmudic period, with his *Herut ha-Prat* ('Freedom of the Debtor's Person in Jewish Law', 1964). His first students continued this methodology, with books by Nahum Rakover on agency (1972) and Shmuel Shilo on *Dina de-Malkhuta Dina*, and Hebrew University dissertations by S. D. Revital on Partnership (1970), M. Corinaldi on Bailment (1972), E. C. Benzimra on Necessity and Duress (1975), B. Z. Eliash on the Law of Interest (1977), I. Warhaftig on Contract (1977), S. Lerner on Bailment (1980), and S. Ettinger on Self-Help (1982). In this context one may mention also the books of Sh. Warhaftig on Labour Law (1969) and Contract (1974).

Nevertheless, for the purposes of research into the law of the talmudic period, it may be better to dedicate research specifically to the sources of that period, using such critical philological methods as may assist in the understanding of the legal points. Asher Gulak, the first modern scholar of Jewish law (cf. s. 2.3 above), dedicated several of his writings to the study of the law of the talmudic period, hoping that it would serve as a proper basis for the study of later ages, notably in his books on Land Law (1929), Obligation and Its Guarantees (1939), and *Das Urkundenwesen im Talmud* (which was translated into Hebrew in 1994). In these books Gulak uses critical methodology, intensively comparing the talmudic material with contemporary legal systems (Roman and Hellenistic).

Jewish law in the talmudic period is the central focus of the work of Shalom Albeck, who has provided volumes on Torts (1965), Property and Contract (1976), Law Courts (1980), and more recently, a general introduction to the law of the period (1999). His method of study, though related to this specific period, is purely dogmatic, seeking the general principles which he takes the detailed rules of the law consistently to exemplify. Albeck approaches the Talmud as a whole, paying little attention to textual variations, layers, and so on. He denies any changes within talmudic law, regarding apparent differences as reflecting the application of unchanging principles to differing circumstances.

On the other hand, the greater number of scholars interested in our period apply a rather more philological approach. One may locate the beginnings of this in those parts of E. Shochetman's book on *Illegal Acts in Jewish Law* dedicated to the talmudic period. B. Lifshitz's 1979 Hebrew University dissertation (*Kam Leh Bəˀ Dəˀ Rabbah Mineh*) critically reviews the apparent Mishnaic law that a person does not suffer a capital punishment and a civil payment for the same act; his later book (1989) reveals and describes the different schools of thought in relation to these legal institutions in the talmudic era (and what happened to them later on). The same approach is taken in his 1993 book on Employee and Independent Contractor, and in other articles.

More or less related to the same school, in that they reveal the discrepancies, differences of mind, changes and development within the talmudic literature, and their effect upon later halacha, are the dissertations of (amongst others) P. Segal on

Liability under Divine Jurisdiction (Hebrew University, 1986), A. Edrei on The Liability of Heirs for the Debts of the Deceased (Hebrew University, 1993), D. Henschke on the tannaitic and talmudic treatment of the 'Mishnah Rishonah' of the Law of Bailment (1997), and A. Radziner on 'Dine Qenasot' in Talmudic Law (Bar-Ilan University, 2001).

The legal literature of the Tannaim and Amoraim is studied also from the jurisprudential point of view, particularly by H. Ben-Menachem (1987, 1991), who addresses the problem whether Jewish law, when examined by modern general jurisprudence, is to be considered as a legal system at all (see also s. 5 below). Recently he has been engaged in research into the phenomenon of controversy in Jewish law (1991–3).

3.3 Medieval Jewish Law

The Gaonic period (seventh through early eleventh centuries) commends itself as a starting-point for the Jewish Middle Ages because it marks two related, significant shifts in rabbinic Jewish culture from its late antique to medieval form: the beginning of the Babylonian Talmud's pre-eminent position in Jewish thought, life, and practice; and the organization of Jewish life as a corporate minority in an exclusivist Muslim (and hence non-pagan) society.

3.3.1 *Medieval Jewish Law as Part of the Overall History of Jewish Law*

Chaim Tchernowitz (*Rav Tza'ir*) and Menachem Elon are systematizers who surveyed medieval Jewish law as part of their overall interpretations of the history of Jewish law. Tchernowitz's *Toldot ha-Poseqim*—conceptualized as a sequel to his *Toldot ha-Halakha*—was informed throughout by his interpretation of the medieval Jewish legal enterprise as a tension between two points of view. The *mafsiqim* (literally 'those who cut off') sought to sever the link between talmudic interpretation and halachic decision-making by extracting the legal rulings from the Talmud and creating special collections (codes) from which to derive the halacha. The *marchivim* (literally 'those who expand'), by contrast, wished to retain the link between talmudic interpretation and halachic decision-making. Tchernowitz's distinction between the *mafsiqim* and *marchivim* indicates that he saw medieval Jewish law as the product of the major legal works of major legal decisors. His approach to these works and their authors was therefore essentially biographical and analytic. Working inductively by means of close studies of the principal works of the major legal decisors, he extracted and explicated the (often) implicit codificatory methodologies they employed.

Menachem Elon also utilized a biographical and analytic approach to medieval Jewish law in his magnum opus: *Jewish Law* (1994) is a systematic, broadly chrono-

logical review of Jewish law from talmudic times to the present, interpreted through
the lens of legal positivism. Drawing on Sir John Salmond's tripartite division of
the sources of law into historical, literary, and legal (see further Jackson 2001), Elon
presents medieval Jewish law most completely in his treatment of the literary sources
of Jewish law. Moving chronologically through the three major literary sources of
Jewish law in the Middle Ages—commentaries and *novellae*, codes, and responsa—
Elon discusses the major works and their authors and methodologies, but without
the extraordinary detail characteristic of Tchernowitz.

3.3.2 *Scholarship on Jewish Law in the Gaonic Period*

The study of Jewish law in the Gaonic period, like that of the period of the Talmud,
builds upon the more general scholarship on the literature and history of the period
(e.g. Assaf 1955 and the up-to-date and comprehensive survey by Robert Brody 1998).

Biographical and/or analytic studies of the methodologies of particular Gaonim
have been and continue to be of major interest in scholarship on Jewish law in the
Gaonic period, beginning with Shlomo Yehudah Rappaport's studies (1904) of
Sa'adia, Hai, and Nissim Gaon in the nineteenth century. The five-volume work
of I. H. Weiss (1924) was also characterized by an interest in halachic biography.
Weiss classified Jewish legal scholars by their relative strictness or leniency, and
according to how they utilized their predecessors' work in deriving their own legal
rulings. Of more recent interest are Shraga Abramson (1974), Tsvi Groner (1985),
and David Sklare (1996). Closely related to such studies are philological analyses
and/or reconstructions of the halachic works of particular Gaonim. Notable
examples of this category are Shraga Abramson (1990), Tirzah Meacham (1999),
and Robert Brody's study of the responsa of R. Natronai Gaon (1994). In his series of
articles reconstructing and publishing fragments of Samuel b. Hofni Gaon's works
on suretyship and the adjoining landowner's right of first refusal, Gideon Leibson
also employs a comparative-law perspective— comparing the Gaon's rulings with
parallel provisions in contemporaneous Islamic legal works (Leibson 1984–6, 1987,
1989, 1991, 1996).

In a related vein, the reconstruction of Gaonic legal texts based on materials
found in collections from the Cairo Genizah is also an ongoing—and far from
complete— subject of scholarly work. The Cairo Genizah has proven to be a fertile
source of literary and documentary materials dating from the tenth through the
thirteenth centuries (see Brody 1998: 32–3) and was instrumental to S. D. Goitein's
reconstruction of Jewish communal and economic life in the Mediterranean world
of the period (Goitein 1967–88, 1973). The potential of the Genizah to contribute to
our understanding of Jewish law in the Gaonic period was illustrated early by
A. E. Harkavy's 1887 publication of a collection of Gaonic *responsa* based on Genizah
materials. Louis Ginzberg's (1928–9, 1968) and Binyamin Menashe Lewin's (1922–44,
1934) work of identifying, analysing, and publishing Gaonic texts and textual

fragments from the Cairo Genizah has led to the discovery of texts that would otherwise have been lost, such as the enigmatic *Sefer Metivot*, a work much used by R. Isaac Alfasi (the 'Rif', 1013–1103). Mordecai Margaliot's Genizah studies (1973) greatly illuminated the world of post-talmudic Palestinian legal literature. Much more work needs to be done to identify, publish, and analyse Gaonic legal texts from the Cairo Genizah. An aid in this effort is the recently published catalogue by Neil Danzig (1997) of the halachic and non-halachic materials found in the Adler collection of Genizah fragments at the Jewish Theological Seminary in New York, thus making that material more accessible for study. Simchah Emanuel has recently published a collection of Gaonic responsa (1995a) based on a Geniza fragment and on a manuscript found in the former Soviet Union.

Reconstruction of the biographies, methodologies, and legal texts of particular Gaonim or of the Gaonic period generally does not exhaust the scholarship on Jewish law in the Gaonic period. Analysis of the codificatory methodologies and use of prior sources in particular Gaonic legal works and the preparation of critical editions of extant Gaonic legal materials have been lively scholarly occupations. Mention should be made of Azriel Hildesheimer (1971–87), Chaim Tykocinski (1960), S. K. Mirsky (1959–77), and Neil Danzig (1999).

Scholarship on Gaonic responsa deserves a special mention because of the centrality of the responsa literature to the development of Jewish law throughout the medieval period (and beyond). To date, the only comprehensive index of Gaonic responsa is Joel Müller's outdated study (1891). Recently published bibliographic aids for Gaonic responsa may be found in Tsvi Groner's bibliography (1985) and in Danzig (1988) and Kimelman (1984/6).

There are scholarly desiderata in the field of Jewish law in the Gaonic period that may be satisfied by application of the biographical, comparative law, philological, or analytic approaches we have discussed. Such desiderata include the preparation of a new critical edition of the *Seder Tannaim ve-Amoraim* (to replace that of Kahana 1935), preparation of a comprehensive introduction to the *Halakhot Gedolot* and an updated comprehensive index to all the Gaonic responsa, increased attention to the principles of legal decision-making developed and employed in the Gaonic period, and a systematic investigation of the legal rulings introduced by the term '*ve-hilkheta*' in the Babylonian Talmud (there is a scholarly consensus that these legal rulings are post-talmudic interpolations into the talmudic text, probably stemming from the Gaonic period). We will defer until later (s. 3.3.6) a discussion of the new methodologies that may be employed.

Before moving on to the scholarship on medieval Jewish law in the Ashkenazic and Sephardic/Provençali worlds, two important recent contributions to the study of the literatures of these worlds should be noted. The first of these, Simcha Emanuel's 'Kitvei Yad u-Sefarim 'Ivriyyim ba-Sifriyot ha-'Olam' (1995), highlights the existence of manuscript fragments of Jewish sources found in libraries, archives, monasteries, and even private hands in Europe— which Emanuel collectively terms 'the European "Genizah"'. The second contribution is Ya'akov S. Spiegel's valuable work (1996), in which he explores the influence of printing on the practice of annotating major works such as the Babylonian Talmud and Maimonides' *Mishneh Torah*, and therefore on the presentation and reception of those works (see further Beit-Arie 2000, on the question of how the form and reproduction of medieval Jewish texts affected their substance and reception). Emanuel and Spiegel's works are important because the study of medieval Jewish law is inextricably tied to the literature in which that law is contained and from which it is extracted. Newly found texts, lost texts, the impact of a later scribe on a text from an earlier period, and the impact of new technology on the transmission and reception of medieval Jewish legal texts, must all be taken into account in the study of medieval Jewish law.

3.3.3 *Jewish Law in Ashkenaz from the Eleventh to the Sixteenth Centuries*

The biographical and analytic approach to the study of Jewish law remains key to scholars working on this period. Avigdor Aptowitzer (1924–5; see also Devaletsky 1976, 1989) utilized this method in publishing the multi-volume *Sefer Ravya* ('Ravya' is the acronym for R. Eliezer b. Yoel ha-Levi, one of the luminaries of twelfth-century Ashkenaz) and his own comprehensive work (1938). Aptowitzer's *Mavo le-Sefer Ravya* (like Danzig's later *Mavo le-Sefer Halakhot Pesuqot*) is a model of a comprehensive introduction to a halachic work. Aptowitzer presents the life of his subject, R. Eliezer b. Yoel ha-Levi, his ancestry, the nature and content of the *Sefer ha-Ravya*, and its halachic methodology. He also collected the later sources in which the work was cited, as well as the scattered references to various Ashkenazic customs found throughout the *Sefer ha-Ravya*. Irving Agus utilized the biographical method in his study (1970) of R. Meir of Rothenburg, as did Avraham Grossman in his excellent studies (1989, 1995b) of the early sages of Germany and France; Ephraim E. Urbach in his magisterial study of the Tosafists (1954/86, see also Faur 1975); Yedidiah Dinari in his (1984) study of the leading Ashkenazic sages of the late Middle Ages (see also Rosensweig 1975; Yuval 1988; Woolf 2001); and Yonah Ben-Sasson (1984). Israel Ta-Shema has also recently pursued a variation of this biographical method (2000), in which he analyses the methodologies of talmudic commentary of the great medieval talmudic commentators of Ashkenaz, Spain, Provence, and Italy. One major lacuna in the biographical and analytic study of medieval Ashkenazic sages is that there is as yet no detailed analysis of the halachic methodology of R. Asher b. Yehiel (the 'Rosh'), though particular aspects of his biography and work have been addressed (Freimann 1918; Zafrany 1980; Washofsky 1988; Richter 1992).

Ta-Shema also analyses the development of particular Jewish legal institutions and issues historically, through a chronologically and geographically organized analysis of the key halachic and other pertinent sources, beginning with the Talmudim. This historical method is valuable because it shows the process of halachic decision-making at work, by showing how medieval authorities read the Talmudim and their own predecessors. In his collected essays (1994, 1996a) Ta-Shema explores such varied subjects as Jewish judicial autonomy, the influence of philosophical considerations on legal decision-making, the development of principles of adjudication, the appearance of a professional literature written by ritual specialists in high-medieval Ashkenaz who were not necessarily halachic scholars, and various issues pertaining to Jewish relations with non-Jews.

Another aspect of Ta-Shema's work deserves separate attention because it highlights the growing concern of scholars of medieval Jewish law with the interplay between halacha and kabbalah (see now Hallamish 2000). Following the lead of Jacob Katz, who contributed greatly to the scholarship in this area with his essays on the subject (1986), Ta-Shema (1995) studied the presence of Ashkenazic customs in the *Zohar* (a thirteenth-century mystical work of Spanish provenance).

Jacob Katz was also a deft practitioner of the historical approach to the study of medieval Jewish law (1961). He combined a deep familiarity with the content and inner logic of rabbinic literature—especially responsa—with a historian's feel for the larger world that exists outside of texts. He too analysed Jewish legal topics through a historical approach to the pertinent texts, beginning with the relevant talmudic sources and then moving chronologically through the other relevant sources: his *Goy Shel Shabbat* is a methodological model for its use of responsa for the reconstruction of Jewish legal history. Possessed of methodological self-awareness, he avoided what he saw as key methodological flaws: the extraction from halachic sources of facts without consideration of the overall process of halachic determination itself, and the opposite mistake of constructing the history of a halacha solely on the basis of halachic texts, without looking at popular practices or other factors external to the halacha (see Katz 1986: 175–6; trans. in Katz 1998; 1984: 11–14).

Haym Soloveitchik shares with Katz a methodological preference for the historical study of Jewish legal texts, and favours areas of the law that show a marked discontinuity between the present and the past (though he has also penned an excellent methodological introduction to the use of responsa—especially early Ashkenazic responsa—as historical sources: 1990). In his 1985 work Soloveitchik emphasized that his interest lies in studying the medieval scholars' discontinuities with the Talmudim: those areas of Jewish law in which the medievals had to direct normative behaviour with little or no talmudic guidance (see also Soloveitchik 1972, 1978, 1987, 1998; but see against the latter Grossman and Ta-Shema 2000). Soloveitchik looks for patterns of difference in the approaches of different sages to these areas of law, and for answers to the difficult question of how elements of the external world have been incorporated into the halachic institution under study while nevertheless retaining the status of that halachic institution as part of God's Law in the eyes of scholar and ordinary Jew alike. In *Halakha, Kalkalah, ve-Dimui ʿAtzmi* and elsewhere, Soloveitchik is interested in how Ashkenazic Jewry maintained its self-image as a holy people faithful to its divine mission and ancestral traditions in the wake of external changes which forced it to behave in ways that seemed to conflict with its Law (see also Soloveitchik 1987). This interest was present as well in some of Jacob Katz's work (see e.g. Katz 1984).

The publication of medieval Ashkenazic texts and guides to medieval Ashkenazic legal literature has also been a scholarly concern. Irving Agus (1954) published responsa authored by Tosafists, while Shlomo Eidelberg published those of R. Gershom Me'or ha-Golah (1955; Eidelberg also wrote essays on Ashkenazic history, including legal history, now collected in 1999). Menachem Elon and his students (Elon 1965, 1973b; Shochetman and Lifshitz 1997) have published guides to medieval Ashkenazic responsa, which greatly facilitate the study of that literature.

3.3.4 *Jewish Law in the Sephardic World and Provence*

The biographical method has also been extensively employed in studies of Sephardic and Provençali scholars (Hershman 1943; Epstein 1968; Goldman 1970; Werblowsky 1977; Twersky 1980b; Soloveitchik 1980; Septimus 1982; Benedict 1985; Benayahu 1991; Ta-Shema 1992), although the detailed study of the methodologies of major figures such as R. Isaac Alfasi (the 'Rif'), contemporaneous early Spanish sages, and much Sephardic and Provençali legal writing remain to be done (but see, for the moment, Wald 1992–4; Ha-Kohen 1992–4). Yehudah Galinsky's recent doctoral dissertation (1999) is an especially noteworthy example of the way such studies ought to be carried out. Galinsky's work is divided into two parts. The first explores the historical circumstances of the composition of R. Jacob ben Asher's *Arba'ah Turim*, while in the second part Galinsky undertakes a close literary analysis of section *Orach Hayyim*. Close literary analysis and an analytic reconstruction of methodology also characterize Boyarin's study (1989) of the analytic talmudic exegesis of the school of R. Isaac Campanton.

Maimonidean scholarship deserves separate mention because of Maimonides' unique significance in the history of Jewish law. The issues that have hitherto dominated *Mishneh Torah* research are Maimonides' relationship to his prior sources and his codificatory methodology (see Blidstein 1990). Noteworthy studies of Maimonides' codificatory methodology include those by Chaim Tchernowitz (Rav Tza'ir) (1946) and Jacob Levinger (1965; see also Cohen 1935; Rakover 1985). Isadore Twersky's introduction to the Code of Maimonides (1980a) is a comprehensive introduction to the structure, content, halachic methodology, and historical context of Maimonides' *Mishneh Torah* (although Twersky pays scant attention to the interesting Islamic literary parallels to aspects of Maimonides' codificatory work; see also Twersky 1982, 1990). Looking beyond the four corners of the work, Jose Faur added a comparative law perspective to his study of the first book of the

Mishneh Torah (the *Sefer ha-Maddaʿ*, or 'Book of Knowledge') (1978). By locating the work in the Islamic legal cultural context, Faur opened the door to a new appreciation of the *Mishneh Torah* as a product of its time and place (cf. Leibson 1984/6, 1987, 1989, 1991, 1996; Kraemer 1996; Lazarus-Yafeh 1981/2; see also Rosenthal 1970: 70–96, who explicitly draws the connection between the Islamic *kitab al-ʿilm* and Maimonides' *Sefer ha-Maddaʿ*). More recently, Blidstein has turned to consideration of specific topics in Maimonidean halacha, exploring and explicating Maimonides' public law (1983) and his views on prayer (1994). Additional work of this sort is a scholarly desideratum.

Publishing new editions or translations of major Sephardic and Provençali legal works, or helpful guides to the principal works, are also ongoing areas of scholarly activity (e.g. Dimitrovsky 1990); see also Passamaneck's 1983 translation and commentary on R. Joseph Karo's codification of the laws of sale. Shochetman (1985/6) has published a compilation of the sources relied on by R. Jacob ben Asher and R. Joseph Karo in their respective works.

3.3.5 *Scholarship on Particular Topics in Medieval Jewish Law*

In reviewing scholarship on particular topics in medieval Jewish law, it is helpful to distinguish between scholars working within and outside the *Mishpat ʿIvri* school. Scholars working outside that school are essentially historians highly skilled in the analysis of halachic sources, who bring their halachic and historical expertise to bear on the topics they study. Jacob Katz, Haym Soloveitchik, Israel Ta-Shema, Irving Agus, and Avraham Grossman have principally utilized historical (including biographical) and/or comparative methods. Finkelstein (1924) has provided a philological and historical analysis of communal enactments, and Falk (1966) considered R. Gershom's reforms in family law against the background of their Christian environment. For historical studies utilizing the responsa literature, see Kahana (1973) and Passamaneck's 1974 monograph on insurance law; for an example of comparative method, see Rabinowitz (1956), where he attempted to demonstrate, *inter alia*, the influence of medieval Jewish law on Frankish and Lombard law, especially in areas of civil law such as forms of security and their documentation. The recent book on inheritance by Yosef Rivlin (1999) contains much on the Gaonic period, and includes a substantial appendix of relevant documents from the Cairo Genizah.

Simchah Assaf (1922, 1924) and David Shohet (1931), on the other hand, used a 'synthetic' method in their studies of Jewish courts and judicial punishments in the Middle Ages. In their works, they studied halachic sources not to demonstrate the historical development of legal institutions, but in order to paint synthetic pictures of them. Shohet used the Talmud, Gaonic literature, and Ashkenazic responsa in order to study, *inter alia*, the synagogue, communal taxation, evidence, and trial procedure. Assaf studied, *inter alia*, attitudes toward Gentile courts, the appointment of judges, and the establishment of courts of appeal. This methodology resembles the 'dogmatic-analytic' model employed at present by some members of the *Mishpat 'Ivri* school (s. 4.1 below).

3.3.6 *Future Directions for Research in Medieval Jewish Law*

The above review of the scholarship on medieval Jewish law (s. 3.3.2) has pointed out the additional work that remains to be done utilizing the traditional methods of scholarship: notably, the publication of more Genizah materials, further study of the methodologies of particular halachic authorities from all times and places, and the production of a comprehensive index of all Gaonic responsa. Nevertheless, there are three fairly new directions which deserve mention: (1) more study of particular medieval Jewish legal institutions using a historical-anthropological model; (2) the introduction of feminist methodologies into the study of medieval Jewish law; and (3) literary-rhetorical criticism of responsa and of the codes.

The need for wider application of the historical-anthropological approach to the study of medieval Jewish law flows naturally from our consideration of particular topics in medieval Jewish law in s. 3.3.5. Ivan Marcus (1990: 121–5, 1996; see also le Goff 1980) has pointed out the rich gains to be had for medieval Jewish studies generally by an application of Clifford Geertz's notion (1966) of 'thick description' of a culture and the metaphor of 'reading' a culture in order to extract from it layers of meaning. Jewish laws pertaining to food taboos, purity rituals, and the life-cycle are rich grounds for the application of anthropological method. Jewish law was not simply the province of the elite scholars who interpreted it, applied it, and adjudicated in accordance with it, but was also the patrimony of ordinary people whose beliefs, customs, and even superstitions must be part of a thorough scholarly reconstruction of the law (cf. Kahana 1973: 439–44, for a treatment of some folkloristic elements in the responsa literature).

The second major new direction the study of medieval Jewish law should take is the introduction of feminist methodologies. Although feminist analysis of biblical and classical rabbinic literature is well under way (Hauptman 1997; Valler 1999), feminist analysis of medieval Jewish law is still in its infancy. Little of the scholarship about Jewish women in the Middle Ages (see now the on-line bibliography of Tallan 2000) is informed by the insights of feminist theory. Writing in the context of biblical studies, Fiorenza (1984: 15) pointed out that feminist scholarship utilizes a 'hermeneutics of suspicion' that 'takes as its starting point the assumption that biblical texts and their interpretations are androcentric and serve patriarchal functions'. Interestingly, there is no article on feminist analysis of medieval Jewish legal texts in Davidman and Tanenbaum (1994) or Adelman's (1995) study of seduction, surrogacy, and rape in early modern Italian Jewish families. Of particular interest is Judith Baskin's collection (1991), as well as her essay on women (1994), and Talya

Fishman's study of gender-specific commandments in the *Sefer ha-Qaneh* (1992). As examples of scholarly desiderata, we may suggest:

- a feminist analysis of the laws of *niddah* (the menstruant) in the Middle Ages (for the talmudic period, see Charlotte Fonrobert 2000);
- a feminist analysis of responsa pertaining to women (for a non-feminist study, see Epstein 1970), especially a study comparing the views of different medieval authorities (from a non-feminist perspective, Grossman (1995a) compares the attitudes of Ashkenazic and Sephardic authorities on the issue of violence against women); and
- more studies seeking out examples of women who behaved in ways not considered usual for women in their time and place (see Ta-Shema 1996b; Jordan (1978, 1988, 1993) has treated the subject of Jewish women moneylenders in medieval Europe from an economic-history perspective; see also Tallan (1991, 1992) on the position of Jewish widows).

The genre of responsa is the largest of the post-talmudic rabbinic literary genres. The fact that the responsum is a learned answer by a halachic authority to a legal query from a specific person in a particular community, time, and place makes this genre a suitable one for the application of literary-rhetorical criticism: a form of analysis that studies how the respondent uses style and legal and literary technique in order to convince his audience that his reading of the law is the most persuasive. The first scholar to propose the turn to literary-rhetorical study of responsa was Haas (1985), but Frankel (1865), Lauterbach (1905), and Freehof (1955) may be regarded as forerunners. Recently Washofsky (1994) has elegantly laid out the theoretical underpinnings and provided an example of such a study, and another example of such a study (Menache 1996) appeared shortly thereafter. A book-length study of responsa fully steeped in the existing historical and textual scholarship on the genre, and also utilizing the method of rhetorical criticism, is a scholarly desideratum; for a summary of the earlier scholarship on responsa, see Elon (1994: 1454–5).

Scholarly work should also be directed to studying the codes as works of legal literature, with attention paid to their structure and content and how these reveal the codifier's intended audience (as was done by Galinsky (1999) in his study of the section *Orach Hayyim* of the *Arba'ah Turim* of R. Jacob b. Asher) and ideology. For example, how do the arrangement and selection of halachot on a Jew's ritual behaviour during the day shed light on a codifier's construction of the ideal religious Jew? How do these constructions change (or not) in various codes stemming from different times and places? Revealing the large-scale, latent structures of thought at the heart of the legal codes is a necessary complement to the necessary work of studying particular halachot.

4. DOGMATIC APPROACHES AND JEWISH LAW IN THE STATE OF ISRAEL

4.1 Dogmatics in Halacha and the Mishpat Ivri Movement

The object of a dogmatic approach is to state the law binding at a particular period (*ius cogens*) on the basis of those sources (textual and institutional) taken to be authoritative. Both *halacha* and *mishpat 'ivri* have their traditions of dogmatics (for halacha, indeed, it is the principal concern), but their conceptions of dogmatics are different in at least this respect: halachists have no necessary background or training in secular law; their conceptual framework is entirely within the talmudic tradition. While those with authority to make halachic decisions—*poskim*—take full account of the 'codes' of halacha—principally the *Yad Hachazaka* of Maimonides (twelfth century), the *Arba'ah Turim* of R. Yaakov, the son of Rosh (fourteenth century), and the *Shulhan Aruch* of R. Yosef Karo (sixteenth century), together with the vast body of *responsa* literature, the Talmud remains of predominant importance. Such a giant and lively body of knowledge cannot be imprisoned in rules, and is still the main source of learning in traditional yeshivot. In such circles the historical-philological method is regarded as an unacceptable means of determining the halacha: there is reluctance even to take account of textual criticism based on talmudic manuscripts, against traditional readings (Bleich 1993). Rather, traditional halacha utilizes an ahistorical, harmonizing form of dogmatics, following the precedent of the Talmud itself.

Despite the fact that Jews living in the post-emancipation West no longer have jurisdiction over civil law matters affecting their lives, Orthodoxy is far from willing to cede authority over all such matters to the secular power: the principle of *dina demalkuta dina* has major limitations, in this respect.

Mention may here be made of three areas where many Jews (and not only in Orthodox circles: both the Conservative and Reform movements in the United States issue their own responsa: see e.g. Golinkin 1996 for the responsa of Louis Epstein and the many volumes of Reform responsa by Solomon Freehof) look to their halachic authorities for dogmatic solutions to contemporary problems, despite the fact that those problems are also regulated by the secular law of the states in which they reside.

(1) The first is the law of succession: the halacha accords priority to the scheme of intestate succession stated in the Bible, in the context of the case of the daughters of Zelophehad (Numbers 27: 1–11); though rabbinic law devised forms of testate succession, which came ultimately to provide something close to the modern will with (in common law countries at least) its principle of freedom of testation, this was achieved by a form/fiction of gift designed to avoid the appearance of open

conflict with the biblical distribution rules. Reliance upon a civil will, it has been argued, therefore conflicts with the halacha. Dayan Grunfeld (1987), amongst others, has offered a form of Jewish will designed to take effect before the civil will, so that the latter (from the viewpoint of Jewish law) in effect simply provides implementation of measures which are valid according to halachic forms. The area of inheritance has given rise also to concern with issues of gender equality: the halacha gives an estate to male to the exclusion of female heirs (of the same class), the latter being confined to rights of maintenance (even though these are given priority to rights of succession). At the foundation of the State of Israel, Chief Rabbi Herzog attempted to enact a *takkanah* which would have inserted in every *ketubah* a clause providing for gender equality in inheritance (Greenberger 1991). The proposed *takkanah* failed to gain acceptance from the other halachic authorities. This raises a dogmatic issue of a rather different kind: who has the authority to enact reforms in contemporary Jewish law? In practice, any such reforms require a 'consensus', but the origins and nature of this requirement of consensus still require clarification.

(2) It is this issue which also afflicts perhaps the most controversial and widely discussed issue in contemporary halacha: the problem of the *agunah*, the wife refused a *get* (bill of divorce) by her husband, even when ordered by a rabbinic court to give one. This issue, too, has provoked much dogmatic writing within halachic circles (most recently, Broyde 2001).

(3) Finally, there is much contemporary halachic writing seeking dogmatic solutions to modern problems of bioethics. Traditional halachic definitions of death in terms of cessation of independent respiration and heartbeat have been challenged by the use in medical practice of criteria based upon electrical activity in the brain or brain-stem. Though versions of these criteria have gained acceptance amongst some Orthodox medical circles, the issue remains controversial (Bleich 1995: 316–50). There are cases where the overriding value of the sanctity of life appears to come into conflict with patient autonomy, and this has given rise to new debate regarding the very methodology of such dogmatic studies in contemporary halacha (Sinclair 1989; Dorff 1992, 1998; Shatz 1997).

The very fact that there is now a body (albeit a minority) of dogmatic halachic literature written in English is perhaps a significant indication of the fact that there is a non-specialist audience for this approach. Whether this audience will remain a purely passive recipient of the statements of its authorities remains to be seen.

Scholars associated with the *Mishpat 'Ivri* school are essentially lawyers highly skilled in the analysis of halachic sources, who conceptualize and study Jewish law as a legal system like other legal systems. In the studies of this school, the 'dogmatic' and 'historic' methods appear in two guises. The first is the 'dogmatic-historical' method, the second the 'dogmatic-analytic'. Practitioners of the 'dogmatic-historical' method first use 'dogmatic' study to identify all of the pertinent textual sources relating to a given legal topic or institution, and subject them to a thorough legal analysis. This dogmatic study is then followed by 'historic' study of these sources in order to discern the extent and nature of continuity and change in the legal institution under study. The method was first named as such by A. H. Freimann in his study of medieval Jewish marriage (1944)—a topic further developed in this tradition by Falk (1966) and Berger (2001)—although it had already been used by Asher Gulak (1926), where he utilizes a dogmatic approach to identify all the types of legal documents in use after the talmudic period, but treats each type of document and the area of law it represents separately, exploring historical development within each topic. Gulak utilized a similar methodology (1922/1967). One weakness of *Yesodei ha-Mishpat ha-ʿIvri* is Gulak's assumption that legal institutions discussed in the Talmud may be assumed to have functioned during the talmudic period in the same way as they did in the Middle Ages. The 'dogmatic-historical' method was subsequently given full methodological expression by Elon in his 1999 book on Human Dignity and Freedom (a revised version of his 1964 study of Freedom of the Debtor's Person) and Shmuel Shilo in his monograph (1975). It was strongly criticized by England (in Jackson ed. 1980: 21–65, to which Elon there replied: ibid. 66–111).

Practitioners of the 'dogmatic-analytic' method identify the pertinent textual sources pertaining to their area of study, and then subject them to rigorous and exclusively halachic/legal analysis. Much has been and can still be written on the strengths and weaknesses of these methods. Shochetman (1981: 18) explains that the dogmatic-historical method may be appropriate for studying areas of Jewish law in which 'developments and changes occurred which had their origin in the changing causal factors of the conditions of time and place'. But, he continued, this method has nothing to contribute to a study like his own (on illegal acts in Jewish law), 'in which changes of the aforementioned type did not occur in the course of the generations, *and if we find differences in the opinions of sages as to these and other problems, they only stem from the different methods of commentary on the talmudic sugya and other sources of Jewish law, and from a different analysis of those sources*' (emphasis supplied). Shochetman does not allow for the likelihood that different methods of talmudic commentary, commentaries on codes, and new methods of halachic analysis may themselves be due to 'the changing causal factors of the conditions of time and place'. Halachic analysis does not occur in a sociological or historical vacuum (see e.g. Boyarin 1989). Scholars in the dogmatic-analytic tradition of *mishpat ivri* tend to be less interested in external influences on the halacha or on historical development. The 'dogmatic-analytic' method is applied, notably, by Shochetman (1981) on Illegal Acts, and is utilized to some extent by Nahum Rakover (compare his work on Copyright (1991) with his more historical approach in his (1972) study on Agency).

4.2 Jewish Law in the State of Israel

Despite the aspirations of religious Zionism, Jewish law was not adopted as the legal system of the State of Israel. The existing Mandatory law became the law of the state, and as a result, only personal status matters affecting Jews remained within the sole jurisdiction of the rabbinical courts (Rabbinical Courts Jurisdiction (Marriage and Divorce) Law, 1953). The law applied in these courts, however, is traditional halacha and not *mishpat 'ivri*. For a general introduction to Jewish law in Israel, see Sinclair (1996).

From its inception, the bench of the Israel Supreme Court always included a judge well versed in Jewish law. A notable example from the early years of the state was Moshe Silberg, who became its Deputy-President in 1965. Silberg, who studied in Lithuanian talmudic academies and at the universities of Marburg and Frankfurt, pursued the *mishpat 'ivri* method of study in his academic writings (1927, 1961) and applied it in several of his judgements in civil and personal status law.

There have been two major debates on the correct approach to the study of Jewish law in modern Israel. Clearly, an Orthodox perspective would frown upon any attempt to use historical research in order to isolate legal principles within the halacha and grant them an enhanced normative status, even if this status is in theory only. Such an enterprise is too reminiscent of Frankel's Historical School and the Conservative movement's methodology. At the same time the isolation of fundamental legal principles using a doctrinal 'all-period' approach to halachic sources— the dogmatic-historical method as it was called by Gulak—was an important element in the Israeli *mishpat 'ivri* enterprise. Since the major scholars involved in *mishpat 'ivri* in the late 1970s were Orthodox, the debate provoked by the charge that the dogmatic-historical method was, in fact, that of the Conservative movement was a lively one. The leading exponent of the dogmatic-historical method is Menachem Elon, Professor of Jewish Law at the Hebrew University and former Deputy-President of the Supreme Court of the State of Israel. Elon is an ordained Orthodox Rabbi who received his diploma from the Tel-Aviv School of Law and Economics in 1948 and went on to receive a doctor of laws degree from the Hebrew University. He was the Director of the Institute for Research in Jewish Law at the Hebrew University and, in addition to many articles, published the leading textbook (Elon 1994) on Jewish law in use today. During his period on the bench he made extensive use of Jewish law material in his judgements.

In applying the dogmatic-historical approach, Elon distinguished between two different roles within the halachic tradition. The first was that of the authoritative decisor (*posek*), whose job it was to make practical halachic rulings on specific cases in real life. *Mishpat 'ivri* is not to be identified with this enterprise and its practitioners do not identify themselves with this role. The second is that of the scholar (*lamdan*), whose function it is to explicate the halacha and clarify it from both a doctrinal and a systemic perspective. This is the role of the *mishpat 'ivri* scholar, and it is best fulfilled in the State of Israel by the dogmatic-historical method since the results are academically sound and may, therefore, be recommended for incorporation by the state's legal system. The adoption of the role of the *lamdan* also avoids the charge that the *mishpat ivri* scholar is flying in the face of the mainstream Orthodox view of the halachic tradition as an 'all or nothing' enterprise, the definition of which is entirely in the hands of an accepted Orthodox authority (see Elon 1980: 86–91).

This approach was attacked by Yitzhak Englard (1980), an Orthodox Professor of Tort Law at the Hebrew University, who has himself recently been appointed a Justice of the Israel Supreme Court. Englard criticized the dogmatic-historical approach on both academic and theological grounds. Many of the academic objections are debatable and have been thoroughly analysed (together with the approach of S. Albeck) by Jackson (1980) in a theoretical discussion of the views of the protagonists in this debate. More fundamental, in the view of the present writer, are the following two points in Englard's critique. First, he argues that the religious character of Jewish law is lost in the process of concentrating on legal doctrine rather than on the spiritual input of the halachic authority issuing a specific ruling. Jewish law thereby loses its very soul, its essence. Second, he observed that there is 'a close affinity between Elon's approach and that of Boaz Cohen, who personally was very much committed to Conservative Judaism [see Cohen 1959: 26 ff.] . . . Hence, what Boaz Cohen would like to achieve inside the halakhic system itself, Menachem Elon prefers to implement in the framework of *mishpat 'ivri*. Whatever may be the exact difference between the two, one thing they clearly have in common: their approach is clearly tainted with personal ideology' (1980: 52 f.). Elon replied that Englard is not entirely innocent of ideology either, and that any study in the humanities or law is bound to involve a measure of personal ideology. It is noteworthy that both of Englard's points take us back to the issue of rabbinic authority debated between R. Ezekiel Landau and R. Moses Sofer described above (s. 2.2). Contemporary researchers from all modern streams of Judaism, both in Israel and the diaspora, use a wide range of methodologies in their work, and the Englard–Elon debate has now receded into the background. It may still, however, serve as a reminder of the close connection between ideology and academic work in this field.

The second major debate (not unrelated to the first) took place in the Supreme Court in the aftermath of the Foundations of Law Act, 1980. Mandatory legislation, which continued in force after the establishment of the State of Israel, had created an official link between Israeli and English law: the courts were to apply 'the substance of the common law, and the doctrines of equity in force in England' where otherwise there would be a gap in the law (the so-called 'lacuna' clause: Art. 46 of the Palestine Order in Council 1922). In 1980 the Knesset replaced this with an instruction that the judge should turn to the 'principles of justice, equity, freedom and peace of the heritage of Israel' for the answer to such questions (though the concept of a 'lacuna' was now defined rather restrictively). At the time of the establishment of the state, Jewish law had been insufficiently developed by the proponents of the *mishpat 'ivri* movement for its adoption as the state law and the existing Mandatory system was adopted by the new state on grounds of expediency alone. Supporters of the *mishpat 'ivri* agenda hoped, therefore, that the 1980 law would serve to promote large-scale absorption of Jewish law into the legal system of the state. Justice Elon was again the most prominent proponent of this view, which had also been attacked by Englard (1968) on both analytical and ideological grounds. However, times had changed and Jewish law was now rejected by the judiciary not by default but rather on grounds of principle. In two Supreme Court hearings in the case of *Hendeles* v. *Kupat Am Bank*, it was decided by the majority that the scope of the 1980 law was extremely limited and basically more of a symbolic legislative flourish than a meaningful piece of legislation. Jewish law was rejected as being out of touch with the temper of the times and inaccessible to the general legal reader. Elon J. found himself in a significant minority in both hearings (F.H. 13/80, P.D. 35 (2) 785). The major opponent of the expansion of the role of Jewish law as a binding force in Israeli law was now Aharon Barak, the current President of the Supreme Court and an outstanding Israeli jurist. The programmatic limb of the *mishpat 'ivri* programme has, therefore, been virtually amputated although the courts continue to use halachic sources in ethically sensitive areas such as medical ethics (see Sinclair 1997). In this context, it is noteworthy that the English Court of Appeals in its recent decision on the separation of Siamese twins referred to Jewish law in its justification of the defence of necessity in the context of a potential murder charge (*Re A (Children)* 2001 2 WLR 480).

In the wake of the judicial rejection of any formal role for Jewish law in the Israeli legal system, the justification for the existing practice of making Jewish law a compulsory course in Israeli law schools has become problematic. This current debate regarding the study of Jewish law in Israel has yet to be resolved, but in the interim two points seem relevant. The first is that the trend in contemporary legal education seems to be moving away from purely professional studies and to be advancing instead in the direction of interdisciplinary and comparative work. In this type of atmosphere, the practical application of *mishpat 'ivri* does not seem as crucial to its academic viability as it once seemed. Indeed, it is ideally suited to an interdisciplinary and comparative role in the light of its long history and very different systemic structure to that of Israeli law. Also, its texts are in Hebrew, which makes it more accessible to the average Israeli law student and researcher than other comparable systems. The second point is that in the post-Zionist age, when Israelis are searching for an identity which must, by definition, include a Jewish component, any vehicle for debating the nature of that identity in a serious fashion must be a welcome addition to the academic curriculum. In that respect, *mishpat 'ivri* is a prime candidate for the law school syllabus.

Academic study of Jewish law in the Israeli context is not confined to the *mishpat ivri* approach. The very fact that Israel proclaims itself (in its Declaration of Independence, cf. the 1994 Human Dignity and Freedom Law) as both a Jewish and a democratic state prompts questions regarding the relationship between these two sets of values and the manner in which the tension between them is played out in the sphere of law (Edelman 1994; Margolin 1999); a particular example of this was the *cause célèbre* of 'Brother Daniel' (Oswald Rufeisen) under the Law of Return, where a legal issue regarding the identity of a Jewish-born Catholic priest prompted discussion of the character of the Jewish identity of the state itself: whether the Jewish culture it sought to preserve was simply a continuation of diaspora (rabbinic) Judaism, or whether it was the locus for a new start, involving a revival of prophetic ideals (Landau 1971; Jackson 1993; see Sinclair 2001 for later cases).

5. COMPARATIVE AND PHILOSOPHICAL APPROACHES

The comparative and philosophical approaches are less prominent than the historical and dogmatic in the study of halacha and Jewish law. As far as halacha (as opposed to *mishpat ʿivri*) is concerned, the comparative approach is virtually unknown. Halacha is concerned with the tradition from the inside, and takes account of foreign legal systems only insofar as they impinge upon Jewish law, and with the significance which halacha itself accords to such historical contact: it may, for example, take account of foreign law in its own conflict of law rules (Jackson 1981: 168, on *Tosefta Baba Kamma* 4: 2); or it may regard the rule of a foreign legal system as posing a threat justifying a particular response from the halacha (*tsorekh hashaʿah*). In academic circles, on the other hand, the comparative approach has proved more popular. Its use in respect of biblical law has been noted above (s. 3.1), as has its use by the early pioneers of talmudic law (s. 2.3); more recently, comparison between Roman law and early Rabbinic law, designed primarily as exercises in comparative law (the possibility of historical influence in one direction or the other being of secondary concern), has generated the occasional monograph (such as Yaron 1960) and various articles—notably, a number by David Daube (e.g. 1961; see also the bibliography in Jackson 1974: 7–15), and the two-volume collection of articles by Boaz Cohen (1966). There is increasing interest in the comparison of Jewish and Islamic law (ss. 3.3.2, 3.3.4, 3.3.5 above), including comparison of the systematics of the two systems, particularly their methods of reasoning (Brunschvig 1976; Wegner 1982; Jackson 2001b). There is a sense, however, in which all *mishpat ʿivri* work is tacitly comparative, insofar as the juristic qualification and methodological orientation necessary for *mishpat ʿivri* work predisposes the researcher to 'translate' material into the concepts and methods of Western, secular law.

The application of philosophical approaches highlights the distinction between halacha and *mishpat ʿivri*: philosophical approaches to the former stress theological issues internal to the religion, and often amount to a philosophy of *mitsvot* and an analysis of the spiritual effect of their performance (Hirsch 1962; J. B. Soloveitchik 1983, 1986); there is also interest in the tensions within the halacha between rationalism and revelation, often focusing upon the writings of Maimonides. Novak (1983, 1998), in particular, has sought to relate this to a version of the natural law tradition in Western philosophy, though this approach remains controversial in halachic circles (Bleich 1988). The predominant approach of the *mishpat ivri* movement has been 'positivist', partly because of the possibility which positivism provides for authorization of development through both legislation and juristic/judicial interpretation, the former stressed by Elon (1994), the latter by Lamm and Kirschenbaum (1979). Elon (1994) adopted Salmond's account of the 'sources' theory of law, structuring his presentation of Jewish law around a distinction between legal, literary, and historical sources, but whether Jewish law can be accommodated within the basic tenets of legal positivism has been doubted (Jackson 2001a). The attack on legal positivism by Ronald Dworkin has also attracted the interest of philosophers of Jewish law, who ask whether the Talmud endorses the conception of 'one correct answer' (Ben-Menahem 1987). Ben-Menahem (1991) has studied the extent to which rabbinic law courts make decisions not in accordance with the halacha, relating this to the tradition found in the Bible of direct divine inspiration to the judge (1996). This leads him to a version of the philosophy of Jewish law closer to legal realism. On these issues, reference may be made to a two-volume symposium in *The Jewish Law Annual* (vols. 6–7), and to the collection of Golding (1994).

Suggested Reading

For a general overview of the history and major trends in the scientific study of Jewish law, see Elon (1994); see also B. S. Jackson in Abramson and Parfitt (1994). A chronological introduction to Jewish law may be found in Hecht *et al.* (1996), providing for each period an account of the political and jurisdictional background, the general character of the sources, evidence of legal practice, the principal authorities, the characteristic features of the substantive halacha, and bibliography. The journal *Tradition* exemplifies, in English, the dogmatic approach as applied in halachic (rather than *mishpat ʿivri*) circles. For the latter, the main organ has been the *Shenaton Ha-Mishpat Ha-ʿIvri* of the Institute for Research in Jewish Law at the Hebrew University (founded by Professor Elon). *The Jewish Law Annual*, published in English since 1978, has been more 'catholic' in providing a platform for all the approaches surveyed in this article— including the, at times related, issues of the status of Jews in the laws of the states in which they reside. *The Jewish Law Annual* also carries a Survey of Recent Literature, which provides abstracts, arranged topically, of articles on Jewish law subjects (including biblical law); a large section of them is now consolidated on the internet: http://www.mucjs.org/JLAS/abstracts.htm. The major bibliographies in the field, however, are those of Rakover (1975–90, 1990) and Weisbard and Schonberg (1989).

BIBLIOGRAPHY

ABRAMSON, G and PARFITT, T. eds. 1994. *Jewish Education and Learning: Published in honour of Dr. David Patterson on the Occasion of His Seventieth Birthday.* Chur.

ABRAMSON, S. 1974. *'Inyanot be-Sifrut ha-Geonim.* Jerusalem.

—— 1990. *Ha-Rav Shmuel b. Hofni (Gaon Sura): Peraqim min Sefer Mavo ha-Talmud.* Jerusalem.

ADELMAN, H. 1995. 'Servants and Sexuality: Seduction, Surrogacy and Rape: Some Observations Concerning Class, Gender, and Race in Early Modern Italian Jewish Families.' In *Gender and Judaism: The Transformation of Tradition.* 81–97. Tamar Rudavsky ed. New York.

AGUS, I. 1954. *Teshuvot Ba'alei ha-Tosafot.* New York.

—— 1970. *R. Meir of Rothenberg: His Life and His Works as Sources for the Religious, Legal, and Social History of the Jews of Germany in the Thirteenth Century.* New York.

AHAD HA'AM, 1957. 'Ancestral Heritage.' [Hebrew.] In *Kol Kitvei Ahad Ha'am.* 271–3. Tel/Aviv.

ALBECK, S. 1965. *General Principles of the Law of Tort in the Talmud* [Hebrew]. Tel/Aviv.

—— 1976. *The Law of Property and Contract in the Talmud* [Hebrew]. Tel/Aviv.

—— 1980. *Law Courts in Talmudic Times* [Hebrew]. Ramat-Gan.

—— 1999. *Introduction to Jewish Law in Talmudic Times* [Hebrew]. Ramat-Gan.

APTOWITZER, A. 1924–5. *Sefer Ravya.* 4 vols. Jerusalem.

—— 1938. *Mavo le-Sefer ha-Ravya.* Jerusalem.

ASSAF, S. 1922. *Ha-'Onshin Aharei Hatimat ha-Talmud.* Jerusalem.

—— 1924. *Batei Din ve-Sidreihem Aharei Hatimat ha-Talmud.* Jerusalem.

—— 1955. *Tequfat ha-Geonim ve-Sifrutah.* Jerusalem.

BASKIN, J. ed. 1991. *Jewish Women in Historical Perspective.* Detroit.

—— 1994. 'From Separation to Displacement: The Problem of Women in *Sefer Hasidim.'* *AJS Review* 19/1: 1–18.

BEIT-ARIE, M. 2000. 'Publication and Reproduction of Literary Texts in Medieval Jewish Civilization: Jewish Scribality and its Impact on the Texts Transmitted'. In *Transmitting Jewish Traditions: Orality, Textuality, and Cultural Diffusion.* 225–47. Y. Elman and I. Gershoni eds. New Haven.

BEN-MENAHEM, H. 1987. 'Is There Always One Uniquely Correct Answer To a Legal Question in the Talmud?' *Jewish Law Annual* 6: 164–75.

—— 1991. *Judicial Deviation in Talmudic Law.* Chur.

—— 1996. 'The Judicial Process and the Nature of Jewish Law'. In *An Introduction to the History and Sources of Jewish Law.* 421–37. N. S. Hecht, B. S. Jackson, *et al.* Oxford.

—— HECHT, N., and WOSNER, S. eds. 1991–3. *Controversy and Dialogue in Halakhic Sources*. 2 vols. Boston.

BEN-SASSON, Y. 1984 *Mishnato ha-ʿIyunit Shel ha-Rema*. Jerusalem.

BENAYAHU, M. 1991. *Yosef Behiri*. Jerusalem.

BENEDICT, B. Z. 1985. *Merkaz ha-Torah ba-Provens*. Jerusalem.

BERGER, M. 2001. 'Two Models of Medieval Jewish Marriage: A Preliminary Study.' *JJS* 52/1: 59–84.

BLEICH, J. D. 1988. 'Judaism and Natural Law.' *The Jewish Law Annual* 7: 5–42.

—— 1995. 'Of Cerebral, Respiratory and Cardiac Death.' In *Contemporary Halakhic Problems*. iv. 316–50. New York.

BLEICH, M. 1993. 'The Role of Manuscripts in Halakhic Decision-Making: Hazon Ish, His Precursors and Contemporaries.' *Tradition* 27/2: 22–55.

BLIDSTEIN, G. J. 1990. 'Where Do We Stand in the Study of Maimonidean *Halakha*?' In *Studies in Maimonides*. 1–30. Isadore Twersky ed. Cambridge, Mass. and London.

BLIDSTEIN, Y. 1983. *ʿEqronot Mediniyyim be-Mishnat ha-Rambam: ʿIyunim be-Mishnato ha-Hilkhatit*. Ramat-Gan.

—— 1994. *Ha-Tefillah ba-Mishnato ha-Hilkhatit Shel ha-Rambam*. Jerusalem.

BLOCH, M. 1879a. *Das mosaisch-talmudische Besitzrecht*. Budapest.

—— 1879b. *Das mosaisch-talmudische Polizeirecht*. Budapest.

—— 1879–1906. *Shaʿarei Torat Hatakanot*. Vienna. 7 vols. repr. Jerusalem: 1970–1.

—— 1890. *Das mosaisch-talmudisch Erbrecht*. Budapest.

—— 1893. *Der Vertrag nach mosaisch-talmudischem Rechte*. Budapest.

—— 1901. *Das mosaisch-talmudische Straftgerichtsverfahren*. Budapest.

—— 1904. *Die Vormundschaft nach mosaisch-talmudischem Recht*. Budapest.

BOYARIN, D. 1989. *Ha-ʿIyun ha-Sefaradi: le-Farshanut ha-Talmud Shel Megorshei Sefarad*. Jerusalem.

BRODY, R. 1994. *Teshuvot Rav Natronai bar Hilai Gaon*. 2 vols. Jerusalem.

—— 1998. *The Geonim of Babylonia and the Shaping of Medieval Jewish Culture*. New Haven.

BROYDE, M. J. 2001. *Marriage, Divorce and the Abandoned Wife in Jewish Law*. Hoboken, NJ.

BRUNSCHVIG, R. 1976. 'Herméneutique normative dans le Judaïsme et dans l'Islam.' In *Atti della Accademia Nazionale dei Lincei*. Serie VIII, Rendiconti, Classe di scienze morali, storiche e filologiche, vol. 30. fasc. 5–6. Roma.

CARMICHAEL, C. M. 1985. *Law and Narrative in the Bible. The Evidence of the Deuteronomic Laws and the Decalogue*. Ithaca and London.

—— 1992. *The Origins of Biblical Law: The Decalogues and the Book of the Covenant*. Ithaca, NY.

CHAJES, Z. W. 1952. *The Student's Guide through the Talmud*. Trans. and ed. J. Shachter. London.

CHIRICHIGNO, G. C. 1993. *Debt-Slavery in Israel and the Ancient Near East*. Sheffield.

COHEN, B. 1935. 'The Classification of the Law in the *Mishneh Torah*.' *JQR* 25/4: 519–540.

—— 1959. *Law and Tradition in Judaism*. New York.

—— 1966. *Jewish and Roman Law*. 2 vols. New York.

COHN, H. 1972. *The Trial and Death of Jesus*. London.

CRÜSEMANN, F. 1996. *The Torah: Theology and Social History of Old Testament Law*. Edinburgh.

DANZIG, N. 1988. 'Teshuvot ha-Geonim "Shaʿarei Teshuvah" u-Sheelot u-Teshuvot min ha-Shamayim".' *Tarbiz* 58/1: 21–48.

DANZIG, N. 1997. *Katalog Shel Sridei Halakha u-Midrash me-Genizat Kahir be-ʾOsef E.N. Adler she-be-Sifriyat Beit ha-Midrash la-Rabbanim ba-Amerikah*. New York and Jerusalem.

—— 1999. *Mavo le-Sefer Halakhot Pesuqot*. 2nd edn. New York and Jerusalem.

DAUBE, D. 1961. 'Derelictio, Occupatio and *Traditio*: Romans and Rabbis.' *Law Quarterly Review* 77: 382–9.

—— 1947. *Studies in Biblical Law*. Cambridge. Repr. 1969, New York.

—— 1956. *The New Testament and Rabbinic Judaism*. London.

—— 1992. *Collected Works of David Daube*. Vol. 1: *Talmudic Law*. C. M. Carmichael ed. Berkeley.

DAVIDMAN, L. and TANENBAUM, S. eds. 1994. *Feminist Perspectives on Jewish Studies*. New Haven and London.

DEVALETSKY, D. 1976. *Sefer Ravya ('Avodah Zarah)*. Bnei Brak.

—— 1989. *Sefer Ravya (Teshuvot)*. Bnei Brak.

DIMITROVSKY, H. Z. 1990. *Teshuvot ha-Rashba*. 2 vols. Jerusalem.

DINARI, Y. 1984. *Hakhmei Ashkenaz be-Shilhei Yemai ha-Beinayim*. Jerusalem.

DORFF, E. N. 1992. 'A Methodology for Jewish Medical Ethics.' In *The Jerusalem 1990 Conference Volume*. 6: 35–57. B. S. Jackson and S. M. Passamaneck eds. Atlanta, Ca.

—— 1998. *Matters of Life and Death: A Jewish Approach to Modern Medical Ethics*. Philadelphia and Jerusalem.

DOUGLAS, M. 1966. *Purity and Danger*. London.

EDELMAN, M. 1994. *Courts, Politics and Culture in Israel*. Charlottesville, Va.

EIDELBERG, S. 1955. *Teshuvot Rabbenu Gershom Maor ha-Golah*. New York.

—— 1999. *Medieval Ashkenazic History: Studies on German Jewry in the Middle Ages*. Brooklyn, NY.

ELON, M. 1964. *Herut ha-Prat be-Darkhei Geviyyat Hov ba-Mishpat ha-ʿIvri*. Jerusalem.

—— 1965. *Mafteah ha-Sheelot ve-ha-Teshuvot: Sheelot u-Teshuvot ha-Rosh*. Jerusalem.

—— 1973a. *Ha-Mishpat ha-ʿIvri: Toldotav, Meqorotav, ʿEqronotav*. 3 vols. Jerusalem.

—— 1973b. *Mafteah ha-Sheelot ve-ha-Teshuvot: ha-Mafteah ha-Histori (Sheelot u-Teshuvot ha-Ritba, Sheelot u-Teshuvot Zikhron Yehudah)*. Jerusalem.

—— 1980. 'More about Research into Jewish Law.' In *Modern Research in Jewish Law*. Bernard Jackson ed. Leiden.

—— 1981. *Mafteah ha-Sheelot ve-ha-Teshuvot Shel Hakhmei Sefarad u-Tzefon Afrika*. Jerusalem.

—— 1994. *Jewish Law: History, Sources, Principles*. 4 vols. Philadelphia and Jerusalem. (Translation of Elon 1973a.)

—— 1999. *Kevod ha-Adam ve-Heruto be-Darkhei ha-Hotzaah la-Poʿal*. Jerusalem.

EMANUEL, S. 1995a. 'Kitvei Yad u-Sefarim ʿIvriyyim ba-Sifriyot ba-ʿOlam.' *Madaʿei ha-Yahadut* 35: 5–29.

—— 1995b. *Teshuvot Geonim ha-Hadashot*. Jerusalem.

ENGLAND, I. 1968. 'The Problem of Jewish law in a Jewish State.' *Israel Law Review* 3: 254–78.

—— 1980. 'Research in Jewish Law: Its Nature and Function.' In *Modern Research in Jewish Law*. 21–65. B. S. Jackson ed. Leiden.

EPSTEIN, I. 1968. *Studies in the Communal Life of the Jews of Spain as Reflected in the Responsa of Rabbi Solomon ben Adreth and Rabbi Simon ben Zemach Duran*. New York.

———— 1970. 'The Jewish Woman in the Responsa 900 C.E.–1500 C.E.' In *The Jewish Library 3: Woman*. Leo Jung ed. London.

FALK, Z. W. 1964/2001. *Hebrew Law in Biblical Times*. Jerusalem. 2nd edn. Winona Lake.

———— 1966. *Jewish Matrimonial Law in the Middle Ages*. London.

———— 1972/8. *Introduction to Jewish Law of the Second Commonwealth*. 2 vols. Leiden.

FAUR, J. 1975. 'The Legal Thinking of Tosafot: An Historical Approach'. *Dine Israel* 6: 43–77.

———— 1978. '*Iyunim ba-Mishneh Torah la-Rambam*. Jerusalem.

FINKELSTEIN, L. 1924. *Jewish Self-Government in the Middle Ages*. New York.

FIORENZA, E. S. 1984. *Bread Not Stone: The Challenge of Feminist Biblical Interpretation*. Boston.

FISHBANE, M. 1985. *Biblical Interpretation in Ancient Israel*. Oxford.

FISHMAN, T. 1992. 'A Kabbalistic Perspective on Gender-Specific Commandments: On the Interplay of Symbols and Society.' *AJS Review* 17/2: 199–245.

FITZPATRICK-MCKINLEY, A. 1999. *The Transformation of Torah from Scribal Advice to Law*. Sheffield.

FONROBERT, C. 2000. *Menstrual Purity: Rabbinic and Christian Reconstructions of Biblical Gender*. Stanford.

FRANKEL, Z. 1846. *Der gerichtliche Beweis nach talmudischen rechte*. Berlin.

———— 1859. *Darkhei Hamishnah*. Leipzig.

———— 1865. *Entwurf einer Geschichte der Literatur der nachtalmudischen Responsen*. Breslau.

———— 1870. *Mavo Hayerushalmi*. Bratislava.

FREEHOF, S. B. 1955. *The Responsa Literature*. Philadelphia.

FREIMANN, A. 1918. 'Ascher ben Jechiel'. *Jahrbuch der Judisch-Literarischen Gesellschaft* 12: 237–318.

———— 1944. *Seder Qiddushin ve-Nissuin Aharei Hatimat ha-Talmud: Mehqar Histori-Dogmati be-Dinei Yisrael*. Jerusalem.

FRIEDMAN, M. A. 1980. *Jewish Marriage in Palestine: A Cairo Geniza Study*. 2 vols. New York and Tel Aviv.

GALINSKY, Y. 1999. 'Arba'ah Turim ve-ha-Sifrut ha-Hilkhatit Shel Sefarad ba-Meah ha-14: Aspektim Historiyyim, Sifrutiyyim, ve-Hilkhatiyyim.', Unpublished Ph.D. diss., Bar-Ilan University.

GANS, E. 1822–3. 'Die Grundzüge des mosaisch-talmudischen Erbrechts.' *Zeitschrift für die Wissenschaft des Judenthums* 1: 419–71.

GEERTZ, C. 1966. 'Religion as a Cultural System.' In *Anthropological Approaches to the Study of Religion*. 1–46. Michael Banton ed. London.

GINZBERG, L. 1968. *Geonica*. 2 vols. New York.

———— 1928–9. *Ginzei Schechter*. New York.

GOITEIN, S. D. 1967–88. *A Mediterranean Society: The Jewish Communities of the Arab World as Portrayed in the Documents of the Cairo Geniza*. Vols. 1–5. Berkeley.

———— 1973. *Letters of Medieval Jewish Traders*. Princeton.

GOLDING, M. P. ed. 1994. *Jewish Law and Legal Theory*. Aldershot.

GOLDMAN, I. 1970. *The Life and Times of Rabbi David Ibn Ali Zimra*. New York.

GOLINKIN, D. ed. 1996. *The Responsa of Professor Louis Ginzberg*. New York.

GREENBERGER, B. 1991. 'Rabbi Herzog's Proposals for Takkanot in Matters of Inheritance.' In *The Halakhic Thought of R. Isaac Herzog*. 49–112. B. S. Jackson ed. Atlanta, Ga.

GRONER, T. 1985. *The Legal Methodology of Hai Gaon*. Chico, Cal.

GROSSMAN, A. 1989. *Hakhmei Ashkenaz ha-Rishonim*. Jerusalem.

GROSSMAN, A. 1995a. 'Alimut Klapei Nashim be-Hevrah ha-Yehudit ha-Yam Tikhonit be-Mei ha-Beinayim.' In *Eshnav le-Hayyeihen Shel Nashim ba-Hevrot Yehudiyot.* 183–208. Y. Azmon ed. Jerusalem.

——1995b. *Hakhmei Tsarfat ha-Rishonim.* Jerusalem.

——and TA-SHEMA, I. 2000. *Yisrael Mul ha-Tslav: Gezerot Tatnu ba-Historiya u-ba-Historiographiya.* Jerusalem.

GRUNFELD, I. 1987. *The Jewish Law of Inheritance.* Southfield, Miss.

GULAK, A. 1922. *Yesodei ha-Mishpat ha-Ivri.* Berlin. Repr. 1967, Tel Aviv.

——1926. *Otzar ha-Shtarot.* Jerusalem.

——1929. *Leheker Ha-Mishpat Ha-'ivri biTekufat ha-talmud. Dinei Karkaot.* Jerusalem.

——1935. *Das Urkundenwesen im Talmud.* Jerusalem.

——1939. *Toledot Hamishpat Beyisrael Bitkufat Hatalmud: Hahiyuv Veshibudav.* Jerusalem.

——1969. 'On the Legal Order of Our National Life'. [Hebrew.] In *Hamishpat Haivri Umedinat Yisrael.* ed. J. Bazak. Jerusalem.

HA-KOHEN, A. 1992–4. 'Ha-Talmud ha-Yerushalmi be-Torat Hakhmei Sfarad ha-Rishonim.' *Shenaton ha-Mishpat ha-'Ivri* 18–19: 113–76.

HAAS, P. J. 1985. 'The Modern Study of Responsa.' In *Approaches to Judaism in Medieval Times.* ii. 35–71. David Blumenthal ed. Chico, Cal.

HALLAMISH, M. 2000. *Ha-Qabbalah ba-Tefillah ba-Halakha u-ba-Minhag.* Ramat-Gan.

HARKAVY, A. E. 1887. *Zikaron la-Rishonim ve-Gam la-Aharonim.* Berlin.

HAUPTMAN, J. 1997. *Re-Reading the Rabbis: A Woman's Voice.* Boulder, Col.

HECHT, N. *et al.* 1996. *An Introduction to the History and Sources of Jewish Law.* N. Hecht, B. S. Jackson, D. Piattelli, S. M. Passamaneck, and A. M. Rabello eds. Oxford.

HENSCHKE, D. 1997. *Mishnah Rishonah BeTalmudam Shel Tanaim Aharonim.* Ramat-Gan.

HERSHMAN, A. M. 1943. *Rabbi Isaac ben Sheshet Perfet and His Times.* New York.

HILDESHEIMER, A. 1971–87. *Sefer Halakhot Gedolot.* 3 vols. Jerusalem.

HIRSCH, S. R. 1962. *Horeb: A Philosophy of Jewish Laws and Observances.* 2 vols. London.

JACKSON, B. S. 1972. *Theft in Early Jewish Law.* Oxford.

——1974. *Studies in Jewish Legal History in Honour of David Daube.* London.

——ed. 1980. *Modern Research in Jewish Law.* Leiden.

——1980. 'Modern Research in Jewish Law—Some Theoretical Issues.' In Jackson ed. (1980): 136–57.

——1981. 'On the Problem of Roman Influence on the Halakah and Normative Self-Definition in Judaism.' In *Jewish and Christian Self-Definition.* ii. 157–203 (text), 352–79 (notes). E. P. Sanders ed. London.

——1993. 'Who is a Jew?: Some Semiotic Observations on a Judgment of the Israel Supreme Court.' *International Journal for the Semiotics of Law/Revue Internationale de Sémiotique Juridique.* 6/17: 115–46.

——2000. *Studies in the Semiotics of Biblical Law.* Sheffield.

——2001a. '*Mishpat Ivri, Halakha* and Legal Philosophy: *Agunah* and the Theory of "Legal Sources"'. In *JSIJ – Jewish Studies, an Internet Journal* 1 (2002) 69–107, at http://www.biu.ac.il/JS/JSIJ/1-2002/Jackson.pdf

——2001b. 'A Semiotic Perspective on the Comparison of Analogical Reasoning in Secular and Religious Legal Systems.' In *Pluralism in Law.* 295–325. A. Soeteman ed. Dordrecht.

JORDAN, W. C. 1978. 'Jews on Top: Women and the Availability of Consumption Loans in Northern France in the Mid-Thirteenth Century.' *JJS* 29: 39–56.

——1988. 'Women and Credit in the Middle Ages: Problems and Directions.' *Journal of European Economic History* 17/1: 33–62.

——1993. *Women and Credit in Pre-Industrial and Developing Societies*. Philadelphia.

KAHANA, K. ed. and trans. 1935. *Seder Tannaim ve-Amoraim*. Frankfurt am Main.

KAHANA, Y. Z. 1973. *Mehqarim ba-Sifrut ha-Teshuvot*. Jerusalem.

KATZ, J. 1961. *Exclusiveness and Tolerance: Studies in Jewish-Gentile Relations in Medieval and Modern Times*. London.

——1984. *Goy Shel Shabbat*. Jerusalem.

——1986. *Halakha ve-Qabbalah*. Jerusalem.

——1998. *Divine Law in Human Hands: Case Studies in Halakhic Flexibility*. Jerusalem.

KIMELMAN, A. 1984/6. 'Luah 'Ezer le-Perushim mi-Tequfat ha-Gaonim (mi-Eretz Yisrael, Bavel u-Kairouwan)'. *Shenaton ha-Mishpat ha-'Ivri* 11–12: 463–587.

KRAEMER, J.L. 1996. 'Hashpaat ha-Mishpat ha-Muslimi 'al ha-Rambam.' *Te'udah* 10: 225–44.

LAMM, N. and KIRSCHENBAUM, A. 1979. 'Freedom and Constraint in the Jewish Juridical Process.' *Cardozo Law Review* 1: 99–133.

LANDAU, A. F. ed. 1971. *Selected Judgments of the Supreme Court of Israel, Special Volume*. Jerusalem.

LANDAU, E. and SOFER, M. 1958. *Darkhei Hahoraah no.6, Kol Kitvei Maharaz Hayyut* 1.

LAUTERBACH, J. Z. 1905. 'She'elot u-Teshubot.' In *Jewish Encyclopedia*. xi. 240–50. New York and London.

LAZARUS-YAFEH, H. 1981/2. 'Bein *Halakha* ba-Yahadut la-*Halakha* ba-Islam.' *Tarbiz* 51: 207–25.

LE GOFF, J. 1980. *Time, Work, and Culture in the Middle Ages*. Trans. A. Goldhammer. Chicago.

LEIBSON, G. 1984/6. 'Shnayim she-'Arvu: Mehqar Hashvaati bein Rav Shmuel ben Hofni Gaon, ha-Rambam, ve-Sifrut Muslimit Maqbilah.' *Shenaton ha-Mishpat ha-'Ivri* 11–12: 337–92.

——1987. 'Arevut la-Guf be-Sefer ha-'Arevut le-Rashbah be-Teshuvot ha-Geonim, ba-Rambam, u-ba-Sifrut ha-Muslimit ha-Maqbilah.' *Shenaton ha-Mishpat ha-'Ivri* 13: 121–84.

——1989. 'Peraqim me-Sefer ha-'Arevut ve-ha-Qablanut le-Rav Shmuel ben Hofni Gaon.' *Tarbiz* 58: 377–412.

——1991. 'Islamic Influence on Medieval Jewish Law? Sepher ha-'Arevuth of Rav Shmuel Ben Hofni Gaon and its Relationship to Islamic Law.' *Studia Islamica* 73: 5–23.

——1996. 'Peraqim Nosafim me-Sefer ha-Masranut le-Rav Shmuel ben Hofni Gaon.' *Qovetz 'al Yad* 13: 43–89.

LEVINGER, J. 1965. *Darkhei ha-Mahshavah ha-Hilkhatit Shel ha-Rambam*. Jerusalem.

LEWIN, B. M. 1922–44. *Ginzei Qedem*. 6 vols. Haifa and Jerusalem.

——1934. *Metivot*. Jerusalem.

LIFSHITZ, B. 1989. *'Asmakhta: Hiyyuv ve-Qinyan ba-Mishpat ha-'Ivri*. Jerusalem.

——1993. *Oved VeKablan—Bein Kinyan Levein Hitchayvut*. Jerusalem.

LOEWENSTAMM, S. E. 1977/80. 'Exodus 21: 22–25.' In *Vetus Testamentum* 27: 352–60. Repr. in his *Comparative Studies in Biblical and Ancient Oriental Literatures*. 517–25. Neukirchen-Vluyn 1980.

MARCUS, I. 1990. 'Medieval Jewish Studies: Toward an Anthropological History of the Jews.' In *The State of Jewish Studies*. 113–27. S. J. D. Cohen and Edward L. Greenstein eds. Detroit.

MARCUS, I. 1996. *Rituals of Childhood: Jewish Acculturation in Medieval Europe.* New Haven and London.

MARGALIN, R. 1999. *Medinat Yisrael Kemedinah Yehudit Vedemokratit.* Jerusalem.

MARGALIOT, M. 1973. *Hilkhot Eretz-Yisrael min ha-Geniza.* Jerusalem.

MARSHALL, J. W. 1993. *Israel and the Book of the Covenant: An Anthropological Approach to Biblical Law.* Atlanta, Ca.

MAYER, S. 1862–76. *Die Rechte der Israeliten, Athener und Romer, mit Rucksicht auf die neuen Gezetsgebungen.* Leipzig.

MEACHAM, T. 1999. *Sefer ha-Bagrut le-Rav Shmuel ben Hofni Gaon.* Jerusalem.

MELAMMED, R. L. 1997. 'He Said, She Said: A Woman Teacher in Twelfth-Century Cairo.' *AJS Review* 22/1: 19–35.

MENACHE, S. ed. 1996. *Communication in the Jewish Diaspora: The Pre-Modern World.* Leiden.

MICHAELIS, J. D. 1768. *Abhandlung von den Ehegesetzen Mosis, welche die Heyrathen in die nahe Freundschaft untersagen.* Göttingen.

—— 1770–5. *Mosaisches Recht.* 6 vols. Frankfurt.

—— 1778. *Mosaisches Peinliches Rechts nebst einer Vergleichung des heutigen Peinlichen Rechtes mit demselben.* Braunschweig u. Hildesheim.

MILGROM, J. 1975. 'The Missing Thief in Leviticus 5:20 ff.' *Revue internationale des droits de l'antiquité* 22: 71–85.

—— 1981. 'Sancta Contagion and Altar/City Asylum.' *Supplements to Vetus Testamentum* 32: 278–310.

—— 1983. *Studies in Cultic Theology and Terminology.* Leiden.

—— 1992. *Leviticus.* Garden City, NY.

MIRSKY, S. K. 1959–77. *Sheiltot de-Rav Ahai Gaon 'im Shnei Perushim Qadmonim.* 5 vols. Jerusalem.

MÜLLER, J. 1891. *Mafteah le-Teshuvot ha-Geonim.* Berlin. Repr. 1959.

NOVAK, D. 1983. *The Image of the Non-Jew in Judaism: An Historical and Constructive Study of the Noahide Laws.* New York.

—— 1998. *Natural Law in Judaism.* Cambridge.

OTTO, E. 1988. *Wandel der Rechtsbegründungen in der Gesellschaftsgeschichte des antiken Israel. Eine Rechtsgeschichte des 'Bundesbuches' Ex XX 22–XXIII 13.* Leiden.

—— 1991. *Körperverletzungen in den Keilschriftrechten und im Alten Testament.* Neukirchen-Vluyn.

—— 1993/6. 'Town and Rural Countryside in Ancient Israelite Law: Reception and Redaction in Cuneiform and Israelite Law.' *Journal for the Study of the Old Testament* 57: 3–22. Repr. in *The Pentateuch. A Sheffield Reader.* 203–21. J. W. Rogerson ed. Sheffield 1996.

PASSAMANECK, S. M. 1974. *Insurance in Rabbinic Law.* Edinburgh.

—— 1983. *The Traditional Jewish Law of Sale: Shulhan 'Arukh Hoshen Mishpat, Chapters 189–240.* Cincinnati.

PIATTELLI, D. 1979. 'An Enquiry into the Political Relations between Rome and Judaea from 161 to 4 B.C.E.' *Israel Law Review* 14/1: 195–236.

RABELLO, A. M. 2000. *The Jews in the Roman Empire: Legal Problems, from Herod to Justinian.* Aldershot.

RABINOWITZ, J. J. 1956. *Jewish Law: Its Influence on the Development of Legal Institutions.* New York.

RAKOVER, N. 1972. *Ha-Shlikhut ve-ha-Harshaah ba-Mishpat ha-'Ivri.* Jerusalem.

——1975–90. *A Bibliography of Jewish Law*. 2 vols. Jerusalem.

——1985. *Maimonides as Codifier of Jewish Law*. Jerusalem.

——1990. *The Multi-Language Bibliography of Jewish Law*. 2 vols. Jerusalem.

——1991. *Zekhut ha-Yotzrim be-Meqorot ha-Yehudiyyim*. Jerusalem.

RAPPAPORT, S. Y. 1904. *Yer'iot Shlomo*. Warsaw. Reprinting studies originally published in the periodical *Bikkurei ha-'Ittim* 1828–31.

RICHTER, D. 1992. *Die Responsen des Rabbi Ascher ben Jechiel (Rosch)*. Zurich.

RIVLIN, J. 1999. *Inheritance and Wills in Jewish Law* [Hebrew]. Ramat-Gan.

ROSENSWEIG, B. 1975. *Ashkenazic Jewry in Transition*. Waterloo, Ont.

ROSENTHAL, F. 1970. *Knowledge Triumphant: The Concept of Knowledge in Medieval Islam*. Leiden.

ROTH, J. 1986. *The Halakhic Process: A Systemic Analysis*. New York.

SAALSCHÜTZ, J. 1848. *Das mosaische Recht, mit Berücksichtigung des spätern Jüdischen*. Berlin.

SCHIFFMAN, L. 1975. *The Halakhah at Qumran*. Leiden.

——1983. *Sectarian Law in the Dead Sea Scrolls: Courts, Testimony and the Penal Code*. Chico, Cal.

SCHWIENHORST-SCHÖNBERGER, L. 1990. *Das Bundesbuch (Ex 20, 22–23, 33). Studien zu seiner Entstehung und Theologie*. Berlin.

SELDEN, J. 1631. *De Successionibus*. London.

——1640. *De Jure Naturali et Gentium*. London.

——1646. *Uxor Ebraica*. London.

SEPTIMUS, B. 1982. *Hispano-Jewish Culture in Transition: The Career and Controversies of Ramah*. Cambridge, Mass.

SHATZ, D. 1997. 'Concepts of Autonomy in Jewish Medical Ethics.' *The Jewish Law Annual* 12: 3–43.

SHILO, S. 1975. *Dina de-Malkhuta Dina*. Jerusalem.

——1982. 'The Contrast Between *Mishpat 'Ivri* and *Halakha*'. *Tradition* 20: 2: 91–100.

SHOCHETMAN, E. 1981. *Ma'aseh ha-Baah ba-'Averah*. Jerusalem.

——1985–6. *Meqorot ha-Tur ve-ha-Beit Yosef: Hoshen Mishpat*. Jerusalem.

——and LIFSHITZ, B. 1997. *Mafteah ha-Sheelot ve-ha-Teshuvot Shel Hakhmei Askhenaz, Tsarfat, ve-Italya*. Jerusalem.

SHOHET, D. 1931. *The Jewish Court in the Middle Ages*. New York. (Repr. 1974.)

SILBERG, M. 1927. *Dienstvertrag und Werkvertrag in talmudischen Rechte*. Frankfurt.

——1961. *Kah Darko Shel Hatalmud*. Jerusalem. Trans. B. Z. Bokser: *Talmudic Law and the Modern State*. New York 1973.

SINCLAIR, D. B. 1989. *Tradition and the Biological Revolution*. Edinburgh.

——1996. 'Jewish Law in the State of Israel.' In *An Introduction to the History and Sources of Jewish Law*. 397–419. N. Hecht. B. S. Jackson, S. Passamaneck, D. Piatelli, and A. Rabello eds. Oxford.

——1997. 'Jewish Law in the State of Israel.' *The Jewish Law Annual* 12: 253–66.

——1998. 'Halakhic Methodology in the Post-Emancipation Period: Case Studies in the Responsa of R. Yechezkel Landau.' *Le'ela* 45: 16–22.

——2001. *Law, Judicial Policy and Jewish Identity in the State of Israel (Jewish Law Association Studies XI)*. Binghamton.

SKLARE, D. 1996. *Samuel b. Hofni Gaon and His Cultural World: Texts and Studies*. Leiden.

SOLOMON, N. 1993. *The Analytic Movement: Hayyim Soloveitchik and his Circle*. Atlanta, Ca.

SOLOVEITCHIK, H. 1972. 'Pawnbroking: A Study in *Ribbit* and of the Halakah in Exile'. *Proceedings of the American Academy for Jewish Research* 38–9: 203–68.

—— 1978. 'Can Halakhic Texts Talk History?' *AJS Review* 3: 153–96.

—— 1980. 'Rabad of Posquières: A Programmatic Essay.' In *Studies in the History of Jewish Society.* Jerusalem.

—— 1985. *Halakha, Kalkalah, ve-Dimui 'Atzmi.* Jerusalem.

—— 1987. 'Religious Law and Change: The Medieval Ashkenazic Example.' *AJS Review* 12/2: 205–21.

—— 1990. *Sheelot u-Teshuvot ke-Maqor Histori.* Jerusalem.

—— 1998. 'Catastrophe and Halakhic Creativity: Ashkenaz—1096, 1242, 1306, and 1298.' *Jewish History* 12: 71–85.

SOLOVEITCHIK, J. B. 1983. *Halakhic Man.* Philadelphia.

—— 1986. *The Halakhic Mind.* New York.

SPIEGEL, Y. S. 1996. *'Amudim be-Toldot ha-Sefer ha-'Ivri: Hagahot u-Magihim.* Ramat-Gan.

SPRINKLE, J. M. 1994. *The Book of the Covenant—A Literary Approach.* Sheffield.

TA-SHEMA, I. 1992. *R. Zerahya ha-Levi Ba'al ha-Maor u-Bnei Hugo: le-Toldot ha-Sifrut ha-Rabbanit ba-Provens.* Jerusalem.

—— 1994. *Minhag Ashkenaz ha-Qadmon.* Jerusalem.

—— 1995. *Ha-Nigla she-ba-Nistar: le-Heqer Sheqi'ei ha-Halakhah be-Sefer ha-Zohar.* Tel Aviv.

—— 1996a. *Halakha, Minhag u-Metziut ba-Ashkenaz 1100–1350.* Jerusalem.

—— 1996b. 'Ma'amad ha-Nashim ha-Mitnadvot Leqayyeim Mitsvot she-ha-Zeman Graman.' In Ta-Shema (1996a): 262–79.

—— 2000. *Ha-Sifrut ha-Parshanit la-Talmud.* Jerusalem. Vol. 1.

TALLAN, C. 1991. 'Medieval Jewish Widows: Their Control of Resources.' *Jewish History* 5/1: 63–74.

—— 1992. 'Opportunities for Medieval Northern-European Jewish Widows in the Public and Domestic Spheres.' In *Upon My Husband's Death: Widows in the Literature and Histories of Medieval Europe.* 115–27. Louise Mirrer ed. Ann Arbor, Mich.

—— 2000. 'Medieval women in History, Literature, Law and Art, A Bibliography', at http://www.brandeis.edu/hirjw/pdf/tallan.pdf

TCHERNOWITZ, C. (Rav Tza'ir) 1943–50. *Toldot ha-Halakha.* 4 vols. New York.

—— 1946. *Toldot ha-Poseqim.* New York.

TWERSKY, I. 1980a. *Introduction to the Code of Maimonides (Mishneh Torah).* New Haven.

—— 1980b. *Rabad of Posquières: A Twelfth-Century Talmudist.* Philadelphia.

—— 1982. *Studies in Jewish Law and Philosophy.* New York.

—— 1990. *Studies in Maimonides.* Cambridge, Mass.

TYKOCINSKI, C. 1960. *Taqqanot ha-Geonim.* New York, Tel-Aviv, and Jerusalem. German original: *Die Gaonischen Verordnungen.* Berlin 1929.

URBACH, E. E. 1954/86. *Ba'alei ha-Tosafot: Toldoteihem, Hibbureihem, Shitatam.* Jerusalem. 5th edn. 1986.

—— 1986. *The Halakhah: Its Sources and Development.* Ramat-Gan.

VALLER, S. 1999. *Women and Womanhood in the Talmud.* Atlanta, Ga.

WALD, S. G. 1992–4. 'le-Derekh Shimusho Shel ha-Rif bi-Meqorot ha-Talmud ha-Bavli.' *Shenaton ha-Mishpat ha-'Ivri* 18–19: 199–214.

WARHAFTIG, S. 1969. *Dinei 'Avodah ba-Mishpat ha-'Ivri.* 2 vols. Tel Aviv.

—— 1974. *Dinei Hozim ba-Mishpat ha-'Ivri.* Jerusalem.

WASHOFSKY, M. 1988. 'R. Asher b. Yehiel and the *Mishneh Torah* of Maimonides: A New Look At Some Old Evidence.' In *Approaches to Judaism in Medieval Times*. iii. 147–157. David R. Blumenthal ed. Atlanta, Ga.

——1994. 'Responsa and Rhetoric: On Law, Literature, and the Rabbinic Decision.' In *Pursuing the Text: Studies in Honor of Ben Zion Wacholder*. 360–409. John C. Reeves and John Kampen eds. Sheffield.

WEGNER, J. R. 1982. 'Islamic and Talmudic Jurisprudence: The Four Roots of Islamic Law and Their Talmudic Counterparts.' *American Journal of Legal History* 26: 25–71.

WEISBARD P. H. and SCHONBERG, D. 1989. *Jewish Law: Bibliography of Sources and Scholarship in English*. Littleton, Col.

WEISS, I. H. 1924. *Dor Dor ve-Dorshav*. 5 vols. Berlin and New York.

WELCH, J. W. 1991. *A Biblical Law Bibliography*. Lampeter.

WERBLOWSKY, R. J. Z. 1977. *Joseph Karo: Lawyer and Mystic*. Philadelphia.

WESTBROOK, R. 1988. *Studies in Biblical and Cuneiform Law*. Paris.

WOOLF, J. 2001. 'Between Diffidence and Initiative: Ashkenazic Legal Decision-Making in the Late Middle Ages (1350–1500).' *Journal of Jewish Studies* 52/1: 85–97.

YARON, R. 1960. *Gifts in Contemplation of Death in Jewish and Roman Law*. Oxford.

YUVAL, Y. 1988. *Hakhamim be-Doram: ha-Manhigut ha-Ruhanit Shel Yehudei Germania be-Shilhei Yemai ha-Beinayim*. Jerusalem.

ZAFRANY, D. 1980. 'Darkhei ha-Horaah Shel ha-Rosh', unpublished Ph.D. diss., Tel Aviv University.

ZURI, J. 1921–2. *Mishpat Ha-Talmud*. Warsaw.

CHAPTER 27

BIBLE INTERPRETATION

MICHAEL FISHBANE

INTRODUCTION: TOPIC AND TERMS

CLASSICAL and traditional Jewish culture is fundamentally a text culture—formed, informed, and reformed by Scripture (the Hebrew Bible) and its interpretation. This Scripture has always served as the centre or source of all legal and intellectual meaning or purpose, no matter how limited its own explicit formulations or how developed its subsequent clarifications, qualifications, and revisions. Scripture is thus the acknowledged and uncontested core of authority in traditional Judaism, and variously deemed divine or sacred in all its parts. By contrast, disagreement and contestation arise over the source and status of its ongoing interpretations, which are variously asserted to be divine or human. The nexus between Scripture and its exegetical traditions is therefore crucial, and the claim by different groups to be the proper bearers of Scripture and its interpretation becomes the claim to be the true heirs of ancient Israel and the embodiments of its divine destiny. Because of the pre-eminence of biblical interpretation for the life of a 'Scriptural culture', the teacher stands in a pivotal position in its genealogical chain—be that for continuity and clarification or for renewal and reformation. Accordingly, allegiance to a founding teacher and his tradition of interpretation marks Jewish text cultures in all their historical variety. The normative patterns of Judaism are inseparable from this phenomenon, and it is equally evident in its schismatic and sectarian offshoots.

The seeds of this 'text culture' and its first flowering are in Scripture itself. Carefully and critically examined, the Hebrew Bible provides explicit testimony for an emergent exegetical culture, which explained words and phrases, adjusted laws and rulings, re-evaluated themes and theologies, and reapplied prophecies and oracles over many centuries (Fishbane 1985). In some instances, the new interpretations are incorporated into the original older strata; sometimes they are formulated in new strata or genres; and in still other cases the relationship between the layers must be inferred across diverse textual and generic divides on the basis of similar terminology or their strategic variation. Moreover, it is increasingly evident from the post-exilic sources that different circles of interpretation with professional interpreters existed; that differences in cultic practice and theology were the basis of rival contestations, whereby earlier textual rules or formulations were cited and reinterpreted to serve different political or polemical purposes. And finally, beyond the occurrence of technical terms for interpretation, it is clear that Torah study and interpretation was increasingly valorized as a religious duty and spiritual preoccupation (Fishbane 1985: 384–8; id. 1989: 70–1). Hence, even if later rabbinic developments of interpretation can arguably be linked to phrases or formulations similar to Greek or Roman rhetoric (Daube 1949; Lieberman 1962: 47–68), it is nevertheless plausible to assert native roots for the ongoing Jewish preoccupation with Scriptural interpretation, and to see in Israelite antiquity a fundamental pattern of Jewish culture in its earliest outlines and delineations—long before the closure of the Scriptural canon and the new types of reception and re-use of authoritative tradition it generated. Moreover, the use of authoritative traditions for ongoing group identity and differentiation is another remarkable feature of Jewish text cultures that finds its origins in the scriptures of ancient Israel. As one follows these forms and patterns in the emergent and vigorous sectarian rivalries evident in the Qumran scrolls, and in the school rivalries preserved in the early rabbinic literary strata, one comes to confirm the much later insight of Spinoza, that Scripture had begun to develop into a 'hieroglyph' or sacred writing: at first, we may say, as a network of holy scriptures whose words and phrases could provide the basis for new cultural codifications; and later, increasingly, as a vast Holy Scripture whose sounds and signs are an infinite code of divine truth. The interpreter thus becomes the interlocutor of a divine speech whose meanings may only be approximated in human terms.

New appreciation for the significance and sweep of Bible interpretation in Jewish culture over the centuries cannot be separated from the hermeneutical revolution that has penetrated all areas of the humanities and social sciences in the twentieth century—a revolution that has given a new regard for and interest in the phenomenon of language, both oral and written, and the ways that cultures are formed through their powers of creativity, revision, and formulation. Similarly, the related growth of semiotics has given new dimensions to the understanding of meaning-making, of the issues of competence and conflict of interpretation, and the specificity and concreteness of units of meaning and significance. The extension of these and related considerations to texts and literary canons has given new stimulus to the study of Bible interpretation—beyond such older concerns which focused on how Jews projected or protected their identity and ideology through exegesis; and it has also provided the framework for a new appreciation for the concreteness and textuality of Jewish thought, beyond older attitudes that denigrated both the characteristic absence of philosophical abstractions in much Jewish creativity and the often unwieldy variety of teachings on any given idea or subject. Realizing anew that Jewish Bible interpretation is rooted in the concrete words and phrases of Scripture, scholarship in this century has begun to re-evaluate the phenomenon of Bible interpretation as a language about a language and to appreciate the close connection between thought and exegesis in Jewish culture. The benefits for the study of the history and character of Jewish ideas and religion follow directly.

Naturally, any survey or overview of this topic is subject to difficulties of period-ization and categorization; and any typification and evaluation of the central issues is freighted with great difficulties. There is no one way to present the subject, and one can only hope that each attempt will both instruct and induce new thinking on these matters, providing a service to the neophyte and a stimulus to the initiate. Choices and characterizations have been made at every juncture.

The present treatment of Bible interpretation in twentieth-century scholarship begins in the aftermath of the post-Talmudic period, roughly with the rise to power and eminence of the great rabbinic academies in Babylon in the ninth century CE, and the challenge to their interpretation of Scripture that is evident in the Near East at that time. It will then also investigate later phases of the subject at several instructive junctures in the medieval and early modern periods, taking aspects of the subject into contemporary times. Complementing this diachronic dimension, and the thematic and analytical approaches involved (Part I), a separate perspective on typical and innovative methods is provided, as much to see what is new and distinctive about scholarship in this century as to stimulate and suggest new lines of investigation (Part II). Further considerations will then be added in conclusion, to broaden and stimulate the ongoing study of Bible interpretation (Part III).

But just what is the field or area of Bible interpretation, as we mark it off for evaluation? What are the fixed and fuzzy boundaries that we must bear in mind at this point, both obvious and obscure?

Over the centuries, Jewish Bible interpretation has meant the explication, trans-lation, apprehension, application, and re-use of the Hebrew Scriptures within and for the ongoing Jewish community, in its many historical forms; it has meant both the understanding of the text for its own sake and on its own terms, and its actualization for the sake of the people and their own self-identity. Life, law, and apologetics have drawn upon Scripture as their central source; and its reinter-pretation has provided both a knowledge of the past and ideals and hope for the present and future. Hence Jewish Bible interpretation has studied the text of

Scripture for Jews and Judaism, and not as a series of documents bearing on or witnesses to ancient Israel within Near Eastern antiquity. Arguably, it is precisely this point that marks a difference between the modern critical study of the Hebrew Bible and earlier types of Bible interpretation—even where the latter privileged the plain-sense of the text and was characterized by a critical spirit; for the fact that Scripture could be read as a stratum of language and meaning independent of rabbinic terms and tradition, did not mean that this level of meaning was separate from the overall Jewish nature and value of the text. To the extent that modern Jewish Bible scholars see themselves as a link in this larger chain of interpretation, and regard their labour *also* as a contribution to an understanding of this core document of Judaism and Jewish civilization, with its bearing on the people's ongoing self-identity and values, the boundary between Biblical scholarship and Bible interpretation is blurred. Scholars of the history of Jewish Bible interpretation must bear this in mind as a real possibility, distinct and peculiar to the modern age.

I. Bible Interpretation and Patterns of Exegetical Culture

One of the foundational achievements of twentieth-century Jewish Bible interpretation is the monumental research of Moshe Zucker on the work of Rav Saadia Gaon, who was the head of the talmudic academy of Sura in the ninth century, and at once the acknowledged champion of rabbinic tradition and intractable foe of early Karaism (which advocated an unbridled approach to the meaning of Scripture). His penetrating studies of old and new sources have thoroughly revised understanding of the Gaon's *tafsir* (or Arabic translation), in both its versions (Zucker 1959), as well as the principles, purposes, and intellectual achievements of his great Bible commentary, particularly the Book of Genesis (id. 1984). The cultural complexity of Saadia's work can now be more fully and accurately appreciated for the way it simultaneously absorbs Islamic principles of interpretation; rebuts Karaite explanations of various laws, terms, and calendrical principles; promotes a concordance between the meaning of the text and rabbinic tradition; and innovates ways to save the surface level of Scriptural anthropomorphisms while also penetrating to a deeper truth. The pivotal role of the Bible commentator in mediating meaning to the community, while promoting a new pedagogy and apologetic, can now be viewed in its subtlety and strategies—and just this has been taken up by other researchers. It also shows at first hand how Jewish life has to be seen as a complex but productive absorption of challenging ideas, and that its culture is a living dialectic with critiques from within and without. At stake in Saadia's day was the very meaning and status of Scripture, and whether it was best and most truthfully interpreted through reason and rabbinic tradition or by an altogether independent rational inquiry ('Search Scripture well' was a Karaite watchword). Nor was this a wholly abstract or intellectual project; for it was and remains the case that Jewish communities are formed and reformed within the orbit of Scripture and its positive application to life. The very concrete and practical results of the conflict of Bible interpretations are powerfully perceived through this paradigmatic instance, and these have not been lost on historical scholarship. It is one thing to differ about meaning within a framework of shared hermeneutical assumptions; it is quite another when the truth of method is deemed a matter of unbridgeable difference.

The reconstruction of Saadia's opponents from his writings (Davidson 1915) has given us a new appreciation for a whole range of critical questions on Bible interpretation; and an analysis of other polemical dimensions of Saadia's work has stimulated much new work on the Karaites and their extensive exegetical labours (S. Poznanski 1908). From a comparative point of view, these latter inquiries offer both a perspective on the Islamic influences on, or the internal stages of, the rise of Scripturalism in such sectarian Jewish circles (Ben-Shammai 1992), and also how such Scripturalist groups developed their own traditions of Bible interpretation. Moreover, broad comparisons between the exegetical literature of the Karaites and the much earlier Qumran community has stimulated study of the theme of the 'return to the Scriptures' in ancient Jewish sectarianism (Ben-Shammai 1993). In addition, the close study of numerous similar exegetical terms and attitudes in both groups have raised intriguing questions about their historical and conceptual relationships (Wieder 1962; Paul 1969). Such inquiries complement the fact that 'in some cases the parallelisms between Aramaic translations [of the Bible, like Targum Yerushalmi I] and unaccepted rabbinic views on the one hand and Karaite views on the other seem to be more than mere coincidence' (Ben-Shammai 1992: 13; and evidence in Itzchaky 1982: 60 f., 241 f., 251–3, 563–5, 656 f., 706 f.)—a topic whose halachic and exegetical dimensions await further study.

These important comparative perspectives must be widened and deepened; and much of this will necessarily await the publication and analysis of critical editions of Geonic Bible exegesis (both the work of individuals, like Samuel ben Hofni; and of groups, like the compendia known as 'Daat Zeqenim'), and the works of Karaite scholars (like Yefet ben Eli's commentary on the Bible; see Ben-Shammai 1976) and groups (like commentaries of the 'Mourners of Zion'; Frank 1995).

A second foundational achievement bearing on Bible interpretation in this century was the path-breaking research of Samuel Poznanski on the Jewish commentators of northern France in the twelfth and thirteenth centuries. Integrating and extending the research of earlier generations, Poznanski gave the first significant conspectus of the school of Rashi (R. Shelomo Yitzhaki), and the work of such well-known figures as Rashbam (R. Samuel ben Meir), R. Joseph Kara, and R. Joseph Bekhor Shor, as well as a first appreciation of R. Eliezer of Beaugency, and an edition of his commentary on the Book of Ezekiel and 'the Twelve' minor prophets (S. Poznanski 1913). This study summarized and set forth a whole research agenda: it sought to indicate what was distinctive and common among these plain-sense minded commentators; it took up matters of style, language, terminology, and ideology; it emphasized the use and study of manuscripts for a full and accurate portrait of the work of this school; and it dealt with matters of reception history and circles of transmission. It would certainly be fair to say that all these are among the defining topics of this field, and that Poznanski's study remains the touchstone for the subsequent refinements (particularly in the meaning and use of exegetical terms and techniques) that have been made over the years, and even a stimulus for perceiving new topics to be treated (particularly in the area of religious and cultural ideas, and a fuller or comparative approach to Bible research in Christian Europe).

Like the study of the rise of Bible interpretation in Geonic times, with its inner structure of concerns, but also its response to the challenge which Karaism gave to a renewed emphasis on the plain-sense of the Hebrew Bible in rabbinic circles, Bible study in northern France is also a pivotal paradigm for appreciating the complex inner development of Jewish interpretation (having native roots in the works of several plain sense minded grammarians and lexicographers) and a renewed emphasis on the plain sense of Scripture that developed in tandem with the external challenges and achievements of Christian Bible scholarship (newly focused on the true and original meaning of the biblical text, the *Hebraica Veritas*, as against its understanding and interpretation through Church tradition). But to properly realize this perspective, earlier scholarly attitudes had to be revised. Formerly, one salient approach was to treat Jewish life and study in France and the Rhineland at this time as wholly insulated against outside cultural or religious influences; as piously focused on its own inner agenda of spiritual and legal topics; and as dominated by the rabbinic curriculum that had developed within the academies of the region (S. Poznanski 1913: pp. xx f.).

But this past consensus has been countered by a number of considerations that require a more nuanced and comparative view of Jewish Bible study in northern France. The study of Beryl Smalley on *The Study of the Bible in the Middle Ages* (Smalley 1941; rev. edn. 1952) has been of seminal influence in this regard. Her research not only documented the new emphasis on the literal sense of Scripture in the monastic and cathedral schools of the twelfth century; it also put special focus on the work of the Victorines generally, and that of Andrew of St Victor in particular—who himself attests to having 'been instructed on the literal sense of the Pentateuch by the Jews (*ab Hebreis*)' (ibid. 100), and whose contemporary, Bartholomew, Bishop of Exeter, also makes clear that these encounters involved debate and 'disagreement', since 'the Jews... take all the Old Testament literally, whenever they can find a literal sense, unless it gives manifest witness to Christ.

Then they repudiate it, saying that it is not in the Hebrew Truth, that is in their books' or otherwise attempt to reinterpret it or deflect it (ibid. 142). Both of these testimonies give succinct and precious proof of complex relations between contemporary Jewish and Christian Bible scholars, involving both text study and polemic; many studies reinforce the point (Dahan 1989; id. 1990). Indeed, just as these testimonies show that the Christians had a double agenda (to study the literal truth of Scripture and to convince Jews of its Christological references or hints), so do they also suggest that Jewish knowledge of the plain sense of Scripture had its own double aspect—for this was at once an internal exegetical tradition (that had developed in the rabbinic academies and was acknowledged by outsiders), and a means for Jews to defend their claim to be the authentic heirs and interpreters of the Hebrew Bible on a common 'rational' ground (altogether independent of rabbinic tradition).

The commentaries of R. Joseph Kara show in particular just how much the increased impact of Christian polemics had on the formulation of the plain-sense of Scripture. For it is not in general that he advocates his compatriots to 'subjugate yourself to Scripture' (*kefof 'atzmekha la-Miqra*; see *ad* Isa. 1: 27); but he repeatedly notes that his remarks may serve as a 'rejoinder to the heretics' and that one should engage in 'wily plain-sense interpretations' (*peshatim shel armumiyut*; see *ad* Gen. 45: 28) in order to rebut verses treated by Christian polemicists as proving the rejection or debasement of the people Israel, or the base immorality of its forebears. The frequency and often hard-pressed nature of these plain-sense readings not only attest to the skill of this commentator, but also to the mood and pressure of the times (Grossman 1986). At the same time, this stimulus can also yield positive principles of interpretation, as when Kara (in efforts to rebut claims of divine rejection) finds several examples of the principle that wherever one finds cases of divine rebuke one will often find statements of compassion nearby, and formulated in related terms (ibid. 44 f.; cf. *ad* Hos. 2: 1). Such instances are deemed proof positive of God's ongoing love for the people. Such features highlight the contentious spirit of the times.

But enmity and rival arguments are only part of the story. On closer inspection, one can also perceive traces of creative influence. Indeed, in some cases the links between the two religious communities offer a series of similarities that suggest a shared spirit of the age—despite doctrinal differences.

In addition to a common search for the best biblical manuscripts and versions (Grabois 1975), Jews and Christians developed study and exegetical techniques that mirror each other in quite striking ways—even using similar terminology. For example, just as in Christian circles there was a notable development of the recitation or reading of Scripture (*lectio divina*) into an aspect of the 'academic lecture course' (Smalley 1941: 156), and the 'reader' was called a *lector*, it is at about this time in French Jewish circles that pedagogical manuals like *Sefer Ḥuqei Ha-Torah* stress that 'teachers must not instruct their pupils by heart, but from a written text', and the biblical teacher or student of Scripture bears the title *qara*, or 'reader'. Moreover, one can also observe similar instructional techniques and emphases. For example, in Christian circles the new pedagogical emphasis of the *trivium* on the study of words (the *res verborum*) and attention to their grammatical sense (*sensus*) corresponds remarkably to the type of Jewish lexical glosses known as *pitronot* (Banitt 1966). Similarly, the concern for literal explanation (or the *sensus literalis*) in Christian exegesis recalls the Jewish term *nimmuqim* (Touitou 1982: 62), and the penetration into the deeper (often doctrinal) meaning of the passage (the *sententia*) recalls the explanations of Rashbam in his commentary on Ecclesiastes regarding the true or 'profound' meaning of wisdom in that text (Japhet 1985: 66–7). And finally, if we add to this the fact that the Christian educational style emphasized the method of question and disputation (*questio* and *disputatio*) initiated by the teacher and followed up by student study among themselves (*collatio*), just as did contemporary Jewish education—as we can readily observe in the Tosafists' comments on the Bible (and Talmud), and by the exhortation found in the aforementioned *Sefer Ḥuqei Ha-Torah* (that 'The teachers must train their youths to ask each other questions daily, at evening, in order to sharpen their wits')—then it is clear that we have common currents in both cultural worlds.

These and many other features hardly indicate that these two communities were totally isolated from one another, and only met on the icy field of formal or literary polemics. Much more do we have before us the indicators of a complex and interrelated intellectual universe, which has aptly been presented as a part of what C. H. Haskins first called the 'Renaissance of the Twelfth Century' (Touitou 1984). To be sure, much more work is needed in order to fill in the details and give a more calibrated portrait of the shared mental world of different northern European Bible scholars at this time. But in comparison with the emphasis of earlier generations on religious polemics and cultural isolation, even these selected examples of 'affinities' between Jewish and Christian Bible study must be celebrated as a shift in scholarly attention and attitude (Kamin 1991: 12*–26*). It should be added that there are indications of similar affinities in the Spanish cultural sphere. Recent studies of the exegesis of Naḥmanides have suggested that such native terms as *tziyurei debarim* are palpable Jewish attempts to approximate the Christian term *figurae*; and that the interest in showing how the acts of the patriarchs and others are 'signs' (*simanim*) or prefigurations of similar actions among their descendants is very much like the regnant Christian interest in typologies connecting themes and acts in the Old Testament to others in the New one (Funkenstein 1993: 98–121). What is particularly striking about this case is the suggestion of Christian influence but the thorough Jewish transformation. For if Christian typologies suggest a prophetic fulfillment and correlation between the two Testaments (and thus a supersessionist spirit), the comparative case of Jewish types shows rather a historical prefiguration (of characters and acts) and their correlation within the Hebrew Bible itself (and thereby confirming its inner unity and coherence). Such comparisons have much to teach regarding the two religious communities and their self understanding through Scriptural interpretation.

Surely one of the intellectual tensions shared by both Jews and Christians at this time is the relationship of *ratio* to *auctoritas*, of independent human reason and inquiry to the authority of received tradition. On the Jewish side, the vaunted interest in the plain or straightforward meaning of the sentences of Scripture came to mark a type of exegetical inquiry that did not always jibe with tradition. The resultant sense of this mode of Bible study was known as the *peshat*. This term (in various forms) is already found in Talmudic literature, and several significant attempts were made in the last half of this century to define the terminology, assess its semantic range, and note its differences from the distinctly traditional mode of exegetical inquiry known as *derash* (Loewe 1964; Gelles 1981; Kamin 1980 and 1986). A particular benefit of these studies has been their contribution to the discussion about the diverse meanings of *peshat* in Rashi and his school, and also of the ways that this sense of Scripture was variously independent of tradition, integrated with it, or set against it in one way or another. For Rashi himself, for example, the *peshat* meant the contextual sense of a sentence on its own terms or even with the help of midrashic tradition; whereas for his grandson, Rashbam, the *peshat* marked the independent straightforward sense of Scripture, even where this meaning contradicted the rabbinical *derash*, which he knew and valorized as the authoritative meaning of the biblical text for Jewish traditional life. Hence, both Rashi and Rashbam are Scripturalists, but in qualified and different ways; and the same could be said of other exegetes of this school, like R. Joseph Kara and R. Eliezer of Beaugency. Moreover, these different approaches to the basic Scriptural sense led to different sensibilities regarding history, narrative sequence, literary form, composition, redaction, and the meaning and function of textual details and lacunae. In recent years such topics have become the independent subject of research on several major exegetes (Lockshin 1989; Harris 1997). Since these new interests draw upon modern literary poetics and theory, they deepen Poznanski's programmatic catalogues of terms, themes, and phrases.

The interest of commentators in the *peshat*-sense of Scripture, and its differentiation from the rabbinical *derash*, is not limited to the northern French sphere but recurs elsewhere during this period. Typical of this phenomenon is the work of R. David Kimḥi of Provence, who developed his own 'way of *peshat*', and who, because of his work in biblical grammar and lexicography, evinces a sensibility for the syntax, style, and narrative thread of literary units which stands over against the methods of rabbinic interpretation and the *darshanim* (preachers) of his day (Talmage 1975: 54–134). Of a quite different sort are the grammatical, stylistic, and historical elements that are found in the wide-ranging oeuvre of R. Abraham ibn Ezra—whose itinerant life led him from his native Spain to Italy and elsewhere; and while there is, increasingly, a subtle appreciation of his commentaries on selected topics, themes, and books (Simon 1965, 1985, 1991), no synthetic and comprehensive study has yet to be written on this seminal scholar. Such an inquiry would also take into account other contemporary scholars of the Spanish exegetical tradition (like ibn Balʿam), who were also interested in the plain sense of Scripture (Poznanski 1924; Goshen-Gottstein 1992), as well as the various and challenging Karaite commentators of his era. Ibn Ezra's well-known antipathy to the rabbinical *derash* aside, his own mode of *peshat* shows the need for a comparative treatment of the subject. Such a study would necessarily have to build on various other sources that have been under-utilized for an appreciation of the stylistic features of Scripture at this time. This would include the observations found in the lexicographical work of R. Jonah ibn Janaḥ (of Spain); in the *Sefer Hakhra ʿot* of R. Jacob Tam (of northern France); and in a host of *peshat* glosses taught by R. Judah He-Ḥasid (of the Rhineland) to his son, (Marcus 1989: 7*–13*), as well as those in such works as R. Jacob of Vienna's *Peirushim u-Pheshatim* and in R. Jacob D'Illesca's *Imrei Noam*. Moreover, such a comparative study would include the hugely important commentaries of Nahmanides, with an emphasis on his attitude towards the *peshat* and uses of the *derash*. In short, a fully differentiated examination of the *peshat* and its connections to the *derash* in medieval Jewish Bible exegesis interpretation is a major desideratum for Jewish studies, one that will provide a rich and important area of research for the future.

This said, the question remains as to whether the best or only approach to comparative study of medieval Bible interpretation should be according to geographical regions; for recent work has posited that a more thematic or semantic orientation towards the range of commentators might yield a quite different and possibly even more intriguing classification of the data. Such linguistic terms as 'meaning-maximalism' and 'meaning-minimalism' have thus been suggested as providing an instructive and heuristic way to view shifts between Saadia and Rashi, and to organize the interpretations of other many commentators (Steiner 1992, 1998). The notion of 'omnisignificance' has also been proposed as a helpful prism into the concerns and character of certain exegetes (Elman 1993). We need not get stuck on these terms *per se*, for it should be obvious that they or their like are only the means for a better understanding of the subject, and not ends in themselves. Moreover, such considerations should not be restricted to the study of commentators dealing with the plain sense. The category of allegory might also be productively correlated with one or another of these rubrics, and such an alignment may prove instructive for understanding better the diverse phenomenon of philosophical allegory and its relationship to other modes of biblical interpretation. This aside, there would still remain the task of determining the extent to which the notion of allegory (and the sense of fixed meanings) may also be applied to certain cases of theosophical exegesis found in books like the *Zohar* (Talmage 1986). We are only at the beginning of such determinations, as well as analysing the various means and modes of esoterism in biblical commentaries (Wolfson 1989). The terms, techniques, and mentalities of Jewish mystical exegesis is also a vast field that has not been fully charted and explored (Idel 1986; Wolfson 1987, 1993; Fishbane 1998: 105–22, 211–16). The paired categories of 'meaning-minimalism' and 'meaning-maximalism' (or their like) may prove helpful or instructive in this area as well.

A third major juncture in the history of Bible interpretation has been reconsidered during the past century. It is the period inaugurated by Benedict Spinoza, in the seventeenth century, when another phase of Scripturalism emerged—this time motivated by a new type of rationalism that demystified the sanctity of Scripture and the techniques of traditional exegesis; and also at this time another joint (Jewish–Christian) enterprise of textual inquiry developed, though this one was often sparked by various types of post-traditionalism that sought to study Scripture as one would any other book (on its own terms, as Spinoza advocated, or through a critical-historical spirit). Hence, even if Scripture became in some circles a document to be studied without benefit of tradition, *Scriptura sola*, its value for these communities of critical interpretation varied considerably. For one thing, it was not a clear given that such communities wanted to be reconstituted in religious or traditional terms—and this because the new turn to Scripture was part of an intellectual project that hoped to depart from certain traditional beliefs and give its readers a new sense of historical and cultural origins. The older presumptions that Holy Scripture encoded hidden truths behind its plain sense and all-too-human imagery, also bowed before this new type of critique. This work now embodied the 'scriptures' of an ancient culture, and its content was just what its plain sense suggested—no more and no less (Strauss 1928). Indeed, if the new Bible interpretation thus valorized the human aspects of 'scripturality' in a new way, this was part and parcel of new appreciations for the human aspects of religion and tradition then being celebrated and studied.

To the extent that Jewish Bible interpretation retained its historical task of being a teacher of Scripture for the religious community, this new spirit of inquiry had to yield more than analytic scepticism or mere information; and to the degree that this Bible interpretation retained its historical task as a defender of Scripture and its cultural legacy, attempts had to be made either to harmonize the older tradition with the newer critical spirit or to discover new ways of reading Scripture and being instructed by it. Several strategies are typical of modern Judaism, and these continue or revise older cultural forms.

1. A first strategy is Bible translation. We commented earlier on the *tafsir* of Rav Saadia Gaon, and its cultural role in promoting and defending both Scripture and rabbinic tradition at a time of cultural crisis. In the eighteenth century Moses Mendelssohn's new translation of the Bible into German, and its accompanying commentary (or *Bi'ur*), also had pedagogical and cultural goals in mind. Contemporary scholarship has assessed its context and cultural achievement anew (Breuer 1996: 77–222; Sorkin 1996: 31–89). Borne by the spirit of the times, Mendelssohn and his cultural collaborators shared with their Christian contemporaries a search for

the best textual versions of Scripture. But they also had specifically Jewish concerns in mind. For one, their hope was that this translation of Scripture could help its readers acquire a literary German unavailable to them in their traditional schools and communities, and thus help give them the cultural skills beneficial for their political and cultural enfranchisement. For another, both the translation and its comments often incorporated traditional interpretations where these were deemed necessary both to promote and to protect certain traditional Jewish values or actions. The combined result was that Scripture served as a means for transmitting tradition and its virtues while also promoting aspects of a shared wider culture—in short the classic features of Jewish Bible interpretation, now in a modern guise.

The strategies and concerns of the Buber–Rosenzweig Bible translation (1925–65) were related, for all the technical differences. On the one hand, their work revalor-ized the content of Scripture for a secular Jewish community by presenting it in a style that evoked certain German cultural sensibilities (particularly the pietistic nuances of a Lutheran type); but this translation also utilized the full scope of traditional Jewish exegesis, and was extraordinary attentive to recurrent theme-words or verbal roots recurring in the text (details that reflected the translators' attunement to ancient and medieval Jewish exegesis). In this way, Buber and Rosenzweig hoped to confront the modern secular spirit of the Jew with an old-new religious language and instruct him in a new sensibility. The fact that this was conveyed through Scripture restored this ancient text to cultural value without promoting either a formal traditionalism or a commitment to any of its theological elements or values (Buber and Rosenzweig 1994/1936, *passim*; Fishbane 1989: 81–111). By contrast, the translators of the Hebrew Scriptures produced by the Jewish Publication Society (1917, 1965, 1985), for all their philological acumen, miss this cultural mark and mode of pedagogy. Repeatedly, the diverse strata of biblical language and literature are levelled into a contemporary demotic; the key words in the original Hebrew (that mark inner textual links and correlations) are not always rendered in similar ways in their English version); and the regular use by the translators of the traditional Jewish commentaries in order to resolve textual difficulties is obscured by the subtitle which states that the translations have been made 'According to the Traditional Hebrew Text'. Readers might therefore conclude that tradition was being safeguarded simply by the use of the Massoretic Text, and that the objective plain sense of the ancient words was thereby guaranteed. It is notable, in this regard, that more popular and altogether inexpert translations of the Hebrew Scriptures by assertively traditional publishers (like 'Art Scroll') have had a striking appeal upon a broad spectrum of the Jewish public—and this is not least because the reader gets an 'Englished' Scripture along with the palpable ring (and even the interpolations) of Jewish interpretative traditions. This reception of such very 'Jewish' translations is a visceral rejection of *Scriptura sola*, and is of consider-able interest to the cultural historian of Jewish Bible interpretation in the twentieth century. The task of presenting Scripture on its own terms, while ever mindful of the historical role of translations in the transmission of cultural knowledge and identity, remains.

2. We now turn to a second cultural strategy: Bible commentary. Under this rubric we stress those products of Bible interpretation that have been produced for Jewish life and thought, products that seek to explain the text but also to clarify its distinctive character. This form of cultural pedagogy often had a strong polemical tone, designed for protection against the dangers of assimilation, criticism, and ignorance. Precisely these factors are spelled out in a series of public letters sent by Solomon Schechter to England, and published in 1901 in the London *Jewish Chronicle*. 'It must be clear to everybody', he wrote, 'that the new century does not open under very favourable auspices for Judaism ... [O]ur Scriptures are the constant object of attack, our history is questioned, and its morality is declared to be an inferior sort.' Accordingly, his clarion call at the beginning of the twentieth century was loud and clear: '[I]t is ... of supreme importance that we repossess ourselves of our Scripture.' Not surprisingly, Joseph Hertz, who was educated at Schechter's Jewish Theological Seminary of America in New York, and latter became the Chief Rabbi of the British Empire, took up these cudgels repeatedly; they also served as the armature of the defence he provided for Anglophone Jewry in the extraordinarily influential Bible commentary that he edited and dominated, *The Pentateuch and Haftorahs* (Oxford, 1929–36 in 5 vols., and Soncino, 1938, in 1 vol. and frequently reprinted).

In this work, the perceived dangers of 'Higher Criticism' were rebutted and the authority of an inspired Mosaic authorship espoused (despite differences among Hertz's collaborators); the benefits of archaeology were selectively adduced and the presumed dangers of science deflected; the superior character of Jewish morality was championed and the problems of paganism and its cultural offshoots made clear (in a Jewish revision of Matthew Arnold's Hellenism versus Hebraism polemic); and a version of Maimonidean rationalism pervades the explanation of biblical miracles, sacrifices, and other topics. At the same time, Hertz did make frequent though selective use of modern (and non-Jewish) biblical criticism, where it served his larger purposes of promoting the need for a secular education; but his uncompromising stance was in the defence of Rabbinism and tradition, and in sounding an alarm against immorality and the possible infusion of Christian elements into Judaism (as advocated by Claude Montefiore). Generations have learned their Judaism from this tendentious work; since, as always, but especially in contemporary times, the synagogue provides the primary place for the espousal of Jewish values and information. For better and for worse, the 'Hertz Humash' (Pentateuch) is a series of sermons (large and small) and its pages a bully-pulpit.

One attempt at rectifying and transforming this state of affairs is the Bible commentary project planned in the last decade of this century by the Rabbinical Assembly of America, and published in late 2001. Entitled *Etz Hayim*, to signal that the Bible is a vast 'tree of life' whose organic offshoots have influenced and produced the vastness of rabbinic Judaism, this work (edited by D. Lieber and his associates) is distinguished by the fact that the core of the '*peshat*' section of the commentary is based on the longer scholarly volumes of the Jewish Publication Society Bible Commentary on the Torah (by Sarna, Levine, Milgrom, and Tigay, 1989–96) and the Haftarot (Prophetic Lectionaries; by Fishbane, 2002). This ensures a critical and responsible presentation of the ancient sources. In addition, there is a '*derash*' section that culls comments from the full range of rabbinic oral tradition (both legal and homiletical), thereby demonstrating how Scripture has and may speak to different generations while helping the reader realize that the ongoing life of the Bible is distinct from its original historical levels and meaning. Comments dealing with practical halachah are also provided, as well as addenda instructing the readership in a variety of theological topics. Such features provide a new pedagogical package for the synagogue, and attempt to fulfill the older ideals of Bible interpretation in a contemporary idiom. However, polemics have been eschewed, and many of the 'difficult' moral and cultural topics of Scripture are faced squarely; with traditional answers offered but also re-evaluated. The aim is thus to provide a new intellectual basis for traditional Jewish values and identity in the open and porous culture of the twenty-first century. It auspiciously closes one era and opens another.

3. A third strategy in the contemporary engagement with Bible interpretation involves the rehabilitation of medieval Jewish commentaries. Particularly influential is the work of Nechama Leibowitz over many decades in the third quarter of the century. Both in oral form and 'stencils' distributed worldwide (in Hebrew), and later in book form (in Hebrew and English), Leibowitz provided a new pedagogy of the Pentateuch for modern Orthodox readers who had difficulties in accepting the assumptions and conclusions of modern critical Bible scholarship and who preferred the traditional commentaries. In her unique style, she provided a way to read and respond to all the detailed nuances of Scripture through a modern-traditional mode of question and answer that made use of the medieval commentaries as 'models' of moral, theological, and literary concern. This rehabilitated an engaged reading of these commentaries and freed them from being historical documents only, and allowed them to instruct in a multivalent way. Hence a mode of traditional Bible interpretation was revived—one that could allow moderns to rethink questions of value and meaning without levelling the meaning of the text or challenging its authority. While no overall principles of reading are offered here, and comments are focused on specific verses and topics, a distinct pedagogical voice and religious concern is everywhere evident and engaging.

4. A fourth strategy of engagement with Scripture attempts to rehabilitate the Bible as a unique or distinctive document for modern readers. Spinoza, as was noted above, provided a cultural turning-point in the appraisal and reading of Scripture with his critique of any claim that the text was not written 'in the language of men', or that this language concealed or encoded deeper dimensions of divine instruction. It is notable that Leo Strauss, who provided the most influential study of this subject

and its meaning for modern religion in the century (Strauss 1965 [translation of 1928 German edn.]), also articulated a mode of reading Scripture that focused on its non-philosophical but uniquely concrete and narrative manner of thought (Strauss 1997: 359–76 [1981 edn.]; 377–405 [1967 edn.]). This valorized the values and world-view and language of Scripture for the modern reader, and offer a model of reflection other than those of philosophical theology (which had been critiqued earlier in this century). The Bible interpretation of Martin Buber and Franz Rosenzweig must also be viewed in this light, for they saw in Scripture a contemporary challenge to the abstractions of German idealism and very much of a witness to the concrete immediacy and importance of language in a morally and theologically engaged life. To be sure, both thinkers valorized some of the specific values and teachings of Scripture; but the larger import and purpose of their work was to emphasize its deeper structures, particularly the 'dialogical character' of existence and its challenges of response and responsibility—the ways that Hebrew Scripture instructs one to be a person in the full sense. For Joseph Soloveitchik, the rabbinic 'doyen' of Jewish Orthodoxy in America, this instruction often comes through diverse textual models. In one of his most celebrated and influential essays, 'The Lonely Man of Faith', written in 1965, he analysed the first two chapters of the Book of Genesis as revealing two types of individuals—the noble rational creature, who is engaged with the broad and challenging world of nature and culture, seeking to ameliorate and abet humanity as a whole; and the religiously faithful creature, who is engaged in the sanctification of existence, and sets his stakes within a more limited community of prayer and practice. In a manner totally different from Strauss's treatment of these chapters, Soloveitchik provides yet another method of Bible interpretation for the modern person that bypasses the issues of critical-historical scholarship. In producing a reading of Scripture that suggests two models of personhood and community, and thus provides a biblical justification for universal commitments alongside parochial ones, one of the historical features of Jewish Bible interpretation is realized in a new way: a reinforcement of the Jewish people from within, and an engagement with the broader world beyond.

II. Models in the Contemporary Study of Bible Interpretation

In this section I wish to shift attention to some of the models that may be discerned in the scholarly study of Bible interpretation during this century. The purpose is to isolate them on their own terms, and thus give a different perspective on what has in fact been achieved. It is my hope that a clarification of these models may generate new work along the same or similar lines. In the final section, this discussion will be supplemented by suggestions for new types of research.

Four models shall be distinguished here: the study of special topics; of specific interpreters and their schools; the collection of materials into compendia; and the consideration of the multiple levels of Bible interpretation.

Topics

Different approaches have been influential or innovative. Starting at the basic level of individual words or phrases, one approach has been the study of a term having important cultural significance, like the messianic meaning of 'Shiloh' (Gen. 49: 10) in Jewish and Christian exegesis (A. Poznanski 1904). Such an avenue of research provides a window into an influential term and provides a comparative mapping of exegetical strategies and standpoints; but it can tend to be static in nature or redundant if the range of materials and their contexts are not rich enough. Of greater potential is the examination of a phrase, like 'Be fertile and increase, fill the earth and master it' (Gen. 1: 28) in Jewish and Christian exegesis over the centuries, from antiquity to the present (Cohen 1989). Since the hermeneutical possibilities are varied in Jewish literature, for example, and the phrase has been variously reinterpreted in homiletical, legal, philosophical, and mystical literature, a diachronic approach provides a significant perspective on the textuality of Jewish thought over the centuries. And further, because of the diverse history of the applications of this phrase down to contemporary times, when it has been both vigorously championed and vilified by proponents of different ecological and birth-control orientations, a diachronic approach becomes an important resource 'for cultural and intellectual historians' (ibid. 3). Indeed, such a study of key biblical phrases over time is a significant subset of tradition-history within the wider context of the history of Western religious thought.

Where scholars have focused on a whole book, one significant new method has been to focus on diverse approaches to its authority, purpose, and authorship—as, for example, has been done with respect to the Book of Psalms in the hands of Saadia, Salmon ben Yerucham, Yefet ben Eli, Moses ibn Giqatillah, and Abraham ibn Ezra (Simon 1991 [1982]). Numerous valuable issues arise from this diachronic and comparative approach, which offers new insights into such matters as medieval Jewish views of poetry, prayer, and prophecy, and their place within the history of Rabbinite and Karaite ideas. Along these lines, the examination of an even wider swathe of medieval commentaries on the Book of Esther (Wallfish 1993), exemplifies how the history of interpretation is also a contribution to Jewish and general intellectual history (notably perspectives on anti-Semitism; on Gentiles; on Persia through medieval eyes; on a foreign court; and on the idea of monarchy). Both studies excel in their use of unknown and unused manuscripts, whose retrieval and study has revolutionized scholarship in the field of Jewish Bible interpretation, as has already been noted with respect to Zucker's study of Saadia and his contemporaries, and the work of S. Poznanski on Eliezer of Beaugency.

Interpreters and Schools

One of the major interpreters whose work has been the subject of numerous textual and cultural studies is Rashbam (see earlier). Among these, most notable and exemplary is the study by Sara Japhet of his commentary on the Book of Job (Japhet 2000). Here we have significant treatments of the technicalities of manuscript evaluation and use; of Rashbam's notion of *peshat* in particular and his method of commentary overall; of literary and linguistic features in the commentary of Job; and finally, an examination of the author's beliefs and ideas. Taken as a whole, these chapters contribute a new synthetic model of scholarship, showing just how a medieval interpreter should be treated and evaluated. Such close, analytic studies will provide the foundation for the integrative treatment of the 'School of Rashi' (and others) yet to be written. In retrospect, the propaedeutic value of S. Poznanski's foundational study looms large.

Another important 'School' whose history of interpretation remains to be written is the Provençal family of authors: Joseph, Moses, and David Kimhi. A growing number of the works of these men have been published and analysed over the century; and we even have an edition of their treatments of the Book of Proverbs (Talmage 1990). This will provide an added basis for a comparative study of the several authors of this school and their commentaries; and one may even hope that the net will be widened to include the treatment of this book by interpreters of other schools and regions, like R. Jonah Gerondi. Such studies will provide the basis for new perspectives on Jewish wisdom literature and ethics in the Middle Ages.

Compendia

The voluminous work on Bible commentators by Ezra-Zion Melammed straddles the preceding and present categories (Melammed 1975, and enlarged in 1978). Tracing the history of interpretation from rabbinic antiquity, and focusing particularly on such medieval authors as Rashi, Rashbam, Abraham ibn Ezra, David Kimhi, and Nahmanides, the author provides a compendious collection of valuable data— treating matters of language and style; uses of sources and strategies of interpretation; and diverse theological and historical factors unique to the writers. The detailed catalogues of data are of major importance, compiled with both a traditional and critical alertness to textual elements. But in the end, Melammed's work exceeds in scholarly diligence what it delivers by way of analysis or evaluation. What we have are the vast materials for a comprehensive study, but not the study itself. Evaluated historically, Melammed's work is a curio of sorts, a most traditional collection of analytical data produced in the context of a modern university (being the product of seminars given at the Hebrew University) and published by an academic press.

Also a notable exemplar of traditional interests and critical considerations is perhaps one of the greatest and least-studied works of Bible interpretation produced during this century: the extraordinary compendium of commentaries and studies by Menahem Kasher, known by the title *Torah Shelemah* (in 44 vols. 1927–95). No summary can do justice to this massive work, in which the verses of the first four books of the Pentateuch are annotated by a broad and diverse selection of commentaries from the full range of ancient rabbinic literature (Talmud and midrash; canonical and extra-canonical), and supplemented by detailed expositions of pertinent textual and exegetical issues found throughout Geonic literature and in the works of later medieval authorities and commentators. These selections and comments are presented on the basis of new manuscript finds, and are critically analysed and presented with a wealth of documentation, along with a host of addenda dealing with of topics of interest to the student of medieval Bible interpretation. In an altogether traditional manner, the organic interconnection of the history of Jewish Bible exegesis unfolds; and with an often singular blend of critical acuity and traditional argumentation, the opinions of specific commentators and commentaries are sifted and evaluated. This encyclopedic work is sorely in need of full-scale academic study, in which its overall achievements for Jewish learning need to be considered, and its many contributions to critical Jewish scholarship need to be sorted and studied and honoured. Until this is done, Kasher's 'Torah *completum*' will remain incomplete.

Levels of Interpretation

Jewish Bible study over the centuries was marked by various levels of interpretation. We have already referred to the methods of *peshat* and *derash*, and to the fact that they themselves are variable in method and meaning and interrelationship from antiquity on, and especially throughout the Middle Ages. Other levels of interpretation are known in addition, and these are often signalled by the words *remez* and *sod*, which are often translated as 'hint' and 'mystery' respectively, and are indicative of the allegorical and mystical senses of Scripture. However, as is increasingly realized by many studies, mystical exegesis could use allegory and be marked by the term *remez*; and philosophical or other esoteric exegesis (like the compositional or astrological secrets in the works of Abraham ibn Ezra) could be indicated by the term *sod*. Based on a pun in the Zohar, these four levels of Bible interpretation have been known by the acronym PaRDeS, which thus indicates the 'Garden' or 'Paradise' of interpretation and a hierarchical series of senses leading from the outer 'body' of Scripture to its inner 'soul' and 'super-soul'. However, quite different versions and terms for the four fold method of Scriptural interpretation are also found in the thirteenth century, like the 'four ways in which the interpreters of the Torah are accustomed to walk' mentioned in the Introduction to an early version of *Sha'ar ha-Shamayim* by Isaac ibn Latif. In addition to some of the better-known terms, this writer uses the word *mashal* to indicate the allegorical meaning of some prophetic visions and *derash* to probably mean the mystical sense of Scripture. Clearly the terminology was fluid and variable among many authors.

All this notwithstanding, it has been tempting for scholars to follow W. Bacher's view that the emergence of the fourfold method of Scripture emerged at this time under the influence of Christian exegesis (Bacher 1891: 38)—and that the Jewish series *peshat, derash, remez,* and *sod* correspond to the Christian one of *littera, allegoria, tropologia,* and *anagoge*. But this series of terms is not at all comparable; there is a significant difference given to the weight of the different terms in the two systems; and Christian influence in this domain of exegesis is not necessarily the dominant or sole factor. Given these various considerations, it is best to think of a dual approach to the question of the emergence of a fourfold scheme of Jewish exegesis at this time: 'an inner development of [the] Jewish religion at a given moment needed a new approach' and 'the Christian theory may have furnished the idea of a fourfold system'; moreover, given the variability of the terminology, it is suggestive to think of the acronym PaRDeS as an innovative and 'programmatic' pun—'a late thirteenth century battle-cry in favour of the validity of kabbalistic exegesis' (van der Heide 1983: 148, 153–4).

It is thus best not to get stuck on the fourfold system, and to remember that different schemata could be used by different interpreters depending on their interests and emphasis (for example, Ibn Ezra mentions five methods of exegesis and rejects three out of hand; and such commentators as Joseph ibn Giqatilla, Abraham ibn Ezra, and Gersonides all use a threefold approach, but their terminology and concerns differ widely). A full catalogue and examination of the terminology of Jewish Bible interpretation is therefore a desideratum for future researchers. The boon of such work will extend to the history of Jewish religious ideas and attitudes, as one may already discern from an analysis of the word *peshat* and its relationship *sod* in the *Zohar* (Wolfson 1993). Other studies on the history and uses of the word PaRDesS in mystical circles provide a valuable angle on the history of religious ideas and the way levels of exegesis were part of a hierarchy of spiritual initiation (Idel 1995).

III. New Agendas and Possibilities for Research

The preceding discussions have focused on achievements already accomplished or that can or should be extended. There is no further need to repeat the importance of and need for ongoing publication of the many exegetical works still in manuscript; of doing critical analyses of persons and schools, both major and marginal, and detailing the techniques and thematics involved; and of extending the work of synthesis to broader cultural realms. In these concluding comments, I wish merely to mention several topics that await future study, and that are, in my opinion, matters of academic and cultural importance. I begin with some technical spheres and end with the history of ideas.

Three areas of investigation may be suggested for development. The first involves the lexicographical oeuvre of such scholars as R. Jonah ibn Janaḥ and R. David Kimḥi, and the need to comb through this material for its exegetical insights into the *peshat* of certain passages as well as for matters of style and hints of emendation or exegetical substitution found there (typically camouflaged under such phrases as '*x* is like *y*'). This material is a virtually untapped well of insights.

A second area of promising study would involve the study of compilatory commentaries. S. Poznanski already observed this phenomenon (calling them *yalqutim*, or 'anthologies') in a discussion of the anonymous commentaries on the Books of Esther, Lamentations, and Ruth (Poznanski 1913: p. lxxxix); but his opinion was not favourable and the topic has languished. Recent re-evaluation of the commentary of R. Joseph Kara on the Book of Job opens the question anew and shows very positive possibilities for research (Japhet 1993).

Finally, a call must be made to develop the area of super-commentaries. These works need to be culled, compared, and analysed. Numerous works await discovery. A case in point is the work of Abraham ibn Ezra, whose lexical notes and 'secrets' have intrigued many interpreters in the Middle Ages, who were scholars and commentators in their own right (like R. Joseph ibn Caspi). Some of these studies have benefited from fine critical editions, like the important work by R. Joseph ben Eliezer (Tov Elem), *Tzafenat Paʿneah* (ed. Herzog, 1911 and 1930; in 2 vols.); but a vast amount still awaits scholarly treatment, as one can observe simply by the bibliographical listing found in R. Judah ibn Mosconi's introduction to *'Even ha-ʿEzer*. In this regard, it would also repay examining many of the comments of David Kimḥi on selected passages (like Gen. 1: 1–3) or entire books (like Psalms), for the light they shed on the opinions of Ibn Ezra. Similarly, a close study of Nahmanides' evaluations of the opinions of Rashi and Ibn Ezra, and their contrastive presentation, would very much widen the scope of such future work on super-commentaries (Septimus 1983).

At the broader level of themes and ideas it is time to begin to anticipate a work on the 'Jewish Study of the Bible in the Middle Ages' (and even beyond, including a systematic study of such 'quasi-medievals' as R. Elijah ben Solomon, the Gaon of Vilna (eighteenth century), and the neglected work of R. Meir Leibush 'Malbim' (nineteenth century). Such a work would need to develop a morphology of the types of exegesis; consider sources and influences; and expand tools for comparative analysis of Christian commentaries on a wide scale. In this vein, one would need to rethink the whole question of comparison within Jewish exegetical literature (both diachronic and synchronic) and between it and other cultures. One may hope that this will contribute to an understanding and appreciation of the Jewish exegetical imagination, and take its place in a future morphology of exegesis considered from a typological and history of religions perspective. Both projects may be beyond the scope of individual scholars and require the collaboration and support of research institutes. They will certainly bring the study of Bible interpretation into wider intellectual arenas and expand its theoretical horizons.

In all these ways, the next generation of scholars will contribute to the relationship of the history of interpretation to the history of thought and religion. The text-centred nature of Jewish thought will be considered, as well as the interrelationship between the expression of ideas and the constraints of exegesis. Such research would proceed in obvious ways, by considering the place of biblical exegesis in classical rabbinic thought, and expand to almost untapped areas like Bible interpretation in the *Zohar*. But other intriguing areas of intellectual creativity based on the Bible and its exegetical applications could include such topics as medieval Hebrew poetry (and such poets as R. Solomon ibn Gabirol, R. Judah Halevi, and R. Moses ibn Ezra); ethical and philosophical literature (as, for example, the role of the Bible and its interpretation in Baḥya ibn Pakuda's *The Duties of the Heart*); polemical tracts (as in the influential *Sefer Nitzaḥon Yashan*); and legal compendia (as in the fairly exclusive use of Scripture for exegetical proof and authority in Maimonides' *Mishneh Torah*).

The role of scholarship is to clarify the various distinct levels and uses and modes of Bible interpretation, so that the organic but stratified dimensions of Judaism as a text-culture may best be appreciated. The task of the academy is to do this without apologetics and with a clear and discerning eye. There can be no rush to generalizations and no reliance on the received or regnant canons of preferred authors or topics. Properly done, the study of Jewish Bible interpretation will help establish the layers of the Jewish imagination and culture, in their historical developments and in their abiding continuities. The benefits of this labour will not accrue to scholarship alone, but will extend beyond the academy to the culture at large. It is my view that scholarship as a whole must see its task as part of a larger cultural pedagogy, and that Jewish studies in particular must take up this responsibility.

Suggested Reading

There is at present no basic introduction to Jewish Bible interpretation in English. For this one may substitute several studies on terms and topics, and well as surveys of trends and authors. Recommended in the category of terms and topics are the essays by Greenberg (1987), Fishbane (1987), and Rawidowicz (1974). Helpful and instructive surveys can be found in Bacher (1903) and the *Encyclopedia Judaica*, Vol. 4 (1971): 889–915. See also the essay by Rosenthal (1969).

Bibliography

Bacher, W. 1891. 'L'Exégèse biblique dans le Zohar.' *Revue Des Études Juives* 22: 33–46, 219–29.

—— 1903. 'Bible Exegesis.' In *The Jewish Encyclopedia*. iii. 162–74.

Banitt, M. 1966. 'Les Poterim.' *Revue Des Études Juives* 125: 21–33.

—— 2000. 'The French Glosses in the Commentary [of Rashbam] to Job.' [Hebrew]. In Japhet (2000): chap. 6.

Ben-Shammai, H. 1976. 'Recensions and Versions of Yefet ben 'Eli's Commentary on the Bible.' [Hebrew]. *Alei Sefer* 2: 17–32.

—— 1992. 'The Karaite Controversy: Scripture and Tradition in Early Karaism.' In *Religionsgespräche im Mittelalter*. 11–26. B. Lewis and F. Niewöhner eds. Wiesbaden.

—— 1993. 'Return to the Scriptures in Ancient and Medieval Jewish Sectarianism and in Early Islam.' In *Les Retours aux écritures: fondamentalismes présent et passes*. 319–39. E. Patlagean and A. Le Boulluec. Louvain and Paris.

Breuer, E. 1996. *The Limits of Enlightenment: Jew Germans, and the Eighteenth-Century Study of Scripture*. Cambridge Mass. and London.

Buber, M. and Rosezweig, F. 1994. *Scripture and Translation*. Trans. L. Rosenwald. Bloomington and Indianapolis. German edn.: *Die Schrift und ihre Verdeutschung*. 1936

Cohen, J. 1989. *'Be Fertile and Increase, Fill the Earth and Master It': The Ancient and Medieval Career of a Biblical Text*. Ithaca, NY and London.

Dahan, G. 1989. 'Juifs et Chrétiens en Occident Médiéval. La Rencontre autour de la Bible (XII⁰–XIV⁰ Siècles', *Revue de Sythese* 110: 3–31.

—— 1990. *Les Intellectuels Chrétiens et les Juifs au Moyen Âge*. Paris.

Daube, D. 1949. 'Rabbinic Methods of Interpretation in Hellenistic Rhetoric.' *Hebrew Union College Annual* 22: 239–64.

Davidson, I. 1915. *Saadia's Polemic Against Hiwi al-Balkhi*. New York.

Elman, Y. 1993. ' "It is No Empty Thing": Nahmanides and the Search For Omnisignificance.' *Torah U-Madda Journal* 4: 1–83.

Fishbane, M. 1985. *Biblical Interpretation in Ancient Israel*. Oxford.

—— 1987. 'Hermeneutics.' In *Contemporary Jewish Religious Thought*. 353–61. A. A. Cohen and P. Mendes-Flohr eds. New York.

—— 1989. *The Garments of Torah: Essays in Biblical Hermeneutics*. Bloomington and Indianapolis.

FISHBANE, M. 1998. *The Exegetical Imagination: On Jewish Thought and Theology* Cambridge Mass. and London.

FRANK, D. 1995. 'The *Shoshanim* of Tenth-Century Jerusalem: Karaite Exegesis, Prayer, and Communal Identity.' In *The Jews of Medieval Islam: Community, Society, and Identity.* 199–245. D. Frank ed. Leiden.

FUNKENSTEIN, A. 1993. *Perceptions of Jewish History.* Berkeley.

GELLES, B. J. 1981. *Peshat and Derash in the Exegesis of Rashi.* Leiden.

GOSHEN-GOTTSTEIN, M. 1992. *R. Judah ibn Bala'm's Commentary on Isaiah.* M. Goshen-Gottstein ed., with the assistance of M. Perez. Ramat-Gan.

GRABOIS, A. 1975. 'The Hebraica Veritas and Jewish–Christian Intellectual Relations in the Twelfth Century.' *Speculum* 50: 613–34.

GREENBERG, M. 1987. 'Exegesis.' In *Contemporary Jewish Religious Thought.* A. A. Cohen and P. Mendes-Flohr. New York.

GROSSMAN, A. 1986. 'The Jewish–Christian Polemic and Jewish Bible Commentary in the Twelfth-Century.' [Hebrew.] *Zion* 51: 29–60.

HAILPERIN, H. 1963. *Rashi and the Christian Scholars.* Pittsburgh.

HARRIS, R. 1997. 'The Literary Hermeneutic of Rabbi Eliezer of Beaugency.' Unpublished Ph.D diss. Jewish Theological Seminary of America.

HERTZ, JOSEPH H. 1929–36. *The Pentateuch and Haftorahs.* 5 vols. J. H. Hertz ed. London and New York. 1 vol. edn. London 1938.

IDEL, M. 1986. 'Infinities of Torah in Kabbalah.' In *Midrash and Literature.* 141–57. G. Hartman and S. Budick eds. New Haven and London.

—— 1995. 'PaRDeS: Some Reflections on Kabbalistic Hermeneutics.' In *Death, Ecstasy, and Other Worldly Journeys.* 249–68. J. J. Collins and M. Fishbane eds. Albany, NY.

ITZCHAKY, E. 1982. 'The Halakha in Targum Yerushalmi I (Pseudo-Jonathan) and its Exegetic Methods.' [Hebrew]. Unpublished Ph.D. diss., Bar-Ilan University.

JAPHET, S. 1985. *The Commentary of R. Samuel ben Meir Rashbam on Qoheleth.* S. Japhet and R. Salters eds. and trans. Jerusalem and Leiden.

—— 1993. 'The Nature and Distribution of the Compilatory Commentaries in the Light of Rabbi Josoph Kara's Commentary on the Book of Job.' In *The Midrashic Imagination. Jewish Exegesis, Thought, and History.* 98–130. M. Fishbane ed. Albany, NY.

—— 2000. *The Commentary of Rabbi Samuel Ben Meir (Rashbam) on the Book of Job* [Hebrew]. Jerusalem.

KAMIN, S. 1980. 'Rashi's Exegetical Categorization with Respect to the Distinction Between Peshat and Derash.' *Immanuel* 11: 16–32.

—— 1986. *Rashi's Exegetica Categorization* [Hebrew]. Jerusalem.

—— 1991. *Jews and Christians Interpret the Bible* [Hebrew and English]. Jerusalem.

KANARFOGEL, E. 1993. 'On the Role of Bible Study in Medieval Ashkenaz.' In *The Frank Talmage Memorial Volume.* i. 151–66. B. Wallfish ed. Haifa.

KASHER, M. 1927–95. *Torah Shelemah* [Hebrew]. 44 vols. Jerusalem.

LAWEE, E. 1995. 'On the Threshold of the Renaissance: New Methods and Sensibilities in the Biblical Commentaries of Isaac Abarbanel.' *Viator* 26: 283–319.

LIEBERMAN, S. 1962. *Hellenism in Jewish Palestine.* New York.

LOCKSHIN, M. I. 1980. *R. Samuel ben Meir's commentary on Genesis: An Annotated Translation.* Lewiston.

LOEWE, R. 1964. 'The "Plain" Meaning of Scripture in Early Jewish Exegesis.' *Papers of the Institute of Jewish Studies* 1: 140–86.

Marcus, I. G. 1989. 'Exegesis for the Few and for the Many: Judah He-Hasid's Biblical Commentaries.' *Jerusalem Studies in Jewish Thought* 8: 1*–24*

Melammed, E.-Z. 1975/1978. *Bible Commentators* [Hebrew]. 2 vols. Jerusalem.

Paul, A. 1969. *Écrits de Qumran et sects juives aux premiers siècles de l'Islam: recherches sur l'origine du Qaraisme*. Paris.

Poznanski, A. 1904. *Shiloh, ein Beitrag zur Geschichte der Messiaslehre*. Leipzig.

Poznanski, S. 1908. *The Karaite Literary Opponents of Saadiah Gaon*. London.

——1913. *Kommentar zu Ezechiel und den XII kleinen Propheten von Eliezer aus Beaugency… und mit einer Abhandlung über die nordfranzösischen Bibelexegeten eingeleitet*. Warsaw. [Introduction in Hebrew].

——ed. 1924. *The Arabic Commentary of Ibn Bal'am on the Twelve Minor Prophets*. Philadelphia.

Rawidowicz, S. 1974. 'On Interpretation.' In *Studies in Jewish Thought*. 45–80. N. N. Glatzer ed. Philadelphia.

Rosenthal, E. I. J. 1969. 'The Study of the Bible in the Middle Ages.' In *The Cambridge History of the Bible*. ii. 252–79. G. W. H. Lampe ed. Cambridge.

Septimus, B. 1983 '"Open Rebuke and Concealed Love": Naḥmanides and the Andalusian Tradition'. In *Rabbi Moses Nahmanides (Ramban): Explorations in His Religious and Literary Virtuosity*. 11–34. I. Twersky ed. Cambridge, Mass.

Simon, U. 1965. 'The Exegetic Method of Abraham ibn Ezra, as Revealed in Three Interpretations of a Biblical Passage.' [Hebrew]. *Bar-Ilan Annual* 3: 92–138.

——1985. 'Ibn Ezra Between Medievalism and Modernism: The Case of Isaiah XL–LXVI.' *Supplements to Vetus Testamentum* 36: 257–71.

——1991. *Four Approaches to the Book of Psalms: From Saadia Gaon to Abraham ibn Ezra*. Albany, NY. (Hebrew original 1982).

Smalley, B. 1941. *The Study of the Bible in the Middle Ages*. Oxford. Revised edn. Oxford 1952.

Sorkin, D. 1996. *Moses Mendelssohn and the Religious Enlightenment*. Berkeley.

Steiner, R. C. 1992. 'Meaninglessness, Meaningfulness, and Super-Meaningfulness in Scripture: An Analysis of the Controversy Surrounding Dan 2:12 in the Middle Ages.' *JQR* 82: 431–49.

——1998. 'Saadia vs. Rashi: On the Shift from Meaning-Maximalism to Meaning-Minimalism in Medieval Biblical Lexicography.' *JQR* 88: 213–58.

Strauss, L. 1965. *Spinoza's Critique of Religion*. Trans. of German version [1928] with new Preface. New York.

——1997. *Jewish Philosophy and the Crisis of Modernity: Essays and Lectures in Modern Jewish Thought*. K. H. Green ed. Albany, NY.

Talmage, F. 1975. *David Kimhi: The Man and the Commentaries*. Cambridge Mass. and London.

——1986. 'Apples of Gold: The Inner Meaning of Sacred Texts in Medieval Judaism.' In *Jewish Spirituality. From the Bible to the Middle Ages*. 313–55. A. Green ed. New York.

——1990. *The Commentaries on Proverbs of the Kimhi Family* [Hebrew]. F. Talmage ed. Jerusalem.

Touitou, E. 1982. 'The Exegetical Method of Rashbam Against the Background of the Historical Reality of his Age.' [Hebrew]. In *E.-Z. Melammed Jubilee Volume*. 48–74. Ramat-Gan.

——1984. 'La Renaissance du 12e siècle et l'exégèse biblique de Rashbam.' *Archives Juives* 24: 3–12.

VAN DER HEIDE, A. 1983. 'PARDES: Methodological reflections on the theory of the Four Senses.' *JJS* 24: 147–58.

WALLFISH, B. 1993. *Esther in Medieval Garb: Jewish Interpretations of the Book of Esther in the Middle Ages*. Albany, NY.

WIEDER, N. 1962. *The Judean Scrolls and Karaism*. London.

WOLFSON, E. 1987. 'Circumcision, Vision of God, and Textual Interpretation: From Midrashic Trope to Mystical Symbol.' *History of Religions* 27: 189–215.

—— 1989. 'By Way of Truth: Aspects of Nahmanides' Kabbalistic Hermeneutic.' *Association for Jewish Studies Review* 14: 103–78.

—— 1993. 'Beautiful Maiden Without Eyes: *Peshat* and *Sod* in Zoharic Hermeneutics.' In *The Midrashic Imagination. Jewish Exegesis, Thought, and History*. 155–203. M. Fishbane ed. Albany, NY.

ZUCKER, M. 1959. *Rav Saadya Gaon's Translation of the Torah* [Hebrew]. New York.

—— 1984, *Saadya's Commentary on Genesis* [Hebrew]. Edited with introduction, translation, and notes by M. Zucker. New York.

CHAPTER 28

MYSTICISM

PHILIP S. ALEXANDER

THE SCHOLEMIAN PARADIGM

FEW fields, if any, in the study of Judaism have been dominated by one man as Gershom Scholem (1897–1982) has dominated mysticism. Scholem's debt to his nineteenth- and early twentieth-century predecessors should not be minimized, but there can be no dispute that before his time mysticism was ill-defined, marginalized, and even vilified within the historiography of Judaism. In a life of unremitting scholarship, Scholem not only brought to light large quantities of new evidence relating to individual mystics and movements (the harvest of tireless searching for unpublished manuscripts), but more importantly he mapped the field as a whole: he articulated for the first time Jewish mysticism as a discipline, defining its limits, its methodology, its place within the history of Judaism, and its relation to other academic fields. His work attracted many talented younger researchers, some of whom he trained himself, and who have formed an influential school. The fact that Jewish mysticism today is one of the liveliest areas of Jewish studies is largely to his credit (Dan 1987).

For present purposes the most important item in Scholem's massive œuvre is his *Major Trends in Jewish Mysticism* (Scholem 1946). This contains an expanded text of lectures which he gave in 1938 at the Jewish Institute of Religion, New York. Two editions were published, one in 1941 and a somewhat revised version in 1946. *Major Trends* offers an overview of Jewish mysticism from its beginnings in the early Talmudic period down to modern times. Scholem presents a *genealogy* of Jewish mysticism. He demonstrates the existence of an evolving *tradition*, unified by the constant reinterpretation of 'canonic' texts (such as the *Heikhalot* literature and *Sefer Yetzirah*), and the reiteration of key theosophical concepts, myths, and symbols (which he tends to label as 'Gnostic'). One stage, he argues, emerges from the other in a dynamic evolutionary process, which constitutes a vital strand in the history of Judaism. Scholem published *Major Trends* in mid-career: it summarized some twenty years of his own research, and it established the framework within which he carried out his later work: he was never again to attempt such a high-level survey of the whole subject (though see Scholem 1974). *Major Trends* created the Scholemian paradigm from which all subsequent research in the field has started. There are signs that this paradigm is crumbling, but it remains dominant and must form the basis of the present essay. The essay falls into two parts. First, following broadly *Major Trends*, it surveys briefly the detailed phases in the history of Jewish mysticism, noting specific areas where Scholem's views have been supplemented, corrected, or contested. Second, it considers overarching questions regarding the tradition as a whole (the limits and the nature of Jewish mysticism, methodology, and mysticism's place in Judaism), which Scholem's work provokes, in order to assess the extent to which Scholem's paradigm still holds, and to get some idea of where the subject may be going.

THE GENEALOGY OF JEWISH MYSTICISM

Heikhalot Mysticism

According to Scholem, the first phase in the development of Jewish mysticism begins in the early Talmudic period with what he calls Merkavah Mysticism. This mysticism is expounded in treatises such as *Heikhalot Rabbati*, *Heikhalot Zutarti*, and *Sefer Heikhalot*, also known as *3 Enoch* (Alexander 1983), which record visions of the heavenly world based loosely on Ezekiel's vision of God's Throne-Chariot, the Merkavah (Ezekiel 1), and other prophetic theophanies in the Hebrew Bible (e.g. Isaiah 6 and Daniel 7). The texts, for the most part in Hebrew, are marked by highly distinctive ideas, style, and vocabulary. In particular they depict God's heavenly throne (the *Kisse' ha-Kavod*) as located in the innermost of seven concentric palaces or temples (*Heikhalot*), whose doors are guarded by fearsome angels. The adept can only get past these angelic gatekeepers, and enter the throne-room to see God's glory and join in the celestial *Qedushah*, if he knows the correct passwords, consisting of mystical names of God. Scholem argued that this literature emanated from conventicles of practising mystics, known as *Yoredei Merkavah*, 'Descenders to the Chariot'

(Kuyt 1995), who flourished within rabbinic society in the Talmudic period, and whose teachings and practices were alluded to and pronounced dangerous in Babylonian Talmud Hagigah 11b–16a.

Though known in the nineteenth and early twentieth centuries, this literature had not been much studied. Most scholars tended to follow Heinrich Graetz (Graetz 1859) and date it to the Gaonic period. Scholem in *Major Trends* pushed it back into Talmudic times and linked it with Gnosticism. In a subsequent study, *Jewish Gnosticism, Merkabah Mysticism and Talmudic Tradition* (Scholem 1965), he defended this thesis in depth, arguing that elements of the *Heikhalot* texts can be dated as early as the second century CE, and that the conceptual and terminological parallels with contemporary Gnosticism were strong enough to warrant classifying *Heikhalot* mysticism as a Jewish form of Gnosticism.

Since *Major Trends*, *Heikhalot* literature has been one of the most flourishing areas in the study of Jewish mysticism (see e.g. Schäfer 1988 and 1992; Morray-Jones 2002), and all aspects of Scholem's account have been subjected to close scrutiny and criticism. It has been argued that Scholem misconstrued the literary character of the *Heikhalot* texts, tending to assume that the various treatises were clearly defined literary entities which could be dated to a particular time and place, and brought into literary relationship with each other. In actual fact, their redactional identity is weak, and their form and content varies greatly from manuscript to manuscript. The amorphous and chaotic character of the great *Heikhalot* manuscripts makes writing a history of the *Heikhalot* movement more difficult than he supposed (Schäfer 1987). Scholem may also have underestimated the extent to which the *Heikhalot* texts were modified by copyists in the Middle Ages. He rather assumed that the manuscripts accurately preserve material from Late Antiquity. However, the texts exist only in medieval copies made by scribes who were intensely interested in their content and who may have substantially edited them.

Scholem's view of the relationship between the *Heikhalot* literature and the Talmud has also been challenged. He believed that the *Heikhalot* texts contain a reasonably reliable account of esoteric teachings alluded to in classic rabbinic literature (especially Bavli Hagigah 11b–16a) under the title of the Account of the Chariot (*Ma'aseh Merkavah*). If this is correct, then it supports a dating of the material to the Talmudic era. However, some have argued that the relationship between the *Heikhalot* literature and the Talmud is essentially midrashic: *Heikhalot* is trying to fill out and make sense of the cryptic allusions in the Talmud to *Ma'aseh Merkavah*. If this is the case, then it implies that the bulk of the *Heikhalot* texts are post-Talmudic (Urbach 1967; Halperin 1980).

Though some had maintained that the *Heikhalot* texts are essentially literary fantasy, Scholem was convinced that they reflected genuine mystical praxis and originated in conventicles of practising mystics. Most recent scholarship agrees with him on this point: there is simply too much apparently genuine magic and theurgy to explain everything in terms of literary artifice (Lesses 1998). However, there is an issue as to whether or not Scholem somewhat overstressed ascent to heaven as the core of the praxis. The *Heikhalot* texts do talk about ascents, as in the Great Séance passage in *Heikhalot Rabbati* (Wolfson 1994: 74–124), but they also describe (as Scholem acknowledged) an alternative praxis which involves conjuring an archangel such as the *Sar Torah* (Prince of Torah) down to earth to reveal secrets. How the *Sar Torah* traditions (which are less easy to read as 'mystical') fit in with the ascent traditions remains a matter of dispute (Schäfer 1992; Swartz 1996).

Scholem reacted strongly against Graetz's view that *Heikhalot* mysticism was something alien to rabbinic Judaism—an import from outside. He pointed out that, although the Talmud expresses reservations about the teachings of the *Yoredei Merkavah*, the *Heikhalot* mystics themselves were keen to parade their rabbinic credentials. *Heikhalot* mysticism, he maintained, was located at the heart of rabbinic society, and was fundamentally a rabbinic phenomenon. This was consistent with his general view of the nature of Judaism as a complex, dynamic tradition in which mysticism plays a central role. However, scholars who see rabbinic Judaism as defined essentially by the halachic standpoint of the Mishnah have remained unconvinced that *Heikhalot* mysticism is anything other than a marginal, problematic, paradoxical movement.

No aspect of Scholem's account of *Heikhalot* mysticism has provoked more fierce debate than his claim that it can be classified as Jewish Gnosticism. Scholem was inclined to characterize Jewish mysticism as a whole as 'Gnostic' in character, and it strengthened his views about the centrality of mysticism within Judaism if he could show that mediaeval Jewish 'Gnosticism' did not originate in the Middle Ages, but had roots in Talmudic-period Jewish 'Gnosticism' in the Middle East. But the term 'Gnosticism' is problematic: scholars have failed to reach much agreement on its definition, and some would argue that it should be abandoned altogether. Moreover, *Heikhalot* mysticism lacks some of the major characteristics of the so-called Gnostic systems, notably a radical dualism which opposes an unknown good God dwelling in the pleroma to an evil demiurge who rules over the world of matter (Deutsch 1995). There is considerable force in these objections, yet the designation of *Heikhalot* mysticism as Jewish Gnosticism retains a useful purpose. It helps to contextualize it. The numerous parallels in language, structure, ideas, and praxis between the *Heikhalot* texts and Gnostic literature indisputably place these close together on the religious spectrum of Late Antiquity (Alexander 1984 and 1999).

The *Sefer Yetzirah*

The *Heikhalot* literature, as we noted, belongs to a type of esoteric inquiry which the Talmudic authorities dubbed *Ma'aseh Merkavah*. But there was another topic, which they also deemed dangerous and unfit for public discussion, concerned with the opening chapters of Genesis and known as *Maʿaseh Bereʾshit* (the Account of Creation). One work dealing with this subject, the *Book of Creation* (*Sefer Yetzirah*), was to have an enormous impact on the development of Jewish mysticism. Scholem fully recognized *Sefer Yetzirah's* importance, but devoted only a few impressionistic pages to it in *Major Trends*.

Almost everything about this little text is problematic, but it was precisely its obscurities which gave it such potential. In highly charged, inventive Hebrew it describes the origin and structure of the cosmos. It offers two systems of cosmology, one based on the ten primordial numbers, which it calls *Sefirot*, the other based on the twenty-two letters of the Hebrew alphabet. The former inspired the medieval mystical cosmogonies, the latter lies behind much medieval mystical praxis which involves manipulating the letters of the Hebrew alphabet. The work is usually thought to have been written in Palestine in the third or fourth century CE, but it could be dated to almost any century between the second and the seventh. It survives in different recensions, and there is little agreement as to its original form. But above all, its genre is unclear. Though the medieval mystics believed it contained deep, mystical doctrine, it is unlikely that its author intended it as a mystical tract. On the face of it, it is a work of science—an attempt to explain in rational terms the structure of reality. It offers a kind of atomic theory: the vast complexity of the world is seen as the expression of different combinations of twenty-two fundamental elements, symbolized by the letters of the Hebrew alphabet. Just as we can make an infinite variety of words and sentences out of the basic sounds of speech, so God made the world by combining in different ways a small number of basic elements. Certainly the earliest commentators on the work (e.g. Saadya, Shabbatai Donnolo, Judah ha-Levi, Judah ben Barzilai of Barcelona) took it basically in a rational, philosophical way. It was not until the late twelfth century that it began to be read as a mystical text in the circles of the Hasidei Ashkenaz and among the theosophists of southern France and Spain (Dan 1993a; 1999: 36–45).

Besides its profundity and obscurity, there were a number of other features of the text which favoured such a reading. First, it hints at some relationship between its teachings and *Maʿaseh Merkavah*: the primordial numbers seem to be identified with the Holy Creatures (the *Hayyot*) of Ezekiel's vision (Hayman 1987). Second, at the end it implies that study of its lore will lead to enlightenment and closeness to God. And third, its theory of the twenty-two letters has obvious practical implications. If there is indeed some profound resonance between the sounds of the Hebrew alphabet and the structure of reality, then humans by manipulating those sounds can affect the cosmos. Indeed, the heady possibility is opened up that, like God, they can create. Later Jewish magic was to claim that the *Sefer Yetzirah* contained the secret of the supreme act of *imitatio dei*, the creation of a *golem* (a homunculus or android: see Idel 1991; Schäfer 1995). In the *Sefer Yetzirah's* theory of language the interests of 'science', 'magic', and 'mysticism' converge. The *Sefer Yetzirah* and the *Heikhalot* literature are the foundation documents of the Jewish mystical tradition. They, and possibly other esoteric texts written in the Middle East in Late Antiquity, were transmitted westwards, by channels which still remain largely hidden, to Italy, the Rhineland, Southern France, and Spain, where they formed the platform on which the vast edifice of medieval Jewish mysticism was raised.

The Hasidei Ashkenaz

The inclusion of a chapter in *Major Trends* on the Pious of Germany (the *Hasidei Ashkenaz*) was not the least of the many innovations of the work. Prior to Scholem medieval German-Jewish Hasidism had attracted little attention in general, and still less in the context of the history of Jewish mysticism: Jewish mysticism meant *par excellence* the *Zohar* and the Spanish Kabbalah. Ashkenazi Hasidism flourished for only a short time (1170–1240) in the Rhineland communities of Mainz, Speyer, and Worms. It drew its leadership from the remarkable Qalonymus family: Rabbi Samuel ben Qalonymus, 'Hasid, Saint, and Prophet', his son Rabbi Judah the Pious (d. 1217), and his cousin and disciple Rabbi Eleazar ben Judah of Worms (d. *c*.1230). Its major literary monument was the rambling *Sefer Hasidim*, which Scholem described as 'an edition of the literary testaments of the three founders and in particular of the writings of Jehudah the Hasid' (Scholem 1946: 83). It is clear that Scholem is not over-impressed with the theosophical acumen of the Hasidei Ashkenaz: he notes their lack of metaphysical originality and doctrinal coherence. What he stresses as important is their ethical and spiritual teaching. The Hasidei Ashkenaz developed an elaborate doctrine of prayer involving a system of 'intentions' (*kavvanot*), which they believed would bring them into contact with the divine realm. They strove to attain a state of 'piety' (*hasidut*) which went beyond what was required by halachic norms. To this end they spurned the world and mortified the flesh through penitential acts (*sigufim*), and generally adopted a martyrological attitude towards life, being ready every day to 'sanctify the name of God'—a legacy, doubtless, of the trauma inflicted on the Rhineland Jewish communities by the massacres of the First Crusade.

After *Major Trends* Scholem paid comparatively little attention to the Hasidei Ashkenaz, possibly because theosophical mysticism dominated his thinking, and the Rhineland Hasidim were more theurgically inclined. However, the field which he opened up was worked by others (e.g. Dan 1968; Marcus 1981; Liss 1997; Abrams 1997). A number of issues emerged, some of which have still to be resolved. It now seems clear that what Scholem had regarded as a more or less unified movement was actually a collection of rather diverse schools and writers, who may not all have been aware of each other's thinking. The historically dominant group was the circle of Judah the Pious, but there were others. One of the most important of these was the

Unique Cherub Circle, so called because it used the term 'unique cherub' (*ha-keruv ha-meyuhad*) to designate the anthropomorphic manifestation of God. From quotations in the writings of Rabbi Elhanan ben Yaqar of London it is clear that the school was in existence in the early thirteenth century, and the surviving texts, all of which are anonymous or pseudepigraphic, suggest that its ideas must have evolved over a number of generations. In other words, it was contemporaneous with the circle of Judah the Pious. But although already in the thirteenth century its teachings were being attributed to Judah, it was independent of his school. We cannot be sure exactly where it was located. Northern France is just as plausible as the Rhineland proper (Dan 1999).

It is uncertain what social realities lie behind the literature of the Hasidei Ashkenaz. Passages in the *Sefer Hasidim* describe vibrant Hasidic communities, but the extent to which these actually existed is unclear. Most research assumes that the accounts are factual, but Dan has stressed their idealizing tendencies. Noting that there is no external corroboration of the existence of these communities, he argues that 'these sections of Sefer Hasidim should be regarded as imaginary; they reflect Rabbi Judah's social dream, which is preached using the literary device of answers to questions which were never asked, referring to situations which were never actual' (Dan 1993b: 99; cf. Marcus 1993). This is not to say that the teachings of Hasidei Ashkenaz would have had no social impact. They are elitist and demanding, presenting ideals which could not in practice have been attained by the majority of Jews. They had the potential to introduce conflict and schism. *Sefer Hasidim* adopts a sharply confrontational tone towards those who do not accept Rabbi Judah's demands, calling them 'wicked' and other such derogatory names.

The relationship of Ashkenazi Hasidism to its historical setting in the Rhineland remains a matter of dispute. Scholem was impressed by an essay by Yitzhaq Baer on 'The Religious-Social Tendency of the *Sefer Hasidim*', in which he argued that Rhineland Hasidism owed something to contemporary Christian, particularly Franciscan, spirituality (Baer 1938). Certainly there are aspects of its teachings, such as the mortification of the flesh, which are prima facie surprising in the context of Jewish spirituality. The hypothesis of Christian influence cannot be said to have been fully tested. However, more recent research (and indeed the later thinking of Baer himself) has tended to stress the continuities of Ashkenazi Hasidic ethics and spirituality with earlier Jewish tradition (e.g. Schäfer 1990).

Theosophical Kabbalah in Spain and Provence

The period 1150 to 1300 witnessed the emergence in Provence and Spain of a powerful theosophical mysticism in Judaism which culminated in the appearance of the mighty *Book of Splendour* (*Sefer ha-Zohar*). Scholem discusses the *Zohar* at length in *Major Trends*, but says almost nothing about the developments which led up to it, noting in his preface to the second edition that the beginnings of Kabbalism from 1150 to 1250 required a more thorough treatment than could be presented within the framework of general lectures. He was to devote a great deal of painstaking research to the diverse and difficult sources for the early Kabbalah, but in the end he felt he was able to introduce order into the chaos. His order was characteristically linear and genealogical (Scholem 1987).

The key was to be found in an enigmatic mystical midrash known as the *Book of Radiance* (*Sefer ha-Bahir*). Scholem typically stressed the 'Gnostic' character of this work. It is concerned with the divine world, which it designates in Hebrew *male'* or *melo'*, 'fullness' (a possible calque of the Greek *pleroma*) and which it characterizes in terms of ten *ma'amarot*, reminiscent in some respects of the Gnostic *aeons*. It develops the early rabbinic doctrine of the *Shekhinah* as a feminine aspect of the Godhead, and creates a powerful sexual mythology which again recalls myths about female divine figures (such as *Sophia*) in early Gnosticism. Significantly, it is this female aspect of the *pleroma* which is identified as the source of evil. Like early Gnosticism, the *Bahir* is intensely dualistic and carries back the origins of evil into the Godhead itself. The radicalism of the *Bahir* is perhaps most strikingly demonstrated in its advocacy of the transmigration of the soul (*gilgul ha-nefesh*)—a doctrine categorically rejected by earlier authorities such as Saadya. The *Bahir* is pseudepigraphically attributed to a great master of *Heikhalot* lore, Nehuniah ben ha-Qanah. Its real author, as well as its date and provenance, are unknown. Scholem argued that it was composed in Provence in the second half of the twelfth century and that it was the first book of the theosophical Kabbalah.

The *Bahir*, Scholem claimed, stimulated theosophical speculation in the rabbinic schools of Languedoc and Provence, evidence for which can be found in traditions attributed by later Kabbalists to the great Talmudist, the Ravad, Rabbi Abraham ben David of Posquières (1120–98), and above all in the writings of his son, Isaac the Blind. This speculation was then carried across the Pyrenees to Gerona, where it was further developed in a circle of Kabbalists to which Ezra ben Solomon, Azriel ben Menahem, and the great Nahmanides belonged. From Gerona Kabbalistic teaching spread northwards to Castile to the school of the Cohen brothers (Jacob and Isaac, and their student Moses of Burgos). The tradition reached a triumphant climax in Castile in the circle of the *Zohar*, whose two principle thinkers were Moses de Leon and Joseph Gikatilla. To one side of this primary line of evolution Scholem identified another school, the Circle of Contemplation (*Hug ha-'Iyyun*), named after its most indicative treatise, the *Book of Contemplation* (*Sefer ha-'Iyyun*). Though also concerned, like the other Kabbalists, with problems of theosophy and cosmogony, the *'Iyyun* Circle propounded a radically different mystical theology, which owes little to mainstream thought. Scholem attributed to it thirty-two little tracts (a corpus subsequently augmented by Mark Verman: see Verman 1992), all of them anonymous or pseudepigraphic. He suggested that the Circle of Contemplation flourished in Provence at the beginning of the thirteenth century.

The crowning glory of the theosophical Kabbalah was the *Zohar*, the importance of which Scholem signalled by devoting to it two whole chapters in *Major Trends*. This sprawling work, comprising some twenty separate treatises written largely in a stilted and artificial Aramaic, is implicitly attributed to the second-century CE Palestinian rabbinic authority Simeon bar Yohai and his disciples (Tishby 1989; Liebes 1993a; Giller 2001). In keeping with its obviously diverse literary character, some nineteenth-century scholars had assumed that the final work combined texts of very different date and origin. Scholem at first subscribed to this view, but after further painstaking study revised his opinion and argued incisively that almost all the component treatises of the *Zohar* had been written by one man, Moses de Leon, in the closing decades of the thirteenth century. The two major exceptions, the *Ra'aya Meheimna* and the *Tiqqunei ha-Zohar*, had been composed by one of Moses de Leon's disciples shortly after the completion of the main text. The *Zohar*, the most influential work in the history of Jewish mysticism, displays astonishing inventiveness and literary power (Wineman 1998). It attempts, like no other Kabbalistic writing, to anchor its teachings about the *Ein Sof* (the hidden God) and the *Sefirot* (the emanated divine attributes) in Scripture. Indeed, it takes the biblical narratives as one huge symbolic description of the upper world: the text of the Scripture is one long mystical name of God. The *Zohar*'s maturity can only be explained by placing it at the end of a period of intense development stretching back 150 years to the *Bahir*, whose name it seems to echo. It everywhere presupposes a system, but nowhere comprehensively expounds it. It did not need to: its readers already had the key in the speculations of the earlier Kabbalists of Spain and Provence. The *Zohar* offered the first totally comprehensive mystical theology of Judaism. Its influence was enormous, and it provided the starting-point for future developments.

Scholem's account of the theosophical Kabbalah is a *tour de force*, but further research has uncovered problems. A consensus is emerging that he may have strung out the tradition in too linear and genealogical a fashion (Dan 1987: 186–7). In fact the different schools may have been more contemporaneous and overlapping with each other, and a more dynamic, interactive, less evolutionary model may better explain their relationship. The dating of the *Bahir*, the linchpin of Scholem's account, remains disputed. Parallels with the writings of Maimonides, which Scholem tended to dismiss, suggest that it may have been composed considerably later than the late twelfth century, and the absence of *clear* echoes of its language and ideas in the early south French Kabbalists throws some doubt on his location of it in that region (Verman 1992: 167). The Circle of Contemplation has been reinvestigated by Verman, and he has concluded that it belongs to Spain and not France (Verman 1992; 1993). This relocation has considerable implications, because it suggests that this school of mystics was operating at the same time as the 'mainstream' schools in precisely the same region, but with little or no regard to them. Scholem had tried to solve the problem of the ʿIyyun Circle by placing it in southern France early on in the history of theosophic Kabbalah, before, arguably, the mainstream tradition had become dominant. Verman's provenance and dating, however, are more compatible with a picture of contemporaneous mystical circles developing their ideas, sometimes in agreement, sometimes in opposition, and sometimes in ignorance of each other.

Graetz had argued that the upsurge of Kabbalah in the thirteenth century marked a recrudescence within Judaism of pagan, polytheistic elements in reaction to the pure monotheism taught by philosophers such as Maimonides (Dan 1987: 147–8). Scholem here, as elsewhere, strongly rejected Graetz's view, which he saw as perpetrating a grave injustice against the Kabbalah. There could be no dispute that Kabbalah was in some sense a response to philosophy. Leading Kabbalists such as Nahmanides took the anti-Maimonidean side during the Maimonidean controversy, and Scholem himself freely acknowledged the use of philosophical ideas by the *Bahir* and other writings of theosophical mysticism. But to reduce the Kabbalah to an anti-rationalist reaction to philosophy he considered a gross travesty of the facts. The mystical tradition had an integrity of its own. The Kabbalah in Provence and Spain went back to ancient Jewish sources. Here the *Bahir* was again of pivotal importance to his case.

Though he held that this work, as we now have it, was composed in the late twelfth century, he believed, following certain medieval traditions, that behind it stood an ancient Jewish Gnostic work, which had been transmitted from the east through the circles of the Hasidei Ashkenaz to southern France, thus neatly linking into his 'genealogy' of Jewish mysticism both Rhineland Hasidism and ancient Jewish Gnosticism. Scholem pointed to similarities between sections of the *Bahir* and an eastern Jewish mystical treatise dating possibly to the Gaonic period known as *Raza Rabba* (*The Great Secret*), which is quoted in thirteenth-century Rhineland Hasidic texts. But the alleged early eastern origins of the *Bahir* remain a subject of dispute. There was a possible alternative source for the outburst of 'Gnostic' speculation in the Jewish communities of southern France, viz., contemporary Catharism which was flourishing in the same region at exactly the same time. Scholem looked into possible Cathar links but was unimpressed. As with philosophy, so with Catharism, he was reluctant to tie theosophic Kabbalah too closely to contemporary conditions, and thus run the risk of diminishing its Jewish authenticity. The last word has been certainly not yet been said on this issue.

Ecstatic Kabbalah: Abraham Abulafia

Abraham Abulafia (1240–*c*.1291), though their contemporary and fellow-country-man, expounded a type of mysticism, commonly known as 'prophetic' or 'ecstatic' Kabbalah, which was very different from that of the Spanish theosophists (Scholem 1946: 119–55). Abulafia stressed the importance of certain practices and techniques (such as combination and permutation of the letters of the Hebrew alphabet, particularly of the names of God), through which he believed union with the Divine (identified as the Active Intellect of the philosophers) could be achieved. The enlightened state of consciousness which these techniques and practices induced he called 'prophecy'. To attain to prophecy was not only to gain illumination but personal redemption as well, and to enjoy in the present the experience of the world to come. Abulafia knew the doctrines of the Spanish theosophists, but he emphatic-ally rejected 'the way of the *Sefirot*'. The antipathy was mutual, and it was probably the opposition of the theosophists that drove him from Spain, never to return, in 1273. He wandered around the Mediterranean studying, writing, and teaching, a peripatetic existence that helped spread his ideas. The sources of Abulafia's thought were also somewhat different from those of the theosophists. Like them, he drew on the *Sefer Yetzirah*, but he stressed its practical rather than its speculative, cosmo-gonic side. Maimonides' *Guide of the Perplexed* also influenced him, and he adopted and developed important aspects of the praxis of the Hasidei Ashkenaz. His mystical system can be characterized as an idiosyncratic but highly coherent and effective blend of elements drawn from Maimonidean philosophy and Rhineland Hasidism.

Moshe Idel has devoted a series of major studies to Abulafia which offer import-ant new insights into his work and his place in the history of Jewish mysticism (Idel 1988b, 1989, and 1993). He argues that Scholem, and even more his followers, have—whether wittingly or unwittingly—marginalized Abulafia. Earlier in his research into Jewish mysticism Scholem had shown a strong interest in Abulafia, and had included an important chapter on him in *Major Trends*. Later, however, he largely ignored him because, claims Idel, he defined Jewish mysticism increasingly restrict-ively in terms of mythology and theosophy. Idel contends that Abulafia influenced later Jewish mystics (e.g. Moses Cordovero and Hayyim Vital in sixteenth-century Safed) to a much greater degree than one would suppose from reading Scholem. The numerous manuscripts of his writings that survive attest to his popularity. In fact he classically represents a non-'Gnostic' strand that has been present in Jewish mysti-cism from the earliest times down to the present day.

Abulafia was a charismatic figure, and his mystical system is intimately bound up with his biography. In contrast to the anonymity of many major medieval Jewish mystical texts, Abulafia's personality intrudes strikingly into his writings. He be-lieved that he had been called to be the Messiah, but his concept of messianism was complex and to a degree contradictory. He did not reject the idea of an eschato-logical Messiah who would redeem Israel as a whole. He predicted that the Messiah would come in 1290 when he (Abulafia) was 50. His early search for the River Sambation was linked to the classic eschatological scenario, for legend had it that it was from beyond the Sambation that the lost Ten Tribes would be gathered in. His disastrous attempt in 1280 to meet the Pope, which almost cost him his life (Idel 1998: 97–100), implies that he envisaged for himself some sort of *political* messianic role. However, the overwhelming thrust of his writings is to emphasize the possibil-ity through his mystical praxis of achieving personal redemption here and now. His function as a teacher was messianic—to lead his followers to personal salvation. He thus plays the role of the classic Gnostic Redeemer. But each individual also has to become his own messiah. In a remarkable passage Abulafia identifies the Messiah not only with the eschatological deliverer but also with the human intellect and with the divine Active Intellect (ibid. 65–77). The human intellect is redeemed by union with the Active Intellect, a state it achieves through Abulafia's way of the Divine Names. But the human intellect in turn redeems the lower human spiritual faculties. This doctrine of personal, 'noetic' redemption involves a remarkable spiritualiza-tion of messianism, a kind of realized eschatology, which may have been picked up and developed in later Hasidic theology (see below). Its originality should not, however, be overestimated. Arguably, it amounts to little more than an idiosyncratic variation of the soteriology of Maimonides, who also believed that prophecy, which is achieved through union with the Active Intellect, constitutes the condition of personal salvation.

Jewish Sufism

One of the most surprising omissions from *Major Trends* is any treatment of Jewish Sufism. In the thirteenth and fourteenth centuries, more or less contemporary with Rhineland Hasidism and the emergence of the Spanish Qabbalah, there existed in Egypt a remarkable school of Jewish Sufis led by members of the family of Mai-monides. The central figures were Maimonides' son Abraham (1186–1237), grandson Obadiah, and David Maimonides (b. 1335). Abraham regarded the Muslim Sufis as the spiritual heirs of the Hebrew prophets, especially Elijah, and in his *Comprehen-sive Guide for the Servants of God* (*Kifayat al-ʿAbidin*) he advocated the adoption of their practices as a way of attaining perfection and union with God. Obadiah, in his *Treatise of the Pool* (*al-Maqala al-Hawdiyya*), and David Maimonides, in his *Guide to Detachment* (*al-Mursid ila t-Tafarrud*), further elaborated a Jewish version of the Sufi *via mystica*. Rosenblatt (1927–38), Rosenthal (1940), Vajda (1955), Goitein (1953–4, 1964, and 1967), and above all Fenton (1981a, 1981b, 1984, and 1987), have done sterling work in editing, translating, and interpreting this tradition, but it remains under-researched, particularly in the context of the history of Jewish mysticism.

It is hard to see any valid reasons for excluding it from consideration. The fact that the key texts are in Arabic may have deterred some scholars. There may also have been a feeling that Jewish Sufism was so heavily derivative, so unoriginal, as to be of little interest from the perspective of Jewish mysticism: it is better treated as a footnote to the history of Islamic mysticism. Egyptian Jewish Sufism, though to some extent following in the footsteps of significant Jewish writers such as Bahya ibn Paquda, whose *Direction to the Duties of the Heart* (*al-Hidaya ila Fara'id al-Qulub*) draws heavily on Sufi ideas, cannot easily be related to earlier Jewish tradition, or to the genealogy of Jewish mysticism set out in *Major Trends*. As we noted earlier, the phases of Jewish mysticism which Scholem traces evolve organically out of each other, and all can be traced back to the foundational documents, the *Heikhalot* texts and the *Sefer Yetzirah*. There is no evidence that this earlier tradition had any impact on Jewish Sufism. There may also be a sense that Jewish Sufism is so ethical or philosophical in content that it belongs more properly to the history of Jewish ethics or philosophy than to mysticism. But none of these arguments is fully persuasive. The Egyptian Jewish Sufis sociologically present a profile remarkably similar to that of the Hasidei Ashkenaz. They were a small, reformist group led by the spiritual and political elite of the local Jewish community, which seems to have retained some sort of identity through three or four generations. Like the Hasidei Ashkenaz, its impact on the Jewish community remains unclear. Absolute distinctions between Jewish 'ethics' and 'philosophy' on the one hand, and Jewish 'mysticism' on the other, are hard to defend. If *Islamic* Sufism is mysticism, then surely so also is *Jewish* Sufism. The absence of Jewish Sufism from the agenda of the study of Jewish mysticism has probably led to a substantial underestimation of the contribution of Arabic-speaking Jews to the subject, and obscured the possibility that Muslim mystics (such as Ibn 'Arabi) may have influenced the Jewish tradition.

Safed and Lurianic Kabbalah

Few historians would deny that sixteenth-century Safed marks an important stage in the history of Jewish mysticism, but for Scholem it was absolutely pivotal, for from it, he believed, emerged the next two phases, Sabbatianism and Hasidism. Without Safed there would have been no Sabbatianism and no Hasidism, at least not in the form in which we know them. For Scholem, the key to understanding Safed is the expulsion of the Jews from Spain in 1492. This led to a diffusion of the Spanish Kabbalah, as Spanish scholars fled to other lands: the Safed mystical circles were composed mainly, though not exclusively, of Sephardis. But the trauma of the expulsion also created a crisis in thought, which was felt deeply even by Jews who were not caught up directly in the events. The expulsion was a catastrophe, comparable to the destruction of the Temple in 70 CE: it demanded a strong, religious response. The crisis was aggravated by the problem of the Marranos. Significant numbers of wealthier Spanish Jews converted to Christianity to avoid the edict. Their apostasy did not in the end save them, for it brought them under the authority of the Inquisition, which (in many cases probably rightly) doubted the sincerity of their Christianity. Many fled abroad, and once in safety sought to return to Judaism, but their return was painful: the Jewish communities were bitterly divided over how they should be received, and over what acts of penitence they should perform. The expulsion from Spain not only sent the Spanish Jews into exile, but made Jews feel exiled and vulnerable everywhere.

Scholem argued that the expulsion led to a heightened messianism. Interest in messianism is evident in Spain from the 1450s, before the expulsion, but it undoubtedly intensified after it. This messianism transformed the Kabbalah and was, Scholem claimed, central to the doctrine and practice of the Safed circles. One of the distinctive characteristics of Safed was the emergence of a range of practices, from personal devotions to new liturgies and new ways of performing the standard prayers, all aimed at hastening the redemption (Fine 1984). Safed was messianically active, not in any political sense, but in the sense of devoting itself to an all-consuming religious and mystical praxis that would bring the Messiah. This theurgical emphasis is reminiscent of the Hasidei Ashkenaz, but may also owe something to Jewish or even contemporary Muslim Sufism. However, the Safed Kabbalists were more successful than the Hasidei Ashkenaz in creating a powerful theoretical framework of myth and theology which gave meaning to their rites. Safed witnessed a marriage of myth and ritual possibly unparalleled in the history of Judaism. The doctrines of the Safed mystics were, Scholem maintained, highly metaphorical: they involved projecting onto the cosmic plane their own bitter experiences of catastrophe and exile. The Safed circles were much exercised with the problem of evil (Tishby 1984), and in the case of Isaac Luria traced its origin back to the primordial catastrophe of the 'breaking of the vessels' (*shevirat ha-kelim*). They dwelt much on the theme of the exile of the *Shekhinah* and its eventual remarriage with the higher aspects of the Godhead. They were involved in *Tiqqun*, the process by which the world would be mended, evil overcome, and cosmic harmony restored.

The two most influential of the Safed theorists were Moses Cordovero and Isaac Luria Ashkenazi. Cordovero was the most famous Safed Kabbalist in his day. His *Pomegranate Orchard* (*Pardes Rimmonim*) was widely accepted as the most comprehensive and authoritative introduction to the Kabbalah. He presents himself essentially as a systematizer and commentator on the *Zohar*, but there was much unremarked originality in his work. Luria, however, was more obviously daring and innovative. He was a charismatic, the subject of an extensive hagiography, one of the true saints of Judaism, who in the brief two years at Safed before his premature death at the age of 38 made a deep and lasting impression. His fame subsequently eclipsed that of Cordovero, and in retrospect his image is now indelibly stamped on Safed. His great cosmic myth, stretching from the primordial act of divine contraction (*tzimtzum*), which made possible the existence of the world, through the first aborted creation and the 'breaking of the vessels', to the second creation, its troubled history, and the final restoration of all things, was, Scholem claimed, one of the most influential in the history of Judaism. There is a strong tension in Safed between the forces of innovation and conservatism. The ideas are daring, but they tend significantly to reinforce tradition. Safed is an interesting example of radical orthodoxy.

Despite its acknowledged importance, Safedian mysticism remains surprisingly under-researched. Scholem's account raises serious questions. Particularly problematic is the extent to which he linked its messianism and Luria's 'catastrophic' theology to historical events. Scholem was too sophisticated a historian of Judaism to assume that messianism is inevitably bound up with persecution or disaster. He was well aware that it is an abiding phenomenon, and the way in which it waxes and wanes cannot easily be correlated with history (Scholem 1971). However, in the case of Safed he does treat the movements in thought as direct reflexes of historical events and experiences. He offers a deeply historicist reading, which may underestimate the degree to which the 'innovations' of Safed were anticipated in the *Zohar* and earlier pre-expulsion Kabbalistic texts, and can be seen as 'natural' developments of thought (Idel 1993: 138–41; 1998: 126–82). He may also have got caught up in a rather circular argument, which resulted in him selecting and foregrounding within the immense complexity of Safedian mysticism precisely those elements which seem to refer metaphorically to historical events. Thus it is arguable that messianism is actually not all that important in Luria's overall thought, and that it is prominent only at a certain stage in his intellectual development.

It is difficult to move beyond Scholem's account because much of the basic research, on which any advance must be predicated, remains to be done. Literary analysis of the primary sources is still at an early stage. Apart from a few scraps, none of Luria's own texts survive (he was not primarily a writer): we have to rely on the transmission of his teaching through his disciples, Hayyim Vital, Joseph ibn Tabul, Israel Sarug, and Menahem Azariah of Fano. But these do not even agree with themselves, let alone with each other (Meroz 1993). Recovering the historical Isaac Luria is every bit as difficult as recovering the historical Jesus. The difference is that the quest for the historical Luria lacks anything remotely comparable to the sophisticated literary and historical analyses that have been carried out on the Gospels. The sociology of the Safed groups also cries out for investigation. For perhaps the first time in the history of Jewish mysticism a vivid and believable picture emerges from the written sources of the composition and dynamics of the groups that stand behind them. The most enlightening analysis of this material remains Werblowsky's classic monograph on Joseph Caro (Werblowsky 1977), but clearly more can be said. Finally, further work needs to be done to clarify how Lurianic Kabbalah spread through the Jewish world. Following Scholem, Dan (1987:

244–6) suggests that by the early seventeenth century Lurianic Kabbalah had become the common theology of Judaism. There is good evidence to back this claim, which is important for Scholem's analysis of Sabbatianism, but how did Lurianic Kabbalah spread? That Italian Kabbalists who were in contact with Safed played a role in disseminating it in Europe seems clear, but how was it spread in the Muslim world, particularly in those areas which were the main theatre of Shabbatai's activity?

Sabbatianism

One of the most arresting and controversial claims that Scholem made in *Major Trends* was that seventeenth-century Sabbatianism, far from being a marginal, heretical movement, whose Messiah had committed the unforgiveable sin of conversion to another faith (Islam), was in fact integral to the development of Jewish mysticism, and to the history of Judaism in modern times. The problems of Sabbatianism greatly exercised Scholem, and called forth his most sustained research and most impressive monograph, *Sabbatai Sevi: The Mystical Messiah*—widely acknowledged as one of the seminal works of modern Jewish historiography (Scholem 1973). Scholem's views stimulated other scholars (see Dan 1987: 286–312; Liebes 1993b; Idel 1998: 183–211)—paradox has a curious fascination for the academic mind!—and it is probably true to say that Sabbatianism is one of the fields in the study of Jewish mysticism where most real progress has been made, though starting, it must be admitted, from a position of deep ignorance. Scholem rescued Sabbatianism from the opprobrium and obscurity into which it had been cast within Judaism, in an act of collective amnesia induced by the bitter controversies of the seventeenth and even more of the eighteenth centuries.

The two main figures of the movement were Shabbatai Zevi (1626–76), the Messiah himself, and Nathan of Gaza (1643–80), his prophet. Shabbatai had a profoundly charismatic personality, which impressed many who met him. Psychologically he was unstable, and subject to violent mood-swings which Scholem and others interpreted as evidence of manic depression. He proclaimed himself Messiah in his home town of Izmir in 1656, but although he attracted something of a following, his movement did not become a major force in the Jewish world until he met Nathan of Gaza. In 1665 Nathan recognized Shabbatai as Messiah and vigorously promoted his messianic claims. His success was spectacular: news that the Messiah had come spread like wildfire and put Jews in a fever of messianic expectation. Then came the debacle of Shabbatai's conversion. But this by no means ended the movement: indeed, Scholem argued, the real historical importance of Sabbatianism manifested itself only after this scandalous event. The conversion was interpreted by the hard-core Sabbatians as the culmination of a series of paradoxical acts performed by the Messiah. It was all part of his mysterious mission: he had voluntarily entered the realm of evil to redeem the divine sparks concealed there. Sabbatianism continued after Shabbatai's death. There were crypto-Sabbatians throughout the eighteenth century, even at the very heart of the rabbinic establishment, as the rabbinical authority Jacob Emden alleged. His accusation that the respected scholar Jonathan Eibeschütz (c.1690–1764) was a crypto-Sabbatian is now widely accepted by historians to have been justified. Sabbatianism also continued in offshoots such as Frankism, led by the even more bizarre and paradoxical Polish Messiah Jacob Frank (1726–91), who regarded himself as a reincarnation of Shabbatai and who, following in Shabbatai's footsteps, apostasized from Judaism. In 1759 he and his followers publicly underwent a mass conversion to Catholicism.

Scholem's brilliant analysis of Sabbatianism raises profound questions which go to the very heart of the historiography of Judaism. He saw Sabbatianism as a turning-point in Jewish history, marking the real end of the Jewish Middle Ages and the beginning of modernity. He argued that there was a significant correlation between Sabbatianism and the rise of Haskalah, the Jewish Enlightenment of the eighteenth century. Sabbatian antinomianism helped destroy from within the walls of the intellectual ghetto in which Jews lived, and accustom them to more radical, daring ways of thinking. That Sabbatianism played this role in certain cases may well be true, but the evidence remains largely anecdotal. Indeed, it is hard to see at this remove in time how it could be anything other than circumstantial and anecdotal. A complex constellation of political, social, and intellectual forces created the Jewish Enlightenment, which was only one aspect of the beginnings of Jewish modernity. That Sabbatianism was a major factor in these developments cannot be said to have been proved.

Scholem argued that Sabbatianism was intimately bound up with the Lurianic Kabbalah. It was the spread of Lurianism, with its strong messianic emphasis, that created the conditions in which Sabbatianism could flourish. Certainly the speed with which Sabbatianism first spread, and the readiness of Jews from very different backgrounds and societies across the world to accept Shabbatai's messiahship, is startling and baffling. Some historians had suggested that the Chmielnicki pogroms of 1648 had made the Jews susceptible to messianism, but as Scholem pointed out this is hardly an adequate explanation, since Sabbatianism was readily embraced by Jews in lands remote from the massacres, whereas the Jews of Poland, who were most closely affected, showed a marked resistance to Shabbatai's claims. Certainly Lurianic Kabbalah played an important role in Sabbatian theology, though more in the thinking of Nathan than of Shabbatai (Shabbatai himself seems to have been influenced more by the *Zohar* and other non-Lurianic sources), but to see Lurianism as the dominant factor in the spread of Sabbatianism is problematic. There must have been a multiplicity of causes, depending on the place, the person, and the community. The presence of Marranos in many parts of the Jewish world may have played a part. It is not hard to imagine why Marranos would have been particularly drawn to Shabbatai's message (they showed themselves in general susceptible to new, radical ideas), and been more forgiving when he converted, more open to alternative explanations, feeling that their own shameful behaviour was in some sense paradoxically vindicated by his.

Hasidism

Scholem's account in *Major Trends* of modern Hasidism, which he calls 'the latest phase' in the development of Jewish mysticism, is comparatively brief, synthetic, and impressionistic, partly, as he hints, because he feels that this is the best known, most widely studied, and accessible of all the Jewish mystical movements (see Hundert 1991 for some of the earlier literature). He basically published the lecture he had delivered without revision. Nevertheless, in *Major Trends*, and in a handful of later studies, he propounded a number of theses about Hasidism which have figured largely in contemporary debate. He argued that there was a significant link between Hasidism and Sabbatianism, just as there was a link between Sabbatianism and Lurianic Kabbalah. Hasidism emerged and spread in areas (Podolia and Volhynia) where Sabbatian influence was strong, and he speculated that the early Hasidic movement may have drawn some of its membership from crypto-Sabbatian circles. He also found evidence that Israel Baal Shem Tov (the Besht), the 'founder' of Hasidism, and other early Hasidic masters, knew and treasured crypto-Sabbatian texts.

He detected Sabbatian influence, both negative and positive, in a number of key areas of Hasidic thought. Negative influence could be seen in the role of messianism in Hasidism. Sabbatianism had been an intensely and destructively messianic movement. Hasidism had reacted against this, and although, like Sabbatianism, it drew on the powerfully messianic Lurianic Kabbalah, it played down—or to use Scholem's precisely nuanced term, it 'neutralized'—messianism. Scholem did not deny that messianic ideas were present in early Hasidic texts (they feature in the famous letter of the Besht to his brother-in-law), but he argued that they do not play a central role. There is no emphasis on national redemption (*gĕ'ullah kelalit*) at the end of history: the coming of the Messiah is relegated to a remote future. Instead stress is placed on the notion of *devequt*, the individual's adhesion to God here and now, which constitutes a personal redemption (*gĕ'ullah peratit*). Scholem also argued that one of Hasidism's distinctive ideas, the notion of the great leader, the *Zaddiq*, who mediated between heaven and earth was derived from Sabbatianism, though once again an element of neutralization comes in, since in Hasidism there was not just one *Zaddiq* (the Messiah) but many, whose intercessions were exercised primarily on behalf of their own followers.

There have been massive strides in the study of Hasidism since *Major Trends* (e.g. Weiss 1985; Schatz-Uffenheimer 1993; Idel 1995; Rapoport-Albert 1996; Rosman 1996). Its history has been clarified. It is now generally accepted that later hagiography has over-simplified the role of the Besht in the emergence of the movement. The historical sources for the origins of Hasidism are extremely problematic. The standard 'life' of the Besht, *The Praises of the Baal Shem Tov* (*Shivhei ha-Besht*), was not published until after his death, and what historical reality, if any, lies behind its pious tales it is hard to tell. It is now widely agreed that the Besht was only one of a number of similar charismatic leaders, and that there already existed circles of Hasidim when he appeared on the scene. The sociology of the movement has been studied. There is an abundance of material on which a sociological analysis can be based. Hasidism's relationship with the dominant rabbinic elite (the *Mitnaggedim*) was fraught, and led to bitter and potentially schismatic struggles which did not die down until the nineteenth century, and indeed have flared up again from time to time. Many of the Hasidic dynasties, grouped round a particular Rebbe, and forming close-knit and often vibrant communities, are well documented. One interesting feature has been that, although Hasidism as a whole lacks any central leadership and is made up of separate and sometimes conflicting groups, it retains a sense of a common identity *contra mundum*, based on a shared Hasidic heritage and certain common ideas and social structures.

Various aspects of the theology of Hasidism have been investigated in depth (Elior 1982 and 1993; Loewenthal 1990). The movement is actually theologically very diverse and innovative, less uniform theologically than Scholem's *Major Trends* might lead one to suppose. Scholem argued that Hasidism may be characterized as a popularizing of Kabbalah, the stripping away of elements not readily understandable to 'the laity'. In fact, within the Hasidic traditions (notably the highly intellectual Habad) there seems to be an inner and an outer doctrine. The inner doctrine is couched in language as impenetrable as that of the most technical Kabbalah. There is vigorous debate as to where the essence of Hasidism lies. Is it to be found, as Buber thought, in the folksy tales which have done so much to create a romantic image of Hasidism in the Jewish world (Buber 1960), or in the more difficult, less accessible theological writings? The role of messianism in Hasidism remains a subject of sharp disagreement. Scholem's thesis about its neutralization has been heavily criticized. Tishby and others have suggested that he underestimated the messianic element in early Hasidism (Tishby 1967). Idel has argued that Scholem worked with too narrow a definition of messianism: the fact that the apocalyptic type of messianism is not prominent in the early Hasidic sources does not mean that messianism was totally absent (Idel 1998: 212–47). Of interest in this context is the recent upsurge of messianism in the Lubavitch tradition centred on the figure of Menahem Mendel Schneerson—one of the most charismatic and influential Jewish religious thinkers of the late twentieth century. It is unclear to what extent this messianism has been imported, so to speak, from outside, or marks the emergence into the light of day of subterranean messianic streams that had always been present in the movement.

BEYOND THE SCHOLEMIAN PARADIGM?

Having examined briefly Scholem's detailed picture of the development of Jewish mysticism, we turn finally to consider some broader issues which his analysis has raised.

The Scope of Jewish mysticism

Scholem did not claim in *Major Trends* to be writing a comprehensive history of Jewish mysticism: the lectures, as his title modestly indicated, only dealt with selected, albeit 'major', trends. There were obvious gaps (e.g. the early Kabbalah in Provence and Spain), some of which Scholem himself later filled in. However, it can hardly be denied that one effect of *Major Trends* was to focus attention on certain areas to the exclusion of others. We have already noted Scholem's neglect of Jewish Sufism. But there are similar cases. In his emphasis on Sabbatianism and Hasidism he largely ignored what might be called 'orthodox' Kabbalah, represented by figures such as Moses Hayyim Luzzato, the Vilna Gaon, and Rabbi Hayyim of Volozhin, all of whom were (and remain) immensely influential in certain Kabbalistic circles. His claim that the origins of the mystical tradition can be carried back no earlier than the second century CE is also looking very questionable. It is now clear that significant elements of *Heikhalot* mysticism can be found in the Second Temple period. There are clear antecedents in Second Temple apocalyptic to the *Heikhalot* ascents to heaven and descriptions of the heavenly world (Gruenwald 1980). More intriguing still are the parallels to *Heikhalot* mysticism in the Songs of the Sabbath Sacrifice and other Dead Sea scrolls (Davila 2000). These parallels are sufficiently striking to suggest a common origin for the Qumranian and *Heikhalot* traditions, perhaps in theosophical speculation among priests in the Jerusalem Temple prior to 70 CE (Elior 1997). *Major Trends* was selective, but it was selective for a purpose. By limiting himself to certain movements Scholem was able to establish a tight dialectical pattern, in which one movement emerges historically in reaction to another, all within the broad framework of halachic Judaism. But it is arguable that if all the missing elements are factored in, and if it can be shown that actually the origins of

Jewish mysticism pre-date the origins of rabbinic Judaism (at least as strictly defined), then Scholem's neat schema falls apart. The paradigm created by *Major Trends* may not be able to accommodate the missing material.

The Nature of Jewish Mysticism

Questions can also be raised as to whether Scholem represented accurately the essence of Jewish mysticism. The mystical traditions are very diverse, but tradition-ally they have been classified as falling into two broad types—the contemplative (*kabbalah 'iyyunit*) and the practical (*kabbalah ma'asit*). The former is strongly theosophical: it is concerned with the nature of the Godhead and the structure of the heavenly world, with creation and the origins of evil, with the constitution of man, with Torah and redemption. It is essentially a mystical *theology*, and it has strong affinities with philosophy. The other is concerned with mystical practices, rituals, and incantations. It comes close to, and indeed from time to time shades into, *magic*. Scholem was, of course, well aware of these two types of material within the tradition, but he tended to privilege the contemplative over the practical. He saw as central to the development of Kabbalah a body of 'Gnostic' (i.e. in this context, effectively, theosophical) myths, symbols, and teachings, which was transmitted through obscure channels from Jewish mystics in the Middle East in Late Antiquity to the Hasidei Ashkenaz, the author of the *Bahir*, and Spanish Kabbalists such as the author of the *Zohar*. Scholem was not the only one to stress the theosophical, contemplative side of Jewish mysticism. There has always been a strong sense, even within the tradition, that the *Zohar*, which is predominantly theosophical, represents the quintessence of mysticism.

Moshe Idel, however, who has done more than anyone else to challenge the Scholemian paradigm, has proposed a variation on the traditional classification which gives greater weight to the practical side. He also distinguishes two major types—the theosophical-theurgical and the ecstatic—in *both* of which praxis is central. The theosophical-theurgical type, of which the *Zohar* may be taken as representative, 'encompasses two central subjects: theosophy—a theory of the elaborate structure of the divine world—and the ritualistic and experiential way of relating to the divinity in order to induce a state of harmony'. As he notes, this is a highly theocentric form of religiosity which, 'while not ignoring the needs of the human being, tends to conceive of religious perfection as instrumental for exerting effective influence on high.' It was, in practice, highly congruent with rabbinic halachah, since the means of attaining perfection, and so influencing the heavenly world, was identified with the performance of the *mitzvot*. The ecstatic type, classically represented by Abraham Abulafia, 'is highly anthropocentric, envisioning the mystical experience of the individual as itself the *summum bonum*, regardless of the possible impact of this mystical status on the inner harmony of the Divine' (Idel 1988a: p. xi). Ecstatic Kabbalah is fundamentally anomian: its praxis is not focused on the observance of the *mitzvot*, but on the performance of highly technical mystical exercises which result in altered states of consciousness. This is a fruitful distinction, provided it is recognized that these are ideal types, and that many actual Jewish mystical systems will combine elements from both. The history of Jewish mysticism can be reasonably configured as a dialectic between these two polarities.

Methodology in the Study of Jewish Mysticism

Scholem, though a stern critic of the philosophy of the Wissenschaft des Judentums, nevertheless embraced its critical methods. His conclusions may have been revolutionary, but his approach was not: he used the standard techniques of historical, philological, and literary criticism to uncover the history of Jewish mysticism. He did so presumably out of choice. A man who could debate as an equal with Walter Benjamin, or who (though not himself a Jungian) was a regular contributor to the Eranos conferences, was clearly capable of great hermeneutical sophistication. He seems, however, to have believed passionately in the validity of the historical-critical approach, and to have felt that it was precisely what was needed, given the state of the field in which he had chosen to work. This comes out strongly in his criticism of Martin Buber's exposition of Hasidism. Hasidism fascinated Buber, and he increasingly saw it as a vivid Jewish validation of his own dialogical philosophy (Buber 1960). His approach was highly intuitive: through the Hasidic tales he entered into a kind of dialogue with the Hasidic masters, and sought imaginatively to think his way into their world, to see things through their eyes. Once he had got, so to speak, beneath their skin, he felt he could grasp the essence of Hasidism, and mediate its outlook as freely and authoritatively as if he himself had been a Hasidic master. The result was a warm, romantic picture of Hasidism which proved attractive to both Jewish and non-Jewish intellectuals. Scholem objected that Buber's account lacked historical reality. He had not subjected himself sufficiently to the rigours of dispassionate, historical inquiry. He had failed properly to document his sources, and had relied too heavily on the Hasidic tales to the neglect of the Hasidic theological writings. He had basically made Hasidism over in his own image (Scholem 1971: 228–50).

Scholem's criticisms were well received among academic historians of Judaism, though they did little to dent the influence of Buber's account of Hasidism in the wider world. However, attempts to declare Scholem the outright victor in this debate may yet prove to be premature. Scholem's approach was actually deeply conservative. The historical-critical method which he espoused has in the past fifty years been subjected to ferocious criticism. Its presuppositions have been exposed, and it has been shown to be less 'objective' and 'scientific' than it claimed to be. Scholem's own ideological agenda has become better understood (see below), and it has been argued that in many ways he too used Jewish mysticism as the vehicle of his own philosophy. Buber's dialogical approach can be seen, with some justification, as more daring and innovative, and as anticipating important features of postmodernist hermeneutics. Postmodernist approaches have, as yet, had relatively little impact on the study of Jewish mystical texts: positivist, historical criticism still rules the field. Even feminist readings of the texts remain rare, despite the fact that their widespread use of erotic and sexual imagery (Abrams 1997; Wolfson 1995b), as well as the absence of women in Jewish mysticism (contrast Christian mysticism), cry out for a feminist critique. (The occasional prominent women on the wilder fringes of Hasidism or Frankism are the exceptions that prove the rule.) As a result, the field as a whole at the moment looks rather intellectually isolated. Generally lacking are thorough comparative studies (though see Davila 2001), or serious attempts to utilize theoretical insights from the phenomenology of religion. This lack of integration into wider academic discourse is probably a major reason why Jewish mysticism, unjustifiably, receives relatively little attention in general discussions of mysticism or religion.

One scholar who has made a sustained effort radically to rethink Jewish mysticism from a more phenomenological standpoint is Moshe Idel. Two of his methodological proposals deserve a brief mention. Idel criticizes Scholem and other historicists for what he calls 'proximism'—the belief that any given movement within Jewish mysticism (such as Hasidism) is fundamentally to be explained in terms of a reaction to contemporary social conditions and historical events. This idea is deeply embedded in classical historiography, and is well illustrated by Scholem's dialectical, Hegelian account of the development of Jewish mysticism from the medieval Kabbalah, through Lurianism and Sabbatianism, to Hasidism. Idel proposes a more 'panoramic' approach, which starts with a survey of the full range of the textual resources actually available to the founders of a movement such as Hasidism, and traces how elements of these were combined to form a mystical point of view (Idel 1995: 1–30; 1996). This approach is certainly a useful tool for discovering the role played by neglected or obscure texts in the development of Jewish mysticism. However, it should not be applied in an ahistorical fashion. Jewish mysticism cannot be reduced to a movement in a Platonic world of ideas, divorced from political and social realities. Faced with a 'smorgasbord' of texts, motifs, and symbols, a mystical thinker will pick and choose to construct his own system, but the dominant influence on his choice is still likely to be his social and political situation.

Idel's other methodological innovation he calls 'reconstructionalism' (Idel 1988a: 32–4). He argues that many of the conceptual structures of the medieval Kabbalah were already present within Judaism in the Talmudic period. He grants that they are often not found actually articulated in the classical-period texts, but he claims that there are hints of their existence—discrete motifs and symbols which form an integral part of these conceptual structures in the medieval systems. The effect of this approach, which is most obviously applicable to pre-Kabbalistic mysticism, is to carry back central elements of the Kabbalah, hitherto regarded as medieval, into Late Antiquity. The Kabbalah thus becomes less revolutionary and innovative than it appears to be: more of it can be derived by 'subterranean channels' from ancient sources than had previously been supposed. The concrete examples by which Idel has exemplified the reconstructionist approach raise many issues. There are clear dangers of anachronism. Intuition plays a larger part in the reasoning than many scholars can comfortably accept. And serious questions can be asked about how Idel understands the hermeneutics of the medieval Kabbalists, and their use of classic sources. It is absolutely typical of rabbinic midrash that it attempts to validate *new* ideas from earlier, authoritative texts, whether biblical or rabbinic, and the cleverer the midrash the more it will *seem* that the ideas are actually there. It is hard to see how a reconstructionist approach, if universalized, could avoid the ahistorical conclusion that the major conceptual structures of rabbinic theology expounded in midrash (e.g. the doctrine of the *Shekhinah*) were actually present in Judaism in the biblical period.

The Place of Mysticism Within Judaism

Scholem's work posed acutely the question of the place of mysticism within Judaism. Nineteenth-century historians such as Graetz had famously denigrated mysticism, seeing it as the unwelcome eruption into Judaism of pagan, polytheistic ideas. Scholem, as part of his ideological onslaught on Wissenschaft tried to show that mysticism had actually been central to the development of Judaism. Its daring innovations, its openness to new ideas, had acted as a necessary counterpoise to the rigidities of the halachah. It had introduced into Judaism as a religious system a degree of flexibility which had allowed it to respond creatively to the challenges of history. The growing sense that mysticism had played a central and very positive role in Jewish history became bound up with Scholem's quest for his own Jewish identity and his involvement with Zionism. He lived through a brilliant renaissance of Jewish culture, and he felt that the mystical tradition was one of the well-springs from which Judaism could be renewed in his own time (Biale 1982; Handelman 1991).

Not everyone, however, agrees with Scholem's understanding of the place of mysticism in Judaism. Elie Schweid has argued that Scholem seriously overestimated its importance (Schweid 1985). Where Graetz prioritized the Halachah (defined in a rationalist fashion), and Scholem the Kabbalah, Schweid tried to claim that the essence of Judaism was to be found in *Musar* (the ethical tradition).

He simply could not accept that highly destructive, anomian movements, such as Sabbatianism, played a positive role in the history of Judaism. Debates over the 'essence' of Judaism are of limited value, and have a tendency to obscure the complexity of the tradition, with all its inner contradictions and conflicts. However, one criticism of Scholem does seem justified: he understood the polarity between Kabbalah and halachah in far too stark and simplistic a fashion. His location of mysticism within Judaism depends on construing halachah (in a manner curiously reminiscent of contemporary German Protestant theology) as a rigid legalism. But halachah has within it powerful mechanisms of flexibility and renewal, and conversely Kabbalah, for all its intellectual daring, often in practice sides with the forces of reaction and conservatism rather than of innovation and change.

The study of Jewish mysticism is at present in a state of flux. Scholem's magnificent and beguiling paradigm is coming under growing pressure, and is showing signs of buckling under the strain. Its basic premises are under attack, and in many detailed areas it is being heavily supplemented, corrected, and contested. Whether the cumulative effects of all this pressure will be simply to modify it or totally to deconstruct it, and what new synthesis, if any, will emerge to take its place, remains to be seen. The successor to *Major Trends* has still to be written.

SUGGESTED READING

For an introduction to the general study of Jewish mysticism, the following are of use: Scholem (1946, 1973, 1974, and 1987); Dan (1987); and Idel (1988a and b).

BIBLIOGRAPHY

ABRAMS, D. 1997. *Sexual Symbolism and Merkavah Speculation in Medieval Germany: A Study of the Sod ha-Egoz Texts.* Tübingen.

ALEXANDER, P. S. 1983. '3 Enoch.' In *The Old Testament Pseudepigrapha.* i. 223–316. J. H. Charlesworth ed. Garden City, NY.

—— 1984. 'Comparing Merkavah Mysticism and Gnosticism.' *JJS* 35: 1–18.

—— 1999. 'Jewish Elements in Gnosticism and Magic c.70 CE to c.270 CE.' In *Cambridge History of Judaism.* iv. 1052–78, 1210–19. W. Horbury, W. D. Davies, and J. Sturdy eds. Cambridge.

BAER, Y. 1938. 'The Religious-Social Tendency of the *Sefer Hasidim.*' [Hebrew]. *Zion* 3: 1–50.

BIALE, D. 1982. *Gershom Scholem: Kabbalah and Counter-History.* Cambridge, Mass.

BUBER, M. 1960. *The Origin and Meaning of Hasidism.* Trans. M. Friedman. New York.

DAN, J. 1968. *The Esoteric Theology of Ashkenazi Hasidism* [Hebrew]. Jerusalem.

—— 1987. *Gershom Scholem and the Mystical Dimension of Jewish History.* New York and London.

DAN, J. 1993a. 'The Religious Meaning of *Sefer Yetzira*.' [Hebrew]. *Jerusalem Studies in Jewish Thought* 11: 7–36.

—— 1993b. 'Ashkenazi Hasidism, 1941–1991: Was There Really a Hasidic Movement in Medieval Germany.' In Schäfer and Dan (1993): 87–102.

—— 1999. *The 'Unique Cherub' Circle: A School of Mystics and Esoterics in Mediaeval Germany.* Tübingen.

DAVILA, J. 2000. 'The Dead Sea Scrolls and Merkavah Mysticism.' In *The Dead Sea Scrolls in their Historical Context.* 249–64. T. H. Lim ed. Edinburgh.

—— 2001. *Descenders to the Chariot: The People Behind the Hekhalot Literature.* Leiden.

DEUTSCH, N. 1995. *The Gnostic Imagination: Gnosticism, Mandaeism and Merkabah Mysticism.* Leiden.

ELIOR, R. 1982. *The Theory of Divinity of Hasidut Habad: Second Generation* [Hebrew]. Jerusalem.

—— 1993. *The Paradoxical Ascent: The Kabbalistic Theosophy of Habad.* Albany, NY.

—— 1997. 'From Earthly Temple to Heavenly Shrines: Prayer and Sacred Song in the Hekhalot Literature and Its Relation to Temple Traditions.' *JSQ* 4: 217–67.

FENTON, P. B. 1981a. 'Some Judaeo-Arabic Fragments by Rabbi Abraham ha-Hasid, the Jewish Sufi.' *JSS* 26: 47–72.

—— 1981b. *The Treatise of the Pool: al-Maqala al- Hawdiyya by 'Obadyah b. Abraham b. Moses Maimonides.* London.

—— 1984. 'The Literary Legacy of David II Maimuni.' *JQR* 75: 1–56.

—— 1987. *Deux traités de mystique juive.* Paris.

FINE, L. 1984. *Safed Spirituality: Rules of Mystical Piety, the Beginning of Wisdom.* Mahwah, NJ.

—— ed. 1995. *Essential Papers on Kabbalah.* New York.

GILLER, P. 2001. *Reading the Zohar: The Sacred Text of the Kabbalah.* Oxford.

GOITEIN, S. D. 1953–4. 'A Jewish Addict to Sufism in the Time of Nagid David II Maimonides.' *JQR* 44: 37–49.

—— 1964. 'New Genizah Documents on Abraham Maimonides and His Pietist Circle.' [Hebrew.] *Tarbiz* 33: 232–56.

—— 1967. 'Abraham Maimonides and his Pietist Circle.' In *Jewish Medieval and Renaissance Studies.* 145–64. A. Altmann ed. Cambridge, Mass.

GRAETZ, H. 1859. 'Die mystische Literatur in der gaonäischen Epoche.' *Monatsschrift für die Geschichte und Wissenschaft des Judentums.* 8: 67–78, 103–18, 140–53.

GREEN, A. 1997. *Keter: The Crown of God in Early Jewish Mysticism.* Princeton.

GRUENWALD, I. 1980. *Apocalyptic and Merkavah Mysticism.* Leiden and Cologne.

HALPERIN, D. J. 1980. *The Merkabah in Rabbinic Literature.* New Haven.

—— 1988. *The Faces of the Chariot: Early Jewish Responses to Ezekiel's Vision.* Tübingen.

HANDELMAN, S. A. 1991. *Fragments of Redemption: Jewish Thought and Literary Theory in Benjamin, Scholem and Levinas.* Bloomington, Ind.

HAYMAN, P. 1987. 'Sefer Yetzira and the Hekhalot Literature.' *JSJT* 6: 71–85.

HUNDERT, G. D. 1991. *Essential Papers on Hasidism: Origins to Present.* New York and London.

IDEL, M. 1987. *The Mystical Experience of Abraham Abulafia.* Trans. J. Chipman. Albany, NY.

—— 1988a. *Kabbalah: New Perspectives.* New Haven and London.

—— 1988b. *Studies in Ecstatic Kabbalah.* Albany, NY.

——1989. *Language, Torah and Hermeneutics in Abraham Abulafia*. Trans. M. Kallus. Albany, NY.

——1991. *Golem: Jewish Magical and Mystical Traditions on the Artificial Anthropoid*. Albany, NY.

——1993. 'The Contribution of Abraham Abulafia's Kabbalah to the Understanding of Jewish Mysticism.' In Schäfer and Dan (1993): 117–44.

——1995. *Hasidism: Between Ecstasy and Magic*. Albany, NY.

——1996. 'Martin Buber and Gershom Scholem on Hasidism: A Critical Appraisal.' In Rapoport-Albert (1996): 389–403.

——1998. *Messianic Mystics*. New Haven and London.

KUYT, A. 1995. *The 'Descent' to the Chariot: Towards a Description of the Terminology, Place and Nature of the Yeridah in Hekhalot Literature*. Tübingen.

LESSES, R. M. 1998. *Ritual Practices to Gain Power: Angels, Incantations and Revelations in Early Jewish Mysticism*. Harrisburg, Pa.

LIEBES, Y. 1993a. *Studies in the Zohar*. Trans. A. Schwartz, S. Nakache, and P. Peli. Albany, NY.

——1993b. *Studies in Jewish Myth and Messianism*. Trans. B. Stein. Albany, NY.

——1995. *On Sabbatianism and its Kabbalah: Collected Essays* [Hebrew]. Jerusalem.

LISS, H. 1997. *El'azar ben Yehuda von Worms: Hilkhot ha-Kavod. Die Lehrsätze von der Herrlichkeit Gottes*. Tübingen.

LOEWENTHAL, N. 1990. *Communicating the Infinite: The Emergence of the Habad School*. Chicago.

MARCUS, I. G. 1981. *Piety and Society: The Jewish Pietists of Medieval Germany*. Leiden.

——1993. 'The Historical Meaning of the *Hasidei Ashkenaz*: Fact, Fiction or Cultural Self-Image.' In Schäfer and Dan (1993): 103–16.

MEROZ, R. 1993. 'Faithful Transmission versus Innovation: Luria and his Disciples.' In Schäfer and Dan (1993): 257–76.

MORRAY-JONES, C. R. A. 2002. *A Transparent Illusion: The Dangerous Vision of Water in Hekhalot Mysticism: A Source-Critical and Tradition Historical Inquiry*. Leiden, Boston, and Cologne.

RAPOPORT-ALBERT, A. ed. 1996. *Hasidism Reappraised*. London and Portland.

ROSENBLATT, S. 1927–38. *The Highways to Perfection of Abraham Maimonides*, 2 vols. New York and Baltimore.

ROSENTHAL, F. 1940. 'A Judaeo-Arabic Work Under Sufic Influence.' *HUCA* 15: 433–84.

ROSMAN, M. 1996. *The Founder of Hasidism: A Quest for the Historical Ba'al Shem Tov*. Berkeley and Los Angeles.

SCHÄFER, P. 1987. 'The Problem of the Redactional Identity of "Hekhalot Rabbati".' [Hebrew.] *JSJT* 6: 1–12.

——1988. *Hekhalot-Studien*. Tübingen.

——1990. 'The Ideal of Piety of the Ashkenazi Hasidim and its Roots in Jewish Tradition.' *JH* 4: 9–23.

——1992. *The Hidden and Manifest God: Some Major Themes in Early Jewish Mysticism*. Trans. A. Pomerance. Albany, NY.

——1993. 'Merkavah Mysticism and Magic.' In Schäfer and Dan (1993): 59–78.

——1995. 'The Magic of the Golem: The Earthly Development of the Golem Legend.' *JJS* 36: 361–75.

SCHÄFER, P. and DAN, J. eds. 1993. *Gershom Scholem's Major Trends in Jewish Mysticism 50 Years After.* Tübingen.

SCHATZ-UFFENHEIMER, R. 1993. *Hasidism as Mysticism: Quietist Elements in Eighteenth Century Hasidic Thought.* Trans. J. Chipman. Princeton and Jerusalem.

SCHOLEM, G. 1946. *Major Trends in Jewish Mysticism.* 2nd edn. New York.

—— 1965. *Jewish Gnosticism, Merkavah Mysticism, and Talmudic Tradition.* 2nd edn. New York.

—— 1969. *On the Kabbalah and Its Symbolism.* Trans. R. Mannheim. New York.

—— 1971. *The Messianic Idea in Judaism.* New York.

—— 1973. *Sabbatai Sevi, the Mystical Messiah.* Trans. R. J. Z. Werblowsky. Princeton.

—— 1974. *Kabbalah.* Jerusalem.

—— 1987. *Origins of the Kabbalah.* Trans. A. Arkush; R. J. Z. Werblowsky ed. Princeton.

SCHWEID, E. 1985. *Judaism and Mysticism According to Gershom Scholem: A Critical and Programmatic Discussion.* Trans. D. A. Weiner. Atlanta, Ga.

SWARTZ, M. D. 1996. *Scholastic Magic: Ritual and Revelation in Early Jewish Mysticism.* Princeton.

TISHBY, I. 1967. 'The Messianic Idea and Messianic Trends in the Growth of Hasidism.' [Hebrew.] *Zion* 32: 1–45.

—— 1984, *The Doctrine of Evil and the 'Kelippah' in Lurianic Qabbalism* [Hebrew]. Jerusalem.

—— 1989. *The Wisdom of the Zohar.* 3 vols. Trans. D. Goldstein. Oxford.

URBACH, E. E. 1967. 'The Traditions Concerning Mystical Teaching in the Era of the Tanna'im.' In *Studies in Mysticism and Religion Presented to Gershom G. Scholem on his Seventieth Birthday.* 1–28 [Hebrew Section]. R. J. Z. Werblowsky and Ch. Wirszubski eds. Jerusalem.

VAJDA, G. 1955. 'The Mystical Doctrine of Rabbi Obadyah, Grandson of Moses Maimonides.' *JJS* 6: 213–55.

VERMAN, M. 1992. *The Books of Contemplation.* Albany, NY.

—— 1993, 'The Evolution of the Circle of Contemplation.' In Schäfer and Dan (1993): 163–80.

WEISS, J. 1985. *Studies in Eastern European Jewish Mysticism.* D. Goldstein ed. Oxford.

WERBLOWSKY, R. J. Z. 1977. *Joseph Karo: Lawyer and Mystic.* Philadelphia.

WINEMAN, A. 1998. *Mystic Tales from the Zohar.* Princeton.

WOLFSON, E. R. 1994. *Through A Speculum That Shines: Vision and Imagination in Mediaeval Jewish Mysticism.* Princeton.

—— 1995a. *Along the Path: Studies in Kabbalistic Myth, Symbolism and Hermeneutics.* Albany, NY.

—— 1995b. *Circle in the Square: Studies in the Use of Gender in Kabbalistic Symbolism.* Albany, NY.

CHAPTER 29

....

JEWISH LITURGY AND JEWISH SCHOLARSHIP: METHOD AND COSMOLOGY*

....

LAWRENCE A. HOFFMAN

THE state of Jewish liturgy as a modern discipline has received treatment in many quarters (e.g. Hoffman 1995). This article too describes liturgical study in Judaism, but first a word should be said about just what Jewish liturgy is. Judaism is a liturgical religion in that it calls for the recitation of prescribed prayers at prescribed times and in prescribed ways (Hoffman 1991: 13–15). Private prayer is always permitted, of course; and some private prayers (accompanying food, for example) are actually demanded. But Jewish liturgy is overall public, a communal recitation of specific prayers in specific ways. Still, Jews understand these liturgical requirements differently, and by now various 'movements' (akin to Christian denominations or confessions) have codified them differently. But all Jews agree on the organization of Jewish liturgy into a book of daily and Sabbath prayers (known as a *siddur*, meaning 'order') and holiday collections (*machzor*, a Hebrew noun implying an annual cycle). There exist also specialized prayer collections, most notably the *Haggadah* (meaning 'recitation') for the Passover eve meal (the *seder*).

* The author dedicates this essay to Stephen and Barbara Friedman in gratitude for their friendship and support over the years.

The liturgy is mostly post-biblical, and with few exceptions, the major rubrics were in place by 200 CE. But the mode of prayer was oral, so that variable wording, depending on the prayer-leader, was used to express the fixed flow of prayer topics (Hoffman 1997: i. 3–5). That wording was heavily influenced by biblical rhetoric, and a lectionary of biblical readings still remains central, so the centrality of the Bible was never lost. But the Bible was read with rabbinic eyes, and prayers were largely couched in a unique rabbinic literary genre called a blessing (or benediction—b'rakhah in Hebrew).

The prayer corpus grew steadily, some blessing versions remaining and others dropping by the wayside, until (in the ninth century) what was the norm in Babylonia (modern-day Iraq) was committed to writing in a semi-canonical way by Rav Amram Gaon (Hoffman 1979). Only with the printing press, however, did the collection get finally fixed, by which time considerable medieval material had been added. In modern times, liberal movements have added to or subtracted from what early printers codified.

The overriding question—often unexplored—has been what paradigm to use in studying a unique type of literature that has evolved over time and still changes today; a literature, moreover, that exists not for private reading or meditation but for repeated public recitation, like (as we shall see) drama. This essay traces that question: it asks how Jewish liturgy has been or should be studied; but further, it seeks an overall scheme to explain that study. More than just chronicling the changing questions and answers to which the liturgy has been subjected, it links changes of method to cosmology: that branch of theology that imagines the condition of the universe.

Technically the 'doctrine of God', theology may be taken also to include anthropology ('doctrine of human nature') and cosmology ('doctrine of the universe'). The latter includes such perennial philosophical questions as: 'What is out there' (what Hilary Putnam describes as 'the furniture of the universe': Putnam 1987); whether there is anything 'out there' at all; or whether there even is an 'out there'. Cosmology, then, is the assumptions about the kind of place in which human beings find themselves. Clifford Geertz calls it a 'world-view', by which he means, 'the picture [people in any given culture] have of the way things in sheer actuality are, their most comprehensive ideas of order' (Geertz 1973: 89). These notions are, in part, culturally given and historically determined. Since scholars too inhabit cultures, however, their world-view determines the advisability of one form of knowledge over another. In sum, we shall see that all traditionalist Jewish study, including study of liturgy, presupposed a pre-modern cosmology where, far from being differentiated into discrete realms, the universe is seen instead as a single interactive whole governed by divine fiat and will. The revolutionary rise of science, however, divided the universe into fields governed by disciplines, causing the pre-modern method to be replaced by a scientific approach. The scientific study of liturgy drew on the scientific paradigm both for its overall goal—an objective description of reality—and for its own specific task subsumed under that goal: a thorough objective description of that part of reality known as liturgy.

But the scientific paradigm can be divided into sub-streams, each with its own pre-assumed cosmology. Nineteenth-century 'Wissenschaft', which invented the modern 'field' of liturgy, is historicist and philological in essence, corresponding to that era's world-view that combined evolutionism, nationalism, and romanticism. We then see a form-critical response, rooted in an equally romantic notion of an essence that lies even before and behind written records. Finally, after the Shoah, Jewish Wissenschaft was merged with a Zionist ideology of a world where all Jewish culture, like all remaining Jews, required being salvaged.

A new view—some would call it postmodern—now predominates: a participational universe where meaning is negotiated at the horizon of meeting between the individual and the experienced world. This view has accentuated the 'meaning' of liturgy to those who use it; it raises questions about the meaning of meaning.

THE STUDY OF JEWISH LITURGY: A DISCIPLINE IN SEARCH OF A HOME

Liturgy is an anomaly, in that Jews who use it tend nonetheless not to recognize it as a familiar Jewish subject. Traditional scholarship discusses it, as it does topics like dietary laws (*kashrut*), say, or the civil law of damages (*n'zikin*), all three being matters of talmudic concern, and therefore grist for the rabbinic mill. But prayer *per se* was never considered its own independent topic; and prayers received no special attention from generations of rabbis who discussed all manner of things, all considered part of a larger seamless whole.

Here is where traditional Jewish cosmology entered. Traditional investigations assumed an undifferentiated cosmos, established by God and governed by Jewish law. Any given talmudic page may thus switch back and forth among topics, deducing regulations over prayer from what moderns would consider unrelated subjects. The traditional Jewish mind, however, viewed them as anything but unrelated. Rather, they were seen as mutually intersecting realms arising from the unified universe that the one true God had brought into being. What connected them were hermeneutic principles that linked their textual discussions together.

Concern with Jewish liturgy as a discrete field of study is, therefore, a modern phenomenon, dependent on this all-embracing cosmology being sliced up into separate 'servings' of reality, each its own field of inquiry. It is, in fact, so recent that it is not even clear what Hebrew word to use for it. *Tefillah* is sometimes apt (Levi

1963), but ambiguous, since *tefillah* more properly denotes the act of prayer (as in, 'It is time for *tefillah*'), or a specific prayer (the *Amidah*), but not prayers in general. The plural *tefillot* means 'prayers', but not the collective, 'prayer' (Rabeinu Yehudah bar R. Yakar 1979). *Pulkhan* can be used for 'worship', but not for what 'liturgy' generally implies: the literature that comprises Jewish prayer. 'Liturgy' comes from the Greek *leiturgia*, meaning 'public works', of which appropriately solicitous prayer to the gods was a prime example; but the parallel *avodah* (which means the same thing) properly denotes the now-defunct Temple cult, a sub-topic within the field of liturgy, but hardly the field as a whole. No wonder, at least in discussion, one hears 'liturgiah', a modern Hebraism that betrays the fact that liturgy as a separate discipline is a modern invention by scholars, who discovered prayers as a specific kind of literature, and needed a word to describe it.

The changeover from the pre-modern paradigm, which knows no discrete disciplines, to the modern scientific view, which knows no knowledge without them, betrays different underlying views of cosmology, but these are not as clear-cut as they may seem. The pre-modern conception of an undifferentiated universe—presupposed already by the Talmud—approaches a view attributed to 'primitive' peoples (Douglas 1966: 73–93). But equally, it is akin to the way advanced scientific disciplines intersect; or the way that modern physics seeks the secrets of nature in a unified field theory. Indeed, the rabbinic quest for a unified 'Jewish' field theory, as it were, is evident in the many attempts to summarize all of Torah in the fewest possible precepts (Mak. 23b–24a). So both the scientific and the rabbinic mind seek the application of common laws that underlie the diversity of appearance. But they differ on the source of the laws in question. For science, they are postulates of mathematical systems that are observed as working within the natural order. For the Rabbis, they are hermeneutical principles that are applicable to texts so as to deduce appropriate human interaction with the natural order. This is not a trivial difference. Science looks for the governing principles of the universe; traditional Jewish inquiry focuses on how men and women should treat the universe.

Cosmology matters, then. The focus on liturgy as a scientific discipline had to await the internalization of a modern scientific world-view that sees nature as harbouring secrets for human inquiry. It required at least some form of the view (religious or not) attributed by Bertolt Brecht to a monk who advises Galileo, 'God made the physical world, God made the human brain. God will allow physics' (Brecht, *Galileo*, scene 8). If the Bible was God's first book, nature was God's second opus, written in mathematical letters that Galileo, Kepler, and Copernicus thought they were mastering (Heisenberg 1983: 9). As long as traditional Judaism eschewed the second book (nature) for the first one (Torah), it investigated human interaction with the environment, not the environment itself as its own objectively observed phenomenon. Scientifically speaking, prayers are part of that environment. Rather than focusing on an objective scientific study of those prayers, then, traditional Jews asked how Jews should pray.

Whatever questions the rabbis had about a prayer's origins or structure tended to arise only within the context of determining its use. For instance, the rabbis of the Talmud (Ber. 28b.) attribute our familiar *Amidah* to Rabban Gamaliel, but not because they cared about the *Amidah*'s history in and of itself. The issue was, rather, the status of the benediction over heretics, and how we know what to do with a prayer-leader who skips over it. Similarly (Meg. 17b), they justify healing as the topic of the *Amidah*'s eighth blessing by the need for a baby boy to heal from his eighth-day circumcision—again, a demonstration of the priority the rabbis give to how prayers must be said. Or finally, to cite a medieval and not just a talmudic case, take Rashi's justification of the 'seven blessings' (*sheva berakhot*) of the wedding ceremony (Ket. 8a). A scientific mind-set would demonstrate the probability that the Talmud's list of these blessings is probably a relatively random collection of early alternatives, not 'seven [required] blessings' at all (Hoffman 1996: 136–8). The final two blessings, for instance, are mutually redundant, praying in somewhat different language for the joy of bridegroom and bride. But wanting to preserve his understanding of them as a canonized set of blessings that must all be said, Rashi relates each of the last two blessings to a different sort of marital bliss: the happiness a couple finds in the environment, and the joy each member of the couple realizes in the other. The overriding issue is 'What prayers do we say, and how do we say them?' Liturgy is part of the general rabbinic project to reveal the mind of God in God's first book, the Torah. It is a halachic category, not a scientific discipline.

The Rise of Disciplines

The word 'discipline' corresponds to the classification scheme by which universities describe what their resident experts do. But what discipline one practises depends on what is in vogue as a title at any given time. The first universities of Bologna, Paris, and Oxford used disciplines traceable to the 'seven liberal arts' of the Middle Ages: the trivium (grammar, rhetoric, and logic) and the quadrivium (arithmetic, geometry, astronomy, and music). With the Renaissance, the trivium was rounded out with poetry, history, and political and moral philosophy. The seventeenth-century scientific revolution split the physical sciences off from the liberal arts, ultimately creating the European university system of the nineteenth century, with its modern disciplines of what we would call the liberal arts: languages, literature, history, and the like (Hargreaves 1963; Kagan 1999; Tapper and Salter 1992). Had Jews never been exposed to universities, it is hard to say what 'disciplines' (if any) Judaism would now have. But the point is moot, since nineteenth-century Jews did encounter academe, whence it subsequently repackaged Jewish tradition for academic consumption. This Jewish search for disciplines emerged from an assumed scientific cosmology, according to which scientists were supposed to unravel the evolution of the universe. So Jewish scientists learned to unpack their texts anew: no longer to find rules on how to live in the universe, but instead, to find the truths of the universe. The particular corner of the 'universe' that their texts would reveal was the nature of Jewish culture. The point is, they now reread their texts scientifically and objectively, their goal being an understanding of the texts, but no longer the will of God that the texts might transmit.

At stake was concern for both method and material, in that method, as expressed by a novel paradigm of study, was applied to the material of Jewish texts. In neither case, for Jews, did liturgy fare well.

As to method, the most significant decision was to adopt the historicist notion of textual evolution, a clear reflection of the cosmology that typified scientific romanticism (Abrams 1953). Pre-modern Jewish study had viewed all of Jewish literature synchronically. True, the Bible enjoyed its own favoured status, and within the Bible, Torah loomed pre-eminently, but the Bible meant what the rabbis said it did. It is true also that different rabbinic eras were specified by name, the earlier ones being seen as more knowledgeable than the ones that came later, but a scientific sense of historical evolution was altogether new. It implied that biblical and post-biblical studies would have to be sharply delineated; medieval and modern would not be confused. Within the broad eras that pre-moderns had conceived—the *amoraim*, for instance—individual generations would be distinguished, often classed according to who had taught them, so that historical schools could be imagined as extending through time. The rabbis had casually juxtaposed Mishnah (second-century Palestine), Maimonides (twelfth-century Egypt), and Rashi (eleventh-century France) without regard for the historical context of each. Modern scientific scholars avoided such 'category' errors; they focused their expertise on more and more circumscribed fields—talmudic literature, say, but not medieval commentaries on what that literature 'meant'.

Here is where liturgy as material failed to match historicism as method. Liturgy spanned time-periods, so that, unlike Talmud, say, or medieval commentaries, it belonged both nowhere and everywhere on a historical chart. Prayers and prayer are ancient; a prayer book is not. Where, then, does liturgy belong? There are some similar anomalies elsewhere in Jewish studies, but none quite so stark—responsa, for instance, that make their first appearance in the Geonic period and continue thereafter all the way to today. But responsa can be broken down into any given jurist's opinions (like the ruling of the Warren Court, or of Lord Denning). Moreover, with few exceptions, largely Geonic, responsa are not anonymous, while prayers are usually folded into the received text without regard for authorship or context. The liturgy, then, is all of a piece, the way responsa are not. Even poetic additions (*piyyutim*) are frequently of unknown authorship; all the more so, the set of standardized prayers in which such poetry is inserted, such as the first morning blessing before the *Sh'ma* (the *yotser*), which is patently an edited assemblage of once-diverse material, but sewn carefully together without regard to provenance of the parts.

Consider the problem with dating the familiar Passover prayer, *Dayyenu*, a litany-like recollection of God's acts of salvation from the Exodus to the erection of the Temple. Unlike the *Yotser*, this is a poem, presumably composed by a single individual. But by whom? And when? The tenth-century Gaon, Saadiah, describes it as optional, from which we might infer that it is relatively recent. But Melito, Bishop of Sardis, writes a similar Christian (and anti-Jewish) litany in the second century, so *Dayyenu* may be an early response to Melito. We need not unravel this mystery once and for all (even if we could). The point is simply the futility of applying historicist methods to liturgical material, which very often (as here) is so unsusceptible to a historical solution that a single poem, well known for centuries, can be variously dated with somewhat equal probability anywhere from the second to the tenth centuries (Hoffman 1987: 195; Yuval 1999a: 104–5).

If models from the secular university failed to provide the right categories, we might wonder why the concept of Jewish liturgy arose altogether. The answer is the parallel evolution of Christian studies. What rabbinics is for Jews, patristics is to Christians. But whereas the rabbis are overwhelmingly concerned with law, the Fathers are fascinated by liturgy. Rabbinic texts therefore provide liturgico-legal commentary, but not the description of prayers that we get in early Christian writing. Even the rabbinic legal material is sparse. Of the Mishnah's sixty-three tractates, only one (*Berakhot*) deals ostensibly, as its main topic, with the daily and Shabbat statutory public service, and over half of that prefers topics related to mealtime prayer or occasional blessings, like seeing a rainbow or hearing bad news. The Passover *Seder* gets only one chapter out of ten in the tractate on Passover. High holiday liturgy cannot even be reconstructed from the Mishnah, so tiny is its coverage there. We almost never get full texts of early prayers; nothing at all akin, say, to the Didache's celebrated Table Prayers, or the Eucharist of Hippolytus (Jungmann 1948: 12, 22–3; Klauser 1979: 16–17), both of which hail from the period that parallels the Mishnah. What liturgical descriptions we have in tannaitic litera-ture are usually cultic events long gone: the *Sukkot* water celebration, for example (Suk. 5: 2–4), the Second Tithe confession (M. Ma'aser Sheni 5: 10–13), the First Fruit affirmation (M. Bik. 3: 1–6), or the Ma'amad fast-day liturgy (M. Ta'an. 2: 1–4). Jews have nothing like the Christian pilgrim Egeria's fourth-century diary (Wilkinson 1981), which is less a travelogue of the holy land than a guide to the holy worship she encountered there. Partly, we assume, this is a matter of chance, and partly not. There are talmudic traditions, after all, of travellers from Palestine observing diverse liturgical customs in Babylonia—Rav's observation of the use of the half *Hallel* there on Rosh Chodesh, for instance (Ta'an. 28b); and notations of liturgical diversity between the two great centres are available in the early post-talmudic or Geonic era (Mueller 1970). So it is not as if Jews paid no attention to what the liturgy was. But unlike the Christian parallel, the topic is rarely the evolving set of prayer texts, so much as it is the halachic issues of when a prayer gets said, who says it, and how—issues that arise not about the nature of reality but about human action within it.

Christians organize knowledge differently than do Jews. Theology is central. Liturgy is the way the faithful act out theological truths. A historicizing agenda was not superimposed on this theological material until the Vatican's brief openness to modernism at the turn of the twentieth century—an easier task than in the Jewish case, if only because of the exceptional documentation by the Fathers and their successors. The Eucharist itself could be traced to the alternative accounts in the Gospels and to 1 Corinthians 11; baptism too reached back at least to references in Mark 1: 4 and John 3: 22, its full theological justification for infants coming from Augustine (354–430). Other rituals that would eventually become sacraments were slotted in later on the historical spectrum (Osborne, OFM 1999: 5–9). Christian historical analysis even developed into a 'liturgical movement', a series of liturgical innovations, based on the new-found rationale of historical consciousness.

But history remained subservient to theology. Theology was said to be transhistorical, composed of truths that are eternal. When historicism necessarily questioned eternal truth, a 'new theology' (La Nouvelle Theologie) arose to argue that truths may indeed be historically determined, but no less valid. For Jews, the same issues arose with regard to halachah. Whereas once it could be imagined that legal precedent was unconditioned by time, the study of history now stipulated the context under which halachah had evolved. The *Kulturkampf* between the timeless and the time-conditioned thus impacted on Judaism and Christianity differently. Christians felt the conflict theologically; Jews did so halachically. Sometimes the same issues would arise for both groups: the right of women to lead prayers, for instance. But the terms of the debate would vary, Christians using a theological rationale and Jews a halachic one. When Christians found the need to shelter liturgy somewhere in a list of academic disciplines, it seemed logical to consider liturgy as a sub-category of theology, to slot liturgy professors into the theological departments, and to develop a cross-discipline called liturgical theology. Jews never found the need to shelter liturgy anywhere. The topic had never existed for them. Jewish scholars pursued liturgical topics, but only insofar as they were part of the larger study of rabbinics.

Two liturgical masters epitomize both parallels and differences in the application of history to liturgy: Josef A. Jungmann (1889–1975) and Ismar Elbogen (1874–1943). Elbogen was born earlier and did not live as long. He was forced from Germany in 1938, after informally directing the fabled Hochschule für die Wissenschaft des Judentums in Berlin, and working with Stephen Wise across the Atlantic to send European Jewish scholars to America and freedom. Jungmann taught theology at Innsbruck until the Anschluss, when the Nazis closed his institution; he made his way to Vienna, and then spent the rest of the war in the surrounding countryside composing his two-volume masterwork, a painstaking historical study of the Mass in the Roman Catholic Church, first entitled *Missarum Sollemnia*, but then provided with the English appellation, *The Mass of the Roman Rite: Its Origins and Development* (Jungmann 1951). In the tempestuous Nazi era, the lives of the two men could not have been different, but both men paid tribute to history in the titles of their work. Elbogen too is best known for a liturgical classic, *Jewish Liturgy in its Historical Development* (Elbogen 1913). Both authors thus embraced history, and they both did so with religious motivation. Elbogen, a modernist and reformer in his own right, also oversaw the development of what he hoped would become a German *Einheitsgebetbuch*, a 'Book of Common Prayer'. For him, liturgical history would demonstrate the way prayer should be conducted. Jungmann was a Jesuit priest, intent on absorbing the lessons of history so as to protect the time-honoured theological truths of the Church. But Elbogen was not just a liturgist: he was a master of rabbinics and a historian, who would come to America and write a seventh volume bringing Graetz's history up to date (Elbogen 1944). Jungmann remained a theologian, who wrote also a posthumously published 'historical, theological and pastoral survey' of the Mass (Jungmann 1975).

Jungmann and Elbogen came to history with different agendas. Jungmann was trained historically so as to defend the faith. He was part of a post-First World War reaction to an 1896 publication that had used history to attack the church's dogmas (Osborne 1987: 103). Elbogen adopted the same historical method but proactively, not reactively: he believed it justified his stand as a religious reformer. Jungmann, therefore, retained ties to theology departments, leaving behind a school of followers who pursued liturgy as a Christian academic discipline. Elbogen left behind a marvellous synthesis of the historical method applied to liturgy; but he neither founded nor continued an academic school of thought with regard to liturgy. After him, as before, Jewish liturgical research was subsumed under the larger canopy of rabbinics. Liturgy was still in search of an identity of its own. The question underlying the issue of identity remained the same: what kind of thing is liturgy, anyway?

FROM HISTORICISM TO FORM CRITICISM AND BEYOND

With Elbogen, Jews can be said to have such a thing as liturgical study—even though liturgy was still not seen as its own discipline. And Elbogen was the crowning point of a longer development, the study of rabbinic texts generally, within which liturgical texts were but part of a larger whole awaiting the scientist's unravelling gaze.

The founder of modern Jewish research, Leopold Zunz (1794–1886), best illustrates the method (Zunz 1832).

Historicism was linked to the nationalist concept of the *Volk*. In part, Jews fit this nationalist mould: they were a people. But whereas other peoples occupied ancestral lands, Jews had been expelled from theirs (by nations or by God, depending on one's theology). Jewish historians like Heinrich Graetz stretched the nationalist scheme to apply to Jews as well, by describing the fortune of Jews in all the areas where they had at one time or another resided. But he could do so as a Hegelian, measuring the evolution of spirit that underlay Jewish peregrinations. He also furthered the research programme set largely by Leopold Zunz, whose goal was the reorganization of Jewish literature into the building-blocks of culture. Peoples had a land, a language, and a culture which their language expressed. If Jews failed the test of land, they at least met the twin marks of language and culture.

But once again, it was not clear where liturgy fit in. Literature was supposed to be studied historically. After charting a people's literature by time and place of composition, one would have a sequential literary narrative of a people's cultural evolution. Zunz therefore marked off talmud from midrash, for instance; and isolated genres and schools of midrash. But again, the liturgy proved elusive. Since literature was supposed to mirror history, prayers were approached as responses to historical challenges. But as evidence, the stuff of prayers is hardly as rich a source as documents that purport to say precisely what is going on, and often why. As we have seen, liturgy is a composite work where editors have blurred the seams that separate one century's output from another. Its layered documentation reminded early scholars of the Bible, however, so that biblical criticism could be applied to separate one liturgical stratum from another. In this way, liturgy would reveal history like any other historical document.

The best example is the *Amidah*. Zunz noticed first that the opening and closing benedictions are cited in the Mishnah (RH 4: 2) by name, whereas the middle blessings, if referred to at all, are known only by their opening words. That must mean that they had been composed sufficiently early for them to attract abstract titles by the fourth decade of the second century, when Rabbi Akiba, who uses their names, died. Zunz then divided the middle blessings into those that seemed personal (petitions for health or divine pardon, for instance) and those that expressed nationalistic sentiments (requests for messianic redemption). Surely personal prayer is primal, he imagined, so must pre-date nationalistic expression. But prayers for Israel the nation had to reflect specific historical circumstances, so Zunz set about the imaginative task of linking the content of any given benediction with an historical event—a petition to 'restore our judges', for instance, was said to be a response to the Roman dissolution of the Sanhedrin. Eventually, Zunz had a time-line on which he could array the growth of the *Amidah* from its origins all the way to Rabban Gamaliel II, whose final redaction of the prayer was described in the Talmud. He had also to explain why this prayer known as the *Shemoneh Esreh*

('The Eighteen Benedictions') had nineteen, rather than eighteen, parts. But the Talmud itself had answered that question by attributing the twelfth blessing (actually a malediction against heretics) to Gamaliel himself, and explaining it as an addendum to his original eighteen. Zunz elsewhere approached sources critically. Here, he accepted the talmudic report as it stood.

In similar fashion, Zunz dispensed with the rest of the liturgy. The morning liturgical rubric known as the *Tachanun*, for instance, contains a seven-paragraph prayer beginning *Vehu rachum*, 'God is merciful...'. The entire piece is highly redundant, to the point where whole paragraphs could be shuffled or even excised with no loss of meaning. Who would have written such an elaborate exercise in gratitude?

Here, Zunz located a tradition attributing the composition to rabbinic émigrés who escaped the war with Rome by sailing a raft across the Mediterranean and landing in Spain, where they began what would become the Spanish Golden Age (Zunz 1865). This is a legend that Zunz knew better than to believe, especially since the prayer is unknown prior to the Geonic era. But gratuitously, he accepted the notion of Spanish provenance, then sought an episode in Spanish-Jewish history to explain the prayer. Zunz scoured the early years of Spanish Jewry until he located some seventh-century anti-Jewish legislation by the Visigothic kings Scintilla and Receswinth. Saved from potential disaster in their reign, Jews must have composed *Vehu rachum*, and then developed the attractive legend that linked their creation to the fall of the Temple.

It is all of a piece then: physical scientists mapped aeons in rock formations; Freud charted the growth of the human psyche; and liturgical scholars measured evolution of prayer texts, as part of the growing density of post-biblical Jewish culture.

Once more we find evidence of cosmology's impact on liturgical method. Knowingly or not, Jewish scientists of text used evolutionary metaphors to govern their approach. They saw culture as a living organism that grows from a tiny genetic essence, but then is subject to accretions that, by definition, do not belong to the purified prayer as it was intended embryonically to be. The putative 'original text' (the Urtext) had become the liturgical holy grail.

In that regard, the quintessential challenge for liturgical reconstruction was the *Amidah*, because of its apparent extra benediction and its evident evolution to the point of containing nineteen benedictions. Zunz had found the Urtext in its first and last three blessings, and the personal, as opposed to the political, intermediary benedictions. The ultimate claim came from Louis Finkelstein, who (among other things) purported to be able to match the use of divine appellations to specific rabbis. This and other stylistic desiderata led him to posit a simple blessing as the crux of Judaism's primary exemplar of prayer: 'Blessed are You, Eternal our God and God of our fathers, God of Abraham, God of Isaac and God of Jacob, great mighty and awesome God on high, maker of heaven and earth, hear our prayer and have mercy upon us. Blessed are you, Eternal One, who hears prayer' (Petuchowski 1970: 91–177).

But why should liturgy develop from the simple to the complex? And why should the original crux of a prayer (assuming there is one) be privileged as more authentic than, say, a prayer full-grown to reflect the views of many authors and compilers? Only the cosmology of nineteenth-century evolutionists requires such a view.

And that view was increasingly under attack in another quarter: biblical study itself. We saw above that the composite nature of liturgical texts suggested linkages with the Pentateuch, which had been revealed as a highly edited whole with independent sources that could be disentangled from each other. In the case of the Torah, that may still turn out to be the case. But other books of the Bible, the Psalms, for instance, seemed less likely to fit the documentarists' paradigm. Assuming that the Psalms were used cultically, it seemed logical to posit an oral origin for them. That they were eventually written down, sometimes as composite documents, said nothing about the original oral creation that could well have been in use for centuries prior to their written canonization.

Not just Psalms but the rest of the Bible too was being exposed to just such considerations by a school of thought that came to be known as form-criticism. To some extent associated with Scandinavia, and driven in part by fundamentalist Protestant attempts to retain divine authorship, biblical critics who had attended only to the written text were said to have missed the very goal of their enterprise: the original Bible, which had been committed to writing only very late. Since oral origins are by definition unrecoverable, biblical scholars needed to change the set of questions being asked. Their new agenda would impact similarly on liturgy which, being 'cultic' in its essence, is all the more akin to psalms, and likely also, then, to have existed for centuries prior to being written down.

A liturgical critique of this sort is associated with the name of Joseph Heinemann. Like other traditional Jewish scholars, Heinemann felt at home in all of rabbinics, and wrote as much on aggadah and Targum as he did on liturgy. His liturgical mentor was Arthur Spanier (1884–1944), the head of the Hebraica and Judaica division of the Prussian State Library until his dismissal as a 'non-Aryan' in 1935. After a brief stay in Sachsenhausen, Spanier emigrated to Holland, but died anyway in Bergen-Belsen.

Thanks to Heinemann, over one hundred years of speculation regarding the identification of a Urtext was exposed as largely a waste of time. The best that can be said of early liturgy is that certain rubrics are mentioned in the Mishnah, so must have existed in some forms at least by 200 CE. By chance, we know the wording by which some people once expressed those rubrics, but there is not, and never was, a single Urtext for them. Heinemann thus reversed philological expectations. As he saw it, liturgy went from complexity to simplicity. It began with many different prayer versions that circulated simultaneously. These were eventually edited into the relative simplicity of a single set of wording that was canonized in a standard written prayer book. He did not study this final canonization process, which occurred in Geonic Babylonia (ninth century) and thus fell outside the time-frame in which his interests lay; that last step would be detailed only in 1979 (Hoffman 1979). The prayer book, as we know it, was compiled as a *responsum* to enforce local Babylonian cultural hegemony (at the expense of rival Palestinian traditions) on new Jewish communities in western Europe. Its author, Amram (*c.*860), is unrelenting in his opposition to Palestinian customs. A further step was taken by Saadiah Gaon (*c.*920), whose prayer book was intended to counter Karaite criticism, and to demonstrate rabbinic Judaism's linguistic, structural, and philosophical purity— these beings aesthetic matters favoured by the surrounding Muslim culture. Later geonim, especially Sherira and Hai (*c.*1000), adopted a stance of permissiveness regarding liturgical customs that deviated from Babylonian norms, so as to retain the loyalty of outlying Jewish communities that no longer required Babylonian guidance and might have broken off economic and cultural relationships with the aging Geonic centre.

Heinemann demonstrated the implausibility of this liturgy's having an ancient Urtext. It began with many different verbal variants, some (like the Protestant free-prayer tradition today) composed on the spot for a single oral 'performance', others repeated until memorized and passed down as fixed versions available for use and re-use. Much of this later material eventually crystallized into different versions or rites, which were even further synthesized into Amram's prayer book or a rival Palestinian tradition, no longer extant but still evident in fragments found in the Genizah. Other forms still must have fallen into desuetude and been lost forever.

But even as Heinemann dismissed the search for original texts, he did not wholly shift emphases. For one thing, he still focused on antiquity, as if Jewish authenticity harks back to its pristine rabbinic origins. An Urtext was gone, but a romanticized early era prior to printing was still imagined. His major liturgical work (Heinemann 1966), entitled *Prayer in the Time of the Tannaim and the Amoraim*, is a privileging of origins, hardly an encyclopedic vision of Jewish prayer in all times and places. And, good rabbinist that he was, Heinemann remained focused on texts. No longer able to ask his texts to reveal their evolution, he developed new questions for them. Since even oral prayers have to be performed somewhere, Heinemann tried pairing prayers with institutional settings. He assumed that different formal patterns betrayed the settings in question: direct addresses to worshippers (such as the priestly blessing from Numbers 6: 24–6) must have been used in the Temple, for instance.

Heinemann's alternative programme has itself proved to be a dead end, as Heinemann himself probably knew. Rather than ask how old a text was, he sought to distinguish its formal characteristics which he thought would correspond to discrete institutions in ancient Israel. But as little as we know about the texts, we know even less about the institutions. And Heinemann himself saw that the prayers as we have them usually display more than one set of formal criteria, so that even if we knew the institutions in question, and even if we knew people prayed at them, and even if single styles did characterize specific institutions, it would still be impossible to assign what we now have with any degree of certainty.

Even after Heinemann, however, historicist philology did not fold up its tents and steal silently away into the night. The late E. D. Goldschmidt (1895–1974), perhaps the most thorough textual scholar ever to apply his skill to liturgy, remained convinced of its validity. Like Spanier, Goldschmidt too worked as a librarian in the Prussian State Library until 1935, but left for Palestine rather than Holland and was spared Spanier's fate. His liturgical interests—indeed, his commitment to Jewish scholarship in general—commenced only upon leaving Germany. His celebrated reconstruction of the Haggadah's history (Goldschmidt 1960) remained fully within the philological mould, but with Goldschmidt we encounter yet another development, associated with the modern State of Israel, and arising from a commitment to scientific study of text, on one hand, and a cosmology best described as Zionist, on the other.

The Zionist Paradigm

A discussion of Zionist influence on scholarship requires a description that is independent of specific 'Zionisms'—transcending Herzl's political Zionism or Ahad Ha'am's cultural Zionism, for instance. For my purposes here, 'Zionism' denotes the cultural attitude that pervaded Israel following 1948, characterized by a sense of the unity of the Jewish People and its cultural productions. Airlifts of Yemeni (and later Ethiopian) Jews followed from this ideology that saw world Jewry after the Shoah as one and united. Accordingly, the National Library took as its duty the collection and preservation of the cultural record of all Jews, everywhere.

This attitude reflects a new cosmology: the particularist yet universal sense of Jewish Peoplehood, particularist in the sense that it is Jewish welfare that is at stake, but universal in the sense that the Jewish people transcends all historical and geographical manifestations of it. Its centre is Israel, where Jewish culture is 'ingathered' no less than the living remnants of the people who produce it.

Goldschmidt's heroic labour is Zionist, in that he sought to uncover and preserve the liturgical output of the Jewish People. His historical reconstruction of the Haggadah was part of a larger oeuvre, best seen in his life-long studies of Jewish rites. He was, at his best, a reconstructor of traditions: recovering manuscripts from Jerusalem's National Library and piecing together scientific copies of the way Jews once prayed in the Balkans, say, or in Provence (Goldschmidt 1979). His last great contributions were reconstructions of the liturgy for Rosh Hashanah, Yom Kippur, and Sukkot (Goldschmidt 1970, 1981)—he died before completing the holiday cycle—each a thick tome, providing in effect the liturgical culture of the Jewish

People in the very Ashkenaz that Hitler had destroyed, but whose cultural hallmarks would be retained forever.

That Goldschmidt devoted much of his life to *piyyutim*, the poetic insertions into the liturgy, deserves special attention in the context of a Zionist paradigm. *Piyyutim* were the centre even of Zunz's enterprise. Think of Zunz and his fellow Wissenschaft colleagues as 'literateurs', the way restaurant-owners are 'restaurateurs'. Think of them as opening a literary establishment called 'The Culture of Our People', where cultural consumers could partake of their literary legacy. Scholarly articles about that literature were the functional equivalent of restaurant menus that organize food. They classified the works of the past into relevant categories, dating them like good wine, evaluating as 'advanced or superstitious' the periods in which they were produced, differentiating 'major' works (the main cultural courses) from 'minor' ones (good as a side dish, perhaps, but not much more), and, above all, making sure that those who visit the establishment will not misjudge it as a medieval slop-house where any old thing gets served, without even suitable regard for knowing its age, the garden in which it grew, and how well the it had been preserved. *Piyyutim* were the *pièce de résistance*, because, as poetry, they were the height of human culture: and common to Jews, Zunz would have emphasized, not just to Germans. Zunz therefore devoted specific attention to the *piyyutim*, as the best demonstration that Judaism had its own culture in which Jews might take pride.

As we see from Goldschmidt, Zionist liturgists were never totally removed from the original philological project. But they had abandoned the evolutionary elitism that insisted on measuring the worth of each literary specimen they encountered. Midrash, that is, did not have to be 'major' or 'minor', and prayers were not 'better' just because they were 'old'. The issue was no longer authenticity. Post-Shoah Zionist scholars took for granted that Jews had a culture. Whereas Zunz and his generation had to demonstrate it, Zionists had only to save it. They emulated the philologists in scientific rigour, but only to rescue, not to rate, the cultural output that they found.

They also shared the philologists' special love of *piyyutim*, but again, for their own reasons. They did not seek out poetry only because it is the form of literature that is quintessentially cultural—the Jewish equivalent of Goethe and Schiller, say. Rather, *piyyutim* are first and foremost a product of Eretz Yisrael. While Babylonian Jewry had very largely eschewed them, Palestinians had developed a golden age of the *piyyut*, culminating in the work of Yose bar Yose, Yannai, and Eliezer Kalir, some-where around the fifth and sixth centuries. Attention to *piyyutim* went hand in hand with the early state's adulation of the Bible and its revival of the Hebrew language, since *piyyutim* are literarily dependent on biblical phraseology and represent the first instance in which Hebrew was creatively enriched by poets who found the Bible's heritage lacking.

Goldschmidt was hardly alone, then, in his attention to scientific manuscripts of liturgical expression, especially *piyyutim*. He was joined by a whole host of patient researchers (also from Eretz Yisrael) who combed the Genizah fragments or other manuscript evidence, reconstructing this poem or that, and demonstrating the cultural richness of the Jewish People. Of them all, Ezra Fleischer deserves particular acclaim, for his own work (which is too vast to describe fully) and for his mentorship to an entire generation of scholars who have continued the task of making available the Payyetanic legacy of the past. In 1990 Fleischer even revived the issue of origins, denying the form-critical critique and arguing that Jewish liturgy is largely the result of Gamaliel II (Fleischer 1990). Most scholars, however, continue to accept Heinemann's claim that there is no single Urtext to be found (Reif 1991; Langer 1999, 2000).

Along with *piyyutim* has come also the reconstruction of the old Palestinian rite, the prayers and customs of Jews who inhabited the Land prior to the Crusades (Fleischer 1988). More work remains to be done, and one suspects that will always be the case, since there is always another manuscript to be sewn together, transcribed, edited, and catalogued. Unlike the philological quest for an Urtext, the search for liturgico-literary activity is never-ending; its validity cannot be denied, since it is independent of any necessary theory of Jewish liturgical development. It is its own reward, with or without the Zionist sentiment that produced it.

Broadening the Field

The most major change to have occurred in the last decade or two, even for those who still do historical reconstruction, is the refusal to limit attention to the earliest historical period as if it alone were sacrosanct. This expansion of interest beyond the formative era of the rabbis is seen everywhere. Reuven Kimelman (1994), for instance, has applied a literary analysis not just to Psalm 145 (the *Ashrei*), but also to the sixteenth-century poetic gem *Lekha Dodi*. Israel Yuval (1999) and Israel Ta-Shma (1992) have focused on medieval liturgical customs—sometimes in dialogue with Christianity. Joseph Tabori (1996) writes specifically on talmudic halachah, but also (1992–3, 1994) provides us with an ongoing comprehensive bibliography of liturgical writing, indicating by its content the proper breadth that the field ought to encompass. Ruth Langer's major work too, thus far (1990), analyses halachic debate, but in dialogue with custom; and her later work (1998) applies symbolist anthropology to the synagogue Torah ritual. Another broadening of scope is the pursuit of women's liturgy, especially for the early modern period in eastern Europe and Italy, where prayers in Yiddish and Italian are common (Weissler 1998; Cardin 1992).

When Elbogen wrote his 1913 liturgical masterpiece, liturgical reform was foremost in his mind, for he was already working on plans for his *Einheitsgebetbuch*. But the organization of his book underscores his historicist bias: origins are determinative; medieval poetry adds textual beauty; only eventually does the liturgy evolve into something modern, which is to say (for Elbogen), 'Reform'. But modern reform is only a latter-day footnote to the historical and poetic foundation. It consumes thirty pages in the English edition of Elbogen's master-piece—whereas the history and analysis of the received text gets 295. The current move toward decentring antiquity has carried with it a new emphasis on the present as worthy of study in its own right. Eric L. Friedland's lifelong work in nineteenth- and twentieth-century liturgical reform, for example, was hitherto seen as second-ary to the main issues of origins. No longer: his contributions are now collected for wider scrutiny (1997). Similarly, David Ellenson, noted expert in Jewish religious thought, has turned increasingly to the analysis of modern liturgies as reflections of identity.

A parallel trend has been the dissemination of knowledge through popular works that once would have been declared too unscholarly even to discuss in a review such as this. But the move toward popularization is significant. Ideologically, one might link it to postmodernist critiques on scholarship, but I hesitate to do so, because that very justification would convert the phenomenon of which I speak into its opposite: a clever scholarly stratagem that is really traditional scholarship in popular disguise. The trend is partly a result of market forces: we have slowly become accustomed to books like Allan Bloom's *The Closing of the American Mind* (1987), Stephen Haw-king's *A Brief History of Time* (1988), and Harold Bloom's *Shakespeare: The Invention of the Human* (1998). All three books—just a sample of many—became best-sellers despite the fact that non-technical audiences could hardly have followed everything the authors had to say.

But this new emphasis on popular scholarship is not just the market at work. It too reveals shifts in cosmology: the feminist erasure of hierarchies, for instance. More important, it heralds the break-up of the arbitrary divisions of knowledge into discrete disciplines with which this essay began. In a celebrated essay of 1983, Clifford Geertz heralded the appearance of 'Blurred Genres'. Formerly hermetic scholarly circles were now talking to one another, finding metaphors to describe their work in terms understandable beyond their own circle. 'One waits', Geertz concluded, 'only for quantum theory in verse or biography in algebra.' Geertz's subtitle proclaimed the news that the tendency was nothing short of 'A Reconstruc-tion of Social Thought', driven by 'the move toward conceiving of social life as organized in terms of symbols.... The woods [he concluded] are full of eager interpreters' (Geertz 1983).

So, too, with liturgy. This repackaging of knowledge is now producing books on prayer designed for general audiences but not, on that account, unscholarly—for instance, *Minhag Ami: My People's Prayerbook* (Hoffman 1997–), the newest comprehensive liturgical publication, that includes the insights of scholars across the ideological divide, in determining the meaning of Jewish liturgy for our time.

'Meaning' is the cosmological key. At stake is the growing recognition of a participational universe in which science defines and invents, as much as it discovers, reality. Realist art that 'pictures' what is already out there has become modern art that pictures what 'out there' might yet become. Brute facts are not entirely 'brute'; they are constructed, the way readings of literature are. In today's intellectual environment, liturgy provides an alternative construction of reality. It is one of the ways that people make sense of their lives.

But they do it in community, and in accordance with an inherited liturgical script. My own work (1987), therefore, increasingly treats the acted-out liturgy as a sacred drama of identity, and the liturgist as interpreter of meaning—a drama critic who explains what the play is about. As Durkheim already knew, shared ritual spells out shared identity. Liturgists are field anthropologists inquiring after the meaning of Jewish worship for the Jews who do it. They observe the entire performance, including such non-textual items as ritual art and ritual action that tell us more about what is going on than the textually recorded word does. Sometimes eyewitness commentary confirms insights, the way an anthropologist's speculation is confirmed by a native informant. Sometimes we are left with the critic's interpretive take on the liturgical event: it is compelling or not.

When, for instance, medieval Italian Jews place a boy about to be circumcised on a 'chair of Elijah', while welcoming him with *Barukh Haba*, 'Blessed be he that cometh', there is reason to believe that they are acting out their hope that he is the long-awaited messiah. Here we have a critical interpretation of the ritual-as-drama, similar to what one reads in a review of a play—the critic observes the performance and asks what it conveys. The interpretation cannot be judged by absolutist criteria of 'right' or 'wrong' in the same sense that an internally coherent system like mathematics yields correct or incorrect solutions. Rather, ritual as art form gives us what Suzanne Langer (1942) called 'presentational truths', whereby the interpretation is either 'felicitous' or not: it works or it doesn't. If it does, it is because it is coherent with what else we know about the play; it is heuristically helpful in making sense out of the performance. This is a kind of functional truth, in the sense used by William James, Thomas Dewey, and more recently Richard Rorty. Interpretations can be more or less true, not just absolutely so. The liturgist starts with an interpretation from the performance as a whole, and sees how far that view can be pressed without its running out of confirmatory evidence or being forced into a caricature that no longer convinces.

Take the 'reading' that the circumcised child is potentially the messiah. Does this 'reading' successfully make sense of other disparate data? It does. We find also that medieval Haggadah art conflates the image of the messiah with Elijah. So the child placed on Elijah's chair is also the messiah. Then we hear of a fourteenth-century

Italian custom of greeting the child as 'brother of seven, or father of eight'—an oblique reference to the boy as David or Jesse. So artistic and textual evidence concur in a 'reading' of the ritual that is coherent with its attendant art, Italian messianism of the time, and so forth. This is not the place to argue for or against this particular case; it is chosen only because it illustrates the holistic study of liturgy as a meaningful human enterprise.

But meaning is a nuanced thing (Hoffman 1993). Sometimes liturgical meaning is entirely idiosyncratic, a remnant of childhood memories, perhaps, that is shared by no one but a single individual. Of greater interest, perhaps, is public meanings: the things many people agree about, whether or not they are rooted in proper Jewish sources—as most American Jews associate the Seder with 'family time', but ignore the official themes associated with redemption. Liturgists ferret out public meanings implicit in sacred performances. Participants may recognize them only when presented with them—as an audience may nod knowingly when a critic explains what the play they just saw was intended to mean.

There is yet a third kind of meaning, however: the official meanings that the 'experts' proclaim as real. With official meaning, we enter into the realm of theology. But we still lack a systematic look at liturgical theology, that is, a coherent study of the official meanings about God, the world, and human nature that the liturgy provides.

The debate between the text-centred approach and my own is not over the use of texts to get our information. Often that is all we have. The question is whether prayer books are texts, or whether they only look like texts but should be treated as something else. Surely, we can say a lot about these books as texts; but do we want to? Stefan Reif does, and he explains why in his lengthy history which traces European rites based largely on their textual dependencies (1993). When he is done, he has a map of ritual dissemination from the two classic Jewish centres of influence (Palestine and Babylonia) and a network of criss-crossing lines that connect the various rites according to how they have influenced each other. This is literary textual study at its best.

But is that all we can ask? My own approach, by contrast, treats rites as ritual statements of identification. I thus ask social, not literary, questions. When community A borrows a poem from community B, it ultimately may signify that the members of A and of B shared a specific aspect of Jewish identity. German Reform Jews, for instance, borrowed Spanish poetry. A text-oriented scholar wants to know the extent to which Ashkenazi (German) liturgy is now Sephardi too (influenced by Spanish liturgy). I ask what it is that attracted German Jews to Spanish poetry, and what they were saying about their own identity as a consequence. Through the way a community prays, it defines who it is.

CONCLUSION: JEWISH LITURGY AS A DISCIPLINE?

We began by wondering how Jewish Liturgy is its own discipline. It now turns out that if it is a discipline, it is a very postmodern one, in the sense that it asks how Jews construct the meaning of their lives. New paradigms do not necessarily displace old ones; they build on them. The scientific rigour of the philologists is as important as ever; the reconstruction of *piyyutim* and rites is raw data without which we would be nowhere.

With the abandoning of the model by which only origins matter, and with the understanding that every communal ritualizing deserves attention for what it says about Jewish identity, liturgy is becoming a 'post-discipline' with enormous potential.

SUGGESTED READING

The standard summary work is still Elbogen (1913). The English version (1993) includes updated notes based largely on the form-critical critique by Heinemann, whose own work (1966) is available in an English version (1977). A more recent general history by Reif (1993) is especially good on the medieval dissemination of rites. An encyclopedic history can be found in Hoffman (1995). The best current popular work in English is Hammer (1994). The formation of the standard prayer book is detailed in Hoffman (1979). On methodology, cf. Reif (1993), and Sarason (1978 and 1982). A series of excellent articles comparing Jewish and Christian liturgy is carried in Bradshaw and Hoffman (1991–9). These are compared theologically by Hoffman (2000). Tabori (1992–3, 1994) maintains an ongoing bibliography of liturgical studies. The only relatively current scholarly history of the High Holiday Liturgy is in Hebrew (Goldschmidt 1970), as a preface to the scientifically edited text. For the Haggadah, Goldschmidt (1960) remains the best edition, but considerable other literature exists: e.g. Guggenheimer (1998), which provides English commentary and diverse versions of the text. See also vols. 5 and 6 of Bradshaw and Hoffman (1999). *Piyyutim* are surveyed best in Fleischer (1975), and in English, Weinberger (1998). For scientific editions of classic texts, see Rav Amram Gaon (Goldschmidt 1971), Siddur Rav Saadja Gaon (Davidson *et al.* 1963), and Siddur Maimonides as well as various medieval rites (Goldschmidt 1979). The Genizah material is best summarized in Fleischer (1988). Individual *piyyutim* may be traced through Davidson (1924). The current debate on reviving the search for an 'original text' can be followed through Fleischer (1990) and his respondents (Reif 1991; Langer 1999, 2000). The standard source for prayer book reform in Europe is Petuchowski (1968). American liturgies are listed and annotated in Wachs (1997). On contemporary prayer books, see also Friedland (1997). For the symbolist anthropological method, see Hoffman (1987) and Langer (1998). From a literary perspective, see Kimelman (1994). For halachah (law) and minhag (custom), cf. Langer (1980), Ta Shema (1992), and (on the Passover Seder) Tabori (1996). Women's prayer from Eastern Europe is described in Weissler (1998), and an eighteenth-century Italian MS for women appears (with translation) in Cardin (1992).

Contemporary commentary to the liturgy from all ideological perspectives is collected in Hoffman (1997–   ).

BIBLIOGRAPHY

ABRAMS, H. 1953. *The Mirror and the Lamp*. Oxford.

BRADSHAW, P. F. and HOFFMAN, L. A. 1991–9. *Two Liturgical Traditions* [series]. Notre Dame, Ind.

CARDIN, N. B. 1992. *Out of the Depths I Call to You*. Northvale, NJ.

DAVIDSON, I. 1924. *Otsar HaShirah VehaPiyyut*. 4 vols. Repr. New York 1970.

——ASSAF, S., and JOEL, B. I. eds. 1963. *Siddur Rav Saadja Gaon*. Jerusalem.

DOUGLAS, M. 1966. *Purity and Danger*. London.

ELBOGEN, I. 1913. *Der Jüdische Gottesdienst in seiner geschichtlichen Entwicklung*. English edn. *Jewish Liturgy in its Historical Development*. 1993.

——1944. *A Century of Jewish Life*. Philadelphia.

FINKELSTEIN, L. 1925–6. 'The Development of the Amidah.' *JQR* 16. Repr. in *Contributions to the Scientific Study of Jewish Liturgy*. 91–177. Jakob J. Petuchowski ed. New York. 1970.

FLEISCHER, E. 1975. *Shirat HaKodesh Ha'Ivrit bimei Habenayim*. Jerusalem.

——1988. *Tefillah UMinhagei Tefillah Erets-Yisra'eliim BiTekufat HaGenizah*. Jerusalem.

——1990. 'Lakadmoniut Tefillot Hachovah Beyisrael.' *Tarbiz* 59: 397–445.

FRIEDLAND, E. L. 1997. *Were Our Mouths Filled With Song*. Cincinnati.

GEERTZ, C. 1983. *Local Knowledge*. New York.

GOLDSCHMIDT, E. D. 1960. *Haggadah Shel Pesach V'Toldoteha*. Jerusalem.

——1970. *Machzor LaYamim HaNora'im*. 2 vols. New York.

——1971. *Seder Rav Amram Gaon*. Jerusalem.

——1979. *Mechkarei Tefillah UFiyyut*. Jerusalem.

——1981. *Machzor Lasukkot*. New York.

GUGGENHEIMER, H. 1998. *The Scholar's Haggadah*. Northvale, NJ.

HAMMER, R. 1994. *Entering Jewish Prayer*. New York.

HARGREAVES, W. N. 1963. *A History of Academical Dress in Europe until the 18th Century*. Oxford.

HEINEMANN, J. 1966. *HaTefillah BiTekufat haTannaim vehaAmoraim*. Jerusalem. Trans. and updated for English readers by R. Sarason, *Prayer in the Talmud*. Berlin 1977.

HOFFMAN, L. A. 1979. *The Canonization of the Synagogue Service*. Notre Dame.

——1987. *Beyond the Text*. Bloomington, Ind.

——1991. 'What is a Liturgical Tradition?' In *The Changing Face of Jewish and Christian Worship in North America*. Paul F. Bradshaw and L. A. Hoffman eds. Notre Dame.

HOFFMAN, L. A. 1993. 'How Ritual Means: Ritual Circumcision in Rabbinic Culture and Today.' *Studia Liturgica* 23/1: 78–97.

——1995. 'Jewish Liturgy and Jewish Scholarship.' In *Judaism in Late Antiquity*. Part I. Jacob Neusner ed. Leiden.

——ed.1997–   . *Minhag Ami: My People's Prayerbook*. 6 vols. [to date]. Woodstock, Vt.

——2000. 'Jewish and Christian Liturgy.' In *Christianity in Jewish Terms*. 175–89. Tikva Frymer-Kensky *et al*. eds. Boulder, Col.

JUNGMANN, J. A. 1951. *The Mass of the Roman Rite: Its Origins and Development.* 2 vols. Repr. Westminster, Md. 1986.

—— 1975. *The Mass: An Historical, Theological and Pastoral Survey.* Collegeville, Minn.

KAGAN, D. 1999. 'What is Liberal Education?' In *Reconstructing History: The Emergence of a New Historical Society.* E. Fox-Genevese and E. Lasch-Quinn eds. New York.

KIMELMAN, R. 1994. 'Mavo Lelekha Dodi ueleKabbalat Shabbat.' *Mechkarei Yerushalayim B'mach'shevet Yisra'el.* 14: 394–454.

—— 1994. 'Psalm 145: Theme, Structure and Impact.' *JBL* 113: 23–44.

KLAUSER, T. 1979. *A Short History of the Western Liturgy.* Oxford.

LANGER, R. 1990. *To Worship God Properly.* Cincinnati.

—— 1998. 'From Study of Scripture to a Reenactment of Sinai: The Emergence of the Synagogue Torah Service.' *Worship* 72/1: 43–67.

—— 1999. 'Revisiting Early Rabbinic Liturgy: The Recent Contributions of Ezra Fleischer.' *Prooftexts* 19/2: 179–94.

—— 2000. 'Considerations of Method: A Response to Ezra Fleischer.' *Prooftexts* 20/3: 381–7.

LANGER, S. K. 1942. *Philosophy in a New Key.* New York.

LEVI, E. 1963. *Yesodot HaTefillah.* Tel Aviv.

MÜLLER, J. 1970. *Chilluf Minhagim bein Bavel Věeretz Yisra'el.* Repr. from 1878. Jerusalem.

OSBORNE, K. B. OFM. 1987. 'Eucharistic Theology Today.' *Worship* 61: 2.

—— 1999. *A Theology for the Third Millennium.* New York.

PETUCHOWSKI, J. J. 1970. *Contributions to the Scientific Study of Jewish Liturgy.* New York.

—— 1978. *Theology and Poetry.* London.

—— 1968 *Prayerbook Reform in Europe.* New York.

PUTNAM, H. 1987. *The Many Faces of Realism.* La Salle, Ill.

REIF, S. C. 1991. 'Al Hitpatchut HaTefillah HaKadumah BeYisrael.' *Tarbiz* 60: 677–81.

—— 1983. 'Jewish Liturgical Research: Past Present and Future.' *JJS* 34: 162–70.

—— 1993. *Judaism and Hebrew Prayer.* Cambridge.

SARASON, R. 1978. 'On the Use of Method in the Modern Study of Jewish Liturgy.' In *Approaches to Ancient Judaism: Theory and Practice.* 97–172. W. S. Green ed. Missoula, Mo.

—— 1982. 'Recent Developments in the Field of Jewish Liturgy.' In *The Study of Ancient Judaism. I. Mishnah, Midrash. Siddur.* J. Neusner, ed. New York

SCHEINDLIN, R. P. trans. 1993. *Jewish Liturgy: A Comprehensive History.* Philadelphia.

TA SHEMA, I. 1992. *Minhag Ashkenaz Hakadmon.* Jerusalem.

TABORI, J. 1992–3. 'Riv'on Bibliografi.' *Kiryat Sefer* [addendum] 64.

—— 1994. 'Nispach: Reshimat Ma'amarim Beinyanei Tefillah uMoadim.' Bar Ilan.

—— 1996. *Pesach Dorot.* Israel.

TAPPER, T. and SALTER, B. 1992. *Oxford, Cambridge and the Changing Idea of the University.* Buckingham.

WACHS, S. R. 1997. *American Jewish Liturgies.* Cincinnati.

WEINBERGER, L. J. 1998. *Jewish Hymnography.* London.

WEISSLER, C. 1998. *Voices of the Matriarchs.* Boston.

WILKINSON, J. 1981. *Egeria's Travels to the Holy Land.* Rev. edn. Warminster.

YEHUDAH BAR R. YAKAR [Rabeinu]. 1979. *Perush HaTefillot vehaBerakhot.* Jerusalem.

YUVAL, I. J. 1999a. 'Easter and Passover As Early Jewish–Christian Dialogue.' In *Passover and Easter: Origin and History to Modern Times.* 104–5. Paul F. Bradshaw and L. A. Hoffman eds. Notre Dame.

—— 1999b. 'Passover in the Middle Ages.' In *Passover and Easter: Origin and History to Modern Times.* 127–260. Paul F. Bradshaw and L. A. Hoffman eds. Notre Dame.

ZUNZ. L. 1832. *Die gottesdienstlichen Vorträge der Juden.* Hebrew edn., Albeck, Chanokh. Trans. *HaDerashot beYisra'el.* Jerusalem 1954.

—— 1865. *Literaturgeschichte der synagogalen Poesie.* Repr. Frankfurt 1920.

CHAPTER 30

JEWISH PHILOSOPHY AND THEOLOGY

PAUL MENDES-FLOHR

THE academic study of Jewish philosophy and theology is bedevilled by definitional and methodological ambiguities. The definitional quandary is illustrated by the *magnum opus* of Salomon ibn Gabirol (*c.* 1020–57), *Mekor Hayyim* (Fountain of Life). This work, which had circulated in a Latin translation under the title *Fons Vitae*, was only in 1845 discovered by sheer chance to be authored by Ibn Gabriol, when an abridged Hebrew translation of the original Arabic manuscript surfaced at the Bibliothéque Nationale in Paris. Entitled *Mekor Hayyim* and ascribed by the translator to Ibn Gabirol, the translation allowed Salomon Munk (1803–67), a scholar of Arabic and Hebrew literature of the Golden Age of Spain, to identify the renowned Spanish Hebrew poet and philosopher as the author of *Fons Vitae*. Hitherto it was held to be the work of a Christian (or alternatively a Muslim) author, and as such it exercised a profound influence on the likes of Duns Scotus, St Bonaventura, and Matthew of Aquasparta. Munk's discovery that such a seminal volume, prized by the Doctors of the Church—the Franciscans especially regarded its author as a great authority—was, in fact, the work of a Jew met with near ecstatic joy within the Jewish community. Under its Hebrew name Ibn Gabirol's philosophical treatise was immediately incorporated into the canon of Jewish philosophy. But the curious history of the work raises serious methodological questions. Had the Jewish provenance of its author not been discovered, would *Mekor Hayyim* have continued to be regarded exclusively as an important disquisition (*qua Fons Vitae*, of course) of medieval Christianity? And conversely, now that its author is known to have been a Jew, does it cease to be significant in the history of Christian philosophy? Further, *Mekor Hayyim*, which sought to bring to light a fundamental cleavage between the Neoplatonic and biblical views of creation, is utterly bereft of any specific Jewish content and terminology. The author does not refer to biblical individuals or events, nor does he quote Hebrew Scripture, Talmud, or other rabbinical writings. Yet virtually every study of Jewish philosophy assigns *Mekor Hayyim* pride of place. Surely, national pride aside, one must ask by which criteria is the volume, originally written in Arabic and with no expressed Jewish character, to be deemed a work of Jewish philosophy.

In addressing such questions, there are scholars who hold that the very concept of Jewish philosophy is dubious. For if by its nature philosophy addresses universal truth-claims, then it cannot be modified by any delimiting national, ethnic, or religious attribute. Similarly it would be problematic to speak of Russian mathematics, Chinese physics, or Peruvian astronomy—unless that is, one meant to denote by such adjectives a specific approach associated with mathematicians from Russia, or a concept of physics developed by physicists from China, and so on. But there is no distinctive school of philosophers of Jewish origin. Scholars are hard put to define a distinctive *Jewish* approach to philosophy. And should the rubric 'Jewish philosophy' be used to refer to the ethnic and religious affiliation or origin of a given philosopher, then one would perforce question what would be the significance of such a designation, other than its sociological, historical, and cultural interest, which, of course, is extraneous to philosophy proper. To be sure, the national attribute may simply be a linguistic or geopolitical marker. Accordingly, one speaks of Italian, Polish, South African, or Czech philosophy, not as specific schools but rather as philosophy pursued in the countries designated by these adjectives, or in the languages of those countries. But such a designation is not applicable to Jewish philosophers, since many did not write in Hebrew or any other Jewish national language. In the Middle Ages some of the most prominent Jewish philosophers, such Ibn Gabriol and Maimonides, wrote in Arabic, and later in the modern period Jewish philosophers would write in European languages such as English, French, German, Italian, Polish, Russian, and Spanish. And until the establishment of the State of Israel, Jewish philosophers did not dwell, or have the option to reside, in a Jewish national territory.

In light of the seemingly inherent and therefore intractable difficulties of defining Jewish philosophy, some scholars prefer to speak of the philosophy or—more cautiously—the philosophies of Judaism. But here too there are ambiguities. Does this term denote a philosophical view unique to Judaism, or philosophical reflections on Judaism, its religious doctrines and values? The latter conception has been defined as 'the thinking and rethinking of the fundamental ideas involved in Judaism, that is, in coherent relation one with another so that they form an intelligible whole' (Roth 1999: 8). Although this definition would apply to many medieval Jewish philosophers, it does not cover those, such as Abraham ibn Ezra, Gersonides,

Ibn Gabriol, or Maimonides, who were exercised by issues of general philosophical concern that were not specifically Jewish.

The first histories of Jewish philosophy sought to circumvent the terminological, and thus definitional, conundrums by employing a broad conception of Jewish religious philosophy, which would include philosophical works that addressed both universal metaphysical questions and issues distinctive to Judaism. Simon Bernfeld (1860–1940) wrote, in Hebrew, a compendious two-volume history of Jewish religious philosophy entitled *Daat Elohim. Toledot ha-Philosophiyah ha-Datit be-Yisrael* (Knowledge of God: The History of Religious Philosophy in Israel), published in Warsaw (1897). Defining religious philosophy as the reconciliation of theistic faith with the principles of reason, he actually presents a catalogue of Jewish religious views from the Bible and the Talmud—the authors of which did not necessarily regard themselves as beholden to the scrutiny of reason—followed by a very brief review of the Alexandrian Jewish philosophers, and a much more detailed survey of the teachings of the medieval philosophers. Bernfeld's exposition of the medievals, which constitutes the major focus of his history, commences with Sa'adiah Gaon, the tenth-century head of the famed Babylonian rabbinical college of Sura, and concludes with the seventeenth-century sage of Amsterdam, Benedict (Baruch) Spinoza. The inclusion of the renegade thinker, who, although banned by the elders of his synagogue, remained unrepentent throughout his life about his heretical views, in Bernfeld's pantheon of Jewish philosophers highlights the methodological issues that continue to confound the academic study of Jewish philosophy. Born and educated as a Jew, Spinoza's signficance in the history of *general* philosophy is universally celebrated. Similarly, the influence of the writings of medieval Jewish philosophers—particularly Hasdai Crescas (d. 1412) and Maimonides (1135–1204)—on some of his principal concepts is now widely acknowledged. But ethnic and intellectual origins do not *eo ipso* render Spinoza's philosophy Jewish. He himself would have denied that his philosophical naturalism was compatible with the religion of his forefathers. Bernfeld's embrace of Spinoza as a Jewish philosopher may be seen as reflecting his own affiliation with Zionism. Indeed, he concludes his survey of the history of Jewish *religious* philosophy—after a chapter on the Enlightenment philosopher Moses Mendelssohn (1724–86) and another providing a very adumbrative and thus fragmentary review of post-Mendelssohnian Jewish religious writers—with a rather detailed analysis of the thought of his mentor and the *spiritus rector* of cultural Zionism, Ahad Ha'am (Asher Ginsburg, 1856–1927), who, as one who sought to recast Judaism as a secular national culture, would hardly qualify as a religious philosopher.

To avoid the issues raised by considerations of including within the ambit of Jewish philosophy Spinoza and other 'heterodox' Jews, most nineteenth- and early twentieth-century historians of Jewish philosophy limited their purview to that of the medievals. Employing a restricted definition of Jewish philosophy, David Neumark (1866–1924) embarked on an ambitious project to write the history of Jewish philosophy in the Middle Ages in ten volumes. He completed but three volumes before his early death. Published as *Die Geschichte der jüdischen Philosophie des Mitellalters, nach Probleme dargestellt* (1907, 1910), these volumes were followed by a revised and expanded Hebrew version, *Toledot ha-Philosophiyah be-Yisrael* (1921, 1929). Eschewing the diachronic approach of Bernfeld—and before him the shorter chronological surveys of Munk (1857) and Joel (1876), that were essentially histories of the ideas held by certain philosophers of the Middle Ages—Neumark offered an analytical delineation of the issues, each the subject of a separate volume, that exercised medieval Jewish philosophy. He explained the conception guiding his history in a lecture delivered in January 1908 upon assuming the chair of Jewish Philosophy at Hebrew Union College, Cincinnati, which, having just left a position at a Reform rabbinical seminary in Berlin, he delivered in German. Framing his remarks under the question 'What is the philosophy of Judaism?', he observed:

The philosophy of Judaism cannot be—and actually is not—different from philosophy in general.... Judaism itself is not philosophy, for it is more than a philosophy—it is a practical system of life, based on a definite conception of the world, and thus on a definite philosophic system of thought. [But] Judaism is not philosophy, for it is more: it is a religion.... Thus the philosophy of Judaism is the system of thought that represents the theoretical conception of the world and of life peculiar to the Jewish religion—the conception on which the Jewish system of living is based.... It is the function of Jewish philosophy to trace the development of the Jewish religion in antiquity—in the days when prophecy fought single-handed against paganism, and in the days when a fermentation was caused by the first contact with Greek philosophy. The purifying effect of this fermentation was recognizable even at that time, in the last two centuries of the old and the first five of the new era; but it came out with full force only later. We call this function *the presentation of the history of Jewish dogma from the philosophic point of view*. The second task is the examination of the second union of Jewish prophecy with Greek philosophy, which we may call the *logical* union, in contradistinction to the first, the psychological. This function we call the *history of Jewish philosophy of the Middle Ages*. (Newmark 1929: 2–6)

He went on to note that, in his judgement, there is still a task for Jewish philosophy, namely, 'the exposition of the philosophic system that supports the theoretical doctrines of Judaism' (ibid. 6). In conjunction with this task, 'Jewish philosophy must show that there is another road to knowledge besides that of natural science ... this is the moral-philosophic road, which gave rise to Judaism, and which was rediscovered by Kant' (ibid.). These latter remarks, reflect Neumark's commitment to Reform Judaism and his conception of the faith of Israel as a continuously evolving religion, whose enduring essence is ethical monotheism, which throughout the ages Jewish philosophers regarded as their task to defend, explicate, and refine.

In a trenchant review of the first two German volumes of Neumark's history, Isaac Husik (1876–1939) faulted the work as apologetic, flawed by an obtrusive theological bias. Like philosophy, scholarship, he declared, cannot compromise its commitment to truth. 'Philosophy qua philosophy [cannot] have a given basis forced upon it. Philosophy will be of value so long, and only so long, as it keeps itself independent of any special religious or other dogmatic doctrines.' Hence, to be true to itself philosophy cannot allow itself to be enlisted in any cause extraneous to itself, not even for the sake of ethical monotheism. Philosophy is essentially the affair of the human being as human being, not of the Jew as Jew. The history of Jewish philosophy was necessarily antiquarian. This reflected Husik's conviction that in modern world, in the words of his intellectual biographer, Leo Strauss, 'Jewish philosophy is not merely nonexistent but impossible' (Strauss 1997: 247). In adopting a self-consciously antiquarian approach to study of medieval Jewish philosophy, Husik thus sought to reveal the inevitable antinomies in constructing a Jewish philosophy. Medieval Jewish philosophers, he argued, assumed the eternal, unimpeachable veracity of Judaism as the revealed word of God. From the perspective of philosophy this posture is but a 'naive dogmatism'. Hence, Husik concluded, 'the attempt of the medieval Jewish philosophers to establish Judaism on a philosophical basis could not, from the nature of the case, have been a success'; the task which they set themselves was 'hopeless'. Beholden to an authority extraneous to reason, the medievals—and by implication, their modern epigoni—could not be deemed genuine philosophers. The medievals, of course, were sincere in their assumption that the truths of revealed faith and reason are ultimately compatible. Jewish philosophy was, then, possible in the Middle Ages and is impossible in the modern age, because the medieval thinkers had 'an intellectual naiveté which we have lost forever'. Husik traced that naiveté to the absence in medieval thought of historical and literary criticism, which when pursued consistently and with intellectual probity must perforce undermine the authority of revealed faith. At the conclusion of his highly acclaimed history of medieval philosophy, Husik formulated the implications of these observations in a somewhat gnomic fashion: 'There are Jews now and there are philosophers, but there are no Jewish philosophers and there is no Jewish philosophy' (Husik 1916: 432). There was, of course, in the Middle Ages such a breed. But in modern times 'there have appeared philosophers among the Jews ... but they ... philosophized without regard to Judaism and in opposition to its fundamental dogmas.' (ibid. 431 f.). In passing, it should be noted that, despite his reservations, Husik esteemed the achievement of medieval philosophers for acknowledging the authority of reason and preventing Judaism from falling prey to superstition and obscurantism.

Appointed in 1911 a lecturer in medieval philosophy at the University of Pennsylvania, Husik was the first scholar to teach Jewish philosophy at a secular institution of higher learning in the United States. He was soon followed by Harry Austryn Wolfson (1887–1974), who from 1915 held an appointment at Harvard University in 'Hebrew literature and philosophy'. Wolfson essentially shared Husik's view of Jewish philosophy, although he would evaluate its accomplishments differently. He divided philosophy into three periods: Greek, Scriptural, and Non-Scriptural.

The Greek philosophers made no reference to Scripture, that is, revealed truth and knowledge. Scriptural philosophers—Jewish, Christian, and Muslim—regarded philosophy as the handmaid of God's revealed Word as recorded in Scripture.

Religious philosophies without a scriptural preamble, such as those with which we are nowadays acquainted, were unknown throughout the Middle Ages. To medieval philosophers of various [theistic] creeds, religion was not an outward survival of primitive times, which, with the magic wand of philosophy, they tried to transform into something serviceable.... It was to them a certain set of inflexible principles, of a divinely revealed origin, by which philosophy, the product of erring human reason, had to be tested and purged and purified. (Wolfson 1947: i. p. v)

What emerged from this encounter between reason and revelation, enhanced by the sublime values and vision of Scripture, Wolfson opined, was perhaps the most lively and engaging chapter in the history of the human spirit. Initiated by Philo of Alexandria, Scriptural philosophy flourished for sixteen-hundred years until 'Spinoza launched a grand assault upon it, and if [it] did not completely disappear as a result of that assault, it no longer held a dominant position' (ibid. ii. 457). Noting that Spinoza's early philosophic studies were nurtured by an extensive reading in the works of his medieval Jewish predecessors, Wolfson quipped that 'Benedictus is the first of the moderns; Baruch the last of the medievals' (Wolfson 1934: i. p. vii). Freed of its moorings in Scripture, post-Spinozan philosophy must be deemed emphatically secular, despite any abiding veneer of religion. For Wolfson, in the modern period there is no genuine religious philosophy, and hence Jewish philosophy has also ceased to exist. Since the seventeenth century we no longer live in a world of Scripture; revealed knowledge no longer makes a serious claim on the way we think and organize our lives. Wolfson thus dismisses the 'verbal theism' to which many modern philosophers continue to adhere as a self-deception. Palpably uncomfortable with the biblical faith in a personal God, these philosophers set out to construct the concept of God anew as the fundamental principle governing existence— variously conceived as the *élan vital*, the ground of being, the universal nisus, and the like—that, in effect, deprived God of an autonomous will and a miraculous, revelatory presence. Hence, Wolfson wonders 'how many of the things offered as God by lovers of wisdom today are [only] polite but empty phrases for the downright denial of God' (Wolfson 1961: 271).

Leo Strauss (1899–1973) drew radically different conclusions from the attempt to forge an alliance between revelation and reason. As diametrically opposed principles, they were bound to clash. The Scriptural philosophy which Wolfson celebrated, Strauss regarded as an oxymoron. A truly believing Jew could not be a philosopher, certainly not a consistent adherent of reason. Although one may dwell in Athens and Jerusalem, one may not have simultaneous allegiance to each. There are no religious philosophers, but only philosophers who employ religion (to appease and educate the masses), and theists who calculatedly conscript philosophy to advance the cause of religion. Rare among the medievals were philosophers who acknowledged the impassible boundary between faith and reason. Strauss singles out the fourteenth-century Spanish philosopher Gersonides (Levi ben Gershom) as a rare but illuminating exception. Torah was expressly for him one matter, philosophy another. He understood that each functioned in a separate sphere. Gersonides was thus a philosopher and a Jew, but not a Jewish philosopher. 'The history of what others call Jewish philosophy is for Strauss the history of certain philosophers who were Jewish by political affiliation and certain Jews who exploited philosophical arguments for religious ends. It is a history fraught with conflict, deception, and perplexity; yet it is, in his judgement, particularly worthy of our attention, for it exposes the powerful tensions at the foundation of our Western civilization', strained as it is by the competing pull of Athens and Jerusalem (Harvey 1997: 31).

Strauss's first systematic critique of the very notion of a Jewish philosophy—*Philosophy and Law* (1935)—was directed at Julius Guttmann (1880–1950), who had recently published a monumental monograph, *Die Philosophie des Judentums* (1933). What aroused Strauss's ire was Guttmann's conviction that philosophy, although not autochthonous to Jewish culture, had, when used to scrutinize the principles of Judaism, served to refine and elevate Jewry's understanding of its religious vocation. So conceived, Jewish philosophy—or rather the Philosophy of Judaism—did not cease with the Middle Ages. It continues, as indeed it should, through the modern period. Thus Guttmann's history concludes with a section entitled 'Jewish Philosophy of Religion in the Modern Era'.

The history of the philosophy of Judaism is the story of how various systems of thought were employed for 'the interpretation and justification of the Jewish religion' (Guttmann 1964: 4). This is not an apologetic exercise, however. At the core of Judaism is a firm and confident affirmation of the fundamental meaningfulness of life, a faith grounded in the biblical conception of God, which for Guttmann was best captured by the notion of ethical monotheism. God is pre-eminently known by virtue of his moral will, by which he rules nature and history. 'This idea of God [was] not the fruit of philosophic speculation but the product of the immediacy of the religious consciousness' (ibid. 5). Biblical faith is primed not by an abstract idea of God, but by an intense experience of the fact that, as the Ruler of the Universe, God is the source of life and of all that is good and just. This experience is sustained by entering into a relationship with God: 'This relationship is an ethical-voluntaristic one between moral personalities, between an "I" and a "Thou.".... Communion with God is essentially a communion of moral wills' (ibid. 6). Though God's moral will is accessible to human comprehension, the Bible also bears witness to God's utter incomprehensibility as manifest in the experience of seemingly unjustifiable suffering, an experience that 'paradoxically becomes the ground for trust in the meaningfulness of his providence, a providence of love and justice which is no less meaningful for remaining impenetrable to human understanding' (ibid. 18). Biblical faith thus constituted, according to Guttmann, a religious philosophy, albeit one that was conceptually inchoate and unsystematic. 'It is a religious philosophy in a sense peculiar to the monotheistic revealed religions which, because of their claim to truth and by virtue of their spiritual depth, could confront philosophy as an autonomous spiritual power' (ibid. 4). Hence, Guttmann does not believe that the term 'Jewish philosophy' applies to any and all metaphysical speculation articulated by Jews. He reserves the term for philosophic reflection promoting the Judaic point of view. In historical perspective, he points out that the confrontation with other systems of thought, especially Greek philosophy, obliged Jewish thinkers to present Judaism as a universal truth and place it in opposition to truths taught by philosophy. In the medieval period, which dominates Guttmann's history, the principal task assumed by Jewish philosophers was to demonstrate the compatibility of biblical faith as a revealed truth with the precepts of reason; in the modern age the effort of Jewish thinkers has concentrated on determining the relation between religion and philosophy, and defining the proper place and value of Judaism in contemporary culture (cf. Scholem 1976).

In light of the overarching religious concerns of Jewish philosophers, Louis Jacobs has argued that, at least until the modern period, the very notion of Jewish philosophy is, 'in reality, a misnomer. The medieval thinkers pursued theology rather than philosophy in that, despite being undoubtedly influenced by Greek thinking, they began and ended with faith. They were religious believers writing for religious believers. What they sought to offer their readers was a reasoned defense of Jewish beliefs even if in the process they arrived at very unconventional attitudes' (Jacobs 1972: 1106). But this observation, sound as it might be, raises the cardinal question of why Jews, at least until the modern period, did not speak of theology, even though they were in fact pursuing it. It is noteworthy that, although the Greek term 'philosophy' was incorporated with due dignity into the traditional Jewish lexicon, the term 'theology' was not. Why, then, philosophy and not theology? One obvious answer is that Jews did not engage in theology as it was understood in the Middle Ages—namely, as a systematic delineation and clarification of the principles of faith; their pre-eminent concern then, was not theology but a philosophical justification of the truth-claims of Judaism. Indeed, Jacobs reached his conclusion by projecting a relatively modern conception of theology—a sustained, rational discourse on God and his relationship to humans and the universe—on to the project of medieval Jewish thinkers. Yet there may be a more profound explanation, which Jacobs himself implicitly acknowledges when he notes that a Jewish interest in theology per se was born of the debates on the doctrinal principles of Judaism that dogged the Jews as they sought entry into modern Europe, and the need of Jews to explain their faith before the tribunal of enlightened and not-so-enlightened Christian opinion. 'From the days of Moses Mendelssohn onward the scope of Jewish thought in the Western world embraced theology. The closer contacts with Christian thought brought in their wake a fresh consideration of the vexed question of dogma in Judaism; of the true significance of ethical monotheism, of the relationship between Judaism and Christianity and between religion and culture, and the meaning of revelation' (ibid. 1108).

   Born of a need to explain the Jewish articles of faith, then, Jewish theology had from its inception an overwhelmingly apologetic motive. Significantly, the first to speak expressly of a Jewish theology was one of the founding fathers of Reform Judaism, Abraham Geiger (1810–74). Noting an exigent need for the then-nascent movement to elaborate the doctrines that differentiated it from both Christianity and traditional Judaism, Geiger gave priority to creating a Jewish theology based on historical criticism. Accordingly, he founded in 1834 the *Wissenschaftliche Zeitschrift für jüdische Theologie* (Scientific Journal for Jewish Theology), to which Jewish scholars throughout Europe, and especially from Germany and France, contributed articles clarifying Jewish principles of faith from a critical-historical perspective and in light of contemporary cultural realities. For Geiger, theology was not purely an intellectual exercise; it had a distinct practical dimension, to articulate for Jews their religious and moral duties in the context of a modern, open society. 'Theology is knowledge of the religious truths and the corresponding [form of] life. It is every person's task to attain this knowledge' (Geiger 1875: 4). Jewish theologians are, then, not only charged with a theoretical task but also a practical one of assisting their fellow Jews, most of whom do not have the privilege or the tools to engage in sustained historical and theological reflection, in achieving the requisite appreci-ation of 'the religious truths and the corresponding life [conducted] in accordance with the teachings of Judaism' (Geiger 1875: 4). The flowering of Jewish theology under the aegis of Reform Judaism, as Jacobs duly notes, had the 'incidental result' of obliging 'Orthodox leaders...to treat theological problems seriously' (Jacobs 1973: 1109). Jewish theological reflection was not limited to Reform and Orthodox thinkers, though. Virtually all currents of Judaism—even those that came to expression in the thought of Martin Buber (1878–1965) and Franz Rosenzweig (1886–1929), who were not affiliated to any particular expression of organized Judaism—felt compelled to pause and consider anew the principles of faith guiding their religious commitments (cf. Bergman 1963).

   Jewish theology was also stimulated by the radical shift in the images of know-ledge governing Western thought (cf. Mendes-Flohr 1999). The modern tendency to deprive religious claims of their epistemological dignity—a tendency initiated by Spinoza in his critique of biblical religion, the *Tractatus Theologico-politicus* (1670), and deepened a century later by Kant's systematic dismantling of the basis of classical metaphysics— led to a radical separation of faith and reason. No longer were they deemed allies in the quest for truth; faith was demoted to a question of the heart and individual inclination. Religious thought in general retreated to theology, in which it sought to defend, if not the epistemological and metaphysical claim of theism, then its enduring ethical significance and existential meaning (as refracted through such theological constructs as creation, revelation, and redemption). No longer regarding themselves as exclusively bound to reconciling faith and reason,

Jewish religious thinkers, especially in the twentieth century, allowed themselves freely to tap an array of non-rational resources, such as the often-audacious theological speculations of midrash, kabbalah, and hasidism (cf. Heschel 1955). The ever-increasing secularization of Jewish life and the crystallization of ideologies to accommodate this change (such as Jewish socialism and Zionism) had a particular impact on Jewish theology; as Arthur A. Cohen put it, the contours of Jewish theology were shaped by the need, which grew in urgency in the face of mass emigration and growing anti-Semitism, to attend to the needs of 'the natural and supernatural Jew' (Cohen 1962). The intersection of the natural reality of the Jews and their supernatural vocation acquired a tragic acuity in the wake of the Shoah (cf. Cohen 1981; Fackenheim 1970; Katz 1993, 1997).

In heeding the call of the double dimension of Jewish existence, Cohen himself not only pursued theology but also wrote fiction exploring the spiritual and cultural landscape of the modern Jew (cf. Stern and Mendes-Flohr 1998). The modern world has, of course, encouraged a wide variety of expressions of Jewish reflection, secular and religious, or, as in the case of Cohen, a blend thereof.

In order to square the circle linking all periods and expressions of Jewish reflection, Nathan Rotenstreich (1913–93) recommended the inclusive concept *Machshavah Yehudit* (Jewish Thought). To accommodate the intended scope of this term, he offered a sociological definition that highlights contextual parameters. 'Jewish thought', which embraces philosophy and theology, but also secular ideologies and creative expressions such as fiction and poetry, is defined as a body of ideas reflecting on issues of concern, broadly understood, to Jews as Jews, and primarily addressed to Jews (Rotenstreich 1945).

The multivalent character of the concept of Jewish thought, designed to complement the rather circumscribed notion of Jewish philosophy, eventually led to the establishment at the Hebrew University of Jerusalem of two separate but parallel departments: the Department of Jewish Philosophy and Kabbalah (*Ha-Chug le-Philosofia Yehudit ve-Kabbalah*), and the Department of the History of Jewish Thought (*Ha-Chug le-Toledot ha-Machshavah ha-Yehudit*). The former tended to limit its purview to medieval sources, emphasizing rigorous philological and text-critical methods. The latter, with a pronounced preference for the methods of intellectual history, had a larger thematic scope, extending—at least in principle—from an examination of the ideational structure of the Bible, to a consideration of modern ideological movements such as Jewish socialism and Zionism. Between these two poles, courses were devoted to the thought-world of Hellenistic Jewry and that of the Talmudic sages; and, generally leaving the philosophical and mystical writings of the Middle Ages to the care of the department of Jewish Philosophy and Kabbalah, the next station was perhaps the *Musar* or ethical literature of the late Middle Ages, and the Lithuanian *yeshivot* of the early nineteenth century; and further, the full thrust of modern Jewish thought in all its manifestations, from the Haskalah to religious reform and the philosophical and theological systems that followed in their wake. Hence, the boundaries between the Department of the History of Jewish Thought and that of Jewish Philosophy and Kabbalah were often blurred, especially when the former would teach the philosophers of Reform Judaism, Samuel Hirsch and Solomon Formstecher; the idiosyncratic philosopher of revelation, Ludwig Steinheim; the neo-Orthodox Shimshon Raphael Hirsch; or the twentieth-century mystic Abraham Kook. The study of the existential religious thinkers Martin Buber and Franz Rosenzweig was also in the domain of the Department of the History of Jewish Thought, and not that of its 'rival' Department of Jewish Philosophy and Kabbalah, which, as noted, tended rather jealously to delimit its scholarly attention to the Middle Ages. This division, perhaps unwittingly, supported the thesis that Jewish philosophy is exclusively a child of the Middle Ages. Were this, indeed, the rationale for the division, then the question was necessarily broached regarding the nature of the writings of the aforementioned nineteenth- and twentieth-century thinkers. If their work was not to be regarded as philosophy, then perhaps it was theology. In this context it should also be noted that, since its founding, the Hebrew University has consciously barred Jewish 'theology' from its classrooms, lest it offend the custodians of traditional Judaism. Was, then, the Department of the History of Jewish Thought a ruse allowing Jewish theology to enter, so to speak, through the back door? Decidedly not—but the lack of clear definitional boundaries surely invited such suspicions.

Needless to say, each of the two departments had its own faculty and curriculum. It seemed that the twain would never meet. Yet in the late 1970s it was suddenly decreed that the two departments should merge. Yielding to administrative and financial considerations, the university's governing authorities found that it was no longer feasible to maintain two departments whose labours seemed overlapping to many. The new department created by union of the two was called *Ha-Chug le-Machshevet Yisrael*, the Department of the Thought of Israel (i.e. of the Jewish People; the Hebrew is not as infelicitous as the English). Behind the circuitous history of departmental organization of Jewish philosophy and theology at the Hebrew University is, as one might expect, also a clash of personalities and scholarly styles. But the definitional and methodological ambiguities regarding the study of Jewish philosophy and theology surely allowed the battle-lines between the contending parties to be cast in theoretical terms. The result of the merger of the two departments, and the attendant conjoining of faculty and research agendas, was the emergence of a tolerant, elastic conception of the field and its methodological criteria. This tendency to entertain a plurality of voices has since increasingly characterized the academic study of the intellectual history of the Jewish people. (cf. Cohen 1962; Frank and Leaman 1997; Jospe 1997; Katz 1993; Levy 1987; Seeskin 1990).

Suggested Reading

The definitional and methodological ambiguities attendant on the study of Jewish philosophy have in recent years gained increasing attention. With the rapid expansion of academic programmes in Judaica, several symposia devoted to the topic have been held. The proceedings of two such symposia, sponsored by the International Center for the University Teaching of Jewish Civilization, Jerusalem, are Fackenheim and Jospe (1996) and Jospe (1997). Jospe (1988) critically reviews the various positions articulated in earlier symposia conducted in Hebrew, analysing them in comparison to conceptions of Jewish philosophy propounded by Guttmann and other prominent scholars of earlier generations. Levy (1987) offers a systematic and comprehensive analysis of the question in the title of the aforementioned study. A brief but judicious discussion of the same issues is presented by Sirat in the introduction to her 1985 book. Also valuable is Daniel Frank's introductory essay to Frank and Leaman (1997). Contemporary Continental European scholarly approaches, especially in France, Germany, and Italy, to the study of Jewish philosophy are reviewed by Giuseppe Veltri in Brenner and Rohrbacker (2000).

The issues facing and defining the conceptual landscape of modern Jewish theology are brilliantly analysed by Scholem (1976: 261–97). For a collection of essays on more than a hundred central concepts and issues in Jewish religious thought, each written by a different scholar, see Cohen and Mendes-Flohr (1987; rev. edn. 1989). In the same volume Cohen provides an incisive analysis of the state of contemporary Jewish theology (ibid. 971–9). The writings of twenty of the leading Jewish theologians and cultural critics of the second half of the twentieth century are critically presented in Katz (1993). For a very useful reader of selected essays on major Jewish philosophical trends, biblical, Talmudic, medieval, modern, and contemporary, see Frank *et al.* 2000.

Bibliography

BERGMAN, S. H 1963. *Faith and Reason: An Introduction to Modern Jewish Thought.* Trans. A. Jospe. New York.

BRENNER, M. and ROHRBACKER, S. eds. 2000. *Wissenschaft vom Judentum. Annähverungen nach der Holocaust.* Berlin.

COHEN, A. A. 1962. *Natural and Supernatural Jew: An Historical and Theological Introduction.* New York; 2nd. rev. edn. New York 1979.

——1981. *The Tremendum: A Theological Interpretation of the Holocaust.* New York.

——and MENDES-FLOHR, P. 1987 [1989]. *Contemporary Jewish Religious Thought: Original Essays on Critical Concepts, Movements and Beliefs.* New York.

FACKENHEIM, E. L. 1970. *God's Presence in History.* New York.

——and JOSPE, R. eds. 1996. *Jewish Philosophy and the Academy.* Madison and London.

FRANK, D. H. and LEAMAN, O. eds. 1997. *History of Jewish Philosophy.* London and New York.

——— and MANEKIN, C. H. 2000. *The Jewish Philosophy Reader.* London and New York.

GEIGER, A. 1875. 'Einleitung in das Studium der jüdischen Theologie' (1849). In *Nachgelassene Schriften*. ii. 1–32. L. Geiger ed. Berlin.

GUTTMANN. J. 1964. *Die Philosophie des Judentums*. Munich 1933. English trans. *Philosophies of Judaism. A History of Jewish Philosophy from Biblical Times to Franz Rosenzweig*. Trans. D. W. Silverman, Intro. R. J. Zwi Werblowsky. New York. Repr. New York 1973.

HARVEY, W. Z. 1997. 'Historiographies of Jewish Philosophy: The Place of Maimonides and Lévinas.' In Jospe (1997): 27–36.

HESCHEL, A. J. 1955. *God in Search of Man: A Philosophy of Judaism*. Philadelphia; 2nd edn. with intro. by S. Heschel. New York 1987.

HUSIK. I. 1916. *A History of Medieval Jewish Philosophy*. New York; 2nd edn. Philadelphia 1940. Pbk edn. New York 1958.

JACOBS, L. 1972. 'Theology.' In *Encyclopedia Judaica* xv. 1103–10. Jerusalem.

JOEL, M. 1876. *Beiträge zur Geschichte der Philosophie*. Breslau.

JOSPE, R. 1988. *What is Jewish Philosophy?* Tel Aviv.

—— ed. 1997. *Paradigms in Jewish Philosphy*. Denver, Madison, and London.

KATZ, S. T. 1975. *Jewish Philosophers*. New York.

—— ed. 1993. *Interpreters of Judaism in the Late Twentieth Century*. Washington DC.

—— 1997 'The Shoa.' In Frank and Leaman (1997): 854–74.

LEVY, Z. 1987 *Between Yafeth and Shem: On the Relationship between Philosophy and General Philosophy*. American University Studies Series 5, Philosophy, Vol. 21. New York.

MENDES-FLOHR, P. 1999. 'Wesensbilder im modernen jüdischen Denken.' In *Wissensbilder. Strategien der überlieferung*. 221–39. U. Roulff and G. Smith eds. Berlin.

MUNK, S. 1857. *Mélanges de philosophie juive et arabe*. Paris.

NEWMARK, D. 1929. 'The Philosophy of Judaism and How it should be Taught.' Lecture delivered in 1908 printed in D. Newmark, *Essays in Jewish Philosophy*, 1–29. Vienna.

PINES, S. 1977. *Studies in the History of Jewish Philosophy: The Transmission of Texts and Ideas*. [Hebrew]. Jerusalem.

ROTENSTREICH, N. 1945. *Jewish Thought in Modern Times* [Hebrew]. 2 vols. Tel Aviv. 2nd edn. 1966.

ROTH, L. 1999. *Is there a Jewish Philosophy? Rethinking Fundamentals*. London and Portland, Oreg.

SCHOLEM, G. 1976. 'Reflections on Jewish Theology.' In *On Jews and Judaism in Crisis: Selected Essays*. 261–97. W. J. Dannhauser ed. New York.

SEESKIN, K. 1990. *Jewish Philosophy in a Secular Age*. New York.

SIRAT, C. 1985. *A History of Jewish Philosophy in the Middle Ages*. Cambridge.

STERN, D. and MENDES-FLOHR, P. eds. 1998. *An Arthur A. Cohen Reader: Selected Fiction and Writings on Judaism, Theology, Literature, and Culture*. Detroit.

STRAUSS, L. 1933. *Philosophie und Gesetz*. Berlin.

—— 1997. 'Preface' to *Issac Husik, Philosophical Essays: Ancient, Medieval and Modern*. pp. vii–xli. M. Nahm and L. Strauss eds. Oxford 1952. Repr. in *Jewish Philosophy and the Crisis of Modernity. Essays and Lectures in Modern Jewish Thought*. 235–66. L. Strauss ed. Intro. K. H. Green. Albany, NY.

VELTRI, G. 2000. 'Jüdische Philosophie. Eine philosophisch-bibliographische Skizze.' In *Wissenschaft vom Judentum. Annäherungen nach dem Holocaust*. 134–63. M. Brenner and S. Rohrbacker eds. Berlin.

WOLFSON, H. A. 1934. *The Philosophy of Spinoza: The Unfolding of the Latent Processes of His Thought.* 2 vols. Cambridge, Mass. and New York. Repr. 1969.

——1947. *Philo: Foundations of Religious Philosophy in Judaism, Christianity, and Islam.* 2 vols. Cambridge, Mass.

——1961. 'Sermonette: The Professed Atheist and Verbal Theist.' In *Religious Philosophy: A Group of Essays*, 270–1. Cambridge, Mass.

CHAPTER 31

JEWISH WOMEN'S STUDIES

TAL ILAN

INTRODUCTION

WOMEN's studies, as a discipline within Jewish studies, is relatively new. It appeared in the 1970s, in the wake of a similar development within other fields of academia particularly in the United States—a move that was later to be designated 'second-wave feminism'. The question of women's status within Judaism, as within any human society, is, however, not new. In Jewish sources it is as old as the story of creation in the first chapters of Genesis, with the description of woman's secondary creation and her implication in the original sin and fall from grace. This story, as well as similar stories related by contemporary cultures (such as the Greek Pandora myth), grounded in theology, and ultimately justified as god-given, women's inferior and subordinate status in society vis-à-vis men. The human condition practically everywhere (to a greater or lesser extent) is, and has always been, one in which women are subordinated to men, and most written cultures have produced documents justifying this condition. Only over the last 200 years has this truism come under criticism, particularly in the cultures of the West (i.e. Christian Europe and America), with the advent of ideas about humanism, equality, and democracy.

FIRST-WAVE FEMINISM

First-wave feminism was a movement that flourished at the turn of the twentieth century, but its roots can be identified deep in the nineteenth century. It was a political movement that fought for the equalization of women's legal and political rights and ended in the West after the Second World War with recognition of the theoretical legal and personal equality between persons of all genders, and with the institution of women's universal suffrage. It was largely a political movement and, since at the time the politics of the Jews were not yet directed at the level of governments and houses of representatives, law-courts, and voters' lists, the influence of this movement on Judaism was relatively marginal. Of course, first-wave feminism also grounded its political agenda in a feminist ideology. As an intellectual movement it produced many writings, which aimed to justify in theory as well as practice the indubitable veracity of human equality. These ideas easily rubbed off on Jewish scholarship. The debate about Jewish attitudes to women and to the status of women was taken up in the second half of the nineteenth century, and is evident in the writings of many Jews the world over (see primarily Pappenheim in Umansky and Ashton 1992: 148–9). However, Jewish scholars' feminist urge in first-wave feminism was greatly diminished by a strong feeling of compulsion to defend Judaism against its detractors. Thus, the Jewish British author, Grace Aguilar, who in 1845 published a thick volume containing sketches of biblical and post-biblical women, implied in her introduction that part of the urge to write the book came in response to Christian attacks on Judaism's approach to women:

Christians themselves... write for the Christian world. Education and nationality compel them to believe that 'Christianity is the sole source of female excellence;'—that to Christianity alone they owe their present station in the world, their influence, their equality with man, their spiritual provision in this life, and hopes of immortality in the next;—nay more, that the value and dignity of woman's character would never be recognised, but for the religion of Jesus, that pure, loving, self-denying doctrines were unknown to women; she knew not even her relation to the Eternal; dared not look upon him as a Father, Consoler, and Savior till the advent of Christianity... Yet we cannot pass such assertions unanswered, lest from the very worth and popularity of these works in which it is promulgated, the young and thoughtless daughter of Israel may believe it really has foundation, and look no further than the page she reads. How or whence originated the charge that the law of Moses sunk the Hebrew female to the lowest state of degradation, placed her on a level with slaves or heathens, and denied her all mental and spiritual enjoyment we know not; yet certain it is that the most extraordinary and unfounded idea obtains credence even in this enlightened age.

... We see no proofs of the humanising and elevating influence of Christianity either on man or woman until the Reformation opened the BIBLE, the whole BIBLE to the nations at large.... (Aguilar 1845: 2–3)

Aguilar's assertion here indicates that the issue which has since plagued Jewish feminist scholarship, and continues to play a most prominent role in second-wave feminism in crippling its development, was already at play in the middle of the nineteenth century. Between loyalty to the feminist cause and loyalty to Judaism, scholars of Jewish women have almost universally chosen their national and religious group identity over and against gender solidarity. Aguilar, and others of her generation, judged Jewish attitudes to women according to less stringent criteria than they used in judging other societies. They were more willing to excuse deviant behaviour on the ground that the hardships of Jewish history had made it impossible for the Jews to improve their minds, and thus their legislation on women, to the degree that their European contemporaries had meanwhile achieved (e.g. Kayserling 1879; Hurwitz 1885; Remy 1897; and see further Levenson, in Rudavsky 1994: 99–111).

First-wave feminism produced many women scholars, historians, philosophers, and theologians (for a bibliography, see Wachstein 1931). In the period following the Second World War, first-wave feminism was silenced and to a great extent forgotten. Writings about women, and particularly writings by women, were suppressed and left to collect dust in libraries. This phenomenon is not unique to Jewish studies (Schüssler Fiorenza 1993: 1–21; Melman, in Zertal 1993: 18–33). The rediscovery by second-wave feminism of works written by women that never became part of the academic cannon, has elicited a deep suspicion in the integrity of the academic institutions. Women studies have gained over the last three decades an enormous influence in western universities, as well as many adherents among the prominent members of academia. Yet it continues to promote itself as, and use the rhetoric of, a marginal and subversive movement. This strategy is (consciously or unconsciously) motivated by the historical awareness that a smug feeling of achievement and triumphalism, as had obviously prevailed in the wake of the women suffrage legislation, will back-fire, with a consequent loss and suppression of many achievements.

SECOND-WAVE FEMINISM

Since in the West, theoretically women and men are deemed legally and politically equal, second-wave feminism as an activist movement in this part of the world monitors the deviations and hidden agendas that prevent women from attaining this theoretical equality. Aside from this, second-wave feminism is mainly an academic, intellectual movement, which sets as a goal for itself the critique of the institutional systems of oppression that keep women 'in their place'. In its wake a new critical interest has arisen in the position of Jewish women, and the remainder of this essay will be devoted to a survey of the kinds of insights and criticism to which it has exposed its subject.

PATRIARCHY

Feminist critique has labelled practically all human societies as patriarchal. This means that they promote a system that favours the patriarch, the male head of the household, as lord and master of his subordinates—wife/wives, children (of both sexes), and in some societies other dependants such as (male and female) servants, clients, or slaves. In such a system all males—children, servants, clients, even slaves—have a potential to become patriarchs and rule over their own individual household. Women, however, lack this capacity. This is true for Jews as well as Gentiles (Ozick, in Heschel 1983: 120–51). Feminist scholars have singled out patriarchy as the single most influential factor in determining women's position.

Feminist scholars of Judaism have amply demonstrated that Judaism from its inception was a thoroughly patriarchal society (e.g. Cantor 1995). This has been elucidated particularly for both biblical and rabbinic Judaism, which together form the foundation of Jewish life over the last two millennia. It was shown that biblical Judaism recognized and promoted polygyny; that biblical marriage was a commercial transaction between the father of the bride and the future husband, in which a commodity (woman) changed hands for a price. Feminist critics claimed that biblical society placed special value on virginity and recognized as unquestionable a husband's exclusive rights over his wife's sexual activities. Wives had no equivalent claim on their husband's sexuality. Moreover, biblical society created women's vulnerability and need for male protection in the face of male predators. Instead of censoring and punishing male sexual transgression, they punished the victim in various legislative moves. For example, a raped woman was forced to marry the rapist (Deuteronomy 22: 29; see Frymer-Kensky, in Matthews et al. 1998: 79–96).

Feminist critique has further shown that the development of rabbinic Judaism changed biblical approaches to women in scores of ways, but did nothing to diminish its patriarchal nature. A few examples: divorce, which interested the biblical author little, was made in the post-biblical period into a unilateral activity, available only to the husband. The Jewish marriage settlement—the Ketubbah—an innovation, which recognized the wife's rights in face of divorce or widowhood, named the husband as the sole actor in his wife's property as long as he lived (Biale 1984).

Critiquing Jewish patriarchy was not performed in a vacuum. It was influenced and inspired by feminists critiquing other oppressive patriarchal forms in other historical and contemporary societies. However, while a critique of the patriarchy of the Athenian society in classical Greece, for example, carries with it very few contemporary implications, many Jews still live by, and consider as god-given, the codes of law embedded in the Hebrew Bible and rabbinic literature. In this it resembles, more than anything, the critique of Christian patriarchy which grew out of, and developed side by side with, Jewish patriarchy. Very soon Jewish feminists found themselves on the defensive. They discovered that they were not free to critique the oppressive aspects of Judaism, since their work was being used against their tradition. Christian feminists picked up the results of their work, and then used Jewish patriarchy comparatively, in order to uphold and exalt the improved form of this system developed by the Christian church (Plaskow, in Beck 1982: 250–4). Jewish and Christian scholarship became a battlefield. Jewish feminists were willing to endorse a critical stance toward their culture and heritage in an internal struggle over the issue of what it means to be Jewish and female within their own communities. At the same time, they could not but put up a united defensive front against the external assault of Christian feminism that brought old anti-Semitism in a new guise through the back-door of feminist scholarship. Thus the art of what I call, for want of a better term, 'comparative patriarchy' came into existence. Jewish feminists claimed passionately that Jewish patriarchy was not really so bad, and when compared with those of its neighbours, Greeks, Egyptians, Persians, even Christians, it stood up very well (e.g. Boyarin 1993; Hauptman 1997; and other examples in Ilan 1995: 2–16).

This debate is but one example of the way the study of women brings to the fore the by-now well-known fact that there is no 'objective' scholarship. All scholars— scientists and theologians, philosophers and doctors—speak from a given social location. Feminist scholarship, in Jewish studies as well as in other disciplines, has acted as a catalyst in urging scholars to recognize and acknowledge their hidden agendas.

PRIVATE AND PUBLIC

Feminist scholarship has helped recognize that patriarchal systems tend to divide the world between public and private spaces. This division was then gendered, designating men as public and women as private. Thus men allocated for themselves such activities as war, politics, and social interaction, while assigning to women the confined spaces of the household, where they were expected to remain concealed from the gaze of other men and to raise their children.

Judaism is, in this respect, no exception. For example, for the Hebrew law-code of the Bible it is inconceivable to imagine the Temple cult as consisting of female as well as male priests (Brenner 1985). Women's participation in the Temple cult was only marginal at the best of times, and is presented in the rhetoric of the Hebrew Bible as non-existent (Grossman, in Grossman and Haut 1992: 17–20). Furthermore, Israeli biblical kingship is by definition male. The biblical author views any encroachment of this space by women as an aberration (2 Kings 11). Feminist critique of Judaism revealed this pattern as continuing throughout history. Rabbinic literature exempts Jewish women from participation in the main cultic commandments of Temple-less Judaism, such as daily prayer, donning phylacteries, residing in the Sukkah, and a host of other activities. Jewish women have been kept marginalized in the synagogue worship, which replaced the Temple after its destruction, by restricting them to the women's gallery where they serve as spectators rather than full participators in the service (Grossman and Haut 1992).

Most conspicuous among the activities from which women were excluded was the study of Torah—the most prestigious activity in a Jew's life, according to the scale of values developed by rabbinic literature and brought to perfection in later generations. Feminist observations on the division between public and private spaces in Jewish history have shown that the esteem in which Judaism held Torah study has somewhat altered the definition of public and private spheres in Jewish history. Thus, over the years it became acceptable in Jewish society for a man who wished to achieve the ideal of learning to depend upon his wife for economic support. Scholars have noted that this specifically Jewish division, between public (learning men) and private (working women), has produced a role-reversal between men and women in traditional Jewish societies. The conventional division between private and public in the critique of patriarchy in other Western societies tended to concentrate on the European bourgeois concept of the single, male bread-winner, and his cultured home-maker wife. In Jewish society, however, particularly in Eastern Europe of the late Middle Ages and the early modern period, women were often found in public spaces such as shops and market-places, conducting business while their husbands studied. This role-reversal, not unnoticed by non-Jewish society, became a subject of scorn and derision by Gentile observers, and has also sometimes been criticised by Jews. It has been noted that while women were allowed a certain measure of freedom in their economic activities, the strict division of public and private spaces has been maintained. Women continued to be exempt from the study-house, the real scene of empowerment in Jewish culture (Boyarin 1997).

ANDROCENTRISM: MARGIN AND CENTRE

Next to patriarchy, a most important critical term in feminist theoretical reading of society is androcentrism. An androcentric perception of reality is one in which the man is in the centre. His interests and views dominate the texts from which we read the past. He is the subject of history, literature, philosophy, theology, law, and so on. Women are but one of the objects of his interest, and are thus marginal to the world-view of practically all texts produced in the past. Feminist criticism has put at the top of its agenda the exposure and displacement of androcentrism. It reasons that since women are, and always have been, half of humanity, accepting these andro-centric texts as they are written means accepting human history as his-story—a term invented by feminist criticism to define male history separately from her-story, that is, women's history.

Exposure of the text's androcentrism is intended to alert the reader to the one-sided view this promotes and to the fallacies and misconceptions that may arise from its acceptance at face value. Exposure, however, is only half the task. It points out the failings of past readings, but it does nothing to correct them. Toward this end displacement is required. One of the strategies adopted by feminist criticism is to displace his-story by her-story. This requires a re-imagination of the texts as though the margin becomes the centre; as though women, rather than men, are the full subjects of the inquiry. It requires a great leap of faith, since the texts themselves, which are our only remnants of the past, have completely silenced women's voices. Thus, many feminists refuse to take this additional step, maintaining that there is no way to reclaim the lost past.

Jewish feminism is entangled in these same difficulties. Although several scholars acknowledge that there is a slight possibility that some texts in the Hebrew Bible retain a feminine voice (Bloom 1990; Brenner and Dijk-Hemmes 1993), and others hold that some of the writings of the Apocrypha were, possibly, composed by women (Kraemer, in Levine 1992: 221–42), practically all agree that the huge and influential body of rabbinic literature is from start to finish the composition of men. Later medieval and modern Jewish literature of all sorts, being less anonymous, makes the task of identifying women's voices therein easier. The critique of andro-centric Jewish texts thus takes two distinct directions.

Exposing Androcentric Approaches

A close reading cannot support the assumption that Jewish texts speaking in the name of Israel refer to the entire Jewish people. Judith Plaskow showed this conclusively, when she read the verse Exodus 19: 15, preparing Israel for the revelation of the Torah. This verse, she had argued, clearly excludes women from the collective of Israel because it states: 'Be ready by the third day; do not go near a woman.' Obviously those who should be ready for the revelation at Sinai do not include women (Plaskow 1990: 25). Other examples are not hard to find. The prayer incumbent on every person (ʾadam) in Israel every morning, blessing God for not making him a woman, clearly indicates that ʾadam 'person' in this case refers only to males (tBerakhot 7: 8). The talmudic definition of what it means to abrogate the Torah includes, next to transgressing the Sabbath and refraining from circumcising sons, also engaging in sexual relations with (literally penetrating) menstruating women (bMeila 17a). Obviously this definition cannot include women among the transgressors.

All feminist readings begin by exposing these tendencies. A reading of this sort produces the literature that I designate here 'feminine images'. This sort of analysis begins with the assumption that women in all literature poetry, prose, philosophical discourses, legal discussions, historical accounts, and so on are represented by the male author as stereotypical, displaying traits that they believe are specifically feminine. This is, of course, particularly true when biological functions associated with women are presented, such as virginity, menstruation, or giving birth. In stories told about persons who possess these capabilities, naturally women are involved. However, Jewish writings, as well as non-Jewish writings, also present as feminine traits other characteristics which are not intrinsically tied up with women, but are clearly culture-bound. A whole range of culture-bound traits is evident in Jewish writings that describe the feminine. These include aspects which the dominant culture considers as positive, such as modesty, humility, love of peace, and abhorrence of violence. They also include a wide range of feminine images which are viewed as inherently negative, such as jealousy, talkativeness, inquisitiveness, love of gossip, sexual permissiveness, and so on.

Exposing the androcentric character of these images takes on different forms within different disciplines (e.g. Lacks 1980). Their use in prose and even historiographic writing exposes the prejudices of the author toward his female subjects. Their use as metaphors, parables, symbols and literary tropes in poetry, philosophical, and even psychological discourse discloses how gendered language works to create the world of the writer. For example, feminine images of the virgin or the menstruating woman are used figuratively, in line with patriarchal values, in order to represent purity and impurity (e.g. Fonrobert 2000: 16–19, 224, n. 19). Metaphors of a patriarchal abusive marriage are related in order to describe systems of hierarchical domination, particularly between God and Israel (Graetz 1998: 35–52). Likewise, images of loose women and sexual promiscuity serve to describe and denigrate concepts within a philosophical discourse (Shapiro, in Peskowitz and Levitt 1997: 158–73). Scholarship of this sort describes the way gender works in creating a world-view of the society which produces the texts under discussion. It says little if anything about real women. In order to do that, one must move from the first step of exposing the androcentric character of the texts to the second step, which seeks to displace this androcentric discourse by placing women in the centre of a feminist reconstruction of the past.

Displacing the Androcentric Discourse

The desire to displace the androcentric discourse takes many forms. In a historical discourse the feminist attempts a reconstruction of women's past (and lost) role in the historical events of the past. In various literary endeavours, they attempt to discover the lost feminine voice. These two approaches are achieved through a number of techniques.

Silencing and Hidden Voices—Suspicious and Subversive Readings

Feminist critics maintain that the dominant masculine culture has, in its major cultural texts, silenced any individual feminine voice. All assumptions about the inclusivity of the voices these texts transmit, maintain these critics, should be approached with extreme suspicion. It should be assumed, on the contrary, that these voices were raised in dialogue with and in response to other voices that have meanwhile been silenced (see e.g. Fonrobert 2000: 160–209). Suspicious reading requires an attempt to reconstruct the points of view and opinions to which our texts responded. Obviously the silenced voices include many groups of the losers in history, but women are certainly among them and it is the feminist reader's task to attempt to identify these hidden voices and reconstruct them. Thus, for example, when feminists read rabbinic legal discussion, they suggest it would be useful to inquire why a certain restrictive piece of legislation is found at a certain point in time, not before and not after. What was it that women said or did then in order to induce this sort of response? (Ilan 1997: 166–9; 186–9.) Similarly, when a minority opinion is heard within this polyphonic literature, voicing opinions that may be identified as less repressive to women, feminists suggest that one should identify here other historical strands of Judaism, which were eventually pushed aside. Some of them can sometimes be identified with known historical groups or movements (Ilan 1999: 11–81).

It should be noted, however, that discovering silenced voices is a difficult endeavour, and can be very frustrating, because silencing processes can be very effective. Thus many scholars tend to concentrate on historical women who are much more conspicuously visible.

Token Women

Despite the silencing process, in every age and in every generation certain women achieved fame or notoriety. These women—prophets (e.g. Deborah), queens (e.g. Shelamzion-Alexandra), scholars (e.g. Beruriah), religious leaders (e.g. the Maiden of Ludmir), authors (e.g. Grace Aguilar), poets (e.g. Rahel Luzato Morpurgo), philosophers (e.g. Hannah Arendt), and others—were never typical of their times and usually constitute the exception that proves the rule. Yet, because of their unusual achievements, more about these women has come down to us through the ages, and more substantial information about them can be employed in order to say something meaningful about women of the Jewish past. Thus, in the period that proceeded second-wave feminism compositions that sketched the lives of such women were very popular (e.g. Aguilar 1845; Kayserling 1879; Remy 1897; Weiss-Rosemarine 1940). In this context it is interesting to note that already scholars of first-wave feminism, who have now become the topics of feminist inquiry themselves, tended to favour women of the past as models of intrinsic interest for their own study. Thus, in the *Jewish Encyclopedia*, published between 1901 and 1906, Henrietta Szold, the future founder of Hadassah, who was at the time the Secretary of the Jewish Publication Society (Dworkin, in Koltun 1976: 164–70), wrote most of the entries on Jewish women (e.g. Grace Aguilar in i. 274–5; Fanny Arenstein in ii. 133; Beruriah in iii. 109–10; Henriette Herz in vi. 366–7; Sara Copia Sullam in xi. 583–4; and others). Bertha Pappenheim, the foremost Jewish feminist of *fin de siècle* Vienna and Germany, founder of the Jewish Women's Movement in Germany (Kaplan 1979: 29–57), translated the memoirs of Glückel of Hameln from Yiddish into German in 1910 (Pappenheim 1910). Nina Salaman, the daughter of Arthur Davis, one of the compilers of the Jewish prayer book in English, and herself a religious poet (Umansky and Ashton 1992: 147), published in 1924 a study of the poetry of the eighteenth-century poetess Rahel Luzato Morpurgo (Salaman 1924). Finally, Hannah Arendt, the foremost Jewish philosopher of the mid-twentieth century, whose interests included Jewishness and its intrinsic Otherness, chose to devote a lengthy study to the most notable Jewish apostate of the late eighteenth and early nineteenth century—Rahel Levin Varenhagen (Arendt 1957). The urge to engage these unusual women has not entirely died down with second-wave feminism: sketches of individual women (Fink 1978; Taitz and Henry 1996), as well as studies and biographies (e.g. Burns 1987; Davis 1995; Hertz, in Baskin 1999: 193–207; Umansky 1983) are still being composed.

Women's Writing

The most obvious source for women's voices is the writings of Jewish women. These, however, only become visible late in the Middle Ages (Baskin 1994). Before their voices are actually heard, however, traces of lost voices can already be found. Thus, for example, we know from half of a correspondence published in 1623, the letters of Ansaldo Ceba to Sara Copia Sullam, that this Italian Jewish women of the sixteenth-to-seventeenth century was a woman of letters. Yet her own letters to this man are, alas, lost (Remy 1897: 140–52). Also from the late Middle Ages, a large body of religious compositions—prayers in Yiddish intended for women, known as *tkhines*—have come down to us. Yet some of these prayers were clearly written by men for women. Others were written by women (Weissler 1998: 9–10). What is one to do with the bulk of the material, which is anonymous? Should it be treated methodologically as women's voices or not?

Beginning with the memoirs of Glückel of Hameln from the seventeenth century, Jewish women become more visible. Toward the end of the nineteenth century many Jewish women wrote political essays, journalist reports, diaries, memoirs, prose, and much poetry (Hyman 1995: 64–5, n. 24). In England several Jewish women joined the mainstream novel culture of the nineteenth century, in which Gentile women (such as George Eliot) were also active (Galchinsky 1996). One issue that has been tackled by feminist scholars is why the male literary establishment more easily acknowledged women poets than women who wrote prose (Rattok and Diment 1994). Another issue discussed broadly is the languages of women's literature. Traditionally Yiddish was viewed as a woman's language. Feminist studies have monitored the slow process through which this concept was eroded (Sokoloff *et al.* 1992; Seidman 1997; Parush 2001: 227–40; on early women writers in Hebrew, see Berlovitz 1984). A major discussion within Jewish studies is whether literature composed in Hebrew is Jewish literature merely by virtue of the language in which it is written. This issue deeply concerns women writers, because these succeeded in becoming successful authors in Hebrew just as that language was losing its key position as the prime signifier of Jewish literature. Of a similar nature is the question whether literature produced by Jewish women in English (and other non-Jewish languages), such as that by Gertrude Stein, is Jewish by virtue of the religious/cultural affiliation of its author, or should perhaps be ignored in the canon of Jewish studies (e.g. Bloom 1998).

Feminist scholars who research modern Judaism also endeavour to bring forth more feminine voices that are still retrievable from private and public archives, by publishing, translating, and writing commentaries on many unknown or forgotten works written by women (e.g. Umansky and Ashton 1992).

Women Studies and Gender Studies

The primary interest of the discipline 'women studies' was the lot of women—half of humanity (and half of the Jewish people) that had been silenced by the other half. However, very soon scholars incorporated women studies into wider contexts. Thus, for example, the oppression of women was viewed in the wider context of multiple forms of oppression based not just on gender but also on class, race, and sexual preferences. The supposedly clear boundaries between male and female became blurred when scholars pointed out that dominance defined manliness and subordination femininity. Thus Jewish studies scholars have pointed out that the oppression of the Jews often took the form of ridiculing Jewish men as feminine (Hyman 1995: 134–69; Boyarin 1997: 1–29). In the nineteenth century this stance was taken up by the Jews themselves, and accepted ruefully (Seidman, in Peskowitz and Levitt 1997: 40–8) or combated by creating alternatives to Jewish maleness (Harrowitz and Hyams 1995). In a reverse symmetry some Jewish scholars have adopted this representation, viewing it positively (Neusner 1993; Eilberg-Schwartz 1994: 163–96). Women are not the problem, claim these voices—it is gender.

Most (but not all) feminist scholars are women. This is true for Jewish women studies as for other areas. However, gender scholars are evenly divided between men and women. Not surprisingly, gender studies have created a paradigm shift within the discipline. They have taken to dealing with the differences—social as well as biological—between men and women. They are interested in the interaction between the sexes. Gender studies have particularly promoted sexuality studies and family studies—areas in which men and women are equally represented (even when not equally active). The shift in scholarly interest created by the move toward gender studies is partly dictated by the sources themselves, which lend themselves more easily to analysis of areas in which women were traditionally seen as legitimate participants—sex and the family. It is, however, also partly the result of the scholars' own interests. It is not surprising that once men enter the arena they tend to re-place themselves in the centre. Jewish studies have also seen this paradigm shift. Since the 1990s studies on the Jewish family have multiplied (Cohen and Hyman 1986; Kraemer 1989; Shamgar-Hendelman and Bar-Yosef 1991; Cohen, S. 1993; van Henten and Brenner 2000). Studies on Jewish sexuality have also increased (D. Biale 1992; Eilberg-Schwartz 1992; Boyarin 1993; Satlow 1995). One book, published in Hebrew, actually combines sex and family (Bartal and Gafni 1998).

A REVIEW OF THE LITERATURE

Biblical Times

The Hebrew Bible is the Scripture of the Jews. It is also the first history book of the Jewish people. Yet it must not be forgotten that it is also the scripture of Christians. Thus, many second-wave feminist biblical scholars are Christian women and men, operating from within Christian theological seminaries. The first feminist exegetical composition to discuss the Hebrew Bible, still as part of first-wave feminism, was Elizabeth Cady Stanton's *Women's Bible* of 1895 (Schüssler Fiorenza 1993: 1–21). The earliest feminist attempts of second-wave feminism both to uncover silenced women's voices and critique biblical patriarchy, was attempted by Christian women (Trible 1978; 1984). Christian feminists initiated the first second-wave Women's Bible Commentary (Newsom and Ringe 1992). Meanwhile, however, the project has become a joint venture. Christian and Jewish, American, European, and Israeli feminists are now co-operating in the feminist critique of the Hebrew Bible. The foremost project of this nature is Athalya Brenner's Feminist Companion to the Bible—a series in which the most up-to-date scholarship on the various books of the Bible is collected. Brenner had published a first series of eleven books, which is both a compilation of older studies and completely new ones. She is now in the process of publishing a second similar series. The division of the volumes in the series is according to the biblical compositions, but it is of particular interest because it makes a feminist statement about the Hebrew canon. Thus, Brenner's series has no volume devoted to the Book of Joshua, on the assumption that feminist interpretation has nothing to say about this violent male book. On the other hand, the volume on the Book of Esther also includes commentaries and studies on two extra-biblical Jewish compositions on women—Judith and Susannah. These three compositions conform to the same literary genre, but their canonical status is completely different. While for the Jews Esther is scripture, Judith and Susannah are not. They were canonized by the Catholic church, but the Jews considered them 'external books' and declared that whoever reads in them will lose his place in the world to come (mSanhedrin 10: 1). Both the exclusion of Joshua from, and the inclusion of Judith and Susannah in, the Feminist Companion to the Bible suggest another important feminist strategy of questioning the boundaries of the canon. This strategy is of particular significance with relation to scripture, which is supposedly God-given, but it is important in the critique of all literary canons valued by the societies feminists study, as will be shown repeatedly below in this review.

Jewish feminist scholars have from a very early stage of second-wave feminism fallen out with their Gentile counterparts over Judaism's role in the suppression of Goddess worship (Daum, in Beck 1982: 255–61). First-wave feminism had created the theory of Matriarchy. Before Patriarchy, claimed Bachofen in his famous study *Muterrecht*, goddesses and women ruled the earth (Bachofen 1861). Although it is highly doubtful whether such a system ever existed, and although the initiators of this theory wished to describe a linear development from a backward female society to a more advanced male one, second-wave feminists have adopted some of the claims of this theory. Accordingly, biblical Israelite monotheism was a newly created religious system in which a single male god was likened to the head of a patriarchal household. He was served by a host of male priests. Suppression of goddess worship eliminated all female participation in the cult (Frymer-Kensky 1992).

Recent feminist studies have looked into the possible alternatives to the lost Goddess in the Jewish religion. The best substitute suggested has been

'Lady Wisdom', who is personified and gendered in the biblical Book of Proverbs, and portrayed as God's companion in creation (Proverbs 8: 22–31). Subsequent developments of this apotheosis are evident in the Jewish apocryphal literature (Hadley and Lang, in Brenner 1997: 360–423).

The Hebrew Bible is a book. Its writings can be subjected to a host of literary interpretations and criticisms. Feminist scholars have applied various modern literary and psychoanalytical theories of interpretations and produced a wide array of exciting cross-cultural, intertextual, and deconstructive readings of the text (e.g. Bal 1987, 1988; Pardes 1992). Feminist scholars have also, meanwhile, moved away from the simplistic assumption that—more than a book—the Hebrew Bible is a history of the Israelites. Feminist biblical scholars have looked beyond the biblical text to the results of the works of archaeologists, in the hope of reconstructing Jewish women's lives (e.g. Meyers 1988). The assumption embedded in such a search is that ancient artefacts and documents written for daily use rather than for posterity may better preserve a record of women's lives than do the highly rhetorical texts preserved in the literary documents. This approach, however, has its limitations. For one thing, inanimate objects are no less silent than silenced women. They require interpretation. Another point to be taken into consideration is that inscriptions carry their own brand of rhetoric, and legal documents are often merely repeated formulae.

Post-Biblical and Rabbinic Judaism

The history of Israel in the biblical period was characterized by the domination of powers that came from the east. The biblical law-code was influenced by old Akkadian law-codes. The Assyrians and then the Babylonians and Persians overran the Land of Israel. The post-biblical period was dominated by powers from the west—Greece and then Rome. Throughout the entire period, although Judaism already began to develop its unique diaspora character, almost all Jews, even those not living in their lands, were found under the sway of Greece and Rome. It was a period that saw Judaism undergo many transformations and then give birth to Christianity. Naturally, the history of Jews in this period too is of great interest to Christian scholars. Some of the most important Jewish sources for this period were only preserved by the Christian church. These include the Apocrypha, the writings of the philosopher Philo, and those of the historian Josephus. Feminist analysis of these sources is ever a joint Jewish–Christian venture (e.g. Levine 1992). A feminist interpretation of the rhetoric of many of these works has been partially undertaken (for Ben Sira, by Trenchard 1983; for Philo, by Sly 1990; for Josephus, by Ilan 1999: 86–125 and bibliography there; see also on Jubilees, Halpern-Amaru 1999). These studies usually demonstrate to what extent ancient Jewish thinkers were imprisoned

within their own rhetorical, occasionally misogynistic (= women hating), conceptions of women.

In the wish to escape rhetoric and misrepresentation, feminist scholars of post-
biblical times too have been drawn by the allure of archaeological finds: inscriptions
(Brooten 1982; Kraemer, in Baskin 1999: 46–72), papyri, and inanimate objects
(Peskowitz 1997). In this sphere, however, there is still much to be done. Although
the literature of the Dead Sea sect is immense, and has drawn much scholarship over
the last twenty years, and whilst scholars have began to probe the issues of gendered
imagery in the texts as well as to discuss the possibility that women were also present
at Qumran (see in Ilan 1999: 38–42), no thorough feminist analysis on this sect has
been produced. Furthermore, the Dead Sea documents have yielded, aside from the
literature of the Qumran sect, many documentary papyri recording the legal lives of
Jews south of the Dead Sea from the period between the destruction of the Temple
and the Bar Kokhba revolt. Although these documents include marriage contracts,
divorce bills, and much other material relevant to women, and two archives
belonging to women were discovered among the documents (Babatha's and Salome
Komaise's), no feminist study of these documents has yet been undertaken (for now,
see Ilan 1999: 217–62).

Unlike the Hebrew Bible, which is Scripture to both Christians and Jews, the post-
biblical period points to a differentiation in interests. Christian theologians who
study the Judaism of this period do so in order to gain a good background for the
New Testament. Jews, on the other hand, study the New Testament as just another
document relevant to the period under discussion. This discrepancy has been
particularly evident in relation to women studies. The main theory developed by
Christian feminists was that Jesus's message was a feminist one (Swidler 1976). In
order to establish this theory, it was necessary to paint Judaism in the worst possible
light (Kellenbach 1994). To this end, a selective and historically incorrect use of
rabbinic literature was undertaken. Sayings about women were chosen indiscriminately, and read out of context, ignoring early and late, normative and deviant,
minority and majority. This attitude obviously had to be combatted.

Rabbinic literature is what became a second Scripture to the brand of Judaism
that triumphed after the destruction of the Second Temple. It was produced by a
Jewish all-male elite in a special type of study house, which sprang up in various
parts of the world in late antiquity. The scope of rabbinic literature is vast and its
influence on the Jewish world-view, Jewish customs and law, and Jewish thinking
has been all-encompassing. Jewish feminists have shown an interest in rabbinic
literature from the start, an interest very different from that of Christian feminists.
They were not interested in denigrating its approach to women, but rather in
exploring its ramifications for women's position in Judaism to this day. They did,
however, encounter difficulties in approaching and tackling rabbinic literature, for
many reasons. It is written not in one, but in fact in two inaccessible languages
(Hebrew and Aramaic). But the formal linguistic problem is the least of the feminist

scholar's difficulties. Rabbinic literature was, from the start, composed in a way that was only understood by initiates into the system. It was written in shorthand expressions, half-sentences and half-verses, in which the unquoted half of the verse is the decisive one. For an initiate the language and terminology eventually become accessible, but women, let alone feminist scholars, were never initiated into the system. Part of the problem of feminist rabbinic interpretation is the need to struggle alone with texts, which the establishment refused to disclose or discuss with the scholar. Nevertheless, in recent years several feminist studies have tackled these enigmatic texts. Not surprisingly, men wrote some of them (Boyarin 1993; Satlow 1995; Cohen 1998). However, women too have meanwhile joined this venture (Wegner 1988; Ilan 1997; Hauptman 1997; Peskowitz 1997; Valler 1999; Fonrobert 2000). Since the literature is so vast, includes so many compositions, and covers such a long period of time, there is still much to be done. Aside from uncovering texts never discussed by feminists, the study of rabbinic literature requires that one search various manuscripts of the texts and discover, through variant readings, information that has been suppressed over time (Ilan 1997: 51–84).

Side by side with rabbinic literature, the vast poetic literature of the *piyyut* also came into existence. This literature is full of rich imagery and much of it is gendered. It still awaits a feminist analysis.

The Middle Ages

Beginning with rabbinic literature, Jewish and Christian feminist interests part company. Jewish feminists who probe the lives of Jewish women, who inquire into attitudes to women, and look into feminine imagery in the Middle Ages work alone. The types of sources they resort to are very different from those of antiquity, owing to the major changes that Jewish history underwent in this period. Medieval Jews were a diaspora people. They were scattered in many lands, spoke many languages, and were influenced by many different cultures. Mainly they were divided by virtue of being under the sway of two divergent religious powers—Christianity and Islam.

Surprisingly, not much has been written about women's history in the Middle Ages from a feminist perspective. Thus, for example, in Carlebach's collection on Jewish women in Germany, the section about the Middle Ages is decidedly devoid of a feminist agenda (Grossman and Toch, in Carlebach 1993: 17–48). Recently A. Grossman's magnum opus on medieval women has added much in the way of vital information on the period (Grossman 2001). The author of this work, however, resorts to comparing patriarchies of Jews in the Christian world and those living under the sway of Islam. A good case in point is the issue of wife-battering, a topic that becomes visible in medieval Jewish writings and has, thus, raised feminist interest. Jewish women were probably also battered prior to the Middle Ages. At the time, however, this was simply not an issue. By contrast, in the halachic and philosophical writings of medieval Jews the issue is often raised. In his comparative analysis of Oriental and European Jews, Grossman has noted that rabbis living in European Christian countries opposed wife-beating, while rabbis who lived in Muslim countries upheld it as normative. He explained the influence of the local cultures on this attitude (Grossman 2001: 373–97). However, Boyarin has rightly rejected this explanation as displaying a Eurocentric bias against Muslim culture (Boyarin 1997: 162–9). In any case, a more detailed discussion by Graetz shows the entire premise to be incorrect (Graetz 1998: 93–119). Grossman also noted that Jews under Christian rule practiced monogamy. Jews under Islam, he showed, endorsed polygamy and were less critical of divorce. This he assigned to the divergent influences of the two cultures (Grossman 2001: 118–55; 443–56). He concluded that Jewish women under Christian influence had greater freedom and personhood (ibid. 495–502; also Levine Melamed, in Baskin 1999: 128–41).

The most important repository of material about Jewish communities in the Middle Ages comes from the Cairo Genizah. Anyone who writes about Jewish women of the times refers to the Genizah documents. Yet scholars still cite the works of S. D. Goitein, published in the 1950s and 1960s (especially Goitein 1978) as the authoritative discussion of the topic. In some respects one can describe Goitein as a proto-feminist because of the topics that interested him, and because of the questions he asked of the texts he read. Thus, for example, he claimed that the biblical Song of Songs could have been written by a woman (Goitein, in Brenner 1993: 58–66, originally published in Hebrew in 1957). It is remarkable, however, that aside from sporadic articles (e.g. Kraemer, in Atzmon 1995: 161–81), no feminist investigation of these documents has been attempted to date. Similarly, the medieval responsa literature is an enormous corpus of material relevant to women's lives. Indicative is Baskin's citation of Epstein's 1934 article on the issue of women in the responsa as the most recent relevant literature (Epstein, in Jung 1934: 123–52; see Baskin, in Baskin 1999: 120). Grossman's work has added much to the discussion of responsa literature, but not to the Genizah material.

Many important Jewish authors and scholars, and many important Jewish movements flourished in the Middle Ages. The following paragraphs will outline what has been done in the field of feminist analysis with relation to medieval writings, and what is still missing.

Many Jews in medieval Spain wrote secular poetry. One of the many topics of this literature was women and romantic love. These poems have now been collected and discussed (Scheindlin 1986). Individual studies discuss individual tractates devoted to the image of women: Fishman discussed Judah ibn Shabbtai's *Misogynist* (Fishman 1988); Melamed analyzed Judah Abarvanel's *Dialoghi d'Amore* (Melamed 2000); Rosen, in two separate studies, discussed the transsexual fantasies of two medieval Jewish authors (Rosen 1996; 2000). Gynaecological studies are clearly associated with gender studies. Many gynaecological treatises have survived from antiquity. However, Jewish women as a gynaecological subject only become visible in the Middle Ages, as has recently been shown (Barkai 1998). In the field of Jewish religious movements of the Middle Ages, Sefer Hasidim, the manifesto of Hasidei Ashkenaz, has received a feminist discussion (Brochers 1998) and the writings of the Kabbalists have similarly been exposed to a thorough gender analysis (Fishman 1992; Wolfson 1995).

However, much has yet to be done. For example, Shapiro has shown that there is much in way of gender to critique in the writings of Maimonides (Shapiro, in Peskowitz and Levitt 1997: 158–73), yet no systematic feminist reading of his writings is available. Similarly, no one has suggested a feminist reading for Rashi's commentary to the Talmud, or for the various prominent medieval commentaries such as that by Nahmanides.

The Modern Period

The Middle Ages end, according to traditional historiography, with the discovery of the New World, or with the Christian Reformation, or with the fall of Constantinople to the Turks. In other words, the modern period begins some time at the end of the fifteenth and the beginning of the sixteenth centuries. Feminists usually claim that traditional periodization is androcentric, and does not reflect women's concerns. Nevertheless, with the advent of the traditional 'Modern World' there is an explosion of information about Jewish women, and with it studies tracing and critiquing the information. Studies of modern Jewish women's history, much more than historical studies of earlier Jewish women, are recognized as a legitimate discipline. I shall begin by surveying such historical studies.

The sixteenth century was characterized for the Jews by the aftermath of the Spanish expulsion: the resettlement of the Jews in other European countries, and the persecution by the Inquisition of Jews who converted but remained secretly faithful to their religion. Levine Melammed's study traces women's role in the preservation of Jewish life under such difficult conditions (Levine Melammed 1999). Her work is based principally on archival material of the Spanish Inquisition. Other Jews chose to emigrate and resettle. Resettled Jewish women, most of whom chose the Ottoman Empire as their refuge, are the subject of Lamdan's study (Lamdan 2000), based mainly on early modern responsa literature. Jewish communities in Eastern Europe also became significant in the seventeenth century. Weissler (1999) discusses women's spiritual life within the Yiddish culture of Eastern Europe in detail.

The beginnings of the modern period saw many religious upheavals within Judaism, the messianic movement of Shabtai Zvi and the rise of Hasidism being the most prominent (on the latter see Rapoport-Albert 1988). A thorough feminist investigation of both movements has not yet been written.

Modernity brought with it new concepts for the Jews: emancipation, assimilation, religious reform, racial persecution, and large waves of immigration. The study of women in all these developments has been vigorously pursued. Assimilation and conversion among upper-class Jewish women in eighteenth-century German society is the topic of many studies. These discuss the way gender influenced the options with which wealthy Jewish women were confronted (primarily Hertz 1988). In nineteenth-century Germany assimilation did not necessarily imply conversion, but it was still a complex, gendered project which involved issues of identity (Kaplan 1991). The complex interplay of gender and assimilation is the topic of Hyman's comprehensive study of women and modernity (Hyman 1995).

Religious reform was one way in which Judaism countered assimilation and conversion. Women as well as men were active in the machinations of reforming Jewish religion. The question of women's fuller participation in Jewish religious practices became a topic toward the end of the nineteenth century. The issue has been tackled by Umansky (in Baskin 1999: 337–63), who has also shown how one woman, Lily Montagu, almost single-handedly reformed British Jewry (Umansky 1983). Women's aspiration to become rabbis and join the Jewish religious leadership is one important aspect of this issue, and has been handled by many scholars (e.g. Weidman Schneider 1984: 48–59; Nadel, in Rudavsky 1994: 123–34).

Religious reforms were only one avenue through which Jews sought to solve what had become known as the 'the Jewish question'. Jews were exceptionally active in other ideological and utopian movements of the nineteenth and early twentieth centuries, which set out to reform the world outside of—and occasionally in spite of—religion. Jewish women as much as (and sometimes more than) Jewish men were active in socialist movements all over Europe and the United States. Names like Rosa Luxemburg or Emma Goldman spring to mind in this context (Shepherd 1993). Jewish women were also active within Jewish communities, particularly as leaders of philanthropic societies, occasionally all female (Kaplan 1979; Kuzmack 1990; Rogow 1993; Las 1996). These organizations often became a tool for enhancing Jewish women's cause in education, community leadership, and political suffrage.

The end of the nineteenth century saw the rise of the two most influential directions in twentieth-century Judaism—mass immigration to the United States and Zionism. Women were obviously active in both. Since much of the scholarship on Jewish women is being written in the United States, the first of these topics, immigration and resettlement, with its implications for women and gender, is being extensively discussed (Baum *et al.* 1976; Marcus 1981; Perry 1987; Weinberg 1988; Glen 1990; Cantor 1995: 207–441). One book even documents the specific psychotherapy engendered by being both Jewish and female in America (Siegel and Cole 1991). An entire encyclopaedia is devoted to American Jewish women's experience (Hyman and Dash-Moore 1998).

Zionism saw some of the boldest attempts at gender equality universally, and certainly within Judaism. Together with a break with tradition, adoption of socialist ideals, and a disavowal of the diaspora, utopian ideas of new men and women were made possible. Yet a critical look at this bold attempt discloses that the rhetoric of equality was never attained or even earnestly attempted (Bernstein 1987, 1992).

Obviously the most salient event in Jewish history in the twentieth century has been the Holocaust. Jewish men and women both died indiscriminately at the hands of the Nazi exterminators. To begin with, it seemed to scholars almost sacrilegious to claim that there are any gender differences associated with the Holocaust. Recently, however, voices have been heard claiming that even the Holocaust was experienced differently by men and women (e.g. Kaplan 1998). The impact of the Holocaust has had a lasting effect on all Jewish studies, including women studies (e.g. Jacoby et al. 1994).

Most of these studies of the modern period concentrate squarely on the experiences and development within the lives of Jewish women of European (Ashkenazi) descent. Yet one should not lose sight of the fact that a large segment of the Jewish women population lived during the modern period under the sway of Islam. Little, though, has been written to cover this topic (e.g. Malino, in Baskin 1999: 248–69), and it still awaits many serious studies and discussions.

The foundation of the State of Israel is another major event in the Jewish history of the twentieth century. In Israel Jewish women from a variety of backgrounds and cultures are gathered, and the study of their relative positions, hopes, expectations, and aspirations in life are the subject of much sociological and anthropological observation (e.g. Sered 1992; El-Or 1994; Atzmon and Izraeli 1993). Next to these, many studies are also devoted to the Israeli woman as she is portrayed in modern Israeli literature (e.g. Fuchs 1987).

This brings us to the issue of Jewish women and literature in the modern period. This issue takes on many aspects. As we have seen above, it involves the slow penetration of discussion of Jewish women into the field of Jewish literature, whether written in Hebrew, Yiddish, or other languages. It also involves the way that women (= Jewish women) are portrayed in (the generally male) Jewish literature (Aschkenasy 1986). In this context, it is of special interest to note the way Jewish women have fared as subjects in literary works of Gentiles (Bitton-Jackson 1982). Another issue that has recently been raised in this context is the Jewish woman as reader and intended audience (Parush 2001).

The question of whether a Jewish philosophy actually exists is a serious one. While most Jewish thinkers of the Middle Ages developed their theories within a Jewish context, Jewish philosophers of the modern period rarely saw their project as Jewish. Universally influential thinkers such as Baruch Spinoza, Karl Marx, Sigmund Freud, and Walter Benjamin were Jews, although their theories seldom addressed specifically Jewish themes. Feminist thinkers have called attention to the writings of these scholars, to their gendered agendas, and to the need to explore them with feminist critical tools (Tirosh-Rothchild, in Davidman and Tenenbaum 1994: 85–119). Perhaps because of its subject-matter, and its overtly gendered agenda, much has been written from a feminist perspective about the work of Freud (e.g. Gilman 1993; Boyarin 1997). The works of other thinkers, primarily Marx, have not been subjected to a similar close feminist reading; this is probably a desideratum.

One should not end such an overview of Jewish women studies without referring to two other important resources for Jewish women. Several journals, beginning with *Lilith*, which first appeared in the United States in 1975, are devoted to the topic. Other journals have since appeared, devoted to Jewish women: *Bridges* in 1990, *Jewish Woman's Literary Annual* in 1996 (both in the United States), and *Nashim* (also in English) in 1998 in Israel. In addition, an annotated and updated bibliography on Jewish women is being continually published (Cantor 1987; Masnik 1996).

SCHOLARLY RESPONSES TO FEMINIST SCHOLARSHIP

Not all quarters of Jewish scholarship have welcomed Jewish feminist studies. In many universities and other academic institutions these studies have been simply ignored, and if not in writing, then at least orally many feminist scholars have been maligned and patronized. The one sector in Jewish society that has taken upon itself to protect in writing the vestiges of traditional Judaism from the alleged destructive power of feminism is Orthodoxy. Orthodox scholars' main claim is that Judaism is a religion in which men and women have different (but not necessarily hierarchical) roles. They further claim that, since the Torah is God-given, we as mere humans, even if we are confronted with what we perceive as injustice, cannot understand God's grand plan. We are not in a position to change the Jewish law—halachah. Much literature has been produced in these circles, most of it apologetic, repetitive, and with few new insights (e.g. Meiselman 1978; Appleman 1979; Brayer 1986; Rapel and Rapel 1989; Berkovitz 1990). Women too, though in a far less scholarly fashion, contribute to this trend (Kornbluth and Kornbluth 2000). Yet, within the Orthodox community other voices are also being heard (Greenberg 1981).

Suggested Reading

A good introduction to the issue of Jewish women's history is the collected essays edited by Baskin (1999). More specifically, for each historical period: biblical times are covered by Meyers (1988); the post-biblical period by Ilan (1995); the Middle Ages by Grossman (2001); and the modern period by Hyman (1995). A good collection of articles on women's writings is that of Baskin (1994). Patriarchy and Jewish women is covered by Cantor (1995). An excellent collection of essays on Jewish women studies within the various academic disciplines is that of Davidman and Tenenbaum (1994).

Bibliography:

AGUILAR, G. 1845. *The Women of Israel or Characters and Sketches from the Holy Scripture and Jewish History.* London.

APPLEMAN, S. 1979. *The Jewish Woman in Judaism.* Hicksville, NY.

ARENDT, H. 1957. *Rahel Varenhagen: The Life of a Jewess.* London.

ASCHKENASY, N. 1986. *Eve's Journey: Feminine Images in Hebraic Literary Tradition.* Philadelphia.

ATZMON, Y. 1995. *A View into the Lives of Women in Jewish Societies* [Hebrew]. Jerusalem.

——and IZRAELI, D. eds. 1993. *Women in Israel: A Sociological Anthology.* New Brunswick.

BACHOFEN, J. J. 1861. *Das Mutterrecht: Die Gynaikokratie der alten Welt nach ihrer religiösen und rechtlichen Natur.* Stuttgart.

BAKER, A. 1993. *The Jewish Woman in Contemporary Society: Transitions and Traditions.* London.

BAL, M. 1987. *Lethal Love: Feminist Literary Interpretations of Biblical Love Stories.* Bloomington, Ind.

——1988. *Murder and Difference: Gender, Genre and Scholarship on Sisera's Death.* Bloomington, Ind.

——ed. 1989. *Anti-Covenant: Counter-Reading Women's Lives in the Hebrew Bible.* JSOT Supplement Series 22. Sheffield.

BARKAI, R. 1998. *A History of Jewish Gynaeocological Texts in the Middle Ages.* Leiden.

BARTAL, I. and GAFNI, I. eds. 1998. *Sexuality and the Family in History: Collected Essays* [Hebrew]. Jerusalem.

BASKIN, J. R. ed. 1994. *Women of the Word: Jewish Women and Jewish Writing.* Detroit.

——ed. 1999. *Jewish Women in Historical Perspective.* 2nd edn. Detroit.

BAUM, C., HYMAN, P., and MICHEL, S. eds. 1976. *The Jewish Woman in America.* New York.

BECK, E. T. ed. 1982. *Nice Jewish Girls: A Lesbian Anthology.* Watertown, Mass.

BERKOVITS, E. 1990. *Jewish Women in Time and Torah.* Hoboken, NJ.

BERLOVITZ, Y. 1984. *Stories of the First Aliyah Women* [Hebrew]. Israel.

BERNSTEIN, D. 1987. *The Struggle for Equality: Urban Women Workers in Prestate Israeli Society.* New York.

BERNSTEIN, D. ed. 1992. *Pioneers and Homemakers: First Wave Feminism in Pre-State Israel.* Albany, NY.

BIALE, D. 1992. *Eros and the Jews: From Biblical Israel to Contemporary America.* New York.

BIALE, R. 1984. *Women and Jewish Law: An Exploration of Women Issues in Halakhic Sources.* New York.

BITTON-JACKSON, L. 1982. *Madonna or Courtesan? The Jewish Woman in Christian Literature.* New York.

BLOOM, H. 1990. *The Book of J.* New York.

BOYARIN, D. 1993. *Carnal Israel: Reading Sex in Talmudic Culture.* Berkeley.

—— 1997. *Unheroic Conduct: The Rise of Heterosexuality and the Invention of the Jewish Man.* Berkeley.

BRAYER, M. B. 1986. *The Jewish Woman in Rabbinic Literture.* Hoboken, NJ.

BRENNER, A. 1985. *The Israelite Woman: Social Role and Literary Type in the Biblical Narrative.* Sheffield.

BRENNER, A. and DIJK-HEMMES, F. van. 1993. *On Gendering Texts: Female and Male Voices in the Hebrew Bible.* Leiden.

BRENNER, A. A. ed. 1993–2000. *A Feminist Companion to the Bible.* Sheffield:
    1993a—*Song of Songs* (1—First Series).
    1993b—*Genesis* (2—First Series).
    1993c—*Ruth* (3—First Series).
    1993d—*Judges* (4—First Series).
    1994a—*Samuel and Kings* (5—First Series).
    1994b—*Exodus to Deuteronomy* (6—First Series).
    1995a—*Esther, Judith, and Susanna* (7—First Series).
    1995b—*The Latter Prophets* (8—First Series).
    1995c—*Wisdom Literature* (9—First Series).
    1996—*The Hebrew Bible in the New Testament* (10—First Series).
    1997—with C. Fontaine. *Reading the Bible: Approaches, Methods and Strategies* (11—First Series).
    1998a—with C. Fontaine. *Wisdom and Psalms* (1—Second Series).
    1998b—*Genesis* (2—Second Series).
    1999a—*Judges* (3—Second Series).
    1999b—*Ruth and Esther* (4—Second Series).
    2000a—*Exodus to Deuteronomy* (5—Second Series).
    2000b—*Song of Songs* (6—Second Series).
    2000c—*Samuel and Kings* (7—Second Series).

Bridges: A Journal for Jewish Feminists and Our Friends (1990–   ).

BROCHERS, S. *Jüdisches Frauenleben im Mittelalter: Die Texte des Sefer Chasidim.* Judentum und Umwelt 68. Frankfurt am Main.

BROOTEN, B. J. 1982. *Women Leaders in the Ancient Synagogue: Inscriptional Evidence and Background Issues.* Brown Judaic Studies 36. Chico, Cal.

BURNS, R. 1987. *Has the Lord Indeed Spoken Only through Moses? A Study of the Biblical Portrait of Miriam.* Atlanta, Ga.

CADY STANTON, E. ed. 1895. *The Woman's Bible.* New York.

CANTOR, A. 1987. *The Jewish Woman 1900–1985: A Bibliography.* Fresh Meadows, NY.

—— 1995. *Jewish Women/Jewish Men: The Legacy of Patriarchy in Jewish Life.* San Francisco.

CARLEBACH, J. ed. 1993. *Zur Geschichte der jüdischen Frau in Deutschland.* Berlin.

COHEN, A. 1998. *Rereading Talmud: Gender, Law and the Poetics of Sugyot.* Brown Judaic Studies 318. Atlanta, Ca.

COHEN. S. J. D. ed. 1993. *The Jewish Family in Antiquity.* Brown Judaic Studies 189. Atlanta, Ca.

COHEN, S. M. and HYMAN, P. E. 1986. *The Jewish Family: Myths and Reality.* New York.

DAVIDMAN, L. and TENENBAUM, S. eds. 1994. *Feminist Perspectives on Jewish Studies.* New Haven.

DAVIS, N. Z. 1995. *Women on the Margins: Three Seventeenth Century Lives.* Cambridge, Mass.

EILBERG-SCHWARTZ, H. ed. 1992. *People of the Body: Jews and Judaism from an Embodied Perspective.* Albany, NY.

——1994. *God's Phallus (and Other Problems for Men and Monotheism).* Boston.

EL-OR, T. 1994. *Educated and Ignorant: Ultraorthodox Jewish Women and their World.* Boulder, Col.

FINK, G. 1978. *Great Jewish Women: Profiles of Courageous Women from the Maccabean period to the Present.* New York.

FISHMAN, T. 1988. 'A Medieval Parody of Misogyny: Judah ibn Shabbetai's "Minhat Yehudah sone hanashim".' *Prooftexts* 8: 89–111.

——1992. 'A Kabbalisitic Perspective on Gender-Specific Commandments: On the Interplay of Symbols and Society.' *AJS Review* 17: 199–245.

FONROBERT, C. E. 2000. *Menstrual Purity: Rabbinic and Christian Reconstructions of Biblical Gender.* Stanford.

FRYMER-KENSKY, T. S. 1992. *In the Wake of the Goddesses: Women, Culture and the Biblical Transformation of Pagan Myth.* New York.

FUCHS, E. 1987. *Israeli Mythogynies: Women in Contemporary Jewish Fiction.* New York.

GALCHINSKY, M. 1996. *The Origin of the Modern Jewish Woman Writer: Romance and Reform in Victorian England.* Detroit.

GILMAN, S. L. 1993. *Freud, Race and Gender.* Princeton.

GLEN, S. A. 1990. *Daughters of the Shtetl: Life and Labor in the Immigrant Generation.* Ithaca, NY.

GOITEIN, S. D. 1978. *A Mediterranean Society.* vol. 3. Berkeley.

GRAETZ, N. 1998. *Silence is Deadly: Judaism Confronts Wifebeating.* Northvale, NJ.

GREENBERG, B. 1981. *On Women and Judaism: A View from Tradition.* Philadelphia.

GROSSMAN, A. 2001. *Pious and Rebellious: Jewish Women in Europe in the Middle Ages.* [Hebrew]. Jerusalem.

GROSSMAN, S. and HAUT, R. eds. 1992. *Daughters of the King: Women in the Synagogue.* Philadelphia.

HALPERN-AMARU, B. 1999. *The Empowerment of Women in the Book of Jubilees.* Leiden.

HARROWITZ, N. and HYAMS, B. eds. 1995. *Jews and Gender: Responses to Otto Weininger.* Philadelphia.

HAUPTMAN, J. 1997. *Rereading the Rabbis: A Woman's Voice.* Boulder, Col.

HENTEN, J. W. and VAN BRENNER, A. eds. 2000. *Families and Family Relations as Represented in Early Judaisms and Early Christianities: Texts and Fictions.* Leiden.

HERZ, D. 1988. *Jewish High Society in Old Regime Berlin.* New Haven.

HESCHEL, S. ed. 1983. *On Being a Jewish Feminist.* New York.

HURWITZ, S. Y. 1885. *The Hebrew Woman and the Jewess: The Status and Condition of Women in Israel in Family and Society During the Biblical and Talmudic Periods* [Hebrew]. Berditchev.

HYMAN, P. E. 1995. *Gender and Assimilation in Modern Jewish History: The Roles and Representations of Women*. Seattle.

—— and DASH-MOORE, D. 1998. *Jewish Women in America: An Historical Encyclopedia*. New York.

ILAN, T. 1995. *Jewish Women in Greco-Roman Palestine: An Inquiry into Image and Status*. Tübingen.

—— 1997. *Mine and Yours are Hers: Retrieving Women's History from Rabbinic Literature*. Leiden.

—— 1999. *Integrating Women into Second Temple History*. Tübingen.

JACOBY, J., SCHOPMANN, C., and ZENA- HENRY, W. eds. 1994. *Nach der Shoa geboren: Jüdische Frauen in Deutschland*. Berlin.

Jewish Woman's Literary Annual (1996–   ).

JUNG, L. ed. 1934. *The Jewish Library Third Series: The Jewish Woman: Background— Foreground—Prospects*. New York.

KAPLAN, M. 1979. *The Jewish Feminist Movement in Germany: The Campaigns of the Jüdischer Frauenbund, 1904–1938*. Westport, Conn.

—— 1991. *The Making of the Jewish Middle Class: Women, Family and Identity in Imperial Germany*. New York.

—— 1998. *Between Dignity and Despair: Jewish Life in Nazi Germany*. New York.

KAYSERLING, M. 1879. *Die jüdischen Frauen in Geschichte, Literatur und Kunst*. Leipzig.

KELLENBACH, K. VON. 1994. *Anti-Judaism in Feminist Religious Writings*. Atlanta, Ga.

KOLTUN, E. ed. 1976. *The Jewish Woman: New Perspectives*. New York.

KORNBLUTH, T. and KORNBLUTH, D. 2000. *Jewish Women Speak about Jewish Matters*. Southfield, Mich.

KRAEMER, D. ed. 1989. *The Jewish Family: Metaphor and Memory*. Oxford.

KUZMACK, L. G. 1990. *Woman's Cause: The Jewish Woman's Movement in England and the United States*. Columbus.

LACKS, R. 1980. *Women and Judaism: Myth, History and Struggle*. Garden City, NY.

LAMDAN, R. 2000. *A Separate People: Jewish Women in Palestine, Syria and Egypt in the Sixteenth Century*. Leiden.

LAS, N. 1996. *Jewish Women in a Changing World: A History of the International Council if Jewish Women (ICJW) 1899–1995*. Jerusalem.

LEVINE, A.-J. 1992. *'Women Like This': New Perspectives on Jewish Women in the Greco-Roman Period*. Atlanta, Ca.

LEVINE MELAMMED, R. 1999. *Heretics or Daughters of Israel*. New York.

Lilith: The Independent Jewish Women's Magazine (1975–   ).

MARCUS, J. R. ed. 1981. *The American Jewish Woman, 1654–1980*. Cincinnati.

MASNIK, A. S. 1996. *The Jewish Woman: An Annotated Selected Bibliography 1986–1993*. New York.

MATTHEWS, V. H., LEVINSON, B. M., and FRYMER- KENSKY, T. eds. 1998. *Gender and Law in the Hebrew Bible and the Ancient Near East*. JSOT Supplement Series 262. Sheffield.

MEISELMAN, M. 1978. *Jewish Women in Jewish Law*. New York.

MELAMED, A. 2000. 'Women as Philosopher: The Image of Sophia in Y. Abarvanel's Dialoghi d'Amore.' [Hebrew.] *JS* 40: 113–30.

MEYERS, C. 1988. *Discovering Eve: Ancient Israelite Women in Context.* New York.

Nashim: Journal of Jewish Women's Studies and Gender Issues (1998–   ).

NEUSNER, J. 1980. *A History of the Mishnaic Law of Women.* 5 vols. Leiden.

——1993. *Androgynous Judaism: Masculine and Feminine in the Dual Torah.* Macon, Ga.

NEWSOM, C. A. and RINGE, S. H. eds. 1992. *The Women's Bible Commentary.* Louisville, Ky.

PAPPENHEIM, B. 1910/1994. *Die Memoiren der Glückel von Hameln (aus dem jüdisch-Deutschen von Bertha Pappenheim).* Weinheim.

PARDES, I. 1992. *Countertraditions in the Bible: A Feminist Approach.* Cambridge, Mass.

PARUSH, I. 2001. *Reading Women: The Benefit of Marginality in Nineteenth Century Eastern European Jewish Society* [Hebrew]. Tel Aviv.

PERRY, E. I. 1987. *Belle Moskowitz: Feminine Politics and the Exercise of Power in the Age of Alfred E. Smith.* New York.

PESKOWITZ, M. B. 1997. *Spinning Fantasies: Rabbis, Gender and History.* Berkeley.

——and LEVITT, L. eds. 1997. *Judaism Since Gender.* New York.

PLASKOW, J. 1990. *Standing Again at Sinai: Judaism from a Female Perspective.* San Francisco.

RAPEL, Y. N., RAPEL, B., and RAPEL, H. eds. 1989. *The Pearl: Memorial Volume for Peninah Rapel: The Jewish Women in Education, Family and Society* [Hebrew]. Jerusalem.

RAPOPORT-ALBERT, A. 1988. 'On Women in Hasidism, S. A. Horodecky and the Maid of Ludmir Tradition.' In *Jewish History: Essays in Honour of Chimen Abramsky.* 495–525. A. Rapoport-Albert and S. J. Zipperstein eds. London.

RATTOK, L. and DIMENT, C. eds. 1994. *Ribcage: Israeli Women's Fiction (A Hadassah Anthology).* New York.

REMY, N. 1897. *The Jewish Woman.* Cincinnati. German original 1891.

ROGOW, F. 1993. *Gone to Another Meeting: The National Council of Jewish Women 1893–1993.* Tuscaloosa.

ROSEN, T. 1996. '"Like a Woman": Gender and Genre in a Love Poem by Isaac Ibn Khalfun.' *Prooftexts* 16: 5–13.

——2000. 'Circumcised Cinderella: The Fantasies of a Fourteenth-Century Jewish Author.' *Prooftexts* 20: 87–110.

RUDAVSKY, T. ed. 1994. *Gender and Judaism.* New York.

SALAMAN, N. 1924. *Rahel Morpurgo and the Contemporary Hebrew Poets in Italy.* London.

SATLOW, M. 1995. *Tasting the Dish: Rabbinic Rhetorics of Sexuality.* Brown Judaic Studies 303. Atlanta, Ga.

SCHEINDLIN, R. P. 1986. *Wine Women and Death: Medieval Hebrew Poems on the Good Life.* Philadelphia.

SCHÜSSLER FIORENZA, E. ed. 1993. *Searching the Scripture: A Feminist Introduction.* New York.

SEIDMAN, N. 1997. *A Marriage Made in Heaven: The Sexual Politics of Hebrew and Yiddish.* Berkeley.

SERED, S. S. 1992. *Women as Ritual Experts: The Religious Lives of Elderly Jewish Women in Jerusalem.* New York.

SHAMGAR-HENDELMAN, L. and BAR-YOSEF, R. eds. 1991. *Families in Israel* [Hebrew]. Jerusalem.

SHEPHERD, N. 1993. *A Price Below Rubies: Jewish Women as Rebels and Radicals.* London.

SIEGEL, R. J. and COLE, E. eds. 1991. *Jewish Women in Therapy: Seen But Not Heard.* New York.

SLY, D. 1990. *Philo's Perceptions of Women.* Brown Judaic Studies 109. Atlanta, Ga.

SOKOLOV, N. B., LAPIDUS LERNER, A., and NORRIS, A. eds. 1992. *Gender and Text in Modern Hebrew and Yiddish Literature.* New York.

SWIDLER, L. 1976. *Women in Judaism: The Status of Women in Formative Judaism.* Metuchen.

TAITZ, E. and HENRY, S. 1996. *Remarkable Jewish Women: Rebels, Rabbis and Other Women from Biblical Times to the Present.* Philadelphia.

TRENCHARD, W. C. 1983. *Ben Sira's View of Women: A Literary Analysis.* Brown Judaic Studies 38. Chico, Cal.

TRIBLE, P. 1978. *God and the Rhetoric of Sexuality.* Philadelphia.

—— 1984. *Texts of Terror: Literary-Feminist Readings of Biblical Narrative.* Philadelphia.

UMANSKY, E. 1983. *Lily Montagu and the Advancement of Liberal Judaism: From Vision to Vocation.* Studies in Women and Religion 12. New York.

—— and ASHTON, D. eds. 1992. *Four Centuries of Jewish Women's Spirituality: A Source Book.* Boston.

VALLER, S. 1999. *Women and Womanhood in the Talmud.* Brown Judaic Studies 321. Atlanta, Ga.

WACHSTEIN, B. 1931. *Literatur über die jüdische Frau (mit einem Anhang: Literatur über die Ehe) Wien.* Veröffentlichungen der Bibliothek der israelitischen Kultsgemeinde Wien 7. Vienna.

WEGNER, J. R. 1988. *Chattel or Person: The Status of Women in the Mishnah.* New York.

WEIDMAN SCHNEIDER, S. 1984. *Jewish and Female: Choices and Changes in Our Life Today.* New York.

WEINBERG, S. S. 1988. *The World of our Mothers: The Lives of Jewish Immigrant Women.* Chapel Hill, NC.

WEISS-ROSEMARINE, T. 1940. *Jewish Women Through the Ages.* New York.

WEISSLER, C. 1998. *Voices of the Matriarchs: Listening to the Prayers of Early Modern Jewish Women.* Boston.

WOLFSON, E. R. 1995. *Circle in the Square: Studies in the Use of Gender in Kabbalistic Symbolism.* Albany, NY.

ZERTAL, I. ed. 1993. *Women's Time (Zmanim: A Historical Quarterly 46–7)* [Hebrew]. Tel Aviv.

CHAPTER 32

DEMOGRAPHY

SERGIO DELLAPERGOLA

CONCEPTS AND INTERPRETATIVE
FRAMEWORKS

PARAPHRASING historiography's *cause celèbre*, scholars have suggested that 'there is no Jewish Demography, only Demography'. The scientific study of Jewish population, also known as Demography of the Jews or Jewish Demography, does not actually claim the status of a distinct discipline. It is an area of specialization focusing on the changing size and composition of Jewish populations and on the determinants and consequences of such changes. This chapter outlines some of the main concepts, interpretative frameworks, and methodological issues in the field, followed by a short outline of substantive patterns and applied uses of available knowledge.

The main scientific rationale for the study of Jewish populations rests with the growing interest in understanding the demography of religious, ethnic, and cultural groups and minorities (or subpopulations). Such insights are increasingly perceived as a fundamental element in general analyses of population and society. The study of Jewish demography hence provides a valuable contribution to the development of population studies, and of the social sciences in general. At the same time, demographic changes provide an important and occasionally indispensable background for an appraisal of Jewish history and cultural experience. Hence, the study of Jewish demography is organically tied to the development of Jewish studies. Furthermore, as an applied and practical outcome, Jewish population studies may provide Jewish communal bodies and institutions with the database needed in order to run Jewish community services and plan their future. Relevant examples can be provided of how Jewish population trends interact with the supply and functioning of Jewish community services.

Clearly, variations in Jewish population size and composition reflect the action of both biological-demographic variables—as in the case of populations in general—and of identificational-cultural variables—as in the case of other minority groups or subpopulations defined by some normative or symbolic criteria. The study of Jewish demography therefore requires a knowledge and an understanding of *quantitative* research methods, though it often deals with *qualitative* research questions. To concisely define our subject-matter, for any given region or territory the size of Jewish population at a given time reflects the size of the same Jewish population at a previous time, as well as the net balances of three different types (or components) of change during that time interval:

- births versus deaths of Jews;
- immigration versus emigration of Jews (if world Jewish population is considered, migrations do not play a direct role on size and can be ignored); and
- accessions to the Jewish population (through formal conversions or otherwise) versus secessions.

These same factors of transformation also continuously affect the composition of the Jewish population according to a variety of characteristics such as age, sex, places of origin, seniority in the community of residence, and so on. Further changes of significance to population composition derive from socio-demographic processes that do not directly touch upon population size. Pertinent examples are marriage and other changes in marital status, geographical mobility within a given territorial division, educational and occupational changes, and other forms of social mobility. Of special interest for Jewish population studies are intervening changes in Jewish identity, attitudes, and behaviour. Changes in population composition regarding any of these variables may importantly affect the likelihood of the occurrence of each above-mentioned determinant of change thus indirectly influencing population size. The study of Jewish demography is thus concerned with the analysis of the various structural and dynamic aspects of population size and composition and of their mutual interactions. Moreover, population studies considers how demographic trends are affected by, or affect other, non-demographic processes of political, institutional, economic, biological, and other natures.

The study of Jewish society can be undertaken from nearly any disciplinary angle. So far, too little effort has been invested in producing integrated studies relying on several disciplinary perspectives, or at least trying to create a fruitful multidisciplinary dialogue. Population studies bring to this dialogue a consolidated body of concepts and techniques. These tools offer definite advantages concerning measurement of individual and collective behaviour inherent in population change. Such measurement techniques provide comparatively objective and verifiable results. Interpreting the emerging results, however, goes far beyond measurement and calls for a much broader, multidisciplinary array of factors. The recent postmodernist propensity to critically read supposedly value-neutral analysis as militant narrative has brought about, in our view, a weakening of the relative strengths inherent in each different discipline, particularly in the social sciences. Reduction of the diverse modes of disciplinary analysis to brands of legitimate but nonetheless subjectively biased literature detracts from the power of determination of sophisticated research methods and analytic tools developed over time. Once faith is lost in the discriminating power of cogent theory and method, adjudication tends to downgrade a set of specialized criteria, to controversy about political correctness and authors' pecking-order. Demography has remained comparatively unscathed by these debates. The problem cannot be avoided, however, that researchers are often part of the populations they are describing. The challenge of being involved in the processes investigated may entail emotional attitudes rooted in personal beliefs and experiences. Examples may be provided by recent debates about the prevailing stability or erosion of contemporary Jewish populations. An effort towards equanimity and objectivity is one of the chief imperatives demanded of analysts if the product of their work is to be classified as social science rather than personal manifesto.

Studying Jewish socio-demographic change requires, in the first place, some conceptual grounding concerning the nature of the main variable of reference. We need briefly to address the question 'what are the Jews?'—not to be confused with the more famous 'who is a Jew?' issue (see below). Jews are posited here as one modality within the broader class of groups defined by *religio-ethnic identities*, often abridged under the rubric of *ethnicity*. Recent debates suggest three main approaches regarding ethnicity's basic nature and societal role. In the particular case of the Jewish group, these may be defined as:

- *Consolidationist*: views Jewish populations as discrete objects for conceptual definition and empirical measurement;
- *Situational*: views Jewish populations as groups that can be recognized and studied but not really quantified—the elusive product of ever-changing exogenous circumstances and endogenous attitudes; and
- *Manipulative*: views Jewish collectives as essentially generated by the calculated interventions of elites or special-interest groups and lacking serious claim to empirical reality or even legitimacy.

The opinion followed here is that Jewish communities in the diaspora and in Israel in the past or present do constitute a target for empirical investigation. Jewish populations are composed of identifiable people according to specified criteria for inclusion and exclusion, featuring definite perceptions of group boundaries and collective identity, and unique and recognizable patterns of social and demographic composition and mobility. This paradigm suggests a powerful, relevant, and necessary approach to establishing the theoretical and empirical foundations for scientific investigation and public discourse on Jewish population.

Jewish ethnicity originates from the encounter of a particular set of people with a particular set of cultural and symbolic contents. Whether such a peculiar encounter is necessary or sufficient to create and permanently support existence of a population is one of the matters to be ascertained through systematic research. Questions that extend beyond the limits of this essay are whether a viable Jewish culture would be possible in the absence of a Jewish population, and whether a definite Jewish population would be possible in the absence of any Jewish culture in its midst. We postulate here that the two complementary dimensions of a population and its cultural identity need to overlap in some recognizable manner, though not necessarily according to fixed criteria across time and space. Sustained or even growing interest in things Jewish (including Jewish studies) on the part of Jews and non-Jews alike does not provide much information on the status of contemporary Jewry as a coherent, original, functional, and viable community. On the other hand, symptoms of demographic and identity erosion that may appear in different sections of the Jewish population do not impinge on the resilience and attractiveness of Jewish civilization. Clearly, trends associated with the two English meanings of the Hebrew word *Yahadut*—Judaism and Jewry—may take antithetical courses and in any case should not be confused, as they often are. Jewish population studies cannot ignore Judaism, but they essentially deal with Jewry.

In this context, Jews are a case of a subpopulation that may come into being through a limited number of alternative processes of *ethnogenesis*: ideational innovation, primary immigration, incorporation of new territory into a pre-existing geographical area of reference, or innovative merger of pre-existing groups. Such subpopulations may exist and develop over time through three already noted biologic-demographic processes, whose net product we may call *ethnomaintenance*: the balance of births and deaths, the balance of immigration and emigration, and the balance of accessions and secessions. The latter type of change does not affect people's physical presence but rather their willingness to identify with a specific religious, ethnic, or otherwise culturally defined group. The same sub-populations may reach a point of *ethno-extinction* following any of a fixed set of processes: total emigration, cession of territory, total assimilation, a totally negative vital balance, or genocide. While each of these circumstances of change can be shown to have occurred in the course of Jewish history, none should be posited as part of a deterministic paradigm concerning the eventual or final product of demographic transformations. The actual paradigm in the socio-demographic study of Jews and of similar subpopulations concerns the multiplicity of mechanisms at work, not the expected results of their working.

Jewish population studies hence stand at the centre of a continuous interaction between a painstaking effort to discover little facts related to the private lives of many individuals, and the need to weave them together into a meaningful pattern related to a broader theoretical outlook. One has selectively to collect and analyse data to describe situations, and at the same time build, expand, validate, or disprove conceptual frameworks. In the literature issued since the late nineteenth century, and with renewed energy throughout the last decades of the twentieth century, both approaches emerge, although fact description and in-depth analysis are not always clearly brought together. Examples of major questions to be dealt with include why were the Jews *forerunners* in several important social and demographic transitions—such as historical declines in mortality and fertility leading to rapid population growth and later to population stagnation—and *late joiners* in some other respects—such as the more recent changes in the role and structure of the nuclear family or the convergence of Jewish population geography to more general distributive patterns.

Interpretation of these and other issues in Jewish population and society clearly calls for a *comparativistic* frame of reference. Three major types of relevant comparisons in the study of Jewish populations are:

- the same Jewish population observed at repeated points in time;
- different Jewish populations observed at the same time;
- Jews and relevant non-Jewish populations observed synchronically.

Because of the limitations of data available, such a broad comparativistic approach can rarely be implemented, with negative repercussions on the scope of research.

Along with comparative design, at least three more major parameters are needed to validate Jewish demographic research. First is the possible range between *all-inclusiveness* versus *time-place-issue specificity*. Thinking of the great complexity of Jewish socio-historical experience, one can hardly hope to reach any definitive conclusions about *the Jews* of a given country, let alone an entire continent or the whole world, without deep command of historical change, geographic variation, and thematic complexity. This in turn requires systematic reference to a full array of diverse and more focused investigations. Across the existing Jewish demographic literature one does find a few major works of synthesis, along with many valuable monographs of a more specialized character. Yet most of the available materials tend to be quite limited in scope.

A related concern can be more generally expressed through the apparent contradiction between essentially *fact-oriented, descriptive* versus *theoretically oriented, analytic* work. Opposite extremes concern here, on the one hand, the intense accumulation of facts and figures without a clear indication of socio-historical direction and meaning; and on the other hand, sweeping generalizations based on narrow databases in terms of time perspective, geographic coverage, and thematic depth. There clearly is no contradiction between facts and theory; yet much of the existing Jewish demographic literature may have given the impression of a lack of appropriate balance between the two elements.

A further dialectical aspect concerns the characterization of investigative focus between *general disciplinary* versus *particularistic communal*. Different choices of target audience imply quite different thematic foci, technical approaches, and levels of discourse. The ultimate contents of Jewish population studies must unequivocally submit to the close scrutiny of general demographic and sociological disciplinary criteria. At the same time, the final relevance of research cannot ignore the benefits carried in terms of the relevance for the Jewish community and generally for society.

As already noted, one of the major aims of research is to help create an understanding of the empirically observed facts in the light of some broader conceptual frameworks. One framework quite popular in the past was that of *race* versus *environment*, reflecting scientific theories of the nineteenth century, especially the interest in physical anthropology. The ensuing infamous exploitation of the concept of human race for political purposes has rendered this approach obsolete and disreputable. It should be noted, however, that the genetic study of isolated and migrant populations continues to be a serious and relevant aspect of contemporary scholarship dealing with a great variety of groups, including the Jews. Renewed impetus in this area of investigation related to the genome project has opened new vistas, in particular concerning mutual validation between conventional historiography, other disciplines in the humanities and social sciences such as linguistics and migration studies, and biochemical analysis of the human body at the DNA level.

Another major interpretative paradigm focuses on the differences between Jews and other groups in the light of the respective *minority* versus *majority* status. Minority status—a long-standing feature for most of world Jewry—played a significant role in promoting societal differences between Jews and non-Jews. These differences related to legal, economic, social, psychological, and other individual and collective patterns. The same differences, in turn, were directly or indirectly tied to population trends. Members of a minority group generally were exposed to a different set of constraints and incentives than were members of the majority (and most often, dominating) group. Usually the minority's range of options was more limited, leading to a comparatively lesser degree of differentiation in its compositional characteristics, concentration in certain sectors of society, and the sharing of various socio-economic and psychological traits with other members of the same minority. These features plausibly explained the earlier timing and faster rhythm of demographic change observed among Jewish populations. Some of these mechanisms can also be hypothesized to stand behind the significant socio-demographic differences which exist between Jews in the diaspora, where they constitute small minorities of the total population, and in Israel, where they constitute the majority.

Various attempts to characterize the main thrust of modern and contemporary Jewish socio-demographic trends have emerged from recent research. Such alternative characterizations have animated recurring debates about the policy implications of Jewish demography (see below). One issue is that of *distinctiveness* versus *conformity*, that is, whether in the final analysis the apparent peculiarities of Jewish population trends reflect a unique and original blend of patterns and explanations, or can merely be explained as a slightly modified version of the experience of other populations. The question is not only whether the general levels or frequencies of features such as mortality, marriage, fertility, or geographical mobility are different among Jews and non-Jews. One also needs to ascertain whether the same peculiarities persist after control for an adequate number of further socio-demographic variables, in other words, whether the modes of interaction between different socio-demographic variables are significantly different among Jews and other control groups.

In this context, Jewish population trends can be explained by the changing equilibrium between the two major categories of *structural* versus *cultural determinants*. Structural determinants may be posited to play an important role in determining rational behaviours aimed at maximizing one's own material welfare; cultural determinants may be seen at work mainly in relation to emotional or spiritual fulfillment not necessarily connected with utilitarian reward. Neither type of variables seems to be sufficient, though both are necessary to provide a full and balanced understanding of Jewish population trends—or for that matter, of population trends in general. Of particular interest here is the scrutiny of what traditional Jewish culture and communal institutions have to say and to do with attitudes and behaviours whose ultimate effect can be measured demographically. The changing demographic dynamics of Jewish populations is better interpreted as a reflection of structural *and* cultural change among the Jews.

The further attempt to distinguish between *quantitative* versus *qualitative* correlates and implications of Jewish population trends, suggests that the total number of Jews, regardless of their degree of identification, has lesser societal meaning than the intellectual and spiritual quality of those who choose to be actively involved with the Jewish community. On the other hand, quantity appears to be strictly related to quality, as it affects a variety of processes fundamental to the viability of a Jewish community. One example is the extension of marriage markets and the amount of effort required to find compatible spouses within the Jewish group. Another case is the scale available to local communities to support an articulated network of Jewish cultural and leisure activities, thus offering a meaningful collective frame of reference to individual Jews.

A major debate, often imbued with value judgement, has involved those who mostly read in the recent Jewish population trends a pattern of *continuity* versus *erosion*. The failure of Jewish populations in the diaspora to replace themselves demographically, because of low fertility rates, and the growing incidence of assimilation and out-marriage accompanied by declining frequencies of conversion to Judaism, provided evidence for the erosion hypothesis. The persistence of large masses of Jews in numerous urban metropolitan areas in Western countries, and the distinctive social and professional environments which continue to characterize the daily life of many of them, offered the main basis for the continuity tenet. Recent research findings, such as those from the 1990 National Jewish Population Survey (NJPS) in the United States, have suggested new and sharper terms of reference for this ongoing debate. The new data indicates that the complex of bio-demographic and identificational factors of Jewish continuity has come to experiencing unprecedented challenge. It is not only a matter of creating a Jewish community locally, which may be and still is achieved in spite of the possible weakening of Jewish cultural life. Rather, the sense of global Jewish peoplehood and solidarity is at stake, as well as the demographic ability to produce a new generation of Jews and to transmit them a corporate identity that will be passed on to a further generation.

The possibility, supported by empirical observation, that different demographic courses emerge among Jewish populations in terms of *Israel* versus *the diaspora* leads not only toward a changing quantitative balance between the two typological components of World Jewry, but also to an understanding of the reasons for and resilience of such differences. While at the end of the 1940s Israel barely included 5 per cent of world Jewish population, international migration reinforced by patterns of family demography raised that share to 37 per cent in the year 2000. Following the same course, before the mid-twenty-first century Israel might hold not only the largest Jewish community on earth but also a majority of world Jewish population, which would constitute a revolutionary step in a diaspora-oriented Jewish history of 2000 years.

Whether such transition will actually occur depends very much on the further assessment of the respective roles of Israel and the diaspora (especially America and the other more developed countries) on a global or world-system scale of *core* versus *periphery*. In many respects, Israel may be posited as the current ethno-cultural core of the world Jewish population. Cultural determinants of demographic trends operate more intensively in Israel than elsewhere. In the diaspora the more strongly identified sections in the respective Jewish communities coexist with peripheral fringes that are declining or fading away. Migrations between Israel and diaspora may be characterized by a trade-off between ideological and socio-economic motives. But Israel's future viability on the international scene, its capacity to attract further large-scale migration, keep a hold on its own population, and pursue sustained demographic growth, heavily depends on its ability to join the core of more developed countries from its current economic and political semi-peripheral position.

One overarching interpretative question is which is the more fruitful and relevant theoretical approach: a general, *outer-oriented*, or a more specific, *inner-oriented*, one. Two extreme versions maintain, respectively, an absolutely *self-directed* course in Jewish society (such as in Jewish mystic interpretations), or their total *dependency* on external circumstances (as in the case of Marxist explanations). Conceptual and substantive reasoning shows the two approaches to be complementary rather than opposed, a combination of *macro-social* and *micro-social* determinants being required when exploring the path of causation. Indeed, while all socio-demographic events occur at the individual or at the household level, the causation chain leading to their occurrence relates individuals and households to collective frames of reference of a higher hierarchic order. Population composition by a variety of personal characteristics is a crucial factor in demographic behaviours. Individual characteristics also directly or indirectly reflect the influence of broader determinants, such as religious and social norms and institutions, legal frameworks, economic development, levels of modernization, political regimes, available technologies, environmental constraints, and other variables that shape at one and the same time the lives of many contemporaries.

Most socio-demographic processes can be statistically explained by an appropriate set of proximate determinants (or intermediate variables). One typical example is viewing birth rates as the joint product of couple-formation frequencies, natural fertility levels, and fertility control. However, these proximate determinants are themselves the dependent variables of a more complex explanatory chain. First and foremost is the community of orientation through or by which individual strategies and behaviour are often learnt, mediated, or influenced. The role of community constraints may have major effects on individual behaviour. Religio-ethnic communities are in turn affected by the overall character of national societies of which they happen to be part. A major constant throughout history is the Jews' exposure to contextual circumstances perceived at the level of national-territorial divisions. With increasing incidence in the course of time the latter are being affected by sweeping trends of a broad international if not global nature. Wide geographical dispersion and the progressive deepening of globalization trends make it essential to address world system structure and change as a basis for understanding the position of Jews internationally and locally. A systematic approach to causation needs to tie together these various hierarchic levels with the complex of main motivating factors.

Summing up and keeping in mind the whole relational chain linking the individual to the global system, major types of explanatory factors to be considered in interpreting social and demographic trends affecting Jewish population include:

- the complex of *distinctive* religious imperatives, ethnic values, social norms, ancestral traditions, popular beliefs, local customs, and community institutions particular to a given group;
- the modes of legal and other *interaction* between that group and the rest (the majority) of society;
- the circumstances *shared* by the specific group and the majority concerning the general character of society, its patterns of modernization, economic resources, modes of production, social structures and stratification, political institutions, level of technology, and climatic conditions.

Several more specific types of determinants should be considered in relation to the different desirability, feasibility, and availability of sociodemographic events among Jews versus others, and regarding patterns of variation at the community level:

- the group's unique *traditional culture and organization* with special reference to religious and social norms relevant to specific demographic and social events, as well as community frameworks and institutions established to implement those norms;
- the group's legal status or—more relevant to the contemporary situation— subjective perceptions of its own *dominance/dependence* versus the majority of society or other minorities within it;
- the group's *social class stratification*, implying significant inter- and intra-group differences in perceived interests and access to resources;
- the group's available *knowledge* on the given sociodemographic process, whether acquired through formal education or other channels;
- group-specific *biological constraints* of genetic or other nature, particularly in relation to inherited properties that may enhance or hinder exposure to various types of event.

Demographic trends draw on non-demographic processes such as the general state of world and regional economies, global cultural change, and political and military affairs. The combination of these factors and their mutual interactions with demography may determine the future size and characteristics of the Jewish population in Israel and elsewhere—hence the nature of the broader Jewish experience worldwide. The emerging insights may provide important feedbacks to a general appraisal of demographic processes worldwide.

METHODOLOGICAL ISSUES

Definitions

A major problem in Jewish population estimates periodically circulated by individual scholars or Jewish organizations is a lack of coherence and uniformity in the definition criteria followed—when the issue of defining the Jewish population is addressed at all. The very definition of the target population, embodied in the paradigmatic 'Who is a Jew?' question, constitutes a major and ever elusive issue in the field of Jewish population studies—in an extended time perspective, and particularly in the contemporary period. To appraise Jewish population trends appropriately, one needs to address the broadest possible meaningful definition of the collective. As a general rule, the study of modern and contemporary Jewish populations tends to rely on *operative* rather than on *normative* definitions of the target population. It is important that data-collectors allow for wide and flexible analytic opportunities to data-users who may later decide on definitional typologies according to their own assumptions and research goals. Yet to make the study of any finite population meaningful and worthwhile we need working definitions, and definitions imply certain standards, the alternative being an amorphous approach unable to generate analytic conclusions of any sort.

Halachah (Jewish rabbinical law) provides a clear and authoritative definition of 'who is a Jew'. However, for empirical research purposes it is not usually possible to undertake the stringent controls involved in ascertaining the Jewish identity of each individual according to such legal criteria. Therefore, the Jewish population is usually defined in censuses or surveys according to subjective criteria, such as self-identification, or based on the more or less accurate proxies offered by easily categorized variables, such as *religion* or *ethnic origin*.

Feudal society may have provided an environment in which social categories tended to be relatively rigid and stable. Identification of individuals with specific sectors of society, including religious groups, usually followed clear rules. So did passages, where feasible, from one population group to another, including accessions to, or (more likely) secessions from the Jewish community. In modern and contemporary societies, on the other hand, patterns of identification between individual self and a meaningful collective frame of reference (such as religion, or ethnic or cultural group) have tended to become more complex and fluid, reflecting the diffusion of subtle processes of cultural, ideological, and psycho-social change. Contemporary patterns of Jewish identity have been especially affected. One important complicating factor in contemporary societies is the increasing frequency of intermarriage. Intermarriage provides the major context for the growing number of individuals whose Jewish identification may be the object of controversy between different religious or legal authorities. More significantly, in the context of the same process, many individuals prefer not to—or do not know whether or when to—identify with the Jewish group, whether or not they might be entitled to do so according to some objective rule. While instances of confused or multiple identities have become more frequent, the socio-demographic boundary of Jewish populations has become increasingly flexible, porous, and blurred.

The existence of various possible types of *core* population and of variously defined types of *periphery* within the *enlarged* collective has become routinely acknowledged in recent research, the mutual relationship and dynamics between the parts being an aspect of primary interest in the analysis of the whole.

The *core Jewish population* approaches a conventional concept of a Jewish population. It includes all those who are ready to identify with the Jewish group, and those of actual Jewish origin who are now indifferent or agnostic, but do not formally identify with another religious group; those who, when asked, identify themselves as Jews, or, if the respondent is a different person in the same household, are identified by him/her as Jews. This is an intentionally comprehensive and pragmatic approach. Such definition of a person as a Jew, reflecting *subjective* feelings, broadly overlaps but does not necessarily coincide with halachah or other normatively binding definitions. It does *not* depend on any measure of that person's Jewish commitment or behaviour—in terms of religiosity, beliefs, knowledge, communal affiliation, or otherwise. Included in the *core* Jewish population are all those who converted to Judaism by any procedure, or joined the Jewish group informally and declare themselves to be Jewish. Persons of Jewish descent who adopted another religion are excluded, as well as other individuals who did not convert out but currently refuse to acknowledge their Jewish identification. In Israel personal status is subject to the ruling of the Ministry of the Interior which relies on rabbinical authorities.

Two additional operative concepts must be considered in the study of Jewish demography.

The *extended* Jewish population includes the sum of (a) the *core* Jewish population and (b) all other persons of Jewish parentage who are *not* Jews currently (or at the time of investigation). These non-Jews with Jewish background, as far as they can be ascertained, include: (i) persons who have themselves adopted another religion, even though they may claim still to be Jews ethnically; (ii) other persons with Jewish parentage who disclaim to be Jews. It is customary in socio-demographic surveys to consider the religio-ethnic identification of parents. Some censuses, however, do ask about more distant ancestry.

The *enlarged* Jewish population, in addition to all those who belong in the *extended* Jewish population, also includes all of the further non-Jewish members (spouses, children, etc.) in mixed households. For both conceptual and practical reasons, this definition does not include any other non-Jewish relatives living elsewhere in exclusively non-Jewish households. Ideally, socio-demographic processes should be analysed with respect to both *core* and *enlarged* Jewish populations, each of which provides a meaningful, albeit different, framework for analysis.

Unfortunately, much recent research has confused these various definitional concepts. It should be noted that an *enlarged* Jewish population may be growing at the same time there is a decline in the respective *core* Jewish population.

The Law of Return, Israel's distinctive legal framework for the acceptance and absorption of new immigrants, awards Jewish new immigrants immediate citizenship and other civil rights. According to the current, amended version of the Law of Return, a Jew is any person born to a Jewish mother, or converted to Judaism (regardless of denomination—Orthodox, Conservative, or Reform), who does not have another religious identity. By a ruling of Israel's Supreme Court, conversion from Judaism, as in the case of some ethnic Jews who currently identify with another religion, entails loss of eligibility for Law of Return purposes. The law *per se* does not affect a person's Jewish status, which as noted is adjudicated by Israel's Ministry of

Interior and rabbinical authorities. The law extends its provisions to all current Jews and to their Jewish or non-Jewish spouses, children, and grandchildren, as well as to the spouses of such children and grandchildren. As a result of its three-generation time perspective and lateral extension, the Law of Return applies to a wide population, one of significantly wider scope than the *core, extended,* and *enlarged* Jewish populations defined above. It is actually quite difficult to estimate what the total size of the *Law of Return* population could be, although some notion of its possible extent is attainable for the major countries.

Some would argue that the highly fluid and voluntaristic patterns of identification of contemporary Jewish populations make unfeasible any attempt to quantify the number of Jews locally or globally. Even if one rejects this position, Jewish population figures and estimates should always be taken as orders of magnitude, surrounded by variable (and sometimes significant) margins of error. While reflecting improvements and corrections, Jewish population estimates highlight the increasing complexity of the socio-demographic and identificational processes underlying the definition of Jewish populations, hence the estimates of their sizes. This is the more so at a time of enhanced international migration often implying double counts of people on the move. Consequently, the analyst has to come to terms with the paradox of the *permanently provisional* character of Jewish population estimates.

Sources of Data

The study of Jewish population has no definite time framework. It overlaps with Jewish history from the origins to our day and beyond. Clearly, quite different situations characterize the documentary basis of Jewish demography in different historical periods. The types and quality of available sources of data have determined the more or less reliable or speculative character of Jewish population studies, and have deeply affected the character and conclusions of research in the field over time.

Where direct and unequivocal information is lacking, three different approaches combined may usefully assist in the attempt to posit at least basic orders of magnitude of a Jewish population, or to outline the likely direction of major intervening changes. First, information of demographic relevance as transmitted by early Jewish tradition can provide a chronology of the major events affecting the rhythm of evolution of the Jewish population in the past, or even a typological sense of the quantities involved. Secondly, verified historical evidence relating to neighbouring or similar populations may provide yardsticks with which to infer parallel changes that may have affected Jewish populations. Thirdly, judicious use of mathematical models describing plausible ranges in the expected patterns of population dynamics and structure under given assumptions may assist in the critical assessment of what might have been possible or impossible under known circumstances.

In the course of time, and especially since the modern era, the amount of reliable information concerning demographic processes of the Jews has tended to grow. Yet, even in the contemporary period, the scientific study of Jewish populations is hindered by exacting methodological problems. A primary difficulty concerns the availability and quality of data. Relevant sources may be numerous, but socio-demographic data were and continue to be very scattered, often not very reliable, and lacking altogether in certain respects. Hence, the possibility to develop system-atic comparisons between different places and over extended periods of time—an imperative research need given the global character of the Jewish experience—is rather limited.

The great geographical dispersion of world Jewry implies exposure in the past and present to many different political regimes and legal arrangements. This in turn affects two basic aspects of modern and contemporary data sources on Jewish populations:

- whether or not the Jews are classified as one among other religious or ethnic groups in census or civil register statistics collected and released by official state or local authorities; and
- the degree of institutional centralization of the Jewish community in a certain place, and the proportion of Jewish population formally affiliated with any Jewish institutions.

Often, in the past, lists of heads of households, records of vital events, genealogies and other materials kept within Jewish communities—often at the request of ruling authorities—provided sources of demographic documentation. With the emerging and consolidation of centralized states, official population censuses, registers, or civil status records, where available, provided good sources of information on the characteristics of Jewish populations, as well as of other religio-ethnic groups. Over the last hundred years, though, major international migrations tended to flow from countries with a tradition of collecting Jewish population statistics to countries lacking such data. One of the side effects of the Shoah was the destruction of large Jewish populations for which detailed demographic data were routinely collected. Nowadays, about 75 per cent of diaspora Jews live in countries where, due to separation of Church and State or for other reasons, no official statistics on the Jewish group are available. In this context, the State of Israel today constitutes the major exception, with detailed and reliable demographic and socio-economic data constantly supplied by its Central Bureau of Statistics.

Centralized listings of Jewish households kept by some contemporary Jewish community organizations provide a useful, though infrequent, database for re-search purposes. Demographic data are sometimes available from registers of Jewish vital events, such as marriages, births, and burials. Based on these sources, trends can sometimes be reconstructed over extended time periods. But most large contemporary Jewish communities in the diaspora have no such central listings or record-keeping. Thus the study of Jewish demography has come to depend mostly on a variety of private or public research initiatives. General social surveys sometimes include a question on religion or ethnic origin. But Jews usually are scant minorities in such surveys, leaving little margin for meaningful analyses of Jewish population characteristics. Jewish-sponsored surveys involving larger numbers of Jewish households have been undertaken in several countries, and even more often in selected local communities, through specially drawn samples representative of the target population, and direct interviewing through specially designed questionnaires. Such studies have provided detailed demographic, socio-economic, and identificational profiles of the selected Jewish communities—beyond the limited array of topics typically covered by official censuses. Unfortunately, lack of uniformity regarding basic concepts, definitions, survey techniques, questionnaire contents, and format of analysis, have detracted from the scientific and practical value of many of these studies.

Human society, and world Jewry within it, perpetually and rapidly changes. The unfolding mutations in Jewish demography, socio-economic stratification, and identification over cohorts, periods of time, and life-cycles call for regular stocktaking, backward evaluation, and forward projection. Combined use of comparable data collected at successive points in time is needed for constructing historical series as well as retrospective adjustments of information obtained from previous sources. Single snapshots devoid of historical context or isolated insights devoid of comparative context may create many good questions but few good answers. Contents-wise, investigators should focus on a body of indicators already tested in previous research in order to infer conclusions over as long as possible a time span—even if in the long run the significance of some of these indicators may decline in the appraisal of a community's profile. New indicators should be added to old ones as their relevance emerges over time. Operationalization of a Jewish population should not, though, be driven by a philosophy that 'anything goes'. It is analytically significant whether measured behaviours and attitudes—no matter how innovative and unconventional—still meet recognizable Jewish community relevance.

While the amount and quality of documentation on Jewish population size and characteristics is far from satisfactory, in recent years important new data and estimates have become available for several countries through official population censuses and Jewish-sponsored socio-demographic surveys. National censuses yielded results on Jewish populations in the Soviet Union (1989), Switzerland (1990), Canada, South Africa, Australia, and New Zealand (both in 1991 and 1996), Brazil, Ireland, the Czech Republic, and India (1991), Romania and Bulgaria (1992), the Russian Republic and Macedonia (1994), Israel (1995), Belarus, Azerbaijan, Kazakhstan, and Kyrgyzstan (1999), and Latvia (2000). The UK 2001 census included a new optional question on religion. Permanent national population registers, including information on the Jewish religious or national group, exist in several European countries (Switzerland, Norway, Finland, Estonia, Latvia, and Lithuania), and in Israel.

Independent sociodemographic studies have provided most valuable information on Jewish demography and socio-economic stratification, as well as on Jewish identification. The largest of such studies so far have been the NJPSs in the United States (1970–1 and 1990). Similar surveys were conducted over the last decade in South Africa (1991 and 1998), Mexico (1991), Lithuania (1993), the United Kingdom and Chile (1995), Venezuela (1998–9), Hungary, the Netherlands, Guatemala and Moldova (1999), and Sweden (2000). Several further Jewish population studies were separately conducted in major cities in the United States and in other countries. Additional evidence on Jewish population trends can be obtained from the systematic monitoring of membership registers, vital statistics, and migration records available from Jewish communities and other Jewish organizations in many countries or cities, notably in the United Kingdom, Germany, Buenos Aires, and Saõ Paulo. Detailed data on Jewish immigration routinely collected in Israel help to assess changing Jewish population sizes in other countries.

A new round of official censuses and Jewish surveys is expected to highlight the demographic profile of large Jewish communities at the dawn of the new millennium, primarily the new US National Jewish Population Survey (2000–1), the censuses of Canada and Ukraine (2001), and the census of Russia (2002).

Research Resources

Global dispersion of the Jews has had deep implications for the possibility to develop effective research facilities and to undertake systematic projects in the field of Jewish population studies. The most significant early modern attempts to create a unified profile of Jewish population trends (under the concept of 'Jewish statistics') may be traced to Leopold Zunz (1823) and to Alfred Nossig (1886–7). The Bureau für Demographie und Statistik der Juden, led in Berlin by Arthur Ruppin, provided for a while a central research facility, including publication of the *Zeitschrift für Demographie und Statistik der Juden* (1905–31, with a few interruptions) and several monographs.

After the Second World War the Hebrew University of Jerusalem became one of the major centres stimulating research on Jewish population globally, mainly through the Division of Jewish Demography and Statistics founded by Roberto Bachi at the Institute of Contemporary Jewry (1959). The Division holds extensive documentation and bibliographic files. Between 1970 and 2001 it published twenty-nine volumes in the series Jewish Population Studies (JPS) and numerous Research

Reports and Occasional Papers. It organizes sessions in Jewish Demography in the framework of the World Congress of Jewish Studies held in Jerusalem every four years.

In the United States, since the 1980s important research activities have been carried out at the North American Jewish Data Bank sponsored by the Council of Jewish Federations (now United Jewish Communities) at CUNY Graduate Center in New York, and at the Center for Modern Jewish Studies at Brandeis University, Waltham, Massachusetts. Each of these centres is a depository of large amounts of documentation on Jewish populations. Research units operate at central Jewish community institutions in the United Kingdom (the Board of Deputies) and Argentina (AMIA). To be sure, much of the progress made in the study of Jewish population, as in any other investigative field, derives from independent scholarship by authors with the support of the respective higher learning organizations but not necessarily as part of specialized research units or projects.

Much remains to be done to improve co-ordination and the quality of Jewish population research. One persistent challenge is the need to create the basis for systematic and periodic updating of the data that exist locally, nationally, and internationally, instead of the sporadic efforts typical of the past. Better documentation is the necessary baseline for improved conceptual-theoretical frameworks, which are necessary to strengthen Jewish population studies as an area of research and teaching. Following a 1987 Jerusalem Conference on Jewish Population, some important new steps were taken toward greater co-ordination of research initiatives and concepts. An International Scientific Advisory Committee (ISAC) was formed and a new round of Jewish population surveys based on common concepts and a common core questionnaire was launched in several countries. The data-collection efforts of more recent years, the intensive and rather intriguing Jewish population trends they have revealed, and the debate—academic and public—they have generated augur well for the continuing expansion of research and analysis in the field of Jewish demography, and for improved quality of the outcome.

SUBSTANTIVE PATTERNS

Historical

While an analysis of the actual patterns of change of modern and contemporary Jewish populations is beyond the scope of this chapter, some of the fundamental processes can be mentioned. All along the course of Jewish demographic history, an intriguing overlap appears between the concepts of *people* and *population*. Though Jewish history cannot be reduced to a sequence of demographic events, the historical impact of demographic processes such as mass migrations, significant increases, or drastic reductions cannot be undervalued.

Since the beginnings of Jewish transmitted collective history, relevant textual testimony illustrates the unique demographic saga of the Jews. We cannot elaborate here on the details and reliability of such early demographic accounts as reported in biblical tradition and other early sources—or, for that matter, on the whole issue of the origin of the Jews. What, however, ancient sources do exemplify are three relevant and fundamental principles that affect long-term demographic experience of the Jews:

• ups and downs in population size and the unequal pace of growth of Jewish population as a whole over time;
• differential growth of different sections of the Jewish population at any given point in time, affecting the compositional characteristics of the whole group; and
• international migration as a large-scale process repeatedly affecting the geography and characteristics of the Jews, hence the location of the main centres of Jewish civilization.

After staying predominantly concentrated in the Middle East and Western Europe across the Middle Ages and the early modern period, fluctuating around an estimated level of 1 million or less, world Jewish population started growing toward the end of the seventeenth century. Jews attained comparatively very high yearly growth rates during the second half of the nineteenth century, the momentum of population growth remaining high after the First World War. An all-time peak of about 16.5 million Jews obtained on the eve of the Second World War and the Shoah. Most of Jewish population growth was concentrated in Eastern Europe, whose Jewish communities emerged as the largest regional component of world Jewry. Rapid growth also created at one and the same time the human pool and the constraining determinant for large intercontinental migration that, mainly since the 1880s, generated the new major centres of Jewish settlement in North America, in other Western countries, and in Palestine.

The main determinant of rapid Jewish demographic increase was the comparatively early transition from higher to lower mortality levels, which anticipated by several decades similar trends among the total population of the same countries. Later, Jewish birth rates declined too, once again anticipating similar developments among surrounding populations. Parallel distinctive Jewish population trends and differentials can be observed in a variety of regional environments, though substantial time-lags separate the onset and tempo of these changes in the more modernized communities in Europe versus the more traditional ones in Asia and Africa. Among the direct and indirect consequences (through international migration) of these late nineteenth- and early twentieth-century population trends was a radical change in the geography and internal cultural balance of world Jewry.

After the loss of over one-third of its global size through the Shoah, Jewish population followed two distinct courses. Jews in Israel featured continued intensive immigration, the absorption and integration of heterogeneous migration, and overall convergence of the diverse demographic behaviors of immigrants and their children. This created a comparatively young population, with a persisting family orientation, and moderately high fertility levels and growth rates. Jews in the diaspora, on the other hand, with some local variation, displayed low or very low fertility rates, growing singlehood, divorce and mixed marriage, a negative balance of new accessions versus secessions (including children of mixed marriages), and population aging. The ensuing negative balance between Jewish births and Jewish deaths tended to cause numerical decline.

Contemporary

At the turn of the twenty-first century world society, and world Jewry within it, has witnessed intensive and dramatic transformations, including the fall of the Berlin Wall and the reunion of Germany, the end of the Soviet Union as a global superpower, the renewal of large-scale Jewish migration, war in the Persian Gulf and the Balkans, peace initiatives and political instability in the Middle East, diplomatic recognition of the State of Israel by the Catholic Church, the Rabin assassination, and terrorist attacks of unprecedented scale. Many of these historical events can be subsumed under a general process of *globalization* involving political, economic, and cultural dimensions. Operative contraction of time and space, and greater interdependence among different and distant components of world society, such as political-military interests, industrial production, international trade, and most significantly media and communication networks, generated global shocks and aftershocks in real time. Gaps in standards of living and human opportunities continued to prevail at the global, regional, national, and local levels, stimulating large waves of geographical mobility across all possible geographic levels, and generating growing ethnocultural heterogeneity. As part of the continuing drive of modernization, society moved toward increasing secularization. Yet, contrary to assumptions about the end of ideology—let alone the end of history—large masses of people were more than ever involved in a keen quest for spiritual meaning. Perhaps deluded by the promises of modernization and a more neutral and affluent society, many sought gratification in religious values and ethnic identities, underscoring growing degrees of ideological tension and bloody conflict.

These general aspects of globalization carried momentous consequences for Jewish population and society. Toward the last quarter of the twentieth century two quite different Jewish population patterns of Israel and the diaspora tended to produce zero population growth among a world Jewry estimated at less than 13 million globally. Jews were once again the forerunners in anticipating a population slow-down in the more developed countries. Among the robust and resilient socio-demographic trends that developed over time among world Jewry, four deserve special attention:

- at its current zero population growth, world Jewry did not recover—nor will in the foreseeable future—its pre-Shoah size. In the longer term, a stable or smaller Jewish presence in a huge and competitive political, economic, and cultural global market-place implied a weaker position in the face of assertive and often aggressive competition;
- world Jewry became increasingly polarized between Israel and North America. The Jewish presence in Asia and Africa virtually ended, and Europe and Latin America represented declining shares of the global Jewish collective, especially among younger age-groups;
- the persistence of Jewish identification among the collective's most peripheral fringes raised serious doubts. This suggested growing difficulties in the struggle to provide one definition— all-inclusive, accepted by broad consensus, and analytically meaningful—for the whole of the Jewish people;
- a growing role for Israel emerged within world Jewry regarding the demographic balance and in the much broader sense of Israel's expected share of investment and responsibility in the running of world Jewish affairs.

Parallel and coherent socio-demographic change appeared among Jewish minorities in many different societal contexts. The latter ranged from the world's leading economic and political power, the United States of America, to its distant and in some respects antithetical counterpart, the former Soviet Union, through the other main centres of Jewish presence in the Western world. These common traits included extremely high rates of concentration in large metropolitan areas, high levels of educational attainment, professional specialization, delayed marriages, growing rates of intermarriage, low levels of fertility, and aging. If demographic process is posited as a dependent variable in a chain of other socio-economic and cultural determinants, after allowing for the differences still prevailing across nations demographic convergence suggested a great measure of symmetry or even similarity in the position of Jewish minorities vis-à-vis society's majority.

Over time, Jews often fulfilled an intermediary or middleman role between dominant holders of political and economic power and more or less anonymous dependent masses. This applied to such different types as Jewish traders of agricultural products in the Eastern European *shtetl*, Jewish immigrant textile craftspersons in Western cities, Jewish administrators in French North African colonies, or even Jewish officers in the Soviet apparatus. Jews as social buffers were exposed to significant stress under normal circumstances, and to dramatic pressures on the occasion of social and political revolutions against the established order. Major consequences resulted for the daily routine of socio-demographic behaviours, obviously more so at the time of major upheavals. The emerging prominent role, in the United States and elsewhere, of Jews as intellectuals, professionals, top managers, and even political representatives translated into new and more sophisticated societal functions, still bridging between the most powerful pace-setters in society and the majority of other citizens. In a general context of greater acceptance, and having moved significantly from providers of goods and services to providers of culture and know-how—somewhat removed from direct confrontation with non-Jewish customers— the risk of major dislocations diminished. But while Jews turned from unsatisfied dreamers of social change into people inherently interested in preserving the existing societal order, the time of definitive emancipation from any special personal and corporate concern had not come yet.

Under the prevailing circumstances, some of the emerging socio-demographic trends were powerfully erosive to Jewish continuity, while others led to continuity under deeply transformed conditions. The crucial ongoing transformation—the gradual transition of the Jewish people from the emblematic case of a diaspora to a more Israel-centred configuration—did not occur following mass migration to Israel, as hoped by the original proponents of Zionism. The underlying cause rather lay in the Israeli Jewish population's continuing ability to reproduce itself in cultural and demographic terms versus the Jewish diaspora's at least partial default to follow suit. The emerging results were nonetheless revolutionary in a long-term historical perspective. Demographic trends gradually produced a *normalization* of the Jewish people, in the sense that a majority of Jews might eventually reside in the territory historically and symbolically referred to as homeland, with a minority more or less concentrated or scattered elsewhere. This would make Jews more similar to other nations and their respective diasporas. Clearly, full normalization was conditional upon a peaceful and stable solution of the Israeli–Arab political conflict. Peace was a prerequisite to socio-economic development in the Middle East and for Israel to close the gap still severing it from the leading and more developed group of nations at the world system's core. Among other benefits, peace would improve Israel's chances of retaining more of its immigrants and also of its native population, thus sustaining the country's Jewish population growth.

The logic of some of the demographic trends currently at work among world Jewry is deeply rooted in history, as in the case of large-scale international migration. On the other hand, the declining weight of conventional nuclear families and the increasing impact of mixed marriage on Jewish demography and identification reflect a Jewish rejoinder to relatively recent and diffuse general societal trends. The momentum typical of demographic trends makes it quite unlikely that sudden and radical changes will occur in the short run. Even if they do, it would take quite some time before the consequences are seen in the composition and dynamics of Jewish populations.

Contextual indicators of the quality of life available to Jews at the global, regional, national, and metropolitan-area levels strongly and positively correlated with the changing numbers of Jews and their share of total population. The intensity and direction of past Jewish international migration was consistent with these general trends. The more recent drive toward global socio-economic integration had intriguing socio-economic effects on Jewish communities in many Western countries. Consequences were negative or worse for many middle-class Jews who only recently had significantly improved their social standing. The position of Jewish communities became increasingly dependent on unpredictable circumstances, sometimes of a cyclical nature, whose roots were far away from current places of residence. The growing reliance of Jewish communities on the support of a handful of powerful donors and economic groups greatly helped the course of Jewish life in the first place, but eventually resulted in a serious setback under worsening financial conditions—primarily in Latin America but also elsewhere. Growing needs perceived at the Jewish institutional level were not matched by comparable growth in available resources, due, among other reasons, to growing support by Jewish donors to causes that were not specifically Jewish.

More open opportunities for interaction with a receptive general societal environment exposed Jews to the competition of an unprecedented array of attractive cultural alternatives. Over time Jewish identification massively drifted from religious commitment, to ethnic bond, to cultural residue—hence, from much more to much less binding and mutually exclusive valence. These changes translated into transformed individual perceptions of the meaning of Jewish collective association—from all-encompassing existential framework, to meaningful reference group, to empty statistical category. At the same time, Jewish communities across the world were increasingly exposed to the inducements of a variety of Jewish religious and other spiritual influences, mostly centred in Israel and the United States, and increasingly competing with one another. In this context, the predicament of Jewish communities at the crossroads of the struggle for continuity also depended on the struggle for hegemony between the Jewish world's competing cultural centres over variously identified Jewish peripheries.

Future demographic change will predictably reflect the Jewish population's age composition resulting from past trends. The leading scenario for the future points to a Jewish people increasingly concentrated in North America and in Israel, with Israel possibly becoming the single largest Jewish community during the first two decades of the twenty-first century. The sharp age-structural differences that separate Israel and the diaspora have already made Israel the largest reservoir of Jewish youth and the principal and most challenging target for Jewish education. On the other hand, over the forthcoming decades the issue of aging will become a crucial and problematic focus for Jewish community service in the diaspora. Fewer economically productive individuals will be responsible for ensuring decent living conditions to a growing share of dependent elderly Jews. In Israel, the evolving demographic balance of Jews and Palestinians, within the territorial framework of Israel's pre-1967 borders, and more so over the whole territory between the Mediterranean Sea and the River Jordan, suggests enormous challenges to the very existence of a Jewish state. The prevailing prospect of a constant and significant reduction in the share of Jews out of total population calls for careful evaluation and strategic decisions.

APPLIED USES

Policies

As noted, understanding of population trends is a prerequisite for any serious attempt to develop Israeli and Jewish community policy planning. Our bias toward a concept of a Jewish society that can be empirically documented and understood also implies a belief about possibly steering society toward a more desirable course through adequate policy interventions. This requires that the inherent logic of ongoing processes be well understood, even more than their immediate results, if useful lessons are to be learnt to help us cope with future developments under the same or somewhat different circumstances. Several major analytic issues emerging from the substantive Jewish population trends just outlined have stimulated controversy and policy response: significant challenges to the Jewish collective stem from low levels of demographic reproduction; uncertainties in the socio-economic sphere; the weak (if any) cultural reproduction among large, more or less peripheral sections of the Jewish collective; and declining levels of internal coherence, consensus, and solidarity.

A false alternative, recently discussed along with plans for a new major Jewish survey in the United States, opposes *data collection* to *policy implementation*. Clearly, only through accumulating different and interrelated research approaches may we generate insights on population and society of comprehensive applicability. This involves a combination of complementary national and local observations exploiting different disciplinary techniques, such as large-scale statistical samples, selected samples tailored to clarify particular issues or the characteristics of specific sub-groups, longitudinal follow-up studies of selected panels, contents analysis of relevant texts, in-depth investigation of small focus groups, individual oral histories, and more. Serious policy analyses need to rely on a comprehensive, multidisciplinary research strategy.

Different readings of research findings have helped in creating the popular though inappropriate dichotomy of the *pessimist* versus the *optimist* analyst. In this respect, contrasting opinions may conceal analysts' different basic postures in the face of primary research goals. Interpretative controversies of the last twenty years about the main thrust of Jewish demography have partly reflected different analytic paths chosen—oriented to viewing Jews as one modality within the primary frame of reference of national societies (particularly in America), or within the primary defining framework of world Jewry. These different approaches have translated into different readings of research findings, emphasizing the general societal salience of group identifications versus specific patterns and implications for the Jewish group. The nature of analytic conclusions about the Jewish group suggested by either approach may be quite different, and so may the inherent policy recommendations.

Actually, besides the healthy function of a critical attitude to data, research findings viewed by some as problematic recently motivated, during the 1990s, a thorough reshaping of the whole Jewish community system in the United States and its priorities. A new institutional framework emerged, empowered to devise new educational and cultural strategies aimed at enhancing American Jewry's resilience in the face of society at large. Such interventions evidently need to be grounded on a clear and honest appraisal of the current status of Jewish society and on reasonable levels of expectation regarding the impact of policy interventions.

In Israel, population policies have been a constant subject of interest to successive governments. Targets such as incentives to Jewish fertility, or to preserving a definite Jewish majority within Israel's population, though, were pursued at a more declarative than systematic level. On the other hand, encouragement of Jewish immigration and Jewish population dispersal over Israel's territory was a constant feature in Israel's social policies. Other non-governmental organizations, primarily the Jewish Agency for Israel, fulfilled a determinant role in the implementation of immigration (*aliyah*) policies. At the end of the 1980s the Jewish Agency and the Government of Israel jointly formed an Association for Demographic Policy of the Jewish People, aimed at promoting research and policy interventions on Jewish population in Israel and in the diaspora, but its impact was limited and short lived.

Teaching

Jewish population studies have been taught as a separate topic regularly at the Hebrew University's Institute of Contemporary Jewry, and occasionally in the framework of Jewish Studies or general Social Sciences (typically Sociology) programmes. The Jews' early demographic transition may provide an exemplary case-study in the context of a broader discussion of modernization. Discussion of demographic issues may usefully highlight other facets of the modern Jewish experience in the framework of a Modern Jewish History course. Analysis of demographic trends in the late eighteenth to early twentieth centuries may usefully be associated with an examination of the social significance of traditional Jewish culture for Jewish populations and communities.

Mass international migration—a consequence of the demographic and social transformations of the nineteenth century, and a cause of the dramatic shift of Jewish centres of gravity in the contemporary world—constitutes a central chapter in the modern Jewish experience. This entails crucial transitions among Jews, from economic and cultural marginality to proximity to the core of global decision-making, and from a traditional and rather segregated to an open and more diverse environment, with special reference to regional patterns in continents of origin and destination. Discussion of Jewish migration is paramount to understanding the emerging and growth of American Jewry, or the decline of Jewish communities in Eastern Europe, Asia, and Africa. Any survey of the modern Jewish Yishuv in Palestine during the late Ottoman period and the inter-war British Mandate, and of the state of Israel as a major centre of Jewish life, must centrally consider the multiple demographic aspects of immigration and immigrant absorption.

Suggested Reading

There exists an extensive literature dealing, if only cursorily, with Jewish population issues. Over the last two centuries several more specialized publications developed the fundamental research methods, description and interpretation of Jewish demography. Among the earliest attempts to create a modern approach to the study of Jewry is Zunz (1823). Later efforts to define the relevant subject-matter, sources, and technical problems include Nossig (1886–7), Robison and Starr (1943), Schmelz and Glikson (1970), Schmelz (1976), and Ritterband et al. (1988). For reviews of long-term Jewish demographic history see Baron (1971) and Della-Pergola (2001). Analyses of main sociodemographic trends over the nineteenth and twentieth centuries include Lestschinsky (1926, 1929–30, and 1948) Ruppin (1930), Bachi (1976), Schmelz (1981b), DellaPergola (1983 and 1999), and Goldscheider and Zuckerman (1984). For a recent emphasis on gender, see DellaPergola (2000). Analyses of the determinants and characteristics of Jewish international migration can be found in Hersch (1931), Kuznets (1975), Eisenstadt (1954), Sicron (1957), and DellaPergola (1998). Major studies of Jewish fertility include Ritterband (1981) and Peritz and Baras (1992). Socio-economic characteristics of the Jews are discussed in Kuznets (1960). Different views about the socio-demographic evolution of American Jewry are presented in Goldstein and Goldscheider (1968), Goldscheider (1986), Cohen (1988), Goldstein (1992), and Rebhun (2001). For a study of the demography of Jews in the Soviet Union, see Altshuler (1987) and Tolts (2001). The emerging demography of Jews in Israel is analysed in Bachi (1977), Friedlander and Goldscheider (1979), Schmelz, DellaPergola and Avner (1991), Goldscheider (1992), DellaPergola (1993), and Goldscheider (1996). A standard source of data is the yearly publication of the Israel Central Bureau of Statistics (*Statistical Abstract of Israel*). Reviews of expected future Jewish population trends are included in Schmelz (1981a), DellaPergola et al. (2000), and DellaPergola (2001). Evaluations of Jewish populations policies and of the politics of Jewish population studies may be found in: DellaPergola and Cohen (1992) and Hart (2000). A journal entirely devoted to Jewish population studies was the *Zeitschrift für Demographie und Statistik der Juden*, published in Berlin. The Hebrew University's Institute of Contemporary Jewry issues the *Jewish Population Studies* series (Jerusalem, 29 vol. by 2001). Detailed reviews of research findings and population updates have appeared regularly in the *American Jewish Year Book* (New York), where further detailed references may be found.

BIBLIOGRAPHY

ALTSHULER, M. 1987. *Soviet Jewry Since the Second World War: Population and Social Structure*. Westport, Conn.

BACHI, R. 1976. *Population Trends of World Jewry*. Jerusalem.

—— 1977. *The Population of Israel*. Jerusalem.

BARON, S. W. 1971. 'Population.' In *Encyclopaedia Judaica*. xiii. 866–903.

COHEN, S. M. 1988. *American Assimilation or Jewish Revival?* Bloomington and Indianapolis.

DELLAPERGOLA, S. 1983 *La trasformazione demografica della diaspora ebraica*. Torino.

—— 1993. 'Demographic Changes in Israel in the Early 1990s.' In *Israel Social Services 1992–93*. 57–115. J. Kop ed. Jerusalem.

—— 1998. 'The Global Context of Migration to Israel.' In *Immigration to Israel: Sociological Perspectives*. 51–92. E. Leshem and J. Shuval eds. New Brunswick and London.

—— 1999. *World Jewry Beyond 2000: The Demographic Prospects*. Oxford.

—— 2000. 'Jewish Women in Transition: A Comparative Sociodemographic Perspective.' In *Jews and Gender: The Challenge to Hierarchy. Studies in Contemporary Jewry, An Annual* 16: 209–42. J. Frankel ed.

—— 2001. 'Some Fundamentals of Jewish Demographic History'. In *Papers in Jewish Demography 1997*, pp. 11–33 S. DellaPergola and J. Even. eds. Jerusalem.

—— and COHEN, L. eds. 1992. *World Jewish Population: Trends and Policies*. Jerusalem.

—— REBHUN, U., and TOLTS, M. 2000. 'Prospecting the Jewish Future: Population Projections, 2000–2080.' *American Jewish Year Book* 100: 103–46.

EISENSTADT, S. N. 1954. *The Absorption of Immigrants*. London.

FRIEDLANDER, D. and GOLDSCHEIDER, C. 1979. *The Population of Israel*. New York.

GOLDSCHEIDER, C. 1986. *The American Jewish Community: Social Science Research and Policy Implications*. Atlanta, Ca.

—— ed. 1992. *Population and Social Change in Israel*. Boulder, Col.

—— 1996. *Israel's Changing Society: Population, Ethnicity, and Development*. Boulder, Col.

—— and ZUCKERMAN, A. S. 1984. *The Transformation of the Jews*. Chicago.

GOLDSTEIN, S. 1992. 'Profile of American Jewry: Insights from the 1990 National Jewish Population Survey.' *American Jewish Year Book* 92: 77–173.

—— and GOLDSCHEIDER, C. 1968. *Jewish Americans: Three Generations in a Jewish Community*. Englewood Cliffs, NJ.

HART, M. B. 2000. *Social Science and the Politics of Modern Jewish Identity*. Stanford.

HERSCH, L. 1931. 'International Migration of the Jews.' In *International Migration* ii. 471–520. W. Wilcox. ed. New York.

Israel Central Bureau of Statistics. *Statistical Abstract of Israel*. Jerusalem, yearly publication.

KUZNETS, S. 1960. 'Economic Structure and Life of the Jews.' In *The Jews: Their History, Culture and Religion.* 2nd edn. 1597–666. L. Finkelstein ed. New York.

—— 1975. 'Immigration of Russian Jews to the United States: Background and Structure.' *Perspectives in American History* 9: 35–124.

LESTSCHINSKY, J. 1926. 'Probleme der Bevölkerungs-Bewegung bei den Juden.' *Metron* 6/2: 1–157.

—— 1929–30. 'Die Umsiedlung und Umschichtung des jüdischen Volkes im Laufe des letzten Jahrhunderts.' *Weltwirtschaftliches Archiv* 30: 123–56; 32: 563–99.

—— 1948. *Crisis, Catastrophe and Survival.* New York.

NOSSIG, A. 1886–7. *Materialien zur Statistik des jüdischen Stammes.* Vienna.

PERITZ, E. and BARAS, M. 1992. *Studies in the Fertility of Israel.* Jerusalem.

REBHUN, U. 1993. 'Trends in the Size of American Jewish Denominations.' *CCAR Journal: A Reform Jewish Quarterly* 40: 1–11.

—— 2001 *Migration, Community and Identification: Jews in Late 20th Century America* [Hebrew]. Jerusalem.

RITTERBAND, P. 1981. *Modern Jewish Fertility.* Leiden.

—— KOSMIN, B. A., and SCHECKNER, J. 1988. 'Counting Jewish Populations: Methods and Problems.' *American Jewish Year Book* 88: 204–21.

ROBISON, S. M. and STARR, J. 1943. *Jewish Population Studies.* New York.

RUPPIN, A. 1930. *Soziologie der Juden.* Berlin.

SCHMELZ, U. O. ed. 1976. *Demography and Statistics of Diaspora Jewry 1920–1970: Bibliography.* Vol. 1. Jerusalem.

—— 1981a. *World Jewish Population: Regional Estimates and Projections.* Jerusalem.

—— 1981b. 'Jewish Survival: The Demographic Issues.' *American Jewish Year Book* 81: 61–117.

—— and GLIKSON, P. 1970 *Jewish Population Studies, 1961–1968.* Jerusalem and London.

—— DELLAPERGOLA, S., and AVNER, U. 1991. *Ethnic Differences Among Israeli Jews: A New Look.* Jerusalem.

SICRON, M. 1957. *Immigration to Israel 1948–1953.* Jerusalem.

TOLTS, M. 2001. 'Jewish Demography of the Former Soviet Union.' In *Papers in Jewish Demography 1997.* 109–39. S. DellaPergola and J. Even eds. Jerusalem.

ZUNZ, L. 1823. 'Grundlinien zu einer künftigen Statistik der Juden.' *Zeitschrift für die Wissenschaft des Judentums* 1: 523–32.

CHAPTER 33

....

ART, ARCHITECTURE, AND ARCHAEOLOGY

....

LEE I. LEVINE

THE EMERGENCE OF ART, ARCHITECTURE, AND ARCHAEOLOGY AS RECOGNIZED DISCIPLINES IN JEWISH STUDIES

....

THIS chapter addresses three related, though not identical, academic fields of study that crystallized only in the twentieth century. Beforehand, it had generally been assumed, whether for political, social, or religious reasons, that Jews eschewed art and architecture, either because they were visually uncreative, preferring the audile to the visual, or owing to the restrictions imposed on them by the Second Commandment (Bland 1999: 13–70).

However, there emerged in the Post-Emancipation era an awareness that, in the course of their history, particularly in the later Middle Ages and modern times, Jews had produced an impressive array of artistic, mostly ceremonial, objects worthy of appreciation and display. This realization that a uniquely Jewish art and architecture existed in the past crystallized in the late nineteenth and twentieth centuries, finding expression, *inter alia*, in the establishment of Jewish museums throughout Europe, America, and Israel.

The Modern Era

The subjects of study in the realm of Jewish art in the medieval and modern eras may be divided into the following categories:

(1) life-cycle—e.g. circumcision (*Sandak*'s Chair, Elijah's Chair, knife), marriage (*ketubbot*, wedding rings, and divorce documents), and death (funerary headstones);

(2) annual cycle—e.g. Sabbath (kiddush cups, hallah covers, havdalah sets), Passover (haggadot, seder plates, cup of Elijah), Hanukkah (candelabra, tops [*dreidels*]);

(3) synagogue appurtenances—e.g. art and architecture of the synagogue building (building design and features, entrances, windows, furnishings, etc.), ornaments for the Torah scroll, decorations for and around the ark (curtain [*parokhet*], lectern, eternal light, etc.);

(4) books—e.g. illustrated Scroll of Esther and biblical manuscripts, decorated title-pages of Jewish books;

(5) paintings of biblical or post-biblical events and figures.

Analyses of the above items often emphasize one or more of the following issues: iconography; style; contextualizing an item or a specific phenomenon in a particular historical setting; Jewish–Christian or Jewish–Muslim interaction, often involving questions of influence; the development of a particular item over time and in different societies (e.g. the Torah ark). The question of how to define Jewish art has been particularly vexing and has often been revisited by scholars (R. Cohen 1993; and see below).

The study of Jewish art and architecture in the last half-century has been concentrated in Israel. Most universities in Israel have academic programmes in the field, either on the undergraduate and graduate levels or both, or at the very least offer courses on a regular basis. Outside Israel the only institution that offers recognized academic degrees in Jewish Art is the Jewish Museum of New York, in co-operation with the Jewish Theological Seminary of America. Elsewhere in North America, occasional courses in Jewish Art and Architecture are offered sporadically in connection with Jewish museums (e.g. New York, Chicago, Los Angeles) or certain colleges and universities (e.g. Stern, Wayne, Rutgers, Cincinnati, and Johns Hopkins). In Europe many Jewish museums or historical institutes offer such courses (e.g. in London, Paris, Brussels, Amsterdam, Berlin, Heidelberg, Vienna, Warsaw, Vilna, and St Petersburg). Recently the internet has become a valuable tool for tapping into an infinite variety of websites sponsored by universities, museums, and galleries that offer a wealth of information on modern and ancient Jewish art and architecture.

Late Antiquity

In order to provide the background for understanding many of the issues in Jewish art and architecture in later periods, we will focus in the present chapter on the ancient period, particularly on Late Antiquity (i.e. the third to the seventh centuries CE), when a distinctly Jewish art and architecture first took shape. As was the case with medieval and modern Jewish art and architecture, the realization that such fields of study were relevant to antiquity as well was confirmed during the first half of the twentieth century owing to substantive strides made in the field of archaeology. The first excavation organized under Jewish auspices, in this case the Palestine Exploration Society (later renamed the Israel Exploration Society), was that of N. Slouschz, who discovered an ancient synagogue in Tiberias in 1921. This event marked the beginning of what might be termed Jewish archaeology, that is, excavations uncovering the Jewish past in the post-biblical period. At the very beginning of the century, from 1905 to 1907, two German scholars, H. Kohl and C. Watzinger, conducted a detailed survey of eleven Galilean synagogues, the results of which appeared in their *Antike Synagogen in Galilaea* (1916), a work that remains indispensable to this day.

Some years later, a slew of excavations brought to light previously unimaginable evidence for the existence of a developed Jewish art and architecture in antiquity. The 1929 excavation at Bet Alpha and the discovery of the magnificent remains from Dura Europos in Syria (1932) began this process, and were followed in rapid succession by synagogue finds at Hammat Gader, Gerasa, Huseifa, Eshtemoa, and Jericho, culminating in the 1936 discovery of the Bet She'arim necropolis in south-western Galilee. A further milestone was reached in mid-century with the publication of E. Goodenough's monumental thirteen-volume *Jewish Symbols in the Greco-Roman Period* (1953–68), which provided conclusive evidence for a well-developed Jewish art and architecture in Israel and the diaspora during the Roman and Byzantine periods.

As these fields continued to develop in the twentieth century, the amount of scholarly material increased geometrically. In the 1930s most writings focused on numerous excavation reports of varying length and detail, which included analyses of significant archaeological finds. The discovery of the frescos at Dura Europos attracted almost immediate attention, generating studies throughout the 1930s and 1940s (see e.g. Gutmann 1973a; Sukenik 1947; Wischnitzer 1948) and culminating in C. Kraeling's monumental official final report (1956) and volumes 9–11 of Goodenough's *Jewish Symbols*, devoted to this topic, that appeared almost a decade later in 1964.

The publication of a volume on Jewish art and architecture, edited by C. Roth (1961), signalled a new stage in the field, in offering a survey by leading experts covering the entire range of Jewish history. Valuable as this volume was at the time (and it remains useful to this day), it was soon regarded as 'outdated' owing to the rapid pace of archaeological discoveries in subsequent years, a tempo that continues to the present time. The magnificent mosaic floor of the Hammat Tiberias synagogue was discovered in 1961, as was the synagogue at Ostia, Rome's port; in the next year the imposing Sardis synagogue was excavated. In the wake of the 1967 war intensive excavations were mounted in Jerusalem, the West Bank (Herodium, Jericho, and renewed investigations in and around Qumran), and the Golan. In the last-mentioned region no fewer than twenty-five synagogues have been discovered to date, of which only three were known beforehand.

The pace of scholarly activity increased markedly in the last third of the twentieth century, in part owing to the formalization of the study of Jewish art and archaeology in institutions of higher learning. Foremost among these was the Hebrew University of Jerusalem, where the study of Jewish art and architecture became an integral part of the Art History and the Archaeology departments. One of the first expressions of this focus was the pioneering publication of an extensive bibliography of Jewish art by L. A. Mayer (1967). Graduates of these departments eventually established similar programmes in other Israeli universities (Tel-Aviv, Haifa, Bar-Ilan, and Ben-Gurion). Moreover, the Hebrew University's Institute of Archaeology has published scores of final excavation reports in its Qedem series, and the Art History department, under B. Narkiss, founded the *Journal for Jewish Art* (later renamed *Jewish Art*) in 1974, as well as the Center for the Research of Jewish Art in 1979. One result was the organization of international conferences and research projects devoted to Jewish art that served to further the study of this field.

During the last half of the twentieth century similar initiatives facilitated the development of Jewish archaeology. The founding of the *Israel Exploration Journal* in 1950 provided an important English-language platform for archaeological discoveries in Israel. In the 1960s the Israel Exploration Society became an active player in archaeological affairs, sponsoring annual archaeological conferences that attracted thousands of participants and publishing archaeological reports as well as the highly regarded periodical *Eretz-Israel* (with Hebrew and English sections). The Society also began publishing at this time a popular archaeological journal in Hebrew, *Qadmoniot*, that provided an accessible forum and attractive format for disseminating archaeological discoveries, studies, state-of-the-field surveys, as well as lively discussions and debates. Moreover, the Israel Antiquities Authority regularly publishes short excavation reports (in *Hadashot Arkheologiyot* in Hebrew and in *Excavations and Surveys in Israel* in English), as well as a Hebrew and English series of longer reports in '*Atiqot*. These organizational and institutional efforts were, in turn, conducive in raising public awareness of and interest in the archaeology of Israel and in attracting a younger generation of scholars to the field.

While it would be foolhardy to try and name all those who have played a major role in the study of Jewish art, architecture, and archaeology to date, a number of figures from previous generations do, nevertheless, stand out for their unique contribution and deserve mention as having been pivotal in these areas (noting here only the deceased).

The pioneering scholar in Israel to have addressed issues of Jewish archaeology, architecture, and art on a sustained basis was E. L. Sukenik, the first professor of archaeology at the Hebrew University of Jerusalem. Sukenik excavated the Bet Alpha and Hammat Gader synagogues, and soon published the results of these excavations in volume-length reports (1932 and 1935 respectively). He also wrote an important overview of the state of synagogue studies entitled *Ancient Synagogues in Palestine and Greece* (1934), which remained a classic for years to come. Sukenik's volume on the Dura Europos finds (1947) is still the only extensive scholarly treatment in Hebrew.

The publication of important studies on the Dura Europos synagogue in the 1950s and 1960s opened a new chapter in the study of Jewish art. Outstanding among these publications is Kraeling's final excavation report (1956), which is both a detailed and thorough presentation of the finds as well as an exhaustive discussion of his and others' interpretations. Besides eschewing any claim to an overall, all-encompassing theme or themes (see below) in his study of the synagogue frescos, Kraeling posits an integral relationship between the third-century Dura finds and rabbinic literature. Consequently, he draws heavily from this literary corpus to interpret the finds.

One cannot overemphasize the pivotal role of E. Goodenough in the development of the field. His mammoth project (1953–68) not only brought together a wealth of examples of Jewish art from antiquity that few could have imagined existed beforehand, but his theory as to its meaning (i.e. the existence of a pervasive Jewish mysticism, which was independent of and opposed to rabbinic culture) generated much discussion and almost total opposition throughout the scholarly world for over a decade (Smith 1967). There existed a profound irony in Goodenough's efforts; his grand theory, in the service of which all the material in these volumes had been mobilized, was rejected by almost everyone. Despite the fact that Goodenough made it clear that he had not intended merely to compile all this material for its own sake, but rather to support his theory, it was indeed this vast array of evidence that made such a lasting impression on his readers. In ways unforeseen by him at the time, Goodenough has had a profound effect to this day, not only on the study of Jewish art but on that of Jewish culture and religion as well. One of the implications of his theory was that rabbinic culture had a limited impact on the Jews of Late Antiquity and that Jewish art simply did not reflect the world of the sages. While his alternative explanation, as noted, has won few adherents, he succeeded in posing the questions and raising the issues that have remained central to these fields of research for decades and have served as a goad to others to find alternative explanations.

Two prominent Israeli archaeologists at the Institute of Archaeology of the Hebrew University of Jerusalem also deserve mention. N. Avigad made significant contributions to the study of Jewish art and architecture through his major excavations, first at Bet She'arim in the 1950s (Avigad 1976) and subsequently in the Jewish Quarter of Jerusalem's Old City following the 1967 reunification of the city (Avigad 1983). In addition, Avigad published an authoritative study of the funerary monuments in Jerusalem's Qidron Valley (1954).

M. Avi-Yonah was primarily an art historian, and his numerous articles on synagogue mosaic floors and specific artistic motifs, as well as his synthetic analyses of Jewish art and architecture in Late Antiquity, gained for him a position of prominence in these fields. Perhaps one of Avi-Yonah's most important legacies was his conceptualization (similar to, and at about the same time as, that of Goodenough) of the division of ancient Palestinian synagogues in three distinct stages (Avi-Yonah 1961; see below). This theory remained dominant for several decades, but it is interesting that in the wake of the Franciscans' excavations at Capernaum challenging this theory, it was Avi-Yonah himself who, in an article written just before his death in 1974, raised the possibility of rethinking its validity (Avi-Yonah 1973).

DEFINING JEWISH ART AND ARCHITECTURE

In order to clarify the parameters of our discussion, it is necessary first to determine what we mean by 'Jewish' art and architecture. Any such definition must take into account the fact that Jews were not particularly innovative in their material culture; what they produced was certainly comparable to that of the surrounding cultures (e.g. Greece and Rome) and, needless to say, to what they themselves produced in the religious, theological, and literary realms. Although Jewish creativity in the material realm was most often expressed in the forms and patterns adopted and adapted from the non-Jewish context, a recognizable and substantial Jewish art and architecture did nevertheless emerge for the first time in Late Antiquity.

A number of possible definitions might be adopted with respect to Jewish art and architecture. On the one hand, a maximalist approach would advocate that anything made or used by Jews should be understood *ipso facto* as Jewish art and architecture. Such a definition would include anything a Jew produces, be it for other Jews or non-Jews, or anything a Jew uses, be it the product of another Jew or a non-Jew. In this regard, Jewish art and architecture would be similar to that of Etruscan, Greek, or Roman art.

A minimalist position, on the other hand, would posit that only a uniquely Jewish object or motif of specific Jewish connotation (i.e. *sui generis* vis-à-vis the surrounding society) ought to be considered as an expression of Jewish art and architecture. Thus, the representation of a menorah would be considered Jewish, but not the zodiac signs or floral and geometric patterns that also appear in non-Jewish contexts. The use of biblical imagery, then, would constitute an exception; while reference to the Hebrew Bible should clearly be considered of inherent Jewish interest, by Late Antiquity it would not have been a unique Jewish concern, as Christian art made use of the Old Testament as well. Thus, in minimalist terms, Jewish art would be comparable to Christian and Islamic art, although the latter are quantitatively far richer in remains.

However, neither of these alternatives is entirely satisfactory. The former appears to be too inclusive, the latter too restrictive. A third approach seeks the middle ground, defining Jewish art and architecture as that intended for use in a distinctly Jewish setting, either a communal building, cemetery, or some other context that serves the wider Jewish community. In this vein, any art used in synagogues would be considered Jewish art, as would that found in Jerusalem's necropolis, the Jewish catacombs in Rome, or the Bet She'arim cemetery in the Galilee.

Yet, like all compromises, this definition is not entirely satisfactory either. One may, for example, ask whether the Doric capitals of the Jerusalem Temple were 'Jewish' by virtue of their context, or if the floral designs on a synagogue mosaic floor should be regarded as such. Contrastingly, ceremonial objects in a domestic context would clearly be considered Jewish art. Nevertheless, despite these difficulties, most scholars have opted for a flexible application of this last alternative. Such a determination affords a large amount of material to work with when trying to understand Jewish art and architecture (along with the accompanying inscriptions) and their significance in antiquity.

PRINCIPAL TYPES OF REMAINS

Below is a brief survey of the various types of remains that constitute what is understood as Jewish art and archaeology in the period of Late Antiquity.

Jewish Art

Aside from the Tabernacle-Temple artefacts, there was very little specifically Jewish art during the First and Second Temple periods. Only toward the very end of the latter, that is, in the first centuries BCE and CE, do we first encounter unique Jewish artistic representations, and even then they were restricted mainly to the menorah, which appears only four times (not including the famous Arch of Titus replica), and then in a priestly context. The coins minted during the First and Second Revolts against Rome (66–74 and 132–5 CE respectively) seem to bear a series of Temple-related artefacts: the four species used in the Temple on Sukkot; amphorae, musical instruments such as the trumpet, lyre, and harp that were part of the Temple ritual; as well as the Temple façade itself. Coin designs minted by earlier Jerusalem authorities (under the Persians, Hasmoneans, and Herodians) that might also be considered Jewish, given their official status, display both figural (e.g. owl, Persian official) and non-figural (cornucopia, wreath, star) motifs borrowed from the surrounding cultures (Meshorer 1982: i. 13–34, 60–8).

All this changed dramatically in Late Antiquity, both in funerary contexts and especially in the synagogues, where decorations appear on stone carvings (of capitals, lintels, doorposts, and façades), mosaic floors, and frescos. Most significant, perhaps, are the use of biblical scenes (see below) and the ubiquitous appearance of Jewish symbols. The representation of the menorah is the most predominant motif, but other symbols, such as the Temple façade, Torah shrine, incense shovel, *shofar*, *lulav*, and *ethrog*, are also common.

The meaning and significance of this last-noted cluster of symbols have long been debated (Levine 2000a: 213–19). One popular theory maintains that they were intended primarily to recall the Jerusalem Temple—the façade representing the Temple itself, and the menorah, *shofar*, *lulav*, *ethrog*, and incense shovel symbolizing the accoutrements once used there. If this interpretation is to be accepted, then the clear implication is that the Temple's memory was of paramount importance in many Byzantine Jewish communities. The appearance of this motif in the synagogue could be viewed, then, as triggering a memory of that institution at the very least, and, at most, as reflecting a desire that the synagogue be considered some sort of continuation of the Temple's sanctity and religious significance (Hachlili 1988: 234).

A second approach regards these religious symbols within the context of the synagogue itself. The façade is thus interpreted as representing the synagogue's Torah shrine, while the other symbols are said to represent the various objects found in the synagogue or used in the synagogue service. By Late Antiquity, for instance, the *shofar* and *lulav* undoubtedly had become integral parts of synagogue worship during the Sukkot holiday (Dothan 1983: 33–9, 69; Fine 1997: 112–17).

A third approach, intriguing though not without its own problems, associates four of these symbols with the important holiday season during the month of Tishri, when three major Jewish festivals occur in rapid succession: Rosh Hashanah (the New Year), Yom Kippur (the Day of Atonement), and Sukkot (the Feast of Booths): *shofar*—Rosh Hashanah; incense shovel—Yom Kippur; *lulav* and *ethrog*—Sukkot (Bratslavi 1969).

Another interpretation of this cluster of Jewish symbols is more inclusive and flexible in nature. Rather than viewing all of these symbols as reflecting one particular institution or time framework, it is claimed that they may allude to several contexts simultaneously. Thus, these symbols may actually point to both the Temple and synagogue at one and the same time by amalgamating their representative symbols (Kühnel 1987: 107–11).

A variation of the last approach views these symbols as representing two basic concepts in Judaism—the Temple and the Torah. Certain symbols are clearly associated with the Temple setting, others would seem to indicate the sanctity of the Torah shrine. Since these two dimensions are often associated with one another, starting with the placing of the two stone tablets bearing the Ten Commandments together with Moses' Torah (Deut. 31: 9, 26) in the Wilderness Tabernacle and later, in the First Temple, this combination may have found expression in the synagogue as well.

Whatever their specific significance and meaning, the widespread use of these symbols in a synagogue context certainly gave vivid expression to the institution's religious ethos and undoubtedly enhanced it. The not-specifically Jewish motifs that appear in synagogue settings (e.g. the zodiac) will be discussed below.

Jewish Architecture

Given the fact that Jews developed a somewhat distinctive architectural style only in Late Antiquity, the amount of material in this category is limited. The two Temples in Jerusalem, built by Solomon and Herod, both utilized non-Jewish building techniques, styles, and patterns. Solomon relied heavily on Phoenician architectural types and artisans, and Herod on Hellenistic-Roman models and perhaps workmen as well. Nevertheless, each building was adapted to the needs and requirements of the Jewish cult, be it in the number and nature of the courtyards, the ceremonial artefacts in the sanctuary itself, or the fact that no images of a deity were to be found in these precincts.

The most important and numerically most significant remains, besides funerary evidence, come from the more than 100 synagogues discovered in Israel and the thirteen from the diaspora. Archaeological finds of synagogue buildings derive from all parts of the Roman Empire, from Dura Europos (Syria) in the East to Elche (Spain) in the West. Between these geographical extremities, synagogue remains have been found at Gerasa in Provincia Arabia, Apamea in Syria, Sardis and Priene in Asia Minor, Aegina in Greece, Stobi in Macedonia, Plovdiv in Bulgaria (ancient Philippopolis), Ostia and Bova Marina in Italy, and Hammam Lif (Naro) in North Africa. Besides the buildings themselves that have been preserved in varying degrees, these remains contain dozens of artistic depictions and hundreds of inscriptions. With regard to Byzantine Palestine, the overwhelming majority of evidence comes from the Galilee and Golan; in the former Jewish settlement is well attested in the literary sources. In addition, synagogues dating to the fifth–seventh centuries have been found along the coastal area and in communities located on the periphery of the Judaean hills.

In the first half of the twentieth century an all-inclusive conceptualization developed with regard to synagogue architecture of Roman-Byzantine Palestine. Articulated in several stages—first by Kohl and Watzinger, then by Sukenik, and finally by Avi-Yonah and Goodenough—it was based on a combination of historical, architectural, and artistic considerations. Kohl and Watzinger argued that the monumental Galilean synagogues were to be dated to the turn of the third century, at the time of Rabbi Judah I. It was assumed that the Jewish community by that time had recovered from the traumatic repercussions of the rebellions of the previous century-and-a-half and was now in a position—politically and economically—to erect such impressive structures. Rabbi Judah's political and religious stature, together with his apparently excellent relations with the Roman authorities, presumably facilitated this development. Moreover, the artistic similarities between these Galilean synagogues and contemporary pagan public buildings provided concrete evidence for this specific historical context. Kohl and Watzinger meticulously described and analysed these architectural and artistic remains, having contextualized them in Roman Syria of the second and third centuries CE.

Following the discovery of additional synagogues in the early 1930s, and especially that of Bet Alpha in 1929, Sukenik, having noted the striking resemblance between the apsidal synagogue with its mosaic floors and the Byzantine basilical church, went a step further and posited a later, basilical-type synagogue (Sukenik 1934: 27–37; 1949: 7–23). Whereas the Galilean-type synagogue was assumed to have existed earlier, at the turn of the third century, the basilical type flourished from the fourth to seventh centuries. The discovery of a synagogue with a totally different plan at Eshtemoa eventually led to the suggestion that there existed a third, transitional, synagogue model. Referred to as the broadhouse, or interim-type, it was assumed to have linked the two other ones. Thus, by mid-century a full-blown theory of the architectural development of the synagogue of Palestine in Late Antiquity had crystallized and the institution was alleged to have evolved linearly from one type to another between the second/third and seventh centuries CE. In this neat scheme typology was wedded to chronology. One of the major developments in the last half of the twentieth century has been the challenge posed to this theory in light of recent finds (see below).

CENTRAL ISSUES IN THE STUDY OF
JEWISH ART AND ARCHITECTURE

Interpreting Specific Scenes

Much effort has been invested in trying to explain individual depictions or repre-sentations appearing in Jewish art. Generally speaking, such studies have focused on the following topics:

1. *Biblical scenes or figures (besides those at Dura Europos).* Such depictions include the 'Aqedah (Bet Alpha and Sepphoris), Noah (Gerasa), David (Gaza and perhaps Merot), Daniel (Na'aran and Susiya), and Aaron with the Tabernacle altar and ritual objects (Sepphoris). Discussions revolved around the reasons for such depictions, and whether the selection was arbitrary or bore religious meaning.

2. *Jewish symbols.* As mentioned above, a relatively small repertoire of Jewish symbols appears in synagogue and funerary settings, either in an inclusive and fairly set pattern, individually, or in some combination (Hachlili 1988: 234–85; 1998: 311–78). These symbols are often clustered together beside a façade, which, as we have noted, has been interpreted in several ways; some representations indeed look like the façade of a building or temple (e.g. Bet Shean), while others are clearly intended as a chest or ark. The depictions on the gold glass fragments from Rome and that of the Hammat Tiberias synagogue fit this latter alternative well.

3. *Zodiac and Helios.* Undoubtedly this is the most startling and enigmatic motif, appearing in no less than six Palestinian synagogues; interestingly, though, never in the diaspora. Was this motif regarded as pagan and, if so, what was it doing in the middle of a synagogue floor? If it was not viewed as such, which is undoubtedly the case, then what was its purpose? The crux of the problem is really not so much the zodiac but the representation of the sun god Helios together with his attributes (the halo, sun rays, globe, and sceptre). To date, there has been no dearth of suggestions, ranging from the merely decorative, to representing the calendar, God's power as creator or ruler of the world, an archangel (as described in the fourth-century *Book of Secrets*, or *Sefer Ha-Razim*), or, finally, God Himself. Within this wide gamut of theories—ranging from the conservative to the radical—many variations have been suggested (Hachlili 1977). Moreover, in the process of substan-tiating one theory or another, many sources have been invoked, from the Bible, Philo, and Josephus, to the numerous varied rabbinic compositions ranging from the second to twelfth centuries, as well as to the above-noted *Sefer Ha-Razim* and even the thirteenth-century *Zohar*. While creativity is much in evidence in this respect, certainty remains elusive.

Aside from the three topics noted above, that have been especially attractive to scholars, the meaning of other elements appearing in Jewish art has also been the subject of inquiry. This would include representations of animals (e.g. eagles, lions, birds, and oxen) and inanimate objects (baskets, fruit, bread, grapes, etc.). Such an approach, most often associated with Goodenough and his determination to find symbols everywhere, is quite problematic methodologically. Are we to assume that all such objects bore significance, or could it be that some, many, or most were chosen only for aesthetic reasons? And perhaps, these representations were interpreted in a different way by various people (the artist, synagogue patrons or leaders, or members of the congregation from one generation to the next)? Scholars have been at odds over these issues for generations, and undoubtedly will continue to be so in the future.

Deciphering Major Programmatic Compositions

The remains of four relatively well-preserved synagogues (Bet Alpha, Dura Europos, Hammat Tiberias, and Sepphoris) have been the focus of most scholarly attention with respect to the study of Jewish art in antiquity. As such, they present a challenge and offer an opportunity to explain not only a single item or panel, but an entire composition. Do the walls of Dura or the floor of Bet Alpha or Sepphoris represent a well-conceived, overall plan, an all-encompassing programmatic conception intended to convey a specific message or a cluster of messages? Or, alternatively, is each panel to be interpreted independently and the sum total to be seen as merely a collection of disparate themes? Even those opting for an overriding idea have reached no consensus; over the years, scholars have presented vastly contrasting interpretations as to the collective meaning of these depictions. In the following paragraphs we look more closely at each of the above synagogues.

Bet Alpha

Are the three panels containing the 'Aqedah scene, zodiac, and Helios, and the array of Jewish symbols to be read individually or as some kind of sequence leading from the entrance-way to the bima? Wischnitzer, for example, viewed the three panels as representing the holiday of Sukkot (1955a); Wilkinson interpreted them as representing the various Temple courtyards and the Temple interior, the movement being to ever-greater holiness (1978); Goodenough posited that they represent the ascent of the soul from a state of earthly purification to the heavenly and then mystical worlds (1953–68: viii. 167–218); and Goldman, in a slight variation, understood them as the movement to the sacred heavenly portal (1966).

Dura Europos

The frescos of this synagogue present a far more challenging task as regards overall composition. Dura preserves a relatively large corpus of material, with as many as fifty to sixty different panels along the synagogue's four walls. One's assessment is hampered, however, by the fact that only about 60 per cent of the original number has survived. Thus, any suggestion as to an overall pattern, or whether the panels had several basic themes, can only be regarded as tenuous. Despite these obstacles, many have tried their hand. Suggestions include a messianic theme (Wischnitzer 1948), a mystical one (Goodenough 1953–68: vols. ix–xi), and an anti-Christian polemic (Weitzmann and Kessler 1990: 153–83; Kessler 2000). Some suggest that different themes are highlighted in each of the three registers: historical, liturgical, and moralizing, respectively (du Mesnil de Buisson 1939: 13–17); or the three crowns of Torah, priesthood, and royalty noted in Mishnah Avot 4, 17 (Sonne 1947). Gutmann, focusing on the middle band, claimed that its message is liturgical and that the various panels trace the peregrinations of the holy ark in Israel's history, beginning with the Wilderness Tabernacle; the register was intended to accompany the synagogue's Torah-reading ceremony (1973a).

As might be expected, a number of scholars have concluded that there is, in fact, no overriding theme or comprehensive programme dictating the selection of the bands at Dura, other than the desire to represent important events in the Bible, particularly those reflecting God's protection of Israel—a kind of artistic *Heilsgeschichte* (Rostovtzev 1938: 100–34; Bickerman 1965). According to this approach, each individual depiction or set of depictions has its own meaning and significance.

Sepphoris

The seven registers of this mosaic floor are likewise unique in synagogue art. The excavators have suggested that the overarching theme is one of Promise—as represented by the 'Aqedah scene, and Redemption—as indicated by the Tabernacle-Temple scenes (Weiss and Netzer 1996: 34–9). The connecting link between these two foci is Helios and the zodiac, which represent the power of God as ruler of the cosmos who, in this capacity, will assure the transition from the one to the other. B. Kühnel has advocated a somewhat different interpretation, assuming that the Tabernacle-Temple motif reflects the continuity of the cult that anticipates redemption, with the Binding of Isaac ('Aqedah) serving as the historical incident that points in this direction and the zodiac alluding to the natural world that also works in concert with God's plan (2000).

The Hellenistic or Synchronic Dimension

The study of Hellenization, the term most often used to describe the impact of the larger surrounding culture on the Jews in the Graeco-Roman world, has been one of the most fruitful areas of inquiry over the past several generations (Levine 1998: 3–32). It usually involves the overall effect that this larger cultural matrix—what is often referred to as the synchronic dimension—had on Jewish life, not always on a conscious level. Often these dynamics involved a complex process of adoption and adaptation of various components from the outside culture and their impact on the Jewish material, social, cultural, and religious realms.

The realms of Jewish architecture and art are particularly persuasive in this respect. Since the Jews, as noted, never possessed a developed architectural or artistic tradition of their own, in either the private or public domain, they borrowed heavily from the regnant styles of contemporary society. A visit to the Museum of the Diaspora at Tel-Aviv University offers a striking demonstration of this fact in its exhibit of miniature replicas of a score-or-so of synagogue buildings from throughout the ages, each constructed and decorated in the tradition and style of the predominant culture of the time.

Thus, while many Galilean and Golan synagogues boasted a monumental façade, with a single or tripartite entrance, as well as stone reliefs on lintels, doorposts, friezes, Syrian gables, windows, and arches, such elements are also well attested in Roman public buildings and especially temples of second- and third-century Syria, as well as in a number of Byzantine churches from that region (Foerster 1987, 1992). Given the extensive imitation of external architectural models, it was nearly impossible to distinguish a synagogue from a non-Jewish edifice merely by its exterior. This is corroborated not only by archaeological remains, but is also reflected in Bavli Shabbat 72b, wherein the sages debated whether one who bowed in deference before a pagan temple, thinking it was a synagogue, was guilty of committing an intentional or unintentional sin. While the halachic aspects of this rabbinic discussion are not relevant to our purposes, the historical reality behind such an example is germane. The rabbis clearly imagined a scenario wherein someone walking along the streets of a town or city would be unable to differentiate between a pagan temple and a synagogue merely on the basis of the building's exterior. The story confirms what is evident from archaeological finds, namely, the striking similarity in external features of Jewish and non-Jewish buildings. This, in fact, was the assumption of Kohl and Watzinger and others who have attempted to reconstruct the façade and interior of Galilean synagogues.

The same indebtedness to contemporary architectural models also holds true with respect to the plans of basilica-type Byzantine synagogues. Patterned after contemporary Christian churches, many of these synagogues featured a courtyard (atrium), tripartite entrances leading into a narthex, and three portals leading into the main hall containing a nave, two side aisles, and apse (or *bima*) positioned in the direction of the building's orientation, or focus (Tsafrir 1987). Such borrowing is clearly attested by the synagogue's adoption of the church's chancel screen (Foerster 1989). In its Christian milieu, this architectural element, built of stone slabs fitted into the grooves of posts, served as a parapet for separating the clergy and altar from the congregation. Unlike the church setting, however, a screen had no discernible function in the synagogue, where no comparable partition existed between clergy (i.e. prayer leaders, preachers, or Torah-readers) and congregation. Thus, the appearance of the chancel screen in a Jewish context seems to be a striking example of the incorporation of a foreign architectural element that, as far as we know, had no practical purpose within the synagogue setting. Once borrowed, however, the synagogue chancel screen was often fashioned similarly to its Christian counterpart, with Jewish symbols (instead of Christian ones), floral and geometric decorations, and dedicatory inscriptions. Whether the synagogue chancel screen subsequently acquired its own symbolic meaning, for example, as marking off sacred space in imitation of the Temple balustrade, is debatable (Branham 1995).

In light of the extensive artistic remains from both Byzantine Palestine and the diaspora, the available information is rich and varied, ranging from instances of slavish imitation of foreign models to those of remarkable originality. In terms of technique (mosaics, frescos, stone mouldings) and types of representations (floral, faunal, geometric, figural), the Jewish communities of this era had little in their own tradition from which to draw, and outside influence was considerable. Jewish creativity often expressed itself in the selection of motifs. Blatantly pagan representations were, for the most part, eschewed, and neutral patterns were more easily assimilated. As a result, geometric and floral patterns are especially common in synagogues, although more neutral figural representations, such as animals, birds, and fish, were also quite ubiquitous (Hachlili 1988: 317–46).

Three specific instances of artistic borrowing in synagogues of Byzantine Palestine are particularly instructive. The first is the remarkable similarity between the mosaic floors of the synagogues in Gaza and nearby Maʿon (Nirim) on the one hand, and that of the Shellal church on the other—all three dating to the sixth century CE. These three sites are so close to one another geographically, and their patterns and motifs so similar (an amphora with vine tendrils flanked by birds or animals forming rows of medallions containing depictions of animals, birds, and other objects), that Avi-Yonah suggested that all three floors may have originated in the same Gazan workshop (Avi-Yonah 1981: 389–95). Although this particular suggestion has met with some reservations, there is little disagreement as to the remarkable resemblance between these floors (Hachlili 1987; Stone 1988; Ovadiah 1995). Another example of a common motif is the Temple façade of a sixth-century church on Mount Nebo. Foerster has suggested that the artisan of the synagogue at Susiya in southern Judaea may have borrowed the architectural representation of the façade from this church (or its source) (1990: 545–52). Finally, Bregman has argued that the ram motif in the ʿAqedah scene of the Bet Alpha synagogue was borrowed from a Christian exemplar, wherein the 'hanging' ram was originally intended as a prefiguration of Jesus on the cross (1995).

If synagogue decorations in Palestine can be readily traced to pagan and Christian models, the situation in the diaspora is even clearer. Given the occasionally substantial amount of comparative material from the immediate surroundings, it seems that synagogue decoration invariably reflects the styles and patterns of its local context. This is dramatically confirmed at Dura Europos, where the paintings of the synagogue are paralleled by wall paintings in many local religious buildings (a church, mithraeum, and other pagan temples). The mosaics of the Elche synagogue are similar to those of Roman villas in the region; the different building styles used over the centuries in Roman Ostia, for instance *opus reticulatum, opus vittatum,* and *opus listatum,* are evidenced in the local synagogue's walls and provide, *inter alia,* rather conclusive evidence for dating. Moreover, the Naro mosaics feature motifs common in Roman Africa (Levine 2000a: 232–87).

The Jewish–Christian Nexus

Numerous studies over the past few decades have made it quite clear that there were many similarities between the synagogue and church in the Byzantine period. This was true architecturally, as many synagogues were built according to the basilical plan then in vogue among churches (see above), and also bore similar artistic motifs (Ovadiah 1977; Tsafrir 1987). Moreover, it has been generally agreed that some sort of dialogue took place, directly or indirectly, between Jews and Christians over issues of faith and biblical interpretation (Visotzky 1995; Hirshman 1996). However, H. Kessler has recently combined these two strands, suggesting that much Jewish art is, in reality, a polemic against Christian claims. In this vein, he interprets many of the Dura synagogue panels (a church was built near the synagogue already in 232 CE) and Sepphoris mosaics (Weitzmann and Kessler 1990; Kessler 2000). Several other scholars have followed Kessler's lead in this regard (Kühnel 2000; Revel-Neher 2000).

The Byzantine–Christian nexus is likewise apparent in the widespread use of Jewish symbols in Late Antiquity. Note has already been taken above of the cluster of these symbols (menorah, *shofar,* etc.) that before the third century CE was rarely, if ever, invoked, and then only in a very few instances, at least with respect to the menorah. Late Antiquity, however, witnessed a deluge of examples. In contrast, the menorah appeared in only a small number of contexts in Second Temple Jerusalem. Following a hiatus of about two centuries, when there seems to have been some ambivalence regarding its depiction, it reappears in many contexts, becoming the dominant Jewish symbol for the next four or five centuries. The menorah is represented in hundreds of instances by itself and together with other Jewish artefacts, such as the Torah shrine, *shofar, lulav,* and *ethrog.* The menorah's centrality holds true for both the diaspora and Palestine, in cemeteries as well as synagogues. In the latter, it is found carved on stone capitals, columns, lintels, and chancel screens, painted on walls, and depicted on mosaic floors; it also appears on a variety of small objects such as gold glass, household objects, seals, amulets, and oil lamps.

The appearance of the menorah as a widespread Jewish symbol should not be divorced from the larger Byzantine-Christian context (Levine 2000b). When compared to the earlier Roman period, the use of symbols now appears to have been more ubiquitous than ever before, and while Christianity spearheaded this development with all the imperial and ecclesiastical means at its disposal, the Jews could hardly have remained unaffected. The menorah is the most salient example of religious objects that were now being depicted, although the Torah shrine, *lulav*, *ethrog*, and *shofar* were also mobilized for this purpose.

A second contextual factor to be taken into consideration in explaining the popularity of the menorah in the Byzantine period is the widespread use of the cross. By the fourth and the fifth centuries the cross appeared everywhere—in Christian buildings, at burial sites, and in homes—and was worn by individuals as well. Its purpose was to serve as a reminder of Jesus, his message, redemption generally, and Jesus's eschatological presence in particular; it also served an apotropaic purpose. The use of the menorah, in part as a Jewish response to the cross, is not simply a theoretical possibility. On a number of archaeological finds we find the menorah precisely where a cross would have been depicted in a Christian context. For example, a menorah was incised on a chancel screen at Hammat Gader, as was a cross on a chancel screen at Masu'ot Yitzhaq, and lamps hung from *menorot* in Na'aran, as they did from a cross in North Africa. Crosses decorated late Byzantine oil lamps as well as glass jugs and jars from Byzantine Jerusalem and elsewhere in precisely the place where *menorot* appear.

Just as the widespread use of inscriptions by Jews in Late Antiquity reflects wider Byzantine practice (Foerster 1981: 33–40), so too may have been the case in the realm of symbolic artistic expression. The use of symbols as a means of reinforcing group identity seems to have been a hallmark of this period for both Christians and Jews. We are only now beginning to realize the extent of Jewish–Christian interaction in all walks of life during this period, whether hostile or supportive, destructive or fructifying. Within the synagogue context, Byzantine architectural and artistic patterns and motifs were frequently adopted. Even in the case of such a uniquely Jewish symbol as the menorah, the synchronic dimension is clearly a crucial factor in accounting for its widespread appearance in this period as the Jewish symbol par excellence.

The Dating of Synagogues in Roman-Byzantine Palestine

One of the major changes over these past few decades has been in the dating of various synagogues, and particularly of several synagogue-types. In tracing the development of synagogue architecture as understood in the early twentieth century, we noted the gradual emergence of the classic three-stage theory. However, this neat compartmentalized reconstruction—coupling typology with chronology—has been seriously undermined over the past quarter-century by numerous archaeological discoveries (Meyers 1987; Seager 1989; Groh 1995). The results of the Franciscan excavations at Capernaum placed the Galilean synagogue building in the late fourth and fifth centuries. Soon after, the excavation findings from the synagogues at Khirbet Shema' and Meiron—located some 600 metres from each other—dated both of these structures to the latter half of the third century. Each of these buildings represents a dramatically different architectural style according to the old theory; Meiron is a quintessentially Galilean-type structure, Khirbet Shema' a broadhouse or so-called transitional type. Nevertheless, they were both built at the same time and in the same region.

The excavation results from Nabratein demonstrate that the extant building, known for over a century as a Galilean-type structure, was in fact the third stage of a synagogue dating from the sixth century. Such is the explicit attestation of its lintel inscription, which was found in the nineteenth century but only deciphered by Avigad in the mid-twentieth. The inscription reads as follows: 'To the count of 494 years after the destruction of the Temple, (this synagogue) was built during the office of Hanina ben Lizar and Luliana bar Yudan' (Avigad 1960).

Until these recent excavations, and because of the regnant chronological assumptions of the time, no one accepted this epigraphical evidence at face value, namely, that the synagogue was built in 564 CE. Thus, the term 'built' was interpreted as 'repaired'. Now that we know that this last stage was built several centuries after the earlier one, and according to a somewhat different plan, it is clear that much more than a repair was involved.

Throughout the 1970s and 1980s several other excavations were conducted at already-identified Galilean synagogues—Horvat 'Ammudim, Gush Halav, and Chorazim. The finds from the first two sites point to a mid- to late third-century date of construction, at the earliest; those from Chorazim indicate a fourth–fifth-century date. Moreover, the results of a number of excavations in the Golan in the 1980s date the time of construction of synagogues there to the fifth and sixth centuries CE. The discovery of a Galilean-type structure at Merot in the mid-1980s placed another nail in the coffin of the older traditional scheme, as the earliest stage of this building was clearly and unequivocally set in the late fourth to early fifth centuries. Most recently, Magness, basing her theory on ceramic evidence, has dated a series of Galilean-type synagogues to the fifth–sixth centuries (2001).

Thus, the linear approach equating each type of building to a specific historical period can rightly be put to rest. Diversity reigned in synagogue art and architecture, as it did in other aspects of Jewish society.

The Local Factor in Understanding Art and Architecture

The social implications of what has just been described with regard to the diversity of synagogue architecture should be obvious. Local tastes and proclivities were the decisive factors in determining what a synagogue looked like and how it functioned. This is eminently clear from the material remains of ancient synagogues, wherein diversity is the norm. In fact, no two synagogues, even those of the same type and located in geographical proximity, are exactly the same. All sorts of differences are apparent, both architectural plans and artistic representations. This fact is quite evident when comparing the three Palestinian synagogues of Bet Alpha, Hammat Tiberias, and Sepphoris. Whatever the similarities, the differences between them regarding iconography and the selection, representation, and placement of the various panels are even more pronounced. A striking example of this marked diversity among synagogues is evident in the Bet Shean area. To date, we know of five contemporaneous synagogue buildings that functioned in sixth-century Bet Shean (Levine 2000a: 198–206). No other urban setting boasts such a concentration of remains, having not only a geographical but also a chronological propinquity. The synagogues referred to are Bet Shean A, just north of the city wall; Bet Shean B, near the south-west city-gate; Bet Alpha, to the west; Ma'oz Hayyim, to the east; and Rehov, to the south. However, despite the fact that all these buildings functioned at one and the same time, they were, in fact, remarkably different from one another in a variety of ways.

Literary sources can contribute here to our understanding of this phenomenon, fully reinforcing this impression of diversity and local autonomy. The synagogue was created by the local Jewish community in response to its need for a central institution that would provide it with a range of services. As a result, the synagogue became firmly rooted in Jewish communities of Late Antiquity as the communal institution par excellence. Also governed by the local community, synagogue officials, for the most part, do not appear to have been subordinate to any outside authority. The synagogue was referred to as bet 'am ('house of [the] people'—Bavli Shabbat 32a), and it is in this capacity that it functioned. The Mishnah views this communal dimension in the following fashion: 'And what things belong to the town itself? For example, the plaza, the bath, the synagogue, the Torah chest, and [holy] books' (Mishnah Nedarim 5, 5). It was the townspeople or their chosen representatives who had ultimate authority over synagogue matters. Thus, in addressing the issue of whether or not to sell communal property, the Mishnah (Megillah 3, 1) states that it was the local population (bnei ha'ir) that should make that decision, while the Tosefta (Megillah 2, 12), according to Rabbi Judah, notes that local officials should act on the institution's behalf, but only after the local townspeople grant them the requisite authority.

The control exercised by the community included the hiring and firing of synagogue functionaries. One account notes that the synagogue community of

Tarbanat (on the border between the Lower Galilee and the Jezreel Valley) dismissed Rabbi Simeon when the latter proved unwilling to comply with their requests (Yerushalmi Megillah 4, 5, 75b).

Figural Art in Jewish Tradition

The abundance of Jewish art from the Byzantine period synagogue tells us much about the institution and its adaptation by different communities. The forms of expression range from simple geometric and floral shapes to animal and human figures. The latter representations are quite varied, at times consisting only of birds ('En Gedi, Ma'oz Hayyim), an assortment of animals (Ma'on [Nirim], Gaza, Bet Shean B, Yafia, Chorazim), and, not infrequently, human figures.

The ubiquity of such figural representations in synagogue art, as well as in the necropolis of Bet She'arim, has indeed revolutionized our understanding of Jewish attitudes toward this type of artistic expression (Levine 1985). Before the archaeological discoveries at Bet Alpha and Dura Europos, it had been assumed that Jews did not engage in figural art, or at least did so only on rare occasion. The apparent prohibition of the Second Commandment, together with a number of Josephus' accounts regarding Jewish aversion to figural representations in the late Second Temple period, particularly in Jerusalem (e.g. Josephus, *Antiquities* 17. 149–63), essentially determined this perception. However, with the steady accumulation of archaeological material over these last few generations, this issue has been completely re-evaluated, resulting in a far more complex picture (Avigad 1976: 275–87).

Today we can safely conclude that Jews in the biblical and early Second Temple periods did, in fact, make use of a variety of figural representations. Examples from the biblical period include the cherubs over the holy ark, those woven into the Tabernacle curtain (*parokhet*), Solomon's use of cherubs and animal figures in his Temple and palace decorations, and the twelve oxen supporting the large basin in the Temple courtyard (Exod. 25: 20; 1 Kgs. 7: 23 ff.). Moreover, the bronze serpent attributed to Moses, the golden calves in the northern sanctuaries of Dan and Beth-el, as well as innumerable figurines and seal engravings (e.g. of lions, horses, gazelles, cocks, snakes, and monkeys) found at Israelite sites and dating primarily from the eighth and seventh centuries BCE, all point to a generally permissive attitude toward this art form in the First Temple era (Num. 21: 9; 1 Kgs. 12: 26–33). From the late Persian and early Hellenistic periods, the 'Yehud' coins minted in Jerusalem featured a wide variety of figural representations, including owls, eagles, a leaping winged animal, a Persian king, a divine figure sitting on a winged wheel, a warrior, a young man, and depictions of Ptolemy and Berenice (Meshorer 1982: i. 13–34). Even at the turn of the second century BCE, the Tobiad Hyrcanus used a variety of carved animal reliefs when building his estate east of the Jordan River.

However, beginning in the late Hellenistic or Hasmonean period, the pendulum swung sharply in the opposite direction. Strict avoidance of figural depictions became the norm in Jewish society for about 300 years, commencing with the rise of the Hasmonean state and lasting until the aftermath of the Bar-Kokhba revolt (c.150 BCE–150 CE). The reasons for this radical about-face with respect to figural representation are not entirely clear. Various suggestions have been offered: (1) a traumatic reaction to the 167 BCE desecration of the Temple by Antiochus IV, which included coercive pagan worship; (2) a more stringent position in this regard reflecting the attitude of the Sadducees, who were generally in control of affairs in Jewish Palestine in the late Second Temple period (except for the era of Salome, 76–67 BCE, when the Pharisees dominated); (3) Hasmonean policy, which aimed, in part, at cultivating unique Jewish modes of expression, may well have affected art forms as well; and (4) a more general Jewish reaction to Hellenization and the threat of foreign influences.

The reintroduction of figural representation beginning in the late second and third centuries CE is far from exceptional in the wider perspective of Jewish history. In fact, this change reflects yet another shift of the pendulum with regard to Jewish attitudes toward figural representation owing to internal needs and in response to the wider cultural, social, and political contexts in which the Jews of Palestine now found themselves. Here, too, a number of suggestions (not necessarily mutually exclusive) have been offered to explain the reintroduction of figural motifs: the ever-increasing Hellenization of the Jewish population; the Jews' increasing minority status which made the need for social, economic, and cultural accommodation to the outside world even more pressing; the decline of paganism and the view that such images are not necessarily a threat to Jews and Judaism.

The Rabbis and the Synagogue: How Much Control and Influence?

The nature and extent of rabbinic involvement in and influence on the synagogue of Late Antiquity are of cardinal importance, not only for understanding how the synagogue functioned, but also for gaining a perspective on the status of the sages generally in Jewish society of Late Antiquity (Goodenough 1961; Levine 1992a; S. J. D. Cohen 1992; Hezser 1997: 214–24).

In studies of Jewish history in the Graeco-Roman and Byzantine eras, it has traditionally been assumed that the sages were the dominant religious and social force within Jewish society. This has been asserted with regard to the Pharisees in the pre-70 era, and to the talmudic sages in the post-destruction period of Roman Palestine (Alon 1977: 22). Moreover, some have carried this assumption over to the diaspora and have applied it to such far-flung places as Rome, Aphrodisias, Asia Minor generally, and Dura Europos. Kraeling (1956: 351–60), followed by K. Schubert (1992) and others, have assumed that the Dura artist (or artists) was influenced by rabbinic midrashic traditions; J. Reynolds and R. F. Tannenbaum (1987: 25–37) detect the influence of rabbinic cultural values and institutions in the Aphrodisias inscription, and L. Feldman (1993: 69–74) assumes that rabbinic Judaism was well known in Asia Minor.

At the same time, there has been a counter-trend these past decades advocating a much more circumspect view of rabbinic influence. Two important studies, appearing in the 1950s and stemming from entirely different perspectives, have had a powerful influence on the discussion of Pharisaic and rabbinic status in antiquity. One was Smith's path-breaking article claiming that the Pharisees were just one of a number of pre-70 sects, and not the dominant force in the religious life of the masses (Smith 1956). At the same time, Goodenough's *Jewish Symbols* argued that Jewish artistic remains prove that the rabbis of later antiquity were a marginal group with little or no impact on wider Jewish society (1953–68: xii. 184–98). The questions raised by these seminal studies have remained central to the scholarly agenda up to the present.

However, the degree of rabbinic influence is far more complex than any sweeping and facile generalization. First of all, not all rabbis were cut from the same cloth. They differed from one another in personality, socio-economic standing, social context (e.g. urban versus rural), and degree of religious stringency; some were more involved in the political and social issues or in communal life, others decidedly less so. Moreover, there were often varied attitudes among them toward the non-rabbinic world, be it the Jewish or non-Jewish one. The cataclysmic changes that affected the Jews at large in the first four or five centuries CE had major repercussions on the rabbinic class as well. This period was distinguished by a major shift in the attitudes of many sages regarding their involvement in the wider Jewish community—for example, between the second century on the one hand, and the third and fourth on the other. This change relates not only to the rabbis' overall attitude toward communal affairs, but also to their actual participation in these areas (Levine 1989: 23–42; 1992a).

Besides differences between various rabbis, one must also keep in mind which aspects of Jewish art and architecture in particular might have come under their influence. Are we speaking of the actual physical building, its architectural style and plan, or are we dealing with the various artistic designs that include biblical scenes as well as the Helios-zodiac motif? One could expand this to include a synagogue's administrative and political leadership, responsibility for its many activities (educational, social, judicial etc.), and specifically its religious dimension. One might expect there to have been more rabbinic involvement in certain aspects (e.g. the liturgical) than in the financial or administrative realms.

Geographical distinctions must also be borne in mind when speaking about the rabbis' influence on or involvement in Jewish communal life. Some areas may have been more affected by rabbinic values and practices than others. For example, are the Galilee or the geographical areas of rabbinic activity in Babylonia comparable in this respect to other regions in Palestine or Babylonia? And what of areas where there is almost no evidence of a rabbinic presence, such as the Roman diaspora?

In short, there is no simple solution to the issue of rabbinic influence on, if not control of, Jewish art and architecture. On the one hand, the rabbis were far from all-dominant in Jewish life at the time—either politically, socially, or even religiously. On the other hand, rabbinic influence was clearly in ascendance between the second and the ninth–tenth centuries, when it was given institutional backing under Islamic rule. Given this trajectory, exactly where rabbinic leadership stood in Late Antiquity is impossible to determine; as we have suggested, it undoubtedly varied from place to place and from one dimension of synagogue and communal life to another. Further refinement of our understanding of this issue remains a primary desideratum.

It is quite clear that the more intensive study of architecture and art over the past few generations has contributed enormously to our knowledge of Jewish life and society in Late Antiquity. The amount of available material has increased significantly with every succeeding excavation, and now constitutes a rich trove of evidence. New areas of study have opened up as a result of these finds and have also enriched our understanding of Jewish life, both in Roman-Byzantine Palestine and the diaspora.

But, as we have seen above, it is not only a matter of enhancing our perception of this era by now being able to relate to its material culture as well—although that in itself is no mean achievement. Of no less import are the profound implications of this material for a wide range of topics in Jewish history and religion, some of which we have noted above. Although this archaeological material is, almost by definition, fragmentary and fortuitous, and by itself cannot offer a comprehensive picture of Jewish life, it still has the potential to illuminate many dimensions of ancient society by corroborating information known from other sources. However, over and above complementing the literary sources, it should be clear that these finds, in their own right, have also succeeded in raising a battery of fundamental issues regarding our understanding of major components of Jewish life in the cultural, religious, and institutional spheres. As might be expected in such cases, there is no unanimity in the scholarly world as to the precise nature of these implications, but the issues are, nevertheless, on the table. Anyone who strives to understand the full range of Jewish life in this era must take full cognizance of these sources of information and their manifold implications.

SUGGESTED READING

Jewish art: Roth (1961), Grossman (1995), Sed-Rajna (1997), Kampf (1990), R. Cohen (1993), Moore (1993), Gutmann (1987). *Jewish architecture*: Wischnitzer (1955b and 1964), Krinsky (1985), Meek (1995), Scott Lerner (2000). *Late Antiquity*: The two most comprehensive treatments of Jewish art and architecture are Goodenough (1953–68), and the more recent summary in Hachlili (1988 and 1998). Helpful collections of studies on aspects of Jewish art and architecture can be found in Chiat (1982), Gutmann (1973b), Levine (1981), and Levine and Weiss (2000).

BIBLIOGRAPHY

ALON, G. 1977. *Jews, Judaism and the Classical World*. Jerusalem.

AVERY-PECK, J. and NEUSNER, J. eds. 2001. *Where We Stand: Issues and Debates in Ancient Judaism*, iv: *The Special Problem of the Synagogue*. Leiden.

AVIGAD, N. 1954. *Ancient Monuments in the Qidron Valley*. [Hebrew]. Jerusalem.

——1960. 'A Dated Lintel-Inscription from the Ancient Synagogue of Nabratein.' *Bulletin of the Louis M. Rabinowitz Fund for the Exploration of Ancient Synagogues* 3: 49–56. Jerusalem.

——1976. *Beth She'arim*, iii. New Brunswick, NJ.

——1983. *Discovering Jerusalem*. Nashville, Tenn.

AVI-YONAH, M. 1960. 'The Mosaic Pavement of the Ma'on Synagogue.' *Bulletin of the Louis M. Rabinowitz Fund for the Exploration of Ancient Synagogues* 3: 25–35. Jerusalem.

——1961. 'Synagogue Architecture in the Late Classical Period.' In Roth (1961): 151–90.

——1973. 'Ancient Synagogues.' *Ariel* 32: 29–43.

——1981. *Art in Ancient Palestine*. Jerusalem.

BICKERMAN, E. 1965. 'Symbolism in the Dura Synagogue: A Review Article.' *Harvard Theological Review* 58: 127–51.

BLAND, K. 1999. *The Artless Jew: Medieval and Modern Affirmations and Denials of the Visual*. Princeton.

BOTTINI, G. T. *et al.* eds. 1990. *Christian Archaeology in the Holy Land—New Discoveries: Essays in Honour of V. F. Corbo, OFM*. Jerusalem.

BRANHAM, J. 1995. 'Vicarious Sacrality: Temple Space in Ancient Synagogues.' In Urman and Flesher (1995), i. 319–45.

BRATSLAVI, Y. 1969. 'Symbols and Mythological Figures in Ancient Galilean Synagogues.' [Hebrew]. In Hirschberg (1969): 106–29.

BREGMAN, M. 1995. 'The Riddle of the Ram in Genesis Chapter 22: Jewish–Christian Contacts in Late Antiquity.' In Manns (1995): 140–4.

BROSHI, M. ed. 1977. *Between Herman and Sinai—Memorial to Amnon* [Hebrew]. Jerusalem.

CHIAT, M. J. S. 1982. *Handbook of Synagogue Architecture*. Chico, Cal.

COHEN, R. 1993. 'Jewish Art in the Modern Era.' In Wertheimer (1993): 228–41.

COHEN, S. J. D. 1992. 'The Place of the Rabbi in Jewish Society of the Second Century.' In Levine (1992b): 157–73.

DAVIS, M. ed. 1956. *Israel: Its Role in Civilization*. New York.

DOTHAN, M. 1983. *Hammath Tiberias: Early Synagogues and the Hellenistic and Roman Remains*. Jerusalem.

DU MESNIL DE BUISSON, R. 1939. *Les peintures de la synagogue de Doura-Europas, 245–256 après J.-C.* Rome.

FELDMAN, L. 1993. *Jew and Gentile in the Ancient World: Attitudes and Interactions from Alexander to Justinian*. Princeton.

FINE, S. ed. 1996. *Sacred Realm: The Emergence of the Synagogue in the Ancient World*. New York

—— 1997. *This Holy Place: On the Sanctity of the Synagogue during the Greco-Roman Period*. Notre Dame.

FOERSTER, G. 1981. 'Synagogue Inscriptions and Their Relation to Liturgical Versions.' [Hebrew]. *Cathedra* 19: 12–40.

—— 1987. 'The Art and Architecture of the Synagogue in Its Late Roman Setting.' In Levine (1987): 139–46.

—— 1989. 'Decorated Marble Chancel Screens in Sixth Century Synagogues in Palestine and their Relation to Christian Art and Architecture.' In *Actes du XIe Congrès d'Archéologie Chrétienne*. 1809–20. Rome.

—— 1990. 'Allegorical and Symbolic Motifs with Christian Significance from Mosaic Pavements of Sixth-Century Palestinian Synagogues.' In Bottini *et al.* (1990): 545–52.

—— 1992. 'The Ancient Synagogues of the Galilee.' In Levine (1992b): 289–319.

GOLDMAN, B. M. 1966. *The Sacred Portal: A Primary Symbol in Ancient Judaic Art*. Detroit.

GOODENOUGH, E. 1953–68. *Jewish Symbols in the Greco-Roman Period*. Bollingen Series, 37. 13 vols. New York.

—— 1961. 'The Rabbis and Jewish Art in the Greco-Roman Period.' *Hebrew Union College Annual* 32: 269–79.

GROH, D. E. 1995. 'The Stratigraphic Chronology of the Galilean Synagogue from the Early Roman Period through the Early Byzantine Period (ca. 420 C.E.).' In Urman and Flesher (1995), i. 51–69.

GROSSMAN, G. C. 1995. *Jewish Art*. New York.

GUTMANN, J. 1973a. 'Programmatic Painting in the Dura Synagogue.' In Gutmann (1973b): 137–54.

GUTMANN, J. ed. 1973b. *The Dura-Europos Synagogue: A Re-Evaluation (1932–72)*. Missoula, Mont.

—— 1987. *The Jewish Life Cycle*. Leiden.

HACHLILI, R. 1977. 'The Zodiac in Ancient Jewish Art: Representation and Significance.' *Bulletin of the American Schools of Oriental Research* 228: 61–77.

—— 1987. 'On the Gaza School of Mosaicists.' [Hebrew]. *Eretz Israel* 19: 46–58.

—— 1988. *Ancient Jewish Art and Archaeology in the Land of Israel*. Leiden.

—— ed. 1989. *Ancient Synagogues in Israel*. BAR International series, 499. Oxford.

—— 1998. *Ancient Jewish Art and Archaeology in the Diaspora*. Leiden.

HEZSER, C. 1997. *The Social Structure of the Rabbinic Movement in Roman Palestine*. Tübingen.

HIRSCHBERG, H. ed. 1969. *All the Land of Naphtali* [Hebrew]. Jerusalem.

HIRSHMAN, M. 1996. *A Rivalry of Genius: Jewish and Christian Biblical Interpretation in Late Antiquity*. Albany, NY.

HORBURY, W. and NOY, D. 1992. *Jewish Inscriptions of Graeco-Roman Egypt*. Cambridge.

JACOBY, D. and TSAFRIR, Y. eds. 1988. *Jews, Samaritans and Christians in Byzantine Palestine* [Hebrew]. Jerusalem.

KAMPF, A. 1990. *Chagall to Kitaj: Jewish Experience in 20th Century Art*. London.

KESSLER, H. 2000. 'The Sepphoris Mosaic and Christian Art.' In Levine and Weiss (2000): 64–72.

KOHL, H. and WATZINGER, C. 1916. *Antike Synagogen in Galilaea*. Leipzig.

KRAELING, C. 1956. *The Excavations at Dura-Europos*. viii/ i: *The Synagogue*. New Haven. Repr. New York 1979.

KRINSKY, C. H. 1985. *Synagogues of Europe: Architecture, History, Meaning*. New York.

KÜHNEL, B. 1987. *From the Earthly to the Heavenly Jerusalem: Representations of the Heavenly City in Christian Art of the First Millennium*. Rome.

—— 2000. 'The Synagogue Floor Mosaic in Sepphoris: Between Paganism and Christianity.' In Levine and Weiss (2000): 31–43.

LEVINE, L. I. ed. 1981. *Ancient Synagogues Revealed*. Jerusalem.

—— 1985. 'The Finds from Beth-Shearim and Their Importance for the Study of the Talmudic Period.' [Hebrew]. *Eretz Israel* 18: 277–81.

—— ed. 1987. *The Synogogue in Late Antiquity*. Philadelphia.

—— 1989. *The Rabbinic Class of Roman Palestine in Late Antiquity*. Rev. edn. Jerusalem and New York.

—— 1992a. 'The Sages and the Synagogue in Late Antiquity: The Evidence of the Galilee.' In Levine (1992b): 201–22.

—— 1992b. *The Gailiee in Late Antiquity*. New York and Jerusalem.

—— 1998. *Judaism and Hellenism in Antiquity*. Seattle.

—— 2000a. *The Ancient Synagogue: The First Thousand Years*. New Haven.

—— 2000b. 'The History and Significance of the Menorah in Antiquity.' In Levine and Weiss (2000): 131–53.

—— and WEISS, Z. eds. 2000. *From Dura to Sepphoris: Studies in Jewish Art and Society in Late Antiquity*. Journal of Roman Archaeology Supplementary Series, 40. Portsmouth, RI.

MAGNESS, J. 2001. 'The Question of the Synagogue: The Problem of Typology.' In Avery-Peck and Neusner (2001): 1–48.

MANNS, F. ed. 1995. *The Sacrifice of Isaac in the Three Monotheistic Religions*. Jerusalem.

MAYER, L. A. 1967. *Bibliography of Jewish Art*. Jerusalem.

MEEK, H. A. 1995. *The Synagogue*. London

MESHORER, Y. 1982. *Ancient Jewish Coinage*. 2 vols. Dix Hills, NY.

MEYERS, E. M. 1987. 'The Current State of Galilean Synagogue Studies.' In Levine (1987): 127–37.

MOORE, C. 1993. *The Visual Dimension: Aspects of Jewish Art*. Boulder, Col.

NOY, D. 1995. *Jewish Inscriptions of Western Europe*, ii: *City of Rome*. Cambridge.

OVADIAH, A. 1977. 'Mutual Influences between Synagogues and Churches in Byzantine Palestine.' [Hebrew]. In Broshi (1977): 163–70.

OVADIAH, A. 1995. 'The Mosaic Workshop of Gaza in Christian Antiquity.' In Urman and Flesher (1995), ii. 367–72.

REVEL-NEHER, E. 2000. 'From Dream to Reality: Evolution and Continuity in Jewish Art.' In Levine and Weiss (2000): 53–63.

REYNOLDS, J. and TANNENBAUM, R. F. 1987. *Jews and God-fearers at Aphrodisias: Greek Inscriptions with Commentary.* Proceedings of the Cambridge Philological Society, Supplement 12. Cambridge.

ROSTOVTZEV, M. 1938. *Dura Europos and its Art.* Oxford.

ROTH, C. ed. 1961. *Jewish Art: An Illustrated History.* New York.

SCHRECKENBERG, H. and SCHUBERT, K. eds. 1992. *Jewish Historiography and Iconography in Early and Medieval Christianity.* Assen.

SCHUBERT, K. 1992. 'Jewish Pictorial Traditions in Early Christian Art.' In Schreckenberg and Schubert (1992): 171–88.

SCOTT LERNER, L. 2000. 'The Narrating Architecture of Emancipation.' *Jewish Social Studies: History Culture, and Society* 6/3: 1–30.

SEAGER, A. 1989. 'The Recent Historiography of Ancient Synagogue Architecture.' In Hachlili (1989): 85–92.

SED-RAJNA, G. 1997. *Jewish Art.* New York.

SMITH, M. 1956. 'Palestinian Judaism in the First Century.' In Davis (1956): 73–81.

——1967. 'Goodenough's "Jewish Symbols" in Retrospect.' *Journal of Biblical Literature* 86: 53–68.

SONNE, I. 1947. 'The Paintings of the Dura Synagogue.' *Hebrew Union College Annual* 20: 255–362.

STONE, N. 1988. 'Notes on the Shellal Mosaic ('Ein Ha-Besor) and the Mosaic Workshops at Gaza.' [Hebrew.] In Jacoby and Tsafrir (1988): 207–14.

SUKENIK, E. L. 1932. *The Ancient Synagogue of Beth Alpha.* Jerusalem.

——1934. *Ancient Synagogues in Palestine and Greece.* London.

——1935. *The Ancient Synagogue of el-Hammeh (Hammath-by-Gadara).* Jerusalem.

——1947. *The Synagogue of Dura Europos and Its Frescoes* [Hebrew]. Jerusalem.

——1949. 'The Present State of Ancient Synagogue Studies.' *Bulletin of the Louis M. Rabinowitz Fund for the Exploration of Ancient Synagogues* 1: 7–23.

TSAFRIR, Y. 1987. 'The Byzantine Setting and its Influence on Ancient Synagogues.' In Levine (1987): 147–57.

URMAN, D. and FLESHER, P. V. M. eds. 1995. *Ancient Synogogues: Historical Analysis and Archaeological Discovery.* 2 vols. Leiden.

VISOTZKY, B. 1995. *Fathers of the World: Essays in Rabbinic and Patristic Literatures.* Tübingen.

WEISS, Z. and NETZER, E. 1996. *Promise and Redemption: A Synagogue Mosaic from Sepphoris.* Jerusalem.

WEITZMANN, K. and KESSLER, H. 1990. *The Frescoes of the Dura Synagogue and Christian Art.* Washington, DC.

WERTHEIMER, J. ed. 1993. *The Modern Jewish Experience: A Reader's Guide.* New York.

WILKINSON, J. 1978 'The Beit Alpha Synagogue Mosaic: Towards an Interpretation.' *Journal of Jewish Art* 5: 16–28.

WISCHNITZER, R. 1948. *The Messianic Theme in the Paintings of the Dura Synagogue.* Chicago.

—— 1955a. 'The Beth Alpha Mosaic: A New Interpretation.' *Jewish Social Studies* 17: 133–44.

—— 1955b. *Synagogue Architecture in the United States: History and Interpretation.* Philadelphia.

—— 1964. *The Architecture of the European Synagogue.* Philadelphia.

CHAPTER 34

MUSIC

PHILIP V. BOHLMAN

INTRODUCTION—JEWISH MUSIC IN DIALOGUE WITH JEWISH STUDIES

THE growth of Jewish studies has made it possible to talk about Jewish music in entirely new and even radically different ways. Discourse about music within Jewish worship, ritual, and everyday life has traditionally posed complex ontological questions, not only about the nature of music as separable from other religious and cultural practices, but also about the presence of any trait within music that is identifiable as Jewish. Jewish studies has changed all that. Since the 1970s the study of music has developed as one of the most productive areas of research in Jewish studies itself, and since the early 1990s discussions about Jewish music have assumed a position as one of the most challenging arenas for research and debate in musicology and ethnomusicology. Both 'music' and 'Jewish music' have emerged as distinctive ontological concepts within the discursive metaphysics that underlies the formation of modern Jewish studies as a field and as a set of disciplines.

It is the aesthetic independence of 'music' that Jewish studies opens up, in other words a metaphysical distinctiveness of music as the product of physical and cultural systems, which nonetheless participates in the articulation of Jewishness. At each stage of the growing engagement between Jewish studies and the study of Jewish music, there has been an immediate and far-reaching reformulation of basic ontological questions. The issue is no longer the pedantic question: Is there such a thing as Jewish music? Modern Jewish musical scholarship asks instead: What kind of Jewish music is this? Rather than searching for an elusive, unifying trait that establishes a singular Jewish music that is in some way unlike any other music, musical scholarship informed by Jewish studies addresses—and surely also celebrates—the ways pluralism, difference, and cultural otherness generate questions about the variety of Jewish musics and musical practices.

For the purposes of this chapter the subdisciplines and subfields of musical scholarship that have entered into productive dialogue with Jewish studies will be included under the larger disciplinary umbrella of 'Jewish music research'. At the beginning of the twenty-first century there is as yet no general consensus about a unitary field, but there is growing application of the term 'Jewish music research' to common scholarly endeavours and the institutions in which they take place (e.g. the Jewish Music Research Centre at the Hebrew University of Jerusalem). It is significant that most scholars contributing to contemporary Jewish music research were trained as musicologists and ethnomusicologists, with only a very small number whose education was centred in religious studies, or even in liturgics. The emphasis that such acts of naming the field and its institutions signals clearly falls on music.

The shift from Judaism and Jewish practice to music and musical practice has unfolded slowly during a period of about two centuries, but accelerated rapidly in the second half of the twentieth century, during which Jewish music research has virtually exploded. Beginning in the early nineteenth century, coeval with the gains in emancipation won through the Haskalah it is possible to sketch the intellectual history of Jewish music research, if schematically, according to five periods, with the first two pre-dating the discursive engagement with modern Jewish studies, the third marking a catalytic period of transition, and the final two representing modern Jewish music research:

Period 1 (c.1830s–90s)—cantorial and liturgical studies of music in the synagogue and Jewish religious life;

Period 2 (c.1860s–1920s)—folkloric and ethnographic collections of Jewish folk music;

Period 3 (c.1920s–50s)—comparative musicology (vergleichende Musikwissenschaft) redeploys Jewish music in relation to other types of music;

Period 4 (c.1950s–90s)—ethnomusicological and ethnological studies of musical differences between and among Jewish communities;

Period 5 (c.1970s–present)—poststructuralist and postmodernist engagements with identity in music and the constructedness of music.

Modern Jewish music research takes place largely within four disciplinary concentrations. Each concentration depends on its own institutions, which in turn determine musical repertories and pedagogical approaches, but all are distinguished by considerable inclusivity and interdisciplinarity. The four disciplinary concentrations are: (1) theology; (2) history; (3) ethnology/folkloristics; and (4) ethnomusicology/cultural studies. Jewish music research within theological institutions (e.g. seminaries, rabbinical or cantorial schools, and university religion departments) concerns itself with traditional repertories, often for practical purposes, but still rallies perspectives from Jewish studies. Historical methods range from the establishment of canonic repertories by Jewish composers to the examination of stereotype and prejudice in canonical non-Jewish repertories of Western art music (e.g. J. S. Bach and Richard Wagner). Ethnologists and folklorists include music as one of numerous cultural practices that provide the foundations for Jewish customs, community, and life in general. Ethnomusicology and music research within cultural studies are by far the disciplinary concentrations most actively engaged with modern Jewish studies, and it is hardly surprising that it is within these concentrations that Jewish music research itself grew most rapidly at the end of the twentieth century. These four concentrations, in fact, illustrate the diverse ways in which Jewish music research has expanded at a pace and in directions paralleling the expansion of Jewish studies itself.

ONTOLOGIES OF JEWISH MUSIC

The new fields of musical research influenced by Jewish studies spawned new ontologies of what Jewish music was or could be. Some of these ontologies added new perspectives to traditional understanding of Jewish musical practices. Others took radically different stances by consciously transforming and abandoning traditional models. Uniting the new fields of Jewish music research was a common concern for rethinking the very fundamental ontology of Jewish music itself.

Jewish music is no longer imagined or defined as a single object, but rather is assumed to have many forms and to reflect many different subjectivities within and without Jewish society. These ontological distinctions are often very different one from another, but the influence from Jewish studies has been to emphasize just what it is that differences have in common. The modern ontologies of Jewish music clearly reflect a shift away from concern about music itself and toward the ways in which music is woven into a much larger set of cultural practices. In simplest terms, Jewish studies has deflected the focus of Jewish music research from text toward context.

In contrast, ontological stances, usually on a popular level, that dismissively claimed Jewish music to be music created by, if not used by, Jews, have also had to withstand an entirely new set of claims from scholars working in Jewish studies. There is no reason why Jewish music, according to the new ontological claims, need be created, performed, or even used by Jews. Again, object and subjectivity were ontologically independent, but paradoxically for the opposite reason: Jewish music, at least hypothetically, need not depend on Jewish musicians or even Jewish society. Studies of traditional music (e.g. folk music) began to identify and chart the spread of Jewish practices into non-Jewish society, often reflecting long histories of exchange across the boundaries that presumably separated Jewish and non-Jewish worlds.[1] Similarly, musicologists have posed new questions about the employment of Jewish themes in works by non-Jewish composers, from Benedetto Marcello in eighteenth-century Venice to Max Bruch and Maurice Ravel in the nineteenth and twentieth centuries.

The most basic and restrictive ontology of Jewish music is text- and language-based. The fundamental issue is not that all music with Hebrew, Yiddish, Ladino, or Judaeo-Arabic texts is Jewish, but rather that texts in these Jewish languages convey something Jewish to music, be it accentual and metric patterns, be it the melodic shape or phrase structure that specific texts engender. The language-based ontology exerted a particularly strong influence in the aesthetic debates accompanying the creation of a modern Jewish art music during the transition from the Yishuv to statehood in Israel (c.1930–60). Using language as the primary criterion, nonetheless, necessarily excludes as much as it includes, for it makes no room for instrumental music or for works in other languages, or even in translations from Jewish languages.

The second ontology relies on criteria that identify Jewish music within sacred practice or within secular repertories with ancillary connections to ritual or religious practice. In his ten-volume *Thesaurus of Hebrew Oriental Melodies* (1914–32), Abraham Zvi Idelsohn divided his collections between examples recorded 'in the synagogue' and those collected elsewhere. What proved most interesting in this anthology, which continues to serve as the monument for modern Jewish music research, is that music with little connection to sacred practice (e.g. instrumental music from the Arab art-music tradition) entered the field of study through association with the synagogue. Revivals of Jewish music—notably in the rise of Jewish choruses and klezmer music since c.1980—also rely largely on this ontology. The multifunctional character of klezmer music, for example, has widely been established as Jewish through putative 'definitions' of klezmer music as 'Jewish wedding music' (see e.g. Rubin and Ottens 1999).

A third ontology is based on distinctions between self and other, that is, between what is Jewish and what is not. Whereas such distinctions would seem to limit Jewish music and to rely on a consensus of how self and other are different, it also generates a vocabulary and a discourse for addressing Jewish music with specific and general categories.

---

[1] See e.g. Bohlman and Holzapfel (2001), which remaps the *longue durée* of Ashkenazic music in Europe by documenting the considerable evidence for a common traditional music culture shared by Jews and non-Jews.

The fourth ontology serves as a counterpart to the third because it encourages understanding the presence of difference within Jewish experience. Implicitly, difference does not arise from within, but it enters from outside Jewish society. Difference, therefore, accounts for non-Jewish influences and, by extension, the transformations of Jewish music in the diaspora. Accounting for difference has been particularly important in the twentieth century as an antidote to the insistence that there be some basic structure that would make real Jewish music sound alike on some level. At the beginning of the twenty-first century most scholars of Jewish music recognize that Jewish musics in different communities, places, or social contexts need not sound at all alike.

Most recently, ontologies of Jewish music have interpreted Jewish music as metonymically representational of Jewish society. Concepts such as *nusach* have been adapted from traditional text-based applications—*nusach* literally refers to the textual rootedness of biblical passages—to explain the distinctiveness of modern and postmodern cultural contexts.[2] Accordingly, music acquires its Jewishness by changing and adapting constantly and demonstrating a capacity to assume new forms and styles, which nonetheless embody the desire to express Jewishness.

IDENTITY

During the course of the twentieth century Jewish music research increasingly tackled questions about the identity of Jewishness in music. The intensified concern about the identity of Jewishness in music stemmed from a sense that it could be lost, indeed, had been lost through assimilation, diaspora, and the destruction of the Holocaust. The processes of ingathering that followed the Holocaust, especially in Israel but also in North America, raised the possibility that the vestiges of what had been lost could be salvaged and restored. The several positions toward Jewish identity were activist and constructivist. In other words, the advocates of such positions took as their ultimate goal that discovery of the essential elements of Jewishness in music was only the first step in employing those elements to turn change in a positive direction. Jewish music not only reflected Jewish identity: it could be used to construct and strengthen identity.

Three major disciplinary transformations paralleled the shift toward identity in Jewish music. With considerable residue from the nineteenth century, the initial

---

[2] Jeffrey Summit (2000) uses *nusach* to portray five different Boston Jewish communities in the 1990s, demonstrating the ways in which melodic and repertorial choices explicitly expressed patterns of self-identity in American society.

disciplinary transformation turned around philological models. As with Jewish music itself, identity was treated as an object, which somehow encapsulated traits of authenticity, for example, the modal structures embedded in cantillation and liturgy, which by extension yielded scales and melodic structures that were marked as Jewish (e.g. *shteiger* in Eastern European vernacular repertories, such as klezmer or Yiddish folk song). The philological paradigm allowed scholars to construct theoretical systems, and to compare these systems in such a way that patterns of internal consistency across the diaspora and in the Yishuv could be displayed. The theoretical systems were further consistent across history, thus making them frameworks for claims about authenticity. Paradoxically, it was similar philologically driven claims about authenticity that had led to nineteenth- and early twentieth-century anti-Semitic claims about Jewishness in music, the most notorious of which was Richard Wagner's 1850 treatise, *Das Judentum in der Musik*. Typical of philological positions toward textual purity, anti-Semitic arguments held that the musical object contained only enough ontological space for a single, authentic identity. Though it seems ironic today, the anti-Semitic use of philological arguments to determine Jewishness in music were frequently countered by Jewish treatises—some of the most notable of which also bore the name *Das Judentum in der Musik*—which employed virtually the same approaches to debunk the validity of the philological models portraying Jewish identity as polluting.

The philological paradigm, with its emphasis on identity in text, was opposed by a social-scientific paradigm, with a sharply focused emphasis on identity in context. With the advent of recording devices in the early decades of the twentieth century, folklorists and ethnomusicologists were able to collect and compare multiple variants of the same piece, thus raising questions about the different forms of Jewish identity that the variants exposed. Social-scientific approaches to identity, therefore, shifted attention away from authenticity, denying even that discovering and identifying authentic variants were possible. Jewish identity accrued through practice and accommodation, the performance of music in Jewish cultural contexts. In many ways, social-scientific approaches were no less systemic than philological approaches, but the systems used in comparison lay outside, rather than inside, the structure of the music itself.

The final transformation has resulted from a more general move toward post-structural and, to some extent, postmodern approaches in the humanities. The humanistic paradigms have produced a shift largely away from authenticity, taking, instead, hybridity and the constructivist response to hybridity as norms. Jewishness in music, therefore, has undergone a process of pluralization, which recognizes the presence of various forms of Jewish identity *and* non-Jewish identity in music. American liturgical practices that were previously deemed 'assimilated' have been described in more postmodern terms as 'Jewish responses' to the American experience (Summit 2000). Israeli popular-music styles, such as those performed by late twentieth-century worldbeat stars like Ofra Haza and Dana International, acquire the potential to juxtapose numerous Jewish identities—Yemenite, Judaeo-Arabic, 'Oriental', Israeli underclass, Mediterranean, among others—while mixing these with postmodern global and local identities that serve as indices to everything from historicist meditations on the Holocaust to hybridized expressions of sexual identity. The keyword in the ways Jewish music and identity are connected is, indeed, 'mix', used to reflect the ways in which postmodern Jewish identity is layered into music much in the same way that recording studios mix and remix pieces before releasing them. The result, regarded by some as positive, by others as negative, is that music accommodates a previously unimaginable plethora of Jewish identities at the beginning of the twenty-first century.

HISTORY

During the second half of the twentieth century Jewish music history has not only been rewritten, but its very nature has been subjected to a sweeping reconceptualization. Prior to the twentieth century histories of Jewish music distinguished between music that did not change and that which did change. The conditions for historical stasis were clear: Jewish music was anchored in the practices of the Temple prior to its destruction in 70 CE and should aspire to return to those practices. The conditions for change were even clearer: the diaspora introduced the potential for influences from the outside. The response to Jewish studies during the twentieth century has been to pluralize Jewish music histories, in other words, to recognize that both the past and the present determine how the centripetal pull of stasis and the centrifugal push of change form a critical counterpoint within Jewish music historiography.

There are roughly five traditions of Jewish music historiography, which, on one hand, overlap in certain ways but, on the other, arise from the different ways in which Jewish music reflects the influences of Jewish studies. If there is a historiography that might be regarded as indigenous to the professional world of Jewish music, it is represented by the genealogical tradition of *hazzanim*, especially the cantors of the European and American Ashkenazic synagogue. Historically, cantors have acquired musical style and repertory from their teachers, since the eighteenth century through both oral and written traditions. The term *hazzanut* possesses the double sense of 'cantorial tradition'—what is sung—and 'lineage of cantors'— those who do the singing. Transmission of the *hazzanut* is itself a form of performing Jewish music history. Since the early nineteenth century cantors have taken considerable pains to write about their repertories and their transmission, for example, in journals such as *Der jüdische Kantor* and *Die österreichisch-ungarische Cantoren-Zeitung*, which appeared at the end of the nineteenth century in Hamburg and Vienna respectively. At the end of the twentieth century professional cantorial organizations had assumed many of the same functions, creating networks for the transmission of old and new music, and honouring the past through the creation of new traditions (see Slobin 1989).

Philological studies of Jewish music engendered another historiographic tradition. Philologists established the authority of tradition by establishing the authenticity of textual transmission (see e.g. Walbe 1975; Grötzinger 1982; Flender 1992). Philological methods were not only influential in theological domains, but were in fact especially vital for the emergence of the study of Jewish folk song in the late nineteenth century. The German philologist Gustaf Dalman was one of the first scholars to interpret the ways in which the transmission of texts in Yiddish provided the historical path along which popular musicians from Eastern Europe had created cosmopolitan practices in Central Europe at the end of the nineteenth century (Dalman 1891). The St Petersburg circle of Jewish music and folk music, active from the closing decade of the nineteenth century until the First World War, turned philological methods to more historicist goals, collecting what would be the first modern monument to Yiddish song (Ginsburg and Marek 1901). Philological methods continue to contribute substantially to the historiographic traditions of modern Jewish music research, especially that supported by the collections at the Jewish Music Research Centre of the Hebrew University.[3]

Social-scientific methods have also produced an historiographic tradition. One of the pioneers in this tradition was Karl Salomo Krauss (1859–1938), who founded and edited ethnological journals in the late nineteenth century (e.g. *Am Urquell*), which served, among other purposes, as a repository for field collections of Jewish folk songs. By far the most influential ethnographer was Max Grunwald (1871–1953), founder of the Gesellschaft für jüdische Volkskunde in the 1880s and editor of several important journals, especially the *Jahrbuch für jüdische Volkskunde*, which was published from 1898 to 1929. The ethnographer's influence on Jewish music historiography is felt in the ways the collections used folk music to portray a much more complete picture of modern Jewish history by clarifying the vitality of contemporary practices. Jewish music, moreover, appears as a complex of diverse cultural practices, not just song in the synagogue and home, but also ritual, dance, and professional entertainment. This historiographic tradition survives in the early twenty-first century, especially in the scholarly work encouraged by the Jewish Folklore and Ethnology section of the American Folklore Society.

Jewish music historiography has also adapted methods and approaches from historical musicology, the general term used to describe the study of European art

---

[3] The most comprehensive bibliography of sources for the study of Hebrew writings on music, Adler (1975), weaves philology and historiography together almost seamlessly.

music. Musicologists have succeeded in identifying Jewish composers, such as Salamone Rossi (*c.*1570–*c.*1628) or Arnold Schoenberg (1874–1951), whose works signify distinctively Jewish contributions to critical moments in European music history. Don Harrán's magisterial studies of Rossi, for example, have emphasized the ways in which Rossi responded to the demands of both the Gonzaga court and the Jewish community in Mantua, but did so in ways that illustrate the presence of Jewish music in the transition from the Renaissance to the Baroque (Harrán 1999). Alexander Ringer similarly examines the ways in which Arnold Schoenberg's foundational role in the articulation of modernism in music derived in no small measure from the Jewishness of his biography (Ringer 1990). Jewish and non-Jewish music histories thus intersect, sometimes productively, sometimes not.

Modern Jewish music historiography increasingly grows from an engagement with modern nationalism. An increasing number of music histories are based on the nation-building project of Israel. One approach relies on more traditional 'life and work' studies, in which Israel's history emerges as a collective biography of its composers and musicians (cf. Gradenwitz 1996 and Fleisher 1997). Another approach, more indebted to developments in Jewish studies, interprets Israel's music as a complex of practices that responds to modernity (cf. Bohlman 1989 and Hirshberg 1995). The emphasis on music in Israel has not only shifted historiography from its more exclusive engagement with the past to a noticeable attempt to understand the 'new generations', it has also created a conceptual field that has significantly challenged previous limitations on what Jewish music was and could be. In Israel, the basic question may no longer be whether music is Jewish at all, but rather how diverse, even disconnected, musical practices facilitate participation in the global agendas of the postcolonial nation state.

THE PLACE OF JEWISH MUSIC

Prior to the rise of Jewish studies and its transformative impact on the ontologies of Jewish music, there prevailed a widespread belief that the place in which music took place defined and limited music as Jewish. Family practices, for example, located musical practice in the spaces of domestic ritual (e.g. *zemirot* or *Tischlieder* performed by the gathered family on Shabbat). The space of the synagogue underwent transformation each week through the musical greeting 'Lecha dodi,' sung by worshipers as *shechina*, the sabbath bride, symbolically entered the synagogue from the west and literally reoriented worship toward *mizrah*, the east. The performance of music thus charted the ritual and historical geography through its concentrated localization of community. The influence of Jewish studies has been to unleash a radical realization and remapping of Judaism's cultural geography, in such ways that it would account for the contested terrains of modernity.

Jewish music had historically contested space through an almost dialectical tension of dualisms that possessed both synchronic and diachronic qualities. Musical practices in the Temple in Jerusalem, with its large and hierarchical choral and instrumental ensembles, and the maintenance of music through a professional class of ritual specialists, the Levites, contrasted with the modest, non-specialist vocal practices of the synagogue. The synagogue–Temple dichotomy produced a powerful set of metaphors for suturing ancient to modern history. The synagogue, too, generated a set of contested musical spaces. Within the synagogue, that tension articulated and maintained gender distinctions, before and during the modern reforms of the sanctuary that would permit women's voices to be heard. The space outside the synagogue, moreover, was the domain of non-sacred and non-Jewish musical practices, for which the synagogue itself became a filter and zone for translation and assimilation. Dualisms also undergirded vernacular and secular musical practices, for example, in the canonic repertories of narrative ballads that grew as both Ashkenazic and Sephardic communities responded to the changes accompanying early modern Europe, not least among them the impact of print technology, which led to the reproduction of Jewish folk-song repertories. Jewish folk ballads in the Ashkenazic lands and in the Mediterranean portrayed the tension at the borders between the Jewish community and its non-Jewish neighbours as symbolic of the encroachment of modernity. Modernity as a complex field of metonymic tension opened up new spaces for Jewish music, but also within Jewish music, exploding those spaces for the stylistic mix of the twentieth century.

In the second half of the twentieth century Jewish music research became broadly concerned with how music both instantiated and represented the Jewish community. Community was understood at once in traditional terms (e.g. as *kehilla*, with linguistic and cultural differences distinguishing one tradition from another) and in modern, nationalist terms. Influenced by liturgical scholarship stemming from the Wissenschaft des Judentums, on one hand, and from Vergleichende Musikwissenschaft ('comparative musicology'), on the other, the emphasis on specifying musical difference as a phenomenological force shaping modern Judaism increasingly took community as its point of departure. A. Z. Idelsohn's *Thesaurus of Hebrew-Oriental Melodies* (1914–32) constructed its monument to Jewish music as a historical whole on the individual foundations in communities across the diaspora.[4] With the dominance of ethnomusicology in Jewish music research after 1948, community studies underwent a further transformation to ethnic studies, in which the musical practices of Jewish communities in Israel were compared synchronically

---

[4] Vol. 1, for example, is an anthology of Yemenite Jewish music, vol. 2 of Moroccan Jewish music, etc.

to each other, but diachronically to the diasporic practices that had proffered a community its individuality prior to immigration.

Ethnomusicological attempts to remap the cultural geography of modern Jewish history intensified with each new wave of immigration to Israel, but also with the shifting patterns for migration and emigration in the diaspora. By working at the borders of changing communities, musical scholars also questioned the very nature of those borders, asking particularly whether they functioned primarily to contain and enforce authenticity, or whether they were permeable and catalytic. Jewish music was identified in the spaces beyond the community, in many instances, beyond Judaism itself. Modernism in twentieth-century European art music, for example, became a site for interpreting the Jewish influences stemming from Jewish composers experimenting at the frontiers of music history. The collapse of musical modernism, too, stimulated new directions in Jewish music research, especially in the intensive study of music created and performed at the geographical core of the Holocaust, in the concentration camps. The impetus of modern Jewish music research, influenced by cultural studies as well as Jewish studies, increasingly moves beyond traditional borders altogether, remapping Jewish music in the most public spaces of a globalized geography.

TODAYNESS IN JEWISH MUSIC

The sea-change in Jewish music research at the end of the twentieth century shifted the scholarly focus from the religious work to the cultural work of Jewish music. The shift of focus, furthermore, paralleled the methodological realignment from religious studies to cultural studies. As radical as such realignments were, they did not entirely result in the abandonment of religion, that is, of the textual presence of Judaism in music, but rather they increasingly treated religion as one of several cultural factors shaping Jewish identity and history, and Jewish responses to modernity.

Realigning the methodologies of Jewish music research to address the cultural work of music initially affected those areas in which the gap between religious and cultural studies was minimal. One of the most sweeping realignments, for example, affected the enormous textual bias that historically limited ontologies of Jewish music. Rather than discussing Jewish music entirely in connection with textual sources, scholarly attention began to address the physical nature of performance and the ways in which concepts of Jewish music expressed bodily origins. The relation of body to music, however, was hardly without significant precedents in the historical discourses about Jewish music. Ironically, it had been Maimonides (1135–1204) who had first articulated a clear aesthetics of music that located it in the organs of perception, thus recognizing that humans responded to music physically.[5] By locating the perception of and response to music in the body and by calling for a series of prohibitions that, for example, would restrict one from listening to musical instruments or to the voices of women, Maimonides also recognized that the power of music lay not in the immutability of its texts but rather in the interpretative capacity of the physical being. Maimonides' restrictions raised ontological questions that would influence Jewish thought from his own day until the present. The severe restrictions he placed on the perception of women's voices, which he believed derived from the Babylonian Talmud, have remained a major justification for separating the women's gallery from the main sanctuary in the synagogue. Whereas Maimonides' restrictions provide the basis for proscriptions against musical instruments, they also recognize the ways in which instruments were thought to possess a high degree of corporeality, in other words, to embody human sound (see Farmer 1941 and Adler 1966).

Ethnomusicological and folkloristic studies of the effects and affects of Jewish music often take arguments made to restrict music and invert these to theorize the extensive presence of music in places where it is, theoretically at least, forbidden. To take one of the most familiar repertories of modern Jewish secular music as an example, klezmer has won a crucial presence in popular and scholarly studies in Jewish music research, despite its almost total embodiment of restricted categories: musical instruments; music for entertainment and dance; crossing gender boundaries; use of vernacular, non-Jewish languages. It is because the questions of embodiment, however, are so complex that klezmer becomes acceptable and, at the turn of our century, virtually emblematic of the cultural work that Jewish music does. Music is both connected to and channeled through the body of the *klezmer*, literally the 'vessel of song'.[6] Although attempts to define klezmer tend to impose unnecessarily restrictive meanings on its religious identity, there can be no question that the cultural identity of klezmer reflects a long history of change within and without Ashkenazic communities. Though treated as 'typically Jewish', there can be little doubt that klezmer musicians historically performed outside the Jewish community, and that non-Jewish musicians, not least among them Rom (or 'Gypsy') musicians, were active performers of klezmer. Contemporary perspectives on klezmer, for example, those dealing with the klezmer revival in Europe since the fall of communist governments in Eastern Europe during 1989–90, must reckon

---

[5] Maimonides developed his own aesthetics of music in a cultural context (medieval Iberia) extensively influenced by Islam, which privileges listening (*sāmaᶜ*) to music in contrast to the performance and production of sound.

[6] The term 'klezmer' may apply to both the music and the performer. Instrumentalists, therefore, who play klezmer are called *klezmorim*, further indicating the blurred distinction between music and those who perform it.

with the postmodern reality that klezmer thrives as much outside as inside Jewish communities (cf. Salmen 1991 and Slobin 2000).

No area of Jewish music research has responded more radically to the influences generated at the intersection of Jewish and cultural studies than popular-music studies. The crucial issue, as the brief excursus into klezmer music has just revealed, is hybridity, the musical fusion of the Jewish with the non-Jewish. On one hand, hybridity by definition negates ontologies of Jewish music that rely on authenticity and that serve to justify text-based models. On the other, the concern of popular-music studies for the global proliferation of hybridity has led to the extensive remapping of Jewish music far beyond Jewish communities, Israel, and the diaspora.[7] Studies of Jewish popular music have almost entirely liberated themselves from any overriding concern for Jewishness. Jewishness needs to exert itself as but one of many identities, perhaps even as an identity that was historically present but that has been masked or pushed aside in the postmodern mix. The effect of the explosion of research devoted to Jewish popular music has ironically been to enable scholars to discern and discover Jewish music in places where it was previously thought not to reside, for example, in historical and contemporary traditions of popular Islamic music. At the beginning of the twenty-first century there are virtually no restrictions whatsoever on the identity of Jewish popular music in the global culture where it wins its audiences.

INSTITUTIONS OF JEWISH MUSIC RESEARCH

Formal scholarly programmes devoted to Jewish music research exist almost exclusively in Israel and the United States. In Israel, Jewish music research dominates all areas of ethnomusicology and historical musicology, forming the focus for most music programmes at universities and research institutions. In the United States, Jewish music research takes place at universities with research posts and professorships held by specialists in Jewish music, who may or may not have been appointed because of their specialties. Scholarship and teaching in both the United States and Israel have benefited from extensive exchange and cross-fertilization. American

---

[7] In the most widely successful guides to global pop, the *Rough Guides* to world music, there are three entries on Jewish popular music: Dubi Lenz's article on Israel (1999); Judith Cohen's article on Sephardic music (1999); and an article on 'USA—Klezmer' (2000), by Simon Broughton, the chief editor of the series. Moti Regev and Edwin Seroussi were the first to complete a comprehensive monograph devoted entirely to Israeli popular music (in preparation).

scholars, for example, frequently take research leaves or spend part of their graduate studies in Israel. A high proportion of Israeli scholars have received their Ph.Ds from American doctoral programmes in advanced musical scholarship.

The two national traditions differ because of the ways in which they approach the specialized topic of Jewish music. In Israel, where the arrival of immigrants remains unabated even at the beginning of the twenty-first century, the scholarly impetus remained one of collecting, archiving, comparing, and classifying a more restricted object recognized as Jewish music. In the United States, scholars, especially ethnomusicologists, have favored interdisciplinary exchange, both within and without Jewish studies. The major Israeli academic programmes in Jewish music research are located in the music departments at Bar-Ilan University, the Hebrew University, and Tel Aviv University, with specialized research institutions and archives in Jerusalem at the Hebrew University (Jewish Music Research Centre) and at the Jewish National and University Library (Phonoteca). Among the American universities with active programmes in Jewish music research are Chicago, Eastman School of Music, Harvard, and Wesleyan, with both practical and scholarly undertakings also at Hebrew Union College and the Jewish Theological Seminary.

European institutions have more tentatively responded to the growth of Jewish music research in the second half of the twentieth century. There has been no seamless transition from the dominance of philological approaches, especially in the German-language universities of Central Europe. Nascent programmes in the United Kingdom, such as that at the School for Oriental and African Studies, University of London, where Alexander Knapp holds the Joe Loss Readership in Jewish Music, offer great promise, but these tend to depend on the activities of individual scholars and individual donors. More to the point, Jewish music research has been slow to take root in European traditions of musicology, which has similarly been slow to abandon methodologies that privilege the past over the present, thus blocking the interdisciplinary influences of ethnomusicology. Ironically, it is the growing presence of globalized world musics in general that is opening other areas of research that have begun to create new possibilities for scholarly approaches to Jewish music in Europe.

Epilogue in the Form of a Prologue

To some extent Jewish music research has not changed in the ways that other forms of modern music research have in response to influences such as poststructuralism, postmodernism, and cultural studies, even though these have exerted an influence on the larger field of Jewish studies. Notwithstanding its growing presence in the secular academy, and the increased dissemination of scholarly and other serious writings on Jewish music to a broader public, Jewish music research has attracted only a handful of non-Jewish scholars. The issue here is not only whether Jewish music research has failed to achieve some of the same breadth as other areas of Jewish studies, not to mention modern cultural studies, but also whether the transformation of attitudes about what Jewish music is—the shift from traditional to modern ontologies of Jewish music—has produced tangible resistance to Jewish studies itself. Stating these issues as a question, one might ask: Just how complete and extensive is the dialogue between Jewish studies and Jewish music research?

The answer to this question will be evident to any reader who spends much time with works in Jewish studies, even the present *Handbook*: Jewish music scholarship remains largely unrecognized by Jewish studies. At the end of the present chapter on 'Music' this observation is likely to appear as a paradox. On one hand, I have argued throughout the chapter that the influence of Jewish studies on understanding what Jewish music is has been profound. Jewish music scholarship has expanded rapidly, paralleling the growth of Jewish studies and intersecting with the many disciplines intersecting with Jewish studies. On the other hand, Jewish music remains a strange object of study, as if it does not fit in the broader field of Jewish studies, as if it is available only to specialists whose interests are more constrained than interdisciplinary. The question that remains to be answered during the future period of expansion and development for both Jewish studies and Jewish music research is whether the rapprochement that many scholars have sought can ever happen, or whether a persistent disciplinary and discursive impasse will continue to mark crucial, yet almost intangible, issues of metaphysics and identity embodied by Jewish music.

SUGGESTED READING

Publications of Jewish Music

Publications of Jewish music have traditionally functioned (1) to facilitate practice, and (2) to enhance preservation. Musical professionals, especially cantors, were quick to take advantage of technological advances in publishing. Jewish publishers, in fact, were active in the first stages of music publishing in early modern history, especially in Italy but also elsewhere in Europe. Publications of *hazzanut* intentionally transformed oral tradition into written tradition so that it would serve practice. By the nineteenth century music appeared in small and large editions, published by Jewish presses, several of whom were specializing in music. By the beginning of the twentieth century Jewish music research could draw upon archives established from what had become a flourishing industry. Some of these archives and collections—for example, Eduard Birnbaum's (1855–1920) vast collection of Jewish music, gathered in Königsberg, where he served as cantor and music director—continue to serve as the foundation for music collections today.[8] Transcontinental Music is only the best-known of contemporary music publishers, devoted exclusively to publishing historical and new works of Jewish liturgical music.

The publication of anthologies of Jewish vernacular music paralleled other ethnographic and folkloristic endeavours to collect and preserve, but were in some ways restricted by particularly Jewish concerns for rescuing the past. The collecting projects sponsored by the Gesellschaft für jüdische Volkskunde or the St Petersburg Society for Jewish Folk Music may have emulated other folk-music projects, but they envisioned their publications in quite different ways. If they were more restricted to Jewish communities in early twentieth-century Europe, they also stimulated some notable experiments in publication, among them the establishment of the Jibneh-Juwal Edition as a subsidiary of Vienna's venerable Universal Edition, one of the leading music publishers in the world. Early twentieth-century publishers with special programmes in Jewish studies, such as Jüdischer Verlag and Schocken, published rather extensively in Jewish music, often bringing out anthologies with variants from different parts of the diaspora and, after the First World War, increasingly from mandatory Palestine.

The historical traditions of publishing Jewish music, particularly because of their tendency to monumentalize, have responded to the influences of Jewish studies either tentatively or not at all. To state the situation more succinctly: Jewish music is rarely published with non-Jewish consumption or reception in mind. This is true even of modern publishing series in the diaspora and in Israel, for example, the print and sound-recording series that appear under the aegis of the Jewish Music Research Centre at the Hebrew University. On one hand, publications of Jewish music explicitly emphasize the Jewishness of their contents, implicitly anchoring these in a traditional canon. On the other hand, printing music by mainstream presses for mainstream performance and consumption has rarely opened possibilities for the publication of Jewish music, unless its appeal, hence marketability, extends beyond the more traditional functions of practice and preservation. There are some exceptions, notably the growing number of series devoted to music by Holocaust composers,[9] but it remains an open question as to whether such exceptions prove or ultimately alter the rule.

Publications about Jewish Music

There are only a very few comprehensive surveys of Jewish music that reflect, to greater or lesser degrees, the influence of Jewish studies. A. Z. Idelsohn's comprehensive study of the history of Jewish music (1929), though shaped by the historical and comparative paradigms of the 1920s, has served as a touchstone and point of departure for most histories of Jewish music in the twentieth century, during which time it regularly appeared in reprint editions. Two surveys by distinguished Israeli scholars, Israel Adler and Amnon Shiloah, together

[8] Birnbaum's collection is held at the Hebrew Union College in Cincinnati, where it has served scholars as influential as A. Z. Idelsohn and Eric Werner. The Birnbaum Collection supports research in Cincinnati, but also at the Hebrew Union College in New York City and for its School of Sacred Music.

[9] B. Schott in Mainz and Universal Edition in Vienna were among the first major musical publishers to make compositions by Holocaust composers available in modern editions. CD series, such as London/Decca's 'Entartete Musik', produce modern recordings, often utilizing the new editions of works by Holocaust composers.

provided a framework for studying Jewish music in the final decades of the century. Employing a historical and philological approach, Adler (1995) stressed the importance of gathering disparate sources and identifying the connections among archival sources. Combining the philological approaches of Middle East studies with the ethnographic methods of modern ethnomusicology, Shiloah (1992) accounted for the vast diversity of musics within Jewish communities throughout the world and throughout diasporic history. Irene Heskes has published several comprehensive annotated bibliographies and surveys of resources for Jewish music research (see esp. 1985). The entry on 'Jewish Music' in the second edition (2001) of the *New Grove Dictionary of Music and Musicians* contains a wealth of details, from which readers can garner a comprehensive sense of where Jewish music research is taking place at the beginning of the twenty-first century.

Monographs and journals contain the most influential work in contemporary Jewish music research. Several scholars, notably Kay Kaufman Shelemay (1998) and Mark Slobin (2000), have written numerous monographs, which together constitute comprehensive and innovative approaches to Jewish music. The influence of other scholars (e.g. Edwin Seroussi on Sephardi music) arises from a sustained series of articles in ethnomusicology and Jewish studies journals.

The core of research in Jewish music may well not be centralized, but rather spread across the rather large number of journals and yearbooks. Traditional Israeli publications, such as *Yuval* and *Orbis musicae*, have been joined by *Israeli Studies in Musicology* (since 1978). In the United States, *Musica Judaica* has been the most accessible journal for the entire field, with scholars who take a more ethnographic perspective publishing in journals such as the *Jewish Folklore and Ethnology Review*. By and large, journals and monograph series in the broader disciplines of Jewish studies have not welcomed contributions from scholars in Jewish music research, claiming that Jewish music is too specialized for Jewish studies. At the beginning of the twenty-first century, the tendency of Jewish studies to regard music as too specialized, quite understandably, remains one of the greatest paradoxes faced by Jewish music research.

BIBLIOGRAPHY

ADLER, I. 1966. *La Pratique musicale savante dans quelques communautés juives en Europe aux 17ième et 18ième siècles.* Paris.

—— 1975. *Hebrew Writings Concerning Music in Manuscripts and Printed Books from Geonic Times up to 1800.* Munich.

—— 1995. *The Study of Jewish Music: A Bibliographical Guide.* Jerusalem.

BOHLMAN, P. V. 1989. *'The Land Where Two Streams Flow': Music in the German-Jewish Community of Israel.* Urbana, Ill.

—— and HOLZAPFEL, O. 2001. *The Folk Songs of Ashkenaz.* Middleton, Wisc.

BROUGHTON, S. 2000. 'USA—Klezmer.' In *World Music: The Rough Guide.* ii. 581–92. S. Broughton and M. Ellingham eds. London.

COHEN, J. 1999. 'Jewish Music—Sephardic.' In *World Music: The Rough Guide.* i. 370–7. S. Broughton *et al.* eds. London.

DALMAN, G. H. 1891. *Jüdischdeutsche Volkslieder aus Galizien und Russland.* 2nd edn. Berlin.

FARMER, H. G. 1941. *Maimonides on Listening to Music.* London.

FLEISHER, R. 1997. *Twenty Israeli Composers: Voices of a Culture*. Detroit.

FLENDER, R. 1992. *Hebrew Psalmody: A Structural Investigation*. Jerusalem.

GINSBURG, S. M. and MAREK, P. S. 1901. *Evreiskie narodnye pesni v Rossii*. St Petersburg.

GRADENWITZ, P. 1996. *The Music of Israel: From the Biblical Era to Modern Times*. 2nd and rev. edn. Portland, Oreg.

GRÖTZINGER, K. E. 1982. *Musik und Gesang in der Theologie der frühen jüdischen Literatur: Talmud, Midrasch, Mystik*. Tübingen.

HARRÁN, D. 1999. *Salamone Rossi: Jewish Musician in Late Renaissance Mantua*. New York and Oxford.

HESKES, I. 1985. *The Resource Book of Jewish Music: A Bibliographical and Topical Guide to the Book and Journal Literature and Program Materials*. Westport, Conn.

HIRSHBERG, J. 1995. *Music in the Jewish Community of Palestine 1880–1948: A Social History*. Oxford.

IDELSOHN, A. Z. 1914–32. *Hebräisch-orientalischer Melodienschatz*. 10 vols. Berlin, Vienna, Leipzig, and Jerusalem.

—— 1929. *Jewish Music in Its Historical Development*. New York.

'JEWISH MUSIC.' 2001. In *The New Grove Dictionary of Music and Musicians*. xiii. 24–112. S. Sadie ed. London.

LENZ, D. 1999. 'Israel: A Narrow Bridge.' In *World Music: The Rough Guide*. i. 363–9. S. Broughton *et al.* eds. London.

REGEV, M. and SEROUSSI, S. In preparation. *Israeli Popular Music* [tentative title]. Berkeley.

RINGER, A. L. 1990. *Arnold Schoenberg: The Composer as Jew*. Oxford.

RUBIN, J. and OTTENS, R. 1999. *Klezmer-Musik*. Cassel.

SALMEN, W. 1991. '... *denn die Fiedel macht das Fest': Jüdische Musikanten und Tänzer vom 13. bis 20. Jahrhundert*. Innsbruck.

SHELEMAY, K. K. 1998. *Let Jasmine Rain Down: Song and Remembrance Among Syrian Jews*. Chicago.

SHILOAH, A. 1992. *Jewish Musical Traditions*. Detroit.

SLOBIN, M. 1989. *Chosen Voices: The Story of the American Cantorate*. Urbana, Ill.

—— 2000. *Fiddler on the Move: Exploring the Klezmer World*. New York and Oxford.

SUMMIT, J. 2000. *The Lord's Song in a Strange Land: Music and Identity in Contemporary Jewish Worship*. New York and Oxford.

WALBE, J. 1975. *Der Gesang Israels und seine Quellen: Ein Beitrag zur hebräischen Musikologie*. Hamburg.

CHAPTER 35

JEWISH THEATRE

AHUVA BELKIN
GAD KAYNAR*

THE HISTORY OF THE JEWISH THEATRE

UNTIL quite recent times, the Jew has never been *homo theatralis*. Although Jews
were known as the People of the Book, and despite the very rich literature attached
to Judaism, the dramatic genre never became an integral part of Jewish civilization,
and theatre as an institution was never a part of its cultural life. This may be in part
because the Bible and the book of oral law—the Talmud and later rabbinical
writings—contain vehement exhortations against the theatre. In Judaism, jesters
are identified with idleness and heresy. The confrontation between the true believer
and the heretic who is presented as a jester is introduced in the first verse of Psalm 1:
'Blessed is the man that walketh not in the counsel of the ungodly, nor standeth in
the way of sinners, nor sitteth in the seat of the scornful.' 'Scornful' is a mistrans-
lation of *latzim* in the Hebrew source, which actually means jesters, and the seats
mentioned in the rabbinical gloss are the seats of the theatre. However, critics differ
on the reasons for the absence of Jewish theatre. Ritual, theological—the monotheistic nature of the Jewish faith—and philosophical factors, world-view, historical
development, the social structure, and political circumstances—all are considered

---

* The section on Jewish theatre was written by Ahuva Belkin. The section on Israeli theatre was
written by Gad Kaynar.

by different schools of thought as impediments to the evolution of Jewish theatre (Belkin 1997: 45–59).

From the sixteenth century onward, however, Jews began to become involved in the theatre in two quite distinct ways. The influence of the Renaissance spawned budding attempts at literary dramatic writing in Hebrew, while popular tradition coupled with the *Purimspiel* bred a folk theatre in Yiddish, which was the language of the people. From the late nineteenth century, and well into the early twentieth century, when the Jewish theatre was becoming professional and established, Jewish scholars began their search for the ancient roots of Jewish involvement with the theatre.

However, as early as the sixteenth century, Leone de'Sommi Portaleone (Yehuda Sommo, 1527–92), the extraordinary Jewish man of the theatre—playwright, actor, director, producer, and choreographer, and member of the Jewish community in Mantua—claimed in his treatise *Quatro dialoghi in materia di rappresentazioni sceniche* that it was the Jews and not the Greeks who were the first to write dramas. (Marotti 1968). De'Sommi considered the Book of Job to be a tragedy, and he held that theatre arts had originated among the Jews in antiquity. This treatise—the first of its kind in the annals of the theatre—includes many new perceptions and revolutionary ideas on theatre as a whole, and establishes de'Sommi as the founder of the modern theory of stage arts.

Studies by later scholars on Jewish histrionic art have frequently been designed to give the impression of the continuous development of the dramatic genre in Jewish culture since antiquity. These researchers attempted to establish some sort of natural evolution of drama in Jewish culture by reference to various surviving documents and relics: a fragment of a classical drama—*Exodus*—written by the Alexandrian Jew Ezekiel in the second century BCE (Jacobson 1983); a few Jewish thespians in the service of the Roman theatre; and numerous condemnations of theatre, which suggest that theatre was indeed being performed and attended. However, when we look more deeply at the studies devoted to this subject, we realize that such a continuous tradition never existed; rather, only a handful of dramas were written in disparate places and times, and none of them were ever staged.

In order to emulate other nations, writers sought to discover an authentic dramatic genre. They fashioned their Jewish material after styles and traditions that were prevalent in the cultures in which they lived. Thus they wrote comedies and pastorals in the Renaissance and Baroque Italian style, in the spirit of the Spanish mystery plays, the *autos sacramentales*, or adopting the structure of the Spanish *commedia*. Most of these plays were never staged. Except for the works of Leone de'Sommi Portaleone, the others reflect little if any experience in writing for the living theatre. Ever since J. Schirmann attributed to de'Sommi the earliest Hebrew play—*Tsahut Bedihuta Dekidushin* (*The Comedy of Betrothal*), he has been widely accepted as the first Hebrew playwright (Schirman 1965). The play represents, quite paradoxically, the pinnacle of Hebrew drama up until the eighteenth century. Prior to that, a play by Moshe Zaccuto (1625[?]–98), *Yesod Olam*, had been considered to occupy that place (Melkman 1969), while the Jews of Amsterdam regarded the work of Josef Felix Penso della Vega, *Asirei HaTikva* (*Prisoners of Hope*), written in 1667 after the fashion of the Spanish *autos*, as the first dramatic piece in Hebrew (Schirman, 1979). This trend reached its pinnacle in the works of Moses Hayyim Luzzatto, who wrote his plays *Maaseh Shimshon* (*The Life of Samson*, 1727), *LaYesharim Tehila* (*Praise of the Righteous*, 1743), and *Migdal Oz* (*Tower of Strength*, upon which a rabbinical ban was imposed and which was only published in 1837) according to his own theory of drama in the wake of Quintilian and the Humanists, using the prevailing genres of his time—allegory and pastoral. Luzzatto influenced the Hebrew dramaturgy of the Enlightenment, and many others tried to copy his style.

Tentative beginnings, such as those made by de'Sommi during the Italian Renaissance or by the Baroque poet Luzzatto, by no means represent the epilogue and prologue of an era in Jewish theatre. They are but landmarks, barely connected. Given the great gaps in the times and places of their appearance, these sporadic endeavours in fact attest to the absence of a Jewish theatrical tradition. The authors were mostly unaware of their predecessors or their contemporaries. It was therefore impossible for Jewish drama to have developed gradually in a continuous, linear fashion, as theatrical traditions in other cultures had done. These intermittent works were flashes, inspired and influenced by the cultural centres where their authors were living at the time. There is no evidence of an evolving style; each play is an isolated work, rather than a link in the chain that creates a tradition. Although a substantial part of Jewish theatrical activity up to the eighteenth century took place in Italy, Italian research hardly ever concerned itself with monographs dedicated to Jewish theatre.

During the Enlightenment and the national revival period, dramatic writing in Hebrew became more prevalent. However, these plays were written by poets and authors who were seldom engaged in actual professional stage work, and their pieces were not usually intended to be performed (Shaked 1970).

Alongside this dramatic writing in Hebrew, which had little to do with the actual theatre and its interaction with an audience, there existed a lively Jewish folk theatre in Yiddish. Since the sixteenth century the *Purimspiel* had constituted a popular theatre independent of the literary poetic tradition, and had developed into a continuous tradition. The earliest documentation in which we can find the term *Purimspiel* is in Gumprecht's poem on the Book of Esther (Stern 1922).

The feast of Purim, with its carnivalesque popular customs and spirit of anarchy, chaos, and the breaking of taboos, was manifested in inebriation, games, clowning, and merrymaking centred on the denigration and abuse of the arch-villain Haman from the Book of Esther. The temporary lifting of all social prohibitions enabled the emergence of these representations. Like other folk genres, the *Purimspiel* did not follow a discernable evolutionary path, unlike the conventional theatre of the time. Once the genre had crystallized into the pattern of a play, its development stopped and it began to rely on tradition. The tradition of the *Purimspiel* lasted as long as it continued to reflect a life that had remained unchanged for hundreds of years.

Seemingly without any apparent connection to its predecessors—either to the *Purimspiel* experience or to the sporadic literary drama of the Enlightenment—a Jewish theatre as an independent institution, without connection to any festival, was created by Avraham Goldfaden in the 1870s. Goldfaden (1840–1908), self-named 'the father of the Jewish theatre', pioneered the staging of plays on Jewish subjects for Jewish audiences. His plan to stage his poems was first realized in a dramatic show in Simon Mark's open-air beer garden in Jassy, Romania, and this became the first Jewish play to be performed on a professional stage. This led to intense theatrical activity, from performances by a modest cast of two men to large troupes that included actresses, and from makeshift boards to a permanent theatre staging grand spectacles complete with music, dance, and scenery. The actors who worked with Goldfaden went on to create additional ensembles, and the waves of Jewish emigration towards the end of the nineteenth century brought the Jewish histrionic endeavour into the New World. Between 1881 and 1925 nearly three and a half million Jews, mostly of East European decent, emigrated to the United States. The majority of these Yiddish-speaking emigrants settled in eastern cities. Yiddish theatre was established in New York in 1882, and spread across the continent, offering a rich spectrum of productions and quickly becoming immensely popular with the Jewish immigrant community. For many years the Jewish theatre in America—mainly in the United States and Argentina—was more than mere entertainment or an element of culture; for the masses, it was a way of life.

JEWISH THEATRE STUDIES

Any attempt to discuss schools of research in Jewish theatre is bound to reach a dead end. The idiosyncratic development of the Jewish theatre, the absence of continuity in time or space, the limited scope of activities, and the different languages it used—all these have influenced approaches to the study of Jewish theatre, which has never been granted its rightful place in scholarship. The development of Jewish theatre research as an independent discipline reflects the sporadic development of Jewish theatre (Hirshhoyt 1971: 7–38). Neither has ever followed the beaten path, nor materialized in specific regions or in academic institutions. The axe that fell on Europe Jewry so suddenly and brutally in the 1930s and 1940s destroyed and dispersed these early theatrical buds. Some researchers moved to America, Israel, and other countries, and archives were often only partially transferred. To this day, Jewish theatre has not been crystallized into a scholarly, separate discipline; there are no university departments or research institutes in the academic world that are wholly concerned with Jewish theatre. Instead, a few scholars within various departments such as literature, drama, theatre, Yiddish, or Judaic studies study the subject sporadically.

Moreover, until the twentieth century theatre research in general was an integral part of literary research and was not regarded as a discipline in its own right. When theatre research began to enjoy a more independent status, most scholars were interested in the 'golden ages' of the theatre and in its classic writers, so that attention was focused upon Greek tragedy and comedy, Shakespeare and the Elizabethans, Lope de Vega and Calderon in Spain, and so forth. Later, when researchers also became interested in other periods and lesser playwrights, they were mainly concerned with 'well-made' plays staged by established companies, which they analysed according to established poetic principles.

In this environment the Jewish folk theatre received scant, if any, attention. Since the language of the folk theatre was Yiddish, the genre is barely mentioned in studies of Hebrew literature. Scholars here, like their colleagues from other cultures, tended to view these early theatrical events as mere preludes to the later, highbrow (or: superior) dramatic activity. Hebrew scholars were happy to fill the void in theatrical activity with the pioneers of Hebrew drama (such as Luzzatto and his cultural descendants), never considering whether their plays were ever performed on stage. Monographs on Jewish and Hebrew literature by the writers of the Jewish Enlightenment only occasionally and very briefly refer to dramatic texts, and never to their theatrical potential.

In the 1860s Avraham Papirna published a book which broke new ground in Hebrew dramatic criticism (Papirna 1868). He too was only interested in the drama of 'high culture' and in the classic dramatic poets of world literature. Compared to them, the early Hebrew playwrights were negligible. A brief survey of the development of Hebrew drama appeared in the early 1920s in *Israel's Literature* by Moshe Steinschneider (Steinschneider 1902). In this study, folk plays on the themes of the Book of Esther, the Selling of Joseph, and David and Goliath are described as an intermediate genre between poetry and drama, and Steinschneider designates them 'religious drama'. By classifying them thus, Steinschneider justifies the fact that these plays were allowed to be 'admitted into the community'. 'Proper' drama, he claims, is that which was influenced by the new winds blowing through European literature. Other scholars not only criticized the folk genre but found it downright distasteful. E. Shulman calls the *Purimspiel* a 'sullied spectacle' (Shulman 1913); Max Erik, who discusses the literary Yiddish genre, relates to the *Purimspiel* as 'primitive' (Erik 1928); and Israel Zinberg brands *Purim* players as ignoramus simpletons, who destroyed the dramatic achievement of the Jewish people with their obscenities and vulgar bawdiness (Zinberg 1943). To these scholars, the *Purimspiel* was a literary degeneration rather than the relic of a popular performance. The published texts of the Jewish folk theatre were condemned as 'evil and horrible' or, at the very best, as 'bad weeds'.

The traditional association of drama research with written texts has caused scholars to neglect the study of theatrical expressions that lacked a written literary style. However, in recent decades popular theatre has been attracting more interest, and a number of monographs have appeared on Jewish folk theatre, some of which deal with its local manifestations.

Several Yiddish scholars, driven by a strong sense of mission to record a vanishing culture, as well as by a premonition of doom for the future of Europe's Jews, managed to assemble an important collection of folklore items. M. Steinschneider took an interest in the *Purimspiel* folk play, and catalogued his findings on Purim folklore in Steinschneider (1902–4). Noyakh Prilutski (born in Bredichev in 1882), jurist, journalist, critic, and folklorist of the Yiddish language and culture, collected folklore items, popular songs, epigrams, and maxims as well as *Purimspiels*, and published them with historical, philological, and ethnographic comments (Prilutski 1912). In 1921, in Bialistok, he published his *Yiddish teater 1905–1912*, a collection of essays on artists, playwrights, and various performances. S. Weissenberg (1867–1928), the Jewish ethnographer and anthropologist from Yelisvetgard (Harson Russia), lamented the disappearance of the Jewish popular theatre from the Jewish cultural scene in the early twentieth century, and transcribed his hometown's traditional *Purimspiel* to save it from oblivion. In 1904 he recorded, in a Latin transcription that was based upon popular Yiddish, the folk play that had been passed down from generation to generation in his community (Weissenberg 1904).

The foundations for the modern Jewish Yiddish theatre that were laid by Goldfaden in Eastern Europe in the 1870s, together with the development of Jewish theatre as an important part of Jewish cultural life in the United States, resulted in Yiddish theatre becoming widespread over the two continents and led to a great deal of writing on the theatre. Jubilee albums of Yiddish theatres and companies (e.g. Scheyn 1964), together with memoirs and biographies of stars, actors, producers, and impresarios, many of whom had moved from Europe to America, offer an abundance of raw material for research into the emergence of Jewish theatre at the end of the nineteenth and beginning of the twentieth centuries. Jewish theatre activities from that period onwards are well documented, albeit by eyewitnesses and first-hand sources who sometimes offer contradictory versions. A few memoirs have been published, such as Kaminska (1973), Kobrin (1925), Tomashefsky (1937), Veykhert (1961), Yablokoff (1968–9), and Z. Turkov (1951). Zilbertsvayg recorded Liberesku's memoirs (Zilbertsvayg 1928) from interviews with him, and did the same for Avraham Goldfaden and Zigmund Mogulesko (Zilbertsvayg 1936). The actor Mukdoyni's criticism (Mukdoyni 1927) reflect the blossoming of Polish Jewish theatre. Many more memoirs are scattered in newspapers and periodicals in different countries and in many languages. The actor A. Teytlboym (Teytlboym 1929) wrote on various general theatrical issues and about several other actors. N. Oyslender (Oyslender 1940) describes Jewish theatre in Russia. In 1968 the Alveltlikhn Yidishn Kultur-Kongress published Herman Yablokoff's memoirs, introduced by I. Manger (1968–9). This book constitutes a source for Jewish theatre documents in Poland. Yonas Turkov (1953) collected memoirs of Jewish actors who perished in the Holocaust. The second part of N. Bukhvald's work (Bukhvald 1943) deals with the Jewish theatre in America. A. Goldberg (Goldberg 1961) compiled twenty-five plays of playwrights from Axenfeld to Khaver-Pover, presenting several acts of each. His short annotation is concerned only with the playwrights' biographies. A survey of different phenomena in the Jewish theatre can be found in Mukdoyni (1953). Y. Shatsky (Shatsky 1940b) edited a most valuable collection on documents of Goldfaden's life and work. The literary society of YIVO in Buenos Aires issued a collection of some of Goldfaden's writings (Goldfaden 1972; and see also Turkov 1969).

Although this literature mostly lacks any scholarly, historical, or genre perspective, it is rich in authentic material, which constitutes a wealth of information for research into Jewish theatre. However, this subjective, prosopographic literature gives us a partial and somewhat misleading picture. The activities of these pioneers were mythologized as a result of pathos, exaggeration, the tendency to romanticize the past or to justify the memorialists' own choices and views, none of whom attempted an analysis of the Jewish theatre itself. This literature seldom engages in comment or critical analysis of the drama or its production. Lacking the perspective needed for an overall view of the historical development of Jewish theatre, the enthusiastic writers among the founding fathers of Jewish theatre were motivated mainly by a sense of new beginnings and of a national mission.

Until the Second World War there was scant difference between the European and the American approach to the study of Jewish theatre. Some scholars lived in America but published their studies in Europe, and vice versa. Many critics moved from Europe to the United States, where they published their findings and memoirs.

The real impetus for Jewish theatre studies came about when theatre studies was separated from literature and became an independent discipline. Anthropological theories relating to the origins of theatre and 'lowbrow' folk culture began to be seen as a subject deserving of research in various disciplines.

One of the first books to deal with the Yiddish theatre was by Y. Mestel (Mestel 1943). This useful book, while lacking continuity, tackles basic questions such as the economics of the Jewish theatre in America, the star system, the repertoire, stage direction, and so forth. Other anthologies of essays on various subjects, such as Veykhert (1922), Mukdoyni (1927), and Bukhvald (1943), were compiled from articles in newspapers and periodicals and deal with specific productions or theatrical aspects.

Despite the relatively recent birth of Yiddish theatre and the consequent lack of historical perspective, two early twentieth-century scholars, Bernard Gorin and Isaac Schiffer, independently of each other undertook the task of writing the history of the Jewish theatre. Bernard Gorin (pseudonym Yitskhok Goydo) was born in 1868 in Lida, Vilnius, and gained experience and a broad knowledge of both Jewish and world theatre in his work as a journalist and critic for *Die Zukunft*, a monthly magazine on Yiddish literature and theatre in Europe. In 1894 he emigrated to America, where he served as editor of the bi-weekly *Theatre Journal* from 1901 to 1903. Gorin published a well-known book which offers a survey of theatre from antiquity to modern Yiddish theatre, and which was the first book written on the history of Jewish theatre (Gorin 1929). Its subtitle, 'Two thousand years of Jewish theatre', indicates his attempt to show the roots and unbroken tradition of Jewish histrionic art from antiquity.

Aware of the new theories regarding the origin of theatre, he was prompted to search for similar developments in Jewish culture. He postulated that Jewish theatre was an original creation precisely because it emerged in a theatrical vacuum, at the very time when classical theatre was in decline. The Jews, to his mind, may well have been the only people who staged any theatre at all in early medieval days, by dramatizing the Book of Esther. His hypothesis locates the origins of Jewish theatre in improvisations on the abuse of Haman in the synagogue courtyard that slowly grew into a dramatic form and developed into the *Purimspiel* as early as the ninth century. He holds that, despite their primitive nature, these performances were closer to mature drama than were the hymns to Dionysus that marked the origins of Greek drama. Gorin was not a historian, however, and his *Geschichte* is a somewhat popularist book, lacks a systematic discussion, and does not rely on documentation or source material. His account of the development of Jewish theatre offers no evidence of any link connecting the ritual with the drama. There are neither texts nor any other proofs attesting to the existence of such plays being recited every year as Haman was symbolically burned at the stake. Nor do we have any evidence to show how these supposed texts developed into the *Purimspiel*. As discipline-oriented historical research, Gorin's book suffers from certain methodological imperfections. The bulk of the book deals with American Jewish theatre, which he himself reviewed as a theatre critic, and it is this that provides a historical document and vivid testimony on the theatre in America up until 1910.

Gorin's book frequently serves as a basic survey textbook for the study of Jewish theatre, and it is much quoted. However, although one cannot deny his great contribution as the pioneer of Jewish theatre criticism and as the person who put theatre into context as an art form, Gorin's effort fails to provide the still-awaited comprehensive written history of Jewish theatre.

The emergence of a new institutionalized Jewish theatre also awoke the enthusiasm of Y. Shiper (born in Turnev, Galicia, in 1884), who had studied law and philosophy at the Universities of Krakov and Vienna, and become interested in

Yiddish folklore and theatre. Using the scholarly methods of an accomplished historian, he wrote a three-volume work on *The History of Yiddish Theatre: Art and Drama From Ancient Times to 1750* (Schiper 1923), which was at that time a unique scholarly book. Schiper wanted to challenge the hypothesis that saw theatre up to the nineteenth century as simply entertainment, and he set out to write his history beginning with the question of whether we should start the history of Jewish theatre from Goldfaden, or whether a continuous tradition from the early folk theatre had indeed existed. He concluded his research with the period a hundred years before the beginning of the first modern theatre in the nineteenth century. In this pioneering monograph the author, an outstanding historian, treats all the popular manifestations of Jewish theatre. The material and records he gathered enable us to study the subject in great depth.

Schiper's first assumption was that the repertoire of the Jewish folk theatre had grown under the influence of Polish festive, semi-dramatic activities and of the *Fastnachtspiel* performed in Germany, and that it had nothing to do with Purim customs. He later revised his argument and, using a comparative method, linked the Jewish folk theatre, the *Purimspiel*, to customs of the Purim holiday. His awareness of theories of the 'Cambridge School of Anthropology', according to which the origin of Greek drama lay in fertility rituals and myths, led him to investigate the origin of Jewish theatre using the model of the Ritual School. He posited a connection between ancient witchcraft rituals and primitive activities related to the belief in evil spirits, demons, and ghosts, and the Jewish folk theatre in which Haman represents the demon. However, this line of development, which implies a Judaic magic cult, led to a dead end. There is no solid evidence in Judaism to indicate the evolution from a theatrical cult to ritual theatre and hence to drama.

In the theories he developed, and in establishing historical facts, Schiper referred to primary sources concerning Jewish involvement in the theatre since the first century CE, and analysed the texts in the context of their time. He perceived the theatre in its broadest sense and included cantors, singers, jesters, fools, and dialogic literature as categories of theatre activity. His work includes both published pieces and orally transmitted material. These items, coupled with various intimations and the power of his imagination, helped him to construct a continuous line of Jewish theatre through the ages.

Since the publication of Schiper's book on Jewish theatre in 1923, no other academic books with a historical scholarly approach to the subject have been published, and his remains the only overview of Jewish theatrical entertainment up until the establishment of modern Jewish theatre in the late nineteenth century.

The researcher and historian Yankev Shatzky was responsible for another important development in the study of Jewish theatre, first in his native Poland and later in the United States, where he emigrated. Shatzky, a highly qualified historian, applied accepted scientific methodology to the study of Jewish theatre—and in so doing elevated Jewish theatre to the level of a recognized academic discipline. He was aware of the shortcomings in scholarship in Gorin's and Schiper's publications, and he objected to that kind of synthetic history. While he dismissed Gorin's book, he gave Schiper more credit and wrote a detailed review of his book, in which he nevertheless drew attention to many documents that Schiper had failed to notice. In 1930 he published those documents in *Klenere arbaitn zu der geshichte fun Yidishen teater* (*A Small Contribution To the Annals of Jewish Theatre*). Nevertheless, Shatzky was influenced by Schiper's work, and in his review he raised the idea of establishing a permanent archive dedicated to the study of Jewish theatre. Shatzky collected a great deal of invaluable material (Shatsky 1940a). His articles on Dutch Jewry throw new light on the link between folk celebration and the theatre (Shatsky 1940c, 1943, 1945). The important scientific institution 'Yivo' (Yidisher Visnshaftlekher Institut), founded in 1925 in Vilna, Poland, as the 'Yiddish Scientific Institute for the Study of East European Jewry and the Yiddish Language, Literature, and Folklore', also served as a repository for theatre research, and it was this institute that founded the Ester Rokhl Kaminska Teater Musey (Esther Rachel Kaminsky Theatre Museum).

The idea of encouraging research through an annual publication of studies on Jewish theatre, drama, and criticism never materialized, however. The only volume to appear was edited by Shatzky and published by the Ester Rokhl Kaminska Teater Musey (Shatsky 1930). It constitutes a major collection of records on various aspects of Jewish theatre. Some material that was originally intended for publication in subsequent volumes was eventually printed in the May–June 1940 edition of the *Yivo Blater.*

The same year that saw the establishment of Yivo also saw the founding of the Museum of Jewish Theatre in New York, and a year later the Museum published the *Goldfaden-Buch* (*Goldfaden Book*, 1926). It contains, among other items of interest, some primary sources collected by Shatzky, as well as an extensive bibliography. Various other compilations offer source material for the study of certain aspects of Jewish theatre. Zalmen Zilbertsvayg undertook the task of gathering all available information on artists connected with the Jewish theatre from the beginning of the nineteenth century: these include actors, playwrights, translators, directors, critics, and theatre managers. The fruits of his efforts appear in six volumes of the *Leksikon fun Yidishn teater* (*Lexicon of Jewish Theatre*) (Zilbertsvayg 1959) Many theatre artists and scholars contributed to the lexicon. Yankev Mestel was co-editor of the first two volumes. The lexicon provides a rich source of material on the history of Jewish theatre and the biographies of its artists, including descriptions of the *Purimspiel* tradition taken from the literature and memoirs of the time. Nevertheless, despite the excellent authority of its contributors—all leading historians and critics, such as Shatzky, Mukdoyni, and others—the *Leksikon* lacks accurate references and mingles authentic material with a medley of episodes and anecdotes that, like most memoirs, suffer from an excess of fantasy, exaggeration, and self-aggrandizement.

As yet, no fundamental research on the development of style or on performance aspects of Jewish theatre has been published. In 1987 David Schneider summed up the situation of modern Yiddish drama research by calling it the 'Cinderella of Yiddish literature', neglected by critics of theatre and literature alike (Schneider 1991).

Since the Second World War research into Jewish theatre has been conducted mostly in Israel and the United States, with some work being done in Europe. From the 1940s New York became a leading force in Jewish political, intellectual, and artistic life. After the destruction of European Jewry and the relocation of Yivo headquarters to New York, research into Yiddish theatre was mainly carried out in America, where that theatre developed. A few studies are particularly worthy of mention. Marvin L. Seiger's well-informed and extensive dissertation deals with 'Yiddish Theatre in New York City to 1892' (1960), and Sandrow (1977) embraces the entire history of the Jewish theatre. More recently, Edna Nahshon, a prominent scholar of Jewish theatre, has published a useful monograph (Nahshon 1998).

In 1966 A. Yaari published his bibliographical compilation of some 1,396 Hebrew plays, which includes the earliest written works from Jewish theatre. S. Avisar (1996) complements Yaari's study by presenting the plots of the plays, some analysis, and introducing some Yiddish plays. The first volume of Avisar's volume, which is subtitled *From Its Beginning Until the End of the Nineteenth Century*, will apparently be followed by a second one dedicated to the twentieth century.

Despite the undeniable significance of the works mentioned above, no systematic or comprehensive study of Yiddish theatre has yet been published. The study of Hebrew drama and Jewish folk theatre takes place mainly in Israel. In 1945 Duvshani published a bibliography of Hebrew drama in the Enlightenment period (Duvshani 1945).

The study of early Hebrew theatre has been part of the general literary research at the Hebrew University, Jerusalem. J. Shirmann, the prominent scholar of Hebrew poetry, took special interest in early Hebrew drama. As mentioned earlier, his research established Leone de'Sommi as the first Hebrew playwright. His articles on the few Hebrew playwrights up to the Haskalah were compiled in Shirmann (1979), see also the seminal article Shirmann (1965); while his disciple, Yonah David, conducted a comparative research on Moses Hayyim Luzzatto's plays (David 1972). In his 1970 study Gershon Shaked deals with the structure, artistic methods, characterization, and dialogue of the Hebrew historical play during the Jewish enlightenment, which started in the 1880s (Shaked 1970).

Having been neglected for decades, the *Purimspiel* became the subject of a comprehensive landmark study by Chone Shmeruk of the Hebrew University. A remarkable collection of *Purimspiel* plays is included in his book (Shmeruk 1979). Without this edifying, scholarly, and monumental work, a study of the *Purimspiel* would have been an almost impossible task. Shmeruk deciphered the manuscripts and early prints of homogenous data—the biblical plays—and devoted a special appendix to the *Purimspiel* in which he characterizes the plays that have survived in writing. The texts are presented in the original Yiddish and Shmeruk's commentaries are in Hebrew. The appendix offers the first attempt to present a systematic research into the beginnings of the *Purimspiel*, as well as features of its scenic scheme.

In all the published works on Jewish theatre, plays by classical writers such as Mendele Mocher Sforim and I. L. Peretz were studied from a purely literary angle. The only exception to this trend was Weitzner (1994).

During the last two decades of the twentieth century scholars at Tel Aviv University began to pay greater attention to Jewish theatre and to experiments in performance style. The Theatre Studies Department at Tel Aviv University examines Jewish theatre from the point of view of theories on the media, considers various categories of and experimentation with actual performances, and mounts performances of plays from early Jewish theatre. The department has held international festivals on Jewish theatre (1981, 1985), and a conference (1988) on Leone de'Sommi and the theatrical activities of the Jews of Mantua under the Gonzagas, which yielded a book on Leone de'Sommi with articles by such international experts as Alfred Golding, Massimo Ciavolella, Georges Banu, Dunbar Ogden, Shimon Levy, Cristina dal Molin, and others (Belkin 1997). De'Sommi's dialogues were translated into French by André Strichan and a comprehensive bibliography on De'Sommi has been published by the Theatre Studies Department. The Tel Aviv University theatre has staged plays by Leone de'Sommi, Zaccutto, and Wolfson as well as other Jewish plays, from the sixteenth century to contemporary works.

Several studies by Ahuva Belkin of Tel Aviv University offer a new approach to the *Purimspiel* as a theatrical genre, its origins, and the context of this genre in other communities. In her 1985 article, which is based to a great extent on iconographical evidence, a tentative period is suggested for the beginning of the *Purimspiel* (Belkin 1985). In Belkin's book (Belkin 2002), Turner's scheme of a processional rite of passage associated with seasonal changes and their accompanying festivals, which were considered liminal events, is applied to Jewish theatre. Turner's research into the experience of a tribal community that had lost its non-reflective character and been reinvented in the form of self-conscious creativity of leisure, the liminoid, provides an effective model for analysis of the Purim festival and its theatrical genre. Belkin suggests that the *Purimspiel* emerged in the diaspora from a new spirit of resentment and frustration, which stimulated new ways to express the liminal experience.

In recent years the study of Jewish theatre has enjoyed a certain revival. In 1998 an international workshop, the first of its kind, brought to Oxford, England, some fifty scholars from various disciplines to discuss the subject mainly from literary and historical points of view. In 2002 an International conference was held at University College London for discussion of historical, genre, and media issues relating to the Jewish theatre.

THE HISTORY OF ISRAELI THEATRE:
1889–2001

The extent of performative activity in Israel is impressive for a country with no theatrical tradition and a population of merely 4.5 million Jewish and Hebrew-speaking inhabitants. Between 1970 and 1990 Israel held first place in the world in theatre attendance per capita (Lev-Ari 1999: 366). The season 2000–1 saw twelve subsidized public repertory theatres play to packed halls, as well as many fringe companies and festivals, from the annual Acco Festival for Alternative Theatre to the festival for one-person shows, TheatroNetto. Over forty professional theatre performances occurred nightly in Tel Aviv alone.

This meteoric growth derives from existential rather than artistic reasons. From its early days, Hebrew theatre and drama played a major role in generating the communal identity of a society 'relentlessly preoccupied with defining itself and justifying its existence' (Kaynar 1996a: 298). Its most important task between 1889 and 1914 was teaching the Hebrew language to the steadily growing community of Zionist settlers (Norman 1966: 34; Rokem 1996a: 53). Its second instrumental function was to revive representationally the connection between the immigrant 'New Jew' and his 'native' soil and mythical biblical and historical ancestors.

Theatre and theatricality also furnished the *Chalutzim* (pioneers) with an outlet for their yearning yet critical attitude to their Orthodox origins and parental home. This was accomplished either through the *Massechet*, a kind of oratorio for moderators and chorus, originating in the kibbutzim in the 1920s to mark a diasporic religious feast with rural origins, or through translated Yiddish melodramas or satirical-grotesque portrayals of the *Shtetl* (e.g. Sholem Aleichem's *The Treasure*), justifying renunciation of the past. Concomitantly, the young Hebrew stage also mounted an avant-garde turn-of-the-century repertoire—Ibsen, Strindberg, Shaw, Chekhov, and others.

The first theatrical performance in Hebrew took place in 1889 at the Lemel School, Jerusalem. The stylized school production, *Zerubavel*, by Moshe Leib Lilienblum, translated and adapted by the Hebrew teacher David Yelin, dealt with the motif of the Exiles' return from Babylon. Like other school productions at that time, it reified the links between the performance's pedagogic frame, tendentious allegorical form, and didactic, nationalistic content.

The various semi-professional groups operating in Jerusalem, Jaffa, and the new settlements between 1905 and 1914 were followed by three companies with more demanding artistic standards: the Hebrew Theatre (1920–7), the Eretz-Israel—or Land of Israel—Theatre, the TAI (founded in Berlin, 1923, by Menachem Gnessin, specializing in Habimah's Jewish repertory), and the Art Theatre (1926–7). These paved the way for the institutionalization of Hebrew theatre in Eretz-Israel.

The first professional workers' theatre, artistically sustained by 'the doctrine of the Moscow Art Theatre', was the Ohel (A Tent, 1925–69), founded by Moshe Halevy, a former member of Habimah in Moscow (Halevy 1955: 100–1). Ohel's initial repertoire reflected a synthesis between the traditional Jewish diaspora, proletarian pathos, and the renewed Hebrew culture.

By the mid-1920s—with three repertory theatres and two satirical stages (Hakumkum (The Teapot) 1927–8, and the successful Hamatate (The Broom) 1928–54)—tiny Tel Aviv was becoming the pseudo-cosmopolitan hub of theatrical life. And yet this intensifying theatrical activity would probably nonetheless have dwindled into provincialism, and lost its crucial national function, had not, paradoxically, the *Moscow* Theatre Habimah (The Stage)—proclaimed the National Theatre in 1958—gained an international reputation for its stylistic inventiveness rather than its Jewish-Zionist repertoire (Kaynar 1998).

The Bolshevist revolution facilitated the realization of earlier attempts (in 1909, and 1913–14) by Nachum Zemach, Habimah's founder, to form a professional Hebrew Art Theatre in Russia. Habimah operated within the framework of the Moscow Art Theatre (MAT), under the patronage and supervision of Konstantin Stanislavsky and the artistic direction of his prize student, the Armenian Yevgeny Vakhtangov. The five points in Habimah's founding manifesto display a balanced equilibrium between the ideological and the aesthetic, the Zionist and the universal goals. The new theatre should be: 1. Hebrew-speaking; 2. biblical-historical; 3. an institution of moral education; 4. a national theatre in Palestine; 5. a high-art theatre.

The first productions merged Stanislavsky's method of emotional veracity and Vakhtangov's idiosyncratic expressionist style with Jewish-Zionist eschatology, for example: David Pinsky's *The Eternal Jew*, directed by Vsevold Mchedelov (1919 and 1923); Vakhtangov's mythical production of *The Dybbuk* (1922); and *The Golem*, H. Leivik's allegory on power-drunkenness and false messianism, directed by B. Vershilov (1925).

The intercultural interaction between Habimah's early Jewish repertiore and its overridingly Gentile directors enriched its artistic output, as outstandingly demonstrated by Vakhtangov's expressionist staging of ethnographer Shlomo An-Ski's *The Dybbuk: Between Two Worlds*, translated from Yiddish by the national poet, Haim Nachman Bialik, and performed over a thousand times in forty-five years with Hanna Rovina in the original female lead. This *Liebestod* tragedy depicts a lovers' revolt against imposed Jewish marriage customs and material middle-class values, and attracted irreconcilable anthropological, psychoanalytic, Marxist, and Zionist interpretations.

Habimah was forced to leave Russia in January 1926, and went on a series of artistically successful but financially ruinous tours throughout Europe, Eretz Israel, and the United States (1926–31), where the company split, leaving the ardent Zionist founder Zemach and several minor actors behind. In 1931 Habimah settled in Tel Aviv. The cornerstone for its permanent building was laid in 1935.

A crucial debate among Jewish cultural leaders over Habimah's artistic and ideological future was held in November 1929 in Berlin. Bialik advocated a biblical theatre devoted to the cause of glorifying Jewish history and tradition. The 'internationalist' philosopher Martin Buber thought that Habimah should be 'part of the mainstream of the global and universal' (Levy 1979: 106). Most of Habimah's actors, who operated as a collective, sided with Buber, as reflected in the repertoire of the 1930s and 1940s.

The Eretz-Israel theatre repertoire in the pre-State period falls into four categories (Rokem 1996a: 70–83; Shoham 1989a): 1. *Biblical Plays*: e.g. Aharon Ashman's successful melodrama *Michal, Daughter of Saul* (Habimah, 1941), dealing with David's wife unrequited love for her husband; 2. *Jewish Diaspora Drama*; 3. *Indigenous Drama*: only three plays in this category were produced by the established theatre before 1940. The tide turned with Ashman's *This Earth* (Habimah, 1942), which belongs to the genre of the affirmative *Machazot Hahityashvut* (Settlement Drama), intended to boost spectator morale by glorifying the Zionist revolution in structural terms of a pagan ritual (Ofrat 1980: 80); 4. *Non-Jewish Plays*: predominantly German and Russian dramas, impregnated by the theatres and audiences' consciousness of Fascist and anti-Semitic escalation in Europe. Thus a public trial was held against Leopold Jessner's production of Shakespeare's 'anti-Semitic' *The Merchant of Venice* at Habimah (1936), again proving the supreme position of ideological considerations in Hebrew theatre (Fichman 1936: 8).

The repercussions of the tense political situation in the final pre-State years, and the ensuing economic problems of Habimah and Ohel theatres, were aggravated by the immediate popularity of the Cameri Theatre, established in 1944 by the young actor and director Yosef Passovky (Milo). The Cameri appealed to the younger, native-born spectators, as well as to the *Bildungstheater* audience, with its variety of styles and dramatic cultures, and its introduction of contemporaneous, realistic Anglo-Saxon drama in crisp, colloquial translations.

The Cameri Theatre also inaugurated the new Israeli drama, written by native-born authors of the young generation of freedom-fighters. The premiere of Moshe Shamir's *Hu halach bassadot* (*He Walked in the Fields*)—on 31 May 1948, two weeks after the declaration of the State of Israel—was 'a point of departure' for any discussion of the Israeli theatre (Rokem 1996a: 82; Feingold 1999). The self-sacrificing protagonist Uri engendered and incarnated the myth of the immaculate *Sabra* and the cult of the fallen war-hero (the *Akeda* motif, i.e. the sacrificial offering of the sons). The play also heralded the Israeli socio-aesthetic paradigm of a Hebrew drama's performance as identification rite with communal Israeli values. It served as incentive for similar semi-documentary war-melodramas, such as Yigal Mossinsohn's *Bearvot hanegev* (*In the Plains of the Negev*, Habimah, 1949). The darker, more critical aspects of the play, unnoticed by the patriotic audience in 1948, are illuminated by Kaynar (1999).

The only exception to this wave of mythical self-glorification was Nathan Sha-cham's *Hem Yagiu Machar* (*They Will Arrive Tomorrow*, Cameri, 1950). This play constituted the metaphoric prototype of the dual depth structure informing Israeli drama, which vacillates between vindication of any atrocities committed for survival's sake against Arabs or other 'Others', and fidelity to the intrinsically Jewish humanist ethos of the prophets.

The homogeneous ideological and organizational structure of pre-State Hebrew theatre has changed drastically over the fifty-four years of Israel's existence, paralleling the growth and tense ethnic heterogeneity of the population, deepening rifts between nationalist-expansionist views and conformist attitudes towards the Palestinians and local Arabs, conflicts between separatist Orthodox and secular cosmopolitan sectors over the spiritual character of the State, and the gradual erosion of Zionist ideals. The centralist structure of Israeli theatre typified by the hegemony of Habimah and the Cameri (the Municipal Theatre of Tel Aviv since 1970), as well as by the supremacy of Tel Aviv as cultural capital, has remained intact. However, processes of geographic, polysystemic, and pluralistic reorganization of theatrical activity have challenged the power of these theatres. The 1950s produced important fringe companies such as Zira (credited with one of the first world premieres of *Waiting for Godot*, 1955), Zuta, and Zavit. The militant, socially conscious line and realistic style characterizing some of these companies infiltrated the mainstream policy in the early 1970s, when Oded Kotler's Actors' Stage joined the Haifa Municipal Theatre, established by Yosef Milo in 1961 as a typical mid-European *Stadttheater*. Under Kotler and American-born director Nola Chilton, this theatre contributed most to the takeover of local drama in the period 1975 to 1980, and to the upsurge—between 1980 and 1987—in provocative political drama.

Three major public repertory theatres were established in the early 1970s: the Jerusalem Khan Theatre, the Beer-Sheva Theatre, and the National Children and Youth Theatre. The expanding theatrical map was enriched in 1980 by the establishment of the Beit Lessin Theatre in Tel-Aviv, and the Russian immigrants' theatre (Gesher, 1991), which under director-manager Yevgeny Arie became the finest non-commercial art theatre in the country. A number of politically assertive Israeli-Arab theatres in Jaffa, Haifa, and Nazareth (alongside Palestinian performative institutions in East Jerusalem and Ramalah) were formed following the first *Intifada* uprising (1987–99). The initially small and conventional fringe scene attained maturity with enterprises such as Rina Yerushalmy's Itim company, the Acco (and subsequently the Kabri and Shlomi) Theatre Centres, Teatron Mekomi (A Local Theatre), Teatron Notzar (A Created Theatre), as well as alternative centres and schools (in Tel Aviv and Jerusalem), which in the 1990s developed unique theatrical idioms, inspired by international models of Performance Art and interdisciplinary theatre.

The narrow scope of Hebrew pre-State dramaturgy gave way to a plethora of genres:

1. *Biblical and Historical Drama* is manipulated as a religiously connoted prism for the critique of political and moral problems, for example: Nissim Aloni's *Achzar mikol haMelech* (*Most Cruel the King*, Habimah, 1953), warning against the dangers of separationism and internal *Kulturkampf*; Aharon Meged's *Haona haBoeret* (*The Burning Season*, Habimah, 1967); and Gilad Evron's *Yehu* (Habimah, 1992); or of existential questions, for example: Yaakov Shabtai's *Keter baRosh* (*A Crown in the Head*, Cameri, 1969), and Hanoch Levin's *Yissurei Iyov* (*The Torments of Job*, Cameri, 1980).

2. *Holocaust Drama*, generally either contemplating the Shoah's shifting repercussions on Israeli society or using it as a socio-political metaphor. The Holocaust is negated in 1940s and 1950s drama as an arch-image of impotence, and juxtaposed with the sublime reality-convention of the *Sabra* (e.g. Aharon Meged's *Hanna Senesh*, Habimah, 1958), while in the 1960s the world of the victims and Nazi accomplices emerges as the analogous alter ego of the rootless cult of the titanic *Sabra*, for example in M. Shamir's *Hayoresh* (*The Heir*), Haifa Theatre, 1963, and Ben Zion Tomer's *Yaldei hatzel* (*Children of the Shadows*), Habimah, 1963. The 1973 Yom Kippur War, which shattered the invincible image of Israel, catalyzed the phase of regarding the Holocaust and Israeli experiences as metonymical and interchangeable. The best-known play of the period is Yehoshua Sobol's *Ghetto* (Haifa Theatre, 1984), for the first time daring to present the symbiotic relations and reversible roles of the Nazi victimizer and Jewish victim, thereby reflecting on Israel's contested belligerency against Lebanon and the occupied territories. Similar political attitudes were advocated by Motti Lerner's *Kastner* and Shmuel Hasfari's *Kiddush* (both Cameri, 1985). The Acco Theatre Center's stunning theatrical event *Arbeit macht frei MiToitland Europa* (*Work Liberates from the Dead Land Europe*) in 1991 marked the beginning of the fourth stage of Holocaust dramaturgy, in which the second and third generations exposed and reacted to the imprints of the Holocaust experience on the sociopolitical *Weltanschauung* and ethical norms of Israeli society.

3. *Zionist and Post-Zionist Drama* is characterized by a slow transition from the self-glorifying Independence War melodrama, to an interim confronting the diminishing Zionist spirit—by criticism in Aharon Meged's *Hedva veAni* (*Hedva and I*, Habimah, 1954); denouncing society's betrayal of the freedom-fighters in Yoram Matmor's Pirandellian *Machaze Ragil* (*A Regular Play*, Cameri, 1956); or resorting to kitsch-nostalgia in an idealization of the pioneers' courage by Nathan Alterman in *Kineret Kineret* (Cameri, 1961)—and finally to reckoning plays that dissect the national myths, exploring their built-in defects conducing to the disintegration of Israeli society, such as Yehoshua Sobol's *Leil haEssrim* (*The Night of the Twentieth*, Haifa Theatre, 1976), and Hillel Mittelpunkt's *Gorodish, ohaYom haShevii* (*Gorodish, or The Seventh Day*, Cameri, 1993).

4. *Social and Political Drama*, distinguished by realistic-documentary or satirical-grotesque styles, as well as left-wing positions. The young dramatists of Israel's formative era (early 1950s) were primarily enraged by the 'counter-revolutionary'

symptoms of the new society. Corruption, bureaucracy, careerism, social inequality, and racial discrimination are criticized in shallow, realistic works, like Nathan Shacham's *Kera li Siomka* (*Call Me Siomka*, Cameri, 1950), Ephraim Kishon's *Shemo Holech Lefanav* (*His Name Precedes Him*, Habimah, 1953) and *Shachor algabei Lavan* (*Black on White*, Habimah, 1956), Yigal Mossinsohn's *Kazablan* (Cameri, 1954) and *Zerok oto laKelavim* (*Throw Him to the Dogs*, Habimah, 1958). The turnaround in theatre's approach to society was the Six Day War. Whereas pre-1967 Israeli drama was basically positive toward the realized ideal of the 'New Jew', post-1967 protest plays adopted an asocial and agnostically deconstructive position (Yaari 1996: 151–2). Hanoch Levin's satirical revues *At veAni vehaMilchama haBaah* (*You and Me and the Next War*, 1968) and *Ketchup* (1969), performed in fringe theatres, and *Malkat Ambatia* (*A Bathtub Queen*), mounted in 1970 by the institutionalized Cameri Theatre, and swiftly closed due to public outcry, as well as Levin's censored *HaPatriyot* (*The Patriot*, Neve-Tzedek Theatre, 1982), denouncing the Lebanon War, did not shrink from recurring profane and provocative devices to slaughter the most sacred cows of the Israeli collective value-system: the ideal of the 'justified war', the cult of the fallen hero and bereavement, admiration for the military, and sanctification of land at the expense of life and ethics. In Yosef Mundy's *Ze misstovev* (*It Turns*, 1970) the allegorical megalomaniac Herzl torments the humanist epitome of Jewish intelligentsia, Kafka. Mundy's *Moshel Yericho* (*The Governor of Jericho*, Cameri, 1975) depicts the racist and demeaning side of Israeli conduct towards the Palestinians. In the early 1970s Nola Chilton created a succession of 'living newspaper' documentaries propagating a spectrum of social causes in 'the other Israel'. Danny Horowitz's *Cherli Ka Cherl*, at the Khan (1977), offered a parody on the *Sabra* myth. Other dramatists—such as Hillel Mittelpunkt, Avraham Raz, Miriam Kainy, Yitzchak Laor, Motti Lerner, and Ilan Hatzor, and most notably Yehoshua Sobol—in *Nefesh Yehudi* (*A Soul of a Jew*, Haifa Theatre, 1982), and *Palestinait* (*The Palestinian Woman*, Haifa Theatre, 1985)—employ tactics of thwarting the accepted 'photographic' conventions from within, thereby upsetting the positive self-image of Israeli society traditionally reasserted by them.

5. *Universal-Existentialist Drama* is inextricably connected with the theatrical, self-referential phantasmagorias of the poets laureate of Hebrew drama, Nissim Aloni and Hanoch Levin, but its attributes also resonate in plays by Yosef Bar-Yosef and Yaakov Shabtai. Aloni's signature play *HaNessicha haAmerikait* (*The American Princess*, Teatron Haonot, 1962) delineates, through the detached narrative of a dethroned and romantic monarch's murder by his opportunist son, the cultural and normative deformation of Israeli society. This small lyrical-ironic masterpiece marks Aloni's ongoing influence on Israeli drama and theatre, as an antidote to the prevailing flat, journalistic dramaturgy.

Dramatist and director Hanoch Levin (1943–99) was undoubtedly the most prominent and prolific (with sixty works) theatre practitioner to emerge from the aftermath of the Six Day War. In the domestic neighbourhood comedies that followed his first satirical revues, Levin unravels the repulsive diasporic myths underlying the apotheosized Jewish-Israeli family, and develops his image of humankind as a beastly hierarchy of humiliaters and humiliated, motivated exclusively by their basest drives and thanatosic fears. Levin's final dramas comprise legendary-universal phantasmagorias or 'Spectacles of Doom' (Yaari 1996: 164–9). In *Requiem* (Cameri, 1999) he composed his own funeral oration, and *HaBachyanim* (*The Weepers*, Cameri, 2000)—based on *Agamemnon*—was conceived on his deathbed.

6. *Women's Dramaturgy, Personal Theatre, and Performance Arts.* The interconnected historical and theatrical developments of the 1990s, from the Oslo Peace Accord to Rabin's murder and the second *Intifada*, present a complete renunciation of communal ideals along with their formal objective correlatives. The personal, cosmopolitan, and humane note is most clearly evident in the upsurge of women's—not necessarily feminist or gender-conscious—dramaturgy and directing, either in more established patterns (e.g. in plays by Shulamit Lapid, Edna Mazia, and Anat Gov); in stylized, poetic-dramatic and theatrical texts, such as Yossefa Even-Shoshan's *HaBetula miLudmir* (*The Virgin of Ludmir*, Khan Theatre, 1997), and Ravid Davara's *HaSsirpad shel haShachen* (*The Neighbour's Thistle*, Habima, 1999); or in highly subjective Performance Art projects, such as Rina Yerushalmi's *Bible Project* (Cameri, 1996, 1998), or Y. Even Shoshan's *Beriah* (*Creation*, Acco Festival, 2001).

The idealistic, committed, and selfless Hebrew theatre of the early settlement period in the Land of Israel has thus reached the extreme opposite pole, as has indeed the entire Zionist ideology imbued in it, both generated by and generating it. Both, however, are still engaged in the same quest for identity by Israeli society.

ISRAELI THEATRE STUDIES

The overriding absence of performative practice and of theatre studies in the Jewish communities in Europe resulted in almost no academic research throughout the entire pre-State era, of either the universal or the Jewish and Hebrew theatre or theatrical event. Scholastic debates were mostly confined to the ideologically instrumental functions ascribed to the theatre by the Emancipation and the Zionist movements, or to the complex questions concerning the interaction of Bible and drama. Most of the related articles appeared in *Bamah* (*Stage*), a Habimah-affiliated periodical established in 1933, that served—as declared in the editorial column of the first issue—as 'a literary platform for the stage arts' (*Bamah* 1, May 1933: 3). The new discipline of Theatre studies (*Theaterwissenschaft*) had little impact on either the Humanist scholars at the Hebrew University (founded in 1925), or the theatre critics. Intellectuals such as Dov Sadan, Baruch Kurzweil, J. Shirmann, Shimon Halkin, Leah Goldberg, and others brought their classical mid-European schooling to bear upon discussions of the Hebrew drama as literary, philosophical, and ethnographic texts, with a strong didactic-programmatic emphasis. The performative and histrionic dimensions received only marginal attention. The lack of theatrically oriented and authoritative documentation of the evolution, structure, artistic policy, and practice of the budding Hebrew theatre lends special significance to the numerous impressionist memoirs by veterans of the semi-professional and professional theatre ensembles established in Tel Aviv in the first three decades of the twentieth century, and by the founders of the Habimah and Ohel theatres (e.g. Hanoch 1937, 1946; Gnessin 1946; Vardi 1950; Baratz, in Tversky and Even-Shoshan 1954; Halevy 1955; Baratz, in Even-Shoshan 1958; Bertonov *et al.* 1962 and Bertonov 1969; Binyamini, in Lahad and West 1962; Finkel 1968, 1971, 1976, 1977, 1978, 1980, 1984, 1985, 1993; Robins 1968; Gor, in Lahad and West 1970; Klausner 1971; Kutai 1972; Gabai 1983; Rovina, in Gai 1995), as well as to reviews by the journalists, belles-lettrists, and poets who functioned as the first theatre critics (e.g. Fichman 1936; Goldberg 1951; Gur 1957, 1958a, 1958b, 1961, 1965, 1968, 1970).

The second generation of scholars, who began to publish in the 1950s and 1960s, constituted a mixed group of native Israeli graduates of the Hebrew University and immigrants from Europe and the Anglo-Saxon world. These savants—including such prominent academics as Gershon Shaked, Dan Miron, Hillel Barzel, Dvora Gilula, Uri Rapp, Chaim Shoham, Eli Rozik, Ben-Ami Feingold, Yosef Melkman, and Ben-Ami Feingold—were initially indebted to literary or sociological schools. They, however, displayed a focused and generically disposed interest in Hebrew drama sustained by formalist and structuralist analytic tools, and infused by cosmopolitan influences (such as the Cambridge School, Czech, French, and German Structuralism, American New Criticism, Classical Drama studies, Socio-theatrical research, etc.), and committed to predominantly aesthetic criteria. The academic indifference to the necessity of recording the annals of the Jewish and Hebrew theatre relegated this role to cultural publicists and theatre columnists (such as Michael Ohad, Mendel Kohansky, Uri Keysari, Raphael Bashan, Moshe Nathan, Boaz Evron, Immanuel Bar-Kadma, and others).

The Department of Theatre Studies at Tel Aviv University—the largest such department in Israel, comprising theoretical studies, acting, directing, dramatic writing, dramaturgy, and stage design, as well as community theatre and production—was inaugurated in 1958, and now offers doctorates in Theatre studies. The Department of Theatre Studies at the Hebrew University, Jerusalem, was opened in 1970, and the university of the third major city in Israel, Haifa, launched its Theatre Department in 1995–6, with a full-scale syllabus of theoretical and practical studies. A Theatre studies' programme is also offered by the Kibbutzim College of Education, and lately too by an increasing number of colleges and teacher-training colleges. These developments mark a general rise in interest in performance-oriented Theatre studies, as is also attested to by the 200 theatre departments in high schools throughout the country, by the services provided by two large theatre archives (the Israeli Documentation Center for the Performing Arts at Tel-Aviv University, and the Israel Gur Theatre Archive and Museum at the Hebrew University in Jerusalem) as well as the Theatre Museum in Tel Aviv, and by the three major theatre periodicals: *Bamah*, edited by Dvora Gilula, which resumed activity in the 1950s; *Teatron—An Israeli Quarterly for Contemporary Theatre*, edited by Gad Kaynar and Haim Nagid (1998); and *JTD*, the annual *Haifa University Studies in Theatre and Drama* (1995). The faculty in the various theatre departments are widely published and internationally acclaimed, and several of their members (who belong to the Israeli Association of Theatre Studies) are also engaged in practical theatre work as directors, actors, dramaturgs, and designers. Present-day scholars such as Shimon Levy, Dan Urian, Freddie Rokem, Ahuva Belkin, Linda Ben Zvi, Eli Rozik, Yehuda (Jean-Bernard) Moraly, Shulamit Lev-Aladgem, Dror Harari, Nurit Yaari, Zvi Serper, Jeanette R. Malkin, Zvi Jagendorf, Avraham Oz, Erela Brown, Shosh Avigal, Immanuel Ben Amos, Shimon Lev-Ari, Gideon Shunami, Dorit Yerushalmi, Rony Mirkin, Haim Nagid, Dvora Gilula, Shifra Schoneman, Gad Kaynar, and many others, represent a large variety of research branches and approaches—structural, rhetoric, semiotic, receptionist, phenomenological, and anthropological—and most of them clearly disengage their performative vocabulary, aesthetic premises, and para-theatrical investigations of the Israeli theatre and drama from any commitment to ideological tenets and teleology (although several of them, such as Avraham Oz, Ben-Ami Feingold, and Yitzchak Laor, have strong political viewpoints).

Discourse on the Bible as theatre and theatre in the Bible constituted the major controversial topic during the pre-State and early Statehood years. The writers Haim Nachman Bialik and Yaakov Fichman, as well as the critic Israel Segal, among others, contended that the Bible yields ample evidence of theatricality in style and content. Bialik presented the 'classical' claim that since much of the biblical narrative is patterned on dialogue, with minimal intervention on the part of the narrator, it suggests 'signs of dramatic acting' (Bialik 1933: 13). These impressionistically formulated views have recently obtained epistemological substantiation (Levy 1992: 21–45; 2000: 145–253). Israel Segal concurred, but emphasized the spectacular-theatrical aspects, although 'there was no theatre in the modern sense in the Land of Israel until the Hellenistic period' (Segal 1935: 33). Yaakov Fichman was much more unequivocal in his contention that 'the Bible is essentially dramatic' (Fichman 1941: 3). The contesting view, however, is stated in equally strong terms. Philosopher Israel Eldad-Sheib postulated that the Bible is an epic-narrative work, and consequently that 'the dramatic form does not occur in the Bible' (Eldad-Sheib 1961: 9). He saw the Book as constituted upon a dramatic outlook, but excluded drama in the artistic sense. The literary critic Baruch Kurzweil (1970) supported this view from his peculiar perspective and, based on Karl Jaspers, maintained that the Bible might eventually mobilize dramatic techniques, but for purely literary and moralistic purposes. A no less heated debate addressed the question of whether the Bible was indeed eligible to serve as source for dramatic adaptation. Critic Eliezer Zuperfein raised a typical objection in noting the extreme difficulty of staging biblical characters in a manner that would not 'desecrate their sanctity, and blur their image as crystalized in the people's imagination throughout the ages' (Zuperfein 1937: 46).

The establishment of the State of Israel marked the departure of Israeli research from fundamentalist and instrumental postulates concerning biblical drama and theatre. It rendered the pragmatic national goals of Hebrew stage art obsolete by apparently realizing and incorporating them. The Bible as drama and as a stimulus for contemporary meaningful adaptations became simply another aesthetic category among the various dramatic types or theatrical modi being studied. This gradual transition led from the early attempts to explore the embodiment of mobilized ideological meanings in generic and structural dramatic forms (Shaked, Shoham, Ofrat), to exegeses of the non-committed aesthetic style of the individual dramatist and play, as well as of a work's structural, semiotic, semantic, rhetorical, and performative strategies (Sternberg, Perry, Levy, Nagid). In later years (roughly 1960s to 1980s) this scholarly 'profanation' of the holy script epitomized the combative agnostic position of secular dramatists and critics alike in their *Kultur-kampf* against social, intellectual, and legislative attempts to impose the norms of the religious and largely nationalist minority on the secular majority. From the 1990s onwards the changing approach to Bible–Theatre dialectics became impregnated by the general post-Zionist and postmodern trends in Israeli society, art, and scholarship, most notably after Itzhak Rabin's murder and the disintegration of the Oslo peace process, as reflected, for instance, in the Proceedings of the IFTR annual conference, 1996 (Levy 1999).

The major publication that epitomizes the epistemological transition from pre-State to statehood is Shaked (1970). This is the seminal work of Gershon Shaked of the Hebrew University in Jerusalem, the leading scholar of Hebrew literature and drama, and recipient of the Israel Prize. Shaked categorizes biblical drama in the theologically indifferent typology of historical works, in order to discern 'how the unmediated ideational meaning of the play... reveals to us inter alia the historical consciousness of the age' (ibid. 19). The biblical plays of the pre-State Period by M. Shoham, N. Bistrizky, H. Seckler, A. Ashman, and others are synoptically examined from this *Zeitgeist*-oriented perspective as 'a theatrical spectacle and as a structure expressing dramatic tension', by employing 'general criteria applicable to any artistic work such as: impact, unity, complexity, etc.' (ibid. 10). This predilection for aesthetic deliberations at the expense of ideological and historical considerations informs Shaked's own later work, such as Shaked (1992), which includes analyses of new 'secular' Israeli plays (L. Goldberg's *Mistress of the Castle*, N. Aloni's *The*

American Princess, and H. Levin's *Yaakobi and Leidental*), regarded as decontextualized autonomous units. *The Drama of the 'Native Born' Generation in Israel* (1989), by Haim Shoham—Shaked's coeval—entirely blurs the distinctions between biblical dramatic parables and his monographic-poetic interpretations of other plays based on actual reality. Shoham emphasizes 'the confrontation between the dramatist and his world and environment, as embodied in the final work' (Shoham 1989a: 10).

The secular-'agnostic' interpretive standpoint has typified Israeli research since the late 1960s. Formalist, rhetorical, narratological, and textualized reader-conscious methodologies underlie the path-breaking interpretations by Meir Sternberg and Menachem Perry of the 'absorbency' of the biblical text, and its subtle and ironic uses of dramatic markers in the service of literary rhetoric and manipulation of the readers' standpoints.

Native-born Gideon Ofrat, in his 1975 work, makes a clean break with the non-dramatic conception of the Bible: 'Even when the Israeli dramatist of the 1960s resorts to the Bible as a source for his allegory, the Bible is no more than a myth' (Ofrat 1975: 17), as attested, for instance, by Ofrat's interpretation of Nissim Aloni's major first play, *Most Cruel the King* (Habima, 1953)—which depicts the initial phase of struggle between the monarchies of Judea and Israel (c.1000 BCE)—as a psychological realistic drama, about 'the political reality of the young State of Israel' (ibid. 48). Ofrat's book is a milestone in Israeli dramatic criticism. It is the first chronological analysis of paradigms for the main genres in Hebrew drama from the Independence War to the mid-1970s. Furthermore, Ofrat classified Hebrew drama in accordance with universal categories of modern genres, thus paving the way for a new generation of scholars with a keen awareness of the local drama and theatre's substructural and intertextual links with global aesthetics and scholarship.

Chaim Shoham's *Theatre and Drama in Search of an Audience* (Shoham 1989b) is a complex and intriguing application of this approach. It focuses on theatrically conscious and meta-theatrical drama, and employs performatively minded, mythopoetic, and receptionist perspectives. Quoting Ingarden, Pavis, Szondi, Fischer-Lichte, and others, Shoham's semiotic methodology leads up to a theory of how the theatrical text programmes the addressee's reactions in the theatrical event.

Shimon Levy's studies (Levy 1992, 2000) constitute a synthesis between the apotheotic conception of the Bible in pre-State research and the 'profane' disregard for the uniqueness of the Scriptures as dramatic/theatrical materials in later years. Levy—an eminent scholar of Beckett, German theatre, and Israeli drama—conceives of the narrative biblical texts, read in the light of modern doctrines such as feminism, as dramatic. The characters are regarded as fully aware *dramatis personae* and performers (including the protagonist, God), and both performative syntax and lexis are seen as stage instructions and markers for scenic divisions, decor, costumes, extra-scenic reality, and so on, yet without denying their religious and transcendental imports.

One of the symptoms typifying the break with mobilized-tendentious conceptions of Hebrew theatre is the increasing particularism in research as it asserts itself in the exploration of specific genres rather than in historical mega-trends. A case in point is Alexander (1985), where he delineates the emergence of 'destructive' satire, its confrontations with official censorship, and final victory over it. The study itself, however, with its emphasis on the indispensability of Saturnalian and obscene elements in Israeli satire (ibid. 23–6), is the epistemological correlative of the empirical transition from the earlier affirmative satire of Ephraim Kishon and his colleagues in the 1950s and early 1960s, to the 'Sabra satire which sets out to examine the very foundations of this reality' (ibid. 70)—a transition highlighted by Hanoch Levin's political revues as a protest against the euphoric social climate after the Six Day War.

Whereas Alexander still appropriates a universal generic vocabulary (in his introduction, which outlines a synoptic poetics of satire), generic research in recent years betrays a subliminal subversive tenor, attesting first and foremost to renunciation of the past mute commitment to Hebrew drama and theatre. One of the last vestiges of this commitment is Ben-Ami Feingold's recent generic-historical-receptionist book, which admits to swimming against the prevailing 'subversive, critical, or so called "postmodern" currents' (Feingold 2001: 9). In his 1998 study, Gideon Shunami of Bar-Ilan University examines the most popular genre on the reality-addicted Israeli stage—the docudrama—as applied to the Holocaust, while focusing, as empirical examples, on the canonical Soviet, German, and American paradigms (Shunami 1998). Avraham Oz, the first Chair of the new Theatre Department of Haifa University and a renowned Shakespearean scholar representing the extreme left in Israeli criticism, is more explicit in his reservations against Israeli theatre. Striving to define 'the links between the theatrical event and the ceremonial and symbolic level of political events in reality' (Oz 1999: 11–12)—according to thematic-ideological parameters such as 'The Conserving Theatre', 'The Arousing Theatre', and 'The Prophetic Theatre'—Oz confines his references to Israeli theatre to the short preface and the epilogue, in which he elucidates the difficulties of the local dramaturgy in coming to grips with the dire consequences of the local dramatist's uneasy preoccupation with the Ur-myths of Israeli society—annihilation and revival. Oz contends that 'Theatre-making [in Israel has become] a function of...marketing calculations...', and 'the ideational-aesthetic value is no more relevant...'. Consequently, 'the local theatrical reality has neutralized the danger of doing injustice to a discourse, whose main issue are the ceremonies of Israeli reality, on stage as well as in politics and in the media'. (ibid. 10–11).

This transcendence of ideological-thematic criticism encouraged the development of novel methodologies, mostly interdisciplinary and intertextual, in the field of theatrical and textual interpretation, as exemplified by a collection of studies in honour of Moshe Lazar, edited by Nurit Yaari (2000). Lazar was the founder of the Tel Aviv Faculty of the Arts. This anthology offers new approaches and research subjects expounded by the university's theatre scholars: the hermeneutic interrela-tions of visual art and theatre (Ahuva Belkin); cinematic transposition of drama (Hadassa Shani); creative interpretation (Eli Rozik); applied dramaturgy (Gad Kaynar); casting as an interpretative means (Tom Lewy); comparative dramatology (Nurit Yaari). If Israeli theatre is discussed at all in this publication, it is only as a sustaining means to universally applicable theoretical ends.

The diminishing role of Israeli theatre as an ideological agent, along with the diversification of theatrical and para-theatrical activity, has not yet found its corresponding counter-formulation in research. Only a meagre and random corpus of publications reflects these empirical developments. In this category one should mention two works by Yossi Alfi (Alfi 1983, 1986), both focusing on one of Israel's most unique theatrical phenomena, issuing from the country's multi-cultural society with its distinct socio-economic stratification; Amir Orian's book (Orian 1989), offering an alternative method for instructing actors, and thus also being one of the few Hebrew publications on experimental theatre; or *Psychodrama* by Eynia Artzi (1991), which reflects the ever-growing interest in Moreno's teachings and in therapeutical theatre practices in general. Dan Redler's book (Redler 1992) is, astonishingly enough, the only work in Hebrew on any technical aspect of the theatrical apparatus, despite the high competence of Israeli theatre craftsmen in this field, not to mention the fact that directing, stage, costume, and lighting design are taught at both Tel Aviv and Haifa universities, as well as at the Kibbutzim College of Education.

The ground-breaking publications on Theatre in Education are exceptional in this context of meagre output of publications in the field of applied and instrumen-tal theatrical practices. This is mainly due to the efforts of Shifra Shonmann, head of the Laboratory for Research in Drama and Theatre in Education at Haifa University, and Dan Urian, who for years headed the Theatre in Education programme of Oranim College, and joined the School of Education and the Department of Theatre Studies at Tel Aviv University several years ago (Schonmann 1995; Urian *et al.* 1996).

Owing to the short history of Israeli theatre and Hebrew drama, there was a distinct lack of scientifically disposed studies in this field until the 1990s. A number of publications—memoirs, memorabilia, monographs, lexical reports, biblio-graphic lists of artists and plays, and compilations of impressionist journalistic essays—rendered a significant contribution to the understanding of partial phe-nomena and circumscribed periods in the annals of performative and dramatic chronology. However, no comprehensive or systematic attempts to present an academically sustained historiography were made. Zara Shakow's *The Theatre in Israel* (1963), the work of an American amateur theatre director predominantly associated with kibbutz performances in the 1950s and early 1960s, is a typical example of these sporadic and segmental enterprises. The short book (143 pages) is an ambitious but unscholarly and somewhat biased overview of various aspects of

Israeli theatre of that period, some of which remained unmentioned in later studies, such as the *Telem* movement (Theatre for New Immigrants), the short-lived Children Theatre companies of the State's early decades, and so on. In contrast to Shakow's book, Yaffe *et al.* (1964) regards theatre as an exclusively high-culture mainstream art with predominantly sociological functions. The patronizing and didactic attitude of the contributors—critics Haim Glikstein, Boaz Evron, Mendel Kohansky, and Lea Goldberg; actors Yehoshua Bertonov and Miriam Bernstein-Cohen; and the director Yossef Milo—is prefigured by the editors' introductory remark that they are striving to bring the theatre closer to the broad audience, and the public to the theatre, as well as by the publication's eclectic structure, which ranges from general questions of repertory and the state of local drama addressed to the 'uninitiated', to banal and gossipy interviews with actors.

Mendel Kohansky, former theatre critic of Israel's influential English newspaper *the Jerusalem Post*, ventured a first attempt of its kind to provide a synoptic and complete chronicle of the Hebrew theatre (Kohansky 1969). The book, like the publications on the history of Israeli theatre that followed it in the 1990s, was first published in English, which betrays the Anglophone orientation of Israeli theatre and theatre research in the context of their self-depreciative subjugation to the hegemony of foreign cultures. Kohansky disclosed his journalistic disposition, as well as the testimonial, 'oral history' approach of the book, by admitting that the material was based on 'contacts with many men and women of all three generations of the Hebrew theatre' (ibid. p. x). The survey, covering the period from the establishment of Habimah in 1917 to the end of the 1960s (in the English version; the Hebrew edition continues to 1973), is meticulous, yet mostly uncritical and bereft of any serious attempt to classify and analyse the data, to point out generic attributes and intertextual links, or to explore the socio-aesthetic contextualization of the facts. Yet precisely for this reason the book manages to avoid the pitfall of overlooking aesthetics for the sake of delving into ideological themes, and for the first time presents a kind of module, which reflects the prevailing hierarchy of theatre institutions and practice in reality and phenomenological reality-convention. Thus, for instance, it excludes the thriving activity on the independent fringe scene both in the pre-State period and in the 1950s and 1960s, except where this is shown to have influenced the mainstream (ibid. 178–87).

Linda Ben-Zvi's book *Theater in Israel* (Ben-Zvi ed. 1996) is the first compendium of articles to explore the multifaceted world of dramatic and theatrical activity in Israel from an epistemological perspective, intending 'to investigate the historical, ideological, political, sociological, cultural and aesthetic background of Israeli theater by drawing together scholars, theater critics, playwrights, directors and actors from the Jewish and Arab communities' (ibid. 8). The uniqueness of this book, again written in English and published outside of Israel, also asserts itself in the fact that almost every methodological approach and mode represented in it professes the performative idiom and orientation of current theatrical research in

Israel, without thereby dispensing with the inevitable awareness of ethnic, socio-logical, political, and ideological considerations.

The book is divided into five parts. Shosh Avigal and Freddie Rokem provide the necessary socio-historical co-ordinates within which subsequent insights into spe-cific issues can be accommodated. Avigal's survey of Israeli theatre development and structure is based on the thesis (which underlies most of the book's essays) that, in an inverted relation to universal practice, 'traditionally, Israeli drama has concerned itself with the themes of national identity. Individual problems were seen as only a reflection of collective values... the political is the norm' (ibid. 9–10). Rokem, in his account of the evolution of theatre in Eretz Israel (Palestine), complements this view by maintaining that from a Zionist point of view the pragmatic functions of theatre dominated at the expense of its aesthetic function: 'This theater had to find the means to change the regnant image of Jewish life and the Jew as well as developing its own artistic resources, starting with a form of the Hebrew language that would actually be spoken on the stage and also understood by the spectators...' (ibid. 52). Similar socio-theatrical and historiographic perspectives are manifested in the narrower and more segmental explorations in this part: Gershon Shaked traces the theatrical and societal evolution through the shifting images of the actors, or rather actresses, who incarnated the spectators' ideals, and the late Shoshana Weitz provided a critical summary of a sociological study of the Israeli theatre in 1990, commissioned by the Center for Cultural Research and Information, an organ that up to its closure in the late 1990s offered an efficient and accurate source of data about Israeli theatrical activity, organization, repertory, financial resources, infra-structure, and audience attendance. This data stimulated a series of official reports and articles commissioned by the government, by S. Avigal, S. Weitz, Giora Rahav, Gita Seltzer, and others in other publications, reflecting the growing emphasis given by contemporary Israeli theatre, as compared to its inceptive years, to production value, entertainment and commercialization.

Part 2, the analytic section, attempts to create a canon of Israeli dramatists by focusing on the work of the prominent playwright trio, Nissim Aloni (ibid. 119–32, 133–50), Hanoch Levin (ibid. 151–72, 173–200), and Yehoshua Sobol (ibid. 201–4)—thus relegating other important dramatists (such as Yosef Bar-Yosef, Shmuel Hasfari, Ilan Hatzor, Danny Horowitz, Miriam Kainy, Shulamit Lapid, Motti Lerner, Edna Mazia, and Hillel Mittelpunkt) to an inferior ranking. It is nevertheless a noteworthy homage to Israeli drama, since several of these dramatists had never before attracted any scholarly attention, and even the leading triumvirate has merited only a few full-scale studies. Only one book—by the late journalist Moshe Nathan (Nathan 1996)—deals exclusively with Aloni's self-referential and allusive drama. The uncontested bard of Israeli theatre, Hanoch Levin, has to this very day been granted only one comprehensive study, by the journalist, poet, and theatre lecturer Haim Nagid. Nagid scrutinizes Levin's biography and analyses most of the plays performed in his lifetime, challenging the prevailing view that Levin 'always writes the same play' by showing that, although one can detect a deep structure that underlies the *opus magnum*, 'each play creates its own idiosyncratic uniqueness through a non recurring blend of subject, plot, structure and stylistic texture' (Nagid 1998: 8). Several books on the thirty-years career of Levin are in preparation (by Avraham Oz, Yitzchak Laor, and the editors Shimon Levy and Nurit Yaari), but for the time being only one additional collection has been published: a compilation of reviews on Levin productions by the *Haaretz* critic Michael Handelsaltz (Handelsaltz 2001). The voluminous work of Yehoshua Sobol, despite its compass, its controversial political intent/content, the large body of articles in which it has been discussed, and the broad international recognition that it has won, has not yielded even a single published study in Hebrew (in contrast to German, for instance). This meagre harvest betrays, more than anything else, the paradoxical situation of Hebrew drama between spectatorial popularity and the gradually disappearing Jewish and academic mistrust of the theatrically designated text.

Part 3 of Ben-Zvi's 1996 collection discusses specific themes and strategies, and foregrounds the socio-aesthetic approach that has become the typical hallmark of Israeli theatrical research due to the relations of symbiosis, interpolation, interaction, and mutual dependence prevailing between Israeli society and histrionic art. Dan Urian—undoubtedly the most prolific, erudite, and consistent representative of this school—attempts a sociological reading ('sociocritique') of dramatic and theatrical texts dealing with the fragile, vulnerable, historically and phenomenologically burdened relationship between the Jewish majority and the Arab/Palestinian minority. The article is a prolegomenon to Urian's 1996 book (Urian 1996a), which explores dramatic texts from the early days of Jewish settlement in Palestine, depicting the Arab persona as both exotically attractive and ominous, through various stages of its characterization as 'a comic figure in Israeli theatre, an undermined character, mainly because of the negligible position of the "Arab Question" on the Israeli society's agenda', until the early 1990s, the period of the first *Intifada* and the Oslo Accord, in which 'the depiction of the Arab as a realistic character reveals a shift from an ethnocentric and stereotypical approach to an acknowledgement of the "other", and an attempt to deal with his humanity' (Urian 1996b: 12) Urian pursues the same socio-aesthetic and ethnocentric approach in a later work (Urian 1998).

Ben-Ami Feingold (Feingold 1996) discerns the strategies that enable the spectator to come to grips with universal moral questions raised by the Holocaust, while abstaining from realistic depictions that tend to desecrate the sanctity of the event. The sacred position of the Holocaust in Israeli consciousness accounts for the fact that Feingold's (1989) and Barzel's (1995) are the only Hebrew books dedicated to the dramatic representation of the Holocaust. Only fairly recently, along with the performative vogue (launched by Dudi Mayan's 'sacrilegious' *Arbeit macht frei MiToitland Europa* at the Acco Theatre Center, 1991) of strategically profaning the Holocaust in order to thereby criticize its perverting effect on the Israeli psyche and ethos, have we begun to encounter in Israeli research an emerging counter-trend of dealing in provocative analytic and ideological terms with the *stage* representation of the Holocaust (see e.g. Rokem 2000: 56–76). This new direction, however, is still confined to articles published in German and English anthologies such as *Nach der Shoah: Israelisch-deutsche Theaterbeziehungen seit 1949* (Bayerdörfer 1996), and *Staging the Holocaust* (Schumacher 1998), including, among others, a small group of Israeli scholars (Shimon Levy, Freddie Rokem, Lea Hadomi, Dan Laor, Jeanette R. Malkin, and Gad Kaynar). Kaynar relativizes the performative manifestations of the Holocaust by presenting them as a shifting, socio-politically bound factor engendering a series of 'stations' in the development of Israeli Holocaust theatre, thus leading to the conclusion that we are actually dealing with Holocausts (that is, 'Holocausts' in the plural) drama (Kaynar 1996b: 200–16). This approach is pre-figured in his seminal article in *Theater in Israel*: ' "Get Out of the Picture, Kid in a Cap": On the Interaction of the Israeli Drama and Reality Convention' (Ben-Zvi ed. 1996: 285–301). Kaynar claims that due to the vital significance of the theatre for the still fluctuant communal identity and deficient existential self-justification of Israeli society, as a pluralistic ethnic conglomerate of 'immigrants, who are always on the verge of becoming potential emigrants' (ibid. 298), the relations between the performance of Israeli drama and Israeli reality conventions may be described as those of reciprocal generation.

Theater in Israel also distinguishes itself in respect of dealing with gender in Israeli drama and histrionics, as well as with the position of woman as the 'Other' in a patriarchal society on and off stage. Shosh Avigal's polemic essay on gendered stereotypes in Israeli society as reflected in local drama, is supplemented by her interview, in Part 5 of the book, with the militant playwright Miriam Kainy (ibid. 355–60). Avigal's article is a harbinger of a growing interest in women's theatre and feminist reading of Israeli drama and performance by female researchers such as Erella Brown, Jeanette R. Malkin, Dorit Yerushalmi, Sharon Aharonson-Lehavi, Orly Hatzor, Karin Heskia, and others. The problem of women in Israeli society and theatre is associated with the representation of the largest 'Others' sector in Israeli society, namely the Palestinians. Their voice was heard only in one previous book (Horowitz 1993), where Arab actresses Bushra Qaraman, Siham Gazala, and Iman Aoun refer to their dual, ethno-gendered stigmatization, in the context of a sympo-sium with over forty scholars and practitioners of Palestinian theatre and drama. This symposium attempted to correct another deficiency in Israeli theatre scholar-ship: the absence of live depth-interviews with dramatists and stage artists, which *Theater in Israel*'s final chapter attempts to rectify by enabling dramatists Danny Horowitz, Miriam Kainy, and Yehoshua Sobol, directors Nola Chilton, Rina Yer-ushalmi, and Yossi Yzraely, actor Muhammad Bakri, and dramaturg Katya Sosonsky to express their views and present their work.

The Israeli-British scholar Glenda Abramson's *Drama and Ideology in Modern Israel* (a sequel to her 1979 book) reinstates the once-predominant extra-aesthetic thesis that 'Hebrew drama perpetuated its original function within the social debate, both as a reflection of and an "active intervention" in Israeli social and political life' (Abramson 1998: 10). In accordance with her left-wing stance, Abramson tendentiously subordinates the aesthetic and rhetorical layers of the syntagmatically-diachronically propounded Hebrew drama to ideological and thematic deliberations. She returns to the anachronistic content–form dichotomy by admitting that she is more concerned 'with what the playwrights are saying than their manner of saying it' (ibid. 12). It is thus hardly surprising that the playwright to whom she accords disproportionally painstaking attention is the most ideologically minded of Israeli dramatists, Yehoshua Sobol. Thus, the old *dybbuk* of enlisted, 'message'-haunted dramatic criticism still seems to pursue certain scholars of Israeli theatre history, even after it had apparently been overcome by more cosmopolitan, intertextual, and performatively oriented approaches.

The articles by Shimon Lev-Ari, director of the Israeli Documentation Center for the Performing Arts at Tel Aviv University, offer authoritative sources for the socio-historiography of the Hebrew pre-State and Israeli theatre. They appear in Shavit (1999), a work considered to be a highly reliable and updated source for Israeli historiography, presenting the top scholars in each field. Lev-Ari renders a heuristically structured and extremely well-documented summary of the development of theatre in the pre-State years (to be completed in additional volumes of this vast oeuvre). The scrutiny comprises, *inter alia,* subjects that have rarely been treated before, such as: 'The Audience—Its Range and Stratification' (ibid. 365–6), 'The Professional Standing of Actors and Directors' (ibid. 435), and 'The Development of the Secondary Theater, 1928–1948' (ibid. 593–617).

To date, very few historical or historiographic studies on specific theatrical institutes in Israel have appeared, although Israel's statehood years have witnessed the publication of anniversary books on the major theatres at regular ten-year interval. As the national theatre, Habimah has naturally been accorded the most *Festbücher,* although only a handful of these Hebrew publications can be regarded as being of scientific value. The first of these was published in 1937, edited by the theatre's ardent chronologist Gershon Hanoch. Published on the theatre's twentieth anniversary, the main merit of this informative book, which outlines Habimah's short annals and provides a list of its repertoire, lies in the authentic reflection of the programmatic perspective of the theatre in its early years. In a sequel, Hanoch introduces a semi-epistemological approach by presenting his survey in subdivisions: (a) The Beginning; (b) Existential Conditions; (c) Method and Style; (d) Organization and the Collective; (e) The Repertory Problem (Hanoch 1946). Ben-Ari's *Habimah* (1957), written by one of the theatre's founders (who stayed behind in the United States), differs from most of the numerous memoirs offered by the institution's veterans, in furnishing the reader with a consequential analysis of the theories and implementation of the theatre's renowned first directors. Emanuel Levy's study (Levy 1979) is the first academic endeavour to account for the political,

ideological, and artistic roles of Habimah over a span of sixty years. Levy's somewhat outmoded socio-theatrical methodology sees the master-key for the artistic
course of the theatre in the unequivocal belief that 'the institutional setting shaped
not only the activities and organization of the Habima, but also the content that it
presented' (ibid. p. xvii). Levy offers detailed and well-documented information
about crucial turning-points that shaped the history of the theatre, such as the
company's pragmatic vacillation, in its formative years, between Jewish and Russian
identity. He also contextualizes the theatre's history and characteristics by comparing Habimah with its rivals (the Yiddish theatre movement, the Ohel, and the
Cameri Theatre). Haim Shoham analyses Habimah's repertory according to the
criteria of reception analysis, aimed at proving the thesis that as long as Habimah
fostered the Jewish subject, 'the theatre stood in the center of national revival.…
However, once the "normal", universal wave, based on the assumption that there is
nothing unique about the Jewish subject, takes the upper hand, the theatre turns
into an entertainment stage, and its negotiation with the audience is no longer
sustained by that historical partnership' (Shoham 1989c: 83).

   To date there has been no full-scale study of the first workers' theatre, Ohel. In this
context the autobiography of Moshe Halevy, one of Habimah's founders and
entrepreneur of the Ohel (Halevy 1955), acquires special importance as a source of
unique first-hand data and ideologically imbued insights concerning the two
pioneering professional Hebrew theatres. It is complemented by the work edited
by Y. Gabai (1983), the theatre's veteran actor, fourteen years after the theatre's
closure. Its special contribution consists in providing a comprehensive list of the
actors, other artists, and even—in accordance with the company's extreme socialist
outlook—stagehands and wardrobe staff, who had been active in the theatre since
its foundation in 1925. A rare contribution to the study of the aesthetics of the early
Hebrew theatre is Norman (1931). This is evidently the earliest instance of performance analysis of a Hebrew production in Hebrew. Norman analyses Halevy's expressionist production of *Jacob and Rachel* in minute detail, describing the geometrics of
the mis-en-scène and decor, depicting the acting (delving even into the subtleties of
intonation and vocal inflexion), commending the Israeli aroma of the Hebrew
translation by A. Shlonsky, and pondering over lighting issues. The reflections of
the composer, S. Rosovsky on the Bible as inspiration for theatre music round off
this edifying and unique booklet. Half-a-century later (1983), Haim Shoham analysed in the same vein *Batia*, a paradigmatic 1940 stage adaptation at the Ohel of an
Israeli short story, dealing with a prototype of a Zionist settlement during the
Second *Aliya* period. Shoham's innovative study combines a semiotic and theatrically minded approach with a historic orientation and a consideration of the
aesthetic and extra-aesthetic norms of the times.

   Privileged with two volumes professing modern theatrical rather than literary
approaches, the Cameri Theatre of Tel Aviv fared better than its predecessors as an
object of academic study. The somewhat self-flattering, superficial, and non-reflex-

ive works of Tamuz (Tamuz 1958) and Alfi (1984), were followed in the 1990s by two anthologies that marked a clear transition in the methodology of historiographic writing on the Israeli theatre: Meshulach (1997) and Kaynar *et al.* (1999), based on the proceedings of a conference organized by the Theatre Department of Tel-Aviv University in 1994. The nostalgic approach of the past is toned down and counterpoised in these compilations through what Rokem (after Uri Rapp) defines as 'touristic' distance (Kaynar *et al.* 1999: 1–2), and by a polyphonic and eclectic interplay of differently oriented scholars exploring various aspects of the activity of the theatre—primarily regarded as a typical *Stadttheater* rather than as a vehicle for transporting socio-political messages—in all its artistic, administrative, technical, and receptionist complexity.

Gad Kaynar's historical chapter in the Meshulach collection (Kaynar 1997) argues—and elaborates in the subsequent publication—that the Cameri's revolt consisted in its policy of 'conformity relevance', reflected in the repertory's shifting attitudes towards the theatre's target audience in unison with the changes in Israeli society over the years. Avraham Oz scrutinizes the Shakespearean repertory of the Cameri throughout its existence, reifying the organic integration of the canon within the artistic agenda through the transition from 'reverend' interpretations in the 1950s (such as Milo's *As You Like It* and *Romeo and Juliet*) to a free interpretive play, with abundant local allusions and actual references, in the 1990s (in Omri Nitzan's political *The Merchant of Venice*, and Rina Yerushalmi's postmodern *Romeo and Juliet*). Elyakim Yaron demonstrates how the indigenous dramaturgy affected the entire image of the evolving Israeli reality, while Emanuel Ben-Amos's article on *He Walked in the Fields in 1948* (Ben-Amos 1997) substantiates this general observation through a work-in-process analysis of the seminal native-born play. Shimon Levy rounds up this line of exemplified reasoning by ascribing to the Cameri the role of moulding Israeli identity as much as being moulded by it. Lighting designer and theatre architect Ben-Zion Munitz, explores the degree to which the physical configuration of the stages dictated the types of scenographic spaces used in Cameri productions in relation to the textually intrinsic dramatic spaces. Shosh Weitz pursues this trend of breaking new analytic ground by presenting extra-conceptual issues in her article on the Cameri as municipal theatre. Weitz reaches the pessimistic conclusion that the Cameri has lost its artistic and ideological autonomy, not because of any censorial intervention of the city, but because of the immense changes that took place in the engulfing theatrical and cultural scene during the period under scrutiny (1970–95). As an appendix the editor provides a full register of the Cameri theatre's productions from 1944 to 1996.

Kaynar *et al.* (1999) is by and large constituted on the same structural principles, and divided into three capital sections—History and Policy; Works, Artists, and Genres; and the City, the Theatre, and the Audience—yet it probes in a more differentiated manner into particular topics. These include socio-artistic and repertory questions, such as the ideological aesthetics of the theatre (Corina Shoef), the anatomy of the Cameri's 1958 crisis and recovery (Kaynar and Rokem), and a thesis concerning the extreme moderation of the Cameri's repertory (Shimon Levy); discussions on distinct stylistic trends: children theatre (Razi Amitai), the musical at the Cameri (Dan Almagor), and the ideological selection and interpretation of the classics on the Cameri stage (Bilha Bloom); explorations of spatial and visual aspects: the techno-aesthetic significance of the theatre's transition from one venue to the other (Ben-Zion Munitz), and the visual iconography of Ruth Dar, the designer of Hanoch Levin's productions at the Cameri (Orna Ben Meir); analyses of performances and directing syntax: an interpretation of Levin's *Mouth Open* (Shimon Levy), and an interview with Rina Yerushalmi, Israel's leading alternative *auteur*, who in the 1990s occupied the theatre's experimental niche (Eli Rozik); as well as a socio-urban reading of the municipal theatre as a communal theatre (Peter Harris).

The increasing number of bibliographies and anthologies of Hebrew theatre and drama emphasizes the thriving theatrical activity and the extent of theatre research in Israel. Ruth Klinger's study (Klinger 1946) is a first and unique attempt to survey the creative artists of pre-State Israel, and altogether includes 600 annotated entries; Avraham Adar (1980) pursues this endeavour from a retrospective and more synoptic viewpoint. The most authoritative bibliographies of Hebrew dramaturgy are: Avraham Yaari (1957); Michael Wilf (1969), which lists the plays in chronological order of performance, and provides invaluable information (including otherwise inaccessible materials), such as reviews, discussions, and previews in daily newspapers; Ezra Lahad's systematic bibliography of original and translated Hebrew drama (Lahad 1989); and Weil (2000), which is the first publication of its kind to appear in English. Shimon Levy and Corina Shoef's forthcoming publication (Levy and Shoef 2002) reveals the maturation of Hebrew drama, and includes synopses, production data, and criticism. The two major anthologies of Israeli drama in English translation are S. Herbert Joseph (1983), which includes the plays *He Walked in the Fields*, *The First Sin*, *Difficult People*, *The Night of the Twentieth*, *Cherli Ka Cherli*, and *Naim*; and Michael Taub (1993), which comprises *The Sorrows of Job*, *Jewish Soul*, *The American Princess*, *Possessions*, *Difficult People*, and *Buba*.

SUGGESTED READING

In the field of Jewish Theatre Studies, see Belkin (1997 and 2002); Gorin (1929); Schiffer (1923); Schirmann (1979); Shatski (1930); Shmeruk (1979); and Zylbercweig (1959). For Israeli Theatre Studies, see Abramson (1979); Ben-Zvi (1996); Joseph (1983); Kaynar *et al.* (1999); Kohansky (1969); E. Levy (1979); S. Levy (2000); Ofrat (1980); Rokem (2000); Shaked (1970); Taub (1993); Urian (1998); and Weil (2000).

BIBLIOGRAPHY

ABRAMSON, G. 1979. *Modern Hebrew Drama*. London.

——1998. *Drama and Ideology in Modern Israel*. Cambridge.

ADAR, A. 1980. 'Teatronim, Lahkot, Sachkanim uVamaim' (Theatres, Companies, Actors and Directors). In *The First Twenty Years: Literature and Arts in Tel-Aviv 1909–1929*. 51–99. A. B. Yaffe ed. Tel Aviv.

ALEXANDER, D. 1985. *Leitzan heChatzer vehaShalit* (The Jester and the King; Political Satire in Israel: A Temporary Summary 1948–1984). Tel Aviv.

ALFI, Y. 1983. *HaTeatron haKehilati* (The Community Theatre). Jerusalem.

——1984. *Arbaim Shana laTeatron haCameri* (The Cameri at Forty). Tel Aviv and Ramat-Gan.

——1986. *Teatron uKehila* (Theatre and Community: Methods in the Application of Community Theatre). Jerusalem.

ALMAGOR, D. 1999. 'HaMachazemer al Bimat haCameri' (The Musical on the Cameri Stage). In Kaynar *et al.* (1999): 103–20.

ALTSHULER, M. ed. 1966. *Di Yidishe Teater in Sovietnfarband*. Jerusalem.

AMITAI, R. 1999. 'HaTeatron liYeladim sheleyad haTeatron haCameri' (The Cameri's Children Theatre). In Kaynar *et al.* (1999): 121–9.

ARTZI, E. 1991. *Psychodrama*. [Hebrew] Tel Aviv.

AVIGAL, S. 1969. 'Patterns and Trends in Israeli Drama and Theater, 1948 to Present.' In Ben-Zvi (1996): 9–50.

AVISAR, S. 1996. *HaMachaze vehaTeatron halVri vehaldi* (A History of Hebrew and Yiddish Theatre). Jerusalem.

BARZEL, H. 1995. *Drama shel Matzavim Kitzoniyim* (Drama of Extreme Situations). Tel Aviv.

BAYERDÖRFER, H. P. ed. 1996. *Nach der Shoah: Israelisch-deutsche Theaterbeziehungen seit 1949*. [German and English] Theatralia Judaica II. Tübingen.

BELKIN, A. 1985. 'Habit de Fou in Purim Spiel?' *Assaph* Sec. C, 2: 40–55.

——1997. 'Citing Scripture for a Purpose—The Jewish Purimspiel as a Parody.' *Assaph* C, No. 12.

——ed. 1997. *Leone de' Sommi and the Performing Arts*. Tel Aviv.

——2000. '*Ut Pictura Theatrum*: Adoration of the Magi by Leonardo da Vinci.' In Yaari ed. (2000): 115–34.

——2002. *The Purimspiel—Studies in the Jewish Folk Theatre* [Hebrew]. Jerusalem.

BEN-AMOS, E. 1997. '*Hu Halach baSsadot* be-1948: "Shchol, Zikaron veNechama"' (*He Went in the Fields* in 1948: 'Bereavement, Memory and Consolation'). In Meshulach (1997): 141–5.

BEN-ARI, R. 1957. *Habimah* [Hebrew]. New York.

BEN MEIR, O. 1999. 'Ikonografia Chazutit baAvodata shel Ruth Dar leMachazotav shel Chanoch Levin' (Visual Iconography in Ruth Dar's Work on Hanoch Levin's Plays). In G. Kaynar *et al.* eds. (1999) 155–62.

BEN-ZVI, L. ed. 1996. *Theater in Israel*. Ann Arbor, Mich.

BERTONOV, J. 1969. *Orot miBaad laMassach* (Light Behind the Curtain). Tel Aviv.

——*et al.* eds. 1962. *Menachem Binyamini—Korotav VeTafkidav* (Menachem Binyamini—His Biography and Roles). Tel Aviv.

BIALIK, H. N. 1933. 'Darchei haTeatron HaIvri' (The Paths of the Hebrew Theatre). *Bamah* 2: 3–13.

BLUM, B. 1999. 'Sipur shel Hissardut: haBechira vehaParshanut shel Machazaut Kanonit' (A Survival Story: The Choice and Interpretation of Canonical Drama). In Kaynar *et al.* (1999): 131–42.

BROWN, E. 1996. 'Politics of Desire: Brechtian "Epic Theater" in Hanoch Levin's Postmodern Satire.' In Kaynar *et al.* (1999): 173–200.

BUKHVALD, N. 1943. *Teater*. New York.

DAVID, Y. 1972. *Moses Hayyim Luzzatto's Plays*. Jerusalem.

DUVSHANI, M. 1945. 'A Bibliography of Hebrew Drama in the Enlightenment Period.' *Bamah* (Aug.).

ELDAD-SHEIB, I. 1961. 'HaTanach KiDrama' (The Bible as Drama). *Bamah* 64: 9–14.

ERIK, M. 1928. *Die geshikhte fun der Yidisher literatur fun di eltste zeitn biz der Haskala tkufah.* Warsaw.

ERNST, S. 1930. 'Textn un kveln zu der geshikhte fun teater' farveilungen un maskeraden bi yidn.' In Shatsky (1930): i. 1–37.

EVEN-SHOSHAN, S. ed. 1958. *Ina Govinska-Baratz, al bamat hateatron* (Ina Govinska-Baratz, on the Theatre's Stage). Tel Aviv.

FEINGOLD, B. A. 1989. *Hashoah bateatron hayissraeli* (The Theme of the Holocaust In Hebrew Drama). Tel Aviv.

—— 1996. 'Hebrew Holocaust Drama as a Modern Morality Play.' [Hebrew.] In Ben-Zvi (1996): 269–83.

—— 1999. 'The Cameri Theatre—The Beginning.' In Kaynar *et al.* (1999): 9–24.

—— 2001. *Tashach baTeatron* (Israeli Theatre and the 1948 War of Independence). Tel Aviv.

FICHMAN, Y. 1936. 'On Classical Theatre.' [Hebrew]. *Bamah* 1–12: 8.

—— 1941. 'Liveayat haMachaze haMekori ('On the Problem of Original Drama'). *Bamah* 31: 3–4.

FINKEL, S. 1968. *Bama uKlaim* (On Stage and Backstage: Autobiography of an Actor). Tel Aviv.

—— 1971. *Bimevoch Tafkidai* (In the Maze of My Roles). Tel Aviv.

—— 1976. *Beshulei hassach hakol: livetei Shlichut Omantutit* (Marginal Notes). Tel Aviv.

—— 1977. *Gilgulim: Leket miNof haKrashim'* (Transformations). Tel Aviv.

—— 1978. *Hannah Rovina*. Tel Aviv.

—— 1980. *Aharon Meskin veAgadat 'haGolem'* (Aharon Meskin and 'The Golem' Legend). Tel Aviv.

—— 1984. *'Sof Mischak'* (Endgame). Tel Aviv.

—— 1985. *Nitzozot: Dyokan uDemuyot* (Sparks: A Profile and Characters). Tel Aviv.

—— 1993. *Hashlamot: Otobiographia—Hemshech* (Supplements—An Autobiography—Continuation). Tel Aviv.

GABAI, Y. ed. 1983. *Teatron 'Ohel'—Sipur haMaasse* ('Ohel'—The Plot). Tel Aviv.

GAI, C. 1995. *HaMalka Nassah baOtobus: Rovina vehaBimah* (Hanna Rovina). Tel Aviv.

GNESSIN, M. 1946. *Darki im haTeatron haIvri: 1905–1926* (My Way with the Hebrew Theatre: 1905–1926). Tel Aviv.

GOLDBERG, A. 1961. *Unzer dramaturgie—Leinbuch in Yidisen Drame*. New York.

GOLDBERG, L. 1951. *Problems of the Hebrew Theatre*. Bamot.

GOLDFADEN, A. 1972. *Oisgeklibene Shriftn*. Buenos Aires.

GORIN, B. 1929. *Di geshikhte fun yidishn teater*. New York.

GUR, I. 1957. *HaMessachakim Evion vaMelech* (The Players of Beggar and King). Jerusalem.

—— 1958a. *Actors in the Hebrew Theatre*. Jerusalem.

——1958b. *HaTeatron haIvri—Tziyunei Derech.* (The Hebrew Theatre—Landmarks). Tel Aviv.

——1961. *Pinkas Teatroni* (A Theatrical Notebook). Jerusalem.

——1965. *Demuyot baTatron haIvri* (Figures in the Hebrew Theater). Jerusalem.

——1968. *Maamad Tarbuti laTeatron beYissrael* (A Cultural Status for the Theatre in Israel). Jerusalem.

——1970. *Nofei Sifrut veTarbut: Massot uRezshimot* (Vistas in Literature and Culture). Jerusalem.

——1982. *Pirkei haMachaze haMekori beYissrael* (Chapters on Original Israeli Drama). *Bamah* 91–2.

HALEVY, M. 1955. *Darki alei Bamot* (My Way on Stages). Tel Aviv.

HANDELSALTZ, M. 2001. *Hanoch Levin alpi Darko* (The Theatre of Hanoch Levin). Tel Aviv.

HANOCH, G. 1937. '*Habima*': *Theatron Ivri beEretz-Yissrael* ('Habimah': A Hebrew Theatre in Eretz-Israel). Tel Aviv.

——1946. *Habimah Bat Kaf-He* (Habima at 25; Historical Highlights). Tel Aviv.

HARRIS, P. 1999. 'Teatron Ironi keTeatron Kehilati' (Municipal Theatre as Community Theatre). In Kaynar *et al.* (1999): 183–92.

HIRSHHOYT, Y. 1971. 'Di Historiker Funem Yidishn Teater.' In Manger, Turkov, and Perenson (1968).

HOROWITZ, D. 1993. *Kemo Gesher Takua* (Like a Troubled Bridge: Conversations with the actors Muhammad Bakri, Salwa Nakkara-Haddad, Makram Khuri, Khawlah Haj and Salim Daw). Raanana.

JACOBSON, H. 1983. *The Exagoge of Ezekiel.* Cambridge.

JOSEPH, S. H. 1983. *Modern Israeli Drama: An Anthology.* London and Toronto.

KAMINSKA, I. 1973. *My Life My Theatre.* C. Leviant ed. and trans. New York.

KAYNAR, G. 1996a. ' "Get Out of the Picture, Kid in a Cap": On the Interaction of the Israeli Drama and Reality Convention.' In Ben-Zvi (1996): 285–301.

——1996b. ' "What's Wrong With The Usual Description of the Extermination?!": National Socialism and The Holocaust as a Self-Image Metaphor in Israeli Drama: Aesthetic Conversion of a National Tragedy into Reality-Convention.' In Bayerdörfer ed. (1996): 200–16.

——1997. 'Hateatron haCameri—Chamishim haShana haRishonot' (The Cameri—the First Fifty Years). In Meshulach (1997): 12–31.

——1998. 'National Theatre as Colonized Theatre: The Paradox of Habima.' *Theatre Journal* 50/1: 1–20.

——1999. '*He Walked in the Fields* and its Position in the Israeli Theatre.' *Jewish Studies* 4/39: 67–76. Jerusalem.

——2000. 'Applied Dramaturgy: The Conception behind the Conception.' In Yaari (2000): 221–42.

—— and ROKEM, F. 1999. 'Anatomia shel Mashber veHitosheshut: Sicha im Yaacov Agmon' (Anatomy of Crisis and Recovery). In Kaynar *et al.* (1999): 57–68.

—— —— and ROZIK, R. eds. 1999. *HaCameri: Teatron shel Zeman uMakom* (The Cameri: A Theatre of Time and Place). Tel Aviv.

KLAUSNER, M. 1971. *Yoman Habimah* (The Habimah Diary). Tel Aviv.

KLINGER, R. 1946. *Sefer haOmanut vehaOmanin beEretz-Yissrael* (The Book of Art and Artists in Eretz-Israel). Tel Aviv.

KOHANSKY, M. 1969. *The Hebrew Theatre: Its First Fifty Years.* Jerusalem.

KOBRIN, L. 1925. *Erinerungen fun a yidishn dramaturg: A fertl yarhundert yidish teater i Amerika* (Reminiscences of a Yiddish Dramatist: A Quarter Century of Yiddish Theatre in America). 2 vols. New York.

KURZWEIL, B. 1970. '*Bamaavak al Erchey haYahadut*' (The Struggle for Jewish Values). 3–25. Tel Aviv.

KUTAI, A. 1972. *Hayim uVama* (Life and Stage: 50 Years of Theatre—Memories, Impressions, Methods). Tel Aviv.

LAHAD, E. 1989. *Hamachaze haIvri beMakor uvtargum: Bibliographica* (The Original and Translated Hebrew Play). Jerusalem.

——and WEST, B. eds. 1962. *Menachem Binyamini: Ish haTeatron haIvri* (Menachem Binyamini: Man of the Hebrew Theatre). Tel Aviv.

——— eds. 1970. *Michael Gor.* Tel Aviv.

LEV-ARI, S. 1999. 'Kehal haTzofim—hekefo veribudo' (The Audience—Its Extent and Stratification). In Shavit ed. (1999).

LEVY, E. 1979. *The Habima—Israel's National Theater 1917–1977.* New York.

LEVY, S. 1992. *Mekatrim baBamot* (The Altar and the Stage). Tel Aviv.

——1997. 'Hazehut haYissraelit: haGirssa haCamaerit' (Israeli Identity: The Cameri Version). In Meshulach (1997): 192–6.

——1999. 'HaMetinut haKitzonit: Iyun baRepertuar shel haTeatron haCameri' (Extreme Moderation: A Scrutiny of the Cameri's Repertory). In Kaynar *et al.* (1999): 68–75.

——1999. 'Peurei pe baTeatron (haCameri)' (*Mouth Open* at the [Cameri] Theatre). In Kaynar *et al.* (1999): 143–53.

——ed. 1999. *Theatre and Holy Script.* Brighton.

——2000. *The Bible as Theatre.* Brighton.

——and SHOEF, C. 2002 (forthcoming). *101 Hatzagot Canon haTeatron haYissraeli* (101 Canonical Performances of the Israeli Theatre). Tel Aviv.

LEWY, T. 2000. 'Casting As An Interpretative Means.' In Yaari ed. (2000): 243–56.

MANGER, I. TURKOV, Y., and PERENSON, M. eds. 1968. *Yidisher Teater in Eyrope tsvishn beyde veit milkhomes.* New York.

MAROTTI, F. ed. 1968. *Leone de' Sommi, Quatro Dialoghi in Materia di rappresentazioni sceniche.* Milan.

MELKMAN, J. 1967. 'Moshe Zaccuto's Play "Yesod Olam".' *Studia Rosenthaliana* 2/3.

MESTEL, Y. 1943. *Undzer Teater* (Our Theatre). New York.

MESHULACH, R. ed. 1997. *HaCameri shel Tel Aviv: 50 Shnot Teatron Yissraeli* (The Cameri of Tel Aviv: 50 Years of Israeli Theatre). Tel Aviv.

MUKDOYNI, A. 1927. *Teater.* New York.

——1953. *Shmuesn vegn teater.* Buenos Aires.

MUNITZ, B.-Z. 1997. 'Chalal haBama vehaTechnologia—haHebet haRepertuari' (Stage Space and Technology—The Repertory Aspect). In Meshulach (1997): 197–201.

——1999. 'HaRepertuar haSzenografi: Hashpaat Chalal haBama vehaTechnologia al Itzuv haBama' (The Scenographic Space: The Influence of Stage Space and Technology on the Stage Design). In Kaynar *et al.* (1999): 91–6.

NAHSHON, E. 1998. *Yiddish Proletarian Theatre: The Art and Politics of the Artef, 1925–1940.* Westport, Conn.

NAGID, H. 1998. *Sechok utzmarmoret* (Laughter and Trembling). Tel Aviv.

NATHAN, M. 1996. *Kishuf neged Mavet* (Magic Against Death: The Theatre of Nissim Aloni). Z. Shatzky ed. Tel Aviv.

NORMAN, I. 1931. *Yaacov veRachel baOhel* (Jacob and Rachel at the Ohel). Jerusalem.

——ed. 1966. *Bereshit Habima: Nachum Zemach—Meyassed Habimah beChason uveMaase* (Habima's Genesis: Nachum Zemach Habima's Founder in Vision and Deed). Jerusalem.

OFRAT, G. 1975. *Hadrama haYissraelit* (The Israeli Drama). Herzeliya.

——1980. *Adama, Adam, Dam* (Earth, Man, Blood: The Myth of the Pioneer and the Ritual of Earth in Eretz-Israel Settlement Drama). Tel Aviv.

OYSLENDER, N. 1940. *Yidisher Teater 1887–1917.* Moscow.

ORIAN, A. 1989. *HaMaagal haPatuach* (The Open Circle). Tel Aviv.

OZ, A. 1997. 'Shakespeare baTeatron haCameri' (Shakespeare at the Cameri Theatre). In *Meshulach* (1997): 133–9.

——1999. *HaTeatron haPoliti* (Political Representations in the Theatre: Prejudice, Protest, Prophecy). Tel Aviv.

PAPIRNA, A. J. 1868. *Drama in General and Hebrew Drama in Particular.* Odesa [Hebrew].

PERRY, M. and STERNBERG, M. 1968. 'HaMelech beMabat Ironi'. (An Ironic Look at the King). *Hasifrut* 2: 251–61.

PRILUTSKI, N. 1912. *Zamlbikher far yidishn folklor, filologye un kulturgeshikhte.* Warsaw.

RAHAV, G., WEITZ, S., and SELTZER, G. 1982. *The Development of a New Theatre Audience in Israel: The History and Development of 'Omanut Laam'* [Hebrew]. Tel Aviv.

REDLER, D. 1992. *Teurat Bamah* (Stage Lighting). Tel Aviv.

ROBINS, T. 1986. *Tamar Robins: Sachkanit haBimah* (Tamar Robins: Actress—'Habimah'). Tel Aviv.

ROKEM, F. 1996a. 'Hebrew Theater from 1889 to 1948.' In Ben-Zvi (1996): 50–84.

——1996b. 'Yehoshua Sobol—Between History and the Arts: A Study of *Ghetto* and *Shooting Magda* (*The Palestinian Woman*).' In Ben-Zvi (1996): 201–24.

——2000. *Performing History: Theatrical Representations of the Past in Contemporary Theatre.* Iowa City.

ROZIK, E. 1996. 'Isaac Sacrifices Abraham in *The American Princess*.' In Ben-Zvi ed. (1996): 133–50.

——1999. 'HaTeatron: Limzo etAtzmecha betoch haKevutza haShlema' (The Theatre: Finding Yourself in the Entire Group: An Interview with Rina Yerushalmi, 23 Feb. 1997). In Kaynar *et al.* (1999): 163–80.

——2000. 'Creative Interpretation in Theatre.' In Yaari ed. (2000): 189–220.

SANDROW, N. 1977. *Vagabond Stars.* New York.

SCHEYN, Y. 1964. *Moskovskiĭ gosudarstvennyĭ erreĭskiĭ teatr imeni S.M. Mikhoelsa.* Paris.

SCHIPER, Y. 1923. *Geshikhte fun yidisher teater: kunst un drame fun die elteste zeitn biz 1750* (The History of Yiddish Theatre: Art and Drama From Ancient Times to 1750). Warsaw.

SCHIRMANN, J. 1965. 'Introduction to Leone de'Sommi.' [Hebrew.] In *Tzakhuth Bedihuta Deqiddushin* (A Comedy of Betrothal). 1–14. Y. Sommo. Jerusalem.

——1979. *Studies in the History of Hebrew Poetry and Drama* [Hebrew]. Jerusalem.

SCHNEIDER, D. 1991. 'Critical Approach to Modern Yiddish Drama.' In D. Kerler ed. *History of Yiddish Studies.* iii. 103–115. Chur and Reading.

SCHONMANN, S. 1995. *Teatron haKita* (Theatre of the Classroom). Tel Aviv.

SCHUMACHER, C. ed. 1998. *Staging the Holocaust.* Cambridge.

SEGAL, I. 1935. 'Perakim al Mekoriyut haOmanut haIvrit' (Chapters on the Originality of Hebrew Art). *Bamah* 7: 33–7.

SEIGER, M.L. 1960. 'Yiddish Theatre in New York City to 1892'. Diss., University of Michigan.

SHAKED, G. 1970. *HaMachaze haIvri haHistori biTekufat haTechiya.* (The Hebrew Historical Drama in the Twentieth Century). Jerusalem.

—— 1992. *Al Sipurim uMachazot: Perakim biYessodot haSsipur vehaMachaze.* (Elements of Short Stories and Plays). Jerusalem.

—— 1996. 'Actors as Reflection of Their Generation: Cultural Interactions between Israeli Actors, Playwrights, Directors, and Theaters.' In Ben-Zvi (1996): 85–100.

SHAKOW, Z. 1963. *The Theatre in Israel.* New York.

SHANI, H. 2000. 'Expressions of Self-Reference in Ancient Greek Tragedy and Their Transition onto the Screen.' In Yaari ed. (2000): 147–68.

SHATSKY, Y. ed. 1930. *Archiv far der geschikhte fun yidishn teater un drame.* Vol. I. Vilna.

—— 1940a. 'Geshikhte fun yidishn teater.' In *Algemeyne entsiklopedye.* ii. 298 Paris.

—— ed. 1940b. *Hunderd yor Goldfaden.* New York.

—— 1940c. 'Drame un teater bi di sfaradim in Holand.' *Yivo Blater* 16/2: 135–49.

—— 1943. 'Purim-spiln un lazim in Amsterdamer Ghetto.' *Yivo Blater* 19: 212–20.

—— 1945. 'Teater farveilungen bi di Ashkenazim in Holand.' *Yivo Blater* 21: 303–22.

SHAVIT, Z. ed. 1999. *The History of the Jewish Community in Eretz-Israel Since 1882: The Construction of Hebrew Culture in Eretz-Israel* [Hebrew]. Part I. Jerusalem.

SHIRMANN, J. 1979. *Studies in the History of Hebrew Poetry and Drama.* Jerusalem.

SHMERUK, C. 1979. *Machazot Mikraim beYiddish 1697–1750* (Yiddish Biblical Plays 1697–1750). Jerusalem.

SHOHAM, H. 1983. *Batia by Z. Shatz: The Staging of Kibbutz-first-stages at the 'Ohel', the Workers Theatre of Israel* [Hebrew]. Haifa.

—— 1989a. *HaDrama shel 'Dor baAretz': Etgar uMetziut baDrama haYissraelit.* (The Drama of the 'Native Born' Generation in Israel: Challenge and Reality in Israeli Drama). Tel Aviv.

—— 1989b. *Teatron uDrama Mechapssim Kahal.* (Theatre and Drama in Search of an Audience). Tel Aviv.

—— 1989c. 'Habimah Messochachat im Kehala—Shanim shel Dialog veMonolog' ('Habima Talks with its Audience—Years of Dialogue and Monologue') In Shoham (1989b): 77–111.

—— 1996. 'The Drama and Theater of Nissim Aloni.' In Ben-Zvi (1996): 119–32.

SHOEF, C. 1999. 'HaTeatron haCameri veha "Omanut leShem Omanut" ' (The Cameri Theatre and the 'Art for Art's Sake'). In Kaynar *et al.* (1999): 49–56.

SHULMAN, E. 1913. *Sefat-Yehudit Ashkenazit VeSifruta* (The Jewish Ashkenazi Language and its Literature). Riga.

SHUNAMI, G. 1998. *HaTeatron haTeudi* (The Documentary Theatre: The Holocaust and Contemporary History in Political Drama). Tel Aviv.

STEINSCHNEIDER, M. 1902–4. 'Purim und Parodie.' In *Monatsschrift fur die Geschichte und Wissenschaft des Judentums* 46 (1902): 176–87, 275–80, 372–6, 473–8, 567–82; 47 (1903): 84–9, 169–80, 279–86, 360–70, 468–74; 48 (1904): 242–7, 504–9.

STERNBERG, M. 1977. 'Structure of Repetition in Biblical Narrative.' [Hebrew.] *Hasifrut* 25: 109–38.

—— 1983. 'Language, World and Perspective in Biblical Narrative Art: Free Indirect Discourse and Modes of Covert Penetration.' [Hebrew]. *Hasifrut* 32: 31–88.

——1987. *The Poetics of Biblical Narrative*. Bloomington, Ind.

TAMUZ, B. 1958. *Sefer haTeatron haCameri beChag heAssor 1944–1954* (The Cameri Theatre's 10th Anniversary Book 1944–1954). Tel Aviv.

TAUB, M. 1993. *Modern Israeli Drama in Translation*. Portsmouth, N.H.

TEYTLBOYM, A. 1929. *Teatralya*. Warsaw and New York.

TOMASHEFSKY, B. 1937. *Mayn Lebens-geschichte* (Book of My Life). New York.

TURKOV. Y. 1953. *Farloshene shtern* (Extinguished Stars). Buenos Aires.

——1969. *Goldfaden un Gordin: Essays and Biographies*. Tel Aviv.

TURKOV. Z. 1951. *Fragmentn fun Mayn Lebn* (Fragments of My Life). Buenos Aires.

TVERSKY, Y. and EVEN-SHOSHAN, S. eds. 1954. *Avraham Baratz, Oman haBama* (Abraham Baratz, the Stage Artist). Tel Aviv.

URIAN, D. 1996a. *Demut haArvi baTeatron haYissraeli* (The Arab in Israeli Theatre). Tel Aviv.

——1996b. 'The Image of the Arab on the Israeli Stage.' In Ben-Zvi ed. (1996): 227–68.

——1998. *Yahaduto shel haTeatron haYissraeli* (The Judaic Nature of Israeli Theatre). Tel Aviv.

——KNOLL-YAHALOM, V., and SCHONMANN, S. 1996. *Drama veChinuch*. (Drama in Education: Writing, Acting, Watching). Tel Aviv.

VARDI, D. 1950. *Bederech Hiluchai* (On My Path). Tel Aviv.

VEYKHERT, M. 1922. *Teater un Drame*. Warsaw.

——1961. *Zichronot—Warsha 1918–1939* (Memoirs—Warsaw 1918–1939). Vols. 1 and 2. Tel Aviv.

WEIL, A. ed. 2000. *Israeli Drama: Synopses of Selected Hebrew Plays*. Jerusalem.

WEISSENBERG, S. ed. 1904. 'Dus Pirimspiel—Du Spielt die Rolle Humen und Mordche.' *Mitteilungen der Gesellschaft für judiche Volkskunde* 13/1: 4–27.

WEITZ, S. 1989. *A Cultural Bridge: The Arts in the Service of Society, Community, and Israel–Diaspora Relations* [Hebrew]. Tel Aviv.

——1996. 'From Combative to Bourgeois Theater: Public Theater in Israel in 1990.' In Ben-Zvi ed. (1996): 101–16.

——1999. 'Mitarbut Gevohah leTaassiyat Tarbut' (From High Culture to Culture Industry: The Cameri Theatre of Tel Aviv). In Kaynar *et al.* (1999): 193–205.

——1997. 'Hateatron haIroni shel Tel-Aviv' (The Municipal Theatre of Tel-Aviv). In Meshulach (1997): 203–6.

WEITZNER, J. 1994. *Sholem Aleichem in the Theatre*. Madison, Wisc.

WILF, M. 1969. *HaMachazaut haYissraelit haMekorit, tashach-tashkach* (The Original Israeli Drama, 1948–1968). Tel Aviv.

YAARI, A. 1957. *Hamachaze Haivri haMekori vehaMeturgam meReshito vead Yameinu. Bibliographia* (The Hebrew Play—The Original and Translated From Its Inception Until Today. Bibliography). Jerusalem.

YAARI, N. 1996. 'Life As a Lost Battle: The Theater of Hanoch Levin.' In Ben-Zvi ed. (1996): 151–72.

——ed. 2000. *On Interpretation In the Arts: Interdisciplinary Studies in Honor of Moshe Lazar*. Assaph Book Series. Tel Aviv.

——2000. 'Staging Dying: Hanoch Levin versus Aeschylus on Human Suffering.' In Yaari ed. (2000): 327–43.

YABLOKOV, H. 1968–9. *Arum der velt mit Yidish teater* (Around the World with Yiddish Theatre). New York.

YAFFE, B., BERTONOV, S., and KATZ, Y. 1964. eds. *Omanut haBamah beYissrael* (Stage Art in Israel). Tel Aviv.

YARON, E. 1997. 'Chamishim Shenot Machazaut Ivrit' (Fifty Years of Hebrew Drama). In Meshulach ed. (1997): 146–91.

ZILBERSSVAYG, Z. 1928. *Hintern Forhang*. Vilna.

——1936. *Abraham Goldfaden un Zigmund Mogulesco*. Buenos Aires.

——ed. 1959. *Leksikon fun yidishn teater* (Lexicon of Yiddish Theatre). 5 vols. New York.

ZINBERG, I. 1943. *Di geshikhte fun der literatur bi Yidn*. Vol. 6. New York.

ZUPERFEIN, E. 1937. 'Al haDrama haTanachit' (On the Biblical Drama). *Bamah* 13: 45–8.

CHAPTER 36

JEWISH AND ISRAELI FILM STUDIES

MOSHE ZIMERMAN

DESPITE the problems inherent in defining the scope of creations associated with the Israeli cinema,[1] it is relatively easy to define the cinema's boundaries and to delineate the writers (of essays, books, and anthologies) who deal with it. This is not the case when attempting to define Jewish cinema or deciding what constitutes writing about Jewish cinema. Later in this paper this issue will be discussed extensively, along with some of the side issues that derive from it. Before this, however, the history of writing on Israeli cinema will be reviewed, since this will shed much light on the difficulties involved in reviewing writing on Jewish cinema.

---

[1] For example, should we consider *Tsabar* (Alexander Forer, 1932)—whose themes and aesthetics correspond with those of the Israeli cinema, which was filmed in Palestine by a primarily local crew featuring a primarily local cast, but whose director was not Israeli—an Israeli film? And what of other foreign productions, such as *Exodus* (Otto Preminger, 1960) and *Shoah* (Claude Lanzmann, 1985), both of which had a major effect on Israeli cinema? My tendency is to say that they are Israeli films, though the opposite could certainly be claimed. There are also the issues of international co-productions, which are devoid of any substantive connection with Israeli cinema, e.g. *God's Gun* (Frank Kramer, 1977), where an Israeli production company was a partner in the production; or foreign films like *The Emperor's New Clothes* (David Irving, 1986), which an Israeli production company produced in Israel. In cases such as these, it seems clear that they are not Israeli.

ISRAELI FILM AND FILM STUDIES

The first essays on cinema published in Palestine were probably those written by Hemda Ben-Yehuda, which were published on two separate occasions (during the course of the summer of 1900) in *Hatzvi*. *Hatzvi* was the newspaper edited and published by Hemda's husband, Eliezer Ben-Yehuda, the father of modern Hebrew. The essays dealt with an Italian traveller, Colora Salvatore, and the first screening of films in Palestine. Salvatore was something of a cinema troubadour who arrived in Palestine with a mule, on whose back he hauled a film projector and a few cans of film. He roamed the length and breadth of the country intent on exhibiting the new miracle to whoever was willing to watch. From Ben-Yehuda's reports we learn that one of the films he screened dealt with the Dreyfus Affair. She described the sensation of viewing this film as follows:

If you were not at Rouen during the Dreyfus trial, go to the moving pictures and you will see the defendant standing before his judges, just as he was, with all the movements and postures, the excited face, the look in his eyes, everything, everything. You will also see him meet his wife, and many other things. You will marvel and have much pleasure, as nothing has been invented yet that is as beautiful and wondrous as the moving pictures.

We do not have the full list of films that Salvatore brought with him to Palestine, but we do know that there were only a very few and he was, therefore, compelled to leave Palestine after only a short time. He left in search of other audiences, leaving behind him only the term 'moving picture', which was coined by Ben-Yehuda especially for the occasion.

Because of the scarcity of cinema events, practically nothing was written about it between 1900–8, when the first movie theater ('Oracle') opened in Jerusalem in the Olympia Hotel. Activities at the Oracle and the public response to them were naturally covered by Hemda Ben-Yehuda (in *Hatzvi*, Fall 1908). She described how 'Jews, Christians and Arabs' together enjoyed the 'living photographs of the moving pictures' (among them the film *The Dreyfus Incident*—a relatively late version, compared to the one on the Dreyfus trial viewed in 1900), viewed to the accompaniment of the music of a 'small orchestra.' A week later Ben-Yehuda reported that some yeshiva students, who became very angry as a result of the screening, shouting 'Wicked! Whores! Scandal!' The reporter was not content with merely reporting the event, but also sought the response of Rabbi Lipa, the yeshiva's rabbi. Rabbi Lipa denounced the act saying: 'The students should have stayed at home and studied all day, all night, all month, and all year, till their dying day; and cinema? *Tfu* (spit)! An abomination!'

In the following years (up to 1914), *Hatzvi* continued to be the main source reporting on the slow penetration of cinema into Palestine. Among other things, it reported on the opening of a movie theatre in Jaffa, run by two gentlemen named

Laurence and Shoenberg, who advertised their activities on 'large and detailed posters' (Ben Yehudah 1909a); and that at the Purim ball of the Sephardi congregation in Jaffa, films were screened between readings of Haim Nahman Bialik's poem 'Small Letter' and the playing of the dance band (Ben Yehuda Spring 1909b).

In 1911, in the wake of producing the first Zionist film (*The First Film of Palestine*), the Hebrew cinema won mention in both a book and the foreign press. The twenty-minute-long film was produced by a British Jew—Morey Rosenberg—who documented his travels in Palestine, focusing on industry in Haifa, the Druze villages on Mount Carmel, Tiberias, Mount Meron, and especially various sites in Jerusalem (the Bezalel Art Academy, new housing for immigrant Yemenites near the Arab village of Silwan, the teacher's seminary founded by David Yellin in Beit Hakerem, the Wailing Wall). The first mention of the film—describing the shooting of an impressive sequence (the visit to Bezalel)—appeared in the memoirs of the institution's founder, Boris Schatz (Schatz 1924). From this work we learn that Schatz had become a cinema aficionado and had even started making practical plans to establish a film-production company in Palestine, to be called 'Menorah' (ibid. 82). The second mention is a direct result of the impact of the film, which was screened before Jewish and non-Jewish audiences in Switzerland, the United States, Russia, Germany, Holland, South Africa, and other countries. This impact was expressed, among other ways, in enthusiastic articles that appeared in Jewish papers such as the *Jewish Chronicle*, *Die Welt*, and in a series of articles written by an Arab-Palestinian journalist, Abu El-Hassan, in the newspaper *Palestine*, published in Jaffa (cf. Beeri 1980). El-Hassan reviewed the propaganda aspects of Rosenberg's film and pleaded with the Palestinian-Arab leadership to initiate a counter-film. Toward this end, he recommended inviting a European production company to photograph 'sights of Palestine', first and foremost the 'two sacred mosques and also all Moslem sites and buildings and views of Palestine' (Schatz 1924: 272–3). The film, so he hoped, would be widely screened, mainly in Egypt, thus providing a fitting answer to the Zionist propaganda in Rosenberg's film. As far as is known, Abu El-Hassan's recommendations were never implemented. Four additional films shot in Palestine at the beginning of the second decade of the twentieth century won local and international acclaim (cf. Harel 1956).

The first of these would, at a later date—in the first historical review written on Israeli film—be considered 'the first film produced in Eretz Israel'. It was photographed by Akiva Arie Weiss, one of the initiators and founders of the city of Tel Aviv. Weiss owned many businesses, one of which was a film and camera distribution agency for 'Sata Brothers'. Weiss received a small financial grant from the Jewish National Fund and used one of the Sata Brothers' cameras to shoot his film (cf. Harel 1956; Gross and Gross 1991: 12). The raw footage was sent to a European laboratory to be developed and a new company ('New Light') was formed (1 April 1914) to deal with distribution. The film, however, was lost (probably on a ship that sank on its way to Palestine) and the company was thus prevented from operating for the purpose for which it was conceived. For those interested in what was or can be written on Hebrew cinema, a number of files containing documents related to the film still remain (located mainly in the Tel Aviv Municipal Archives). These files contain the first real documentation of cinematic activity in Palestine.

The second of the films was a full-length feature directed by Sidney Olcott (*From the Manger to the Cross*, 1913). The plot dealt with Jesus's life and was primarily shot at sites where, according to Christian tradition, the central occurrences in his life took place.[2] This was the first film shot in Palestine whose distribution was conducted routinely, with reviews and promotional articles (which can be found in various archives in the United States).

The third film was called *From Jewish Life in Eretz Israel*. It was an eighteen-minute film shot in Palestine in the spring of 1913. Its uniqueness lies in its being the first movie whose filming was covered in the press, in a letter written by a public figure (Meir Dizengoff, mayor of Tel Aviv), and in a book of memoirs written by a Zionist who viewed it in the diaspora. The press reviews consisted of two articles, 'Cinema on the Farmers of Rishon LeZion' (*Hapoel Hatsair*, Spring 1913) and 'Rishon Le'zion' (*Haherut*, 29 May 1913). These reviews revealed that a group of Russian merchants were behind the making of the film, and that they had sent a representative and a film photographer to Palestine to shoot Palestinian vistas, new and ancient Jewish settlements, and Jewish and Zionist institutions. A more thorough check of the reviews reveals that each newspaper emphasized the aspect closest to its heart. *Hapoel Hatsair*, with a Zionist-Socialist orientation, focused on photos of farm-work (picking grapes and various tasks at a winery, the harvest, almond picking, and even children working in a school garden) performed by Jews. *Haherut*, the paper of the young Sephardi community, emphasized the film's nationalist-propaganda achievement. Accordingly, the article began by declaring: the film '*Eretz Israel* is destined to spread around the world—in some months it will be seen in all corners of the earth, in Japan, China, and even in holy Russia'. The review ended defiantly: 'And all those who hate us throughout the world shall see that the people of Israel still live in Israel, under the patronage of the Ottoman government.'

The significance of Dizengoff's letter (1913, Jewish National Fund file 29.3 at the Central Zionist Archives), written in favour of the film and calling on readers to support it, lies in its being one of the first documents to show that the pioneer leaders and institutions were interested in cinema and understood the necessity and obligation of promoting it.

---

[2] Olcott specialized in historical films and was also known for his involvement in one of the first copyright law claims in the history of cinema: as director of the first cinema version of *Ben-Hur* (1907), he was sued by the book's copyright owners, who saw themselves damaged by the film. One of the reasons he chose to shoot a film on the life of Jesus was in order to avoid another claim. No one could claim copyright ownership of the New Testament.

Yaacov Davidon recalls seeing the film and notes how viewers received it 'with indescribable enthusiasm'. 'Tears of happiness shone in the eyes of salvation-hungry Jewish viewers', he writes (Davidon 1983: 227). This youthful recollection is important not only because it exists; it is important as well because it caused Davidon to become a prominent cinema-owner in Palestine and one of the most important documenters of the development of the screening sub-system in Israeli cinema.[3]

The fourth film, *Egypt-Palestine the Holy Land* (1914), was shot by a Polish director, Stanislav Sabel, in 1913. It was produced at the initiative of a Polish film production company ('Cosmo-Film') whose Jewish owner, Henrik Finkelstein, believed that the film would offer a taste of Palestine to Polish Jews (who then numbered three to four million), and would, therefore, be highly successful. The uniqueness of this film—in terms of what was written about it—is that it was mentioned in a number of sources dealing with the history of Polish cinema, for example, in the filmography edited by Dr Vladislav Yavsivitzky (Yavsivitzky 1925) and published in 1966 (Bnashkiviz 1966).[4] These sources—which testify to the fact that the director did not manage to return to Poland with the photographed material before the outbreak of the First World War, and therefore developed, and possibly also edited, the film in Moscow—again raise the (relatively simple) topic of what is Eretz-Israel cinema and the (complicated) problem of what is Jewish cinema. These questions arise because of the need to determine whether a film like *Egypt-Palestine the Holy Land*, is an Eretz-Israel or Jewish film. It is composed of elements similar to those found in other Eretz-Israel films of the era, yet at the same time it is considered part of the Polish film industry and positions the Jewish presence in Palestine as its main theme.

Immediately after the filming of the four above-mentioned films and just before the outbreak of the First World War, the Eden Cinema opened its doors in Tel Aviv. It was the first institute in the screening sub-system that managed to operate continuously over a long period (more than fifty years). The importance of this occasion lies in the controversy that revolved around it among the Tel Aviv populace, community leaders, and the press, and in the way the controversy ended

[3] The source of the terms 'system' and 'sub-system' is the multiple-system theory developed by Itamar Even-Zohar in many essays (see 1978), based on the dynamic functionality that occupied many researchers at the beginning of the century, especially those working within the framework of Russian Formalism (see Erlich 1965, Tynjanov 1971, Jakobson 1971, and Shiklovsky 1965) and Czech structuralism (Mukarovsky 1970, Steiner 1970). The theory describes the dynamics that exist in a specific cultural system and in each of its parts as a meeting between processes that occur in the present with those that occurred in the past and affect the present. Thus, it makes it possible to describe the system as multiple-stage individual activity in which at times one system component takes part, while at others many of its components (sub-systems) participate. Six such components exist in cinema: finance, production, technical infrastructure, distribution, screening, and brokering.

[4] This filmography, and the fact that it includes a film that some sources associate with the Israeli cinema, again point to the problems involved in defining Jewish cinema.

(cf. Klein 1975; Beeri 1980). The source of the controversy—evidence of which can be found in extensive correspondence stored in the Tel Aviv Municipal Archives[5] and in the archives of various newspapers—was the fear that a movie theatre would ruin the rural character of Tel Aviv, and that the electric-generator used to operate it would cause an ecological nuisance through its noise and gasoline fumes. There was also concern that the theatre would bring a lower class of people (since only they visit the cinema!) into a peaceful neighbourhood. The community leaders voted decidedly in favour of seeing the new art form as part of their world. Although they mistakenly gave the movie theatre's owners a thirteen-year monopoly on screening films in the city, they contributed to the birth of an additional (through random, for the meantime) activity: journalistic reviews of films.

The First World War inhibited the growth of the film industry and reports about it. The war's end, however, marks a point of accelerated development in both, expressed by the 'birth' of a local director (Yaacov Ben-Dov), who regularly produced films in Palestine, and the appearance of a Zionist leader (Zeev Jabotinsky) who struggled to elevate the cinema's status among supporters of Zionism. Ben-Dov, who produced approximately twelve films[6] between 1917 and 1930, created a precedent by providing his audiences with programmes that enabled them (and cinema researchers) to understand what he had filmed and the rationale that stood behind his pictures. His third film (*Return to Zion*, 1920) was especially important. Unlike his previous films, in which items were organized chronologically according to when they were photographed, in this third film he divided the photographed items into three parts with a common story structure: 'Pioneers'—describing Zionist activity in developing the country; 'Moments'—describing the pioneers' social life during their free time; and 'The High Commissioner in Palestine'—describing Zionism's political optimism upon the arrival of the first British governor, Sir Herbert Samuel. This trio of subjects (Zionist activity, the folklore accompanying it, and the political climate in Palestine) would from this time forward form the main narrative framework of Israeli films.

Several sources about Israeli cinema came about as a result of Ben-Dov's activities. From these, one can learn about the development and state of cinema in Palestine from this time onward. There are legal protocols, the first of which documents a claim by Ben-Dov against distributors who lost a negative copy of his first film (*Liberated Judea*, 1919);[7] personal diaries, the first of which was written by William Topkis, an American Jew who wanted to produce a documentary that

---

[5] I have indicated where the correspondence can be found in order to portray the growth of Israeli cinematic research (which is part of the brokerage sub-system) in a manner that not only makes it possible to present research already conducted, but also identifies where the raw documents for future research can be found.

[6] Much can be learned about Ben-Dov's activity in documents located in Jewish National Fund file 29.3 in the Central Zionist Archives (CZA) in Jerusalem.

[7] The protocols of the trial can be found in files 1357, 1851 in the Jerusalem Municipal Archives.

would encourage Jewish tourism to Palestine (Ben-Dov helped him and in 1923 also photographed the film, which was called *The Awakening Eretz Israel*). Topkis came away with the impression that Ben-Dov was an 'excellent artist' who 'needs financial aid' to realize his talent (cf. Geffen 1980: 72–94). Ben-Dov was a pioneer in writing memoirs of the film industry.[8] He also prepared an organized archive of his films and left it, arranged in an orderly manner, to those who followed in his footsteps.[9] In addition, he created a presence that generated monographic articles dedicated to his work (e.g. Levin 1985). As opposed to most of his comrades in the Zionist leadership (and especially his arch political rival, Ben-Gurion, who sabotaged not a little the penetration of cinema into Jewish-Zionist culture[10]), Zeev Jabotinsky understood the power of cinema and wrote considerably in its praise (Jabotinsky 1948a, 1948b). He himself wrote a melodramatic Zionist script for a long feature film[11] called *Balm in Gilead*, telling the love story (man for woman and man for nation) of two native-born Jews, Amnon and Tamar, who combine practical studies (Tamar—medicine) and creative beauty (Amnon—establishing a pioneer perfume factory) with love for Greater Eretz-Israel (in one of whose regions, the Gilead, Amnon finds the plant from which he extracts his perfumes). Jabotinsky conducted an extensive correspondence with the Jewish National Fund but did not manage to convince them to finance the film.[12] His disappointment with the Fund's attitude caused Jabotinsky to condemn the Zionist institutional attitude to cinema in rather sharp language: 'In the circles of the educated', he wrote, 'agreement has not yet been reached that cinema is also literature and even the most important branch of literature in our time' (Jabotinsky 1948b).

In 1927, immediately upon the expiration of the monopoly given to the Eden Cinema to screen films in Tel Aviv, many entrepreneurs rushed to build and operate movie theatres,[13] now required by the city whose population had grown from 2,000, when the monopoly was first granted, to 50,000. These movie theatres made writing regular film reviews a necessity, and reviews began to appear on 1 February 1927,

[8] Ben-Dov's memoirs were written in 1930 and are quoted in Natan and Yaacov Gross (1991: 21–2).

[9] The archive was sold to Baruch Agadati, who used it extensively in his film *This Is Not a Legend* (1934). There is debate on the date of sale: Menahem Levin (1985: 134) claims it was 1924, while Natan and Yaacov Gross (1991: 29) argue for 1930.

[10] This can be demonstrated by the following story: when Ben-Gurion visited the United States for the first time as Israel's prime minister in 1950, he was invited to the premiere of the film *Samson and Delilah* (based on a novel, *Samson*, written by Jabotinsky). When asked his opinion of the film, Ben-Gurion replied that he could not offer one, as he had not seen a film for twenty years.

[11] The script—originally written in English on leftover pages in a notebook that Naftali Blumenthal sent from Tel Aviv to his revered leader—appears in a Hebrew version of Jabotinsky's writings (1949). It is the first Israeli script extant.

[12] From the correspondence (in Jewish National Fund file 29.3 at the CZA) one can learn much about Zionist institutes, institutional production bodies, and the attitude of public funds to films.

[13] Such as the Ophir (opened in 1927), Gan Rina (1928), Beit Ha'am (1929), Mugrabi (1930), Migdalor (1931), and Rimon (1932).

with an article by Avigdor Hameiri ('Chaplin the Artist'), printed in *Ha'aretz*. Indeed, Hameiri felt a need to open his article with an apology—'I do not care if I am publicly denounced...but for seven or eight years now...I have run to see Charlie Chaplin every chance I get.' He informed his readers that, as of the current article, he would be writing reviews in the paper regularly. Soon enough all the dailies began publishing film reviews—a very significant step that represents the coming of age of cinema and its inseparability from the developing culture system in Palestine.

As a result of the increased number of cinemas, a multitude of films were produced in a variety of genres—newsreels, advertisements, documentaries, and short and long feature films[14]—by a series of producers[15] who built their casts from actors performing on the stages of the best of the country's theatres (such as Habima and Haohel). All of these are documented, not only in the newspapers, but also in the first publication[16] that dealt with cinema[17] and in the memoirs of Natan Axelrod.[18] This documentation shows that going to the movies had become a regular activity in Palestine. From the period of its inception (1927–1935) onward, the cinema went through six additional phases.

1936–44: Throughout this period the cinema underwent a crisis caused by the inability of most production companies to raise the funds needed to purchase equipment for filming talking movies. They also suffered from the difficult security situation in the country following the Great Arab Revolt (1936–9); and because the British, starting with the outbreak of the Second World War, supplied movie theatres free of charge with newsreels describing the war's events. Even so, this period made two contributions to the development of Hebrew cinema: intensive photography of Jewish settlement activity in the framework of settlements established in a day (called 'Tower and Stockade' settlements), and the publication of the first magazine dedicated exclusively to cinema (*Kalnoa*, 1939–52), edited by Gershon Komrov, who also wrote considerably in the newspapers.

---

[14] The most important among them are: *It Happened in My Days* and *Oded the Wanderer* (1932), *The Dream of My People, Work*, and *Tsabar* (1933), and *This Is a Country* and *Celebrating a New Life* (1934). The divisions into different genres of these films will be discussed later.

[15] e.g. Natan Axelrod, Baruch and Itzhak Agadati, Yerushalayim Segal, Helmar Larski, A. I. Blum, Yehuda Liehman, and Alexander Forer.

[16] *Light Cinema*, a periodical that dealt with culture, art, and news and was published in 1931–5.

[17] In this vein, for instance, in the October 1932 issue of the periodical an article by Shlomo Ben-Israel ('Secrets of the Damp Room') can be found in which he describes the modifications made to Axelrod's laboratory on the occasion of photographing the first full-length Hebrew feature film, *Oded the Wanderer*.

[18] Axelrod was undoubtedly the most prominent film-maker operating in Palestine up to 1948. His memoirs, despite their importance, are the property of his family and have not yet been published. Even though the memoirs fail as a result of being overly egocentric (he emphasizes his own work and scoffs at everyone who worked with him), this does not detract from their importance.

1944–8: This was the period when the Hebrew cinema extracted itself from crisis through the money invested in films that dealt with the distress of Jewish Holocaust survivors and their immigration and absorption in Palestine. These were films made in the hope of convincing the world to support the creation of a Jewish state in Palestine. The films produced[19] are of the utmost importance, since they moulded the attitude towards immigrants in the cinema and in Israeli society for many years to come (more will be written about this later).

1948–60: These years saw the foundation of two state and public institutes (the National Film Service and the Cinema Division of the Histadrut Labor Federation) that produced documentaries about the absorption of the waves of immigrants, especially those arriving in Israel from eastern countries after the founding of the State. These films were screened before audiences in order to influence them. Few feature films were produced during this period (about one a year), and those that were produced utilized the motifs of the previous era and the documentaries of that time. Two publication were also founded: *Olam Hakolnoa*, that continued the tradition of combining gossip and reviews as its predecessor (*Kalnoa VeKolnoa*); had done; and *Omanut Hakolnoa* (1958–63), edited by David Greenberg, which was the first publication to regard cinema as an art form.

1961–77: These were the years that saw the establishment of the long feature film. During this period, the poetic aspects of the Israeli feature film were formulated and the genre in which it would deal was finally developed. At the same time, the stature of documentary film-making declined, and documentary production was relegated almost entirely to television (which began broadcasting at the end of the 1960s). Television slowly aided this genre to return to its former stature, as it tried to present the problematic characteristics of Israeli society. During this period, cinema became an academic subject and the Israel Film Institute was founded. The Institute published *Kolnoa* magazine (1974–81). Most of the writers were graduates of the Institute's Cinema Department (and were involved in their student years in publishing an internal publication, *Close-Up*, that was more or less a predecessor of *Kolnoa*) and their colleagues, who had fought together to make the Israeli cinema less commercial and more artistic. The publication of the first anthology to discuss the theoretical aspects of cinema in 1975 was part of this trend (Keler 1975).

1978–90: These years saw the struggle to turn cinema into an art form bear fruit, and the face of Israeli feature films was totally transformed. There were primarily

---

[19] Feature films such as *The Big Dream* (1946), *My Father's House* (1947), *Tomorrow Will Be a Wonderful Day* (1948); documentaries such as *The Illegals* (1947) and *The Forgotten Children* (1947); and propaganda films like *Do You Hear Me?* (1947). Raw material on the production process of these films can be found in the Jewish National Fund file KKL/1636/121, in the CZA in Jerusalem, in an extensive essay on the preparations for shooting and producing the film *My Father's House*, by Baruch Dinar in the periodical *Galgal* (11 July 1946), in a review of the film in the *Palestine Post* (25 Oct. 1946), and of *Tomorrow Will Be a Wonderful Day* in the periodical *Cinema* (30 Sept. 1948).

two changes: first, films ceased to identify with Zionist ideology and became critical towards it; secondly, they began to focus on integration between young and old people (in youth films) or on people who were unidentified with any specific sector (in candid-camera films). At the same time, film-makers once again began making interesting documentaries outside the framework of television programming (which reached a pinnacle of success in that media between 1978 and 1983). At this time (1982) a periodical called *Cinematheque* began appearing, and the fact that it is still published today (2001) gives hope to all who consider regular discussion on cinema—not only in reviews and through journalistic coverage—essential in creating a national film culture. In addition, towards the end of this period (1986–90), a semi-academic periodical, *Sratim*, whose editorial policy was to establish seriously researched writing on cinema, began to appear. Books published on and by film directors[20] completed this trend.

1990 and Beyond: As a result of the introduction of cable and commercial TV into the local cinema system, these years have seen a substantial growth in Israeli public exposure to local and foreign films. At the same time there has been a substantial growth in the number of books on Israeli cinema (e.g. Spoto 1991; Gabler 1993; Kazan 1994; Bresson 1999; Gianett 2000; Mast and Kawin 2002). If the history of Israeli cinema is divided into one era that pre-dates documentation (1896–1927) followed by seven historic eras (1927–2001), it becomes apparent that only the fourth period (1944–48) included within it an initial attempt to describe the development of Israeli cinema. It was Yehuda Harel (Harel 1956) who confronted the challenge involved in a methodical presentation of the history of Israeli cinema. The pioneering nature of this study is also expressed in the two most common failures of research on Hebrew film-making: that of focusing on some of the processes and films that form the cinematic system and of reviewing them from a narrow (personal and/or ideological) perspective. In Harel's case it is relatively easy to explain these failures. Harel worked for Axelrod's Carmel Film Company for many years, and he therefore greatly emphasized his employer's contribution to the development of Hebrew cinema. At the same time, he de-emphasized the role played by many of Axelrod's competitors (Baruch Agadati, for example). A similar problem can be found in Margot Klausner's attempts (summarized in Klausner 1974), where her tendency to emphasize her own activity (her partnership in producing the film, *Towards a New Life*, in 1934, and founding Herzlia Studios at the beginning of the 1950s) is even greater than Harel's, even though sixteen years had passed since he published his book. In the years between these first two historical reviews—which rely more on memoirs than on historical research— only two additional significant occurrences can be mentioned: first, the attempts of the periodical, *Omanut Hakolnoa*, to deal somewhat more thoroughly with

---

[20] e.g. Green (1985), Truffaut (1987), and four books on Bunuel, Truffaut, Losey, and Resnais, published in 1986–7 by Keter.

various matters relating to Israeli cinema;[21] and the publication of a long interview with David Perlov—one of the leading documentary directors in Israel—by Moshe Natan in *Keshet*, one of the most important literary periodicals in Israel in the 1960s.

The period when Klausner's conservative book was published also paradoxically coincided with a revolution that occurred in the attitude towards writing on Israeli cinema following the publication of *Kolnoa* (see above). This journal was edited by the director of the Israel Film Institute, Nahman Ingber, one of the most important intellectuals working in the brokerage sub-system of Israeli film. Under Ingber's leadership the journal became a stage for a large group of reporters and interviewees,[22] who represent three trends: the beginning of academic-oriented writing about cinema;[23] the creation of a forum for intensive discussion of Israeli cinema by giving wide expression to creators (directors, scriptwriters, producers, actors) who worked within its framework;[24] and the emergence of a struggle to change the character of Israeli cinema by changing 'government policy on the issue of encouraging the Israeli film' so as to enable the creation of 'personal, artistic cinema devoid of destructive commercial pressures'.[25]

The book that represents the beginning of academic writing on Hebrew-Israeli cinema is Ora-Gloria Arzooni's *The Israeli Film* (Arzooni 1983). Although it was a

---

[21] This can be demonstrated by an example relating to the time when the periodical was published, and one relating to the time before its appearance. The first was a debate on the film *Hot Sands* in issue 21 (1960), over whether the film's distribution should be halted since it dealt with Israelis—who were not portrayed positively—travelling to a dangerous site outside Israel (Petra, Jordan). The fear was that many viewers would be tempted to risk their lives in an attempt to reach Petra themselves. The second was an extensive review in the Oct. 1963 issue of the process of producing the film *Oded the Wanderer*, written by the film's director Haim Halahmi.

[22] e.g. Shoshana Avigal, Michelangelo Antonioni, Gideon Bachman, Natan Gross, Boaz Davidson, Daniel Dayan, Nisim Dayan, Uri Zohar, S. Izhar, Elihu Katz, Ram Levi, Yehuda Ne'eman, Rahel Ne'eman, Amos Oz, Roman Polanski, Sever Plotsker, David Pavlov, Nisim Kalderon, Uri and Irma Klein, Amram Klein, Ranan Shor, Roni Sher, Eli Tavor, and many others.

[23] e.g. a comparative analysis of two of Fellini's films, *Satyricon* and *La Dolce Vita*, made by Daniel Dayan—in later days a prominent writer on semiotics in cinema; or articles by Natan Gross on the beginnings of the film industry in Israel, that later became the basis for a book (1991) that he wrote with his son Yaacov; and also an article by Amram Klein (1975) on the first cinema screenings in Israel.

[24] The main importance of this discussion lies in the debate it aroused regarding the legitimacy of producing films whose sole purpose was commercial success, and in the first attempts of writers like Nisim Dayan (1976), Ranan Shor (1978), and Yehuda Ne'eman (1979) to characterize the major genres that were formed in Israeli feature films (national, integration, and personal). The periodical can claim to have defined a sub-genre that dealt with the relationships between Eastern and Ashkenazi Jews in the years 1964–78 (called 'Burekas films'), and to have first outlined the characteristics of a personal sub-genre of films that tried to be an antithesis to the Burekas film (and was eventually called the 'new sensitivity').

[25] The quotation is from a manifesto published in a periodical by a group of young directors. With the perspective of a quarter of a century, it can be seen that this struggle was of foremost interest to the periodical's editors, and it is not by chance that shortly after having achieved their goal—a change in the Israeli cinema support system, by the founding of the 'Foundation for Encouraging Quality Cinema' in 1979—the periodical faded out and eventually ceased publication (1981).

vanguard work, it did not greatly influence the development of orderly research of Israeli cinema, for two reasons. Because it attempts to review the development of Hebrew cinema and theatre over a period of some sixty years (1912–73), its treatment is somewhat shallow. In addition, the book was not translated into Hebrew and remained trapped within the English-language ghetto—whose walls still, apparently, form a barrier for the general public and possibly also for the Israeli cinema elite.

Another example is L. Beeri's essay (1980), whose academic quality and broad scope can be demonstrated best by comparing it to a piece by Amram Klein, published in *Kolnoa* only five years previously (Klein 1975). While Klein's five-page essay searched for a proper means to review the development of the screening subsystem in the Hebrew film industry, Beeri (1980) performs a similar task across twenty pages, demonstrating clear control of the procedures of responsible academic writing. An even greater commitment to the academic format appears in an essay by Menahem Levin in 1985 (Levin 1985), and this trend can also be found in *Sratim* (1986–90), a journal edited by Oshra Schwartz and Amir Rotem. All articles were accompanied by notes and bibliography, and it even ran a regular feature that reviewed important articles in academic publications relating to cinema. The articles in *Sratim* are of great importance, since they were to form the basis for most of the academic books on Israeli cinema that would be published in the final decade of the twentieth century and the beginning of the twenty-first century.

The periodical *Cinematheque*—which first appeared in 1982 and which has continued up to the present time (end of 2001)—has provided a regular forum in which writings on Israeli cinema can be published. More than 200 essays dealing with Israeli cinema have appeared, and some of the articles are of pioneering importance and great value. Another phenomenon, the first signs of which appeared in *Sratim* and *Cinematheque*, is the publication of articles dealing with films on the Holocaust—one of the prominent issues in the Israeli film industry at the end of the 1980s. This period also saw the publication of books of memoirs (e.g. Davidon 1983) that describe chapters from the past without pretending to present an organized historical review.

At the beginning of the 1990s a series of books marked a significant breakthrough in the study of Israeli cinema. The first of these was by Igal Burstyn (Burstyn 1990). The book, which deals with the reciprocal relations between ideology and aesthetics in Israeli cinema (it analyses the manner in which faces are described/presented/acted in Israeli films from the beginning, and the underlying ideology this reveals), is of utmost importance because of the way it deviates from the social-political analysis that had characterized most books on Israeli cinema written up till then.

The second book, *East/West* by Ella Shohat (1989), was based on her doctoral thesis. The book was based mainly on the theories on 'Orientalism' developed by Edward W. Said (e.g. Said 1978, 1985); Shohat uses these theories to show how the concept of a 'primitive and backward' East has always shaped Israeli cinema, and how it especially affected the manner in which Eastern Jews and values were portrayed. Although many critics claimed that her account was one-sided and her point of view exaggerated, many others saw her book as one of the more important and significant works on Hebrew cinema.

The Hebrew Film—Chapters in the History of Moving Pictures and the Cinema in Israel, edited by N. and Y. Gross (Gross and Gross 1991), was the third of the important studies of Israeli cinema to appear in the 1990s. As its name implies, it is a book that deals with a variety of subjects without referring to sources or documents, and without taking into account the duty of the 'historian' to combine all of these into one consistent story. Even so, one can find some valuable elements in the book—especially in those parts that discuss pre-State days, which contain a massive amount of raw material on the pre-State cinema, and in the personal memoirs of Natan Gross in the chapters that describe the cinema in the early State years, which he witnessed as a Polish immigrant who wanted to become part of the local film industry.

The central theme of the fourth of these books, by Nurit Gertz (Gertz 1993), is an analysis of five full-length feature films adapted for the screen from novels or short stories. Two historical chapters (chaps. 1 and 5) describe the movie world in whose framework the adaptations were made. The book makes an important contribution by defining the status of the cinema within the Israeli cultural system, and by analyzing the reciprocal relationship between it and other cultural branches (especially literature) in this system. And even though this portrayal grants clear hegemony to literature over cinema, which is described as a medium that makes 'concessions' to the public in relation to the symbolism, the complex narrative structure, and the political and philosophical considerations of its literary sources, Gertz broadens the debate and makes a significant contribution to the Israeli cinema bookshelf. A similar contribution is made by Nitzan Ben-Shaul (Ben-Shaul 1993). Like Daniel Bar-Tal, Ben-Shaul discusses how 'the Masada Syndrome', which causes Israelis to feel that their very existence is constantly under threat, determines Israeli behaviour, and how various Israeli films (e.g. The Silver Platter and Beyond the Walls, 1984), express existential anxieties and points of view that are not 'realistic'.

A contribution of a totally different nature comes from Meir Schnitzer (Schnitzer 1994), who reviews all the feature films produced in Israel from the beginning of the 1930s to the beginning of the 1990s. This is an album-format book that supplies important information to anyone interested in getting a quick (but representative) aerial snapshot of the Israeli feature-film industry, along with some general explanation in the forewords to the period chapters (1930–60, 1960–70, 1970–80, 1980–90, 1994–) into which the book is divided. These, along with the book's foreword and a review by Schnitzer on each film, mark his book as more popular than academic, but this does not prevent its being one of the most useful tools available to anyone wishing to familiarize himself with, or do research on, Israeli cinema.

Another tool is provided by Hillel Tryster (1995), in a book primarily dedicated to the period that pre-dates the historical documentation of Israeli cinema. The kind of contribution it makes can be seen in the chapter 'Joseph Gal-Ezer: A Force for Film', in which a 'hero' is revealed whose role in the development of Hebrew cinema was previously unknown. Tryster credits Gal-Ezer with many accomplishments, the most important being that he convinced Keren Hayesod (the Palestine Foundation Fund) to support film production on a regular basis. Gal-Ezer is presented as a man who, by the beginning of the 1920s, already believed that Palestine could become a centre for Zionist and international film production.

In 1998 the Hebrew bookshelf was enriched by a pioneering anthology edited by Nurit Gertz, Orly Lubin, and Yehuda Ne'eman (Gertz, Lubin, and Ne'eman 1998). The essays cover several areas: a fresh presentation of the personal model; ideology in Israeli cinema; the Holocaust; man; postmodernism; religion; and aesthetics. The anthology is witness to the scope of research conducted and the number of active researchers who have appeared in the last quarter of the twentieth century. Additional evidence of this can be found in Ariel Schweitzer's book (Schweitzer 1998), which elaborately portrays the personal Israeli cinema—created in Israel between the middle of the 1960s and the end of the 1970s under the auspices of the 'French new wave'. The importance of this work is that it described and analysed many films (e.g. *Woman Instance* and *The Skirt*, 1969) that had never before been the subject of academic scrutiny, and gave a new and profound perspective to personal cinema as a whole.

Miri Talmon (2001) sheds light on a new, previously nearly unresearched aspect of film which deals with the role of youth movies and nostalgia films in Israeli cinema. The book reveals the extent to which these genres were deeply embedded in the Israeli cinema, against the accepted view that they came into being at the end of the 1970s, and it shows the role filled by nostalgia in the moulding and design of Israeli society in general, and its effect on the Israeli male in particular, who was expected to act according to a specific code dictated by Zionism in trying to fashion a New Jew (the *tsabar*). A more extensive treatment of these issues can also be found in Moshe Zimerman's books (Zimerman 2001a, b), that attempt to show how the three central Zionist myths (immigration, assimilation (melting-pot), and the *tsabar*) are essential ingredients for anyone wishing to understand Israeli cinema and society. The manner in which these myths were vulgarized after the Holocaust, causing the cinema and society to apply heavy pressure on the Jewish Holocaust survivors to transform themselves quickly into part of Israeli society, forms a base for Zimerman's third book (2002), which focuses on revealing the different stages in Israeli society's confrontation with the Holocaust. The myths are also central to the final chapter of his book on Tel Aviv (2001b), which describes the development of Israeli cinema up to 1948, and serve as a covert platform for introducing a number of creators and creations with Tel Aviv at their core.

These books constitute an intensified flow of works on cinema, and make essays on Israeli cinema a regular part of anthologies and prominent periodicals published in Israel and abroad (e.g. Gutkind-Golan 1990; Avisar 1996; Zimerman 1998, 1999; Ne'eman 1999; Lubin 1999; Gertz 1999). More remains to be done, such as the establishment of a central film archive, but it can be said that Israeli cinema research has come of age.

JEWISH FILM

As has already been suggested, a survey of writing about Jewish cinema is much more complicated than one of writing about Israeli cinema, because of the difficulty of defining 'Jewish cinema'. This can be exemplified by a number of questions, such as: are artists like Woody Allen—whose films are sometimes considered to be Jewish cinema (cf., e.g., Shechner 1983; Adler and Feinman 1975)—really creating Jewish movies, so that what is written about them is in effect writing on Jewish cinema? What distinguishes these directors from others, like Otto Preminger, Billy Wilder, Fritz Lang, and even Steven Spielberg (before and after *Schindler's List*), whose Jewishness leaves no mark on their films? By the same token, were Jewish producers—like those who set up many of the Hollywood studios and financed part of French movie-making before the Second World War—who shaped the production systems they controlled in accordance with their sensitivities, needs, and desires, partners in the creation of cinema with a Jewish dimension? Are books written about them, which emphasize their Jewishness and its influence on the systems (films and studios) they created, to be considered books about Jewish cinema?[26] Should every film that deals with Jews or is based on a Jewish literary or dramatic work be classified as 'Jewish cinema'?

The way out of this labyrinth of questions—only some of which have been presented here—would seem to be to abandon the attempt to define 'Jewish cinema' in favour of a description of what has been written (explicitly or implicitly) about groups of films that have Jews at their centre and/or for which the Jewishness of their creators is important for their 'correct' exegesis and 'full' understanding. Even if we can imagine some other classification or other groups of films that could be defined as Jewish, it seems logical to categorize films as 'Jewish', on the basis of what has been written about them, in five groups:

---

[26] e.g. Neal Gabler's *An Empire of Their Own: How the Jews Invented Hollywood* (1988), whose title alone suggests the degree of its relevance to the present issue; or Edward Baron Turk's book on Marcel Carné (1992), which describes, inter alia, the role played by (other) Jewish producers (and professionals) in shaping Carné's films.

1. Writing that focuses on films made as part of national cinema industries, which help us to see how films documented Jews, or how Jews were perceived by at least some members of that nation.

2. Attention to the Jewish presence in cinema during particular periods in the history of the cinema (French Poetic Realism and the European 'retro' cinema) and of general history (the Holocaust), or in various genres (the western, gangster films, war movies, comedies).

3. Writing that surveys the manner in which Judaism influenced the work of various figures (e.g. directors, producers, and screenwriters) who were active in different cinema industries, or film-makers who view their Jewishness (or whose Jewishness is viewed by others) as a key element in their work or understanding their work.

4. Attention to the manner in which Jews are presented in films based on the works of Jewish authors (e.g. Isaac Bashevis Singer and Sholem Aleichem), in branches of Jewish cinema (generally Yiddish) in various countries, and in films set in various historical eras (the Bible, the Second Temple period, the Middle Ages, the Second World War[53]). This helps in understanding how Jews were perceived in the periods with which the films deal (or were made).

5. Writing that analyses the Jewish presence in the cinema world, with the objective of studying the way this has been perceived over the years since the birth of cinema.

In attempting to describe the writing that belongs to these groups we shall discover that some of it (as will be noted explicitly) can be assigned to several groups, or can be associated with another group altogether. This fact, though, does not make the classification valueless. So let us begin.

1. National Cinema Industries

Most of the writing that focuses on films made in national cinema industries deals with the Jewish presence in the American movie world. There are several reasons for this: scholarly study of the cinema began in the United States; this scholarly study grew to larger proportions and acquired greater legitimacy in the United States than in other countries; many scholars all over the world deal with American cinema because of its vast influence throughout the world. Nevertheless, there are not very many books that deal with the Jewish presence in American cinema or in certain periods thereof. Among the most important are Fox (1976); L Friedman (1982); Erens (1984); L Friedman (1987); Rogin (1996). What all of these have in common is a survey (generally by decade) of the history of the Jewish presence in American cinema.

This presence began in the first decade of the twentieth century (to be more precise, in 1903), during which period there was nothing special or unique about the presentation of Jews.[27] Only toward the end of the decade (in the first screen version of *The Merchant of Venice*, 1908) is it possible to begin to identify a typical Jewish representation, which continued to develop during the next decade and which crystallized chiefly around three prominent archetypes. The first of these is the 'ugly Jew', modelled chiefly on stereotypes (such as greed, a lack of ethical and aesthetic feelings, and exploitation) that had been prevalent in the depiction of Jews during the Middle Ages and most of the modern era (especially the nineteenth century). This process was particularly conspicuous in the successive remakes of classic dramas (such as *The Merchant of Venice*, which appeared in screen versions in 1908, 1912, 1913, and 1914) and popular novels (notably *Oliver Twist*, versions and adaptations of which were released in 1909, 1910, 1912 (two versions), 1916, 1921, and 1922).

The second archetype is the 'old' Jew, practical and successful, found in films like *The Yiddisher Cowboy* (two versions, 1909 and 1911), *Foxy Izzy* (1911), and *Murphy and the Mermaids* (1914). These 'ghetto films', as Patricia Erens labels them, depict Jews who, despite their traditional ways (appearance, dress, and behaviour), are clever enough to overcome those who try to trick or harm them.

The third archetype is that of the 'modern Jew', as in *A Woodland Christmas in California* (1912), *Cohen Save the Flag* (1913), *Judith of Bethulia* (1913), *The Song of Solomon* (1914), *The Missing Diamond* (1914), and *A Daughter of Israel* (1914). In these films, Jews are generally depicted as manual labourers and merchants who fit into the 'new' American milieu, but also as bold fighters who do not hide their Jewishness (*Cohen Save the Flag*), or as individuals who belong to an industrious and enlightened historical people (*Judith of Bethulia*).

In the 1920s, the anti-Semitic image vanished almost completely (evidently because of the rise of the major Hollywood studios, most of which were founded by Jewish producers), but the other two models survived. They were joined by a few other stock characters: the successful Jewish businessman—as in *A Tailor-Made Man* (1922) and *Abie's Imported Bride* (1925)—who fully integrates into the American capitalist world; the famous figure whose Jewish origins were an important part of his life—as in *Prime Minister Disraeli* (1929), one of the first movies to win an Academy Award; comic Jews, as in *Humoresque* (1920), *Potash Perlmutter* (1923), *Cohen and the Kellys* (1926), films which show that humour is frequently the most prominent sign of the normal integration of an ethnic group into society at large. A film like *The Jazz Singer* (1927), in addition to being the first talkie, describes a Jew who abandons the world of tradition and (using the same talents that would have made his way in the society he left) blends into the modern world. Jews in ancient history, as in Cecil B. DeMille's *The Ten Commandments* (1923) and *King of Kings* (1927), are depicted with almost no connection to either the historical or the

---

[27] Examples are *Cohen's Advertising Scheme* (1904), created by Edison's production company, and *Old Isaac the Pawnbroker*, directed by D. W. Griffith in 1907.

contemporary Jew, in response to the cinematographic needs of Hollywood and the values that its magnates thought they should be providing to, or even inculcating into, the American public. True, we can trace the roots of this phenomenon back to *Judith of Bethulia*, but books that deal with the Jewish presence in American cinema ascribe only to films of the 1920s the elements that characterized this type of film from that time on—in works such as DeMille's *Samson and Delilah* (1949), his remake (forty-three years on) of *The Ten Commandments* (1956), and *Ben Hur* (1959).

In the 1930s Jews also became culture heroes representing values worthy of emulation—for example, in films like *The House of Rothschild* (1934)—as well as the objects of an anti-Semitic hatred that must be dealt with before it generates catastrophe. As examples of the latter trend, various books cite *Street Scene* and *Counselor-at-Law* (based on the successful 1933 plays by Elmer Rice) and Charlie Chaplin's *The Great Dictator* (1940). Discussions of these films focus on the fact that they were an early warning of the grave results that could come about as a result of anti-Semitism; unfortunately they miss the immense damage latent in these films (especially Chaplin's) by virtue of the fact that they lulled their audiences more than they cautioned them. Because they followed the Hollywood formula, which usually requires a happy ending, and always dispels the audience's anxieties, they created the illusion that it would be a simple matter to suppress anti-Semitism in general and Hitler in particular (I shall return to this point later).

Two other important developments occurred in the 1930s: Yiddish theatre and films based on it emerged into the limelight,[28] and Jewish interests ceased to be adequately protected by Hollywood's self-imposed censorship.

In the 1940s and 1950s, and even into the early 1960s, the trends of the twenties and thirties, which continued to characterize most American films that dealt with Jews, were augmented by three other trends that attempted to deal with Jewish existence in the aftermath of the Holocaust. Films like *Crossfire* (1944), *Gentleman's Agreement* (1947), and *The Young Lions* (1958) tried to show how widespread anti-Semitism was in broad circles of American society, and how eliminating it would permit those Jews who wished and were able to live like everyone else to become an integral part of that society. Films like *The Pawnbroker* (1965) attempted to explain why the Jews (before the Holocaust and all the more so after it) are pushed into becoming distrustful of their surroundings, cynical, and stubborn. In such films as *Exodus* (1960), *Judith* (1964), and *Cast a Giant Shadow* (1966), Jews in Israel were seen as an inseparable part of the Jewish people, and treated as a model for how Jews should conduct themselves in general, especially after the Holocaust. Today, with hindsight, we can say that these films were—each in its own way—also an expression of the need to avoid dealing with the Holocaust head-on, by denying or

---

[28] According to Spiegel (1983), whose article will be discussed later, 61 Yiddish films were made in New York between 1924 and 1961—most of them during the 1930s.

repressing its true meanings. This phenomenon dwindled in the late 1960s and the 1970s, after the first serious attempts to grapple with the Holocaust and the distinctive nature of American-Jewish identity.

To the books that cover the history of the representation of Jews in American cinema we must add articles and essays that deal with the topic, and relate to the Jewish representation in American cinema in general or in particular periods. Among these may be noted Miriam Hansen's *Babel and Babylon: Spectatorship in American Silent Film* (Hansen 1994), which deals (in part) with the Jewish presence in American silent films and distinguishes those made before the First World War, which Hansen, following Patricia Erens, calls 'ghetto films', from those made after. Whereas the former, for Hansen, 'dramatize conflicts between traditional values and American customs and attitudes' and highlight (and accept) the difficulties Jews experienced in blending into American life, the latter present (and encourage ideologically) Jews' participation in the American melting-pot, which includes all the ethnic groups that immigrated to the United States (Hansen 1994: 70–6). A similar approach, but covering a much longer period (from the start of the century until after the Second World War), can be found in Michael Rogin's *Ethnicity and the American Cinema* (1991), which deals with the depiction of Jewish integration into American society as compared with that of various other ethnic groups.

The manner in which this process is presented in films that dealt with Jews, from the beginning of the century, was also the starting-point for Alan Spiegel's comprehensive essay (Spiegel 1983). Spiegel, however, returns to this point not in order to consider the cinematic documentation of the Jews' integration into America, but to describe and analyse the change in how they have been depicted in American cinema from the late 1960s on (more precisely, the decade from the late 1960s to the late 1970s). At the centre of his essay are movies like *Funny Girl* (1968), *Goodbye Columbus* (1969), *Fiddler on the Roof* (1971), *The Way We Were* (1973), *Lenny* (1974), *The Apprenticeship of Duddy Kravitz* (1974), *Funny Lady* (1975), *Hester Street* (1975), *Next Stop, Greenwich Village* (1976), *A Star Is Born* (1975), *Interiors* (1979), and several films of Mel Brooks and Woody Allen that focused on the personal stories of children or grandchildren of the Jewish immigrants who came to America, and attempted to draw both an individual and a collective biography of their road through American society. This biography was created by Jewish directors and screenwriters like Brooks and Allen, Carl Reiner, Neil Simon, Paddy Chayefsky, Elaine May, Arnold Shulman, Marshal Brickman, Jules Feiffer, and Paul Mazursky, and performed by Jewish actors and actresses like Barbra Streisand, Alan Arkin, Richard Benjamin, George Segal, Elliot Gould, Walter Matthau, Richard Dreyfus, Dustin Hoffman (and, of course, also Brooks and Allen), who contributed their personal experiences and private worlds to the films (which they sometimes initiated or produced). We need only mention a few of the stereotypical 'Jewish mothers' who appeared in these films, and about whom Philip Roth wrote in his essay 'Some

New Jewish Stereotypes' (Roth 1977), to demonstrate the abundant confidence (both in the legitimacy of their Jewish identity and in the absence of anti-Semitism) that typifies the attitude of the artists responsible for these films.

Other surveys of the representation of Jews in national film industries—such as the French (discussed in the following section), the Australian (e.g. Freiberg 1993), and the Swedish (e.g. Wright 1998)—are few and marginal for countries other than the United States, France, and Israel. This phenomenon is spotlighted by the almost total omission of such references in books about the German cinema (cf. Saunders 1994, which attempts to wade cautiously between the two most famous books on German expressionism—Kracauer 1947, which linked Weimar cinema and the rise of Hitler, and Eisner 1969, which considered the aesthetics of this current—without ever mentioning how this cinema dealt with Jews or Judaism; so, too, in books about the new German cinema of the 1970s and 1980s, like Sandford 1980. And when one finally does find references to Judaism in a book about German cinema—for example, in Silberman 1995—they can be described as almost insulting in their brevity, as they appear only in respect of artists whose careers were damaged by the fact that they had made films that expressed great antipathy for Jews during the Third Reich (without considering the nature or significance of these films). As for Soviet cinema, the anthology on Chaplin, edited by P. Tatasheva and S. Achushkow (1945), which included articles by Eisenstein, Bleiman, and Kuznetsov (among the leading theoreticians of Soviet cinema), presented Chaplin's 'Jewishness' (in his films in general and in *The Great Dictator* in particular)[29] as the spearhead of the struggle against fascism; while Josephine Woii (2000) presents revolutionary changes—such as the repression or the flowering of culture and the cinema in the Soviet Union—as inseparably linked to anti-Semitic (or anti-anti-Semitic) processes that took place in Soviet society. The treatment of the 'Jewish presence' itself in Soviet films is scarcely addressed.

2. Cinema Periods and Film Genres

Even though it would have been possible to imagine abundant writing about the Jewish presence in various historical periods and genres, there are only two historical periods (Poetic Realism and 'retro' cinema) and a semi-genre/semi-era (Holocaust films) about which a serious amount has been written. A systematic perusal of the two most important books about the history of the French cinema—Abel (1984) and Crisp (1993)—reveals that Jews did not become an influence in French cinema until just before the Second World War. That was when one first heard—as is noted

[29] Chaplin was not Jewish, but from time to time there have been claims that he was of Jewish extraction and that this influenced the themes of his films.

in Crisps's book and in Turk 1992—critical voices opposed to the negative role of Jewish producers and of directors influenced by them in the French cinema. During the Occupation these voices became louder. Evidence of this can be found in remarks by Lucien Rebatet on Marcel Carné (Rebatet 1941: 87), and in the periodical *Le Film* (16 June 1941), where he wrote that 'Carné and his Jews made the French cinema wallow in degrading fatalistic determinism' Turk (1992: 87). rejects this position, but recounts how such accusations caused Carné to join the cinema industry guild (the Comité d'organisation de l'industrie cinématographique), established by the Germans during the Occupation to prevent Jews from working in the industry, and thus briefly to lose the opportunity to work with the screenwriter Jacques Prévert, with whom he had made several important films of Poetic Realism and whose association with Carné was described as a legend-making partnership.

Crisps's volume puts Carné's story into its overall historical context and explains why French cinema in the 1960s went back to deal with the trauma left behind in the collective memory by the occupation. A number of films, such as Claude Berril's *The Two of us* (1966), announced the new trend, but the official launch was Marcel Ophuls's *The Sorrow and the Pity* (1969), which sparked great interest. A long interview with Ophuls was published in *CINEMA 71* (no. 157, June 1971). The script from which it was shot was published in *L'Avant-scène du cinéma* (nos. 127–8, July–Sept. 1972). Hoffman (1975) wrote that the film was a watershed in the use of the cinematic medium to convey intellectual messages. Ferro (1977: 162) stated that the place of the film in the history of documentary films was on a par with the Bolshevik Revolution. Henri Rousseau (1991) pointed to the revolution set off by the film in the historical discourse and the rent it tore in the veil of silence that had enveloped part of what took place during the Second World War. Rousseau divided the many 'retro' films that burst through that hole into four groups: 'prosecutorial', which sought to uncover the truth about the Occupation period; 'chronological', which presented experiences (mainly of children) during that time; 'aesthetic', which used the Occupation as a platform for films that emphasized the artistic side; and 'exploitative', which used the Occupation to make perverted profit-oriented films.

The various currents of this stream set off a furious debate. Michel Foucault published a manifesto against the 'retro' film (Foucault 1974), out of fear that it would work against the intentions of its creators and replace dealing with the present with a flight into the past. Régine (Michal) Friedman contributed three articles (Friedman 1979, 1984, and 1990), in which she argued that such films should be analysed not only in the context of the past, but also from the point of view of the artist while making the film and the perspective of viewers when they watch it. Naomi Green (1995) contended that the retro films do not aim at, and certainly do not succeed in, reconstructing the past, but rather present a desirable picture of it in the hope of it serving as a model for the future. Michel Ciment and

Joseph Losey (1985) support Friedman's approach (Ciment 1985). Colette Milon's interview with Claude Lalouche, 'Un patchwork de bons sentiments' (1981), supports Naomi Green (Milon 1981). Ariel Schweitzer (2000) maintains that retro films rule out any attempt to model universal rules of behaviour that people might be required to follow. Jeanine Frank adopts Friedman's approach to the retro film, and notes, in parallel, that Claude Lanzmann's *Shoah* was a sign of its death and the beginning of a new era in which the Holocaust is presented as a mythical memory that must be dealt with in other than historical terms. (Frank 2000).

As for American cinema, Sam B. Girgus wrote in his *Hollywood Renaissance* (Girgus 1998: 171–2) to the effect that the film was only a stage in Elia Kazan's quest for identity: as the son of an immigrant, he wanted to understand why many Europeans, including Jews, wanted to reach America. Avisar (1988) argues that such a focus on the drama of personal identity is characteristic of many American Holocaust films, and illustrates his point with the statement that the film *The Diary of Anne Frank* 'preferred the action of the spiritually triumphant classical drama over the actual crushing experience of the Holocaust' (Avisar 1988: 120). Criticism of film's attempts to portray the Holocaust using the familiar models of the past is typical of early treatment of the subject: examples are H. H. Wollenberg (1949); André Bazin (1952a)—where Holocaust films are compared with Fritz Lang's *Metropolis* of 1927—and his article 'The Vanishing Jew of Our Popular Culture' (1952b), noting the public's reluctance to look at authentic pictures of the Holocaust. We can supplement these essays with texts that dealt with the Holocaust in the context of a discussion of Second World War movies: Lewis Jacobs (1967/8); J. Morella, E. Z. Epstein, and J. Griggs (1973); and Roger Manvell (1976).

The first treatment of the Holocaust itself can be identified in books and essays about non-American films that dealt with the Holocaust, such as Moskowitz (1959); Armes (1968); Josef Skvorecky (1971); Adler (1971); and Novak (1974). These texts, and others, which covered Polish, French, and Czech films, highlighted the fact that films showed few Nazis, did their utmost to camouflage the Jewishness of their protagonists, and attempted to achieve their goal through the 'irony of distancing' (Monaco 1978: 20). The Holocaust was still hard to depict, and was easier to deal with indirectly, by considering its impact on those who had experienced it directly or lived in its shadow after it was over.

Toward the end of the 1970s the Holocaust began to be depicted in a more concrete fashion. 'Retro' films and others, such as *The Garden of the Finzi-Contini* (1970), *The Night Porter* (1974), *Cabaret, The Man in the Glass Booth, The Eighty-First Blow, Seven Beauties* (1975), *Mr. Klein* (1976), *The Last Chapter, Holocaust* (teledrama, 1978), *The Tin Drum, Confidence (Bizalom), The Last Sea* (1979), *Image Before My Eyes, The Last Metro* (1980), *Mephisto* (1981), and *Sophie's Choice* (1982), garnered box-office success, recognition (Academy Awards), or were poetic trailblazers. These films were followed by books, periodicals, and essays, like Neil

Hurley's *Theology Through Film* (1976), and Judith Doneson's 'The Jew as a Female Figure in Holocaust Film' (1978)—a pioneering treatment of how women are depicted in Holocaust films, published in the first issue of *Shoah: A Review of Holocaust Studies and Commemoration*. Susan Sontag (1980) and Brian Winston (1981) both dealt with the propaganda aspects of films made in Nazi Germany in a much more methodical and profound way than did Hull (1969). Paul (1983) noted that the attention paid to the Holocaust is not merely historical, but also 'a manner of discourse, in which the portrayal of past events is a medium through which the filmmaker speaks to the audience of today about realities that concern them' (p. 83). Langer (1983) writes about the 1978 television mini-series *Holocaust*: 'The upset ending of *Holocaust*, minimizing the negative impact of all that has gone before, typifies the absence of insight and the externalization of horror that makes the entire production meretricious in its confrontation with disaster: wormwood and gall are mollified by aromatic spices from the Orient' (1986, 1983: 229).

Many of the defects that Langer (Langer 1986 [1983]) noted in *Holocaust* were successfully avoided by Claude Lanzmann in *Shoah* (1985). Many agree on this point, including Avisar (1988: 24–32) and most of the contributors to the anthology *Spielberg's Holocaust* (Loshitzky 1997). The film and its screenplay mark a turning-point in films about the Holocaust and its impact can be felt in subsequent writing on the subject. Among works to be noted are Hanson (1986); Doneson (1987); Avisar (1988); Koch (1989); Langer (1991); the articles by Anton Kaes and Yael Feldman (1992); the relevant articles in *The Netherlands and Nazi Genocide* (Colijn and Little 1992); André Colombat (1993); the anthology, *The Art of Memory: Holocaust Memorials in History* (Young 1994); and Nir 1996.

3. Creators of Cinema

Works deal with the influence of their Jewishness on the creators of cinema in different ways. Gabler 1988, which describes the growth of the American movie industry, sees the Jewish origins of its founders as a key motivator of their actions. Almost every essay and book on Woody Allen points to the influence of his Jewishness on his films (e.g. Adler and Feinman 1975: 9): 'Almost all of the Allen humor is rooted in those Brooklyn Jewish beginnings. There's the standard, for example, listening to the news while his mother knits a chicken.' Authors dealing with influence of Jewishness on film-makers tend to fall into two groups: those who deal with the Hollywood managers who built up the American film world; and those who look at the influence of their Jewishness on directors, scriptwriters, and so on. The first group includes Bergman (1971); Weinberger (1972); Erens (1975); Tugend (1975); Suber (1979); and Clarens (1980). The second includes Madsen (1973); Morris

(1975); B. Gross (1975); Hirt-Manheimer (1975); Simone Signoret's *La Nostalgie n'est plus ce qu'elle était* (1976); Corliss (1978); Dmytryk (1978); Campbell (1978); Tynan (1978); Walden (1980); Shechner (1983), and Pinsker (1983) and McBride (1997).

4. Jewish Sources for Films

Relatively little has been written about films based on Jewish works, on Yiddish cinema, and about films about Jews in various historical periods. On film adaptations of Jewish texts, one can mention, for instance, Robert Warshaw (1970), which describes the change that took place in material that tackled the Jewish milieu in America as it was transferred from stage to screen.

The little that has been written on Yiddish cinema—which includes films like *Yiddishe Gliken* (based on Sholem Aleichem; Soviet Union, 1925), *Uncle Mozes* (based on Sholem Asch; United States, 1932), and *Yid'l with a Fiddle* and *A Brivele der Mamma* (Poland, 1936 and 1938)—includes Michele Aaron (2000) and Davis (2001). The video *Almonds and Raisins: A History of the Yiddish Cinema*, produced by Ergo Media (in 1986), enables viewers to gain a reasonable acquaintance with the history of the Yiddish cinema.

As for films that depict Jews of various historical periods, Cripps (1975), and the books by Kenneth Short (1981) and Miriam Hanson (1994), all deal with how movies depicted the stages in Jewish immigrants' integration into American society during the first decades of the twentieth century. Perhaps so little has been written about the topics covered in this section because Jewish history since the Second World War has pushed them to the sidelines, while promoting to the main ring films dealing with the Holocaust and the State of Israel, as is indirectly maintained by Alan Spiegel (1983).

5. The Jewish Presence

There is very little writing on how Jews have been depicted through cinema as a whole. One can point to works like Sig Altman (1971) or the general survey *Cinéma et Judéité*, written by Michel Ciment for *Cinéma Action* (1986). Several works, such as Rovit (1976), shed light on the central issues relevant to the depiction of Jews in the cinema. With some stretching of boundaries one could include Robert F. Wilson's 'From Novel to Film: De-Sinistering *The Boys from Brazil*' (1979) as relevant here, because of its attention to fundamental questions that relate to how Jews are depicted in films based on literary works, but this does not significantly expand the pool of works that deal with the issue.

Two other categories might be included here. Melville Shevelson (1971), describes the author's experiences when filming *Cast a Giant Shadow* (1966) in Israel. Shevelson describes in humorous detail the many problems that beset the production, and thereby suggests the question: how did it happen that people quite similar to those who founded the giant movie empires in America did not manage to set up a parallel film industry in Israel? The second category is much more important, and concerns the historical and ethical significance of certain 'Jewish' films like *The Great Dictator* (Chaplin, 1940) and *To Be or Not to Be* (Lubitsch, 1942). The first buds of a discussion of these films can be found in texts referred to above (such as Insdorf 1979 and Avisar 1988), but they seem to miss the importance of the point they raise. I have referred above to the damage done by *The Great Dictator* in causing the Nazi menace not to be taken with appropriate seriousness by people in the United States. Even if this claim seems to be overblown and exaggerated, it contains the seeds of a discussion that should be developed. This view is reinforced by remarks made by Anita Shapira, in her 'Historiography and Memory: The Case of Latrun 1948' (in Shapira 1997: 46):

In parallel with the expansion of the areas of historical research, the growth in the number of scholars...the improvement of research tools...academic historiography is losing its influence—even that limited amount it used to have—in shaping the picture of the past engraved in the public imagination. I maintain that the collective memory is not shaped by professional historians, but by a series of 'agents of memory,' who fashion the picture of the past in accordance with the needs of the present and its distresses.... The press, the novel, poetry, cinema, television—they have greater power in painting the picture of the past than do the careful and measured words of well-documented research, to the point of relegating it to the margins of public awareness.

Shapira's view of historiography is, I believe, a fitting conclusion to this survey.

SUGGESTED READING

On Jewish films in the United States, see Fox (1976) and, more generally, Erens (1984). For an introduction to Israeli film studies, see Arzooni (1983), Shohat (1991), and Schnitzer (1993).

BIBLIOGRAPHY

AARON, M. 2000. 'The Queer Jew and Cinema: From Yidl to Yentel and Back and Beyond.' *Jewish History and Culture* 3/1: 23–44.
ABEL, R. 1984. *French Cinema: The First Wave 1915–1929*. Princeton, New Jersey.
ADLER, B. and FEINMAN, J. 1975. *Woody Allen: Clown Prince of American Humor*. New York.
ADLER, R. 1971. *A Year in the Dark*. New York.
ALTMAN, S. 1971. *The Comic Image of the Jew*. Rutherford, NJ.

ARMES, R. 1968. *The Cinema of Alain Resnais.* New York.

ARZOONI, O. G. 1983. *The Israeli Film: Social and Cultural Influences 1912–1973.* New York and London.

AVISAR, I. 1988. *Screening the Holocaust: Cinema's Image of the Unimaginable.* Bloomington, Ind.

—— 1996. 'Israeli Cinema and the Ending of Zionist Ideology.' In *Israel in the Nineties.* 153–69. F. Lazin and G. Mahler eds. Gainesville, Vg.

AXELROD, N. forthcoming. *Memories.* Jerusalem.

BAR-TAL, D. 1984. 'The Massed Syndrome: A Case of Central Belief.' *Discussion Paper 3.* Tel Aviv.

BARRY, D. 2001. 'The Era of Yiddish Film.' *Manna 71.*

BAZIN, A. 1952a. 'Les Ghettos Concentrationnaires.' *Cahiers du Cinéma.* Feb.

—— 1952b. 'The Vanishing Jew of our Popular Culture.' *Commentary* 14 July.

—— 1981. *French Cinema of the Occupation and Resistance: The Birth of a Critical Esthetic.* New York.

BEERI, L. 1980. 'Films and Cinema Halls.' In *The First Twenty Years: Literature and Art in 'Little Tel Aviv'.* 272–94. A. B. Joffe ed. Tel Aviv.

BEN-ISRAEL, S. 1932. 'Secrets of the Damp Room.' *Kolnoa* Oct. pp. 5–8.

BEN SHAUL, N. 1993. *Expression of the 'Siege Syndrome' in Israeli Films.* Ann Arbor, Mich.

BEN YEHUDA, H. 1900. 'The Dreyfus Trial's Diary.' *Hatzvi.* 18 Sivan, p. 4.

—— 1908. 'The "Oracle" in Olympic Hotel.' *Hatzvi.* 8 Heshvan, p. 3.

—— 1909a. 'The Cinema Comes to Jaffa.' *Hatzvi* 23 Shvat, p. 4.

—— 1909b. 'The Purim Celebrations in Jaffa.' *Hatzvi* 19 Adar, p. 5.

BERGMAN, A. 1971. *We're In the Money.* New York.

BNASHKIVIZ, Y. 1966. *History of Polish Cinema.* Warsaw.

BOWLES, S. E. 1979. *Sidney Lumet.* Boston.

BRESSON, R. 1999/75. *Notes sur le Cinematographe.* A. Schweitzer Introduction and Preface. Jerusalem.

BURSZTYN, I. 1990. *Face as Battlefield.* Tel Aviv.

CAMPBELL, R. 1978. 'The Ideology of the Social Consciousness Movie: Three Films of Daryl F. Zanuck.' *Quarterly Review of Film Studies* 3/1: 51–4.

CHAPLIN, C. 1964. *My Autobiography.* New York.

CLARENS, C. 1980. *Crime Movies.* New York.

CIMENT, M. 1985. *Conversations with Losey.* New York and London.

—— 1986. 'Cinema et Judéité.' *Cinema Action.* Paris.

'Cinema on the Farmers of Rishon LeZion' [no author given] 1913. Article in *Hapoel Hatsair.* Spring, 1913.

COHEN, S. B. ed. 1983. *From Hester Street to Hollywood: The Jewish-American Stage and Screen.* Bloomington, Ind.

COLIJN, G. J. and LITTEL, M. S. eds. 1992. *The Netherlands and Nazi Genocide: Papers of the 21st Annual Scholars' Conference.* New York.

COLOMBAT, A. P. 1993. *The Holocaust in French Film.* New Jersey and London.

CORLISS, R. 1978. 'Paul Mazursky: A Poet for People Like Us.' *New Times* 3 Apr. pp. 53–8.

CRIPPS, T. 1975. 'The Movie Jew as an Image of Assimilation 1903–1927.' *Journal of Popular Film* 4: 190–207.

CRISP, C. 1993. *The Classic French Cinema 1930–1960*. Bloomington, Ind.

DAVIDON, Y. 1983. *Forced Love*. Tel Aviv. [Hebrew].

DAVIS, B. 2001. 'The Era of Yiddish Film.' *Manna* 71 Spring.

DESSER, D. and FRIEDMAN, L. D. 1993. *American-Jewish Filmmaker: Tradition and Trends*. Chicago.

DINAR, B. 1946. 'At Last They Found the Actors.' *Hagalgal* 11/7: 4–11.

DMYTRYK, E. 1978. *It's a Hell of a Life But Not a Bad Living*. New York.

DONESON, J. E. 1978. 'The Jew as a Female Figure in Holocaust Film.' *Shoah: A Review of Holocaust Studies and Commemoration* 1: 11–3.

—— 1987. *The Holocaust in American Film*. Philadelphia, New York, and Jerusalem.

—— 1992. 'Feminine Stereotypes of Jews in Holocaust Film: Focus on the Diary of Anne Franck.' In Colijn and Littel (1992).

EISNER, L. 1969. *The Haunted Screen*. London.

ERENS, P. 1975. 'Gangsters, Vampires, and J.A.P'S: The Jew Surface in the American Movies.' *Journal of Popular Film* 4: 208–23.

—— 1984. *The Jewish Image in American Cinema*. Bloomington, Ind.

ERLICH, V. 1965. *Russian Formalism: History—Doctrine*. Paris.

EVEN-ZOHAR, I. 1978. *Papers in Historical Poetics*. Tel Aviv.

FELDMAN, Y. 1992. 'Whose Story Is It Anyway?' In Friedlander (1992): 223–39.

FERRO, M. 1977. *Cinema et histoire*. Paris

FINARO, E. ed. 1982–2002. *Cinematheque*. Tel Aviv.

FOUCAULT, M. 1974. 'Anti-Retro.' *Cahiers du Cinéma* 251–2: 5–15.

FOX, S. 1976. *Jewish Film in the United States: A Comprehensive Survey and Descriptive Filmography*. Boston.

FRANCK, J. 2000. 'Representation of the Holocaust in French Movies: 1945–1985'. Unpublished MA diss., Tel Aviv University.

FREIBERG, F. 1993. 'Lost in Oz? Jews in the Australian Cinema.' *Generation* 3/4: 19–22.

FRIEDLÄNDER, S. ed. 1992. *Probing the Limits of Representation: Nazism and the 'Final Solution'*. Cambridge.

FRIEDMAN, L. D. 1982. *Hollywood's Image of the Jew*. New York.

—— 1987. *50 Greatest Jewish Movies: A Critic's Ranking of the Very Best*. New York.

FRIEDMAN, R. M. 1979. 'Les Juif et les camps dans le cinéma retro.' *Les Nouveaux Cahiers* 58.

—— 1984. 'Exorcising the Past: Jewish Figures in "Contemporary Films".' *Journal of Contemporary History* 19/3: 512–27.

—— 1990. 'The Periods of French Resistance Films: The Case of the Red Poster.' *Film and History* 20/3: 51–61.

GABLER, N. 1993 [1988]. *An Empire of Their Own: How the Jews Invented Hollywood*. Tel Aviv.

GEFFEN, M. 1980. '"A Visit to the Father Land": William Topkis' Diary.' *Catedra* 13: 72–94.

GERTZ, N. 1987. 'Away Went the Gang.' *Sratim* 3.

—— *Motion Fiction: Israeli Fiction in Film*. Tel Aviv.

—— 1994. 'From Destruction to Redemption: Israeli Literature and Cinema.' *Shofar* 13/1: 55–67.

—— 1999. 'From Jew to Hebrew: The Zionist Narrative in the Israeli Cinema of the 1950s and 1940s.' *Israel Studies* 4/1: 72–99.

GERTZ, N., LUBIN, O., and NEEMAN, J. 1998. *Fictive Looks—On Israeli Cinema*. Tel Aviv.

GIANETTI, L. 2000. *Understanding Movies*. Tel Aviv.

GIRGUS, S. B. 1998. *Hollywood Renaissance: The Cinema of Democracy in the Era of Ford, Capra, and Kazan*. Cambridge.

GREEN, E. ed. 1985. *Movies Makers on Movie Making*. Tel Aviv.

GREEN, N. 1995. 'La vie en rose: Image of the Occupation in French Cinema.' In *Auschwitz and After: Race, Culture and 'The Jewish Question' in France*. 283–98. L. D. Kritzman ed. New York.

GREENBERG, D. ed. 1957–63. *Amanut Hakolnoa*. Tel Aviv.

GROSS, B. 1975. 'No Victim She: Barbra Streisand and the Movie Jew.' *The Journal of Ethnic Studies* 3/1: 28–40.

GROSS, N. and GROSS, Y. 1991. *The Hebrew Film—Chapters in the History of Moving Pictures in Israel*. Jerusalem.

GUTKIND-GOLAN, N. 1990. 'The Heikhal Cinema Issue.' In *Religious and Secular: Conflict and Accommodation Between Jews in Israel*. C. S. Liebman ed. Jerusalem.

HAMEIRI, A. 1927. 'Chaplin the Artist.' *Ha'aretz* 1 Feb. Tel Aviv.

HAMPTON, B. B. 1970. *History of the American Film Industry From its Beginning To 1931*. New York.

HANSEN, M. 1994. *Babel and Babylon: Spectatorship in American Silent Film*. Cambridge.

HANSON, M. 1986. 'La Choah et la mode retro.' *Les Nouveaux cahiers* 84.

HAREL, Y. 1956. 'Thirty Years of Israeli Cinema.' In *The Cinema from its Beginning to the Present Day*. 216–40 Tel Aviv.

HIRT-MANHEIMER, A. 1975. 'From Jews to Jaws.' *Davka* Fall: 32–40.

HOFFMANN, S. 1975. *The Sorrow and the Pity: Chronicle of a French City Under the German Occupation*. London.

HULL, D. S. 1969. *Film in the Third Reich*. Berkeley and Los Angeles.

INGMAR, N., KLEIN, U., KLEIN, I., and NATAN, M. eds. 1974–81. *Kolnoa* (Magazine). Tel Aviv.

INSDORF, A. 1979. 'Take Two: To Be or Not to Be.' *American Film* Nov. 80–1.

—— 1989. *Indelible Shadows: Film and the Holocaust*. New York.

JABOTINSKY, Z. 1948a. 'On America.' In *Jabotinsky's Writings*. Vol 6: 183–204. Jerusalem.

—— 1948b. 'What One Reads What One Thinks.' In *Jabotinsky's Writings*. Vol 6. Jerusalem: 309–18.

—— 1949. 'Scent Of the Gilead.' In *Jabotinsky's Writings* Vol. 7: 55–112. Jerusalem.

—— 1950. *Samson*. Jerusalem.

JACOBS, L. 1967–8. 'World War II and the American Film.' *Cinema Journal* Winter. pp. 32–8.

JAKOBSON, R. 1971. *Selected Writing*. Vols. 1 and 2. Paris.

JOFFÉ, A. B. 1953. *Charlie Chaplin: Étude Biographique et Critique*. Merchavia.

—— ed. 1980. *The First Twenty Years: Literature and Art in 'Little Tel Aviv'*. Tel Aviv.

KAES, A. 1989. *From Hitler to Heimat: The Return of History as Film*. Cambridge.

—— 1992. 'Holocaust and the End of History.' In Friedlander (1992). 206–22.

KAZAN, E. 1994 [1988]. *A Life*. Tel Aviv.

KELER, H. ed. 1975. *A Legendary World: An Anthology of the Cinema*. Tel Aviv.

KLAUSNER, M. 1974. *The Dream Industry*. Tel Aviv.

KLEIN, A. 1975. 'The First Film Show.' *Kolnoa* 5: 75–80.

KOCH, G. 1989. 'The Aesthetic Transformation of the Image of the Unimaginable in Claude Lanzmann's Shoah.' *October* 48 (Spring): 28–38.

KOMROV, G. ed. 1939–52. *Kolnoa* (Magazine). Tel Aviv.

—— 1948. 'Adama.' *Kolnoa* 30 Sept. Tel Aviv. pp. 1–5.

KRACAUER, S. 1947. *From Caligari to Hitler: A Psychological History of the German Film.* Princeton.

KRITZMAN, L. D. ed. 1995. *Auschwitz and After: Race, Culture and 'The Jewish Question' in France.* New York.

LANGER, L. L. 1983. 'The Americanization of the Holocaust on Stage and Screen.' In Cohen (1983): 213–30.

—— 1991. *Holocaust Testimonies: The Ruins of Memory.* New Haven.

LANZMANN, C. 1985a. *Shoah.* Paris.

—— 1985b. *Shoah: An Oral History of the Holocaust.* New York.

LEAHY, J. 1986. *The Cinema of Joseph Losey.* Jerusalem.

LEVIN, M. 1985. 'Yaacov Ben-Dov and the Beginning of the Film Industry in Eretz-Israel.' *Catedra* 38: 127–34.

LEYDA, J. 1973. *Kino: A History of the Russian and Soviet Film.* New York.

LIEBMAN, C. S. 1990. *Religious and Secular: Conflict and Accommodation Between Jews in Israel.* Jerusalem.

LIEHM, M. and LIEHM, A. J. 1977. *The Most Important Art: Eastern European Film After 1945.* Berkeley.

LOSHITSKY, Y. ed. 1997. *Spielberg's Holocaust: Critical Perspectives on 'Schindler's List'.* Bloomington, Ind.

LUBIN, O. 1999. 'Body and Territory: Women in Israeli Cinema.' *Israel Studies* 4/1: 175–87.

MCBRIDE, J. 1997. *Steven Spielberg: A Biography.* New York.

MADSEN, A. 1973. *William Wyler.* New York.

MALKIN, Y. ed. 1973–75. *Close-Up* (Magazine). Tel Aviv.

MANVELL, R. 1975. *Films of Second World War.* New York.

MAST, J. and KAWIN, B. F. 2002 [1996]. *A Short History of the Movies.* Tel Aviv.

MAY, R. 1935. *Charlie Chaplin in time: souvenirs recueillis par Claire Goll.* Paris.

MILON, C. 1981. 'Un patchwork de bons sentiments.' *Combat Socialiste* 3: 19–27.

MILTON, S. 1985. 'The Camera as Weapon: Documentary Photography and the Holocaust.' In *The Wiesenthal Center Annual.* Vol. 1: 35–42.

MONACO, J. 1978. *Alain Resnais.* New York.

MORELLA, J., EPSTEIN, E. Z., and GRIGGS, J. 1973. *The Films of World War II.* New York, NJ.

MORRIS, C. 1975. 'Roger Corman: The Schlemiel as Outlaw.' In *The Kings of Bs.* 77–92. T. McCarthy and C. Charles Flynn eds. New York.

MOSKOWITZ, G. 1959. 'The Uneasy East.' *Sight and Sound* 27: 18–24.

MUKAROVSKY, J. 1970. *Aesthetic, Function, Norm and Value as Social Facts.* Ann Arbor, Mich.

NATAN, M. 1968. 'Conversations with David Perlov.' *Keshet* (Autumn). Tel Aviv.

NEEMAN, J. 1999. 'The Dead Mask of the Moderns: A Genealogy of New Sensibility Cinema in Israel.' *Israel Studies* 4/1: 100–28.

NIR, Y. 1996. 'Jews as Powerful Victims: Ambivalent Attitudes in Retrospective Cinema.' In *Major Changes Within the Jewish People in the Wake of Holocaust*. 27–40. Jerusalem

NOVAK, A. 1974. *Film and Filmmakers in Czechoslovakia*. Prague.

OPHULS, M. 1972a. 'Le Chagrin et la pitié.' *L'Avant-scene du cinema* 127–8 (juillet–septembre). Paris.

—— 1972b. *The Sorrow and the Pity*. Trans. M. Jonston. New York.

PAUL, D. W. ed. 1983. *Politics, Art and Commitment in the East European Cinema*. London.

PINSKER, S. 1986 [1983]. 'Mel Brooks and the Cinema of Exhaustion.' In Cohen (1983): 245–56.

PRATLEY, G. 1969. *The Cinema of John Frankenheimer*. New York.

RADOMSKY, S. ed. 1952–92. *Olam Hakolnoa* (Magazine). Tel Aviv.

REBATET, L. 1941. *Les Tribus du cinéma et du theatre*. Paris.

'RISHON LE ZION' [no author given] 1913. Article in *Haherut*. 29 May 1913.

ROGIN, M. 1991. *Ethnicity and the American Cinema*. Chicago.

—— 1996. *Black face, White Noise: Jewish Immigrants in the Hollywood Melting Pot*. Berkeley and Los Angeles.

ROSKIES, D. G. 1984. *Against the Apocalypse: Response to Catastrophe in Modern Jewish Culture*. Cambridge, Mass.

ROTH, P. 1977. 'Some New Jewish Stereotypes.' In *Reading Myself and Others*. 75–90. New York.

ROVIT, E. 1976. 'Jewish Humor and American Life.' In *Howe*. I. Herzog ed. New York.

ROUSSO, H. 1991 [1987]. *The Vichy Syndrome: History and Memory in France Since 1944*. Cambridge, Mass.

SAID, E. W. 1978. *Orientalism*. New York.

—— 1983. *Orientalism Reconsidered*. Cambridge, Mass.

SANDFORD, J. 1980. *The New German Cinema*. New York.

SAUNDERS, T. J. 1994. *Hollywood in Berlin: American Cinema and Weimar Germany*. Los Angeles.

SCHATZ, B. 1924. *Built-Up Jerusalem*. Paris.

SCHORR, R. 1988. 'Des Terres Desertiques aux Terres de la Nuit: 40 ans de cinéma en Israel.' *Ariel* 71–2: 106–27.

SCHNITZER, M. 1993. *Israeli Cinema—Facts/Plots/Directors/Opinions: The First Complete Lexicon of Israeli Films 1932–1993*. Tel Aviv.

SCHWARZ, O. and ROTEM, A. eds. 1985–2000. *Sratim*. Tel Aviv.

SCHWEITZER, A. 1998. *Le Cinéma israelien de la modernité*. Paris.

SCHWIZER, A. 2000. 'Pasqualin, les camps et la morale de la jungle.' *Vertigo* 20.

SETH, C. and DRAY, P. 1984. *Hollywood Films of the Seventies: Sex , Drugs, Violence, Rock 'n' roll and Politics*. New York.

SHAPIRA, A. (1997) *New Jews, Old Jews* [Hebrew]. Tel Aviv.

SHECHNER, M. 1986 [1983]. 'Woody Allen: The Failure of the Therapeutic.' In Cohen (1983). 231–44.

SHEVELSON, M. 1971. *How To Make a Jewish Movie*. Englewood Cliffs, NJ.

SHIKLOVSKY, V. 1965 [1917]. 'Art as Technique.' In *Russian Formalist Criticism*. L. T. Lemon ed. New York and Lincoln.

SHOHAT, E. 1989. *East/West and the Politics of Representation.* Austin, Tex.

—— 1991. *The Israeli Cinema: History and Ideology.* [Hebrew]. Tel Aviv.

SHORT, K. R. M. 1981. *Jews in Feature Film History.* Knoxville, Tenn.

SIGNORET, S. 1976. *La Nostalgie n'est plus ce qu'elle etait.* Paris.

SILBERMAN, M. 1995. *German Cinema: Text in Context.* Detroit, Mich.

SKVORECKY, J. 1971. *All the Bright Young Men and Women: A Personal History of the Czech Cinema.* Trans. M. Schonberg. Toronto.

SONTAG, S. 1975. 'Persona: The Film in Depth.' In *Ingmar Bergman: Essays in Criticism.* 92–110. S. Kaminsky ed. New York.

—— 1980. *Under the Sign of Saturn.* New York.

SPIEGEL, A. 1983. 'The Vanishing Act: A Typology of the Jew in the Contemporary American Film.' In Cohen (1983): 257–75.

SPOTO, D. 1991. *The Dark Side of a Genius: The Life of Alfred Hitchcock.* Tel Aviv.

STEINER, P. ed. 1970. *The Prague School—Selected Writing.* New York.

SUBER, H. 1979. 'Politics and Popular Culture: Hollywood at Bay 1933–1953.' *American Jewish History* 67/4: 22.

TALMON, M. 2001. *Israeli Graffiti: Nostalgia, Groups, and Collective Identity in Israeli Cinema.* Tel Aviv.

TATASHEVA, P. and ACHUSHCOW, S. eds. 1945. *Chaplin.* Moscow.

TRUFFAUT, F. 1987 [1975]. *Les Films de ma vie.* Tel Aviv.

TRYSTER, H. 1995. *Israel Before Israel: Silent Cinema in the Holy Land.* Jerusalem.

TUGEND, T. 1975. 'The Hollywood Jews.' *Davka Magazine* Fall: 4–8.

TURK, E. B. 1992. *Child of Paradise: Marcel Carné and the Golden Age of French Cinema.* Cambridge.

TYNAN, K. 1978. 'Mel Brooks: Frolics and Detours of a Short Hebrew Man.' *New Yorker* Oct. 30.

TYNJANOV, J. 1971. 'On Literary Evolution.' In *Reading in Russian Poetics.* 120–37. L. Matejka and A. Pomorska eds. London and Cambridge, Mass.

WALDEN, D. 1980. 'Neil Simon: Towards Chapter III.' *Melus* 7/2: 77–85.

—— 1986 [1983]. 'Neil Simon's Jewish-Style Comedies.' In Cohen (1983): 152–66.

WARSHAW, R. 1970. 'Clifford Odets: Poet of the Jewish Middle Class.' In *The Immediate Experience.* 92–104. New York.

WEINBERGER, D. 1972. 'The Socially Acceptable Immigrant Minority Group: The Image of the Jew in American Popular Films.' *North Dakota Quarterly* 40: 60–8.

WILSON, R. F. 1979. 'From Novel to Film: De-Sinistering The Boys From Brazil.' *Film/Literature Quarterly* 7/4: 322–4.

WINSTON, B. 1981. 'Was Hitler There?' *Sight and Sound* (Spring). 8–14.

WOLL, J. 2000. *Real Images: Soviet Cinema and the Thaw.* New York.

WOLLENBERG, H. H. 1949. 'The Jewish Theme in Contemporary Cinema.' *Penguin Film Review* 8: 28–32.

WRIGHT, R. 1998. *The Visible Wall: Jews and Other Ethnic Outsiders in Sweden.* Chicago.

YAVSIVTZKY, V. 1925. *Material for the Annals of Cinema in Poland.* Warsaw.

YOUNG, J. ed. 1994. *The Art of Memory: Holocaust Memorials in History.* New York.

ZIMERMAN, M. 1998. 'Avec la Joie et le Plaisir.' *Champs Visuelle* 11: 60–74. Paris.

——1999. 'The Development of Hebrew Cinema in the Jewish Settlement.' In *History of the Jewish Community in Eretz-Israel Since 1882—Part One.* 573–92. M. Lisak and Z. Shavit eds. Jerusalem.

——2001a. *Signs of Movies: History of Israeli Cinema in the Years 1896–1948.* Tel Aviv.

——2001b. *Tel Aviv Was Never Small.* Tel Aviv.

——2002. *Leave My Holocaust Alone: The Impact of the Holocaust on Israeli Cinema and Society.* Haifa and Lod.

CHAPTER 37

ANTI-SEMITISM RESEARCH

WOLFGANG BENZ

ANTI-SEMITISM—a term that came into use in the last third of the nineteenth century—in modern usage refers to all anti-Jewish statements, tendencies, resentments, attitudes, and actions, regardless of whether they are religiously, racially, socially, or otherwise motivated (Nipperdey and Rürup 1972–92: 129–153; Hoffmann 1994: 293–317). Ever since the experience of National Socialist ideology and dictatorship, anti-Semitism has been understood as a social phenomena which serves as a paradigm for the formation of prejudices and the political exploitation of the hostilities that ensue from them.

It is not a coincidence that anti-Semitism research in Germany holds a special position. The Centre for Anti-Semitism Research at the Technical University in Berlin, founded in 1982, is the only academic institute dedicated solely to this subject. The following chapter focuses primarily on the perspectives of this institute and the problems of anti-Semitism research from a German standpoint. There are, however, a number of other institutes which also address anti-Semitism research—either in connection with Jewish studies or the history and impact of the Holocaust—on a social-scientific basis, within other disciplines, or as part of current educational aims.

There are two Israeli institutions, in particular, that have made important contributions to international research: the Vidal Sassoon International Centre for the Study of Anti-Semitism at the Hebrew University of Jerusalem has, since 1982, organized many conferences and established itself as an important centre for international academic discourse. Additionally, as part of the Felix Posen Biblio-graphic Project, it has created a database containing over 30,000 titles related to every aspect of anti-Semitism. The second institution, the Stephen Roth Institute for the Study of Contemporary Anti-Semitism and Racism at Tel Aviv University (since 1991 under the auspices of the Wiener Library), has developed a database to keep track of contemporary anti-Semitism and extremist right-wing groups, and based on this has, since 1993, published in co-operation with the Anti-Defamation League (New York) the annual report *Antisemitism Worldwide*, which lists related manifestations and incidents according to country.

Why, in addition to political education and various forms both of public clar-ification and defensiveness, is academic research conducted on anti-Jewish resent-ments? (The term here encompasses the entire historical spectrum spanning from prejudice to genocide: see Benz and Bergmann 1997). What distinguishes research on anti-Semitism from 'Jewish studies'? The following chapter will attempt to provide both answers and to make distinctions. In order to do this, however, it is necessary first to define the field and to outline its methods and disciplines, or more precisely, to identify the many diverse themes and subjects that make up the field of anti-Semitism research.

Anti-Semitism research, unlike, for example, studies in medieval history or cultural sociology, is not a scholarly discipline that exists as part of a larger whole within the canon of university departments. There is only one university (the Technical University of Berlin) at which anti-Semitism research has been established as an independent department, but anti-Semitism is both researched and combated in many different disciplinary contexts and constellations (religious studies and theology, psychology and sociology, ethnology and art history, philoso-phy and history, just to name a few), albeit often without methodological tools and sometimes with more zeal than skill. This assertion, naturally, requires illustration. And it will also be necessary to consider the specific nature of anti-Semitism research in scholarship.

In regard to recent history, for which there are people still living who can tell of their experiences (in this case, the experience of persecution), there is a tendency to see witnesses as sufficiently qualified to explain past events. In other words, when in doubt, the public usually grants to historical witnesses and to the people who were personally affected by past events a larger degree of competence in relaying and analysing these experiences than they do the historian, who addresses the subject from a scholarly perspective. Just as the witnesses assume as their natural right the responsibility of providing explanations and definitions to the younger generation, so the victims of anti-Semitism are usually regarded as automatically competent to define and analyse the origins, motives, and consequences of anti-Jewish hostility (and not only that which they have experienced). But it is very important even here—in explaining anti-Semitism as a form of prejudice and examining its consequences—to draw distinctions, and to separate personal experience with anti-Semitism from the scholarly investigations of hostility towards Jews.

Discrepancies occasionally develop which are difficult to bridge, between, on the one hand, the importance and essentialness of authentic autobiographical sources, both to research on anti-Semitism and to contemporary history in general, and on the other hand, the aim of providing a definitive explanation of the described phenomena. To try to conduct research on anti-Semitism without contact and dialogue with people who can share with scholars their experiences of anti-Semitism is, of course, virtually impossible. Anyone who is seriously involved in work on prejudice research and Jewish history is clear on that point. But it must be recognized that the tension between critical, scholarly distance, the empathy of researchers, and the personal experience of victims characterizes the field to a considerable degree and constitutes its social relevance.[1]

The scholarly preoccupation with anti-Jewish hostility, without regard for its origins, motives, or traditions, occurs on an interdisciplinary level, with many different branches of scholarship working together and using different methods. The subject of prejudice against minorities attracts the interest of various disciplines without requiring them to submerge themselves into a new field. Naturally, co-operation is necessary between the different disciplines and their specific subjects, which include themes as various as the literary metaphor, the national-cultural image of Jews (Rohrbacher and Schmidt 1991), the semantic stereotype, the historical connotation, and the religious construct, just to name a few. Through the different methodologies, these phenomena can be illuminated to provide a more complex explanation based on different perspectives. A variety of methodological approaches is thus a prerequisite of anti-Semitism research. But the task still remains to provide a definition of the field.

Many people, driven by ethical convictions and upright attitudes, feel themselves called upon to explain the phenomenon of hostility towards Jews, to diagnose its causes and prescribe therapy in order to heal civilized society of an evil whose symptoms include intolerance, racism, social bigotry, and xenophobia. This interest and zeal stems from the historical catastrophe which converted existing resentments against the Jewish minority into politics and which culminated in the exterminating excesses of the Holocaust. In this naive approach to the problem, the fact is often overlooked that every science requires methods and theories, and that empathy and political will do not suffice.

---

[1] This is symptomatically demonstrated by the questions that researchers of anti-Semitism are often asked concerning their personal motivation and background. The expected responses ('repentance' by those whose relatives were involved in National Socialism, 'revenge' by those who lost family in the Holocaust, or 'sense of mission' by those who feel personally moved by the history, are diametrically opposed to the setting of the question: whether it is posed in a German national context or among Holocaust survivors. Whatever the case, it is the question that defines the field for the audience.

History and literary studies are the disciplines which traditionally make contributions to research on anti-Semitism based on method and content. Studies of motives and images of Jews are the classical subjects of literary studies. From the modern understanding of interdisciplinary research, non-literary references are used to examine literary imagery, and thanks to this approach, which overcomes the positivistic-naive understanding of metaphors (Klüger 1994), important findings have been made on the unreal images of Jews as they effect anti-Semitic resentments (Heil and Wacker 1997). Shylock and Nathan, Ahasuerus and the 'beautiful Jewess', as paradigms of Jewish existence have been defined by recent research as artistic literary figures, which do not correspond—as was previously falsely believed to the non-literary reality (see Körte 1998: 140–50).

Once the Frankfurt Institute for Social Research was established in the early 1940s, social scientists began to make 'anti-Semitism' the subject of studies which (from exile), provided explanatory models that are still effective today (Bergmann and Erb 1998: 103–20). Both qualitative and quantitative studies which use scales to measure anti-Semitism and authoritarianism, as well as the foundations set by general prejudice research, have their origins in these approaches. Although the emphasis of focus in the subjects addressed by social science has shifted to ethnic relations and minority problems, the impulses it provides are still influential for the more narrowly defined study of anti-Semitism and, with respect for the differences of subject and the developed terminology, are still fruitful for the further understanding of it. Naturally the usefulness of measurements and comparisons are limited when, for example, anti-Semitic incidents are statistically calculated and documented without the researched subject ever being sufficiently defined. A worldwide statistic of offences provided by press reports without any methodological controls or standards has no scholarly relevance beyond the attention paid to it by the media.

The most important methods of social research are opinion polls, conducted either periodically or just once, on attitudes regarded as either representative or as individual. They ask questions, for example, about the attitude of Germans to the State of Israel, to the Holocaust, to the problem of restitution, to the immigration of Jews from the states of the former Soviet Union. Or they focus on the profile of individual groups, such as violent youths or people who vote for right-wing extremist parties. Biographical research works with various types and techniques of interviews; media analysis serves as a quantitative or qualitative method of discourse analysis, paying special attention to press publications, pamphlets, fliers, and other material of ideological content. Psychoanalysis, through its focus on individuals, serves the field of Holocaust research by addressing phenomena such as trauma, survival syndrome, or the inter-generational delegation of guilt complexes following genocide. Social psychology, on the other hand, takes into consideration group relations, specific prejudices, and exclusion and discrimination in group conflicts.

Studies on group relations which use the participatory observation method within the framework of an ethnological study in the field of anti-Semitism research can also prove insightful, if the empirical research in the field of investigation is precisely defined.

Having broadly outlined some of the interests and methods of a number of disciplines, the question remains as to how adequately to define and narrow down the field of anti-Semitism. Even the most common expressions of hostility toward Jews are various, with different traditions overlapping. Adding to the old, familiar, and continually reanimated forms, such as the endless reproductions of the 'Protocols of the Elders of Zion' (see Sammons 1998), new variations emerge from different regions and time-periods. Take, for example, the resurrection of open hostility towards Jews following the end of the communist system—a most astounding phenomenon in present-day Eastern Europe. More than five decades after the end of the Holocaust, and eight decades after the collapse of tsarist Russia, anti-Semitism is propagated and exploited in daily politics in the former Soviet Union and in what was once its satellite states, as if the clock had been turned back. Infiltration fantasies and world conspiracy theories, stereotypes with religious roots, national ethnic traditions passed on over generations, and even revived legends of ritual murder and blood accusations are once again a component of public discourse in Russia, Poland, Hungary, the Balkans, Ukraine, and White Russia (Hausleitner and Katz 1995).

In order to explain these developments, it is necessary first to inquire into the roots and traditions of anti-Semitism in the ethnic and national cultures, religions, and mentalities of each country. Secondly, the fate of Jews in the region, their role before communist rule was established, and the history of persecution are also of central interest. The mechanisms of repression and the strategies for coming to terms with the Holocaust are also indicators in Eastern Europe of the public attitude towards Jews, as well as towards its own history. Connected to this is the third point, namely, the function of anti-Semitism in identity-searching during the transitional period following the collapse of the communist system. Finally, social indicators are also to be considered.

The clandestine forms of Jewish hatred which mark Stalinism (one thinks of the Doctor Trials in Moscow, the Slansky Trial in Prague, and the purges in East Berlin in the early 1950s) are also a part of the anti-Semitic tradition in Eastern Europe. But they played no special role in current issues in the way that the ideologically determined political exploitation of anti-Zionism found expression in present-day hostility towards Israel. It should not be overlooked, however, that these latent forms of anti-Semitism were present even before the emergence of *Perestroika* and *Glasnost*. Hence there arises the theory that old traditions which originated in Russia under the Tsar, or in the church and cleric, in Poland were revived, and after merging with a (weaker) strain of tradition from the communist era, have now come to embody new meanings for the present. Due to the simple construction of anti-Semitic prejudice and its easy universal application, anti-Jewish feelings play a special role in the process of identity formation in Eastern Europe. All concrete observations have indicated this.

Anti-Semitism research must incorporate nationalism and the nation-state as an essential parameter in its analysis of exclusion and discrimination of Jewish (and other) minorities. Western society requires other models of interpretation, with German society falling into a category of its own. The German Democratic Republic (GDR), according to opinion polls, fares better than the old Federal Republic on questions about attitudes towards Jews. These results, of course, must be measured against the reality of xenophobia in East Germany, the readiness of its citizens to use violence against 'foreigners', and the preconditions which are formed on the basis of knowledge, awareness, and problem-reflection (see Wiltenberg *et al.* 1995: 88–106; Mertens 1995: 89–100, and 1998: 208–25).

Post-National Socialist anti-Semitism in the old Federal Republic can be explained as a consequence of feelings of guilt and shame, but also as a reflex against the restitution and reparation payments. (In the GDR, in contrast, the experience of anti-Zionist propaganda directed at Israel became the essential factor.) In France, alongside revisionist currents and Auschwitz denial, anti-Jewish ethnocentric anti-egalitarian tendencies which use traditional argumentation have also been identified (Commission Nationale Consultative des Droits de L'Homme 1997).

Jewish experiences during and after the National Socialist persecution suggest that anti-Jewish resentments persisted after the genocide in the form of unreflective religious and ethnically derived anti-Semitism, as a practised prejudice, and as political calculation: in the liberated concentration camp at Dachau, the Christian Polish prisoners announced that they would use violence to prevent a Jewish religious ceremony from taking place. The modest celebration had to be conducted under the protection of the US army (Eichhorn 1988: 207–18).

One might add some considerations here on the power of these prejudices in this event and reflect upon how the clearly shared suffering during the National Socialist persecution did nothing to improve or reform human nature, nor to eliminate the potency of any of its hostile imagery. Hostility towards Jews in Poland, which had a long and wretched tradition well before the emergence of German National Socialism, continued to be virulent even after the National Socialist occupation had ended. The violent acts and pogroms that occurred between June 1945 and July 1946 in Poland, reaching a climax in Kielce, where forty people died in a pogrom, speak for themselves. People who had returned to their homes after being released from the concentration camps were persecuted and murdered because they were Jews, and because hostile images and atavistic accusations of guilt were converted directly into action (Friedrich 1997: 115–47).

The persecution in Kielce was triggered by the ancient accusation of ritual murder (Erb 1993), and caused the first exodus of Polish Jews following the Holocaust. Attacks and acts of murder motivated by anti-Semitic feelings and directed at survivors of the National Socialist persecution were daily occurrences: a total of between 1,500 and 2,000 Jews lost their lives in Poland in 1945–6. These Jews had returned to their past home to find that their possessions and property had been appropriated by their Polish neighbours, and that their presence was totally un-desired. They became definitive 'displaced persons', who left Poland to find safety in Germany, from where they hoped to be able to emigrate to a secure refuge.

But there were also Jews who stayed and who constituted the small remains of a community that had been exterminated in the Holocaust during the German occupation. Most of them, 20,000 people (90 per cent of the Jewish citizens who still lived in Poland), left the country in 1968 in a second exodus. They were driven out of their homeland as victims of an anti-Zionist campaign that began in 1967, with Israel's June War providing the pretext. The official Polish slogan: 'The removal of all Zionist elements from the state and party', was in accord with the policies of the Soviet bloc which regarded Israel as the ultimate enemy. In March 1968 Polish nationalist feelings came into conflict with the communist party line when the government banned the play *Dziady* by the Polish national poet Adam Mickiewicz, because the audience had applauded too enthusiastically during the anti-Russian scenes. Police and representatives of the working class were mobilized against students who protested the ban. 'The Jews' were stigmatized as the culprits, as the enemy of the worker and farmer state, and as agitators and troublemakers (see the 1998 conference findings in Kosmala 1999).

The above example shows how anti-Semitism research functions in the field of political history through the deconstruction of ideas that are based on enemy myths. It also illustrates how social history, in deciphering prejudices, identifying underlying forces, and analysing motives of social developments and decision-making, also contributes. The post-war pogroms in Poland can be explained as emotional group reactions, which in crisis situations were directed by traditional behavioural patterns: assigning of blame, exclusion, and collective aggression.

The interdisciplinary character of anti-Semitism research requires not only pluralist methods, but also a number of interpretative models. The wide selection of theories on anti-Semitism correspond to the many manifestations of the phenomena. Historical interpretations, which go back to the anti-Judaism of pagan antiquity (see Gager 1983; Feldman 1993; Yavetz 1997; Schäfer 1997) and early Christianity (Evans and Hagner 1993), serve in many ways as forerunners. The significance of 'modern anti-Semitism' in the nineteenth century is presented by historical research as a reaction to the crises of modernity (Rürup 1975; Erb and Bergmann 1989; Volkov 1994), in which many different influences, traditions, and structures played a joint role in the reaction of middle-class society to social restructuring and problems of self-value and legitimacy. The crisis theory can be applied to various epochs, to the phase of industrialization, just as well as to the period after the First World War and even (in part) to reunified Germany. These periods of crisis are each marked by a considerable degree of social tension, producing frustrations and aggressions which require a vent, and which search for appropriate objects to hold guilty and accountable (scapegoat theory). The fear of individual or collective loss of status is essential to the crisis model: in the period following the fall of communism in the 1990s, foreigners in Eastern Europe and former Soviet states (both asylum-seekers and long-time residents) became the object of aggression, taking on the role that the Jews had filled in the crisis of modernity at the close of the nineteenth century.

Theories of psychology and psychoanalysis have long been an established part of anti-Semitism research (see Simmel 1993; Rensmann 1998; Strauss and Bergmann 1987–93). Information on the authoritarian character and approaches to the inter-action between frustration and aggression could not have been attained without the findings of Freudian psychoanalysis. From sociology we have the interpretative models of group theories (authority conflict, education trauma, inner-conflict frustration), which define anti-Semitism through structures of prejudice that find expression in the relationship between the (Jewish) minority and majority society in conflict situations. Competitive relations originating from social and ethnic conflict play an important role in these interpretative models. They are particularly helpful in interpreting conflicts that are ideologically determined, but which have their origins in a competitive relationship, as, for example, is often the case with xenophobia.

The experience or fear of privation (often in connection with an impending loss of status), is central to the perception of social positions and influences behaviour towards minorities, who are considered less important. The deprivation theory deduces from this that the existence and effect of prejudice is derived from what is perceived as the upward social mobility of minorities (when immigrants appear to be better off), and is based on an underlying fear that the social status of one's own group is suffering. These emotions then find expression through negative stereo-types.

Because explanations based on a single motive do not do justice to the complex phenomena of anti-Semitism, we must use the various disciplines, methods, and theories in combination. Anti-Semitism, due to its long history and its multitude of manifestations, serves as the exemplary phenomenon for research on group conflict and social prejudices. The current migration changes and the new formation of societies with large ethnic minorities in Europe are a repetition, in their structure, of the many conflicts and problem areas that we know from the history of Jews and non-Jews living together. It is for this reason that anti-Semitism research cannot restrict itself to the narrow realm of hostility toward Jews. The field must expand, and go beyond the investigation of special resentments and their effects to include general and broad problems of prejudice and discrimination, the exclusion of minorities, and xenophobia. Migration processes and minority conflicts are thus, as general and broad theoretical approaches, just as much a part of anti-Semitism research as are the histories of discrimination and persecution of individual sociological, ethnic, religious, and political minorities. The aim here is to achieve a comprehensive prejudice research which can integrate every appropriate field of research of a paradigmatic nature. Comparative studies, therefore, in accordance with their multitude of methods, are highly valued as an important component of anti-Semitism research.

From this perspective, the term 'anti-Semitism' can be broadly understood as a research strategy which also addresses phenomena such as the persecution of Sinti and Roma, the discrimination of minorities such as 'asocials', and exclusionary ideologies that incorporate biological determinism, Social Darwinism, or racist anti-egalitarian tendencies. Youth violence, right-wing extremism, and hatred of foreigners are also subjects for anti-Semitism research that demand both answers to complex problems and analysis of the multitude of hostile images and prejudices in a social and cultural context.

The primary and classical field of anti-Semitism research remains, however, the history of anti-Jewish hostility, but this is naturally closely intertwined with the history of Jews and their interaction with majority societies (here is the link to Jewish studies). The social history of Jewish and non-Jewish communities living together spans centuries and nations, forming an intellectual, religious, and cultural historical complex that includes subjects of ritual and religion, inquiries into the Christian ban on usury, and both local and regional Jewish policies. It also investigates religious life in the Middle Ages and social movements of the Christian majority in the modern age in light of their impact on the Jewish minority (Berger 1996; Limor *et al.* 1996; Chazan 1997; Horbury 1998). The perpetuation of anti-Semitism in history shows it to be a continuous companion of Jewish experience (Almog 1980; Wistrich 1991). However, when the long-term perspective is put aside and specific circumstances are analysed, the Jewish component becomes a factor of a specific, local history requiring a contextual examination (for Late Antiquity: Stemberger 2000; for the Middle Ages: Nirenberg 1996). Therefore, anti-Semitism remains a 'persisting question' (Fein 1987), but reveals, in historical perspective, many changing facets. Recent studies have tried to emphasize both continuities and discontinuities in the history of Jew-hatred by discerning specific characters. Gavin Langmuir divided in chronological order 'realistic', 'xenophobic', and thoroughly 'chimeric' elements—like the blood-libel legends which began to spread in the mid-twelfth century (Langmuir 1990a: 311–52; but see also Reisigl and Wodak 2001). The history of emancipation in the nineteenth century is also a field of interest in anti-Semitism research, as is the development of modern racial anti-Semitism and its exploitation by illiberal anti-modern political movements. Both lead to the history of the Holocaust which, as the central subject of the twentieth century, forms its own field within historical anti-Semitism research, and which is broadened further by comparative genocide research. The resultant effects of anti-Jewish hostility are also a part of the history of anti-Semitism. For this reason, emigration and exile research and the social history of 'displaced persons' are also addressed within the history of anti-Semitism. The analysis of how the German majority society has come to terms with its past ('Vergangenheitsbewältigung') is, with regard to its many political, cultural, and psychological manifestations, also a component of this research as it is linked to the effects of historical and empirical interpretative models.

Given the historical facts and the current manifestations of anti-Jewish feeling, it is not necessary to stress the social necessity of anti-Semitism research. Prescriptions for preventing hostile excesses directed at minorities, for reducing the willingness to employ violence, and for combating intolerance are constantly in demand, but there are no quick solutions. The path leading from education to insight is long and offers no shortcuts. It is impossible to quickly heal resentments or to immunize against prejudice. Does the answer lie in more education about Judaism, about foreign peoples, about minorities? This well-meaning idea was often practised as a remedy against anti-Semitism, but without success, for the simple reason that anti-Semites are not interested in Jewish reality but rather in the release of their feelings through invented hostile images and in the political effect of these resentments. This is true also for xenophobia that is born out of a fear of privation and all its related manifestations.

One of the tasks of anti-Semitism research is to provide clarification on the connections and motives of social resentments as a way to prevent their finding violent expression. It is essential that the connections between aggression against minorities, hatred for foreigners, and anti-Semitism be recognized and made comprehensible. Insight into the effectiveness of prejudice is attained through the recognition that hostile images are exclusionary and create a common bond within the majority society. This feeling of unity which opens minorities to attack and reduces them to the inferior status of outsider is only of limited positive value. When Jews are defined as foreign, when asylum-seekers are denounced as criminals, when foreigners are perceived as threatening to the social peace and to the vested rights of citizens, it is a reflection of the aggressions and fears of the majority which need a vent and must be overcome. Anti-Semitism is not a prejudice against a single minority that can be isolated from the social context. Rather, it is the prototype of social and political resentments and hence an important indicator of the current state of society. Recognizing this is the first step to overcoming it. Anti-Semitism research can make a contribution towards this recognition.

The description of its methods and aims has made clear that anti-Semitism research has little to do with studies devoted to Jewish culture, religion, and intellectual achievement. As prejudice research, it is primarily interested in the behaviour and attitudes of different majority societies, and strictly speaking, it does not even require knowledge of the discriminated minority. The culture of the Sinti and Roma need not be described, nor Jewish customs or literature explained, in order for the focus, the prejudice of the majority against this minority, to be effectively analysed and interpreted. Naturally knowledge about the minority, which is the target of resentments and aggressions, is an advantage, but it is not a part of the *conditiones sine qua non*. It has thus been emphasized here that anti-Semitism research and Jewish studies are not interconnected, nor dependent on one another.

Jewish history, however, is a different story, to the degree that it addresses not only the history of the victims of aggression, but also the history of emancipation as an example of discrimination overcome. The history of Jews, their interaction with non-Jewish majority societies, their persecution and extermination, serves anti-Semitism research as a paradigm. For this reason, study of anti-Semitism remains indispensable (Heil 1998: 121–39).

Suggested Reading

The best introductions to the study of anti-Semitism are Almog (1980), Langmuir (1990b), Wistrich (1991), and Simmel (1993).

Bibliography

ALMOG, S. ed. 1980. *Antisemitism Through the Ages*. Oxford.

Antisemitism Worldwide 1993. *Annual Report edited by the Stephen Roth Institute For the Study of Contemporary Antisemitism and Racism*. Tel Aviv and Nebraska.

BENZ, W. and BERGMANN, W. eds. 1997. *Vorurteil und Völkermord. Entwicklungslinien des Antisemitismus*. Freiburg.

BERGER, D. 1996. 'Anti-Semitism. An Overview.' In *History and Hate: The Dimensions of Antisemitism*. D. Berger ed. Philadelphia.

BERGMANN, W. and ERB, R. 1998. 'Sozialwissenschaftliche Methoden in der Antisemitismusforschung. Ein Überblick.' *Jahrbuch für Antisemitismusforschung* 7: 103–20.

CHAZAN, R. 1997. *Medieval Stereotypes and Modern Antisemitism*. Berkeley and Los Angeles.

Commission Nationale Consultative des Droits de L'Homme 1998. 'La Lutte contre le racisme et la xenophobie. Exclusion et Droits de L'Homme.' Paris.

EICHHORN, D. M. 1988. 'Sabbath Service in Dachau Concentration Camp. Report on the First week in May 1945 by a US Military Rabbi.' *Dachau Review* 1: 96–105.

ERB, R. ed. 1993. *Die Legende vom Ritualmord. Zur Geschichte der Blutbeschuldigung gegen Juden*. Berlin.

—— and BERGMANN, W. 1989. *Die Nachtseite der Judenemanzipation. Der Widerstand gegen die Integration der Juden in Deutschland 1780–1860*. Berlin.

EVANS, C. A. and HAGNER, D. A. eds. 1993. *Anti-Semitism and Early Christianity: Issues of Polemic and Faith*. Minneapolis.

FEIN, H. ed. 1987. *The Persisting Question: Sociological Perspectives and Social Contexts of Modern Antisemitism*. Berlin.

FELDMAN, L. H. 1993. *Jew and Gentile in the Ancient World: Attitudes and Interactions From Alexander to Justinian*. Princeton.

FRIEDRICH, K. -P. 1997. 'Antijüdische Gewalt nach dem Holocaust. Zu einigen Aspekten des Judenpogroms von Kielce.' *Jahrbuch für Antisemitismusforschung* 6: 115–47.

GAGER, J. F. 1983. *The Origins of Anti-Semitism: Attitudes Toward Judaism in Pagan and Christian Antiquity.* New York and Oxford.

HAUSLEITNER, M. and KATZ, M. eds. 1995. *Juden und Antisemitismus im östlichen Europa.* Wiesbaden.

HEIL, J. 1998. 'Antisemitismus, jüdische Geschichte und Jüdische Studien.' *Jahrbuch für Antisemitismusforschung* 7: 121–39.

—— and WACKER, B. eds. 1997. *Shylock? Zinsverbot und Geldverleih in jüdischer und christlicher Traditon.* Munich.

HOFFMANN, C. 1994. 'Christlicher Antijudaismus und moderner Antisemitismus. Zusammenhänge und Differenzen als Problem der historischen Antisemitismusforschung.' In *Christlicher Antijudaismus und Antisemitismus. Theologische und Kirchliche Programme Deutscher Christen.* 293–317. L. Siegele-Wenschkewitz ed. Frankfurt am Main.

HORBURY, W. 1998. *Jews and Christians in Contact and Controversy.* Edinburgh.

KLÜGER, R. 1994. *Katastrophen. Über deutsche Literatur.* Göttingen.

KÖRTE, M. 1998. 'Das "Bild des Juden in der Literatur". Berührungen und Grenzen von Literaturwissenschaft und Antisemitismusforschung.' *Jahrbuch für Antisemitismusforschung* 7: 140–50.

KOSMALA, B. ed. 1999. *Die Vertreibung der Juden aus Polen 1968.* Antisemitismus und politisches Kalkül. Berlin.

LANGMUIR, G. 1990a. 'Toward a Definition of Antisemitism.' In *Toward a Definition of Antisemitism.* 311–52. Berkeley and Los Angeles.

—— 1990b. *History, Religion, and Antisemitism.* London.

LIMOR, O. *et al.* eds. 1996. *Contra Iudaeos: Ancient and Medieval Polemics Between Christians and Jews.* Texts and Studies in Medieval and Early Modern Judaism 10. Tübingen.

MERTENS, L. 1995. 'Antizionismus: Feindschaft gegen Israel als neue Form des Antisemitismus.' In *Antisemitismus in Deutschland. Zur Aktualität eines Vorurteils.* 89–100. W. Benz ed. Munich.

—— 1998. 'Alltäglicher Antisemitismus in der deutschen Provinz? Der Fall Gollwitz.' *Jahrbuch für Antisemitismusforschung.* 7: 208–25.

NIRENBERG, D. 1996. *Communities of Violence: Persecution of Minorities in the Middle Ages.* Princeton.

NIPPERDEY, T. and RÜRUP, R. 1972–92. 'Antisemitismus.' In *Geschichtliche Grundbegriffe. Historisches Lexikon zur politisch-sozialen Sprache in Deutschland.* i. 129–153. O. Brunner, W. Conze, und R. Koselleck eds. Stuttgart.

REISIGL, M. and WODAK, R. eds. 2001. *Discourse and Discrimination: Rhetorics of Racism and Antisemitism.* London and New York.

RENSMANN, L. 1998. *Kritische Theorie Über den Antisemitismus. Studien zu Struktur, Erklärungspotential und Aktualität.* Hamburg.

ROHRBACHER, S. and SCHMIDT, M. 1991. *Judenbilder. Kulturgeschichte antijüdischer Mythen und antisemitischer Vorurteile.* Reinbek.

RÜRUP, R. 1975. *Emanzipation und Antisemitismus. Studien zur 'Judenfrage' der bürgerlichen Gesellschaft.* Göttingen.

SAMMONS, J. L. 1998. *Die Protokolle der Weisen von Zion. Die Grundlage des modernen Antisemitismus–eine Fälschung. Text und Kommentar.* Göttingen.

SCHÄFER, P. 1997. *Judeophobia: Attitudes Toward the Jews in the Ancient World.* Cambridge, Mass.

SIMMEL, E. ed. 1993. *Antisemitismus.* (Originally *Anti-Semitism. A Social Disease.* New York and Boston. 1946) Frankfurt am Main.

STEMBERGER, G. 2000. *Jews and Christians in the Holy Land: Palestine in the Fourth Century.* Trans. R. Tuschling. Edinburgh.

STRAUSS, H. A. and BERGMANN, W. eds. 1987–93. *Current Research on Antisemitism.* 3 vols. Berlin and New York.

VOLKOV, S. 1994. *Die Juden in Deutschland 1780–1918.* Munich.

WILTENBERG, R., PROSCH, B., and ABRAHAM, M. 1995. 'Struktur und Ausmaß des Antisemitismus in der ehemaligen DDR. Ergebnisse einer repräsentativen Umfrage unter Erwachsenen und einer regional begrenzten schriftlichen Befragung unter Jugendlichen.' *Jahrbuch für Antisemitismusforschung.* 4: 88–106.

WISTRICH, R. S. 1991. *Antisemitism—The Longest Hatred.* London.

YAVETZ, Z. 1997. *Judenfeindschaft in der Antike.* Munich.

CHAPTER 38

JEWISH FOLKLORE AND ETHNOGRAPHY

GALIT HASAN-ROKEM*

FOLKLORE AS A UNIQUE FORM OF CULTURAL CREATIVITY AND EXPRESSION

FOLKLORE is a form of creativity and expression that exists in all the cultures we know. It is characterized by its qualities of *collectivity* and *tradition*, by its *oral mode* of expression, and usually by *anonymity* (Utley 1965). Folklore is created and transmitted among individuals and groups through all the audio-visual interpersonal channels of communication. The material of folklore is by and large created and performed simultaneously, usually in an interactive context. The following historical survey of Jewish folklore through the ages will be preceded by general remarks on the field of folkloristics, to facilitate the application of accepted general terminology to the survey of Jewish folklore.

The *collective* aspect of folklore is expressed both in the immediate interaction established between performer and audience, and in the concept of authority and ownership of the work, that is considered as belonging to the group and not an individual. This group may vary in size and character: it can be a people, an ethnic group, an age or gender group, a religion, profession, family, or political affiliation.

* Translated from the Hebrew by Sara Friedman.

One may speak, for instance, of folklore of children, folklore of actors, Jewish folklore, folklore of Mediterranean Jews, and so on.

The aspect of *tradition* is expressed in the group's concept that their cultural heritage contains traditional values and modes of expression that are transmitted from generation to generation. Folklore is thus one of the means by which the historical-chronological identity of the group is strengthened and its continuity sustained. It thus plays an important role in creating the group's *collective consciousness*, which combines folklore's traditional and collective qualities.

The *oral* aspect of folklore is seen in that folkloric material is performed and transmitted through direct, audio-oral interpersonal contact (Alexander and Govrin 1990). Even when folktales assume written and printed form, this is not a *canonical* version, and they are subject to constant change and appear in numerous versions.

The *anonymity* of most works of folklore is due to their collective ownership and authority; however, in different societies and periods folk artists and storytellers were known by name, though usually their art did not remain linked to their name later.

Society, in which folklore emerges, is served by a range of channels of communication, all forming a single network with internal links. For the purpose of classification and analysis, different cultural genres can be distinguished, each displaying distinct and fixed formal and communicative features. The most general distinction is between the verbal domain of *folk literature*, the visual domain of *folk art* and *material culture*, and the behavioural domain of *custom, ceremony, festival*, and *ritual*.

Within folk literature the following genres can be distinguished: *folk narrative, folk poetry*, and what is known as the *minor genres*. Folk narrative includes the *folktale* and the *legend*. Folktales are located in the world of the imaginary, and tell of anonymous, typological supernatural characters that are not set in time and place. The folktale is replete with decorative and rhetorical devices such as repetition, use of the number three, riddles, and even rhymed prose (Ben-Amos 1992, Hasan-Rokem 2000: 41–3). Folktales can be either realistic novellas featuring motifs of wisdom and the problem of fate, or magical, with motifs of transformation, reversal, and miracle.

The *legend*, on the other hand, is anchored in a social context, its figures are identified, to a greater or lesser degree as to time and place, and they are frequently familiar cultural heroes of the storytelling society. The legend is linked to society's values, including its religious beliefs, and displays few decorative, artistic, or rhetorical devices, concentrating instead on a semblance of verisimilitude (Yassif 1999: 132–44; Hasan-Rokem 2000: 39–40, 147–50). In addition to these two main prose genres, there are animal fables, humorous stories, anecdotes, and jokes (Apte 1992).

Folk poetry is divided into *lyrical poetry, epic poetry*, and *functional poetry* (Finnegan 1977). Lyrical poetry includes love songs, songs of longing, and other poems expressing the individual's sentiments and feelings. Epic poetry can be of extended scope, telling of heroic deeds, wars, and tribal wanderings, or of the myth of creation and other mythological events, or of narrower scope, in the form of a ballad recounting a specific event. Functional poetry spans a wide range, including work songs, for example of sailors, slaves, workers, and so on, and lullabies, wedding and festival songs, or laments.

The minor genres in folk literature are proverbs and riddles, which appear independently in various behavioural contexts, or are embedded within the other forms of folk narrative and poetry (Hasan-Rokem 1982, 1992; Hasan-Rokem and Shulman 1996: 3–9, 316–20).

Visual folklore includes folk art in its various forms, from artistic design of daily implements and work tools, through ritual and religious art, and finally, art for decoration, pleasure, and play. The locations where folk art is created and performed include the home and its surroundings, as well as public areas of a religious, ritual, or official nature (Babcock 1992).

Behavioural folklore is usually comprised of audio-visual elements and combines folk literature and folk art in performances in different contexts (Bauman 1992). Customs are modes of behaviour of fixed form and content, usually related to specific beliefs that strengthen, motivate, and legitimize the customs. Different customs are substantiated by stories that attest to that particular belief. The observance of a custom often includes storytelling or wearing certain apparel manufactured by folk art. Rituals are a fixed continuity of customs exhibiting unity of content as well as formal and aesthetic links involving a variety of participants at different levels of authority and of functional specialization, and of different degrees of voluntary participation (Turner 1969, 1974; Handelman 1996: 38–41).

Customs and ceremonies revolve around two main cycles, the life-cycle and the year-cycle. The rituals of the life-cycle include folkloric enactment of events imbued with cultural significance: birth, weaning, puberty, marriage, childbirth, death, and so on. The ceremonies of the year-cycle are usually festivals that recur annually, in contradistinction to the unique events in an individual's life-cycle. The folkloric expression of the year-cycle includes events imbued with cultural significance, such as agricultural events (sowing, planting, reaping, grape and fruit harvest), and other modes of gaining a livelihood from nature; the constellations (the equinoxes, the solstices, the lunar cycle, etc.); historical points of reference (victories, miracles, disasters, anniversaries of heroes, etc.).

Ritual is the special term designating customs and ceremonies in the religious cultural sphere, though in most cultures there is no clear-cut separation between functional religious folklore and other behavioural folklore.

Folklore plays an important role in other ideological formations and aspects of culture, in addition to religion. At times folklore shaped within a certain cultural institution endows it with a distinction and identity that serves to bolster its position (familial folklore, for example).

At the same time, folklore created within a given cultural institution can also be seen as a challenge, as defiance and subversion of the existence of that very same institution (school folklore, for example).

The study of Jewish folklore through the ages is based both on inherent, internal criteria for the distinction of the folkloristic genres mentioned above, as well as on intercultural comparative criteria.

JEWISH FOLKLORE THROUGH THE AGES

The Bible is the earliest source affording a picture of Jewish folklore, and has become the basis for further Jewish cultural elaboration since about 200 BCE.

While the biblical text in its received edition often displays the mark of an individual author, as in the prophetic books and the psalms, or the mark of a political establishment, as in the historical books, there are nevertheless many texts whose content, form, and style reveal their direct link to literary folk genres. Many stories can be identified as legends, though this might constitute a problem from the viewpoint of anyone who considers the biblical text revealed truth. It must be stressed that the term *legend* does not invalidate the truth content, and refers rather to the means and modes of reporting that content. The legendary characteristics are most in evidence when more than one narrative tradition tell of the same event, such as the creation of Adam and Eve in Genesis, chapters 1 and 2, and the first encounter between Saul and David in 1 Sam. 16. The folkloric nature of the story also emerges from its relation to a wide intercultural tradition that existed in the Mediterranean region in antiquity. The biblical account of the Flood, for instance, has parallels in several narrative traditions of the region and even further (Frazer 1918).

Folk-tales proper do not appear in the Bible, but biblical stories occasionally display motifs that are familiar from the international repertoire of folktales, such as the younger brother who is teased by his elder brothers and who ultimately rises to power (Joseph, David), or a staff that magically turns into a serpent (the staff of Aaron in Pharaoh's court).

Among the minor genres of folk literature, the most common is the proverb. Proverbs appear in the Bible in two collections, the Books of Proverbs and Ecclesiastes. These books contain many typical folk proverbs, though the collections as units exhibit an elitist, even royal style. Among the typical folk sayings in these anthologies are, for instance: 'The simple believes every word' (Prov. 14: 15); 'Go to the ant, thou sluggard; consider her ways and be wise' (Prov. 6: 6), 'Cast your bread upon the waters for you shall find it after many days' (Eccl. 11: 1), and '. . . a bird of the air shall carry the voice' (Eccl. 10: 20). The popularity of proverbs from Ecclesiastes compared with Proverbs to this day, in speech and in folk narratives, may stem from the fact that Ecclesiastes has a fixed slot in the reading cycle of biblical texts in the synagogue (Sabbath of the Feast of the Tabernacles), whereas the Book of Proverbs has none. Proverbs appear in narrative contexts as well, such as: 'Is Saul also among the prophets?' (1 Sam. 10: 11–12; 19: 24), a saying which is explicitly reported to have entered the spoken language of the time.

The genre of the riddle also appears in the Bible, in its account of Samson's wedding banquet. Samson posed a riddle to the Philistines that he alone could answer, as it derived from the image he saw of a carcass of a lion, in which bees were making honey: 'Out of the eater came forth meat, and out of the strong came forth sweetness' (Judg. 14: 14).

Customs in biblical literature appear in the context of the interpretation of dreams, also amply documented in ancient Egyptian and Mesopotamian sources. Joseph is especially noteworthy among biblical interpreters of dreams. Joseph recounted his own dream (Gen.7), then interpreted the dreams of Pharaoh's courtiers (Gen. 40) and finally the dream of Pharaoh himself (Gen. 41). Daniel too interpreted the dreams of Nebuchadnezzar, king of Babylon (Daniel 2–3).

The corpus of rabbinic literature assumed its form at the end of the ancient period, referred to usually in Jewish historiography as the period of the Mishnah and the Talmud, or alternatively, the period of Roman and Byzantine rule in Palestine. Jewish culture from this period is known to us mainly as it existed in Palestine and Babylonia, and to a lesser degree in North Africa. As in the biblical period, here too our knowledge of Jewish folk culture stems mainly from internal Jewish textual sources, and partly also from texts of other cultures, which came into contact with Jews. The folkloristic materials in the rabbinic texts serve as important indices for the intercultural contacts of Jewish culture with neighbouring cultures in this period (Lieberman 1942, 1950). This period, even more than the biblical one, has benefited greatly from archeological evidence providing an important source for corroboration, verification, and, at times, correction of information culled from literary sources.

Folklorists are very fortunate that the compilers of the corpus of rabbinic literature included many elements of folk literature and even described at length genres of behavioural folklore and visual folklore, although to a lesser degree than literature. Folklore in its entirety is mediated in this corpus with reference to the normative framework of halacha, on the one hand, and midrash, the exegesis of biblical texts, on the other, the two cultural traits which dominate the rabbinic literary oeuvre.

The folk literature of the Mishnah, the two Talmuds, and the midrashic literature includes all the different genres. Tales are usually of the realistic kind. The magical folk-tale does not appear in its characteristic form, as we know it either from the European tradition or from the Indian heritage, and from oral Jewish traditions in communities all over the world in the modern period. The absence of the magical folktale genre from rabbinic literature does not indicate its absence from the folk cultural repertoire performed in that period, but only the preferences exhibited by the redactors of these works. There is no lack of magical and supernatural motifs that usually characterize the magical tale, such as a certain herb invested with the power to bring the dead back to life (e.g. Midrash Leviticus Rabbah 22: 5, Palestine, fifth century CE). Such motifs are frequently interpreted in the conceptual world of rabbinic literature as portents of a religious nature, like an empty oven that fills with loaves of bread, or a table-leg that turns to gold, as reward for good deeds and good qualities (Babylonian Talmud, Tractate Ta'anit 25a).

Tales in the form of wisdom literature appear in a collection that contrasts the inhabitants of Jerusalem with those of Athens, the cosmopolitan centre of wisdom famous throughout the ancient world. These stories are based on riddles that the inhabitants of Jerusalem prove to be more quick-witted at solving than the Athenians (Midrash Lamentations Rabbah I, Palestine, fifth century CE; see also Hasan-Rokem 2000: 39–87).

The genre of the animal tale, known in antiquity especially from the tradition of Aesop's fables, is also found in rabbinic literature; however, while the fables of Greece and Rome offered a general, abstract lesson, the midrashic link is usually to a biblical verse. For instance, a tale of a fox who could enter a fenced-in vineyard only by fasting, and then had to fast again in order to make its way out, functions as a parable illustrating the verse Ecclesiastes 5: 14 (Midrash Ecclesiastes Rabbah *ad loc.*, Palestine, fifth century CE). The legend is the main genre in rabbinic literature. Many mythological legends appear in what is known as the extended biblical narrative, such as that describing the serpent in the Garden of Eden as a four-legged creature who could fulfill all the needs and tasks of mankind (Gen. Rabbah 19: 1, Palestine, fifth century, CE).

Biographical stories of holy figures—hagiography—are a primary genre in rabbinic literature. Figures such as Rabbi Judah the Prince and Rabbi Akiva are depicted in light of their leadership, relations with other people, and the study of Torah. There are also novellas, romantic stories of R. Akiva, telling of the love-story between him and Rachel, the daughter of a wealthy man from Jerusalem. R. Akiva is also the protagonist of historical legends about the Bar-Kokhba revolt and of martyrological accounts describing how the Romans put him to death. Many other historical and martyrological legends describe the fate of individuals, either anonymously or by name, such as R. Ishmael, R. Gamaliel, Martha daughter of Boethus, and others, in the time of the destruction of the Second Temple, the Bar-Kokhba revolt, and the period of persecution and hostile decrees.

The dividing line between folk-tale and legend is not always clear-cut, as seen in the stories of voyages and the exaggerated anecdotes of Rabbah Bar Bar Hana, which span a range from mythological motifs, such as an encounter with 'The Dead of the Wilderness', a vision of Mount Sinai, to comical motifs such as a raven who swallowed an alligator or a giant fish with grass growing on its back (Babylonian Talmud, Tractate Baba Bathra 73b–75b).

There are very few examples of folk poetry in rabbinic literature, the exceptions being a lament over the destruction of the temple (Midrash Lamentations Rabbah, Proem 24) and a lament over the dead attributed to the women of the Babylonian town of Shkanziv (Babylonian Talmud, Tractate Moed Katan 28b).

On the other hand, rabbinic literature has a wealth of proverbs. These include typical popular sayings based on metaphors and images from daily life, frequently introduced by the words 'this is what people say', as well as general statements of an ethical-intellectual nature, attesting to their scholarly source. Some 150 proverbs, introduced by the 'this is what people say' formula, are interspersed in rabbinic literature, especially in the Babylonian Talmud. These proverbs are, as a rule, in Aramaic. Several compilations of proverbial lore appear as well, such as in Tractate Baba Kama 92a–93a, where folk proverbs, at times quite lurid and colourful, are collected; here are some examples: 'Poverty follows the poor'; 'Though the wine belongs to the owner, the thanks are given to the butler'; 'A dog when hungry is ready to swallow even its own excrement'; 'Into the well from which you have once drunk water, do not throw clods'; 'Not for nothing did the starling follow the raven, but because it is of its kind'. The best-known collection of sayings in rabbinic literature is Mishnah Aboth, or Sayings of the Fathers, which is also printed in prayer books and is read in all the different communities every Sabbath (in some of them only during the winter months).

In addressing the issue of the Jewish material culture and customs in the period of the Talmud, it is clear that a great deal of material may be gleaned from halachic literature. Most of the customs pertaining to the life-cycle celebrations, such as circumcision (Hoffman 1996), marriage or divorce, and burial, are set out in tractates devoted to a halachic discussion of these topics. Customs that still persist to this day—the fast undertaken by a bridegroom on his wedding day, breaking a glass at the wedding, smelling spices at the *havdalah* prayer at the end of the Sabbath—all of these are already mentioned in talmudic-midrashic sources (Lauterbach 1970). The sages viewed customs as important supplementary material for interpreting biblical texts, the activity of their main halachic endeavour.

The Sabbath and the three pilgrimage festivals also have entire tractates devoted to their observance, in the part of the Mishnah that treats festivals—Moed—and consequently in the two Talmuds as well: Tractates Beitza and Yoma deal with the Day of Atonement; Tractates Shabbat and Erubin both deal with the commandments of the Sabbath; Tractates Rosh Hashana, Sukkah, Megillah, and Pesahim address respectively New Year, the Feast of Tabernacles, Purim, and Passover.

The rabbinic sages also addressed the interpretation of dreams, though they did not compile a systematic document such as the *Oneirokritikon*, the classic dream-book by Artemidoros of Daldis (second century CE). The sages continued the biblical tradition on the one hand, and applied to dream interpretation the methods of interpretation of Scripture as a universal interpretive paradigm on the other. The most detailed and lengthy text dealing with the interpretation of dreams in rabbinic literature is found in Tractate Berakhot 55a–57b, opening with the famous words of the Babylonian sage Rav Hisda: 'an uninterpreted dream is like an unread letter' (Niehoff 1992; Alexander 1995; Hasan-Rokem 2000: 88–107). In the same source appear stories, known to us also from Palestinian sources, which reflect a variety of positions with regard to the truth of the dream's messages. Among other matters, the Tractate describes a ceremony for turning a bad dream into a good one, a practice that reappeared in later traditions and is still performed today. In the context of Jewish culture it is not surprising that this magical ceremony too is to a large extent based on a formulaic reading aloud of biblical verses. Another story explicitly mentions belief in the evil eye and enumerates several ways of preventing its baleful effects. The evil eye is one of the many potent beliefs pervading the Mediterranean and Middle East to this day, regardless of race and religion (Dundes 1980).

From the end of the period of the Mishnah and the Talmud, and following upon the unique work of Rabbi Sa'adiah Gaon, influenced by the flourishing of Islam, there is evidence of Jewish folklore in an ever greater variety of sources: prayer customs as seen in prayer books, halacha as appearing in codices, customs and halachic rulings in the responsa literature that began in the gaonic period and which still continues. A dialectic discourse is still maintained in responsa literature between the interpretive exegesis of biblical texts, as well as rabbinic texts and especially the two Talmuds (with the Babylonian Talmud becoming the more authoritative)—and customs and traditions as they are practised throughout the Jewish world. Questions were put by rabbis of peripheral communities to rabbis in the centres of study, at first in Babylonia, then in North Africa, in Europe, Italy, and Spain, and later in France, Ashkenaz (Germany), and Poland. The questions and replies span the extensive range of Jewish life, from quotidian problems to more speculative and intellectual issues such as messianic beliefs and rulings. Frequently the questions reflect special problems that arise as a result of the living conditions of different communities in the diaspora, including contact and confrontation with the non-Jewish surroundings. The conceptual world of Jewish folk beliefs developed out of cultural interaction with the conceptual world of their environment.

Thus, the texts of the Jews living in Islamic countries contain stories that can be attributed to the literary traditions figuring in Arab and Persian literature, which derive in part from the rich body of Indian tales (Yassif 1999: 265–82). Jewish anthologies from the late Middle Ages onwards contain many stories of Solomon, the wise king and judge, known also as a powerful sorcerer, who goes around the world in disguise like kings in oriental literary traditions such as those that crystallized later in the European tradition as *The Thousand and One Nights*. These stories found their way into Hebrew and Judaeo-Arabic anthologies, alongside Jewish stories that are partly reworkings of biblical plots or rabbinic stories, and partly original literary creations (Stein 1996; Yassif 1999: 276–8). Solomon continues to be one of the most popular biblical figures in Jewish folk narratives to this day, second only to Elijah.

A unique text in medieval Jewish culture in Europe, inasmuch as it reveals in detail the conceptual world of folk beliefs, is the book *Sefer Hasidim*, composed in Germany. It is attributed to Rabbi Judah he-Hasid who lived in the twelfth century in the city of Regensburg in Bavaria, where he spread the unique beliefs he received from his father and teacher Rabbi Shmuel. The lore of the hasidim (German Jewish Pietists) in medieval Ashkenaz combined ethical dicta with mystical teachings about the divine attributes. These beliefs found expression in prayer and strict observance of ascetic mortification. The rich and variegated literary tradition of the hasidim shows complex and firm generic and contextual links with contemporary stories known from Latin anthologies composed in the monasteries in the area. Like the monks and priests, the hasidic rabbis recounted stories of a moral nature, or *exempla*, to their audience (Alexander 1991: 23–5, 104–5, 147–9, Yassif 1999: 283–97). They, too, amazed their listeners with stories of supernatural events—*mirabilia*; like Christian teachers, the rabbis too attested to God's reign on earth through *miracula*, stories of wondrous happenings. Their literary tradition was so intertwined with contemporary German folk tradition that demonic and supernatural figures in their stories had German names, for example, the female demon Striga and the werewolf. Like the world of Christian imagery since the ninth century, and especially from the twelfth century onward, the world developed by Jewish storytellers drew upon powerful and detailed images from the netherworld. Especially prominent were attempts to make contact between the world of the living and the dead in visions and dreams (Hasan-Rokem 1999). The reason for the detailed preoccupation in *Sefer Hasidim* with supernatural elements is the belief that God withdrew from the world after the act of creation, and left his mark on the world in the form of extraordinary phenomena that cannot be explained rationally. R. Judah Hasid (the Pious) commanded that as many stories of these events as possible be recounted. Passages from the Ashkenazic *Sefer Hasidim* appear frequently in the responsa literature, especially from the fifteenth century onward, throughout the Jewish communities. In addition to the ethnographic *Sefer Hasidim* itself, the hasidim of Ashkenaz, especially Rabbi Shmuel and Rabbi Judah Hasid, became heroes in the hagiographic literary collections that started to develop after their death and flourished especially in the fifteenth and sixteenth centuries. *Sefer Hasidim* serves also, together with other texts produced in the same intellectual milieu, as a source for studying Jewish rituals, customs, and education (Marcus 1996; Yuval 1999).

In addition to the ceremonial year-cycle and life-cycle, Jewish customs in the diaspora included the custom of making a pilgrimage to the Holy Land. The pilgrimage had lost its original setting among the other ceremonies of the year-cycle, to be observed on the three pilgrimage festivals as it had been during the First and Second Temple periods, and was also dependent on economic and political circumstances in Palestine. The two most famous Hebrew travelogues, by Rabbi Benjamin of Tudela in Spain and Rabbi Petahia of Regensburg in Germany, show that the Jewish itinerary to the Holy Land in that period concentrated on the holy cities, and especially the tombs of the patriarchs, prophets, and sages. The voyages also included the surrounding countries, such as Egypt, Babylonia, and Syria. The Jewish travellers always made efforts to locate their co-religionists in countries they visited, and reported information as to their numbers, occupation, and general situation in their written accounts. They are also important sources for the long duration of Jewish folk culture, and especially folk religion, in the Holy Land (Reiner 1998).

The development of the most important branch of Jewish mysticism—the kabbalah, in all its nuances—pervaded Jewish folklore with many beliefs and customs. The belief in a Godhead with masculine and feminine components, which mankind must strive to bring closer together for the sake of the redemption of the world, left its mark in many customs that persist to this day. For example: holding the pair of Friday-night loaves close together, and putting the two Sabbath candlesticks together. There were also customs that derived from what was called 'practical kabbalah', such as invoking sacred names for various magical purposes, and inscribing amulets and charms to ward off danger, provoke love, bring healing, and so on. These practices continued Jewish magic practices extant already in Late Antiquity. The particular kabbalistic school of R. Isaac Luria (sixteenth century in Safed) developed the belief in metempsychosis, expressed in many tales. This laid the foundation for the belief in the *dybbuk*, the wandering spirit of the deceased that cannot find peace in a new reincarnation and therefore invades the body of a living person. From the seventeenth century onward there are descriptions of ceremonies of exorcism of a *dybbuk* and demons that troubled human beings. Another supernatural being widely attested in medieval Jewish lore is the *golem* android (Idel 1990).

From the second half of the eighteenth century, the hasidic movement founded by Rabbi Israel Ba'al Shem Tov left its mark on customs, stories, and even external appearance and dress, on a large part of East European Jewry, and its influence reached as far as North Africa. For this movement, as for the medieval hasidim, recounting stories was considered a tangible religious commandment, because of the important role played in the movement by its saintly men and charismatic leaders who were the subject of most of the stories (Idel 1994). The first and most famous collection of hasidic stories, *Praises of the Ba'al Shem Tov* (Ben-Amos and Mintz 1970), dealt naturally with the unique biography of the movement's founder. In the course of the nineteenth century more rabbis gained prominence in the movement, and additional collections were devoted to individual saintly men. Even today, members of hasidic groups cultivate their differentiation from each other by their dress, varying, for example, the cut and colour of the caftan and the men's head-covering, which were influenced by fashion trends in Eastern Europe. They also still uphold the customs of holding feasts at, and pilgrimages to, the home of the leader of each hasidic dynasty. Brazlav hasidism is unique in that its founder, Rabbi Nahman, had no heir, but his followers faithfully make pilgrimages to his tomb in Uman in the Ukraine, as they did even in times when political circumstances made access difficult and dangerous.

The folklore of the Jews under the rule of Islam and in the Mediterranean region also emerged out of a reality of intercultural relations with the non-Jewish surrounding peoples (Goldberg 1996). On the one hand, Jewish educational and social institutions ensured the continuity of traditional Jewish cultural values and their adaptation to new conditions, as, for instance, in the centrality of French culture in the Alliance Française schools as a result of the influence of French colonialism. On the other hand, regional-ecological elements and regional culture acted as uniting factors on folk culture among different religious groups. For instance, in the rich folk literature of the Jews of Iraq there is a clear differentiation between 'Jewish' stories, relating to classical Jewish sources, and those showing the influence of the *adab* and the *faraj* wisdom literature and tales from classical and folk sources in Arabic.

In the folk culture of Jewish women, too, which was usually less influenced by written texts, many different influences can be discerned. The language of the proverbs, stories, and folk songs is as a rule in one of the regional Jewish languages, the best-known of which are Yiddish, Judaeo-Arabic, Judaeo-Spanish, and Judaeo-Persian. The folklore of Jewish women is, however, intimately linked also to the classical sources of the Bible and rabbinic literature, witnessing to the manifold channels of oral transmission even of the canonized corpora of texts and wisdom.

Today the tradition of East European Jewish folk culture exists in the general consciousness of folklore scholars and practitioners alike, garbed in a deep experience of loss due to the Holocaust. The very sound of the Yiddish language is by many wrongly interpreted as a sign of folklore, thus distorting and erasing the memory of the rich and varied culture of the Jews of Poland, Russia, the Ukraine, Romania, the Baltic countries, and even Hungary, that expressed itself in Yiddish in all cultural modes, in canonical and non-canonical, folk, popular, and elite culture alike.

West European Jewish folklore has not been as much recognized as has the folklore of East European Jews on one hand (Zborowski and Herzog 1995), and the folklore of the Jews of the Middle East on the other. This can be partly explained by general trends in the history of the discipline of folklore research that have divided the subjectivity of the tradition-bearers and that of the scholars, making the former into objects of research. This trend is currently under harsh criticism by folklorists as well as anthropologists, leading to various forms of dialogical research in which the subjectivity and the authority in the process of research are shared. This enables scholars to study also the folklore of elite groups and of modern urban cultures.

Probably unrelated to this change in the climate and politics of folklore research, the input of Jews in the folklore of the United States has long been acknowledged. American folklore has naturally developed to include great ethnic and regional varieties, often marking a particular tradition with a specific characteristic. Thus, elements of Jewish folklore have been incorporated into the multicultural patchwork of American society. The contribution of the East European American Jews is especially evident in humorous genres, as well as in the show-business-related genres of popular culture, and quite a few Yiddish words and expressions have found their way into the general spoken language.

Life in Israel created a powerful and sometimes explosive encounter between Jewish folk cultures of vastly different types, to say the least. The settlement in Palestine opened the way for a reawakening of ancient traditions, that were known mainly from written texts or as part of pilgrimages. Tales about the graves of the patriarchs, kings, and saintly men, as well as customs linked to the holy places, have flourished. The development of folklore within non-Orthodox, secularist Zionist ideologies may seem paradoxical. Promoting the ideal of a new type of Jew, the antithesis of the diaspora Jew, they cut ties with traditional folklore and as a result with its folkloristic creativity. In the new cultural institutions emerging in new forms of life, such as the kibbutz, the *moshav*, and pioneering youth movements, and in the various military organizations, new forms of folk culture that emphasized the link to the land and manual labour were more or less consciously generated. In this folkloristic creativity it has not been uncommon to foster a certain degree of reference to ancient values, especially biblical ones.

Thus, with regard to the Jewish calendar and festivals, especially the three pilgrimage festivals, Passover, Shavuot, and the Feast of Tabernacles, the renewed settlement in Palestine has emphasized their affinity with the cycle of nature and agriculture. This connection had been relegated to a position of minor importance outside of Israel, especially where the climate was very different and Jews did not make a living from the land. The emphasis on these agricultural elements, as opposed to explicit religious ones like the special prayers for each festival, became the distinctive mark of the emerging Israeli folk culture. Urban Israelis, especially in Tel Aviv, created their own folk culture. In Tel Aviv, especially in the first half of the twentieth century, quite a few holidays took on a carnival aspect and were celebrated with colourful processions: Hanukkah, the 15th of Shevat—the New Year of the Trees; and especially the Purim carnival. Although centrally organized by the municipality, they quickly led to a folk culture displaying clear collective creativity.

Another phenomenon of the emerging Israeli folklore was the emphasis put on events, places, and holidays to which the Jewish tradition had consistently awarded a minor position in the past. Such was the myth of the last stand at Masada, peripheral in earlier Jewish tradition, or the thirty-third day of the Omer (*Lag Ba-Omer*), related to the bravery of Bar Kokhba, who met with criticism even in rabbinic literature, that both became hallmarks of Israeli identity (Zerubavel 1995). The

Israeli Independence Day is of course a new holiday, celebrated by crowds dancing in the streets, picnics and campfires, as well as disco dancing till dawn.

Wars and bloodshed, and the unnatural deaths of many young people, brought about a folk culture of mourning and memorial days, emerging in the educational faculties of the army and in schools as well as in the families of the bereaved themselves. This finds verbal, musical, visual, and clearly also ceremonial expression.

The army is a formative institution of Israeli folk culture over and beyond the culture of mourning. The long stints that Israelis serve in a military framework, whether as regular soldiers or reservists, are evident in their language, humour and even dress, especially among the youth. Another popular custom among Israeli youth, also linked to military service (at least in terms of age-group), is the popular trend of travelling and trekking in far-off countries, especially India, the Far East, and South America.

Alongside the emerging Israeli folklore of Jews that draws in part upon ancient sources and in part is created by new circumstances, there are also characteristic forms of folklore of other ethnic groups. Jewish ethnic groups maintain the practice of particular traditions that are subjected to varying degrees of transformation in the new Israeli reality. Generally speaking, East European Jewish folklore is the one that has most markedly lost its sociological basis, both as a result of the Holocaust and due to the trend of many Jews of East European origin to reject or abandon their folk tradition, whether for ideological reasons before the Holocaust, or for emotional ones following it. Some work is, however, now conducted in this field too (Bar- Itzhak 2001). By contrast, the awareness of oriental and non-European Jews is very much on the rise today (e.g. Salamon 1999). This process comes as reaction and resistance to the domination by European culture of the political and cultural establishment in Israel. Jews of Mediterranean origin were made to feel excluded from political power, and relegated to a cultural periphery. The reorganization of the hierarchy of folk culture in Israel is expressed very strongly in folk music, where oriental music has moved away from the fringe and is now being played in most radio stations together with more 'mainstream' Israeli music.

Folk culture, especially of North Africa, most notably among Moroccan Jewry, has given rise to the cult of saintly men. This cult has formed over the last century-and-a-half and has become a major phenomenon in Israeli folk religion (Bilu 2000). It finds expression in all the domains of folklore. Legends of holy men describe their birth and death and the miracles they worked. First-person accounts, telling of dreams or visions in which a holy man appeared, are especially important. The holy man is usually someone who died and was buried in Morocco many years ago. He now reveals himself for the purpose of renewing his cult and of being buried in Israel. The sites of pilgrimage become cult places that exhibit features of visual folk art: artefacts related to the cult and the holy figures are sold there. These pictures and other artefacts are sometimes believed to be imbued with magical healing powers, or the promise of fruitfulness, matchmaking, love, and means of livelihood. The phenomenon of Moroccan holy men who 'immigrated' to Israel exists alongside, and sometimes with intricate relations to, the practice of visiting local holy grave-sites. The most popular of these are the festive celebration at the grave-site of R. Shimon b. Yohai in Meron, with the participation of different Jewish ethnic groups, the pilgrimages to the grave-site of Honi the Rainmaker, and others. The belief in holy graves occasionally connects with the previous existence of graves on a certain site, holy for other religions in Israel. Examples are the grave of Dan, son of the patriarch Jacob, in the south, and the grave of Ruben, another of his sons, on the coast. The burial-place of King David in Jerusalem belongs to a sacred tradition shared by the three monotheistic religions, and each one is charged with caring for a separate area of the site. The graves of the patriarchs in Hebron are holy for Jews and Muslims alike, and this frequently causes tension between believers.

Scholarship of Jewish Folklore

Folklore, as an independent discipline, did not until recent years play a central part in the study of Jewish culture (Ben-Amos 1990; Kirshenblatt-Gimblett 1990; Hasan-Rokem and Yassif 1990). The intellectual roots of Jewish studies emphasized literature and history, as reflected in written texts and documents. These were considered the appropriate subject of inquiry for their purpose: establishing the existence of the Jewish spiritual-cultural identity with independent and distinctive features. The cultural expression of the Jewish people that was directly related to the canonical literature—reflecting a situation of isolated tension, rejection, and segregation in relation to the surrounding cultures—fitted well into this programme. The exposure and revelation of folk culture, revealing complex interactions with surrounding societies, would have painted a truer and more complete picture of Jewish culture, but would also have blurred its specific characteristics by revealing its parallels in other cultures. The early scholars of Wissenschaft des Judentums, or Jewish studies, were active in Germany when German Romantics in fact created the modern scholarly field of folklore as an inquiry into folk literature in all its forms. It may be exactly the great investment of German nationalist Romanticism in the study of folklore that caused the Jewish scholars to distance themselves from the field, and emphasize dissimilation and the uniqueness of the Jewish culture.

Though some of the most prominent philologists of the Wissenschaft des Judentums raised the need to address folkloristic issues in scholarly study—such as customs, ceremonies, and folk literature—no one applied the scholarly methods that already existed to the study of folk culture in Europe. Max Grunwald, a rabbi in Hamburg, founded the Society for the Study of Jewish Folklore (1897) and was founder and editor of the first journal for the study of Jewish folklore, *Mitteilungen für jüdische Volkskunde* (1898), that was published until the Nazis rose to power in the 1930s. However, Grunwald himself focused mainly on the folklore of the Jews of Eastern Europe and the heirs of the exiles from Spain whom he met when he served as rabbi in Vienna, and avoided studying the folklore of his own immediate society. It seems that the position in which the scholar distances himself from folklore was another obstacle that beset the acceptance of folklore research into the framework of the study of national Jewish culture in the twentieth century.

Among East European Jewry there were some noteworthy figures who applied themselves to the study of folklore as part of the revolutionary social movements that drew upon popular support. They viewed Yiddish culture as the essence of East European Jewish culture. YIVO, the Institute for the Study of Yiddish Culture, was established in Vilna in 1925, and until the Holocaust was the centre of rich folkloristic and ethnographic research. The institute was headed by Reisman, An-ski, and Cahan. YIVO scholars carried out fieldwork of the folklore of far-flung Jewish communities in Russia, the Ukraine, and Poland, and studied verbal and musical traditions as well as material culture, ceremonies, and customs. The activities of YIVO were terminated by the Holocaust, and after a short rehabilitation period after the war the centre and its archives moved to New York.

Among Jews from Mediterranean and Islamic countries, efforts were made to collect stories and proverbs, and to a certain degree also folk music, which usually circulated privately and unofficially.

The study of folklore in Israel is divided into two main periods, with the dividing line being the two central events in Jewish life in the twentieth century: the Holocaust and the establishment of the State of Israel. The early study of Jewish folklore in Palestine consists of travelogues composed in the Middle Ages and afterwards. At the end of the nineteenth century these descriptions took on a quasi-scientific style, in keeping with the spirit of the nascent ethnographic study of that period. Abraham Moshe Lunz, a journalist and public functionary in Jerusalem, was the first Jewish scholar in Palestine at the end of the nineteenth century systematically to record folk culture, especially folk religion, in both Ashkenazi and Sephardic communities in Jerusalem. He reported his findings with annotations of comparative research, drawing especially upon classical Jewish sources.

In the late 1920s and early 1930s scholars of folk culture, with formal training in this field at European universities, began to work in Palestine. Their main point of interest was the study of Jewish communities from the Mediterranean region. Shlomo Dov (Fritz) Goitein studied and published Yemenite oral traditions (Goitein 1970, 1973), before he became the great scholar of the Cairo Genizah treasures; Erich Brauer composed extensive ethnographies of the Jews who had immigrated from Yemen and Kurdistan (Brauer 1934, 1947); Abraham Z. Idelsohn conducted a study of impressive scope on the folk music of oriental Jews (Idelsohn 1992).

In this period the first Hebrew journal on Jewish folklore, *Reshumot*, was established under the editorship of H. N. Bialik, Y. H. Ravnitzky, and A. Druyanov, who arrived in Palestine from Berlin around 1930. The first two especially were also central in the effort of reviving classical Hebrew traditions. Thus Bialik and Ravnizky co-edited the famous compilation of rabbinic narratives and folklore, *The Book of Legends* (Bialik and Ravnitzky 1992), that was partly intended as a 'substitution' for the folklore of the diaspora. A parallel literary project accomplished in Europe was Micha Joseph Ben-Gorion's (Berdyczewsky) anthology *Mimekor Yisrael*, initially published in German as *Der Born Judas*, that extended its scope to medieval and even early modern centuries (Bin Gorion 1990).

In 1936 Rafael Patai finished writing the first doctoral dissertation in folklore at the Hebrew University, on the theme of water in Jewish folklore in the biblical and talmudic periods. In the 1940s folklorists in Israel studied local folklore, historical folklore, and folklore of the Jewish diaspora. In addition to *Reshumot*, there appeared the journals *Edot* and *Yeda-Am* (edited by Yomtov Levinsky). Folklorists applied themselves both to the emerging Israeli folklore as well as to the folklore as reflected in ancient Jewish sources, and they also studied the heritage of the Arab inhabitants. Patai and Levinsky were joined by Dov (Stock) Sadan and later by Haim Schwarzbaum and Dov Noy.

Sadan conducted extensive study of Jewish culture in Eastern Europe, emphasizing folk culture, especially genres of folk speech. Schwarzbaum addressed himself primarily to folk literature from the historical perspective, mainly medieval literature, and the rich interactions between Jewish folklore and Muslim folklore.

The contribution of Dov Noy to the study of Jewish folklore in Israel and its promotion as an academic discipline is vast. Noy has been active at the Hebrew University in Jerusalem as teacher and mentor for a generation of folklorists, who are active today in all the academic institutions of study and research in Israel. His most important project of research is the Israeli Folktale Archive, which he established in 1955, located today at Haifa University, and which houses some 25,000 narrative texts. An archive for proverbs which is comprised to date of 7,500 sayings was established at the Hebrew University in Jerusalem in the 1980s by Noy's student, Galit Hasan-Rokem.

Folklore as a discipline is studied at all the major universities in Israel, though meanwhile only the Hebrew University in Jerusalem trains students in all the domains of folklore: folk literature, folk art, and behavioural folklore (beliefs, customs, and ceremonies). The scholarly journal *Jerusalem Studies in Folklore* is published by the Institute for Jewish Studies at the Hebrew University of Jerusalem, and an inter-university folklore conference is held annually at one of the universities in Israel. There are some illustrious American folklorists who specialize in Jewish

folklore, such as Dan Ben-Amos, Barbara Kirshenblatt-Gimblett, and Yael Zerubavel.

SUGGESTED READING

Bar-Itzhak (2001) has written a book on the folk narratives of Polish Jews based on both
written and oral sources. The narratives are analysed in their Polish-Jewish as well as Polish-
local context. Ben-Amos (1999) contains a comprehensive survey of Jewish folk literature
through the ages. In Ben-Amos and Mintz (1970), the hagiography of the founder of
Hasidism is translated and commented, with an introduction referring mainly to its folk
literary aspects. See also Bialik and Ravnitzky (1992), with an introduction by David Stern.
This book contains a collection of the narratives and popular traditions of rabbinic literature
compiled in thematic order. The second important popular collection of narratives from
rabbinic literature, including medieval and early modern (especially European) traditions, is
found in Bin Gorion (1990). The introduction combines literary, historical, and theological
consideration of the texts. The classical comparative method of J. G. Frazer is applied to the
Old Testament (only its earliest parts), with rich comparative materials from ancient and
tribal cultures (1918). Goitein (1973) contains a collection of Yemeni Jewish narratives based
on the author's ethnographic fieldwork among Yemeni Jews in pre-state Palestine. An
interpretation of Late Antique rabbinic literature, especially the Palestinian Aggadic Midrash
Lamentations Rabbah, from a folk-literary perspective is found in Hasan-Rokem (2000).
Patai (1983) is a comprehensive book on Jewish folklore, including introductory chapters of a
general, as well as a monographic, character, such as an elaborate study of Jewish birth
customs, based on rich bibliographical as well as ethnographical sources. The most comprehensive history of the Hebrew folk narrative to date, ranging from biblical narratives to
present-day oral performances in Israel, is Yassif (1999). Zerubavel (1995) has produced an
analysis of contemporary Israeli symbolical expression, rituals, and celebrations that are
rooted in classical Jewish sources, based on the theoretical concept of collective memory.

BIBLIOGRAPHY

ALEXANDER, P. S. 1995. 'Bavli Berakhot 55a–57b: The Talmudic Dreambook in Context.' *JJS*
46: 230–48.
ALEXANDER, T. 1991. *The Pious Sinner: Ethics and Aesthetics in the Medieval Hasidic Narra-*
tive. Tübingen.
—— and GOVRIN, M. 1989. 'Story-Telling as a Performing Art.' *Assaph: Studies in the Theatre*
5: 45–51.
APTE, M. 1992. 'Humor.' In *Folklore, Cultural Performances and Popular Entertainments: A*
Communications-Centered Handbook. 67–75. R. Bauman ed. New York and Oxford.
BABCOCK, B. A. 1992. 'Artifact.' In *Folklore, Cultural Performances and Popular Entertain-*
ments: A Communications-Centered Handbook. 204–16. R. Bauman ed. New York and
Oxford.
BAR-ITZHAK, H. 2001. *Legends of the Jews of Poland.* Detroit.

——— and S HENHAR, A. 1993. *Jewish Moroccan Folk Narratives From Israel.* Detroit.

B AUMAN, R. 1992. 'Performance.' In *Folklore, Cultural Performances and Popular Entertainments: A Communications-Centered Handbook.* 41–9. R. Bauman ed. New York and Oxford.

B EN-A MOS, D. 1990. 'Jewish Studies and Jewish Folklore.' In *Proceedings of the Tenth World Congress of Jewish Studies.* Division D (Art, Folklore and Music). ii. 1–20.

——— 1992. 'Folktale.' In *Folklore, Cultural Performances and Popular Entertainments: A Communications-Centered Handbook.* 101–18. R. Bauman ed. New York and Oxford.

——— and M INTZ, J. R. eds. 1970. *In Praise of the Baal Shemtov: The Earliest Collection of Legends About the Founder of Hasidism.* Bloomington, Ind.

B IALIK, H. N. and R AVNITZKY, Y. H. eds. 1992. *The Book of Legends: Legends from the Talmud and Midrash.* Trans. W. G. Braude. Intro. D. Stern. New York.

B ILU, Y. 2000. *Without Bounds: The Life and Death of Rabbi Ya'acov Wazana.* Detroit.

B IN G ORION, M. J. 1990. *Mimekor Yisrael: Classical Jewish Folktales.* I. Bin Gorion ed. Trans. I. M. Lask. Intro. and headnotes D. Ben-Amos. Bloomington, Ind.

B RAUER, E. 1934. *Ethnologie der jemenitischen Juden.* Heidelberg.

——— 1947. *The Jews of Kurdistan.* [Hebrew]. Jerusalem.

F INNEGAN, R. 1977. *Oral Poetry: Its Nature, Significance and Social Context.* Cambridge.

F RAZER, J. G. 1918. *Folklore in the Old Testament.* 3 vols. London.

G ASTER, M. 1928. *Studies and Texts in Folklore, Magic, Medieval Romance, Hebrew Apocrypha and Samaritan Archaeology.* 3 vols. London.

G OITEIN, S. D. 1970. *Jemenica. Sprichwörter und Redensarten aus Zentral-Yemen.* Leiden.

——— 1973. *From the Land of Sheba: Tales of the Jews of Yemen.* New York.

G OLDBERG, H. ed. 1996, *Sephardi and Middle Eastern Jewries: History and Culture in the Modern Era.* Bloomington, Ind.

H ANDELMAN, D. 1996. 'Traps of Trans-formation: Theoretical Convergences between Riddle and Ritual.' In *Untying the Knot: On Riddles and Other Enigmatic Modes.* 37–61. G. Hasan-Rokem and D. Shulman eds. New York and Oxford.

——— and S HAMGAR-H ANDELMAN, L. 1991. 'The Presence of the Dead: Memorials of National Death in Israel.' *Suomen Antropologi* 4: 3–17.

H ASAN-R OKEM, G. 1982. *Proverbs in Israeli Folk Narratives: A Structural Semantic Analysis. Folklore Fellows Communications* 232. Helsinki.

——— 1992. 'Proverb.' In *Folklore, Cultural Performances and Popular Entertainments: A Communications- Centered Handbook.* 128–33. R. Bauman ed. New York and Oxford.

——— 1999. 'Communication with the Dead in Jewish Dream Culture.' In *Dream Cultures: Explorations in the Comparative History of Dreaming.* 213–32. D. Shulman and G. G. Stroumsa eds. New York and Oxford.

——— 2000. *Web of Life: Folklore and Midrash in Rabbinic Literature.* Trans. B. Stein. Stanford.

——— and S HULMAN, D. 1996. 'Introduction' and 'Afterword.' In *Untying the Knot: On Riddles and Other Enigmatic Modes.* 3–9, 316–20. G. Hasan-Rokem and D. Shulman eds. New York and Oxford.

——— and Y ASSIF, E. 1990. 'Jewish Folkloristics in Israel: Directions and Goals.' In *Proceedings of the Tenth World Congress of Jewish Studies.* Division D (Art, Folklore and Music). ii. 33–62.

H OFFMAN, L. A. 1996. *Covenant of Blood: Circumcision and Gender in Rabbinic Judaism.* Chicago and London.

IDEL, M. 1990. *Golem: Jewish Magical and Mystical Traditions on the Artificial Anthropoid.* Albany, NY.

——1994. *Hasidism: Between Ecstasy and Magic.* Albany, NY.

IDELSOHN, A. Z. 1992. *Jewish Music: Its Historical Development.* New York.

JASON, H. 1975. *Studies in Jewish Ethnopoetry.* Taipei.

KIRSHENBLATT-GIMBLETT, B. 1990. 'Problems in the Early History of Jewish Folkloristics.' In *Proceedings of the Tenth World Congress of Jewish Studies.* Division D (Art, Folklore and Music). ii. 21–31.

LAUTERBACH, J. 1970. *Studies in Jewish Law, Custom and Folklore.* New York.

LIEBERMAN, S. 1942. *Greek in Jewish Palestine.* New York.

——1950. *Hellenism in Jewish Palestine.* New York.

MARCUS, I. 1996. *Rituals of Childhood: Jewish Acculturation in Medieval Europe.* New Haven.

NIEHOFF, M. 1992. 'A Dream Which is Not Interpreted Is Like a Letter Which is Not Read.' *JJS* 43: 58–84.

NOY, D. 1971. 'The Jewish Versions of the "Animal Languages" Folktale (AT 670)—A Typological-Structural Study.' *Scripta Hierosolymitana* 22: 171–208. Jerusalem.

PATAI, R. 1983. *On Jewish Folklore.* Detroit.

REINER, E. 1998. 'From Joshua to Jesus: The Transformation of a Biblical Story to a Local Myth: A Chapter in the Religious Life of the Galilean Jew.' In *Sharing the Sacred: Religious Contacts and Conflicts in the Holy Land.* A. Kofsky and G. G. Stroumsa eds. Jerusalem.

SALAMON, H. 1999. *The Hyena People: Ethiopian Jews in Christian Ethiopia.* Berkeley and Los Angeles.

SCHWARZBAUM, H. 1968. *Studies in Jewish and World Folklore.* Berlin.

——1979. *The Mishle Shuʿalim (Fox Fables) of Rabbi Berechiah Ha-Nakdan: A Study in Comparative Folklore and Fable Lore.* Kiron.

STEIN, D. 1996. 'A King, a Queen, and the Riddle Between: Riddles and Interpretation in a Late Midrashic Text.' In *Untying the Knot: On Riddles and Other Enigmatic Modes.* 125–47. G. Hasan-Rokem and D. Shulman eds. New York and Oxford.

TURNER, V. W. 1969. *The Ritual Process: Structure and Anti-Structure.* Chicago.

——1974. *Dramas, Fields and Metaphors: Symbolic Action in Human Society.* Ithaca, NY.

UTLEY, F. L. 1965. 'Folk Literature: An Operational Definition.' In *The Study of Folklore.* A. Dundes ed. Englewood Cliffs, NJ.

YASSIF, E. 1999. *The Hebrew Folktale: History, Genre, Meaning.* Trans. J. S. Teitelbaum. Foreword D. Ben-Amos. Bloomington, Ind.

YUVAL, I. J. 1999. 'Passover in the Middle Ages.' In *Passover and Easter: Origin and History to Modern Times.* 127–160. Notre Dame, Ind.

ZBOROWSKI, M. and HERZOG, E. 1995. *Life is with People: The Culture of the Shtetl.* Foreword by M. Mead, with a new Introduction by B. Kirshenblatt-Gimblett. New York.

ZERUBAVEL, Y. 1995. *Recovered Roots: Collective Memory and the Making of Israeli National Tradition.* Chicago.

CHAPTER 39

MODERN JEWISH SOCIETY AND SOCIOLOGY

HARVEY E. GOLDBERG

THE social-scientific study of Judaism is a modern phenomenon just as are the social sciences themselves. It is a realm into which both resources and effort have been invested, but also one without defined borders. A recent study has probed the historical background to the field, focusing on statistical studies in the European setting (Hart 2000). However, there are no clear borders between sociology and anthropology on the one hand, and demography on the other, particularly if one traces the evolution of these disciplines over the nineteenth and twentieth centuries. Also, it is a field that has not always grown in a continuous and cumulative factor but has been 'reinvented' in different places and contexts. Coverage of the topic is like trying to map a delta over time, seeking to keep track of shifting currents and waterbeds that intersect and sometimes flow into one another, but might also seem to disappear only to re-emerge later.

The shifting nature of the enterprise notwithstanding, several themes run through various efforts to study Jews and Judaism in social-scientific terms. First is the need to understand the socio-political and ideological backgrounds to, and motivations for, making Jews the object of scientific study. This also entails probing resistances to the idea or programme, even though these may be hard to document or demonstrate. Another question is whether the impetus to a study of the Jews comes from a particular interest in their situation and development or whether it is linked to broader social-scientific concerns. Related to both of these issues is the question whether those undertaking the research are Jews or Gentiles, and differences within these broad categories are relevant as well. Another significant dividing line is the sociology of modern communities in the diaspora in contrast to the sociology of Israeli society that took shape at the time the state was established. Along different lines, and cross-cutting the above divisions, is whether the sociological study of Jews is only 'synchronic' in its orientation, stressing modern Jewish society and its dynamics, or whether it incorporates the Jewish past in its view of the present. A related topic that is worth tracing is the degree to which historians or other scholars of Jews and Judaism have adopted social-scientific modes of thought into their writings. It is useful to discuss all these themes by placing them in their historical settings, with attention to junctures at which directions and trends were defined.

BACKGROUND AND CRYSTALLIZATION OF A JEWISH SOCIOLOGY

It is often noted that early in the development of the Wissenschaft des Judentums, Leopold Zunz, in a paper from 1823, included a Jewish sociology or 'Statistik' in his view of future Jewish science. At that period of time, 'statistic' referred to the assessment of the political (broadly conceived) characteristics or strengths of a region that involved qualitative description as well as quantitative accounting and analysis (Hart 2000: 348, n. 30). The emphasis was on understanding Jewry today, and not only in terms of its earlier history and literature. Both by virtue of this precedent, and on the basis of development of the social sciences from the late nineteenth century, the study of society based on ethnography, and theorized within social anthropology, should be included alongside, or as an aspect of, 'sociology'. Zunz was a student of Friedrich Karl von Savigny, a mentor to Jacob Grimm who, together with his brother Wilhelm, provided the foundations for the European field of Volkskunde—later rendered into English as 'folklore' (Ben-Amos 1990). Zunz had available to him a model of research stressing the 'folk' sides of Judaism but did not follow or directly promote this line of inquiry. The statistical (in the contemporary sense) approach to Jewish society also waited until the last decades of the nineteenth century before taking shape.

During the nineteenth century an information-base for the emergence of a Jewish statistics, demography, and sociology began to grow. Jewish communities, which often were becoming reorganized within the framework of spreading emancipation in Europe, frequently collected data on their membership or on other Jews in their regions for administrative and philanthropic purposes. This took place while major transformations in Jewish life such as population growth (changing birth- and death-rates), upward mobility and impoverishment, rural–urban migration, and massive movement westward were under way. Marriage between Jews and Christians was a legal possibility in some countries and a noticeable phenomenon in a few places. The nineteenth century was also a time of colonial expansion that in some places, like North Africa and the Middle East, brought Jewish communities in those regions to the attention of their newly emancipated co-religionists in Europe. Various organizations, most extensively the Alliance Israélite Universelle established in Paris in 1860, began to document demographic figures and life conditions in the communities of their concern. This trend gained impetus as representatives of the Alliance, including their schoolteachers, established ongoing contact with these communities (Rodrigue 1993). In the course of the century, the official census data of many European countries also included information separating the religious category of Jews, while in other states no such differentiation was permitted (Hart 2000: 7). It was only at the turn of the twentieth century that a self-conscious trans-regional move to create a 'Jewish statistics' was formulated and institutionalized.

Mitchell Hart (2000) views the emergence of a Jewish social science as closely linked to Zionism (see Efron 1994: 173–4). The effort drew on earlier statistical work that was available, and quickly attracted the involvement and co-operation of non-Zionist groups, but the ideological thrust and major organizational efforts came from the nascent Jewish national movement. It reflected the perspective of people, including Martin Buber, who set up the Democratic Faction in the World Zionist Congress that was opposed to Theodor Herzl's control of the Congress. They advocated a 'cultural' approach in contrast to Herzl's 'political Zionism', and one implication of this stance was a systematic effort to document the status and situation of the Jewish *Volk* as it existed at the time. The concrete expression of this goal was the establishment, in Berlin, of the Verein für jüdische Statistik— Bureau of Jewish Statistics—in 1902.

The Bureau drew inspiration from a speech by Herzl's associate, Max Nordau, delivered at the Congress the previous year. Nordau asserted: 'we [Zionists] must know with greater precision the national material (*Volksmaterial*) with which we have to work.' He mentions anthropological, biological, economic, and intellectual statistics. Zionism thus provided the historically specific circumstances upon which a push for an inclusive social-scientific perspective on Jewish life was launched. Hart enumerates a number of factors feeding into and characterizing this development.

One was the importance of a statistical point of view in European culture that gained ground in the nineteenth century. This enabled new fields, such as sociology, to take root and grow in the intellectual landscape. By turning to these disciplines, Zionist-motivated sociologists brought the prestige of science to their perspective on the movement. At the same time that they made claims for the objective nature and value of statistical assessment, they were arrogating for themselves state-like functions of gathering, organizing, and using systematic information on 'their' population. There was no attempt to hide the ideological side of this programme; they felt they could show that the current situation of the Jews pointed to a Zionist solution rather than the assimilatory orientation characterizing large segments of European Jewry during the nineteenth century. There thus was a basic irony in their position. They wanted to demonstrate the *existence of* a Jewish people in spite of several generations of trends toward assimilation, and, simultaneously, they pointed to the social ills afflicting that people which called for the Zionist programme. From the outset, the sociological study of Jews was highly intertwined with ideological outlooks and practical programmes, and this remained true even when the field was cultivated and mobilized by researchers and scholars with non-Zionist perspectives. We will follow this theme after tracing other developments that highlight ethnographic and anthropological approaches to the study of Jews and Judaism.

INPUTS FROM ETHNOGRAPHY, ANTHROPOLOGY, AND FOLKLORE

A history of the ethnography of Jewish life reveals various settings and motivations that fuelled it. Some 'seeds' are found in the intellectual movement known as Christian Hebraism consisting of the study of the Hebrew Bible and rabbinic literature by Christian scholars (Deutsch 2001). Such study took place in the Middle Ages, but took on new emphases during the Renaissance and the following centuries. Studying Hebrew sources brought some Christian scholars into direct contact with rabbis and Jewish life around them. A major example appears in *The Jewish Synagogue* by Johann Buxtorf, published in Latin in 1604. It combines quotes from Joseph Qaro's *Shulhan Arukh* and material reflecting observations in Buxtorf's own time. The portrayal of Jewish life, in particular the attention to details of ritual, entered into debates between Catholics and Protestants.

Another side to the 'ethnographic perspective' on Jews that emerged at the time of the Renaissance and was taken seriously for a very long time is the notion that peoples in the New World might be descended from Ancient Jews or the Ten Lost

Tribes. How deep-rooted this idea was may be seen in another Christian Hebraic book, Lancelot Addison's *The present state of the Jews (more particularly relating to those in Barbary): wherein is contained an exact account of their customs, secular and religious* (1675). Addison, a clergyman assigned to the English garrison in Tangiers, met local Jews and subsequently wrote about Jewish life. His book appeared in the decades after Jews were formally permitted to resettle in England, and thus had a 'useful' purpose to it (Horowitz 1992). A striking feature of the publication is its frontispiece, which depicts an 'aborigine', in meagre garb and a headdress, holding a banner with the title of the book. No explanation is attached to the illustration, suggesting that the association between Jews and 'barbarians' was familiar to the intended audience. By the end of the eighteenth century there was extended criticism of this idea, but it did not disappear overnight. The appropriateness of Jews for 'anthropological' study took many expressions. Henri Grégoire, whose prize-winning essay 'Are there means of making the Jews more happy and useful in France?' is often cited as reflecting attitudes leading to the emancipation of the Jews, also wrote on the 'intellectual faculties' and 'qualities' of blacks in the West Indies (1808; see Efron 1994: 6–7).

Barbara Kirshenblatt-Gimblett has identified other genres that implicitly contained ethnographic elements (1990). Haskalah oriented education from the late eighteenth century emphasized teaching geography. Geography implied describing the mores, customs, and manners of people in different lands, including other Jewish communities. The Haskalah sought to abet the 'progress' of Jews, so its literature on Jewish groups that it defined as still in need of 'cultivation' coloured their life-ways in negative shades. Kirshenblatt-Gimblett also points to an early nineteenth-century writing mode that she calls 'ethnographic burlesque', because it ridiculed the customs of Jews still practicing 'exotic' customs. She notes that fifty years later there is already in evidence a trend of looking at traditional communities with nostalgia for what has been lost in 'modern' Jewish life, and as a possible source of revival.

By the end of the nineteenth century the ground had been established for the creation of a folkloristics. Max Grunwald, a rabbi in Vienna, is seen as founding the field in his writings in the 1890s (Noy 1982). His programme included both the gathering of contemporary and recent materials that reflected folk life and the study of the popular strata within classic Jewish literature. A turn to the 'folk' as a source of inspiration was also a theme in the work of Solomon Rappoport, more widely known by his pen name Ansky, who conducted ethnographic research in eastern Galicia and neighbouring areas from 1912 to 1916 (Roskies 1992: 257–8). His play *The Dybbuk*, based on a portrayal of life in an Eastern European *shtetl* (small-town), demonstrates the interweaving of ethnography and literature. This overlap of genres has reappeared at various times in the study of Jewish culture.

An assumption common to several of the approaches cited is that Jewish life, or aspects of it, belongs to an earlier time period. This theme has been considered with regard to anthropological writing by Johannes Fabian (1983), who argues that the discipline has constituted its objects as 'non-contemporaneous' with the historical setting of those writing about them. Another expression of this assumption is found in the anthropological analysis of the Hebrew Bible.

The two major figures representing this approach were William Robertson Smith and James George Frazer, who was Smith's student at Cambridge. Smith showed the connection between social life and religious life in Semitic religions (Beidelman 1974; Goldberg 1995). His analysis contributed to understanding the Bible and also influenced Émile Durkheim's sociological theory of religion (1995 [1912]). Smith called upon the anthropology of his day, implying that biblical society could be compared to less-developed forms of society and religion. He carried out his comparative exercise as a committed Christian. Smith accepted the historical framework posited by the continental scholars of the Higher Biblical Criticism, and placed Judaism on an evolutionary ladder between primitive society and Christianity.

It was Smith who drew Frazer's attention to comparative (anthropological) study, leading him to channel his interest in the classical world into the monumental collection *The Golden Bough*. Both men shared a Scottish background, but Smith was a believing Christian while Frazer was not. After Smith died, the person at Cambridge who became closest to Frazer was Solomon Schechter, a Reader of Rabbinics who was also a committed Jew (Ackerman 1992). Frazer told Schechter of his progress in being able to read the Bible in Hebrew as he prepared himself for his three-volume work, *Folklore in the Old Testament* (1918). In *The Golden Bough* Frazer presented comparative work on magic and religion, while *Folklore in the Old Testament* was a springboard to discuss the anthropology of social organization (Strathern 1987). Frazer stated that he was not a man of religious affiliations, but his relationship to religion may have been ambivalent. In the preface to *Folklore* he wrote: 'The annals of savagery and superstition unhappily compose a large part of human literature; but in what other volume [than the Old Testament] shall we find side by side with that melancholy record, psalmists who poured forth their sweet and solemn strains...?' (1918: p. xi). Frazer's rhetorical question implies some sympathy for the literature of the Hebrew Bible, while it also indicates the presence of 'savage and superstitious' elements in it. Smith and Frazer alike had both positive and negative evaluations of the Hebrew Bible, the book eminently linked to the Jews (Eilberg-Schwartz 1990; Feeley-Harnik 1994). Another contemporary aspect of anthropology, however, often designated as race science, was heavily weighted toward the negative side.

Jewish Social Science and
the Question of Race

The notion of the division of mankind into races, and the formulation of a discipline that scientifically investigated the topic, also appeared in the late eighteenth century. The history of the term 'anthropology' (in various European languages) over the course of the nineteenth and twentieth centuries is complex, as is evident when reviewing attempts to apply the field to the study of Jews. Originally, the term included both the investigation of physical features of human populations along with aspects of their 'manners', customs, and so forth. Over the course of the nineteenth century distinctions within the overall field began to emerge. Research on customs and beliefs was called 'ethnology', so in various languages, particularly on the continent, 'anthropology' mainly meant the study of physical or 'racial' characteristics. In England, the term 'social anthropology' was used from early in the twentieth century as distinct from 'physical anthropology', and a similar separation was made in the United States that stressed a sub-field of 'cultural anthropology'.

It is probably not coincidental that a number of Jewish scholars, while not studying Judaism, were prominent in stressing the importance of understanding social and cultural life phenomena in their own right and not as reducible to some more 'basic' level that explains them. The work of German-born Franz Boas, who critically shaped academic anthropology in the United States early in the twentieth century, is best known in this regard (Boas 1940), but Durkheim's insistence on the existence of 'social facts' that required their own discipline of sociology (Durkheim 1951 [1897]) may be placed in opposition to racial notions as well as to psychological reductionism. Max Grunwald's advocacy of a Jewish folklore was explicitly aimed at combating some recent European anthropological portrayals of Jews (Kirshenblatt-Gimblett 1990). These points should be placed in broader context.

With the hindsight of the rise of Nazism and the horrendous results of the Second World War, most social scientists in the mid-twentieth century roundly rejected any sort of racial explanations or other theories that seemed to share similar assumptions. In recent decades, however, historical research has shown that studying what was understood as race, and trying to assess its role in history and behaviour, were respectable parts of social science in the first decades of the twentieth century and not associated only with conservative and nationalistic politics. Scholars with liberal orientations were also interested in the subject (Massin 1996; Hart 2000). While there were those who argued against understanding social life in medical or biological terms, perhaps a more common reaction was to consider these questions as open, or not to focus on sharp analytical distinctions between the racial and cultural aspects of a people's history. This was true of many who were concerned with Jewish life. In Buber's address on 'Jewish Science' to the Fifth Zionist Congress in 1901, he included the Jewish race as one of the topics deserving study (Hart 2000: 39), although at a later date he sought to separate this understanding from the Nazi concern with race theories (Shapira 1993).

During the nineteenth century racial perspectives on understanding groups had gained momentum. The category of 'Semites' was first formulated in the eighteenth century in reference to human language-groups, but gradually came to assume racial connotations and was incorporated into the term anti-Semitism. A similar trend existed with regard to the concept 'Aryan' in the study of Indian history and culture (Trautmann 1997). It has been noted that racial anti-Semitism became prominent precisely when Jews were integrating into European society and losing their religious distinctiveness. Sociologically speaking, this entailed a situation in which Jews dressed like Gentiles and spoke like Gentiles and might not be recognized for who they 'really were' in daily interaction. Racial ideas supported the notion that Jews continued to have special characteristics even though these might not be immediately apparent. In general, the dissolution of social boundaries due to widespread urbanization in nineteenth-century Europe often created anxiety about being able to recognize peoples' origins. This was one factor feeding into the social attractiveness of photography, and that new technology became one central tool in the rapidly expanding discipline of (physical) anthropology (Hart 2000: 176–8).

By the turn of the twentieth century the notion that race was one key to understanding nations and their histories was salient in scientific discourse, even as it also had its critics and opponents. The racial perspective had become active and scientifically acceptable enough for Jews to feel that they had to react to it. By this time many Jews were integrated into European culture and had been educated in its universities, including Eastern European Jews who were attracted to universities in Germany. They could not help but accept the prestige of science and internalize its premises and some of its results, including negative images of Jews and Judaism (Gilman 1991; Stepan and Gilman 1993). In some instances this led to the response of adopting the same scientific tools to present an alternate view of Jews and their history. Jewish scholars who did so were addressing a Gentile audience, but also their fellow Jews.

This response has been discussed both in terms of a Jewish 'race science' (Efron 1994), and in relation to an emerging Jewish social science (Hart 2000). At the time these realms were closely linked. Many Jews engaged in studying the racial statistics of Jews were trained physicians. The shift from individual health to the well-being of the 'collective body' was a step that was persuasive to many. The unexamined metaphor was particularly cogent within a Zionist milieu; Leo Pinsker, trained as a doctor, made the case for Zionism in his classic tract *Autoemancipation*

(1944 [1881]), by analysing anti-Semitism as a pathology that had come to be transmitted by heredity. At the same time, there were also those interested in Jewish race science whose Jewish ideology was primarily oriented to diaspora existence.

One such scholar was Joseph Jacobs, who lived in England for many years but also experienced Jewish life in Australia, and eventually moved to the United States (Efron 1994: 58–90). There he became an editor of the *Jewish Encyclopaedia*, published in 1904. An aim of this pioneering attempt to represent Judaism in America was to confront anthropology and to combat some of the ideas about Jews that it put forth (Schwartz 1992: 108–12; Efron 1994: 89). Jacobs also insisted that an anthropology of the Jews be linked to the broader study of Judaism and its history.

This insistence was a general feature of Jewish race science and social science. Efron (1994) shows how the racial study of Jews inevitably expanded to include ethnography. As scholars began to relate to Middle Eastern Jews, it became apparent how diverse Jews were in physical appearance. Understanding this required describing these groups and placing them within history. If one assumed that Jews were a single 'nation' in the ancient past, what explains their present diversity? Did it reflect heredity or environment, and how was it transmitted? In the first decades of the twentieth century there were still scientists who adhered to the Lamarckian position that acquired characteristics could be inherited, and this seemed an appropriate way of explaining the diversity among Jewish groups (Hart 2000: 11–12). It enabled the claim that Jews changed physically in response to environmental conditions, and then transmitted the new characteristics to the following generations. Thus, the continuity of 'race' was one factor in these discussions, but could never be divorced from the social settings within which Jewish groups found themselves. Its utilization of race concepts notwithstanding, at bottom Jewish social science promoted a *sociological* view of Jewish existence that stressed the ongoing impact of contemporary economic and social conditions, rather than determinants rooted in the group's past (Efron 1994: 166–74; Hart 2000: 26–7).

SOCIAL AND CULTURAL SCIENCE IN RELATION TO JEWISH HISTORY

Given that notions of a racial past of the Jews hovered over explaining modern trends, we may ask how the emerging Jewish social science saw itself in relation to the historically oriented Wissenschaft de Judentums that preceded it. According to Hart (2000: 39–40), the attitude was one of contrast. Wissenschaft scholarship dealt with earlier periods while the social scientists were concerned with the present.

Practitioners of the newer discipline claimed that Wissenschaft grew from an atmosphere of emancipation and individual assimilation, an ideology that they were now abandoning in favour of a collective Jewish future. Earlier scholarship assumed that the road to progress and 'regeneration' of un-emancipated Jewry led to its integration into modern Europe, while Zionist-oriented social science entailed a radical critique of the possibility of Jewry's future there. Buber announced a difference between 'the science of Judaism' and 'Jewish science' (Hart 2000: 39), in which the former studied the religion of the past with detached analysis, while the latter was concerned with a living people and was designed to contribute to its revival.

Buber could relate both to textual traditions and to emerging social concerns, but frequently Wissenschaft scholars and social-science researchers came from different backgrounds. Many of the former had experienced traditional education, including Yeshiva study, and then attended universities in Central or Western Europe where they were trained in philological and historical methods. Many of the latter were products of education in relatively emancipated contexts that lacked immersion in Jewish textual culture. What both schools held in common is that their subject-matter was not cultivated in academic frameworks like universities and research institutes, but was largely studied with the support of funds, and in the framework of institutions, created within Jewish communities. The more recent social science was often carried out as an adjunct to other professional work, particularly that of physicians (Efron 1994). The social scientists criticized work of an earlier generation by pointing to its ideological conditioning and biases, but were not troubled that their own scientific analysis was explicitly harnessed to ideological claims.

Some of the work of the social scientists was published in general journals, in addition to the organs which they had created, most prominently the *Zeitschrift für Demographie und Statistik der Juden*. Arthur Ruppin, a leading Jewish social scientist and the first editor of that journal, invited his teacher, anthropologist Felix von Luschan, to contribute an article to it. Von Luschan represented a liberal trend among race scientists, as did Rudolph Virchow, who was a mentor of Franz Boas (Massin 1996). But Jewish social scientists also could positively evaluate the work of researchers whose formulations had anti-Semitic biases if these carried the prestige of science. The views of economist-sociologist Werner Sombart concerning the link between Jews and modern capitalism went along with a racial theory that saw this linkage continuing from antiquity to the present. This claim was adopted warmly by some Zionist social scientists because it could easily be harnessed to the call to give Jews their own society and state (Efron 1994: 130–1).

It should also be asked to what extent a sociological perspective entered the work of Jewish historians. This took place slowly and unevenly, and sometimes entailed serious debate. Wissenschaft scholars of the mid-nineteenth century, in tune with their times, wrote history with an ideational emphasis and showed the respectable place deserved by *Judaism* in the unfolding of world history. Later in the century Heinrich Graetz expounded what might be called a national (but not yet Zionist) perspective, stressing the specific historical circumstance of different groups of Jews. Another major synthesizer, Simon Dubnow, introduced a more systematic consideration of social conditions. The prominent ideological orientation in his work stressed Jewish autonomous existence in the diaspora, and this entailed attention to the political and social structures supporting that existence. Salo W. Baron, perhaps the last generalist among Jewish historians, also moved in this direction as is evident in his multi-volume oeuvre entitled the *Social and Religious History of the Jews* (1957–83). To what extent this work really offered new perspectives informed by sociology may be questioned (Katz 1955), but it did emphasize directions not adequately developed in earlier writings. There were also explicit criticisms by Jewish historians of the application of sociological models to the subject of their discipline (Alon 1958).

Some Judaic scholars were open to the field of folklore as potentially contributing to the understanding of classic Jewish texts and possibly to the regeneration of Jewish identity in new social and political conditions. This probably assumed a distinction between that field as representing the *Volk* in 'civilized' (even if traditional) societies, and the discipline anthropology that dealt with 'primitive' societies (Patai 1983: 17 [1945]). Buber's concern with Hasidic lore may be viewed in this light, as well as the collation of talmudic and midrashic materials by Bialik and Ravnitzky (1988 [1925]). Above, the connection between Solomon Schechter and Sir James Frazer at Cambridge was mentioned. When Schechter moved to New York to head the Jewish Theological Seminary of America (JTSA) in 1903, he cited Frazer on the Hebrew Bible in a major address (1959: 47). One of Schechter's key appointments was talmudist Louis Ginzberg, who devoted much scholarly effort, formulated in accessible prose, to his multi-volume *Legends of the Jews* (1909–38). Ginzberg considered himself, among other things, a student of folklore (E. Ginzberg 1966: 181). It may even be that Frazer's oeuvre served as an inspiration to this effort, even though their ideological commitments were different. Some of the volumes of *Legends of the Jews* were translated from German by Paul Radin, an anthropologist who studied with Franz Boas. Radin was the son of a rabbi, and his brother Max, who taught law at the University of California, Berkeley, also wrote on Jewish topics (1915). A folklore perspective on classic texts was not then paralleled by ethnographic research on contemporary Jews. But correspondence between Ginzberg and Max Radin shows interest in the sociological approach of Max Weber to Judaism.

JEWISH SOCIETIES IN
SOCIOLOGICAL THEORY

This raises the question of the place of Jewish history and Jews in the development of sociological theory. Weber, initially an economic historian, developed a now well-known theory about the role of the Protestant ethic in the rise of capitalism. To highlight this thesis, he continued in a comparative direction, examining the religions of Ancient India and Ancient China and also probing the background to Protestantism in the Hebrew Bible and Ancient Judaism (1952 [1917–19]). Weber was an erudite scholar who learned biblical Hebrew as well as drawing upon the historical writings of his day. His analyses went hand in hand with the development of a sophisticated set of categories examining various ways in which religion interacted with society.

Weber's contribution is often contrasted with those of Karl Marx and of Werner Sombart, who was Weber's contemporary. Marx stressed the control of the means of production as the central variable shaping other aspects of society and culture, while Weber, accepting many of Marx's ideas, also showed the importance of other factors in economic development. Sombart disagreed with Weber, arguing that Jews were a major force in developing modern capitalism (1969 [1913]). As noted, his economic history was linked to a negative racial view of Jews, while a major premiss of Weber's sociology was the importance of a value-free analysis.

Discussions of Jews also appear in the work of another classic figure in the history of modern sociology: Émile Durkheim. In his *Suicide* (1951 [1897]), that demonstrated the existence of 'social facts' requiring a sociological level of explanation, Durkheim contrasted the degree of solidarity found in Protestant and Catholic society, and also found that Jews, like Catholics, were characterized by higher solidarity which accounted for a lower suicide rate. In *The Division of Labor in Society* (1964 [1893]), which outlines the major features of modern societies in relation to earlier ones, he cites the Bible frequently. Here, the Ancient Hebrews serve as examples of general categories and theories that he is attempting to establish. In contrast to Weber, Durkheim did not mobilize his sociological armoury to provide an in-depth portrait of Jewish society at any particular period. In *The Elementary Forms of Religious Life* (1995 [1912]), now viewed as a foundational text both in sociology and anthropology, Durkheim continued to provide scattered mentions of Judaism, often side by side with examples from Christianity.

JEWS IN THE DEVELOPMENT OF
MODERN SOCIAL SCIENCE

That text, which hammers home the links between religion and the structure of society, has made many readers ask about the importance of Durkheim's Jewish background, and opens up the general question of the role of modern Jewish history in the development of social thought. For example, Durkheim sees a notion of, and relation to, 'the sacred' as the kernel of religion, and defines 'the sacred' as something utterly 'separate' from everyday life. Readers familiar with Jewish sources cannot help wonder about the connection between this definition and an interpretation of the Hebrew stem QDSh (holy) as 'that which is set aside' (Babylonian Talmud, Qiddushin 2b), although Durkheim nowhere cites such a specific source. Durkheim's father was a rabbi, and this fact has provided various interpretations on possible connections between his background and his theories. The complexity of the question may be seen in a number of directions along which links between Durkheim's Jewishness and his sociology have been explored.

Durkheim advocated the full integration of Jews into French society. His secular philosophy and politics articulated during the Third Republic, when the ties between Catholicism and the state were loosened institutionally, dovetail with a theoretical search for a new basis of social solidarity and express an ideology shared by many Jews at the time (Moore 1986). But to what extent did he think that such integration required relinquishing ties to the Jewish collectivity? Several authors (Cuddihy 1974: 25–6; Hart 2000: 131–2) mention the seemingly forced interpretation Durkheim placed on the finding that suicide rates among Jews were significantly lower than among Protestants, even though Jews showed many characteristics of modern social individuation such as extended education. He claimed that Jews absorbed notions of modernity without deeply internalizing them, but only utilizing them, so that they did not erode traditional ties of solidarity that provided immunity to suicidal tendencies. One might wonder how Durkheim viewed himself in this regard. His way of life was that of an agnostic, but he did not sever ties with Jewish organizations concerned with the welfare of Jews (Hyman 1979: 56–7, 59). Pierre Birnbaum (1995) cites the Dreyfus Affair as challenging previously held views by Durkheim, and other French sociologists who were Jewish, on the ultimate possibility of a neutral, rational French society. Another study (Strenski 1997) places the sociology of Durkheim and his students in a somewhat similar context, while stressing other dilemmas they faced within it such as intellectual theories that denigrated Jews or their place in history. Durkheim was prepared to move beyond Judaism and search for the foundations of a modern secular society, but may have resisted views that his own religious past was inferior to anyone else's. While not fitting the rubric of a 'Jewish social scientist', he also responded to challenges of combating 'science' that devalued Judaism. He was probably more aware than is evident in his writings of Jewish Wissenschaft scholarship in neighbouring Germany, but his intellectual strategy was to take new insights regarding the Jewish past and to formulate them in terms of general theory.

Durkheim's story shows how the search for Jewish influence in modern cultural phenomenon is intricate and full of guesswork. Nevertheless, the prominence of Jews in the development of social theory in the nineteenth to twentieth centuries is a topic that may yield more insights. In this realm, the careful and comparative documentation of absences may be as revealing as that of presences. It was not unusual for some Jewish intellectuals, like those now labelled the 'Frankfurt School' in Germany of the 1920s, to disavow the relevance of their background for appreciating their theories, but there too the story is a varied and complex one (Cuddihy 1974: 153–4; Jacobs 1997).

Absences also featured in scholarly positions with an anti-Semitic aspect. An example is Austrian Catholic ethnologist Wilhelm Schmidt and his adherence to the theory of Primitive Monotheism, that claimed that notions of a High God were sometimes found in the most 'primitive' societies. It has been noted that this theory fitted a world-view anchored in Genesis and the story of the Fall of Man; Adam was a monotheist, but his descendants degenerated both morally and religiously. But there was also an anti-Semitic bias in this position (Hauschild 1997). Ignoring Jews was a way of depriving the Ancient Hebrews of any originality, challenging the assumption that European civilization stood on two bases: one the 'classical' world, and the other the Hebraic tradition. More broadly, the vigorous search for the Aryan roots of Europe was often a strategy of erasure of the history of Jewish influences. Growing out of the same intellectual milieu, one may also document the elimination of Jews, including several who had an interest in Jewish life, from the fields of ethnology and Völkerpsychologie in Germany (ibid.; Bunzl forthcoming, 2003).

The period of National Socialism and its atrocities eventually placed all social-science perspectives that were based on some notion of race under a cloud, if not a taboo. The social-science research that considered viewing Jews as even partially defined by biological continuity was largely ignored after the Second World War, only to be unearthed by the historical research cited. In a broad developmental view, intellectual positions that challenged the relevance of race for understanding society and history represented the avenue of advancement. But the complete elimination of physical or biological explanations required the theoretical formulation of the factors capable of accounting for group definitions and continuity in behaviour over time. Such advance took place around the turn of the twentieth century in a variety of disciplines, often with important contributions made by researchers of a Jewish background. In addition to Durkheim's stress on 'society', and Boas's emphasis on 'culture', already mentioned, one can point to Freud's 'discovery' of the symbolic in *The Interpretation of Dreams* [1900], or the philosophical work of Ernst Cassirer. The implication of these perspectives is that all of human culture is potentially available to all members of the human species. While not universally accepted when they were first put forth, the aftermath of the World War at mid-century set the stage for these becoming the basic notions on which contemporary Western social science was built (e.g. Lévi-Strauss 1958).

Sociology of the Jews after the Second World War

The post-war situation created a new setting for the sociological study of the Jews. It was necessary for a tradition of social research to reconstitute itself in a new context, which mainly meant work in North America (which had become the main demographic center of active Jewish life). This was not an effort that was undertaken entirely *de novo*. Since the beginning of the twentieth century the American Jewish Committee put out the *American Jewish Yearbook* in collaboration with the Jewish Publication Society of America. There had been one outstanding study of Jewish life in America published in the 1920s, Louis Wirth's *The Ghetto* (1998 [1928]). This work placed American Jewish experience against the background of ghetto existence over the centuries in Europe. An introduction to a reissue of the book stresses how it was unique in its day: a study of Jews published by a major university press, at a time when Jewish studies, whether concerning earlier historical periods or contemporary trends, were close to non-existent in American universities (Diner 1998). Wirth, who became a tenured professor at the University of Chicago, did not continue academic work in that direction. The envisioned future for Jews implied by his analysis was acceptance by and assimilation into American society. Assimilation was also the implied view of anthropologist Franz Boas, who in the 1920s was one of less than a handful of Jewish 'full professors' at Columbia University. Boas had criticized racial views of the Jewish people, but paid almost no attention to the culture of Jews (Glick 1982). In this regard, his views dovetailed with those of Maurice Fishberg, a physician and physical anthropologist who worked in the framework of Jewish institutions, and with whom Boas collaborated to some degree (Hart 2000: 158). Our reading of Boas today mostly reflects his silence about Jewish culture, while

Fishberg explicitly saw assimilation as the preferred solution to the Jewish problems of Jewish immigrants in America.

The period after the Second World War, however, set the stage for a new agenda for the organized Jewish community and for Jewish social sciences. How to forge such a tradition anew was not clear. Race was no longer available as a topic hinting at the existence of a Jewish collectivity beyond the specific histories of Jewish groups, but anthropology had a new task. In 1939 Salo Baron, under the auspices of the Conference on Jewish Relations, founded the journal *Jewish Social Studies*. In the early volumes (1–4), four articles by anthropologists were included. One was a paper that Boas delivered at a conference on race in Europe. Another was an obituary of Edward Sapir, a noted linguist and anthropologist, who died in 1939 but had co-operated with Max Weinreich of YIVO (Jewish Institute of Social Research) in Vilna (Kirshenblatt-Gimblett 1996). At the same period, Louis Finkelstein became President of the JTSA and launched plans for the multi-volume anthology: *The Jews: Their History, Culture and Religion* (1949), which became one of the major academic statements about Judaism for over two decades. Finkelstein could not easily find a person to write on the sociology of the Jews. An adequate section on this topic, consisting of six chapters, was only achieved in the third edition (Finkelstein 1960: p. xxxv).

At the time of war and through the 1950s, the sociological study of American Jewry was a project growing out of the concerns of national Jewish organizations and community 'federations'. It continued to deal with some of the central issues that had concerned the earlier work in Europe—the basis of Jewish demography such as migration, occupational distribution, and intermarriage (Hart 2000: 229). By this time many Jews were three-generation Americans, were socially mobile, and evidenced a relative demographic stability in and around major cities. Part of this 'stability', however, entailed the large-scale move to the suburbs after the Second World War. There, issues of cultural continuity, education, and identity determined by individual choices came to the fore. Research sought to document emerging trends and understand how Jews could be both American and Jewish.

Findings and answers were formulated by sociologists and other writers with a sociological slant. Oscar Handlin (1954), historian of American immigration, documented Jews maintaining a sense of collective existence, while the content of their lives differed little from that of other middle-class Americans. Sociologist Marshall Sklare supplied a portrait of Conservative Judaism, subtitling his book: *An American Religious Movement* (1955). This branch of Judaism enjoyed significant growth during the post-war move to the suburbs. Sklare highlighted its contribution to Jews being able to follow their traditions while feeling part of America, but also showed the compromises that its religious leaders had to make. Another sociologist, Milton Gordon, distinguished various phases of acculturation and assimilation, thereby indicating how Jews could adopt many American patterns but not disappear as a separate group (1964). Essayist Will Herberg authored *Protestant—Catholic—Jew*

(1955), calling the work religious sociology. He claimed that in America it was important to have a religion, and that now all three faiths were acceptable expressions of American life. These books had impacts well beyond academia. They were discussed by rabbis in pulpits who condemned Handlin's 'agnosticism' concerning an American Jewish future and celebrated Herberg's formulation. Another oft-quoted statement in that context derived from a study of immigration by Hansen (1948), that did not focus on Jews but created the aphorism that 'what the second generation wants to forget, the third generation wants to remember'. This generalization was not necessarily confirmed by data with regard to the Jews (Heilman 1982: 142–3), but became a 'sociological truth' repeated by leadership committed to Jewish continuity.

A New Anthropology and Comparative Perspectives

In the 1950s there also developed a social anthropology of Jewish life. Against the background of the Second World War, Mark Zborowski and Elizabeth Herzog interviewed individuals in the United States who had grown up in *shtetl* communities and created a portrait of Jewish small towns in Poland (1995 [1952]; see Kirshenblatt-Gimblett's introduction). Another study focused on a collective kibbutz in Israel (Spiro 1958). Later in the decade, several anthropologists from the United States travelled to Israel and documented the lives of Jews in Middle Eastern settings (Weingrod 1966; Willner 1969; Zenner 1963). That subject will be mentioned below when discussing sociology in Israel.

The regrouping of efforts to study Jews and Judaism from social-scientific perspectives was a transnational phenomenon. Jewish sociologists in England were consulted in the development of the discipline in Israel (Eppel 1994). In 1958 the *Jewish Journal of Sociology* was established in London, edited by Maurice Freedman, a noted anthropologist specializing in China. The journal published (and publishes) contributions relating to Jewish life in all regions of the world. Within Europe, Jewish life took on new characteristics after the war. While radically affected by the Second World War, several countries later received Jewish immigration from North Africa in the 1950s–60s (France, Italy), and in the 1980s–90s from the former Soviet Union (Germany). There have been studies in France, for example, reflecting both the classic conceptions of Jewish integration into French society (Schnapper 1983), and issues stemming from the more recent immigration from North Africa (Bahloul 1996). On the background of both migration and the

Holocaust, the sociology of memory emerged as a major theme (Valensi and Wachtel 1991), often in a context that bridges continents (Kugelmass 1992). At the same time, Jews in Europe evidenced the far-reaching diversification of self-definitions that characterizes much of contemporary Jewry (Webber 1994). The same is true of smaller Jewries in 'peripheral' areas, which have been studied both with regard to sociopolitical and cultural processes (e.g. Medding 1968; Cimet 1997; Gilman and Shain 1999).

THE 1960S AND BEYOND

In the 1960s United States politics and values were severely questioned, a development that affected Jews and Judaism. The growing political consciousness of American blacks highlighted issues of ethnicity, and the Vietnam War made Americans more aware than in the past of the problems of colonialism. New perceptions of US foreign policy created sympathy for Palestinian Arabs who came under Israeli military control during the 1967 war. Jews were sensitive to seeing Israel in the role of an oppressor, and one reaction was to focus on realms in which realities seemed to consist of simple contrasts. Such an arena was provided by the Soviet Union, that suppressed religious life and prohibited emigration. The situation of Soviet Jewry first became the rallying cry of the Jewish Defense League, that reflected the atmosphere of the 1960s in advocating 'Jewish Power', and thereby challenged the dominant mode of Jewish middle-class accommodation to America (Dolgin 1977). Another development, relevant to the internal content of Judaism, was the *havura* movement spearheaded by young Jews who challenged the formality and passive atmospheres of the large suburban synagogues established by their parents' generation. The prayer groups they formed were, among other things, sites for the expression of feminist awareness and participation (Prell 1989; Weissler 1990). The greater acceptance of ethnic distinctiveness that developed in America also contributed to restraining the numerical decline of orthodoxy, and was also evident in a trend of 'returning to' orthodox ways of life on the part of those who did not grow up in them (Heilman 1976; Davidman 1991; Soloveitchik 1994: 79). This diversification stimulated ethnographic work. Studies of aging Jews documented both the bridges and the gaps between the vanishing remnants of Eastern European Judaism (Myerhoff 1980; Kugelmass 1986) and their descendants, while other projects closely monitored some of the new developments. Two edited collections discussed American Jewry while emphasizing ethnographic perspectives, pointing to the diversity of expressions that were emerging in the postmodern mood (Kugelmass 1988; Zenner 1988).

The more conventional sociological surveying of trends within Jewry continued as well. In addition to the data made available through census tracts or other official bodies, Jewish organizations supported research that utilized up-to-date methods of sampling and survey research. With the expansion of Jewish studies in American universities that began in the 1960s, the sociology of Jews began to grow as well. Still, Heilman (1982) claimed that the majority of sociological research about Jews was conducted by Jews and written for them. Perhaps this reflects the reality that most funding for this research came from within the organized Jewish community. A similar observation is relevant to the formulation of a Jewish political science (Elazar 1976). The 'case of' the Jews, however, did appear in general discussions of immigration and ethnicity in American society (Glazer and Moynihan 1963). Consciousness of the Second World War informed the social-psychological research on discrimination in terms of the 'authoritarian personality' (Adorno *et al.* 1950), which received theoretical inspiration from the disbanded 'Frankfurt School', and was partially sponsored by the American Jewish Committee. From the late 1960s, 'ethnic studies' became prominent on the campus scene, giving Jews legitimacy to delve into their own past and current reality. Paradoxically, this widely shared cultural mood provided justification for each group to turn inward. The interest of organizationally sponsored research, of course, was not in a comparative perspective, but in assessing 'the situation' of American Jews in various realms. Demographic and economic data were relevant to new social challenges like a growing elderly population. Measuring attendance at various forms of Jewish schools was important in tracking how the content of Judaism was being transmitted. The topic that attracted the most widespread attention was intermarriage.

In 1991 the Council of Jewish Federations published a co-ordinated National Jewish Populations Survey assessing trends among American Jews, hoping to attain accurate and in-depth readings in a variety of areas. The official summary reported an intermarriage rate among younger people of over 50 per cent. There were dissenting interpretations that claimed the figure was lower, and which also questioned methods of interviewing, definitions used, and technical features of the survey's data analysis. One argument was that growing intermarriage indeed was linked to the loss of Jews, but that those who remained connected to Judaism were more committed than earlier generations. The degree to which these findings attracted public Jewish attention is striking, including accusations of ideological influences on interpretations of the survey (Cohen 1994, 1995; Goldstein *et al.* 1995). The links between scholarly interpretations of Jewish life and the stance of researchers continued to be noted throughout the decade (Lederhendler 1998).

The United States also provided the arena for a 'critical' Jewish studies that built upon cultural studies, combining textual analyses, anthropological insights, and critical theory (Boyarin and Boyarin 1997). Typically, the object of criticism was Zionism and Israel in relation to Palestinian society, when the former were compared to more traditional versions of Judaism (J. Boyarin 1990). This comparison implied an idealization of diaspora existence, particular that of Eastern Europe (D. Boyarin 1997). The approach keenly sought to establish a representation of Judaism within critical discourse. One question arising from this work is the way that terms once closely linked to Jewish existence (and usually coined by Gentiles), such as Ghetto, Holocaust, or Diaspora, are transferred into general concepts in social analysis.

There were also further steps, in both America and Israel, to connect sociological analysis to Jewish history. A major figure in this realm was Jacob Katz (1955, 1961), even though his method was at first resisted by many historians. S. D. Goitein testifies that his approach to medieval Mediterranean Jewry was influenced by anthropology (1988: 498–501). The linkage was also attempted from the perspective of the sociology of religion (Sharot 1976), or by showing the relevance of contemporary anthropology to historical and present-day Jewish settings (Goldberg 1987). Today, some scholars boldly incorporate anthropological analysis into Jewish history (Marcus 1996).

Sociology and Israeli Society

The post-Second World War period, and the creation of the State of Israel, form the background to the crystallization of sociology in Israel. There are two figures that might be viewed as links between the Jewish social science in Europe and developments in Palestine before the state was established. One is Arthur Ruppin, who migrated there in 1907 and was prominent in the Zionist land-acquisition programme. While active in practical affairs, Ruppin continued research and was appointed to the Institute of Jewish Studies of the new Hebrew University in 1925. His course on the Sociology of the Jews included modern Jewish history before an appointment was made in that field. It began by presenting data on Jewish physical anthropology (Ruppin 1930–1). Ruppin's memoirs stress his role as a scientist, admonishing politicians to pay more attention to scientific findings (1971: 74), while he himself was 'a-political by nature' (ibid. 236). He was a founder of Brit Shalom, that argued that Zionist leaders were ignoring the Arab question. Within the university, his appointment appears as an exception; later attempts to encourage anthropology within the university did not succeed (Patai 1992: 456–8). Ruppin died in 1943 and was not replaced.

The second figure was Martin Buber, who migrated to Palestine in 1938. The historians of Judaism there were wary of his mixture of scholarship and ideology, and he was not appointed to the Institute of Jewish Studies at the University. He did give courses on the Sociology of Culture, which were the background to the

Department of Sociology established in 1950. Two of his students, Shmuel N. Eisenstadt and Yonina Talmon-Garber, helped forge a sociology that shifted away from philosophy and incorporated a systematic empirical basis. Both studied in England, where they met leading sociologists and social anthropologists. The department was incorporated into a Faculty of Economic and Social Science that was to provide an educational base for civil servants in the new state. The sociology that emerged from this setting exhibited few of the broad concerns about Jewry characterizing Buber and Ruppin. The remarks that follow discuss features of Israeli sociology with potential or actual points of comparison with the sociology of Jews abroad.

Two systematic foci of Israeli sociology in the 1950s were kibbutz society (Talmon 1972), and the immigration that more than doubled the Jewish population of the country during its first three-and-a-half years (Eisenstadt 1954). The kibbutz movement, while small in number, had played a pivotal role in implementing the values of the Zionist ideology, and projected a vision that in principle was to shape the whole society. The immigrants, by contrast, constituted an unknown set of influences that potentially could alter the direction of Israeli Jewish society as it had developed thus far. Both phenomena were met by a sociology that paid minimal attention to history.

A major paradigm in studying the kibbutz was to examine to what extent that communal form met, in social reality, its own collectivist ideals. The very definition of these ideals involved overturning ways of life that characterized Jews in the diaspora. With regard to the 'absorption of immigrants', the emphasis was on how the immigrants changed to adapt to the new society. Immigrants coming from Europe were positively viewed in terms of 'a relatively great "neutralization" of the social influences of the countries of origin of the immigrants' (Eisenstadt 1950). Even the very immediate past of the Holocaust, whose historical impact was stressed later on, did not then appear in analyses of Israeli society. Parallel to this, the main claim with regard to Middle Eastern immigrants was that their specific histories were only marginally relevant to their new roles and social trajectories in Israeli society. Part of this view was to criticize anthropological approaches to the study of immigration because they highlighted the specific cultures of each group rather than the task of understanding changing Israeli society (Ben-David 1952). This was ironic, for much of the research on kibbutzim and immigrant agricultural villages (*moshavim*) was modelled upon anthropological fieldwork.

The basic orientation in studying immigration was that of 'modernization'. The cultures of the immigrants were a focus of study only insofar as they impeded or abetted that goal (Goldberg 1978). Viewed in terms of 'traditionality', a regnant notion in modernization studies, social research in Israel paid little attention to the religious backgrounds of immigrants or how their Jewish identities were being affected by their new setting. Early sociological study of religion focused on problems of religion and state and on the place of *haredim* (ultra-orthodox) in a situation of autonomous Jewish statehood. Studying the 'moderate' religiosity of those identified with Zionism became a sociological focus only after the 1967 war when this became linked to the political struggles over territory (Aran 1991).

The criticisms that the next generation of sociologists directed toward early work was not concerned with issues of Jewish history and identity, but stemmed from general developments within the social sciences after the 1960s. At that time a department of Sociology and Anthropology was created at the recently autonomous Tel Aviv University, as well as in new smaller universities, breaking the monopoly of academic sociology by the Hebrew University department (Marx 1980). Israelis trained abroad (and new immigrants) joined these departments and reflected the emerging critical orientation of the social sciences abroad. Older paradigms were challenged, emphasizing how 'absorbing immigrants' entailed economic exploitation and how conflicts in Israeli society were as salient as the integrative elements. It was also claimed that the first generation of Israeli sociology itself was a reflection of the initial hegemony of European derived old-timers, rather than an independent stance critical of social processes (Smooha 1978; Bernstein 1980; Shenhav and Kunda 1992; Ram 1995). Most recently, both historical and sociological perspectives have reassessed the evolving relationship of the Israeli state and Jewish society to Palestinian Arabs, both within and without its borders. The growing appreciation of diversity within the society and the move away from former encompassing models has brought about a greater recognition of ethnography in studying Israeli society (Abuhav et al. 1998).

The conflicting tasks, internal fragmentation, and the loss of a 'centre' of Israeli society are now prominent in analysis (Horowitz and Lissak 1990; Kimmerling 2001). The electoral rise of the Sephardi ultra-orthodox party, SHAS, is one component of this perception, along with the rapid political impact of 'Russian' Jews within a decade of their immigration. The most general challenge presented by evolving social realities is that the establishment of an independent state, and the success of 'ingathering the exiles', has had effects far more complex than that of creating a single national culture. In one sense, contemporary Israel has internalized the historical dilemmas of many post-emancipation diaspora communities.

This perhaps sets the stage for more study of issues and trends that link Israel and North America, or for considering other diaspora communities (Liebman and Cohen 1990; Gilman and Shain 1999). Examples of such issues, some of which already have attracted some research, are Jewish feminism, trips to Israel within diaspora Jewish education, or the importance of understanding middle-of-the-road religious approaches (Kopelowitz 1998; Cohen and Eisen 2000). Methodological issues are also entailed in this development. In both Israel and the United States there is now an interest in supplementing survey studies of religious behaviour and identity with qualitative assessment of the diversity of life-ways that contemporary Jews forge for themselves (Liebman and Katz 1997).

Broadly viewed, the idea of 'Jewish social science' may appear as a contradiction in terms. As a discipline relevant to all humanity, the social sciences should brook no ethnic qualifiers. Viewed historically, rather than through tight definitions, there has been a synergetic relationship between attempts to formulate general perspectives on society and culture, often on the part of Jews, and research focused on Jews that draw upon the 'universal' social sciences. In this manner, social-science disciplines have constituted an important avenue of Jews' interpretations of their experiences in the modern world.

Suggested Reading

An account of the historical background to the emergence of Jewish social science in the early decades of the twentieth century is found in Hart (2000). Goldscheider and Zuckerman (1984) provide a comparative analysis of modern demographic and socio-political developments in European and European-derived Jewry over most of the twentieth century, while a complementary perspective on Middle Eastern Jewry is found in Goldberg (1996). Kugelmass's collection of essays on American Jewry (1988), relates ethnographic studies to earlier work, while Cohen and Eisen's recent study (2000) discusses both statistical and qualitative trends. Two views of Israeli society and sociology are found in Horowitz and Lissak (1989) and in Kimmerling (2001), the former representing classic Israeli sociology and the latter more recent viewpoints.

Bibliography

ABUHAV, O., HERTZOG, E., GOLDBERG, H., and MARX, E. eds. 1998. *Yisrael: Antropologia Meqomit*. Tel Aviv.

ACKERMAN, R. 1992. 'J. G. Frazer and the Jews.' *Religion* 22: 135–50.

ADORNO, T., FRENKEL-BRUNSWIK, E., LEVINSON, D. J., and SANFORD, N. T. 1950. *The Authoritarian Personality*. New York.

ALON, G. 1958. 'The Sociological Method in Researching *Halakha*.' [Hebrew]. *Studies in Jewish History* 2: 181–227. Tel Aviv.

ARAN, G. 1991. 'Jewish-Zionist Fundamentalism.' In *Fundamentalisms Observed*. 265–345. M. Marty and S. Appleby eds. Chicago.

BAHLOUL, J. 1996. *The Architecture of Memory: A Jewish–Muslim Household in Colonial Algeria, 1937–1962*. New York.

BARON, S. W. 1957–83. *Social and Religious History of the Jews*. 2nd edn 18 vols. New York.

BEIDELMAN, T. O. 1974. *W. Robertson Smith and the Sociological Study of Religion*. Chicago.

BEN-AMOS, D. 1990. 'Jewish Studies and Jewish Folklore.' In *Proceedings of the Tenth World Congress of Jewish Studies*, Division D. ii. 1–20.

BEN-DAVID, J. 1952. 'Ethnic Differences or Social Change?' [Hebrew]. *Megamot* 3: 171–83.

BERNSTEIN, D. 1980. 'Immigrants and Society—A Critical View of the Dominant School of Israeli Sociology.' *British Journal of Sociology* 31: 246–64.

BIALIK, H. Y. and RAVNITZKY, Y. H. 1988. *Sefer ha-aggadah: The Book of Jewish Folklore and Legend.* Selected, translated and annotated by Ch. Pearl. Tel Aviv.

BIRNBAUM, P. 1995. 'French Jewish Sociologists Between Reason and Faith: the Impact of the Dreyfus Affair.' *Jewish Social Studies* NS 2: 1–35.

BOAS, F. 1940. *Race, Language and Culture.* New York.

BOYARIN, D. 1997. *Unheroic Conduct: The Rise of Heterosexuality and the Invention of the Jewish Man.* Berkeley.

BOYARIN, J. 1990. *Storm from Paradise: The Politics of Jewish Memory.* Minneapolis.

—— and BOYARIN, D. eds. 1997. *Jews and Other Differences: The New Jewish Cultural Studies.* Minneapolis.

BUNZL, M. N. D. 2003 forthcoming, '*Völkerpsychologie* and German-Jewish Emancipation.' In *Worldly Provincialism: German Anthropology in the Age of Empire.* H. Glenn Penny and M. Bunzl, eds. Ann Arbor, Mich.

CIMET, A. 1997. *The Ashkenazi Jews in Mexico: Ideologies in the Structuring of a Community.* Albany, NY.

COHEN, S. M. 1994. 'Why Intermarriage May *not* Threaten Jewish Continuity.' *Moment* Dec.: 54–7, 89, 95.

—— 1995. Rejoinder to Goldstein *et al.* (1995). *Moment* Apr.: 68–9.

—— and EISEN, A. 2000. *The Jew Within: Self, Family and Community in the United States.* Bloomington, Ind.

CUDDIHY, J. M. 1974. *The Ordeal of Civility: Freud, Marx, Lévi-Strauss, and the Jewish Struggle with Modernity.* New York.

DAVIDMAN, L. 1991. *Tradition in a Rootless World: Women Turn to Orthodox Judaism.* Berkeley.

DEUTSCH, Y. 2001. '"A View of the Jewish Religion"—Conceptions of Jewish Practice and Ritual in Early Modern Europe.' *Archiv für Religionsgeschichte* 2: 273–95.

DINER, H. 1998. 'Introduction to the Transaction Edition.' In Wirth (1998).

DOLGIN, J. 1977. *Jewish Identity and the JDL.* Princeton.

DURKHEIM, É. 1951. *Suicide: A Study in Sociology.* Ed. G. Simpson, trans. J. Spaulding and G. Simpson. New York.

—— 1964. *The Division of Labor in Society.* New York.

—— 1995. *The Elementary Forms of Religious Life.* Trans. K. Fields. New York.

EFRON, J. 1994. *Defenders of the Race: Jewish Doctors and Race Science in Fin-de-Siècle Europe.* New Haven.

EILBERG-SCHWARTZ, H. 1990. *The Savage in Judaism: An Anthropology of Israelite Religion and Ancient Judaism.* Bloomington, Ind.

EISENSTADT, S. N. 1950. 'The Oriental Jews in Palestine.' *Jewish Social Studies* 12: 199–222.

—— 1954. *The Absorption of Immigrants.* London.

ELAZAR, D. 1976. *Community and Polity: The Organizational Dynamics of American Jewry.* Philadelphia.

EPPEL, E. M. 1994. *Professor Morris Ginsberg (1889–1970): His Life and Work.* Jerusalem.

FABIAN, J. 1983. *Time and the Other: How Anthropology Makes Its Object.* New York.

FEELEY-HARNIK, G. 1994. *The Lord's Table: Eucharist and Passover in Early Christianity.* Washington, DC.

FINKELSTEIN, L. ed. 1960. *The Jews: Their History, Culture and Religion.* 2 vols. New York.

FRAZER, J. G. 1918. *Folklore in the Old Testament.* 3 vols. London.

GILMAN, S. 1991. *The Jew's Body.* New York.

——and SHAIN, M. eds. 1999. *Jewries at the Frontier: Accommodation, Identity, Conflict.* Urbana, Ill.

GINZBERG, E. 1966. *Keeper of the Law: Louis Ginzberg.* Philadelphia.

GLAZER, N. and MOYNIHAN, D. 1963. *Beyond the Melting Pot: The Negroes, Puerto Ricans, Jews, Italians, and Irish of New York City.* Cambridge, Mass.

GLICK, L. B. 1982. 'Types Distinct from Our Own: Franz Boas on Jewish Identity and Assimilation.' *American Anthropologist* 84: 545–65.

GOITEIN, S. D. 1988. *A Mediterranean Society: The Jewish Communities of the Arab World as Portrayed in the Documents of the Cairo Geniza.* Vol. 5: *The Individual.* Berkeley.

GOLDBERG, H. 1978. 'Introduction: Culture and Ethnicity in the Study of Israeli Society.' *Ethnic Groups* 1: 163–86.

——ed. 1987. *Judaism Viewed From Within and Without: Anthropological Studies.* Albany, NY.

——1995. 'The Voice of Jacob: Jewish Perspectives on Anthropology and the Study of the Bible.' *Jewish Social Studies* NS 2: 36–71.

——ed. 1996. *Sephardi and Middle Eastern Jewries: History and Culture in the Modern Era.* Bloomington, Ind.

GOLDSCHEIDER, C. and ZUCKERMAN, A. 1984. *The Transformation of the Jews.* Chicago.

GOLDSTEIN, S. *et al.* 1995. 'Twelve Angry Men and Women' Rejoinder to Cohen (1994). *Moment* Apr.: 66–7.

GORDON, M. 1964. *Assimilation in American Life: The Role of Race, Religion, and National Origins.* New York.

GRÉGOIRE, H. 1808. *De la littérature des nègres ou, recherches sur leur facultés intellectuelles, leurs qualités, morales et leur littérature; suivi de notices sur la vie et les ouvrages des nègres qui se sont distinqués dans les sciences, les lettres et les arts.* Paris.

HANDLIN, O. 1954. *Adventure in Freedom: Three Hundred Years of Jewish Life in America.* New York.

HANSEN, M. 1948. *The Immigrant in American History.* Cambridge, Mass.

HART, M. B. 2000. *Social Science and the Politics of Modern Jewish Identity.* Stanford.

HAUSCHILD, T. 1997. 'Christians, Jews, and the Other in German Anthropology.' *American Anthropologist* 99: 746–53.

HEILMAN, S. 1976. *Synagogue Life: A Study in Symbolic Interaction.* Chicago.

——1982. 'The Sociology of American Jewry: The Last Ten Years.' *Annual Review of Sociology* 8: 135–60.

HERBERG, W. 1955. *Protestant—Catholic—Jew: An Essay in American Religious Sociology.* New York.

HOROWITZ, D. and LISSAK, M. 1989. *Trouble in Utopia: The Overburdened Polity of Israel.* Albany, NY.

HOROWITZ, E. 1992. '"A Different Mode of Civility": Lancelot Addison on the Jews of Barbary.' *Studies in Church History* 29: 309–25.

HYMAN, P. 1979. *From Dreyfus to Vichy: The Remaking of French Jewry, 1906–1939.* New York.

JACOBS, J. 1997. 'A "most remarkable Jewish sect"?: Jewish Identity and the Institute of Social Research in the Years of the Weimar Republic.' *Archiv für Sozialgeschichte* 37: 73–92.

KATZ, J. 1955. 'The Concept of Social History and Its Possible Use in Jewish Historical Research.' *Scripta Hierosolymitana* 3: 292–312.

——1961. *Tradition and Crisis.* New York.

KIMMERLING, B. 2001. *The Invention and Decline of Israeliness: State, Society and the Military in Israel*. Berkeley.

KIRSHENBLATT-GIMBLETT, B. 1990. 'Problems in the Early History of Jewish Folkloristics.' *Proceedings of the Tenth World Congress of Jewish Studies*, Division D. ii. 21–31.

——1995. 'Introduction.' In Zborowski and Herzog (1995).

——1996. 'Coming of Age in the Thirties: Max Weinreich, Edward Sapir, and Jewish Social Science.' *YIVO Annual* 23: 1–103.

KOPELOWITZ, E. 1998. 'Three Sub-Cultures of Conservative Judaism and the Issue of Ordaining Women.' *Nashim* 1: 136–53.

KUGELMASS, J. 1986. *The Miracle of Intervale Avenue*. New York.

——ed. 1988. *Between Two Worlds: Ethnographic Essays on American Jewry*. Ithaca, NY.

——ed. 1992. 'Going Home.' *YIVO Annual* 21 (special issue).

LEDERHENDLER, E. 1998. Review of *Portrait of American Jews* by S. C. Heilman and *Alternatives to Assimilation* by A. Silverstein. *Studies in Contemporary Jewry* 14: 282–5.

LÉVI-STRAUSS, C. 1958. *Race and History*. Paris.

LIEBMAN, C. S. and COHEN, S. M. eds. 1990. *Two Worlds of Judaism: The Israeli and American Experiences*. New Haven.

LIEBMAN, C. S. and KATZ, E. eds. 1997. *The Jewishness of Israelis: Responses to the Guttman Report*. Albany, NY.

MARCUS, I. 1996. *Rituals of Childhood: Jewish Culture and Acculturation in the Middle Ages*. New Haven.

MARX, E. ed. 1980. *A Composite Portrait of Israel*. London.

MASSIN, B. 1996. 'From Virchow to Fisher: Physical Anthropology and "Modern Race Theories" in Wilhelmine Germany.' In *Volkgeist as Method and Ethic: Essays on Boasian Ethnography and the German Anthropological Tradition*. 79–154. George Stocking Jr., ed. Madison, Wisc.

MEDDING, P. Y. 1968. *From Assimilation to Group Survival: A Political and Sociological Study of an Australian Jewish Community*. Melbourne.

MOORE, D. D. 1986. 'David Émile Durkheim and the Jewish Response to Modernity.' *Modern Judaism* 6: 287–300.

MYERHOFF, B. 1980. *Number Our Days*. New York.

NOY, D. 1982. 'Dr. Max Grunwald—The Founder of Jewish Folkloristics.' In *Tales, Songs and Folkways of Sephardic Jews*. Max Grunwald. Folklore Research Center 6. Jerusalem.

PATAI, R. 1983. *On Jewish Folklore*. Detroit.

——1992. *Journeyman in Jerusalem (1933–1947)*. Salt Lake City.

PINSKER, L. 1944. *Writings and Addresses* B. Netanyahu. ed. New York.

PRELL, R. 1989. *Prayer and Community: The Havurah in American Judaism*. Detroit.

RADIN, M. 1915. *The Jews Among the Greeks and Romans*. Philadelphia.

RAM, U. 1995. *The Changing Agenda of Israeli Sociology: Theory, Ideology, and Identity*. Albany, NY.

RODRIGUE, A. 1993. *Images of Sephardi and Eastern Jewries in Transition: The Teachers of the Alliance Israélite Universelle, 1860–1939*. Seattle.

ROSKIES, D. 1992. 'S. Ansky and the Paradigm of Return.' In *The Uses of Tradition: Jewish Continuity in the Modern Era*. 243–60. J. Wertheimer ed. New York.

RUPPIN, A. 1930–1. *Die Soziologie der Juden*. 2 vols. Berlin.

——1971. *Memoirs, Diaries, Letters*. A. Bein ed. London.

SCHECHTER, S. 1959. *Seminary Addresses and Other Papers*. New York.

SCHNAPPER, D. 1983. *Jewish Identities in France: An Analysis of Contemporary French Jewry.* Chicago.

SCHWARTZ, S. R. 1992. *The Emergence of Jewish Scholarship in America: The Publication of the Jewish Encyclopedia.* Cincinnati.

SHAPIRA, A. 1993. 'Buber's Attachment to Herder and German "Volkism".' *Studies in Zionism* 14: 1–30.

SHAROT, S. 1976. *Judaism: A Sociology.* London.

SHENHAV, Y. and KUNDA, G. 1992. 'The Fertile Western Imagination: How Israel's Ethnic Problem is Represented.' [Hebrew.] *Theory and Criticism* 2: 137–46.

SKLARE, M. 1955. *Conservative Judaism: An American Religious Movement.* Glencoe, Ill.

SMOOHA, S. 1978. *Israel: Pluralism and Conflict.* London.

SOLOVEITCHIK, H. 1994. 'Rupture and Reconstruction: The Transformation of Contemporary Orthodoxy.' *Tradition* 28: 64–130.

SOMBART, W. 1969. *The Jews and Modern Capitalism.* Trans. M. Epstein. New York.

SPIRO, M. 1958. *Children of the Kibbutz.* Cambridge, Mass.

STEPAN, N. L. and GILMAN, S. 1993. 'Appropriating the Idioms of Science: The Rejection of Scientific Racism.' In *The Racial Economy of Science.* 170–93. S. Harding ed. Bloomington, Ind.

STRATHERN, M. 1987. 'Out of Context: The Persuasive Fictions of Anthropology.' *Current Anthropology* 28: 251–81.

STRENSKI, I. 1997. *Durkheim and the Jews of France.* Chicago.

TALMON, Y. 1972. *Family and Community in the Kibbutz.* Cambridge, Mass.

TRAUTMANN, T. 1997. *Aryans and British India.* Berkeley.

VALENSI, L. and WACHTEL, N. 1991. *Jewish Memories.* Trans. B. Harshav. Berkeley.

WEBBER, J. ed. 1994. *Jewish Identities in the New Europe.* London.

WEBER, M. 1952. *Ancient Judaism.* Trans. and ed. H. H. Gerth and D. Martindale. Glencoe, Ill.

WEINGROD, A. 1966. *Reluctant Pioneers: Village Development in Israel.* Ithaca, NY.

WEISSLER, CH. 1990. 'Making Davening Meaningful: Worship in the Havurah Movement.' *YIVO Annual* 19: 255–82.

WILLNER, D. 1969. *Nation Building and Community in Israel.* Princeton.

WIRTH, L. 1998. *The Ghetto.* New Brunswick, NJ.

ZBOROWSKI, M. and HERZOG, E. 1995. *Life Is With People.* New York.

ZENNER, W. P. 1963. 'Ambivalence and Self-Image among Oriental Jews in Israel.' *Jewish Journal of Sociology* 5: 214–23.

—— ed. 1988. *Persistence and Flexibility: Anthropological Perspectives on the American Jewish Experience.* Albany, NY.

INDEX